Welcome to the 9th Edition of Camps Australia Wide.

This publication is considered one of Australia's most valuable printed resources for the RV traveller, providing a comprehensive and authenticated guide to free and low cost camping as well as unique outback camping sites throughout Australia.

Once again we have "notched up" a great number of kilometres, checking verifying and visiting existing and new sites, adding photos where possible. Those that we found closed or not suitable have been removed. The result of this "zig zagging" around and across Australia is that there are now over 4000 sites listed in this new edition, the majority of which are overnight stops and camping areas, also included are low cost caravan parks, national parks and station stays.

The maps have been customized as much as possible to make them easier to read, however please note that, due to the scale of the maps, as we add more and more sites it becomes a challenge to fit the icons onto them! We do our best to ensure nothing of importance is covered over.

On another topic, Rubbish! – we have noticed a much larger amount of rubbish being left behind at camp sites, PLEASE put your rubbish in bins if they are provided and if not take it with you to dispose of later. Consider leaving an area cleaner than you find it, we carry rubbish bags and a special tool (a long handled picker, available from hardware stores) to do just that.... A well looked after site does not give the authorities a reason to close it down!

We appreciate your feedback, about the book, the sites and any general RV issues, so please call or email us with any comments or suggestions.

Phone (07) 5474 2542 or email Cathryn at
cathryn@campsaustraliawide.com

Philip & Cathryn Fennell

ACKNOWLEDGEMENTS

Camps Australia Wide Pty Ltd

PO Box 1765 Noosaville
BC Queensland Australia 4566

Phone: (07) 5474 2542 Fax: (07) 5474 1715

Email: info@campsaustraliawide.com

Website: www.campsaustraliawide.com

Ninth edition published February 2017
Reprinted December 2017

ISBN: Camps 9 A4 Paperback   978-0-9925732-4-9
   Camps 9 A4 Spiral Bound   978-0-9925732-5-6
   Camps 9 B4 Spiral Bound   978-0-9925732-6-3

Proprietors of Camps Australia Wide:
Philip and Cathryn Fennell

Compiled, Designed and Published by:
Philip and Cathryn Fennell

Research:
Julie Simpson, Jacqueline Wardle, Cathryn & Philip Fennell

Field Research:
Philip and Cathryn Fennell

Production and Prepress:
Allan and Linda Shearer (Shearer Publishing Systems)
Pauline Gleeson (www.paulinegleesongraphicdesign.com)
Gavin James (www.mapuccino.com.au)

Cover Design:
Pauline Gleeson (www.paulinegleesongraphicdesign.com)

Photography:
Philip Fennell, Cathryn Fennell, Sheng Yee

Base Maps:
Hema Maps Pty Ltd
Printed by C&C Offset Printing Co Ltd, China
Copyright © Camps Australia Wide Pty Ltd 2017

Personal acknowledgements to the many people and organisations for their contribution of information over the years, however small, are listed on page 447.

Cover photo: Speeds Point Campground, SA 508

CONTENTS

ABOUT THIS GUIDE

GPS Co-ordinates used in Camps Australia Wide 9

The format used in Camps 9 is d°m's" (Degrees, Minutes, Seconds).

Most GPS units generally have three GPS format settings. It is important that you select the correct setting in your GPS to match our format. This will ensure you are accurately guided to the site.

Listed below are the three common coordinates formats:

- d.d° (-49.5000°, 123.500°) sometimes called "Degrees".
- d° m.m (49° 30.0, 123° 30.0) sometimes called "Minutes".
- **d° m's" (49° 30 00S, 123° 30 00E) sometimes called "Seconds" (we use this format)**

We now have GPS Point Of Interest (POI) files that have been created by our partner GPSOZ. When these files are loaded into your GPS you can view and select Camps 9 sites from the Custom POI section of your GPS for turn by turn guidance to the selected Camps listing. These files are available as a download only for Garmin, TomTom and Navman and are delivered by email.

Visit our web site www.campsaustraliawide.com for more information about purchasing GPS POI files.

This guide prominently lists Free and Low Cost Camping, National Parks, State Forests, Rest Areas, Station Stays, and Show Grounds.

This guide is NOT a comprehensive Caravan Park Guide, only Caravan Parks where fees are below $25 per night for 2 adults are included, this means the parks are generally in country and remote areas.

Feedback

Our publication relies on consumer feedback to maintain accuracy and content. Your input would be most appreciated. You can email us on talktous@campsaustraliawide.com or can phone us on (07) 5474 2542. A site feedback form is available on our website under the 'Updates' tab. Any information, no matter how small, can be sent in by mail, fax or email. It won't be ignored.

Dump Point List

Because of the ever-increasing concern for the environment a comprehensive Public Dump Point list has been included. These dump points also have GPS co-ordinates to help you find their positions. Any new addition to our list of public dump points would be most welcome.

Seven Principles of Leave No Trace

- Plan ahead and prepare
- Travel and camp on durable surfaces
- Dispose of waste properly
- Leave what you find
- Minimise campfire impacts
- Respect wildlife
- Be considerate of your hosts and other visitors for more information visit www.lnt.org.au

This book

This book is intended to be used as a guide only. The representation on the maps of any road or track is not necessarily evidence of public right of way. Third parties who provide information to the publisher and authors concerning roads and other matters do not assert or imply to the publishers that such information is complete, accurate or current. Whilst the author believes the details contained in the book to be correct at the time of publication and all care has been taken to ensure the information is as accurate as possible, inaccuracies may occur. As such, no responsibility is taken for changes, amendments, additions or alterations to any item and no liability will be accepted for any decisions or actions taken based on information contained in the publication. Conditions in Australia are constantly changing, and as such, Federal, State and Local authorities may make changes to conditions relating to sites listed in this guide, which are subject to closure or change without notice. Please obey any signs and do not insist that you are in the right because it says so in the book. The book is not the absolute authority. It's a guide only!

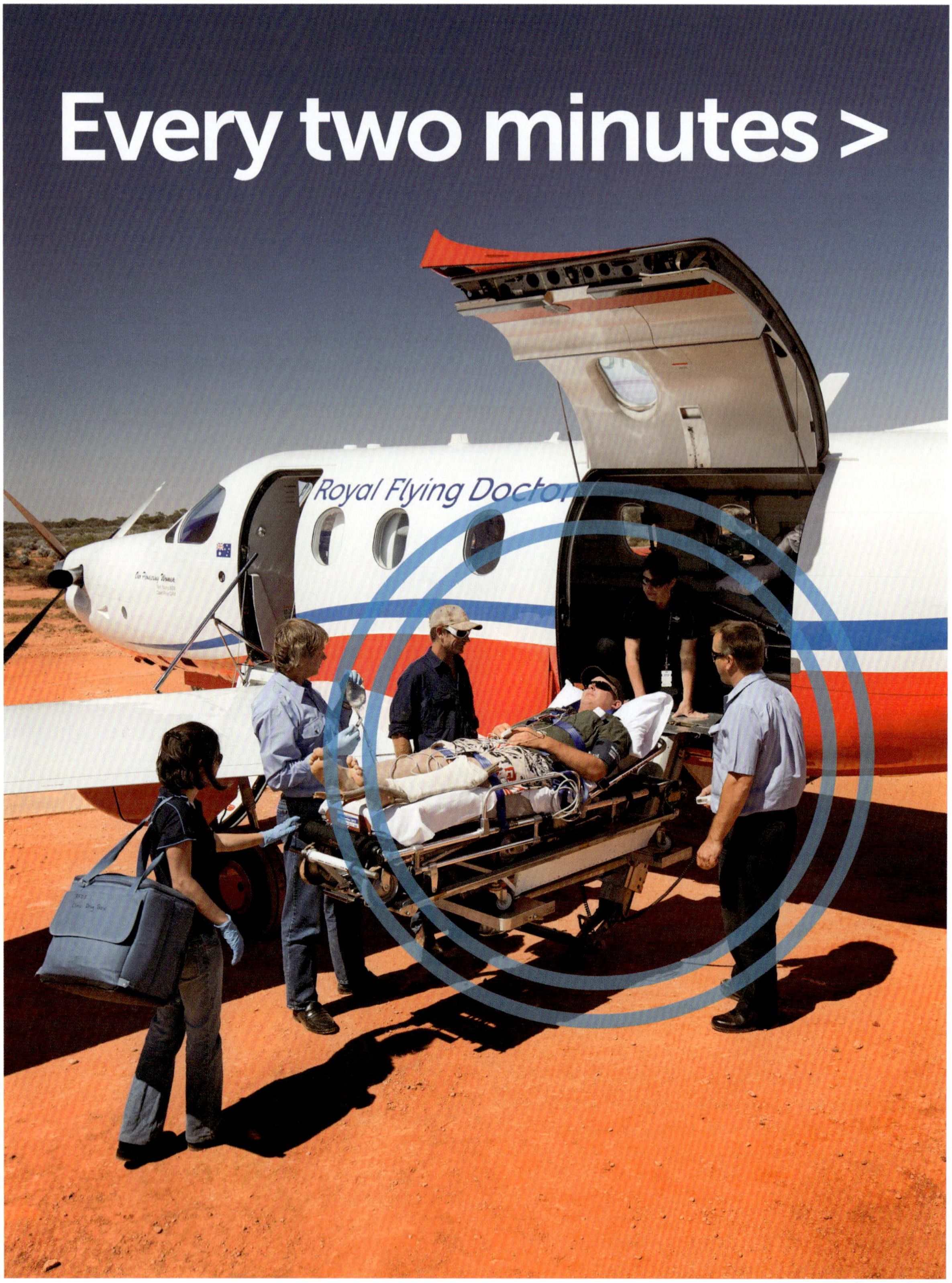

Every two minutes >

The Royal Flying Doctor Service (RFDS) delivers 24-hour emergency aeromedical and primary health care services to more than 290,000 Australians every year – that's one person every two minutes.

The RFDS relies on donations from the community to purchase and medically-equip its aircraft – at a cost of more than $6 million each – and to finance other major health initiatives.

Make a donation today and help keep the Flying Doctor flying.

1300 669 569

www.flyingdoctor.org.au

Royal Flying Doctor Service
The furthest corner. The finest care.

IMPORTANT: UPDATING THIS BOOK

A free user-friendly searchable update service is provided on our website via the 'Updates' tab. Changes will undoubtedly occur, especially over time after the book's release. So it is important to check regularly for updates. Updates for this edition are provided for four years from the date first published.

Step 1

On the Camps Australia Wide website (www.campsaustraliawide.com) select the 'Updates' tab.

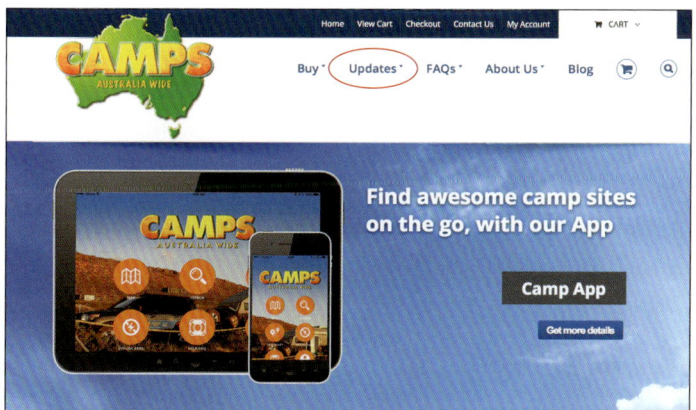

Step 2

Selecting the 'Updates' tab will direct you to the 'Update Service' page which gives you an option to 'Launch Updates Program'. When that is selected, the Updates Program will display in a window floating above the web page.

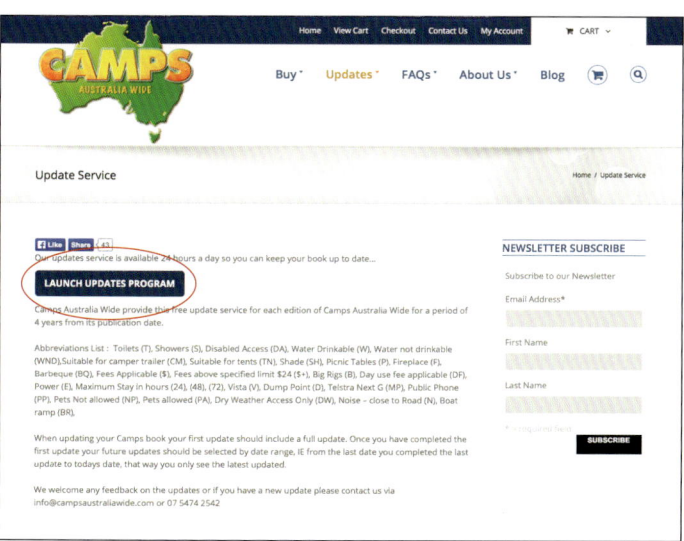

Step 3

The Updates Program window. Here choices are made as to publication, edition, State, and dates.

The first time you do the updates leave the date fields blank. For subsequent updates just enter the date range using the pop-up calendar to show new updates only.

Printing. If the Print button is obscured, simply use the scroll bar to reveal it.

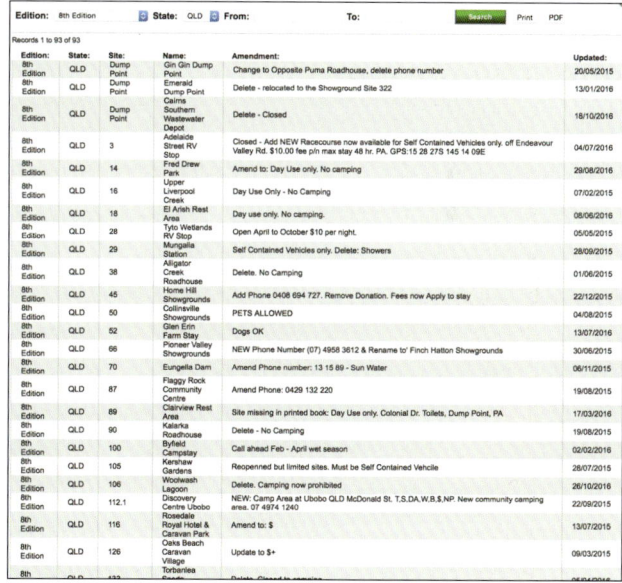

Feedback

Our team always welcomes feedback on existing sites and any new site that you think worthwhile sharing with our fellow travellers. Please email us on talktous@campsaustraliawide.com

HOW TO USE THIS GUIDE

Layout of the guide

The book is divided into different coloured sections for each State or Territory for easier navigation.

The listings, in general, are in a linear order along the highways and roads, running from north to south and east to west, where possible.

Abbreviations Some abbreviations have been used to condense the amount of text throughout the book.

They are:

Dr – Drive		Tce – Terrace	
Rd – Road		St – Street	
Ave – Avenue		cnr – corner	
Hwy – highway		jcn – junction	
km – kilometre		L – left	
R – right		m – metre	
N – north		S – south	
E – east		W– west	
NP – National Park		PO – Post Office	

Map References Maps are by Hema with sites and site numbers from Camps Australia Wide 9 overlaid.

All the sites are referenced to these maps.

Where the number of sites is quite comprehensive, more detailed maps should be used for navigation.

Site Classification Symbols and Map Symbols

The following are used in the listings and on the maps:

Explanation	In Listings	On Maps	
		No Dump Point	With Dump Point
Day Use Only	☀	32	30
Camping and Parking	🌙	155	115
Caravan Parks	🚐	121	
Public Dump Point not at a Listed Site			💧

Site symbols are placed as close as possible to the exact position.

Explanation of terms used in this guide

Rest Area An area usually located close to the highway to enable the traveller to take a break. Some rest areas provide a wide range of facilities, while others are just an area to rest for a while. Overnight camping is permitted at some sites, depending on the relevant authority's regulations. Please take notice of any regulatory signs.

Camp Area An area that has been established for camping overnight or longer, that usually provides at least some basic facilities such as toilets and water, but not necessarily showers or power. A fee is usually charged for most locations.

Camp Spot An area that is not an established camp area, but is adequate for an overnight stay or even longer, usually with limited facilities. A fee may be charged in some instances.

Picnic Area An area that has suitable facilities for a picnic. Overnight stays may be permissible in some cases.

Parking Area An area with limited or no facilities. Overnight stays may be allowed in certain cases.

Caravan Park An established area for short or long term stays, providing a range of facilities and comforts. A fee is payable depending on the quality and number of facilities offered.

Self-contained Vehicle A vehicle that is fully self-contained with respect to shower, toilet, washing, cooking and sleeping facilities and which must have holding tanks for all toilet waste and sullage water sufficient for at least 48 hours' use by the occupants.

Small Vehicle On some site descriptions, we add 'small vehicle only' this generally indicates the entry into the site is tight and parking-camping or turning area is restrict, only Toyota Hi size camper or small camper trailers or Caravan are recommended.

How to locate a site

- If you know the name of a site, go to the Site Index, (alphabetically listed), which gives you the site number and the relevant page number.
- If you want to find sites in any particular area, look at the relevant map for site numbers in that region, then look up those sites in the numerical listing.

There will always be variations in odometer readings and road distance signs, so do allow for those discrepancies when locating sites.

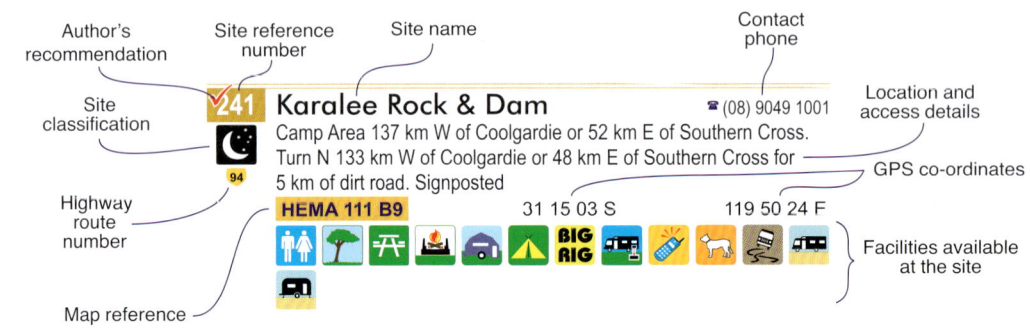

LEGEND – CAMPSITES

The sample below explains how each site is laid out for easy interpretation. Most of the symbols are self-explanatory, but some have been designed to fit certain criteria.

Sample of a Site Listing

Author's recommendation — Site reference number — Site name — Contact phone

Site classification

Highway route number

Map reference

✓ 241 Karalee Rock & Dam ☎ (08) 9049 1001 — Location and access details
Camp Area 137 km W of Coolgardie or 52 km E of Southern Cross. Turn N 133 km W of Coolgardie or 48 km E of Southern Cross for 5 km of dirt road. Signposted — GPS co-ordinates

HEMA 111 B9   31 15 03 S   119 50 24 F — Facilities available at the site

Explanation of Symbols

 Toilets
Outside of caravan parks these may be longdrops or composting types. As these are not always serviced frequently it is advisable to carry your own supply of toilet tissue.

 Disabled facilities
Generally there is at least one dedicated toilet and shower, in some sites this facility is unisex.

 Shade
At the time of viewing this site there was shade available for your vehicle.

 Fireplace
It is advisable to carry your own supply of firewood for fires and barbeques at some of the more isolated camp spots. Most National Parks do not allow firewood collection within the Park boundaries. Please gather deadwood only, do not destroy trees. Ensure you respect all local fire bans and seasonal restrictions.

 Fees applicable
At the time of publication sites with this symbol had a fee below $25 per night for 2 adults. As fees at all sites are subject to change without notice it is strongly recommended that you call and verify the fees before you arrive.

 Day use fee applicable
Primarily charged at State and National Parks, often in addition to any camping fees.

 Fees above specified limit
Sites with this symbol have been included in this edition because of their locations or because they offer something special, even though the cost may be above the upper limit of $24 per night.

 Site suitable for big rigs
We define Big Rigs as rigid vehicles with an overall length of 10 metres or more. There are usually limited sites available for larger vehicles.

 Powered sites
These sites may have a concrete pad and/or grassed area with a power point for your vehicle.

 Pleasant outlook or vista
The site provides over water, valley, or mountain views.

 Mobile phone service
Site has access to Telstra NextG™ Network with a 'Blue Tick Telstra phone'.

Pets
Although pets are allowed at these sites conditions may apply when entering a commercial camping area or caravan park. Some operators now require a fee and/or bond as part of the conditions of entry into the area, and may limit animal size and allow pets only in off-peak periods. It is advisable to call ahead to ensure that your pet is welcome. As a general rule pets must always be on a lead, and must never be left unattended. As always, clean up after your pet!

 Pets NOT allowed

Pets are not allowed at this site.

 Dry weather access only

Roads used to access the site may become impassable during the wet season or after rain and care is advised. Please check with local authorities for conditions. Usually recommended for 4WD only.

 Showers

May be hot or cold and in some isolated areas solar heated only. Some sites have showers available for a gold coin donation.

 Water

Even though it is listed as drinkable it is advisable to boil or filter before use. Please use common sense and limit your use, so that others can enjoy the availability as well.

 Water not drinkable

While this site has a water supply we recommend that you NOT drink it.

 Picnic table

Picnic tables are available and may be shaded at some locations.

 BBQ

At camp sites these are usually wood fuelled. Some caravan parks and national parks provide a free gas or electric barbeque for guests, others may charge a small fee for the use of the facility. Commonsense and etiquette on use and cleaning after use applies.

 Camper trailer

Site is suitable for the setting up of a camper trailer.

 Tent Site

Site is suitable for the setting up of a tent. In a commercial camping area tent sites are usually in an open grassed area (subject to local conditions).

 Maximum stay (hours)

These may be Main Roads rest areas or sites provided by local authorities. Please use these as intended and honour the time limits as sign posted. Improper use of these sites may be detrimental to travellers' future use of the facility.

 Author's Recommendation

The authors at the time of their visit found that these sites were appealing, either because of the site's position or vista or because facilities were above average.

 Dump Point

This symbol advises that the park or site has a central dump point. These dump points are generally provided for the disposal of cassette toilets. For those vehicles with holding tanks you will need to check with the facility operator to ensure that there is access for the disposal of black or grey water.

 Public phone

A public phone is available at this facility or within 100 metres of the site.

 Site close to road

These sites may be noisy depending on the amount of passing traffic and time of day.

 Caravan

Site is suitable for a caravan.

 Camper/Motorhome

Site is suitable for a camper/motorhome (not a Big Rig).

 Boat ramp

This site has boat launch facilities nearby. The ramp may be properly built or may be adapted from local conditions. In most cases they are suitable for small 'tinnies'. Check local conditions for tidal flow and other hazards.

Site Symbols

 Day Use Only   Overnight Camping/Parking   Caravan Parks

Public Dump Points

An example of a public dump point listing and the symbols used for dump points are shown on the introductory page of the Public Dump Point section on page 420.

HELP SAVE THE FREE CAMP SITES!

All travellers have a responsibility to remove their own rubbish, but we also unfortunately need to clean up after other non-considerate travellers who leave rubbish behind.

SIMPLE WAYS TO HELP CLEAN UP!

- Always travel with a 'picker & pack of tough bags'
- If there are no bins to dispose of rubbish
  - Take it with you, to dispose of in a bin.
  - Burn the rubbish (watch for fire bans)
  - Bury the rubbish

PICKER

TOUGH BAGS

Thank you for cleaning up Australia and saving free camping areas

GENERAL COMMENTS

Road Conditions

Some of the sites listed are accessed by roads that may be unsuitable for some vehicles and which may also change due to weather conditions. It is recommended that you enquire from local authorities before travelling on roads of uncertain condition.

Pets

Apart from National Parks and some caravan parks, pets are generally accepted, provided they are under control by their owner. Dogs especially need to be under control, especially around other dogs or people. Where dogs are accepted in caravan parks, it is usually at the manager's discretion and on condition that they are on a leash at all times. Common sense should prevail. Clean up any mess left behind and respect the area.

Generators

These can be a necessary part of travelling, but do have consideration for your neighbour and run them at respectable hours. Be aware of the noise and fumes put out by these machines and park accordingly. Generators are banned in some National Parks. Consult the relevant National Park information for details.

Rubbish

If there are no rubbish bins provided, please take your rubbish with you. Leave an area cleaner than you find it and consider cleaning up after someone else. A well-looked-after site will give the authorities a good reason to keep it open for our use.

Toilet Waste

We have provided a comprehensive 'Public Dump Point' listing starting at page 420. Some Caravan Parks for a fee will allow access and use of their dump point, enquire at the caravan park. If you have to bury your waste in remote areas, make sure it is buried at least 20 centimetres deep and 200 metres away from any waterway, runoff area or camp site.

Firewood

It is advisable to carry your own supply of firewood for fires and barbeques at some of the more isolated camp spots, rather than destroy any remaining trees.

Water

Although the water available at sites should be suitable for drinking, it would be wise to carry sufficient water for drinking as a backup and as an alternative if the water is drinkable but unpleasant.

At all times use common sense with fires, plants, animals and your fellow traveller and protect the environment.

State Regulations

Overnight Camping

There are some differences in the laws relating to overnight camping in rest areas and on private property within each State, and these laws are always changing. Some states and local authorities are quite tolerant of overnight camping, while others will enforce the law and move you on, fine you, or both. Observe any regulatory signs, respect people in authority and use common sense always.

IMPORTANT CONTACTS

Police, Ambulance & Fire Brigade — 000

International emergency Number 112 (mobile phones only)

National Parks and Wildlife Service

Western Australia
Department of Parks and Wildlife (DPAW) Ph: (08) 9219 9000 www.dpaw.wa.gov.au

Queensland
Dept of National Parks, Sport & Racing Ph: 13 74 68 www.nprsr.qld.gov.au

New South Wales
NSW National Parks and Wildlife Service Ph: 1300 072 757 www.nationalparks.nsw.gov.au

South Australia
Dept of Environment, Water and Natural Resources Ph: (08) 8204 1910 www.environment.sa.gov.au/parks

Tasmania
Parks and Wildlife Service Ph: 1300 827 727 www.parks.tas.gov.au

Northern Territory
Parks and Wildlife Commission Northern Territory Ph: (08) 8951 8250 www.parksandwildlife.nt.gov.au

Victoria
Parks Victoria Ph: 13 19 63 www.parkweb.vic.gov.au

Australian Capital Territory
Environment and Planning Development Ph: 13 22 81 www.environment.act.gov.au

Aboriginal Land Permits

Western Australia
Department of Indigenous Affairs Ph: 1300 651 077
On-line Permits: www.daa.wa.gov.au/land/permits

Northern Territory, Central Land Council
Alice Springs Main Office Ph: (08) 8951 6211 www.clc.org.au

South Australia
Maralinga-Tjarutja Admin Office Ph: (08) 8625 2946

Road Conditions

Live Traffic NSW www.livetraffic.com Ph: 132 701

New South Wales (Outback)
Ph: (08) 8082 6660 – 24 hour recorded message

Queensland Ph: 13 19 40

South Australia Ph: 1300 361 033

Road Conditions

Western Australia Ph: 13 81 38

Northern Territory Ph: 1800 246 199

Victoria Ph: 13 11 70

Vehicle Assistance

AANT, NRMA, RAA, RAC,RACQ, RACT, RACV
Ph: 131 111

Royal Doctor Flying Doctor Service

Emergency General Ph: 1300 697 337

NSW Medical & Emergency Calls (Broken Hill) Ph: (08) 8088 1188

Qld Medical & Emergency Calls (Charleville) Ph: (07) 4654 1443

Qld Medical & Emergency Calls (Mt Isa) Ph: (07) 4743 2802

SA & NT South of Tennant Creek Medical & Emergency Calls Ph: (08) 8648 9555

NT (North of Tennant Creek) After Hours Emergency Calls Ph: 000 (112 for mobile phones)

WA Medical & Emergency Calls Ph: 1800 625 800 (Satphones Ph: (08) 9417 6389)

Weather Information

Bureau of Meterology www.bom.gov.au

Other Useful Contacts

DFES Western Australia Ph: 133 337

New South Wales Rural Fire Service Ph: 1800 679 737

Queensland Fire & Rescue Service Ph: 13 74 68

Victoria Country Fire Authority – Fire Restrictions Ph: 1800 240 667

South Australia Country Fire Service Ph: 1300 362 361

Bushfires Council Northern Territory Ph: (08) 8922 0844

Tasmanian Fire Service Ph: (03) 6230 8600

Australian National 4WD Radio Network Ph: (08) 8287 6222, www.vks737.on.net

Birdsville Hotel, Queensland Ph: (07) 4656 3244

Innaminka Hotel Ph: (08) 8675 9901

Spirit of Tasmania - Information and Reservations Ph: 1800 634 906, www.spiritoftasmania.com.au

Pink Roadhouse, Oodnadatta, SA Ph: (08) 8670 7822 www.pinkroadhouse.com.au

Fruit and Quarantine Zones

www.quarantinedomestic.gov.au

Western Australian Quarantine & Inspection Service

Kununurra border checkpoint Ph: (08) 9168 7354

Eucla/Eyre Hwy (WA/SA Border) Ph: (08) 9039 3227

South Australia Fruit Fly & Quarantine Ph: 1300 666 010

Queensland DPI & F Coen Quarantine & Inspection Point Ph: 13 25 23, www.daf.qld.gov.au

HEMA ROAD ATLAS LEGEND

Freeway; Divided Highway
Autobahn
Autoroute; route rapide à chaussées séparées
Autostrada; superstrada
Autosnelweg; hoofdweg met gescheiden rijbanen

Freeway – future
Autobahn – im Bau
Autoroute – en construction
Autostrada – in costruzione
Autosnelweg in aanleg

Major Highway – sealed; unsealed
Durchgangsstraße – befestigt; unbefestigt
Route principale – revêtue; non revêtue
Strada di grande comunicazione – pavimentata; non pavimentata
Hoofdverbindingsweg – verhard; onverhard

Major Road – sealed; unsealed
Hauptstraße – befestigt; unbefestigt
Route de communication – revêtue; non revêtue
Strada principale – pavimentata; non pavimentata
Belangrijke weg – verhard of onverhard

Minor Road – sealed; unsealed
Nebenstraße – befestigt; unbefestigt
Autre route revêtue; non revêtue
Altra strada – pavimentata; non pavimentata
Secundaire weg – verhard of aardeweg

Track, four-wheel drive only
Piste, nur mit 4-Rad-Antrieb befahrbar
Piste, utilisable pour véhicule à 4 roues motrices
Pista, praticabile solo con trazione integrale
Piste, uitsluitend voor 4 x 4

Rough Track, four-wheel drive only
Piste (unwegsam), nur mit 4-Rad-Antrieb befahrbar
Piste rugueux, utilisable pour véhicule à 4 roues motrices
Pista greggio, praticabile solo con trazione integral
Piste moeilijk berijbaar, uitsluitend voor 4 x 4

Walking Track; Gate
Wanderweg; Tor
Sentier; barrière
Sentiero; cancello
Wandelweg; gate

 **44** | 20 24

Total Kilometres   **Intermediate Kilometres**
Entfernung (total) in km   Teildistanz in km
Distance totale en km   Distance partielle en km
Distanza totale in km   Distanza parziale in km
Totale afstand in km   Gedeeltelijke afstand in km

National Route Number/
National Highway Number
Nummer Nationalstraße/ Nummer nationale Durchgangsstraße
Numéro de route nationale/ de route rapide
Numero della strada nazionale/ Numero della strada di grande comunicazione
Wegnummers op nationale/ wegen en expresswegen

State Route Number
Staats-Straßennummer
Numéro de route d'Etat
Nùmero della strada dello stato
Staatswegnummer

Tourist Route
Touristische Route
Route touristique
Strada turistica
Toeristische route

Railway – in use; disused
Bahnlinie – in Betrieb; stillgelegt
Chemin de fer – en service; abandonné
Ferrovia – in esercizio; interrotto
Spoorweg – in gebruik; buiten gebruik

Ferry Route
Fährverbindung
Route de traversier
Traghetto rotta
Veerdienst

State/ Territory Border
Staats-/ Territoriengrenze
Frontière d'Etat/ territoire
Stato/ territorio di confine
Staats-/ Territorygrens

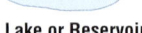 **Pest Free Area**
Pest Freie Zone
Zone de ravageur franche
Zona parassiti franca
Pestvrij gebied

Fruit Fly Exclusion Zone
Fruchtfliegen Ausschluss Zone
Zone exclusive de la mouche des fruits
Zona esclusiva de la mosca della frutta
Fruitvliegvrij gebied

National Park
Nationalpark
Parc national
Parco nazionale
Nationaal park

Other Parks & Nature Reserves
Sonstige Parks und Natur Reservate
Autre parks et réserve naturelle
Altri parchi e riserve
Andere parken en natuurreservaten

Resources Reserve
Ressourcen Schutzgebiet
Zone protégée de ressources
Zona protetta da risorse
Ontginnings Reservaat

Scientific Reserve
Naturwissenschaftliches Schutzgebiet
Zone protégée scientifique
Zona protetta scientifica
Wetenschappelijk Reservaat

State Forest & Timber Reserve
Staatsforst & Holz Reservat
Forêt domaniale
Zona protetta da risorse
Staatsbos en bosbouw reservaat

Aboriginal Land
Aborigines-Gebiet
Région d'aborigènes
Regione d'aborigeni
Gebied van de aborigines

World Heritage Area
Weltkulturerbegebiet (UNESCO)
Site du patrimoine mondial
Luogo dell' patrimonio mondiale
Wereld Beschermd Gebied

Marine Park
Meeresschutzgebiet
Parc marin
Parco marino
Zeereservaat

Prohibited Area
Sperrgebiet
Zone interdite
Area vietata
Afgesloten gebied

Lake or Reservoir
See oder Reservoir
Lac ou réservoir
Lago o lago artificiale
Meer of waterreservoir

Intermittent or Salt Lake
Periodischer oder Salzwassersee
Lac périodique ou d'eau salée
Lago periodico o salato
Periodiek of zoutwatermeer

River – perennial;
non-perennial
Fluß – dauerhaft; periodisch
Rivière – constant; périodique
Fiume – constante; periodico
Rivier – altijd; periodiek

Saline Coastal Flat
Wattgebiet
Salines côtières
Salino castiero platts
Zeekust vlakte

Swamp
Sumpf
Marais
Palude
Moeras

Subject to Inundation
Überschwemmungsgebiet
Sujet aux inondations
Soggette a inondazioni
Kan onderwater lopen

Sandridges
Sanddüne
Dune de sable
Dune di sabbia
Zandruggen

Mangroves
Mangroven
Mangroves
Mangrovie
Wortelbomen

Built up area
Bebaute Fläche
Zone construite
Costruito nell'area
Bebouwde kom

• **BRISBANE**
Capital City
Hauptstadt
Capitale
Capitale
Hoofdstaad

◉ **Cairns**
City
Grossstadt
Ville importante
Città grande o importante
Stad of hoofdplaats

⊙ **Gympie**
Large Town
Stadt
Ville
Città
Stad

• **Tully**
Medium Town
Mittelgroße Stadt
Ville moyenne
Città de medie
Middelgrote Stad

• Samford
Small Town
Kleinstadt
Ville petite
Piccola città
Kleine Stad

∘ Ayton
Locality
Gegend
Localité
Località
Plaats

▪ 'Rostock'
Homestead
Gehöft
Ferme
Masseria
Hofstede

◉ Doomadgee   ⊙ Urlampe
Aboriginal Community –
major; minor
Aborigines Gemeinde – groß; klein
Communauté d'aborigènes
Comunità d'aborigeni
Gebied van aborigines – groot; klein

+ *Mount James*
Mountain/ Hill
Berg/ Hügel
Montagne/ colline
Monte/ colle
Bergen/ heuvel

• *Fruit Bat Falls*
Tourist Point of Interest
Sehenswürdigkeit
Curiosité touristique
Curiosità turistica
Toeristische bezienswaardigheid

• *Lindeman's*
Hunter Valley
Winery
Weinkellerei
Établissement vinicole
Cantina
Wijnmakerij

⚓ Shipwreck   ✿ Lighthouse
Schiffswrack   Leuchtturm
Naufrage   Phare
Naufragio   Faro
Schipwrak   Vuurtoren

Ψ Tower   ▲ Hut
Turm   Hütte
Tour   Hutte
Torre   Capanna
Toren   Hut

—40— **Distance from GPO (km)**
Entfernung zum Hauptpostgebäude (km)
Distance par la route du bureau de poste général (km)
Distanza dalla strada da General Post Office (km)
Afstand uit de algemene postkantoor (km)

 Diesel
Diesel erhältlich
Diesel disponible
Diesel disponibile
Diesel beschikbaar

 Outback Fuel (Diesel and Unleaded)
(not shown on region pages)
Diesel u. bleifreies Benzin bzw.
Diesel et carburant sans plomb
Diesel e benzina senza piombo
Diesel en loodvrij

 Opal (unleaded replacement)
(not shown on region pages)
Opal Bezin erhältlich
Opal disponible
Opale disponibile
Opal

⛳ **Golf Course**
(only shown on suburb/region pages)
Golfplatz
Terrain de golf
Campo da golf
Golfbaan

 Airport; International Airport
Flughafen; Internationaler Flughafen
Aéroport; Aéroport international
Aeroporto; Aeroporto internazionale
Vlieghaven; Vlieghaven internationaal

MAIN KEY MAP

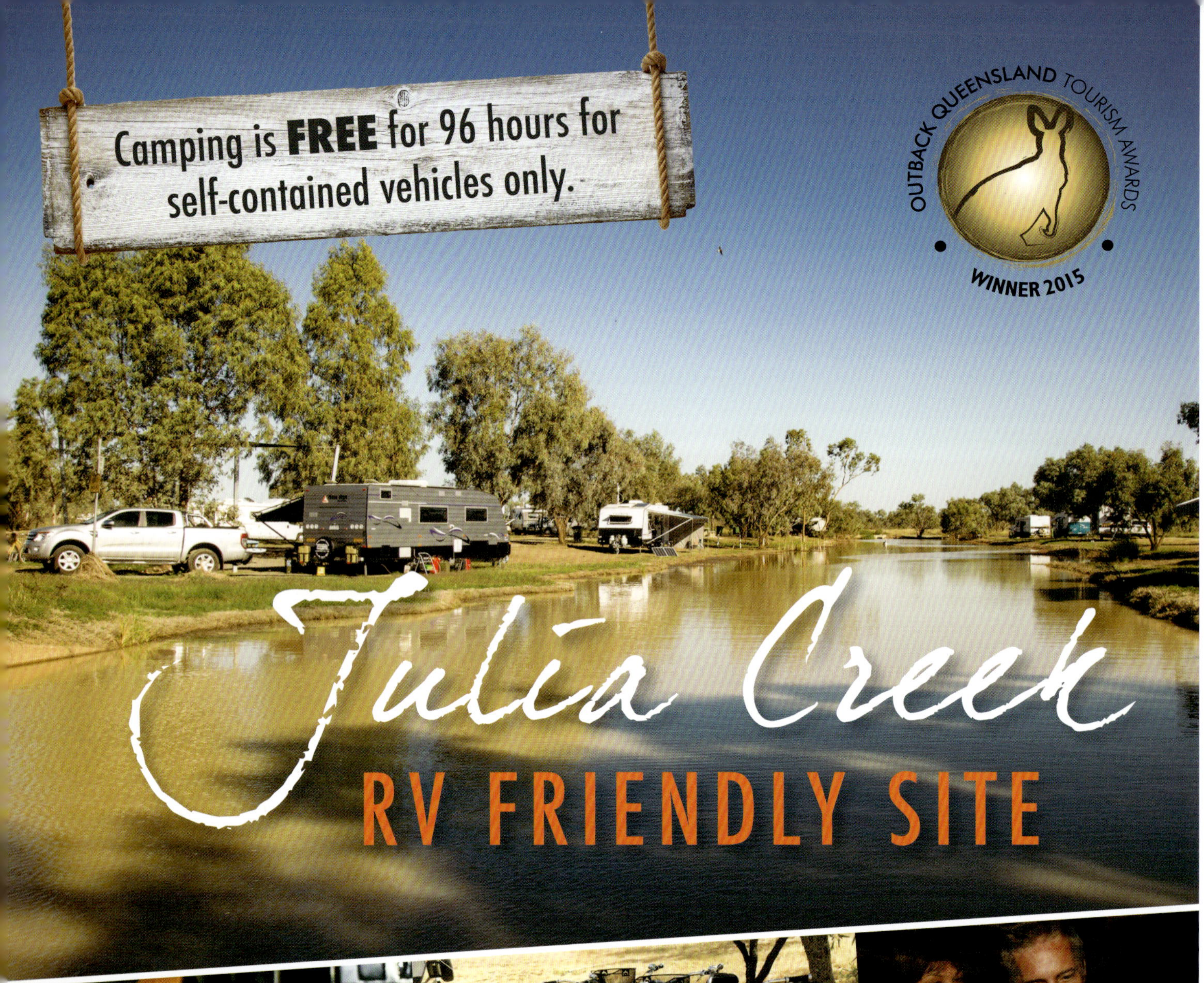

Camping is **FREE** for 96 hours for self-contained vehicles only.

OUTBACK QUEENSLAND TOURISM AWARDS
WINNER 2015

Julia Creek
RV FRIENDLY SITE

Julia Creek Queensland is home to one of the best known RV Friendly Sites. Make sure you're in Julia Creek on a Monday night from April to September for one of our famous bush dinners.

Please obtain a RV Site permit from the Julia Creek Visitor Information Centre:
34 Burke St Julia Creek 4823
(07) 4746 7690
tourism@mckinlay.qld.gov.au
www.atthecreek.com.au

 Julia Creek Visitor Information Centre
 juliacreekqld

WHITEHAVEN BEACH, WHITSUNDAY ISLAND (15 B8)   PHOTO: © ISTOCK.COM/SAM VALTENBERGS

Queensland Government Disclaimer
Contains data provided by the State of Queensland (Department of Environment and Resource Management) [2010]. In consideration of the State permitting use of this data you acknowledge and agree that the State gives no warranty in relation to the data (including accuracy, reliability, completeness, currency or suitability) and accepts no liability (including without limitation, liability in negligence) for any loss, damage or costs (including consequential damage) relating to any use of the data. Data must not be used for direct marketing or be used in breach of the privacy laws.

Distances are shown in kilometres and follow the most direct major sealed route where possible.

Bamaga	2709	2681	2444	1008	2637	2727	2132	1747	2265	2081	2369	2719	1359	1957
Birdsville	1575	1743	1687	841	1506	699	1492	680	1380	1109	1453	1339	741	
Brisbane	366	1673	734	347	1164	937	1807	603	466	122	1325	1339		
Bundaberg	1452	908	591	1044	697	1687	363	640	408	1085	1219			
Cairns	1626	1722	1147	736	1190	1070	1358	1708	348	972				
Charleville	592	514	1049	1157	848	268	612	1278	689					
Goondiwindi	1106	986	1749	652	358	225	1374	1281						
Longreach	793	643	681	698	1042	773	175							
Mackay	1224	334	781	972	388	916								
Mount Isa	1324	1341	1685	906	468									
Rockhampton	560	638	722	856										
Roma	344	1010	873											
Toowoomba	1360	1217												
Townsville	598													
Winton														

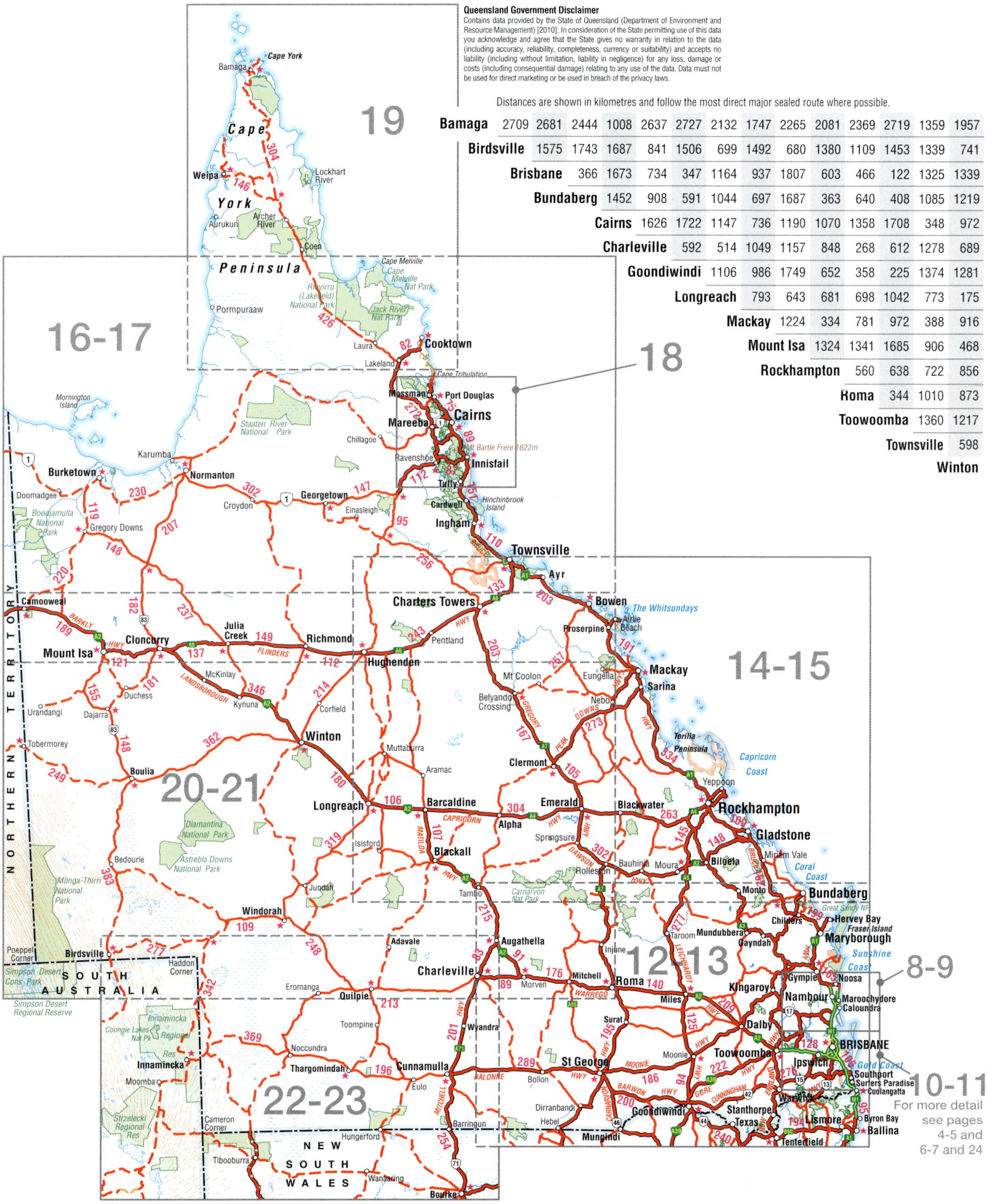

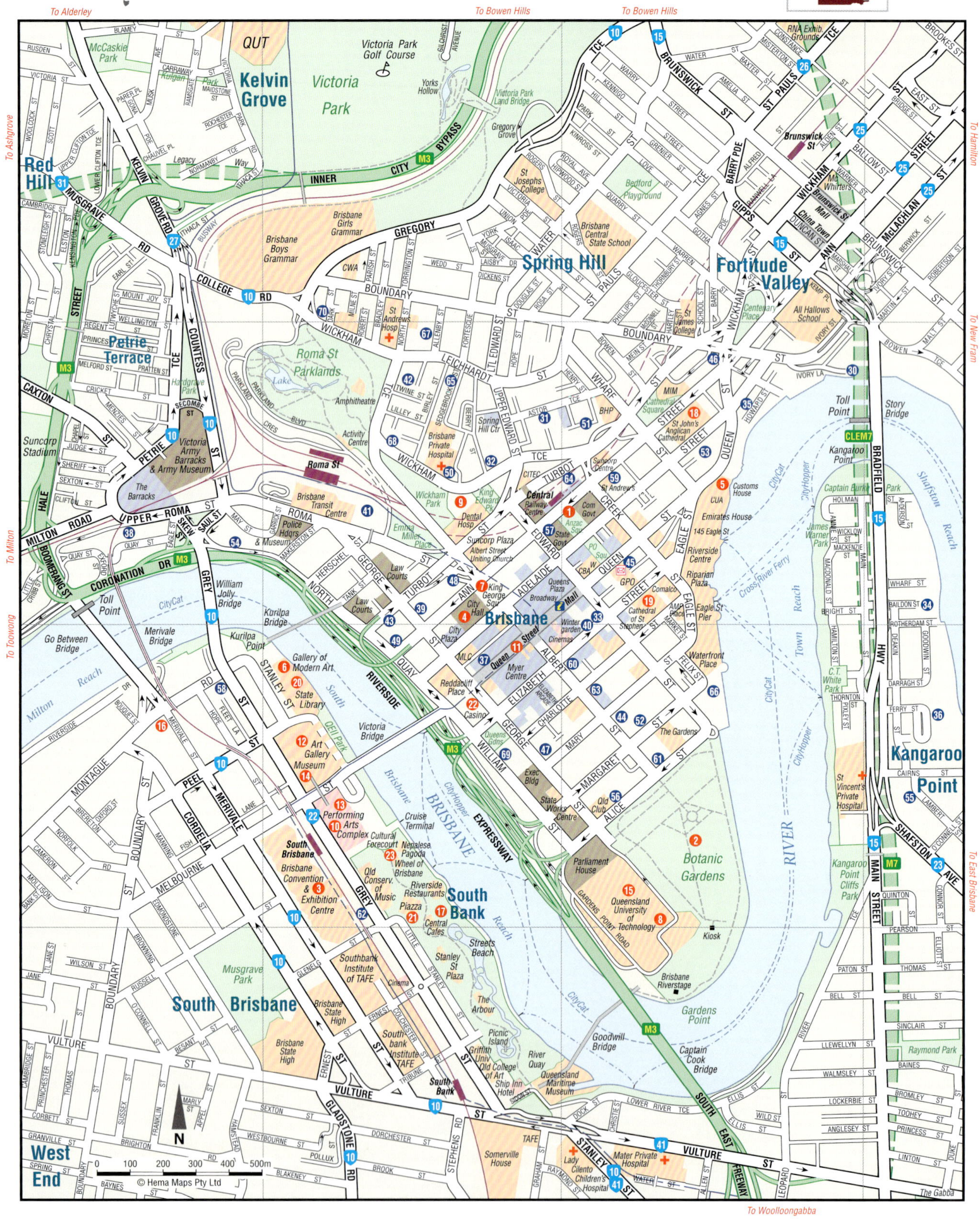

Places of Interest

1 Anzac Memorial B3
2 Botanic Gardens C3
3 Brisbane Convention & Exhib Ctr C2
4 City Hall B2
5 Customs House B3
6 Gallery of Modern Art C2
7 King George Square B2
8 Old Government House C3
9 Old Windmill Observatory B2
10 Performing Arts Complex C2
11 Queen Street Mall C2
12 Queensland Art Gallery C2
13 Queensland Cultural Centre C2
14 Queensland Museum C2
15 Queensland University of Technology C3
16 Queensland Theatre Company C1

17 South Bank C2
18 St John's Cathedral B3
19 St Stephen's Cathedral B3
20 State Library of Queensland C2
21 Suncorp Entertainment Piazza C2
22 Treasury Casino C2
23 Wheel of Brisbane C2

Accommodation

30 Adina Apartment Hotel Brisbane B3
31 Astor Apartments, The B2
32 Astor Metropole Best Western Hotel,The B2
33 Base Brisbane Embassy B3
34 Bridgewater Apartments B4
35 Brisbane Marriott Hotel B3
36 Central Dockside Apartments C4

37 Chifley at Lennons, The C2
38 City Backpackers B1
39 George Williams Hotel B2
40 Hilton Brisbane B3
41 Holiday Inn Hotel Brisbane B2
42 Hotel Grand Chancellor B2
43 Hotel Ibis Brisbane B2
44 iStay River City C3
45 Manor Apartment Hotel, The B3
46 Mantra on Queen B3
47 Marque Hotel, The C2
48 Mercure Brisbane King George Square B2
49 Mercure Hotel Brisbane C2
50 Metro Hotel Tower Mill B2
51 Novotel Brisbane B3
52 Oaks 212 Margaret C3
53 Oaks Aurora B3

54 Park Regis North Quay B1
55 Point Hotel, The C4
56 Quay West Suites Brisbane C3
57 Rendezvous Hotel B2
58 Riverside Hotel C1
59 Rothbury Heritage Apartment Hotel B3
60 Royal Albert Hotel C3
61 Royal on the Park C3
62 Rydges South Bank Hotel C2
63 Sebel Brisbane, The C3
64 Sofitel Brisbane Central B3
65 Spring Hill Centrepoint B2
66 Stamford Plaza Brisbane C3
67 Summit Apartments, The B2
68 Terraces on Wickham B2
69 Treasury Casino & Hotel C2
70 Watermark Hotel Brisbane A2

Freeway	Ferry Route
Major Road	Major Building
Minor Road	Govt Building
Lane / Path	Theatre/Cinema
Railway,Station	Shopping
Busway	Hospital
CLEM7 Tunnel (Toll)	Mall
Post Office	
Accredited Information	

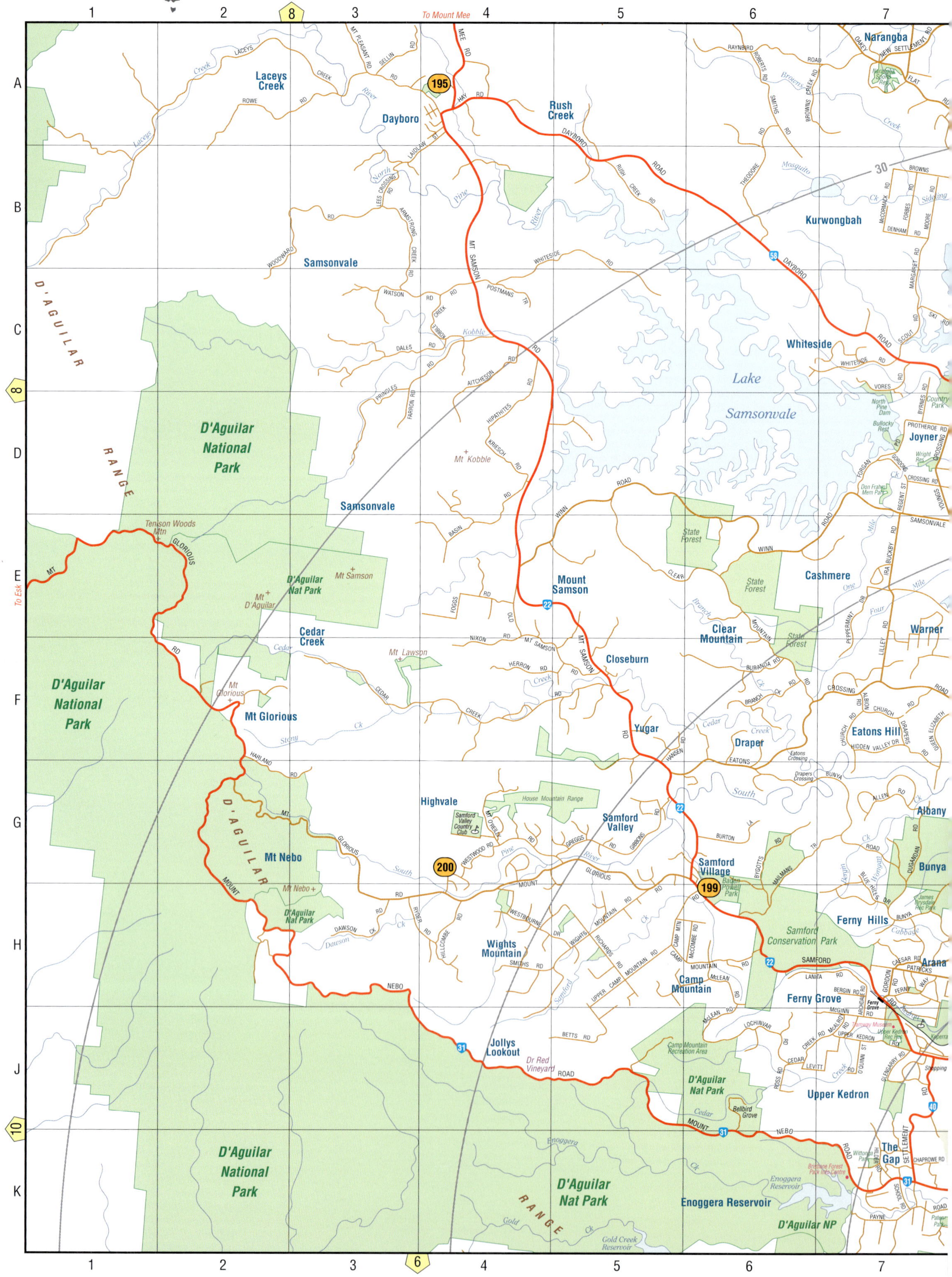

To Mount Mee

Narangba

Laceys Creek

Dayboro

Rush Creek

Kurwongbah

Samsonvale

Whiteside

D'Aguilar National Park

Lake Samsonvale

Joyner

D'Aguilar Range

Tenison Woods Mtn

D'Aguilar Nat Park

Mt Samson

Mt D'Aguilar

Cedar Creek

Mt Lawson

Mount Samson

State Forest

Cashmere

Clear Mountain

Warner

D'Aguilar National Park

Mt Glorious

Mt Glorious

Closeburn

Yugar

Draper

Eatons Hill

Albany

Highvale

Samford Valley Country Club

Samford Valley

Bunya

Mt Nebo

Mt Nebo

D'Aguilar Nat Park

House Mountain Range

Samford Village

Baden Powell Park

Ferny Hills

Samford Conservation Park

Wights Mountain

Camp Mountain

Samford

Arana

Ferny Grove

Jollys Lookout

Dr Red Vineyard

Camp Mountain Recreation Area

D'Aguilar Nat Park

Bellbird Grove

Upper Kedron

The Gap

D'Aguilar National Park

Enoggera Reservoir

Gold Creek Reservoir

D'Aguilar Nat Park

D'Aguilar Range

D'Aguilar NP

To Esk

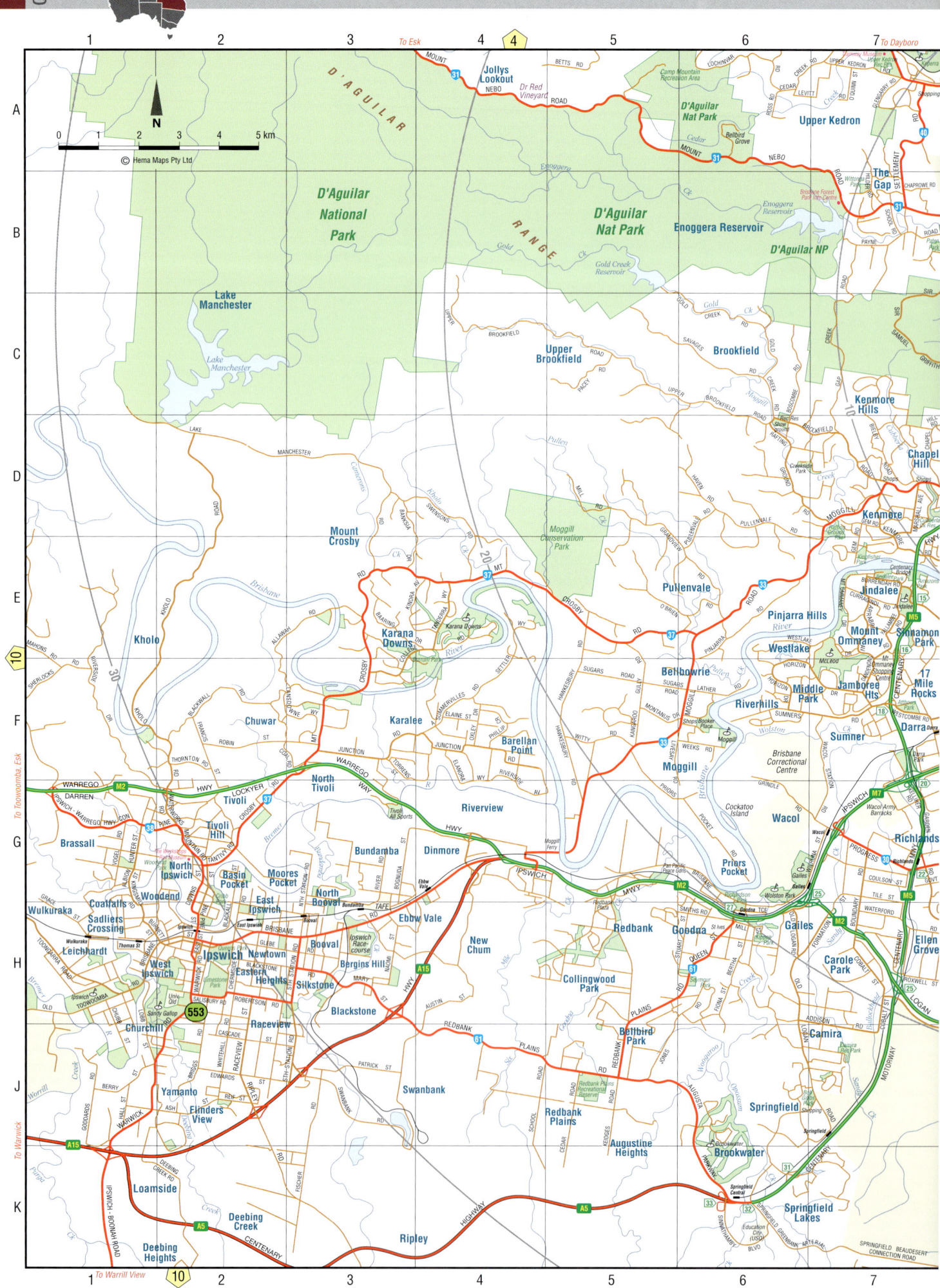

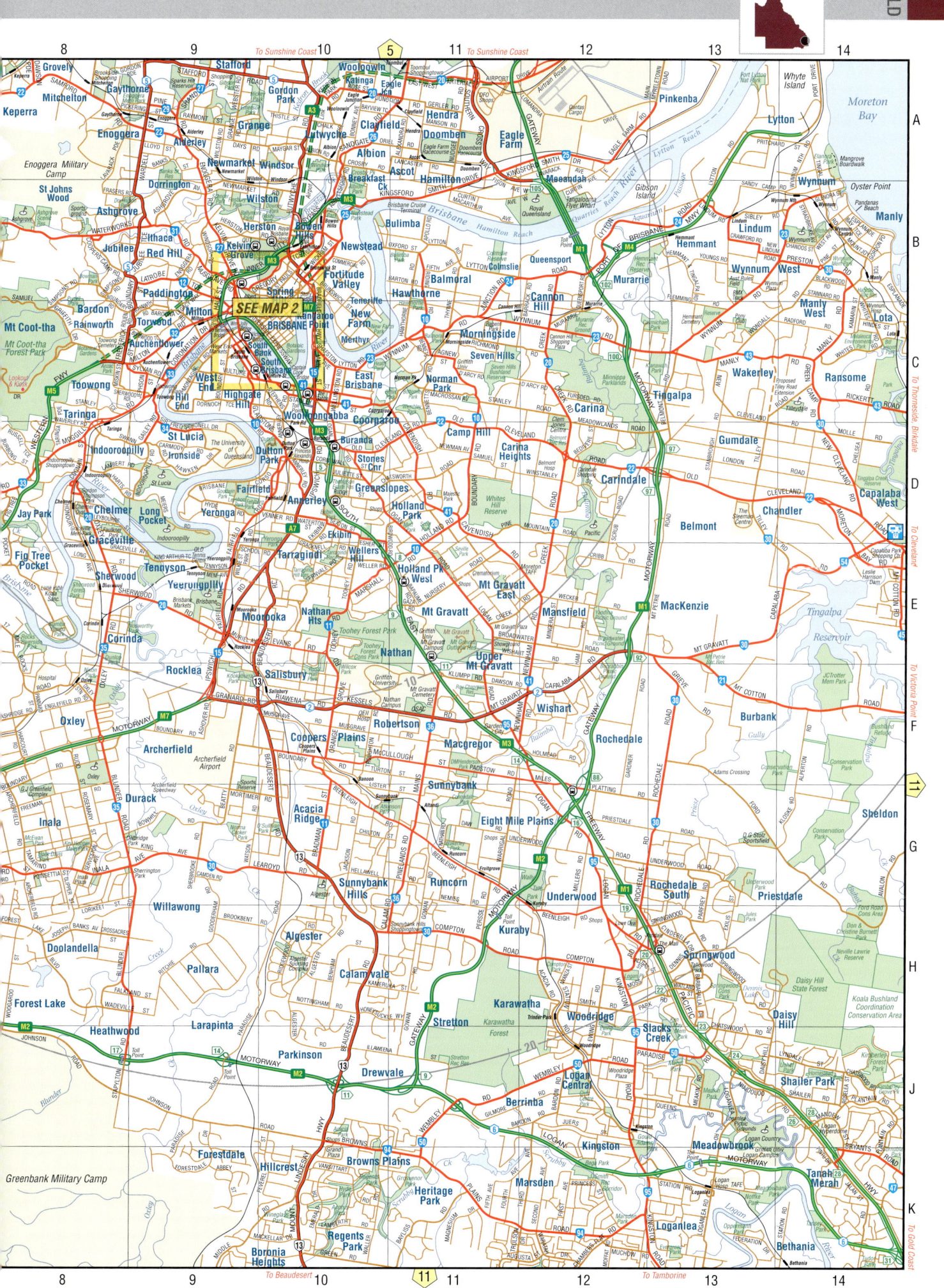

Brisbane Region, Queensland

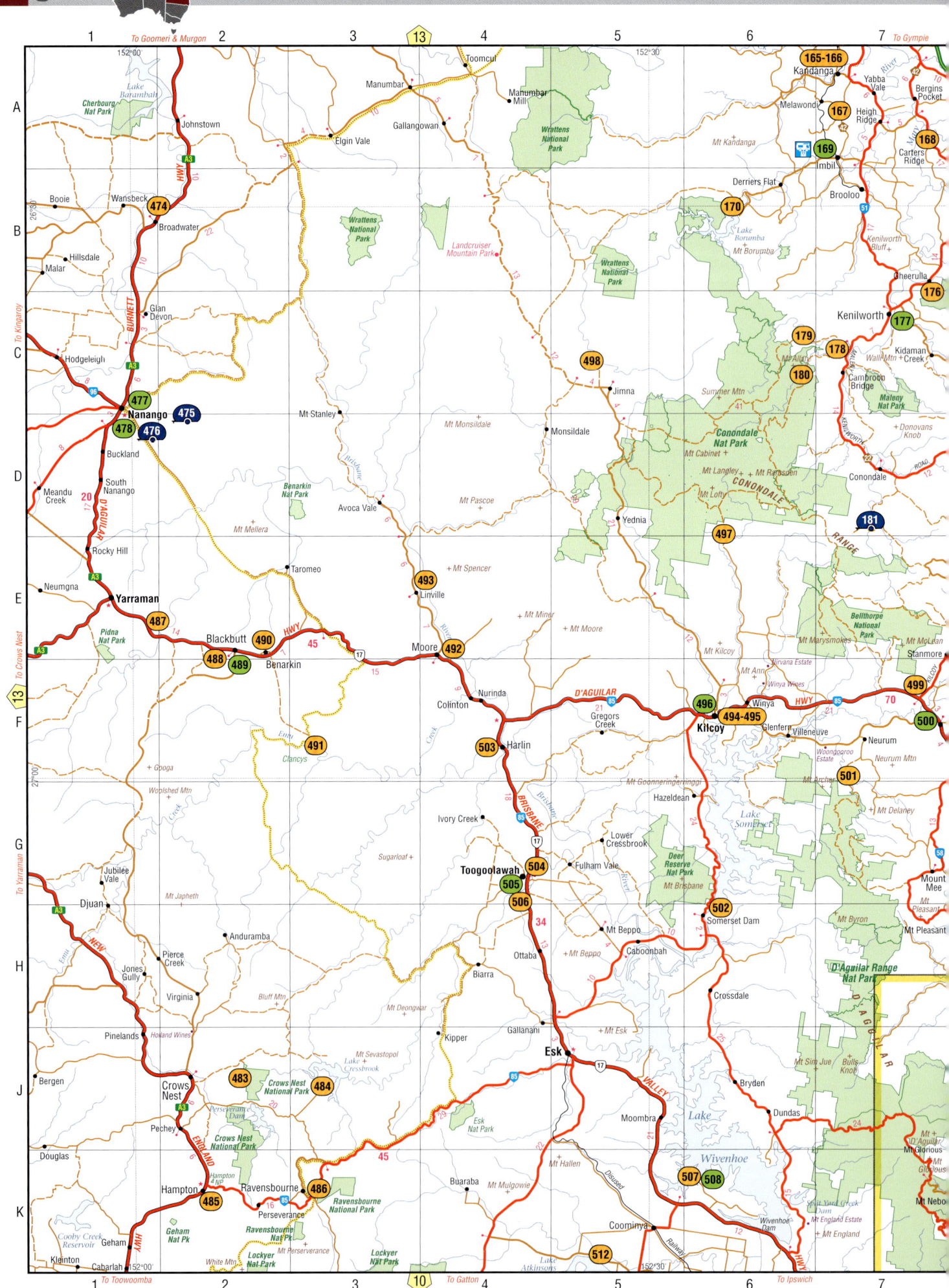

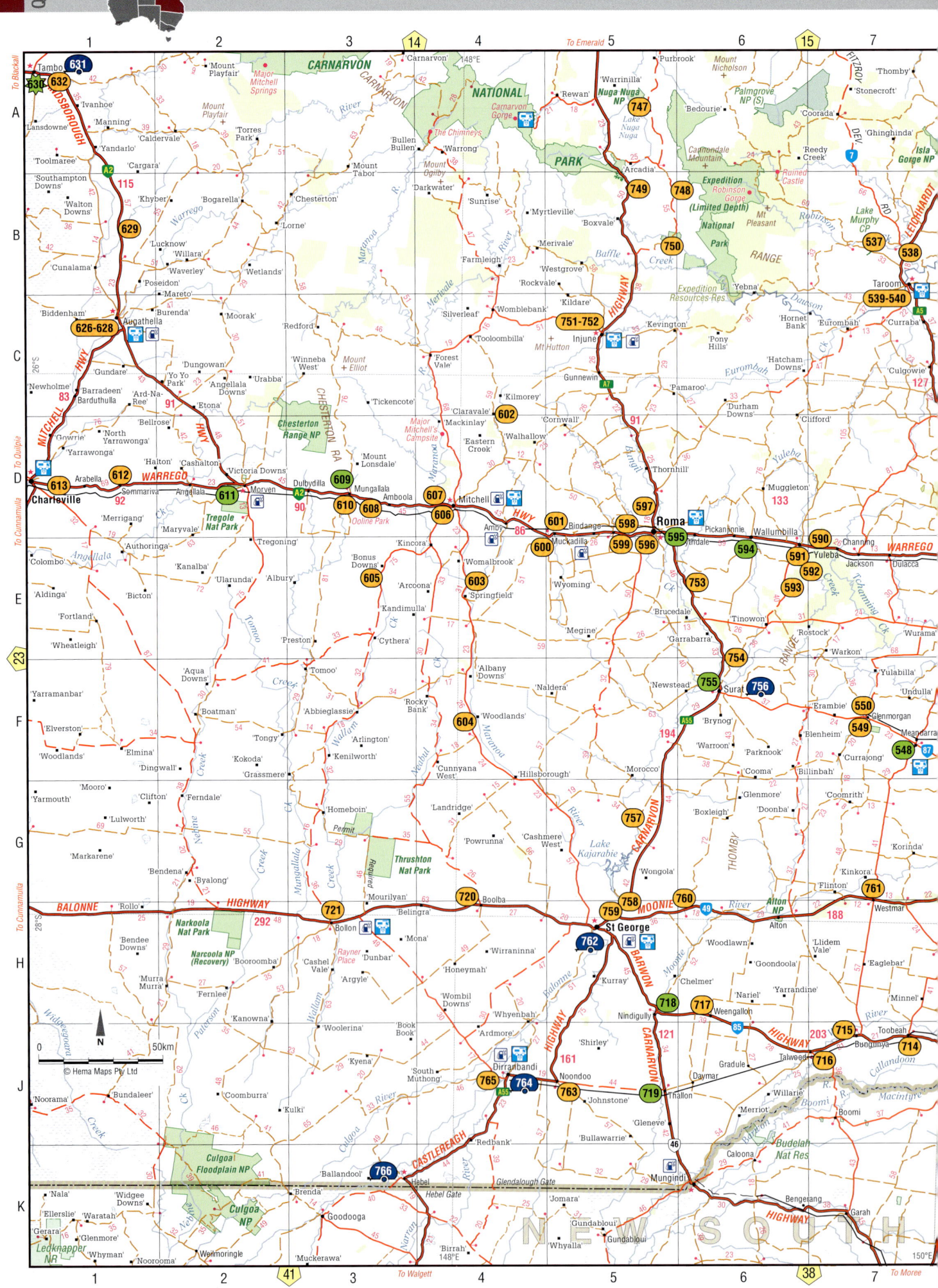

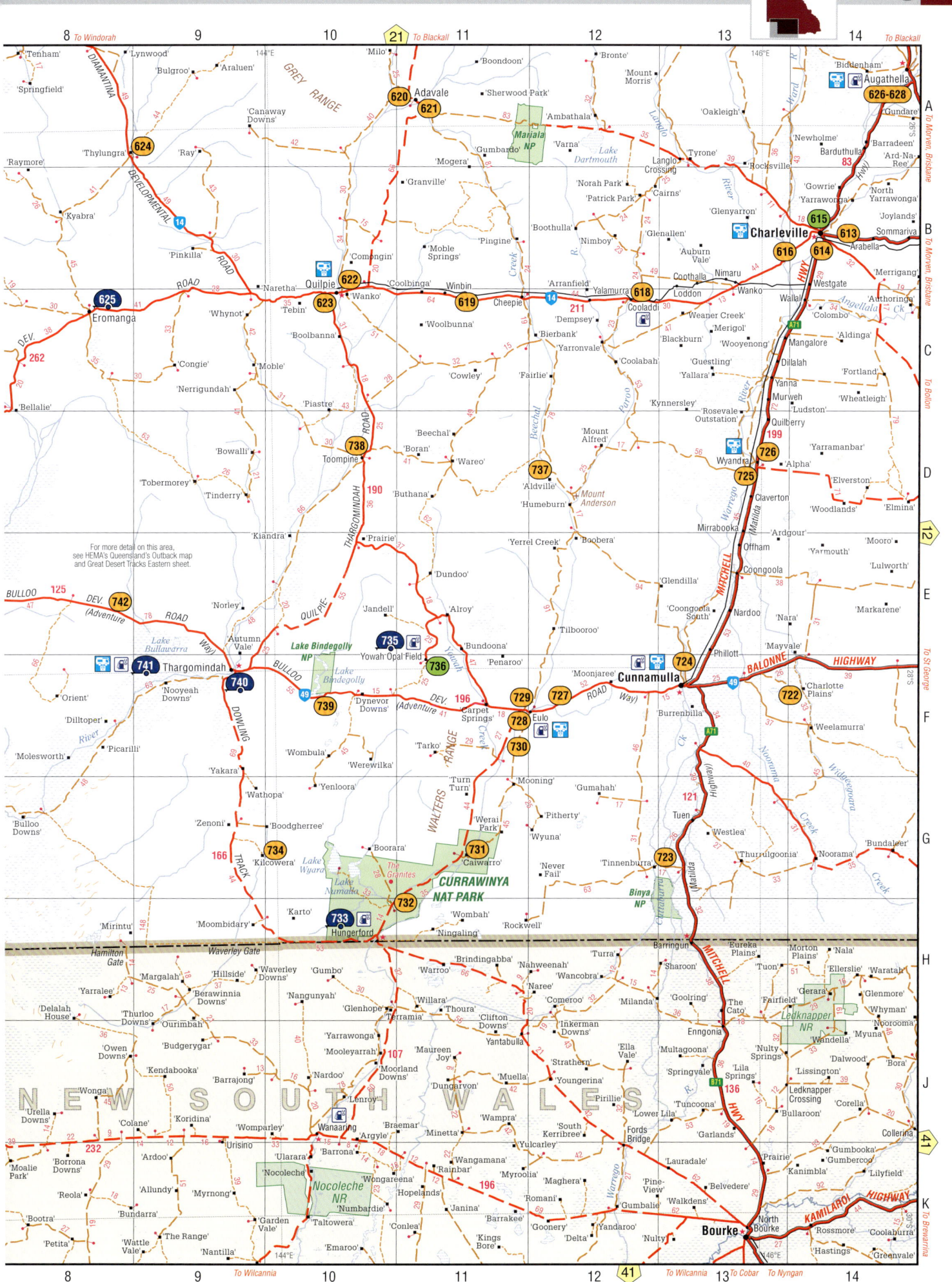

Queensland Highway Index

Queensland Alphabetic Site Index

Queensland Alphabetic Site Index

QUEENSLAND

Mossman to the Gold Coast
Bruce Highway

1 Endeavour River Escape ☎ (07) 4069 5084

Camp Area 17 km N of Cooktown PO. Turn R after Cooktown Airport 5 km along Barretts Creek Rd. Closed during wet season (Dec-Apr)

HEMA 17 B10   15 24 26 S   145 11 24 E

2 Hill Top Farm ☎ (07) 4069 5058

Camp Area 23 km NW of Cooktown via Endeavour Valley Rd

HEMA 17 B10   15 25 05 S   145 05 16 E

3 Cooktown Racecourse RV Stop ☎ (07) 4069 5444

Parking Area at Cooktown, Racecourse Rd off Endeavour Valley Rd. Fees collected. Self Contained Vehicles only. Max stay 7 nights and not exceeding 14 nights in a 30 day period

HEMA 17 C10   15 28 27 S   145 14 09 E

4 Archer Point ☎ (07) 4069 6957

Camp Spot 24 km SE Cooktown. Signposted turnoff 15 km S of Cooktown from Mulligan Hwy onto Archer Point Rd, then 11 km dirt road, narrow & steep in places. 4WD only. Maximum stay 14 days. Permit required

HEMA 17 C10   15 36 11 S   145 19 35 E

5 Lions Den Hotel Campground ☎ (07) 4060 3911

Camp Area at Helenvale on the Bloomfield Rd

HEMA 17 C10   15 42 21 S   145 13 23 E

6 Wujul Wujul Sportsground ☎ (07) 4060 8333

Camp Area at Wujul Wujul. Cape Tribulation Rd. Permit & key required from Bana Yirriji Centre

HEMA 17 C10   15 56 43 S   145 19 27 E

7 Noah Beach Campground ☎ 13 74 68
Daintree National Park

Camp Area 8 km S of Cape Tribulation. Small vehicles only. No caravans permitted. Closed wet season. Bookings required

HEMA 17 D10   16 08 06 S   145 27 05 E

8 Catch a Barra ☎ (07) 4056 1727

Camp Area at Little Mulgrave 14 km W of Gordonvale. 386 Nielson Rd

HEMA 18 F4   17 07 22 S   145 41 57 E

9 The Boulders ☎ (07) 4067 1008

Camp Area 6 km W of Babinda. Limited sites

HEMA 18 G5   17 20 27 S   145 52 14 E

10 Babinda Rotary Park ☎ (07) 4067 1008

Rest Area at Babinda. Just E of town over railway. S end of Howard Kennedy Dr. Hot showers coin operated. Donation appreciated for upkeep

HEMA 18 G6   17 20 54 S   145 55 35 E

11 Bramston Beach Caravan Park & Campground ☎ (07) 4067 4121

Camp Area at Bramston Beach. N end of Evans Rd

HEMA 18 G6   17 21 08 S   146 01 25 E

12 Garradunga Hotel ☎ 0428 563 754

Camp Spot at Garradunga. Free stay with a spend at the bar. Fee for hot showers

HEMA 18 G6   17 27 41 S   145 59 43 E

13 Fred Drew Park

Rest Area 4 km N of Innisfail or 25 km S of Babinda. At Palmerston Hwy turnoff

HEMA 18 H6   17 30 55 S   145 59 37 E

14 Mena Creek Hotel ☎ (07) 4065 3201

Camp Area at Mena. 19 km SW of Innisfail on the Innisfail Japoon Rd. Free camping if order a meal at the hotel. Check in at bar

HEMA 18 J6   17 39 18 S   145 57 22 E

15 Upper Liverpool Creek

Rest Area at Japoonvale. 29 km SW of Innisfail or 14 km W of Silkwood. Beside creek

HEMA 18 J5   17 43 25 S   145 56 01 E

16 Kurrimine Beach Campground ☎ (07) 4030 2222

Camp Area at Kurrimine. N end of Robert Johnstone Pde. Maximum stay 4 weeks. Caretaker on site. No pre-booking taken

HEMA 18 J6   17 46 31 S   146 06 32 E

17 Bingil Bay Campground ☎ (07) 4030 2222

Camp Area at Bingil Bay, 3 km N of Mission Beach. Small vehicles only. Beachfront. Maximum stay 4 weeks

HEMA 18 K6   17 49 40 S   146 06 03 E

18 Tully Showground ☎ 07 4068 2288

Camp Area at Tully Showground, Butler St. Limited sites. Self Contained Vehicles only. Obtain permit from Info Centre

HEMA 18 K5   17 56 02 S   145 55 47 E

19 Tully Gorge Campground ☎ (07) 4066 8601
Tully Gorge National Park
Camp Area 44 km NW of Tully, via Tully Falls Rd. Cold showers. Must pre-book

HEMA 18 J4   17 46 22 S   145 38 59 E

20 Hull Heads Recreation Area
Camp Area at Hull Heads, 21 km SE of Tully. Entry off Luff St. Limited space, caretaker will collect fee

HEMA 17 F11   17 59 42 S   146 04 18 E

21 Murray Falls Campground ☎ 13 74 68
Murray Falls National Park
Camp Area 36 km SW of Tully or 41 km NW of Cardwell. Turn W 16 km S of Tully at Murrigal or 21 km N of Cardwell at Bilyana. 3 km dirt road. Bookings essential

HEMA 17 F11   18 09 11 S   145 48 57 E

22 Bilyana Rest Area
Rest Area 22 km S of Tully or 21 km N of Cardwell

HEMA 17 F11   18 07 07 S   145 54 43 E

23 Five Mile Swimming Hole
Picnic Area 9 km S of Cardwell or 46 km N of Ingham. 700m W of Hwy. Dirt road

HEMA 17 G11   18 19 39 S   146 02 44 E

24 Broadwater Campground ☎ 13 74 68
Abergowrie State Forest
Camp Area 45 km NW of Ingham, via Trebonne along Abergowrie Rd, or turn W off Bruce Hwy 3 km N of Ingham onto Hawkins Creek Rd for 26 km.17 km dirt road. Bookings required

HEMA 17 G11   18 24 59 S   145 56 43 E

25 Wallaman Falls Campground ☎ 13 74 68
Girringun National Park
Camp Area 51 km W of Ingham, via Trebonne. 20 km dirt road. Steep, winding road not suitable for caravans. Bookings required

HEMA 17 G11   18 35 59 S   145 48 00 E

26 Ashton Hotel ☎ (07) 4777 4179
Camp Area at Long Pocket. Behind Hotel. Check in at bar. Amenities available in business hours. Hotel patronage requested. Pets on a leash. Maximum 7 days

HEMA 17 G11   18 31 33 S   146 00 21 E

27 Halifax Hotel ☎ (07) 4777 7436
Parking Area at Halifax. Macrosan St. Limited space. Check in with the publican on arrival

HEMA 17 G11   18 34 49 S   146 17 06 E

28 Tyto Wetlands RV Stop ☎ (07) 4776 4792
Parking Area at Ingham. Tyto Wetlands Info Centre. Cnr Bruce Hwy & Cooper St. Must get permit from Info Centre. Self Contained Vehicles only. Open April to October

HEMA 17 G11   18 39 18 S   146 09 11 E

29 Mungalla Station ☎ (07) 4777 8718
Camp Area at Mungalla Station. 15 km E of Ingham on the Forrest Beach Rd towards Allingham. Signposted at entrance. Pets by arrangement. Self Contained Vehicles only

HEMA 17 G11   18 41 49 S   146 15 52 E

30 Frances Creek
Rest Area 11 km S of Ingham or 98 km N of Townsville

HEMA 17 G11   18 44 52 S   146 08 14 E

31 Jourama Falls ☎ 13 74 68
Paluma Range National Park
Camp Area 29 km S of Ingham. Turn W off Bruce Hwy 24 km S of Ingham or 85 km N of Townsville for 5 km. 3 km dirt road. Cold showers. Bookings required

HEMA 17 G11   18 51 20 S   146 07 35 E

32 Big Crystal Creek Camping Area ☎ 13 74 68
Paluma Range National Park
Camp Area 43 km S of Ingham. Turn W off Bruce Hwy 38 km S of Ingham onto Barrett Rd, then R into Spiegelhauer Rd. 5 km to camping area. Not suitable for large motorhomes, caravans. Bookings required

HEMA 17 H11   18 58 47 S   146 15 25 E

33 Bushy Parker Park
Rest Area at Rollingstone. Turn E off Bruce Hwy just N of Rollingstone, across railway line. Cold showers

HEMA 17 H11   19 02 46 S   146 23 37 E

Notes...

QUEENSLAND

34 Balgal Beach
Rest Area 6 km E of Rollingstone. Turn E off Bruce Hwy 1 km S of Rollingstone. 5 km E of Hwy. N end of town near boat ramp. Limited sites
HEMA 17 H12   19 00 37 S   146 24 18 E

35 Toomulla Beach
Rest Area 68 km S of Ingham or 45 km N of Townsville. Turn E off Bruce Hwy 43 km N of Townsville or 66 km S of Ingham. S end of town Herald St
HEMA 17 H12   19 05 00 S   146 28 34 E

36 Bluewater Park
Rest Area at Bluewater. 80 km S of Ingham or 29 km N of Townsville. Beside creek. Outside cold shower
HEMA 17 H12   19 10 35 S   146 33 05 E

37 Saunders Park
Rest Area at Saunders Beach. Turn E off Bruce Hwy 87 km S of Ingham or 24 km N of Townsville, 1 km N of Yabulu. N side of town. 7 km off Bruce Hwy. No tents
HEMA 17 H12   19 09 14 S   146 36 15 E

38 Alligator Creek Campground   ☎ 13 74 68
Bowling Green Bay National Park
Camp Area 25 km SE of Townsville. Turn W off Bruce Hwy 25 km SE of Townsville or 63 km NW of Ayr. Gate locked 1830 - 0630 hrs. Small vehicles only. Online booking
HEMA 14 A5   19 26 02 S   146 56 46 E

39 Barramundi (Morris) Creek
Parking Area 15 km N of Giru. Via Morris Creek Rd. Self Contained Vehicles only
HEMA 14 A5   19 28 47 S   147 09 05 E

40 Cromarty Boat Ramp
Parking Area 10 km N of Giru. Via Cromarty Creek Rd. Self Contained Vehicles only
HEMA 14 A5   19 28 10 S   147 05 53 E

41 Hotel Brandon Caravan Park   ☎ (07) 4782 5255
Caravan Park at Brandon. 54 Drysdale St
HEMA 14 A6   19 33 14 S   147 21 13 E

42 Plantation Creek Boat Ramp
Camp Spot 12.5 km NE of Ayr. Take Airdmillan Rd to Old Wharf Rd. 5.5 km dirt road
HEMA 14 A6   19 32 05 S   147 30 46 E

43 Burdekin Farm Stay   ☎ 0418 727 425
Camp Area 16 km SW of Ayr. Turn off Hwy 79 km S of Townsville or 8 km N of Ayr onto the airport road (Sandy Corner driver reviver). Follow past airport to T junction, turn L onto Waterview Rd. Follow for 3 km to campground sign. Must call before arrival. Self Contained Vehicles only
HEMA 14 A6   19 37 36 S   147 18 51 E

44 Red Lilly Rural Stopover   ☎ 0428 826 846
Camp Spot at Mt Kelly, 22 km SW of Ayr. 450 Barrett Rd. Turn off Hwy at airport signs, travel past airport to Waterview Rd, Barrett Rd. Self Contained Vehicles only. Donation for upkeep of wetlands
HEMA 14 A5   19 38 11 S   147 18 16 E

45 Home Hill Comfort Stop
Rest Area at Home Hill Comfort Stop. Adjacent to old railway station just W of main street. No tents
HEMA 14 A6   19 39 54 S   147 24 50 E

46 Home Hill Old Showgrounds
Camp Area at Home Hill. Georgees Rd. Self Contained Vehicles only
HEMA 14 A6   19 40 11 S   147 24 58 E

47 Funny Dunny Park
Camp Area 5 km S of Inkerman. Signposted Wunjunga. 15 km dirt road. Maximum stay 4 days in a 2 week period. Donation for use
HEMA 14 A6   19 45 08 S   147 35 45 E

48 Wallace Landing
Parking Area 15 km W of Inkerman. Via Wallace & Peak Rd. Self Contained Vehicles only
HEMA 14 A6   19 44 10 S   147 33 20 E

49 Guthalungra Rest Area
Rest Area at Guthalungra. Shower at service station for a fee
HEMA 14 B6   19 55 24 S   147 50 35 E

50 Bowen River Hotel   ☎ (07) 4785 3388
Camp Area 32 km W of Collinsville, via Strathmore
HEMA 14 C6   20 32 01 S   147 33 21 E

QUEENSLAND

51 Collinsville Showgrounds
☎ (07) 4785 5795
Camp Area at Collinsville. Entry from Railway Rd next to Showgrounds. Self Contained Vehicles only
HEMA 14 C6   20 33 24 S   147 50 57 E

52 Glen Erin Farm Stay
☎ (07) 4786 4899
Camp Area 20 km S of Bowen. Turn W off Bruce Hwy at Mookara Rd for 4 km. Signposted
HEMA 14 B7   20 07 06 S   148 13 21 E

53 Camp Kanga
☎ (07) 4947 2600
Camp Area 24 km W of Proserpine, via Crystal Brook Rd. Reservations essential
HEMA 14 B7   20 21 37 S   148 23 53 E

54 Bloomsbury BP
☎ (07) 4947 5739
Parking Area at Bloomsbury. At rear of service station, fee for shower
HEMA 14 C7   20 42 19 S   148 35 45 E

55 Jaxut Camping Area
Cathu State Forest
☎ (07) 4944 7800
Camp Area 30 km NW of Calen. Turn W off Bruce Hwy 13 km S of Bloomsbury or 18 km N of Calen onto Cathu-O'Connell River Rd. 12 km dirt road, steep in places, not suitable for caravans
HEMA 14 C7   20 47 32 S   148 32 56 E

56 St Helens Gardens Tourist Park
☎ (07) 4958 8152
Caravan Park at Calen. Bruce Hwy. 1 km S of PO
HEMA 15 C8   20 54 15 S   148 46 48 E

57 St Helens Camping Reserve
☎ 1300 622 529
Camp Area 15 km NE of Calen. 1.5 km S of St Helens Beach, via Murrays Rd. Beachfront. Attendant collects fees daily
HEMA 15 C8   20 50 28 S   148 50 38 E

58 Wintermoon Way Camping Oasis
☎ (07) 4958 8390
Camp Area 12 km W of Calen. Via Calen - Mount Charlton Rd
HEMA 15 D8   20 57 47 S   148 41 47 E

59 Boulder Creek
Rest Area 18 km SW of Calen, via Camerons Pocket. 1.5 km dirt road
HEMA 15 D8   21 00 31 S   148 43 10 E

60 Jolimont Caravan Park
☎ (07) 4954 0170
Caravan Park 16 km S of Calen or 6 km N of Kuttabul. Bruce Hwy
HEMA 15 D8   21 00 25 S   148 52 27 E

61 Seaforth Camping Reserve
☎ 0427 373 358
Camp Area at Seaforth. On the Esplanade. Maximum stay 6 weeks
HEMA 15 D8   20 53 58 S   148 57 57 E

62 Ball Bay Camping Reserve
☎ 1300 622 529
Camp Area at Ball Bay. 9 km E of Seaforth. Turn N 3 km W of Seaforth onto Cape Hillsborough Rd & Ball Bay Rd. N end of Ward Esplanade. Outside showers
HEMA 15 D8   20 54 11 S   148 59 44 E

63 Smalleys Beach
Cape Hillsborough National Park
☎ 13 74 68
Camp Area 12 km E of Seaforth. Via Cape Hillsborough Rd & Smalleys Beach Rd. Limited sites for larger vehicles. 1.5 km dirt road. Prebook online
HEMA 15 D8   20 54 51 S   149 01 00 E

64 Leap Hotel
☎ (07) 4954 0993
Parking Area at Hotel. 1954 Bruce Hwy, The Leap. Hotel patronage requested
HEMA 15 D8   21 04 10 S   149 00 57 E

65 The Pinnacle Hotel
☎ (07) 4958 5207
Parking Area at Pinnacle. Check in with publican
HEMA 15 D8   21 08 46 S   148 42 51 E

66 Finch Hatton Showgrounds
☎ (07) 4958 3612
Camp Area at Finch Hatton. W of Mackay. Closed during show week in early June
HEMA 14 D7   21 08 22 S   148 37 51 E

Notes...

QUEENSLAND

67 Platypus Bushcamp ☎ (07) 4958 3204
Camp Area at Finch Hatton Gorge. W of Mackay
HEMA 14 D7   21 04 53 S   148 38 16 E

68 Crediton Hall Campground ☎ 13 74 68
Crediton State Forest
Camp Area 15 km S Eungella. Via Eungella Dam Rd, Crediton Loop Rd, continue 6.7 km to the campground. Steep access road. Not suitable for caravans
HEMA 14 D7   21 12 21 S   148 32 46 E

69 Broken River Bush Camp ☎ 13 74 68
Eungella National Park
Camping Area at Broken River. Via Eungella Dam Rd. 5 km from Eungella, turn L before crossing bridge. Permit required
HEMA 14 D7   21 10 06 S   148 30 16 E

70 The Diggings Camping Area ☎ 13 74 68
Crediton State Forest
Camp Area 9.5 km W of Broken River off the Eungella Dam Rd. 4WD access only, off road campertrailers only. Permit required
HEMA 14 D7   21 10 25 S   148 28 47 E

71 Eungella Dam ☎ 13 15 89
Camp Area 28 km SW of Eungella, via Broken River Rd. 20 km dirt road. Cold showers. 28 day maximum stay (Big Rig access from Peak Downs Hwy via Turrawulla Rd, dry weather access only). Pay fees at self-registration station
HEMA 14 D7   21 09 01 S   148 23 03 E

72 Kinchant Waters Leisure Resort ☎ (07) 4954 1453
Caravan Park 15 km NW of Eton, via North Eton & Kinchant Dam Rd
HEMA 15 D8   21 13 14 S   148 53 34 E

73 General Gordon Hotel ☎ (07) 4959 7324
Camp Area at Homebush, 8 km W of Rosella or 13 km E of Eton
HEMA 15 D8   21 15 45 S   149 04 53 E

74 Moana Caravan Park ☎ (07) 4956 4165
Caravan Park at Alligator Creek via MacKay. 24 km S of Mackay
HEMA 15 D8   21 19 15 S   149 11 30 E

75 The Retreat Hotel ☎ (07) 4954 1239
Camp Area 35 km SW of Eton or 28 km NE of Nebo via Peak Downs Hwy
HEMA 15 D8   21 28 42 S   148 48 40 E

76 The Retreat Hotel Rest Area
Rest Area 35 km SW of Eton or 28 km NE of Nebo. Adjacent to Hotel
HEMA 15 D8   21 28 48 S   148 48 40 E

77 Moonlight Dam ☎ 13 74 68
Homevale National Park
Camp Area 40 km NW of Nebo. Travel 17 km on Suttor Development Rd, turn N into Turrawulla Rd, signposted after passing Homevale-Mount Britton turnoff. 4WD vehicles only. Must pre-book
HEMA 14 D7   21 24 34 S   148 30 13 E

78 Lake Elphinstone ☎ (07) 4944 5888
Camp Spot 136 km SW of Mackay. Turn W off Peak Downs Hwy 86 km SW of Mackay to Elphinstone. 4 km on Suttor Development Rd. Cold shower
HEMA 14 D7   21 32 18 S   148 14 08 E

79 Nebo Rest Area
Rest Area at Nebo. Cnr Bowen St & Peak Downs Hwy.
HEMA 14 E7   21 40 58 S   148 41 34 E

80 Nebo Showground ☎ 1300 47 22 27
Camp Area Bowen St. Must register & pay at council office in Reynolds St before camping
HEMA 14 E7   21 41 02 S   148 41 19 E

81 Isaac River Rest Area
Rest Area 108 km NE of Clermont. 7 km NE of Moranbah turnoff
HEMA 14 E7   22 02 57 S   148 07 53 E

82 Funnel Creek
Camp Spot 92 km SW of MacKay via Sarina Range or 32 km E of Nebo via Marlborough Sarina Rd. Sites S side of bridge
HEMA 15 E8   21 46 42 S   148 55 59 E

83 Rocky Dam Creek
Camp Spot 10 km NE of Koumala. Turn E into Landings Rd just N of Koumala. 6 km dirt road. No entry via N & S Inneston Rds
HEMA 15 E8   21 32 57 S   149 18 00 E

84 Koumala Caravan Park ☎ (07) 4950 3657
Caravan Park at Koumala, 20 km S of Sarina. Mumby St
HEMA 15 E8   21 36 35 S   149 14 49 E

85 Ilbilbie Caltex ☎ (07) 4950 3944
Parking Area at Ilbilbie, at the back of the roadhouse
HEMA 15 E8   21 42 17 S   149 21 26 E

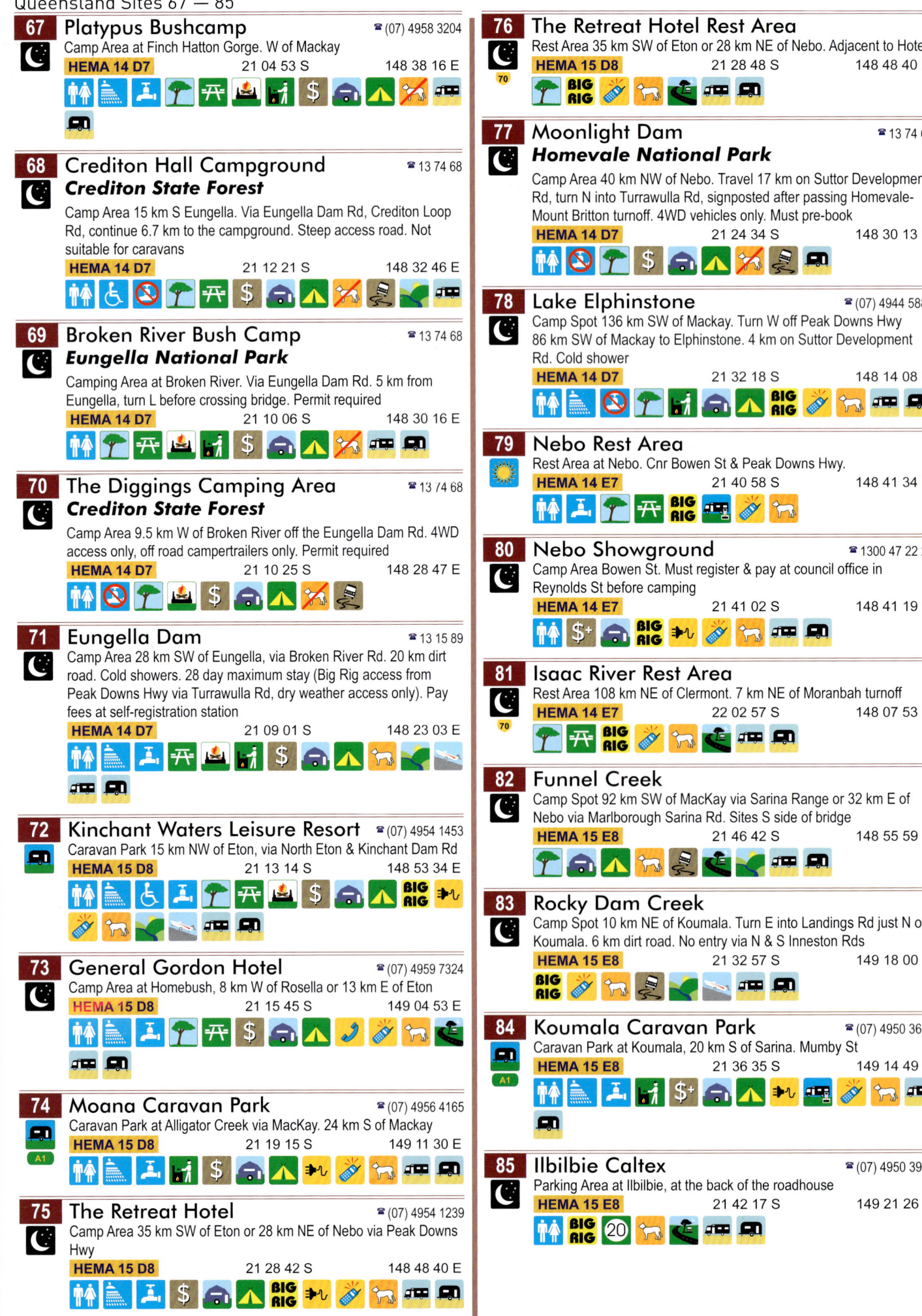

86 Notch Point Road
Camp Spot 11 km E of Ilbilbie via Greenhill Rd & Notch Point Rd. 1 km dirt road. Limited camp spots alongside Marion Creek
HEMA 15 E9   21 43 24 S   149 26 33 E

87 Yarrawonga Park Reserve
Camp Area 14 km E of Ilbilbie. Turn E onto Greenhill Rd, R onto Notch Point Rd, 9 km to gate, then 3 km of narrow rough sandy track. 4WD only
HEMA 15 E9   21 44 28 S   149 28 28 E

✓ 88 Carmila Beach   ☎ 1300 472 227
Camp Area 6 km E of Carmila. Camp site off dirt road for 1 km. Last 300m narrow, sandy track. Pay by phone or online via a smart phone
HEMA 15 E9   21 54 50 S   149 27 47 E

89 Flaggy Rock Cafe   ☎ 07 4950 2148
Parking Area at Flaggy Rock. Self Contained Vehicles only. Fee waived if cafe is patronised
HEMA 15 E9   21 58 13 S   149 26 09 E

90 Flaggy Rock Community Centre   ☎ 0477 545 618
Camp Area at Flaggy Rock, 7 km S of Carmila. 85 Flaggy Rock Rd. Self Contained Vehicles only. Caretaker on site
HEMA 15 E9   21 58 06 S   149 26 37 E

91 Brandy Bottle Camping & Recreation Reserve   ☎ 0423 877 288
Camp Area 17 km S of Carmila or 8 km N of Clairview Northern turnoff. 82943 Bruce Hwy. Limited number of sites, reservations essential. Fee includes golf. Signposted off Hwy
HEMA 15 E9   22 02 49 S   149 29 07 E

92 Clairview Rest Area
Rest Area at Clairview. N end of Colonial Dr, 3 km from town centre
HEMA 15 E9   22 06 17 S   149 31 36 E

93 St Lawrence Recreational Reserve   ☎ 1300 472 227
Camp Area 1 km W of St Lawrence. 5.5 km off Bruce Hwy. Pay by phone or online via a smart phone
HEMA 15 F9   22 21 04 S   149 31 11 E

Notes...

94 Waverley Creek Rest Area
Rest Area 8 km S of St Lawrence turnoff or 64 km N of Marlborough
HEMA 15 F9   22 26 19 S   149 28 30 E

95 Tooloombah Creek Roadhouse   ☎ (07) 4935 6214
Camp Spot at Roadhouse. 42 km S of St Lawrence turn off or 32 km N of Marlborough. Self Contained Vehicles only. Call in at reception before parking
HEMA 15 F9   22 41 18 S   149 37 41 E

96 Marlborough Hotel   ☎ (07) 4935 6103
Parking Area at Marlborough. Head over railway line, turn R into Milman St. Check in with publican on arrival
HEMA 15 G9   22 48 48 S   149 53 18 E

97 Marlborough Caltex   ☎ (07) 4935 6135
Parking Area at Marlborough. Fee for showers. Check in at counter prior to camping. Showers close at 2000 hrs
HEMA 15 G9   22 49 18 S   149 53 29 E

98 Lotus Creek Tourist Centre   ☎ (07) 4950 7135
Caravan Park Tourist Centre on Alternate Hwy 1. 130 km S of Sarina or 120 km N of Marlborough
HEMA 15 F8   22 20 53 S   149 06 09 E

99 Stanage Bay
Camp Area at Stanage Bay. 100 km dirt road. Main camping area at boat ramp. Gold coin donation
HEMA 15 F9   22 08 10 S   150 02 02 E

100 Yaamba Rest Area
Rest Area at Yaamba. Cnr Iris St & Yaamba Rd
HEMA 15 G10   23 08 06 S   150 22 07 E

101 Byfield Campstay   ☎ (07) 4935 1002
Camp Area at Byfield. 53 Castle Rock Rd. Travel 2 km N of Byfield, turn L into Castle Rock Rd, then first on the L. Call ahead wet season Feb-April
HEMA 15 G10   22 49 46 S   150 37 56 E

102 Upper Stony Campground   ☎ 13 74 68
Byfield State Forest
Camp Area 37 km N of Yeppoon. Turn W off Byfield Rd 27 km N of Yeppoon for 11 km of dirt road. 6 tonne load limit bridge. Bookings essential. 4WD vehicles only. Book online or at Byfield Store
HEMA 15 G10   22 53 31 S   150 37 05 E

103 Red Rock Campground ☎ 13 74 68
Byfield State Forest
Camp Area 33 km N of Yeppoon. Turn E off Byfield Rd 32 km N of Yeppoon. 1 km dirt road. Maximum stay 14 days. Book online or at Byfield Store
HEMA 15 G10   22 52 25 S   150 41 05 E

104 Water Park Creek Campground ☎ 13 74 68
Byfield State Forest
Camp Area 39 km N of Yeppoon. Turn E off Byfield Rd 36 km N of Yeppoon for 3 km. 1 km dirt road. Small Vehicles only. Bookings essential. Book online or at Byfield store
HEMA 15 G10   22 50 08 S   150 40 20 E

105 Fardooleys Bush Camp ☎ 0400 361 568
Camp Area 19 km N of Rockhampton via Belmont Rd. Neslein Rd, Glendale. Seasonal. Bookings essential
HEMA 15 G10   23 15 15 S   150 26 38 E

106 Kershaw Gardens
Parking Area at Rockhampton. High St opposite Bob Janes T-Mart. Self Contained Vehicles only
HEMA 15 H10   23 21 27 S   150 31 09 E

107 Bajool Country Hotel ☎ (07) 4934 6120
Parking Area at Bajool. 27 km S of Rockhampton, off Bruce Hwy. Self Contained Vehicles only
HEMA 15 H10   23 39 05 S   150 38 36 E

108 Calliope River Picnic Area
Rest Area 70 km N of Miriam Vale or 27 km S of Mount Larcom. 7 km N of Calliope turnoff. Turn W off Hwy onto Old Bruce Hwy beside Historical Village, follow road to river bank
HEMA 15 J11   23 57 40 S   151 09 09 E

109 Boyne River Rest Area
Rest Area 49 km SE of Mount Larcom or 49 km N of Miriam Vale. 1 km S of Benaraby. Beside river
HEMA 15 J11   24 00 39 S   151 20 26 E

Notes...

110 Futter Creek
Rest Area at Barmundu, 21 km S of Calliope on the Gladstone-Monto Rd
HEMA 15 J11   24 08 17 S   151 11 45 E

111 Boynedale Bush Camp
Camp Area at Boynedale, 31 km S of Calliope. 2 km E of Gladstone-Monto Rd, beside dam. Maximum stay 7 days. Small dogs only on leash
HEMA 15 J11   24 13 02 S   151 15 00 E

112 Discovery Centre Ubobo ☎ 07 4974 1240
Camp Area at Ubobo. McDonald St. Cash only
HEMA 15 J11   24 24 21 S   151 19 10 E

113 The Reef Caravan Park ☎ (07) 4974 7547
Caravan Park 5 km W of Agnes Water. Rocky Crossing Rd
HEMA 15 J12   24 14 50 S   151 51 39 E

114 Workmans Beach Camping Area ☎ (07) 4902 1515
Camp Area 1 km S of Agnes Water, via Springs Rd. Small vehicles only. Maximum stay 42 days. Cold showers
HEMA 15 J12   24 12 45 S   151 54 51 E

115 Corso's Lowmead Hotel ☎ (07) 4156 9138
Parking Area at Lowmead, behind hotel. Must register at the hotel before camping
HEMA 15 K12   24 31 46 S   151 45 14 E

116 Colosseum Creek Motel and Roadhouse ☎ (07) 4974 5244
Camp Area at Colosseum. 16 km S of Miriam Vale or 83 km N of Gin Gin
HEMA 15 K12   24 27 25 S   151 35 15 E

117 Granite Creek (Bernie Christensen) Rest Area
Rest Area 36 km S of Miriam Vale or 63 km N of Gin Gin
HEMA 15 K12   24 36 44 S   151 40 04 E

118 Rosedale Royal Hotel & Caravan Park ☎ (07) 4156 5322
Caravan Park at Rosedale. 55 km NW of Bundaberg
HEMA 15 K12   24 37 44 S   151 54 59 E

119 Norval Park Campground ☎ (07) 4153 8888
Camp Area 48 km N of Bundaberg. Via Bundaberg - Lowmead Rd. Entry via Norval Park Rd & Park Rd. Permit required before arrival, booking by phone or online via Bundaberg Tourism web site. Tent & camper trailers only
HEMA 15 K12   24 36 32 S   152 07 49 E

120 Avondale Homestead Tavern ☎ (07) 4156 1206
Camp Area at Avondale. Large camping area next to the hotel, please check in at the bar
HEMA 15 K12   24 45 48 S   152 09 12 E

121 Binnowee Bush Camp ☎ (07) 4157 8331
Camp Area 20 km W of Bundaberg. Take the Rosedale Rd for 16 km, turn W into Bucca Rd for 3 km. Signposted. Self Contained Vehicles only. Bookings essential
HEMA 13 A12   24 49 42 S   152 11 24 E

122 Gin Gin Rest Area
Rest Area 2 km N of Gin Gin
HEMA 13 A11   24 58 27 S   151 56 45 E

123 Gin Gin Showgrounds ☎ (07) 4157 3223
Camp Area at Gin Gin. N end of town off King St. Caretaker on site
HEMA 13 A11   24 59 16 S   151 57 07 E

124 Wolca Reserve ☎ 1300 696 272
Camp Area 6 km N of Mount Perry. Bania Rd, off Gin Gin-Mount Perry Rd. Permit required. Pay at council office or phone ahead
HEMA 13 A11   25 07 58 S   151 37 08 E

125 Mt Perry Caravan Park ☎ 07 4156 3850
Caravan Park at Mt Perry. 53 km W of Gin Gin
HEMA 13 A11   25 10 29 S   151 38 24 E

126 Mount Perry Showgrounds ☎ 1300 696 272
Camp Area at Mount Perry. Via Monto-Mount Perry Rd S end of town. Maximum stay 7 Days. Pay at council office or phone ahead
HEMA 13 A11   25 11 18 S   151 38 29 E

127 Sharon Nature Park
Rest Area 36 km E of Gin Gin or 15 km W of Bundaberg. 3 km W of Sharon
HEMA 13 A12   24 53 01 S   152 14 34 E

128 Bucca Hotel ☎ (07) 4157 8171
Parking Area 30 km W of Bundaberg. 5 North Bucca Rd
HEMA 13 A12   24 51 33 S   152 05 34 E

129 Hinkler Lions Park
Rest Area at Bundaberg. 4 km SW of PO. Opposite airport
HEMA 13 A12   24 53 49 S   152 18 51 E

130 Wallum Reserve
Rest Area 28 km SW of Bundaberg or 24 km N of Childers, on Isis Hwy
HEMA 13 A12   25 03 32 S   152 13 50 E

131 Booyal Roadhouse ☎ (07) 4126 0173
Parking Area at Booyal Roadhouse. Grassed area next to roadhouse. Self Contained Vehicles only
HEMA 13 B11   25 12 53 S   152 02 24 E

132 Booyal Crossing
Camp Spot 30 km N of Childers or 33 km S of Gin Gin. Turn S into Booyal Dallarnil Rd, then W into Causeway Rd
HEMA 13 B11   25 13 45 S   152 00 34 E

133 Paradise Dam ☎ (07) 4127 7278
Camp Area 35 km NE of Biggenden. Turn N off Isis Hwy into Gooroolba Biggenden Rd at Biggenden. Follow signs
HEMA 13 B11   25 21 17 S   151 55 10 E

QUEENSLAND

134 Apple Tree Creek Rest Area
Rest Area 7 km N of Childers or 49 km SE of Gin Gin
HEMA 13 B12   25 13 09 S   152 14 18 E

135 Childers Rest Area
Rest Area at Childers. Crescent St. Behind PO. Self Contained Vehicles only
HEMA 13 B12   25 14 06 S   152 16 44 E

136 Iron Ridge Park   ☎ (07) 4126 8410
Caravan Park at Redridge. 1472 Goodwood Rd 16 km NW of Redridge. Mobile 0437 264 478
HEMA 13 A12   25 10 06 S   152 22 29 E

137 Brierley Wines   ☎ (07) 4126 1297
Camp Area 7 km SE of Childers. 574 Rainbows Rd. Turn S into Taylors St in town, which becomes Rainbows Rd. Free to customers. Booking required & must be on site by 1500 hrs. Open Tue to Sun. Self Contained Vehicles only
HEMA 13 B12   25 17 15 S   152 17 23 E

138 Howard RV Stop
Parking Area at Howard. Steley St. Self Contained Vehicles only
HEMA 13 B12   25 19 04 S   152 33 47 E

139 Torbanlea Racecourse & Sports Complex
Camp Area at Torbanlea. Torbanlea - Pialba Rd
HEMA 13 B13   25 20 47 S   152 35 59 E

140 Hervey Bay RV Stop Info Centre   ☎ 1800 811 728
Parking Area at Hervey Bay. Cnr Urraween Rd & Hervey Bay Rd. Self Contained Vehicles only
HEMA 13 B13   25 17 59 S   152 48 34 E

141 Lenthall Dam   ☎ (07) 4129 4833
Camp Area 21 km SW of Howard. Turn W off Bruce Hwy 12 km S of Howard or 16 km N of Maryborough, for 2 km, then 7 km NW along rough dirt road. Cold showers. Limited spaces, pre-booking of sites required
HEMA 13 B12   25 24 14 S   152 32 00 E

142 Wongi Waterholes Camping Area   ☎ 13 74 68
Wongi State Forest Recreation Area
Camp Area 21 km SW of Howard. Turn W off Bruce Hwy 12 km S of Howard or 16 km N of Maryborough, for 9 km of dirt road. Cold showers. No camping at lake. Bookings necessary
HEMA 13 B12   25 26 15 S   152 32 37 E

143 Cheery Nomad RV Park & Farmstay   ☎ 0414 754 638
Camp Area 6 km N of Maryborough off Fazio Rd. 113 Lawson Rd
HEMA 13 B13   25 29 34 S   152 42 28 E

144 The Wharf   ☎ 0427 233 081
Parking Area at Maryborough. Wharf St next to Muddy Waters Cafe
HEMA 13 B13   25 32 22 S   152 42 25 E

145 Maryborough Showground & Equestrian Park   ☎ 1300 794 929
Camp Area at Maryborough off the Bruce Hwy. Camping closed during major events. Book & Pay online via their website 2 days before arrival
HEMA 13 B13   25 30 22 S   152 39 46 E

146 Alan & Jane Brown Car Park
Parking Area at Maryborough. Kent St. Self Contained Vehicles only
HEMA 13 B13   25 32 12 S   152 42 01 E

147 Petrie Park RV Camp & Rest Area
Rest Area 2 km NW of Tiaro. Van Doorn Rd, turn W over railway line 1 km N of PO, then immediately R for 200m, then L to E bank of Mary River. Self Contained Vehicles only. Limited space & level ground
HEMA 13 C13   25 42 52 S   152 34 37 E

148 Tiaro Memorial Park
Rest Area at Tiaro. Inman St, behind town park. Cold showers. Toilet 100m across park. Self Contained Vehicles only
HEMA 13 C13   25 43 43 S   152 35 02 E

149 Bauple RV Stop
Camp Spot at Bauple Village. Bauple Dr, 100m from Museum. Self Contained Vehicles only
HEMA 13 C13   25 48 44 S   152 37 08 E

150 Rosendale Park RV Stop
Rest Area at Bauple. Bauple Dr. 500m E of Bruce Hwy. Self Contained Vehicles only
HEMA 13 C13   25 50 23 S   152 35 43 E

Notes...

151 Gunalda Rest Area
Rest Area 2 km N of Gunalda turnoff
HEMA 13 C13 25 59 10 S 152 34 13 E

152 Dickabram Bridge Rest Area
Rest Area at Miva. Miva Rd, next to bridge. Self Contained Vehicles only. Limited space
HEMA 13 C12 25 57 16 S 152 29 40 E

153 Prince Alfred Hotel (The Gundy) ☎ (07) 4129 3182
Camp Area at Gundiah. Check in at hotel bar
HEMA 13 C12 25 49 58 S 152 32 31 E

154 Ross Creek Store Rest Area
Rest Area at Goomboorian. 25 km NE of Gympie or 32 km SW of Tin Can Bay
HEMA 13 D13 26 05 26 S 152 46 02 E

155 Standown Caravan Park ☎ (07) 5486 5144
Caravan Park at Kia Ora. 91 Radtke Rd
HEMA 13 D13 26 02 08 S 152 47 32 E

156 Log Dump Campground ☎ (07) 4121 1800
Tuan State Forest
Camp Area 44 km SE of Maryborough. S on Cooloola Coast Rd for 38 km, turn E into Tinnanbar Rd for 6 km. Small vehicles only. Dirt road. Must be pre-booked
HEMA 13 C13 25 48 38 S 152 55 26 E

157 Hedleys Campground ☎ (07) 4121 1800
Tuan State Forest
Camp Area 44 km SE of Maryborough. S on Cooloola Coast Rd for 38 km, turn E into Tinnanbar Rd for 9 km. Small vehicles only. Dirt road. Beware that the camp area can only be accessed via private property, access fee applies payable to property owner
HEMA 13 C13 25 47 56 S 152 56 51 E

158 Inskip Point Campground ☎ 13 74 68
Camp Area 12 km N of Rainbow Beach. Permit required, must be obtained prior to arrival
HEMA 13 C13 25 49 00 S 153 04 15 E

159 Chatsworth Park
Rest Area 59 km S of Tiaro or 6 km N of Gympie. Self Contained Vehicles Only
HEMA 13 D13 26 08 58 S 152 37 37 E

160 Glastonbury Creek Campground ☎ 13 74 68
Brooyar State Forest
Camp Area 26 km W of Gympie. Turn N at Glastonbury 16 km W of Gympie for 10 km. 6 km dirt road. Must pre book
HEMA 13 D12 26 09 18 S 152 33 05 E

161 Marg McIntosh Park
Rest Area at Upper Widgee, 26 km W of Gympie. 2 km N of Widgee Primary School
HEMA 13 D12 26 11 30 S 152 25 55 E

162 Six Mile Creek Rest Area
Rest Area 6 km S of Gympie or 4 km N of Kybong
HEMA 13 D13 26 13 54 S 152 41 49 E

163 Cedar Grove Campground ☎ 13 74 68
Amamoor State Forest
Camp Area 12 km W of Amamoor, via Amamoor Creek Rd. 5 km dirt road. Must pre-book
HEMA 13 D12 26 21 58 S 152 35 13 E

164 Amamoor Creek Campground ☎ 13 74 68
Amamoor State Forest
Camp Area 16 km W of Amamoor, via Amamoor Creek Rd. 5 km dirt road
HEMA 13 D12 26 21 26 S 152 33 24 E

165 Kandanga RV Stop ☎ (07) 5488 4605
Parking Area at Kandanga. Self Contained Vehicles only. Toilets across road during opening hours, gold coin donation for upkeep appreciated. Showers at swimming pool for a fee
HEMA 8 A7 26 23 13 S 152 40 37 E

166 Kandanga Country Club ☎ 0438 843 195
Parking Area at Kandanga. Bowling Club Rd, enter off the Kandanga Amamoor Rd
HEMA 8 A7 26 23 11 S 152 40 34 E

167 Mary Valley Koolewong Par 3 Golf Course ☎ (07) 5484 5999
Camp Spot 5 km N of Imbil. Head N on Kandanga Imbil Rd for 4.5 km, turn E into Barsby Rd, 800m to entrance on L. Self Contained Vehicles only. Limited sites, phone ahead
HEMA 8 A7 26 25 38 S 152 41 12 E

QUEENSLAND

168 Carters Ridge RV Stop
Parking Area at Carters Ridge. Cnr Jubilee & Poulsen Rd next to RFS shed on grassed area. Store next door. Toilet & BBQ across the road in Mary Fereday Park. Self Contained Vehicles only. Do not park in Mary Fereday Park
HEMA 8 A7   26 27 04 S   152 45 52 E

169 Island Reach Camping Resort ☎ 0438 386 380
Camp Area at Imbil. Yabba Creek Rd. Cash only
HEMA 8 A7   26 27 32 S   152 40 54 E

170 Borumba Campground ☎ (07) 5488 6662
Camp Area at Borumba Dam. 12 km W of Imbil, via Yabba Creek Rd
HEMA 8 B6   26 30 06 S   152 35 17 E

171 Matilda Roadhouse
Parking Area 10 km S of Gympie or 40 km N of Cooroy. Behind roadhouse. Some noise from trucks. Fee for shower payable at roadhouse
HEMA 13 D13   26 18 19 S   152 43 13 E

172 Kin Kin Oval
Camp Area at Kin Kin. Entry at the roundabout Main St. Payment & keys at pub
HEMA 13 D13   26 15 46 S   152 52 30 E

173 Elanda Point Canoe Company ☎ (07) 5485 3165
Camp Area 6 km N of Boreen Point. 1.5 km dirt road, entry at end of road
HEMA 13 D13   26 15 15 S   152 59 57 E

174 Cobb & Co Nine Mile Campgrounds ☎ (07) 5483 5065
Camp Area 10 km S of Gympie or 40 km N of Cooroy. Turn E onto Tandur Rd at Matilda Roadhouse, travel 6 km, then turn S onto Old Noosa Rd for 300m. GPS at gate. Pets on application call ahead to check
HEMA 13 D13   26 17 08 S   152 45 55 E

175 Pomona Showgrounds ☎ (07) 5485 1477
Camp Area at Pomona. Exhibition St. Maximum stay 6 weeks
HEMA 9 A8   26 21 36 S   152 51 28 E

176 Gheerulla Campground ☎ 13 74 68
Mapleton Forest Reserve
Camp Area 10 km E of Kenilworth. Turn SE 23 km W of Eumundi or 8 km E of Kenilworth for 2 km. Very small area. Rough dirt road
HEMA 8 C7   26 34 12 S   152 47 29 E

177 Kenilworth Show & Recreation Grounds ☎ 0438 849 947
Camp Area at Kenilworth. S side of town. Elizabeth St
HEMA 8 C7   26 35 56 S   152 43 34 E

178 Little Yabba Picnic Area
Picnic Area 6 km SW of Kenilworth on Kenilworth - Maleny Rd. Small vehicles only
HEMA 8 C7   26 37 27 S   152 41 25 E

179 Charlie Moreland Campground ☎ 13 74 68
Imbil State Forest
Camp Area 12 km SW of Kenilworth. Turn W off Kenilworth-Maleny Rd 7 km S of Kenilworth. 5 km dirt road
HEMA 8 C6   26 36 59 S   152 39 02 E

180 Booloumba Creek No.4 Campground ☎ 13 74 68
Conondale National Park
Camp Area 14 km SW of Kenilworth. Turn W off Kenilworth-Maleny Rd 7 km S of Kenilworth. 7 km dirt road. High clearance 4WD recommended. Alternative 2WD dry-weather access is via Sundy Creek Rd, Funnels Hut Rd & Booloumba Creek Rd. Not suitable for large vehicles
HEMA 8 C6   26 38 46 S   152 38 52 E

181 Crystal Waters Eco Caravan Park ☎ (07) 5494 4550
Caravan Park at Conondale. 65 Kilcoy Lane, via Aherns Rd off Maleny-Kenilworth Rd
HEMA 8 D7   26 46 54 S   152 43 00 E

182 Maleny Showgrounds ☎ (07) 5494 2008
Camp Area at Maleny. Turn S 1 km W of PO onto Myrtle St for 800m. Pay at Secretary's Office next to Pavillion. Contact prior as showground closed to camping during some events
HEMA 9 D8   26 45 47 S   152 50 44 E

183 Camp Cooroora ☎ (07) 5442 5285
Camp Area 10 km NE of Cooroy. Take the Noosa-Cooroy Rd towards Noosa turn L into Sivyers Rd, turn R into Gumboil Rd, following signs to camp. Bookings essential
HEMA 9 A9   26 22 51 S   152 56 14 E

184 Cooroy RV Stop ☎ (07) 5485 3244
Camp Spot at Cooroy. 17 Mary River Rd, enter at driveway between Car Club & Horse & Pony Club. Self Contained Vehicles only. Must book & pay online, or caretaker will collect
HEMA 9 A8   26 24 49 S   152 54 25 E

185 Cooroys No Worries Caravan Parking ☎ 0427 006 018
Parking Area at Cooroy. 154 Holts Rd. Take Cooroy exit 230B off M1, follow ramp for 200m. Turn R into Mayall St under Hwy & L at Holts Rd. 1.5 km. Entry signposted RH side. Self Contained Vehicles only
HEMA 9 A8   26 26 31 S   152 55 08 E

186 Eumundi Showgrounds ☎ (07) 5442 7224
Camp Area at Eumundi. 1.3 km N of Eumundi on Black Stump Rd. Bookings essential as gates are locked
HEMA 9 B9   26 28 13 S   152 56 34 E

187 Eumundi RV Stop Over ☎ 0412 566 671
Parking Area at Eumundi. Cnr Albert St & Napier St. Fees collected
HEMA 9 B9   26 28 34 S   152 57 13 E

188 Browns Creek Rest Area
Rest Area 2 km N of Yandina. On Old Bruce Hwy. Limited space
HEMA 9 B9   26 32 19 S   152 57 21 E

189 Dunethin Rock Scout Camp ☎ (07) 5446 6246
Camp Area 7 km SE of Yandina or 6 km NW of Bli Bli on the Yandina - Bli Bli Rd. 1 km gravel road from the Yandina entry. Road narrow & steep. Bookings essential
HEMA 9 C9   26 34 42 S   153 00 39 E

190 Beerwah Sportsground ☎ (07) 5494 0513
Camp Area at Beerwah. Entry is via Simpson St off the roundabout. Contact caretaker on arrival
HEMA 9 E9   26 51 50 S   152 57 21 E

191 Coochin Creek Campground ☎ 13 74 68
Beerburrum State Forest
Camp Area 30 km NE of Caboolture. Exit Bruce Hwy at Roys Rd / Bells Creek Rds interchange. 400 metres along Bells Creek Rd turn S into Coochin Rd. Must pre book
HEMA 9 E10   26 52 52 S   153 02 46 E

Notes...

192 Glasshouse Mountains Camping Ground ☎ (07) 5496 9588
Camp Area 4.5 km W of Glasshouse Mountain PO. 2001 Old Gympie Rd, via Coonowrin Rd
HEMA 9 F9   26 54 50 S   152 55 17 E

193 Caboolture Showgrounds ☎ (07) 5495 2030
Camp Area at Caboolture. Beerburrum Rd. 4 km N of Town Centre. Gate 2. Check in with caretaker
HEMA 9 G9   27 04 04 S   152 56 55 E

194 Watson Park Convention Centre ☎ (07) 3204 6544
Seventh Day Adventist Church
Caravan Park at Dakabin. 337 Old Gympie Rd, check in with caretaker 2pm to 5pm only. No alcohol, drugs or tobacco permitted
HEMA 5 B8   27 13 13 S   152 59 21 E

195 Dayboro Showgrounds ☎ (07) 3425 1156
Camp Area at Dayboro. Mt Mee Rd
HEMA 4 A4   27 11 25 S   152 49 25 E

196 Wyllie Park Rest Area
Rest Area 1 km S of Petrie. 755 Gympie Rd, beside North Pine River. Self Contained Vehicles only
HEMA 5 D8   27 16 22 S   152 58 49 E

197 Redcliffe Showgrounds ☎ (07) 3205 0555
Camp Area at Redcliffe. Scarborough Rd. Motorhome must be 30ft or over
HEMA 5 B12   27 13 30 S   153 06 22 E

198 Pine Rivers Showground ☎ 0459 023 346
Camp Area at Lawnton, Gympie Rd. Check in required with caretaker. Closed to campers in August for Show. Maximum stay 21 days. Deposit for key required
HEMA 5 D8   27 17 07 S   152 59 13 E

199 Baden Powell Park Scout Campsite ☎ (07) 3289 2599
Camp Area at Samford. Cash Ave. Booking essential
HEMA 4 G4   27 22 33 S   152 53 25 E

200 Samford Showground ☎ (07) 3289 7057
Camp Area 7 km W of Samford, off Mt Glorious Rd & Showgrounds Dr. Gates usually locked. Contact caretaker. Closed during July for show
HEMA 4 G6   27 22 14 S   152 49 29 E

Cairns to Cloncurry

Kennedy Highway, Gulf and Burke Developmental Roads

201 James Earl Lookout

Rest Area 14.5 km S of Lakeland or 100 km N of Mt Carbine. Limited sites

HEMA 17 C10 15 58 29 S 144 49 44 E

202 Palmer River Roadhouse

☎ (07) 4060 2020

Camp Area at Roadhouse. 31 km S of Lakeland or 113 km N of Mount Molloy. Limited generator power

HEMA 17 C9 16 06 25 S 144 46 37 E

BIG RIG

203 North Palmer River Camping Area

☎ 13 74 68

Camp Area W of Palmer River Roadhouse. If travelling from the north, follow the Old Maytown-Laura Rd until you cross the North Palmer River, then follow the tracks to the right until you reach the signposted turn-off for the camping area. 4WD & off road vehicles only. Pre book E-Permit only

HEMA 17 C9 16 01 01 S 144 17 00 E

204 Mt Carbine Caravan Park

☎ (07) 4094 3160

81

Caravan Park at Mt Carbine. Peninsula Hwy. 300m SE of roadhouse. No cats

HEMA 18 B1 16 31 42 S 145 08 21 E

BIG RIG

205 Bustard Downs

☎ (07) 4094 3094

Camp Area 22 km N of Mount Molloy or 10 km S of Mount Carbine. Turn E into East Mary Rd 21 km N of Mount Molloy. Signposted on East Mary Rd

HEMA 18 B1 16 34 31 S 145 11 31 E

BIG RIG

206 Rifle Creek Rest Area

Rest Area 1 km N of Mt Molloy, 33 km S of Mossman or 41 km N of Mareeba. Cold showers. Donation requested

HEMA 18 C2 16 39 58 S 145 19 42 E

BIG RIG 48

207 Sheoak Ridge

☎ (07) 4092 2003

Camp Area 13 km E of Mount Molloy. Bush Camping must be self sufficient. Sites must be prebooked. Donation for upkeep of sites. Bird watching

HEMA 18 C2 16 38 26 S 145 24 22 E

208 Tableland Caravan Park

☎ (07) 4094 1145

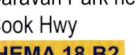

Caravan Park near Julatten. 1045 Rex Hwy. 10.5 km from the Captain Cook Hwy

HEMA 18 B2 16 32 44 S 145 22 59 E

209 Kerribee Park Camping Grounds

☎ (07) 4092 1654

Camp Area 3 km W of Mareeba, 614 Dimbulah Rd

HEMA 18 E2 16 59 34 S 145 23 43 E

BIG RIG

210 Dimbulah Caravan Park

☎ (07) 4093 5242

27

Caravan Park at Dimbulah. Burke Developmental Rd

HEMA 18 F1 17 09 05 S 145 06 20 E

BIG RIG

211 Eureka Creek

Camp Spot 9 km W of Dimbulah. Burke Developmental Rd

HEMA 17 E10 17 11 12 S 145 02 29 E

BIG RIG 20

212 Emu Creek Outback Holiday Station

☎ (07) 4094 8313

Camp Area at Emu Creek Station. 30 km W of Dimbulah on Burke Developmental Rd. Turn N 23 km W of Dimbulah, check in at house. 7 km to station. Dirt road

HEMA 17 E10 17 17 14 S 144 58 34 E

213 Tamarind Gardens Caravan Park

☎ (07) 4094 8201

Caravan Park at Almaden. Schools Rd

HEMA 17 E9 17 20 15 S 144 40 41 E

BIG RIG

214 Chillagoe Rodeo Grounds

☎ (07) 4094 7119

Camp Area at Chillagoe. From Queen St turn W onto Frew St, entrance 700m on R. Pay fees at the Post Office Hotel in Queen St after 10am

HEMA 17 E9 17 09 29 S 144 30 58 E

BIG RIG

215 Chillagoe Observatory & Eco Lodge

☎ (07) 4094 7155

Caravan Park at Chillagoe. 1 Hospital Ave

HEMA 17 E9 17 08 55 S 144 31 39 E

BIG RIG

216 Chillagoe Tourist Village

☎ (07) 4094 7177

Caravan Park at Chillagoe. 21 - 23 Queen St

HEMA 17 E9 17 09 20 S 144 31 28 E

217 Walsh River
Camp Spot 32 km W of Chillagoe on the Burke Developmental Rd
HEMA 17 E9   16 59 24 S   144 17 58 E

218 Walsh River West
Camp Spot 120 km W of Chillagoe or 450 km E of Karumba on the Burke Developmental Rd
HEMA 17 D8   16 32 43 S   143 46 58 E

219 Granite Gorge Nature Park   ☎ (07) 4093 2259
Camp Area 14 km SW of Mareeba via Rankin St & Chewko Rd. Riverside camping. Fee includes entry to 3 gorge walks
HEMA 18 E2   17 02 31 S   145 21 06 E

220 Mareeba Bush Stays   ☎ 0400 978 331
Camp Area 8.2 km SW of Mareeba. From Chewko Rd, turn W for check in at signposted house 16 Paglietta Rd. Maximum stay 5 days. Self Contained Vehicles only
HEMA 18 E2   17 03 27 S   145 22 28 E

221 Ringers Rest   ☎ 0447 136 865
Camp Area 7 km from PO SE of Mareeba, take Kennedy Hwy E turn S into Tinaroo Creek Rd then turn S into Fichera Rd. Camp entry via 2nd gate. Self Contained Vehicles only. Alt phone number 0421 253 259 ring to book
HEMA 18 E3   17 01 55 S   145 27 15 E

222 The Billabong
Camp Area at Kuranda. 186 Mt Haren Rd
HEMA 18 D4   16 50 34 S   145 36 18 E

223 Walkamin Central Van Park   ☎ (07) 4093 3561
Caravan Park at Walkamin. 15 km S of Mareeba or 18 km N of Atherton. S side of town
HEMA 18 E3   17 07 56 S   145 25 41 E

✓224 Rocky Creek Memorial Park & Camping Reserve
Rest Area 23 km S of Mareeba or 12 km N of Atherton. Donation box at toilet block. Self Contained Vehicles only
HEMA 18 F3   17 10 54 S   145 27 19 E

225 Kairi Lions Park
Parking Area at Kairi. Irvine St, opposite hotel. Self Contained Vehicles only. Donation at amenities block
HEMA 18 F3   17 12 57 S   145 32 34 E

226 Platypus Campground   ☎ 13 74 68
Danbulla State Forest
Camp Area 6 km NE of Tinaroo off Danbulla Forest Dr. 3 km dirt road. Small sites not suitable for caravans. Must be prebooked. Lakefront
HEMA 18 F3   17 09 36 S   145 33 38 E

✓227 Downfall Creek Campground   ☎ 13 74 68
Danbulla State Forest
Camp Area 8 km NE of Tinaroo off Danbulla Forest Dr. 5 km dirt road. Must be prebooked. Lakefront
HEMA 18 F4   17 08 52 S   145 35 18 E

✓228 Kauri Creek Campground   ☎ 13 74 68
Danbulla State Forest
Camp Area 10 km NE of Tinaroo off Danbulla Forest Dr. 7 km dirt road. Must be prebooked. Lakefront
HEMA 18 F4   17 08 18 S   145 35 53 E

229 School Point Campground   ☎ 13 74 68
Danbulla State Forest
Camp Area 18 km NE of Tinaroo off Danbulla Forest Dr. 13 km dirt road. Lakefront. Small sites not suitable for caravans. Must be prebooked
HEMA 18 F4   17 08 54 S   145 36 39 E

230 Fong-On Bay Campground   ☎ 13 74 68
Danbulla State Forest
Camp Area 22 km E of Tinaroo off Danbulla Forest Dr. 19 km dirt road. Lakefront. Must be prebooked
HEMA 18 F4   17 09 13 S   145 35 55 E

231 Genazzano Campground   ☎ 0429 351 566
Camp Area 16 km NE of Yungaburra. Take Gillies Hwy E for 9 km, turn N into Powley Rd for 7 km. Open March to November. Bookings required
HEMA 18 F4   17 12 08 S   145 37 01 E

Notes...

QUEENSLAND

232 Wild River Caravan Park ☎ (07) 4096 2121
Caravan Park at Herberton. Holdcroft Dr. E end of town
HEMA 18 G2   17 22 03 S   145 23 20 E

233 Irvinebank Town Common
Camp Spot at Irvinebank. 28 km W of Herberton (12 km dirt road) or 45 km E of Petford. Showers gold coin donation. Open grassed area opposite tavern
HEMA 18 G1   17 25 41 S   145 12 13 E

234 Lakeside Motor Inn & Caravan Park ☎ (07) 4095 3563
Caravan Park at Yungaburra. Tinaburra Dr, follow signs to public boat ramp
HEMA 18 F3   17 15 05 S   145 35 00 E

235 Lake Eacham Tourist Park ☎ (07) 4095 3730
Caravan Park 6 km SE of Yungaburra. 198 Lakes Dr
HEMA 18 F4   17 17 44 S   145 38 07 E

236 Henrietta Creek ☎ 13 74 68
Wooroonooran National Park
Camp Area 22 km SE of Millaa Millaa or 33 km W of Bruce Hwy/ Palmerston Hwy intersection. Must be prebooked
HEMA 18 H5   17 35 56 S   145 45 31 E

237 Ravenshoe Steam Railway Travellers Rest ☎ (07) 4097 6005
Camp Area at Ravenshoe. Just S of town centre, enter from Grigg St. Maximum stay 7 days
HEMA 18 H3   17 36 30 S   145 28 59 E

238 Ravenshoe Millstream Country Club ☎ 0418 778 770
Parking Area at Millstream 8 km W of Ravenshoe via Kennedy Hwy. Please check in with caretaker
HEMA 18 J3   17 38 30 S   145 25 27 E

239 Archer Creek Rest Area
Rest Area 16 km W of Ravenshoe or 28 km E of Mount Garnet. Large area beside creek
HEMA 18 J2   17 38 46 S   145 20 50 E

240 Woodleigh Station ☎ (07) 4097 0204
Camp Area 22 km W of Ravenshoe. Via Kennedy Hwy, turn at white 44 gallon drum, signposted. 3.5 km to station. Bush camp spots also available
HEMA 18 J2   17 38 43 S   145 17 48 E

241 Junction Parking Area
Parking Area 67 km W of Mount Garnet 51 km E of Mount Surprise. Shared with trucks. Tracks out the back to gravel area
HEMA 17 F10   18 08 19 S   144 48 43 E

242 Planet Earth Adventures ☎ 0427 406 230
Camp Area at Mount Surprise
HEMA 17 F9   18 08 49 S   144 19 07 E

243 Greenvale Caravan Park & Cabins ☎ (07) 4788 4155
Caravan Park at Greenvale. 3 Kylee Crt
HEMA 17 H10   19 00 04 S   144 59 00 E

244 Elizabeth (O'Briens) Creek Campground ☎ (07) 4062 3001
Camp Area 30 km NW of Mount Surprise township. Turn onto O'Briens Creek Rd opposite Police Station. Dirt road
HEMA 17 F9   18 02 43 S   144 03 42 E

245 The Einasleigh Hotel ☎ (07) 4062 5222
Parking Area at Einasleigh. Check in with publican, fee for showers & power. Maximum stay 7 days
HEMA 17 G9   18 30 45 S   144 05 40 E

246 Copperfield Lodge Camping & Caravan Park ☎ (07) 4062 5102
Caravan Park at Einasleigh. Baroota St. Open between Easter & Labour day weekend in October. No children allowed
HEMA 17 G9   18 30 35 S   144 05 37 E

247 Oaks Rush Outback Resort ☎ (07) 4062 4100
Camp Area 40 km S of Einasleigh via Georgetown-Mt Garnet Rd, turn S onto Kidston Rd for 19 km. Signposted
HEMA 17 G9   18 49 41 S   144 10 05 E

248 Forsayth Tourist Park ☎ (07) 4062 5324
Caravan Park at Forsayth. First St
HEMA 17 G8   18 35 16 S   143 36 06 E

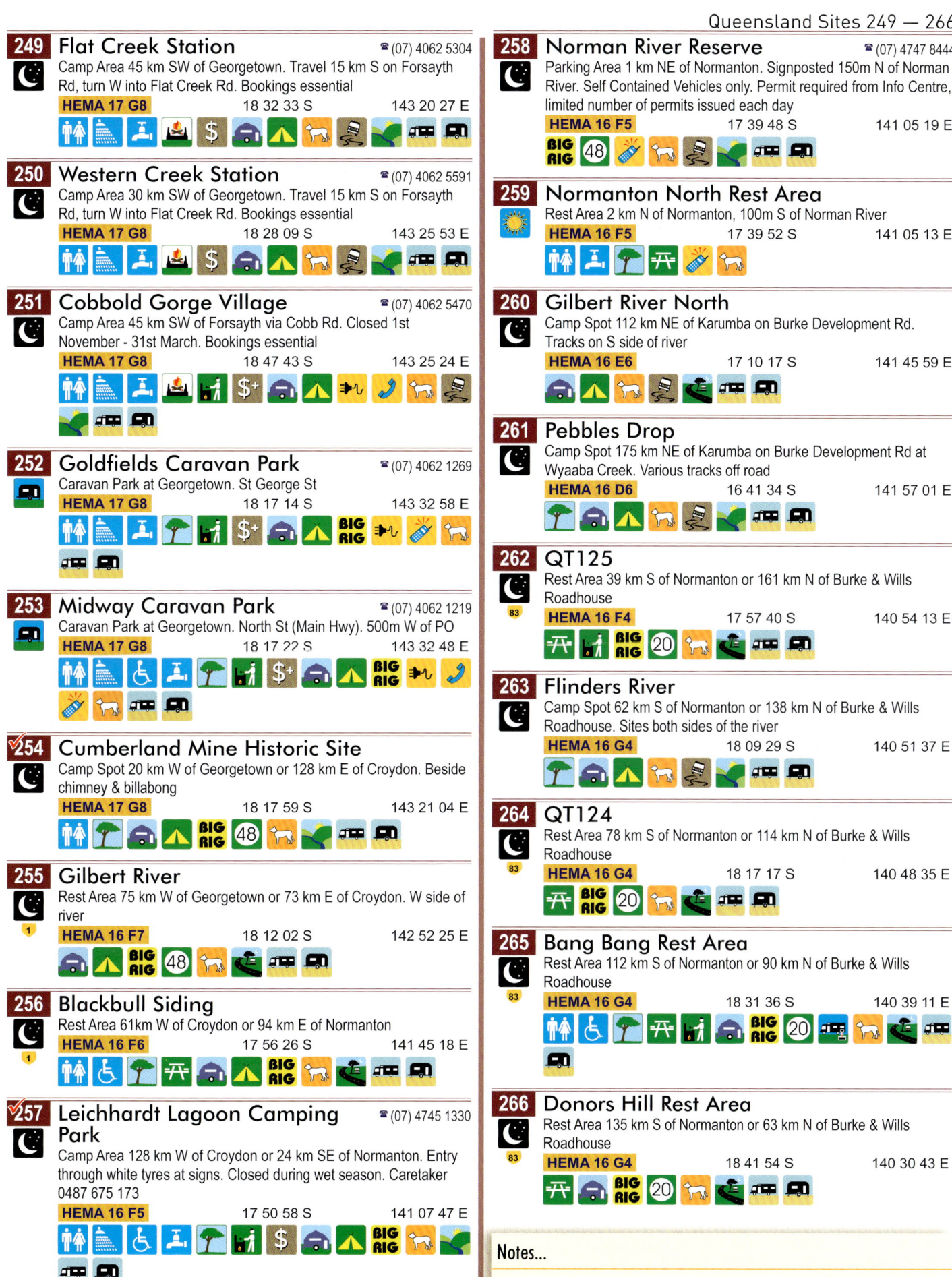

249 Flat Creek Station ☎ (07) 4062 5304
Camp Area 45 km SW of Georgetown. Travel 15 km S on Forsayth Rd, turn W into Flat Creek Rd. Bookings essential
HEMA 17 G8   18 32 33 S   143 20 27 E

250 Western Creek Station ☎ (07) 4062 5591
Camp Area 30 km SW of Georgetown. Travel 15 km S on Forsayth Rd, turn W into Flat Creek Rd. Bookings essential
HEMA 17 G8   18 28 09 S   143 25 53 E

251 Cobbold Gorge Village ☎ (07) 4062 5470
Camp Area 45 km SW of Forsayth via Cobb Rd. Closed 1st November - 31st March. Bookings essential
HEMA 17 G8   18 47 43 S   143 25 24 E

252 Goldfields Caravan Park ☎ (07) 4062 1269
Caravan Park at Georgetown. St George St
HEMA 17 G8   18 17 14 S   143 32 58 E

253 Midway Caravan Park ☎ (07) 4062 1219
Caravan Park at Georgetown. North St (Main Hwy). 500m W of PO
HEMA 17 G8   18 17 22 S   143 32 48 E

✓254 Cumberland Mine Historic Site
Camp Spot 20 km W of Georgetown or 128 km E of Croydon. Beside chimney & billabong
HEMA 17 G8   18 17 59 S   143 21 04 E

255 Gilbert River
Rest Area 75 km W of Georgetown or 73 km E of Croydon. W side of river
HEMA 16 F7   18 12 02 S   142 52 25 E

256 Blackbull Siding
Rest Area 61km W of Croydon or 94 km E of Normanton
HEMA 16 F6   17 56 26 S   141 45 18 E

✓257 Leichhardt Lagoon Camping Park ☎ (07) 4745 1330
Camp Area 128 km W of Croydon or 24 km SE of Normanton. Entry through white tyres at signs. Closed during wet season. Caretaker 0487 675 173
HEMA 16 F5   17 50 58 S   141 07 47 E

258 Norman River Reserve ☎ (07) 4747 8444
Parking Area 1 km NE of Normanton. Signposted 150m N of Norman River. Self Contained Vehicles only. Permit required from Info Centre, limited number of permits issued each day
HEMA 16 F5   17 39 48 S   141 05 19 E

259 Normanton North Rest Area
Rest Area 2 km N of Normanton, 100m S of Norman River
HEMA 16 F5   17 39 52 S   141 05 13 E

260 Gilbert River North
Camp Spot 112 km NE of Karumba on Burke Development Rd. Tracks on S side of river
HEMA 16 E6   17 10 17 S   141 45 59 E

261 Pebbles Drop
Camp Spot 175 km NE of Karumba on Burke Development Rd at Wyaaba Creek. Various tracks off road
HEMA 16 D6   16 41 34 S   141 57 01 E

262 QT125
Rest Area 39 km S of Normanton or 161 km N of Burke & Wills Roadhouse
HEMA 16 F4   17 57 40 S   140 54 13 E

263 Flinders River
Camp Spot 62 km S of Normanton or 138 km N of Burke & Wills Roadhouse. Sites both sides of the river
HEMA 16 G4   18 09 29 S   140 51 37 E

264 QT124
Rest Area 78 km S of Normanton or 114 km N of Burke & Wills Roadhouse
HEMA 16 G4   18 17 17 S   140 48 35 E

265 Bang Bang Rest Area
Rest Area 112 km S of Normanton or 90 km N of Burke & Wills Roadhouse
HEMA 16 G4   18 31 36 S   140 39 11 E

266 Donors Hill Rest Area
Rest Area 135 km S of Normanton or 63 km N of Burke & Wills Roadhouse
HEMA 16 G4   18 41 54 S   140 30 43 E

Notes...

QUEENSLAND

267 Burke & Wills Roadhouse ☎ (07) 4742 5909
Camp Area 207 km S of Normanton or 183 km N of Cloncurry
HEMA 16 H4   19 13 37 S   140 20 49 E

268 Firey Creek
Camp Spot 118 km W of Burke & Wills Roadhouse or 31 km E of Gregory Downs. Various tracks off road
HEMA 16 G3   18 41 45 S   139 31 21 E

269 Gregory Downs
Camp Spot at Gregory Downs. On vacant land NW cnr of Lawn Hill Rd & Wills Developmental Rd. Facilities opposite hotel. No camping on river bank per Council
84
HEMA 16 G2   18 38 51 S   139 15 13 E

270 Adels Grove Camping Park ☎ (07) 4748 5502
Camp Area 88 km W of Gregory Downs. Bookings essential in high season. Dirt road
HEMA 16 G1   18 41 24 S   138 31 54 E

271 Boodjamulla (Lawn Hill) National Park ☎ 13 74 68
Boodjamulla National Park
Camp Area 10 km W of Adels Grove. Bookings essential in high season. Dirt road
HEMA 16 G1   18 42 05 S   138 29 16 E

272 Miyumba Bush Camp ☎ 13 74 68
Boodjamulla National Park
Camp Area 185 km N of Camooweal via "Riversleigh", 48 km S of Adels Grove. 4.2 km S of Riversleigh Fossil site. Open March - Oct. Reservations essential. Dry weather access only
HEMA 16 H2   19 01 06 S   138 43 21 E

273 Beames Brook
Camp Spot 93 km N of Gregory Downs or 27 km S of Burketown, 3 km S of Savannah Way jcn. Tracks off road, small vehicles only
HEMA 16 F2   17 52 37 S   139 20 35 E

274 Tirranna Springs Roadhouse ☎ (07) 4748 3998
Camp Area at Tirranna Springs. 103 km N of Gregory Downs or 34 km S of Burketown
1
HEMA 16 F2   17 53 45 S   139 17 45 E

275 Burketown North River
Camp Spot along river N of Burketown. 6.5 km N of town on Beames St & Truganini Rd. Permit required from Information Centre
HEMA 16 F3   17 43 58 S   139 35 32 E

276 Leichhardt River Falls
Camp Spot 72 km E of Burketown or 154 km W of Normanton
HEMA 16 G3   18 13 15 S   139 52 35 E

277 Tower Layby
Camp Spot 100 km E of Burketown or 126 km W of Normanton
HEMA 16 G3   18 09 09 S   140 05 48 E

278 Little Bynoe River
Camp Spot 189 km E of Burketown or 37 km W of Normanton. Tracks on SW side of river, limited space
HEMA 16 F4   17 52 00 S   140 49 28 E

279 Hells Gate Roadhouse ☎ (07) 4745 8258
Camp Area at Hells Gate Roadhouse
HEMA 16 F1   17 27 18 S   138 21 22 E

280 Terry Smith Lookout
Rest Area 103 km S of Burke & Wills Roadhouse or 78 km N of Cloncurry
83
HEMA 16 J4   20 04 49 S   140 13 39 E

Townsville to Camooweal
Flinders and Barkly Highways

281 Reid River
Rest Area 58 km S of Townsville or 75 km NE of Charters Towers
A6
HEMA 14 A5   19 45 24 S   146 50 02 E

282 Grass Hut Station ☎ (07) 4770 3051
Camp Area Grass Hut Station. 7 km SE of Mingela on the Burdekin Falls Dam Rd. Station signposted on LH side of road
HEMA 14 B4   19 55 28 S   146 40 58 E

283 Ravenswood Showground ☎ (07) 4770 2113
Camp Area 39 km SE of Mingela. Maximum stay 3 months. See caretaker on arrival
HEMA 14 B5   20 05 54 S   146 53 32 E

284 Burdekin Falls Dam Caravan Park ☎ (07) 4770 3177
Caravan Park 77 km SE Ravenswood
HEMA 14 C5   20 38 28 S   147 08 47 E

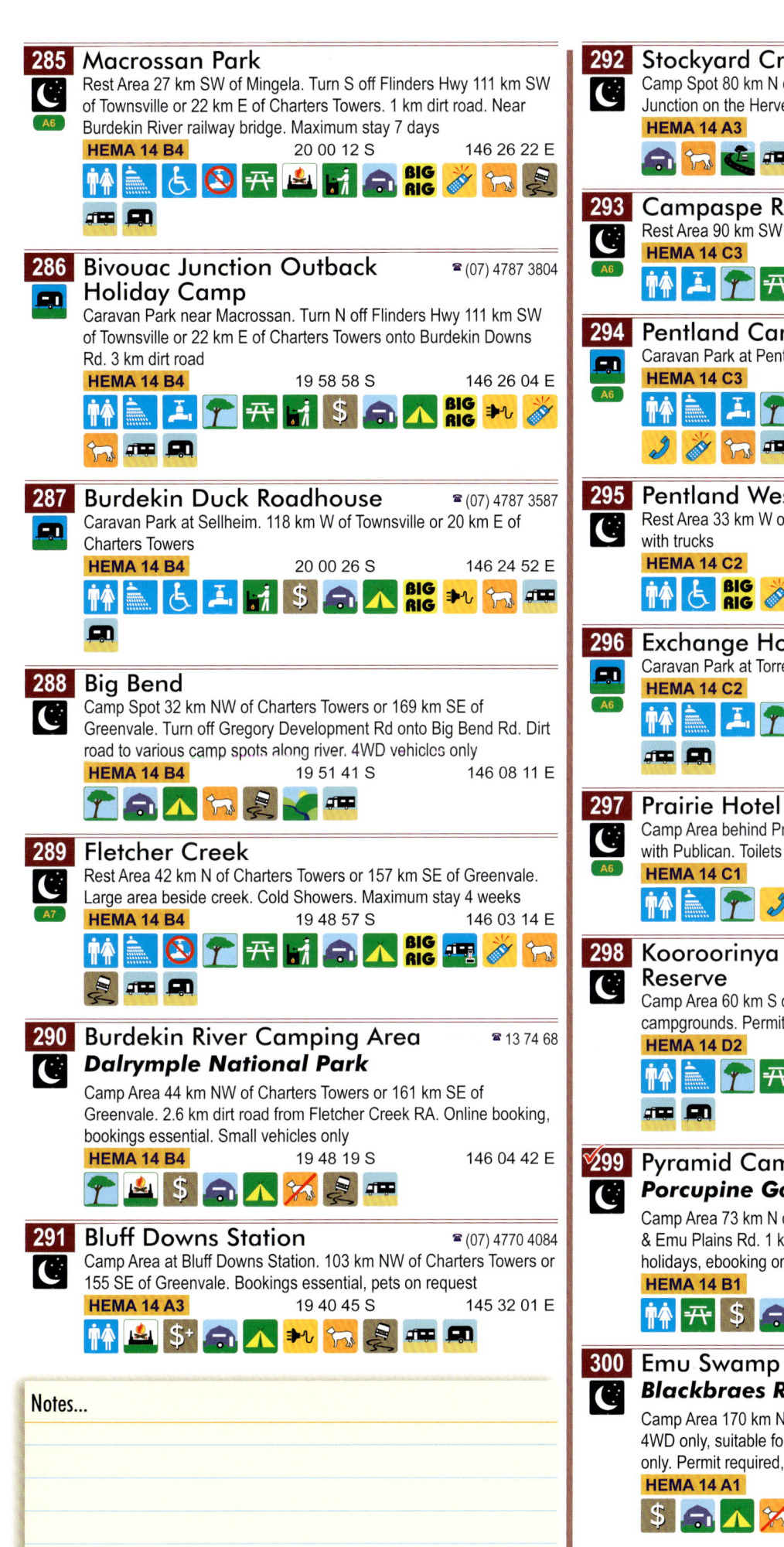

285 Macrossan Park
Rest Area 27 km SW of Mingela. Turn S off Flinders Hwy 111 km SW of Townsville or 22 km E of Charters Towers. 1 km dirt road. Near Burdekin River railway bridge. Maximum stay 7 days
A6
HEMA 14 B4   20 00 12 S   146 26 22 E

286 Bivouac Junction Outback Holiday Camp   ☎ (07) 4787 3804
Caravan Park near Macrossan. Turn N off Flinders Hwy 111 km SW of Townsville or 22 km E of Charters Towers onto Burdekin Downs Rd. 3 km dirt road
HEMA 14 B4   19 58 58 S   146 26 04 E

287 Burdekin Duck Roadhouse   ☎ (07) 4787 3587
Caravan Park at Sellheim. 118 km W of Townsville or 20 km E of Charters Towers
HEMA 14 B4   20 00 26 S   146 24 52 E

288 Big Bend
Camp Spot 32 km NW of Charters Towers or 169 km SE of Greenvale. Turn off Gregory Development Rd onto Big Bend Rd. Dirt road to various camp spots along river. 4WD vehicles only
HEMA 14 B4   19 51 41 S   146 08 11 E

289 Fletcher Creek
Rest Area 42 km N of Charters Towers or 157 km SE of Greenvale. Large area beside creek. Cold Showers. Maximum stay 4 weeks
A7
HEMA 14 B4   19 48 57 S   146 03 14 E

290 Burdekin River Camping Area   ☎ 13 74 68
Dalrymple National Park
Camp Area 44 km NW of Charters Towers or 161 km SE of Greenvale. 2.6 km dirt road from Fletcher Creek RA. Online booking, bookings essential. Small vehicles only
HEMA 14 B4   19 48 19 S   146 04 42 E

291 Bluff Downs Station   ☎ (07) 4770 4084
Camp Area at Bluff Downs Station. 103 km NW of Charters Towers or 155 SE of Greenvale. Bookings essential, pets on request
HEMA 14 A3   19 40 45 S   145 32 01 E

Notes...

292 Stockyard Creek
Camp Spot 80 km N of Charters Towers or 221 km SE of The Lynd Junction on the Herveys Range Development Rd
HEMA 14 A3   19 30 47 S   145 47 15 E

293 Campaspe River Rest Area
Rest Area 90 km SW of Charters Towers or 16 km NE of Pentland
HEMA 14 C3   20 26 28 S   145 31 59 E

294 Pentland Caravan Park   ☎ (07) 4788 1148
Caravan Park at Pentland. Flinders Hwy. E end of town
A6
HEMA 14 C3   20 31 19 S   145 24 03 E

295 Pentland West Rest Area
Rest Area 33 km W of Pentland or 107 km E of Hughenden. Share with trucks
HEMA 14 C2   20 43 47 S   145 10 56 E

296 Exchange Hotel Caravan Park   ☎ (07) 4741 7342
Caravan Park at Torrens Creek. Flinders Hwy
A6
HEMA 14 C2   20 46 12 S   145 01 09 E

297 Prairie Hotel   ☎ 0427 876 750
Camp Area behind Prairie Hotel at Prairie. Flinders Hwy. Check in with Publican. Toilets open during pub hours
A6
HEMA 14 C1   20 52 14 S   144 36 01 E

298 Kooroorinya Falls Nature Reserve   ☎ (07) 4741 7460
Camp Area 60 km S of Prairie on Muttaburra Rd. Signposted to campgrounds. Permit from caretaker
HEMA 14 D2   21 22 04 S   144 38 25 E

299 Pyramid Campground   ☎ 13 74 68
Porcupine Gorge National Park
Camp Area 73 km N of Hughenden, via Kennedy Developmental Rd & Emu Plains Rd. 1 km dirt road. Advanced booking essential in the holidays, ebooking online or at Info Centre Hughenden
HEMA 14 B1   20 20 44 S   144 27 39 E

300 Emu Swamp Campground   ☎ 13 74 68
Blackbraes Resources Reserve
Camp Area 170 km N of Hughenden. 20.5 km from park entrance. 4WD only, suitable for high clearance caravans & camper trailers only. Permit required, closed during wet season
HEMA 14 A1   19 25 03 S   144 09 47 E

QUEENSLAND

301 Hughenden Allen Terry Caravan Park ☎ (07) 4741 1190
Caravan Park at Hughenden. 2 Resolution St. 2 km SW of PO
HEMA 14 C1   20 50 57 S   144 11 46 E

302 Rest Easi Motel & Caravan Park ☎ (07) 4741 1633
Caravan Park at Hughenden. Flinders Hwy
HEMA 14 C1   20 50 55 S   144 11 59 E

303 Hughenden RV Parking Area ☎ (07) 4741 2970
Parking Area at Hughenden. E end of Stansfield St on N side of road, adjacent to showgrounds. Self Contained Vehicles only. Permit required from Info Centre, Grey St
HEMA 14 C1   20 50 41 S   144 12 20 E

304 Marathon Rest Area
Rest Area 65 km W of Hughenden or 47 km E of Richmond. Share with trucks
A6
HEMA 17 K8   20 51 31 S   143 34 07 E

305 Richmond RV Parking Area
Parking Area at Richmond. 300m off Flinders Hwy, via Harris St & Hillier St. Self Contained Vehicles only. Register at Kronosaurus Korner
A6
HEMA 16 K7   20 43 44 S   143 08 36 E

306 Maxwelton Rest Area
Rest Area 50 km W of Richmond or 99 km E of Julia Creek
A6
HEMA 16 K7   20 43 23 S   142 40 42 E

307 Corella Creek Country Stay N Store ☎ (07) 4746 7555
Camp Area at Nelia. 1 Main St. 2 km off Flinders Hwy
A5
HEMA 16 K6   20 39 17 S   142 12 49 E

✓ 308 Julia Creek ☎ (07) 4746 7690
Camp Spot 1.3 km E of Julia Creek. 200m off main road. Camping either side of bridge. Permit required from onsite Camphosts during peak tourist season, or Info Centre. Self Contained Vehicles only
HEMA 16 K6   20 39 21 S   141 45 22 E

309 Julia Creek Caravan Park ☎ (07) 4746 7108
Caravan Park at Julia Creek. Old Normanton Rd. 500m N of PO
HEMA 16 K6   20 39 09 S   141 44 41 E

310 Oorindi Rest Area
Rest Area 69 km W of Julia Creek or 68 km E of Cloncurry
A6
HEMA 16 K5   20 38 32 S   141 06 15 E

311 Wals Camp ☎ (07) 4742 1606
Camp Area 1 km S of Cloncurry. Turn S at bowls club onto Sheaffe & Philips Sts. Follow signs. Mobile 0408 700 302
HEMA 16 K4   20 42 58 S   140 29 47 E

312 Burke & Wills Memorial (Corella River)
Parking Area 44 km W of Cloncurry or 77 km E of Mt Isa
A2
HEMA 16 K4   20 46 56 S   140 06 45 E

✓ 313 Clem Walton Park & Corella Dam
Camp Spot at Corella Dam. 65 km E of Mt Isa or 53 km W of Cloncurry. Turn S off Hwy, through gate, it's only locked if the water is high so check lock. Veer L at first Y jcn. At 2nd Y veer L to Clem Walton Park (1.7 km). Veer R to camp spots by dam. Toilets at Clem Walton
A2
HEMA 16 K3   20 49 36 S   140 02 56 E

314 Fountain Springs Rest Area
Rest Area 60 km W of Cloncurry or 61 km E of Mt Isa
A2
HEMA 16 K3   20 48 01 S   139 59 48 E

315 Mary Kathleen Old Mine Township
Parking Area 63 km W of Cloncurry or 56 km E of Mt Isa. This is private land please respect notices for no litter & no fires
HEMA 16 K3   20 46 29 S   139 58 50 E

316 West Leichhardt Station ☎ (07) 4743 8947
Camp Area at West Leichardt Station. 30 km NW of Mt Isa via Lake Julius Rd. Bookings are essential, pets on request
HEMA 16 K3   20 37 12 S   139 42 00 E

317 Lake Moondarra Picnic Area
Picnic Area at Lake Moondarra
HEMA 16 K3   20 35 17 S   139 34 37 E

318 Gunpowder Rest Area
Rest Area 50 km NW of Mt Isa or 137 km E of Camooweal. Near monument on Barkly Hwy
A2
HEMA 16 K2   20 22 23 S   139 15 50 E

319 David Hall Rest Area
Rest Area 90 km NW of Mt Isa or 99 km E of Camooweal
A2
HEMA 16 K2   20 11 23 S   138 53 52 E

320 Inca Creek Rest Area
Rest Area 119 km NW of Mt Isa or 70 km E of Camooweal
A2
HEMA 16 J2   20 03 58 S   138 45 34 E

QUEENSLAND

321 ✓ **Camooweal Billabong**
Camp Spot at Camooweal. Head W across Georgina River Bridge turn S immediately W of bridge onto dirt road. Follow gravel road for 2 km, tracks for various camping spots next to river
HEMA 16 J1 — A2 — 19 55 15 S — 138 06 33 E

322 **Nowranie Waterhole**
Camooweal Caves National Park ☎ 13 74 68
Picnic Area 21 km S of Camooweal signposted off the Camooweal Urandangi Rd. 19 km dirt road
HEMA 16 J1 — 20 02 37 S — 138 10 19 E

Rockhampton to Cloncurry
Capricorn and Landsborough Highways

323 **Westwood Rest Area**
Rest Area at Westwood, behind the hall
HEMA 15 H10 — A4 — 23 37 18 S — 150 09 23 E

324 **Duaringa Rest Area**
Rest Area at Duaringa. E end of town
HEMA 15 H9 — A4 — 23 43 18 S — 149 40 20 E

325 **Duaringa Hotel & Caravan Park** ☎ (07) 4935 7202
Caravan Park 20 Edward St off Hwy. 1 km off Hwy over railway line
HEMA 15 H9 — 23 42 46 S — 149 40 12 E

326 **Bridgewater Creek Rest Area**
Rest Area 26 km W of Duaringa or 10 km E of Dingo
HEMA 15 H8 — A4 — 23 39 50 S — 149 25 41 E

327 **Dingo Caravan Park** ☎ (07) 4935 9121
Caravan Park at Dingo. Cairns St, off Fitzroy Developmental Rd. N end of town
HEMA 15 H8 — 23 38 33 S — 149 19 48 E

328 **Munall Campground**
Blackdown Tableland National Park
Camp Area in Blackdown Tableland National Park. Turn off is 11 km W of Dingo then campsite is 8 km from Park entrance. Steep winding road suitable for small vehicles only, not suitable for caravans. Bookings essential, E-Permit required
HEMA 15 H8 — 23 47 41 S — 149 04 12 E

329 **Bluff Hotel** ☎ (07) 4982 9158
Parking Area at Bluff. Parking at hotel, free camping if a meal or beverage is purchased from the bar
HEMA 15 H8 — 23 34 56 S — 149 04 13 E

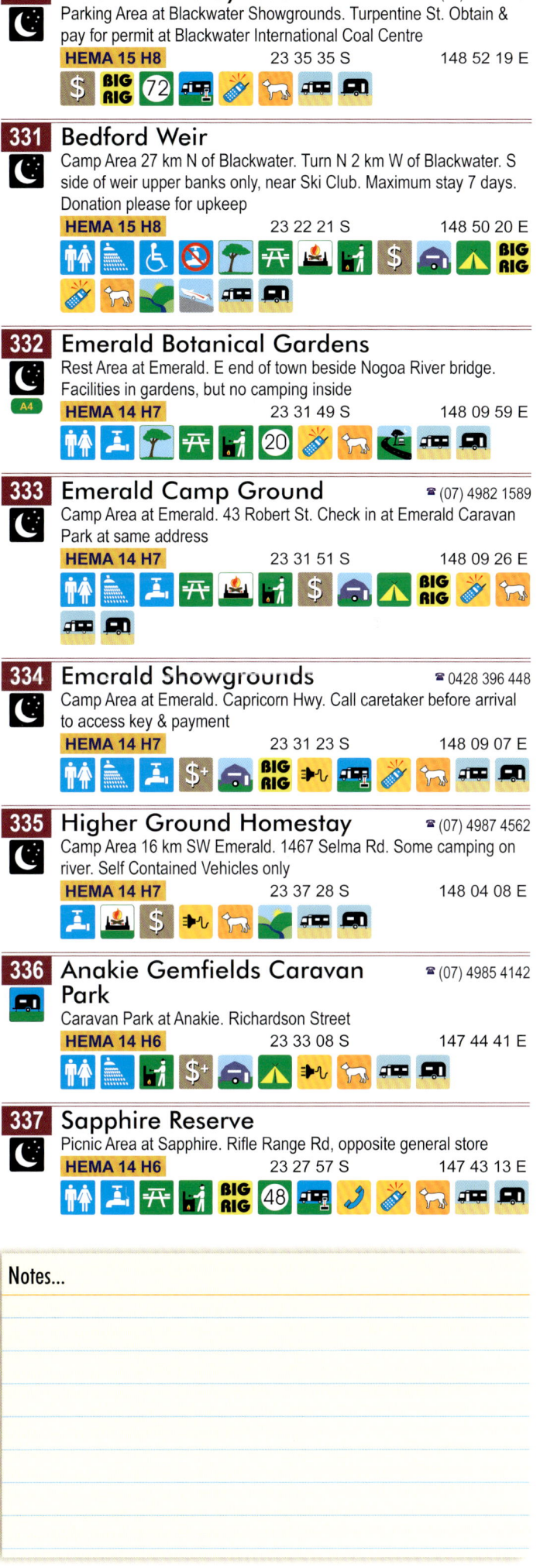

330 **Blackwater Stay Over** ☎ (07) 4982 7755
Parking Area at Blackwater Showgrounds. Turpentine St. Obtain & pay for permit at Blackwater International Coal Centre
HEMA 15 H8 — 23 35 35 S — 148 52 19 E

331 **Bedford Weir**
Camp Area 27 km N of Blackwater. Turn N 2 km W of Blackwater. S side of weir upper banks only, near Ski Club. Maximum stay 7 days. Donation please for upkeep
HEMA 15 H8 — 23 22 21 S — 148 50 20 E

332 **Emerald Botanical Gardens**
Rest Area at Emerald. E end of town beside Nogoa River bridge. Facilities in gardens, but no camping inside
HEMA 14 H7 — A4 — 23 31 49 S — 148 09 59 E

333 **Emerald Camp Ground** ☎ (07) 4982 1589
Camp Area at Emerald. 43 Robert St. Check in at Emerald Caravan Park at same address
HEMA 14 H7 — 23 31 51 S — 148 09 26 E

334 **Emerald Showgrounds** ☎ 0428 396 448
Camp Area at Emerald. Capricorn Hwy. Call caretaker before arrival to access key & payment
HEMA 14 H7 — 23 31 23 S — 148 09 07 E

335 **Higher Ground Homestay** ☎ (07) 4987 4562
Camp Area 16 km SW Emerald. 1467 Selma Rd. Some camping on river. Self Contained Vehicles only
HEMA 14 H7 — 23 37 28 S — 148 04 08 E

336 **Anakie Gemfields Caravan Park** ☎ (07) 4985 4142
Caravan Park at Anakie. Richardson Street
HEMA 14 H6 — 23 33 08 S — 147 44 41 E

337 **Sapphire Reserve**
Picnic Area at Sapphire. Rifle Range Rd, opposite general store
HEMA 14 H6 — 23 27 57 S — 147 43 13 E

Notes...

338 Tomahawk Creek Fossicking Area

Camp Spot 42 km NW of Rubyvale. Take the Rubyvale Clermont Rd for 27km, turn W into Recklaw Park/ Mount Mica turn off. Turn L then L again onto Recklaw Park Track for 17 km. Well signposted. Permit required for fossicking & camping

HEMA 14 H6   23 21 06 S   147 27 35 E

339 Bogantungan Rest Area

Rest Area at Bogantungan. 98 km W of Emerald or 70 km E of Alpha. 400m S of Hwy.

HEMA 14 H5   23 38 53 S   147 17 22 E

340 Drummond Range Lookout

Rest Area 108 km W of Emerald or 60 km E of Alpha. 300m N of Hwy. Unlevel area, steep approach

HEMA 14 H5   23 38 38 S   147 12 16 E

341 Drummond West Rest Area

Rest Area 120 km W of Emerald or 48 km E of Alpha

HEMA 14 H5   23 40 14 S   147 05 27 E

342 Jericho Showground   ☎ (07) 4651 4129

Camp Area 1 km NE of Jericho. At E end of town, turn N just E of railway crossing

HEMA 21 F11   23 35 42 S   146 07 54 E

343 Redbank Park

Camp Area on river bank in Jericho. Turn S off Hwy into Bessemer St, Pasteur St & R into Lyon St. Signposted. Donation appreciated

HEMA 21 F11   23 36 21 S   146 07 47 E

344 Outback Pioneer Centre & Bush Camping   ☎ 0428 503 090

Slygo Station

Camp Area 27 km SW of Jericho or 94 km NE of Blackall on the Jericho-Blackall Rd

HEMA 21 F11   23 46 36 S   145 59 27 E

345 Barcaldine East Rest Area

Rest Area 2 km E of Barcaldine

HEMA 21 F10   23 33 09 S   145 18 26 E

346 Barcaldine Showgrounds   ☎ (07) 4651 5600

Camp Area at Barcaldine. E end of town. Fees payable at Council Office or fees collected by Council staff daily. Closed for camping from 1st Nov - 1st of March

HEMA 21 F10   23 33 02 S   145 17 37 E

347 Lloyd Jones Weir

Camp Area 15 km SW of Barcaldine. Turn W off Landsborough Hwy 5 km S of Barcaldine for 9 km. 1 km dirt road. Donation appreciated

HEMA 21 F10   23 39 00 S   145 12 57 E

348 Aramac Shire Caravan Park & Camping Grounds   ☎ (07) 4652 9999

Camp Area at Aramac. Booker St. Pay fee at Council Office or after hours book return at Aramac Library, Gordon St

HEMA 21 E10   22 58 02 S   145 14 20 E

349 Lake Dunn   ☎ (07) 4651 0565

Camp Area 63 km NE of Aramac. Off Eastmere Rd. Owners collect fees daily

HEMA 21 D11   22 36 16 S   145 40 24 E

350 The Broadwater

Camp Spot 6 km S of Muttaburra via Muttaburra Westside Rd & Broadwater Rd. Bush campsites along Thomson River

HEMA 21 E9   22 39 23 S   144 34 06 E

351 Muttaburra Caravan Park   ☎ (07) 4658 7191

Caravan Park at Muttaburra. Cnr Mary & Bridge Sts

HEMA 21 D9   22 35 36 S   144 33 07 E

352 Pump Hole

Camp Spot 4.5 km E of Muttaburra. Turn N off the Muttaburra-Aramac Rd 3 km E of Muttaburra. 1.2 km dirt road to camp spots

HEMA 21 D9   22 34 59 S   144 33 57 E

353 Nat Buchanan Bridge Rest Area

Rest Area 67 km N of Aramac or 202 km S of Torrens Creek. Just N of Bowen Downs Rd & bridge

HEMA 21 D10   22 27 16 S   145 00 36 E

354 Four Mile Waterhole Camping Area   ☎ 13 74 68

Forest Den National Park

Camp Area in Forest Den National Park. Signposted, 8.5 km to camp area. GPS at entrance. E-Permit required. Not suitable for large caravans, 4WD only

HEMA 21 D10   22 09 19 S   145 09 17 E

355 Rainsby Rest Area

Rest Area 136 km N of Aramac or 134 km S of Torrens Creek

HEMA 21 C10   21 53 43 S   145 11 25 E

356 Shirley Shearing Shed Camping Area
☎ 13 74 68
Moorrinya National Park

Camp Area in Moorrinya National Park. Signposted, 15 km to camp area, follow directional signs. GPS at entrance. 4WD only. E-Permit required

| HEMA 21 C10 | 21 29 36 S | 145 02 54 E |

357 Packsaddle Creek Rest Area

Rest Area 30 km W of Barcaldine or 76 km E of Longreach. Share with trucks

| HEMA 21 F10 | 23 32 07 S | 144 59 46 E |

358 Dartmouth Rest Area

Rest Area 63 km W of Barcaldine or 43 km E of Longreach. Share with trucks

| HEMA 21 F9 | 23 30 44 S | 144 40 13 E |

359 Newstead Creek Rest Area

Rest Area 74 km W of Barcaldine or 32 km E of Longreach

| HEMA 21 F9 | 23 30 08 S | 144 33 06 E |

360 12 Mile Hotel Site Rest Area

Rest Area 20 km S of Ilfracombe or 70 km N of Isisford

| HEMA 21 F9 | 23 39 25 S | 144 30 27 E |

361 Apex Riverside Park

Rest Area 4 km NW of Longreach. 1 km E of Hwy, via River Farms Rd. Fee payable at Info Centre in town

| HEMA 21 F9 | 23 24 37 S | 144 13 47 E |

362 Macsland Rest Area

Rest Area 24 km NW of Longreach or 156 km SE of Winton

| HEMA 21 E9 | 23 16 34 S | 144 07 39 E |

363 Morella Rest Area

Rest Area 68 km NW of Longreach or 112 km SE of Winton

| HEMA 21 E8 | 22 58 31 S | 143 51 36 E |

364 Chorregon Rest Area

Rest Area 112 km NW of Longreach or 68 km SE of Winton

| HEMA 21 E8 | 22 41 28 S | 143 34 24 E |

365 Crawford Creek

Rest Area 132 km NW of Longreach or 46 km SE of Winton

| HEMA 21 D8 | 22 33 29 S | 143 25 30 E |

366 North Gregory Hotel
☎ (07) 4657 0647

Parking Area at Winton. Area behind hotel entry off Oondooroo St. Register at hotel

| HEMA 20 D7 | 22 23 21 S | 143 02 21 E |

367 Long Waterhole

Camp Spot 4 km S of Winton. Turn E off the Winton-Jundah Rd 2 km S of Winton then 2 km of dirt road. Signposted

| HEMA 20 D7 | 22 24 46 S | 143 03 33 E |

368 Mistake Creek

Camp Spot 3.6 km S of Winton via Winton-Jundah Rd. E side of road just S of Western River, tracks to various spots along river

| HEMA 20 D7 | 22 25 14 S | 143 01 56 E |

369 Bough Shed Hole Campground
☎ 13 74 68
Bladensburg National Park

Camp Area 28 km S of Winton. Turn E off the Winton-Jundah Rd 14 km S of Winton onto Opalton Rd for 12 km, then N along River Gums Route for 2 km. Beside creek. 14 km dirt road. Permits required must be pre booked

| HEMA 20 D7 | 22 33 37 S | 142 57 39 E |

370 Opalton Bush Camp

Camp Area at Opalton. 124 km S of Winton

| HEMA 20 E7 | 23 14 45 S | 142 45 46 E |

371 Corfield Rest Area

Rest Area at Corfield. 86 km NE of Winton or 128 km SW of Hughenden. Donation for RFDS to stay

| HEMA 21 C8 | 21 42 51 S | 143 22 27 E |

372 Ayrshire Hills

Parking Area 65 km NW of Winton or 99 km SE of Kynuna

| HEMA 20 D7 | 21 58 17 S | 142 39 40 E |

373 Wanora Downs Rest Area

Rest Area 90 km NW of Winton or 74 km SE of Kynuna

| HEMA 20 C7 | 21 45 20 S | 142 31 07 E |

374 Blue Heeler Caravan Park
☎ (07) 4746 8650

Caravan Park at Kynuna. At Blue Heeler Hotel

| HEMA 20 C6 | 21 34 43 S | 141 55 23 E |

Notes...

QUEENSLAND

375 Kynuna Roadhouse Caravan Park ☎ (07) 4746 8683
Caravan Park at Kynuna. No bookings
HEMA 20 C6   21 34 44 S   141 55 13 E

376 Walkabout Creek Hotel & Van Park ☎ (07) 4746 8424
Caravan Park at McKinlay. Cnr Middleton St & Landsborough Hwy
HEMA 20 C5   21 16 19 S   141 17 23 E

377 Fullarton River North Rest Area
Rest Area 46 km NW of McKinlay or 60 km SE of Cloncurry. 2 km W of Fullarton River. Share with trucks
HEMA 20 B5   21 01 16 S   140 56 24 E

Longreach - Birdsville - Mt Isa

378 Isisford Road Rest Area
Rest Area 121 km S of Longreach or 96 km N of Jundah
HEMA 21 G8   24 14 01 S   143 33 27 E

379 Broadwater Waterhole Camping Area ☎ 13 74 68
Lochern National Park
Camp Area in Lochern National Park. Turn W 100 km S Longreach or 45 km N of Stonehenge onto access road. Follow for 45 km to waterhole t/off. Signposted. Dirt road 4WD recommended
HEMA 21 G8   24 06 19 S   143 21 13 E

380 Stonehenge Caravan Park ☎ (07) 4658 5857
Caravan Park at Stonehenge. Stratford St
HEMA 21 G8   24 21 16 S   143 17 11 E

381 Swan Vale Rest Area
Rest Area 179 km SW of Longreach or 39 km N of Jundah, on Thompson Developmental Rd
HEMA 21 G8   24 35 09 S   143 16 08 E

382 Jundah Caravan Park ☎ (07) 4658 6930
Caravan Park at Jundah. Miles St
HEMA 20 H7   24 49 51 S   143 03 37 E

383 Thomson River
Camp Spot 1 km W of Jundah or 95 km N of Windorah
HEMA 20 H7   24 49 48 S   143 03 04 E

384 Little Boomerang Waterhole Camping Area ☎ 13 74 68
Welford National Park
Camp Area 60 km SE of Jundah on the Barcoo River. Turn W off the Jundah-Quilpie Rd. Campground is approx 10 km from turn off. Signposted. 4WD recommended. Dirt road. Small vehicles only. Must be pre-booked
HEMA 21 H8   25 10 33 S   143 08 23 E

385 Yaraka Town Park ☎ (07) 4657 5526
Camp Area at Yaraka. Behind the town hall next to swimming pool
HEMA 21 H9   24 52 59 S   144 04 43 E

✓386 Cooper Creek
Camp Spot 10 km E of Windorah or 238 km NW of Quilpie. Various sites along riverbank
HEMA 20 J7   25 22 14 S   142 44 46 E

387 Windorah Caravan Park ☎ (07) 4656 3063
Caravan Park at Windorah. 1 Albert St
HEMA 20 J7   25 25 13 S   142 39 09 E

388 JC Hotel Ruins
Camp Spot 75 km W of Windorah or 34 km E of Birdsville Developmental Rd Jcn
HEMA 20 J6   25 22 38 S   141 53 55 E

389 Morney Rest Area
Rest Area 108 km W of Windorah or 95 km E of Betoota on the Diamantina Developmental Rd
HEMA 20 J6   25 22 50 S   141 37 24 E

390 Haddon Corner
Camp Spot 55 km SW of Diamantina Developmental Rd & Birdsville Developmental Rd. Sandy road, caution
HEMA 22 A4   25 59 46 S   140 59 58 E

391 Deons Lookout
Rest Area 200 km W of Windorah or 20 km E of Betoota, on the Birdsville Developmental Rd
HEMA 22 A4   25 43 04 S   140 53 40 E

392 Betoota Rest Area
Rest Area at Betoota
HEMA 22 A3   25 41 36 S   140 44 52 E

393 Cuppa Rest Area
Rest Area 81 km W of Betoota or 85 km E of Birdsville, on the Birdsville Developmental Rd
HEMA 22 A2   25 40 00 S   140 04 01 E

394 Birdsville Windmill
Parking Area 2 km E of Birdsville, on riverbank near windmill
HEMA 22 A1   25 54 22 S   139 22 24 E

395 Cacoory Ruins
Rest Area 81 km N Birdsville or 107 km S of Bedourie. Alternate sites on N side of creek
HEMA 20 H3   25 14 34 S   139 33 30 E

396 Cuttaburra Crossing Rest Area
Rest Area 121 km N of Birdsville or 68 km S of Bedourie
HEMA 20 H3   24 54 49 S   139 38 58 E

397 Monkira Rest Area
Rest Area on Diamantina Development Rd, 121 km E of Eyre Development Rd Jcn or 138 km W of Birdsville Developmental Rd Jcn
HEMA 20 H4   24 49 11 S   140 32 28 E

398 No 3 Bore Rest Area
Rest Area on Diamantina Development Rd. 28 km E of Eyre Development Rd Jcn
HEMA 20 G3   24 28 31 S   139 48 33 E

399 King Creek
Rest Area 22 km S of Bedourie or 2 km N of the Diamantina Development Rd Jcn
HEMA 20 G3   24 31 04 S   139 33 28 E

400 Simpson Desert Oasis Caravan Park   ☎ (07) 4746 1291
Caravan Park at Bedourie. Herbert St, opposite Roadhouse
HEMA 20 G3   24 21 23 S   139 28 16 E

401 Bedourie Caravan Park   ☎ (07) 4746 1040
Caravan Park at Bedourie. Nappa St next to Aquatic Spa, S end of town. Fees payable at Info Centre
HEMA 20 G3   24 21 45 S   139 28 12 E

402 Vaughan Johnson Lookout
Rest Area on Diamantina Development Rd, 88 km N of Bedourie or 107 km S of Boulia. Access via 3 km of steep dirt road. Small vehicles only
HEMA 20 F3   23 41 21 S   139 38 07 E

403 Amaroo Picnic Area
Picnic Area on Diamantina Development Rd. 89 km N of Bedourie or 106 km S of Boulia
HEMA 20 F3   23 40 44 S   139 38 09 E

404 Boulia Caravan Park   ☎ (07) 4746 3320
Caravan Park at Boulia. Winton Rd
HEMA 20 E3   22 54 36 S   139 55 04 E

405 Burke River
Camp Spot 5 km NE of Boulia. Turn N onto Chatsworth-Boulia Rd (known as Cloncurry Rd), then onto Racecourse Rd. Veer L at signs follow track behind racecourse to river
HEMA 20 E3   22 53 24 S   139 56 19 E

406 Old Police Barracks Waterhole
Picnic Area 25 km N of Boulia via Selwyn Rd. 1.5 km E of road, signposted. Dirt road
HEMA 20 E4   22 43 12 S   140 01 52 E

407 Hunters Gorge Camping Area   ☎ 13 74 68
Diamantina National Park
Camp Area 183 km SE of Boulia via Springvale Rd. Signposted, follow track 4 km to Mundawerra Waterhole. 4WD only. Must be pre booked
HEMA 20 F5   23 40 55 S   141 06 08 E

408 Gum Hole Camping Area   ☎ 13 74 68
Diamantina National Park
Camp Area 180 km SE of Boulia via Springvale Rd. Signposted, follow track 4 km to Gumhole. 4WD only. Small vehicles only, limited space
HEMA 20 F5   23 40 21 S   140 59 13 E

409 Old Cork Homestead
Camp Area 160 km SW of Winton. Via Diamantina Ricer Rd. On Old Cork Station, riverside camping
HEMA 20 E6   22 55 26 S   141 52 26 E

410 Hamilton Hotel Historic Site
Rest Area 76 km E of Boulia or 286 km W of Winton
HEMA 20 E4   22 46 23 S   140 34 54 E

411 Lilley Vale
Rest Area 146 km E of Boulia or 216 km W of Winton
HEMA 20 E5   22 36 14 S   141 12 54 E

Notes...

QUEENSLAND

412 Hotel Hilton
Parking Area at Middleton. Opposite the hotel
HEMA 20 D5   22 21 11 S   141 32 59 E

413 Poddy Creek Rest Area
Rest Area 90 km W of Winton or 271 km E of Boulia
HEMA 20 D6   22 12 46 S   142 13 49 E

414 Georgina River
Camp Spot 122 km W of Boulia or 124 km E of Tobermorey Station. Dirt road. Both sides of bridge. 4WD recommended
HEMA 20 E2   22 54 44 S   138 52 19 E

415 Peak Creek
Rest Area 64 km N of Boulia or 84 km S of Dajarra
HEMA 20 D3   22 24 40 S   139 39 47 E

416 Dajarra Campground
Camp Area at Dajarra
HEMA 20 C3   21 41 46 S   139 30 49 E

417 Dangi Bush Resort   ☎ (07) 4748 4988
Camp Area at Urandangie. Free camping if you spend a gold coin in the pub
HEMA 20 C1   21 36 33 S   138 19 00 E

Charters Towers to Banana
Gregory and Dawson Highways

418 Cape River
Parking Area 112 km S of Charters Towers or 91 km N of Belyando Crossing
HEMA 14 C4   20 59 16 S   146 25 13 E

419 Belyando Crossing Service Station Caravan Park   ☎ (07) 4983 5269
Caravan Park at Belyando Crossing. Gregory Developmental Rd. $2 deposit for toilet key. No water hook up available
HEMA 14 D5   21 31 56 S   146 51 31 E

420 Mount Coolon Hotel   ☎ (07) 4983 5530
Camp Area at Mount Coolon
HEMA 14 D5   21 23 06 S   147 20 33 E

421 Belyando South
Parking Area 31 km S of Belyando Crossing
HEMA 14 E5   21 46 20 S   146 58 18 E

422 BP Roadhouse
Parking Area at Clermont. Patronise shop for free showers & parking
HEMA 14 G6   22 48 07 S   147 38 46 E

423 Theresa Creek Dam   ☎ (07) 4983 2327
Camp Area 22 km SW of Clermont. See caretaker
HEMA 14 G6   22 58 16 S   147 33 13 E

424 Bundoora Dam
Camp Area 69 km NE of Capella or 26 km SW of Middlemount. 2nd turn coming from Capella or 1st turn 2.7km from German Creek Mine entrance. Go over railway line 400m to dam. Rough road
HEMA 14 G7   22 57 13 S   148 32 15 E

425 Virgin Rock Rest Area
Rest Area 1.5 km N of Springsure or 63.5 km S of Emerald. W side of road
HEMA 14 J7   24 05 37 S   148 05 48 E

426 Springsure Showgrounds   ☎ 0427 841 612
Camp Area at Springsure. Barcoo St
HEMA 14 J7   24 07 19 S   148 05 02 E

427 Staircase Range Historical Site
Picnic Area 20 km SE of Springsure or 51 km NW of Rolleston. Turn N at historical marker, follow track for 600m to picnic area veering L at Y junction
HEMA 14 J7   24 13 22 S   148 13 18 E

428 Rolleston Caravan Park   ☎ (07) 4984 3145
Caravan Park at Rolleston. Comet St
HEMA 14 J7   24 27 54 S   148 37 21 E

429 Bauhinia Store   ☎ (07) 4996 4146
Camp Area at Bauhinia
HEMA 15 K8   24 34 13 S   149 17 31 E

Notes...

430 Moura Apex River Park

60

Rest Area 66 km E of Bauhinia or 7 km W of Moura. Beside river. Fee for shower. Donation appreciated to upkeep facility

HEMA 15 K9 24 35 58 S 149 54 36 E

BIG RIG

Rockhampton to Toowoomba

Burnett Highway

431 Royal Hotel

(07) 4934 0120

Camp Area at Bouldercombe. Cnr Burnett Hwy & Mount Usher Rd. Toilets in park across the road

HEMA 15 H10 23 34 17 S 150 28 07 E

BIG RIG 48

432 Mount Morgan Motel & Van Park

(07) 4938 1952

17

Caravan Park at Mount Morgan. Cnr Burnett Hwy & Showgrounds Rd

HEMA 15 H10 23 39 37 S 150 23 13 E

BIG RIG

433 Dululu Rest Area

17

Rest Area at Dululu. 70 km SW of Rockhampton or 75 km N of Biloela. Bryant St, S end of town, near tennis courts. Donation requested. No generators allowed

HEMA 15 H10 23 50 54 S 150 15 40 E

BIG RIG 48

434 Wowan Caravan Park

(07) 4937 1542

A5

Caravan Park at Wowan. Don St

HEMA 15 J10 23 54 42 S 150 11 39 E

BIG RIG

435 Goovigen Showground

Camp Area at Goovigen, Stone Cres. Pay fee at Goovigen Hotel

HEMA 15 J10 24 08 44 S 150 17 08 E

BIG RIG 48

436 Country Caravan Park

(07) 4998 1103

Caravan Park at Baralaba. 16 Wooroonah Rd. 500m SW of PO. Limited sites, small vans only

HEMA 15 J9 24 11 08 S 149 48 56 E

437 Baralaba Showgrounds

Camp Area at Baralaba. Entry off Wooroonah Rd

HEMA 15 J9 24 11 06 S 149 48 54 E

BIG RIG

438 Neville Hewitt Weir

(07) 4998 1142

Camp Spot at Baralaba. S end of Stopford St. Beside weir. Coin operated shower. Donation requested

HEMA 15 J9 24 11 07 S 149 48 26 E

BIG RIG 48

439 Queensland Heritage Park

(07) 4992 2400

A3

Camp Area in Biloela. Exhibition Ave. Call into the front office to register

HEMA 15 J10 24 24 17 S 150 29 59 E

BIG RIG 48

440 Callide Dam

Picnic Area 15 km NE of Biloela. Turn S off Dawson Hwy 5 km NE of Biloela. Beside lake

HEMA 15 J10 24 22 26 S 150 36 46 E

BIG RIG

441 Lochenbar Station

(07) 4992 2186

Camp Area at Lochenbar Station. 35 km E of Biloela, via Valentine Plains Rd. 12 km dirt road. Donation requested

HEMA 15 J10 24 27 08 S 150 47 54 E

BIG RIG

442 Lawgi Hall Rest Area

17

Rest Area 27 km SE of Biloela or 66 km NW of Monto

HEMA 15 K10 24 34 05 S 150 39 40 E

BIG RIG

443 Coominglah Range Rest Area

17

Rest Area 75 km SE of Biloela or 22 km NW of Monto. 100m W of Hwy

HEMA 13 A9 24 47 58 S 150 59 04 E

BIG RIG

444 Monto Community Rest Stop

69

Rest Area in Monto. In the Old Railway complex behind Visitor Information Centre off Gladstone-Monto Rd. Self Contained Vehicles only

HEMA 13 A10 24 51 46 S 151 07 15 E

BIG RIG 72

445 Mulgildie Hotel

(07) 4167 2107

17

Parking Area at Mulgildie, 5 km S of Monto. Monal St. Rear of hotel. Contact manager. Fee for showers (business hours only)

HEMA 13 A10 24 57 50 S 151 07 56 E

BIG RIG 24

446 Wuruma Dam

(07) 4165 7200

Camp Area 48 km NW of Eidsvold, via Abercorn. Turn W 19 km N of Eidsvold. 1 km dirt road. Maximum stay 2 weeks

HEMA 13 B10 25 10 52 S 150 59 14 E

BIG RIG

447 Ceratodus Rest Area

17

Rest Area 65 km S of Monto or 11 km N of Eidsvold. Beside Burnett River

HEMA 13 B10 25 16 53 S 151 08 20 E

BIG RIG 20

448 Eidsvold Caravan Park

(07) 4165 1168

17

Caravan Park at Eidsvold. Esplanade St

HEMA 13 B10 25 22 06 S 151 07 23 E

QUEENSLAND

449 **RM Williams Australian Bush Centre** ☎ (07) 4165 7272
Parking Area at Eidsvold. Gayndah Monto Rd. Parking in car park for Self Contained Vehicles only. Payment & permit from the Centre office
HEMA 13 B10   25 22 17 S   151 07 42 E

450 **Lochaber Tourist Park**
Camp Area 20 km N of Mundubbera, 15 km S of Eidsvold. Entrance off Burnett Hwy, camp area 700m from turning. Self Contained Vehicles only. Donations requested
HEMA 13 B10   25 28 33 S   151 12 32 E

451 **Tolderodden Campground** ☎ 13 74 68
Tolderodden Regional Park
Camp Area 4.5 km W of Eidsvold or 82 km E of Cracow. Beside Burnett River. Bookings required
HEMA 13 B10   25 22 36 S   151 05 14 E

452 **Auburn River Campground** ☎ 13 74 68
Auburn River National Park
Camp Area 42 km SW of Mundubbera. Turn W off Mundubbera-Durong Rd 15 km S of Mundubbera or 91 km N of Durong South onto Hawkwood Rd for 20 km, then S for 7 km of dirt road. Bookings required
HEMA 13 C10   25 42 41 S   151 03 10 E

453 **Jaycees Park**
Rest Area 3 km N of Mundubbera, 35 km SE of Eidsvold or 44 km W of Gayndah. 500m E of Mundubbera turnoff
HEMA 13 B10   25 34 24 S   151 18 40 E

454 **Mundubbera Showgrounds** ☎ (07) 4165 4764
Camp Area at Mundubbera. Entry via Bunce St
HEMA 13 B11   25 35 09 S   151 17 50 E

455 **Binjour Range Rest Area**
Rest Area 28 km E of Mundubbera or 17 km NW of Gayndah
HEMA 13 B10   25 32 00 S   151 29 59 E

456 **Zonhoven Park**
Rest Area at Gayndah. E end of town
HEMA 13 B11   25 37 44 S   151 37 33 E

457 **Riverview Caravan Park** ☎ (07) 4161 1280
Caravan Park at Gayndah. 3 Barrow St. 1 km N of PO
HEMA 13 B11   25 37 44 S   151 36 10 E

458 **Mingo Crossing Caravan & Recreation Park** ☎ (07) 4161 6200
Caravan Park at Mingo Crossing. 30 km S of Mt Perry or 40 km N of Gayndah
HEMA 13 B11   25 23 38 S   151 46 38 E

459 **Ban Ban Springs**
Rest Area 28 km SE of Gayndah or 74 km N of Goomeri
HEMA 13 C11   25 40 54 S   151 48 57 E

460 **Mountain View Caravan Park** ☎ (07) 4127 1399
Caravan Park at Biggenden. Walsh St. 1 km W of PO
HEMA 13 B12   25 30 49 S   152 02 25 E

461 **Biggenden RV Stop**
Parking Area at Biggenden. Edward St, Old Railway Station site. Self Contained Vehicles only. Donation box on site
HEMA 13 B12   25 30 44 S   152 02 40 E

462 **Brooweena RV Stop**
Parking Area at Brooweena. Smith Crescent across from Claude Wharton Park. Facilities in park. Self Contained Vehicles only
HEMA 13 C12   25 36 01 S   152 15 50 E

463 **Monica Hodges Park**
Parking Area at Aramara. Self Contained Vehicles only
HEMA 13 C12   25 36 41 S   152 19 22 E

464 **Teebar Sports Ground**
Parking Area at Teebar. Teebar Hall Rd. Self Contained Vehicles only
HEMA 13 C12   25 37 09 S   152 14 00 E

465 **Springvale Park** ☎ (07) 5484 2109
Camp Area 23 km S of Teebar. 875 Yarrabine Rd. Via Brooweena - Woolooga Rd. Bookings essential, cash only
HEMA 13 C12   25 48 50 S   152 11 40 E

466 **Lawless Park (Booubyjan)**
Rest Area 40 km S of Ban Ban Springs or 34 km N of Goomeri
HEMA 13 C11   25 56 40 S   151 57 11 E

467 **Kilkivan Bush Camping Park** ☎ (07) 5484 1340
Camp Area 8 km E of Kilkivan. Turn S 2 km E of Kilkivan onto Rossmore Rd
HEMA 13 D12   26 07 01 S   152 17 25 E

468 Fat Hen Creek
Rest Area 6 km E of Kilkivan or 32 km W of Bruce Hwy jcn
HEMA 13 D12   26 05 24 S   152 17 18 E

469 Munna Creek Hall   ☎ 0429 912 154
Parking Area at Munna Creek. 23 km E of Woolooga
HEMA 13 C12   25 53 48 S   152 28 34 E

470 Kinbombi Falls
Picnic Area 11 km E of Goomeri or 24 km W of Kilkivan. Turn S off Wide Bay Hwy 6 km E of Goomeri or 19 km W of Kilkivan. 5 km to area
HEMA 13 D12   26 13 19 S   152 09 03 E

471 Goomeri Caravan and Bush Camp   ☎ 0418 734 060
Camp Area 3 km E of Goomeri off the Wide Bay Hwy, 2.5 km to the camp area
HEMA 13 D12   26 11 49 S   152 05 35 E

472 Goomeri Showgrounds   ☎ 0419 720 407
Camp Area at Goomeri. Cnr Burnett Hwy & Laird St. S end of town
HEMA 13 D12   26 11 11 S   152 04 09 E

473 Goomeri Roadhouse Caravan Park   ☎ (07) 4168 4203
Caravan Park at Goomeri. Moore St (Burnett Hwy)
HEMA 13 D11   26 11 10 S   152 04 13 E

474 Broadwater Recreational Reserve
Camp Spot 22 km N of Nanango, on Broadwater Access Rd
HEMA 8 B1   26 30 04 S   152 02 12 E

475 Twin Gums Caravan Park   ☎ (07) 4163 1376
Caravan Park at Nanango. Cnr of Scott & Arthur Sts. 1 km S of PO
HEMA 8 C1   26 40 49 S   151 59 54 E

476 Nanango RV & Caravan Park   ☎ (07) 4163 1677
Caravan Park at Nanango. Elk St. A/H 0400 631 677
HEMA 8 C1   26 40 07 S   152 00 03 E

477 Nanango Showgrounds   ☎ (07) 4163 1273
Camp Area at Nanango. Entrance off Cairns St. Closed during events so please call ahead
HEMA 8 C1   26 40 19 S   151 59 34 E

478 Tipperary Flat Park
Rest Area at Nanango. 1.5 km S of PO
HEMA 8 C1   26 40 48 S   151 59 47 E

479 Maidenwell Rest Area
Rest Area at Maidenwell. 27 km SW of Nanango or 19 km N of Cooyar. Opposite hall on Coomba Falls Rd. Donation for showers
HEMA 13 E11   26 50 48 S   151 48 00 E

480 Maidenwell Hotel   ☎ (07) 4164 6133
Camp Spot at Maidenwell. 27 km SW of Nanango or 19 km N of Cooyar. Gold coin donation for showers
HEMA 13 E11   26 50 49 S   151 47 56 E

481 Swinging Bridge Park
Rest Area at Cooyar. Behind Cooyar Hotel. Fee for power. Key from pub. Toilets opposite hotel in Memorial Park
HEMA 13 F11   26 58 54 S   151 49 57 E

482 Cooyar Showgrounds   ☎ (07) 4692 6281
Camp Area at Cooyar. Entry off Cooyar Rangemore Rd. Check in with caretaker. Closed during some events in February & October
HEMA 13 F11   26 59 17 S   151 49 34 E

483 Crows Nest Camping Area   ☎ 13 74 68
Crows Nest National Park
Camp Area 7 km E of Crows Nest, via Three Mile Rd. Permit required
HEMA 8 J2   27 15 15 S   152 06 25 E

484 Lake Cressbrook   ☎ (07) 4688 6540
Camp Area 19 km E of Crows Nest. Self registration at entry
HEMA 8 J3   27 15 42 S   152 11 13 E

485 Chapman Park
Rest Area at Hampton. Visitor Information Centre
HEMA 8 K2   27 21 30 S   152 04 09 E

Notes...

QUEENSLAND

486 Ravensbourne Rest Area
Rest Area 14 km E of Hampton or 32 km SW of Esk
HEMA 8 K3   27 21 36 S   152 10 35 E

Yarraman to Ipswich
D'Aguilar and Burnett Highways

487 Harland Park
Camp Spot 8.6 km W of Blackbutt or 6 km E of Yarraman
HEMA 8 E1   26 52 07 S   152 01 26 E

488 Edelweiss Cafe   ☎ (07) 4163 0872
Parking Area at Blackbutt. Hart St. W end of town. Toilet & shower during cafe hours. Fee for shower
A17
HEMA 8 E2   26 53 11 S   152 05 44 E

489 Blackbutt Showgrounds   ☎ (07) 4163 0633
Camp Area at Blackbutt. Via Hart St, Bowman Rd
HEMA 8 E2   26 52 52 S   152 06 08 E

490 First Settlers Park
Rest Area at Benarkin. 4 km E of Blackbutt or 42 km NW of Toogoolawah. Donation welcomed. Power avaliable for a hourly fee
85
HEMA 8 E2   26 53 18 S   152 08 10 E

491 Clancys Campground   ☎ 1300 130 372
Benarkin State Forest
Camp Area 15 km SE of Blackbutt, via Benarkin Forest Dr. Turn S 4 km E of Blackbutt. 12 km dirt road. Maximum stay 14 days. Small area, 4WD recommended
HEMA 8 F3   26 58 36 S   152 10 19 E

492 Stanley Gates Park
Parking Area at Moore. Main St. Opposite local store
85
HEMA 8 E4   26 53 37 S   152 17 22 E

493 Linville Village
Camp Spot at Linville. Turn through white gates opposite Linville Hotel. Donation welcomed
HEMA 8 E3   26 50 36 S   152 16 33 E

494 Kilcoy Camping Area (Anzac Memorial park)   ☎ (07) 5422 4900
Camp Area at Kilcoy. E end of town at cnr of Seib & William Sts
85
HEMA 8 F6   26 56 31 S   152 34 03 E

495 Kilcoy RV Stop
Parking Area at Kilcoy. Seib St in signed area S of Hope St intersection. Self Contained Vehicles only
85
HEMA 8 F6   26 56 49 S   152 34 05 E

496 Kilcoy Showgrounds   ☎ (07) 5422 4900
Camp Area at Showgrounds. Turn NE 2 km W of Kilcoy off the D'Aguilar Hwy. Caretaker will collect fee
HEMA 8 F6   26 56 37 S   152 32 45 E

497 Yandilla Farm   ☎ (07) 5498 1220
Camp Area 22 km NE of Kilcoy. 1785 Mt Kilcoy Rd. Travel N from Kilcoy on the Kilcoy Murgon Rd, turn E at Mt Kilcoy Rd. Small dogs may be permitted on enquiry. Bookings essential
HEMA 8 D6   26 47 15 S   152 34 26 E

498 Peach Trees Camping Area   ☎ 13 1304
Jimna State Forest
Camp Area 4 km N of Jimna, 44 km N of Kilcoy. Permit required. Four tonne load limit in park
HEMA 8 C5   26 38 15 S   152 26 59 E

✓499 Cruice Park
Rest Area 4 km NW of Woodford or 29 km W of Beerwah at jcn of Kilcoy-Beerwah Rd & D'Aguilar Hwy
53
HEMA 8 F7   26 55 40 S   152 45 33 E

500 Woodford Showgrounds   ☎ 0437 390 862
Camp Area at Woodford. Neurem Rd. Register with onsite caretaker on arrival. Often closed for events, call ahead. Maximum stay 7 nights
HEMA 8 F7   26 56 51 S   152 46 12 E

501 Neurum Creek Bush Retreat   ☎ (07) 5496 3692
Camp Area 14 km W of Woodford. 268 Rasmussen Rd, Neurum. Bookings essential, a $7 site fee applies to all bookings for the first night only
HEMA 8 F7   26 59 54 S   152 41 12 E

502 Somerset Dam Campground   ☎ 0428 180 450
Camp Area at Somerset Dam. 27 km S of Kilcoy or 24 km NE of Esk. Coin operated showers
HEMA 8 H6   27 07 25 S   152 33 03 E

503 Simeon Lord Park
Rest Area at Harlin. Self Contained Vehicles only. Small area
17
HEMA 8 F4   26 58 33 S   152 21 34 E

504 Toogoolawah Drop Zone ☎ (07) 5423 1159
Camp Area 3 km N of Toogoolawah or 12 S of Harlin
HEMA 8 G4   27 04 11 S   152 23 21 E

505 Toogoolawah Showgrounds ☎ 0419 706 617
Camp Area at Toogoolawah Showgrounds. 30 Ivory Creek Rd
HEMA 8 G4   27 04 41 S   152 22 31 E

506 Pol Crandle Park
Parking Area. Entry off Brisbane Valley Hwy. Self Contained Vehicles only
HEMA 8 G4   27 05 48 S   152 22 49 E

507 Captain Logan Camp ☎ 0428 310 740
Wivenhoe Dam
Camp Area at Lake Wivenhoe. Logan Inlet Rd
HEMA 8 K6   27 21 06 S   152 33 05 E

508 Lumley Hill Campground ☎ (07) 5426 4729
Wivenhoe Dam
Camp Area at Lake Wivenhoe. Logan Inlet Rd
HEMA 8 K6   27 20 50 S   152 33 08 E

509 Geoffrey Fisher Bridge
Parking Area 3.5 km N of Fernvale beside river. Self Contained Vehicles only
HEMA 10 B6   27 25 53 S   152 38 23 E

510 Lowood Showgrounds & Caravan Park ☎ 0455 187 201
Camp Area at Lowood. Station St
HEMA 10 B6   27 27 45 S   152 35 01 E

511 Atkinson Dam Scout Camp ☎ (07) 5427 9319
Camp Area at Atkinson Dam. 366 Watson Rd. Off Coominya Connection Road, 12 km W of Lowood
HEMA 10 A5   27 26 35 S   152 27 28 E

512 Atkinson Dam Holiday Park ☎ (07) 5426 4211
Camp Area at Atkinsons Dam. 381 Atkinsons Dam Rd. 18 km W of Lowood
HEMA 10 A5   27 25 12 S   152 27 11 E

Goomeri to Dalby
Bunya Highway

513 Murgon RV Stop ☎ (07) 4189 9387
Camp Area at Murgon. 3 Krebs St. 1 km NE of PO. Deposit for key if using facilities, at info centre
HEMA 13 D11   26 14 32 S   151 56 17 E

514 Wondai Caravan Park ☎ (07) 4169 2555
Caravan Park at Wondai. McKenzie St. Centre of town, next to swimming pool & railway line. $10 deposit for shower & toilet key. Payment & key available from Council Chambers or Wondai Diggers Club
HEMA 13 D11   26 19 10 S   151 52 18 E

515 Wondai RV Stop ☎ (07) 4189 9251
Parking Area. Haly St. Coin operated showers
HEMA 13 D11   26 19 02 S   151 52 26 E

516 Proston Caravan Park ☎ (07) 4168 9272
Caravan Park at Proston. Next to Showgrounds Proston Boondooma Rd. Check in & pay fee at Golden Spurs Hotel, 2 Blake St
HEMA 13 D11   26 09 39 S   151 35 55 E

517 Boondooma Homestead ☎ (07) 4168 0159
Camp Area 81 km S of Mundubbera or 112 km SW of Chinchilla. Off the Mundubbera Durong Rd. Pay fees to caretaker
HEMA 13 D10   26 12 10 S   151 17 35 E

518 Tingoora Rest Area
Rest Area at Tingora. Tingoora-Charlestown Rd, grassed area opposite hotel
HEMA 13 D11   26 21 52 S   151 49 21 E

519 Stuart River Rest Area
Rest Area 19 km W of Tingoora or 44 km E of Durong South
HEMA 13 D11   26 22 22 S   151 38 52 E

520 Wooroolin Rest Area
Rest Area at Wooroolin. Opposite PO. Gold coin for showers
HEMA 13 D11   26 24 38 S   151 48 58 E

Notes...

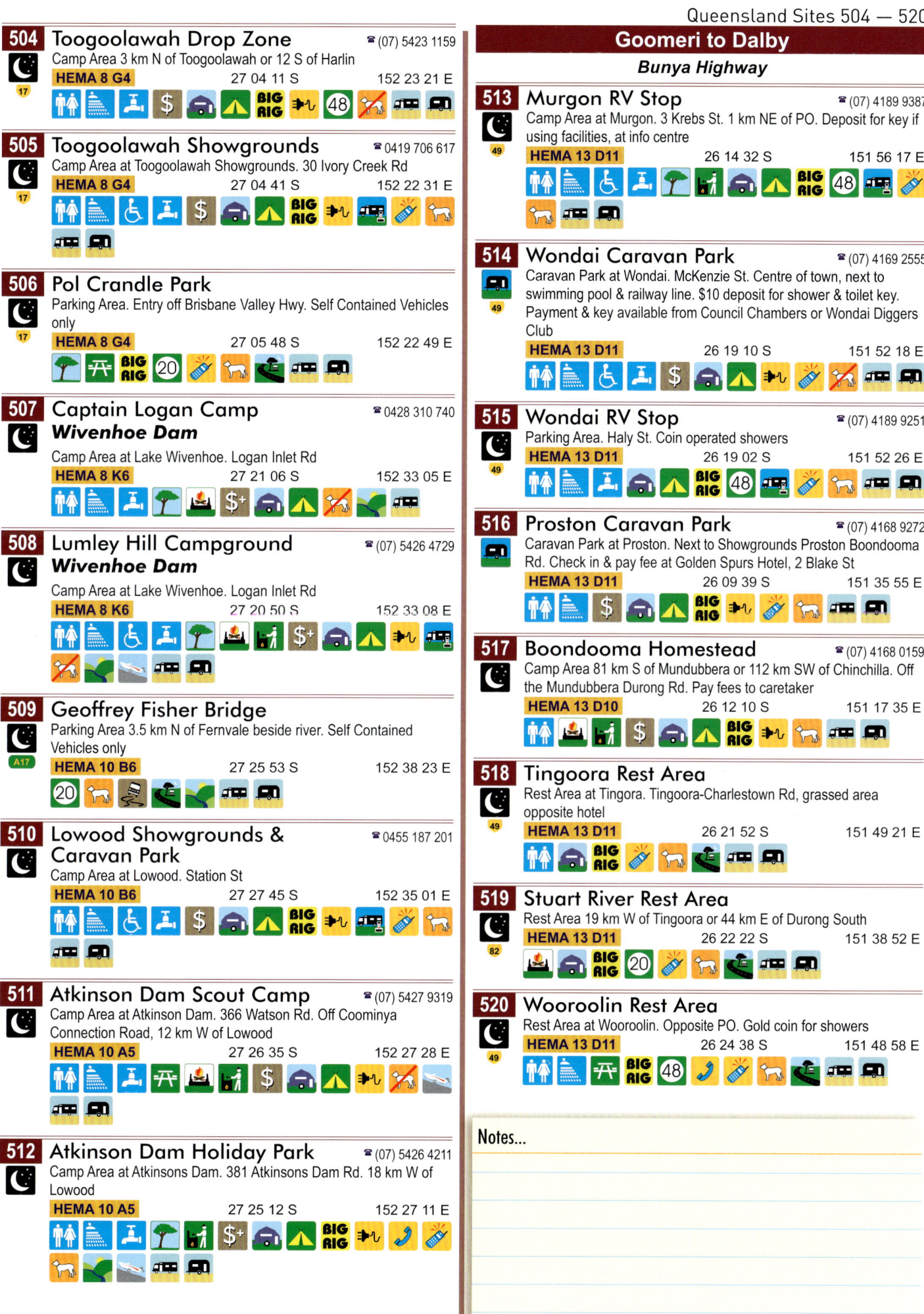

QUEENSLAND

521 Kingaroy Showgrounds Caravan Park ☎ (07) 4162 5037
Camp Area at Kingaroy. 1.5 km from PO. 31 Youngman St. S side of town
HEMA 13 E11   26 32 49 S   151 49 56 E

522 Coolabunia Rest Area
Rest Area 7 km SE of Kingaroy or 17 km NW of Nanango. Small area
HEMA 13 E11   26 34 49 S   151 52 41 E

523 Alwyn Francis Bridge
Rest Area 10 km SW of Kingaroy or 17 km NE of Kumbia. Large area beside river
HEMA 13 E11   26 36 41 S   151 47 00 E

524 Kumbia Apex Park
Rest Area at Kumbia. Opposite Police Station. Coin operated power & shower, powered sites limited
HEMA 13 E11   26 41 32 S   151 39 10 E

525 Kumbia Caravan Park ☎ (07) 4164 4375
Caravan Park at Kumbia. Bell St
HEMA 13 E11   26 41 23 S   151 39 18 E

526 Dandabah Campground
Bunya Mountains National Park
Camp Area 62 km SW of Kingaroy. Permit required must pre book
HEMA 13 E11   26 52 45 S   151 35 52 E

527 Bushland Park Cabins & Camping ☎ 0407 113 514
Camp Area 52 km N of Dalby or 62 km S of Kingaroy on Bunya Mountain Rd
HEMA 13 E11   26 54 48 S   151 37 52 E

528 Bells N Whistles Accommodation Park ☎ (07) 4663 1265
Caravan Park at Bell. Bunya Hwy. 200m S of PO
HEMA 13 E10   26 55 57 S   151 26 49 E

529 Yamsion Rest Area
Rest Area 44 km S of Kumbia or 42 km NE of Dalby on Bunya Mountains Rd
HEMA 13 F11   26 59 05 S   151 34 42 E

530 Glasbys Caravan Park ☎ (07) 4663 4228
Caravan Park at Kaimkillenbun. Moffatt St
HEMA 13 F10   27 03 39 S   151 26 03 E

Rockhampton to Goondiwindi
Leichhardt Highway

531 Junction Park ☎ (07) 4993 1900
Rest Area at Theodore. S end of The Boulevard. Donations requested
HEMA 13 A8   24 57 14 S   150 04 29 E

532 Theodore Recreation Reserve ☎ 0427 367 069
Camp Area at Theodore. The Boulevard. E side of town
HEMA 13 A8   24 56 22 S   150 04 34 E

533 Cracow Heritage Centre ☎ (07) 4993 7900
Camp Area at Cracow. Third Ave. Donation box
HEMA 13 B8   25 17 39 S   150 18 04 E

534 Cracow Hotel ☎ (07) 4993 7118
Camp Spot at Cracow. Across from hotel
HEMA 13 B8   25 17 43 S   150 18 10 E

535 Isla Gorge Campground
Isla Gorge National Park
Camp Area 38 km S of Theodore. Turn W 37 km S of Theodore or 57 km N of Taroom. 1 km dirt road. GPS at entry point
HEMA 13 A8   25 12 05 S   149 58 34 E

536 Glebe Weir ☎ 07 4628 6113
Camp Area 93 km S of Theodore. Turn E 66 km S of Theodore or 28 km NE of Taroom. Honesty box for payment. Maximum stay 4 weeks
HEMA 13 B8   25 27 49 S   150 02 02 E

537 Lake Murphy Conservation Park ☎ 13 74 68
Camp Area 39 km NW of Taroom. Turn NW 76 km S of Theodore or 18 km N of Taroom onto Fitzroy Developmental Rd, then W after 1 km onto Glenhaughton Rd for 11 km dirt road
HEMA 12 B7   25 29 08 S   149 39 36 E

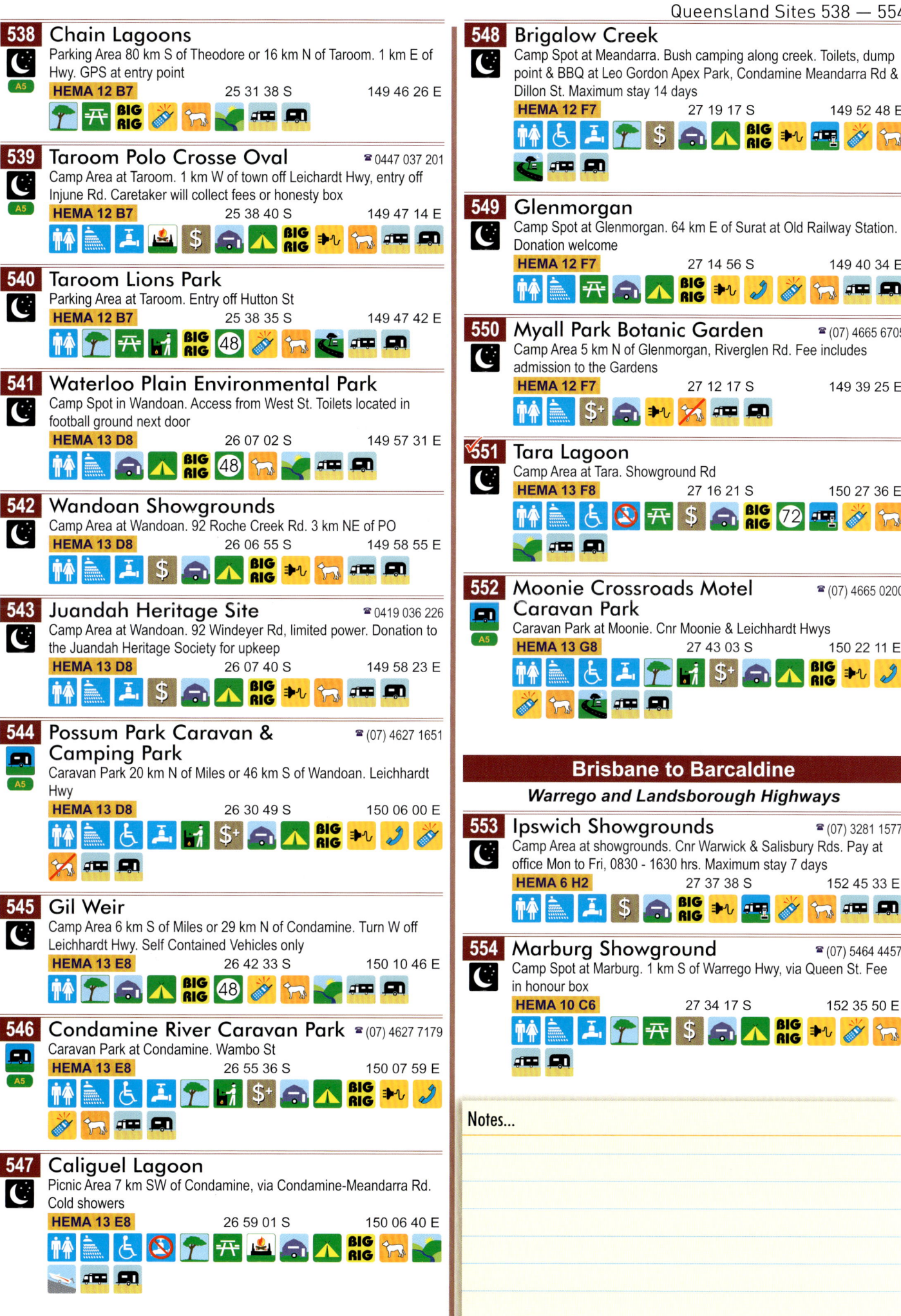

538 Chain Lagoons
Parking Area 80 km S of Theodore or 16 km N of Taroom. 1 km E of Hwy. GPS at entry point
A5
HEMA 12 B7   25 31 38 S   149 46 26 E

539 Taroom Polo Crosse Oval   ☎ 0447 037 201
Camp Area at Taroom. 1 km W of town off Leichardt Hwy, entry off Injune Rd. Caretaker will collect fees or honesty box
A5
HEMA 12 B7   25 38 40 S   149 47 14 E

540 Taroom Lions Park
Parking Area at Taroom. Entry off Hutton St
HEMA 12 B7   25 38 35 S   149 47 42 E

541 Waterloo Plain Environmental Park
Camp Spot in Wandoan. Access from West St. Toilets located in football ground next door
HEMA 13 D8   26 07 02 S   149 57 31 E

542 Wandoan Showgrounds
Camp Area at Wandoan. 92 Roche Creek Rd. 3 km NE of PO
HEMA 13 D8   26 06 55 S   149 58 55 E

543 Juandah Heritage Site   ☎ 0419 036 226
Camp Area at Wandoan. 92 Windeyer Rd, limited power. Donation to the Juandah Heritage Society for upkeep
HEMA 13 D8   26 07 40 S   149 58 23 E

544 Possum Park Caravan & Camping Park   ☎ (07) 4627 1651
Caravan Park 20 km N of Miles or 46 km S of Wandoan. Leichhardt Hwy
A5
HEMA 13 D8   26 30 49 S   150 06 00 E

545 Gil Weir
Camp Area 6 km S of Miles or 29 km N of Condamine. Turn W off Leichhardt Hwy. Self Contained Vehicles only
HEMA 13 E8   26 42 33 S   150 10 46 E

546 Condamine River Caravan Park   ☎ (07) 4627 7179
Caravan Park at Condamine. Wambo St
A5
HEMA 13 E8   26 55 36 S   150 07 59 E

547 Caliguel Lagoon
Picnic Area 7 km SW of Condamine, via Condamine-Meandarra Rd. Cold showers
HEMA 13 E8   26 59 01 S   150 06 40 E

548 Brigalow Creek
Camp Spot at Meandarra. Bush camping along creek. Toilets, dump point & BBQ at Leo Gordon Apex Park, Condamine Meandarra Rd & Dillon St. Maximum stay 14 days
HEMA 12 F7   27 19 17 S   149 52 48 E

549 Glenmorgan
Camp Spot at Glenmorgan. 64 km E of Surat at Old Railway Station. Donation welcome
HEMA 12 F7   27 14 56 S   149 40 34 E

550 Myall Park Botanic Garden   ☎ (07) 4665 6705
Camp Area 5 km N of Glenmorgan, Riverglen Rd. Fee includes admission to the Gardens
HEMA 12 F7   27 12 17 S   149 39 25 E

✓551 Tara Lagoon
Camp Area at Tara. Showground Rd
HEMA 13 F8   27 16 21 S   150 27 36 E

552 Moonie Crossroads Motel Caravan Park   ☎ (07) 4665 0200
Caravan Park at Moonie. Cnr Moonie & Leichhardt Hwys
A5
HEMA 13 G8   27 43 03 S   150 22 11 E

Brisbane to Barcaldine
Warrego and Landsborough Highways

553 Ipswich Showgrounds   ☎ (07) 3281 1577
Camp Area at showgrounds. Cnr Warwick & Salisbury Rds. Pay at office Mon to Fri, 0830 - 1630 hrs. Maximum stay 7 days
HEMA 6 H2   27 37 38 S   152 45 33 E

554 Marburg Showground   ☎ (07) 5464 4457
Camp Spot at Marburg. 1 km S of Warrego Hwy, via Queen St. Fee in honour box
HEMA 10 C6   27 34 17 S   152 35 50 E

Notes...

QUEENSLAND

555 Rosewood Tourist Park & Camping ☎ 0481 382 049
Camp Area at Rosewood. At the showgrounds, Railway St. Maximum stay 7 nights
HEMA 10 C6   27 38 25 S   152 35 58 E

556 Narda Lagoon
Parking Area at Laidley. S end of town Cnr Drayton & Pioneer St
HEMA 10 C4   27 39 01 S   152 23 27 E

557 Laidley Showground ☎ (07) 5465 1284
Camp Area at Laidley. Use McGregor St entrance
HEMA 10 C4   27 38 16 S   152 23 22 E

558 Mulgowie Community Hall ☎ (07) 5465 9127
Camp Spot at Mulgowie 12 km S of Laidley. Beckman Rd. Advance booking required, fee payable at the Mulgowie Hotel
HEMA 10 D4   27 43 48 S   152 21 48 E

559 Centenary Park Camping Ground ☎ 0439 368 561
Camp Area at Thornton. 24 km S of Laidley. Maximum stay 7 nights. Key for access to power via Lake Dyer Camping ground office. Limited powered sites. Bookings essential
HEMA 10 E4   27 47 54 S   152 22 27 E

560 Lake Dyer Caravan & Camping Ground ☎ (07) 5465 3698
Camp Area 1.5 km NW of Laidley off Gatton-Laidey Rd
HEMA 10 C4   27 37 57 S   152 22 40 E

561 Gatton Caravan Park ☎ (07) 5462 1198
Caravan Park at Gatton. 291 Eastern Dr
HEMA 10 B4   27 33 19 S   152 17 19 E

562 Heifer Creek
Rest Area 41 km SW of Gatton or 25 km NE of New England Hwy. On Clifton-Gatton Rd. Beside creek
HEMA 10 D2   27 44 56 S   152 05 23 E

563 Casuarina Camping Area
Glen Rock State Forest ☎ 13 74 68
Camp Area 42 km SW of Gatton. From Gatton take Mt Sylvia Rd via Tenthill to Junction View. Turn E onto East Haldon Rd. Signposted to Park. Permit required. Maximum stay 30 days
HEMA 10 F3   27 53 18 S   152 14 50 E

564 James Hedges Park
Rest Area at Helidon beside Warrego Hwy
HEMA 10 B2   27 33 04 S   152 07 09 E

565 Murphy's Creek Escape Camping Park ☎ 07 4630 5353
Camp Area at Upper Lockyer. 356 Thomas Rd. 14 km N of Helidon or 17 km SE of Cabarlah. Fee for dogs
HEMA 10 B2   27 28 53 S   152 05 35 E

566 Six Mile Country Retreat ☎ 0417 780 194
Camp Area NW of Postmans Ridge. Follow Murphy's Creek Rd, after 0.5 km turn L into Six Mile Creek Rd, follow for 2.9 km, cross creek & camp area is on your R
HEMA 10 B2   27 31 27 S   152 02 16 E

567 Toowoomba Showground ☎ (07) 4634 7400
Camp Area at Toowoomba. 302 Glenvale Rd. Available to motorhomes over 30 ft & travellers with pets. Must register at office. Closed during events
HEMA 10 C1   27 33 36 S   151 53 04 E

568 Goombungee Haden Showgrounds ☎ 0457 183 406
Camp Area at Goombungee. Lau St. NE side of town off Pechey Maclagan Rd
HEMA 13 F11   27 18 19 S   151 51 27 E

569 Biddeston Tractor Pull ☎ 0428 717 493
Camp Area 10 km S of Oakey. 477 Oakey-Crosshill Rd
HEMA 13 G11   27 31 32 S   151 42 16 E

570 Jondaryan Woolshed ☎ (07) 4692 2229
Camp Area 3 km S of Jondaryan. 264 Jondaryan Evanslea Rd
HEMA 13 F11   27 23 32 S   151 34 30 E

571 Bowenville Reserve
Rest Area 5 km S of Bowenville on Bowenville-Norwin Rd
HEMA 13 F10   27 19 40 S   151 27 17 E

572 Cecil Plains Rural Retreat Caravan Park   ☎ 0428 913 779
Caravan Park at Cecil Plains. Taylor St. See notice board for payment & keys
HEMA 13 G10   27 31 59 S   151 11 45 E

573 Cecil Plains Apex Park   ☎ (07) 4695 1399
Picnic Area at Cecil Plains. 1 km E of PO on the Toowoomba-Cecil Plains Rd, beside the Condamine River. Self Contained Vehicles only
HEMA 13 G10   27 31 56 S   151 12 16 E

574 Wilga Campground   ☎ 13 74 68
Lake Broadwater Conservation Park
Camp Area 28 km SW of Dalby. Turn S off Moonie Hwy 20 km SW of Dalby or 92 km NE of Moonie along Lake Broadwater. Register on arrival, no prebooking available
HEMA 13 F10   27 19 55 S   151 05 46 E

575 The Lake Campground   ☎ 13 74 98
Lake Broadwater Conservation Park
Camp Area 30 km SW of Dalby. Turn S off Moonie Hwy 20 km SW of Dalby or 92 km NE of Moonie along Lake Broadwater Rd. Register on arrival. No prebooking available
HEMA 13 F10   27 21 13 S   151 05 34 E

576 Kumbarilla Rest Area
Rest Area 46 km SW of Dalby or 66 km NE of Moonie
HEMA 13 F9   27 19 28 S   150 52 39 E

577 Warra Rest Area
Rest Area 46 km NW of Dalby or 35 km SE of Chinchilla
HEMA 13 E9   26 55 43 S   150 55 10 E

578 Jimbour Rest Area
Rest Area at Jimbour. Next to War Memorial Hall
HEMA 13 E10   26 57 50 S   151 12 59 E

579 Jandowae Showgrounds   ☎ (07) 4668 5268
Camp Area at Showgrounds. Warra St. Caretaker collects fees. Mobile 0458 595 796
HEMA 13 E10   26 47 13 S   151 06 38 E

580 Kogan Memorial Hall   ☎ (07) 4668 1762
Camp Area at Kogan. W side of Memorial Hall. Phone to pay & get the key
HEMA 13 F9   27 02 24 S   150 45 40 E

581 Archers Crossing (South side)   ☎ (07) 4668 9564
Camp Area 24 km S of Chinchilla. Turn S 26 km NW of Warra or 9 km SE of Chinchilla, onto Hopelands Rd for 9 km to school. Turn R for 2 km to Archers Crossing Rd, then 4 km of dirt road to river
HEMA 13 E9   26 47 57 S   150 40 46 E

582 Archers Crossing (North side)   ☎ (07) 4668 9564
Camp Area 11 km SE of Chinchilla. Turn S 28 km NW of Warra or 7 km SE of Chinchilla onto No Through Rd for 4 km of dirt road. GPS at entry point
HEMA 13 E9   26 47 44 S   150 40 40 E

583 Round Water Hole Rest Area
Rest Area 5.5 km NE of Chinchilla on the Chinchilla-Wondai Rd
HEMA 13 E9   26 43 18 S   150 40 03 E

584 Chinchilla Weir   ☎ (07) 4668 9564
Rest Area 9 km SW of Chinchilla on Chinchilla-Tara Rd. Power available for a fee
HEMA 13 E9   26 48 02 S   150 34 52 E

585 Chinchilla Showgrounds   ☎ (07) 4662 7194
Camp Area at Chinchilla. Entrance at Cnr Zeller St & Gaske Ln
HEMA 13 E9   26 45 02 S   150 37 05 E

586 Columboola Country Caravan Park   ☎ (07) 4665 8293
Caravan Park at Columboola. Ryalls Rd
HEMA 13 E8   26 32 46 S   150 19 52 E

587 Miles Crossroads Caravan Park   ☎ (07) 4627 2165
Caravan Park at Miles. 132 Murilla St
HEMA 13 E8   26 39 36 S   150 11 42 E

Notes...

588 Miles Showgrounds ☎ 0419 028 905
Camp Area at Miles. Entry off Hawkins St, contact caretaker on arrival
HEMA 13 E8   26 39 41 S   150 10 56 E

589 Moraby Park
Rest Area 1 km W of Miles. Both sides of the road
HEMA 13 E8   26 39 20 S   150 10 46 E
A2

590 Yuleba East Rest Area
Rest Area 17 km W of Jackson or 7.5 km E of Yuleba
HEMA 12 E7   26 37 16 S   149 27 25 E
A2

✓591 Judds Lagoon ☎ (07) 4623 5155
Camp Spot 3 km SE of Yuleba, turn W onto Forestry Rd just before the town Cemetery then onto Moongool Rd. Signposted
HEMA 12 E6   26 38 12 S   149 23 46 E

592 Old Yuleba ☎ 1300 007 662
Camp Spot 13 SE of Yuleba. Via Forestry Rd & then Moongool Rd for 8.3 km. Signposted Historic Site. 2.1 km dirt road
HEMA 12 E7   26 41 50 S   149 25 59 E

593 The Maryanne
Camp Spot 16 km S of Yuleba on the Yuleba Surat Rd. (The Cobb & Co Way) past the windmill follow track to lagoon & open area
HEMA 12 E6   26 43 48 S   149 19 33 E

✓594 Wallumbilla Showgrounds
Camp Area at Wallumbilla. W end of town
HEMA 12 E6   26 35 14 S   149 11 01 E
A2   72

595 Roma Showgrounds ☎ 0408 988 002
Camp Area at Roma Showgrounds (Bassett Park) Carnarvon Hwy. Only available when all caravan parks in town are full or for large club groups
HEMA 12 D5   26 33 13 S   148 47 06 E

596 Roma Gun Club ☎ 0476 674 514
Camp Area at Roma. Geoghegan Rd
HEMA 12 D5   26 35 39 S   148 46 23 E

597 Ups N Downs Farm Stay ☎ 0407 740 252
Camp Area 7.5 N of Roma. Turn W off the Carnarvon Hwy onto Hartleys Lane 5 km N of Roma
HEMA 12 D5   26 30 48 S   148 46 41 E

598 Meadowbank 'Museum' Farm Stay ☎ 0488 527 355
Camp Area at Meadowbank Station. 60 Bindango Rd Warrego Hwy. 12 km W of Roma, turn N for 2 km. Signposted. Seasonal, only open from Easter - end of October
HEMA 12 D5   26 34 46 S   148 40 48 E
A2

599 Bungeworgorai Creek
Camp Spot 10 km W of Roma or 31 km E of Muckadilla. Entry S of road, E of bridge
HEMA 12 D5   26 35 32 S   148 41 39 E
A2

600 Muckadilla Community Park
Rest Area at Muckadilla. Donation box E side of Community Hall for showers & upkeep of facility
HEMA 12 D5   26 35 07 S   148 23 17 E
A2   24

601 Muckadilla Hotel ☎ (07) 4626 8318
Camp Area at Muckadilla. Fee for power
HEMA 12 D5   26 35 06 S   148 23 06 E
A2

602 Natural Wilderness Experience 'Claravale' ☎ (07) 4623 2721
Camp Area 52 km NE of Mitchell. 500m E of Mitchell on the Warrego Hwy turn N onto Warroonga-Tooloombilla Rd. 25 km of dirt road
HEMA 12 C4   26 08 43 S   148 07 51 E

603 Womalilla Creek
Camp Spot 37 km S of Mitchell or 176 km NW of St George. Near bridge at jcn of Maranoa River & Womalilla Creek
HEMA 12 E4   26 46 20 S   148 01 51 E
48

604 Woodlands Rest Area
Rest Area 91 km S of Mitchell or 114 km N of St George
HEMA 12 F4   27 15 59 S   148 03 16 E

605 Bonus Downs Station ☎ (07) 4623 1573
Camp Area at Bonus Downs Station. 46 km SW of Mitchell on the Mitchell Bollon Rd. Bookings essential. Fee for dogs
HEMA 12 E3   26 42 41 S   147 41 01 E

QUEENSLAND

606 Neil Turner Weir
Rest Area 3.2 km W of Mitchell. Turn N off Warrego Hwy 2 km W of Mitchell. Cnr Alexandra & River St
HEMA 12 D4   26 28 28 S   147 57 21 E

607 Fishermans Rest
Camp Spot 5.5 km W of Mitchell. Turn N off Warrego Hwy 5 km W of Mitchell onto Fishermans Rest Rd
HEMA 12 D4   26 28 49 S   147 55 55 E

608 Ooline Park
Rest Area 36 km W of Mitchell or 9.6 km E of Mungallala. Turn S off Hwy, follow track for 1 km. Limited space, small vehicles only
HEMA 12 D3   26 27 53 S   147 37 49 E

609 Mungallala RV Stop
Camp Spot at Mungallala. Warrego Hwy. 45 km W of Mitchell or 44 km E of Morven. Donation required for use
HEMA 12 D3   26 26 44 S   147 32 29 E

610 Mungallala Hotel   ☎ (07) 4623 6192
Camp Area at Mungallala Hotel. Warrego Hwy
HEMA 12 D3   26 26 46 S   147 32 36 E

611 Morven Recreation Ground   ☎ (07) 4654 8281
Camp Area at Morven. S side of town via Victoria St. $5 donation per night appreciated for upkeep of facilities. Maximum stay 7 days
HEMA 12 D2   26 25 06 S   147 06 58 E

612 Sommariva Rest Area
Rest Area 49 km W of Morven or 39 km E of Charleville
HEMA 12 D1   26 24 51 S   146 37 30 E

613 Charleville Rockpool
Camp Spot 11 km E of Charleville on Warrego Hwy
HEMA 23 B14   26 25 06 S   146 21 05 E

614 The Red Lizard Camping Ground   ☎ (07) 4654 7047
Camp Area 7 km S of Charleville on the Mitchell Hwy
HEMA 23 B14   26 27 45 S   146 14 02 E

615 Charleville Bush Camp   ☎ 0428 545 200
Camp Area 1.5 km NW of Charleville. 77 Adavale Rd. Non Smoking park. Separate generator area. Self Contained Vehicles only
HEMA 23 B14   26 23 20 S   146 13 47 E

616 Ward River
Camp Spot 18 km W of Charleville. Turn NW off Diamantina Hwy 17 km W of Charleville onto old Hwy, follow for 500m. Tracks along river. Signposted "Ward River Fishing"
HEMA 23 B13   26 29 39 S   146 06 01 E

617 Nungil Station   ☎ (07) 4654 0151
Camp Area At Nungil Station 117 km NW of Charleville. Via Charleville Adavale & Langlo Rds. Bookings are essential
HEMA 21 J11   25 44 45 S   145 39 03 E

618 Cooladdi Foxtrap Roadhouse   ☎ (07) 4654 0347
Camp Spot at Cooladdi. 88 km W of Charleville or 122 km E of Quilpie. Camp sites available near pub & river. Fee for shower
HEMA 23 C12   26 38 53 S   145 28 04 E

619 Winbin East Rest Area
Rest Area 159 km W of Charleville or 53 km E of Quilpie
HEMA 23 C11   26 38 15 S   144 47 48 E

620 Adavale Town Camping Area   ☎ (07) 4656 4656
Camp Area at Adavale. Beside Community Hall, Blackall Adavale Rd call into Pub for more info. Donation required
HEMA 23 A11   25 54 29 S   144 35 59 E

621 Adavale Bush Camping   ☎ (07) 4656 4656
Camp Area 1 km W of Adavale off the Charleville Adavale Rd. Collect Map from the pub for other bush camping & fishing spots in the area
HEMA 23 A11   25 54 30 S   144 37 00 E

622 Wanco Station
Lake Houdraman
Camp Spot 7 km NE of Quilpie at Lake Houdraman. Turn N 2 km E of Quilpie onto Adavale Back Rd, follow for 2 km then turn E at grid. 4.5 km dirt road
HEMA 23 B10   26 35 07 S   144 18 22 E

Notes...

QUEENSLAND

623 Quilpie River
Camp Spot at Quilpie. Turn S 1 km E of Quilpie, just W of John Waugh Bridge (Bulloo River). Follow track to camp spots along river near old crossing
HEMA 23 C10   26 36 55 S   144 17 03 E

624 Kyabra Creek Rest Area
Rest Area 116 km NW of Quilpie or 130 km SE of Windorah on Diamantina Developmental Rd
HEMA 23 A9   26 05 50 S   143 26 38 E

625 Eromanga Motel & Caravan Park   ☎ (07) 4656 4885
Caravan Park at Eromanga. Access via King St
HEMA 23 C8   26 40 10 S   143 16 20 E

626 Augathella Warrego River Picnic Area
Picnic Area at Augathella. Opposite hotel
HEMA 21 J12   25 47 43 S   146 34 53 E

627 Ellangowan Hotel   ☎ (07) 4654 5054
Parking Area at Augathella, behind hotel. Please see publican before parking. Fee for showers & power
HEMA 21 J12   25 47 46 S   146 34 58 E

628 Fisherman's Hut
Camp Spot at Augathella. N side of river via Welch St
HEMA 21 J12   25 47 42 S   146 34 47 E

629 Augathella North Rest Area
Rest Area 42 km N of Augathella or 72 km S of Tambo
HEMA 21 J12   25 28 15 S   146 35 42 E

630 Tambo Lake
Rest Area at Tambo. At S entrance to town
HEMA 21 H11   24 52 55 S   146 15 35 E

631 Tambo Caravan Park   ☎ (07) 4654 6463
Caravan Park at Tambo. Next to Football Grounds
HEMA 21 H11   24 53 06 S   146 14 52 E

632 Stubby Bend
Camp Spot 2 km NE of Tambo. First turn right after bridge on Alpha-Springsure Rd. Signposted
HEMA 21 H11   24 52 34 S   146 15 46 E

633 Tambo North Rest Area
Rest Area 25 km NW of Tambo or 75 km SE of Blackall
HEMA 21 H11   24 45 03 S   146 06 20 E

634 Barcoo River Rest Area
Rest Area 59 km N of Tambo or 41 km S of Blackall. Self Contained Vehicles only
HEMA 21 G11   24 34 53 S   145 48 34 E

635 Barcoo River Camp (Blackall)   ☎ (07) 4657 4637
Camp Spot at Blackall. 500m W of PO. Self Contained Vehicles only. Toilets & showers across road
HEMA 21 G10   24 25 29 S   145 27 41 E

636 Monks Tank Camping Area   ☎ 13 74 68
Idalia National Park
Camp Area in Idalia National Park. Turn S off Yaraka Rd at Benlidi Siding, then 54 km to camp area. Signposted. Dirt road, 4WD access only
HEMA 21 H9   24 47 37 S   144 42 16 E

637 Oma Waterhole
Camp Area 17 km SW of Isisford, next to Oma Station. Take St Helens Rd out of Isisford then join Yaraka River Rd. Fee payable at Council Offices
HEMA 21 G9   24 17 11 S   144 18 32 E

638 Yaranigh's Pond
Camp Spot 7 km S of Isisford on the Isisford Emmet Rd
HEMA 21 G9   24 17 59 S   144 28 44 E

639 Barcoo River Nature Park   ☎ (07) 4658 8900
Camp Area at Isisford. E of town beside river. Showers in town park. Fee payable at Council Offices
HEMA 21 G9   24 15 28 S   144 26 36 E

640 Golden West Hotel Caravan Park   ☎ (07) 4658 8222
Caravan Park at Isisford
HEMA 21 G9   24 15 30 S   144 26 29 E

Notes...

641 Douglas Ponds Creek
Rest Area 23 km N of Blackall or 84 km S of Barcaldine. Self Contained Vehicles only
A2
HEMA 21 G10   24 16 34 S   145 20 29 E

642 Lara Wetlands Camping Grounds   ☎ 0457 661 243
Camp Area at Lara Station. Turn W at signpost 79 km N of Blackall or 28 km S of Barcaldine onto access road. 13 km dirt road. GPS at the gate
HEMA 21 F10   23 47 51 S   145 18 31 E

643 Barcaldine South Rest Area
Rest Area 79 km N of Blackall or 28 km S of Barcaldine
HEMA 21 F10   23 48 01 S   145 18 34 E
A2

Brisbane to Rathdowney

Mt Lindesay Highway

644 Hugh Muntz Park   ☎ (07) 3412 3412
Parking Area at Beenleigh. Reisers Rd. Self Contained Vehicles only. Maximum of 3 nights in a 30 day period
HEMA 11 D11   27 43 01 S   153 12 33 E

645 Beenleigh Showgrounds   ☎ (07) 3807 1871
Camp Area at Beenleigh. Entry off Showgrounds Rd. Self Contained Vehicles only
HEMA 11 D11   27 43 14 S   153 12 00 E

646 Tully Memorial Park
Rest Area 6 km N of Jimboomba. Entry via Greenbank Rd, Beryl Parade. Self Contained Vehicles only
13
HEMA 11 E9   27 47 01 S   153 00 44 E

647 Canungra Sports and Recreation Ground   ☎ (07) 5543 5904
Camp Area at Canungra. On RHS past hotel along Lamington National Park Rd. Follow signs to rec grounds
HEMA 11 G10   28 01 18 S   153 09 36 E

648 Sharp Park River Bend Bush Camping   ☎ 0409 550 745
Camp Area 4 km SE of Canungra. On Beechmont Rd, on either side of Coomera River. Bookings essential during peak season. Max stay 3 weeks
HEMA 11 G11   28 02 59 S   153 11 18 E

649 Mt Nimmel Lodge Campground   ☎ 0413 775 752
Camp Area 10 km SW of Mudgeeraba via Austinville. 271 Austinville Rd
HEMA 24 K2   28 08 10 S   153 19 07 E

650 The Settlement Camping Area   ☎ 13 74 68
Springbrook National Park
Camp Area on Carricks Rd. Suitable for small vehicles only, not suitable for caravans. Booking required
HEMA 11 J11   28 11 36 S   153 16 19 E

651 Darlington Park   ☎ (07) 5544 8120
Camp Area 24 km S of Beaudesert, via Kerry Rd. Beside Albert River
HEMA 11 H9   28 11 04 S   153 02 26 E

652 Burgess Park   ☎ (07) 5544 8120
Camp Area 19 km SE of Laravale on Christmas Creek Rd. 3 km S of Hillview
HEMA 11 J9   28 14 20 S   152 59 45 E

653 Stinson Memorial Park   ☎ (07) 5544 0008
Camp Area 27 km SE of Laravale on Christmas Creek Rd. 11 km S of Hillview. Bookings preferred
HEMA 11 J9   28 17 16 S   153 02 13 E

654 Andrew Drynan Park   ☎ (07) 5544 1281
Camp Area 18 km SE of Rathdowney. Turn E 4 km N of Rathdowney onto Running Creek Rd (Lions Tourist Rd). 3.5m clearance, 5 tonne limit, steep grades & sharp curves into NSW via Lions Tourist Rd. Access only from the N due to damaged road S of the camp area
HEMA 11 K9   28 19 08 S   152 55 59 E

655 Rathdowney Caravan Park   ☎ 0467 684 879
Caravan Park at Rathdowney. Running Creek Rd, just E of PO
HEMA 11 J8   28 12 42 S   152 51 55 E

656 Bigriggen Park Reserve   ☎ (07) 5463 6190
Camp Area 9 km W of Rathdowney. Turn W off Mt Lindesay Hwy 1 km S of Rathdowney onto Rathdowney-Boonah Rd for 7 km. S onto Upper Logan Rd for 500m, then R onto Bigriggen Rd. Dirt road
HEMA 10 J7   28 11 53 S   152 46 46 E

Notes...

QUEENSLAND

657 Flanagan Reserve ☎ (07) 5544 3128
Camp Area 14 km W of Rathdowney. Turn S off Rathdowney-Boonah Rd onto Upper Logan Rd (4 km), then Flanagan Reserve Rd. Dirt road. Coin operated showers
HEMA 10 J7   28 12 50 S   152 45 55 E

658 Lake Maroon Holiday Park ☎ (07) 5463 6256
Camp Area at Lake Maroon. 28 km W of Rathdowney or 32 km S of Boonah. 535 Burnett Creek Rd
HEMA 10 H6   28 12 05 S   152 38 43 E

659 Mt Barney Lodge Country Retreat ☎ (07) 5544 3233
Camp Area 19 km W of Rathdowney, 1093 Upper Logan Rd. Dirt road. Bookings essential
HEMA 10 J7   28 16 32 S   152 44 19 E

Toowoomba to Goondiwindi
Gore Highway

660 Yarramalong Weir ☎ (07) 4695 1399
Camp Spot 25 km SW of Pittsworth. From Gore Hwy, turn E 11 km N of Millmerran or 33 km S of Pittsworth onto Leyburn Rd for 11 km, then N onto Yarramalong Rd. 3 km to weir. Signposted
HEMA 13 G10   27 50 07 S   151 27 02 E

661 Walpole Park
Rest Area at Millmerran. In Charles St between Walpole & Charlotte Sts. 400m E of PO. Dump point opposite park. Self Contained Vehicles only
HEMA 13 G10   27 52 17 S   151 16 28 E

662 Millmerran Showgrounds ☎ 0427 957 176
Camp Area at Millmerran Showgrounds. N end of town on Millmerran-Cecil Plains Rd. Entry just past Aerodrome
HEMA 13 G10   27 51 37 S   151 16 40 E

663 Wyaga Creek Rest Area
Rest Area 74 km SW of Millmerran or 64 km NE of Goondiwindi. At Yelarbon turnoff
HEMA 13 H9   28 09 32 S   150 39 23 E

Notes...

Toowoomba to Stanthorpe
New England Highway

664 Federation Park
Rest Area 13 km S of Toowoomba or 71 km N of Warwick, on Drayton Connection Rd
HEMA 10 C1   27 39 09 S   151 53 32 E

665 Shammah Park ☎ 07 4697 1414
Camp Area at Ramsay. 136 Dixon Ln, 24 km S of Toowoomba via New England Hwy. Self Contained Vehicles only. Not suitable for big rigs due to weight restrictions. Maximum stay 14 days. Mobile 0411 753 912
HEMA 10 D1   27 44 28 S   151 56 31 E

666 Nobby Town Park
Rest Area at Nobby. Opposite Rudds Hotel. Limited power available for a fee. Pay at hotel
HEMA 10 E1   27 51 08 S   151 54 13 E

667 Clifton Recreation Grounds ☎ 131 872
Camp Area at Clifton. N side of town in Morton St, via Clark & Devonport Sts. Caretaker on site for payment or Shire Offices. Maximum stay 7 days
HEMA 10 F1   27 55 34 S   151 54 45 E

668 O'Shanley's Pub ☎ (07) 4697 3288
Parking Area at Clifton. Clarke St. Check in with publican, shower available in hotel
HEMA 10 F1   27 55 54 S   151 54 24 E

669 Clifton Golf Club ☎ 0427 973 638
Camp Spot 12 km W of Clifton on the Clifton-Leyburn Rd. Self Contained Vehicles only
HEMA 10 F1   27 56 41 S   151 47 35 E

670 Leyburn Rest Area
Rest Area 66 km SW of Toowoomba or 24 km N of Karara. Across bridge near General Store
HEMA 13 H10   28 00 27 S   151 34 58 E

671 Spring Creek Caravan Park ☎ (07) 4697 3397
Caravan Park 8 km E of Clifton or 9 km N of Allora. New England Hwy
HEMA 10 F1   27 57 00 S   151 59 28 E

672 Allora Showgrounds ☎ 0402 717 836
Camp Area at Allora. Darling St. Maximum stay 7 nights. Alt mobile 0427 100 210
HEMA 10 G1   28 02 19 S   151 59 24 E

673 Allora Rest Area
Rest Area at Allora. N side of town. Access from Herbert St off Allora Dr. Beside Dalrymple Creek
HEMA 10 G1   28 01 45 S   151 58 58 E

674 Killarney Sundown Motel Tourist Park ☎ (07) 4664 1318
Caravan Park at Killarney. 2-4 Pine St
HEMA 10 K4   28 20 29 S   152 17 46 E

675 Cherrabah Homestead Resort ☎ (07) 4667 9177
Camp Area 30 SE of Warwick. 1 Keoghs Rd, Elbow Valley
HEMA 10 K2   28 26 11 S   152 05 34 E

676 Jim Mitchell Park
Rest Area at Dalveen. 40 km S of Warwick or 18 km N of Stanthorpe. Mountain Park Rd
HEMA 13 J11   28 29 21 S   151 58 14 E

677 Blue Topaz Caravan Park & Camping Ground ☎ (07) 4683 5279
Caravan Park 6 km S of Stanthorpe on the New England Hwy
HEMA 13 J11   28 41 50 S   151 54 21 E

678 Country Style Tourist Accommodation Park ☎ (07) 4683 4358
Caravan Park 1 km N of Glen Aplin or 9 km S of Stanthorpe. New England Hwy. Beside river
HEMA 13 J11   28 43 24 S   151 53 19 E

679 Bald Rock & Castle Rock Campgrounds ☎ 13 74 68
Girraween National Park
Camp Area 35 km S of Stanthorpe. Turn E off New England Hwy 7 km S of Ballandean or 11 km N of Wallangarra onto Pyramids Rd for 9 km
HEMA 13 K11   28 49 58 S   151 56 16 E

Notes...

680 Wallangarra Lions Park
Rest Area at Wallangarra
HEMA 13 K11   28 55 18 S   151 55 41 E

681 Broadwater Campground ☎ 13 74 68
Sundown National Park
Camp Area 79 km SW of Stanthorpe or 70 km W of Tenterfield, via Bruxner Hwy & Glenlyon Dam Rd. 5 km E of Glenlyon Dam Rd along Permanents Rd. Small vehicles only. 4 km of gravel road
HEMA 13 K10   28 55 09 S   151 34 36 E

Brisbane to Goondiwindi
Cunningham Highway

682 Kalbar Showground ☎ 0499 970 119
Camp Area at Kalbar. George St. N end of town
HEMA 10 F6   27 56 15 S   152 37 32 E

683 Fassifern Memorial Reserve
Rest Area 5 km NE of Aratula or 16 km S of Warrill View
HEMA 10 F6   27 57 30 S   152 34 46 E

684 Boonah Showgrounds ☎ (07) 5463 4080
Camp Area at Showgrounds. Entry via Melbourne St
HEMA 10 G7   27 59 51 S   152 41 06 E

685 Aratula Hotel Motel ☎ (07) 5463 8100
Parking Area at Aratula. Check in with manager on arrival. Self Contained Vehicles only
HEMA 10 F6   27 58 57 S   152 32 51 E

686 The Gorge Campground ☎ (07) 5526 0683
Camp Area 3 km S of Aratula, via Charlwood Rd & Gorge Rd. Dirt road
HEMA 10 G6   28 00 37 S   152 33 16 E

687 Maryvale Crown Hotel ☎ (07) 4666 1148
Parking Area at Maryvale. 47 Taylor St. Self Contained Vehicles only
HEMA 10 G3   28 04 18 S   152 14 22 E

688 Gladfield Rest Area
Rest Area at Gladfield, Cunningham Hwy
HEMA 10 G3   28 04 26 S   152 11 12 E

689 Gleneden Family Farm ☎ 0429 137 224
Camp Area. 375 North Branch Rd. Turn 650m W of Maryvale or 18 km E of junction of New England and Cunningham Hwys
HEMA 10 G3   28 02 10 S   152 14 57 E

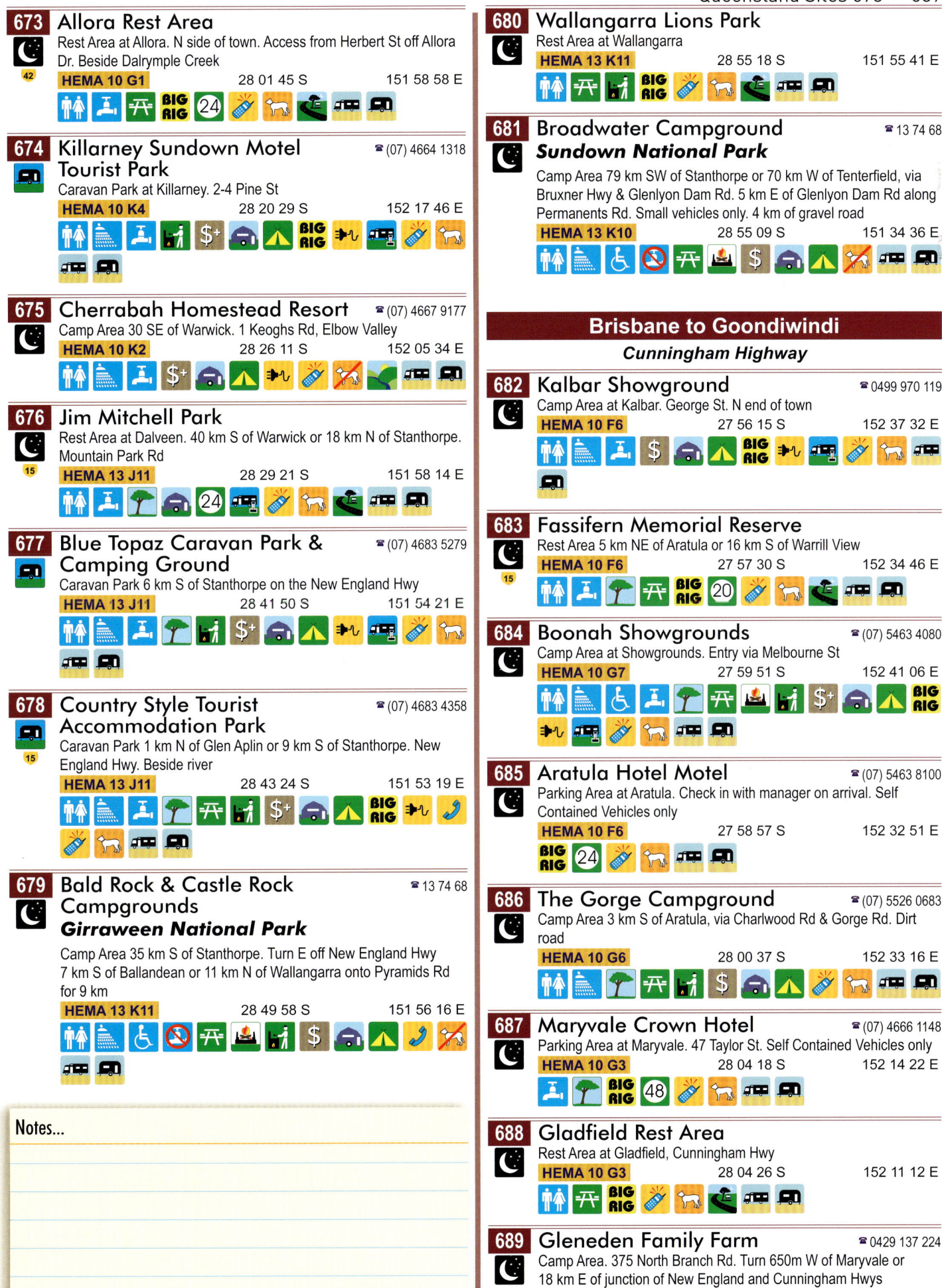

QUEENSLAND

690 Janowen Hills Camping and 4WD Park ☎ (07) 4666 6207
Camp Area 15 km E of Goomburra on Inverramsay Rd
HEMA 10 G3   27 59 44 S   152 15 18 E

691 Goomburra Valley Campground ☎ (07) 4666 6006
Camp Area 20 km E of Goomburra. 2013 Inverramsay Rd . Dog Vaccination Certificate must be sighted upon arrival. Dog bond payable
HEMA 10 F3   27 58 49 S   152 17 37 E

692 Gordon Country ☎ (07) 4666 6179
Camp Area 20 km E of Goomburra. Take Inverramsay Rd out of Goomburra
HEMA 10 F4   27 58 39 S   152 17 52 E

693 Goomburra Forest Retreat ☎ (07) 4666 6058
Camp Area 25 km NW of Goomburra on Forestry Reserve Rd
HEMA 10 F4   27 58 44 S   152 20 16 E

694 Poplar Flat Camping Area
Main Range National Park ☎ 13 74 68
Camp Area 25 km E of Goomburra on Inverramsay Rd into Forest Reserve Rd
HEMA 10 F4   27 58 44 S   152 20 32 E

695 Manna Gum Camp Site
Main Range National Park ☎ 13 74 68
Camp Area 26 km E of Goomburra. E on Inverramsay Rd, into Forest Reserve Rd
HEMA 10 F4   27 58 51 S   152 20 49 E

696 Caltex Truck Stop Roadhouse
Parking Area 6 km N of Warwick
HEMA 10 H2   28 11 05 S   152 03 15 E

697 The Glen
Rest Area 14.5 km S of Warwick or 47 km N of Stanthorpe. Share with trucks
HEMA 10 J1   28 17 14 S   151 56 57 E

Notes...

698 Darling Downs Hotel (Sandy Creek Pub) ☎ (07) 4661 3413
Parking Area 10 km W of Warwick. Turn N off Cunningham Hwy 7 km W of Warwick or 41 km E of Karara onto Sandy Creek Rd for 3 km. Fee for shower
HEMA 10 H1   28 11 01 S   151 56 49 E

699 Washpool Camping Reserve ☎ (07) 4661 7844
Leslie Dam
Camp Area 18 km W of Warwick. Turn S off Cunningham Hwy 9 km W of Warwick or 39 km E of Karara. Beside lake
HEMA 10 J1   28 14 25 S   151 54 59 E

700 Cunningham Rest Area
Rest Area 33 km W of Warwick or 17 km E of Karara
HEMA 13 H11   28 10 10 S   151 43 52 E

701 Glendon Camping Grounds ☎ (07) 4667 4756
Camp Area 38 km W of Warwick or 10 km E of Karara. 222 Glendon Rd, Thane
HEMA 13 H11   28 10 30 S   151 41 48 E

702 Gore Rest Area
Rest Area at Gore, next to store. 63 km W of Warwick or 47 km E of Inglewood. Fee for shower
HEMA 13 H10   28 17 42 S   151 29 19 E

703 Oman-ama Rest Area
Rest Area at Oman-ama. 88 km W of Warwick or 22 km E of Inglewood. E side of servo
HEMA 13 J10   28 23 50 S   151 17 42 E

704 Lake Coolmunda Camping Area ☎ (07) 4652 4171
Camp Area at Lake Coolmunda, 16 km E of Inglewood, via Coolmunda Dam Access Rd. Register & pay at caravan park. Deposit on key payable
HEMA 13 J10   28 25 18 S   151 12 49 E

705 Lake Roadhouse ☎ (07) 4652 4274
Parking Area 13 km E of Inglewood on the Cunningham Hwy. Showers available during operating hours (day only)
HEMA 13 J10   28 24 28 S   151 12 13 E

706 Inglewood RV Stop
Parking Area at Inglewood. N end of town, grassed area just S of McIntyre Brook bridge. Opposite the park. Self Contained Vehicles only
HEMA 13 J10   28 24 42 S   151 05 09 E

707 Texas Caravan Park ☎ (07) 4653 1194
Caravan Park at Texas. Avon St
HEMA 13 K10   28 50 56 S   151 10 08 E

708 Dumaresq River
Picnic Area 1 km S of Texas. Opposite stock inspection station.
Maximum stay 14 days. Self Contained Vehicles only
HEMA 13 K10   28 52 03 S   151 09 51 E

709 Goat Rock Camping Ground & Tourist Park ☎ (07) 4653 0999
Camp Area 16 km S of Texas. 1040 Goat Rock Rd off Bruxner Way
HEMA 13 K10   28 57 43 S   151 06 02 E

710 Carisbrooke Camping & Fishing Reserve
Camp Spot 14.5 km SW of Inglewood on Cunningham Hwy. 300m N
of McDougalls Rd, beside river. N side of road
HEMA 13 J9   28 27 58 S   150 57 32 E

✓711 Yelarbon Recreation Ground ☎ (07) 4675 1224
Camp Area at Yelarbon, 41 km SW of Inglewood. Wyemo St. AH
contact 0438 024 158
42
HEMA 13 J9   28 34 34 S   150 45 24 E

712 Munda Rest Area
Rest Area 69 km W of Inglewood or 21 km E of Goondiwindi
42
HEMA 13 J8   28 29 19 S   150 29 10 E

713 Monte Cristo Rest Area
Rest Area 41 km N of Goondiwindi or 52 km S of Moonie on
Leichhardt Hwy
A5
HEMA 13 H8   28 10 49 S   150 16 49 E

Goondiwindi to Thargomindah
Barwon and Balonne Highways

714 Toobeah Coronation Hotel ☎ (07) 4677 5280
Parking Area at Toobeah. Behind hotel, please check in at the bar
before parking. Free to patrons
HEMA 12 J7   28 25 01 S   149 52 14 E

715 Bungunya Rest Area
Rest Area at Bungunya, 69 km W of Goondiwindi or 87 km E of
Nindigully
HEMA 12 J7   28 25 23 S   149 39 28 E

716 Talwood Sports Ground ☎ (07) 4671 7400
Camp Spot at Talwood, 91 km W of Goondiwindi or 65 km E of
Nindigully. Donation appreciated for upkeep of grounds, please leave
at Talwood Store. Limited power
HEMA 12 J7   28 29 12 S   149 28 08 E

717 Weengallon Rest Area
Rest Area at Weengallon. 40 km W of Talwood or 26 km E of
Nindigully. S side of Hwy
HEMA 12 H6   28 21 29 S   149 03 17 E

✓718 Nindigully
Camp Spot at Nindigully, 1 km S of Barwon Hwy jcn. Camping beside
Moonie River, across from the hotel. Donation for upkeep of facilities
46
HEMA 12 H5   28 21 17 S   148 49 15 E

719 Thallon Recreation Ground ☎ 0427 259 095
Camp Spot at Thallon. Call mobile for access key or see PO during
business hours
46
HEMA 12 J5   28 37 58 S   148 51 59 E

720 Boolba Rest Area
Rest Area 56 km W of St George or 56 km E of Bollon
49
HEMA 12 H4   27 58 10 S   148 02 36 E

✓721 Wallum Creek
Camp Spot at Bollon. Willliam St. beside creek. Donation for upkeep
HEMA 12 H3   28 01 40 S   147 28 41 E

722 Charlotte Plains ☎ (07) 4655 4923
Camp Area. Turn S 135 km W of Bollon or 46 km E of Cunnamulla,
then 15 km dirt road to homestead. Signposted. Advance bookings
preferred
HEMA 23 F14   28 04 55 S   146 10 32 E

723 Warrego River
Camp Spot 95.7 km S of Cunnamulla or 38.7 km N of Barringum.
Turn W 89 km S of Cunnamulla into Tinnenburra Rd for 6.7 km to
bush camping area by river
HEMA 23 G13   28 44 04 S   145 36 38 E

Notes...

724 Bowra Sanctuary ☎ (07) 4655 1238

Camp Area 10 km N of Cunnamulla via the Humeburn Rd. Turn W at signposted gate, then 6 kms to house. Bookings essential limited sites & power. Closed to public summer period Dec to Feb

HEMA 23 F13   27 59 32 S   145 40 22 E

725 Wyandra Camping Ground ☎ (07) 4655 2481

Camp Area at Wyandra, N end of town, behind school. Donations requested

A71

HEMA 23 D13   27 14 37 S   145 58 36 E

726 Wyandra Post & General Store ☎ (07) 4654 9212

Camp Area at Wyandra, N end of town, behind PO & General Store

HEMA 23 D13   27 14 46 S   145 58 48 E

A71

727 Paddabilla Bore

Camp Spot 50 km W of Cunnamulla or 16 km E of Eulo. 300m behind bore

HEMA 23 F12   28 07 02 S   145 11 40 E

728 Eulo Queen Hotel ☎ (07) 4655 4867

Camp Area at Hotel in Eulo. Leo St

HEMA 23 F12   28 09 37 S   145 02 49 E

729 Paroo River

Camp Spot 1.5 km W of Eulo or 128 km E of Thargomindah. Both sides of bridge

HEMA 23 F11   28 09 38 S   145 02 12 E

730 Wandilla Station ☎ (07) 4655 4065

Camp Area at Wandilla Station. 15 km S of Eulo. From Eulo, head S on Pitherty Rd, turn W at the Big Yellow Sponge Bob letterbox

HEMA 23 F11   28 17 04 S   144 59 09 E

731 Corni Paroo Waterhole and Caiwarro Camp Areas
Currawinya National Park

Camp Areas in National Park. Approx 35 km NE of Ranger Station or 72 km S of Eulo. 4WD only, small off road caravans & motorhomes. Toilets at Caiwarro Ruins. Permit required

HEMA 23 G11   28 41 13 S   144 47 12 E

Notes...

732 Ourimperee Waterhole Bush Camping Area ☎ 13 74 68
Currawinya National Park

Camp Area in National Park. Behind Currawinya Woolshed. 25 km N Hungerford Entrance or 105 km S Eulo. 4WD only, small off road caravans & motorhomes. Cold showers. Permit required

HEMA 23 H10   28 52 59 S   144 30 36 E

733 Southern Cross Caravan Park ☎ (07) 4655 4105

Caravan Park at Hungerford. Honesty box provided for outside hours

HEMA 23 H10   28 59 51 S   144 24 35 E

734 Kilcowera Station ☎ (07) 4655 4960

Camp Area at Kilcowera Station. 95 km S Thargomindah or 90 km N of Hungerford. Bookings essential. High clearance 4WD. Open 1st March to 31st October

HEMA 23 G9   28 40 52 S   143 56 14 E

735 Artesian Waters Caravan Park ☎ (07) 4655 4953

Caravan Park at Yowah Opal Field. 87 km NW of Eulo. Bluff Rd

HEMA 23 F11   27 58 15 S   144 38 17 E

736 Yowah Rest Area

Rest Area at Yowah. Gemwood St, first turn L after school. Donation requested

HEMA 23 F11   27 58 01 S   144 37 59 E

737 Aldville Station ☎ 07 4655 4814

Camp Area at Aldville Station. 120 km NW of Cunnamulla or 110 kms W of Wyandra. Advance booking appreciated

HEMA 23 D12   27 17 45 S   145 09 12 E

738 Toompine Hotel ☎ (07) 4656 4863

Camp Area at Toompine Hotel, 76 km S of Quilpie or 120 km N of Thargomindah. Donation requested

HEMA 23 D10   27 13 30 S   144 22 05 E

739 Lake Bindegolly Bush Camping

Camp Spot 34 km E of Thargomindah or 90 km W of Eulo. Turn S 100m W of National Park Rest Area entrance, follow track. Signposted. Do not camp in rest area

HEMA 23 F10   28 05 35 S   144 12 12 E

740 Thargomindah Explorers Caravan Park ☎ (07) 4655 3307

Caravan Park at Thargomindah. Dowling St. 500m W of PO

HEMA 23 F9   27 59 51 S   143 49 11 E

QUEENSLAND

741 Napunyah Caravan Park ☎ (07) 4655 3198
Caravan Park at Thargomindah. 37 Powell St
HEMA 23 F9   27 59 49 S   143 49 31 E

742 Bulloo Development Rd
Parking Area 75 km W of Thargomindah or 63 E of Noccundra turn off
HEMA 23 E8   27 46 24 S   143 21 22 E

743 Wilson River Camp ☎ (07) 4655 4317
Camp Spot at Noccundra. Track opposite hotel. Sites beside river. Facilities at hall
HEMA 22 E7   27 49 16 S   142 35 26 E

744 Noccundra Hotel ☎ (07) 4655 3097
Camp Area at Noccundra. Check in with publican. Limited powered sites
HEMA 22 E7   27 49 04 S   142 35 20 E

745 Jackson Oil Field Rest Area
Rest Area. Cnr of Cooper Development Rd & Adventure Way
HEMA 22 E7   27 37 59 S   142 41 01 E

746 Burke & Wills Dig Tree
Nappa Merrie Station
Camp Area 46 km E of Innamincka or 225 km W of Noccundra on the Adventure Way. Signposted
HEMA 22 E4   27 37 19 S   141 04 24 E

Rolleston to Hebel (NSW border)
Carnarvon and Castlereagh Highways

747 Lake Nuga Nuga ☎ 13 74 68
Nuga Nuga National Park
Camp Area 85 km SE of Rolleston. Access via Arcadia Valley Access Rd, 28 km SE of Rolleston on Dawson Hwy. 58 km gravel road, then W onto Lake Nuga Nuga Access Rd. Dirt road, 4WD recommended. E-Permit required
HEMA 12 A5   24 59 32 S   148 41 04 E

748 Arcadia Valley Escape ☎ (07) 4626 7197
Camp Area 130 km S of Rolleston or 73 km N of Injune via Carnarvon Hwy & Arcadia Valley Rd. Entry via "Sunnyholt" at stone gates, follow signs to camp area. Bookings preferred
HEMA 12 B5   25 18 43 S   148 50 37 E

749 Wallaroo Parking Area
Parking Area 105 km S of Rolleston or 68 km N of Injune. Share with trucks, tracks into bush at rear of parking area
HEMA 12 B5   25 18 09 S   148 39 31 E

750 Lonesome Bush Camping Area ☎ 13 74 68
Expedition National Park
Camp Area 55 km NE of Injune. Travel N for 26 km on Carnarvon Hwy, turn E onto Arcadia Valley Rd, 18 km to campsite, signposted. E-Permit required
HEMA 12 B5   25 29 28 S   148 49 51 E

751 Injune Rodeo Ground ☎ (07) 4626 0503
Parking Area at Injune. 1.6 km S of town, park in fenced off area on southern side of buidings. Self Contained Vehicles only
HEMA 12 C5   25 51 14 S   148 33 28 E

752 Possum Park (Racecourse) ☎ (07) 4626 0503
Camp Area at Injune. Racecourse Rd, off the Carnarvon Hwy. Pay at Info Centre, caretaker will visit
HEMA 12 C5   25 50 49 S   148 33 25 E

753 Croydon Rest Area
Rest Area 31 km S of Roma or 47 km N of Surat
HEMA 12 E6   26 46 47 S   148 56 03 E

754 Toalki Rest Area
Rest Area 65 km S of Roma or 13 km N of Surat
HEMA 12 E6   27 02 04 S   149 04 58 E

755 Surat Fishing & Restocking Club Park ☎ (07) 4626 5058
Camp Area 1 km N of Surat. Just over Balonne River. Gold coin donation
HEMA 12 F6   27 08 57 S   149 04 23 E

756 Surat Caravan Park ☎ (07) 4626 5218
Caravan Park at Surat. Marcus St. Key & payment at Hotel opposite
HEMA 12 F6   27 09 05 S   149 03 59 E

757 Warroo Bridge
Camp Spot 60 km N of St George. Turn W at Wycombe School, 66 km S of Surat or 51 km N of St George for 9 km of dirt road
HEMA 12 G5   27 38 34 S   148 44 28 E

Notes...

QUEENSLAND

758 Beardmore

Camp Spot 15 km N of St George. Turn W off Carnarvon Hwy 103 km S of Surat or 14 km N of St George onto Beardmore Dam Rd for 1 km. Left at 1st grid. Camp beside river

HEMA 12 H5   27 57 25 S   148 40 59 E

759 Kapunda Tourist & Fishing Park   ☎ (07) 4625 5546

Camp Area at St George. 9 km N of PO on Carnarvon Hwy. GPS at gate

HEMA 12 H5   27 59 14 S   148 39 33 E

55

760 Thomby Rest Area

Rest Area 38 km E of St George or 148 km W of Moonie

HEMA 12 H6   27 58 08 S   148 56 17 E

49

761 Westmar Rest Area

Rest Area at Westmar. Adjacent to pub

HEMA 12 H7   27 55 09 S   149 42 55 E

49

762 Kamarooka Tourist Park   ☎ (07) 4625 3120

Caravan Park at St George. 56 Victoria St

HEMA 12 H5   28 02 01 S   148 35 12 E

55

763 Noondoo Rest Area

Rest Area 19.5 km E of Dirranbandi or 76 km S of St George. Share with trucks

HEMA 12 J5   28 36 36 S   148 25 23 E

764 Dirranbandi Caravan Park   ☎ (07) 4625 8707

Caravan Park at Dirranbandi. 45 Kirby St

HEMA 12 J4   28 34 53 S   148 13 44 E

765 Balonne Minor Bridge

Rest Area 3 km W of Dirranbandi, on Dirranbandi-Bollon Rd

HEMA 12 J4   28 35 56 S   148 12 34 E

766 Hebel Caravan Park   ☎ (07) 4625 0920

Caravan Park at Hebel. William St, behind general store

HEMA 12 K3   28 58 18 S   147 47 44 E

Notes...

Cairns to Cape York

This road is seasonal and more suitable to 4WD vehicles, camper trailers and off road caravans. Road conditions phone Main Roads 131 940, Cooktown Shire 07 4069 5444 or RACQ 1300 130 595

767 Ang-Ganrra Aboriginal Community

Camp Spot 61 km NW of Lakeland or 1 km SE of Laura. Signposted

HEMA 19 K5   15 39 01 S   144 32 02 E

768 Quinkan Hotel & Camp Ground   ☎ (07) 4060 3393

Camp Area at Laura. At hotel. Limited power available

HEMA 19 K5   15 33 59 S   144 27 01 E

769 Quinkan Centre Campground   ☎ (07) 4060 3419

Camp Area at Laura. S end of town. Pay at Laura Roadhouse opposite

HEMA 19 K5   15 33 57 S   144 26 57 E

770 Elim Beach Campsite - Eddies Camp   ☎ (07) 4060 9223

Camp Area at Elim Beach. 25km E Hopevale. 4WD recommended

HEMA 19 J7   15 15 37 S   145 16 55 E

771 Horseshoe Lagoon & Welcome Waterhole   ☎ 13 74 68
Rinyirru (Lakefield) National Park

Camp Area in southern area of National Park. Turn off Battle Camp Rd 20km E of Old Laura Homestead, travel 2 km, take left-hand track to Horseshoe Lagoon. 9 km to Welcome Waterhole. Sandy access, 4WD only. Permit required, bookings essential

HEMA 19 J6   15 17 07 S   144 36 45 E

772 Old Laura Homestead   ☎ 13 74 68
Rinyirru (Lakefield) National Park

Camp Area at Old Laura Homestead, southern area of park. Near junction of Lakefield & Battle Camp Rds. 2 sites, either side of the road. 4WD only. Permit required, bookings essential

HEMA 19 J5   15 20 51 S   144 27 02 E

773 Six Mile Waterhole   ☎ 13 74 68
Rinyirru (Lakefield) National Park

Camp Area in southern area of the park. Turn off 12 km N of Old Laura Homestead or 15 km S of new Laura Ranger Base. 3 km sandy access track. 4WD only. Permit required, bookings essential

HEMA 19 J5   15 16 33 S   144 25 39 E

774 Twelve Mile Lagoon Camping Area ☎ 13 74 68
Rinyirru (Lakefield) National Park
Camp Area in southern area of park. Turn off opposite new Laura Ranger Base. 12 km sandy access track. 4WD only. Permit required, bookings essential
HEMA 19 J5   15 10 38 S   144 21 06 E

775 Kennedy Bend Camping Area ☎ 13 74 68
Rinyirru (Lakefield) National Park
Camp Area in southern area of park. 8 km N of new Laura Ranger Base & 25 km S of Lakefield Ranger Base. 4 sites, 4WD only. Permit required, bookings essential
HEMA 19 J5   15 06 59 S   144 18 45 E

776 Old Faithful Waterhole Camping Area ☎ 13 74 68
Rinyirru (Lakefield) National Park
Camp Area in southern area of park. Turn off 16 km N of new Laura Ranger Base or 17 km S of Lakefield Ranger Base. 6 km sandy access track. 3 sites. 4WD only. Permit required, bookings essential. GPS at entrance
HEMA 19 J5   15 03 09 S   144 17 16 E

777 Mick Fienn Waterhole Camping Area ☎ 13 74 68
Rinyirru (Lakefield) National Park
Camp Area in the central part of the park on Normanby River. Turn off 24 km N of New Laura Ranger base or 9 km S of Lakefield ranger base. 9 km to camp. GPS at turnoff. 4WD only, river crossing. Permit required, bookings essential
HEMA 19 J5   14 59 45 S   144 16 00 E

778 Kalpowar Crossing Camping Area ☎ 13 74 68
Rinyirru (Lakefield) National Park
Camp Area in the central part of the park, on Normanby River. Turn off 1 km S of Lakefield Ranger Base. 4WD only. Permit required, bookings essential
HEMA 19 J5   14 56 46 S   144 12 41 E

779 Hann Crossing Camping Area ☎ 13 74 68
Rinyirru (Lakefield) National Park
Camp Area in central part of park. Along Eastern & Western banks of North Kennedy River. 28 km NW of Lakefield Ranger Base or 81 km SE Musgrave Roadhouse. 4WD only. Permit required, bookings essential
HEMA 19 H5   14 45 52 S   144 04 34 E

780 Saltwater Crossing Camping Area ☎ 13 74 68
Rinyirru (Lakefield) National Park
Camp Area in the northern part of park. 32 km NW of Hann Crossing or 53 km E of Musgrave Roadhouse. 4 sites either side of creek. 4WD only. Permit required, bookings essential
HEMA 19 H4   14 37 07 S   143 53 58 E

781 Jowalbinna Rock Art Safari Camp ☎ (07) 4060 3236
Camp Area 36 km SW of Laura. Turn SW 1 km N of Laura. Signposted. 4WD access. Open May-Nov, reservations preferred
HEMA 19 K5   15 45 39 S   144 15 25 E

782 Kennedy River Rest Area
Rest Area 33 km N of Laura or 43 km S of Hann River Roadhouse
HEMA 19 K5   15 25 13 S   144 11 12 E

783 Hann River Roadhouse ☎ (07) 4060 3242
Camp Area at Hann River. 74 km NW of Laura or 62 km S of Musgrave
HEMA 19 J5   15 11 20 S   143 52 22 E

784 Morehead River Rest Area
Rest Area 27 km N of Hann River Roadhouse or 63 km S of Musgrave Roadhouse
HEMA 19 J4   15 01 22 S   143 39 50 E

785 Musgrave Roadhouse ☎ (07) 4060 3229
Camp Area at Musgrave. 62 km N of Hann River Roadhouse or 107 km S of Coen
HEMA 19 J4   14 46 51 S   143 30 14 E

786 Mungkan River Camping Area ☎ (07) 4060 4155
Camp Area at Pormpuraaw. 210 km W of Musgrave. 7.5 km N of township. Permit required from Ranger
HEMA 19 J1   14 51 31 S   141 36 13 E

787 Chapman River ☎ (07) 4060 4155
Camp Area at Pormpuraaw. 210 km W of Musgrave. 2.5 km S of township. Permit required from Ranger
HEMA 19 J1   14 55 00 S   141 37 18 E

788 Lukin River Rest Area
Rest Area 55 km S of Coen or 53 km N of Musgrave Roadhouse. E side on N of the river. Small area
HEMA 19 H4   14 23 43 S   143 21 42 E

Notes...

789 Port Stewart Campground
Camp Area at Port Stewart. 19 km E of Peninsula Development Rd. Register at community offices
HEMA 19 G4 14 04 10 S 143 40 58 E

790 Exchange Hotel ☎ (07) 4060 1133
Camp Area at Coen, behind hotel. Please register at bar
HEMA 19 G3 13 56 37 S 143 11 57 E

791 The Bend
Camp Spot on Peninsula Development Rd. 3 km N of Coen. Bush camping
HEMA 19 G3 13 55 27 S 143 11 38 E

792 Archer River Roadhouse ☎ (07) 4060 3266
Camp Area at Archer River Crossing. 64 km N of Coen or 123 km S of Moreton Telegraph Station
HEMA 19 F3 13 26 16 S 142 56 27 E

793 Chuulangun Aboriginal Corporation Campgrounds ☎ (07) 4060 3240
Camp Area 16 km E of the Peninsula Development Rd, 7 km off the Portland Roads Rd. Permit required
HEMA 19 F3 13 06 27 S 142 57 52 E

794 Batavia Goldfield Ruins
Camp Spot at ruins. Take LH (northern side) track just E of Wenlock River crossing, then veer R at fork, follow narrow track 1 km to ruins. Bush camping around ruins
HEMA 19 F3 13 05 15 S 142 56 48 E

795 Rainforest Campground ☎ 13 74 68
Kutini-Payamu (Iron Range) National Park
Camp Area 130 km NE of Archer River Roadhouse. Camp site near the Portland & Lockhart River Rd jcn. Permit required. 2 small sites. Must be prebooked
HEMA 19 E3 12 42 49 S 143 17 13 E

796 Cooks Hut Campground ☎ 13 74 68
Kutini-Payamu (Iron Range) National Park
Camp Area 130 km NE of Archer River Roadhouse. Camp site near the Portland & Lockhart River Rd jcn. Permit required
HEMA 19 E4 12 42 35 S 143 17 33 E

797 Gordon Creek Campground Sth ☎ 13 74 68
Kutini-Payamu (Iron Range) National Park
Camp Area 135 km NE of Archer River Roadhouse. Camp site near the Portland & Lockhart River Rd jcn. Permit required must be pre booked
HEMA 19 E3 12 42 48 S 143 17 53 E

798 Chilli Beach Campground ☎ 13 74 68
Kutini-Payamu (Iron Range) National Park
Camp Area 170 km NE of Archer River Rd Roadhouse. Permit required must be pre booked
HEMA 19 E4 12 37 52 S 143 25 36 E

799 Merluna Station Stay & Tourist Park ☎ (07) 4060 3209
Camp Area 150 km NW of Coen or 150 km SE of Weipa on the Peninsula Development Rd. Signposted
HEMA 19 F2 13 03 54 S 142 27 01 E

800 Weipa Caravan Park & Camping Ground ☎ (07) 4069 7871
Caravan Park at Weipa. Kerr Point Rd. Bookings essential in high season (June-Sep)
HEMA 19 E1 12 38 20 S 141 51 38 E

801 Moreton Telegraph Station Camping Ground ☎ (07) 4060 3360
Camp Area at Moreton Telegraph Station. 123 km N of Archer River Roadhouse. Limited power
HEMA 19 E3 12 27 13 S 142 38 19 E

802 Bramwell Station ☎ (07) 4060 3300
Camp Area at Bramwell Station. 37 km NE of Moreton Telegraph Station or 8 km SE of Bramwell Junction
HEMA 19 D3 12 08 26 S 142 37 19 E

803 Bramwell Roadhouse ☎ (07) 4060 3230
Camp Area at Bramwell Junction
HEMA 19 D2 12 05 33 S 142 33 37 E

Notes...

804 Captain Billys Landing
☎ 13 74 68
Heathlands Regional Park

Camp Area on Eastern Coast. 32 km narrow winding access track, 4WD, only suitable for high clearance small offroad caravans or campervans, limited turning or passing in places. Large open exposed area. Permit required, bookings essential

HEMA 19 C3 11 37 54 S 142 51 21 E

805 Eliot Falls Camping Area
☎ 13 74 68
Heathlands Regional Park

Camp Area at Eliot Falls. High clearance 4WD only, steep creek crossing. Limited sites for offroad campervans & camper trailers only. Permit required, bookings essential

HEMA 19 C2 11 23 06 S 142 24 43 E

806 Jardine River Ferry Campground & Service Station
☎ (07) 4069 1369

Camp Area on S side of Jardine River at Ferry Crossing

HEMA 19 C2 11 06 14 S 142 16 59 E

807 Alau Beach Campground
☎ (07) 4069 3029

Camp Area At Umagico

HEMA 19 B2 10 53 09 S 142 20 48 E

808 Seisia Holiday Park
☎ (07) 4203 0992

Caravan Park at Seisia. Koroba Rd

HEMA 19 B2 10 50 51 S 142 22 05 E

809 Loyalty Beach Campground & Fishing Lodge
☎ (07) 4069 3372

Camp Area at Loyalty Beach, Seisia

HEMA 19 B2 10 50 05 S 142 23 01 E

810 Cable Beach
☎ (07) 4069 1722

Camp Area at Cable Beach. Bookings & payment at Punsand Bay Camping Resort. Sandy track to sites

HEMA 19 B2 10 43 13 S 142 27 01 E

811 Punsand Bay Camping Resort
☎ (07) 4069 1722

Camp Area at Punsand Bay

HEMA 19 B2 10 43 19 S 142 27 47 E

Notes...

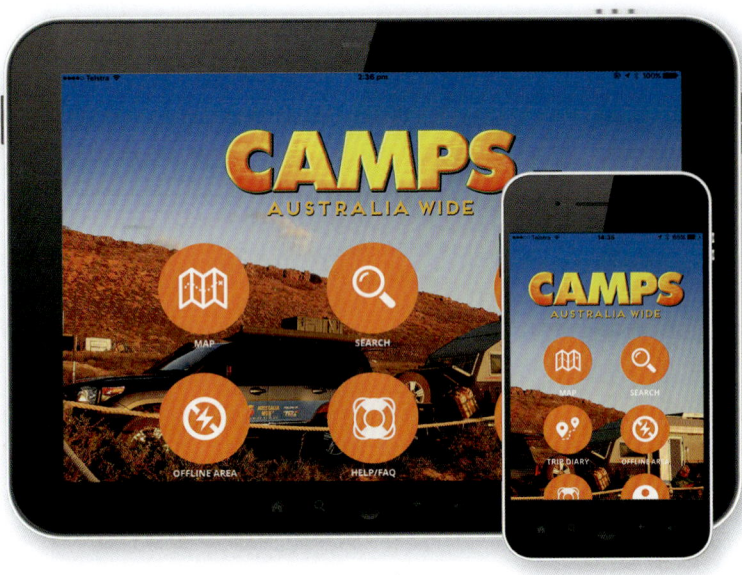
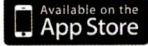 

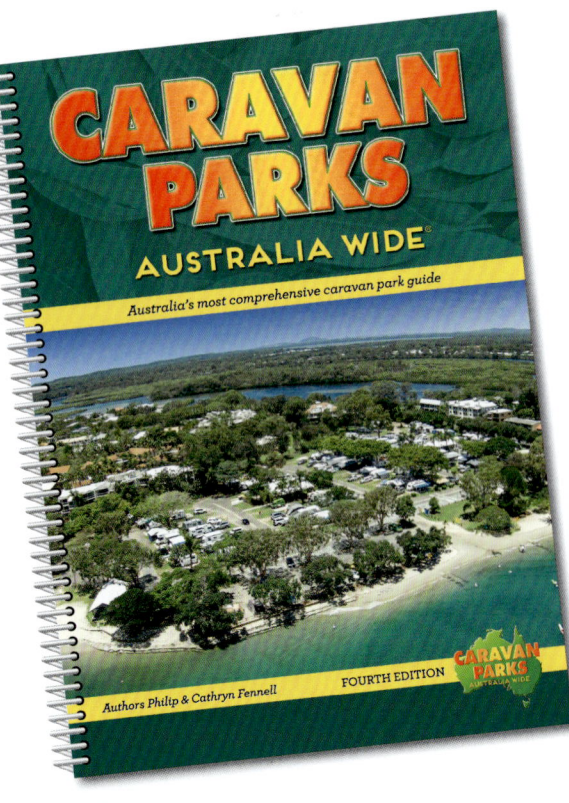

key map

THE THREE SISTER, BLUE MOUNTAINS (34 E4)

PHOTO: © ISTOCK.COM/TOMOGRAF

	Wagga Wagga	Tamworth	Sydney	Port Macquarie	Newcastle	Mildura	Lismore	Grafton	Goulburn	Dubbo	Canberra	Broken Hill	Bathurst	Armidale	Albury
Armidale															993
Bathurst														547	446
Broken Hill													981	1119	832
Canberra												1133	263	810	340
Dubbo											475	775	206	446	537
Goulburn										410	89	1155	174	721	362
Grafton									809	641	899	1314	742	195	1188
Lismore								134	943	775	1048	1448	876	329	1322
Mildura							1576	1442	859	801	807	296	810	1247	617
Newcastle						1188	628	479	358	428	448	1094	355	398	721
Port Macquarie					251	1411	397	248	600	603	671	1276	578	235	944
Sydney				382	159	1029	759	610	205	403	289	1177	196	529	562
Tamworth			414	272	283	1132	444	310	619	331	703	1004	432	115	878
Wagga Wagga		752	465	847	624	564	1224	1075	265	411	243	890	320	857	126
Wollongong	400	492	78	460	237	964	837	688	134	481	224	1255	274	607	526

Distances are shown in kilometres and follow the most direct major sealed route where possible.

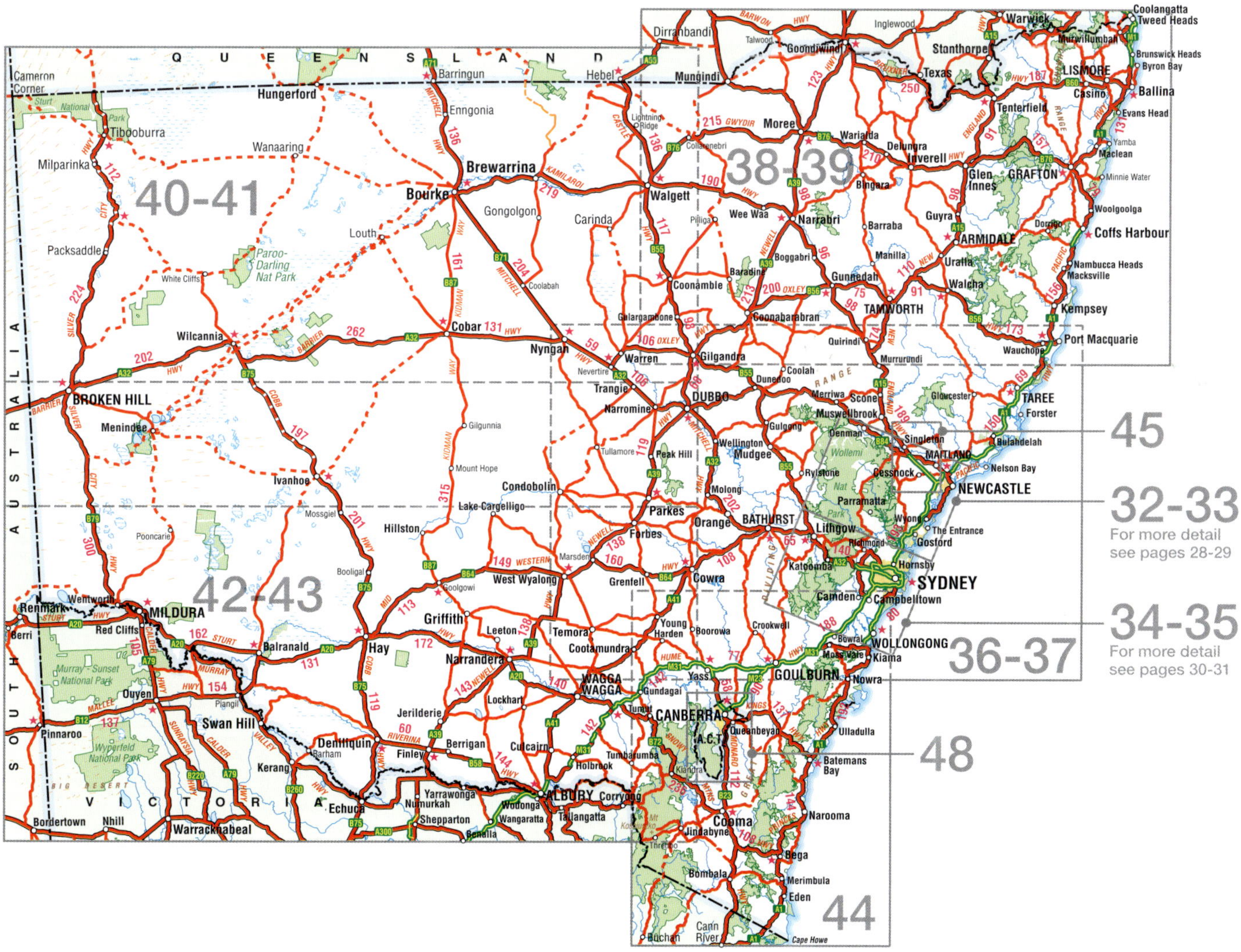

40-41

38-39

42-43

45

32-33
For more detail
see pages 28-29

34-35

36-37
For more detail
see pages 30-31

48

44

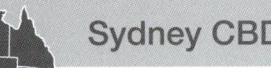

Legend

Freeway/B Double		Major Building	
Major Road		Govt Building	
Street		Theatre/Cinema	
Tunnel/B Double		Shopping	
Lane/Walkway		Hospital	
Railway	*Underground*	Post Office	
Railway Station	*Wynyard*	Tourist Info. Centre	

0 100 200 300 400 500 m
© Hema Maps Pty Ltd

Travel
90 Central Station D2
91 Circular Quay Station B2
92 Kings Cross Station C4
93 Martin Place Station C2
94 Museum Station D2
95 St James C2
96 Town Hall Station C2
97 Wynyard Station B2

Places of Interest
1 Anzac War Memorial D2
2 Art Gallery of NSW C3
3 Australian Museum C3
4 Australian Nat. Maritime Museum C1
5 Bridge Climb Sydney A2
6 Cadmans Cottage A2
7 Chinatown D1
8 Darling Harbour D1
9 Government House B3
10 Harbourside Shopping Centre C1
11 Hyde Park Barracks C3
12 LG IMAX Theatre Sydney C1
13 Mint, The C3
14 Mrs Macquarie's Chair A4
15 Museum of Contemporary Art B2
16 Parliament House B3
17 Powerhouse Museum D1
18 Rocks, The A2
19 Royal Botanic Gardens B3
20 SEA LIFE Sydney Aquarium C1
21 St Andrews Cathedral C2
22 St Marys Cathedral C3
23 St Stephens Church B2
24 Star, The C1
25 State Library of NSW B3
26 Sydney Conservatorium of Music B3
27 International Convention Centre C1
28 Sydney Opera House A3
29 Sydney Tower Eye & SKYWALK C2
30 Sydney Town Hall C2
31 Wharf Theatres A2
32 WILD LIFE Sydney Zoo C1

Accommodation
35 Aarons Hotel Sydney D1
36 Adina Apartment Hotel Harbourside C1
37 Adina Apartment Hotel Sydney C2
38 Amora Hotel Jamison Sydney B2
39 APX Apartments Darling Hbr D1
40 Arts Hotel D4
41 Blue Sydney D3
42 Cambridge Hotel Sydney D3
43 Castlereagh Boutique Hotel C2
45 Four Seasons Hotel Sydney B2
46 Grace Hotel Sydney (The) C2
47 Harbour Rocks Hotel (The) B2
48 Hilton Sydney C2
49 Hyde Park Inn D2
50 Ibis Sydney Darling Harbour C1
51 Ibis Sydney World Square D2
52 InterContinental Sydney B2
53 Langham Sydney (The) B1
54 Mantra 2 Bond Street B2
55 Mantra on Kent C1
56 Menzies Sydney (The) B2
57 Mercure Sydney D1
58 Metro Hotel Sydney Central D2
59 Napoleon on Kent B1
60 Novotel Sydney Central D1
61 Novotel Sydney on Darling Harbour C1
62 Oaks Hyde Park Plaza D3
63 Oaks Maestri Towers C1
64 Old Sydney Holiday Inn A2
65 Park Hyatt Hotel Sydney A2
66 Park Regis City Centre C2
67 Parkroyal Darling Harbour C1
68 Pullman Quay Grand Sydney Harbour B3
69 Pullman Sydney Hyde Park Hotel D3
70 Quay West Suites Sydney B2
71 Radisson Blue Plaza Hotel Sydney B2
72 Radisson Sydney D2
73 Rendezvous Hotel Sydney The Rocks B2
74 Russell Hotel B2
75 Rydges World Square Sydney D2
76 Seasons Harbour Plaza Sydney C1
77 Sebel Pier One Sydney (The) A2
78 Shangri-La Hotel Sydney B2
79 Sheraton on the Park C2
80 Sir Stamford at Circular Quay B2
81 Sofitel Sydney Wentworth B2
82 Swissotel Sydney C2
83 Sydney Boulevard Hotel (The) C3
84 Sydney Harbour Marriott Hotel B2
85 Travelodge Wynyard B2
86 Waldorf Apartment Hotel (The) D2
87 Waldorf Woolloomooloo Waters C4
88 Westin Sydney (The) C2
89 York by Swiss - Belhotel (The) B2

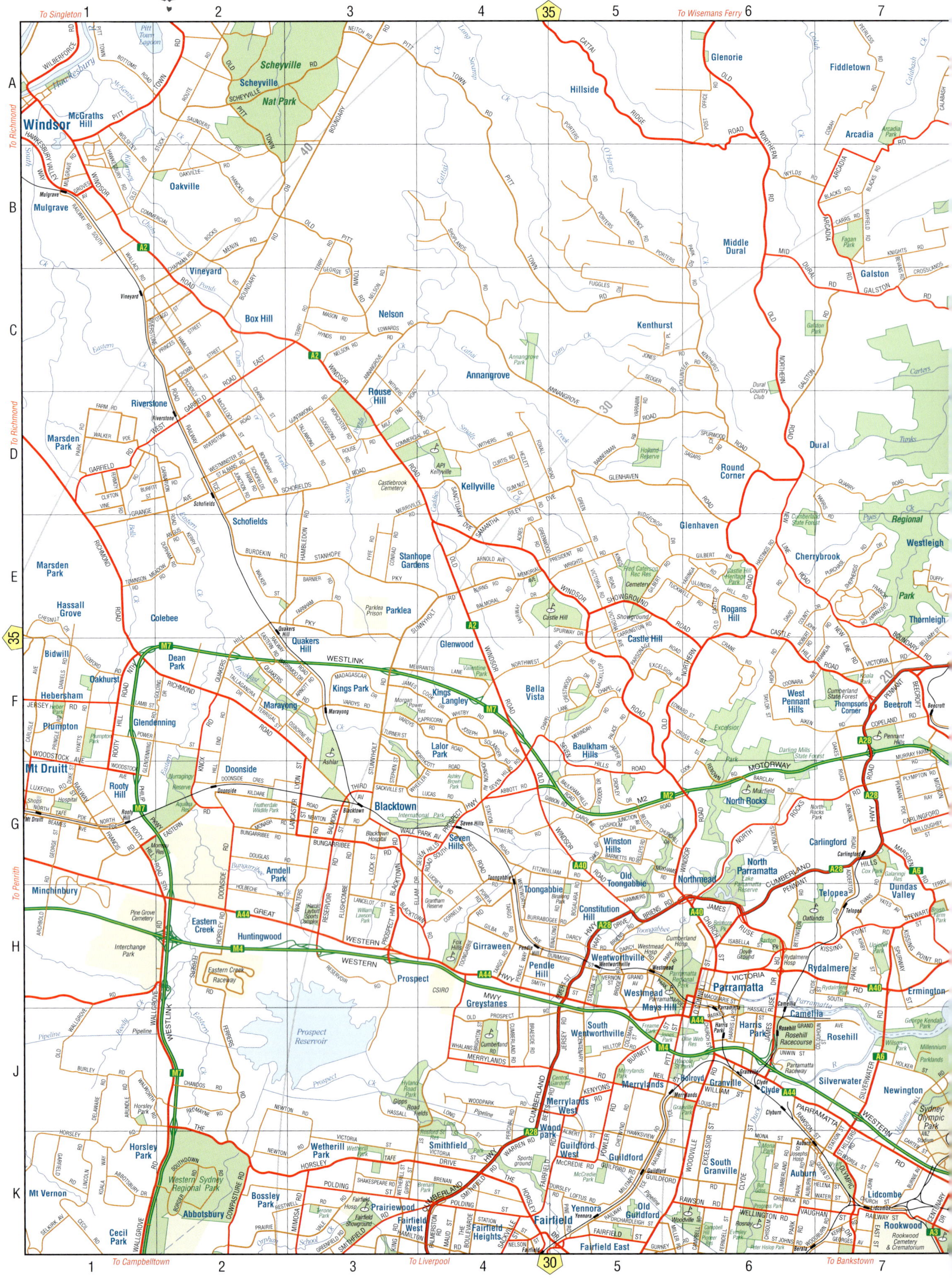
To Singleton
To Wisemans Ferry
To Richmond
To Penrith
To Campbelltown
To Liverpool
To Bankstown
Windsor
McGraths Hill
Mulgrave
Oakville
Scheyville
Scheyville Nat Park
Vineyard
Box Hill
Nelson
Riverstone
Marsden Park
Schofields
Rouse Hill
Annangrove
Kellyville
Hillside
Glenorie
Fiddletown
Arcadia
Middle Dural
Galston
Kenthurst
Dural
Round Corner
Glenhaven
Cherrybrook
Westleigh
Thornleigh
Stanhope Gardens
Parklea
Castle Hill
Rogans Hill
Marsden Park
Hassall Grove
Colebee
Quakers Hill
Glenwood
Bella Vista
West Pennant Hills
Beecroft
Bidwill
Dean Park
Oakhurst
Hebersham
Kings Park
Kings Langley
Plumpton
Glendenning
Marayong
Lalor Park
Baulkham Hills
Mt Druitt
Doonside
Rooty Hill
Blacktown
Seven Hills
Winston Hills
North Rocks
Carlingford
Minchinbury
Arndell Park
Toongabbie
Old Toongabbie
Northmead
North Parramatta
Telopea
Dundas Valley
Eastern Creek
Huntingwood
Constitution Hill
Girraween
Pendle Hill
Wentworthville
Prospect
Greystanes
Westmead
Parramatta
Mays Hill
Harris Park
Camellia
Rydalmere
Ermington
Prospect Reservoir
South Wentworthville
Rosehill
Merrylands
Holroyd
Granville
Clyde
Silverwater
Newington
Merrylands West
Smithfield
Wetherill Park
Horsley Park
Woodpark
Guildford West
Guildford
South Granville
Sydney Olympic Park
Lidcombe
Auburn
Western Sydney Regional Park
Abbotsbury
Bossley Park
Prairiewood
Fairfield West
Fairfield Heights
Fairfield
Yennora
Old Guildford
Fairfield East
Rookwood
Mt Vernon
Cecil Park
Interchange Park
Eastern Creek Raceway
Castle Hill Showground
Regional Park
Pennant Hills

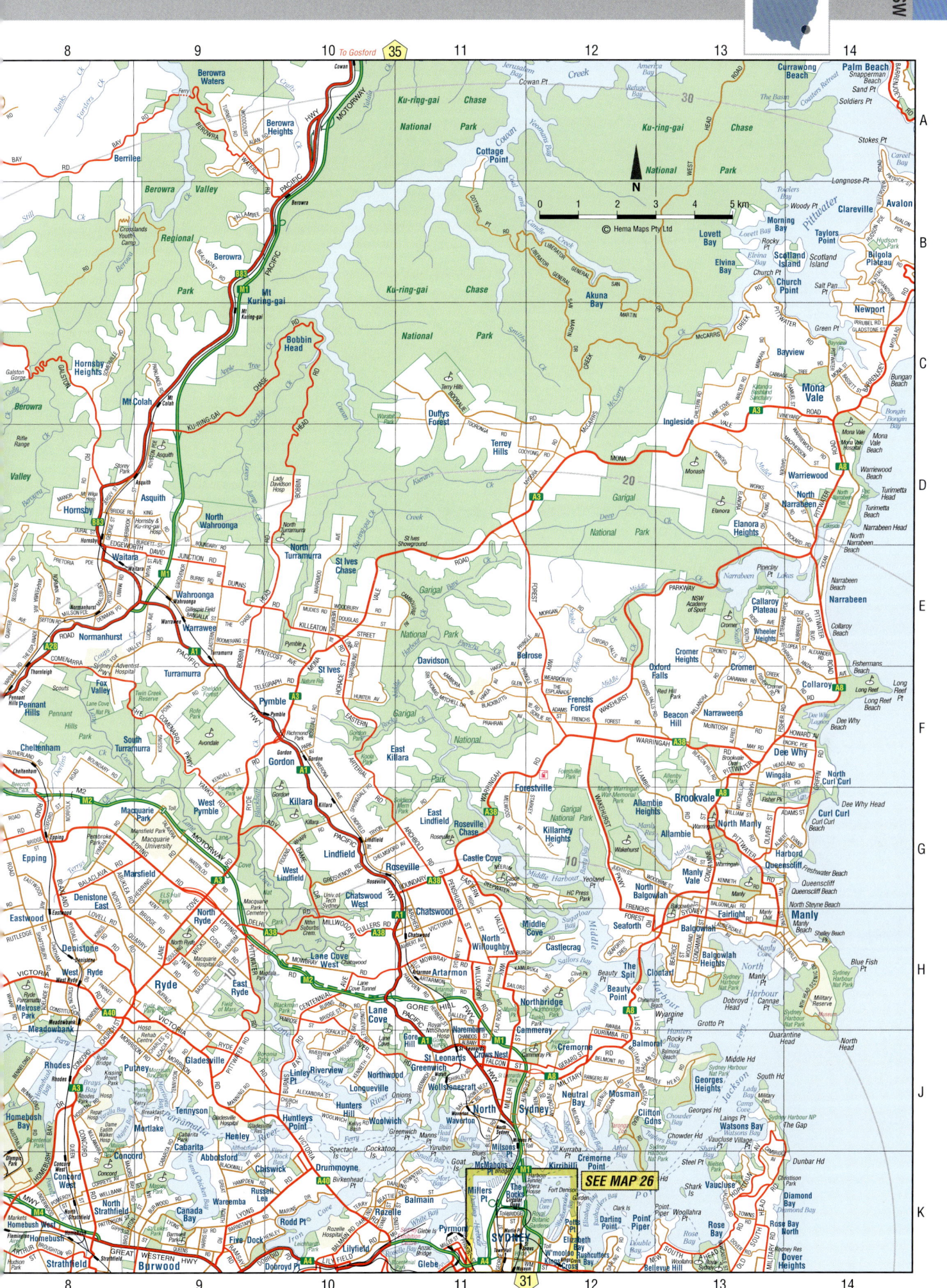

To Mt Druitt
To Penrith
To Gosford
To Camden
To Goulburn, Melbourne
To Wollongong
Prospect Reservoir
South Wentworthville
Harris Park
Rosehill
Silverwater
Newington
Sydney Olympic Park
Merrylands
Merrylands West
Holroyd
Granville
Clyde
Woodpark
Smithfield
Wetherill Park
Horsley Park
Guildford
Guildford West
South Granville
Auburn
Lidcombe
Mt Vernon
Western Sydney Regional Park
Abbotsbury
Bossley Park
Prairiewood
Fairfield West
Fairfield
Fairfield Heights
Yennora
Old Guildford
Cecil Park
Wakeley
Greenfield Park
Edensor Park
St Johns Park
Canley Heights
Canley Vale
Carramar
Fairfield East
Villawood
Chester Hill
Regents Park
Berala
Rookwood
Cecil Hills
Bonnyrigg Heights
Bonnyrigg
Cabramatta West
Cabramatta
Lansvale
Sefton
Birrong
Bass Hill
Chullora
Yagoona
Greenacre
Mt Pritchard
Heckenberg
Busby
Ashcroft
Warwick Farm
Chipping Norton
Georges Hall
Bankstown
Mt Lewis
Punchbowl
Hinchinbrook
Sadleir
Miller
Cartwright
Liverpool
Bankstown Airport
Condell Park
Austral
West Hoxton
Moorebank
Milperra
Roselands
Hoxton Park
Lurnea
Casula
Prestons
Panania
Revesby
Riverwood
Hammondville
Voyager Point
Padstow
Peakhurst
Edmondson Park
The Cross Roads
Chatham Village
Wattle Grove
East Hills
Revesby Heights
Padstow Heights
Glenfield
Holsworthy
Holsworthy Barracks
Pleasure Point
Sandy Point
Picnic Point
Alfords Point
Lugarno
Denham Court
Macquarie Links
Macquarie Fields
Military Reserve
Varroville
Ingleburn
Long Point
Illawong
Bangor
Como
Bonnet Bay
Menai
Bow Bowing
Raby
St Andrews
Minto
Barden Ridge
Woronora Heights
Woronora
Minto Heights
Eagle Vale
Lucas Heights
Loftus
Yarrawarrah
Woodbine
Leumeah
Campbelltown
Engadine
Ruse
Kentlyn
Heathcote
Heathcote National Park
Airds
Bradbury
Audley
National

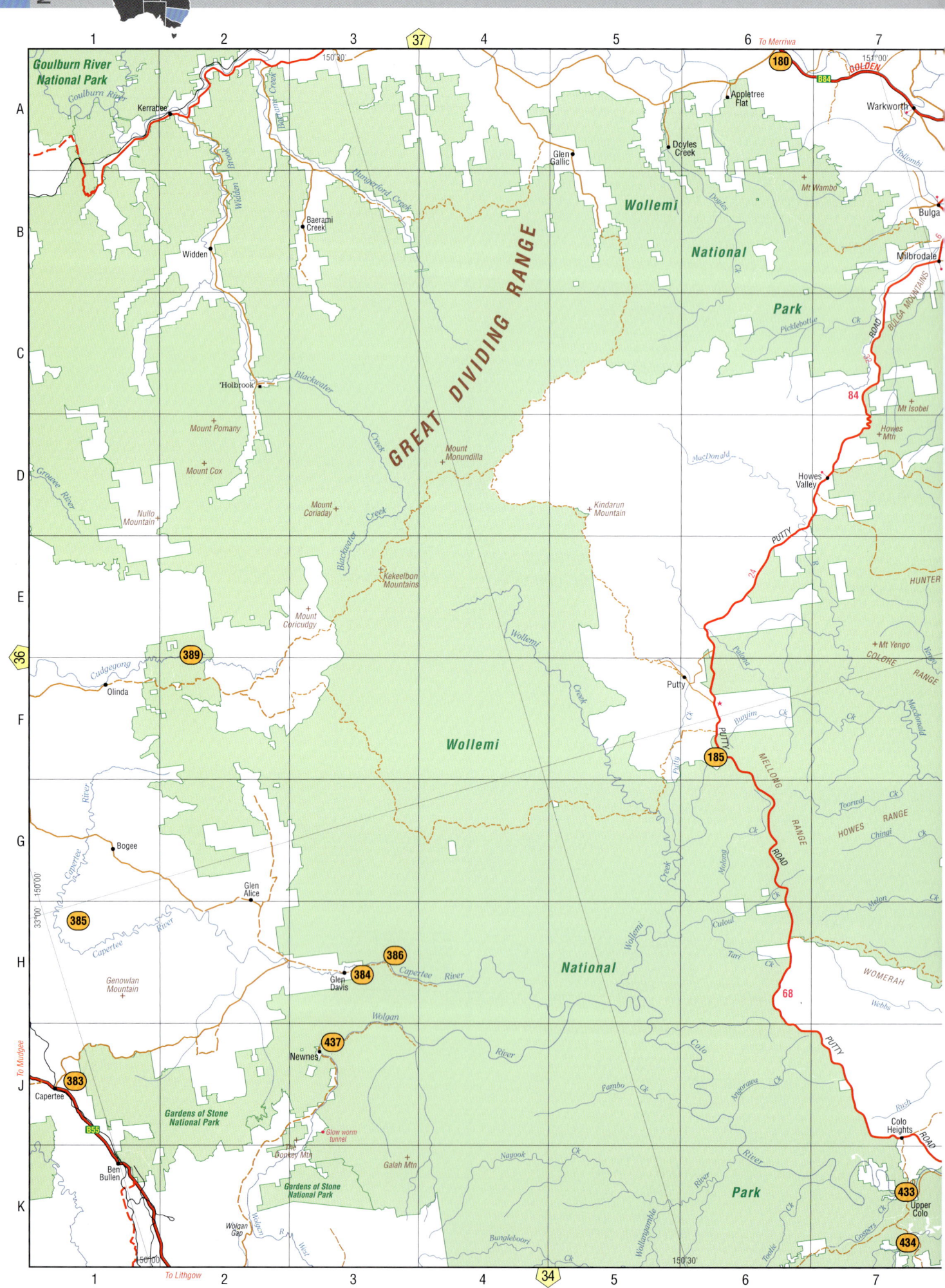

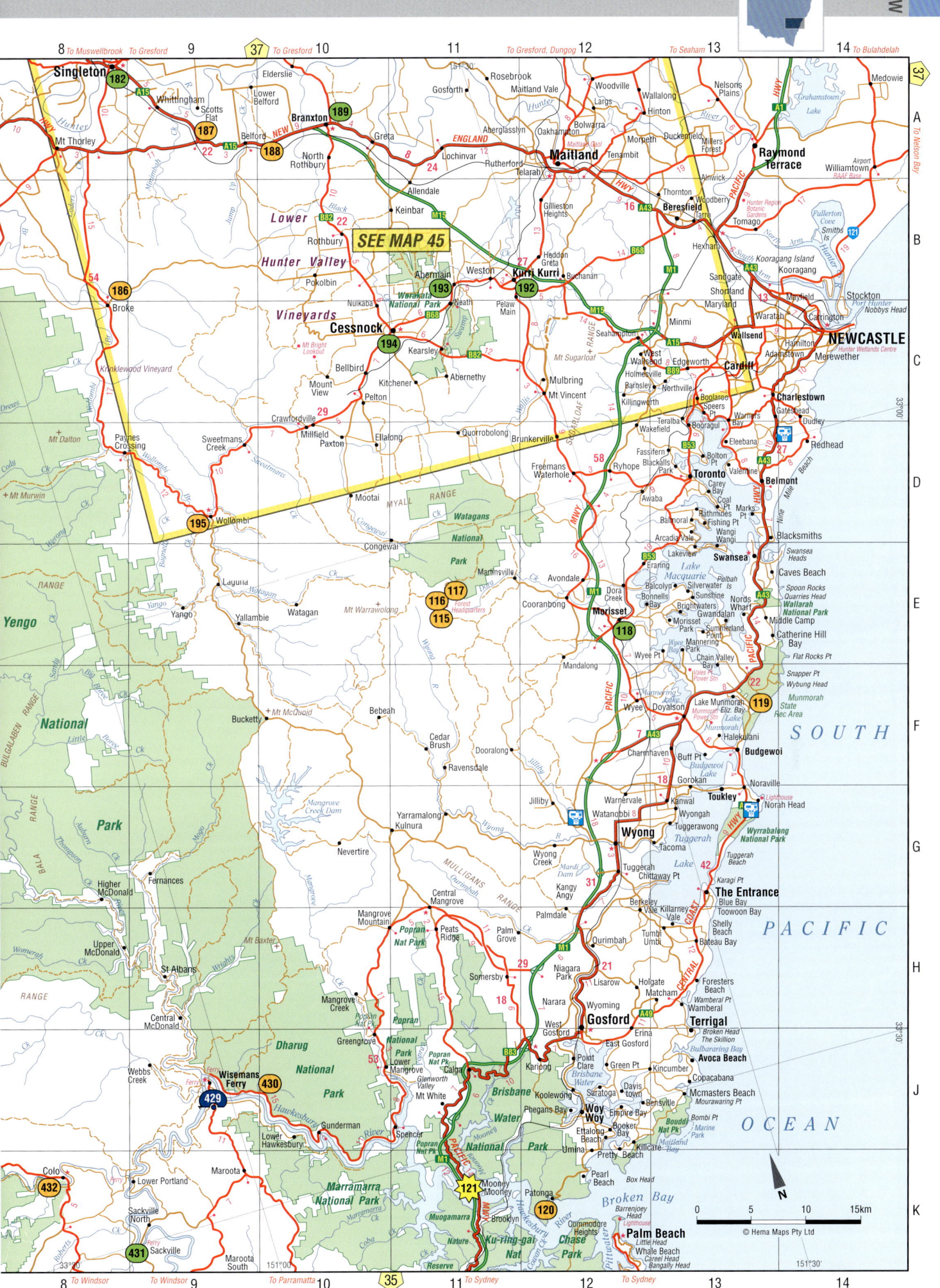

Sydney Region South, New South Wales

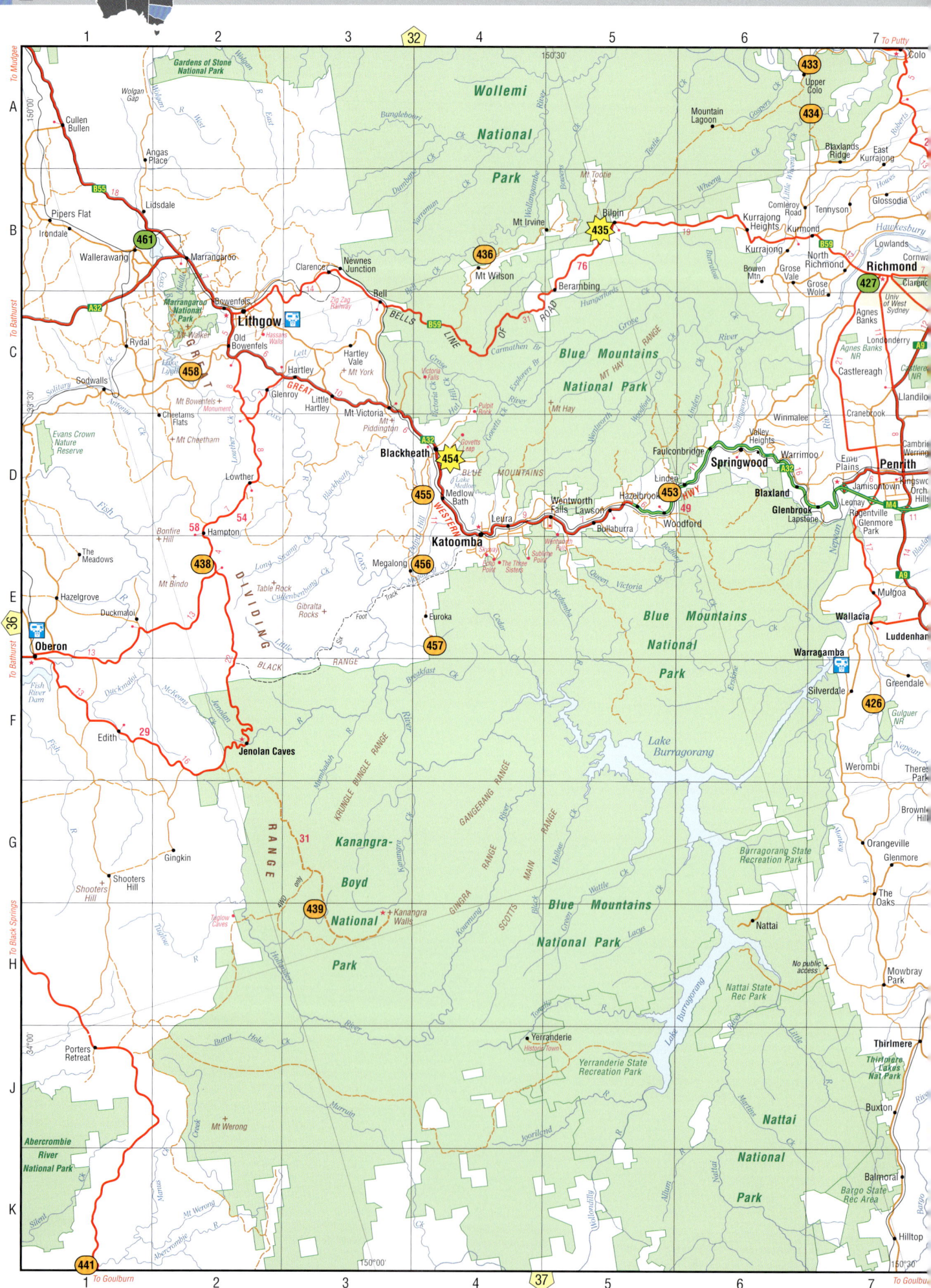

North-East New South Wales

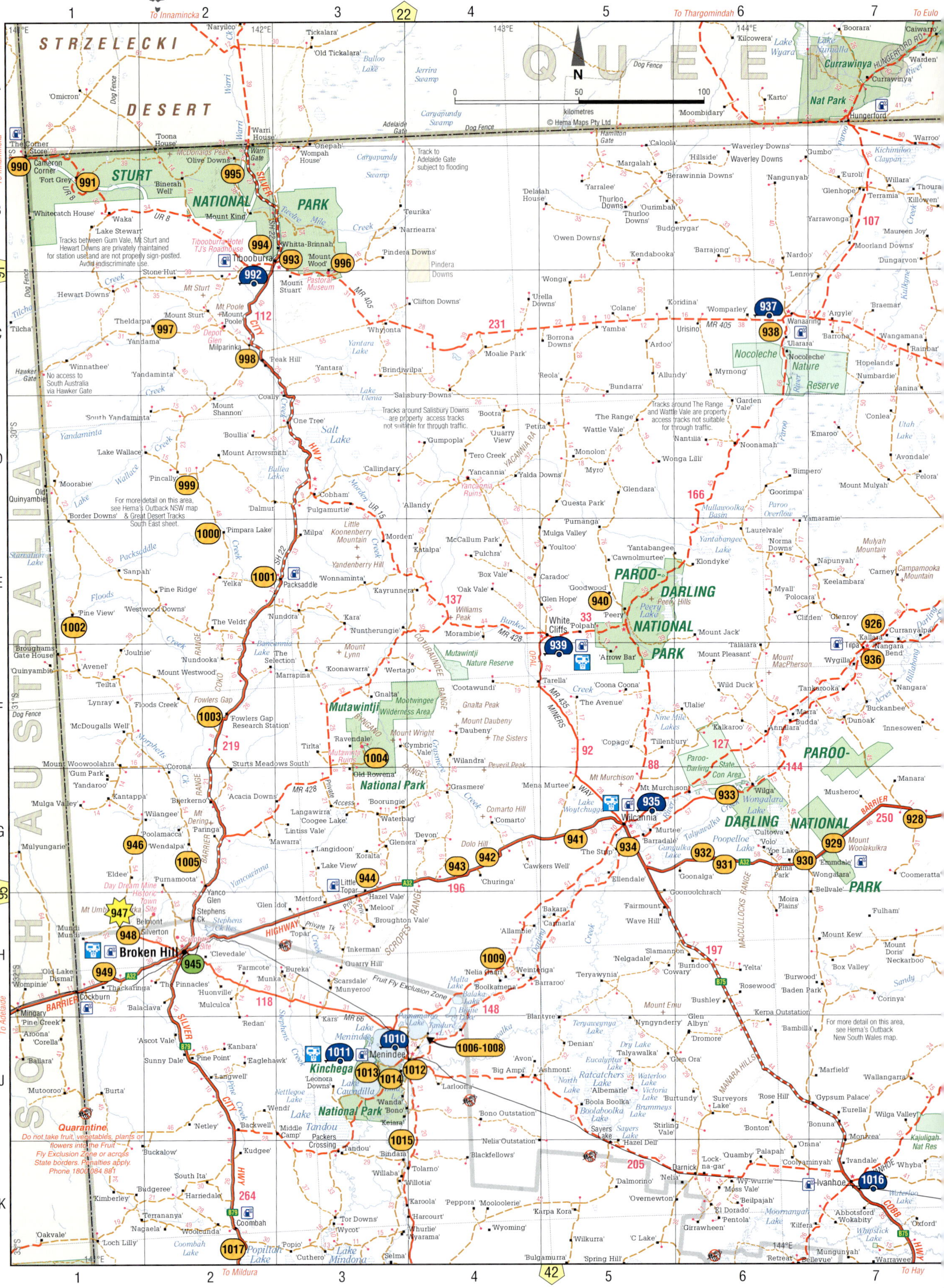

STRZELECKI DESERT

QUEENSLAND

STURT NATIONAL PARK

SOUTH AUSTRALIA

PAROO-DARLING NATIONAL PARK

PAROO-DARLING NATIONAL PARK

Mutawintji National Park

Mutawintji Wilderness Area

Mutawintji Nature Reserve

Nocoleche Nature Reserve

Currawinya Nat Park

Kinchega National Park

Broken Hill

Wilcannia

Menindee

Tibooburra

To Innamincka · To Thargomindah · To Eulo · To Hay · To Adelaide · To Mildura

© Hema Maps Pty Ltd

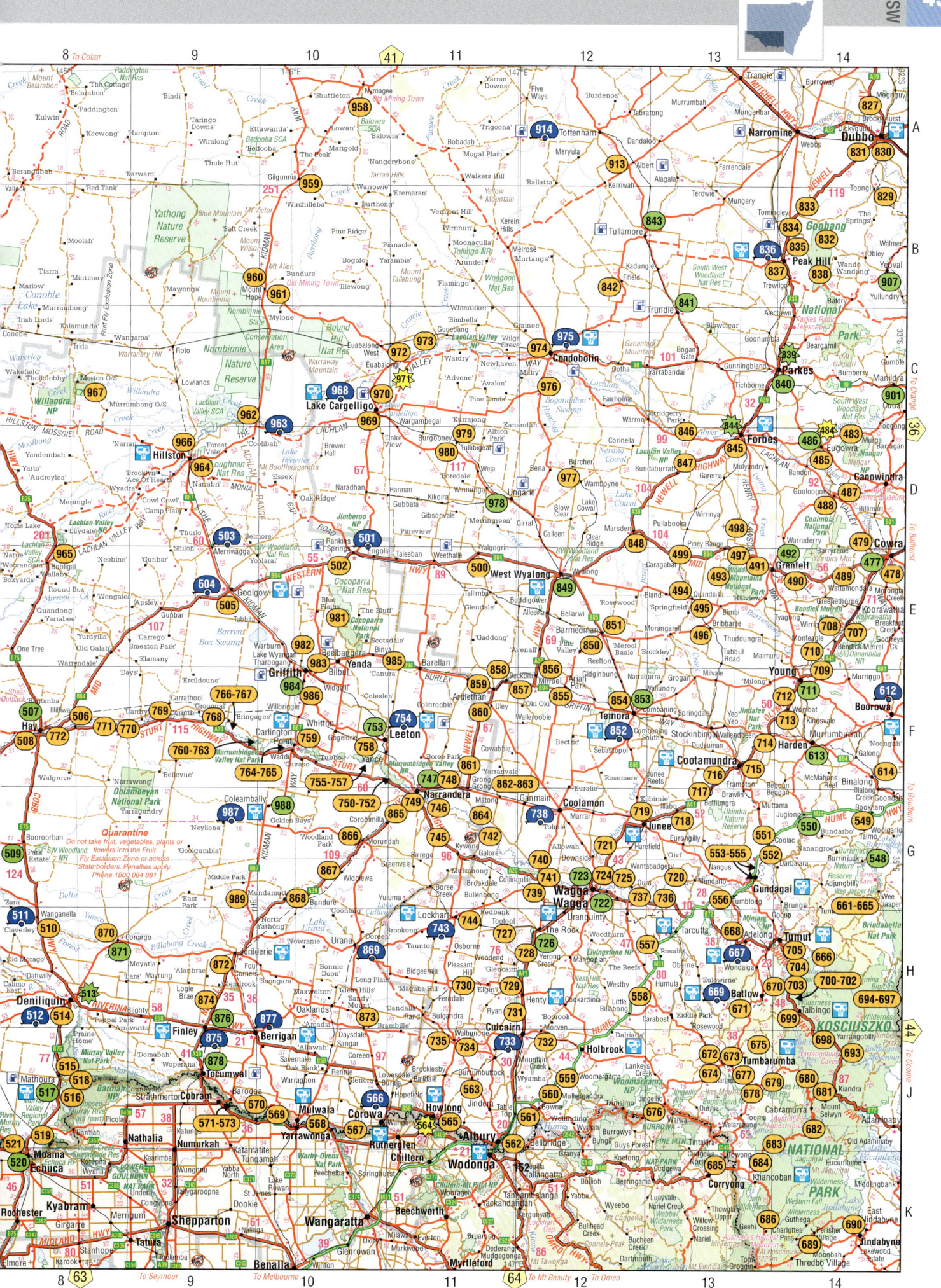

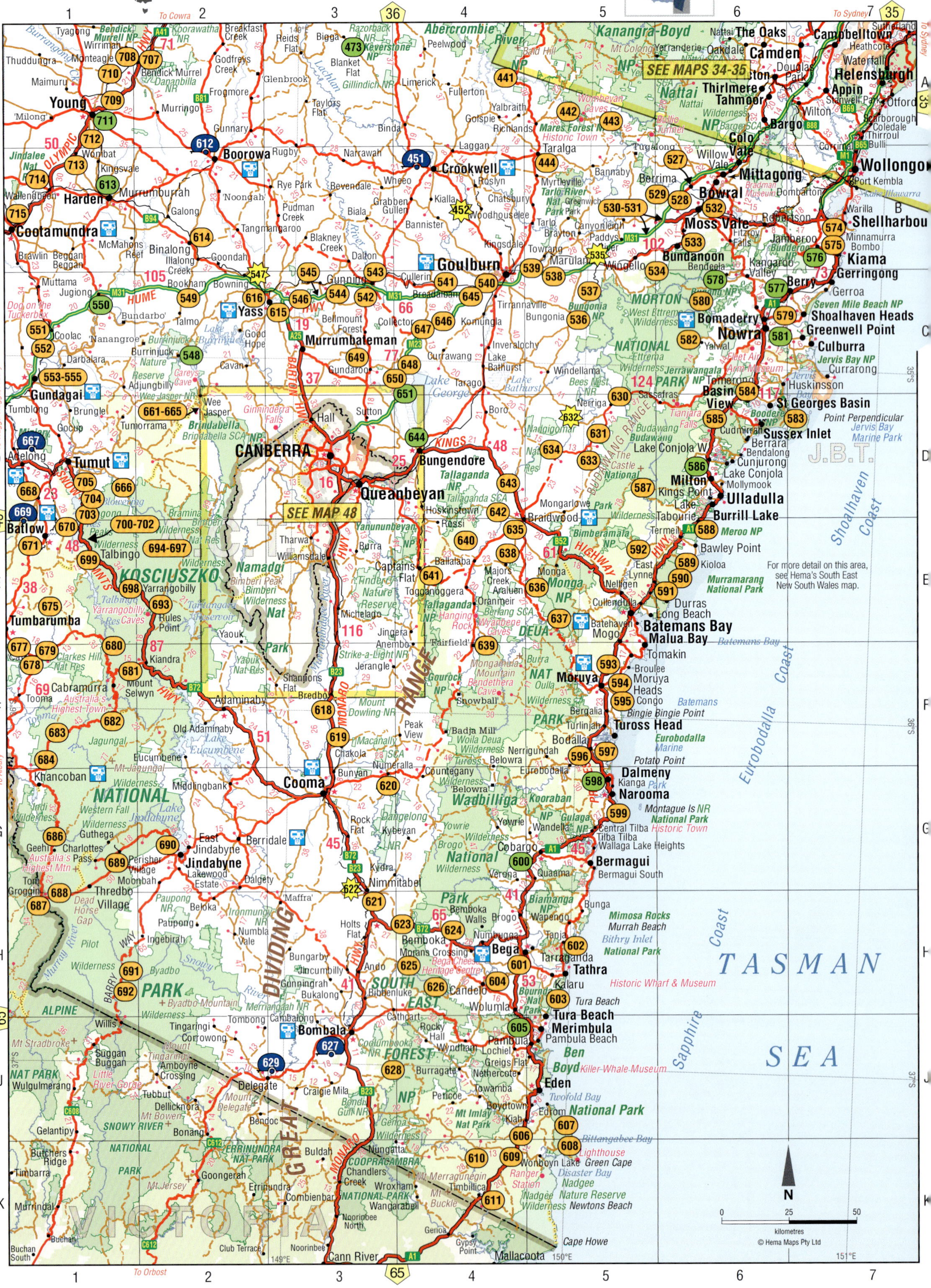

SEE MAPS 34-35
SEE MAP 48
Young
Harden
Cootamundra
Boorowa
Crookwell
Goulburn
Yass
Murrumbateman
Gundagai
Tumut
Batlow
Tumbarumba
Talbingo
CANBERRA
Queanbeyan
Bungendore
Braidwood
Cooma
Jindabyne
Thredbo Village
Bombala
Delegate
Nimmitabel
Bega
Tathra
Merimbula
Pambula
Eden
Bermagui
Narooma
Dalmeny
Tuross Head
Moruya
Batemans Bay
Malua Bay
Ulladulla
Milton
Burrill Lake
Nowra
Bomaderry
Kiama
Gerringong
Berry
Shellharbour
Wollongong
Helensburgh
Campbelltown
Camden
The Oaks
Thirlmere
Tahmoor
Bargo
Mittagong
Bowral
Moss Vale
Bundanoon
Culburra
Greenwell Point
Shoalhaven Heads
St Georges Basin
Sussex Inlet
Basin View
Huskisson
Adelong
Khancoban
Cabramurra
Kosciuszko
Namadgi Nat Park
Wadbilliga National
South East Forest NP
Ben Boyd National Park
Morton National Park
Budawang Range
Deua Nat Park
Monga NP
Great Dividing Range
Alpine National Park
Snowy River National Park
Victoria
Tasman Sea
J.B.T.
Jervis Bay
Batemans Bay
Eurobodalla Coast
Sapphire Coast
Shoalhaven Coast
For more detail on this area, see Hema's South East New South Wales map.
© Hema Maps Pty Ltd
kilometres
0 25 50
N
To Cowra
To Sydney
To Wagga Wagga, Albury
To Albury
To Orbost

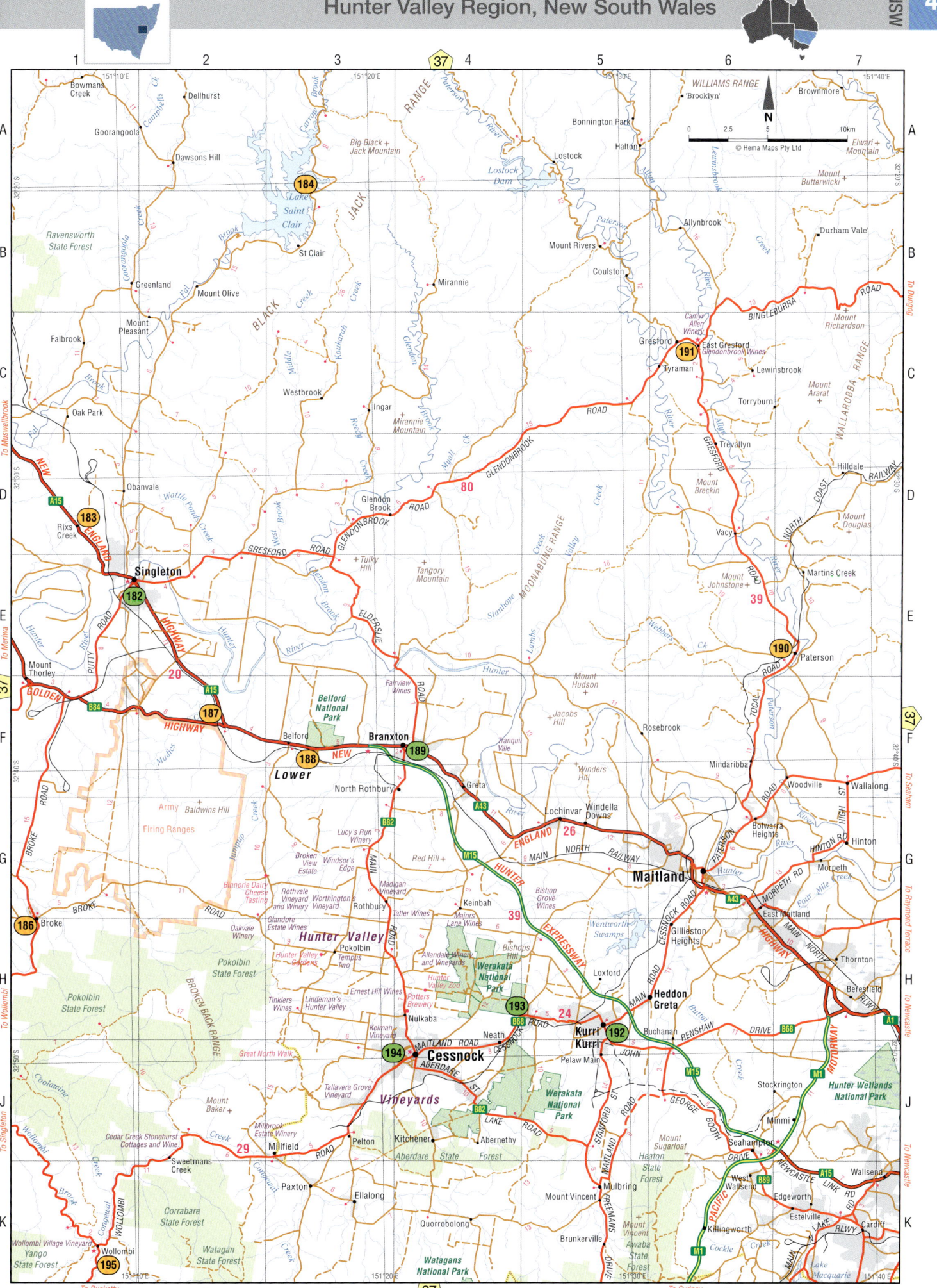

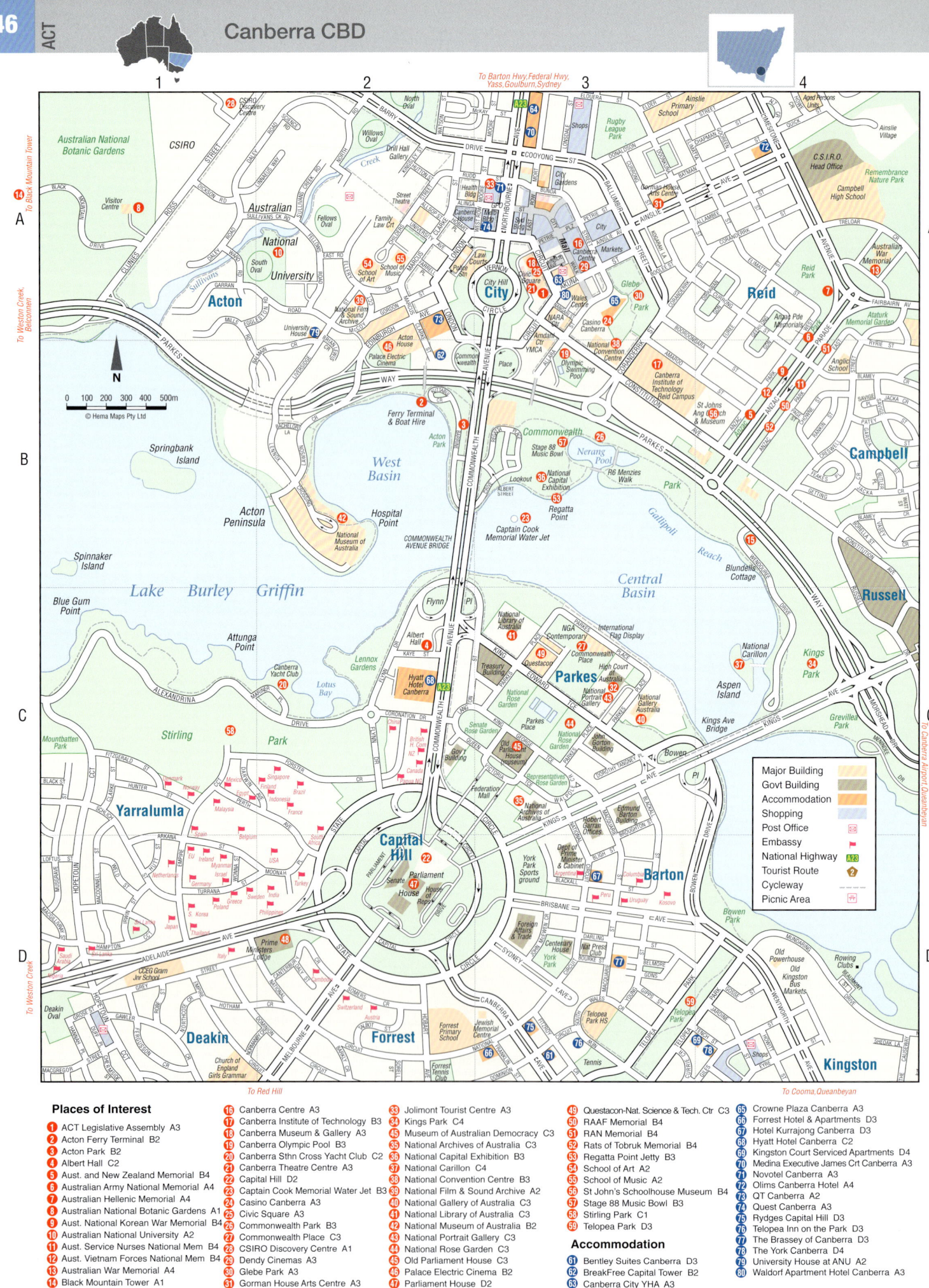

To Barton Hwy,Federal Hwy,
Yass,Goulburn,Sydney

Places of Interest

1 ACT Legislative Assembly A3
2 Acton Ferry Terminal B2
3 Acton Park B2
4 Albert Hall C2
5 Aust. and New Zealand Memorial B4
6 Australian Army National Memorial B4
7 Australian Hellenic Memorial A4
8 Australian National Botanic Gardens A1
9 Aust. National Korean War Memorial B4
10 Australian National University A2
11 Aust. Service Nurses National Mem A4
12 Aust. Vietnam Forces National Mem B4
13 Australian War Memorial A4
14 Black Mountain Tower A1
15 Blundell's Cottage B4

16 Canberra Centre A3
17 Canberra Institute of Technology B3
18 Canberra Museum & Gallery A3
19 Canberra Olympic Pool B3
20 Canberra Sthn Cross Yacht Club C2
21 Canberra Theatre Centre A3
22 Capital Hill D2
23 Captain Cook Memorial Water Jet B3
24 Casino Canberra A3
25 Civic Square A3
26 Commonwealth Park B3
27 Commonwealth Place C3
28 CSIRO Discovery Centre A1
29 Dendy Cinemas A3
30 Glebe Park A3
31 Gorman House Arts Centre A3
32 High Court of Australia C3

33 Jolimont Tourist Centre A3
34 Kings Park C4
45 Museum of Australian Democracy C3
35 National Archives of Australia C3
36 National Capital Exhibition B3
37 National Carillon C4
38 National Convention Centre B3
39 National Film & Sound Archive A2
40 National Gallery of Australia C3
41 National Library of Australia C3
42 National Museum of Australia B2
43 National Portrait Gallery C3
44 National Rose Garden C3
45 Old Parliament House C3
46 Palace Electric Cinema B2
47 Parliament House D2
48 Prime Minister's Lodge D2

49 Questacon-Nat. Science & Tech. Ctr C3
50 RAAF Memorial B4
51 RAN Memorial B4
52 Rats of Tobruk Memorial B4
53 Regatta Point Jetty B3
54 School of Art A2
55 School of Music A2
56 St John's Schoolhouse Museum B4
57 Stage 88 Music Bowl B3
58 Stirling Park C1
59 Telopea Park D3

Accommodation

61 Bentley Suites Canberra D3
62 BreakFree Capital Tower B2
63 Canberra City YHA A3
64 Comfort Inn Downtown A3

65 Crowne Plaza Canberra A3
66 Forrest Hotel & Apartments D3
67 Hotel Kurrajong Canberra D3
68 Hyatt Hotel Canberra C2
69 Kingston Court Serviced Apartments D4
70 Medina Executive James Crt Canberra A3
71 Novotel Canberra A3
72 Olims Canberra Hotel A4
73 QT Canberra A2
75 Quest Canberra A3
75 Rydges Capital Hill D3
76 Telopea Inn on the Park D3
77 The Brassey of Canberra D3
78 The York Canberra D4
79 University House at ANU A2
80 Waldorf Apartment Hotel Canberra A3

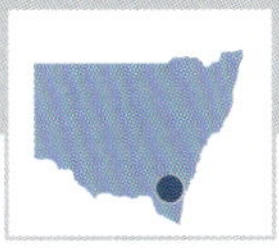

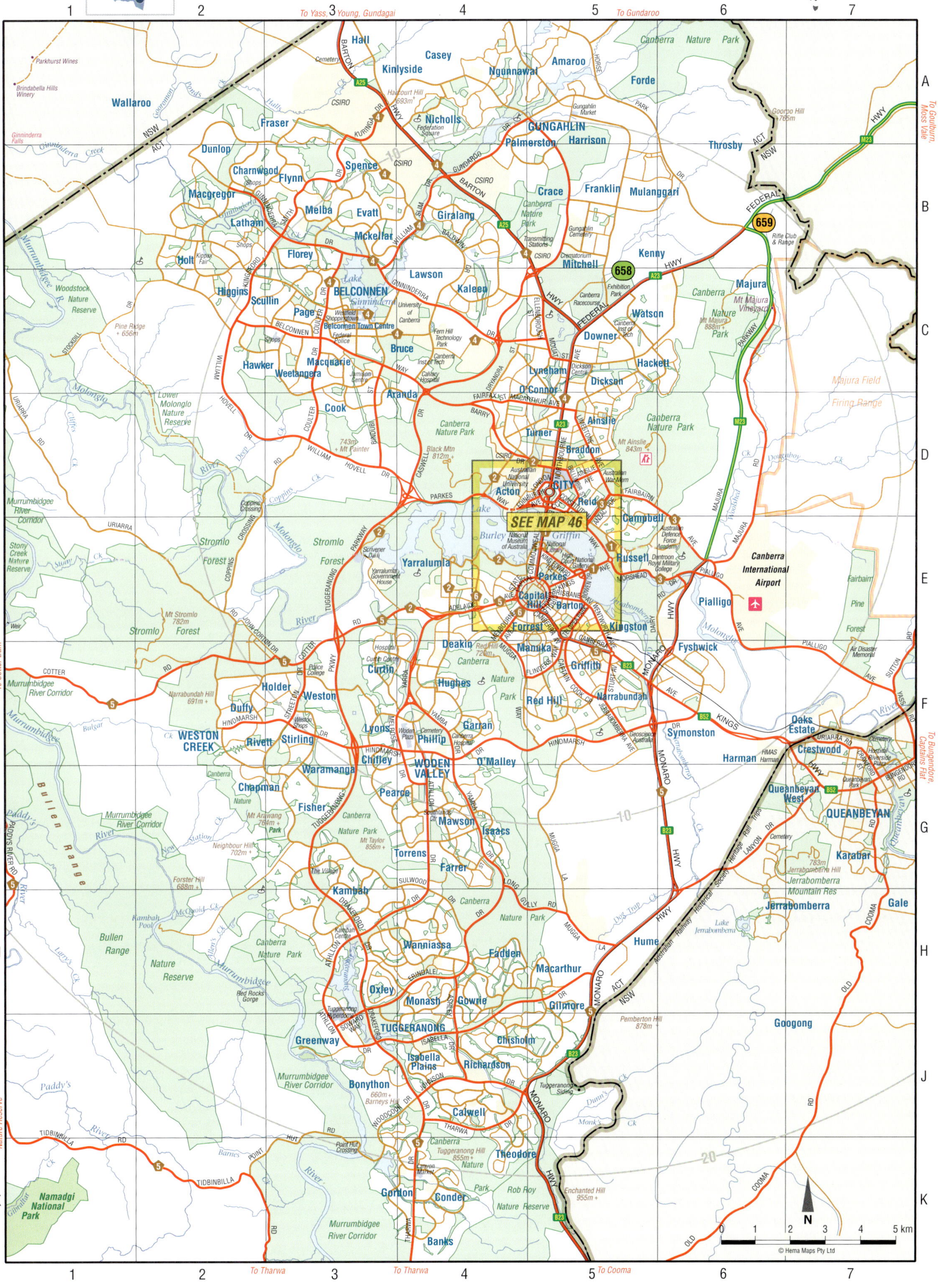

SEE MAP 46

© Hema Maps Pty Ltd

1 | 2 | To Yass | 3 | To Yass 4 | 44 | 5 | 6 | 7 | To Goulburn

NEW

SOUTH

WALES

Brindabella

National

Park

Doctors Hill

WALLAROO RD
MOUNTAIN CREEK RD

BARTON HWY

Hall

Ginninderra Falls

Woodstock NR

Lower Molonglo NR

Mt Black Mtn

Gungahlin

Canberra Nature Park

Lake Ginninderra

A25
658
A23
659

FEDERAL HWY

Sutton

Purrorumba Mtn

Lake George

M23
Ginns Gap
MACS REEF

GUNDAROO RD

Belconnen

HOWELL

Mt Ainslie

Canberra Nature Park

Majura Firing Range

Gorooyarroo NR

NORTON RD

644 B

Devils Peak

Mt Blundell

652

Mt Coree

Uriarra Forest

Stony Creek Nature Reserve

Stromlo

Mt Stromlo Observatory

Stromlo Forest

City

Parkes

CANBERRA

Capital Hill

Lake Burley Griffin

RAAF Fairbairn

Canberra Airport

Kowen Pine Forest

660

Molonglo Gorge NR

KINGS HWY

B52

653 C

Brindabella

Bulls Head

Cotter Hill

Pierces Creek Forest

Cotter Dam

Weston Creek

Woden

Hindmarsh

Draeford

Tuggeranong

DR

Fyshwick

Queanbeyan

Burbong

Cuumbeun NR

Stony Creek NR

Balcombe Hill

CAPTAINS FLAT RD

Cuumbeun NR

Mt Molonglo

D

AUSTRALIAN

Bimberi Nature Reserve

Bendora Dam

Tidbinbilla Nature Reserve

Tidbinbilla Visitor Centre

Canberra Deep Space Communication Complex

Lake Tuggeranong

Erindale Isabella

654

Gibraltar Falls

Tidbinbilla

Murrumbidgee Corridor

Lanyon Homestead

Rob Roy Nature Reserve

Hume

Australian Railway Historical Society heritage rail trips

Googong Reservoir

Mt Molonglo

London Bridge

E 44

Mt Aggie

Mt Franklin

Mt Ginini

CORIN RD

Corin Dam

CAPITAL

Namadgi

Namadgi Visitor Centre

Tharwa

Royalla

Lobb Hill

Googong Hill

Burra Creek Nature Reserve

Burra

Yunununbeyan Nat Park

Yunununbeyan SCA

F

BRINDABELLA RANGE

Bimberi Nature Reserve

Mt Gingera

TERRITORY

National

APOLLO RD

655

Naas

Rocky Crossing

Williamsdale

NEW

Mt Burra

Mt Bullongong

Horseshoe Hill

G

Kosciuszko

Bimberi Peak

Mt Gingera

656

Glendale Crossing

Nursery Hill

SOUTH

Mt Michelago

Tinderry Nature Reserve

H

National

Tantangara Reservoir

Mt Murray

Coronet Peak

National

Park

Mt Morgan

Half Moon Peak

Scabby Range Nature Reserve

Mt Scabby

Mt Kelly

Yankee Hill

Bogong Ck

Booths Hill

BOOTH RANGE

Mt Yarara

Michelago

WALES

Tinderry Peak

TINDERRY RANGE

Mt Woolpack

Boolboolma Crossing

Mt Holland

Jingera

H

Mt Ash Hill

Bradleys

Sentry Box Rock

Mt Gudgenby

Yaouk Peak

Yaouk Nature Reserve

Clear Hill

Black Cow Peak

BOBOYAN DIVIDE

657

CLEAR RANGE

Mt Clear

MONARO HWY

617

Colinton

Mt Colinton

Disused Railway

RANGE

Strike-a-light NR

Burnt School NR

Wallaby Hill

Mt Wangrah

Anembo

Jerangle

Whinstone Hill

J / K

N

0 2 4 6 8 10km

© Hema Maps Pty Ltd

Bugtown

Shannons Flat

1 | 2 | 3 To Adaminaby | To Cooma | 44 | 4 To Cooma | 5 | 6 | 7

SEE MAP 47

New South Wales Highway Index

New South Wales Alphabetic Site Index

New South Wales Alphabetic Site Index

Gold Coast to Sydney
Pacific Highway

1 Tyalgum Sports Ground ☎ (02) 6679 3569
Camp Area at Tyalgum. Entry off Carraboi Tce. Caretaker collects fees
HEMA 39 A13   28 21 11 S   153 12 20 E

2 Murwillumbah Showground ☎ 0423 327 234
Camp Area at Murwillumbah. Entry off Mooball St via Queensland Rd. Maximum stay 7 days. Not available during events
HEMA 39 A13   28 19 24 S   153 23 36 E

3 Hosanna Farmstay ☎ (02) 6677 9023
Camp Area at Stokers Siding. 4 Tunnel Rd. 11 km S of Murwillumbah on the Tweed Valley Way
HEMA 39 A13   28 24 02 S   153 24 33 E

4 Cutters Camp Campground ☎ (02) 6670 8600
Mebbin National Park
Camp Area 13 km S of Tyalgum, via Byrrill Creek Rd. 11 km dirt road. Alternative access from Kyogle Rd & Cadell Rd. Small vehicles only
HEMA 39 A13   28 26 40 S   153 11 41 E

5 Mount Burrell Caravan Park ☎ (02) 6679 7170
Caravan Park at Mount Burrell. Kyogle Rd
HEMA 39 B13   28 29 12 S   153 13 14 E

6 Wadeville Woolies ☎ (02) 6689 7285
Camp Area at Wadeville. 20 km N of Kyogle or 48 km S of Murwillumbah. Turn N onto Link Rd
HEMA 39 B12   28 33 59 S   153 07 40 E

7 Sleepy Hollow Rest Area Southbound
Rest Area 22 km S of Chinderah or 63 km N of Ballina. Southbound only
HEMA 39 A13   28 24 50 S   153 31 31 E

8 Sleepy Hollow Rest Area Northbound
Rest Area 24 km S of Chinderah or 61 km N of Ballina. Northbound only
HEMA 39 A13   28 25 25 S   153 31 14 E

9 Billinudgel Hotel ☎ (02) 6680 1148
Parking Area at Billinudgel. 1 Wilfred St, Limited space & you must be there before 5pm, check in with publican. Fee for shower
HEMA 39 A13   28 30 14 S   153 31 35 E

10 Yelgun Rest Area
Rest Area 32 km S of Chinderah or 50 km N of Ballina
HEMA 39 B13   28 29 31 S   153 31 22 E

11 Tyagarah Rest Area
Rest Area at Tyagarah. 8 km S of Brunswick Heads or 40 km N of Ballina
HEMA 39 B13   28 35 54 S   153 32 41 E

12 Mullumbimby Leagues Club ☎ 0405 198 866
Camp Area at Mullumbimby. Manns Rd. Camping at riverbank, next to Leagues Club. 2 km NE of PO
HEMA 39 B13   28 33 11 S   153 30 52 E

13 Mullumbimby Showground ☎ 0474 100 189
Camp Area at Mullumbimby. Main Arm Rd. 2 km W of PO
HEMA 39 B13   28 32 48 S   153 29 20 E

14 Macas Camping Ground ☎ (02) 6684 5211
Camp Area 3 km W of Main Arm on Main Arm Rd
HEMA 39 B13   28 29 49 S   153 24 39 E

15 Flat Rock Tent Park ☎ (02) 6686 4848
Camp Area at East Ballina. 38 Flat Rock Rd. Tents & camper trailers only
HEMA 39 C14   28 50 37 S   153 36 10 E

16 Alstonville Showground ☎ (02) 6628 0358
Camp Area at Alstonville. Entry is South St cnr Commercial Rd. Contact caretaker
HEMA 39 C13   28 50 23 S   153 26 26 E

17 Wardell Rest Area
Rest Area 14 km S of Ballina or 3 km N of Wardell, South & Northbound
HEMA 39 C13   28 56 07 S   153 28 19 E

Notes...

NEW SOUTH WALES

18 Sandalwood Van & Leisure Park ☎ (02) 6683 4221
Caravan Park at Wardell, 12 km S of Ballina S turnoff or 21 km NE of Woodburn. 978 Pimlico Rd
HEMA 39 C13   28 56 29 S   153 28 21 E

19 Broadwater Stopover Tourist Park ☎ (02) 6682 8254
Caravan Park at Broadwater. 1 - 5 Pacific Hwy
HEMA 39 C13   29 01 12 S   153 25 26 E

20 Sunrise Caravan Park ☎ (02) 6682 8388
Caravan Park at Broadwater. 74 - 92 Pacific Hwy. 1 km N of PO
HEMA 39 C13   29 00 54 S   153 25 49 E

21 Black Rocks Campground
Bundjalung National Park ☎ (02) 6627 0200
Camp Area 24 km SE of Woodburn. Turn E off Pacific Hwy 3.6 km from Woodburn onto Gap Rd. 16 km dirt road
HEMA 39 D13   29 15 02 S   153 21 59 E

22 New Italy Rest Area
Rest Area at New Italy. 12 km S of Woodburn or 38 km N of Maclean. Near museum
HEMA 39 C13   29 09 13 S   153 17 55 E

23 Bundjalung Rest Area
Rest Area 13 km S of New Italy or 27 km N of McLean. Northbound only
HEMA 39 D13   29 15 39 S   153 13 53 E

24 Beekeepers Rest Area
Rest Area 17 km S of New Italy or 23 km N of Maclean
HEMA 39 D13   29 16 56 S   153 12 56 E

25 Woombah Woods Caravan Park ☎ (02) 6646 4544
Caravan Park 36 km S of Woodburn or 8 km N of Harwood, cnr Pacific Hwy & Iluka Rd
HEMA 39 D13   29 21 12 S   153 15 13 E

26 Woody Head Campground
Bundjalung National Park ☎ (02) 6646 6134
Camp Area 4 km N of Iluka. Turn E off Pacific Hwy onto Iluka Rd, follow 13 km over Esk River, then signposted
HEMA 39 D13   29 21 59 S   153 22 16 E

27 Maclean Showground
Camp Area at Maclean. Entry off Cameron St. Self Contained Vehicles only. Fees collected
HEMA 39 D13   29 27 50 S   153 11 58 E

28 Red Cliff Campground
Yuraygir National Park ☎ (02) 6641 1500
Camp Area 5 km N of Brooms Head or 19 km SE of Maclean. Turn E off Pacific Hwy onto Brooms Head Rd. Continue 18 km. Signposted. 1 km dirt road
HEMA 39 E13   29 34 35 S   153 20 06 E

29 Lake Arragan
Yuraygir National Park ☎ (02) 6641 1500
Camp Area 5 km N of Brooms Head or 19 km SE of Maclean. Turn E off Pacific Hwy onto Brooms Head Rd. Continue 18 km. Signposted. 2 km dirt road
HEMA 39 E13   29 34 00 S   153 20 10 E

30 Sandon River Campground
Yuraygir National Park ☎ (02) 6641 1500
Camp Area 10 km S of Brooms Head. Turn W onto Brooms Head Rd 21 km SE of Maclean then onto Sandon River Rd. 9 km dirt road
HEMA 39 E13   29 40 27 S   153 19 37 E

31 The Lawrence Tavern ☎ (02) 6647 7214
Parking Area at Lawrence. Bridge St behind Tavern, please check in with publican. Fee if amenities used
HEMA 39 D12   29 30 09 S   153 05 59 E

32 Grafton Greyhound Racing Club Campground ☎ (02) 6642 3713
Camp Area at Grafton. 70 Cranworth St. W side of town. Pets on application
HEMA 39 E12   29 40 27 S   152 55 32 E

33 Grafton Showground ☎ 0468 482 919
Camp Area at Grafton. Prince St & Dobie St
HEMA 39 E12   29 41 03 S   152 56 24 E

Notes...

34 McPhillips Creek Rest Area
Rest Area 7 km S of South Grafton or 51 km N of Woolgoolga
HEMA 39 E12   29 44 37 S   152 59 29 E

35 Glenugie Road Rest Area
Rest Area 13 km S of South Grafton or 45 km N of Woolgoolga
HEMA 39 E12   29 47 05 S   153 00 31 E

36 Illaroo Campground ☎ (02) 6641 1500
Yuraygir National Park
Camp Area 2 km N of Minnie Water. Turn E off Pacific Hwy 12 km S of South Grafton or 44 km N of Woolgoolga onto Wooli Rd & Minnie Water Rd. Dirt road
HEMA 39 E13   29 45 26 S   153 17 28 E

37 Boorkoom Campground ☎ (02) 6641 1500
Yuraygir National Park
Camp Area 10 km N of Wooli. Turn E off Pacific Hwy 12 km S of South Grafton or 44 km N of Woolgoolga onto Wooli Rd & Diggers Camp Rd. 6 km dirt road
HEMA 39 E13   29 49 12 S   153 17 28 E

38 Diggers Headland Reserve ☎ (02) 6643 0200
Camp Area 11 km N of Wooli. Open School holidays only. Turn E off Pacific Hwy 12 km S of South Grafton or 44 km N of Woolgoolga onto Wooli Rd & Diggers Camp Rd. 7 km dirt road
HEMA 39 E13   29 48 55 S   153 17 19 E

39 3 Creeks Family Campground ☎ 0407 168 014
Camp Area at Kungala. 750 Kungala Rd. 31 km S of Grafton or 85 km N of Coffs Harbour turn W into Kungala Rd. Camp area 7 km along Kungala Rd
HEMA 39 F12   29 56 38 S   153 00 41 E

40 Glenreagh Recreation Reserve ☎ 0427 183 553
Camp Area at Glenreagh. Bridge St
HEMA 39 F12   30 03 08 S   152 58 26 E

41 Corindi Park ☎ 0403 075 335
Camp Area at Corindi Beach. 95 Corindi Dr. Bookings essential, must have own toilet & shower. Must call ahead
HEMA 39 F12   30 00 47 S   153 11 53 E

Notes...

42 Station Creek Campground ☎ (02) 6641 1500
Yuraygir National Park
Camp Area 48 km SE of South Grafton. Turn E 35 km SE of South Grafton or 22 km N of Woolgoolga onto McPhillips Rd for 6 km, then E on Barcoongare Station Creek Rd for 7 km. 13 km dirt road
HEMA 39 F12   29 57 03 S   153 14 48 E

43 Burdett Park
Rest Area 4.5 km E of Bellingen
HEMA 39 G12   30 28 21 S   152 56 04 E

44 Bellingen Showgrounds ☎ 0431 264 836
Camp Area at Bellingen. Entrance on Hammond St opposite Dowle St. Maximum stay 2 weeks. Contact caretaker
HEMA 39 G12   30 26 55 S   152 53 53 E

45 Roses Park
Rest Area at Thora. 14 km W of Bellingen. Donation requested
HEMA 39 G11   30 25 33 S   152 46 43 E

46 Taylors Arm Reserve
Parking Area 27 km W of Macksville. "Pub with No Beer". Toilets & showers at hotel. Gold coin donation
HEMA 39 H11   30 46 04 S   152 42 58 E

47 Gumma Crossing Reserve ☎ (02) 6568 2555
Camp Area 7.5 km E of Macksville. Turn E off Pacific Hwy 200m S of bridge at Macksville onto Partridge St then onto Gumma Rd for 5 km. L at Boltons Crossing Rd. 2 km dirt road. Fairly large area beside Warrell Creek, but narrow access
HEMA 39 H12   30 42 24 S   152 59 00 E

48 Paddy's Rest
Rest Area 5 km S of Warrell Creek or 17 km N of Clybucca
HEMA 39 H12   30 48 47 S   152 52 15 E

49 Stuarts Point Convention Centre ☎ (02) 6569 0576
Camp Area at Stuarts Point. 250 Grassy Head Rd
HEMA 39 H12   30 47 57 S   152 59 15 E

50 Clybucca Rest Area Southbound
Rest Area 7 km S of Stuarts Point Rd intersection or 17 km N of Frederickton intersection
HEMA 39 H12   30 54 34 S   152 55 06 E

NEW SOUTH WALES

51 Clybucca Rest Area Northbound

Rest Area 7 km S of Stuarts Point Rd intersection or 17 km N of Frederickton intersection

HEMA 39 H12   30 54 31 S   152 55 03 E

52 Clybucca BP Roadhouse

Parking Area at Clybucca. Self Contained Vehicles only

HEMA 39 H12   30 56 17 S   152 56 33 E

53 Frederickton Golf Club   ☎ 02 6566 8261

Parking Area at Frederickton Golf Club. Yarrabandinni Rd. Please check in with bar manager. Self Contained Vehicles only

HEMA 39 J12   31 01 50 S   152 52 41 E

54 Kempsey Showgrounds   ☎ (02) 6562 5231

Camp Area at Kempsey. 19 Sea St. Closed for events in April & October, check for specific dates

HEMA 39 J11   31 04 24 S   152 49 45 E

✓55 Trial Bay Gaol Campground   ☎ (02) 6566 6168
Arakoon National Park

Camp Area 4 km E of South West Rocks. Near Trial Bay Gaol. Very expensive in peak season

HEMA 39 H12   30 52 41 S   153 04 16 E

56 Smoky Cape Campground   ☎ (02) 6561 6700
Hat Head National Park

Camp Area 9 km SE of South West Rocks, via Arakoon Rd & Lighthouse Rd. Bush camping in confined area. Near beach

HEMA 39 H12   30 55 45 S   153 04 37 E

57 Hungry Gate Campground   ☎ (02) 6561 6700
Hat Head National Park

Camp Area 3.5 km S of Hat Head via Gap Rd, turn R into Hungry Rd. 3 km dirt road. Not suitable for caravans

HEMA 39 J12   31 04 47 S   153 02 31 E

58 Bloodwood Ridge Rest Area

Rest Area 6 km S of Kempsey. Northbound only. Combined truck bay

HEMA 39 J11   31 09 50 S   152 49 10 E

59 Racecourse Headland Campground   ☎ (02) 6561 6700
Goolawah National Park

Camp Area 8 km S of Crescent Head via Point Plomer Rd. 7 km dirt road. Beside beach. Outside cold showers. Small vehicles only

HEMA 39 J12   31 14 57 S   152 57 37 E

60 Delicate Campground   ☎ (02) 6561 6700
Goolawah Regional Park

Camp Area 10 km S of Crescent Head via Point Plomer Rd. 9 km dirt road. Beside beach. Outside cold showers

HEMA 39 J12   31 15 37 S   152 58 06 E

61 Waves Campground   ☎ (02) 6566 0144

Camp Area 11 km S of Cresent Head. 954 Point Plomer Rd. Bookings preferred

HEMA 39 J12   31 15 43 S   152 58 02 E

✓62 Melaleuca Campground   ☎ (02) 6561 6700
Limeburners Creek National Park

Camp Area 12 km S of Crescent Head via Point Plomer Rd. 14 km dirt road. Beside creek. Outside school holidays contact Point Plumber to open access gate (02) 6583 8805

HEMA 39 K12   31 16 49 S   152 57 45 E

✓63 Point Plomer Campground   ☎ (02) 6583 8805
Limeburners Creek National Park

Camp Area 17 km S of Crescent Head via Point Plomer Rd. 16 km dirt road. Beside beach

HEMA 39 K12   31 18 48 S   152 58 12 E

64 Log Wharf Reserve

Rest Area 1 km S of Telegraph Point or 14 km N of Pacific Hwy/Oxley Hwy jcn. Access via Hacks Ferry Rd, just S of bridge

HEMA 39 K11   31 19 36 S   152 47 46 E

65 Burrawan Rest Area

Rest Area 10 km N of Kew. Northbound only

HEMA 39 K11   31 33 06 S   152 45 17 E

✓66 Kendall Showgrounds   ☎ (02) 6559 4463

Camp Area at Kendall. 23 Batar Creek Rd

HEMA 37 A13   31 38 11 S   152 42 06 E

67 Diamond Head Campground   ☎ (02) 6588 5555
Crowdy Bay National Park

Camp Area 9 km S of Laurieton, via Diamond Head Rd. 5 km dirt road. Cold showers. Beside beach

HEMA 37 B14   31 43 05 S   152 47 39 E

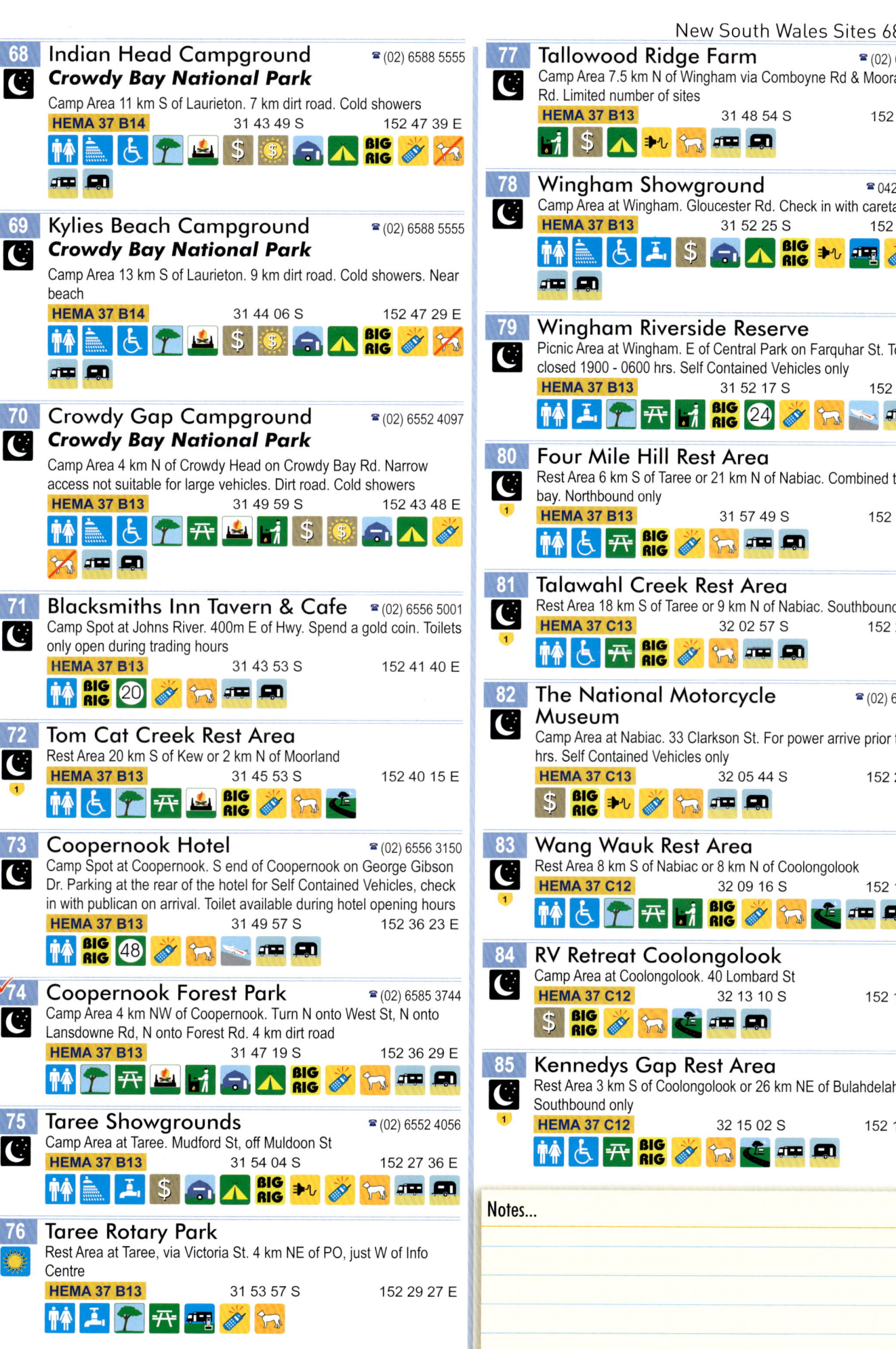

68 Indian Head Campground ☎ (02) 6588 5555
Crowdy Bay National Park
Camp Area 11 km S of Laurieton. 7 km dirt road. Cold showers
HEMA 37 B14   31 43 49 S   152 47 39 E

69 Kylies Beach Campground ☎ (02) 6588 5555
Crowdy Bay National Park
Camp Area 13 km S of Laurieton. 9 km dirt road. Cold showers. Near beach
HEMA 37 B14   31 44 06 S   152 47 29 E

70 Crowdy Gap Campground ☎ (02) 6552 4097
Crowdy Bay National Park
Camp Area 4 km N of Crowdy Head on Crowdy Bay Rd. Narrow access not suitable for large vehicles. Dirt road. Cold showers
HEMA 37 B13   31 49 59 S   152 43 48 E

71 Blacksmiths Inn Tavern & Cafe ☎ (02) 6556 5001
Camp Spot at Johns River. 400m E of Hwy. Spend a gold coin. Toilets only open during trading hours
HEMA 37 B13   31 43 53 S   152 41 40 E

72 Tom Cat Creek Rest Area
Rest Area 20 km S of Kew or 2 km N of Moorland
HEMA 37 B13   31 45 53 S   152 40 15 E

73 Coopernook Hotel ☎ (02) 6556 3150
Camp Spot at Coopernook. S end of Coopernook on George Gibson Dr. Parking at the rear of the hotel for Self Contained Vehicles, check in with publican on arrival. Toilet available during hotel opening hours
HEMA 37 B13   31 49 57 S   152 36 23 E

✓ 74 Coopernook Forest Park ☎ (02) 6585 3744
Camp Area 4 km NW of Coopernook. Turn N onto West St, N onto Lansdowne Rd, N onto Forest Rd. 4 km dirt road
HEMA 37 B13   31 47 19 S   152 36 29 E

75 Taree Showgrounds ☎ (02) 6552 4056
Camp Area at Taree. Mudford St, off Muldoon St
HEMA 37 B13   31 54 04 S   152 27 36 E

76 Taree Rotary Park
Rest Area at Taree, via Victoria St. 4 km NE of PO, just W of Info Centre
HEMA 37 B13   31 53 57 S   152 29 27 E

77 Tallowood Ridge Farm ☎ (02) 6557 0438
Camp Area 7.5 km N of Wingham via Comboyne Rd & Mooral Creek Rd. Limited number of sites
HEMA 37 B13   31 48 54 S   152 22 24 E

78 Wingham Showground ☎ 0427 570 229
Camp Area at Wingham. Gloucester Rd. Check in with caretaker
HEMA 37 B13   31 52 25 S   152 21 43 E

79 Wingham Riverside Reserve
Picnic Area at Wingham. E of Central Park on Farquhar St. Toilets closed 1900 - 0600 hrs. Self Contained Vehicles only
HEMA 37 B13   31 52 17 S   152 22 51 E

80 Four Mile Hill Rest Area
Rest Area 6 km S of Taree or 21 km N of Nabiac. Combined truck bay. Northbound only
HEMA 37 B13   31 57 49 S   152 27 53 E

81 Talawahl Creek Rest Area
Rest Area 18 km S of Taree or 9 km N of Nabiac. Southbound only
HEMA 37 C13   32 02 57 S   152 26 49 E

82 The National Motorcycle Museum ☎ (02) 6554 1333
Camp Area at Nabiac. 33 Clarkson St. For power arrive prior to 1530 hrs. Self Contained Vehicles only
HEMA 37 C13   32 05 44 S   152 23 00 E

83 Wang Wauk Rest Area
Rest Area 8 km S of Nabiac or 8 km N of Coolongolook
HEMA 37 C12   32 09 16 S   152 19 19 E

84 RV Retreat Coolongolook
Camp Area at Coolongolook. 40 Lombard St
HEMA 37 C12   32 13 10 S   152 19 12 E

85 Kennedys Gap Rest Area
Rest Area 3 km S of Coolongolook or 26 km NE of Bulahdelah. Southbound only
HEMA 37 C12   32 15 02 S   152 19 24 E

Notes...

NEW SOUTH WALES

86 Wootton Rest Area
Rest Area at Wootton. On Wootton Way
HEMA 37 C12   32 17 38 S   152 18 14 E

87 Chapmans Rest Area
Rest Area 16 km S of Coolongolook or 13 km NE of Bulahdelah. Share with trucks. Both sides of the road
HEMA 37 C12   32 21 09 S   152 18 51 E

88 Strike a Light Campground
☎ (02) 4997 4981
Camp Area 24 km NW of Bulahdelah, via Cabbage Tree Creek & Strike a Light Rds. 4WD high clearance vehicles only
HEMA 37 C12   32 17 42 S   152 05 29 E

89 Bulahdelah Showgrounds
☎ (02) 4997 4981
Camp Area at showgrounds. Cnr Stuart St & Prince St. Pay fee at Info Centre
HEMA 37 D12   32 24 18 S   152 12 16 E

✓ 90 Bulahdelah Lions Park
Camp Spot at Bulahdelah. 1 km S of PO, entry 600m before bridge on Old Pacific Hwy Rd. Entry only from N bound lane. Self Contained Vehicles only. Donation appreciated please
HEMA 37 D12   32 24 50 S   152 12 21 E

91 Bulahdelah Golf Club
Parking Area at Bulahdelah. Golf Rd. Self Contained Vehicles only. Check in at the Bar
HEMA 37 D12   32 23 34 S   152 13 16 E

92 Bulahdelah Bowling Club
☎ (02) 4997 4365
Parking Area at Bulahdelah. 50 Jackson St, check in at the bar, toilets & showers available during opening hours
HEMA 37 D12   32 24 25 S   152 12 14 E

93 Bungarie Bay Camping Area
Myall Lakes National Park
☎ (02) 6591 0300
Camp Area 18 km E of Bulahdelah. Turn S off The Lakes Way onto Violet Hill Rd, 10 km E of Bulahdelah near Boolambayte. 8 km dirt road. Small area beside lake
HEMA 37 D12   32 27 34 S   152 19 09 E

94 Violet Hill Campground
Myall Lakes National Park
☎ (02) 6591 0300
Camp Area 20 km E of Bulahdelah. Turn S off The Lakes Way onto Violet Hill Rd, 10 km E of Bulahdelah near Boolambayte. 10 km dirt road. Beside lake
HEMA 37 D12   32 28 16 S   152 19 37 E

95 Wallingat River Campground
Wallingat National Park
☎ (02) 6591 0300
Camp Area 15 km N of Bungwahl. Turn N off Lakes Way 2 km E of Bungwahl or 10 km SW of Pacific Palms onto Sugar Creek Rd, then River Rd. 13 km dirt road, not suitable for caravans. Beside river
HEMA 37 C13   32 19 39 S   152 24 10 E

96 Neranie Campground
Myall Lakes National Park
☎ (02) 6591 0300
Camp Area 5 km S of Bungwahl. Turn W off Seal Rocks Rd after 4 km at Fishermans Co-Op Neranie Rd. 1 km dirt road. Beside lake
HEMA 37 D13   32 24 33 S   152 27 08 E

97 Yagon Campground
Myall Lakes National Park
☎ (02) 6591 0300
Camp Area 4 km SW of Seal Rocks, via Thomas Rd
HEMA 37 D13   32 27 11 S   152 29 41 E

98 The Ruins Campground
Booti Booti National Park
☎ (02) 6591 0300
Camp Area 16 km S of Forster or 5 km N of Pacific Palms
HEMA 37 C13   32 18 36 S   152 31 10 E

99 Camp Elim
☎ (02) 6554 0277
Camp Area 11.5 km S of Forster or 9.5 km N of Pacific Palms. 4859 The Lakes Way. Bookings essential as limited sites
HEMA 37 C13   32 16 08 S   152 31 42 E

100 Myall River Camp
☎ 0409 836 828
Camp Area 4 km N of Hawks Nest. Mungo Brush Rd. Fees collected
HEMA 37 D12   32 38 23 S   152 10 44 E

101 Stewart and Lloyds Campground
Myall Lakes National Park
☎ (02) 6591 0300
Camp Area 10 km N of Hawks Nest. Via Mungo Brush Rd. Signposted
HEMA 37 D12   32 36 27 S   152 13 55 E

102 Banksia Green Campground
Myall Lakes National Park
☎ (02) 6591 0300
Camp Area 19.5 km NE of Hawks Nest, via Mungo Brush Rd. Access also via Bombah Pt ferry from Bulahdelah (Crawford St, Ann St, Lakes Rd). Small vehicles only
HEMA 37 D12   32 32 58 S   152 18 26 E

103 Mungo Brush Campground
☎ (02) 6591 0300
Myall Lakes National Park

Camp Area 19 km NE of Hawks Nest, via Mungo Brush Rd. Access also via Bombah Pt ferry from Bulahdelah (Crawford St, Ann St, Lakes Rd)

HEMA 37 D12   32 32 37 S   152 18 37 E

104 Dees Corner Campground
☎ (02) 6591 0300
Myall Lakes National Park

Camp Area 20 km NE of Hawks Nest, via Mungo Brush Rd. Access also via Bombah Pt ferry from Bulahdelah (Crawford St, Ann St, Lakes Rd)

HEMA 37 D12   32 32 19 S   152 18 59 E

105 White Tree Bay Campground
☎ (02) 6591 0300
Myall Lakes National Park

Camp Area 22 km NE of Hawks Nest, via Mungo Brush Rd. Access also via Bombah Pt ferry from Bulahdelah (Crawford St, Ann St, Lakes Rd)

HEMA 37 D12   32 31 41 S   152 19 21 E

106 The Wells Camp Ground
☎ (02) 6591 0300
Myall Lakes National Park

Camp Area 23 km NE of Hawks Nest, via Mungo Brush Rd. Access also via Bombah Pt ferry from Bulahdelah (Crawford St, Ann St, Lakes Rd)

HEMA 37 D12   32 31 29 S   152 19 22 E

107 Korsmans Landing Campground
☎ (02) 6591 0300
Myall Lakes National Park

Camp Area in Myall Lakes National Park. From Pacific Hwy turn S onto Ann St at Bulahdelah, which becomes Bombah Point Rd follow for 12 km then L to Korsmanns Landing

HEMA 37 D12   32 28 36 S   152 17 08 E

108 Browns Flat North Rest Area
Rest Area 19 km S of Bulahdelah or 10 km N of Tea Gardens turnoff. Northbound

HEMA 37 D12   32 32 54 S   152 09 13 E

109 Browns Flat Rest Area
Rest Area 20 km S of Bulahdelah or 9 km N of Tea Gardens turnoff. Southbound only

HEMA 37 D12   32 33 15 S   152 09 01 E

110 Station Creek Rest Area
Rest Area 30 km S of Bulahdelah or 500m N of Tea Gardens turnoff. Northbound only

HEMA 37 D12   32 36 33 S   152 05 43 E

111 12 Mile Creek Rest Area Southbound
Rest Area 500m S of Bucketts Way (Stroud) intersection. Southbound only

HEMA 37 D11   32 39 13 S   151 51 35 E

112 12 Mile Hill Rest Area
Rest Area 17 km N of Raymond Tce. Northbound only

HEMA 37 D11   32 39 44 S   151 50 33 E

113 Medowie Rd Rest Area
Rest Area 12 km SW of Karuah. 1 km S of The Bucketts Way turnoff. Southbound only

HEMA 37 D11   32 40 10 S   151 50 06 E

114 Lemontree Passage Boat Ramp
Parking Area 32 km E of Raymond Tce. Turn N at Salt Ash onto Lemontree Passage Rd & Cook Pde

HEMA 37 D12   32 43 47 S   152 02 22 E

115 Olney HQ Camping Area
☎ 1300 655 687
Olney State Forest

Camp Area 16 km W of Cooranbong, via Martinsville Rd & Watagan Forest Rd. 8 km dirt road

HEMA 33 E11   33 03 47 S   151 19 53 E

116 The Pines Camping Area
☎ 1300 655 687
Olney State Forest

Camp Area 17 km W of Cooranbong, via Martinsville Rd & Watagan Forest Rd. 9 km dirt road

HEMA 33 E11   33 03 47 S   151 20 13 E

117 Casuarina Camping Area
☎ 1300 655 687
Onley State Forest

Camp Area 18 km W of Cooranbong, via Martinsville Rd & Watagan Forest Rd. 9 km dirt road

HEMA 33 E11   33 03 27 S   151 20 04 E

118 Morisset Showground
☎ (02) 4973 2670

Camp Area at Morisset. 40 Ourimbah St. Maximum stay 4 weeks. See caretaker on arrival

HEMA 33 E12   33 06 30 S   151 28 49 E

Notes...

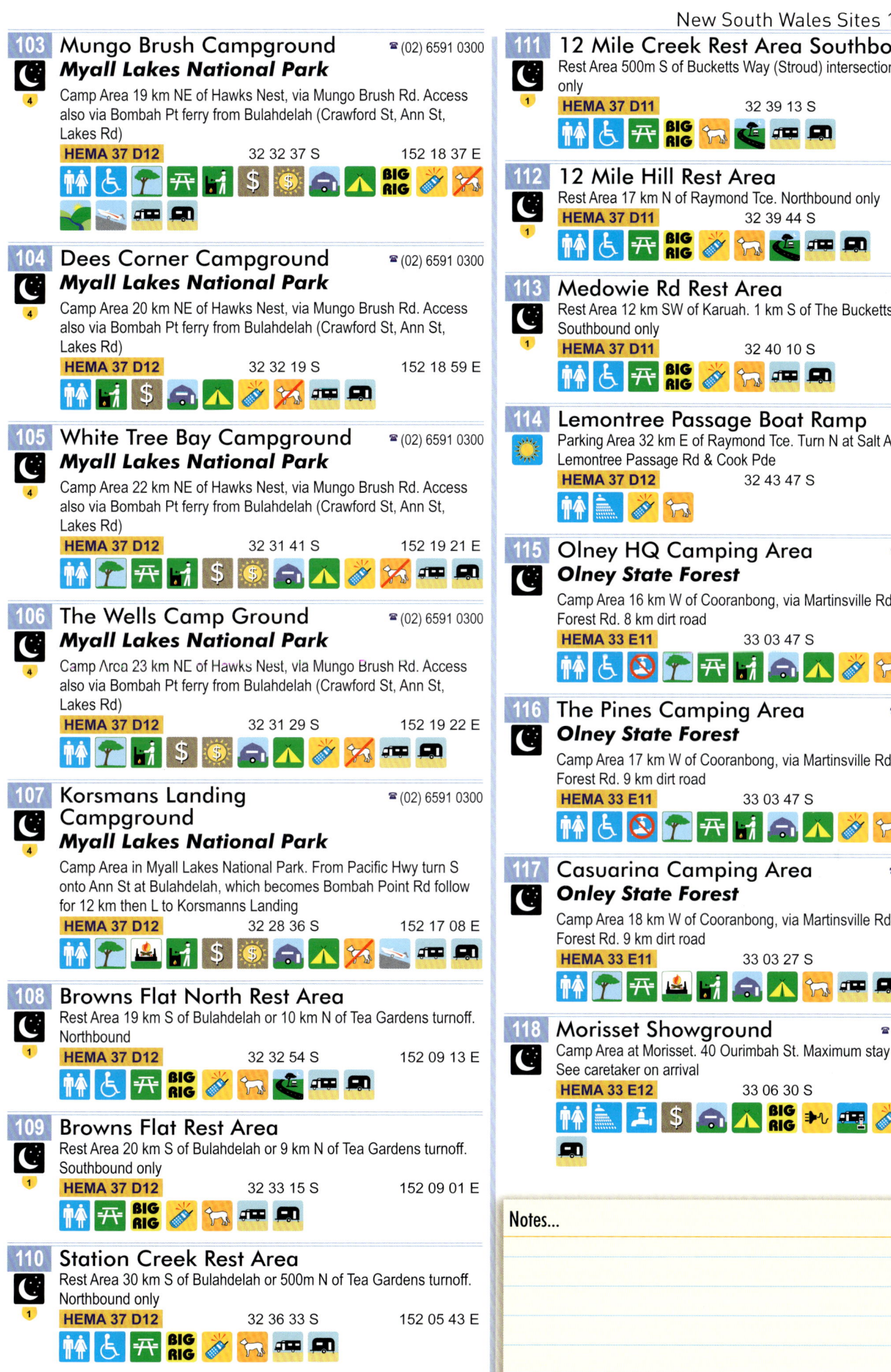

NEW SOUTH WALES

119 Freemans Campground ☎ (02) 4972 9000
Munmorah State Conservation Area
Camp Area 17 km S of Swansea or 23 km N of Wyong, via Elizabeth Bay Dr & Birdie Beach Dr. Limited caravan sites. Bookings essential
HEMA 33 F13   33 12 04 S   151 36 11 E

120 Patonga Foreshore Caravan & Camping Area ☎ (02) 4379 1287
Camp Area at Patonga. Bay St. Steep winding road. Maximum stay 6 weeks
HEMA 33 K12   33 33 14 S   151 16 07 E

121 Mooney Mooney Point Rest Area
Rest Area at Hawkesbury River. N side of bridge. Accessible from North & Southbound lanes
HEMA 33 K11   33 32 02 S   151 11 53 E

Stanthorpe to Newcastle
New England Highway

122 Cullendore High Country ☎ 0459 901 538
Camp Area 42 km NE of Stanthorpe. Via Liston Rd, Cullendore & Cullendore Creek Rds
HEMA 39 A10   28 29 32 S   152 07 21 E

123 Aloomba Lavender Farm ☎ (07) 4686 1191
Camp Area at Liston. 5425 Mt Lindesay Rd. 21 km E of Stanthorpe
HEMA 39 B10   28 37 09 S   152 05 49 E

124 Bald Rock Campground ☎ (02) 6736 4298
Bald Rock National Park
Camp Area 27 km S of Stanthorpe or 29 km NE of Tenterfield. Off Mt Lindesay Hwy, via Bald Rock Rd
HEMA 39 B10   28 50 50 S   152 02 48 E

125 Cypress-Pine Campground ☎ (02) 6736 4298
Boonoo Boonoo National Park
Camp Area 35 km NE of Tenterfield. Off Mt Lindesay Hwy via Boonoo Boonoo Falls Rd
HEMA 39 B10   28 47 55 S   152 10 01 E

126 Basket Swamp Campground ☎ (02) 6736 4298
Camp Area 24 km NE of Tenterfield. Off Mt Lindesay Hwy, via Lindrook Rd, Woollool Woolloolni & Basket Swamp Rds
HEMA 39 C10   28 54 33 S   152 09 11 E

127 Jennings Hotel ☎ (02) 4684 3237
Parking Area at Jennings. 26 Duke St. Small area at back of hotel, check in with publican
HEMA 39 C10   28 55 29 S   151 55 56 E

128 Tenterfield Showground ☎ (02) 6736 3666
Camp Area located at Tenterfield. Miles St. Turn W opposite Info Centre
HEMA 39 C10   29 03 25 S   152 00 55 E

129 Craigs Caravan Park ☎ (02) 6736 1585
Caravan Park at Tenterfield. 102 Rouse St. 800m S of PO
HEMA 39 C10   29 03 40 S   152 00 59 E

130 Bluff Rock Rest Area
Rest Area 11 km S of Tenterfield or 41 km N of Deepwater
HEMA 39 C10   29 09 15 S   152 00 07 E

131 Kookaburra Camping & Caravan Park ☎ 0429 462 473
Caravan Park at Bolivia. 35 km S of Tenterfield or 12 km N of Deepwater. Cnr New England Hwy & Castlerag Rd
HEMA 39 D10   29 20 37 S   151 53 04 E

132 Deepwater Inn ☎ (02) 6734 5111
Camp Spot at Deepwater behind the Old Deepwater Inn. Turn E off Hwy into Cadell St, entry 100m. Please register at bar
HEMA 39 D9   29 26 12 S   151 50 53 E

133 Gunyah - Deepwater River Camping ☎ 0429 462 642
Camp Area at Gunyah. 1 km E of Deepwater. Access via Simpson St off New England Hwy. Follow signs across stock route to property
HEMA 39 D9   29 26 42 S   151 51 01 E

134 Blatherarm Creek Campground ☎ (02) 6736 4298
Torrington State Conservation Area
Camp Area 11 km N of Torrington, via Blatherarm Rd off Silent Grove Rd
HEMA 39 C9   29 14 25 S   151 41 58 E

135 Emmaville Caravan Park ☎ 0429 347 249
Caravan Park at Emmaville. Park Rd
HEMA 39 D9   29 26 51 S   151 36 08 E

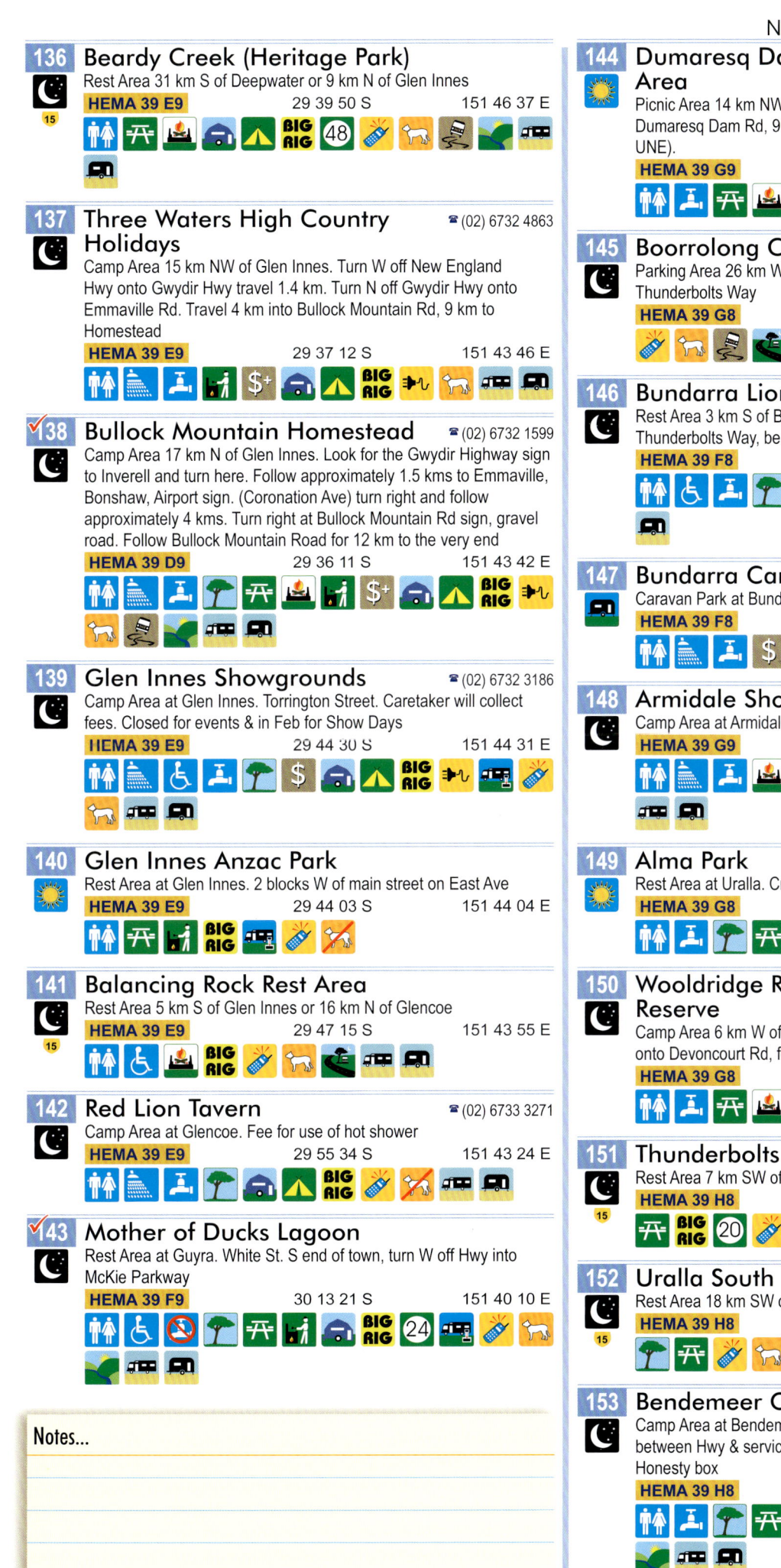

136 Beardy Creek (Heritage Park)
Rest Area 31 km S of Deepwater or 9 km N of Glen Innes
HEMA 39 E9   29 39 50 S   151 46 37 E

137 Three Waters High Country Holidays   ☎ (02) 6732 4863
Camp Area 15 km NW of Glen Innes. Turn W off New England
Hwy onto Gwydir Hwy travel 1.4 km. Turn N off Gwydir Hwy onto
Emmaville Rd. Travel 4 km into Bullock Mountain Rd, 9 km to
Homestead
HEMA 39 E9   29 37 12 S   151 43 46 E

✓138 Bullock Mountain Homestead   ☎ (02) 6732 1599
Camp Area 17 km N of Glen Innes. Look for the Gwydir Highway sign
to Inverell and turn here. Follow approximately 1.5 kms to Emmaville,
Bonshaw, Airport sign. (Coronation Ave) turn right and follow
approximately 4 kms. Turn right at Bullock Mountain Rd sign, gravel
road. Follow Bullock Mountain Road for 12 km to the very end
HEMA 39 D9   29 36 11 S   151 43 42 E

139 Glen Innes Showgrounds   ☎ (02) 6732 3186
Camp Area at Glen Innes. Torrington Street. Caretaker will collect
fees. Closed for events & in Feb for Show Days
HEMA 39 E9   29 44 30 S   151 44 31 E

140 Glen Innes Anzac Park
Rest Area at Glen Innes. 2 blocks W of main street on East Ave
HEMA 39 E9   29 44 03 S   151 44 04 E

141 Balancing Rock Rest Area
Rest Area 5 km S of Glen Innes or 16 km N of Glencoe
HEMA 39 E9   29 47 15 S   151 43 55 E

142 Red Lion Tavern   ☎ (02) 6733 3271
Camp Area at Glencoe. Fee for use of hot shower
HEMA 39 E9   29 55 34 S   151 43 24 E

✓143 Mother of Ducks Lagoon
Rest Area at Guyra. White St. S end of town, turn W off Hwy into
McKie Parkway
HEMA 39 F9   30 13 21 S   151 40 10 E

144 Dumaresq Dam Recreation Area   ☎ (02) 6772 4655
Picnic Area 14 km NW of Armidale. Turn N off Boorolong Rd onto
Dumaresq Dam Rd, 9 km NW of Armidale, via Donnelly St (past
UNE).
HEMA 39 G9   30 25 46 S   151 35 46 E

145 Boorrolong Creek
Parking Area 26 km W of Armidale or 54 km SE of Bundarra on
Thunderbolts Way
HEMA 39 G8   30 28 46 S   151 25 41 E

146 Bundarra Lions Park
Rest Area 3 km S of Bundarra or 73 km NW of Uralla. On
Thunderbolts Way, beside river. Donations welcome
HEMA 39 F8   30 11 36 S   151 04 42 E

147 Bundarra Caravan Park   ☎ (02) 6723 7106
Caravan Park at Bundarra. Court St. Pay at hotel
HEMA 39 F8   30 10 14 S   151 04 35 E

148 Armidale Showgrounds   ☎ 0400 639 630
Camp Area at Armidale. Dumaresq St
HEMA 39 G9   30 30 54 S   151 40 47 E

149 Alma Park
Rest Area at Uralla. Cnr of Hill St & Queen St. Opposite bowling club
HEMA 39 G8   30 38 20 S   151 30 01 E

150 Wooldridge Recreation & Fossicking Reserve
Camp Area 6 km W of Uralla. Take Kingstown Rd for 4.5 km, turn N
onto Devoncourt Rd, follow to end. Cattle grid at reserve entrance
HEMA 39 G8   30 37 45 S   151 28 18 E

151 Thunderbolts Rock
Rest Area 7 km SW of Uralla or 41 km NE of Bendemeer
HEMA 39 H8   30 41 52 S   151 28 07 E

152 Uralla South Rest Area
Rest Area 18 km SW of Uralla or 32 km NE of Bendemeer
HEMA 39 H8   30 45 11 S   151 23 02 E

153 Bendemeer Camping Area
Camp Area at Bendemeer. Access via 800m dirt road, parallel to Hwy,
between Hwy & service station. Behind rodeo grounds. Beside river.
Honesty box
HEMA 39 H8   30 53 14 S   151 09 25 E

Notes...

NEW SOUTH WALES

154 Bendemeer Tourist Park ☎ (02) 6769 6604
Caravan Park at Bendemeer. Havannah St. Single fee rate for solo travellers

| HEMA 39 H8 | 30 52 50 S | 151 09 29 E |

155 Moonbi Park & Lookout
Rest area 6 km N of Moonbi or 11 km S of Bendemeer on Moonbi Lookout Rd

| HEMA 38 H7 | 30 58 34 S | 151 05 57 E |

156 Cockburn River ☎ (02) 6764 5100
Camp Area 11 km E of Kootingal or 2 km W of Limbri, via Kootingal-Limbri Rd. Beside Cockburn River

| HEMA 39 J8 | 31 03 07 S | 151 08 38 E |

157 Tamworth Airport Rest Area
Rest Area 8 km W of Tamworth or 67 km E of Gunnedah. On Hwy opposite airport

| HEMA 38 J7 | 31 04 40 S | 150 51 02 E |

158 The Lorna Byrne Park
Rest Area at Currabubula. Near Currabubula Creek. Toilets at sports oval

| HEMA 38 J7 | 31 15 41 S | 150 44 21 E |

✓159 Woolomin Reserve ☎ (02) 6764 2243
Camp Area at Woolomin. Beside Peel River. Fee for power payable at store. Maximum stay 30 days

| HEMA 39 J8 | 31 18 12 S | 151 08 51 E |

✓160 Bowling Alley Point Rec Reserve
Chaffey Dam
Camp Area 7 km S of Woolomin or 15 km N of Nundle. Maximum stay 7 days. Honesty box

| HEMA 39 J8 | 31 21 38 S | 151 08 00 E |

161 Swamp Creek ☎ (02) 6764 5100
Camp Area 4 km N of Nundle. Beside Peel River on Bowling Alley Point Rd. 2 km dirt road

| HEMA 37 A10 | 31 26 07 S | 151 08 33 E |

✓162 Sheba Dams Reserve ☎ (02) 6764 5100
Camp Area 11 km E of Nundle, via Hanging Rock Rd. 1 km SE of Hanging Rock. Steep climb

| HEMA 37 A10 | 31 29 56 S | 151 11 46 E |

163 Ponderosa Park Campground ☎ 1300 655 687
Hanging Rock State Forest
Camp Area 17 km E of Nundle. Turn N off Hanging Rock Rd after 8 km onto Forest Way. 8 km dirt road

| HEMA 37 A10 | 31 27 49 S | 151 15 25 E |

164 Teamsters Rest Campground ☎ (02) 6764 5100
Camp Area 14 km S of Nundle, via Crawney Rd. Beside Wombramurra Creek. 5 km dirt road

| HEMA 37 A10 | 31 33 24 S | 151 03 22 E |

✓165 Wallabadah Camping Ground
Camp Area at Wallabadah, behind First Fleet Gardens, beside Quirindi Creek. Coach St. Donation box at entrance

| HEMA 37 A9 | 31 32 17 S | 150 49 52 E |

166 Willow Tree Recreation Ground ☎ (02) 6747 1226
Camp Area at Willow Tree. Recreation Rd. Visit info centre to pay for power and get code for facility

| HEMA 37 A9 | 31 38 43 S | 150 43 16 E |

167 Nowlands Gap Rest Area
Rest Area 16 km SE of Willow Tree or 4 km NW of Murrurundi. Southbound only

| HEMA 37 B9 | 31 44 25 S | 150 47 52 E |

168 Murrurundi Caravan Park ☎ (02) 6546 6288
Caravan Park at Murrurundi. 11 Bernard St. 1 km N of PO

| HEMA 37 B9 | 31 45 30 S | 150 49 21 E |

169 Murrurundi Self Contained Vehicle Park ☎ (02) 6546 6288
Camp Area attached to caravan park. Self Contained Vehicles only

| HEMA 37 B9 | 31 45 30 S | 150 49 21 E |

170 Burning Mountain Reserve ☎ (02) 6540 2300
Rest Area 10 km S of Blandford or 23 km N of Scone. 5 km N of Wingen. 200m in from Hwy on sloping parking area

| HEMA 37 B9 | 31 51 21 S | 150 53 58 E |

171 Bunnan Rest Area
Rest Area at Bunnan. High St, N end of town

| HEMA 37 B9 | 32 02 04 S | 150 35 08 E |

172 Scone Caravan Park ☎ (02) 6545 2024
Caravan Park at Scone. New England Hwy. 1 km N of PO. Advance notice required for pets
HEMA 37 B9   32 02 33 S   150 51 56 E

173 Lake Glenbawn Holiday Park ☎ (02) 6543 7193
Caravan Park 13 km SE of Scone or 13 km NE of Aberdeen
HEMA 37 C9   32 06 28 S   150 59 25 E

174 Taylor Park
Rest Area at Aberdeen. N end of town
HEMA 37 C9   32 09 39 S   150 53 17 E

175 Muswellbrook Showgrounds ☎ 0428 493 731
Camp Area at Muswellbrook. Entry off Rutherford Rd. Call ahead to confirm with caretaker
HEMA 37 C9   32 16 51 S   150 53 48 E

176 Gungal Rest Area
Rest Area at Gungal. 11 km NW of Sandy Hollow or 24 km SE of Merriwa
HEMA 37 C8   32 16 24 S   150 30 06 E

177 Battery Rock Rest Area
Rest Area 20 km NW of Sandy Hollow or 15 km SE of Merriwa
HEMA 37 C8   32 12 51 S   150 27 33 E

178 Merriwa Sports Club ☎ (02) 6548 2028
Camp Spot at Merriwa. King George Ave, entry at Golf Course sign. Check in at bar in club for parking directions. Self Contained Vehicles only
HEMA 37 C8   32 08 24 S   150 21 43 E

179 Merriwa RV Stop
Parking Area at Merriwa. Solly's Lane, between Bow St & Vennacher St. Self Contained Vehicles only
HEMA 37 C8   32 08 24 S   150 21 15 E

180 Jerrys Plains Recreation Ground
Camp Spot at Jerrys Plains. S end of town
HEMA 37 D9   32 29 54 S   150 54 34 E

181 Lake Liddell Recreation Area ☎ (02) 6541 2010
Camp Area 16 km S of Muswellbrook or 39 km NW of Singleton. Turn E off Hwy 15, 12 km S of Muswellbrook or 35 km NW of Singleton onto Hebden Rd for 4 km
HEMA 37 C9   32 21 03 S   150 59 48 E

182 Singleton Showground ☎ 0488 722 424
Camp Area at Singleton. Access gates in Church St, directly opposite Dight Ave. Max stay 5 days. Closed for show late September
HEMA 45 E1   32 34 05 S   151 10 19 E

183 Rixs Creek Rest Area
Rest Area 42 km SE of Muswellbrook or 5 km N of Singleton, E side of New England Hwy. Enter via Rixs Rd
HEMA 45 D1   32 31 55 S   151 08 22 E

184 Lake St Clair Campground ☎ (02) 6577 3370
Camp Area 35 km N of Singleton, via Bridgeman Rd. Beside lake
HEMA 45 A3   32 20 04 S   151 17 30 E

185 Grey Gum Cafe ☎ (02) 6579 7015
Camp Area 86 kms S of Singleton or 87 kms N of Windsor on the Putty Rd. Pay for showers
HEMA 32 F6   33 01 49 S   150 40 25 E

186 McNamara Park
Camp Spot at Broke. Beside river
HEMA 45 H1   32 44 52 S   151 06 01 E

187 Singleton East Rest Area
Rest Area 11 km W of Branxton or 11 km SE of Singleton, at jcn of New England Hwy & Golden Hwy
HEMA 45 F2   32 38 33 S   151 13 56 E

188 Pothana Lane Rest Area
Rest Area 5 km W of Branxton or 17 km SE of Singleton, via Belford St S of Hwy
HEMA 45 F3   32 39 30 S   151 17 32 E

Notes...

189 Branxton Oval
Parking Area at Branxton. Entry via John Rose Ave. Self Contained Vehicles only

| HEMA 45 F4 | 32 39 18 S | 151 21 05 E |

190 Paterson Sports Ground
☎ (02) 4938 5029

Camp Area at Paterson. Entry from Webbers Creek Rd

| HEMA 45 E7 | 32 36 12 S | 151 36 40 E |

191 East Gresford Showground
Camp Area at East Gresford on the Gresford-Paterson Rd

| HEMA 45 C6 | 32 25 56 S | 151 33 27 E |

192 Kurri Kurri Central Oval
Parking Area at Kurri Kurri. Allworth St. Self Contained Vehicles only

| HEMA 45 H5 | 32 49 24 S | 151 28 51 E |

193 Abermain Bowling & Recreation Club
☎ (02) 4930 4285

Parking Area at Abermain. Goulburn St. Self Contained Vehicles only

| HEMA 45 H4 | 32 48 26 S | 151 25 36 E |

194 Cessnock Showground
☎ 0412 235 447

Camp Area at Cessnock. Access gates beside indoor sports centre Mount View Rd. Closed Feb & early Mar for show

| HEMA 45 J4 | 32 49 51 S | 151 20 26 E |

195 The Wollombi Tavern
☎ (02) 4998 3261

Parking Area at Wollombi. Parking at hotel, check in with publican for directions

| HEMA 45 K1 | 32 56 19 S | 151 08 25 E |

Woodenbong to Grafton
Summerland Way

196 Koreelah Creek Campground
☎ (02) 6632 0000

Koreelah National Park
Camp Area 35 km NW of Woodenbong. Turn N off the Mt Lindesay Rd 23 km W of Woodenbong or 22 km E of Legume at Old Koreelah onto White Swamp Rd for 12 km. 3 km dirt road. Beside creek

| HEMA 39 A11 | 28 18 30 S | 152 27 58 E |

197 Levuka
☎ (02) 6634 1338

Camp Area 16 km SW of Woodenborg. 6 km W of Woodenborg turn S into Beaury Creek Rd then turn W into Plantation Rd to Levuka. Bookings essential

| HEMA 39 A11 | 28 25 20 S | 152 30 33 E |

198 Woodenbong Campground
☎ (02) 6635 1300

Camp Area at Woodenbong. W end of town next to swimming pool. Pay at either service station or caretaker on site. Fee for showers

| HEMA 39 A11 | 28 23 20 S | 152 36 21 E |

199 Legume
Camp Spot at Legume. Behind Community Hall, Killarney St. Donation please at the shop

| HEMA 39 A11 | 28 24 23 S | 152 18 25 E |

200 Tooloom Falls Campground
Camp Area 6 km S of Urbenville. Turn S off Urbenville-Warwick Rd 3 km SW of Urbenville onto Tooloom Falls Rd. 3 km dirt road

| HEMA 39 A11 | 28 30 46 S | 152 31 36 E |

201 Urbenville Forest Park
☎ (02) 6634 1211

Camp Area at Urbenville. N end of town. Fees collected

| HEMA 39 A11 | 28 28 06 S | 152 32 56 E |

202 Old Bonalbo Pioneers Park
Rest Area 23 km S of Urbenville or 1 km N of Old Bonalbo

| HEMA 39 B11 | 28 38 35 S | 152 35 49 E |

203 Moore Park Nature Reserve
Picnic Area 1.2 km N of Old Grevillia. 32 km SE of Woodenbong or 13 km NW of Wiangaree. Via Findon Creek Rd. Beside Richmond River

| HEMA 39 A12 | 28 26 11 S | 152 52 42 E |

204 Sheepstation Creek Campground
☎ (02) 6632 0000

Border Ranges National Park
Camp Area 17 km NE of Wiangaree, via Lynchs Creek Rd & Tweed Range Scenic Dr. 11 km dirt road

| HEMA 39 A12 | 28 24 47 S | 153 01 23 E |

205 Kyogle Showground
☎ 0459 537 601

Camp Area at Kyogle. N end of town

| HEMA 39 B12 | 28 36 57 S | 153 00 00 E |

206 Bells Bay
☎ (02) 6633 9140

Toonumbar Dam
Camp Area 29 km W of Kyogle, via Afterlee Rd & Dam Access Rd. Some dirt road

| HEMA 39 B12 | 28 37 00 S | 152 47 39 E |

207 Braemar Park
Ellangowan State Forest
Rest Area 28 km S of Casino or 22 km N of Whiporie
HEMA 39 C12   29 05 16 S   153 00 07 E

208 Whiporie General Store   ☎ (02) 6661 9100
Camp Spot at Whiporie. Beside store. Ask owner's permission
HEMA 39 D12   29 16 56 S   152 59 22 E

209 Copmanhurst Primitive Camping Ground   ☎ 1300 886 235
Camp Area at Copmanhurst. Lawrence St. 31 km NW of Grafton via Clarence Way
HEMA 39 E11   29 35 24 S   152 46 50 E

210 Copmanhurst Recreation Reserve   ☎ 0427 449 783
Camp Area at Copmanhurst. Lawrence St
HEMA 39 E11   29 35 23 S   152 46 27 E

211 Lilydale Primitive Camp Ground   ☎ 1300 886 235
Camp Area 12 km from Copmanhurst, via Clarence Way, Winegrove Rd. SW side of Lilydale Bridge
HEMA 39 D11   29 32 46 S   152 40 16 E

212 The Gorge   ☎ (02) 6647 2173
Camp Area on Heifer Station. 2568 Gorge Rd. 27 km from Lilydale Bridge, via Copmanhurst. Dirt Rd. Call ahead before arrival
HEMA 39 D11   29 23 28 S   152 34 18 E

Ballina to Goondiwindi
Bruxner Highway

213 Lismore Showgrounds   ☎ (02) 6621 5916
Camp Area at Lismore. Alexandra Parade, North Lismore. Not available during events, call ahead to check availability. Maximum stay 14 days
HEMA 39 B13   28 47 50 S   153 16 25 E

214 The Channon Village Campground   ☎ (02) 6688 6204
Camp Area at The Channon. 391 The Channon Rd just S of the village
HEMA 39 B13   28 40 42 S   153 16 46 E

215 Rummery Park   ☎ (02) 6627 0200
Whian Whian State Conservation Area
Camp Area 32 km NE of Lismore. Turn N off Dunoon Rd 7 km NE of Dunoon onto Minyon Falls Rd (Nightcap Range Rd) & Peates Mountain Rd for 8 km. 7 km narrow, winding, dirt road. Pre booking essential
HEMA 39 B13   28 35 55 S   153 22 41 E

216 Nimbin Showgrounds   ☎ 0458 872 228
Camp Area at Nimbin. Cecil St. Maximum stay 7 days
HEMA 39 B13   28 35 56 S   153 13 36 E

217 Mallanganee Oval
Camp Spot at Mallanganee. Access via Pine St, behind Bush Fire Brigade Building. Self Contained Vehicles only. Ask at Info Centre, do not take water, town is on tank water
HEMA 39 C11   28 54 29 S   152 43 17 E

218 Bonalbo Caravan & Camping Park   ☎ (02) 6665 1137
Caravan Park at Bonalbo. See onsite caretaker. Mobile 0400 229 291
HEMA 39 B11   28 44 19 S   152 37 43 E

219 Peacock Creek Camping Area   ☎ (02) 6632 0000
Richmond Range National Park
Camp Area 18 km NE of Bonalbo. Turn N off Clarence Way 3 km E of Bonalbo onto Peacock Creek Rd. 13.5 km to campsite. Dirt road. 4WD only when wet
HEMA 39 B11   28 39 36 S   152 42 56 E

220 West of The Range Rest Area
Rest Area 10 km E of Tabulam or 9 km W of Mallanganee, at jcn of Bruxner Hwy & Bonalbo Rd
HEMA 39 C11   28 54 02 S   152 39 15 E

221 Tabulam Racecourse   ☎ (02) 6666 1535
Camp Area 2 km S of Tabulam. On Racecourse Rd & Creek St. Keys & payment at the service station or co-op in town. Campdraft has the site during the June long weekend for private use
HEMA 39 C11   28 54 22 S   152 33 16 E

Notes...

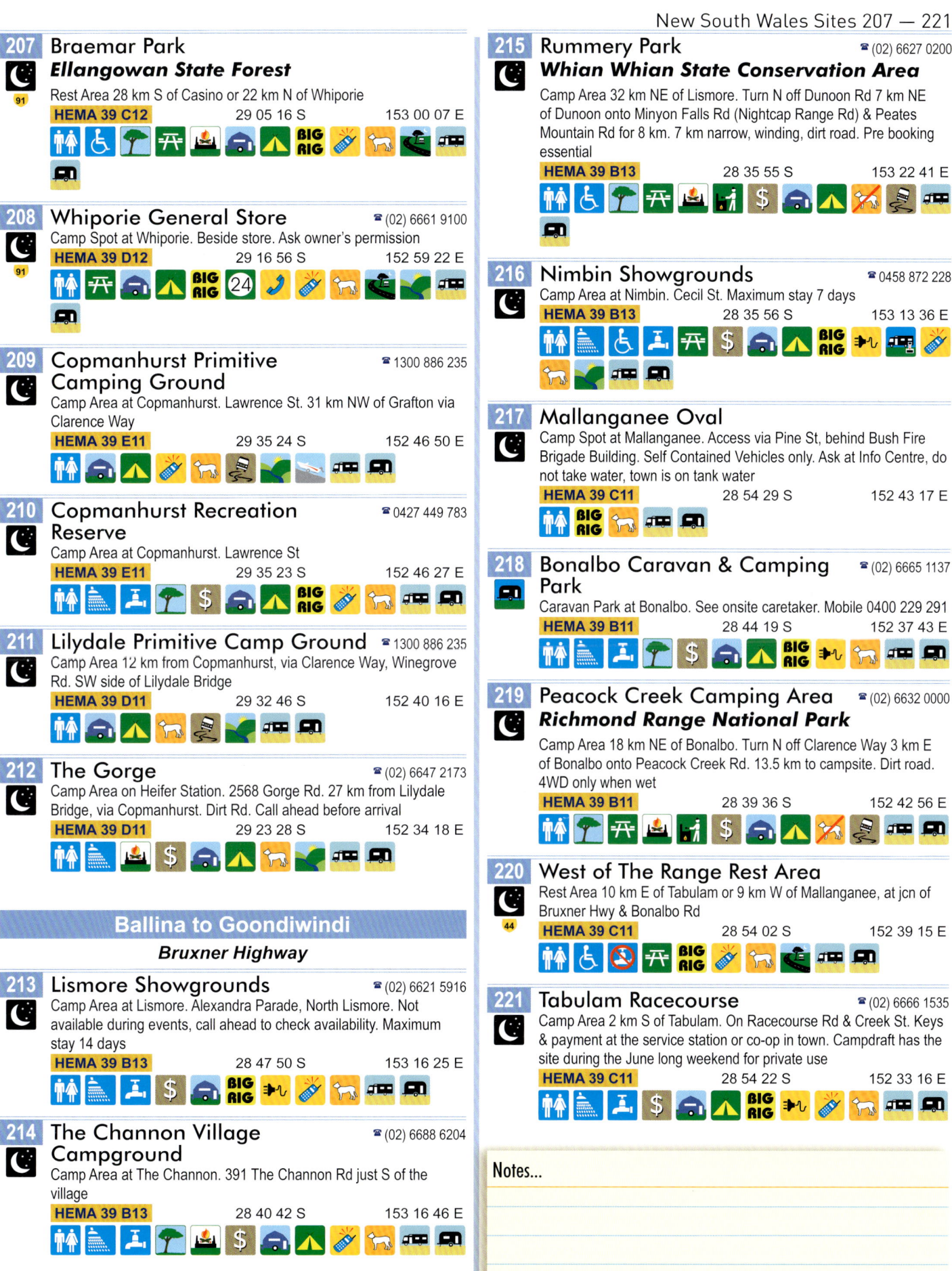

NEW SOUTH WALES

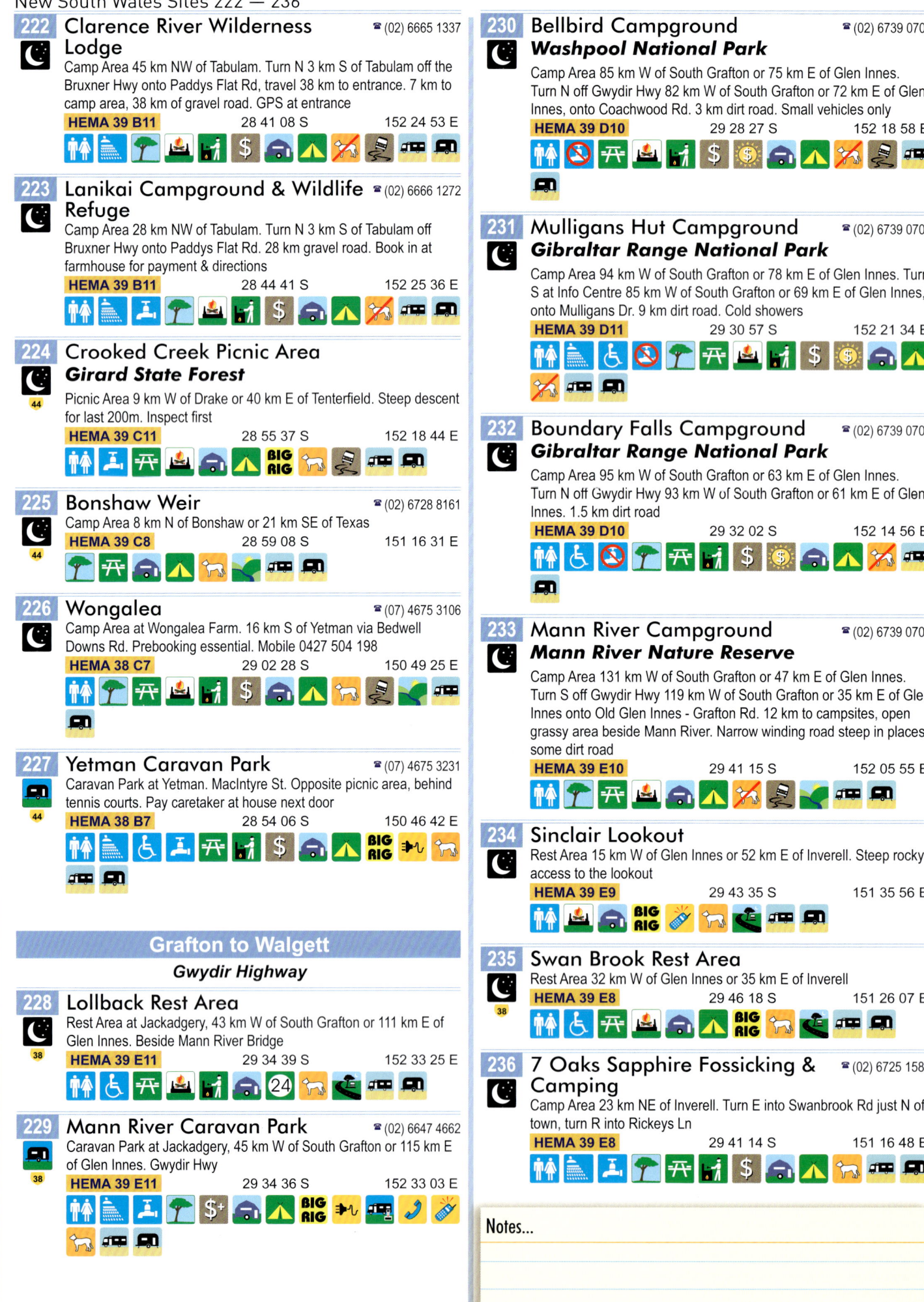

222 Clarence River Wilderness Lodge ☎ (02) 6665 1337
Camp Area 45 km NW of Tabulam. Turn N 3 km S of Tabulam off the Bruxner Hwy onto Paddys Flat Rd, travel 38 km to entrance. 7 km to camp area, 38 km of gravel road. GPS at entrance
HEMA 39 B11   28 41 08 S   152 24 53 E

223 Lanikai Campground & Wildlife Refuge ☎ (02) 6666 1272
Camp Area 28 km NW of Tabulam. Turn N 3 km S of Tabulam off Bruxner Hwy onto Paddys Flat Rd. 28 km gravel road. Book in at farmhouse for payment & directions
HEMA 39 B11   28 44 41 S   152 25 36 E

224 Crooked Creek Picnic Area
Girard State Forest
Picnic Area 9 km W of Drake or 40 km E of Tenterfield. Steep descent for last 200m. Inspect first
HEMA 39 C11   28 55 37 S   152 18 44 E

225 Bonshaw Weir ☎ (02) 6728 8161
Camp Area 8 km N of Bonshaw or 21 km SE of Texas
HEMA 39 C8   28 59 08 S   151 16 31 E

226 Wongalea ☎ (07) 4675 3106
Camp Area at Wongalea Farm. 16 km S of Yetman via Bedwell Downs Rd. Prebooking essential. Mobile 0427 504 198
HEMA 38 C7   29 02 28 S   150 49 25 E

227 Yetman Caravan Park ☎ (07) 4675 3231
Caravan Park at Yetman. MacIntyre St. Opposite picnic area, behind tennis courts. Pay caretaker at house next door
HEMA 38 B7   28 54 06 S   150 46 42 E

Grafton to Walgett
Gwydir Highway

228 Lollback Rest Area
Rest Area at Jackadgery, 43 km W of South Grafton or 111 km E of Glen Innes. Beside Mann River Bridge
HEMA 39 E11   29 34 39 S   152 33 25 E

229 Mann River Caravan Park ☎ (02) 6647 4662
Caravan Park at Jackadgery, 45 km W of South Grafton or 115 km E of Glen Innes. Gwydir Hwy
HEMA 39 E11   29 34 36 S   152 33 03 E

230 Bellbird Campground
Washpool National Park ☎ (02) 6739 0700
Camp Area 85 km W of South Grafton or 75 km E of Glen Innes. Turn N off Gwydir Hwy 82 km W of South Grafton or 72 km E of Glen Innes, onto Coachwood Rd. 3 km dirt road. Small vehicles only
HEMA 39 D10   29 28 27 S   152 18 58 E

231 Mulligans Hut Campground
Gibraltar Range National Park ☎ (02) 6739 0700
Camp Area 94 km W of South Grafton or 78 km E of Glen Innes. Turn S at Info Centre 85 km W of South Grafton or 69 km E of Glen Innes, onto Mulligans Dr. 9 km dirt road. Cold showers
HEMA 39 D11   29 30 57 S   152 21 34 E

232 Boundary Falls Campground
Gibraltar Range National Park ☎ (02) 6739 0700
Camp Area 95 km W of South Grafton or 63 km E of Glen Innes. Turn N off Gwydir Hwy 93 km W of South Grafton or 61 km E of Glen Innes. 1.5 km dirt road
HEMA 39 D10   29 32 02 S   152 14 56 E

233 Mann River Campground
Mann River Nature Reserve ☎ (02) 6739 0700
Camp Area 131 km W of South Grafton or 47 km E of Glen Innes. Turn S off Gwydir Hwy 119 km W of South Grafton or 35 km E of Glen Innes onto Old Glen Innes - Grafton Rd. 12 km to campsites, open grassy area beside Mann River. Narrow winding road steep in places, some dirt road
HEMA 39 E10   29 41 15 S   152 05 55 E

234 Sinclair Lookout
Rest Area 15 km W of Glen Innes or 52 km E of Inverell. Steep rocky access to the lookout
HEMA 39 E9   29 43 35 S   151 35 56 E

235 Swan Brook Rest Area
Rest Area 32 km W of Glen Innes or 35 km E of Inverell
HEMA 39 E8   29 46 18 S   151 26 07 E

236 7 Oaks Sapphire Fossicking & Camping ☎ (02) 6725 1582
Camp Area 23 km NE of Inverell. Turn E into Swanbrook Rd just N of town, turn R into Rickeys Ln
HEMA 39 E8   29 41 14 S   151 16 48 E

Notes...

NEW SOUTH WALES

237 Tingha Gems Caravan & Camping ☎ (02) 6723 3234
Camp Area at Tingha, entry off Swimming Pool Rd
HEMA 39 E8   29 56 45 S   151 12 58 E

238 Green Valley Farm ☎ (02) 6723 3015
Camp Area at Tingha. Jones Rd
HEMA 39 E8   29 59 13 S   151 18 01 E

239 Fossickers Rest Caravan Park ☎ (02) 6722 2261
Caravan Park at Inverell. Lake Inverell Dr, 3 km E of PO. 300m off Gwydir Hwy
HEMA 39 E8   29 47 10 S   151 08 15 E

240 Sapphire City Caravan Park ☎ (02) 6722 1830
Caravan Park at Inverell. 93-103 Moore St
HEMA 39 E8   29 46 32 S   151 07 52 E

241 Inverell Showground ☎ (02) 6722 3435
Camp Area at Inverell. 1 km E of town, enter off Tingha Rd, in between Sporting Complex & Pioneer Village. Limited sites
HEMA 39 E8   29 46 57 S   151 07 14 E

242 Pindari Dam
Camp Area 80 km N of Inverell or 22 km SE of Ashford. Small vehicles only
HEMA 39 D8   29 23 46 S   151 15 36 E

243 Wells Crossing
Camp Area 7 km E of Ashford on the Pindari Dam Rd, beside Severn River
HEMA 39 D8   29 21 44 S   151 08 36 E

244 Ashford Caravan Park ☎ (02) 6725 4014
Caravan Park at Ashford. 57 km N of Inverell. Bukkulla St. Payment in honesty box
HEMA 39 D8   29 19 24 S   151 05 52 E

245 Severn River
Rest Area 4 km N of Ashford
HEMA 39 D8   29 17 52 S   151 07 05 E

✓ **246 Lemon Tree Flat Campground** ☎ (02) 6736 4298
Kwiambal National Park
Camp Area 38 km NW of Ashford. Via Wallangra Rd, Sandy Creek Rd, Limetone Rd. 21 km of unsealed road. Limited caravan sites (6)
HEMA 38 C7   29 08 50 S   150 59 24 E

247 Copeton Dam (Northern Foreshore) ☎ (02) 6723 0250
Camp Area 17 km SW of Inverell, via Auburn Vale Rd. Check ahead for dogs permitted
HEMA 38 E7   29 53 37 S   150 59 50 E

248 Delungra Recreation Ground ☎ (02) 6724 8275
Camp Spot at Delungra. W end of town
HEMA 38 E7   29 39 04 S   150 49 33 E

249 Graman Hotel ☎ (02) 6725 6482
Camp Spot at Graman. Yetman Rd. Large grassed area behind hotel. Check in with publican
HEMA 38 D7   29 28 09 S   150 55 41 E

250 Dumboy Creek Rest Area
Rest Area 4 km NW of Delungra or 25 km SE of Warialda
HEMA 38 E7   29 38 24 S   150 47 51 E

251 Cranky Rock Nature Reserve ☎ (02) 6729 1402
Camp Area 26 km NW of Delungra or 8 km E of Warialda. Turn N off Gwydir Hwy 23 km NW of Delungra or 5 km E of Warialda for 3 km. Pay at kiosk
HEMA 38 D7   29 33 39 S   150 38 46 E

252 The Coolatai Hall
Camp Spot at Coolatai at the Community Hall. Donation box at hall for upkeep & hot showers
HEMA 38 C7   29 15 07 S   150 44 59 E

253 Saleyards Rest Area
Rest Area in Warialda, Gwydir Hwy, E of town
HEMA 38 D6   29 32 44 S   150 34 53 E

254 Cunninghams Rest Area
Rest Area 2 km W of Warialda or 78 km E of Moree. N side of Hwy
HEMA 38 D6   29 32 46 S   150 33 14 E

Notes...

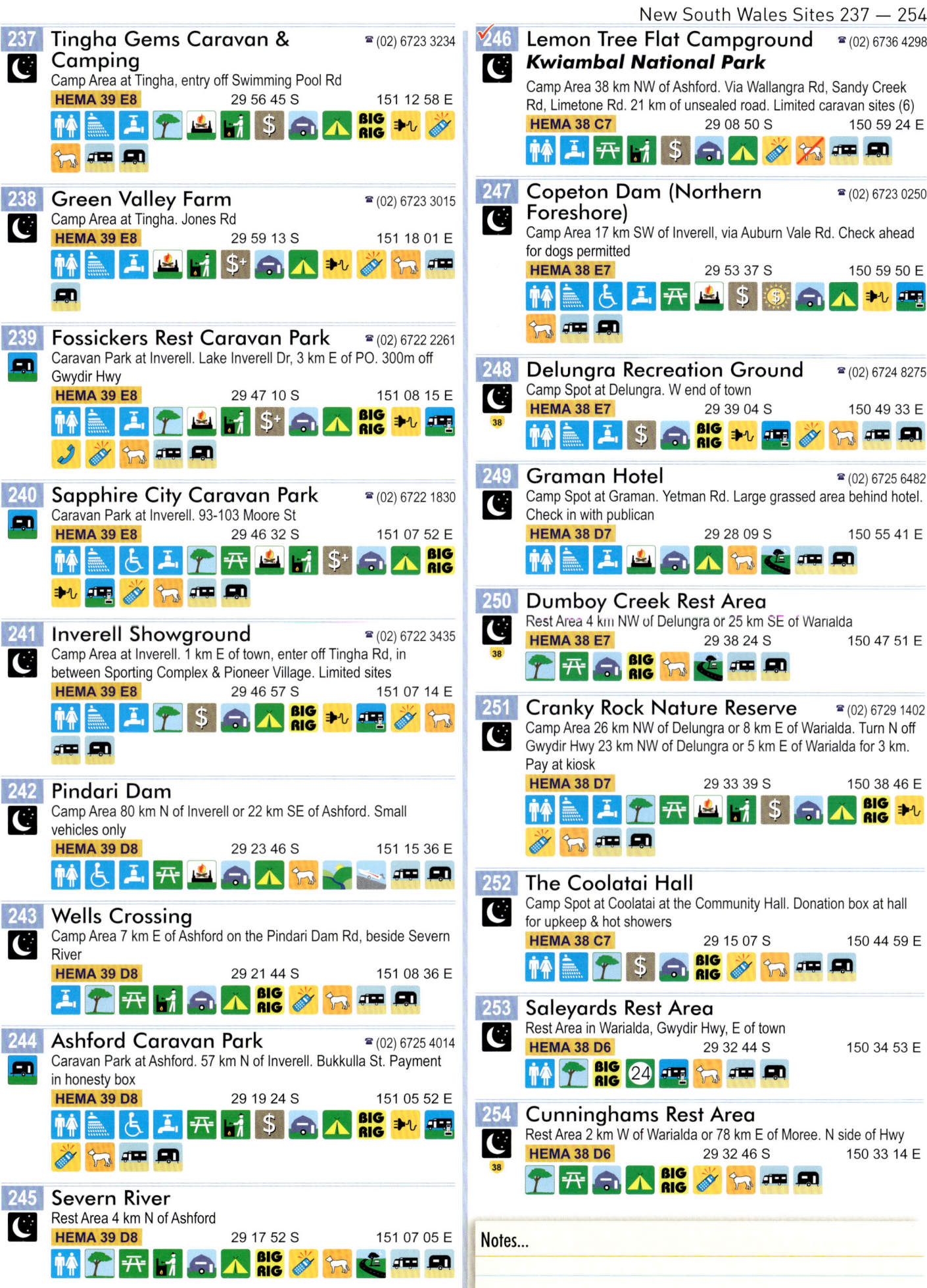

NEW SOUTH WALES

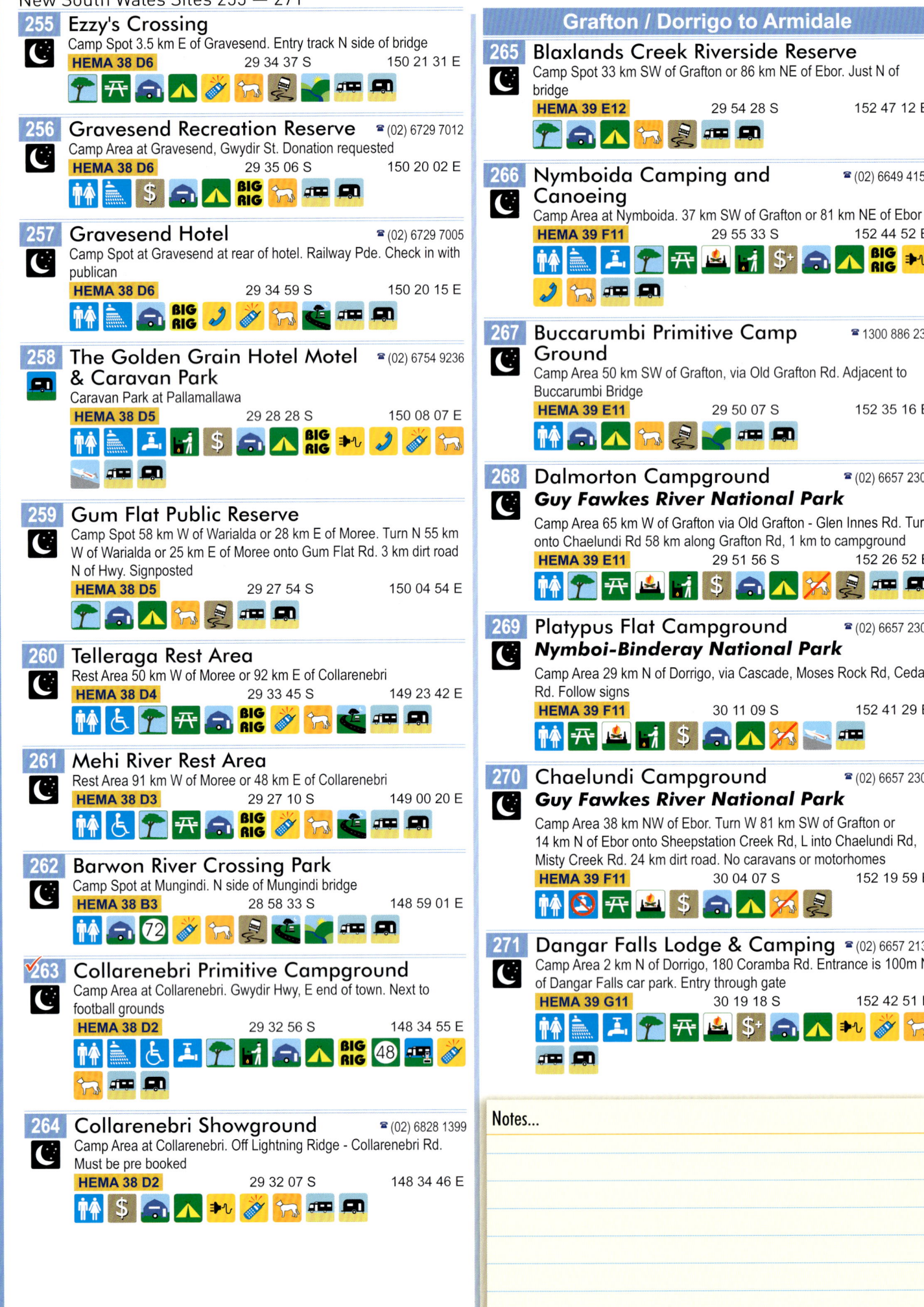

255 Ezzy's Crossing
Camp Spot 3.5 km E of Gravesend. Entry track N side of bridge
HEMA 38 D6   29 34 37 S   150 21 31 E

256 Gravesend Recreation Reserve ☎ (02) 6729 7012
Camp Area at Gravesend, Gwydir St. Donation requested
HEMA 38 D6   29 35 06 S   150 20 02 E

257 Gravesend Hotel ☎ (02) 6729 7005
Camp Spot at Gravesend at rear of hotel. Railway Pde. Check in with publican
HEMA 38 D6   29 34 59 S   150 20 15 E

258 The Golden Grain Hotel Motel ☎ (02) 6754 9236
& Caravan Park
Caravan Park at Pallamallawa
HEMA 38 D5   29 28 28 S   150 08 07 E

259 Gum Flat Public Reserve
Camp Spot 58 km W of Warialda or 28 km E of Moree. Turn N 55 km W of Warialda or 25 km E of Moree onto Gum Flat Rd. 3 km dirt road N of Hwy. Signposted
HEMA 38 D5   29 27 54 S   150 04 54 E

260 Telleraga Rest Area
Rest Area 50 km W of Moree or 92 km E of Collarenebri
HEMA 38 D4   29 33 45 S   149 23 42 E

261 Mehi River Rest Area
Rest Area 91 km W of Moree or 48 km E of Collarenebri
HEMA 38 D3   29 27 10 S   149 00 20 E

262 Barwon River Crossing Park
Camp Spot at Mungindi. N side of Mungindi bridge
HEMA 38 B3   28 58 33 S   148 59 01 E

263 Collarenebri Primitive Campground
Camp Area at Collarenebri. Gwydir Hwy, E end of town. Next to football grounds
HEMA 38 D2   29 32 56 S   148 34 55 E

264 Collarenebri Showground ☎ (02) 6828 1399
Camp Area at Collarenebri. Off Lightning Ridge - Collarenebri Rd. Must be pre booked
HEMA 38 D2   29 32 07 S   148 34 46 E

Grafton / Dorrigo to Armidale

265 Blaxlands Creek Riverside Reserve
Camp Spot 33 km SW of Grafton or 86 km NE of Ebor. Just N of bridge
HEMA 39 E12   29 54 28 S   152 47 12 E

266 Nymboida Camping and ☎ (02) 6649 4155
Canoeing
Camp Area at Nymboida. 37 km SW of Grafton or 81 km NE of Ebor
HEMA 39 F11   29 55 33 S   152 44 52 E

267 Buccarumbi Primitive Camp ☎ 1300 886 235
Ground
Camp Area 50 km SW of Grafton, via Old Grafton Rd. Adjacent to Buccarumbi Bridge
HEMA 39 E11   29 50 07 S   152 35 16 E

268 Dalmorton Campground ☎ (02) 6657 2309
Guy Fawkes River National Park
Camp Area 65 km W of Grafton via Old Grafton - Glen Innes Rd. Turn onto Chaelundi Rd 58 km along Grafton Rd, 1 km to campground
HEMA 39 E11   29 51 56 S   152 26 52 E

269 Platypus Flat Campground ☎ (02) 6657 2309
Nymboi-Binderay National Park
Camp Area 29 km N of Dorrigo, via Cascade, Moses Rock Rd, Cedar Rd. Follow signs
HEMA 39 F11   30 11 09 S   152 41 29 E

270 Chaelundi Campground ☎ (02) 6657 2309
Guy Fawkes River National Park
Camp Area 38 km NW of Ebor. Turn W 81 km SW of Grafton or 14 km N of Ebor onto Sheepstation Creek Rd, L into Chaelundi Rd, Misty Creek Rd. 24 km dirt road. No caravans or motorhomes
HEMA 39 F11   30 04 07 S   152 19 59 E

271 Dangar Falls Lodge & Camping ☎ (02) 6657 2131
Camp Area 2 km N of Dorrigo, 180 Coramba Rd. Entrance is 100m N of Dangar Falls car park. Entry through gate
HEMA 39 G11   30 19 18 S   152 42 51 E

Notes...

272 Dorrigo Showgrounds ☎ (02) 6657 1373
Camp Area at Dorrigo. Entry off Waterfall Way. Self Contained
Vehicles only
HEMA 39 G11   30 20 17 S   152 42 23 E

273 Ebor Rest Area
Rest Area at Ebor. 600m W of town, next to sportsground. Opposite
Ebor Falls turnoff
78
HEMA 39 G10   30 24 29 S   152 20 45 E

274 Ebor Falls Hotel Motel ☎ (02) 6775 9155
Camp Area at Ebor. Behind Ebor Hotel
78
HEMA 39 G10   30 24 11 S   152 20 51 E

275 Native Dog Creek Campground ☎ (02) 6657 2309
Cathedral Rock National Park
17
Camp Area 12 km NW of Ebor or 67 km SE of Guyra, via Ebor -
Guyra Rd. 200m W of Hwy
HEMA 39 G10   30 23 15 S   152 16 06 E

276 Barokee Campground ☎ (02) 6657 2309
Cathedral Rock National Park
Camp Area 14 km SW of Ebor or 38 km E of Wollomombi. Turn W
off Waterfall Way 6 km SW of Ebor or 32 km E of Wollomombi, onto
Round Mountain Rd. 8 km dirt road. Small vehicles only. Not suitable
for caravans
HEMA 39 G10   30 26 38 S   152 15 02 E

✓277 Little Styx River Campground
Camp Area 21 km S of Ebor or 37 km E of Wollomombi. Turn E off
Waterfall Way 11 km SW of Ebor or 27 km E of Wollomombi, onto
Point Lookout Rd.10 km dirt road. At entrance to New England
National Park
HEMA 39 G10   30 30 28 S   152 21 59 E

278 Thungutti Camping Ground ☎ (02) 6657 2309
New England National Park
Camp Area 23 km S of Ebor or 35 km E of Wollomombi. Turn E off
Waterfall Way onto Point Lookout Rd. 11 km dirt road. Tent camping
only
HEMA 39 G11   30 30 02 S   152 23 15 E

279 Oaky Creek Rest Area
Rest Area 16 km SW of Ebor or 22 km E of Wollomombi
78
HEMA 39 G10   30 30 00 S   152 15 14 E

280 Dingo Fence Rest Area
Rest Area 28 km SW of Ebor or 10 km E of Wollomombi
78
HEMA 39 G10   30 30 08 S   152 08 43 E

281 Wollomombi Rest Area
Rest Area at Wollomombi. 1 km NW off Waterfall Way. Toilets at
Memorial Hall
HEMA 39 G10   30 30 42 S   152 02 40 E

282 Wattle Flat Camping Area ☎ 1300 655 687
Styx River State Forest
Camp Area 70 km E of Armidale. Access via Armidale-Kempsey Rd.
Turn N onto Styx River Forest Way, follow signage. 4WD only, small
offroad caravans & campervans
HEMA 39 G10   30 35 01 S   152 12 02 E

283 Georges Junction
Camp Area 83 km SE of Armidale or 46 km W of Bellbrook. Via
Armidale - Kempsey Rd, access road not suitable for caravans
HEMA 39 H10   30 45 06 S   152 11 25 E

284 Blackbird Flat Reserve ☎ (02) 6563 1555
Picnic Area 69 km NW of Kempsey or 68 km SE of Wollomombi near
Comara. 16 km dirt road. Not suitable for caravans
HEMA 39 H10   30 46 20 S   152 22 06 E

285 West Kunderang Wilderness Retreat ☎ (02) 6778 1264
Camp Area 50 km E of Armidale. Off Raspberry Rd. Bookings
essential. Dirt road. Suitable for off-road caravans & camper trailers
only
HEMA 39 H10   30 50 38 S   152 04 36 E

286 Wollomombi Campground ☎ (02) 6777 4700
Oxley Wild Rivers National Park
Camp Area 4 km W of Wollomombi. Turn S off Waterfall Way 2 km
W of Wollomombi or 38 km E of Armidale. Near Wollomombi Gorge.
Narrow entrance way
HEMA 39 G10   30 31 54 S   152 01 40 E

287 Gara River Rest Area
Rest Area 27 km W of Wollomombi or 13 km E of Armidale
78
HEMA 39 G9   30 32 38 S   151 47 39 E

288 Dangars Gorge Campground ☎ (02) 6777 4700
Oxley Wild Rivers National Park
Camp Area 22 km SE of Armidale via Dangarsleigh, Dangars Falls
Rd. 10 km dirt road
HEMA 39 H9   30 40 20 S   151 43 32 E

Port Macquarie-Tamworth-Coonabarabran
Oxley Highway

289 Rocks Ferry Reserve
Rest Area at Wauchope N end of town. River Ferry Rd
HEMA 39 K11   31 27 07 S   152 44 46 E

290 Wauchope Showgrounds ☎ 0475 111 074
Camp Area at Wauchope, enter via High St. Limited sites, reservations preferred
HEMA 39 K11   31 27 28 S   152 43 27 E

291 Brushy Mountain Campground ☎ (02) 6582 3355
Werrikimbe National Park
Camp Area 61 km NW of Wauchope, via Beechwood, Bellangry & Hastings Forest Way. 38 km dirt road. Small vehicles only
HEMA 39 J10   31 08 52 S   152 21 42 E

292 Ellenborough Reserve
Camp Area at Ellenborough. 500m N of Hwy on E side of bridge, beside river. Maximum stay 14 days
HEMA 39 K11   31 26 25 S   152 27 40 E

293 Stockyard Creek Rest Area
Rest Area 82 km W of Wauchope or 83 km SE of Walcha. Just E of Gingers Creek store
HEMA 39 K10   31 24 10 S   152 07 26 E

294 Mooraback Campground ☎ (02) 6777 4700
Werrikimbe National Park
Camp Area 84 km E of Walcha. Turn N off the Oxley Hwy 111 km W of Wauchope or 54 km SE of Walcha onto Kangaroo Flat Rd, Mooraback Rd. 30 km dirt road. Small vehicles only
HEMA 39 J10   31 08 51 S   152 12 54 E

295 Tia Falls Campground ☎ (02) 6777 4700
Oxley Wild Rivers National Park
Camp Area 42 km SE of Walcha. Turn N off Oxley Hwy 128 km NW of Wauchope or 37 km SE of Walcha. 5 km dirt road
HEMA 39 J9   31 09 37 S   151 51 16 E

296 Tia River Rest Area
Rest Area 129 km NW of Wauchope or 36 km SE of Walcha
HEMA 39 J9   31 11 17 S   151 49 51 E

297 Stoney Creek Rest Area
Rest Area 143 km NW of Wauchope or 22 km SE of Walcha
HEMA 39 J9   31 04 35 S   151 46 39 E

298 Apsley Falls Campground ☎ (02) 6777 4700
Oxley Wild Rivers National Park
Camp Area 20 km SE of Walcha. Turn N off Oxley Hwy 146 km NW of Wauchope or 19 km SE of Walcha for 1 km
HEMA 39 J9   31 03 16 S   151 45 45 E

299 Walcha East Rest Area
Rest Area 161 km NW of Wauchope or 4 km E of Walcha
HEMA 39 H9   31 00 13 S   151 37 48 E

300 Woolbrook Rest Area
Rest Area at Woolbrook. 26 km W of Walcha or 26 km E of Bendemeer. 1 km S of Hwy beside river
HEMA 39 H8   30 57 55 S   151 20 50 E

301 Somerton Hotel ☎ (02) 6769 7683
Camp Area at Somerton. Check in at the bar for directions for parking
HEMA 38 H6   30 56 26 S   150 38 26 E

302 Eastern Foreshore Campground ☎ (02) 6769 7605
Lake Keepit State Park
Camp Area 56 km NW of Tamworth. Turn N off Oxley Hwy 46 km W of Tamworth or 29 km E of Gunnedah. 3 km dirt road. Pets only permitted in bush camping area, not caravan park area, must phone ahead for pets
HEMA 38 H6   30 53 20 S   150 31 06 E

303 Red Bank Rest Area
Rest Area 7 km W of Carroll or 12 km E of Gunnedah
HEMA 38 H6   30 59 39 S   150 22 40 E

304 South St RV Park ☎ (02) 6742 1589
Camp Area at Gunnedah. South St, next to showgrounds. Caretaker collects fees
HEMA 38 H6   30 58 44 S   150 14 42 E

305 Donnelly Park
Parking Area at Gunnedah. Via Chandos St, at the cnr Kelvin Rd & Maitland St
HEMA 38 H6   30 58 20 S   150 15 10 E

306 150 Meridian Rest Area
Rest Area 27 km W of Gunnedah or 10 km E of Mullaley
HEMA 38 H5   31 03 46 S   149 59 55 E

307 Mullaley Post Office Hotel ☎ (02) 6743 7820
Camp Area at Mullaley. Oxley Hwy. W end of town
HEMA 38 J5   31 06 01 S   149 54 15 E

308 Oxleys Crossing Rest Area
Rest Area 37 km W of Mullaley or 31 km E of Coonabarabran
HEMA 38 J4   31 07 56 S   149 32 38 E

NEW SOUTH WALES

Walcha to Raymond Terrace
Thunderbolts Way, Bucketts Way

309 Bretti Nature Reserve ☎ (02) 6558 1408
Camp Area 44 km S of Nowendoc or 34 km N of Gloucester. On Thunderbolts Way beside Manning River. Maximum stay 1 month
HEMA 37 B12 31 47 29 S 151 54 56 E

310 Gloryvale Reserve ☎ (02) 6558 1408
Camp Area 55 km S of Nowendoc or 23 km N of Gloucester. On Thunderbolts Way, beside Manning River. Maximum stay 1 month
HEMA 37 B11 31 51 25 S 151 52 42 E

311 Woko Campground
Woko National Park ☎ (02) 6538 5300
Camp Area 33 km NW of Gloucester. Turn W off Thunderbolts Way 59 km S of Nowendoc or 19 km N of Gloucester onto Curricarbark Rd & Flood Detour Rd for 14 km. 10 km dirt road. Beside river
HEMA 37 B11 31 48 05 S 151 47 42 E

312 Barrington Reserve ☎ (02) 6558 4249
Camp Area 1.5 km W of Barrington. W side of bridge, beside Barrington River. Steep dip at entrance. Pay fee at Barrington Store. Maximum stay 14 nights
HEMA 37 B11 31 58 17 S 151 53 59 E

313 Poley's Place ☎ (02) 6558 4220
Camp Area 2 km W of Barrington. 814 Thunderbolts Way
HEMA 37 B11 31 58 05 S 151 53 53 E

314 Gloucester River Campground
Barrington Tops National Park ☎ (02) 6538 5300
Camp Area 38 km W of Gloucester. Turn W off Bucketts Way 9 km S of Gloucester onto Gloucester Tops Rd. 15 km dirt road
HEMA 37 C11 32 03 33 S 151 40 44 E

315 Telegherry Camping Area
Chichester State Forest ☎ 1300 655 687
Camp Area 26 km N of Dungog. From Dungog take Chichester Dam Rd, turn N into Wangat Rd, E into Middle Ridge Rd. Dirt road
HEMA 37 C11 32 13 21 S 151 44 40 E

316 Coachwood Camping Area
Chichester State Forest ☎ 1300 655 687
Camp Area 29 km N of Dungog, take Chichester Dam Rd N into Wangat Rd turn E into Middle Ridge Rd, then into Frying Pan Rd. Dirt road
HEMA 37 C11 32 12 58 S 151 45 39 E

317 Frying Pan Creek Camping Area
Chichester State Forest ☎ 1300 655 687
Camp Area 29.5 km N of Dungog, take Chichester Dam Rd N into Wangat Rd turn E into Middle Ridge Rd E into Frying Pan Rd. Narrow track only suitable for small vehicles. Recommend 4WD to access
HEMA 37 C11 32 13 09 S 151 45 42 E

318 Ferndale Camping Area ☎ (02) 4995 9239
Camp Area 25 km N of Dungog on Chichester Dam Rd. Signposted
HEMA 37 C11 32 14 45 S 151 41 21 E

319 Dobbie Rim Camping Area
Chichester State Forest ☎ 1300 655 687
Camp Area 40 km N of Gresford. Via Allyn River Rd & Allyn River Forest Rd. Signposted. Maximum stay 28 days
HEMA 37 C10 32 09 21 S 151 29 15 E

320 Pademelon Camping Area
Chichester State Forest ☎ 1300 655 687
Camp Area 40 km N of Gresford. Via Allyn River Rd & Allyn River Forest Rd. Signposted. Maximum stay 28 days
HEMA 37 C10 32 09 13 S 151 29 02 E

321 Old Camp Camping Area
Chichester State Forest ☎ 1300 655 687
Camp Area 40 km N of Gresford. Via Allyn River Rd & Allyn River Forest Rd. Signposted. Maximum stay 28 days
HEMA 37 C10 32 09 18 S 151 29 18 E

322 Dungog Showground ☎ (02) 4992 1810
Camp Area at Dungog Showground. Main entrance from Chapman St. Caretaker will collect fees
HEMA 37 D11 32 24 19 S 151 45 03 E

323 Dungog Memorial Bowls, Sport & Recreation Club ☎ (02) 4992 1635
Camp Area at Dungog. 56 Brown St. 5 powered sites, check in at reception
HEMA 37 D11 32 24 08 S 151 45 10 E

Notes...

NEW SOUTH WALES

324 Stroud Showground
☎ (02) 4994 5204
Camp Area at Stroud. 47 km S of Gloucester or 47 km N of Raymond Tce
HEMA 37 D12   32 23 59 S   151 57 51 E

325 Riverwood Downs
☎ 1800 809 772
Camp Area 29 km NW of Stroud via Bucketts Way & Monkerai Rd
HEMA 37 C11   32 16 59 S   151 50 59 E

326 Wharf Reserve
☎ (02) 4996 4231
Camp Spot at Clarence Town. Rifle St
HEMA 37 D11   32 35 27 S   151 46 40 E

327 Williams River Holiday Park
☎ (02) 4996 4231
Caravan Park at Clarence Town. Durham St
HEMA 37 D11   32 34 56 S   151 46 55 E

Kew to Scone

328 Swans Crossing
☎ 1300 655 687
Kerewong State Forest
Camp Area 16 km NW of Kendall. Turn N 4 km W of Kendall off Kendall-Lorne Rd onto Upsalls Creek Rd for 12 km. 10 km dirt road
HEMA 37 A13   31 36 29 S   152 34 55 E

329 Comboyne Showgrounds
☎ (02) 6550 4305
Camp Area at Comboyne. Showgrounds Rd off Main St. Call into general store or CTC centre for details & access information. Sealed road from Wauchope
HEMA 37 A13   31 36 28 S   152 27 58 E

330 Little Plains Sportsground
Camp Area at Elands. 39 km N of Wingham or 24 km W of Comboyne. Ask at shop for directions
HEMA 37 A12   31 37 56 S   152 17 44 E

331 Rocks Crossing Reserve
☎ (02) 6552 1900
Camp Area 43 km NW of Wingham. Access along Nowendoc Rd, via Killawarra & Mount George
HEMA 37 B12   31 46 07 S   152 04 30 E

332 Knorrit Flat Riverside Retreat & Camping Ground
☎ (02) 6550 7541
Camp Area 35 km NW of Wingham, 3109 Nowendoc Rd
HEMA 37 B12   31 47 49 S   152 03 36 E

333 Cundle Flat Farm
☎ (02) 6550 7565
Camp Area 22 km NW of Bundook via Gloucester or 60 km W of Taree via Wingham. Dirt road. Bookings required
HEMA 37 B12   31 48 45 S   151 59 02 E

334 Copeland Reserve
☎ (02) 6558 1408
Camp Area 12 km W of Gloucester on Scone Rd. Maximum stay 1 month
HEMA 37 B11   31 58 21 S   151 51 32 E

335 Camp Cobark
☎ (02) 6558 5524
Camp Area 34 km W of Gloucester. 2677 Scone Rd. Report to office on arrival
HEMA 37 B11   31 55 45 S   151 41 54 E

336 Manning River Campground
☎ 1300 655 687
Barrington Tops State Forest
Camp Area in State Forest. Via Barrington Tops Forest Rd & Pheasant Creek Rd
HEMA 37 B10   31 52 47 S   151 29 27 E

337 Polblue Campground
☎ (02) 6540 2300
Barrington Tops National Park
Camp Area 64 km W of Gloucester, via Barrington, Copeland & Barrington Tops Rd. Dirt road
HEMA 37 B10   31 57 19 S   151 25 28 E

338 Belmadar Park Camping Area
☎ (02) 6546 3165
Camp Area 51 km E of Scone. At Moonan Flat, Ellerston St. Amenity key available from hotel
HEMA 37 B10   31 55 26 S   151 14 13 E

339 Stewarts Brook Recreation Reserve
☎ (02) 6546 1237
Camp Area at Stewarts Brook. From Gundy take Hunter Rd, then turn SE onto Stewarts Brook Rd, follow to reserve, signposted. Maximum 6 weeks, fees payable to caretaker. 10 km dirt road
HEMA 37 B10   32 00 12 S   151 18 29 E

340 Gundy Showgrounds
☎ (02) 6545 8045
Camp Area at Gundy. 23 km E of Scone or 27 km W of Moonan Flat. Keys from general store. Site not available on show-event days
HEMA 37 B9   32 00 46 S   150 59 43 E

Notes...

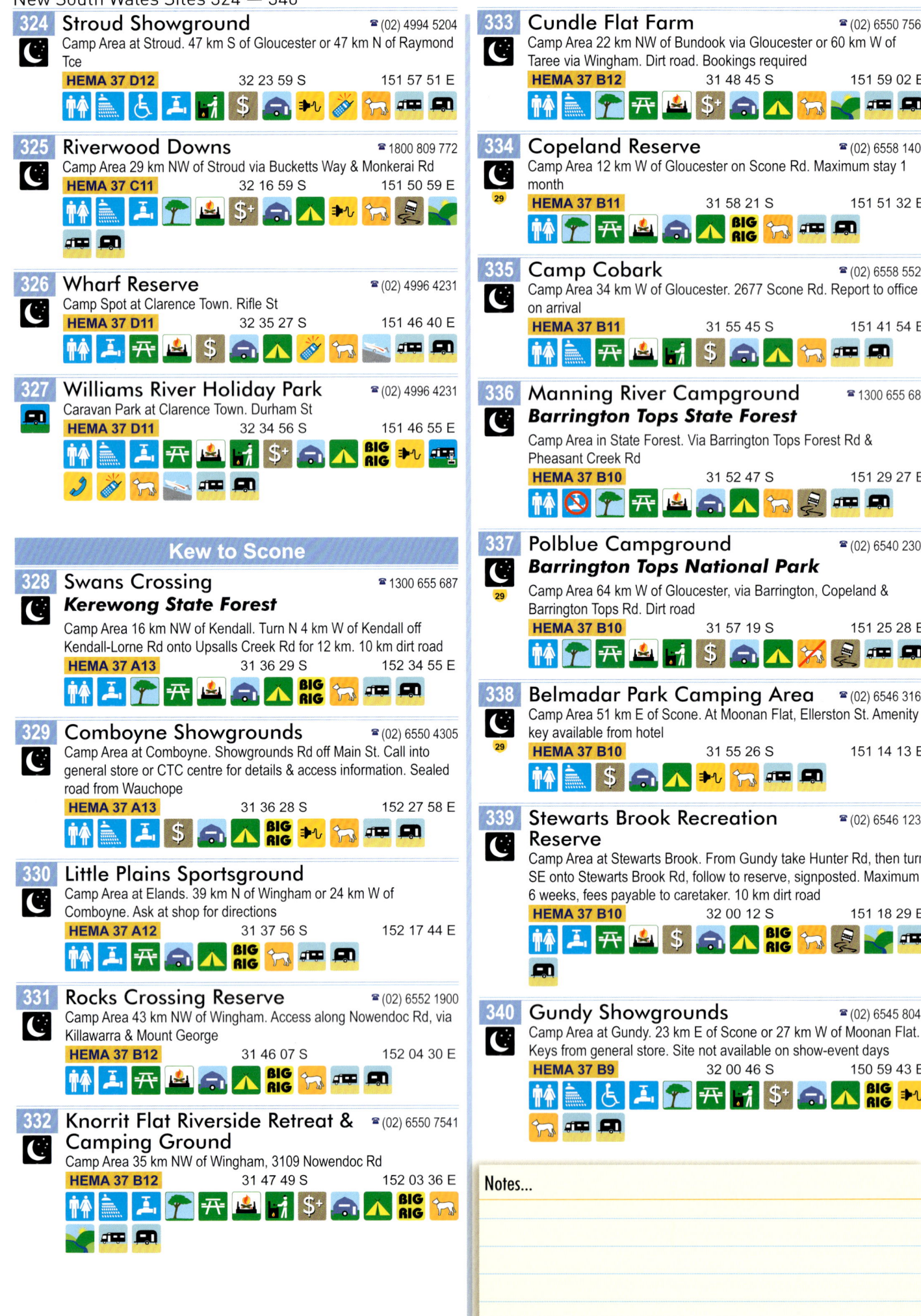

Warialda-Tamworth
Fossickers Way

341 Ti Tree Creek Rest Area
Rest Area 11 km S of Warialda or 31 km N of Bingara
HEMA 38 D6   29 36 50 S   150 32 36 E

342 Myall Creek Rest Area
Rest Area 18 km SW of Delungra or 24 km NE of Bingara
HEMA 38 E7   29 46 30 S   150 43 01 E

343 Bingara Riverside Camping
Camp Spot at Bingara, 3 areas of riverside camping. Information & map for camp areas on board at entrance to S side camp area, Copeton Dam Rd. Maximum stay 7 nights. Self Contained Vehicles only. GPS at entry gate
HEMA 38 E6   29 51 45 S   150 34 45 E

344 Gwydir River Camps   ☎ (02) 6724 0066
Camp Spot 8 km E of Bingara, via Old Keera Rd. Various sites along riverbank
HEMA 38 E7   29 53 26 S   150 37 17 E

345 Allawah 4WD & Camping   ☎ (02) 6724 1240
Camp Area 10 km E of Bingara on the Bundarra - Bingara Rd. Bush camping
HEMA 38 E7   29 54 40 S   150 38 46 E

346 Upper Horton Caravan & Camping Area
Camp Area at Upper Horton. Cobbadah St, next to tennis courts
HEMA 38 F6   30 08 24 S   150 26 36 E

347 Rocky Creek Glacial Area
Camp Spot 36 km SW of Bingara or 67 km NE of Narrabri via Killarney Gap Rd. Some dirt road
HEMA 38 F6   30 02 04 S   150 19 01 E

348 The Ponds Camp
Rest Area 29 km S of Bingara or 32 km N of Barraba
HEMA 38 F6   30 06 39 S   150 35 51 E

349 Barraba Caravan Park   ☎ (02) 6782 1818
Caravan Park at Barraba. Bridge St. N end of town
HEMA 38 G6   30 22 23 S   150 36 36 E

350 Little Creek Reserve   ☎ (02) 6782 1255
Picnic Area 21 km W of Barraba, via Trevallyn Rd. Beside creek
HEMA 38 F6   30 18 38 S   150 26 04 E

351 Barraba Lions Park
Rest Area 5 km S of Barraba or 40 km N of Manilla. Donation box
HEMA 38 G6   30 25 15 S   150 36 59 E

352 Glen Riddle Recreation Reserve   ☎ (02) 6782 1255
Camp Area 17 km S of Barraba. Turn E 9 km S of Barraba or 36 km N of Manilla onto Pera Linton Rd for 8 km
HEMA 38 G7   30 27 01 S   150 41 34 E

✓353 Split Rock Dam   ☎ (02) 6782 1105
Camp Area 39 km S of Barraba. Turn E 30 km S of Barraba or 15 km N of Manilla for 7 km, then N onto Recreation Area Rd. Payment at council office in either Barraba or Manilla. Alt phone (02) 6761 0200
HEMA 38 G7   30 33 50 S   150 40 35 E

354 Warrabah Campground   ☎ (02) 6739 0700
Warrabah National Park
Camp Area 35 km NE of Manilla, via Namoi Rd. 22 km dirt road. Not suitable for caravans, small vehicles only
HEMA 38 G7   30 34 07 S   150 54 55 E

355 Lions Park
Rest Area 7.5 km S of Manilla or 37.5 km N of Tamworth on the Fossickers Way
HEMA 38 H7   30 48 14 S   150 45 12 E

356 Attunga Creek
Rest Area 24 km S of Manilla or 21 km N of Tamworth
HEMA 38 H7   30 55 45 S   150 50 48 E

Quirindi to Bourke
Kamilaroi Highway

357 Braefield Rest Area
Rest Area 9 km N of Willow Tree or 7 km S of Quirindi. Next to railway line
HEMA 38 K7   31 33 54 S   150 41 53 E

358 Quirindi Caravan Park   ☎ (02) 6746 2407
Caravan Park at Quirindi. 15 Rose St
HEMA 38 K6   31 30 37 S   150 41 01 E

359 Caroona Hall   ☎ (02) 6747 4749
Parking Area at Caroona. Next to hall
HEMA 38 J6   31 24 23 S   150 25 29 E

NEW SOUTH WALES

360 Spring Ridge Showground
Camp Area at Spring Ridge. Entry from Tungenbone Rd. Donation box on site

| HEMA 38 J6 | 31 23 45 S | 150 14 42 E |

361 Premer Lions Park
Camp Area midway between Quirindi & Coonabarabran. Donation to Lions Club payable at honesty box

| HEMA 38 K5 | 31 27 09 S | 149 54 03 E |

362 David Taylor Oval
Parking Area at Werris Creek, entry off Parks St. Self Contained Vehicles only

| HEMA 38 J6 | 31 20 28 S | 150 38 56 E |

363 Square Bush Rest Area
Rest Area 34 km NW of Quirindi or 7 km S of Breeza

| HEMA 38 J6 | 31 17 55 S | 150 29 43 E |

364 Gunnedah South Rest Area
Rest Area 11 km N of Curlewis or 7 km S of Gunnedah

| HEMA 38 H6 | 31 01 32 S | 150 16 28 E |

365 Gunnedah North Rest Area
Rest Area 8 km N of Gunnedah or 31 km S of Boggabri

| HEMA 38 H5 | 30 55 22 S | 150 11 15 E |

366 Boggabri South Rest Area
Rest Area 33 km N of Gunnedah or 6 km S of Boggabri

| HEMA 38 H5 | 30 44 41 S | 150 04 35 E |

367 Gins Leap
Rest Area 6 km N of Boggabri or 51 km SE of Narrabri

| HEMA 38 G5 | 30 39 21 S | 150 02 29 E |

368 Pilliga Pub
☎ (02) 6796 4320
Camp Area at the Pilliga Pub. 55 km SW of Wee Waa or 38 km S of Burren Junction

| HEMA 38 F2 | 30 21 07 S | 148 53 04 E |

369 Pilliga Bore Baths
☎ (02) 6799 6760
Camp Spot 1.6 km E of Pilliga on the Wee Waa Pilliga Rd at the Hot Mineral Bore. Pay fee at Pilliga Cafe or Narrabri Info centre. Maximum stay 21 days

| HEMA 38 F2 | 30 21 19 S | 148 54 25 E |

370 Burren Junction Bore Baths
☎ (02) 6828 1399
Camp Area 3 km E of Burren Junction. Self Contained Vehicles only. Baths closed during summer months, campground open all year

| HEMA 38 F3 | 30 06 52 S | 148 59 44 E |

371 Junction City Hotel
☎ (02) 6796 1440
Parking Area at Burren Junction

| HEMA 38 F3 | 30 06 19 S | 148 58 12 E |

372 Alex Trevallion Park
Camp Spot 2 km S of Walgett. E side of Hwy

| HEMA 38 E1 | 30 02 04 S | 148 06 55 E |

373 Walgett Showground
Camp Area at Walgett Showground. Wee Waa St

| HEMA 38 E1 | 30 01 14 S | 148 07 57 E |

374 Pagan Creek Bridge
Camp Spot 6 km N of Walgett. 1.5 km N of the Castlereagh Hwy & Kamilaroi Hwy Jcn

| HEMA 38 E1 | 29 59 15 S | 148 09 16 E |

375 Cumborah Park Reserve
☎ 0418 317 002
Camp Area at Cumborah. Entry to the park is at the S end of the main road. Donation box

| HEMA 41 C13 | 29 44 45 S | 147 46 17 E |

376 Boorooma Creek
Parking Area 75.5 km E of Brewarrina or 56.5 km W of Walgett. N side of the road, entry W of The Big Warrambool Bridge

| HEMA 41 D12 | 30 04 39 S | 147 33 36 E |

377 Culgoa River Campground
☎ (02) 6871 2744
Culgoa National Park

Camp Area 25 km N of Weilmoringle or 60 km W of Goodooga. Turn N 6 km W of Weilmoringle for 17 km, (or turn W 24 km NW of Goodooga for 34 km), then S for 9 km. Rough dirt road

| HEMA 41 A12 | 29 10 11 S | 146 59 51 E |

378 Four Mile Campground
☎ (02) 6830 5152
Camp Area 6 km E of Brewarrina. Via Coolabah - Brewarrina Rd & Billybingbone Brae for 5 km. Follow blue signs. Cold showers

| HEMA 41 C11 | 29 59 06 S | 146 55 02 E |

Notes...

379 Brewarrina Caravan & Camping Park
☎ 0467 064 316
Caravan Park at Brewarrina. Church St
HEMA 41 C11   29 58 00 S   146 51 40 E

380 Beds on the Barwon Campground
☎ 1300 76 50 86
Camp Area at Brewarrina. Burban St. Turn L on Burban St just before the racecourse, follow road for 600m to entry
HEMA 41 C11   29 58 28 S   146 52 31 E

381 Food & Huts by Mt Oxley
Rossmore Station
☎ 0428 723 275
Camp Spot 28 km E of Bourke or 70 km W of Brewarrina. Check in at homestead for directions to camp area. Self Contained Vehicles only. Bush camping
HEMA 41 D10   30 02 51 S   146 12 55 E

382 May's Bend
Camp Spot 13 km NE of Bourke on Mitchell Hwy. Turn E 10 km from Bourke onto dirt road, travel 12.6 km, take R fork at Y Jcn, for further 15 kms. Check with Bourke Info Centre for road conditions (02 6872 1321)
HEMA 41 D10   30 02 20 S   146 01 23 E

Bathurst-Mudgee-Gilgandra-Nevertire

383 Capertee
Parking Area at Capertee. Railway St
HEMA 32 J1   33 08 48 S   149 59 05 E

384 Glen Davis Campground
☎ (02) 6353 1859
Camp Area 35 km E of Capertee or 52 km SE of Rylstone. Signposted off Castlereagh Hwy at Capertee, 26 km dirt road. 10 km dirt road from Rylstone
HEMA 32 H3   33 07 31 S   150 16 55 E

385 Capertee Campground
Capertee National Park
☎ (02) 6370 9000
Camp Area 12 km SW of Bogee. Just N of Bogee turn W into Port Macquarie Rd for 11 km on dirt road. At the locked gate cross river & follow signposts to campground. Must prebook to gain access code
HEMA 32 G1   33 01 08 S   150 01 54 E

386 Coorongooba Campground
Wollemi National Park
☎ (02) 4787 8877
Camp Area in Western Area of National Park. Turn E off Hwy at Capertee. Turn onto Goora St, R onto Nioka St, follow signs. 4WD only, river crossing
HEMA 32 H3   33 07 21 S   150 19 20 E

387 McDonalds Hole Road Rest Area
Rest Area 15 km S of Ilford or 11 km N of Capertee
HEMA 36 E7   33 03 57 S   149 56 08 E

388 Ilford Rest Area
Rest Area at Ilford. Ilford Hall Rd, 400m E of Hwy beside hall
HEMA 36 E7   32 57 47 S   149 51 41 E

389 Dunns Swamp - Ganguddy Campground
Wollemi National Park
☎ (02) 6370 9000
Camp Area 27 km E of Rylstone, via Narrango Rd. Beside lake. 7 km dirt road
HEMA 32 F2   32 50 09 S   150 12 26 E

390 Wallaby Rocks Crossing
Camp Spot 4.6 km W of Sofala on Hill End Rd. E side of Turon River Bridge, camp spots along river. Small vehicles only
HEMA 36 E6   33 04 29 S   149 38 59 E

391 Coles Bridge Camping Area
Camp Area 13 km W of Sofala on Turondale Rd, via Hill End Rd. Turn R over bridge then 200m rough access track
HEMA 36 E6   33 03 33 S   149 37 15 E

392 Ration Point
Camp Spot 3 km E of Sofala, via Upper Turon Rd. Beside river. Small vehicles only
HEMA 36 E6   33 05 30 S   149 42 56 E

✔ 393 Greens Point
Camp Area 6 km E of Sofala via Upper Turon Rd. Beside river
HEMA 36 E6   33 05 44 S   149 43 55 E

394 Wattle Flat Racecourse
Camp Area 3 km E of Wattle Flat on Limekilns Rd
HEMA 36 F6   33 10 33 S   149 42 35 E

395 Wattle Flat Heritage Land (North)
Camp Area 800m W of Wattle Flat. Turn W onto Thompson St. Signposted at entrance, follow signs for campground and BBQ. GPS at gate. Maximum stay 14 days
HEMA 36 F6   33 08 19 S   149 41 08 E

396 Wattle Flat Heritage Land (South)
Camp Spot at Wattle Flat. 1 km SW of Wattle Flat on Peel Rd
HEMA 36 F6   33 08 55 S   149 41 23 E

NEW SOUTH WALES

397 The Village Campground ☎ (02) 6337 8206
Hill End Historic Site
Camp Area at Hill End, 38 km W of Sofala, via Clarke St & Warrys Rd. Coin operated hot showers
HEMA 36 E6   33 02 01 S   149 24 51 E

✓398 Glendora Campground ☎ (02) 6337 8206
Hill End Historic Site
Camp Area at Hill End, 38 km W of Sofala. 1 km NE of town, via Beyers Ave & Lees Ln. Coin operated showers
HEMA 36 E6   33 01 39 S   149 24 34 E

399 Bushlands Tourist Park ☎ (02) 6373 8252
Caravan Park at Windeyer. 1879 Windeyer Rd. Turn W off Hwy 86, 3 km N of Mudgee onto Windeyer Rd. 40 km to Windeyer
HEMA 36 D6   32 47 44 S   149 33 25 E

400 Old Bara ☎ 02 6373 6555
Camp Area 28 km E of Mudgee on Bara Rd via Lue Rd & Hayes Gap Rd
HEMA 36 D6   32 34 39 S   149 48 22 E

401 Mudgee Showground ☎ (02) 6372 3828
Camp Area at Mudgee Showgrounds. Entry from Douro St. See caretaker
HEMA 36 D6   32 36 10 S   149 34 53 E

402 Cudgegong River Park ☎ (02) 6373 0378
Camp Area 36 km W of Mudgee, Burrendong Dam Rd, off Yarrabin Rd
HEMA 36 D5   32 37 37 S   149 15 28 E

✓403 Gulgong Showground ☎ (02) 6374 1255
Camp Area at Gulgong Showgrounds. 1 km S of Gulgong off Mudgee Rd. Entrance on cnr of Grevillia Rd & Guntawang Rd
HEMA 36 C6   32 22 15 S   149 31 41 E

404 Tallawang Rest Area
Rest Area 28 km N of Gulgong or 22 km S of Dunedoo
HEMA 36 C6   32 08 51 S   149 26 38 E
86

405 Goulburn River Reserve The Drip ☎ (02) 6370 9000
Camp Spot 10 km N of Ulan or 14 km S of Turill. Small vehicles only, limited space
HEMA 36 C7   32 12 56 S   149 47 16 E

406 Spring Gully Campground ☎ (02) 6370 9000
Goulburn River National Park
Camp Area 15 km NE of Wollar, via Mogo Rd, Spring Gully Rd. Dry weather only. Not suitable for caravans. Small vehicles only, off road campertrailers only
HEMA 36 C7   32 14 35 S   150 02 43 E

407 Big River Campground ☎ (02) 6370 9000
Goulburn River National Park
Camp Area 22 km NE of Wollar. Via Mogo Rd, Spring Gully Rd & Big River Rd. Not suitable for caravans. Small vehicles only, off road campertrailers only
HEMA 36 C7   32 14 15 S   150 03 20 E

408 Bylong Community Sportsground
Camp Area at Bylong. Bylong Valley Way, opposite shop. Coin operated shower
HEMA 36 C7   32 24 58 S   150 06 52 E

409 Cassilis Park Rest Area
Rest Area 9 km NE of Turill or 7 km SW of Cassilis
HEMA 36 B7   32 03 16 S   149 56 00 E

✓410 Cassilis War Memorial Park ☎ (02) 6376 1002
Camp Area at Cassilis. Uarbry Rd, adjacent to Bowling Club. Pay at Bowling Club. Limited power
HEMA 36 B7   32 00 41 S   149 58 46 E

411 Site Closed

412 The Barracks Campground ☎ (02) 6370 9000
Coolah Tops National Park
Camp Area 35 km NE of Coolah, via The Pinnacle Rd. 15 km dirt road
HEMA 36 A7   31 43 51 S   150 00 54 E

413 The Pines Campground ☎ (02) 6370 9000
Coolah Tops National Park
Camp Area 37 km NE of Coolah, via Hildegarde Rd. Approx 16 km rough unsealed road
HEMA 36 B7   31 44 35 S   150 01 46 E

414 The Black Stump Rest Area
Rest Area 11 km N of Coolah or 42 km SE of Binnaway
HEMA 36 A7   31 44 44 S   149 42 22 E

415 Pumphouse Camping Ground
Camp Area at Binnaway. Cnr Warrumbungle Way & Castlereagh Ave. Fee by the hour for showers & power. Limited powered sites. See notice board for access
HEMA 36 A6   31 32 48 S   149 22 44 E

416 Dunedoo Caravan Park   ☎ (02) 6375 1455
Caravan Park at Dunedoo. Bolaro St. 600m W of PO
HEMA 36 B6   32 00 56 S   149 23 22 E

417 Mendooran Rest Area
Rest Area at Mendooran, beside river. Cold showers
HEMA 36 B5   31 49 28 S   149 06 53 E

418 Breelong Rest Area
Rest Area at Breelong. 17 km E of Gilgandra or 39 km W of Mendooran
HEMA 36 B4   31 48 40 S   148 47 43 E

419 Marthaguy West Rest Area
Rest Area 23 km W of Gilgandra or 14 km E of Collie. Share with trucks
HEMA 36 A4   31 39 28 S   148 26 51 E

420 Warren North Rest Area
Rest Area 44 km W of Collie or 6 km NE of Warren
HEMA 36 A2   31 40 02 S   147 51 30 E

421 Macquarie Caravan Park   ☎ (02) 6847 4706
Caravan Park at Warren. 2 Hospital Rd
HEMA 36 A2   31 41 43 S   147 50 23 E

422 Bob Christensen Reserve   ☎ (02) 6847 6600
Parking Area at Warren. Via Burton St, Dubbo St onto Industrial Access Rd. Self Contained Vehicles only
HEMA 36 A2   31 41 08 S   147 50 01 E

423 Warren Weir
Camp Spot 5 km S of Warren via Wambianna Rd. Nth side of weir. GPS at entrance, follow track to river, bush camping
HEMA 36 A2   31 43 25 S   147 52 00 E

424 Sandy Creek
Rest Area 8 km SW of Warren or 12 km N of Nevertire
HEMA 36 A2   31 44 56 S   147 47 00 E

Greater Sydney Area

425 Bonnie Vale Campground   ☎ (02) 9542 0648
Royal National Park
Camp Area 25 km NE of Waterfall. Near Bundeena. Pre-booking essential. 1300 072 757 for bookings
HEMA 31 K9   34 04 58 S   151 08 08 E

426 Bents Basin Campground   ☎ (02) 4632 4500
Bents Basin State Conservation Area
Camp Area 25 km S of Penrith, via Northern, Greendale Rd & Wolstenholme Rd. Bookings essential
HEMA 34 F7   33 55 58 S   150 38 14 E

427 Wanderest Travellers Park   ☎ (02) 4578 1144
Camp Area at Richmond. 71 Francis St. Fee for power. Self Contained Vehicles only
HEMA 34 B7   33 35 48 S   150 45 18 E

428 Cattai Campground   ☎ (02) 4572 3100
Cattai National Park
Camp Area at Cattai. 800m N of Cattai on the Wiseman Ferry Rd turn W into road leading to the camping ground. Signposted. No caravans, small vehicles only
HEMA 35 B8   33 33 33 S   150 53 24 E

429 NSW Ski Gardens   ☎ (02) 4566 4212
Caravan Park Sydney side of Hawkesbury River. 1.2 km from Wisemans Ferry Township
HEMA 33 J9   33 23 45 S   150 58 57 E

Notes...

NEW SOUTH WALES

430 Mill Creek
☎ (02) 4320 4200
Dharug National Park
Camp Area in Dharug National Park. 6 km E of Wisemans Ferry Crossing, N side of the Hawkesbury River
HEMA 33 J10   33 24 03 S   151 02 42 E

431 Sackville Ski Gardens
☎ (02) 4579 1036
Camp Area at Sackville. 742 Tizzana Rd
HEMA 33 K9   33 29 47 S   150 52 59 E

432 Bielany Camp Colo River
☎ (02) 4575 5311
Camp Area at Colo. 213 Upper Colo Rd
HEMA 33 K8   33 25 26 S   150 48 34 E

433 Upper Colo Reserve
☎ (02) 4560 4444
Camp Area at Upper Colo. Turn off Upper Colo Rd into Colo Heights Rd, L into Hulbert Rd. Caravans not permitted. Campervans subject to approval. Bookings are essential, permit required
HEMA 34 A6   33 25 13 S   150 43 50 E

434 Wheeny Creek Campground
☎ (02) 4588 2400
Wollemi National Park
Camp Area 11 km S of Upper Colo. Via Coleroy Rd. Last 4 kms unsealed. Limited space, suitable for small vehicles only
HEMA 34 A6   33 27 21 S   150 43 02 E

435 Bilpin Reserve
Rest Area 30 km NW of Richmond or 35 km E of Bell. Next to recreation area. Limited space
HEMA 34 B5   33 29 49 S   150 31 01 E

436 Cathedral Reserve
Camp Area at Mt Wilson. Mount Irvine Rd
HEMA 34 B4   33 30 07 S   150 23 26 E

437 Newnes Campground
☎ (02) 4787 8877
Wollemi National Park
Camp Area 35 km NE of Lithgow. Turn NE at Lidsdale, 11 km N of Lithgow, onto Wolgan Rd. 9 km dirt road. Small vehicles only
HEMA 32 J3   33 10 21 S   150 14 19 E

438 Millionth Acre Picnic Area
☎ (02) 6331 2044
Hampton State Forest
Picnic Area 4 km S of Hampton. Intersection of Jenolan Caves Rd & Oberon Rd
HEMA 34 E2   33 40 37 S   150 03 00 E

439 Boyd River Campground
☎ (02) 4787 8877
Kanangra-Boyd National Park
Camp Area 30 km S of Jenolan Caves, via Kanangra Walls Rd. 27 km dirt road
HEMA 34 H3   33 58 16 S   150 03 21 E

440 Black Springs Campground
☎ (02) 6331 2044
Vulcan State Forest
Camp Area at Black Springs. 24 km SW of Oberon or 26 NE of Burraga. Opposite General Store
HEMA 36 G6   33 50 51 S   149 44 38 E

441 Bummaroo Ford
☎ (02) 6336 1972
Abercrombie River National Park
Camp Area 25 km N of Taralga. On Abercrombie Rd at Abercrombie River crossing
HEMA 36 H6   34 11 40 S   149 44 10 E

442 Wombeyan Caves Campground
☎ (02) 4843 5976
Wombeyan Karst Conservation Reserve
Camp Area 33 km NE of Taralga. Near Visitors Centre. 13 km dirt road. Bookings essential for caravans & camper trailers
HEMA 36 J7   34 18 36 S   149 57 58 E

443 Wollondilly River Station
☎ (02) 4888 9207
Camp Area Wollondilly River Station. 50 km W Bowral on Wombeyan Caves Rd. 15 km W of Wombeyan Caves. Dirt road. Small vehicles only
HEMA 36 J7   34 18 28 S   150 04 00 E

444 Taralga Showgrounds
Camp Area at Taralga. Bannaby Rd. Pay at Taralga General Store or Taralga Gifts & Goodies. AH 0425 270 763
HEMA 36 J7   34 24 16 S   149 49 26 E

445 Burraga Dam
☎ (02) 6337 0255
Camp Area 3 km NE of Burraga. Turn N off Arkstone Rd 1.7 km E of Burraga, opposite Jeremy Station. 1.3 km dirt road
HEMA 36 H6   33 56 09 S   149 33 08 E

Notes...

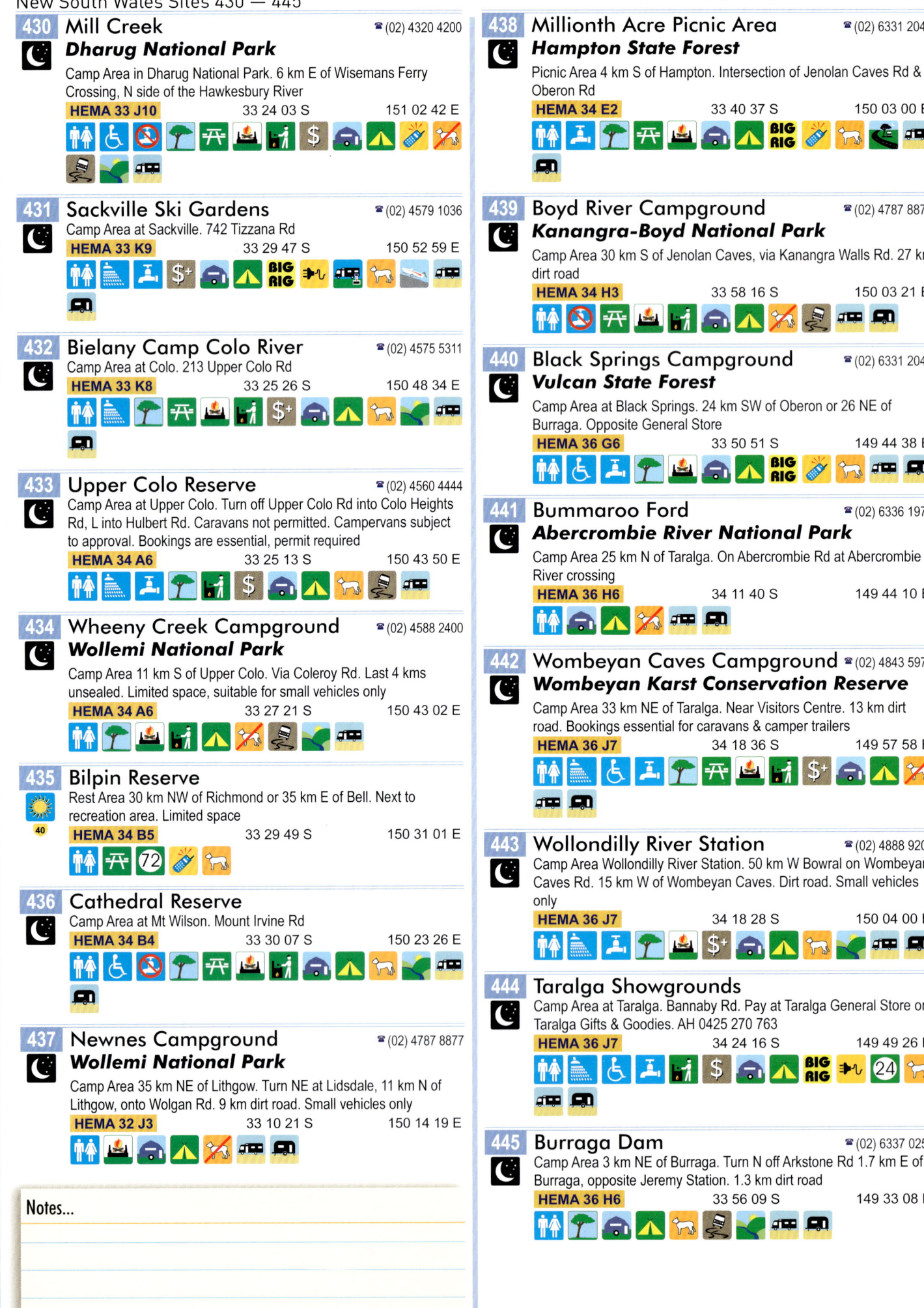

446 Campbells River ☎ 1300 655 687
Camp Area 12 km N of Mount David via Swallows Nest Rd
HEMA 36 G6   33 47 07 S   149 36 17 E

447 Trunkey Creek Showground ☎ (02) 6368 8604
Camp Spot at Trunkey Creek. Church St. Information at hotel
HEMA 36 G6   33 49 03 S   149 19 23 E

448 Abercrombie Caves Campground ☎ (02) 6368 8603
Abercrombie Karst Conservation Reserve
Camp Area 14 km S of Trunkey Creek. 2 km narrow, winding road
HEMA 36 H6   33 54 50 S   149 21 30 E

449 Abercrombie River Camp
Camp Spot 19 km S of Trunkey Creek. S of bridge turn W. Some spots next to river
HEMA 36 H6   33 57 23 S   149 19 13 E

450 Tuena Camping & Picnic Ground ☎ (02) 4834 5235
Camp Area at Tuena. Bathurst Rd. Fee for power please pay at the General Store
HEMA 36 H6   34 00 59 S   149 19 40 E

451 Crookwell Caravan Park ☎ 0408 250 652
Caravan Park at Crookwell. Laggan Rd. Register at Visitor Information Centre or Council office
HEMA 36 J6   34 27 17 S   149 28 03 E

452 Pejar Dam Rest Area
Rest Area at Pejar Dam. S of dam wall. 22 km S of Crookwell or 24 km NW of Goulburn
HEMA 36 K6   34 35 14 S   149 34 47 E

Sydney to Echuca
Great Western, Mid Western, Sturt Highways

453 Bulls Camp Reserve
Rest Area 17 km W of Blaxland or 2 km E of Woodford
HEMA 34 D5   33 43 32 S   150 29 26 E

454 Sutton Park Rest Area
Rest Area at Blackheath. 1.5 km S of PO or 10 km N of Katoomba. Alternative for pets at Whitley Park, 500m towards town
HEMA 34 D4   33 38 48 S   150 17 03 E

455 Blackheath Glen Reserve
Camp Spot 6.5 km S of Blackheath via Megalong Valley Rd
HEMA 34 D4   33 40 30 S   150 16 08 E

456 Old Ford Reserve
Camp Area 15.3 km S of Blackheath. Via Shipley Rd & Megalong Valley Rd
HEMA 34 E3   33 43 54 S   150 14 06 E

457 Dunphy's Camping Area
Camp Area 23 km S of Blackheath via Megalong Rd & Bellbird Ridge Firetrail
HEMA 34 E4   33 47 24 S   150 13 48 E

458 Lake Lyell Campground ☎ (02) 6355 6347
Camp Area 13 km SW of Lithgow. Magpie Hollow Rd
HEMA 34 C2   33 31 30 S   150 04 38 E

459 Flat Rock
Camp Spot 13 km W of Tarana or 7 km E of O'Connell. At Rainville Creek, Mutton Falls Rd, beside Fish River
HEMA 36 G7   33 32 54 S   149 47 31 E

460 Chifley Dam Primitive Camping Area ☎ (02) 6632 1444
Camp Area at Chifley Dam. 20 km S of Bathurst, travel 6 km S of Bathurst along Vale Rd, turn E into Lagoon Rd then Chifley Dam Rd 14 km. Only 4 sites, no pre-booking. Access gates locked after dark
HEMA 36 G6   33 33 43 S   149 38 00 E

461 Lake Wallace
Camp Area at Wallerawang. Barton Ave, beside lake. Turn N off Great Western Hwy 8 km W of Lithgow or 57 km E of Bathurst
HEMA 34 B1   33 24 56 S   150 04 24 E

462 Kremer Park
Camp Area at Portland. Kiln St
HEMA 36 F7   33 21 11 S   149 58 28 E

463 Sunny Corner Recreation Reserve
Camp Spot 7 km N of Meadow Flat. Turn N off Great Western Hwy 26 km W of Lithgow or 33 km E of Bathurst. S end of village, E side of road
HEMA 36 F7   33 23 16 S   149 53 34 E

464 Bathurst Showground ☎ (02) 6331 1349
Camp Area at Bathurst, Kendell Ave. Mobile 0418 637 682
HEMA 36 F6   33 25 05 S   149 35 22 E

NEW SOUTH WALES

465 Lions Club Berry Park
Parking Area at Bathurst, Lions Club Dr, E side of city. Self Contained Vehicles only
HEMA 36 F6   33 25 01 S   149 35 38 E

466 McPhillamy Park
Rest Area 5 km SW of Bathurst. On top of Mt Panorama
HEMA 36 F6   33 27 23 S   149 32 55 E

467 Carcoar Dam   ☎ (02) 6367 3103
Camp Area 12 km SW of Blayney or 16 km NE of Mandurama. Turn S 9 km SW of Blayney or 6.5 km NE of Carcoar onto Carcoar Dam Rd
HEMA 36 G5   33 36 39 S   149 10 47 E

468 Carcoar Rest Area
Rest Area 11 km SW of Blayney or 11 km NE of Mandurama
HEMA 36 G5   33 35 54 S   149 09 53 E

469 Mandurama East Rest Area
Rest Area 3 km E of Mandurama or 19 km SW of Blayney
HEMA 36 G5   33 38 24 S   149 06 06 E

470 Bakers Shaft Reserve
Camp Area 15 km N of Mandurama. Turn W off Mandurama - Burnt Yards Rd after 10 km onto Bakers Rd, then onto Junction Park Rd. 5 km dirt road. Beside Belubula River. 4WD recommended
HEMA 36 G5   33 36 34 S   149 00 43 E

471 Lyndhurst Primitive Campground   ☎ 0427 201 824
Camp Area at Lyndhurst. In recreation ground, entrance off Harrow St. Maximum stay 5 days. Donation box
HEMA 36 G5   33 40 24 S   149 02 20 E

472 Wyangala Waters Holiday Park   ☎ (02) 6345 0877
Camp Area 37 km SE of Cowra, via Darbys Falls. Bookings required for powered sites
HEMA 36 H5   33 57 46 S   148 57 17 E

473 Bigga Recreation Ground
Camp Area at Bigga 81 km SE of Cowra or 56 km NW of Crookwell. Bistro at golf club Friday night, General Store & pub in town centre
HEMA 36 H5   34 04 59 S   149 09 06 E

474 Grabine Lakeside Holiday Park   ☎ (02) 4835 2345
Caravan Park 97 km SE of Cowra or 71 km NW of Crookwell, via Bigga Rd & Grabine Rd. NE side of Lake Wyangala. Some dirt road
HEMA 36 H5   33 57 03 S   149 01 44 E

475 Darbys Falls River Reserve
Rest Area 26 km SE of Cowra or 17 km NW of Wyangala. Beside Lachlan River. 2 km S of township
HEMA 36 H5   33 56 53 S   148 51 45 E

476 Ramage Park
Rest Area 1.5 Km E of Cowra on Mid Western Hwy. Entry from Campbell Rd, across from Europa Park. Self Contained Vehicles only
HEMA 36 G5   33 49 47 S   148 42 36 E

477 Cowra Overnight Rest Area
Rest Area at Cowra, Lachlan Valley Way, 100m S Mid Western Hwy intersection. Self Contained Vehicles only. Dump Point 100m S
HEMA 36 G4   33 50 08 S   148 40 55 E

478 Cowra Showground   ☎ 0428 405 245
Camp Area at Cowra. Entrance off Grenfell Rd. Must register with caretaker
HEMA 36 G4   33 50 00 S   148 40 26 E

479 Farleigh Reserve
Camp Spot 9 km W of Cowra. Farleigh Reserve Rd off Lachlan Valley Way
HEMA 36 G4   33 48 49 S   148 37 15 E

480 Canowindra Caravan Park   ☎ 0428 233 769
Caravan Park at Canowindra. Tilga St. Next to swimming pool. 300m S of PO
HEMA 36 G4   33 34 08 S   148 39 50 E

481 Canowindra Showgrounds   ☎ (02) 6344 1886
Parking Area at Canowindra, entry off Rodd St
HEMA 36 G4   33 33 09 S   148 40 10 E

482 Canowindra Rest Area
Rest Area 2 km W of Canowindra, beside river
HEMA 36 G4   33 33 35 S   148 39 05 E

483 Terarra Creek Camping & Picnic Area   ☎ (02) 6332 7640
Nangar National Park
Camp Area 18 km E of Eugowra or 76 km W of Orange on Escort Way. Turn S 11 km E of Eugowra onto Dripping Rock Rd. Camp sites are 7 km from this point
HEMA 36 F4   33 25 08 S   148 29 54 E

484 Escort Rock Rest Area
Rest Area 5 km NE of Eugowra or 36 km SW of Cudal
HEMA 36 F4   33 24 04 S   148 24 35 E

485 Eugowra Showground   ☎ 0427 639 701
Camp Spot at Eugowra. 1 km E of PO. Noble St
HEMA 36 F3   33 26 01 S   148 23 00 E

486 Byrnes Park
Parking Area at Eugowra. Myall St, adjacent to bridge
HEMA 36 F3   33 25 40 S   148 22 11 E

487 Maisie Thompson Camping Ground
Camp Area at Gooloogong. Power available. Donation requested please
HEMA 36 G4   33 36 47 S   148 26 03 E

488 Gooloogong West
Camp Spot 2 km NW of Gooloogong or 49 km SE of Forbes. Turn N into Grey St 1 km W of Gooloogong. Near old Anglican church site. Beside river
HEMA 36 G4   33 36 31 S   148 25 12 E

489 Bumbaldry Rest Area
Rest Area 23 km W of Cowra or 32 km E of Grenfell
HEMA 36 H4   33 54 06 S   148 28 00 E

490 Murrays Creek Parking Area
Parking Area 45 km W of Cowra or 1.5 km E of Grenfell. Large area, share with trucks
HEMA 36 H3   33 54 29 S   148 15 54 E

491 John Channon Park
Rest Area 1 km W of Grenfell
HEMA 36 H3   33 53 25 S   148 08 43 E

492 Grenfell Old Railway Station   ☎ (02) 6343 1212
Rest Area at Grenfell Old Railway Station. 1 km from PO, W side of town
HEMA 36 H3   33 53 43 S   148 09 21 E

493 Ben Halls Campground   ☎ (02) 6332 7640
Weddin Mountains National Park
Camp Area 20 km W of Grenfell. Turn W off Mid Western Hwy 5.5 km NW Grenfell onto Back Piney Range Rd, follow signs for 23 km then turn L over the grid, follow to campground. Dirt road
HEMA 36 H3   33 54 23 S   147 55 11 E

494 Quandialla Showgrounds   ☎ (02) 6347 1365
Camp Area at Quandialla, bookings essential
HEMA 36 H2   34 00 28 S   147 47 24 E

495 Bland Hotel   ☎ (02) 6347 1253
Camp Spot at Quandialla. 2 Second St, area next to hotel. Check in with publican. Fee for showers, limited power for a fee
HEMA 36 H2   34 00 37 S   147 47 35 E

496 Bribbaree Showgrounds   ☎ 0427 008 285
Camp Area at Bribbaree. Bookings essential
HEMA 36 H2   34 07 16 S   147 51 44 E

497 Bogolong Creek Rest Area
Rest Area 9 km NW of Grenfell or 35 km E of Caragabal
HEMA 36 G3   33 50 58 S   148 05 27 E

498 Ochre Arch Farm   ☎ 0425 760 596
Camp Area at Pinnacle. 13 km N of Piney Range. 761 Goodes Ln. Self Contained Vehicles only. Please call ahead
HEMA 36 G3   33 45 12 S   148 00 54 E

499 Caragabal Rest Area
Rest Area at Caragabal
HEMA 36 G2   33 50 38 S   147 44 23 E

500 Yalgogrin Rest Area
Rest Area 36 km W of West Wyalong or 57 km E of Rankins Springs
HEMA 43 E11   33 50 41 S   146 49 44 E

501 Rankins Springs Caravan Park   ☎ 0447 780 861
Caravan Park at Rankins Springs. Mid Western Hwy
HEMA 43 E10   33 50 29 S   146 15 44 E

502 John Oxley Rest Area
Rest Area 12 km W of Rankins Springs or 44 km E of Goolgowi. Share with trucks
HEMA 43 E10   33 52 22 S   146 11 03 E

Notes...

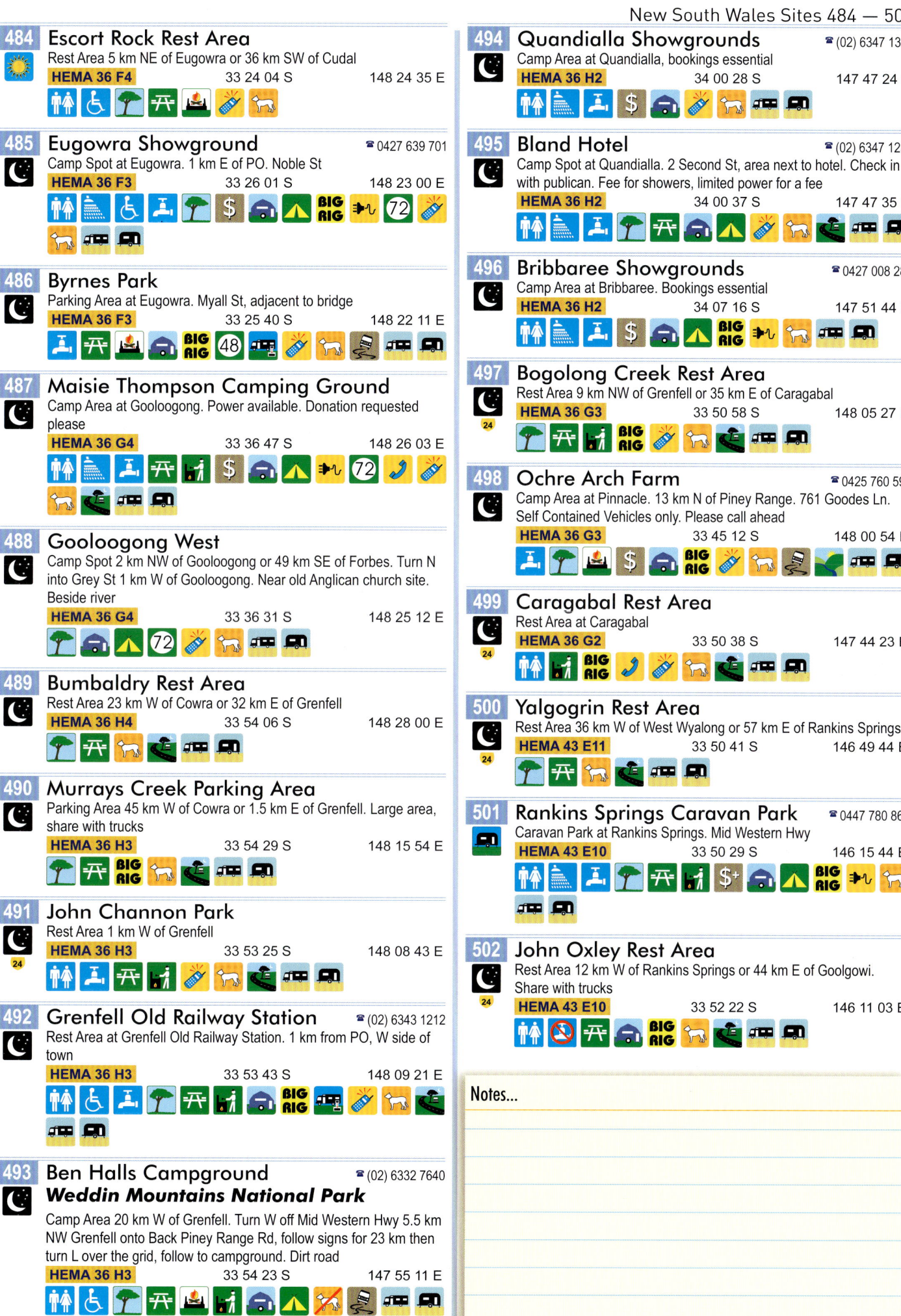

NEW SOUTH WALES

NEW SOUTH WALES

503 The Old School Camping & Caravan Park
☎ (02) 6965 4484
Caravan Park at Merriwagga. Marne St
HEMA 43 E9 33 48 52 S 145 37 38 E

504 Goolgowi Caravan Park
☎ (02) 6965 1900
Caravan Park at Goolgowi. Combo St. 1 km NE of PO. Pay fees & key collection at Council office or Ex-servicemans Club
HEMA 43 E9 33 58 47 S 145 42 22 E

505 Goolgowi Rest Area
Rest Area 1 km W of Goolgowi
HEMA 43 E9 33 59 22 S 145 41 42 E

506 Meriola Reserve
Camp Spot 19 km E of Hay. Turn S off Mid Western Hwy onto Murrumbidgee River Rd 16 km E of Hay or 241 km W of West Wyalong for 3.1 km. Turn S at river sign, through gate, veer L follow track for 1 km to river. Various sites. GPS at gate
HEMA 43 F8 34 28 01 S 145 00 56 E

507 Hay Showground
☎ (02) 6993 1087
Camp Area at Hay. Showground Rd. 1.5 km N of PO. Dump point 200m W
HEMA 43 F8 34 29 51 S 144 50 17 E

508 Sandy Point Reserve
Parking Area at Hay. Turn W off Cobb Hwy just N of bridge onto Brunker St, then S for 1 km to N bank of Murrumbidgee River. Use entry from Water St, near Hatty St for large vehicles
HEMA 43 F8 34 30 55 S 144 50 08 E

✓509 Royal Mail Hotel
☎ (02) 6993 0694
Camp Area at Booroorban. 6 acres of camping grounds. Limited power available
HEMA 43 G8 34 55 54 S 144 45 44 E

510 Wanganella Weir
Camp Spot at Wanganella. Turn SW on N side of bridge (opposite store) follow track for 1 km. Camp spots along river
HEMA 43 H8 35 13 03 S 144 48 26 E

511 Wanganella Creek Camp Park
☎ (03) 5882 3509
Caravan Park at Wanganella. Murray St, behind Pepin Ram Memorial. Call ahead to arrange key from PO
HEMA 43 H8 35 12 57 S 144 48 59 E

512 Deni Car O Tel & Caravan Park
☎ (03) 5881 1732
Caravan Park at Deniliquin. 700m E of PO opposite RSL Club
HEMA 43 H8 35 32 08 S 144 58 07 E

513 Deniliquin Rest Area
Rest Area at Deniliquin. Davidson St. Recreation reserve N side of town
HEMA 43 H8 35 31 31 S 144 58 41 E

514 Willoughby's Beach Campground
Murray Valley National Park
☎ (03) 5483 9100
Camp Area at Deniliquin. Take Memorial Dr past showgrounds to Regional Park entrance. Campground 200m inside gate, various sites
HEMA 43 H8 35 31 53 S 144 58 36 E

515 Gulpa Island Forest
☎ (03) 5483 9100
Camp Spot 3 km E of Mathoura, via Picnic Point Rd & Gulpa Creck Rd. Signposted Gulpa Island Forest Dr, veer R at fork. 1.1 km track to bush camping beside creek
HEMA 43 J8 35 48 41 S 144 54 36 E

516 Porters Creek Camp Ground
Murray Valley National Park
☎ (03) 5483 9100
Camp Area 13 km SE of Mathoura. Turn E 5 km S of Mathoura or 35 km N of Moama. Access via Coolamon Rd, Poverty Creek Rd & Porters Creek Rd. 8 km of dirt road. Bush camping beside creek
HEMA 43 J8 35 53 45 S 144 57 51 E

517 Mathoura Bowling Club
☎ (03) 5880 3200
Camp Spot at Mathoura. Cobb Hwy. Behind Bowling Club, entry from Steven St. Self Contained Vehicles only. Contact manager on arrival
HEMA 43 J8 35 48 34 S 144 53 59 E

518 Edward River Bridge Campground
Murray Valley National Park
☎ (03) 5483 9100
Camp Area 8.5 km E of Mathoura. Off Mathoura - Tocumwal Rd. Bush camping beside Edward River
HEMA 43 J8 35 48 38 S 144 57 45 E

519 Moama North Rest Area
Rest Area 30 km S of Mathoura or 10 km N of Moama
HEMA 43 J8 36 02 08 S 144 46 42 E

520 Rich River Golf Club Resort
☎ (03) 5481 3333
Parking Area at Moama. Twenty Four Ln, via Perricoota Rd. Self Contained Vehicles only. Register at reception, must join as a social member to stay
HEMA 43 K8 36 04 35 S 144 43 35 E

521 Moama (5 Mile) Campground ☎ (03) 5483 9100
Murray Valley National Park
Camp Area 8 km W of Moama, via Perricoota Rd
HEMA 43 J8 36 04 03 S 144 41 30 E

522 Benarca Campground ☎ (03) 5483 9100
Murray Valley National Park
Camp Area 18 km NW of Moama. Take Perricoota Rd (Moama - Barnham Rd) for 15 km, turn S onto Benarca Forest Rd, follow signs to campground
HEMA 42 J7 36 03 15 S 144 37 25 E

523 Wakool River
Camp Spot 11 km E of Wakool or 53 km W of Deniliquin. Turn E just S of Wakool River bridge, follow tracks to camp spots on river
HEMA 42 H7 35 29 58 S 144 27 30 E

Sydney-Albury-Tocumwal
Hume and Riverina Highways

524 Partridge VC Rest Area
Rest Area 42 km S of Campbelltown or 10 km N of Picton Rd. Southbound only
HEMA 35 H8 34 09 22 S 150 44 18 E

525 Coledale Camping Reserve ☎ (02) 4267 4302
Camp Area at Coledale. Lawrence Hargrave Dr. Advance bookings are essential. Minimum stay applies on a seasonal basis, please confirm with the booking office
HEMA 35 J10 34 17 13 S 150 56 54 E

526 Pheasants Nest Service Centre
Rest Area 6 km S of Picton Rd or 8 km N of Yanderra on South Western Fwy
HEMA 35 J8 34 17 00 S 150 38 11 E

527 Berrima Reserve ☎ 1300 657 599
Camp Area at Berrima. Just NW of town, past White Horse Inn. W onto Oxley St, L at fork. No discharge of grey water permitted, no generators & only 4 sites. Permit required
HEMA 44 B6 34 29 09 S 150 19 57 E

528 Gordon VC Rest Area
Rest Area 17 km SW of Mittagong or 33 km NE of Marulan. 7 km N of Illawarra Hwy jcn near Belanglo State Forest turnoff. Northbound only
HEMA 44 B6 34 32 11 S 150 16 49 E

529 Daley's Clearing Campground ☎ 1300 655 687
Belanglo State Forest
Camp Area 10 km W of Moss Vale. Turn W off Hume Hwy 6 km N of Illawarra Hwy jcn onto Bunnygalore Rd & Dalys Rd at Gordon VC Rest Area. Follow Belanglo Rd for 4 km R onto Daleys Rd for 0.9 km
HEMA 44 B6 34 31 38 S 150 14 30 E

530 MacKay VC Rest Area
Rest Area 26 km SW of Mittagong or 27 km NE of Marulan. 2 km N of Illawarra Hwy jcn. 100m off Hwy. Southbound only
HEMA 44 B6 34 34 45 S 150 15 10 E

531 Kingsbury VC Rest Area
Rest Area 28 km SW of Mittagong or 25 NE of Marulan. 6 km S of Illawarra Hwy jcn. Southbound only. 100m off Hwy
HEMA 44 B5 34 37 08 S 150 12 46 E

532 Moss Vale Showgrounds ☎ 0474 186 458
Camp Area at Moss Vale. Entry via Robertson Rd. Bookings are essential. Closed during show week
HEMA 44 B6 34 32 52 S 150 22 53 E

533 Gambells Rest Campground ☎ (02) 4887 7270
Morton National Park
Camp Area 2 km S of Bundanoon, via Church St & Gullies Rd. Dirt road. Bookings essential
HEMA 44 B6 34 40 07 S 150 17 48 E

534 HQ Camp ☎ 1300 655 687
Wingello State Forest
Camp Area 4 km SE of Wingello, via Forest Rd. Dirt road
HEMA 44 B5 34 42 57 S 150 11 20 E

535 Marulan Service Centre
Rest Area 29 km SW of Illawarra Hwy jcn or 42 km NE of Federal Hwy jcn
HEMA 44 B5 34 43 13 S 149 59 42 E

536 Bungonia Park
Parking Area at Bungonia. King St. Donation appreciated for upkeep of park
HEMA 44 C5 34 51 17 S 149 56 36 E

Notes...

NEW SOUTH WALES

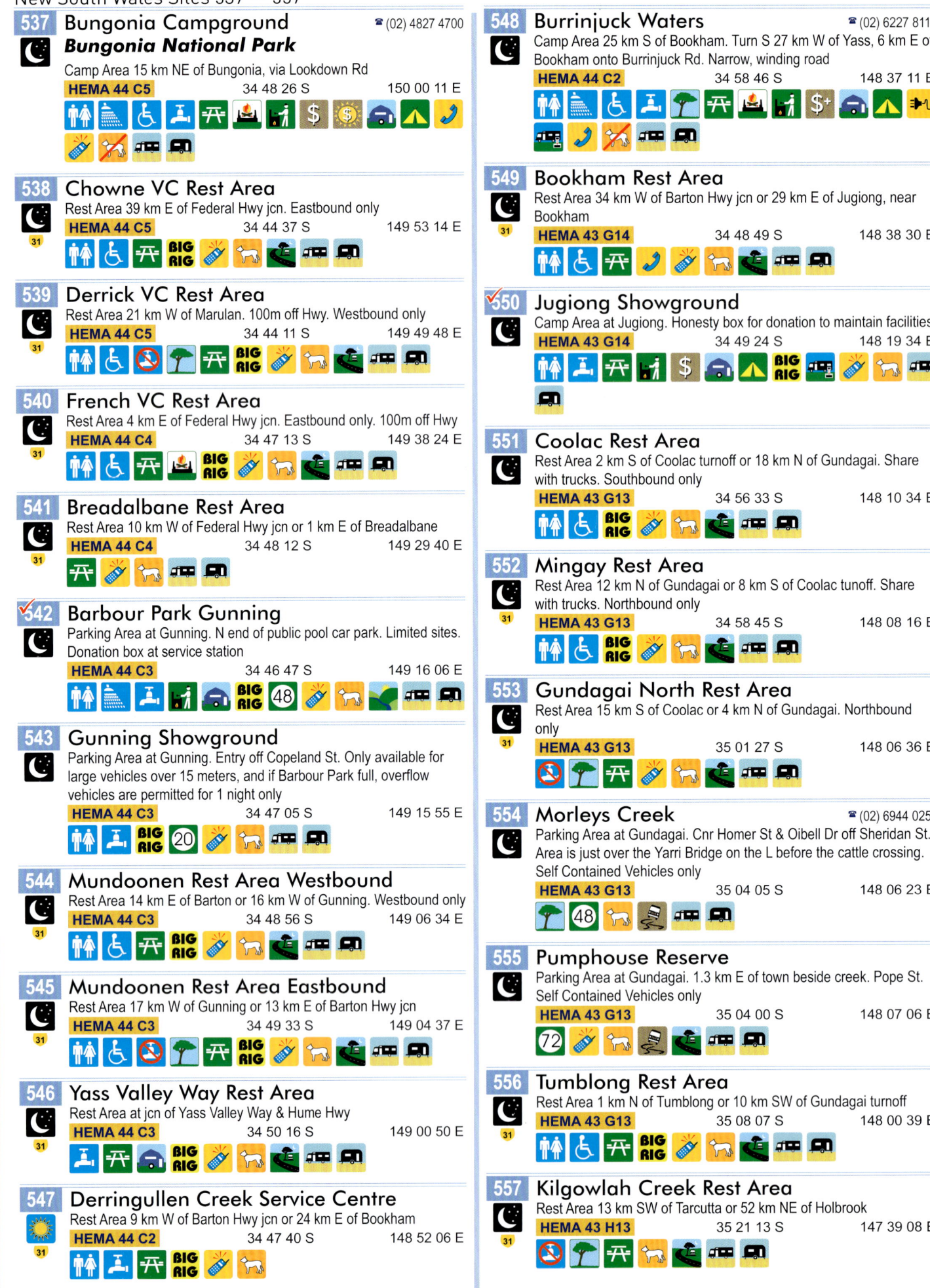

537 Bungonia Campground
☎ (02) 4827 4700
Bungonia National Park
Camp Area 15 km NE of Bungonia, via Lookdown Rd
HEMA 44 C5   34 48 26 S   150 00 11 E

538 Chowne VC Rest Area
Rest Area 39 km E of Federal Hwy jcn. Eastbound only
HEMA 44 C5   34 44 37 S   149 53 14 E

539 Derrick VC Rest Area
Rest Area 21 km W of Marulan. 100m off Hwy. Westbound only
HEMA 44 C5   34 44 11 S   149 49 48 E

540 French VC Rest Area
Rest Area 4 km E of Federal Hwy jcn. Eastbound only. 100m off Hwy
HEMA 44 C4   34 47 13 S   149 38 24 E

541 Breadalbane Rest Area
Rest Area 10 km W of Federal Hwy jcn or 1 km E of Breadalbane
HEMA 44 C4   34 48 12 S   149 29 40 E

✓542 Barbour Park Gunning
Parking Area at Gunning. N end of public pool car park. Limited sites. Donation box at service station
HEMA 44 C3   34 46 47 S   149 16 06 E

543 Gunning Showground
Parking Area at Gunning. Entry off Copeland St. Only available for large vehicles over 15 meters, and if Barbour Park full, overflow vehicles are permitted for 1 night only
HEMA 44 C3   34 47 05 S   149 15 55 E

544 Mundoonen Rest Area Westbound
Rest Area 14 km E of Barton or 16 km W of Gunning. Westbound only
HEMA 44 C3   34 48 56 S   149 06 34 E

545 Mundoonen Rest Area Eastbound
Rest Area 17 km W of Gunning or 13 km E of Barton Hwy jcn
HEMA 44 C3   34 49 33 S   149 04 37 E

546 Yass Valley Way Rest Area
Rest Area at jcn of Yass Valley Way & Hume Hwy
HEMA 44 C3   34 50 16 S   149 00 50 E

547 Derringullen Creek Service Centre
Rest Area 9 km W of Barton Hwy jcn or 24 km E of Bookham
HEMA 44 C2   34 47 40 S   148 52 06 E

548 Burrinjuck Waters
☎ (02) 6227 8114
Camp Area 25 km S of Bookham. Turn S 27 km W of Yass, 6 km E of Bookham onto Burrinjuck Rd. Narrow, winding road
HEMA 44 C2   34 58 46 S   148 37 11 E

549 Bookham Rest Area
Rest Area 34 km W of Barton Hwy jcn or 29 km E of Jugiong, near Bookham
HEMA 43 G14   34 48 49 S   148 38 30 E

✓550 Jugiong Showground
Camp Area at Jugiong. Honesty box for donation to maintain facilities
HEMA 43 G14   34 49 24 S   148 19 34 E

551 Coolac Rest Area
Rest Area 2 km S of Coolac turnoff or 18 km N of Gundagai. Share with trucks. Southbound only
HEMA 43 G13   34 56 33 S   148 10 34 E

552 Mingay Rest Area
Rest Area 12 km N of Gundagai or 8 km S of Coolac tunoff. Share with trucks. Northbound only
HEMA 43 G13   34 58 45 S   148 08 16 E

553 Gundagai North Rest Area
Rest Area 15 km S of Coolac or 4 km N of Gundagai. Northbound only
HEMA 43 G13   35 01 27 S   148 06 36 E

554 Morleys Creek
☎ (02) 6944 0250
Parking Area at Gundagai. Cnr Homer St & Oibell Dr off Sheridan St. Area is just over the Yarri Bridge on the L before the cattle crossing. Self Contained Vehicles only
HEMA 43 G13   35 04 05 S   148 06 23 E

555 Pumphouse Reserve
Parking Area at Gundagai. 1.3 km E of town beside creek. Pope St. Self Contained Vehicles only
HEMA 43 G13   35 04 00 S   148 07 06 E

556 Tumblong Rest Area
Rest Area 1 km N of Tumblong or 10 km SW of Gundagai turnoff
HEMA 43 G13   35 08 07 S   148 00 39 E

557 Kilgowlah Creek Rest Area
Rest Area 13 km SW of Tarcutta or 52 km NE of Holbrook
HEMA 43 H13   35 21 13 S   147 39 08 E

558 Kyeamba Gap Rest Area
Rest Area 34 km SW of Tarcutta or 36 km NE of Holbrook. Northbound only, share with trucks
HEMA 43 H12   35 30 19 S   147 33 50 E

559 Woomargama Rest Area
Rest Area at Woomargama. Woomargama Way, signposted off Hume Hwy
HEMA 43 J12   35 49 58 S   147 14 47 E

560 Mullengandra Rest Area
Rest Area at Mullengandra
HEMA 43 J12   35 53 34 S   147 10 09 E

561 Ettamogah Pub   ☎ (02) 6026 2070
Parking Area at Table Top in hotel carpark. "Buy a stubby holder" covers the fee
HEMA 43 J11   35 58 04 S   147 00 25 E

562 SS&A Club   ☎ (02) 6041 2222
Parking Area at Albury. Entry off Swift St. Self Contained Vehicles only, check in at reception on arrival
HEMA 43 J11   36 04 44 S   146 55 12 E

563 Burrumbuttock Hall
Camp Area at Burrumbuttock. 30 km NW of Albury or 96 km SW of Wagga Wagga. Diagonally opposite General Store, behind the hall. Fee for power. Self Contained Vehicles only
HEMA 43 J11   35 49 59 S   146 48 16 E

564 Howlong Memorial Park
Picnic Area at Howlong. From PO turn S onto Riverina Hwy, then W into Victoria St after 500m. N side of Murray River
HEMA 43 J11   35 58 56 S   146 37 04 E

565 Howlong Lions Park
Rest Area 1 km S of Howlong. S side of river at Leahy Bridge. Camping allowed S side of area as signposted. BBQ & toilets at day use area
HEMA 43 J11   35 59 17 S   146 37 21 E

566 Corowa Caravan Park   ☎ (02) 6033 1944
Caravan Park at Corowa. 84 Federation Ave
HEMA 43 J10   36 00 25 S   146 22 47 E

567 Collendina State Forest   ☎ (03) 5483 9100
Murray Valley Regional Park
Camp Spot 8.5 km W of Corowa or 31 km E of Mulwala.Turn S off Mulwala Corowa Rd onto signposted access track. Bush camping at river. GPS at gate
HEMA 43 J10   36 01 02 S   146 17 57 E

✓568 Kyffins Reserve
Camp Spot 32 km W of Corowa or 7 km E of Mulwala. Spring Rd. Visitors are required to use portable toilets & dispose in the appropriate manner offsite. Camping in marked areas only. Max stay 2 weeks in a 3 month period
HEMA 43 J10   35 58 34 S   146 03 50 E

569 Mulwala Campground (Hinches Beach)   ☎ (02) 6841 4288
Murray Valley Regional Park
Camp Spot 8 km W of Mulwala. Bush camping via Mulwala - Barooga Rd. Signposted. Hinches Beach 4 km from entrance. GPS at gate
HEMA 43 J10   35 57 12 S   145 57 40 E

570 Boomanoomana State Forest   ☎ (02) 6841 4288
Camp Spot 18 km W of Mulwala or 21 km E of Barooga. Bush camping via Mulwala - Barooga Rd. Signposted. Sandy Beach 4.5 km, Little Pebble Beach 4 km from entrance. GPS at gate
HEMA 43 J10   35 55 55 S   145 53 26 E

571 Quicks Beach   ☎ (03) 5483 9100
Murray Valley National Park
Camp Area 4 km SE of Barooga. Turn S off Mulwala - Barooga Rd 34 km W of Mulwala or 2 km E of Barooga onto Quicks Rd
HEMA 43 J9   35 55 37 S   145 42 01 E

572 Paradise Beach   ☎ (03) 5483 9100
Murray Valley Regional Park
Camp Area 2.5 km W of Barooga. Turn S off Cobram - Barooga Rd for 1.8 km. Signposted. Dirt road
HEMA 43 J9   35 55 46 S   145 41 07 E

573 Wattle Tree Beach   ☎ (03) 5483 9100
Murray Valley Regional Park
Camp Area 2 km W of Barooga. Turn S off Cobram - Barooga Rd for 1.1 km then turn R for 0.5 km. Signposted. Dirt road
HEMA 43 J9   35 55 27 S   145 40 27 E

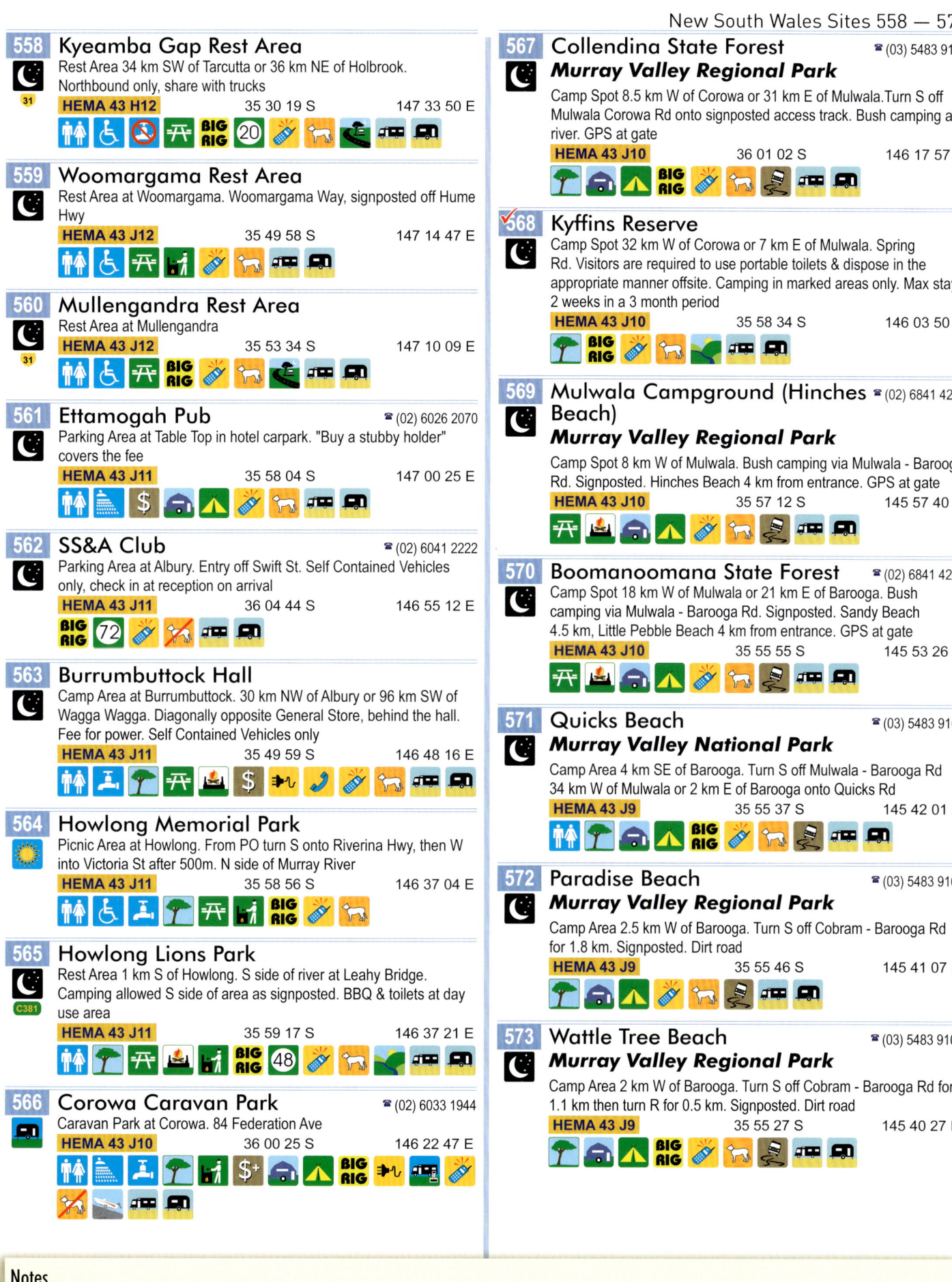

Notes...

NEW SOUTH WALES

Sydney to Victorian Border via Eden

Princes Highway

574 Killalea Campground ☎ (02) 4237 8589
Killalea State Park
Camp Area 6 km S of Shellharbour or 9 km N of Kiama, off
Shellharbour Rd. Gates closed between 1915 - 0430 hrs
HEMA 44 B7   34 36 41 S   150 51 12 E

575 Wirriwin Rest Area
Rest Area 5 km N of Kiama. Northbound traffic only
HEMA 44 B7   34 38 05 S   150 49 56 E

576 Kevin Walsh Oval ☎ 0409 917 092
Camp Area at Jamberoo. Churchill St
HEMA 44 B7   34 38 50 S   150 46 28 E

577 Berry Showground ☎ 0427 605 200
Camp Area at Berry. 500m S of PO. Alexandra St
HEMA 44 C7   34 46 46 S   150 41 46 E

578 Bendeela Recreation Area
Camp Area 7 km W of Kangaroo Valley. Turn W N of Hampden Bridge
onto Bendeela Rd. Short steep access into camp area
HEMA 44 C6   34 44 21 S   150 28 15 E

579 Shoalhaven Zoo ☎ (02) 4421 3949
Camp Area at Nowra. Turn W just N of Nowra Bridge onto Illaroo Rd,
McMahons Rd & Rockhill Rd. Riverfront
HEMA 44 C6   34 52 17 S   150 33 59 E

580 Coolendel Bush Camp ☎ (02) 4421 4586
Camp Area 30 km W of Nowra, via Yalwal Rd & Grassy Gully Rd
(Burrier Rd). 10 km dirt road. Beside Shoalhaven River. Bookings
preferred
HEMA 44 C6   34 50 38 S   150 25 18 E

581 Nowra Showground ☎ 1300 662 808
Camp Area at Nowra. West St. Bookings required
HEMA 44 C6   34 52 30 S   150 35 31 E

582 Yalwal Campground ☎ 1300 662 808
Camp Area at Yalwal, 24 km W of Nowra, via Burrier Rd & Yalwal Rd.
Overlooking Danjera Dam. 17 km dirt road, not suitable for caravans.
Bookings required
HEMA 44 C6   34 55 23 S   150 23 03 E

583 Green Patch Campground ☎ (02) 4443 0977
Booderee National Park
Camp Area 25 km SE of Falls Creek. Access via Iluka Rd off Jervis
Bay Rd. Bookings essential
HEMA 44 D7   35 08 17 S   150 43 17 E

584 Bewong Rest Area
Rest Area 27 km S of Nowra or 38 km N of Ulladulla. Share with
trucks
HEMA 44 D6   35 05 06 S   150 31 59 E

585 Jerrawangala Rest Area
Rest Area 38 km S of Nowra or 23 km N of Ulladulla. Small vehicles
only
HEMA 44 D6   35 08 43 S   150 27 39 E

586 Milton Showground ☎ 0429 934 067
Camp Area at Milton Showgrounds. Croobyar Rd. Please camp in
signposted designated camping areas only
HEMA 44 D6   35 19 09 S   150 25 48 E

587 Yadboro Flat ☎ 1300 655 687
Yadboro State Forest
Camp Area 38 km W of Ulladulla. 8 km S of Ulladulla turn W onto
Wheelbarrow Rd, L into Woodburn Rd, R into Ridge Rd (Yadboro Rd).
Dirt Rd, rough in places, off road caravans & campervans
HEMA 44 D5   35 20 24 S   150 13 01 E

588 Termeil Point Campground ☎ (02) 4454 9500
Meroo National Park
Camp Area at Termeil Point. 14 km S of Ulladulla turn E onto
Blackbutt Rd, travel 2 km to fork, veer R, 600m to camp area. 4WD
only, high clearance off road caravans
HEMA 44 E6   35 27 35 S   150 23 38 E

589 Pretty Beach ☎ (02) 4457 2019
Murramarang National Park
Camp Area 2 km S of Kioloa. Turn E off Hwy at Termeil onto Bawley
Point Rd. Reservations on 1300 072 757
HEMA 44 E6   35 34 06 S   150 22 01 E

590 Pebbly Beach ☎ (02) 4478 6582
Murramarang National Park
Camp Area 8 km E of East Lynne, via Mount Agony Rd 5 km S of
East Lynne. Reservations 1300 072 757
HEMA 44 E6   35 36 26 S   150 19 33 E

NEW SOUTH WALES

591 Depot Beach Campground
☎ (02) 4478 6582
Murramarang National Park

Camp Area 9 km E of East Lynne. Via Mt Agony Rd & North Durras Rd. Reservations 1300 072 757

| HEMA 44 E6 | 35 37 45 S | 150 19 20 E |

592 Shallow Crossing Camp Ground
☎ (02) 4478 1183

Camp Area 21 km N of Nelligan via The River Rd

| HEMA 44 E5 | 35 31 55 S | 150 11 55 E |

593 Waldrons Swamp Rest Area

Rest Area 20 km S of Batemans Bay or 7 km N of Moruya. Shared with trucks

| HEMA 44 F5 | 35 51 54 S | 150 07 09 E |

594 North Head Campground
☎ 0428 633 447

Camp Area 7 km E of Moruya. From Moruya turn E along North Head Dr just N of bridge, then to Bruce Cameron Dr beside airport. Cold showers. Fees higher in peak season

| HEMA 44 F5 | 35 54 11 S | 150 08 55 E |

595 Congo Campground
☎ (02) 4476 0800
Eurobodalla National Park

Camp Area at Congo. 10 km SE of Moruya, via South Head Dr & Congo Rd. Beachside. Cold showers

| HEMA 44 F5 | 35 57 17 S | 150 09 31 E |

596 Brou Lake Campground
☎ (02) 4476 0800
Eurobodalla National Park

Camp Area 14 km S of Bodalla. Turn E 9 km S of Bodalla onto Brou Lake Rd, veer R at fork. 5 km dirt road to camp area. Bush camping, small vehicles only

| HEMA 44 F5 | 36 08 52 S | 150 07 09 E |

597 Bodalla Forest Park Rest Area
☎ (02) 4472 6211
Bodalla State Forest

Rest Area 9 km S of Bodalla or 9 km N of Narooma

| HEMA 44 F5 | 36 09 03 S | 150 05 46 E |

598 Dalmeny Campground
☎ 0428 635 641

Camp Area at Dalmeny. Turn E off Princes Hwy onto Mort Ave 38 km S of Moruya or 5 km N of Narooma

| HEMA 44 G5 | 36 09 46 S | 150 07 38 E |

599 Mystery Bay Campground
☎ 0428 622 357

Camp Area 12 km S of Narooma. Turn SE 10 km S of Narooma or 27 km NE of Cobargo onto Mystery Bay Rd. Cold showers. Fees higher in peak season

| HEMA 44 G5 | 36 17 54 S | 150 08 00 E |

600 Cobargo Hotel
☎ (02) 6493 6423

Parking Area at Cobargo. Princes Hwy. Self Contained Vehicles only. Check in with publican, fee for showers

| HEMA 44 G5 | 36 23 22 S | 149 53 09 E |

601 Bega Showgrounds

Camp Spot at Bega. Upper St. Caretaker on site

| HEMA 44 H5 | 36 40 46 S | 149 50 52 E |

602 Gillards Campground
☎ (02) 4476 0800
Mimosa Rocks National Park

Camp Area 13 km N of Tathra, via Tathra - Bermagui Rd & Gillards Rd. 4 km single lane dirt road care needed. Maximum stay 1 month

| HEMA 44 H5 | 36 39 35 S | 150 00 05 E |

603 Hobart Beach
☎ (02) 6495 5000
Bournda National Park

Camp Area 13 km S of Tathra or 18 km N of Merimbula. Turn E off Sapphire Coast Dr 10 km S of Tathra or 15 km N of Merimbula. 3 km dirt road

| HEMA 44 H5 | 36 47 49 S | 149 56 21 E |

604 Candelo Rest Area

Rest Area at Candelo. Opposite General Store. Williams St

| HEMA 44 H4 | 36 46 00 S | 149 41 42 E |

605 Merimbula Caravan & Motor Home Park
☎ 0428 260 734

Camp Area 6 km W of Merimbula or 4 km N of Pambula Village on Princes Hwy. 2529 Princes Hwy. Self Contained Vehicles only

| HEMA 44 J5 | 36 53 14 S | 149 52 13 E |

606 East Ben Boyd Forest Rest Area

Rest Area 18 km S of Eden or 41 km N of Genoa. Both sides of the road

| HEMA 44 J4 | 37 12 09 S | 149 50 43 E |

Notes...

NEW SOUTH WALES

607 Saltwater Creek ☎ (02) 6495 5000
Ben Boyd National Park
Camp Area 41 km SE of Eden. Turn E 18 km S of Eden or 7 km N of Narrabarba, onto Edrom Rd, Green Cape Rd, Duckhole & Saltwater Rds. 16 km winding dirt road. Limited space for trailers & caravans, small vehicles only. Bookings required Christmas, Easter
HEMA 44 J5   37 10 08 S   149 59 58 E

608 Bittangabee Campground ☎ (02) 6495 5000
Ben Boyd National Park
Camp Area 43 km SE of Eden. Turn E 19 km S of Eden or 7 km N of Narrabarba, onto Edrom Rd & Green Cape Rd. 18 km winding dirt road. Small vehicles only. Bookings required Christmas, Easter
HEMA 44 K5   37 13 04 S   150 00 58 E

609 Scrubby Creek Picnic Area
East Boyd State Forest
Picnic Area 20 km S of Eden or 39 km N of Genoa. 700m W of Hwy. GPS at entrance
HEMA 44 K4   37 13 39 S   149 49 51 E

610 Newtons Crossing Picnic Area ☎ 1300 655 687
Yambulla State Forest
Camp Area 56 km SW of Eden. Turn W into Imlay Rd 25 km S of Eden or 36 km N of Genoa. Follow for 12 km, turn S into Allan Brook Rd, 6 km dirt road to campsite. Last 100m rough track. Small vehicles only
HEMA 44 K4   37 16 03 S   149 40 30 E

611 Wallagaraugh River Rest Area
Rest Area 40 km S of Eden or 19 km N of Genoa. Small vehicles only, limited space
HEMA 44 K4   37 22 10 S   149 43 00 E

Cowra to Cann River
Lachlan Valley Way, Barton and Monaro Highways

612 Boorowa Caravan Park ☎ (02) 6385 3658
Caravan Park at Boorowa. Brial St. 1 km N of PO
HEMA 44 B2   34 26 04 S   148 43 10 E

613 Harden-Murrumburrah Showgrounds ☎ 0488 509 977
Camp Area at Harden-Murrumburrah. Entry off Woolrych St. Call caretaker to pay fees & unlock facilities
HEMA 44 B1   34 32 45 S   148 21 27 E

614 Binalong Rest Area
Rest Area at Binalong, next to swimming pool
HEMA 44 C2   34 40 33 S   148 38 01 E

615 Yass Showgrounds ☎ (02) 6226 1615
Camp Area at Yass. Entry off Grand Junction Rd. Closed during show week mid-March. Honesty box
HEMA 44 C2   34 50 27 S   148 55 18 E

616 Joe O'Connor Park
Parking Area at Yass off Laidlaw St, W side of town. Self Contained Vehicles only
HEMA 44 C2   34 50 10 S   148 54 21 E

617 Colinton Rest Area
Rest Area 15 km S of Michelago or 13 km N of Bredbo
HEMA 48 J5   35 50 16 S   149 09 44 E

618 Bredbo Inn Hotel ☎ (02) 6454 4440
Parking Area at Bredbo. 82 km SE of Canberra or 34 km N of Cooma on the Monaro Hwy
HEMA 44 F3   35 57 03 S   149 08 44 E

619 Numeralla River Rest Area
Rest Area 14 km S of Bredbo or 20 km N of Cooma. Beside river
HEMA 44 F3   36 04 36 S   149 09 33 E

620 Badja Recreation Reserve ☎ (02) 6450 1777
Camp Spot at Numeralla, 22 km E of Cooma. Numeralla Peak View Rd. Beside river
HEMA 44 G3   36 10 25 S   149 21 01 E

621 Nimmitabel Campground ☎ 0427 406 668
Camp Area at Nimmitabel. N end of town. Call caretaker to use amenties block. Fees collected
HEMA 44 G3   36 30 31 S   149 17 04 E

622 Lake Williams
Rest Area at Nimmitabel. S end of town
HEMA 44 H3   36 30 53 S   149 16 56 E

623 Brown Mountain
Parking Area 22 km SE of Nimmitabel or 17 km W of Bemboka. Behind truck parking area
HEMA 44 H4   36 36 31 S   149 25 58 E

624 Bemboka Sports Ground ☎ 0408 020 636
Camp Area 1 km E of Bemboka. Turnoff at Colombo Creek Bridge. Fee for power & shower, phone for key & payment
HEMA 44 H4   36 38 08 S   149 34 41 E

625 Nunnock Campground ☎ (02) 6458 4080
South East Forests National Park

Camp Area in SE Forests National Park. Turn N off Mount Darragh Rd onto Tantawangalo Mountain Rd. N onto New Line Rd, then E into Packers Swamp Rd, then onto Cattlemans Link Trail, follow to campsite. Small vehicles only. 15 km dirt road

HEMA 44 H4   36 42 12 S   149 26 49 E

626 Six Mile Creek ☎ (02) 6458 5900
South East Forest National Park

Camp Area 20 km NE of Cathcart or 12 km W of Candelo on the Tantawangalo Mountain Rd. Dirt road. Small vehicles only

HEMA 44 H4   36 47 11 S   149 32 18 E

627 Bombala Caravan Park ☎ (02) 6458 3817

Caravan Park at Bombala. Monaro Hwy

HEMA 44 J3   36 54 30 S   149 14 20 E

628 Waratah Gully Campground ☎ (02) 6458 5900
South East Forests National Park

Camp Area 19 km SE of Bombala. Via Bucky Springs Rd, Coolangubra Forest Way & Wog Way

HEMA 44 J3   37 00 09 S   149 23 02 E

629 Delegate Caravan Park ☎ (02) 6458 8167

Caravan Park at Delegate. Bill Jeffery's Park, Topping St

HEMA 44 J3   37 02 24 S   148 56 48 E

Tomerong to Braidwood
Trunk Road 92

630 Endrick River Crossing

Camp Spot 55 km W of Tomerong or 5 km NE of Nerriga on Turpentine Rd. 100m N of bridge on N side of the road. Dirt road

HEMA 44 D5   35 05 22 S   150 07 15 E

631 Corang River

Camp Spot 12 km S of Nerriga or 41 km NE of Braidwood. On the Braidwood - Nerriga Rd. Dirt road. N side of bridge beside river

HEMA 44 D5   35 12 21 S   150 03 06 E

632 Oallen Ford

Parking Area 18 km W of Nerriga or 37 E of Tarago, via Oallen Rd. Access 200m E of bridge. Overlooking river

HEMA 44 D5   35 09 06 S   149 57 19 E

633 Wog Wog Campground ☎ (02) 4887 7270
Morton National Park

Camp Area 22 km S of Nerriga or 41 km NE of Braidwood. Turn S off Braidwood - Nerriga Rd 17 km S of Nerriga or 36 km NE of Braidwood onto Mongarlowe Rd. Dirt road

HEMA 44 D5   35 16 06 S   150 02 08 E

634 Charleyong Crossing

Camp Spot 31 km SW of Nerriga or 26 km NE of Braidwood. Turn W off Braidwood - Nerriga Rd 29 km SW of Nerriga or 24 km NE of Braidwood onto Stewarts Crossing Rd, across causeway. Dirt road

HEMA 44 D5   35 14 43 S   149 53 29 E

635 The Service Club ☎ (02) 4842 2108

Parking Area at Braidwood. Cnr Coronation Ave & Victory St. Parking on fenceline only. Self Contained Vehicles only, please support the club

HEMA 44 D5   35 26 34 S   149 47 31 E

Batemans Bay to Canberra
Kings Highway

636 Araluen Creek

Camp Area 24 km S of Braidwood or 3 km N of Araluen Hotel. 200m along Majors Creek Mountain Rd

HEMA 44 E4   35 37 27 S   149 47 37 E

637 Deua River Campgrounds ☎ (02) 4476 0800
Deua National Park

Camp Areas 48 km S of Braidwood along Araluen Rd. Small vehicles only. No caravans

HEMA 44 E5   35 44 52 S   149 55 00 E

638 Majors Creek Recreation Reserve

Camp Spot at Majors Creek, 16 km S of Braidwood. Araluen St. Big rig access via King St

HEMA 44 E4   35 34 08 S   149 44 31 E

639 Wyanbene Caves ☎ (02) 4476 0800
Deua National Park

Camp Area 47 km S of Braidwood, via the Braidwood - Cooma Rd. 7 km dirt road

HEMA 44 E4   35 47 41 S   149 40 59 E

Notes...

NEW SOUTH WALES

640 Lowden Forest Park
☎ 1300 655 687
Tallaganda State Forest
Camp Area 38 km SW of Braidwood. Via the Krawarree Rd to Ballalaba, then Harolds Cross Rd (Parlour Creek), Coxes Creek Rd, into Lowden Forest Rd. Dirt road

HEMA 44 E4	35 30 34 S	149 36 16 E

641 Wilkins Memorial Park
Camp Area at Captains Flat. Foxlow St, S end of town. Small vehicles only. Donation welcome

HEMA 44 E4	35 35 26 S	149 26 46 E

642 Bombay Reserve
Camp Spot 9 km W of Braidwood via Cooma Rd & Bombay Rd. 200m past bridge on R. 100m off road, beside Shoalhaven River

HEMA 44 D4	35 25 37 S	149 42 48 E

643 Warri Camping Reserve
Camp Area 14 km N of Braidwood or 35 km SE of Bungendore. Beside Shoalhaven River

HEMA 44 D4	35 20 39 S	149 44 15 E

644 Bungendore Showground
☎ 0455 174 463
Camp Area 4 km NW of Bungendore on Bungendore - Sutton Rd. Caretaker on site. Maximum stay 7 days

HEMA 44 D4	35 14 30 S	149 24 37 E

Goulburn to Canberra
Federal Highway

645 Kibby VC Rest Area
Rest Area 2 km S of Hume Hwy/Federal Hwy jcn. Southbound only

HEMA 44 C4	34 48 55 S	149 36 14 E

646 Edmondson VC Rest Area
Rest Area 15 km SW of Hume Hwy/Federal Hwy jcn or 62 km NE of Barton/Federal Hwy jcn. Beside Rowes Lagoon, 300m off Hwy

HEMA 44 C4	34 53 46 S	149 30 37 E

647 Gurney VC Rest Area
Rest Area 33 km SW of Hume Hwy/Federal Hwy jcn or 44 km NE of Barton/Federal Hwy jcn

HEMA 44 C4	34 54 42 S	149 26 35 E

648 Badcoe VC Rest Area
Rest Area 37 km SW of Hume Hwy/Federal Hwy jcn or 40 km NE of Barton/Federal Hwy jcn

HEMA 44 C4	35 02 05 S	149 22 40 E

649 Gundaroo Sport & Recreation Ground
Camp Area at Gundaroo. Cork St. Donation please for upkeep at General Store/PO

HEMA 44 C3	35 01 25 S	149 15 57 E

650 Wheatley VC Rest Area
Rest Area 41 km SW of Hume Hwy/Federal Hwy jcn or 36 km NE of Barton/Federal Hwy jcn

HEMA 44 C4	35 04 01 S	149 22 26 E

651 Anderson VC Rest Area
Rest Area 48 km SW of Hume Hwy/Federal Hwy jcn or 29 km NE of Barton/Federal Hwy jcn. 100m off Hwy

HEMA 44 C4	35 06 01 S	149 22 36 E

Australian Capital Territory

652 Blue Range Recreation Area
☎ (02) 6207 2900
Camp Area 42 km W of Canberra via Uriarra Rd, turn N into Blue Range Rd, travel 2.8 km to camp area. Bookings essential, phone or online www.bookings.act.gov.au

HEMA 48 C2	35 17 22 S	148 52 32 E

653 Cotter Campground
☎ 13 22 81
Camp Area 20 km W of Canberra, via Cotter Rd. Beside River. Maximum stay 14 days

HEMA 48 C3	35 19 33 S	148 56 52 E

654 Woods Reserve Recreation Area
☎ 13 22 81
Camp Area 19 km NW of Tharwa, via Tidbinbilla Rd & Corin Rd. Bookings essential. Maximum stay 14 days

HEMA 48 E3	35 28 47 S	148 56 26 E

655 Honeysuckle Campground
☎ (02) 6207 2900
Namadgi National Park
Camp Area 68 km SW of Canberra, via Monaro Hwy turn W onto Angle Crossing Rd, S into Naas Rd, then onto Apollo Rd. Travel 9.5 km to campground. No caravans permitted. Bookings essential

HEMA 48 F3	35 35 00 S	148 58 35 E

656 Orroral Campground
☎ (02) 6207 2900
Namadgi National Park
Camp Area 55 km S of Canberra. Via Boboyan Rd & Orroral Rd. 19 km S of Tharwa. Limited sites for caravans, camper trailers & campervans. Bookings are essential

HEMA 48 G3	35 39 46 S	148 59 21 E

657 Mount Clear Campground ☎ (02) 6207 2900
Namadgi National Park
Camp Area 48 km S of Tharwa off Boboyan Rd. Bookings essential. Small vehicles only, 4WD recommended
HEMA 48 J4   35 51 55 S   149 00 39 E

658 Exhibition Park (EPIC) Camping Ground ☎ (02) 6205 4976
23
Camp Area at Canberra. 8 km N of city centre at cnr of Federal Hwy & Flemington Rd. Closed mid-Dec to mid-Jan, Easter (plus 1 week either side) & mid-Feb to early March
HEMA 47 C5   35 13 47 S   149 09 02 E

659 Hughie Edwards VC Rest Area
23
Rest Area 71 km SW of Hume Hwy/Federal Hwy jcn or 6 km NE of Barton/Federal Hwy jcn. Southbound only
HEMA 47 B6   35 12 40 S   149 11 26 E

660 Kowen Forest ☎ 12 33 81
Camp Area 11 km N of Queanbeyan East via Sutton & Kowen Rds. Bookings essential as gate is locked
HEMA 48 C6   35 17 19 S   149 17 15 E

Snowy Mountains Area
Snowy Mountains Highway

661 Careys Reserve ☎ (02) 6227 9626
Wee Jasper Reserves
Camp Area 4 km N of Wee Jasper. 53 km SW of Yass. Beside Burrinjuck Dam, near Careys Cave. Some dirt road
HEMA 44 C2   35 05 30 S   148 40 20 E

662 Fitzpatricks Trackhead Reserve ☎ (02) 6227 9626
Wee Jasper Reserves
Camp Area 4 km S of Wee Jasper, via Tumut - Nottingham Rd. N at T jcn, then W into reserve. Dirt road
HEMA 44 D2   35 08 20 S   148 40 27 E

✓663 Billy Grace Reserve ☎ (02) 6227 9626
Wee Jasper Reserves
Camp Area 6 km S of Wee Jasper, via Tumut - Nottingham Rd. S at T jcn, then E into reserve. 1 km dirt road. Beside Goodradigbee River
HEMA 44 D2   35 08 14 S   148 41 14 E

664 Swinging Bridge Reserve ☎ (02) 6227 9626
Wee Jasper Reserves
Camp Area 9 km S of Wee Jasper, via Nottingham Rd. Dirt road. Beside Goodradigbee River
HEMA 44 D2   35 09 44 S   148 41 13 E

665 Micalong Creek Reserve ☎ (02) 6227 9626
Wee Jasper Reserves
Camp Area 12 km S of Wee Jasper via Tumut - Nottingham Rd. S at T jcn. Beside Micalong Creek. 7 km dirt road. Cold, outside shower
HEMA 44 D2   35 11 19 S   148 41 10 E

666 Thomas Boyd Trackhead ☎ (02) 6937 2700
Camp Area 23 km SE of Tumut, via Goobarragandra Rd (Laclamac Rd), beside river. 3 km dirt road
HEMA 44 D1   35 22 24 S   148 24 59 E

667 Golden Gully Caravan Park ☎ (02) 6946 2163
Caravan Park at Adelong. Victoria Hill Rd, behind Services Club. Register at club
HEMA 44 D1   35 18 25 S   148 03 55 E

668 Adelong Showgrounds
Parking Area at Adelong. Entry off Cromwell St. Self Contained Vehicles only
HEMA 44 D1   35 18 55 S   148 03 49 E
72

669 Batlow Caravan Park ☎ (02) 6949 1444
Caravan Park at Batlow. Kurrajong Ave. N end of town
HEMA 44 E1   35 31 02 S   148 08 47 E

670 Windy Point Camping Area ☎ 1300 655 687
Blowering Reservoir
Camp Area 20 km NE of Batlow via Blowering Foreshore Rd. Western foreshore, lakeside
HEMA 44 D1   35 29 43 S   148 14 30 E

671 White Gate Rest Area
Rest Area 6 km SW of Batlow or 9 km N of Laurel Hill
HEMA 44 E1   35 31 57 S   148 05 58 E

Notes...

NEW SOUTH WALES

672 Mannus Campsite
☎ (02) 6948 3444

Camp Area 7 km W of Tumbarumba, via Jingellic Rd. Beside Mannus Creek

HEMA 43 J13   35 46 46 S   147 56 44 E

673 Tumbarumba RV Stop

Parking Area at Tumbarumba. Winton St, opposite Police Station. Self Contained Vehicles only

HEMA 43 H13   35 46 34 S   148 00 41 E

674 Lake Mannus Boat Ramp

Camp Spot 12 km W of Tumbarumba. Turn S at Mannus Campsite on Lake Rd, follow dirt road for 5 km to boat ramp

HEMA 43 J13   35 48 40 S   147 58 39 E

675 Paddys River Dam
Bago State Forest
☎ 1300 655 687

Camp Area 23 km NE of Tumbarumba. Via Round Creek Rd, Dog Tree Rd, Perkins Rd. Dirt road

HEMA 43 J13   35 42 44 S   148 10 01 E

676 Jingellic Reserve
☎ (02) 6037 1290

Camp Area at Jingellic. Beside Murray River & hotel. Toilets & showers at hotel for a fee. Dogs must be on lead. Maximum stay 4 weeks

HEMA 43 J13   35 55 44 S   147 42 14 E

677 Henry Angel Track Head
☎ (02) 6948 9100

Camp Area 8 km SE of Tumbarumba or 26 km N of Tooma. Beside river. Maximum stay 4 weeks

HEMA 43 J13   35 49 41 S   148 03 38 E

678 Paddys River Falls
☎ (02) 6948 9100

Camp Area 16 km SE of Tumbarumba or 22 km N of Tooma. Turn S 14 km SE of Tumbarumba or 20 km N of Tooma. Steep winding road, only 4 sites, small vehicles only. Permit required after 1 week

HEMA 43 J13   35 51 32 S   148 06 56 E

679 Paddys River Flats
☎ (02) 6948 9100

Camp Area 18 km SE of Tumbarumba or 16 km N of Tooma. Beside river. Maximum stay 4 weeks, permit required after 1 week

HEMA 43 J13   35 51 06 S   148 08 23 E

680 O'Hares Campground
Kosciuszko National Park
☎ (02) 6947 7025

Camp Area 22 km N of Cabramurra or 48 km SE of Tumbarumba on Elliot Way. Steep & winding road

HEMA 43 J14   35 49 20 S   148 21 55 E

681 Three Mile Dam Campground
Kosciuszko National Park
☎ (02) 6947 7025

Camp Area 6 km W of Kiandra or 12 km NE of Cabramurra. 300m N of road

HEMA 43 J14   35 53 18 S   148 26 56 E

682 Bradley's Hutt
Kosciuszko National Park
☎ (02) 6076 9373

Camp Area 47 km NE of Khancoban or 17 km SE of Cabramurra. E side of road. Steep & winding road

HEMA 43 J14   36 00 57 S   148 22 46 E

683 Clover Flat Campground
Kosciuszko National Park
☎ (02) 6076 9373

Camp Area 25 km NE of Khancoban or 35 km SW of Cabramurra. Steep & winding road, limited space, small vehicles only

HEMA 43 J14   36 04 21 S   148 13 02 E

684 Bradneys Gap Campground
Kosciuszko National Park
☎ (02) 6076 9373

Camp Area 10 km NE of Khancoban or 50 km SW of Cabramurra

HEMA 43 K13   36 09 56 S   148 09 24 E

685 Towong Reserve
☎ (02) 6948 9100

Camp Area 25 km S of Tooma or 1 km E of Towong. Beside Murray River bridge

HEMA 43 J13   36 07 25 S   147 59 49 E

686 Geehi Flats Campground
Kosciuszko National Park
☎ (02) 6076 9373

Camp Area 30 km S of Khancoban or 81 km W of Jindabyne, via Alpine Way. Steep & winding road. Small vehicles only

HEMA 44 G1   36 23 05 S   148 10 51 E

687 Tom Groggin Campground
Kosciuszko National Park
☎ (02) 6076 9373

Camp Area 53 km S of Khancoban or 58 km W of Jindabyne. Steep & winding road. Small vehicles only

HEMA 44 H1   36 32 22 S   148 08 06 E

688 Leatherbarrel Creek Picnic Area
Kosciuszko National Park
☎ (02) 6076 9373

Camp Area 61 km S of Khancoban or 50 km W of Jindabyne. Steep & winding road. Small vehicles only, limited space

HEMA 44 H1   36 31 33 S   148 11 35 E

Notes...

689 **Thredbo Diggings Campground** ☎ (02) 6450 5600
Kosciuszko National Park
Camp Area 92 km SE of Khancoban or 19 km W of Jindabyne, beside Thredbo River. Steep & winding road
HEMA 44 G1   36 26 49 S   148 25 31 E

690 **Adventist Alpine Village** ☎ (02) 6456 2738
Camp Area at Jindabyne. 122 Tinworth Drive. Advance reservations essential
HEMA 44 G2   36 25 51 S   148 35 32 E

691 **Jacobs River Campground** ☎ (02) 6450 5600
Kosciuszko National Park
Camp Area 51 km S of Jindabyne or 37 km N of Suggan Buggan on Barry Way
HEMA 44 H1   36 44 58 S   148 26 38 E

692 **Pinch River Campground** ☎ (02) 6450 5600
Kosciuszko National Park
Camp Area 58 km S of Jindabyne or 31 km N of Suggan Buggan on Barry Way
HEMA 44 H1   36 47 32 S   148 24 27 E

693 **Long Plain Hut Campground** ☎ (02) 6450 5600
Kosciuszko National Park
Camp Area 15 km SE of Yarrangobilly. 10.5 km S of Yarrangobilly turn E into Long Plain Rd for 3.5 km, turn L at signpost, 1 km to camping area near hut. 4WD recommended
HEMA 44 E2   35 41 49 S   148 32 23 E

694 **Cooinbil Hut Campground** ☎ (02) 6947 7025
Kosciuszko National Park
Camp Area 25 km SE of Yarrangobilly. 10.5 km S of Yarrangobilly turn E into Long Plain Rd for 10.5 km, turn R at signpost, 1 km to camping area near hut. 4WD recommended
HEMA 44 E2   35 37 53 S   148 35 49 E

695 **Cooleman Mountain Campground** ☎ (02) 6947 7025
Kosciuszko National Park
Camp Area 30 km SE of Yarrangobilly. 10.5 km S of Yarrangobilly turn E into Long Plains Rd for 17 km, turn R into Blue Waterhole Trail for 2.6 km. 4WD recommended
HEMA 44 E2   35 35 51 S   148 38 23 E

696 **Magpie Flat Campground** ☎ (02) 6450 5600
Kosciuszko National Park
Camp Area 35 km SE of Yarrangobilly. 10.5 km S of Yarrangobilly turn E into Long Plain Rd for 16.5 km, turn R into Blue Waterholes Trail for 8 km. 4WD recommended
HEMA 44 E2   35 37 16 S   148 40 49 E

697 **Blue Waterholes Campground** ☎ (02) 6947 7025
Kosciuszko National Park
Camp Area 35.5 km SE of Yarrangobilly. 10.5 km S of Yarrangobilly turn E into Long Plain Rd for 16.5 km, turn R into Blue Waterholes Trail for 8.5 km. 4WD recommended
HEMA 44 E2   35 37 36 S   148 41 03 E

698 **Yarrangobilly Village Campground** ☎ (02) 6947 7025
Kosciuszko National Park
Rest Area 29 km N of Kiandra or 24 km S of Talbingo turnoff. Beside river
HEMA 44 E2   35 39 07 S   148 27 44 E

699 **Jounama Creek Campground** ☎ (02) 6947 7025
Kosciuszko National Park
Camp Area opposite Talbingo turnoff. 500m E of Hwy. Beside creek
HEMA 44 E1   35 33 56 S   148 19 55 E

700 **Yolde Campground** ☎ (02) 6947 7025
Kosciuszko National Park
Camp Area 5 km N of Talbingo turnoff or 35 km S of Tumut. Small vehicles only
HEMA 44 E1   35 32 18 S   148 17 43 E

701 **Yachting Point Campground** ☎ (02) 6947 7025
Kosciuszko National Park
Camp Area 10 km N of Talbingo turnoff or 30 km S of Tumut
HEMA 44 E1   35 30 39 S   148 16 03 E

702 **Humes Crossing Campground** ☎ (02) 6947 7025
Kosciuszko National Park
Camp Area 15 km N of Talbingo turnoff or 25 km S of Tumut
HEMA 44 E1   35 28 25 S   148 16 34 E

703 **The Pines Campground** ☎ (02) 6947 7025
Kosciuszko National Park
Camp Area 18 km N of Talbingo turnoff or 22 km S of Tumut
HEMA 44 D1   35 26 51 S   148 17 06 E

Notes...

NEW SOUTH WALES

704 Log Bridge Creek Campground ☎(02) 6947 7025
Kosciuszko National Park
Camp Area 22 km N of Talbingo turnoff or 18 km S of Tumut. Turn SE off Hwy, follow road back across Hwy for 1.5 km to main camp area
HEMA 44 D1   35 25 07 S   148 16 23 E

705 Tumut River Rest Area
Rest Area 9 km S of Tumut. Turn S off Snowy Mountains Hwy onto Blowering Dam Access Rd. 1.5 km to rest area next to river. Self Contained Vehicles only
HEMA 44 D1   35 22 23 S   148 15 27 E

706 Site Closed

Cowra to Albury
Olympic Highway

707 Bendick Murrell Rest Area
Rest Area 44 km SW of Cowra or 26 km NE of Young
HEMA 36 H4   34 10 02 S   148 27 33 E

708 Calare Tavern ☎(02) 6383 7203
Parking Area in Bendick Murrell. See publican before parking. Limited space. Fee for shower
HEMA 36 H4   34 09 34 S   148 26 46 E

709 Lions Lookout Rest Area
Rest Area 62 km SW of Cowra or 8 km NE of Young
HEMA 36 J3   34 17 14 S   148 21 16 E

710 Touts Lookout
Parking Area 20 km N of Young. Via Scenic Rd & Monteagle Rd
HEMA 36 H4   34 10 33 S   148 22 47 E

711 Young Showground ☎(02) 6382 2079
Camp Area at Young. Entry from Whiteman Ave. Self Contained Vehicles only. Bookings essential. Mobile 0455 141 801
HEMA 36 J3   34 18 58 S   148 18 50 E

712 Big Spring Creek
Rest Area 8 km S of Young or 23 km NE of Wallendbeen
HEMA 36 J3   34 22 28 S   148 15 35 E

713 Waganbah Oval ☎(02) 6384 3206
Camp Area at Wombat. Entry off Ross St. Please pay fee at the Wombat Hotel
HEMA 36 J3   34 25 42 S   148 14 46 E

714 Mackay Park
Rest Area at Wallendbeen at the roundabout
HEMA 36 J3   34 31 45 S   148 09 46 E

715 Cootamundra Showgrounds ☎0428 555 241
Camp Area at Cootamundra off Pinkerton Rd. See caretaker before parking
HEMA 36 K3   34 38 24 S   148 02 27 E

716 Frampton Reserve Rest Area
Rest Area 12 km SW of Cootamundra or 12 km NE of Bethungra, Cnr of Lismore Rd
HEMA 36 K2   34 42 09 S   147 56 30 E

✓717 Bethungra Dam & Reserve
Camp Area 5 km E of Bethungra. 1 km N of Bethungra Village turn E onto dirt road under viaduct, onto Bethungra Waterworks Rd, follow to dam. 5 km dirt road
HEMA 36 K2   34 45 50 S   147 54 27 E

718 Illabo Rest Area
Rest Area at Illabo. Opposite hotel
HEMA 36 K2   34 48 57 S   147 44 21 E

719 Junee Golf Club ☎(02) 6924 3371
Parking Area at Junee. Golf Ave via Gundagai Rd. Check in at club house
HEMA 43 G12   34 52 19 S   147 35 32 E

720 Sandy Beach Reserve
Camp Area 3 km SE of Wantabadgery on River Rd
HEMA 43 G13   35 04 03 S   147 44 21 E

721 Wallacetown Rest Area
Rest Area 20 km S of Junee or 21 km N of Wagga Wagga. Opposite service station
HEMA 43 G12   34 57 34 S   147 26 54 E

722 Wagga Wagga Showgrounds ☎(02) 6925 2180
Camp Area at Wagga Wagga. Entry via Bourke Rd, Urana St
HEMA 43 G12   35 07 30 S   147 20 51 E

723 Wilks Park
Rest Area at Wagga Wagga. Turn E off Olympic Hwy at Travers St, cross bridge to Hampden Ave. N side of town, E side of Murrumbidgee River. Self Contained Vehicles only
HEMA 43 G12   35 05 59 S   147 22 17 E

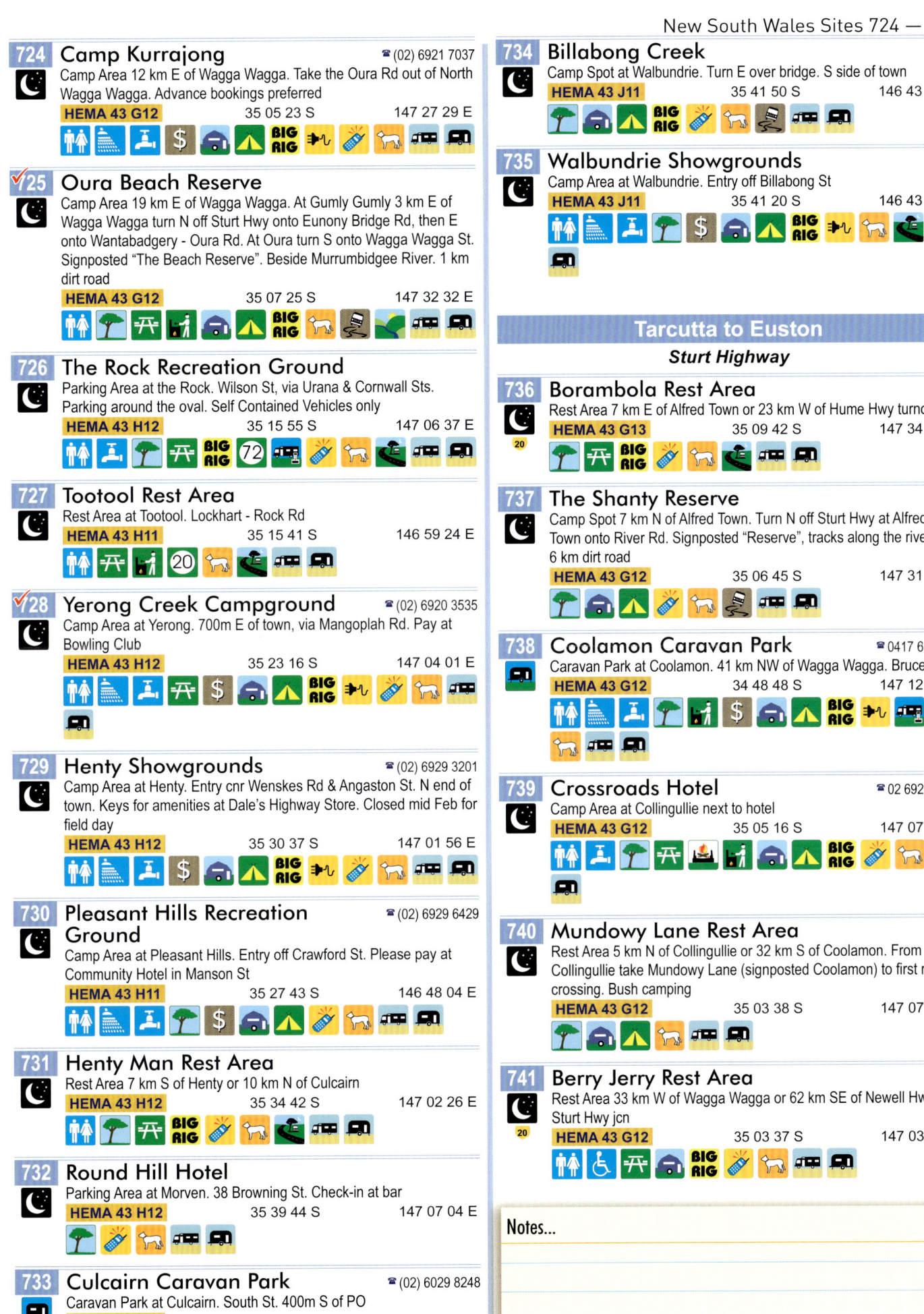

724 Camp Kurrajong ☎ (02) 6921 7037
Camp Area 12 km E of Wagga Wagga. Take the Oura Rd out of North Wagga Wagga. Advance bookings preferred
HEMA 43 G12 — 35 05 23 S — 147 27 29 E

725 Oura Beach Reserve
Camp Area 19 km E of Wagga Wagga. At Gumly Gumly 3 km E of Wagga Wagga turn N off Sturt Hwy onto Eunony Bridge Rd, then E onto Wantabadgery - Oura Rd. At Oura turn S onto Wagga Wagga St. Signposted "The Beach Reserve". Beside Murrumbidgee River. 1 km dirt road
HEMA 43 G12 — 35 07 25 S — 147 32 32 E

726 The Rock Recreation Ground
Parking Area at the Rock. Wilson St, via Urana & Cornwall Sts. Parking around the oval. Self Contained Vehicles only
HEMA 43 H12 — 35 15 55 S — 147 06 37 E

727 Tootool Rest Area
Rest Area at Tootool. Lockhart - Rock Rd
HEMA 43 H11 — 35 15 41 S — 146 59 24 E

728 Yerong Creek Campground ☎ (02) 6920 3535
Camp Area at Yerong. 700m E of town, via Mangoplah Rd. Pay at Bowling Club
HEMA 43 H12 — 35 23 16 S — 147 04 01 E

729 Henty Showgrounds ☎ (02) 6929 3201
Camp Area at Henty. Entry cnr Wenskes Rd & Angaston St. N end of town. Keys for amenities at Dale's Highway Store. Closed mid Feb for field day
HEMA 43 H12 — 35 30 37 S — 147 01 56 E

730 Pleasant Hills Recreation Ground ☎ (02) 6929 6429
Camp Area at Pleasant Hills. Entry off Crawford St. Please pay at Community Hotel in Manson St
HEMA 43 H11 — 35 27 43 S — 146 48 04 E

731 Henty Man Rest Area
Rest Area 7 km S of Henty or 10 km N of Culcairn
HEMA 43 H12 — 35 34 42 S — 147 02 26 E

732 Round Hill Hotel
Parking Area at Morven. 38 Browning St. Check-in at bar
HEMA 43 H12 — 35 39 44 S — 147 07 04 E

733 Culcairn Caravan Park ☎ (02) 6029 8248
Caravan Park at Culcairn. South St. 400m S of PO
HEMA 43 J12 — 35 40 13 S — 147 02 11 E

734 Billabong Creek
Camp Spot at Walbundrie. Turn E over bridge. S side of town
HEMA 43 J11 — 35 41 50 S — 146 43 34 E

735 Walbundrie Showgrounds
Camp Area at Walbundrie. Entry off Billabong St
HEMA 43 J11 — 35 41 20 S — 146 43 12 E

Tarcutta to Euston
Sturt Highway

736 Borambola Rest Area
Rest Area 7 km E of Alfred Town or 23 km W of Hume Hwy turnoff
HEMA 43 G13 — 35 09 42 S — 147 34 54 E

737 The Shanty Reserve
Camp Spot 7 km N of Alfred Town. Turn N off Sturt Hwy at Alfred Town onto River Rd. Signposted "Reserve", tracks along the river. 6 km dirt road
HEMA 43 G12 — 35 06 45 S — 147 31 15 E

738 Coolamon Caravan Park ☎ 0417 610 946
Caravan Park at Coolamon. 41 km NW of Wagga Wagga. Bruce St
HEMA 43 G12 — 34 48 48 S — 147 12 09 E

739 Crossroads Hotel ☎ 02 6920 0166
Camp Area at Collingullie next to hotel
HEMA 43 G12 — 35 05 16 S — 147 07 30 E

740 Mundowy Lane Rest Area
Rest Area 5 km N of Collingullie or 32 km S of Coolamon. From Collingullie take Mundowy Lane (signposted Coolamon) to first river crossing. Bush camping
HEMA 43 G12 — 35 03 38 S — 147 07 18 E

741 Berry Jerry Rest Area
Rest Area 33 km W of Wagga Wagga or 62 km SE of Newell Hwy/ Sturt Hwy jcn
HEMA 43 G12 — 35 03 37 S — 147 03 12 E

Notes...

742 Pipers Reserve

Camp Spot 57 km W of Wagga Wagga or 46 km SE of Newell Hwy/ Sturt Hwy jcn. 10 km N of Galore, turn N onto Weir Rd, then turn R at Riverside Reserve sign. Beside Murrumbidgee River. Dirt road

HEMA 43 G11   34 55 15 S   146 51 39 E

743 Lockhart Caravan Park   ☎ 0458 205 303

Caravan Park at Lockhart. Green St. 300m W of PO

HEMA 43 H11   35 13 13 S   146 42 46 E

744 Lockhart Showgrounds   ☎ 0429 205 288

Parking Area at Lockhart, entry off Treasure St. Self Contained Vehicles Only. Leave fee at lockhart VIC

HEMA 43 H11   35 13 40 S   146 42 36 E

745 Sandigo Rest Area

Rest Area 74 km W of Wagga Wagga or 21 km SE of Newell Hwy/ Sturt Hwy jcn

HEMA 43 G11   34 55 17 S   146 38 54 E

746 Five Mile Reserve

Camp Spot 9 km E of Narrandera, on Old Wagga Rd, via Bolton St & Victoria Ave. N bank of Bundidgerry Creek

HEMA 43 G11   34 45 47 S   146 38 17 E

747 Narrandera Showground   ☎ 0407 105 846

Camp Spot at Narrandera. Elizabeth St. 3 km E of PO. See caretaker

HEMA 43 G11   34 44 57 S   146 33 52 E

748 Narrandera Town Beach

Camp Spot in Narrandera. Enter via Larmer & Hankinson Sts, cross old railway line, turn L onto track to river. Self Contained Vehicles only

HEMA 43 G11   34 45 25 S   146 32 07 E

749 Brewery Flat Reserve

Camp Spot 1 km S of Narrandera on Newell Hwy, turn into Old Brewery Rd. Adjacent sports oval. Self Contained Vehicles only

HEMA 43 G11   34 45 15 S   146 33 00 E

750 Sandy Beach Camp
Murrumbidgee Valley National Park   ☎ (02) 6966 8107

Camp Spot 16 km NW of Narrandera, turn S from Irrigation Way at MIA-Rifle Club sign, follow dirt road & No 2 State Forest green post signs to N bank of Murrumbidgee River

HEMA 43 F11   34 43 16 S   146 27 47 E

751 Markeys Beach Camp
Murrumbidgee Valley National Park   ☎ (02) 6966 8107

Camp Spot 18 km NW of Narrandera. Turn S off Irrigation Way 12 km NW of Narrandera or 7 km SE of Yanco for 6 km to N bank of Murrumbidgee River. Not suitable caravans

HEMA 43 F11   34 42 59 S   146 26 45 E

752 Long Beach Camp
Murrumbidgee Valley National Park   ☎ (02) 6966 8107

Camp Spot 8 km SE of Yanco. Turn S off Irrigation Way 13.5 km NW of Narrandera or 4.5 km SE of Yanco at MIA sign for 1.5 km, then along Long Beach Comeback Track for 1.5 km to N bank of Murrumbidgee River. Not suitable for caravans

HEMA 43 F10   34 39 01 S   146 22 44 E

753 Leeton Showground   ☎ (02) 6953 6481

Camp Area at Leeton. Racecourse Rd. Self Contained Vehicles only

HEMA 43 F10   34 33 49 S   146 23 58 E

754 Oasis Caravan Park   ☎ (02) 6953 3882

Caravan Park at Leeton. Corbie Hill Rd, off Yanco Ave. 2 km S of PO

HEMA 43 F10   34 33 52 S   146 25 22 E

755 Whitton Beach Camp
Murrumbidgee Valley National Park   ☎ (02) 6966 8107

Camp Spot 22 km W of Yanco, via River Rd & Forest Dr. N bank of Murrumbidgee River. Follow No 2 green sign post. Not suitable for caravans

HEMA 43 F10   34 36 59 S   146 11 01 E

756 Middle Beach Camp
Murrumbidgee Valley National Park   ☎ (02) 6966 8107

Camp Spot 6 km SW of Yanco. Turn W 1 km S of Yanco onto Euroley Rd for 4.5 km, then W for 500m at MIA sign. N bank of Murrumbidgee River. GPS at entry

HEMA 43 F10   34 38 07 S   146 22 32 E

757 Euroley Bridge Reserve   ☎ (02) 6841 4288

Rest Area 9 km SW of Yanco, via Euroley Rd. N side of Murrumbidgee River

HEMA 43 F10   34 38 17 S   146 22 32 E

758 Gogeldrie Weir Park   ☎ (02) 6955 9267

Camp Area 22 km W of Leeton. Via Irrigation Way. Turn S onto Murrami Rd 12 km W of Leeton, W onto Whitton Rd, S onto Gogeldrie Rd then E into River Rd. Signposted. Limited powered sites

HEMA 43 F10   34 36 56 S   146 15 29 E

NEW SOUTH WALES

759 Boomerang Beach Camp ☎ (02) 6966 8107
Murrumbidgee Valley Regional Park
Camp Spot 4 km E of Darlington Point. Turn S off Whitton Rd 1.2 km E of PO for 3 km on Beach Rd to N bank of Murrumbidgee River. Follow No 1 green sign post. Not suitable for caravans
HEMA 43 F10   34 34 59 S   146 01 13 E

760 Horries Beach Camp ☎ (02) 6966 8107
Murrumbidgee Valley Regional Park
Camp Spot 4 km W of Darlington Point. Turn W off Kidman Way just N of bridge, opposite caravan park into Willbriggle State Forest, pass sawmill, follow No 1 green sign post for 4 km, then S at sign "Beach" for 200m to N bank of Murrumbidgee River. Not suitable for caravans
HEMA 43 F10   34 33 46 S   145 58 38 E

761 Swaggys Beach Camp ☎ (02) 6966 8107
Camp Spot 7 km W of Darlington Point. Turn W off Kidman Way just N of bridge, opposite caravan park into Willbriggle State Forest, past sawmill, follow No1 green sign post 7 km, then S to N bank of Murrumbidgee River. Not suitable for caravans
HEMA 43 F10   34 33 33 S   145 57 30 E

762 Cookoothama Reserve
Camp Spot 8 km W of Darlington Point. Turn W 3 km N of Darlington Point onto Murrumbidgee River Rd. N bank of Murrumbidgee River
HEMA 43 F10   34 32 47 S   145 56 49 E

763 Nobles Beach Camp ☎ (02) 6966 8107
Murrumbidgee Valley National Park
Camp Spot 15 km W of Darlington Point. Turn W 3 km N of Darlington Point onto Murrumbidgee River Rd. N bank of Murrumbidgee River
HEMA 43 F9   34 33 20 S   145 54 12 E

764 Common Beach
Camp Spot at Darlington Point. From W end of King St, cross grid, then immediate R to S bank of Murrumbidgee River. GPS at entry
HEMA 43 F10   34 33 57 S   145 59 32 E

765 Bunyip Hole Reserve
Camp Spot at Darlington Point. From W end of King St, cross grid, then 2nd track to R, then L at T jcn, then R to S bank of Murrumbidgee River. GPS at entry
HEMA 43 F10   34 33 57 S   145 59 32 E

766 Birdcage Reserve Rest Area
Rest Area 86 km W of Newell Hwy/Sturt Hwy jcn or 86 km E of Hay. Both sides of the road
HEMA 43 F9   34 31 27 S   145 42 08 E

767 Birdcage Reserve
Camp Spot 86 km W of Newell Hwy/Sturt Hwy jcn or 86 km E of Hay. Turn N at sign "Birdcage Reserve" for 400m to S bank of Murrumbidgee River. Dirt road
HEMA 43 F9   34 31 12 S   145 41 56 E

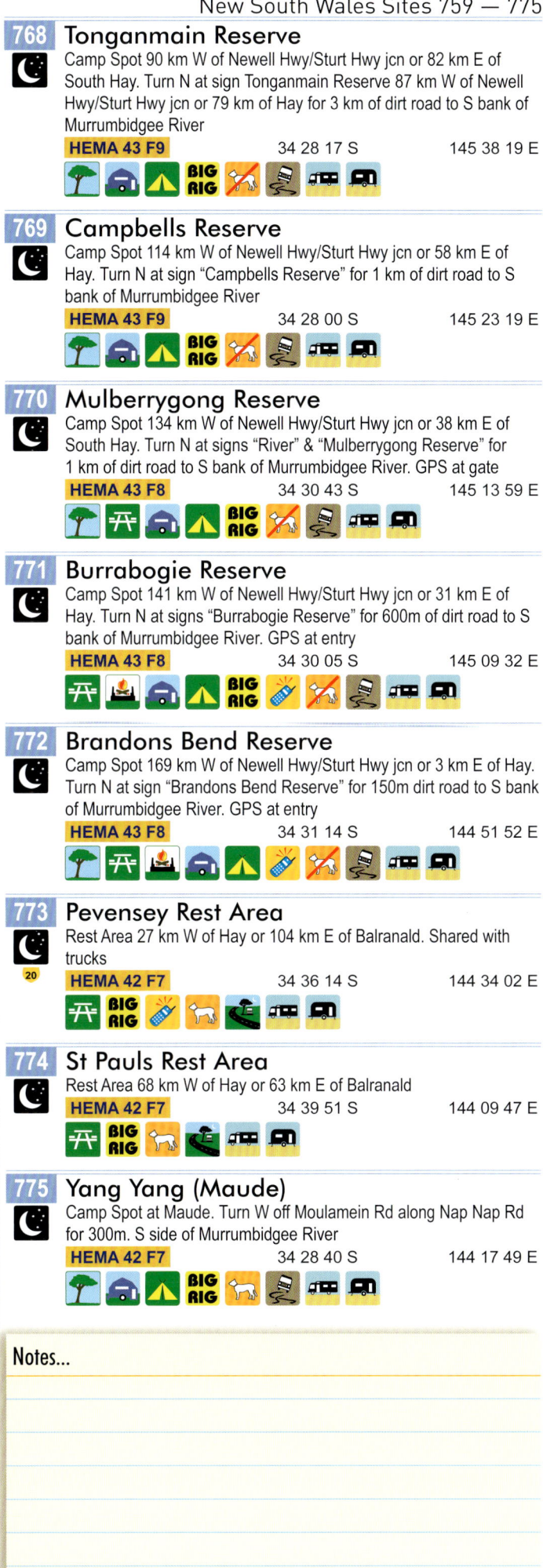

768 Tonganmain Reserve
Camp Spot 90 km W of Newell Hwy/Sturt Hwy jcn or 82 km E of South Hay. Turn N at sign Tonganmain Reserve 87 km W of Newell Hwy/Sturt Hwy jcn or 79 km of Hay for 3 km of dirt road to S bank of Murrumbidgee River
HEMA 43 F9   34 28 17 S   145 38 19 E

769 Campbells Reserve
Camp Spot 114 km W of Newell Hwy/Sturt Hwy jcn or 58 km E of Hay. Turn N at sign "Campbells Reserve" for 1 km of dirt road to S bank of Murrumbidgee River
HEMA 43 F9   34 28 00 S   145 23 19 E

770 Mulberrygong Reserve
Camp Spot 134 km W of Newell Hwy/Sturt Hwy jcn or 38 km E of South Hay. Turn N at signs "River" & "Mulberrygong Reserve" for 1 km of dirt road to S bank of Murrumbidgee River. GPS at gate
HEMA 43 F8   34 30 43 S   145 13 59 E

771 Burrabogie Reserve
Camp Spot 141 km W of Newell Hwy/Sturt Hwy jcn or 31 km E of Hay. Turn N at signs "Burrabogie Reserve" for 600m of dirt road to S bank of Murrumbidgee River. GPS at entry
HEMA 43 F8   34 30 05 S   145 09 32 E

772 Brandons Bend Reserve
Camp Spot 169 km W of Newell Hwy/Sturt Hwy jcn or 3 km E of Hay. Turn N at sign "Brandons Bend Reserve" for 150m dirt road to S bank of Murrumbidgee River. GPS at entry
HEMA 43 F8   34 31 14 S   144 51 52 E

773 Pevensey Rest Area
Rest Area 27 km W of Hay or 104 km E of Balranald. Shared with trucks
HEMA 42 F7   34 36 14 S   144 34 02 E

774 St Pauls Rest Area
Rest Area 68 km W of Hay or 63 km E of Balranald
HEMA 42 F7   34 39 51 S   144 09 47 E

775 Yang Yang (Maude)
Camp Spot at Maude. Turn W off Moulamein Rd along Nap Nap Rd for 300m. S side of Murrumbidgee River
HEMA 42 F7   34 28 40 S   144 17 49 E

Notes...

NEW SOUTH WALES

776 Maude Hotel & Caravan Park
☎ (02) 6993 6112
Caravan Park at Maude
HEMA 42 F7   34 28 25 S   144 18 07 E

777 Willowvale Rest Area
Rest Area 91 km W of Hay or 40 km E of Balranald. Share with trucks
HEMA 42 G6   34 43 23 S   143 55 41 E

778 The Willows Campground
☎ (03) 5020 1764
Yanga National Park
Camp Area in National Park. Turn S off Sturt Hwy 100 km W of Hay or 24 km E of Balranald onto Impimi Rd. Travel 1 km to park entrance, follow track 1.5 km to camping area. GPS at entrance
HEMA 42 G6   34 44 46 S   143 45 05 E

779 Yanga Rest Area
Rest Area 121 km W of Hay or 10 km E of Balranald
HEMA 42 G6   34 42 01 S   143 35 41 E

780 Swimming Pool Car Park
Parking Area in Balranald. Church St, next to blue towers. Self Contained Vehicles only
HEMA 42 F6   34 38 07 S   143 33 43 E

781 Balranald RV Stop
☎ (03) 5020 1599
Parking Area in Balranald behind the Discovery Centre. Entry from River St. Self Contained Vehicles only. Gold coin donation for showers
HEMA 42 F6   34 38 21 S   143 33 52 E

782 Lake Paika Station
☎ (03) 5020 1653
Camp Area 18 km N of Balranald. 1735 Ivanhoe Rd
HEMA 42 F5   34 29 28 S   143 35 16 E

783 Homebush Hotel Campground
☎ (03) 5020 6803
Camp Area at Penarie 28 km N of Balranald or 201 km S of Ivanhoe
HEMA 42 F6   34 24 27 S   143 36 47 E

784 Mamanga Campground
☎ (03) 5020 1764
Yanga national Park
Camp Area 9 km SW Balranald. Via Sturt Hwy & Windomal Rd. Signposted. GPS at entrance
HEMA 42 G6   34 40 40 S   143 31 13 E

785 Wakool River
Camp Spot 17 km NE of Tooleybuc or 36 km SW of Balranald, turn SE on the S side of Wakool River bridge, dirt road to tracks by river
HEMA 42 G6   34 56 47 S   143 28 41 E

786 Kyalite Pub
☎ (03) 5038 2221
Parking Area at Kyalite. Kyalite Rd. Check in at Pub
HEMA 42 G6   34 57 00 S   143 29 00 E

787 Meilman East Rest Area
Rest Area 59 km W of Balranald or 20 km E of Euston. Share with trucks
HEMA 42 F5   34 31 45 S   142 56 17 E

✓788 Lake Benanee
Rest Area 65 km W of Balranald or 15 km E of Euston. Lakefront. Cold shower. Donation requested
HEMA 42 F4   34 31 13 S   142 52 39 E

Goondiwindi to Tocumwal
Newell Highway

789 North Star Road Rest Area
Rest Area 40 km S of Goondiwindi or 84 km N of Moree
HEMA 38 B6   28 50 26 S   150 13 34 E

790 North Star Caravan Park
☎ 0458 530 265
Caravan Park at North Star
HEMA 38 B6   28 55 55 S   150 23 39 E

791 Kiga Bore Rest Area
Rest Area 69 km S of Goondiwindi or 55 km N of Moree. Combined truck stop. Both sides of road
HEMA 38 C5   29 02 18 S   150 03 11 E

792 Gil Gil Creek North Rest Area
Rest Area 83 km S of Goondiwindi or 41 km N of Moree. 2 km N of Gil Gil Creek
HEMA 38 C5   29 09 50 S   150 00 48 E

793 Boolooroo Rest Area
Rest Area 116 km S of Goondiwindi or 8 km N of Moree. Combined truck stop
HEMA 38 D5   29 25 12 S   149 54 15 E

794 Moree Showgrounds
☎ 0428 205 098
Camp Area at showgrounds. Entrance off River St, via Alice St & Warialda St. Caretaker on site. Closed show weeks April
HEMA 38 D5   29 28 07 S   149 50 53 E

NEW SOUTH WALES

795 Boomi Caravan Park & Artesian Spa ☎ (02) 6753 5336
Caravan Park at Boomi. Opposite Police Station, adjacent to artesian pools
HEMA 38 B4   28 43 30 S   149 34 43 E

796 Tookey Creek Rest Area
Rest Area 47 km S of Moree or 51 km N of Narrabri
HEMA 38 E5   29 52 28 S   149 47 19 E

797 Bellata Golf Club ☎ 0417 014 714
Camp Area at Bellata. 800m E off the Newell Hwy on Berrigal Rd. Self Contained Vehicles only. Gold coin donation at the bar
HEMA 38 E5   29 55 08 S   149 47 57 E

798 Edgeroi Rest Area ☎ (02) 6793 8375
Parking Area at Edgeroi. Next to fuel shop
HEMA 38 F5   30 06 48 S   149 47 56 E

799 Wee Waa Showgrounds ☎ 0428 506 363
Camp Area at Wee Waa. Entry off Maitland St. Caretaker will visit to collect fee
HEMA 38 F4   30 13 08 S   149 26 57 E

800 Cameron Park
Rest Area at Narrabri. 700m S of Info Centre. S bank of Narrabri Creek. Beside bridge
HEMA 38 F5   30 19 37 S   149 46 43 E

801 Narrabri Showground ☎ (02) 6792 3913
Camp Area at Narrabri. Entry on Wukuwa St. Turn off Newell Hwy onto Belar St at Eathers Creek Bridge. S of town
HEMA 38 F5   30 20 19 S   149 45 48 E

802 Bark Hut ☎ (02) 6792 7300
Mt Kaputar National Park
Camp Area 50 km E of Narrabri. Access steep & narrow in parts. Some sections of dirt road, but all steep sections are sealed. No caravans allowed in the park, motorhomes up to size of coaster allowed
HEMA 38 F5   30 17 25 S   150 08 35 E

803 Dawsons Spring ☎ (02) 6792 7300
Mt Kaputar National Park
Camp Area 56 km E of Narrabri. Some sections of unsealed road, but all steep sections are sealed. Access steep & narrow in parts. No caravans allowed in the park, motorhomes up to size of coaster allowed
HEMA 38 F5   30 16 51 S   150 09 47 E

804 Yarrie Lake ☎ 0427 666 105
Camp Area 27 km W of Narrabri. Turn W off Newell Hwy 3 km S of Narrabri onto Yarrie Lake Rd, towards Australia Telescope for 19 km then S for 7 km, turn R on Lake Circuit. 1 km dirt road
HEMA 38 G4   30 22 07 S   149 31 05 E

805 Bohena Creek Rest Area
Rest Area 16 km S of Narrabri or 103 km N of Coonabarabran. Share with trucks
HEMA 38 G4   30 26 12 S   149 40 42 E

806 Sir William Bridges Rest Area
Rest Area 25 km S of Narrabri or 95 km N of Coonabarabran
HEMA 38 G4   30 29 41 S   149 38 09 E

807 Schwagers Bore Picnic Area ☎ (02) 6843 1607
Picnic Area 61 km SW of Narrabri or 50 km NE of Baradine, turn SW onto Pilliga Forest Way 27 km SW of Narrabri. Dirt road
HEMA 38 G3   30 36 13 S   149 18 57 E

808 Salt Caves Picnic Area ☎ (02) 6843 4011
Pilliga National Park
Picnic Area 68 km SW of Narrabri or 37 km NE of Baradine, turn SW onto Pilliga Forest Way 27 km SW of Narrabri, then S onto County Line Rd. Dirt road
HEMA 38 H3   30 44 46 S   149 17 28 E

809 The Aloes Picnic Area ☎ (02) 6843 1607
Picnic Area 88 km SW of Narrabri or 23 km N of Baradine, via Pilliga Forest Way. Dirt road. Beside Etoo Creek
HEMA 38 H3   30 44 57 S   149 06 38 E

810 Anzac Park Primitive Campground ☎ (02) 6799 6760
Camp Spot at Gwabegar, Anzac Parade
HEMA 38 G3   30 36 30 S   148 58 15 E

811 Camp Cypress ☎ (02) 6843 1035
Camp Area at Baradine. 1 km W of PO at showground. Lachlan St
HEMA 38 H3   30 56 49 S   149 03 21 E

Notes...

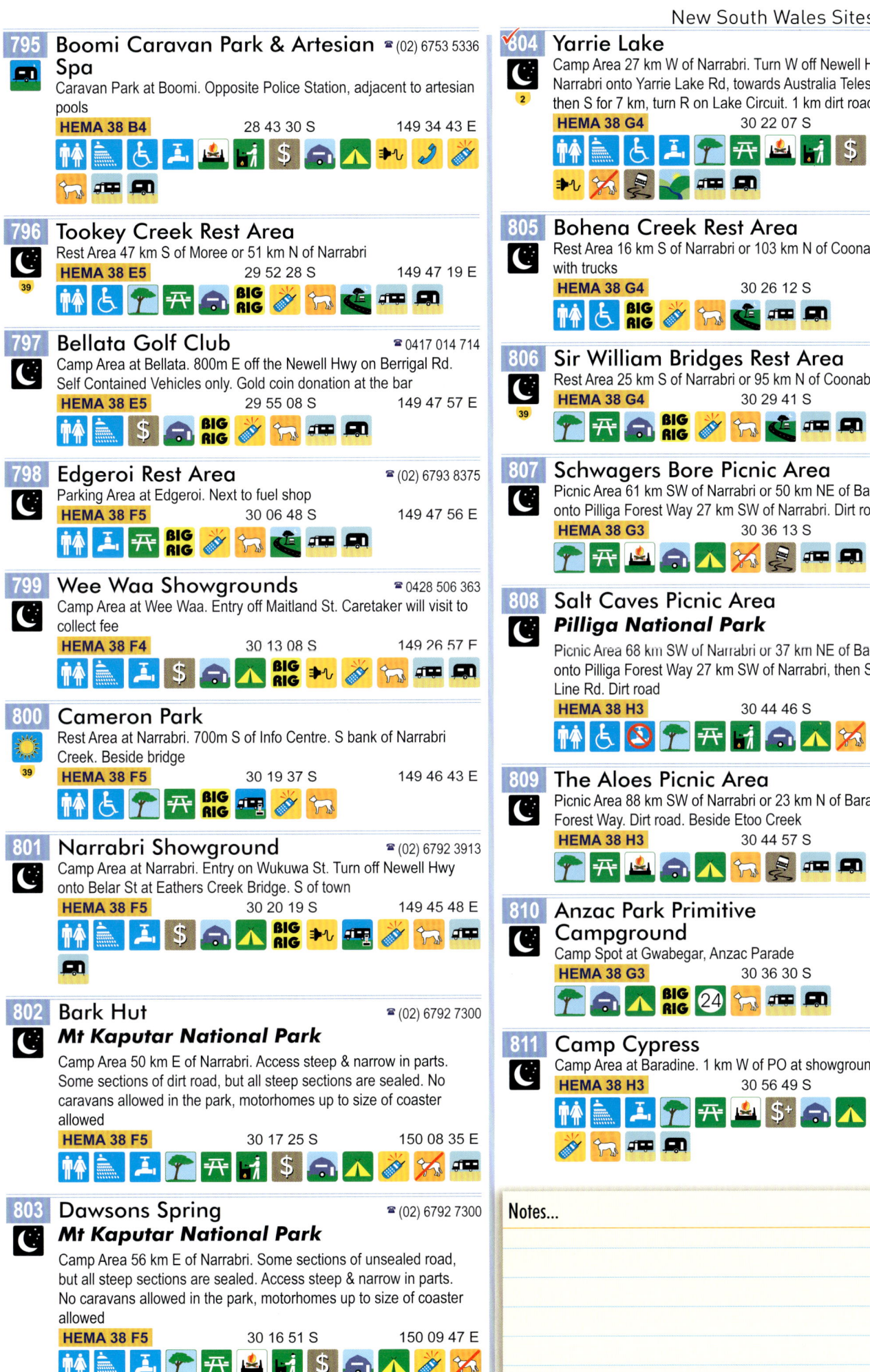

NEW SOUTH WALES

812 Baradine Sports & Recreation Oval
Parking Area at Baradine, Cnr of Darling & Queen Sts
HEMA 38 H3   30 57 01 S   149 03 57 E

813 Yarraman Rest Area
Rest Area 49 km S of Narrabri or 71 km N of Coonabarabran.
Northbound only, share with trucks
HEMA 38 G4   30 41 43 S   149 32 13 E

814 Pilliga Rest Area
Rest Area 52 km S of Narrabri or 68 km N of Coonabarabran
HEMA 38 G4   30 43 22 S   149 31 28 E

815 Yamminba Rest Area
Rest Area 68 km S of Narrabri or 52 km N of Coonabarabran
HEMA 38 H4   30 51 14 S   149 27 26 E

816 Sculptures in the Scrub
Campground & Picnic Area   ☎ (02) 6843 4011
Pilliga National Park
Camp Area 33 km E of Baradine. From Baradine, N on Indian Lane
for 9.5 km, E into No 1 Break Rd for 11 km, S into Top Crossing Rd
for 11 km, E at "Sculptures in the Scrub" sign for 1.5 km. 27 km dirt
road
HEMA 38 H3   30 59 46 S   149 14 03 E

817 Barkala Farmstay   ☎ (02) 6842 2239
Camp Area 34 km NW of Coonabarabran or 105 km SW of Narrabri
via Newwell Hwy. Turn W 23 km N of Coonabarabran into Borambitty
Rd, travel for approx 11 km. Signposted
HEMA 38 J3   31 02 42 S   149 19 04 E

818 Gowan Rest Area
Rest Area 111 km S of Narrabri or 9 km N of Coonabarabran. 2 km N
of Gowan Truck parking bay
HEMA 38 J3   31 13 05 S   149 19 34 E

819 Neilson Park
Rest Area at Coonabarabran. Essex St beside river
HEMA 38 J3   31 16 16 S   149 16 46 E

820 Camp Blackman Campground   ☎ (02) 6825 4364
Warrumbungle National Park
Camp Area 34 km W of Coonabarabran, via John Renshaw Parkway
HEMA 38 J3   31 16 43 S   148 59 30 E

821 Camp Wambelong   ☎ (02) 6825 4364
Warrumbungle National Park
Camp Area 35 km W of Coonabarabran. Large open area beside
creek
HEMA 38 J3   31 16 48 S   148 58 36 E

822 Hickeys Falls
Parking Area 39 km SW of Coonabarabran or 56 km NE of Gilgandra
HEMA 38 K3   31 25 49 S   149 04 01 E

823 Tooraweenah Caravan Park   ☎ (02) 6848 1133
Caravan Park at Tooraweenah. Cnr Bridge St & Aimee St
HEMA 38 J2   31 26 20 S   148 54 39 E

824 Tooraweenah Rest Area
Rest Area at Tooraweenah, 56 km SW of Coonabarabran or 39 km
NE of Gilgandra
HEMA 38 K2   31 28 08 S   148 55 14 E

825 Biddon Rest Area
Rest Area 72 km SW of Coonabarabran or 23 km NE of Gilgandra
HEMA 38 K2   31 33 50 S   148 47 41 E

826 Eumungerie Recreation Reserve   ☎ 0407 015 234
Camp Area 38 km N of Dubbo or 27 km S of Gilgandra. Turn E
off Hwy, 800m turn L just after railway crossing. 300m dirt road
to entrance gate. Report to PO during business hours or refer to
instructions on gate. Cold showers
HEMA 36 B4   31 56 51 S   148 37 20 E

827 Terramungamine Reserve
Camp Spot 3.5 km W of Brocklehurst. Turn W 57 km S of Gilgandra
or 10 km N of Dubbo, onto Burroway Rd. Beside river
HEMA 36 C4   32 10 04 S   148 35 16 E

828 Ballimore Hotel
Parking Area at Ballimore. Parking area opposite hotel. Toilets at
hotel during opening hours or in park next door after hours
HEMA 36 C5   32 11 45 S   148 53 53 E

829 Toongi Hall
Camp Spot located 26 km S of Dubbo. Turn S off Newell Hwy 4 km
SW of Dubbo PO onto Obley Rd. Donation
HEMA 36 C4   32 26 58 S   148 34 59 E

830 Red Earth Estate Vineyard ☎ (02) 6885 6676

Camp Spot 10 km S of Dubbo. 18 Camp Rd. Turn E onto Obley Rd (Western Plains Zoo signs) for 4.5 km, then W onto Camp Rd. 1.5 km to entrance. Self Contained Vehicles only. Purchase of wine expected. Limited sites, bookings required

HEMA 36 C4   32 17 38 S   148 34 56 E

831 Dubbo South Parking Area

Parking Area 15 km SW of Dubbo or 55 km NE of Peak Hill

HEMA 36 C4   32 19 48 S   148 30 29 E

832 Wanda Wandong Campground ☎ (02) 6332 7640

Goobang National Park

Camp Area 30 km SE of Tomingley via the Tomingley - Obley Rd, Gundong Rd

HEMA 36 D4   32 38 17 S   148 22 50 E

833 Tomingley North Rest Area

Rest Area 45 km SW of Dubbo or 25 km N of Peak Hill. Signposted only from the South

HEMA 36 D3   32 31 19 S   148 16 43 E

834 South Tomingley Rest Area

Rest Area 2 km S of Tomingley or 16 km N of Peak Hill

HEMA 36 D3   32 35 42 S   148 13 10 E

835 Lyndabale Rest Area

Rest Area 15 km S of Tomingley or 2 km N of Peak Hill

HEMA 36 D3   32 41 51 S   148 11 26 E

836 Peak Hill Caravan Park ☎ (02) 6869 1422

Caravan Park at Peak Hill. 2 Ween St. N end of town

HEMA 36 D3   32 43 17 S   148 11 27 E

837 Peak Hill Showgrounds ☎ 0429 661 382

Camp Area at Peak Hill, Coradgery Rd

HEMA 36 D3   32 43 42 S   148 10 33 E

838 Greenbah Campground ☎ (02) 6332 7640

Goobang National Park

Camp Area 24 km E of Trewilga. Via Peak-Hill Baldry Rd for 15 km, turn N onto Sawpit Gully firetrail for 5.5 km. Dirt road. Signposted

HEMA 36 D3   32 46 18 S   148 21 11 E

839 Kelly Reserve

Rest Area at Parkes. N end of town. Beside lake

HEMA 36 E3   33 07 28 S   148 10 23 E

840 Parkes Showground ☎ (02) 6862 2580

Camp Area at Parkes. Victoria St. Not available during show August or Elvis Festival 1-14 Jan

HEMA 36 E3   33 07 52 S   148 09 47 E

841 Trundle Showgrounds ☎ (02) 6892 1260

Camp Area at Trundle Showgrounds, Austral St. Must collect key & pay fee at True Value Hardware store. AH phone number 0447 821 098

HEMA 36 E2   32 55 33 S   147 42 06 E

842 Fifield Hotel ☎ (02) 6892 7276

Camp Spot at Fifield, behind hotel. See publican for parking area, limited space. Fee for showers

HEMA 36 D1   32 48 25 S   147 27 28 E

843 Tullamore Showground ☎ (02) 6892 5194

Camp Area at Tullamore. Cornet St, camping at end of road. Keys & registration at Tullamore Hotel

HEMA 36 D2   32 37 39 S   147 34 11 E

844 Forbes Lions Park

Rest Area at Forbes. Cnr of Lachlan St & Junction St. 500m S of PO, beside lake

HEMA 36 F3   33 23 22 S   148 00 14 E

845 Wheogo Park

Rest Area at Forbes. Cnr Junction St & Show St. Self Contained Vehicles only

HEMA 36 F3   33 23 16 S   148 00 05 E

846 Jemalong Weir

Picnic Area 24 km W of Forbes or 76 km E of Condobolin. On Lachlan Valley Way. Entry through gates

HEMA 36 F2   33 23 59 S   147 46 32 E

847 Bundaburrah Rest Area

Rest Area 31 km SW of Forbes or 71 km NE of Wyalong

HEMA 36 G2   33 31 20 S   147 44 00 E

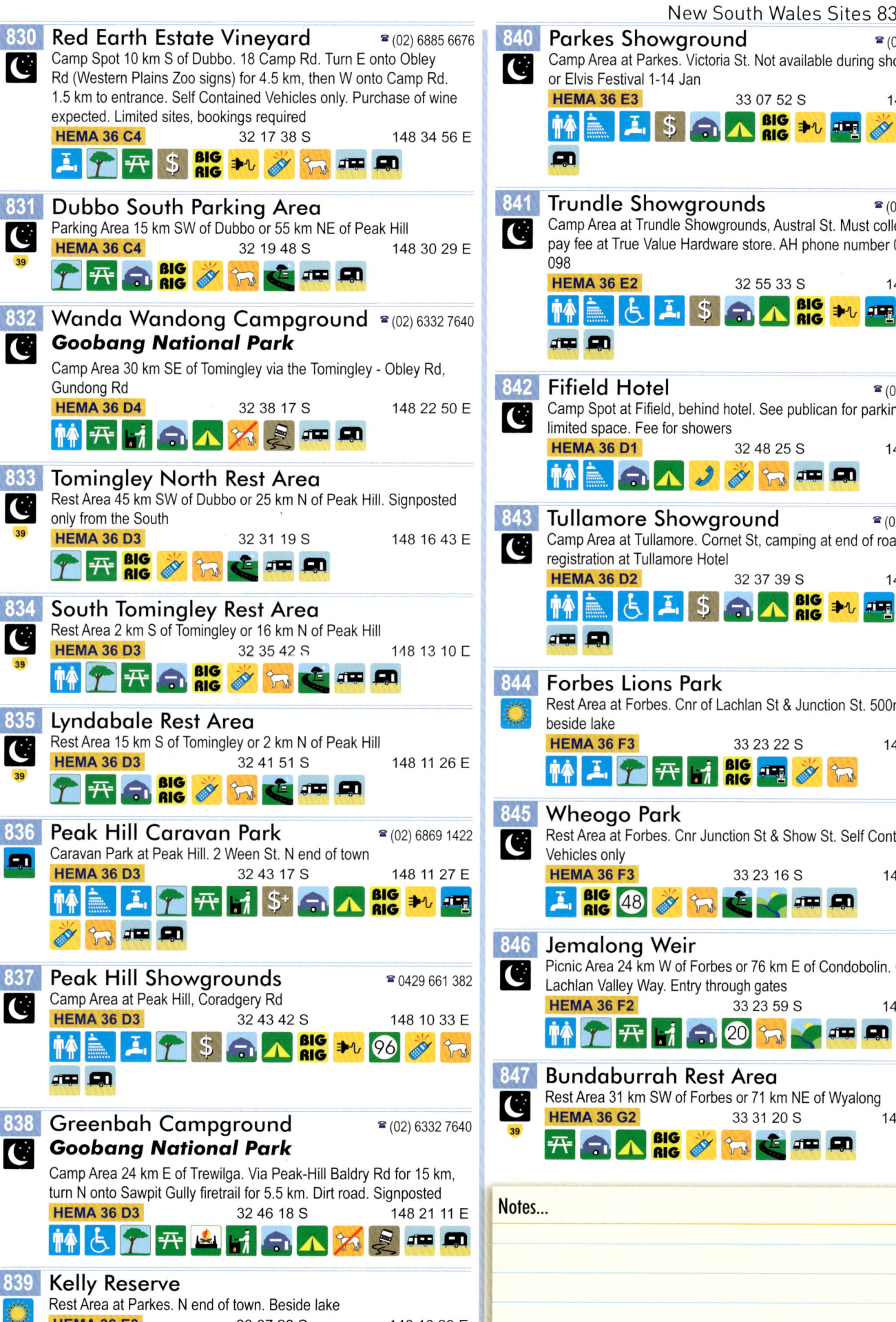

Notes...

NEW SOUTH WALES

848 Marsden Rest Area
Rest Area 67 km SW of Forbes or 35 km NE of Wyalong. 1 km S of Hwy 24 jcn, near Bland Creek
HEMA 36 G2　　　33 45 46 S　　　147 31 14 E

849 West Wyalong Showground
☎ 0428 518 329
Camp Area at West Wyalong. Entry by Duffs Rd only off the West Wyalong Bypass Rd
HEMA 43 E12　　　33 56 18 S　　　147 12 50 E

850 Barmedman Mineral Pool
Camp Spot at Barmedman. Cnr Nobbys Rd & Goldfield Way. Grassed area each side of the pool. Donation welcome. Pool is seasonal
HEMA 43 F12　　　34 08 19 S　　　147 23 10 E

851 Barmedman Recreation Ground
Camp Area at Barmedman. Cnr DeBoors St & Star St. Check notice board for fee payment & contact number or call at hotel
HEMA 43 F12　　　34 08 34 S　　　147 23 16 E

852 Temora Caravan Park
☎ 0418 780 251
Caravan Park at Temora. Junee Rd
HEMA 43 F12　　　34 27 22 S　　　147 32 05 E

853 Temora Showground
☎ 0427 280 339
Camp Area at Temora. Entry via Mimosa St. Caretaker collects fees
HEMA 43 F12　　　34 26 23 S　　　147 31 17 E

854 Temora Free Camp
Parking Area at Temora. Off Parkes St, adjacent to Railway Station. Self Contained Vehicles only. Donation welcome for upkeep
HEMA 43 F12　　　34 26 43 S　　　147 31 42 E

855 Ariah Park Camping Ground
☎ 0458 184 033
Camp Area at Ariah Park. 33 km E of Ardlethan or 39 km W of Temora. 1 km N of Hwy. Coin operated power points
HEMA 43 F12　　　34 21 08 S　　　147 13 09 E

856 Royal Hotel
Camp Area at Mirrool opposite Hotel. 300m W of Hwy. Donation box at toilets
HEMA 43 F12　　　34 18 26 S　　　147 05 19 E

857 Beckom Rest Area
Rest Area 5 km E of Beckom, 52 km S of West Wyalong or 16 km E of Ardlethan
HEMA 43 F11　　　34 20 09 S　　　147 00 53 E

858 Beckom RV Stop
Parking Area in Beckom, opposite Hotel, next to old bowling club
HEMA 43 F11　　　34 19 30 S　　　146 57 41 E

859 Ardlethan Community Park
Rest Area at Ardlethan. On main street, next to bowling club. Power available for a fee. Self Contained Vehicles only
HEMA 43 F11　　　34 21 28 S　　　146 54 09 E

860 Ardlethan Rest Area
Rest Area 14 km S of Ardlethan or 55 km NE of Narrandera
HEMA 43 F11　　　34 26 50 S　　　146 50 20 E

861 Firetail Rest Area
Rest Area 42 km S of Ardlethan or 5 km N of Grong Grong. Share with trucks
HEMA 43 F11　　　34 41 36 S　　　146 47 12 E

862 Grong Grong Park
Rest Area at Grong Grong. Parking adjacent, on roadside. Ask at store, donation welcomed for upkeep
HEMA 43 F11　　　34 44 19 S　　　146 46 59 E

863 Grong Grong Royal Hotel
☎ (02) 6956 2117
Parking Area at Grong Grong, rear of hotel. Check with publican for parking, big rigs check first
HEMA 43 F11　　　34 44 24 S　　　146 46 58 E

864 Berembed Weir
Camp Spot 19 km S of Grong Grong, via Old Narrandera Rd & signposted track, GPS at entry gate. Follow road across weir to campspots. Toilets at picnic area. Beside Murrumbidgee River. 12 km dirt road
HEMA 43 G11　　　34 50 18 S　　　146 50 36 E

865 Gillenbah Rest Area
Rest Area 10 km SW of Narrandera or 100 km NE of Jerilderie. Share with trucks
HEMA 43 G11　　　34 48 54 S　　　146 28 42 E

866 Colombo Creek
Camp Spot 1 km S of Morundah, off The Yamma Rd (Coleambally Rd). Limited space, small vehicles only. Beside creek
HEMA 43 G10　　　34 56 11 S　　　146 17 40 E

867 Widgiewa Rest Area
Rest Area 51 km SW of Narrandera or 59 km NE of Jerilderie
HEMA 43 G10   35 03 21 S   146 10 45 E

868 Bundure Rest Area
Rest Area 71 km SW of Narrandera or 39 km NE of Jerilderie. Share with trucks
HEMA 43 G10   35 09 01 S   146 00 36 E

869 Urana Caravan Park & Aquatic Centre   ☎ (02) 6920 8192
Caravan Park at Urana. Corowa Rd. 1 km S of PO. Beside lake
HEMA 43 H10   35 20 18 S   146 16 23 E

870 Conargo
Parking Area at Conargo. Parking bays adjacent to the tennis courts
HEMA 43 H8   35 18 18 S   145 10 53 E

871 Bills Park   ☎ (03) 5880 1200
Rest Area at Conargo. W end of town, near school
HEMA 43 H8   35 18 24 S   145 10 38 E

872 Jerilderie South Rest Area
Rest Area 8 km S of Jerilderie or 28 km N of Finley
HEMA 43 H9   35 25 01 S   145 41 28 E

873 Daysdale Recreation Reserve
Camp Area at Daysdale. 1 km N of Daysdale Hotel on Federation Way. Donation requested
HEMA 43 H10   35 38 07 S   146 18 17 E

874 Tongaboo Rest Area
Rest Area 27 km S of Jerilderie or 9 km N of Finley
HEMA 43 H9   35 34 24 S   145 36 56 E

875 Finley Lakeside Caravan Park   ☎ (03) 5883 1170
Caravan Park at Finley. Newell Hwy. 2 km N of PO
HEMA 43 H9   35 38 03 S   145 34 49 E

Notes...

876 Finley RV Stop
Parking Area at Finley. Endeavour St by old railway station. Self Contained Vehicles only
HEMA 43 J9   35 38 41 S   145 34 37 E

877 Berrigan Caravan Park   ☎ 0400 563 979
Caravan Park at Berrigan. Jerilderie St. 1 km S of PO
HEMA 43 J9   35 39 37 S   145 48 49 E

878 Town Beach   ☎ (03) 5874 2517
Camp Area at Tocumwal. From Tocumwal - Corawa Rd turn W onto Hennessy St then S on Town Beach Rd. 700m dirt road. Cold showers. Caretaker on site. Maximum stay 6 weeks. Beside river
HEMA 43 J9   35 49 06 S   145 33 43 E

Hebel to Gilgandra
Castlereagh Highway

879 Bore Baths - Lightning Ridge
Rest Area at Lightning Ridge. Cnr Opal St & Pandora St. Hot bore baths
HEMA 41 B13   29 25 22 S   147 59 52 E

880 Crocodile Caravan Park   ☎ (02) 6829 0437
Caravan Park at Lightning Ridge. Morilla St. 500m W of PO
HEMA 41 B13   29 25 45 S   147 58 30 E

881 Lightning Ridge Tourist Park   ☎ (02) 6829 0532
Caravan Park at Lightning Ridge. Harlequin St. 200m SE of PO
HEMA 41 B13   29 25 42 S   147 58 54 E

882 Lorne Holiday Station   ☎ (02) 6829 0253
Camp Area at Lorne Station. 5 km S of Lightning Ridge. Turn off 3 km S on Opal St - Lorne Rd. Mobile 0418 211 024
HEMA 41 B13   29 27 46 S   147 58 34 E

883 The Sheepyard Inn   ☎ (02) 6829 3932
Camp Area at Grawin. Approx 73 km W of Lightning Ridge via Cumborah & Walgett Goodooga Rd. Self Contained Vehicles only
HEMA 41 C13   29 41 20 S   147 37 41 E

884 Glengarry Hilton   ☎ (02) 6829 3983
Camp Area 75 km W of Lightning Ridge via Cumborah & Walgett Goodooga Rd
HEMA 41 C13   29 40 11 S   147 36 56 E

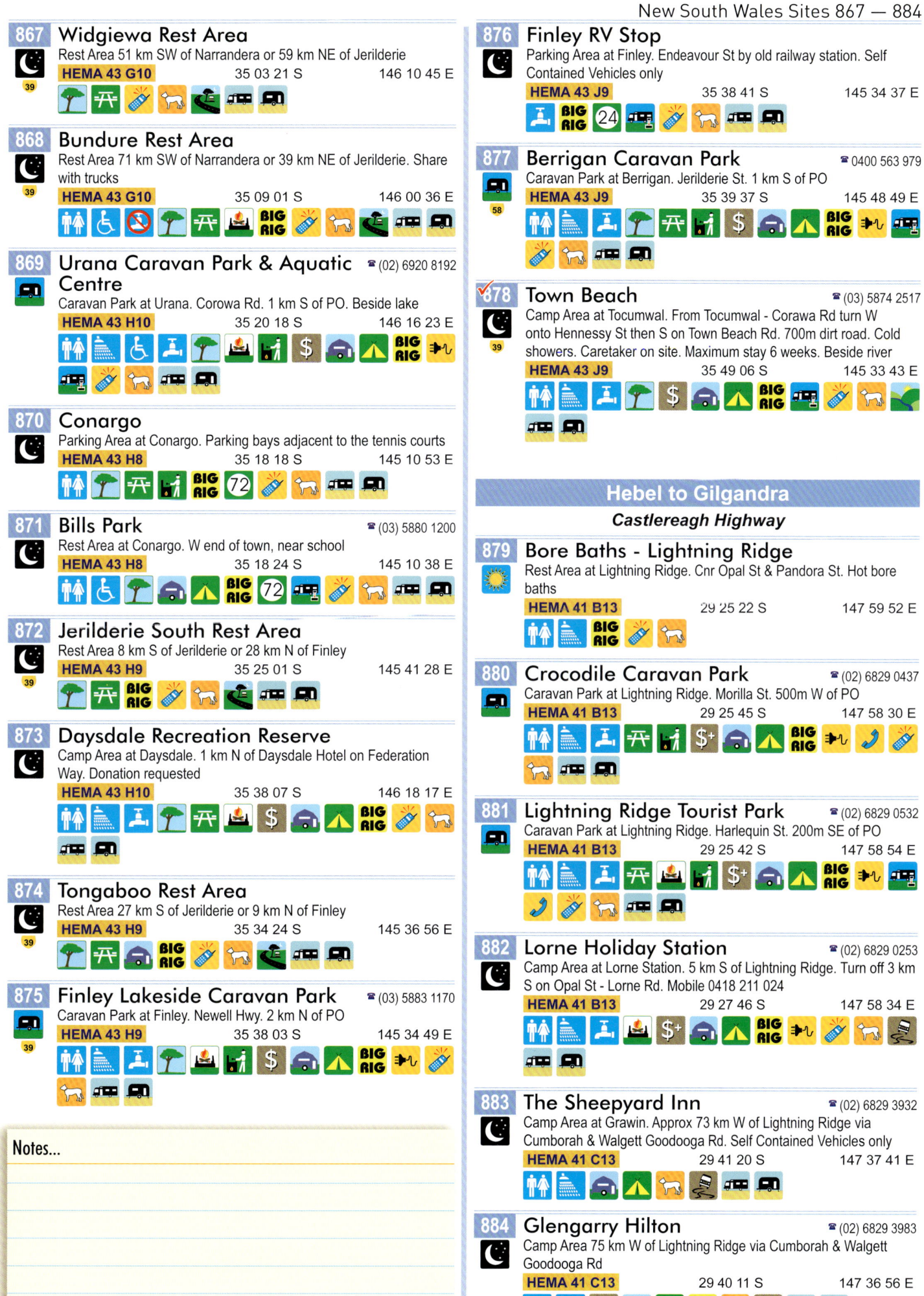

NEW SOUTH WALES

885 Wingadee Rest Area
Rest Area 53 km S of Walgett or 62 km N of Coonamble. 4 km S of Combogolong
55
| HEMA 38 G1 | 30 28 05 S | 148 11 40 E |

886 Nakadoo
☎ 0428 221 861
Camp Area 4 km N of Coonamble, Castleregh Hwy.
| HEMA 38 H1 | 30 55 41 S | 148 22 28 E |

887 Coonamble Showground
☎ 0427 408 183
Camp Area at Coonamble. Castlereagh Hwy. Gold coin donation. Closed during community events June & October
| HEMA 38 H1 | 30 57 58 S | 148 23 17 E |

888 Back Combara
Parking Area at Coonamble. Back Combara Rd, adjacent to the sheep yard. Self Contained Vehicles only
| HEMA 38 H1 | 30 57 28 S | 148 22 40 E |

889 Warrena Weir
☎ (02) 6827 1923
Parking Area at Coonamble, Baradine Rd. Self Contained Vehicles only
| HEMA 38 H1 | 30 57 12 S | 148 23 55 E |

890 Quambone Primitive Camp Site
☎ (02) 6827 1923
Camp Area at Quambone. Mungie St near swimming pool & tennis courts. Keys for pool & courts at Quambone General Store, hours 0800 - 1900 hrs
| HEMA 41 E13 | 30 56 01 S | 147 52 16 E |

891 John Oxley Rest Area
Rest Area 32 km S of Coonamble or 13 km N of Gulargambone
| HEMA 38 J1 | 31 13 36 S | 148 27 25 E |

892 Gulargambone Rest Area
Rest Area 42 km S of Coonamble or 3 km N of Gulargambone
| HEMA 38 J1 | 31 18 20 S | 148 28 08 E |

893 Gulargambone Caravan Park
☎ (02) 6825 1666
Caravan Park at Gulargambone. Skulthorpe St
55
| HEMA 38 J1 | 31 19 51 S | 148 28 12 E |

894 Armatree Hotel
☎ (02) 6848 5805
Camp Area at Armatree. Cnr Myall & Yarran Sts. Check in with publican on arrival
| HEMA 38 J1 | 31 26 55 S | 148 29 01 E |

Bathurst to Broken Hill
Mitchell and Barrier Highways

895 The Rocks Rest Area
Rest Area 20 km W of Bathurst or 34 SE of Orange
32
| HEMA 36 F6 | 33 25 56 S | 149 22 48 E |

896 Macquarie Woods
☎ (02) 6331 2044
Vittoria State Forest
Camp Area 28 km W of Bathurst or 26 km SE of Orange. 2 km N of Hwy via Cashens Lane, Macquarie Woods Drive. Dirt road
| HEMA 36 F6 | 33 24 34 S | 149 18 44 E |

897 Shadforth Reserve
Rest Area 40 km NW of Bathurst or 4 km SE of Lucknow. Cnr of Mitchell Hwy & Millthorpe Rd
32
| HEMA 36 F5 | 33 22 31 S | 149 11 18 E |

898 Colour City Caravan Park
☎ (02) 6393 8980
Caravan Park at Orange. 203 Margaret St. Beside showground
| HEMA 36 F5 | 33 16 19 S | 149 06 33 E |

899 Orange Showgrounds
☎ (02) 6393 8980
Parking Area at Orange. Margaret St. Register at Colour City Caravan Park for allocated parking. Closed during April show
| HEMA 36 F5 | 33 16 19 S | 149 06 34 E |

900 Cudal Caravan Park
☎ (02) 6390 7100
Caravan Park at Cudal. Main St. 400m E of PO
| HEMA 36 F4 | 33 17 03 S | 148 44 39 E |

901 Manildra Showground
☎ 0428 697 685
Camp Area at Manildra. Entry off Orange St. Fees collected.
| HEMA 36 F4 | 33 10 38 S | 148 41 16 E |

902 Ophir Reserve
☎ 1800 069 466
Camp Area 26 km NE of Orange. At Ophir goldfields. Steep sections. Best entry from the S. Obtain permit from Orange Visitor Centre
| HEMA 36 F5 | 33 10 10 S | 149 14 21 E |

903 Gamboola Rest Area
Rest Area 17 km NW of Orange or 17 km SE of Molong
32
| HEMA 36 F5 | 33 09 44 S | 149 00 36 E |

904 Bell River Rest Area
Rest Area 22 km N of Molong or 41 km S of Wellington. E side of Hwy
32
| HEMA 36 E5 | 32 54 42 S | 148 53 27 E |

905 Two Mile Creek Rest Area
Rest Area 31 km N of Molong or 32 km S of Wellington. W side of Hwy
HEMA 36 E5   32 50 03 S   148 54 27 E

906 Cumnock Showgrounds   ☎ 0403 054 754
Camp Area at Cumnock, Baldry Rd. 21 km NW of Molong or 90 km SE of Dubbo. Key at General Store
HEMA 36 E4   32 55 43 S   148 44 46 E

907 Yeoval Showground   ☎ 0427 208 913
Camp Spot at Yeoval. 45 km NW of Molong or 40 km SW of Wellington. Warne St
HEMA 36 D4   32 44 37 S   148 38 42 E

908 Caves Turnoff Rest Area
Rest Area 56 km N of Molong or 9 km S of Wellington. Near Wellington Caves turnoff
HEMA 36 D5   32 37 23 S   148 56 51 E

909 Lake Burrendong Holiday Park   ☎ (02) 6846 7435
Caravan Park 7 km NE of Mumbil or 27 km SE of Wellington, via Burrendong Dam Rd
HEMA 36 D5   32 41 24 S   149 06 29 E

910 Mookerawa Waters Holiday Park   ☎ (02) 6846 8426
Caravan Park 11 km E of Stuart Town or 39 km SE of Wellington
HEMA 36 D5   32 45 58 S   149 09 27 E

911 Ponto Falls
Camp Area 19 km NW of Wellington. Turn W off Mitchell Hwy 10 km NW of Wellington or 11 km S of Geurie. 5 km dirt road. Beside river. Maximum stay 14 days
HEMA 36 C5   32 27 57 S   148 49 12 E

912 Geurie North Rest Area
Rest Area 2 km N of Geurie or 26 km SE of Dubbo
HEMA 36 C5   32 23 17 S   148 48 57 E

913 Rabbit Trap Hotel   ☎ (02) 6892 8201
Camp Area at Albert. 55 km SW of Trangie or 67 km N of Trundle. Cabins also available. Donation for use of showers, limited power available for a fee
HEMA 36 C2   32 21 25 S   147 30 29 E

914 The State Centre Caravan Park   ☎ (02) 6892 4126
Caravan Park at Tottenham. Tullamore Rd. AH 0428 924 126
HEMA 36 C1   32 14 44 S   147 21 50 E

915 Nyngan Leisure & Van Park   ☎ (02) 6832 2366
Caravan Park at Nyngan. S end of town, via Hospital Rd, Old Warren Rd
HEMA 41 G12   31 34 00 S   147 12 29 E

916 Mid-State Shearing Shed Car Park
Parking Area in Nyngan. Nymagee St. Toilets locked at night
HEMA 41 G12   31 33 44 S   147 11 49 E

917 Teamsters Rest Area
Rest Area at Nyngan. Self Contained Vehicles only. Limited space. Toilets nearby locked at night
HEMA 41 G12   31 33 43 S   147 11 40 E

918 Hermidale West Rest Area
Rest Area 1.5 km W of Hermidale
HEMA 41 G11   31 32 53 S   146 42 28 E

919 Florida Rest Area
Rest Area 82 km W of Nyngan or 50 km E of Cobar
HEMA 41 G10   31 31 56 S   146 21 05 E

920 Cornish (Cobar) Rest Area
Rest Area at Cobar. 500m S of Info Centre. Share with trucks, park on grass area behind toilet to keep away from truck parking area. Self Contained Vehicles only
HEMA 41 G9   31 29 57 S   145 50 41 E

921 Newey Reservoir
Parking Area at Cobar. Knight Drive
HEMA 41 G9   31 30 41 S   145 49 49 E

922 Louth Camp Spot
Camp Spot at Louth beside Darling River. Turn W, go over bridge, camping on S side of river. Showers at park opposite hotel for gold coin donation
HEMA 41 E8   30 32 07 S   145 06 45 E

Notes...

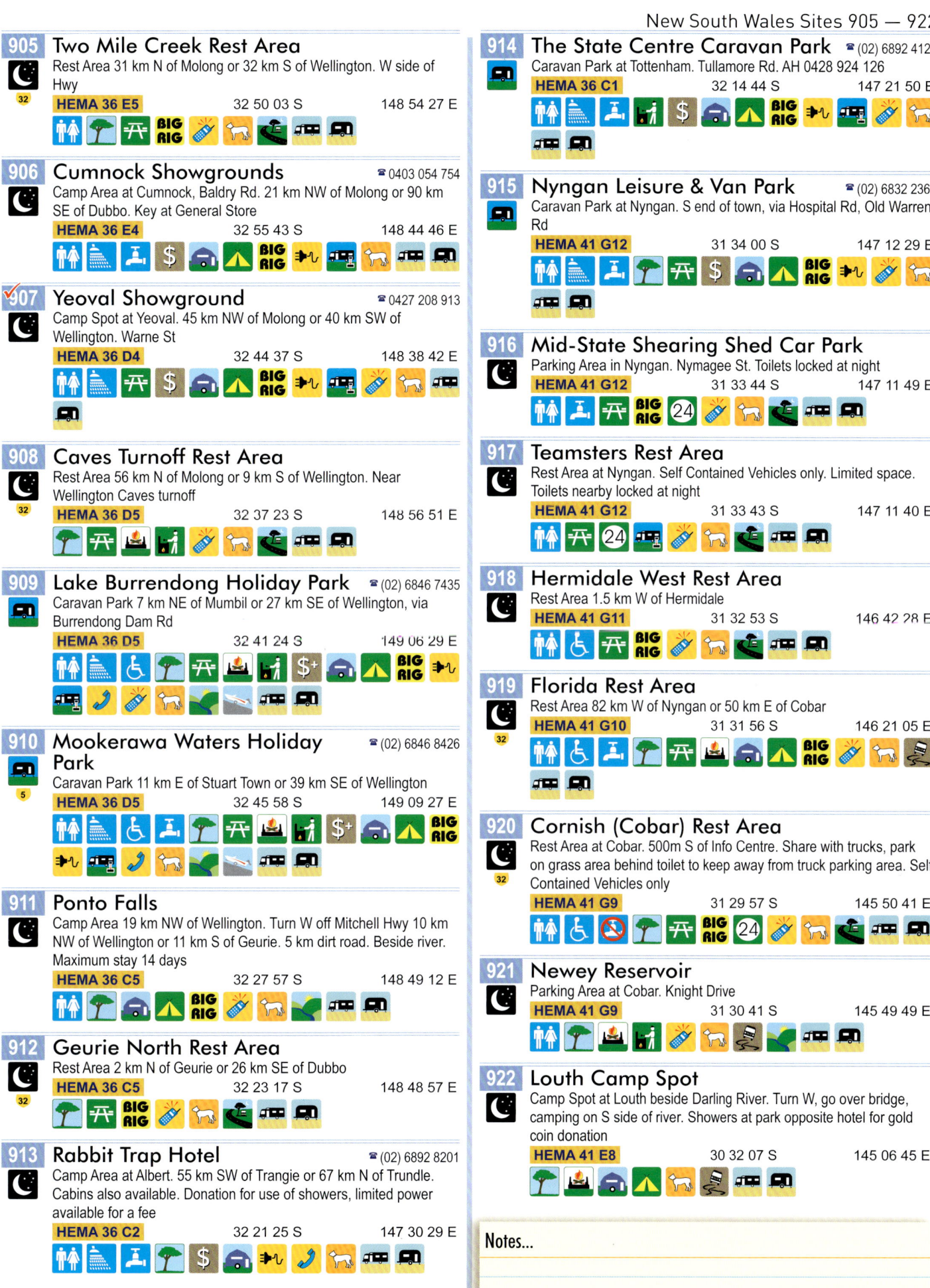

NEW SOUTH WALES

923 Shindy's Inn
☎ (02) 6874 7422
Camp Area at Louth. Bloxham St
HEMA 41 E8   30 32 07 S   145 06 56 E

924 Trilby Station
☎ (02) 6874 7420
Camp Area Trilby Station. 160 km NW of Cobar via Louth or 125 km SW of Bourke via Louth. Western side of the Louth to Tilba Rd. GPS at gate. Unpowered sites riverside
HEMA 41 E8   30 37 14 S   144 55 37 E

925 Idalia Outback River Stay
☎ (02) 6874 7401
Camp Area 43 km SW of Louth or 47 km NE of Tilpa on Western side of Bourke to Wilcannia Rd. 600m from turnoff to homestead office. Pets by prior arrangement
HEMA 41 E8   30 43 51 S   144 46 37 E

926 Kallara Station
☎ (02) 6837 3963
Camp Area at Kallara Station. 208 km NW of Cobar via Louth or 175 km SW of Bourke via Louth. Signed turn off 80 km SW of Louth or 10 km NE of Tilpa on the Western side of Tilpa - Louth Rd. 2 km from turn off to homestead office
HEMA 40 E7   30 53 27 S   144 30 55 E

✓ 927 Meadow Glen Rest Area
Rest Area 63 km W of Cobar or 196 km E of Wilcannia. Tracks off site
HEMA 41 G8   31 33 33 S   145 11 16 E

928 Bulla Park Rest Area
Rest Area 119 km W of Cobar or 140 km E of Wilcannia
HEMA 40 G7   31 33 30 S   144 37 35 E

929 Emmdale Roadhouse
☎ (02) 6837 3979
Parking Area 159 km W of Cobar or 100 km E of Wilcannia. Limited power available
HEMA 40 G7   31 39 11 S   144 16 06 E

930 Baden Park Rest Area
Rest Area 172 km W of Cobar or 89 km E of Wilcannia
HEMA 40 G6   31 42 50 S   144 08 34 E

931 MacCullochs Range Rest Area
Rest Area 204 km W of Cobar or 55 km E of Wilcannia
HEMA 40 G6   31 41 42 S   143 48 53 E

932 Caltigeena Rest Area
Rest Area 212 km W of Cobar or 48 km E of Wilcannia
HEMA 40 G6   31 41 43 S   143 44 23 E

933 Coach & Horses Campground
☎ (08) 8083 7900
Paroo - Darling National Park
Camp Area 52 km NE of Wilcannia or 282 km SW of Bourke on the Bourke - Wilcannia Rd. E side of Darling River
HEMA 40 G6   31 27 23 S   143 49 37 E

934 Warrawong on the Darling
☎ 0437 010 105
Camp Area 3 km S of Wilcannia. Barrier Hwy
HEMA 40 G5   31 34 03 S   143 23 39 E

935 Victory Park Caravan Park
☎ (08) 8091 5803
Caravan Park at Wilcannia. Pay at Council Chambers 0900-1500 M-F or contact carelaker, see notice board
HEMA 40 G5   31 33 36 S   143 22 52 E

936 Tilpa Weir
☎ (02) 6837 3928
Camp Spot 6 km NE of Tilpa on E side of Darling River. 139 km NE of Wilcannia or 186 km SW of Bourke
HEMA 40 F7   30 55 10 S   144 27 29 E

937 Wanaaring Store & Caravan Park
☎ (02) 6874 7720
Caravan Park at Wanaaring 192 km W Bourke or 234 km E Tibooburra
HEMA 40 C6   29 42 09 S   144 08 57 E

938 Wanaaring Town Common
Camp Spot at Wanaaring. 1.3 km E of town, S of Paroo River Bridge
HEMA 40 C6   29 41 51 S   144 09 31 E

939 Opal Pioneer Caravan & Camping Tourist Park
☎ (08) 8091 6688
Caravan Park at White Cliffs. Johnston St. 200m N of PO
HEMA 40 E5   30 50 58 S   143 05 23 E

940 Goodwood Station
☎ (08) 8091 6728
Camp Area 46 km NE of White Cliffs. Via Keraro Rd, turn N onto Wilcannia- Wanaaring Rd for 4 km, then L onto Glendara Rd. 9.7 km to mailbox
HEMA 40 E5   30 42 43 S   143 22 09 E

941 Netallie Rest Area
Rest Area 18 km W of Wilcannia or 176 km E of Broken Hill
HEMA 40 G5   31 34 07 S   143 13 00 E

942 Dolo Rest Area
Rest Area 60 km W of Wilcannia or 136 km E of Broken Hill
HEMA 40 G4   31 40 23 S   142 48 47 E

943 Spring Hill Rest Area
Rest Area 74 km W of Wilcannia or 122 km E of Broken Hill
HEMA 40 G4   31 43 23 S   142 41 09 E

944 Little Topar Roadhouse
Rest Area 128 km W of Wilcannia or 76 km E of Broken Hill
HEMA 40 H3   31 46 47 S   142 13 39 E

945 Broken Hill Racecourse
☎ 0437 250 286
Camp Area 5 km NE of Broken Hill, Racecourse Rd, off Tibooburra Rd. See caretaker before parking. Cash only
HEMA 40 H2   31 54 48 S   141 28 51 E

946 Eldee Station
☎ (08) 8091 2578
Camp Area at Eldee Station. 52 km NW of Broken Hill
HEMA 40 G1   31 40 10 S   141 15 33 E

947 Umberumberka Reservoir
Parking Area 36 km WNW of Broken Hill via Silverton
HEMA 40 H1   31 48 53 S   141 12 33 E

948 Penrose Park
☎ (08) 8088 5307
Camp Area at Silverton, 24 km NW of Broken Hill
HEMA 40 H1   31 52 57 S   141 13 55 E

949 Thackaringa Rest Area
Rest Area 36 km W of Broken Hill or 14 km E of Cockburn
HEMA 40 H1   32 02 44 S   141 07 39 E

Notes...

Barringun to Jerilderie
Kidman Way

950 Bush Tucker Inn
☎ (02) 6874 7584
Camp Area at Barringun. Check in at office. Mitchell Hwy
HEMA 41 A9   29 00 36 S   145 42 44 E

951 Oasis Hotel Enngonia
☎ (02) 6874 7577
Camp Area at Enngonia. Register & pay at the bar for access to secure parking
HEMA 41 B9   29 19 14 S   145 50 46 E

952 Enngonia South Rest Area
Rest Area 70 km S of Barringun or 66 km N of Bourke
HEMA 41 C9   29 35 10 S   145 50 32 E

953 Warrego Pub
☎ (02) 6874 7877
Camp Area at Fords Bridge 70 km NW of Burke or 145 km SE of Hungerford on Bourke - Hungerford Rd Check in with publican
HEMA 41 C9   29 45 09 S   145 25 30 E

954 Kinchela Rest Area
Rest Area 41 km S of Bourke or 120 km N of Cobar
HEMA 41 D10   30 27 27 S   145 56 07 E

955 Dry Tank Campground
☎ (02) 6830 0200
Gundabooka National Park
Camp Area 49 km S of Bourke or 111 km N of Cobar. Turn W onto Ben Lomond Rd for 18 km to campsites. Dirt road
HEMA 41 E9   30 31 04 S   145 42 53 E

956 Yanda Campground
☎ (02) 6830 0200
Gundabooka National Park
Camp Area 46 km S of Bourke or 114 km N of Cobar. Turn W off Louth Rd opposite Telstra tower, follow signs to campground. GPS at turn off
HEMA 41 E9   30 19 28 S   145 36 21 E

957 Curraweena Rest Area
Rest Area 61 km S of Bourke or 100 km N of Cobar
HEMA 41 E9   30 38 16 S   145 52 20 E

958 Four Corners Farm Stay
☎ 0438 683 626
Camp Area 8 km S of Nymagee township on Burthong Rd. Pets on application only. Limited powered sites
HEMA 41 H10   32 09 02 S   146 18 07 E

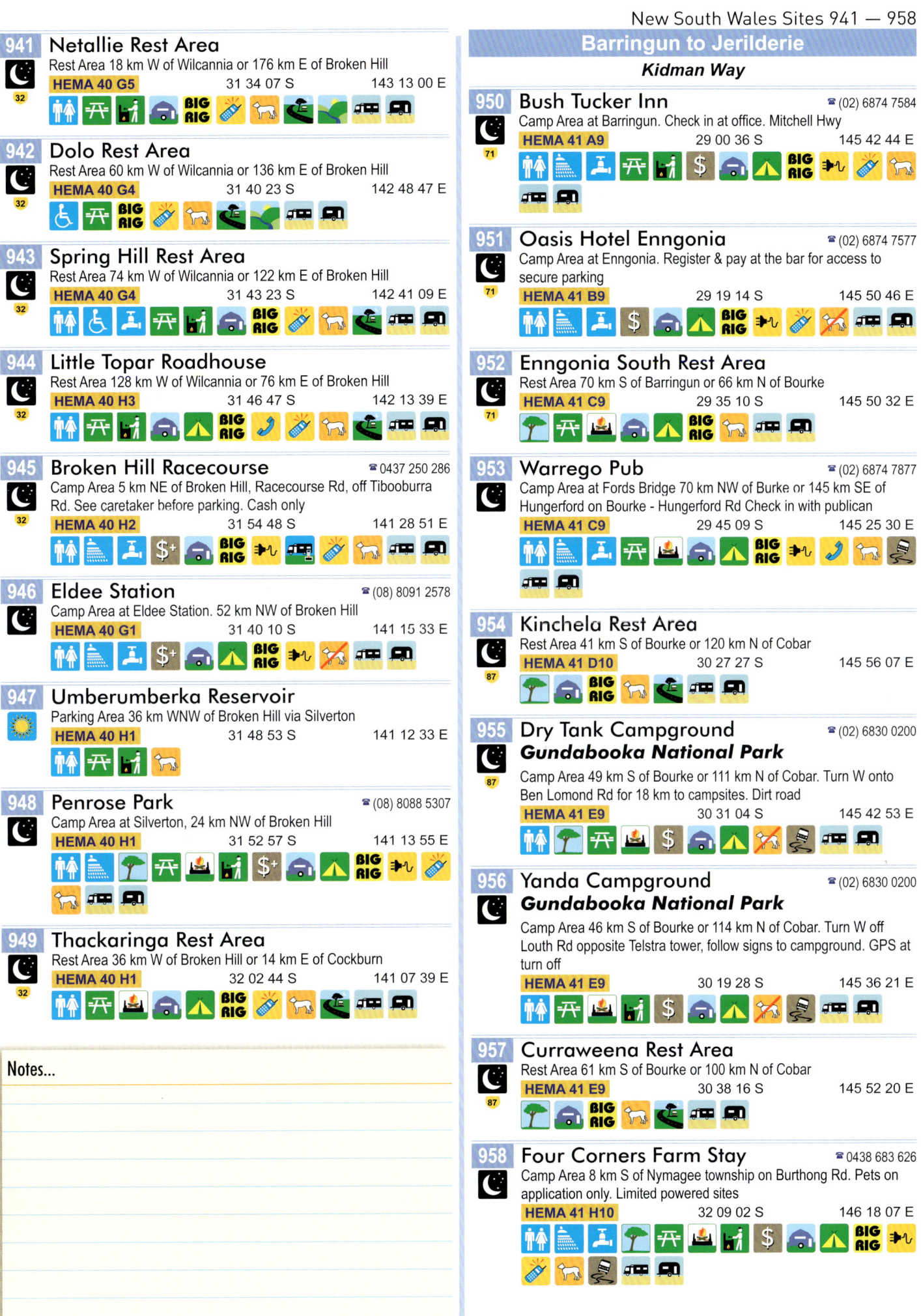

NEW SOUTH WALES

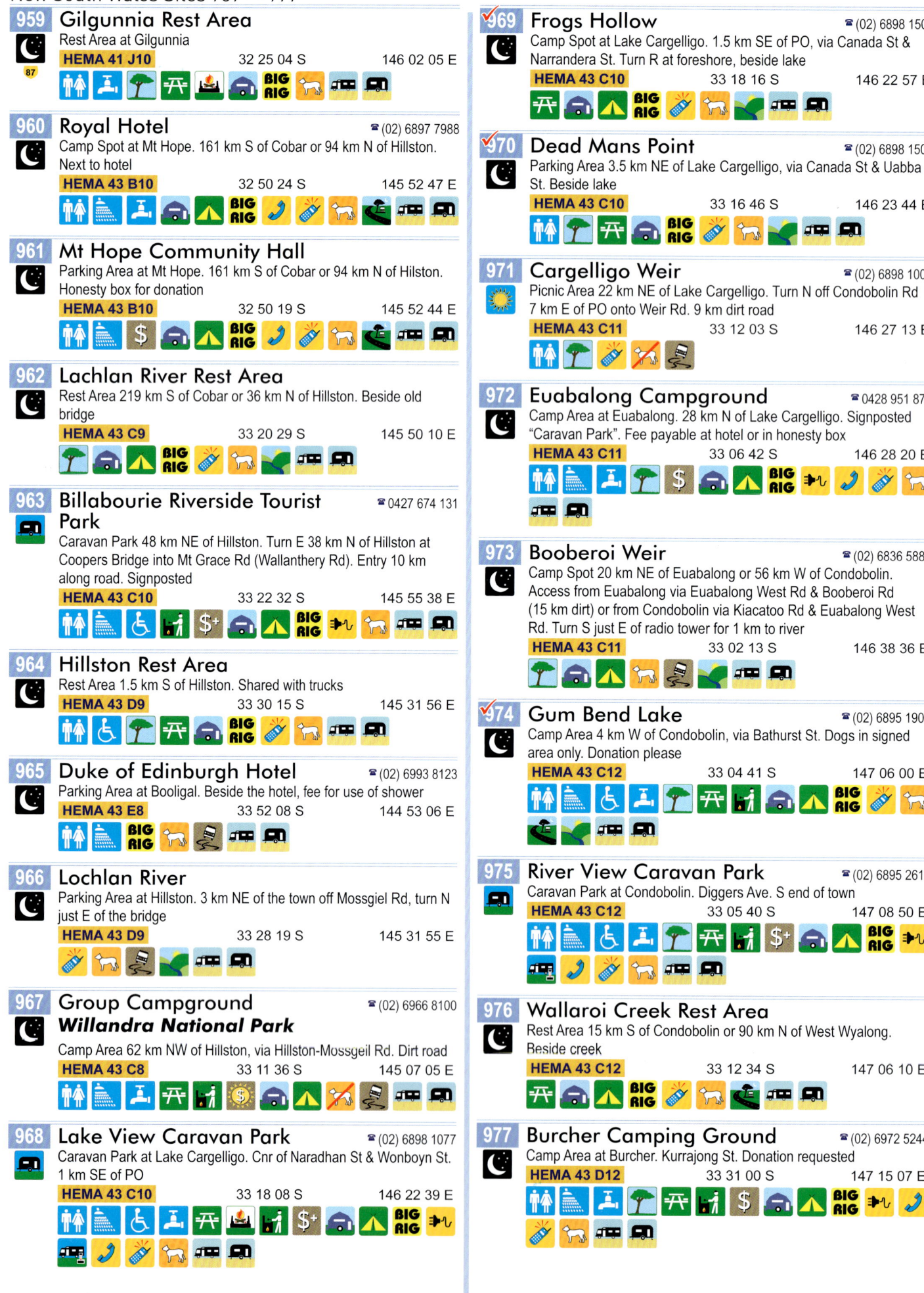

959 Gilgunnia Rest Area
Rest Area at Gilgunnia
HEMA 41 J10   32 25 04 S   146 02 05 E

960 Royal Hotel ☎ (02) 6897 7988
Camp Spot at Mt Hope. 161 km S of Cobar or 94 km N of Hillston. Next to hotel
HEMA 43 B10   32 50 24 S   145 52 47 E

961 Mt Hope Community Hall
Parking Area at Mt Hope. 161 km S of Cobar or 94 km N of Hilston. Honesty box for donation
HEMA 43 B10   32 50 19 S   145 52 44 E

962 Lachlan River Rest Area
Rest Area 219 km S of Cobar or 36 km N of Hillston. Beside old bridge
HEMA 43 C9   33 20 29 S   145 50 10 E

963 Billabourie Riverside Tourist Park ☎ 0427 674 131
Caravan Park 48 km NE of Hillston. Turn E 38 km N of Hillston at Coopers Bridge into Mt Grace Rd (Wallanthery Rd). Entry 10 km along road. Signposted
HEMA 43 C10   33 22 32 S   145 55 38 E

964 Hillston Rest Area
Rest Area 1.5 km S of Hillston. Shared with trucks
HEMA 43 D9   33 30 15 S   145 31 56 E

965 Duke of Edinburgh Hotel ☎ (02) 6993 8123
Parking Area at Booligal. Beside the hotel, fee for use of shower
HEMA 43 E8   33 52 08 S   144 53 06 E

966 Lochlan River
Parking Area at Hillston. 3 km NE of the town off Mossgiel Rd, turn N just E of the bridge
HEMA 43 D9   33 28 19 S   145 31 55 E

967 Group Campground
Willandra National Park ☎ (02) 6966 8100
Camp Area 62 km NW of Hillston, via Hillston-Mossgeil Rd. Dirt road
HEMA 43 C8   33 11 36 S   145 07 05 E

968 Lake View Caravan Park ☎ (02) 6898 1077
Caravan Park at Lake Cargelligo. Cnr of Naradhan St & Wonboyn St. 1 km SE of PO
HEMA 43 C10   33 18 08 S   146 22 39 E

969 Frogs Hollow ☎ (02) 6898 1501
Camp Spot at Lake Cargelligo. 1.5 km SE of PO, via Canada St & Narrandera St. Turn R at foreshore, beside lake
HEMA 43 C10   33 18 16 S   146 22 57 E

970 Dead Mans Point ☎ (02) 6898 1501
Parking Area 3.5 km NE of Lake Cargelligo, via Canada St & Uabba St. Beside lake
HEMA 43 C10   33 16 46 S   146 23 44 E

971 Cargelligo Weir ☎ (02) 6898 1009
Picnic Area 22 km NE of Lake Cargelligo. Turn N off Condobolin Rd 7 km E of PO onto Weir Rd. 9 km dirt road
HEMA 43 C11   33 12 03 S   146 27 13 E

972 Euabalong Campground ☎ 0428 951 875
Camp Area at Euabalong. 28 km N of Lake Cargelligo. Signposted "Caravan Park". Fee payable at hotel or in honesty box
HEMA 43 C11   33 06 42 S   146 28 20 E

973 Booberoi Weir ☎ (02) 6836 5888
Camp Spot 20 km NE of Euabalong or 56 km W of Condobolin. Access from Euabalong via Euabalong West Rd & Booberoi Rd (15 km dirt) or from Condobolin via Kiacatoo Rd & Euabalong West Rd. Turn S just E of radio tower for 1 km to river
HEMA 43 C11   33 02 13 S   146 38 36 E

974 Gum Bend Lake ☎ (02) 6895 1900
Camp Area 4 km W of Condobolin, via Bathurst St. Dogs in signed area only. Donation please
HEMA 43 C12   33 04 41 S   147 06 00 E

975 River View Caravan Park ☎ (02) 6895 2611
Caravan Park at Condobolin. Diggers Ave. S end of town
HEMA 43 C12   33 05 40 S   147 08 50 E

976 Wallaroi Creek Rest Area
Rest Area 15 km S of Condobolin or 90 km N of West Wyalong. Beside creek
HEMA 43 C12   33 12 34 S   147 06 10 E

977 Burcher Camping Ground ☎ (02) 6972 5244
Camp Area at Burcher. Kurrajong St. Donation requested
HEMA 43 D12   33 31 00 S   147 15 07 E

978 Ungarie Showground
Camp Spot at Ungarie. Crown Camp Rd, entrance beyond school, signposted. Collect key from Ampol Service Station, Main St. Gold coin donation
HEMA 43 D11   33 38 07 S   146 58 43 E

979 Tullibigeal Sportsground   ☎ (02) 6972 9176
Camp Spot at Tullibigeal. 44 km SE of Lake Cargelligo or 82 km NW of West Wyalong. Call ahead during office hours to arrange keys
HEMA 43 D11   33 25 00 S   146 43 28 E

✓ 980 Tullibigeal Pioneer Park   ☎ (02) 6972 9176
Rest Area at Tullibigeal, 44 km SE of Lake Cargelligo or 82 km NW of West Wyalong. Donation requested
HEMA 43 D11   33 25 16 S   146 43 40 E

981 Woolshed Flat   ☎ (02) 6966 8100
Cocoparra National Park
Camp Area 25 km NE of Griffith. Access via Beelbangera Rd to Yenda, N along Myall Park Rd (Whitton Stock Route) then E onto Mt Bingar Rd. Signposted. Some dirt road
HEMA 43 E10   34 04 45 S   146 13 26 E

982 Lake Wyangan   ☎ (02) 6962 4145
Camp Area 8 km NW of Griffith. From Main St via roundabout onto Ulong St, L onto Binya St then onto Wyangan Ave. Cold showers only
HEMA 43 E10   34 12 46 S   146 01 02 E

983 Griffith Showgrounds   ☎ 0403 655 123
Camp Area at Griffith. Cnr Merrigal St & Walla Ave. See notice board for caretaker details & payment
HEMA 43 F10   34 17 25 S   146 01 46 E

984 Willow Park   ☎ (02) 6962 4145
Rest Area at Griffith. Walla Ave off Kookora St. 1.5 km W of PO, near TAFE college. Self Contained Vehicles only
HEMA 43 F10   34 17 16 S   146 01 55 E

985 Garoolgan Rest Area
Rest Area at Garoolgan. 40 km E of Griffith or 45 km W of Ardlethan
HEMA 43 E11   34 15 10 S   146 26 56 E

986 Nugan Bend
Rest Area 10 km S of Griffith or 24 km N of Darlington Point
HEMA 43 F10   34 22 08 S   146 02 03 E

987 Coleambally Caravan Park   ☎ (02) 6954 4100
Caravan Park at Coleambally. Kingfisher Ave
HEMA 43 G10   34 47 56 S   145 52 48 E

988 The Coly Club   ☎ (02) 6954 4170
Parking Area at Coleambally. 3 Falcon St, check in at reception. Showers at footy oval
HEMA 43 G10   34 47 52 S   145 52 46 E

989 Yanko Creek Rest Area
Rest Area 30 km N of Jerilderie or 26 km S of Coleambally
HEMA 43 G9   35 08 48 S   145 46 19 E

Tibooburra to Mildura
Silver City Highway

990 Cameron Corner Store   ☎ (08) 8091 3872
Camp Spot at Cameron Corner
HEMA 40 B1   28 59 48 S   140 59 59 E

991 Fort Grey Campground   ☎ (08) 8091 3308
Sturt National Park
Camp Area 109 km NW of Tibooburra, via Tibooburra-Cameron Corner Rd. Dirt road
HEMA 40 B1   29 05 17 S   141 12 45 E

992 The Granites Motel Caravan Park   ☎ (08) 8091 3305
Caravan Park at Tibooburra. Cnr of King St & Brown St
HEMA 40 B3   29 26 02 S   142 00 33 E

993 Tibooburra Aboriginal Reserve Campground   ☎ (08) 8091 3435
Camp Area 1 km from the end of Burgess St. Pay at Land Council office, Briscoe St
HEMA 40 B3   29 26 29 S   142 01 03 E

Notes...

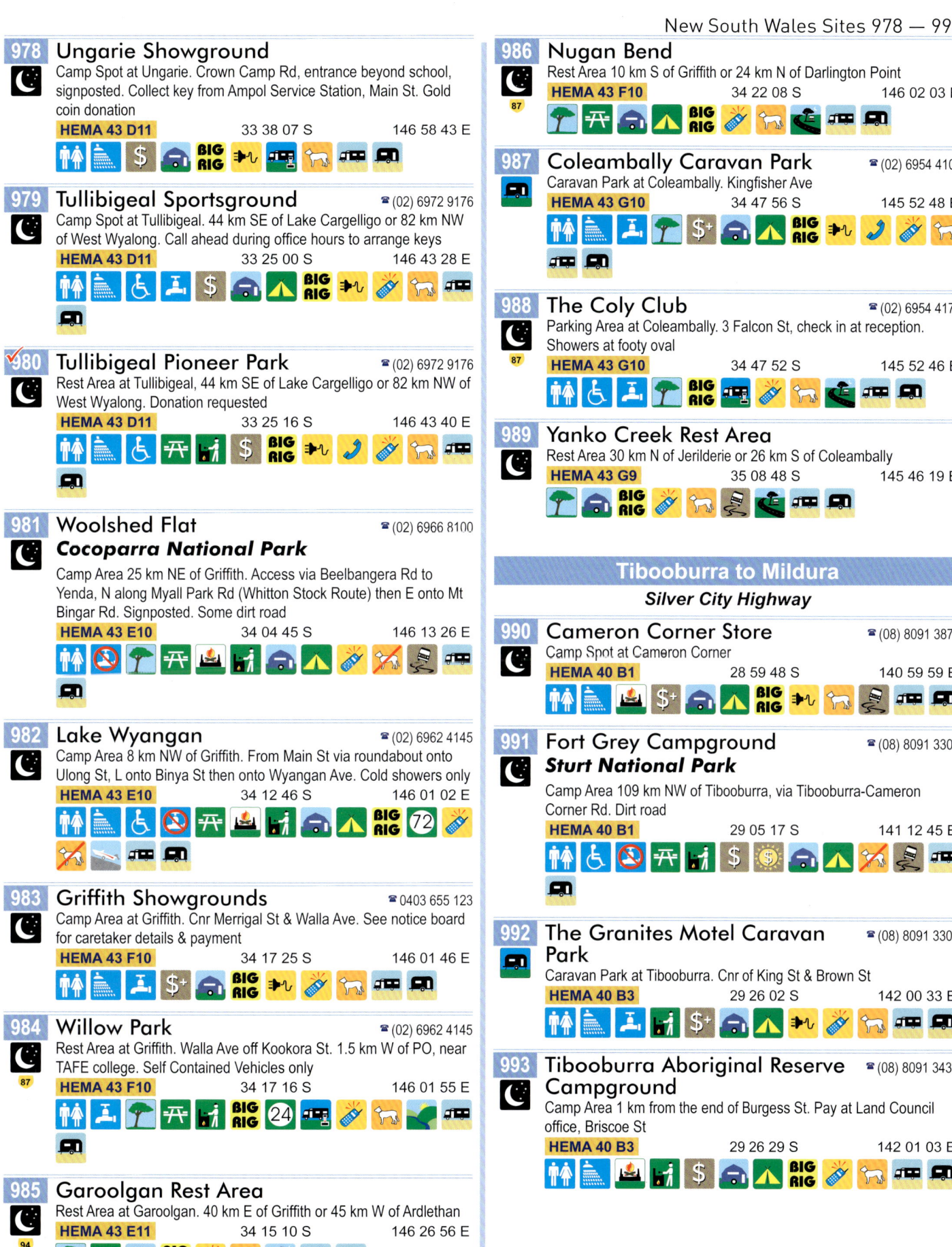

994 Dead Horse Gully Campground ☎ (08) 8091 3308
Sturt National Park
Camp Area 2.5 km N of Tibooburra. Turn W off Silver City Hwy 1 km N of Tibooburra. Signposted
HEMA 40 B3   29 25 02 S   142 00 03 E

995 Olive Downs Campground ☎ (08) 8091 3308
Sturt National Park
Camp Area 55 km N of Tibooburra, via Jump Up Loop Rd. Signposted off Silver City Hwy. Access road can be rough, off road caravans only
HEMA 40 B2   29 03 32 S   141 51 48 E

996 Mt Wood Campground ☎ (08) 8091 3308
Sturt National Park
Camp Area 26 km E of Tibooburra, via Wanaaring Rd & Gorge Loop Rd. Dirt road
HEMA 40 C3   29 28 51 S   142 14 06 E

997 Theldarpa Station ☎ (08) 8091 3576
Camp Area at Theldarpa Station. 45 km W of Milparinka on the Milparinka Hawker Gate Rd
HEMA 40 C2   29 39 17 S   141 28 59 E

998 Milparinka Camping & Caravan Site
Camp Area at Milparinka. Behind Heritage Centre. Pay at hotel or centre
HEMA 40 C2   29 44 18 S   141 53 06 E

999 Pincally Station ☎ (08) 8091 3571
Camp Area at Pincally Station. 70 km S of Milparinka on the Mt Shannon Rd. Bookings required
HEMA 40 D2   30 11 25 S   141 33 13 E

1000 Pimpara Lake Station ☎ (08) 8091 2524
Camp Area at Pimpara Lake Station. 130 km S of Milparinka or 200 km N of Broken Hill. Via Mount Arrowsmith Rd, Pimpara Lake Rd. Bush camping, get directions from homestead
HEMA 40 E2   30 25 19 S   141 44 02 E

1001 Packsaddle Rest Area
Rest Area at Packsaddle. N of roadhouse
HEMA 40 E3   30 36 07 S   141 57 52 E

1002 Pine View Station ☎ (08) 8091 2513
Camp Area at Pine View Station. 180 km NW of Broken Hill. Via Silverton to Hawker Gate Rd. Dirt road
HEMA 40 E1   30 41 46 S   141 04 22 E

1003 Fowlers Gap
Rest Area 66 km S of Packsaddle or 110 km N of Broken Hill
HEMA 40 F2   31 06 07 S   141 42 07 E

1004 Homestead Creek Campground ☎ (08) 8080 3200
Mutawintji National Park
Camp Area 130 km NE of Broken Hill. Turn E 56 km S of Fowlers Gap or 54 km N of Broken Hill onto Broken Hill-White Cliffs Rd. Dirt road
HEMA 40 F3   31 16 56 S   142 17 37 E

1005 Mount Gipps Station ☎ (08) 8091 3537
Camp Area at Mount Gipps Station. 40 km N of Broken Hill. Via Corona Rd. Dirt road. Bookings preferred. Permission required for pets. Open April to October
HEMA 40 G2   31 37 47 S   141 33 25 E

1006 Lake Pamamaroo Campsites ☎ (08) 8091 4274
Camp Spots along Lake Pamamaroo. 16 km NE of Menindee. Turn E off Menindee-Broken Hill Rd 8 km N of Menindee onto Main Weir Rd. Various spots along lake
HEMA 42 A4   32 18 59 S   142 27 58 E

1007 Burke and Wills Campground ☎ (08) 8091 4274
Camp Area 18 km NE of Menindee. Turn E off Menindee-Broken Hill Rd 8 km N of Menindee onto Main Weir Rd. Beside Darling River
HEMA 42 A4   32 18 18 S   142 29 55 E

1008 Main Weir Campground ☎ (08) 8091 4274
Camp Area 19 km NE of Menindee. Turn E off Menindee-Broken Hill Rd 8 km N of Menindee onto Main Weir Rd. Beside Darling River
HEMA 42 A4   32 18 49 S   142 30 26 E

1009 Nelia Gaari Station ☎ (08) 8091 6496
Camp Area at Nelia Gaari Station. Western side of River rd, 80 km E of Menindee or 90 km W of Wilcannia
HEMA 42 A4   32 06 08 S   142 51 04 E

1010 Menindee Lakes Caravan Park ☎ (08) 8091 4315
Caravan Park 5 km NW of Menindee. Menindee Lakes Shore Dr
HEMA 40 J3   32 21 15 S   142 24 12 E

NEW SOUTH WALES

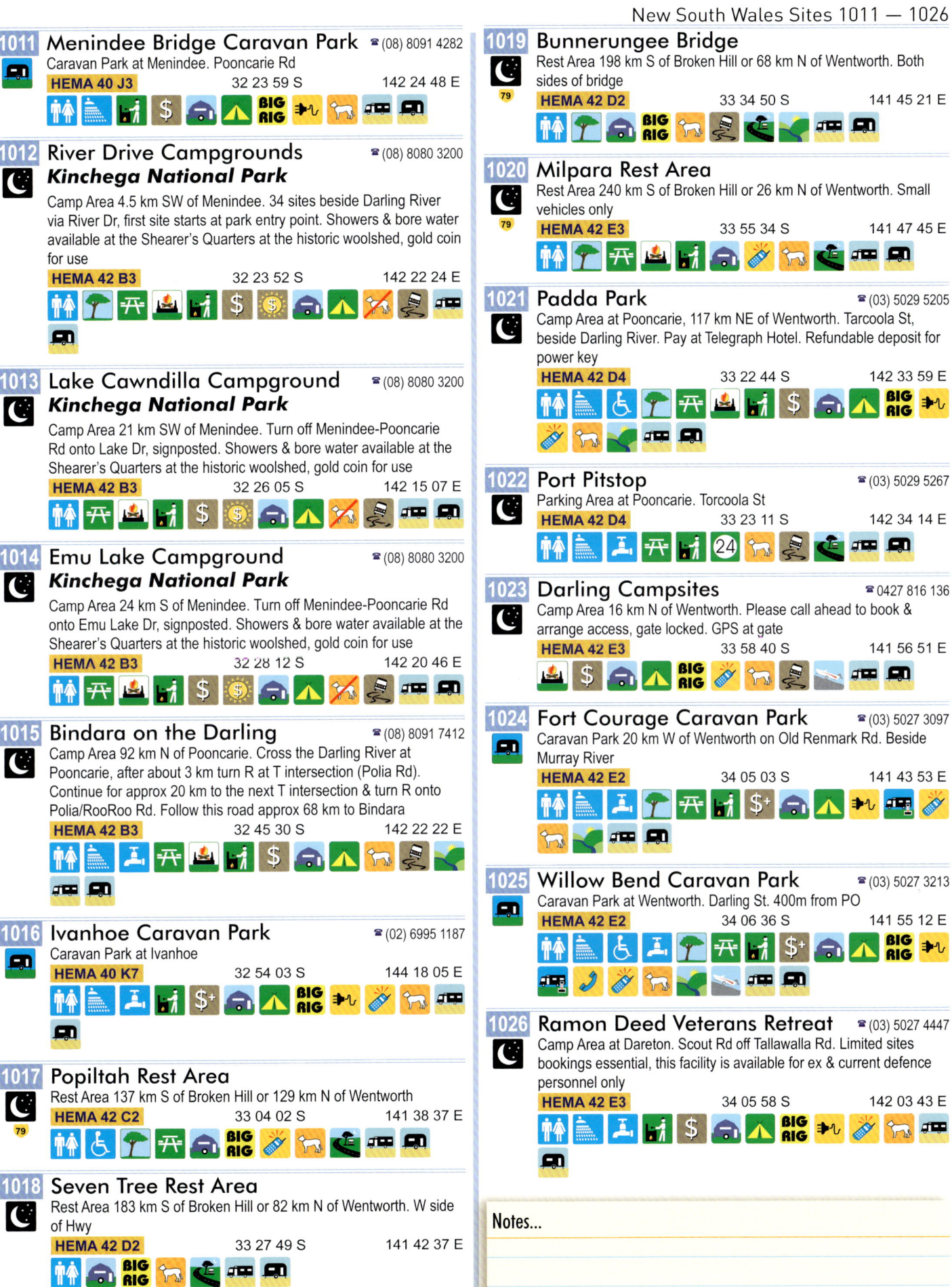

1011 Menindee Bridge Caravan Park ☎ (08) 8091 4282
Caravan Park at Menindee. Pooncarie Rd
HEMA 40 J3
32 23 59 S   142 24 48 E

1012 River Drive Campgrounds ☎ (08) 8080 3200
Kinchega National Park
Camp Area 4.5 km SW of Menindee. 34 sites beside Darling River via River Dr, first site starts at park entry point. Showers & bore water available at the Shearer's Quarters at the historic woolshed, gold coin for use
HEMA 42 B3
32 23 52 S   142 22 24 E

1013 Lake Cawndilla Campground ☎ (08) 8080 3200
Kinchega National Park
Camp Area 21 km SW of Menindee. Turn off Menindee-Pooncarie Rd onto Lake Dr, signposted. Showers & bore water available at the Shearer's Quarters at the historic woolshed, gold coin for use
HEMA 42 B3
32 26 05 S   142 15 07 E

1014 Emu Lake Campground ☎ (08) 8080 3200
Kinchega National Park
Camp Area 24 km S of Menindee. Turn off Menindee-Pooncarie Rd onto Emu Lake Dr, signposted. Showers & bore water available at the Shearer's Quarters at the historic woolshed, gold coin for use
HEMA 42 B3
32 28 12 S   142 20 46 E

1015 Bindara on the Darling ☎ (08) 8091 7412
Camp Area 92 km N of Pooncarie. Cross the Darling River at Pooncarie, after about 3 km turn R at T intersection (Polia Rd). Continue for approx 20 km to the next T intersection & turn R onto Polia/RooRoo Rd. Follow this road approx 68 km to Bindara
HEMA 42 B3
32 45 30 S   142 22 22 E

1016 Ivanhoe Caravan Park ☎ (02) 6995 1187
Caravan Park at Ivanhoe
HEMA 40 K7
32 54 03 S   144 18 05 E

1017 Popiltah Rest Area
Rest Area 137 km S of Broken Hill or 129 km N of Wentworth
HEMA 42 C2
33 04 02 S   141 38 37 E

1018 Seven Tree Rest Area
Rest Area 183 km S of Broken Hill or 82 km N of Wentworth. W side of Hwy
HEMA 42 D2
33 27 49 S   141 42 37 E

1019 Bunnerungee Bridge
Rest Area 198 km S of Broken Hill or 68 km N of Wentworth. Both sides of bridge
HEMA 42 D2
33 34 50 S   141 45 21 E

1020 Milpara Rest Area
Rest Area 240 km S of Broken Hill or 26 km N of Wentworth. Small vehicles only
HEMA 42 E3
33 55 34 S   141 47 45 E

1021 Padda Park ☎ (03) 5029 5205
Camp Area at Pooncarie, 117 km NE of Wentworth. Tarcoola St, beside Darling River. Pay at Telegraph Hotel. Refundable deposit for power key
HEMA 42 D4
33 22 44 S   142 33 59 E

1022 Port Pitstop ☎ (03) 5029 5267
Parking Area at Pooncarie. Torcoola St
HEMA 42 D4
33 23 11 S   142 34 14 E

1023 Darling Campsites ☎ 0427 816 136
Camp Area 16 km N of Wentworth. Please call ahead to book & arrange access, gate locked. GPS at gate
HEMA 42 E3
33 58 40 S   141 56 51 E

1024 Fort Courage Caravan Park ☎ (03) 5027 3097
Caravan Park 20 km W of Wentworth on Old Renmark Rd. Beside Murray River
HEMA 42 E2
34 05 03 S   141 43 53 E

1025 Willow Bend Caravan Park ☎ (03) 5027 3213
Caravan Park at Wentworth. Darling St. 400m from PO
HEMA 42 E2
34 06 36 S   141 55 12 E

1026 Ramon Deed Veterans Retreat ☎ (03) 5027 4447
Camp Area at Dareton. Scout Rd off Tallawalla Rd. Limited sites bookings essential, this facility is available for ex & current defence personnel only
HEMA 42 E3
34 05 58 S   142 03 43 E

Notes...

1027 Curlwaa Caravan Park
☎ (03) 5027 6210

Caravan Park at Curlwaa. 5 km E of Wentworth

HEMA 42 E3   34 06 45 S   141 59 21 E

Nyngan to Bourke
Mitchell Highway

1028 Memorial Park

Rest Area at Girilambone. Turn E of Hwy. See signage for access. Overflow parking at hotel, see publican

HEMA 41 F11   31 14 52 S   146 54 24 E

1029 Willie Retreat Macquarie Marshes
☎ (02) 6824 4361

Camp Area 110 km N of Warren or 76 km S of Carinda on the Carinda - Nyngan Rd, turn E into Gibson Way, entrance 1.5 km on the S side of road. Bush camping also available. Pets by prior arrangement

HEMA 41 E12   30 53 47 S   147 29 08 E

1030 Glenariff Rest Area

Rest Area 26 km NW of Coolabah or 25 km SE of Byrock

HEMA 41 E11   30 49 51 S   146 32 46 E

1031 Mulga Creek Hotel Caravan Park
☎ (02) 6874 7311

Caravan Park at Byrock. Behind hotel

HEMA 41 E10   30 39 47 S   146 24 10 E

1032 Maroona Rest Area

Rest Area 56 km NW of Byrock or 22 km SE of Bourke

HEMA 41 D10   30 14 44 S   146 03 30 E

Euston to Mildura

1033 Mail Route Rest Area

Rest Area 24 km NW of Euston or 47 km SE of Gol Gol. Combined truck stop

HEMA 42 F4   34 27 53 S   142 32 26 E

1034 Bottle Bend Conservation Reserve
☎ (03) 5051 6205

Picnic Area 57 km NW of Euston or 18 km SE of Gol Gol. Turn S 56 km NW of Euston or 15 km SE of Gol Gol at signpost. 2 km dirt road. Beside river. Self Contained Vehicles only

HEMA 42 F4   34 18 12 S   142 17 55 E

1035 Trentham Cliffs Caravan Village
☎ (03) 5024 8545

Caravan Park 7 km SE of Gol Gol or 11 km SE of Mildura. Sturt Hwy

HEMA 42 F3   34 13 29 S   142 14 50 E

1036 Mungo Lodge
☎ 1300 663 748

Camp Area at Arumpo. 150 km NW of Balranald or 110 km NE of Mildura. Dirt road. Reservations essential

HEMA 42 D5   33 44 29 S   143 00 08 E

1037 Main Campground
Mungo National Park
☎ (03) 5021 8900

Camp Area 150 km NW of Balranald or 110 km NE of Mildura. Signposted. Dirt road

HEMA 42 D5   33 44 05 S   143 00 55 E

1038 Belah Campground
Mungo National Park
☎ (03) 5021 8900

Camp Area 136 km NW of Balranald or 142 km NE of Mildura. From Visitor Centre follow signposted directions. Small area, not suitable for caravans

HEMA 42 D5   33 42 46 S   143 10 36 E

Notes...

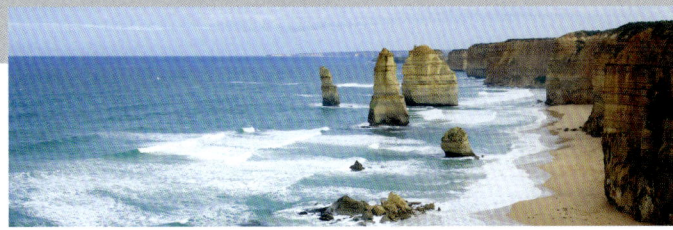

TWELVE APOSTLES, GREAT OCEAN RD (60 H6)

PHOTO: © ISTOCK.COM

key map

Distances are shown in kilometres and follow the most direct major sealed route where possible.

	Ballarat	Bairnsdale	Bendigo	Echuca	Eden (NSW)	Geelong	Hamilton	Horsham	Melbourne	Mildura	Shepparton	Swan Hill	Traralgon	Wangaratta	Warrnambool
Albury	428	333	310	245	542	372	608	524	305	624	178	403	456	77	601
Ballarat		410	118	201	693	88	180	188	116	449	240	307	287	359	173
Bairnsdale			447	578	283	366	590	598	294	859	511	636	123	410	552
Bendigo				92	730	206	298	214	153	426	122	189	324	230	291
Echuca					787	298	390	306	204	379	68	157	405	176	383
Eden (NSW)						649	873	881	577	1127	794	919	386	619	835
Geelong							233	276	72	537	260	395	273	308	186
Hamilton								128	296	436	420	487	497	532	111
Horsham									304	308	336	403	505	444	239
Melbourne										579	188	342	201	236	258
Mildura											447	220	780	555	547
Shepparton												225	389	108	413
Swan Hill													543	333	480
Traralgon														437	459
Wangaratta															532

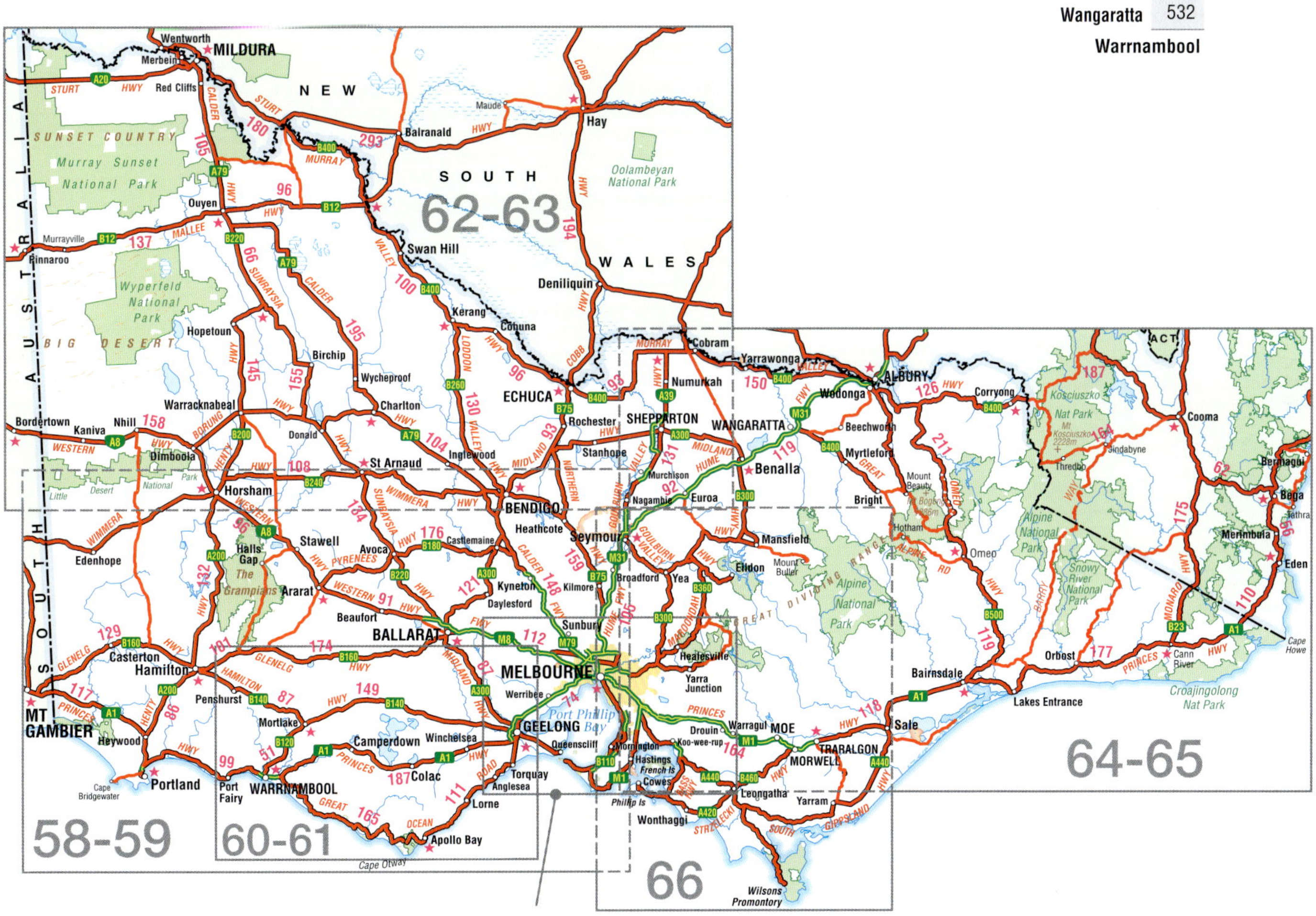

Melbourne CBD

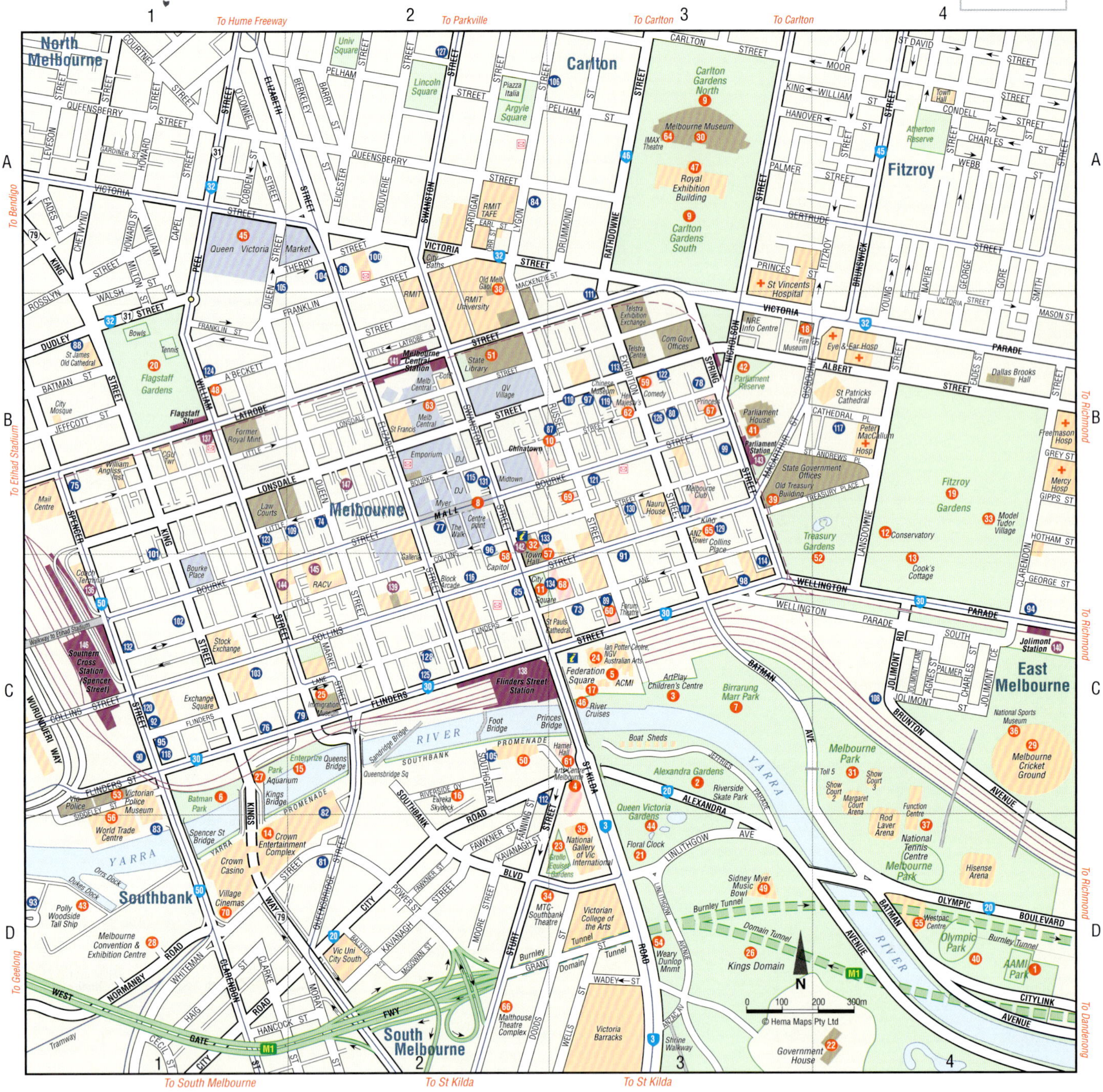

Map Legend

Freeway/Tunnel	FREEWAY
Main Road	
Secondary Road	ROAD
Minor Road	STREET
Lane/Footbridge	
National Route	M1 79
Metropolitan Route	22
One Way Street	
Railway	Underground
Tram	

Park/Garden	
Railway Station	
Major Building	
Government Building	
Theatre/Cinema	
Shopping	
Hospital	+
Post Office	
Accredited Information	

Places of Interest
1 AAMI Park D4
2 Alexandra Gardens C3
3 Artplay Children's Centre C3
4 Arts Centre Melbourne, The C3
5 Aust Ctr for the Moving Image (ACMI) C3
6 Batman Park C1
7 Birrarung Marr Park C3
8 Bourke Street Mall B2
9 Carlton Gardens A3
10 Chinatown B2
11 City Square C2
12 Conservatory B4
13 Cook's Cottage C4
14 Crown Entertainment Complex D1
15 Enterprize Park C2
16 Eureka Skydeck C2
17 Federation Square C3
18 Fire Services Museum B3
19 Fitzroy Gardens B4
20 Flagstaff Gardens B1
21 Floral Clock D3
22 Government House D4
23 Grollo Equiset Gardens D3
24 Ian Potter Centre NGV Australia C3
25 Immigration Museum C2
26 Kings Domain D3
27 Melbourne Aquarium C1
28 Melbourne Convention & Exhibition Cnt (MCEC) D1
29 Melbourne Cricket Ground C4
30 Melbourne Museum A3
31 Melbourne Park C4
32 Melbourne Town Hall B2
33 Model Tudor Village B4
34 MTC - Southbank Theatre D2
35 National Gallery of Victoria International D3
36 National Sports Museum C4
37 National Tennis Centre D4
38 Old Melbourne Gaol A2
39 Old Treasury Building B3
40 Olympic Park D4
41 Parliament House B3
42 Parliament Reserve B3
43 Polly Woodside D1
44 Queen Victoria Gardens D3
45 Queen Victoria Market A1
46 River Cruises C3
47 Royal Exhibition Building A3
48 Royal Historical Society B1
49 Sidney Myer Music Bowl D3
50 Southgate Arts & Leisure Pct C2
51 State Library of Victoria B2
52 Treasury Gardens C4
53 Victorian Police Museum C1
54 Weary Dunlop Monument D3
55 Westpac Centre C1
56 World Trade Centre D1

Theatres
57 Athenaeum Theatre C2
58 Capitol Theatre C2
59 Comedy Theatre B3
60 Forum Theatre C3
61 Hamer Hall C3
62 Her Majesty's Theatre B3
63 Hoyts Melbourne Central B2
64 IMAX Cinema A3
65 Kino Dendy Cinemas B3
66 Malthouse Theatre Complex D2
67 Princess Theatre B3
68 Regent Theatre C3
69 Russell Street Cinemas B3
70 Village Cinemas D1

Accommodation
73 Adelphi Hotel C3
74 Adina Apartment Hotel Melbourne B2
75 Atlantis Hotel B1
76 Best Western Riverside Apts C1
77 Causeway Inn on the Mall B2
78 City Limits Hotel B3
79 Clarion Suites Gateway C2
80 Crossley Hotel, The B3
81 Crown Promenade Hotel D2
82 Crown Towers D2
83 Crowne Plaza Melbourne D1
84 Downtowner on Lygon A2
85 Econo Ledge City Square Motel C2
86 Elizabeth Hostel A2
87 Exford Hotel, The B3
88 Flagstaff City Inn B1
89 Flinders Landing Apartment C3
90 Grand Hotel Melbourne C1
91 Grand Hyatt Melbourne C3
92 Great Southern Hotel, The C1
93 Hilton Melbourne South Wharf D1
94 Hilton on the Park Melbourne C4
95 Holiday Inn Melbourne on Flinders C1
96 Hotel Causeway B2
97 Hotel Grand Chancellor Melbourne B3
98 Hotel Lindrum C3
99 Hotel Windsor, The B3
100 Ibis Hotel A2
101 Ibis Melbourne Little Bourke Street Hotel B1
102 Ibis Styles Kingsgate Hotel C1
103 InterContinental Melbourne The Rialto C1
104 Jasper Hotel A2
105 Langham Melbourne, The C2
106 Lygon Lodge A3
107 Mantra 100 Exhibition B3
108 Mantra on Jolimont C4
109 Mantra on Little Bourke B2
110 Mantra on Russell B3
111 Mantra on the Park B3
112 Mantra Southbank Melbourne C3
113 Melbourne Marriott Hotel B3
114 Mercure Melbourne Treasury Gardens C3
115 Mercure Welcome Melbourne B2
116 Novotel Melbourne on Collins B2
117 Park Hyatt Melbourne B4
118 Pensione Hotel Melbourne C2
119 Punthill Little Bourke Apartments B3
120 Quality Hotel Batman's Hill on Collins C1
121 Quest on Bourke B3
122 Quest on Lonsdale B3
123 Quest on William B1
124 Radisson on Flagstaff Gardens B1
125 Rendezvous Grand Hotel C2
126 Rydges Melbourne B3
127 Rydges on Swanston Melbourne A2
128 Sebel Melbourne Flinders Lane, The C2
129 Sofitel Melbourne on Collins B3
130 Stamford Plaza Melbourne C3
131 Swanston Hotel Melbourne Grand Mercure, The B2
132 Vibe Savoy Hotel Melbourne C1
133 Victoria Hotel, The B2
134 Westin Melbourne, The C3

Travel Information
136 Coach & Bus Terminals C1
137 Flagstaff Station B1
138 Flinders Street Station C3
139 Information Victoria C2
140 Jolimont Station C4
141 Melbourne Central Station B2
142 Met Shop C2
143 Parliament Station B3
144 Qantas Terminal C1
145 RACV Travel C2
146 Southern Cross Station C1
147 YHA Office B2

© Hema Maps Pty Ltd

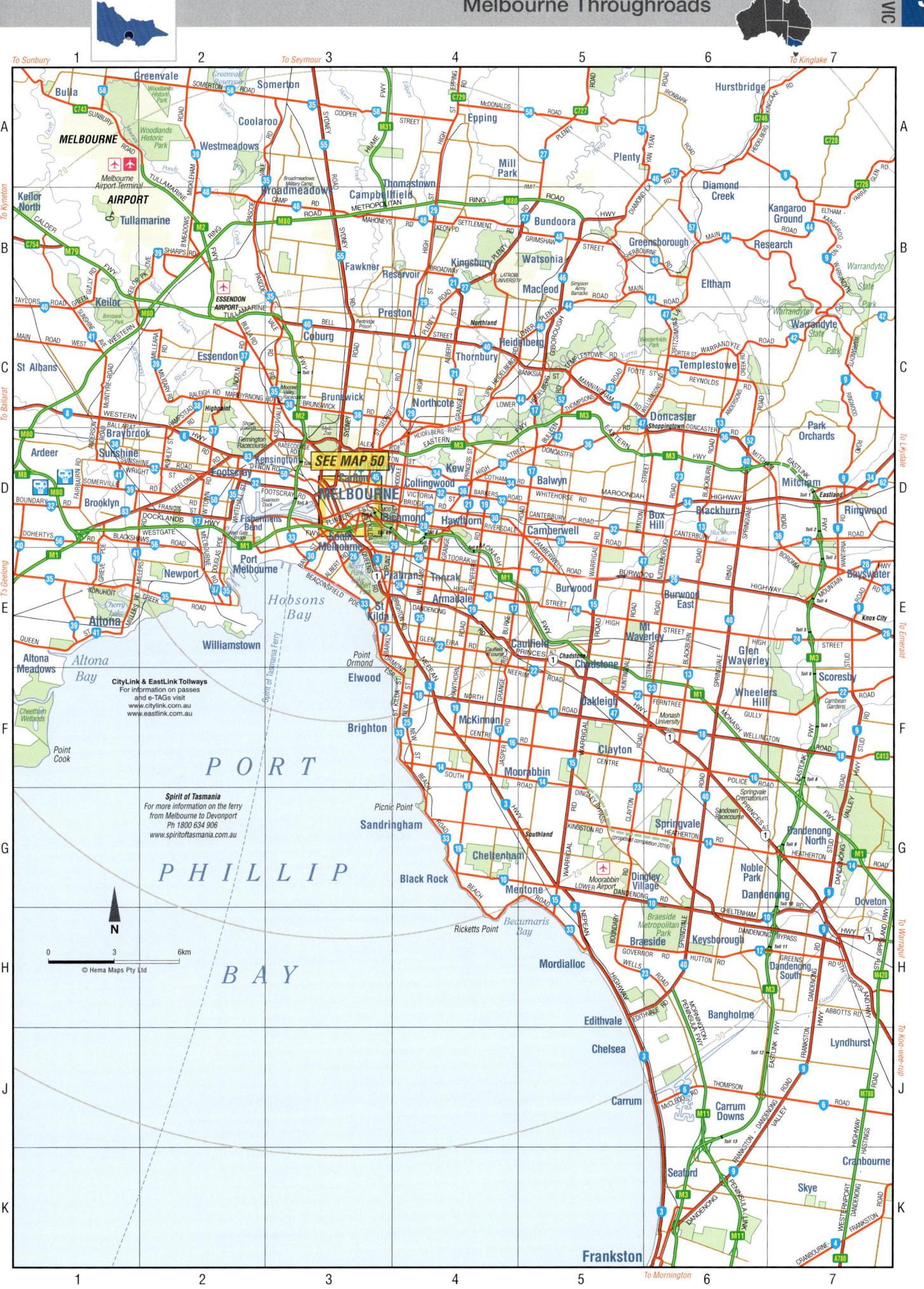

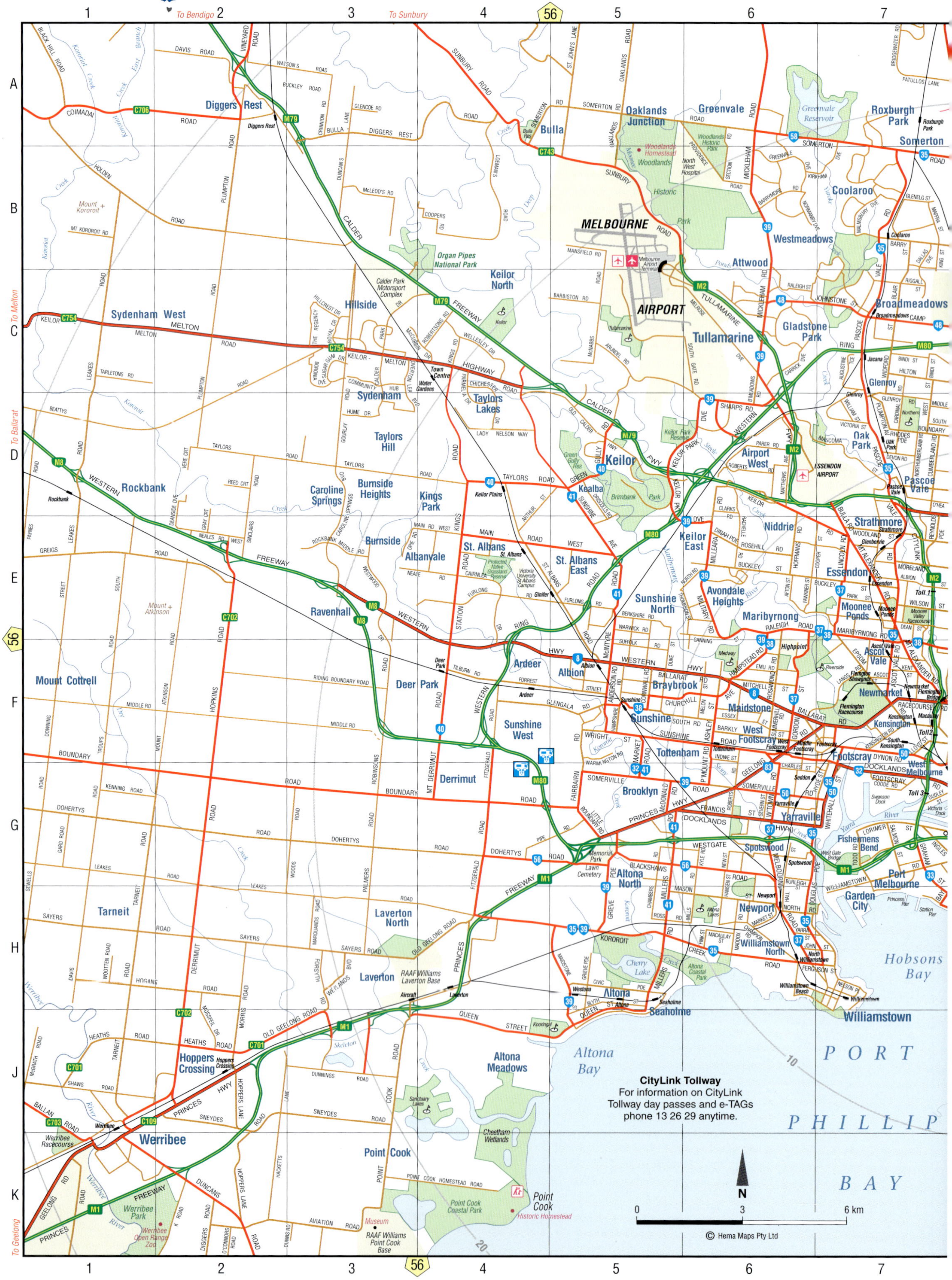

MELBOURNE AIRPORT

CityLink Tollway
For information on CityLink Tollway day passes and e-TAGs phone 13 26 29 anytime.

PORT PHILLIP BAY

Hobsons Bay

Altona Bay

N

0   3   6 km

© Hema Maps Pty Ltd

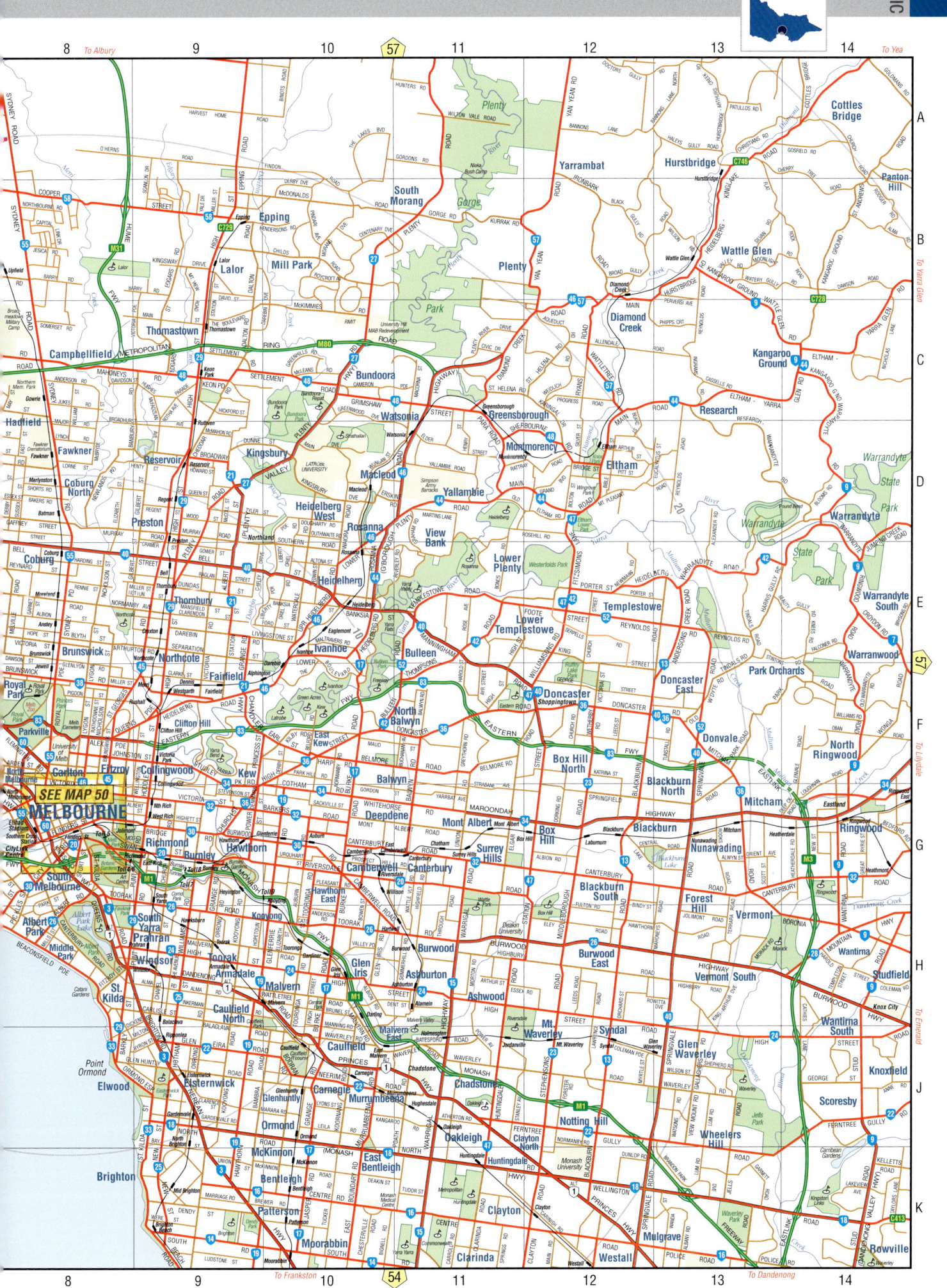

CityLink Tollway
For information on CityLink
Tollway day passes and e-TAGs
phone 13 26 29 anytime.

© Hema Maps Pty Ltd

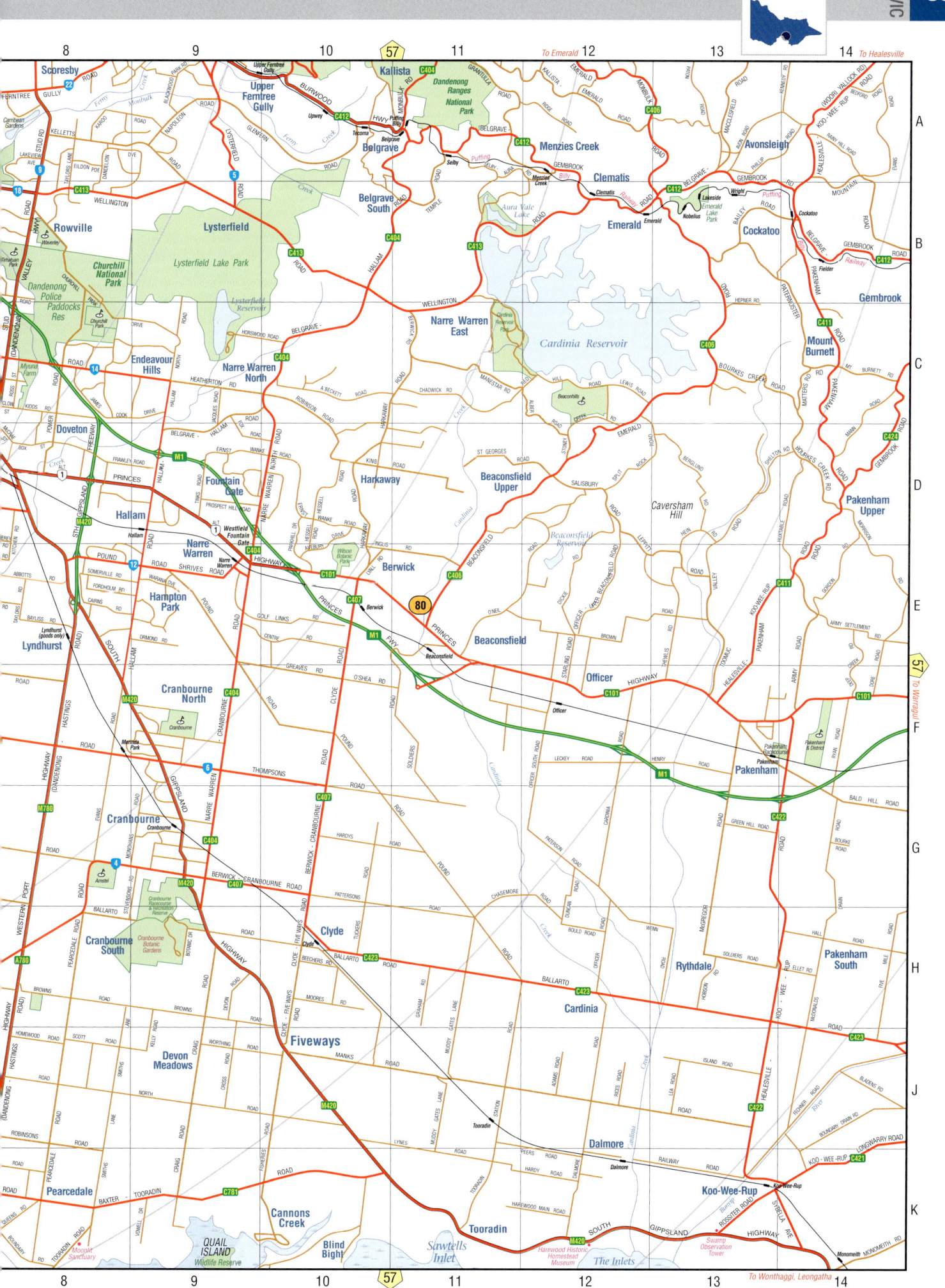

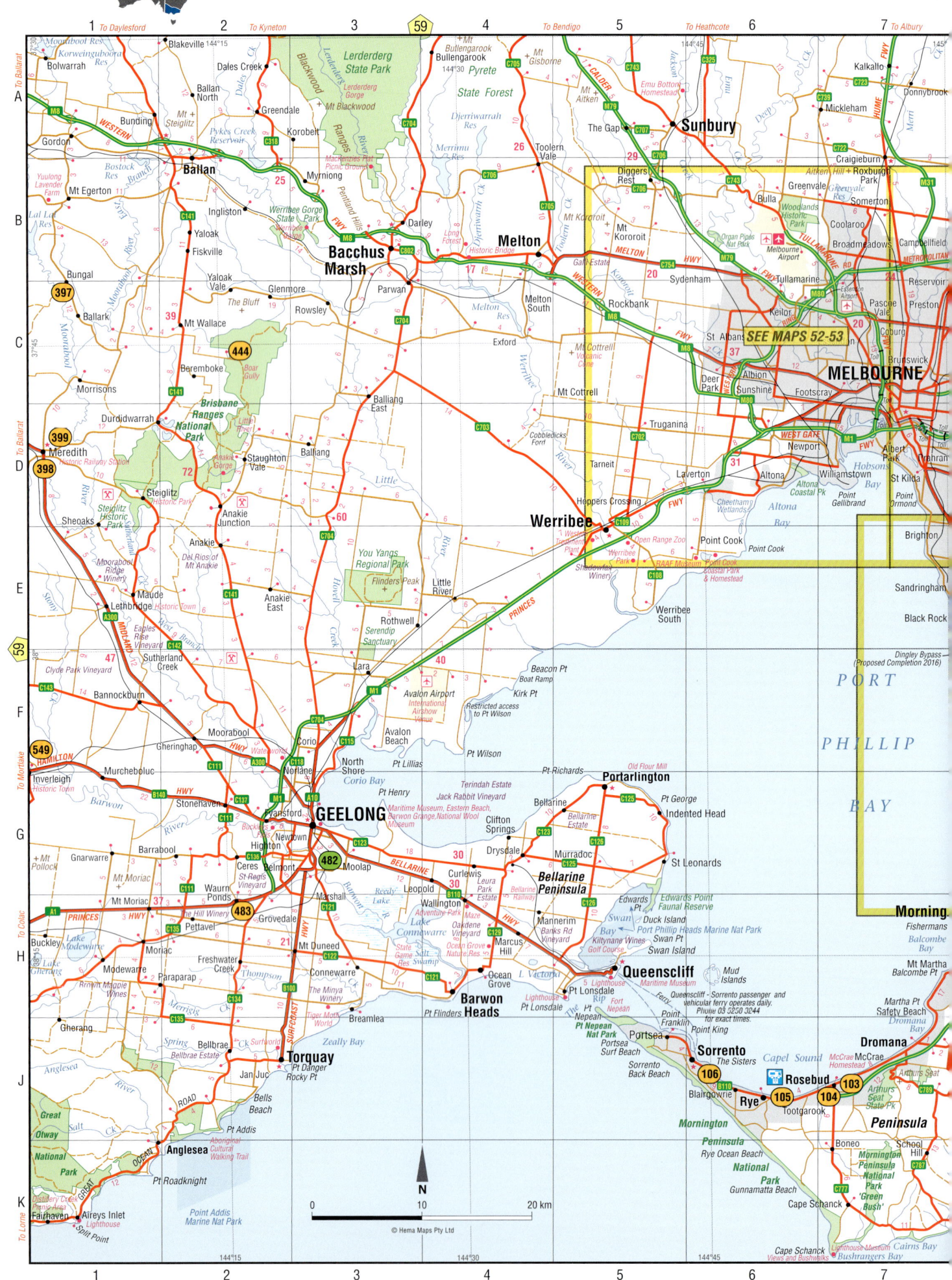

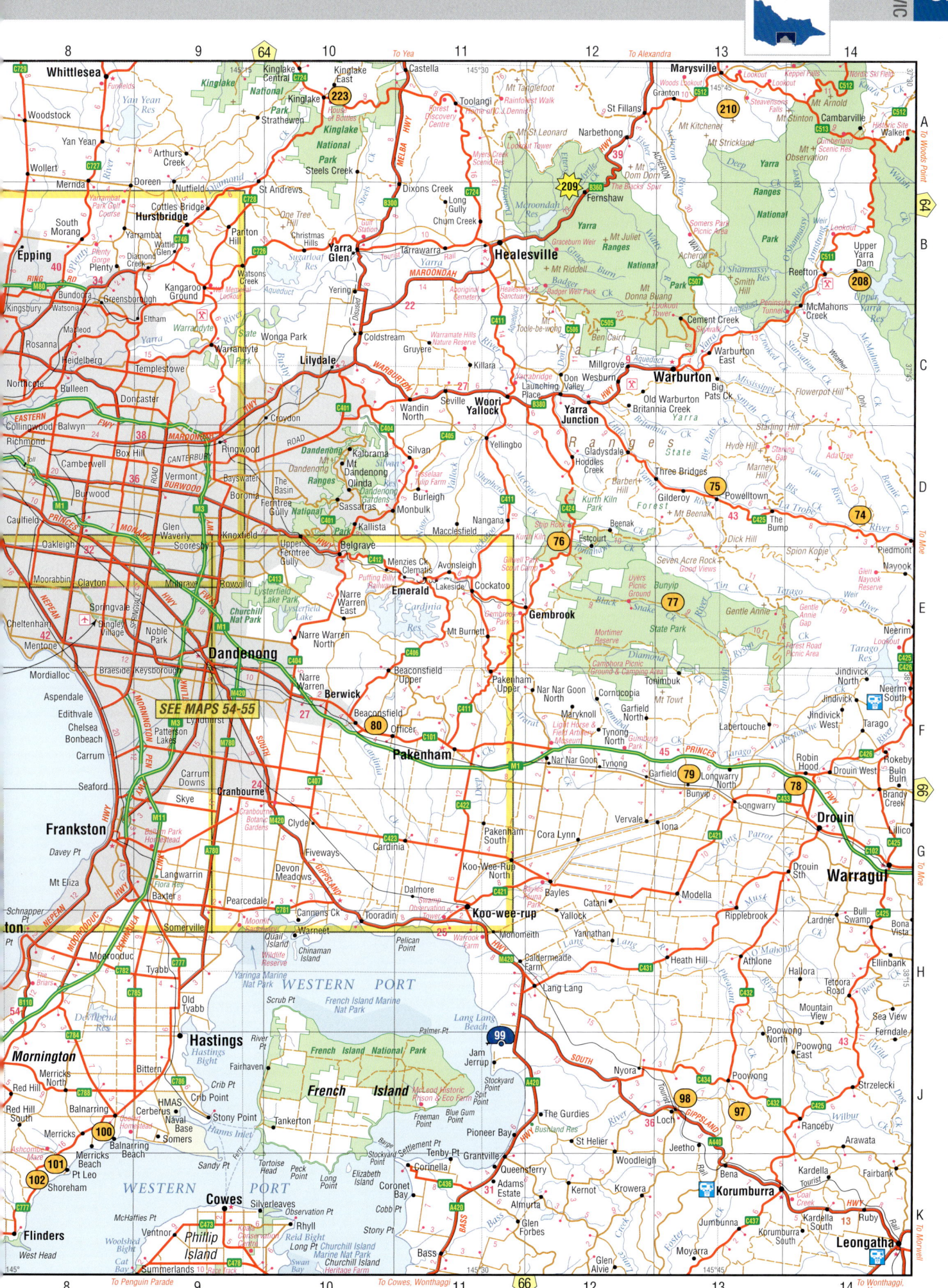

SOUTHERN OCEAN

© Hema Maps Pty Ltd

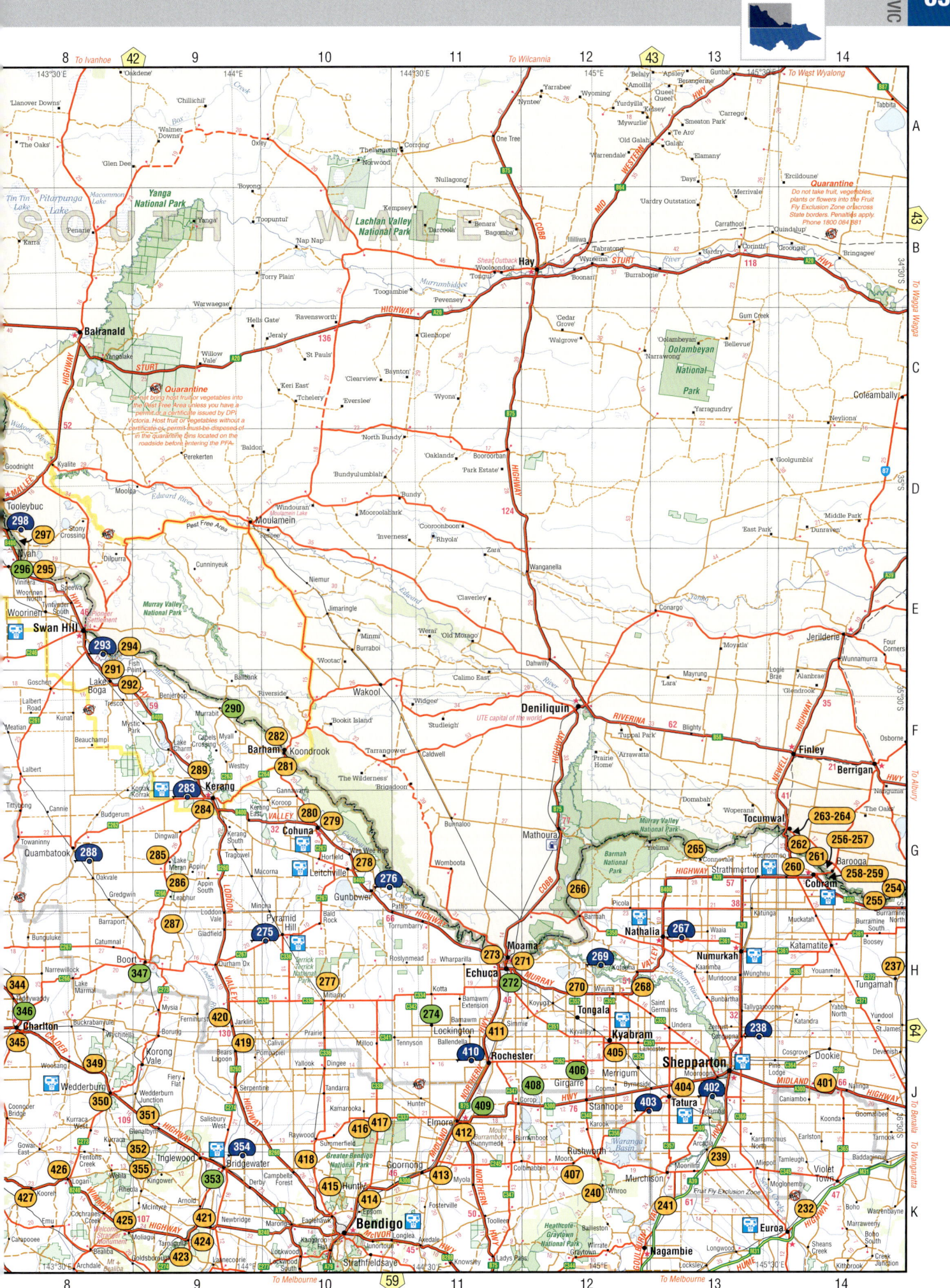

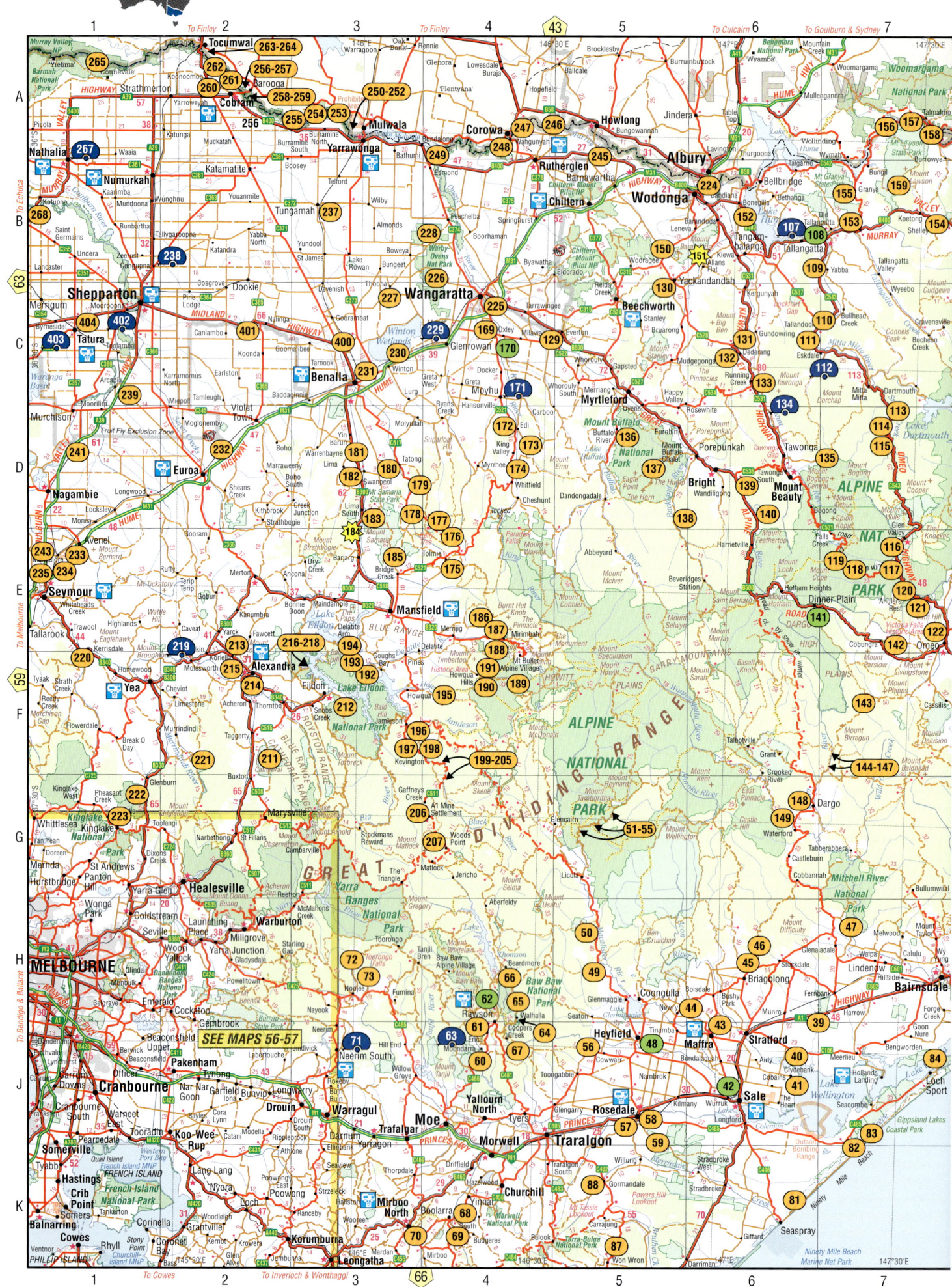

Victoria Highway Index

Victoria Alphabetic Site Index

Victoria Alphabetic Site Index

Victoria Alphabetic Site Index

NSW Border to Melbourne
Princes Highway

1 Wallagaraugh River Retreat ☎ (03) 5158 8211

Camp Area 17 km S of Timbillica. 80 Piesley Rd. Turn E just N of bridge 9 km S of Timbillica or 9 km N of Genoa. 8 km dirt road. Generator power

| HEMA 65 G13 | 37 27 14 S | 149 41 25 E |

✓ 2 Genoa Rest Area

Rest Area 1 km N of Genoa before bridge. Donation welcome

A1

| HEMA 65 G13 | 37 28 21 S | 149 35 27 E |

3 Mallacoota Foreshore Holiday Park ☎ (03) 5158 0300

Caravan Park at Mallacoota, Allan Dr

| HEMA 65 G13 | 37 33 26 S | 149 45 32 E |

4 Thurra River Rest Area (Drummond Creek)

A1

Rest Area 36 km W of Genoa or 11 km E of Cann River. 200m off Hwy

| HEMA 65 G12 | 37 34 10 S | 149 16 15 E |

5 Cann River Rainforest Caravan Park ☎ (03) 5158 6369

Caravan Park at Cann River. 7536 Princes Hwy

| HEMA 65 G12 | 37 33 59 S | 149 08 46 E |

6 Thurra River Campground ☎ (03) 5158 4268
Croajingolong National Park

Camp Area 42 km S of Cann River. At the mouth of the Thurra River near Point Hicks. Dirt road. Not suitable caravans

| HEMA 65 H12 | 37 46 38 S | 149 19 25 E |

✓ 7 Peach Tree Creek Camping Area ☎ 131 963
Croajingolong National Park

Camp Area 27 km S of Cann River. Turn S onto Tamboon Rd for 21 km, then veer R onto Fishermans Track. 6 km to campground. Dirt road. Small vehicles only

| HEMA 65 H12 | 37 44 33 S | 149 08 12 E |

8 Brightlight Saddle Rest Area

Rest Area 19 km W of Cann River or 57 km E of Orbost

A1

| HEMA 65 G11 | 37 35 20 S | 148 57 26 E |

9 Ada River Campground

C616

Camp Area 22 km N of Club Terrace. Turn NW off the Club Terrace-Combienbar Rd 11 km N of Club Terrace onto Errinundra Valley Rd. 12 km dirt road. Beside Little Ada River

| HEMA 65 G11 | 37 24 15 S | 148 53 33 E |

10 Goongerah Campground

Camp Area 25 km S of Bonang or 68 km N of Orbost. Ellery Creek Rd, signposted off Bonang Hwy

| HEMA 65 F10 | 37 20 34 S | 148 42 02 E |

11 Delegate River Streamside Reserve ☎ 13 19 63

C616

Camp Area 9 km SW of Bendoc. Beside Delegate River, via Berdoc-Orbost Rd

| HEMA 65 F11 | 37 11 48 S | 148 49 41 E |

12 McKillops Bridge Campground ☎ 131 963
Snowy River National Park

Camp Area 30 km E of Wulgulmerang or 53 km W of Bonang. Tight winding road not suitable for caravans

| HEMA 65 E10 | 37 05 25 S | 148 24 42 E |

13 Bemm River Rest Area

A1

Rest Area 30 km W of Cann River or 46 km E of Orbost. Toilets 300m off Hwy

| HEMA 65 G11 | 37 37 37 S | 148 53 20 E |

14 Bellbird Hotel ☎ (03) 5158 1239

A1

Rest Area 38 km W of Cann River or 38 km E of Orbost. Toilets at hotel with permission. Fee for shower

| HEMA 65 H11 | 37 39 08 S | 148 49 04 E |

15 Banksia Bluff Campground ☎ (03) 5154 8438
Cape Conran Coastal Park

Camp Area 19 km E of Marlo, via Marlo Rd & Yeerung River Rd. 1.5 km dirt road. Cold showers

| HEMA 65 H11 | 37 47 55 S | 148 44 15 E |

16 Murrungower Rest Area

A1

Rest Area 18 km W of Bellbird or 20 km E of Orbost

| HEMA 65 H10 | 37 41 22 S | 148 37 06 E |

17 Orbost Caravan Park ☎ (03) 5154 1097

A1

Caravan Park at Orbost. 2-6 Lochiel St

| HEMA 65 H10 | 37 42 38 S | 148 27 14 E |

18 Snowy River Rest Area 1
Rest Area 8 km S of Orbost or 8 km N of Marlo. Beside river. Self Contained Vehicles only
C107
HEMA 65 H10   37 44 24 S   148 30 26 E

19 Snowy River Rest Area 2
Rest Area 12 km S of Orbost or 4 km N of Marlo. Self Contained Vehicles only
C107
HEMA 65 H10   37 46 04 S   148 32 13 E

20 Corringle Slips Campground ☎ (03) 5161 1222
Corringle Foreshore Reserve
Camp Area 18 km S of Newmerella, via Corringle Rd. Dirt road
HEMA 65 H10   37 48 00 S   148 31 21 E

21 Tostaree Cottages & Tavern ☎ (03) 5155 7254
Parking Area at Tostaree. Jonsons Rd. Check in with Tavern before parking
HEMA 65 H9   37 44 51 S   148 11 03 E

22 Stonehenge Farmstay Camping Ground ☎ (03) 5155 9312
Camp Area at Buchan South. 9 km N of Nowa Nowa turn N onto Buchan Caves Rd, 15 km to Buchan South Rd, then onto Buchan South Gillingall Rd. Signposted. GPS at gate
HEMA 65 G9   37 31 51 S   148 08 08 E

23 Buchan Caves Camping Reserve ☎ 131 963
Camp Area at Buchan Caves. Buchan Caves Rd
HEMA 65 G9   37 29 43 S   148 09 50 E

24 Wulgulmerang Recreation Reserve ☎ (03) 5155 0253
Camp Area at Wulgulmerang. 133 km NE of Bairnsdale or 112 km SW of Jindabyne
C608
HEMA 65 E9   37 04 06 S   148 15 37 E

25 Suggan Buggan Campground ☎ 131 963
Camp Area 80 km N of Buchan or 87 km S of Jindabyne. Tight winding road in places, not suitable for caravans
HEMA 65 E9   36 57 09 S   148 19 27 E

26 Willis Campground
Camp Area 99 km N of Buchan or 68 km S of Jindabyne. Via Snowy River Rd. Tight winding road in places, not suitable for caravans
HEMA 65 E10   36 53 41 S   148 25 22 E

27 Running Waters Creek Campground
Camp Area 102 km N of Buchan or 65 km S of Jindabyne. Via Barry Way. Tight winding road in places, not suitable for caravans
HEMA 65 D10   36 48 47 S   148 24 16 E

28 Burned Bridge Reserve
Rest Area 12 km E of Lakes Entrance or 10 km W of Nowa Nowa
A1
HEMA 65 H9   37 48 56 S   148 01 50 E

29 ✓ The Glasshouse Camping Area ☎ 131 963
Lake Tyers State Park
Camp Area 22 km SE of Nowa Nowa. Turn S 6 km E of Nowa Nowa or 32 km W of Orbost onto Lake Tyers Rd, follow to end. 16 km dirt road
HEMA 65 H9   37 50 47 S   148 06 33 E

30 Camerons Arm No 1 ☎ 131 963
Lake Tyers State Park
Camp Area 16 km SE of Nowa Nowa. Turn S 6 km E of Nowa Nowa or 32 km W of Orbost onto Tyers House Rd, follow to Camerons Arm No 1 track
HEMA 65 H9   37 46 48 S   148 08 12 E

31 Trident Arm Campground ☎ 131 963
Lake Tyers State Park
Camp Area 18 km SE of Nowa Nowa. Turn S 6 km E of Nowa Nowa or 32 km W of Orbost onto Tyers House Rd, then Lake Tyers Beach Rd, Trident Arm Track. 14 km dirt Rd. Limited space
HEMA 65 H9   37 49 27 S   148 08 05 E

32 Pettmans Beach ☎ 131 963
Lake Tyers State Park
Camp Area at Pettmans Beach. Turn S 6 km E of Nowa Nowa or 32 km W of Orbost onto Tyers House Rd, follow to Pettmans Rd. 12 km dirt rd
HEMA 65 H9   37 49 44 S   148 11 08 E

33 Lake Tyers Camp & Caravan Park ☎ (03) 5156 5530
Caravan Park at Lake Tyers Beach. 558 Lake Tyers Beach Rd
HEMA 65 H9   37 51 30 S   148 04 59 E

Notes...

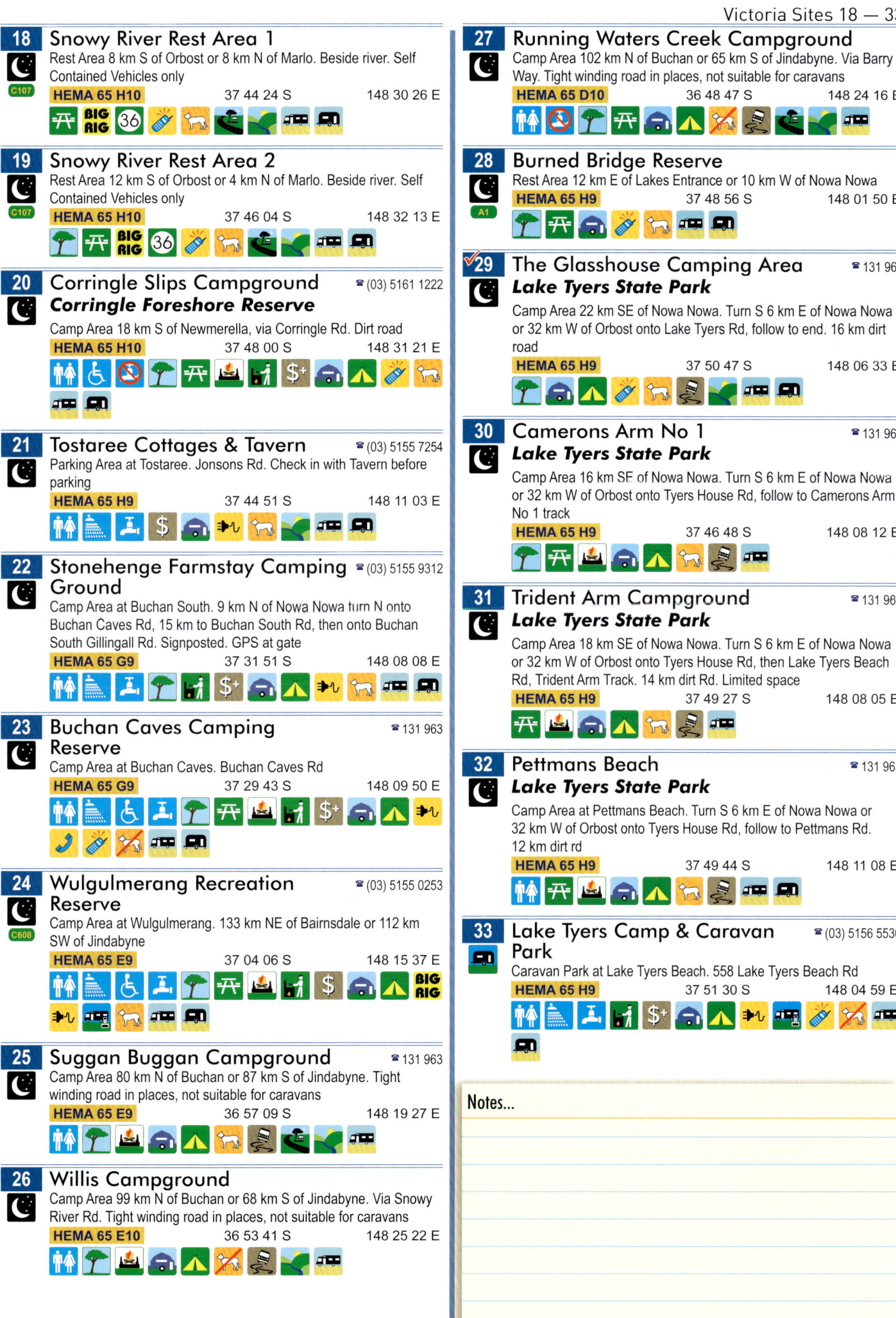

34 Waterwheel Beach Tavern & Cabins ☎ (03) 5156 5855

Parking Area at Lake Tyers Beach. 577 Lake Tyers Beach Rd. Check in with publican

HEMA 65 H9   37 51 26 S   148 05 08 E

35 Lakes Entrance Recreation & Camping Reserve ☎ (03) 5155 1647

Camp Area at Lakes Entrance. 1 Rowe St

HEMA 65 H8   37 52 40 S   147 59 09 E

36 Metung RV Stop

Parking Area at Metung. Rosherville Rd. Small area

HEMA 65 H8   37 52 41 S   147 51 28 E

37 Nicholson River Reserve

Rest Area at Nicholson. W side of bridge beside river

HEMA 65 H8   37 49 02 S   147 44 24 E

38 Eagle Point Caravan Park ☎ (03) 5156 1183

Caravan Park at Eagle Point. 40 School Rd

HEMA 65 H8   37 53 32 S   147 40 53 E

39 Providence Ponds

Rest Area 34 km W of Bairnsdale or 18 km E of Stratford

HEMA 64 H6   37 55 14 S   147 16 25 E

40 Avon River Streamside Reserve

Camp Spot 4 km S of Perry Bridge. Via Springberg Lane

HEMA 64 J6   38 01 49 S   147 14 54 E

41 Marlay Point

Parking Area at Marlay Point. Turn E off Hwy onto Clydebank Rd 8 km S of Stratford or 9 km N of Sale, then onto Marlay Point Rd, follow signs. Grassy area near yacht club

HEMA 64 J6   38 03 40 S   147 14 58 E

42 Sale Showground Caravan & Motorhome Park ☎ (03) 5144 6432

Camp Area at Sale. Maffra-Sale Rd. N end of town

HEMA 64 J6   38 05 31 S   147 03 58 E

43 Maffra Golf Club ☎ (03) 5147 1884

Camp Area at Maffra Golf Club. Via Stratford Rd, Fulton Rd. Behind Clubrooms

HEMA 64 J6   37 57 04 S   147 00 01 E

44 Newry Recreation Reserve

Camp Area at Newry Recreation Reserve. 2 km N of Newry via Newry - Boisdale & Three Chain Rd. Adjacent to golf course. Donation welcomed. Self Contained Vehicles only

HEMA 64 H5   37 54 20 S   146 54 28 E

45 Briagolong Quarry Reserve

Camp Area 4 km N of Briagolong, via Freestone Creek Rd. Beside river. Pay at Briagolong cafe or hotel

HEMA 64 H6   37 48 50 S   147 05 19 E

46 Blue Pools Campground

Camp Area 10 km N of Briagolong. 6 km N of The Quarries Campground. Small vehicles only

HEMA 64 H6   37 46 50 S   147 06 46 E

47 Echo Bend Camping Park ☎ (03) 5157 6317

Camp Area 12 km NE of Glenaladale. 345 Dunbars Rd. Via Bairnsdale-Dargo Rd, Wallers Rd

HEMA 64 H7   37 42 41 S   147 21 52 E

48 Heyfield RV Rest Stop ☎ 0418 108 691

Camp Area 700m SE of Heyfield PO, cnr MacFarlane & Clark Sts. Camping in S area of reserve. Self Contained Vehicles only. Please take away own rubbish

HEMA 66 E6   37 59 06 S   146 47 15 E

49 Paradise Valley Camping Park ☎ (03) 5148 0291

Camping Area 16 km N of Glenmaggie. 51 Gells Rd. Prebooking essential

HEMA 64 H5   37 50 24 S   146 42 31 E

50 Cheynes Bridge

Camp Area 20.5 km S of Licola or 32 km N of Heyfield. Via Licola Rd

HEMA 66 D6   37 45 50 S   146 40 07 E

51 Currawong Camp ☎ 131 963

Alpine National Park

Camp Area 11 km N of Licola on Tamboritha Rd. Beside Wellington River

HEMA 66 D6   37 33 07 S   146 36 44 E

52 Manna Gums Camp ☎ 131 963

Alpine National Park

Camp Area 16 km N of Licola on Tamboritha Rd. Beside Wellington River

HEMA 66 C6   37 31 58 S   146 36 30 E

VICTORIA

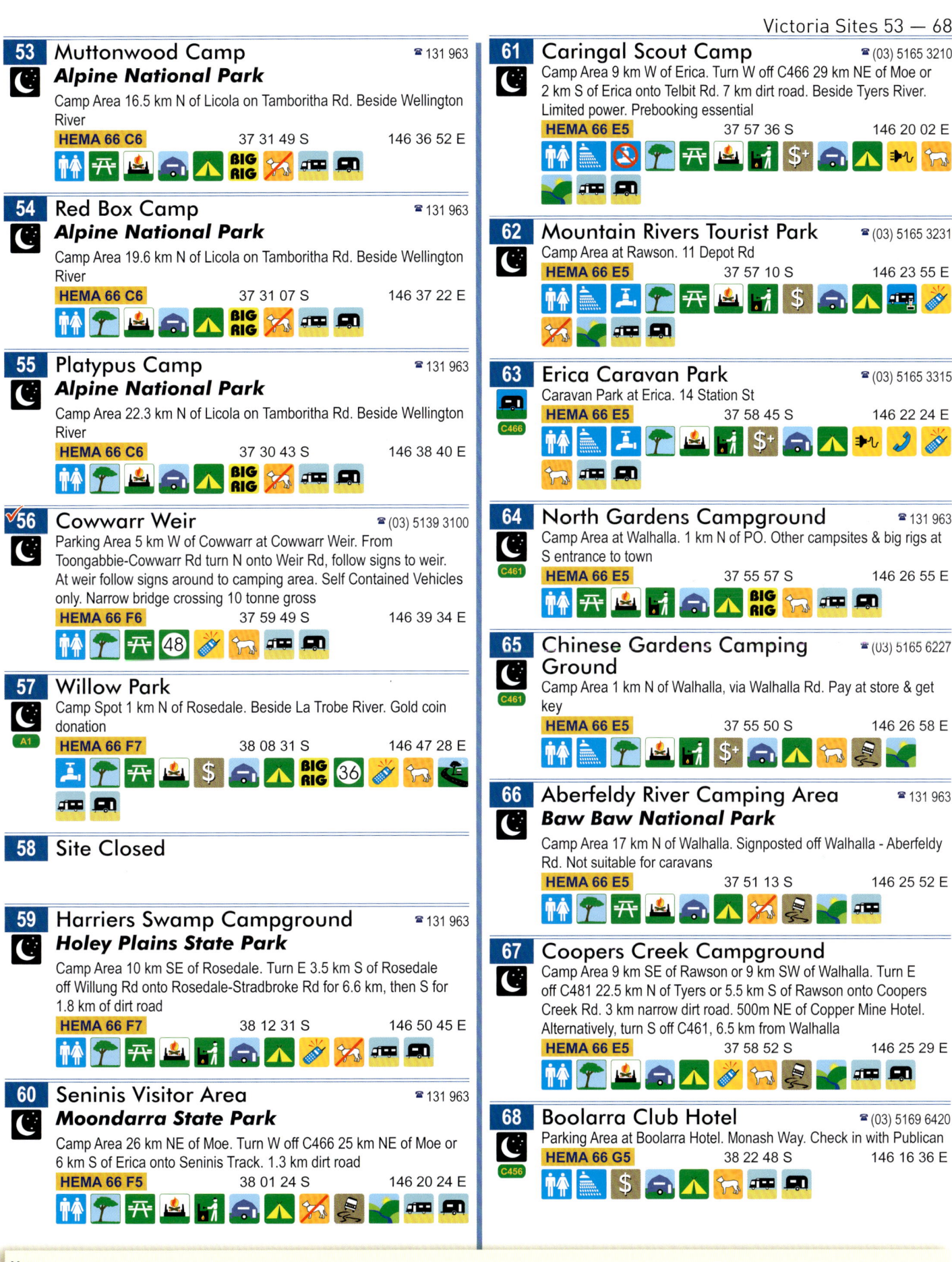

53 Muttonwood Camp ☎ 131 963
Alpine National Park
Camp Area 16.5 km N of Licola on Tamboritha Rd. Beside Wellington River
HEMA 66 C6   37 31 49 S   146 36 52 E

54 Red Box Camp ☎ 131 963
Alpine National Park
Camp Area 19.6 km N of Licola on Tamboritha Rd. Beside Wellington River
HEMA 66 C6   37 31 07 S   146 37 22 E

55 Platypus Camp ☎ 131 963
Alpine National Park
Camp Area 22.3 km N of Licola on Tamboritha Rd. Beside Wellington River
HEMA 66 C6   37 30 43 S   146 38 40 E

56 Cowwarr Weir ☎ (03) 5139 3100
Parking Area 5 km W of Cowwarr at Cowwarr Weir. From Toongabbie-Cowwarr Rd turn N onto Weir Rd, follow signs to weir. At weir follow signs around to camping area. Self Contained Vehicles only. Narrow bridge crossing 10 tonne gross
HEMA 66 F6   37 59 49 S   146 39 34 E

57 Willow Park
Camp Spot 1 km N of Rosedale. Beside La Trobe River. Gold coin donation
HEMA 66 F7   38 08 31 S   146 47 28 E

58 Site Closed

59 Harriers Swamp Campground ☎ 131 963
Holey Plains State Park
Camp Area 10 km SE of Rosedale. Turn E 3.5 km S of Rosedale off Willung Rd onto Rosedale-Stradbroke Rd for 6.6 km, then S for 1.8 km of dirt road
HEMA 66 F7   38 12 31 S   146 50 45 E

60 Seninis Visitor Area ☎ 131 963
Moondarra State Park
Camp Area 26 km NE of Moe. Turn W off C466 25 km NE of Moe or 6 km S of Erica onto Seninis Track. 1.3 km dirt road
HEMA 66 F5   38 01 24 S   146 20 24 E

61 Caringal Scout Camp ☎ (03) 5165 3210
Camp Area 9 km W of Erica. Turn W off C466 29 km NE of Moe or 2 km S of Erica onto Telbit Rd. 7 km dirt road. Beside Tyers River. Limited power. Prebooking essential
HEMA 66 E5   37 57 36 S   146 20 02 E

62 Mountain Rivers Tourist Park ☎ (03) 5165 3231
Camp Area at Rawson. 11 Depot Rd
HEMA 66 E5   37 57 10 S   146 23 55 E

63 Erica Caravan Park ☎ (03) 5165 3315
Caravan Park at Erica. 14 Station St
HEMA 66 E5   37 58 45 S   146 22 24 E

64 North Gardens Campground ☎ 131 963
Camp Area at Walhalla. 1 km N of PO. Other campsites & big rigs at S entrance to town
HEMA 66 E5   37 55 57 S   146 26 55 E

65 Chinese Gardens Camping Ground ☎ (03) 5165 6227
Camp Area 1 km N of Walhalla, via Walhalla Rd. Pay at store & get key
HEMA 66 E5   37 55 50 S   146 26 58 E

66 Aberfeldy River Camping Area ☎ 131 963
Baw Baw National Park
Camp Area 17 km N of Walhalla. Signposted off Walhalla - Aberfeldy Rd. Not suitable for caravans
HEMA 66 E5   37 51 13 S   146 25 52 E

67 Coopers Creek Campground ☎ 131 963
Camp Area 9 km SE of Rawson or 9 km SW of Walhalla. Turn E off C481 22.5 km N of Tyers or 5.5 km S of Rawson onto Coopers Creek Rd. 3 km narrow dirt road. 500m NE of Copper Mine Hotel. Alternatively, turn S off C461, 6.5 km from Walhalla
HEMA 66 E5   37 58 52 S   146 25 29 E

68 Boolarra Club Hotel ☎ (03) 5169 6420
Parking Area at Boolarra Hotel. Monash Way. Check in with Publican
HEMA 66 G5   38 22 48 S   146 16 36 E

Notes...

69 Boolarra Apex Park
Camp Area 8 km SE of Boolarra, via Morwell River Rd. Turn W at Boolarra South sign, then after 30m S into Morwell River Rd
HEMA 66 G5   38 25 45 S   146 18 32 E

70 Cafe Escargot   ☎ (03) 5668 1589
Parking Area at Mirboo North. 10 Old Nichols Rd. SE of town via Grand Ridge East Rd, free overnight parking with a purchase. Self Contained Vehicles only
HEMA 66 G5   38 25 05 S   146 10 17 E

71 Neerim South Caravan Park   ☎ (03) 5628 1248
Caravan Park 4 km E of Neerim South. Neerim East Rd
HEMA 66 F4   38 00 46 S   145 59 25 E

72 Poplars Reserve
Camp Area 9 km N of Noojee, via Loch Valley Rd & Loch Valley Ext Rd. Narrow Road. Beside river. Steep access
HEMA 66 E4   37 49 08 S   145 59 38 E

73 Toorongo Falls Camp Area   ☎ 136 186
Camp Area 9 km NE of Noojee. Turn N off Mt Baw Baw Rd 4 km E of Noojee onto Toorongo Valley Rd. 4 km dirt road. Unlevel area beside river
HEMA 66 E4   37 51 19 S   146 02 28 E

74 Latrobe River Camping Area   ☎ 136 186
Camp Area 15 km W of Noojee. Turn N off C425, 11 km W of C425/C426 jcn or 14 km E of Powelltown. 400m off Hwy on Ada River Rd. Small vehicles only
HEMA 57 D14   37 52 54 S   145 53 35 E

75 Powelltown Rest Area
Rest Area at Powelltown. W end of town
HEMA 57 D13   37 51 38 S   145 44 41 E

76 Kurth Kiln Picnic & Camping Ground   ☎ 131 963
Kurth Kiln Regional Park
Camp Area 8 km N of Gembrook or 23 km S of Launching Place, turn W into Soldiers Rd then 1.8 km of dirt road to Kurth Kiln. Small vehicles only. 4WD recommended
HEMA 57 D12   37 53 59 S   145 34 31 E

77 Nash Creek Campground   ☎ 131 963
Bunyip State Park
Camp Area in Bunyip State Park 65 km E of Melbourne. From Gembrook via Beenak East Rd & Black Snake Creek Rd. 1.4 km E of Dyers Picnic Area. Small vehicles only
HEMA 57 E12   37 56 48 S   145 41 15 E

78 Longwarry North Rest Area
Rest Area on Princes Hwy 2 km W of Robin Hood turn off. Westbound traffic only
HEMA 57 F13   38 05 26 S   145 48 25 E

79 Bunyip Recreation Reserve   ☎ 0459 022 374
Camp Area in Bunyip, 3 km W of Longwarry on Longwarry Nar Nar Goon Rd. Call ahead to book or pay at Top Pub. Camp area located on the grassy area before the Oval
HEMA 57 F13   38 05 59 S   145 43 08 E

80 Akoonah Park   ☎ 0427 057 768
Camp Area at Berwick. Park is 2.5 km SE of Berwick along the Princes Hwy, entry into park via Cardinia St "Gate 5". Bookings advised during peak period. Closed in February each year. Maximum stay 21 days
HEMA 55 E11   38 02 20 S   145 21 51 E

Sale - Leongatha - Dandenong
South Gippsland Highway

81 Gippsland Lakes Coastal Park   ☎ 131 963
Camp Area between Seaspray & Golden Beach. 20 separate numbered camp areas, facilities & sizes vary. Dogs permitted in sites 1-6 only. Showers at Golden Beach
HEMA 64 K6   38 20 26 S   147 14 15 E

82 Golden Beach RV Rest Stop Area
Camp Area at Golden Beach. Self Contained Vehicles only. Donations appreciated
HEMA 64 K7   38 12 40 S   147 23 56 E

83 Paradise Beach Campground   ☎ 131 963
Camp Area 2.5 km N of Golden Beach, via Shoreline Dr
HEMA 64 J7   38 11 39 S   147 25 20 E

84 Emu Bight Campground   ☎ 131 963
The Lakes National Park
Camp Area 5 km E of Lochsport, via Lake Victoria Track. Bookings required
HEMA 64 J7   37 59 44 S   147 30 10 E

85 Reeves Beach Coastal Reserve   ☎ 131 963
Camp Area 10 km S of Woodside. Via Woodside Beach Rd, Balloong Rd & Reeves Beach Rd
HEMA 66 H7   38 34 24 S   146 57 08 E

VICTORIA

86 White Womans Waterhole ☎ (03) 5183 9100
Won Wron State Forest
Picnic Area 5 km E of Won Wron, via Napier Rd. 5 km dirt road
HEMA 66 H6   38 28 55 S   146 46 19 E

87 Won Wron North Rest Area
Rest Area 2 km N of Won Wron or 25 km S of Gormandale
C482
HEMA 66 G6   38 27 32 S   146 43 47 E

88 Gormandale Recreation Reserve ☎ (03) 5197 7200
Camp Spot at Gormandale, 20 km SE of Traralgon. Hyland Hwy
C482
HEMA 66 G6   38 17 32 S   146 42 03 E

89 Tarra River Rest Area
Rest Area 1 km NE of Yarram
B440
HEMA 66 H6   38 33 02 S   146 40 59 E

90 Port Albert Parking Area
Parking Area at Port Albert. 6 overnight bays available. Self Contained Vehicles only
HEMA 66 H6   38 40 22 S   146 41 38 E

91 Agnes River Rest Area
Rest Area 5 km W of Welshpool or 6 km E of Toora
B440
HEMA 66 H5   38 40 18 S   146 23 11 E

92 Franklin River Reserve Rest Area
Rest Area 2 km W of Toora or 10 km E of Foster. Beside river
B440
HEMA 66 H5   38 39 06 S   146 18 00 E

93 Shallow Inlet Campground ☎ (03) 5687 1365
Shallow Inlet Coastal Reserve
Camp Area 8 km W of Yanakie. Turn W off C444 19 km S of Foster or 4 km N of Yanakie onto Lester Rd. Past caravan park. 4 km dirt road. Bush camping adjacent to beach. Open Nov to April inclusive
HEMA 66 J4   38 49 16 S   146 10 18 E

94 Tidal River ☎ 131 963
Wilsons Promontory National Park
C444
Camp Area 63 km S of Foster. Via Wilsons Promontory Rd
HEMA 66 K5   39 01 48 S   146 19 16 E

95 Bear Gully Reserve ☎ 131 963
Cape Liptrap Coastal Park
Camp Area 35 km SW of Fish Creek, via Walkerville-Fish Creek Rd. Turn SE at Cape Liptrap turnoff onto Walkerville South Rd for 3 km, then S along Bear Gully Rd for 5 km to beach. Dirt road. Small vehicles only
HEMA 66 J4   38 53 18 S   145 59 14 E

96 Walkerville Camping Reserve ☎ (03) 5663 2224
Camp Area at Walkerville North. 82 Bayside Dr. Booking essential
HEMA 66 J4   38 50 26 S   146 00 00 E

✓ 97 Bass Valley Camping Ground
Camp Area 8 km N of Bena or 1 km S of Poowong on Bass Valley Rd. Beside Bass River. Toilets only open 1 Oct to 30 April
HEMA 57 J13   38 21 38 S   145 45 52 E

98 Loch Camping Ground ☎ (03) 5659 4441
Camp Area at Loch. 35 Loch-Poowong Rd
A440
HEMA 57 J13   38 22 03 S   145 42 44 E

99 Lang Lang Foreshore Caravan Park ☎ (03) 5997 5220
Caravan Park at Lang Lang. Jetty Lane
HEMA 57 H11   38 18 25 S   145 31 16 E

100 Balnarring Beach Camping Reserve ☎ (03) 5983 5582
Camp Area at Balnarring Beach. Three camping areas. Signposted from Rangers Office. 154 Balnarring Rd. Open Sept-June. Bookings essential
HEMA 57 J8   38 23 24 S   145 07 29 E

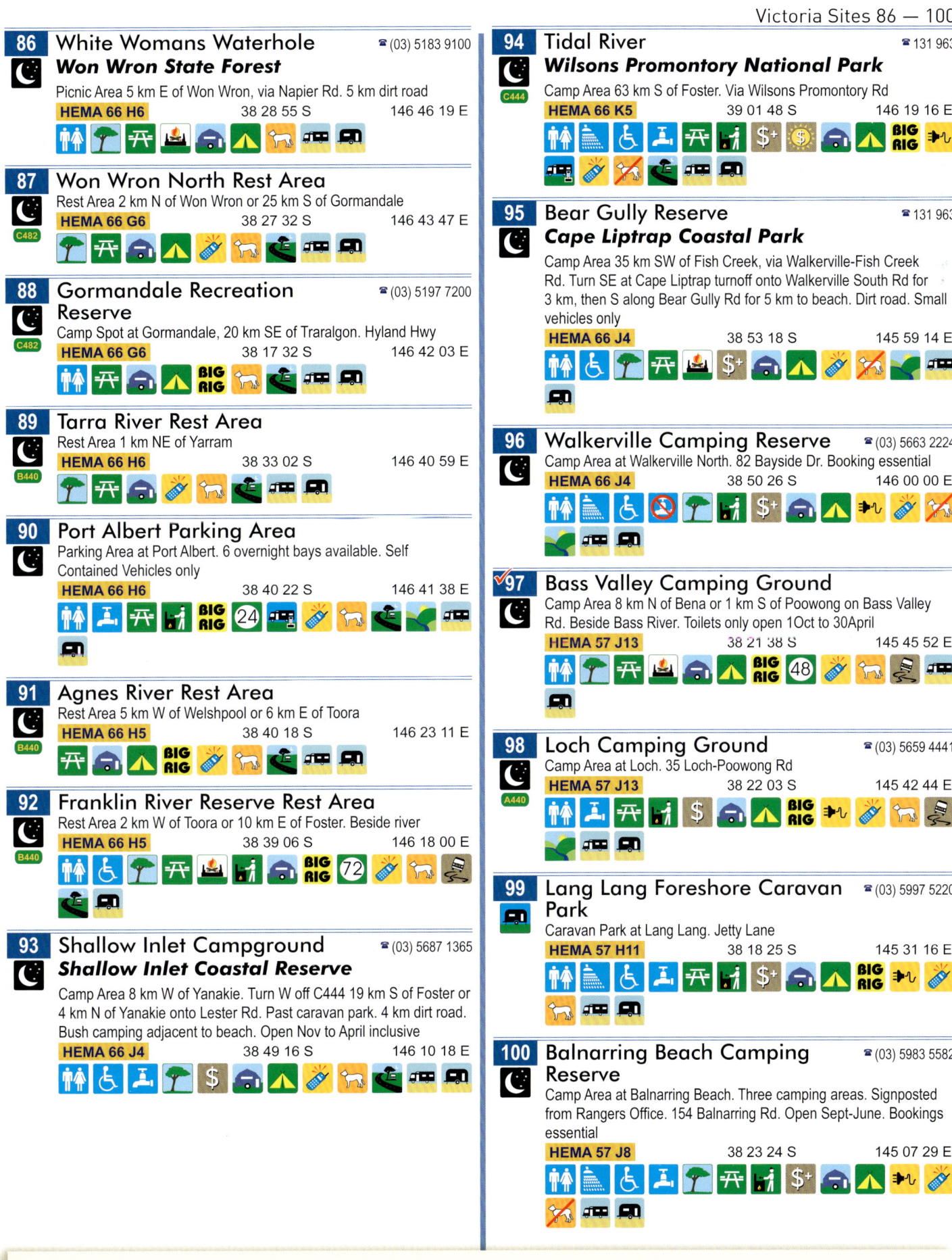

Notes...

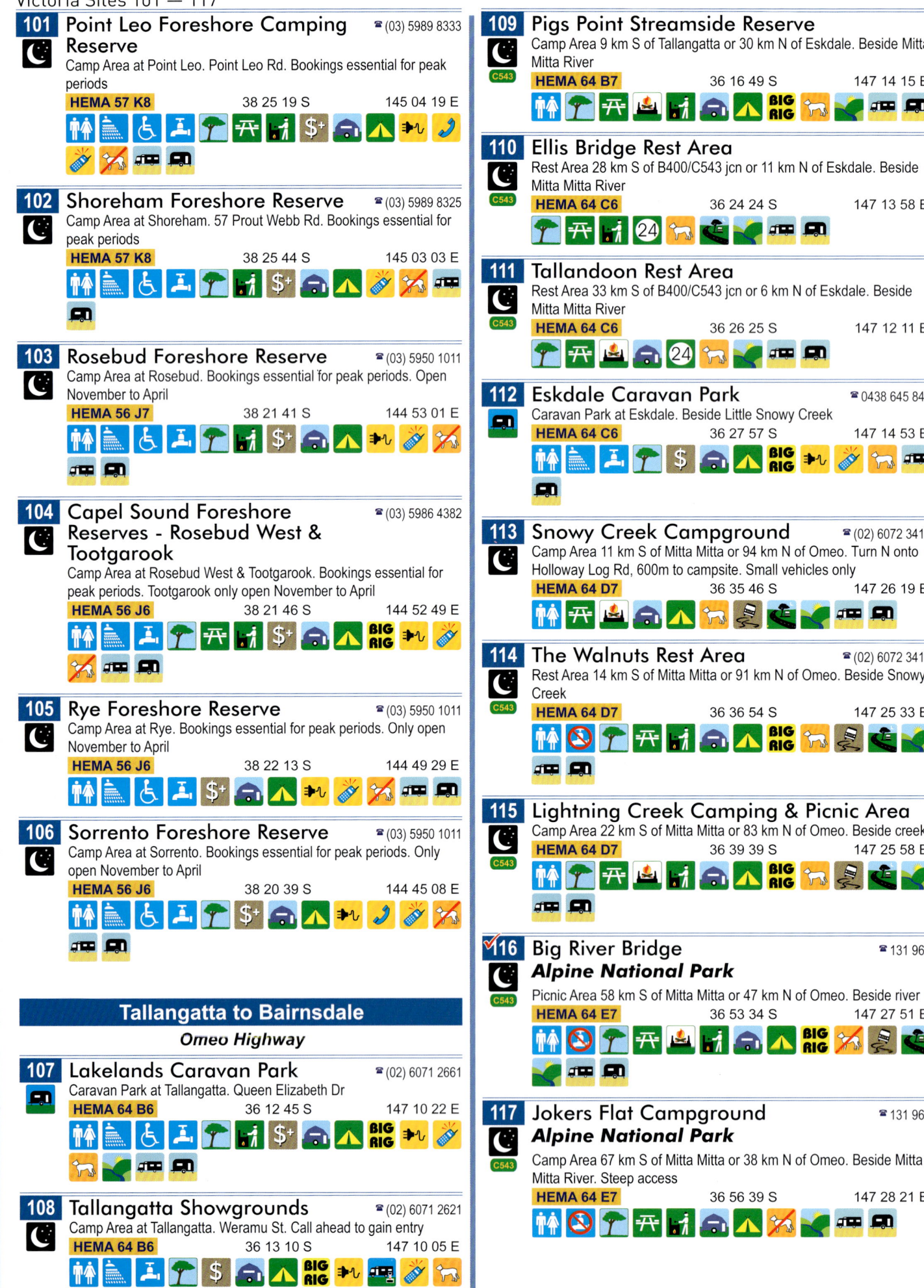

101 Point Leo Foreshore Camping Reserve ☎ (03) 5989 8333

Camp Area at Point Leo. Point Leo Rd. Bookings essential for peak periods

HEMA 57 K8   38 25 19 S   145 04 19 E

102 Shoreham Foreshore Reserve ☎ (03) 5989 8325

Camp Area at Shoreham. 57 Prout Webb Rd. Bookings essential for peak periods

HEMA 57 K8   38 25 44 S   145 03 03 E

103 Rosebud Foreshore Reserve ☎ (03) 5950 1011

Camp Area at Rosebud. Bookings essential for peak periods. Open November to April

HEMA 56 J7   38 21 41 S   144 53 01 E

104 Capel Sound Foreshore Reserves - Rosebud West & Tootgarook ☎ (03) 5986 4382

Camp Area at Rosebud West & Tootgarook. Bookings essential for peak periods. Tootgarook only open November to April

HEMA 56 J6   38 21 46 S   144 52 49 E

105 Rye Foreshore Reserve ☎ (03) 5950 1011

Camp Area at Rye. Bookings essential for peak periods. Only open November to April

HEMA 56 J6   38 22 13 S   144 49 29 E

106 Sorrento Foreshore Reserve ☎ (03) 5950 1011

Camp Area at Sorrento. Bookings essential for peak periods. Only open November to April

HEMA 56 J6   38 20 39 S   144 45 08 E

Tallangatta to Bairnsdale
Omeo Highway

107 Lakelands Caravan Park ☎ (02) 6071 2661

Caravan Park at Tallangatta. Queen Elizabeth Dr

HEMA 64 B6   36 12 45 S   147 10 22 E

108 Tallangatta Showgrounds ☎ (02) 6071 2621

Camp Area at Tallangatta. Weramu St. Call ahead to gain entry

HEMA 64 B6   36 13 10 S   147 10 05 E

109 Pigs Point Streamside Reserve

Camp Area 9 km S of Tallangatta or 30 km N of Eskdale. Beside Mitta Mitta River

C543

HEMA 64 B7   36 16 49 S   147 14 15 E

110 Ellis Bridge Rest Area

Rest Area 28 km S of B400/C543 jcn or 11 km N of Eskdale. Beside Mitta Mitta River

C543

HEMA 64 C6   36 24 24 S   147 13 58 E

111 Tallandoon Rest Area

Rest Area 33 km S of B400/C543 jcn or 6 km N of Eskdale. Beside Mitta Mitta River

C543

HEMA 64 C6   36 26 25 S   147 12 11 E

112 Eskdale Caravan Park ☎ 0438 645 846

Caravan Park at Eskdale. Beside Little Snowy Creek

HEMA 64 C6   36 27 57 S   147 14 53 E

113 Snowy Creek Campground ☎ (02) 6072 3410

Camp Area 11 km S of Mitta Mitta or 94 km N of Omeo. Turn N onto Holloway Log Rd, 600m to campsite. Small vehicles only

HEMA 64 D7   36 35 46 S   147 26 19 E

114 The Walnuts Rest Area ☎ (02) 6072 3410

Rest Area 14 km S of Mitta Mitta or 91 km N of Omeo. Beside Snowy Creek

C543

HEMA 64 D7   36 36 54 S   147 25 33 E

115 Lightning Creek Camping & Picnic Area

Camp Area 22 km S of Mitta Mitta or 83 km N of Omeo. Beside creek

C543

HEMA 64 D7   36 39 39 S   147 25 58 E

✓116 Big River Bridge ☎ 131 963
Alpine National Park

Picnic Area 58 km S of Mitta Mitta or 47 km N of Omeo. Beside river

C543

HEMA 64 E7   36 53 34 S   147 27 51 E

117 Jokers Flat Campground ☎ 131 963
Alpine National Park

Camp Area 67 km S of Mitta Mitta or 38 km N of Omeo. Beside Mitta Mitta River. Steep access

C543

HEMA 64 E7   36 56 39 S   147 28 21 E

118 Buckety Plain Campground ☎ 131 963
Alpine National Park
C543
Camp Area 19 km S of Falls Creek or 18 km W of Omeo Hwy.
Signposted. Steep & winding road
HEMA 64 E7   36 56 20 S   147 19 43 E

119 Raspberry Hill Campground ☎ 131 963
Alpine National Park
C543
Camp Area 18 km S of Falls Creek or 19 km W of Omeo Hwy.
Signposted. Steep & winding road
HEMA 64 E7   36 56 32 S   147 19 05 E

120 C.R.B Campground ☎ 131 963
Alpine National Park
C543
Camp Area 77 km S of Mitta Mitta or 28 km N of Omeo. Beside river
HEMA 64 E7   36 59 16 S   147 29 41 E

121 Anglers Rest ☎ 131 963
Alpine National Park
C543
Camp Area 76 km S of Mitta Mitta or 29 km N of Omeo. Beside
Cobungra River
HEMA 64 E7   36 59 24 S   147 29 23 E

122 Omeo RV Stop
Parking Area at Omeo. Livingstone Park off Creek St, park behind the
RV signage. Self Contained Vehicles only
HEMA 64 E7   37 05 57 S   147 35 24 E

123 Ferny Flat Campground ☎ 131 963
Alpine National Park
C543
Camp Area 26 km N of Omeo via Omeo Valley Rd & Kellys Rd.
Beside Mitta Mitta River. 5.5 km dirt road
HEMA 65 E8   36 53 36 S   147 37 53 E

124 Gibbo River Bush Camping ☎ 131 963
C545
Camp Spot 26.5 km N of Benambra or 97.5 km S of Corryong. From
Benambra 15 km winding dirt road. Not suitable for caravan access
from Corryong. Steep creek crossing at entrance. Large open area
beside river
HEMA 65 D8   36 45 25 S   147 42 15 E

125 Ah Sye's Camping Area ☎ 13 19 63
C545
Camp Area 31 km N of Benambra or 93 km S of Corryong. From
Benambra 20 km winding dirt road. Not suitable for caravan access
from Corryong
HEMA 65 D8   36 43 52 S   147 44 02 E

126 Swifts Creek Caravan & Tourist Park ☎ (03) 5159 4205
B500
Caravan Park at Swifts Creek. McMillan Ave, 500m E of PO. Adjacent
to the Tambo River
HEMA 65 F8   37 15 47 S   147 43 24 E

127 Ensay Recreation Ground ☎ (03) 5157 3227
B500
Camp Area at Ensay. Doctors Flat Rd. To pay & pick up key call land
line or mobile 0419 249 535
HEMA 65 F8   37 22 54 S   147 49 25 E

128 The Little River Inn ☎ (03) 5157 3311
Camp Area at Ensay. Large open grassed area behind hotel, check in
& pay at the bar
HEMA 65 F8   37 21 46 S   147 50 07 E

Wangaratta to Omeo
Great Alpine Road

129 Pioneer Bridges
Rest Area 2 km SW of Everton or 3 km NE of Markwood. Turn S
700m W of Everton onto Markwood Everton Rd. Beside Ovens River
HEMA 64 C5   36 26 32 S   146 31 30 E

130 Dederang North Rest Area
C531
Rest Area 5 km N of Dederang or 13 km S of Kergunyah
HEMA 64 C6   36 26 40 S   147 01 01 E

131 Dederang Hotel ☎ (02) 6028 9325
Parking Area at Dederang, Kiewa Valley Hwy. Check in with publican,
camp area is behind the hotel. Toilets at hotel during opening hours
HEMA 64 C6   36 27 58 S   147 00 46 E

132 Yackandandah Creek ☎ 136 186
Yackandandah State Forest
Camp Area 4.5 km SW of Yackandandah. Take Bell's Flat Rd follow
for 2.5 km on to Service Basin Rd, then into Number One Rd. There
are a number of sites along this road
HEMA 64 C5   36 20 18 S   146 48 24 E

133 Running Creek Rest Area
C534
Rest Area 37 km E of Myrtleford or 1 km W of C531/C534 jcn
HEMA 64 C6   36 32 40 S   147 02 47 E

Notes...

VICTORIA

134 Mongans Bridge Caravan Park ☎ (03) 5754 5226

Caravan Park 13 km N of Tawonga or 18 km S of Dederang. Turn E 12 km N of Tawonga or 7 km S of C531/C534 jcn onto Bay Creek Lane

HEMA 64 C6   36 35 05 S   147 05 37 E

135 Mountain Creek Campground ☎ 131 963

Alpine National Park

Camp Area 11 km E of Tawonga. Via Mountain Creek Rd

HEMA 64 D7   36 41 59 S   147 15 09 E

136 Nug Nug Reserve ☎ 0418 336 272

Camp Area 15 km S of Myrtleford. Turn E off C526, 13 km S of Myrtleford before McGuffies Bridge onto Nug Nug Rd. Turn L after 1 km, then next R. Cold showers

HEMA 64 D5   36 39 42 S   146 42 20 E

137 Lake Catani Campground ☎ 131 963

Mt Buffalo National Park

C535

Camp Area 28 km W of Porepunkah. Closed May to October. Bookings essential

HEMA 64 D5   36 44 07 S   146 48 43 E

✓138 Ah Youngs Camping Area ☎ 136 186

Camp Area 18 km S of Porepunkah. From Porepunkah roundabout turn S onto Buckland Valley Rd, follow for 18 km to campsites along river. 5.6 km dirt road

HEMA 64 D5   36 50 30 S   146 51 04 E

139 Freeburgh Bridge

Rest Area 7 km S of Bright or 16 km N of Harrietville. Turn E off B500 onto Old Harrietville Rd. Camp spots on W side of bridge, entry track 5m from intersection. No camping on E side of bridge in picnic area

HEMA 64 D6   36 45 22 S   147 01 24 E

140 Smoko Camping Area ☎ 136 186

B500

Camp Area 16 km S of Bright or 11.5 km N of Harrietville. Turn E off Great Alpine Rd (opposite house) follow track for 700m veering R to campsite. Beside river

HEMA 64 D6   36 49 39 S   147 04 36 E

141 Scrubbers End Overnight Parking ☎ 1800 444 066

B500

Parking Area at Dinner Plain Alpine Village. Enter via Big Muster Dr & Scrubbers End Ln, E side of village. Permit required in winter

HEMA 64 E6   37 01 28 S   147 14 36 E

142 Victoria Falls Historic Area ☎ 131 963

Alpine National Park

Camp Area 25 km W of Omeo or 90 km SE of Bright. Near Cobungra Station

HEMA 64 E7   37 05 37 S   147 25 30 E

Omeo-Dargo-Bairnsdale

143 Dogs Grave Campground

C601

Camp Area 22 km SW of Omeo or 44 km NE of Dargo. Turn S off B500, 3 km W of Omeo onto Swifts Creek-Omeo Rd for 7 km, then SW onto Upper Livingstone Rd for 6 km, then W onto Birregun Rd for 6 km. Winding dirt road

HEMA 64 F7   37 14 01 S   147 22 51 E

144 Ollies Jumpup Campground

C601

Camp Area 61 km SW of Omeo or 12 km N of Dargo. 5.5 km N of Dargo turn NE onto Upper Dargo Rd. Winding dirt road. Signposted

HEMA 64 F7   37 23 09 S   147 16 39 E

✓145 Jimmy Iversons Campground

C601

Camp Area 63 km SW of Omeo or 10 km N of Dargo. 5.5 km N of Dargo turn NE onto Upper Dargo Rd. Winding dirt road. Beside river. Signposted

HEMA 64 F7   37 23 54 S   147 16 21 E

146 Italian Flat Campground

C601

Camp Area 65 km SW of Omeo or 8 km N of Dargo. 5.5 km N of Dargo turn NE onto Upper Dargo Rd. Winding dirt road. Beside river. Signposted

HEMA 64 G7   37 24 33 S   147 15 53 E

147 Two Mile Creek

C601

Camp Area 66 km SW of Omeo or 7 km N of Dargo. 5.5 km N of Dargo turn NE onto Upper Dargo Rd. Winding dirt road. Beside Two Mile Creek. Signposted

HEMA 64 G6   37 24 31 S   147 15 28 E

148 Dargo River Inn ☎ (03) 5140 1330

Camp Area at Dargo River Inn, Lower Dargo Rd. Some powered sites avaliable

HEMA 64 G6   37 28 16 S   147 15 17 E

✓149 Meyers Flat Campsite

C601

Camp Area 12.5 km S of Dargo. Signposted access, next to Dargo Bairnsdale Rd beside river

HEMA 64 G6   37 30 59 S   147 13 53 E

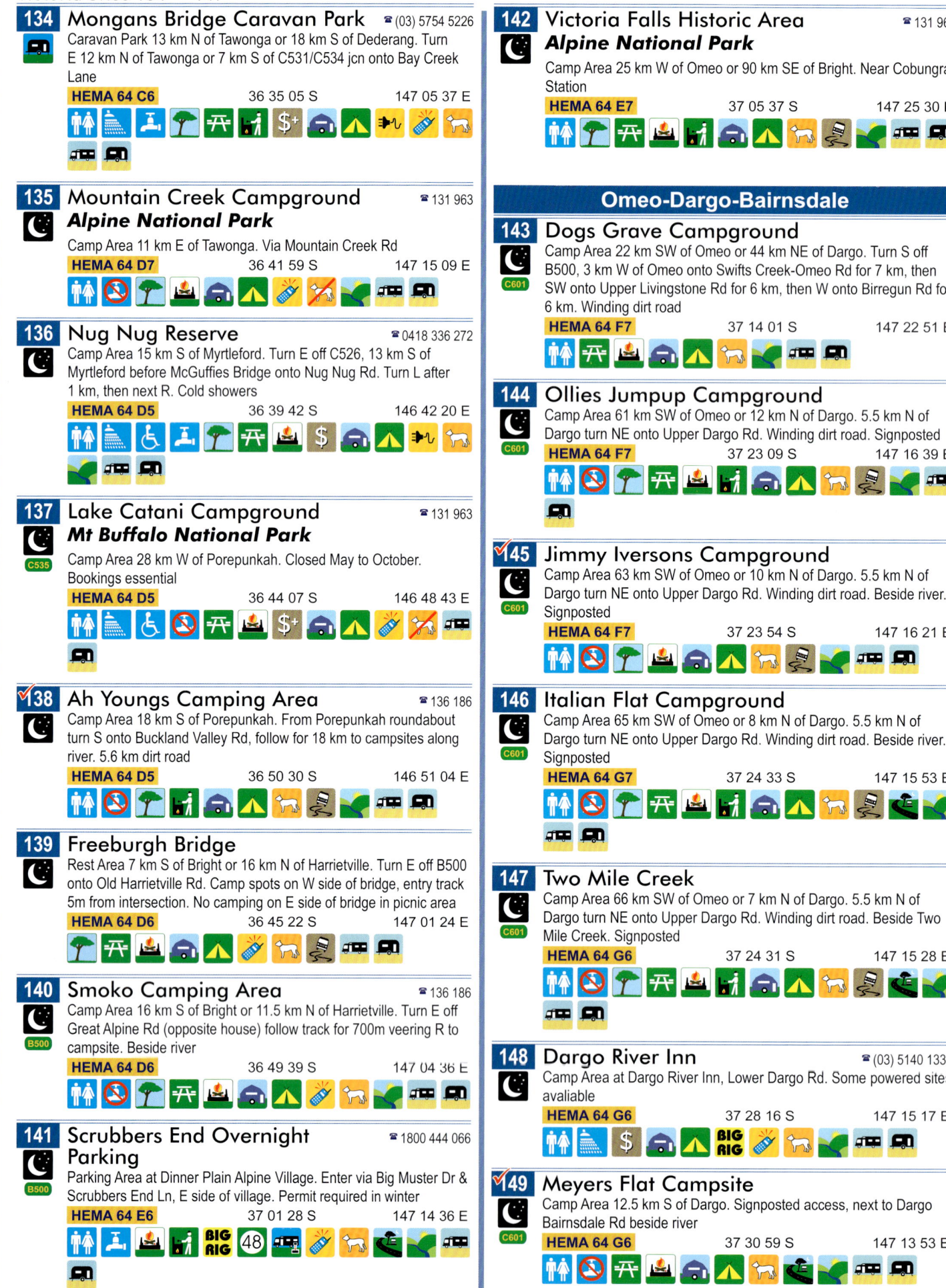

Far North East Victoria

150 Yackandandah North Rest Area
Rest Area 22 km SW of Wodonga or 5 km NW of Yackandandah. Jcn of C532 & C315
C315
HEMA 64 B5   36 16 33 S   146 48 15 E

151 Allans Flat Reserve
Picnic Area 8 km NE of Yackandandah. Turn E off C527 7 km NE of Yackandandah or 13 km SW of Baranduda for 700m. Beside lake
T6
HEMA 64 B6   36 16 27 S   146 54 34 E

152 Ludlows Reserve
Rest Area 5 km SE of Bonegilla or 22 km NW of Tallangatta. Beside Lake Hume. Self Contained Vehicles only
B400
HEMA 64 B6   36 10 16 S   147 02 09 E

153 Tallangatta Creek Rest Area
Rest Area 13 km E of Tallangatta or 2 km W of B400/C546 jcn
B400
HEMA 64 B7   36 11 43 S   147 19 01 E

154 Tom Mitchell Reserve Rest Area
Rest Area 6.5 km E of Koetong or 24 km W of Cudgewa-Tintaldra Rd intersection. Cnr of Murray Valley Hwy & Avondale Rd
B400
HEMA 64 B7   36 10 43 S   147 32 59 E

155 Cotton Tree Creek Campground
Mt Granya State Park   ☎ 131 963
Camp Area 2 km W of Granya. Dirt road
HEMA 64 B7   36 06 53 S   147 18 18 E

156 The Kurrajongs Campground
Mount Lawson State Park   ☎ 131 963
Camp Area 40 km W of Walwa or 16 km NE of Bungil Junction. Via Murray River Rd. Small vehicles only
HEMA 64 A7   35 57 22 S   147 25 11 E

157 Kennedys Reserve
Rest Area 37 km W of Walwa or 23 km NE of C542/C546 jcn. Beside Murray River
C546
HEMA 64 A7   35 57 33 S   147 26 37 E

158 Burrowye Reserve
Camp Area 25 km W of Walwa or 35 km NE of C542/C546 jcn. Beside Murray River
C546
HEMA 64 A7   35 59 15 S   147 31 39 E

159 Koetong Creek Campsites
Mount Lawson State Park   ☎ 131 963
Camp Area 7 km NW of Koetong. Off Mount Lawson Rd & Koetong Creek Track. Small vehicles only
HEMA 64 B7   36 05 54 S   147 26 49 E

160 Walwa Riverside Caravan Park   ☎ (02) 6037 1388
Caravan Park at Walwa. River Rd. 1 km N of PO
HEMA 65 A8   35 57 16 S   147 44 14 E

161 Neils Reserve   ☎ 131 963
Camp Spot 7 km E of Walwa or 17 km NW of Tintaldra. 300m dirt road off Hwy. Beside Murray River
C546
HEMA 65 A8   35 58 22 S   147 48 46 E

162 Clarke Lagoon Reserve   ☎ (02) 6076 2277
Camp Area 19 km SE of Walwa or 5 km NW of Tintaldra. 300m dirt road off Hwy. Beside Murray River
C546
HEMA 65 A8   36 01 27 S   147 54 38 E

163 Clear Water by the Upper Murray Caravan & Tourist Park   ☎ (02) 6077 9207
Caravan Park at Tintaldra. 17 Tintaldra Back Rd
HEMA 65 B9   36 02 47 S   147 55 44 E

164 Corryong RV Parking   ☎ (02) 6076 2277
Parking Area at Corryong. Showgrounds Rd via Strzelecki Way. Next to old tennis courts. Self Contained Vehicles only. DO NOT park in the Rec Reserve
HEMA 65 B8   36 11 36 S   147 54 02 E

165 Indi Bridge Reserve   ☎ (02) 6076 2277
Camp Area 4 km S of Towong Upper, 16 km S of Towong. Upper Murray Rd
HEMA 65 B9   36 14 05 S   148 02 00 E

166 Bluff Creek Campground
Burrowa - Pine Mountain National Park   ☎ 131 963
Camp Area 21 km SW of Tintaldra. Take the Cudgewa-Tintaldra Rd, turn N into Cudgewa N Rd & S into Bluff Falls Rd. Dirt road. Small caravans only
HEMA 65 B8   36 07 19 S   147 46 40 E

Notes...

VICTORIA

167 Nariel Creek Recreation Reserve ☎ (02) 6076 2277
C545
Camp Area 9 km S of Corryong or 24 km N of Nariel Creek. Via Corryong-Benambra Rd. Honesty box
HEMA 65 B8   36 14 32 S   147 49 53 E

168 Staceys Bridge Camping Reserve ☎ (02) 6076 2277
C545
Camp Area 44 km S of Corryong. Via Corryong-Benambra Rd
HEMA 65 C8   36 26 37 S   147 49 45 E

Wangaratta-Mansfield-Healesville
North East Victoria

169 Stan Allan Reserve
C522
Rest Area at Oxley. 300m W of town over bridge. Toilets 100m towards town
HEMA 64 C4   36 26 35 S   146 22 44 E

170 Oxley Recreation Reserve
Rest Area 3 km S of Oxley, via Oxley Meadowcreek Rd
HEMA 64 C4   36 28 14 S   146 23 06 E

171 Moyhu Caravan Park ☎ (03) 5727 9217
Caravan Park at Moyhu. Byrne St
HEMA 64 C4   36 34 37 S   146 22 43 E

172 Edi Turnoff Rest Area
C521
Rest Area 9 km S of Moyhu or 15 km N of Whitfield. Beside King River. Camp in permitted areas only, no generators permitted
HEMA 64 D4   36 38 51 S   146 25 19 E

173 Edi Cutting Reserve
C521
Camp Area 10 km S of Moyhu or 14 km N of Whitfield. 1 km S of Edi turnoff. Dirt track to camps along King River. N area more suited to 2WD & large vehicle access
HEMA 64 D4   36 39 48 S   146 25 11 E

174 Gentle Annie Caravan & Camping Reserve ☎ (03) 5729 8205
Camp Area 24 km S of Moyhu or 2 km N of Whitfield. Turn E 23 km S of Moyhu or 1 km N of Whitfield onto Gentle Annie Ln for 1 km. Beside King River
HEMA 64 D4   36 45 08 S   146 25 27 E

175 Tolmie Recreation Reserve ☎ (03) 5776 2113
C521
Camp Area at Tolmie. 20 km NE Mansfield or 20 km SW of Whitfield. Pay via registration envelopes on site
HEMA 64 E4   36 56 05 S   146 14 14 E

176 Toombullup School Site
Toombullup State Forest ☎ 136 186
C517
Camp Area 6 km NW of Tolmie or 33 km SE of Tatong, along Tolmie-Tatong Rd. Dirt road. Small area 100m off road
HEMA 64 E4   36 53 16 S   146 14 06 E

177 Kelly Tree & Stringybark Creek Campground
Toombullup State Forest ☎ 136 186
C517
Camp Area 11 km NW of Tolmie or 28 km SE of Tatong, via Tolmie-Tatong Rd. Dirt road. Large area 400m off road
HEMA 64 D4   36 52 22 S   146 12 06 E

178 Jones Campground
Toombullup State Forest ☎ 136 186
Camp Area 23 km NW of Tolmie or 16 km SE of Tatong, via Tolmie-Tatong Rd & Jones Rd. Turn W 21 km NW of Tolmie or 16 km SE of Tatong. 3 km dirt road from Tatong
HEMA 64 D3   36 50 22 S   146 08 37 E

179 Dodds Bridge Rest Area
C517
Rest Area 28 km NW of Tolmie or 11 km S of Tatong
HEMA 64 D3   36 47 39 S   146 08 06 E

180 Tatong Reserve
Parking Area 750m S of Tatong on Tatong-Moorngag Rd beside Creek
HEMA 64 D3   36 44 06 S   146 06 03 E

181 Swanpool Reserve
Parking Area at Swanpool, S end of town. Self Contained Vehicles only
HEMA 64 D3   36 44 59 S   146 00 03 E

182 Lima East Creek Rest Area
B300
Rest Area 18 km S of B300/M31 Jcn or 2 km N of Swanpool
HEMA 64 D3   36 43 28 S   145 59 31 E

183 James Camping Reserve
Strathbogie Ranges State Forest ☎ 136 186
Camp Area 13 km SW of Swanpool. From Swanpool turn W onto Swanpool-Lima Rd, then turn S along Lima East Rd for 11 km. 5.5 km dirt road. Beside Black Charlies Creek
HEMA 64 D3   36 50 11 S   145 56 49 E

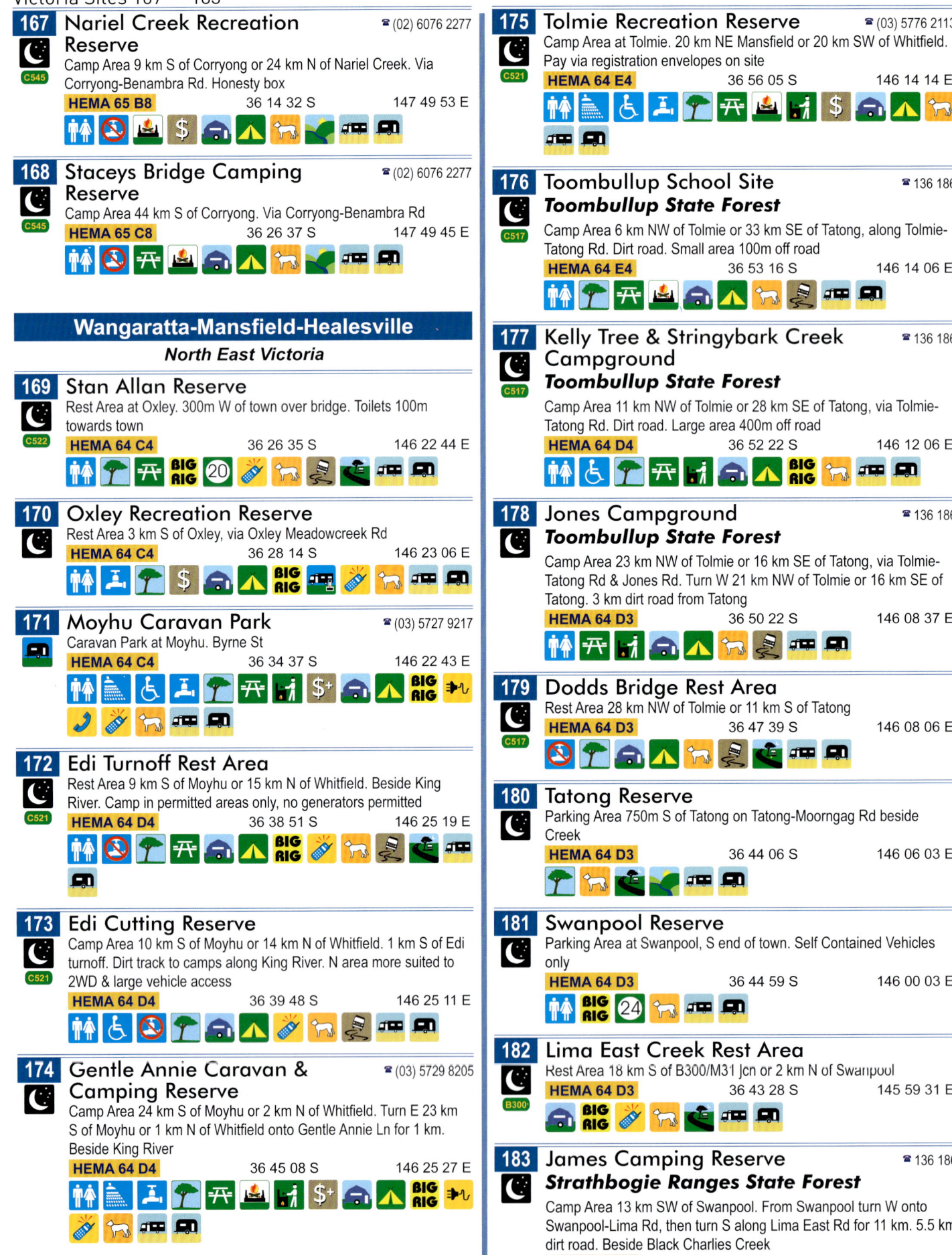

184 Lake Nillahcootie
Picnic Area 13 km S of Swanpool or 26 km N of Mansfield
HEMA 64 D3   36 51 27 S   146 00 16 E

185 Blue Range Camping & Picnic Area
Camp Area 14 km N of Mansfield. Turn N 18 km W of Tolmie or 10 km N of Mansfield onto Blue Range Rd. 4 km dirt road
HEMA 64 E3   36 56 07 S   146 05 42 E

186 Buttercup Creek Camping Area   ☎ 131 963
Camp Area 10 km E of Merrijig or 3 km NW of Mirimbah. Via Carters Rd, turn W at Buttercup Rd. 5 sites over 4 km dirt road
HEMA 66 B5   37 04 05 S   146 20 21 E

187 Carters Mill Camping & Picnic Area   ☎ 136 186
Camp Area 10 km E of Merrijig or 3 km W of Mirimbah. Turn N along Carters Rd for 400m. Unlevel area
HEMA 66 B5   37 06 11 S   146 22 02 E

188 Mirimbah West Rest Area
Rest Area 12 km E of Merrijig or 1 km W of Mirimbah. Small vehicles only
HEMA 66 B5   37 06 31 S   146 23 10 E

189 8 Mile Campground   ☎ 131 963
Alpine National Park
Camp Area 29 km SE of Merrijig. Turn S off C320 2 km E of Merrijig into Howqua Hills Rd. 27 km dirt road, steep in places. Small vehicles only. 4WD recommended
HEMA 66 B5   37 11 54 S   146 25 44 E

✓190 Sheepyard Flat   ☎ 131 963
Camp Area 19 km SE of Merrijig. Turn S off C320 2 km E of Merrijig onto Howqua Hills Rd. 17 km dirt road. Beside river
HEMA 66 B5   37 11 33 S   146 20 46 E

191 Fry's Flat   ☎ 131 963
Camp Area 19 km SE of Merrijig. Turn S off C320 2 km E of Merrijig onto Howqua Hills Rd. 19 km dirt road. Beside river. 4WD only, off road caravans & camper trailers
HEMA 66 B5   37 11 46 S   146 19 48 E

192 Blue Gum Flat   ☎ 131 963
Delatite Arm Reserve
Camp Area 8 km N of Goughs Bay, via Howes Creek Rd (500m before Goughs Bay). Mostly dirt road
HEMA 66 B4   37 10 29 S   145 59 54 E

193 Picnic Point   ☎ 131 963
Delatite Arm Reserve
Camp Area 10 km N of Goughs Bay, via Howes Creek Rd (500m before Goughs Bay). Mostly dirt road
HEMA 66 B4   37 09 43 S   145 59 36 E

194 Ewarts Campgrounds   ☎ 131 963
Delatite Arm Reserve
Camp Area N of Goughs Bay, via Howes Creek Rd (500m before Goughs Bay). Mostly dirt road. 24 campgrounds of various sizes
HEMA 66 B4   37 08 18 S   145 58 38 E

✓195 Running Creek Campground   ☎ 136 186
Camp Area 7 km E of Howqua. From Howqua turn E onto Howqua River Rd. Dirt road, steep in places, numerous sites beside river. Water is from the river
HEMA 66 B5   37 14 11 S   146 13 54 E

196 Doctors Creek Reserve   ☎ 136 186
Camp Area 5 km S of Jamieson or 51 km N of Woods Point. Camping beside river
HEMA 66 C4   37 19 55 S   146 07 50 E

197 Skipworth Reserve   ☎ 136 186
Camp Area 7.5 km S of Jamieson or 48.5 km N of Woods Point. Beside river
HEMA 66 C4   37 20 46 S   146 08 34 E

198 Kevington Hotel   ☎ (03) 5777 0543
Camp Spot next to Kevington Hotel. Pay at hotel. Fee for showers
HEMA 66 C5   37 21 30 S   146 09 41 E

199 Tunnel Bend Reserve   ☎ 131 963
Camp Area 19 km S of Jamieson or 37 km N of Woods Point
HEMA 66 C5   37 22 59 S   146 13 31 E

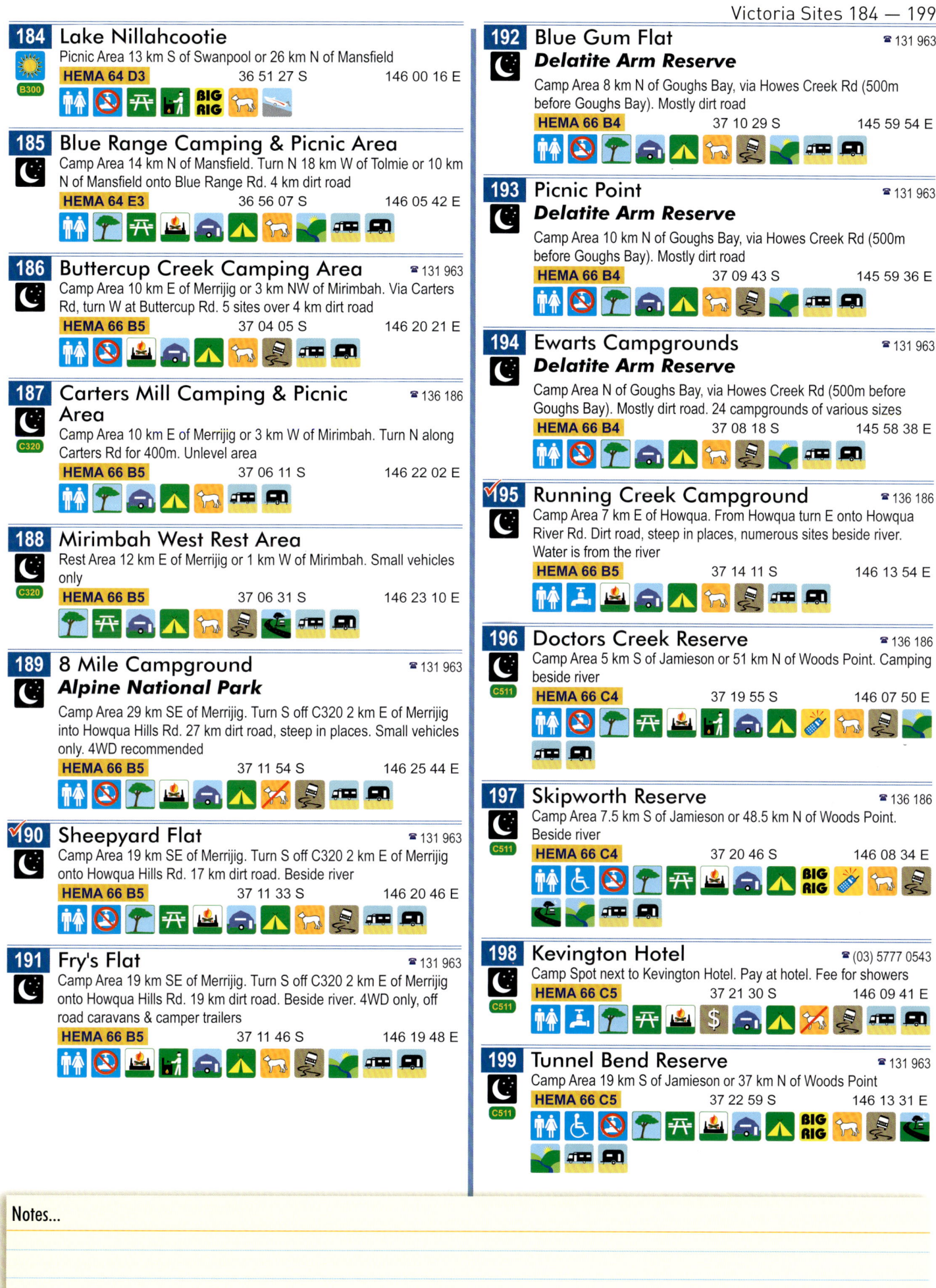

Notes...

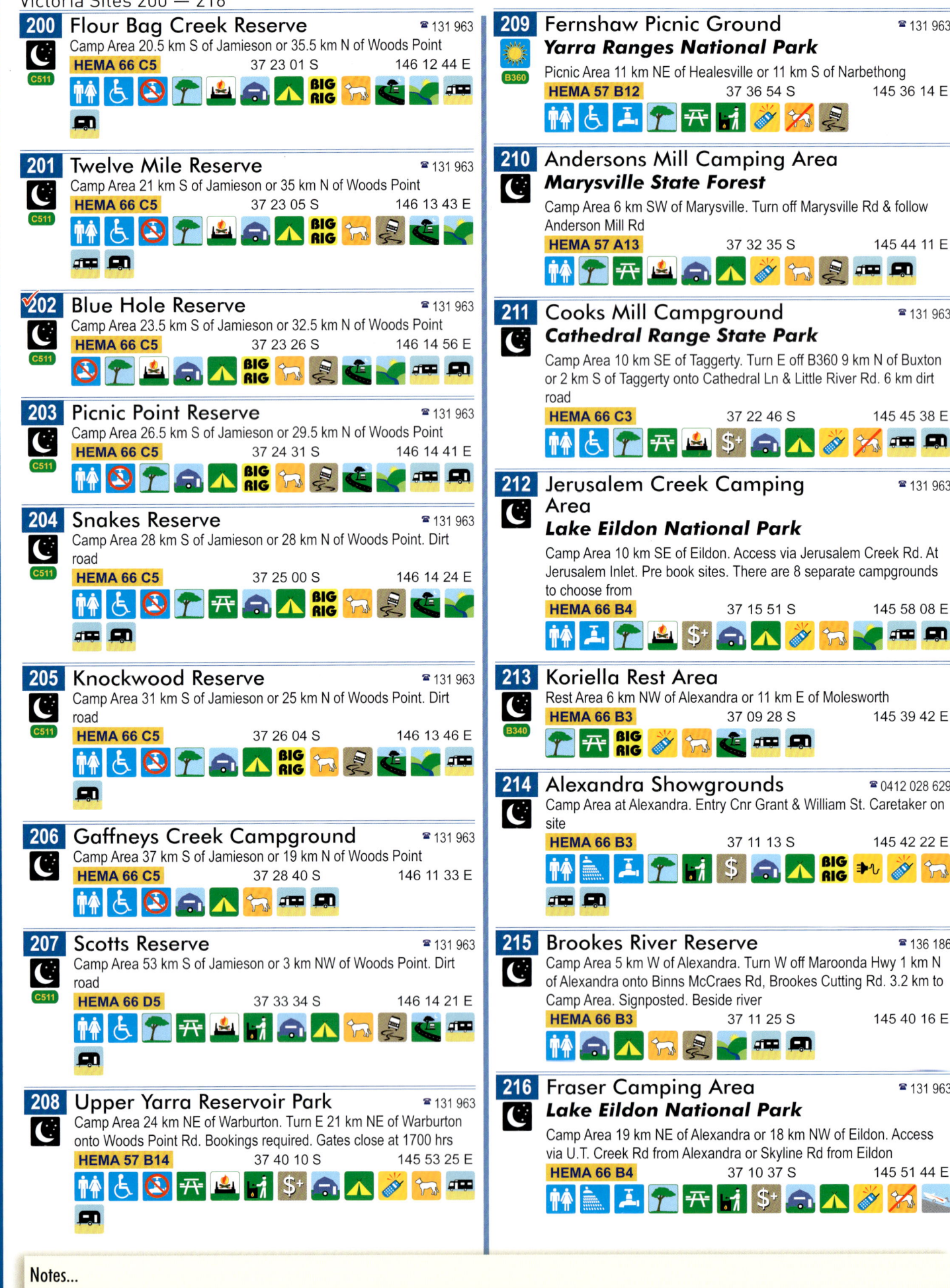

200 Flour Bag Creek Reserve ☎ 131 963
Camp Area 20.5 km S of Jamieson or 35.5 km N of Woods Point
HEMA 66 C5   37 23 01 S   146 12 44 E

201 Twelve Mile Reserve ☎ 131 963
Camp Area 21 km S of Jamieson or 35 km N of Woods Point
HEMA 66 C5   37 23 05 S   146 13 43 E

202 Blue Hole Reserve ☎ 131 963
Camp Area 23.5 km S of Jamieson or 32.5 km N of Woods Point
HEMA 66 C5   37 23 26 S   146 14 56 E

203 Picnic Point Reserve ☎ 131 963
Camp Area 26.5 km S of Jamieson or 29.5 km N of Woods Point
HEMA 66 C5   37 24 31 S   146 14 41 E

204 Snakes Reserve ☎ 131 963
Camp Area 28 km S of Jamieson or 28 km N of Woods Point. Dirt road
HEMA 66 C5   37 25 00 S   146 14 24 E

205 Knockwood Reserve ☎ 131 963
Camp Area 31 km S of Jamieson or 25 km N of Woods Point. Dirt road
HEMA 66 C5   37 26 04 S   146 13 46 E

206 Gaffneys Creek Campground ☎ 131 963
Camp Area 37 km S of Jamieson or 19 km N of Woods Point
HEMA 66 C5   37 28 40 S   146 11 33 E

207 Scotts Reserve ☎ 131 963
Camp Area 53 km S of Jamieson or 3 km NW of Woods Point. Dirt road
HEMA 66 D5   37 33 34 S   146 14 21 E

208 Upper Yarra Reservoir Park ☎ 131 963
Camp Area 24 km NE of Warburton. Turn E 21 km NE of Warburton onto Woods Point Rd. Bookings required. Gates close at 1700 hrs
HEMA 57 B14   37 40 10 S   145 53 25 E

209 Fernshaw Picnic Ground ☎ 131 963
Yarra Ranges National Park
Picnic Area 11 km NE of Healesville or 11 km S of Narbethong
HEMA 57 B12   37 36 54 S   145 36 14 E

210 Andersons Mill Camping Area
Marysville State Forest
Camp Area 6 km SW of Marysville. Turn off Marysville Rd & follow Anderson Mill Rd
HEMA 57 A13   37 32 35 S   145 44 11 E

211 Cooks Mill Campground ☎ 131 963
Cathedral Range State Park
Camp Area 10 km SE of Taggerty. Turn E off B360 9 km N of Buxton or 2 km S of Taggerty onto Cathedral Ln & Little River Rd. 6 km dirt road
HEMA 66 C3   37 22 46 S   145 45 38 E

212 Jerusalem Creek Camping Area ☎ 131 963
Lake Eildon National Park
Camp Area 10 km SE of Eildon. Access via Jerusalem Creek Rd. At Jerusalem Inlet. Pre book sites. There are 8 separate campgrounds to choose from
HEMA 66 B4   37 15 51 S   145 58 08 E

213 Koriella Rest Area ☎ 131 963
Rest Area 6 km NW of Alexandra or 11 km E of Molesworth
HEMA 66 B3   37 09 28 S   145 39 42 E

214 Alexandra Showgrounds ☎ 0412 028 629
Camp Area at Alexandra. Entry Cnr Grant & William St. Caretaker on site
HEMA 66 B3   37 11 13 S   145 42 22 E

215 Brookes River Reserve ☎ 136 186
Camp Area 5 km W of Alexandra. Turn W off Maroonda Hwy 1 km N of Alexandra onto Binns McCraes Rd, Brookes Cutting Rd. 3.2 km to Camp Area. Signposted. Beside river
HEMA 66 B3   37 11 25 S   145 40 16 E

216 Fraser Camping Area ☎ 131 963
Lake Eildon National Park
Camp Area 19 km NE of Alexandra or 18 km NW of Eildon. Access via U.T. Creek Rd from Alexandra or Skyline Rd from Eildon
HEMA 66 B4   37 10 37 S   145 51 44 E

Notes...

VICTORIA

217 Candlebark Campground ☎ 131 963
Lake Eildon National Park
Camp Area 17 km NE of Alexandra or 16 km NW of Eildon. Access via U.T. Creek Rd from Alexandra or Skyline Rd from Eildon
HEMA 66 B4   37 10 36 S   145 50 26 E

218 Devils Cove Campground ☎ 131 963
Lake Eildon National Park
Camp Area 18 km NE of Alexandra or 17 km NW of Eildon. Access via U.T. Creek Rd from Alexandra or Skyline Rd from Eildon. (Only open at Easter)
HEMA 66 B4   37 10 25 S   145 50 21 E

219 Molesworth Caravan & Camping Park ☎ (03) 5797 6278
B300
Caravan Park at Molesworth. Entrance opposite Hall. 300m off Hwy. Limited powered sites
HEMA 66 B2   37 09 49 S   145 32 23 E

220 King Parrot Creek Rest Area
B340
Rest Area 18 km NW of Yea or 20 km SE of Seymour
HEMA 66 B2   37 08 46 S   145 16 01 E

221 Murrindindi Scenic Reserve ☎ 13 61 86
Camp Area 34 km NE of Toolangi. Turn E off B300 at Devlins Bridge onto Murrindindi Rd & Wilhelmina Falls Rd. 6 camping areas. Alternative access from Toolangi via Myers Creek Rd & Murrindindi Rd. Dirt road
HEMA 66 C3   37 23 26 S   145 33 14 E

222 The Gums Campground ☎ 131 963
Kinglake National Park
C724
Camp Area 10 km N of Kinglake. Access via Eucalyptus Rd (Glenburn Rd)
HEMA 66 C2   37 28 08 S   145 23 40 E

223 Kinglake Pub ☎ (03) 5786 1230
Parking Area at Kinglake. Cnr Whittlesea-Kinglake Rd & Kinglake-Glenburn Rd. Check in with publican on arrival
HEMA 57 A10   37 31 49 S   145 20 24 E

Wodonga to Melbourne
Hume Highway
---

224 Wodonga Showgrounds ☎ (02) 6024 1872
Camp Area at Wodonga. Entry via Wilson Street. Limited sites, call phone number on arrival
HEMA 64 B6   36 08 16 S   146 53 37 E

225 Ovens Billabongs
Camp Spot 5 km NE Wangaratta. GPS at turnoff onto dirt road
HEMA 64 B5   36 22 46 S   146 21 44 E

226 Wenhams Camp ☎ 131 963
Warby-Ovens National Park
Camp Area 15 km W of Wangaratta, via Wangandry Rd, Gerret & Booth Rds. Small vehicles only, limited space. 4.4 km dirt Rd
HEMA 64 B4   36 20 27 S   146 12 15 E

227 Thoona Pub ☎ (03) 5765 2224
Parking Area at Thoona. Behind the pub, see hotel before parking. Self Contained Vehicles only
HEMA 64 C3   36 20 20 S   146 04 41 E

228 The Forest Camp ☎ 131 963
Warby-Ovens National Park
Camp Area 21 km NW of Wangaratta or 17 km SW of Peechelba. Turn W 13 km N of Wangaratta or 9 km S of Peechelba along Boweya Rd, then N along Camp Rd after 6 km. Advance booking required
HEMA 64 B4   36 13 19 S   146 10 43 E

229 Glenrowan Caravan & Tourist Park ☎ (03) 5766 2288
Caravan Park at Glenrowan. 2 km N of PO
HEMA 64 C4   36 27 06 S   146 14 13 E

230 Mokoan Rest Area
M31
Rest Area 30 km SW of B500/M31 jcn or 17 km NE of B300/M31 jcn. Both sides of road
HEMA 64 C3   36 29 54 S   146 06 25 E

231 Benalla RV Stop
Parking Area at Benalla. E end of Deas St by the tennis court. Self Contained Vehicles only
HEMA 64 C3   36 33 02 S   145 58 34 E

232 Balmattum Rest Area
M31
Rest Area 7 km NE of Euroa. Northbound only
HEMA 64 D2   36 42 49 S   145 38 07 E

233 Coach Road Rest Area
M31
Rest Area 33 km SW of Euroa or 6 km NE of A39/M31 jcn. Southbound only
HEMA 64 E1   36 56 32 S   145 12 43 E

234 Grass Tree Rest Area
Rest Area 36 km SW of Euroa or 3 km NE of A39/M31 jcn. Northbound only
M31
HEMA 64 E1   36 57 47 S   145 10 50 E

235 Northwood Reserve
Parking Area 5 km from Seymour via Emily St, Manse Hill Rd & Northwood Rd
HEMA 59 B14   37 01 11 S   145 06 53 E

236 Great Divide Rest Area
Rest Area 44 km S of C384/M31 jcn or 6 km N of B75/M31 jcn. Both sides of the road
M31
HEMA 59 D14   37 24 12 S   145 00 56 E

Tocumwal to Seymour
Goulburn Valley Highway

237 Tungamah Lions Park
Parking Area at Tungamah. Bailey St next to creek
HEMA 64 B3   36 10 00 S   145 52 42 E

238 Four Corners Motel & Caravan Park   ☎ (03) 5829 9404
Caravan Park at Congupna. Goulburn Valley Hwy
HEMA 63 J13   36 18 13 S   145 25 55 E

239 Calder-Woodburn Rest Area
Rest Area 25 km S of Shepparton or 33 km N of Nagambie. Northbound
A39
HEMA 64 C1   36 34 24 S   145 20 29 E

✓240 Greens Campground   ☎ 13 19 63
Whroo Historic Reserve
Camp Area 8 km S of Rushworth, via Rushworth-Nagambie Rd & Reedy Creek Rd. 1 km dirt road. Beyond Balaclava Hill Info Centre
HEMA 63 K12   36 38 45 S   145 01 41 E

241 Nagambie North Rest Area
Rest Area 41 km S of Shepparton or 12 km N of Nagambie. Southbound only. Share with trucks
A39
HEMA 64 D1   36 41 43 S   145 12 51 E

242 Major Creek Reserve   ☎ 131 963
Camp Spot 14 km SW of Nagambie. Turn W off Goulburn Valley Hwy 6 km S of Nagambie onto Mitchellstown Rd for 8 km
HEMA 59 A14   36 51 19 S   145 04 01 E

243 Taungurung Country Rest Area
Rest Area 20 km S of Nagambie or 7 km N of Seymour. Southbound
M39
HEMA 59 B14   36 56 54 S   145 08 41 E

244 Dargile Camping and Picnic Area   ☎ 136 186
Heathcote-Graytown National Park
Camp Area 15 km NE of Heathcote. Access via Plantation Rd off Heathcote-Costerfield Rd
HEMA 59 A13   36 51 04 S   144 44 34 E

Wodonga to Mildura
Murray Valley Highway

245 Rutherglen East Rest Area
Rest Area 26 km W of Wodonga or 18 km E of Rutherglen
B400
HEMA 64 A5   36 02 50 S   146 38 04 E

246 Police Paddocks   ☎ 131 963
Gooramadda State Forest
Camp Area 12 km NE of Rutherglen, via Gooramadda Rd (1.7 km E of Rutherglen) & Police Paddocks Rd. Beside Murray River. 1 km dirt road
HEMA 64 A5   35 58 45 S   146 30 34 E

247 Granthams Bend   ☎ 131 963
Camp Area 6 km N of Wahgunyah or 1 km S of Riverina Hwy. Turn E off Federation Way just S of John Foord Bridge, follow track. Signposted
HEMA 64 A4   35 59 08 S   146 24 45 E

248 'Willows' Camping & Recreation Reserve
Camp Area at Wahgunyah. Enter off Short St. Donation per day for Park Projects
HEMA 43 A4   36 00 28 S   146 23 26 E

249 Parolas Bend   ☎ 131 963
Lower Ovens Wildlife Reserve
Camp Area 24 km W of Rutherglen or 7 km SE of Bundalong. Turn N off B400 just E of Ovens River, opposite Riverside Caravan Park, along Parolas Track. Big rigs just inside park entrance. Camping beside Ovens River. GPS at entrance
HEMA 64 A4   36 04 03 S   146 12 10 E

250 Green Bank   ☎ 131 963
Murray River Reserve
Camp Area 5 km W of Yarrawonga. Turn N off B400, 3 km W of Yarrawonga or 34 km SE of Cobram onto Cullens Rd. Left fork at info board
HEMA 64 A3   36 00 35 S   145 58 38 E

251 Chinamans Bend
☎ 131 963
Murray River Reserve
Camp Area 6.6 km W of Yarrawonga. Turn N off B400, 4 km W of Yarrawonga or 33 km SE of Cobram onto Brears Rd. L at gate onto Chinamans Track

HEMA 64 A3　　　36 00 20 S　　　145 58 15 E

252 Forges Beach No2
☎ 131 963
Murray River Reserve
Camp Area 10.6 km NW of Yarrawonga. Turn N off B400, 8 km W of Yarrawonga or 29 km SE of Cobram onto Forges Pump Rd. Signposted along Forges Bend Track. Camping beside river

HEMA 64 A3　　　35 59 35 S　　　145 57 21 E

253 Bruces Beach No2
☎ 131 963
Murray River Reserve
Camp Area 13.2 km NW of Yarrawonga. Turn N off B400, 9 km W of Yarrawonga or 28 km SE of Cobram onto Bruces Rd. L at fork onto Bruces Track

HEMA 64 A3　　　35 57 58 S　　　145 54 52 E

254 Nevins Beach East
☎ 131 963
Murray River Reserve
Camp Area 20.2 km NW of Yarrawonga. Turn N off B400, 14 km W of Yarrawonga or 23 km SE of Cobram onto Thoms Rd. R at info board along Collins Ln & Nevins Track

HEMA 64 A3　　　35 57 20 S　　　145 53 31 E

255 Bourkes Bend No 3
☎ 131 963
Murray River Reserve
Camp Area 22.5 km W of Yarrawonga. Turn N off B400, 19 km W of Yarrawonga or 18 km SE of Cobram onto Burkes Bend Track

HEMA 64 A3　　　35 58 45 S　　　145 49 39 E

256 Big Toms Beach
☎ 131 963
Cobram Regional Park
Camp Area 3 km N of Cobram. Turn N onto Wondah St from C370 (Cobram Baroonga Rd). At end of street take track over the levee. After grid take middle dirt track for 2 km. Camp areas along river. Toilet block 1 km away

HEMA 64 A2　　　35 53 37 S　　　145 38 52 E

257 Little Toms Beach
☎ 131 963
Cobram Regional Park
Camp Area 2.4 km N of Cobram. Turn N onto Wondah St from C370 (Cobram Barooga Rd). Cross over levy at end of road, take middle track for 0.6 km. Signposted

HEMA 64 A2　　　35 54 03 S　　　145 39 24 E

258 Horseshoe Bend
☎ 131 963
Cobram Regional Park
Camp Area 6.8 km E of Cobram. Turn S off Barooga Rd onto River Rd for 4.8 km, then N onto Horseshoe Track. Camping along river

HEMA 64 A2　　　35 55 41 S　　　145 41 45 E

259 Scotts Beach
☎ 131 963
Cobram Regional Park
Camp Area 3.5 km E of Cobram. Turn S off Barooga Rd onto River Rd for 3 km. Camping beside river. Maximum stay 14 days

HEMA 64 A2　　　35 55 36 S　　　145 40 36 E

260 The Big Strawberry
☎ (03) 5871 1300
Parking Area at Koonoomoo. Check in with the cafe. Limited power available for a fee

HEMA 64 A2　　　35 53 19 S　　　145 34 28 E

261 Dead River Beach
☎ 131 963
Murray River Reserve
Camp Area 5.5 km NW of Cobram. Turn N off Cobram-Koonoomo Rd 1.7 km W of Cobram onto Racecourse Rd. Travel to end of road through gate/grid. After 200m take middle track for 500m, then R into Dead River Track. Camping beside river

HEMA 64 A2　　　35 52 49 S　　　145 37 45 E

262 Weiss Beach
☎ 131 963
Cobram Regional Park
Camp Area 13.5 km N of Cobram or 17.5 km S of Tocumwal. Turn E off Cobram Koonoomoo Rd (C357) onto Fresian Rd, then L into Levings Rd, cross levy at end of road & take Cobram Track for 3.5 km. Signposted

HEMA 64 A2　　　35 51 41 S　　　145 35 45 E

263 Finley Beach
☎ 131 963
Tocumwal Regional Park
Camp Area 2.5 km S of Tocumwal. Turn E off A39, 2 km S of Tocumwal along Finley Track. Camping beside river

HEMA 64 A2　　　35 49 22 S　　　145 33 34 E

264 Apex Beach
☎ 131 963
Tocumwal Regional Park
Camp Area 2.5 km SW of Tocumwal. Turn W off A39, 200m S of bridge, signposted "Time-Out Resort", then L over railway line onto Pumps Bend Track for 1 km. Camping beside river

HEMA 64 A2　　　35 48 47 S　　　145 32 54 E

Notes...

265 Barmah National Park ☎ 131 963

Camp Area 20 km W of Tocumwal. Various sites along 112 km frontage of Murray River. Only Barmah Lake has a toilet

HEMA 64 A1   35 51 39 S   145 17 44 E

266 Barmah Lakes Campground ☎ 131 963
Barmah National Park

Camp Area 7 km N of Barmah. Turn N at Hotel onto Moira Lake Rd, follow to park entrance

HEMA 63 G12   35 57 17 S   144 57 32 E

267 Riverbank Caravan Park ☎ (03) 5866 2821

Caravan Park at Nathalia. 1-5 Park St. 1 km E of PO

HEMA 63 H13   36 03 15 S   145 12 35 E

268 McCoys Bridge

Rest Area 18 km S of Nathalia or 8 km E of Wyuna, beside Goulburn River

B400

HEMA 63 H12   36 10 41 S   145 06 58 E

269 Wakiti Creek Resort ☎ (03) 5867 3237

Caravan Park 34 km E of Echuca. Turn N off Murray Valley Hwy 22 km E of Echuca onto Curr Rd for 7 km, then E along Yambuna Bridge Rd for 5 km

HEMA 63 H12   36 08 13 S   145 01 46 E

270 Tongala Turnoff Rest Area

Rest Area 10 km W of Wyuna or 21 km E of Echuca

B400

HEMA 63 H12   36 11 57 S   144 57 05 E

271 Christies Beach Campground ☎ 131 963
Echuca Regional Park

Camp Area 8.5 km E of Echuca. Turn N off Echuca-Bangerang Rd 6 km E of Echuca onto Simmie Rd, 2 km to various camping areas. 2.5 km dirt road. Camping beside river. GPS at entry

HEMA 63 H12   36 07 04 S   144 48 48 E

272 Echuca Rotary Park RV Stop

Parking Area at Echuca. Entry Cnr Rose & Crossen Sts. Self Contained Vehicles only. Donation box on site

HEMA 63 H11   36 08 43 S   144 44 02 E

273 Wharparilla Flora Reserve Rest Area

Rest Area 4 km NW of Echuca or 38 km SE of Gunbower

B400

HEMA 63 H11   36 07 20 S   144 43 09 E

274 Lockington Travellers Stopover ☎ 0447 787 581

Camp Area at Lockington. Call mobile to access facilities. Maximum stay 14 nights, permit required for stays longer than 3 days

HEMA 63 H11   36 16 15 S   144 32 08 E

275 Pyramid Hill Caravan Park ☎ 0438 557 012

Caravan Park at Pyramid Hill. 1 km E of PO. Ring caretaker on arrival

C267

HEMA 63 H10   36 03 19 S   144 07 30 E

276 Gunbower Caravan Park ☎ (03) 5487 1412

Caravan Park at Gunbower, on main Hwy. N end of town 400m from PO

B400

HEMA 63 G10   35 57 20 S   144 21 47 E

277 Terrick Terrick Campground ☎ 131 963
Terrick Terrick National Park

Camp Area 6 km N of Mitiamo. Take Mitiamo Forest Rd N for 4.2 km, E onto Cemetery Track. 1.6 km to picnic access track. Signposted. Small vehicles only

HEMA 63 H10   36 10 05 S   144 14 35 E

278 Travellers Rest Leitchville

Rest Area at Leitchville. 2 King George St, N side of town. Donation for upkeep

HEMA 63 G10   35 54 14 S   144 18 06 E

279 Flora Park

Parking Area Cohuna. Cnr Cohuna Island & Tennis Rd. Self Contained Vehicles Only

B400

HEMA 63 G10   35 48 31 S   144 13 26 E

280 Cohuna Golf Club ☎ (03) 5456 2820

Camp Area 6 km N of Cohuna via Weymouths Rd. Self Contained Vehicles only

HEMA 63 G10   35 46 14 S   144 13 25 E

281 Gunbower State Forest ☎ 131 963
Murray River Reserve

Camp Area 2.5 km SE of Koondrook, via weir along Canoe Trail. Numerous bush camping sites along Vic side of river

HEMA 63 F10   35 39 47 S   144 07 47 E

282 Guttram State Forest ☎ 131 963

Camp Area 4 km NW of Koondrook, via Murray Parade, Cassidy Ln & Brays Ln. Bush camping sites along Vic side of river

HEMA 63 F10   35 36 45 S   144 06 55 E

283 Kerang Caravan & Tourist Park ☎ (03) 5452 1161
Caravan Park at Kerang. 21 Museum Dr. 1 km W of PO
HEMA 63 G9   35 44 13 S   143 54 49 E
B400

284 Kerang Turf Club
Parking Area at Kerang. Park Rd. Self Contained Vehicles only
HEMA 63 G9   35 43 52 S   143 55 31 E

285 Lake Meran
Camp Area at Lake Meran. 21 km S of Kerang on Boort Kerang Rd. Donation requested
HEMA 63 G9   35 52 07 S   143 48 11 E

286 Leaghur ☎ (03) 5452 1266
Leaghur State Park
Camp Area 29 km S of Kerang off Boort Kerang Rd. Two picnic-camp areas in the park, one at entrance, one at S end of Lake Meran Track. GPS at entrance
HEMA 63 G9   35 55 43 S   143 47 02 E

287 Simply Tomatoes ☎ (03) 5455 4237
Camp Area 19 km N of Boort via Boort Kerang Rd, 479 Parkers Rd
HEMA 63 H9   36 01 41 S   143 47 57 E

288 Quambatook Caravan Park ☎ 0428 857 122
Caravan Park at Quambatook. Boort Rd next to Golf Course
HEMA 63 G8   35 51 10 S   143 31 31 E

289 Reedy Lake RV Rest Area ☎ (03) 5456 2047
Parking Area 8.5 km N of Kerang or 12 km S of Lake Charm. 1 km E of Hwy, via Apex Park Rd. Beside lake. Self Contained Vehicles only
HEMA 63 F9   35 41 10 S   143 53 11 E

290 Murrabit Recreation Reserve
Camp Area at Murrabit. Entry off Browning Ave. Caretaker collects fees
HEMA 63 F9   35 31 49 S   143 57 09 E

291 Lake Boga Area 4 Camping ☎ (03) 5037 2386
Camp Area at Lake Boga, Lakeside Dr, NW side of lake. Register and pay at Lake Boga Caravan Park
B400
HEMA 63 F8   35 26 02 S   143 39 09 E

292 Lake Boga Area 5 Camping ☎ (03) 5037 2386
Camp Area at Lake Boga, Lakeside Dr, NW side of lake. Register & pay at Lake Boga Caravan Park
HEMA 63 F8   35 26 19 S   143 39 33 E

293 Pental Island Holiday Park ☎ (03) 5032 2071
Caravan Park 6 km S of Swan Hill. Pental Island Rd
HEMA 63 E8   35 22 38 S   143 36 43 E

294 Loddon Floodway
Camp Spot 19 km SE of Swan Hill. Turn E 2 km S of Swan Hill onto Pental Island Rd for 14 km, then N into Caelli Lane. 3 km dirt road. Small vehicles only
HEMA 63 E8   35 22 40 S   143 41 22 E

295 Nyah-Vinifera Park South ☎ 131 963
Camp Area 10.5 km NW of Beverford or 4.5 km SE of Vinifera. Turn N 7.5 km NW of Beverford or 1 km S of Vinifera via Forest Rd. 3 km dirt road. Various sites along riverbank
HEMA 63 E8   35 11 42 S   143 25 02 E

296 Nyah Recreation Reserve
Camp Spot at Nyah. On riverbank behind Harness Club, River St. Self Contained Vehicles only. Maximum stay 7 days. Honesty box for donations
B400
HEMA 63 E8   35 10 18 S   143 22 53 E

297 Nyah-Vinifera Park North ☎ 131 963
Camp Area between Nyah & Wood Wood. Entry off Bynres Ln. Various camping sites along W bank of river
HEMA 63 E8   35 09 19 S   143 22 56 E

298 Wood Wood Caravan Park ☎ (03) 5030 5444
Caravan Park at Wood Wood. Murray Valley Hwy. Close to river
B400
HEMA 63 D8   35 06 17 S   143 20 44 E

299 Piangil North Rest Area
Rest Area 2 km N of B12/B400 jcn or 45 km S of Boundary Bend. Beside river
B400
HEMA 62 D7   35 02 34 S   143 19 29 E

Notes...

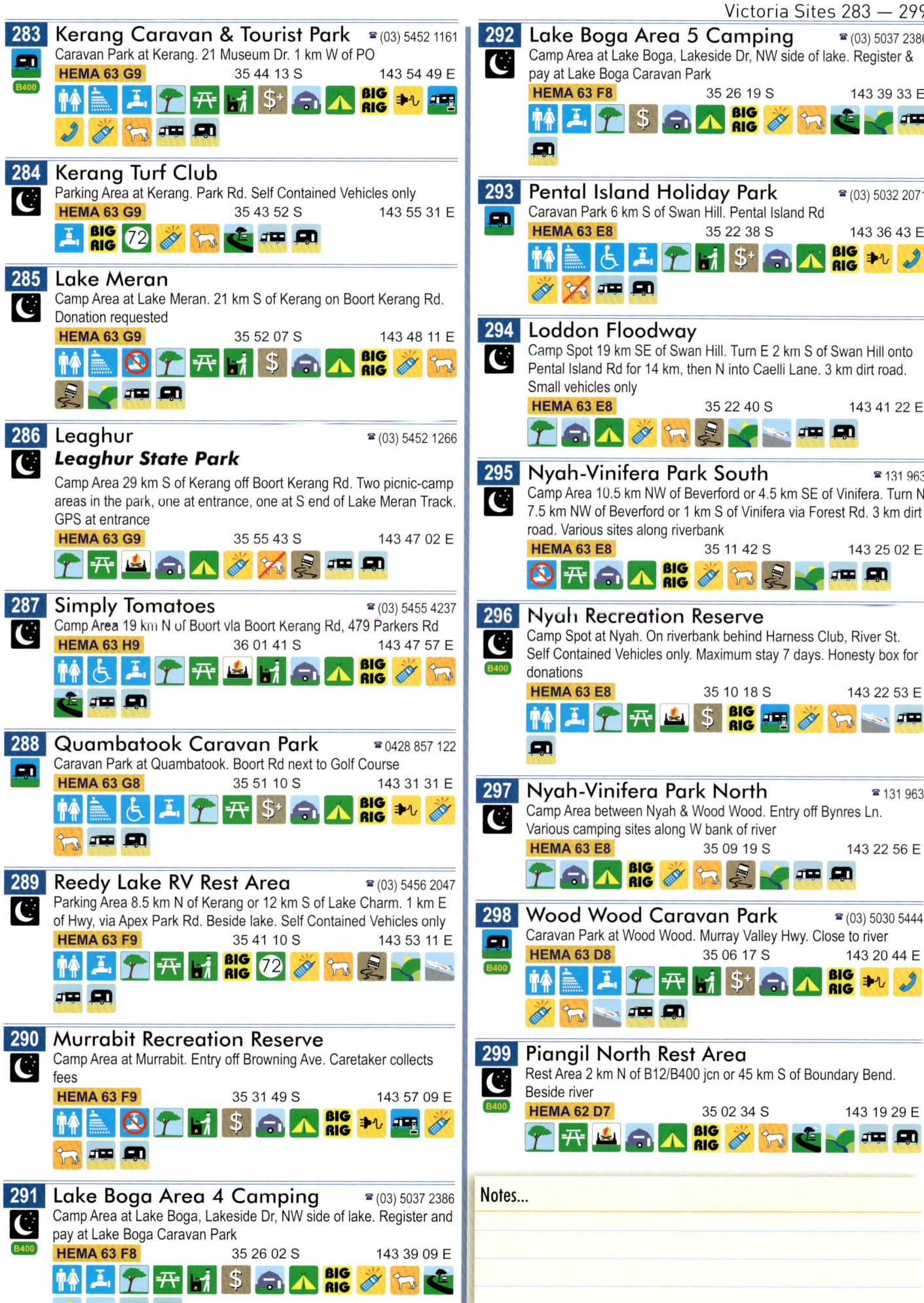

VICTORIA

Victoria Sites 300 — 316

300 Wakool Junction

Camp Area 7 km E of Piambie. Turn E off B400 27 km N of B400/ B12 jcn or 20 km SE of Boundary Bend onto Coghill Rd. Dirt road. Camping beside river. Small vehicles only

HEMA 62 C7 | 34 51 08 S | 143 20 43 E

301 Passage Camp

Camp Area 5 km SE of Boundary Bend. Turn E onto Mills Lane. Veer N at end of lane onto Passage Camp Track. Signposted to Passage Camp. 2 km to river. Small vehicles only

HEMA 62 C7 | 34 43 01 S | 143 11 58 E

302 Boundary Bend General Store & Caravan Park

☎ (03) 5026 8201

Caravan Park at Boundary Bend. 27 Murray Valley Hwy. 300m W of PO

HEMA 62 C7 | 34 42 55 S | 143 08 51 E

BIG RIG

303 Beggs Bend State Forest

☎ 131 963

Camp Spot approx 15 km SE of Robinvale. Take Murray Valley Hwy, turn NE 5 km E of Robinvale onto Tol Tol Rd for approx 5 km to signposted entry. Follow tracks to river. GPS at entrance

HEMA 62 C6 | 34 38 19 S | 142 51 03 E

BIG RIG

304 Walshs Bend Camp

Camp Spot 5 km E of Robinvale. Turn N into Tol Tol Rd for 600m. Turn N onto track, signposted Walshs Bend. Follow dirt track for 2 km to camping areas along river. Beware low branches. GPS at entrance

HEMA 62 C6 | 34 37 16 S | 142 48 45 E

305 Pump Road Camp

Camp Spot 2 km E of Robinvale. Turn N onto Pump Rd (E of Cemetry) for 500m. Bridge has a 2T weight limit. Turn E over water pipes, follow dirt tracks to various spots along river

HEMA 62 C6 | 34 36 25 S | 142 48 10 E

BIG RIG

Mildura to Yamba

Sturt Highway

306 Merbein Caravan Park

☎ (03) 5025 2198

Caravan Park at Merbein. Box St. 1 km NW of PO

HEMA 62 A4 | 34 09 58 S | 142 03 03 E

307 Wallpolla Island

Camp Spot 26 km W of Merbein, via Channel Rd & Old Mail Rd. Dirt road. Camping beside river

HEMA 62 A3 | 34 09 13 S | 141 46 45 E

308 Merrinee North Rest Area

A20

Rest Area 35 km W of Mildura or 22 km E of Cullulleraine

HEMA 62 B3 | 34 15 37 S | 141 49 27 E

BIG RIG

309 Johansen Memorial Reserve

A20

Picnic Area at Cullulleraine. Beside lake

HEMA 62 B3 | 34 16 34 S | 141 36 00 E

BIG RIG

310 Bushmans Rest Caravan Park

☎ (03) 5028 2252

A20

Caravan Park at Cullulleraine. 70 Sturt Hwy, beside lake

HEMA 62 B3 | 34 16 23 S | 141 35 13 E

BIG RIG

311 Lake Cullulleraine Holiday Park

☎ (03) 5028 2226

Caravan Park at Cullulleraine. Off Sturt Hwy beside lake

HEMA 62 B3 | 34 16 40 S | 141 36 00 E

BIG RIG

312 Lock 9

Camp Spot 10 km N of Cullulleraine. Turn N 1 km W of Cullulleraine. 9 km dirt road. Turn W at boat ramp sign, follow track. Camp spots near boat ramp. No camping at Lock car park

HEMA 62 A2 | 34 11 30 S | 141 35 39 E

313 VIC/SA Border Rest Area

A20

Rest Area 113 km W of Mildura or 25 km E of Renmark. Both sides of the road

HEMA 62 B1 | 34 16 26 S | 140 57 52 E

BIG RIG

Tooleybuc to Pinnaroo

Mallee Highway

314 Piangil Rest Area

Rest Area at Piangil. Hall St. Self Contained Vehicles only

HEMA 62 D7 | 35 03 19 S | 143 18 43 E

BIG RIG 24

315 Piangil West Rest Area

B12

Rest Area 9 km W of Piangil or 31 km E of Manangatang

HEMA 62 D7 | 35 03 25 S | 143 13 01 E

BIG RIG

316 Manangatang Travellers Rest

B12

Rest Area at Manangatang. Wattle St. Opposite Hotel, donation welcome for upkeep

HEMA 62 D6 | 35 03 10 S | 142 53 00 E

BIG RIG 24

Notes...

317 Walpeup Wayside Stop

Camp Area at Walpeup. Centre of town. Place camp fees in box at toilet block

HEMA 62 E4   35 08 10 S   142 01 30 E

318 Lake Walpeup Reserve

Camp Spot 14 km SE of Walpeup. Take Walpeup-Patchewollock Rd, turn N into Walpeup Lake Rd then E into Mclivena Rd. 6 km dirt road

HEMA 62 E4   35 11 53 S   142 08 18 E

319 Underbool Rest Area

Rest Area at Underbool. Cotter St. Honesty box for power

HEMA 62 E3   35 10 11 S   141 48 35 E

320 Underbool Recreation Reserve

Camp Area at Underbool Gnarr Rd, N of railway line. Power box & water on W side of grounds, access around oval. Honesty box at toilet block

HEMA 62 E3   35 10 08 S   141 48 47 E

321 Lake Crosbie Campground

Murray Sunset National Park

Camp Area 13.5 km N of Linga. Turn N 60 km W of Ouyen or 76 km E of Pinnaroo. 13 km dirt road. Signposted

HEMA 62 D3   35 03 19 S   141 43 53 E

322 Murrayville East Rest Area

Rest Area 12 km W of Cowangie or 7 km E of Murrayville

HEMA 62 E2   35 15 43 S   141 15 03 E

323 Murrayville Caravan Park

Caravan Park at Murrayville. Reed St. Honesty box. Alternative Mobile 0418 623 670

HEMA 62 E2   35 15 57 S   141 10 54 E

324 Ngallo Park

Camp Area 21 km SW of Murrayville. Turn S off Mallee Hwy onto Ngallo South Rd. E side of road. 3 km dirt road

HEMA 62 E1   35 16 20 S   141 04 10 E

Notes...

Mildura to Melbourne
Calder Highway

325 Kings Billabong Park   ☏ 131 963

Camp Spot 12 km SE of Mildura, via Eleventh St. R into Cureton Ave, then L at sign to Psyche Bends. 4 km dirt road. Camping beside river

HEMA 62 A4   34 15 16 S   142 13 55 E

326 Red Cliffs Caravan Park   ☏ (03) 5024 2261

Caravan Park at Red Cliffs. 8760 Calder Hwy

HEMA 62 B4   34 17 51 S   142 11 11 E

327 Spences Bend

Camp Spot 1 km N of Nangiloc. Camping beside river

HEMA 62 B5   34 27 47 S   142 21 14 E

328 Watts Bend   ☏ 131 963

Camp Spot 2 km S of Colignan. Camping beside river

HEMA 62 B5   34 32 07 S   142 22 16 E

329 Emmerts Bend

Camp Spot 7 km S of Colignan. Veer L at Info board. Camping beside river

HEMA 62 C5   34 34 10 S   142 24 36 E

330 Hattah North Rest Area

Rest Area 51 km S of Red Cliffs or 3 km N of Hattah

HEMA 62 C5   34 44 31 S   142 16 18 E

331 Lake Hattah Campground   ☏ 131 963

Hattah-Kulkyne National Park

Camp Area 6 km E of Hattah. Turn N 5 km E of Hattah for 1 km. Dirt road. Narrow for last 100m. Must pre book

HEMA 62 C5   34 45 10 S   142 20 36 E

332 Lake Mournpall Campground   ☏ 131 963

Hattah-Kulkyne National Park

Camp Area 15 km NE of Hattah. Turn N 5 km E of Hattah for 10 km. 9 km sandy road. Must pre book

HEMA 62 C5   34 42 18 S   142 20 08 E

333 Wemen Rest Area

Rest Area at Wemen, beside river. Small vehicles only

HEMA 62 C6   34 46 56 S   142 38 13 E

334 Hattah South Rest Area

Rest Area 12 km S of Hattah or 22 km N of Ouyen

HEMA 62 D5   34 51 49 S   142 17 58 E

Victoria Sites 335 — 352

335 Blackburn Park
Rest Area at Ouyen. Calder Hwy. 1 km SE of PO
HEMA 62 D5   35 04 24 S   142 19 14 E
A79

336 Lake Tyrrell Rest Area
Rest Area 20 km S of Daytrap Corner or 7 km N of Sea Lake
HEMA 62 F6   35 27 12 S   142 49 44 E
A79

337 Sea Lake Recreation Reserve Caravan Park   ☎ 0427 701 261
Caravan Park at Sea Lake. 71-91 Calder Hwy. Honesty box for payment
HEMA 62 F6   35 30 11 S   142 50 57 E
A79

338 Sea Lake Travellers Rest
Rest Area at Sea Lake, next to Calder Hwy, entry at Caravan Park signs then turn L into parking area
HEMA 62 F6   35 30 12 S   142 50 57 E

339 Green Lake Camping & Caravan Park   ☎ (03) 5070 1058
Camp Area 10 km S of Sea Lake on Birchip Rd
HEMA 62 F6   35 35 48 S   142 50 54 E

340 Kaneira Hotel   ☎ (03) 5077 2330
Parking Area at Culgoa. 24 Main St, grassed area next to Hotel, register with publican. Toilets open during hours. Mobile 0431 188 117
HEMA 62 G7   35 43 00 S   143 06 25 E

341 Torneys Tank Bushland Reserve
Rest Area 3 km S of Culgoa or 39 km N of Wycheproof
HEMA 62 G7   35 44 22 S   143 06 59 E
A79

342 Wycheproof Caravan Park   ☎ (03) 5493 7278
Caravan Park at Wycheproof. Calder Hwy 500m N of PO
HEMA 62 H7   36 04 10 S   143 13 33 E
A79

343 Centenary Park
Parking Area at Wycheproof. Fairview St. Self Contained Vehicles only
HEMA 62 H7   36 04 44 S   143 13 33 E

344 Teddywaddy Rest Area
Rest Area 22 km SE of Wycheproof or 9 km N of Charlton. 100m N of A79/Charlton-Glenloth Rd intersection
HEMA 63 H8   36 12 50 S   143 21 37 E
A79

345 Travellers Rest North Camping Ground   ☎ 0448 276 631
Camp Area 1 km W of Charlton. 100m E of N end of bridge over Avoca River. Dump point across bridge at Travellers Rest Ensuite Park
HEMA 63 H8   36 15 59 S   143 21 02 E
A79

346 Travellers Rest Caravan Park   ☎ 0448 276 631
Caravan Park at 43-45 High St, Charlton. There is also RV parking at the rear on unpowered sites at $10 per night
HEMA 63 H8   36 16 02 S   143 21 05 E

347 Boort Park Showground   ☎ (03) 5455 2282
Camp Area at Boort, Malone St. Self Contained Vehicles only. Donation required
HEMA 63 H9   36 06 37 S   143 43 46 E

348 Wooroonook Lakes
Camp Area 14 km W of Charlton or 27 km E of Donald. 300m W of the C239/C271 (northbound) intersection
HEMA 62 H7   36 15 38 S   143 11 46 E
B239

349 Skinners Flat Reservoir
Picnic Area 27 km SE of Charlton or 6 km NW of Wedderburn. Turn E 26 km SE of Charlton or 5 km NW of Wedderburn. 1 km dirt road
HEMA 63 J8   36 21 58 S   143 35 09 E

350 Hard Hill Tourist Reserve   ☎ (03) 5494 3489
Camp Area at Wedderburn. Wilson St, 600m N of Info Centre. Dump point at Pioneer Caravan Park
HEMA 63 J8   36 24 52 S   143 36 22 E

351 Ryan Creek Rest Area
Rest Area 12 km SE of Wedderburn or 17 km NW of Inglewood
HEMA 63 J9   36 29 12 S   143 42 51 E
A79

352 Kooyoora Park Retreat   ☎ (03) 5438 3428
Camp Area 10 km W of Kurting. Turn W into Brenanah-Kurting Rd at Kurting, travel past the dip sign to T intersection. Signposted. Bookings essential
HEMA 63 J8   36 33 14 S   143 41 33 E

Notes...

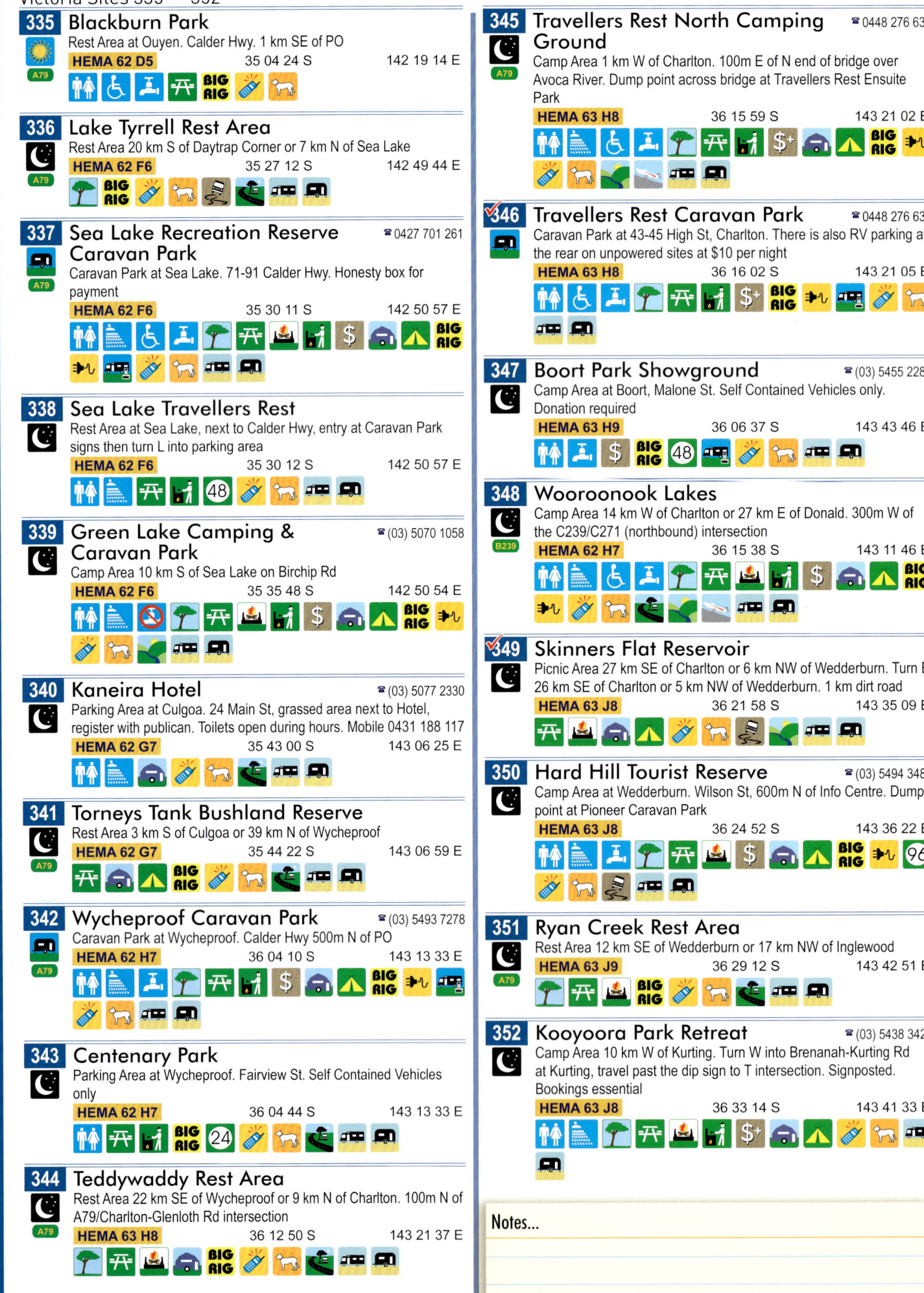

353 Bridgewater Recreation Reserve
Camp Area at Bridgewater. Entry off Bridgewater-Maldon Rd. Self Contained Vehicles only. Donation apreciated. Key for dump point at Bakery in Main St

HEMA 63 K9   36 36 23 S   143 56 41 E

354 Bridgewater Public Caravan Park
☎ (03) 5437 3086
Caravan Park at Bridgewater. Park St. 500m SW of PO

HEMA 63 K9   36 36 19 S   143 56 17 E

355 Melville Caves Campground
Kooyoora State Park
☎ 131 963
Camp Area 21 km W of Inglewood, via Kingower. Turn N 19 km W of Inglewood

HEMA 63 K9   36 36 03 S   143 41 55 E

356 Happy Jacks Recreation Reserve
Camp Spot at Lockwood South. Glen Rd.

HEMA 59 A11   36 50 30 S   144 09 19 E

357 Hamiltons Crossing
Camp Spot 12 km S of Eddington or 2 km N of Baringhup on Baringhup-Eastville Rd. S side of bridge to sites

HEMA 59 B10   36 56 33 S   143 56 01 E

358 Butts Reserve
Maldon Historic Area
☎ 131 963
Camp Area 2 km W of Maldon. From town head N, then W into Franklin St, Mt Tarrengower Rd

HEMA 59 B11   36 59 10 S   144 03 14 E

359 Newstead Racecourse & Rec Reserve
☎ (03) 5476 2360
Camp Area at Newstead. Racecourse Rd. Key for shower at Rural Transaction Centre. Donation box at the Rec Reserve

HEMA 59 C11   37 07 01 S   144 03 23 E

360 Jessie Kennedy Reserve
Rest Area 6 km S of Castlemaine or 5 km N of Guildford

HEMA 59 C11   37 06 37 S   144 11 04 E

361 Vaughan Springs Reserve
Castlemaine Diggings National Heritage Park
☎ 131 963
Camp Area 15 km S of Castlemaine or 8 km E of Guildford. Turn E 9 km S of Castlemaine or 2 km NE of Guildford, via Yapeen along Vaughan Springs Rd. Campground on top level

HEMA 59 C11   37 09 41 S   144 12 51 E

362 Warburton Bridge Reserve
Castlemaine Diggings National Heritage Park
☎ 131 963
Camp Area 18 km S of Castlemaine or 11 km E of Guildford. Turn E 9 km S of Castlemaine or 2 km NE of Guildford, via Yapeen along Vaughan Springs Rd & Vaughan-Drummond Rd. At Loddon River bridge

HEMA 59 C11   37 10 11 S   144 14 16 E

363 Ravenswood Rest Area
Rest Area on Calder Hwy. 19 km N of Castlemaine. Northbound only

HEMA 59 B11   36 54 39 S   144 13 12 E

364 The Oaks
Parking Area 3 km E of Harcourt. E end of Market St from BP servo. Follow sign post to "Picnic Gully" along dirt road. L at "Xmas Tree" sign, then R at "Oak Plantation" sign. Small vehicles only. Low trees

HEMA 59 B12   36 59 54 S   144 17 26 E

365 Leanganook Picnic Area
Mt Alexander Regional Park
☎ 131 963
Picnic Area 13 km SE of Harcourt via Harmony Way & Faraday Sutton Grange Rd

HEMA 59 B12   37 01 02 S   144 18 22 E

366 Elphinstone North Rest Area
Rest Area 10 km S of Harcourt or 8 km N of Taradale

HEMA 59 B12   37 04 14 S   144 18 23 E

367 Sawpit Gully Reserve
Camp Area at Elphinstone. Cnr Bateman St & Hoinsville Rd. Key for power at Store PO

HEMA 59 C12   37 06 06 S   144 20 03 E

368 Taradale Mineral Springs Reserve
Picnic Area at Taradale, next to fire station

HEMA 59 C12   37 08 19 S   144 20 59 E

Notes...

VICTORIA

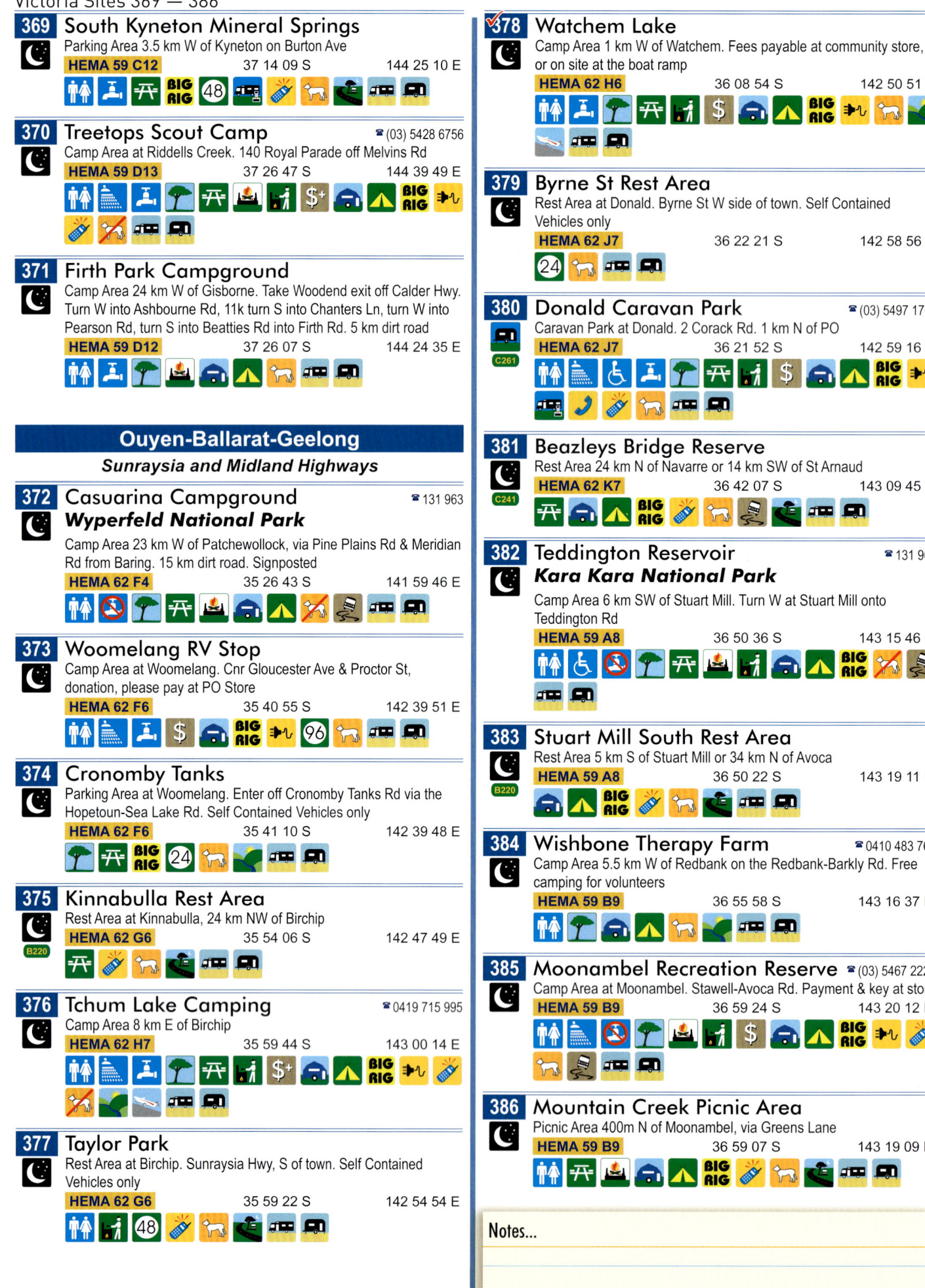

369 South Kyneton Mineral Springs
Parking Area 3.5 km W of Kyneton on Burton Ave
HEMA 59 C12 37 14 09 S 144 25 10 E

370 Treetops Scout Camp ☎ (03) 5428 6756
Camp Area at Riddells Creek. 140 Royal Parade off Melvins Rd
HEMA 59 D13 37 26 47 S 144 39 49 E

371 Firth Park Campground
Camp Area 24 km W of Gisborne. Take Woodend exit off Calder Hwy. Turn W into Ashbourne Rd, 11k turn S into Chanters Ln, turn W into Pearson Rd, turn S into Beatties Rd into Firth Rd. 5 km dirt road
HEMA 59 D12 37 26 07 S 144 24 35 E

Ouyen-Ballarat-Geelong
Sunraysia and Midland Highways

372 Casuarina Campground ☎ 131 963
Wyperfeld National Park
Camp Area 23 km W of Patchewollock, via Pine Plains Rd & Meridian Rd from Baring. 15 km dirt road. Signposted
HEMA 62 F4 35 26 43 S 141 59 46 E

373 Woomelang RV Stop
Camp Area at Woomelang. Cnr Gloucester Ave & Proctor St, donation, please pay at PO Store
HEMA 62 F6 35 40 55 S 142 39 51 E

374 Cronomby Tanks
Parking Area at Woomelang. Enter off Cronomby Tanks Rd via the Hopetoun-Sea Lake Rd. Self Contained Vehicles only
HEMA 62 F6 35 41 10 S 142 39 48 E

375 Kinnabulla Rest Area
Rest Area at Kinnabulla, 24 km NW of Birchip
HEMA 62 G6 35 54 06 S 142 47 49 E

376 Tchum Lake Camping ☎ 0419 715 995
Camp Area 8 km E of Birchip
HEMA 62 H7 35 59 44 S 143 00 14 E

377 Taylor Park
Rest Area at Birchip. Sunraysia Hwy, S of town. Self Contained Vehicles only
HEMA 62 G6 35 59 22 S 142 54 54 E

378 Watchem Lake ✓
Camp Area 1 km W of Watchem. Fees payable at community store, or on site at the boat ramp
HEMA 62 H6 36 08 54 S 142 50 51 E

379 Byrne St Rest Area
Rest Area at Donald. Byrne St W side of town. Self Contained Vehicles only
HEMA 62 J7 36 22 21 S 142 58 56 E

380 Donald Caravan Park ☎ (03) 5497 1764
Caravan Park at Donald. 2 Corack Rd. 1 km N of PO
HEMA 62 J7 36 21 52 S 142 59 16 E

381 Beazleys Bridge Reserve
Rest Area 24 km N of Navarre or 14 km SW of St Arnaud
HEMA 62 K7 36 42 07 S 143 09 45 E

382 Teddington Reservoir ☎ 131 963
Kara Kara National Park
Camp Area 6 km SW of Stuart Mill. Turn W at Stuart Mill onto Teddington Rd
HEMA 59 A8 36 50 36 S 143 15 46 E

383 Stuart Mill South Rest Area
Rest Area 5 km S of Stuart Mill or 34 km N of Avoca
HEMA 59 A8 36 50 22 S 143 19 11 E

384 Wishbone Therapy Farm ☎ 0410 483 763
Camp Area 5.5 km W of Redbank on the Redbank-Barkly Rd. Free camping for volunteers
HEMA 59 B9 36 55 58 S 143 16 37 E

385 Moonambel Recreation Reserve ☎ (03) 5467 2225
Camp Area at Moonambel. Stawell-Avoca Rd. Payment & key at store
HEMA 59 B9 36 59 24 S 143 20 12 E

386 Mountain Creek Picnic Area
Picnic Area 400m N of Moonambel, via Greens Lane
HEMA 59 B9 36 59 07 S 143 19 09 E

Notes...

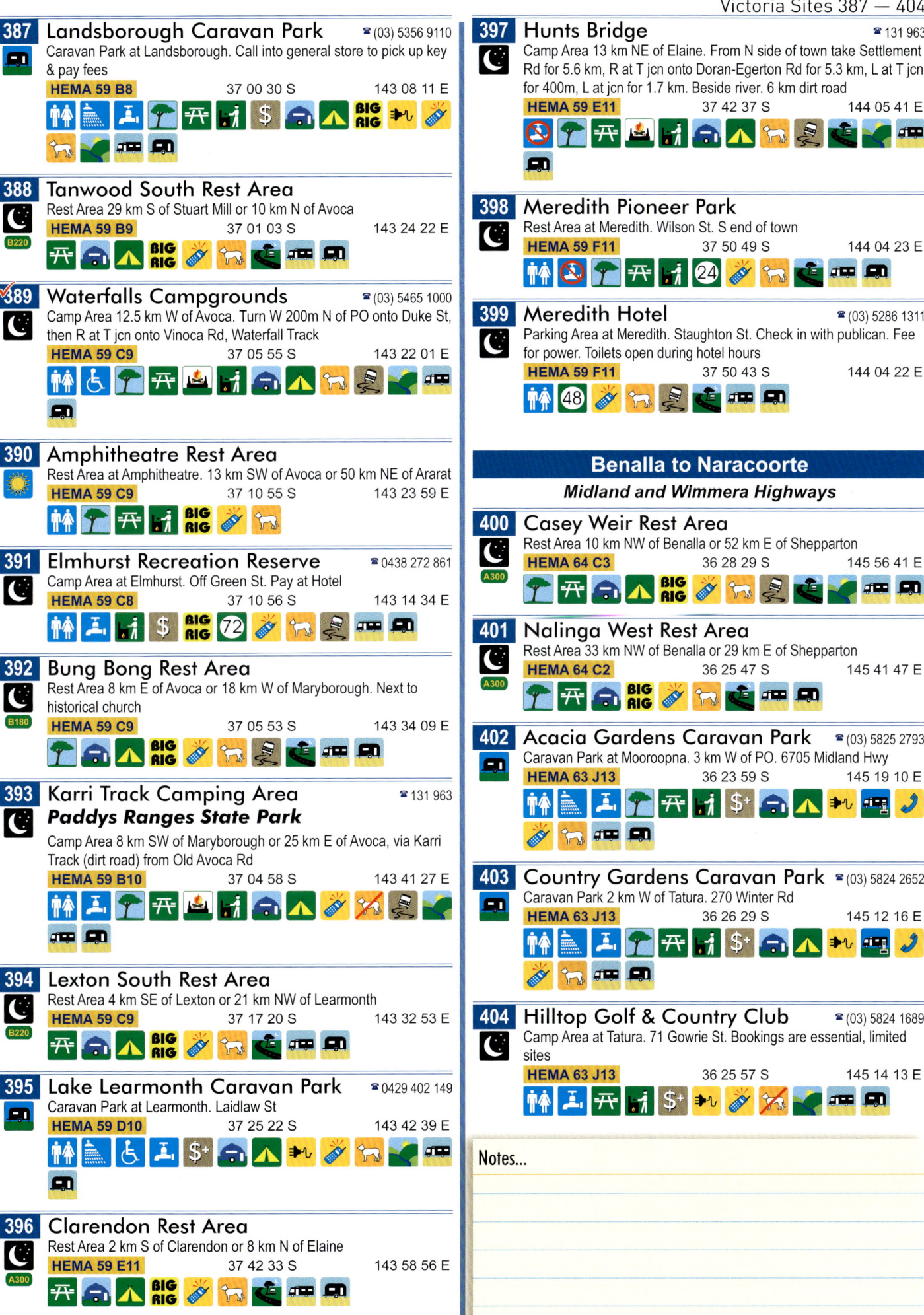

387 Landsborough Caravan Park ☎ (03) 5356 9110
Caravan Park at Landsborough. Call into general store to pick up key & pay fees
HEMA 59 B8   37 00 30 S   143 08 11 E

388 Tanwood South Rest Area
Rest Area 29 km S of Stuart Mill or 10 km N of Avoca
HEMA 59 B9   37 01 03 S   143 24 22 E
B220

389 Waterfalls Campgrounds ☎ (03) 5465 1000
Camp Area 12.5 km W of Avoca. Turn W 200m N of PO onto Duke St, then R at T jcn onto Vinoca Rd, Waterfall Track
HEMA 59 C9   37 05 55 S   143 22 01 E

390 Amphitheatre Rest Area
Rest Area at Amphitheatre. 13 km SW of Avoca or 50 km NE of Ararat
HEMA 59 C9   37 10 55 S   143 23 59 E

391 Elmhurst Recreation Reserve ☎ 0438 272 861
Camp Area at Elmhurst. Off Green St. Pay at Hotel
HEMA 59 C8   37 10 56 S   143 14 34 E

392 Bung Bong Rest Area
Rest Area 8 km E of Avoca or 18 km W of Maryborough. Next to historical church
B180
HEMA 59 C9   37 05 53 S   143 34 09 E

393 Karri Track Camping Area ☎ 131 963
Paddys Ranges State Park
Camp Area 8 km SW of Maryborough or 25 km E of Avoca, via Karri Track (dirt road) from Old Avoca Rd
HEMA 59 B10   37 04 58 S   143 41 27 E

394 Lexton South Rest Area
Rest Area 4 km SE of Lexton or 21 km NW of Learmonth
B220
HEMA 59 C9   37 17 20 S   143 32 53 E

395 Lake Learmonth Caravan Park ☎ 0429 402 149
Caravan Park at Learmonth. Laidlaw St
HEMA 59 D10   37 25 22 S   143 42 39 E

396 Clarendon Rest Area
Rest Area 2 km S of Clarendon or 8 km N of Elaine
A300
HEMA 59 E11   37 42 33 S   143 58 56 E

397 Hunts Bridge ☎ 131 963
Camp Area 13 km NE of Elaine. From N side of town take Settlement Rd for 5.6 km, R at T jcn onto Doran-Egerton Rd for 5.3 km, L at T jcn for 400m, L at jcn for 1.7 km. Beside river. 6 km dirt road
HEMA 59 E11   37 42 37 S   144 05 41 E

398 Meredith Pioneer Park
Rest Area at Meredith. Wilson St. S end of town
HEMA 59 F11   37 50 49 S   144 04 23 E

399 Meredith Hotel ☎ (03) 5286 1311
Parking Area at Meredith. Staughton St. Check in with publican. Fee for power. Toilets open during hotel hours
HEMA 59 F11   37 50 43 S   144 04 22 E

Benalla to Naracoorte
Midland and Wimmera Highways

400 Casey Weir Rest Area
Rest Area 10 km NW of Benalla or 52 km E of Shepparton
A300
HEMA 64 C3   36 28 29 S   145 56 41 E

401 Nalinga West Rest Area
Rest Area 33 km NW of Benalla or 29 km E of Shepparton
A300
HEMA 64 C2   36 25 47 S   145 41 47 E

402 Acacia Gardens Caravan Park ☎ (03) 5825 2793
Caravan Park at Mooroopna. 3 km W of PO. 6705 Midland Hwy
HEMA 63 J13   36 23 59 S   145 19 10 E

403 Country Gardens Caravan Park ☎ (03) 5824 2652
Caravan Park 2 km W of Tatura. 270 Winter Rd
HEMA 63 J13   36 26 29 S   145 12 16 E

404 Hilltop Golf & Country Club ☎ (03) 5824 1689
Camp Area at Tatura. 71 Gowrie St. Bookings are essential, limited sites
HEMA 63 J13   36 25 57 S   145 14 13 E

Notes...

VICTORIA

405 John Pilley Reserve ☎ (03) 5481 2200
Parking Area at Kyabram. Cnr Lake Rd & Fauna Park Dr. Permit required for stays over 2 days. Self Contained Vehicles only
HEMA 63 J12   36 19 19 S   145 02 48 E

406 Girgarre Town Park
Camp Area at Girgarre. On outer grounds of Town Park, cnr Winter & Station Sts, either side of Hall. See notice board for facilities. Not available 2nd Sunday of the month due to markets. Donation please in the box
HEMA 63 J12   36 23 53 S   144 58 48 E

407 Moora Racecourse
Parking Area at Moora. 7 km W of Rushworth or 13 km E of Colbinabbin. Self Contained Vehicles Only. Donation appreciated for upkeep, donation box is on the shed
HEMA 63 K12   36 35 49 S   144 56 46 E

408 Greens Lake Recreation Reserve
Camp Area 16 km W of Stanhope or 24 km E of Elmore. Turn N off Midland Hwy 14 km W of Stanhope or 22 km E of Elmore. 1 km dirt road. Donation please for upkeep for facilities
HEMA 63 J12   36 26 16 S   144 49 42 E

409 Aysons Reserve (Campaspe River) ☎ (03) 5481 2200
Camp Area 8 km NE of Elmore. Turn N off Midland Hwy 32 km W of Stanhope or 5 km NE of Elmore along Burnewang Rd for 3 km. Permit required for stays over 3 days, max stay 28 days
HEMA 63 J11   36 27 34 S   144 40 08 E

410 Rochester Caravan & Camping Park ☎ (03) 5484 1622
Caravan Park at Rochester. 1 Church St. 400m E of PO
HEMA 63 J11   36 21 36 S   144 42 16 E

411 Rochester North Rest Area
Rest Area 11 km N of Rochester or 18 km S of Echuca, beside Campaspe River
HEMA 63 H11   36 16 31 S   144 42 05 E

412 Runnymede Highway Park
Rest Area 47 km N of Heathcote or 5 km SE of Elmore. Beside river
HEMA 63 J11   36 31 25 S   144 37 38 E

413 Englishs Bridge Streamside Reserve ☎ 136 186
Camp Spot 3 km E of Goornong. Turn E off A300 3 km NE of Goornong onto Axedale Rd, then E onto Englishs Rd for 2.5 km. Beside Campaspe River
HEMA 63 K11   36 37 23 S   144 33 42 E

414 Huntly Lions Park
Rest Area at Huntly. S end of town. Small area
HEMA 63 K10   36 40 11 S   144 19 36 E

415 Notley Picnic Area
Greater Bendigo National Park
Camp Area 21 km N of Eaglehawk. Turn E off Bendigo-Pyramid Rd (C336) 12 km N of Eaglehawk onto Evans Rd for 4 km, then S at T jcn along Neilborough-Eaglehawk Rd for 5 km ☎ 131 963
HEMA 63 K10   36 38 59 S   144 15 47 E

416 Rush Dam
Greater Bendigo National Park
Camp Area 27 km W of Elmore or 20 km E of Raywood. Via Millwood & Camp Rds ☎ 131 963
HEMA 63 K10   36 30 26 S   144 20 22 E

417 Mulga Dam
Greater Bendigo National Park
Camp Area 23 km W of Elmore or 23 km W of Raywood. Via Bendigo-Tennyson Rd ☎ 131 963
HEMA 63 K10   36 29 56 S   144 22 23 E

418 Sebastian Recreation Ground
Camp Area at Sebastian. Via Main St, Vogele Rd & Recreation Rd. Park in rec ground around oval not the trotting track. Maximum stay 7 nights. Donation requested
HEMA 63 K10   36 35 32 S   144 11 14 E

419 Bears Lagoon Fruit Fly Rest Area
Rest Area 2 km N of Bears Lagoon or 21 km S of Durham Ox
HEMA 63 J9   36 18 47 S   143 58 28 E

420 Four Post Hotel ☎ (03) 5437 9241
Parking Area at Jarklin. Check in at bar. Toilets only during trading hours
HEMA 63 H9   36 16 08 S   143 58 01 E

421 Newbridge Recreation Reserve
Camp Area at Newbridge. E side of Loddon River on Wimmera Hwy. Pay at hotel
HEMA 59 A10   36 44 25 S   143 54 10 E

422 Laanecoorie River Reserve
Camp Area at Laanecoorie. Main Rd N end on town by Loddon River
C277
HEMA 59 A10   36 49 32 S   143 53 55 E

423 Waanyarra Camping Ground ☎ 136 186
Camp Area 10 km NE of Dunolly or 33 km S of Bridgewater. Turn E onto Waanyarra Cemetery Rd. 2 km dirt road
HEMA 59 A10   36 49 00 S   143 48 02 E

424 Tarnagulla Recreation Park ☎ 0427 387 397
Camp Area at Tarnagulla. 25 Wayman St, off Commercial Rd. Caretaker on site
HEMA 59 A10   36 46 28 S   143 49 42 E

425 Moliagul Rest Area
Rest Area 14 km N of Dunolly or 21 km S of Logan
C240
HEMA 59 A10   36 45 02 S   143 39 50 E

426 Logan Pub ☎ (03) 5496 2220
Parking Area at Logan. 23 km E of St Arnaud or 35 km NW of Dunolly. Behind hotel. Check in with publican
B240
HEMA 59 A9   36 37 17 S   143 29 28 E

427 Kooreh Hall
Parking Area at Kooreh. 36 km SW of Wedderburn or 12 km E of St Arnaud. Donation please
B240
HEMA 59 A9   36 38 28 S   143 23 05 E

428 Avon River
Rest Area 27 km W of St Arnaud or 50 km E of Murtoa
B240
HEMA 62 K7   36 38 25 S   142 58 42 E

✓ 429 Lake Batyo Catyo Campground
Camp Area 22 km NE of Marnoo or 28 km S of Donald, via Donald-Stawell Rd. Then on St Arnaud-Banyena Rd. Last 7 km dirt road
HEMA 62 J7   36 30 58 S   142 56 45 E

✓ 430 Rupanyup Memorial Park
Camp Area at Rupanyup, 63 km W of St Arnaud or 14 km E of Murtoa. Cnr of Wimmera Hwy & Minyip-Rupanyup Rds
B240
HEMA 62 K6   36 37 35 S   142 37 45 E

431 Minyip Wetlands Travellers Rest
Camp Area at Minyip. Cnr Petering St & Stawell-Warracknabeal Rd. Limited power. See notice board for payment details, honesty box
HEMA 62 J6   36 27 23 S   142 35 12 E

432 Murtoa Caravan Park ☎ 0448 511 879
Caravan Park at Murtoa. Beside Lake Marma, Lake St
C237
HEMA 58 A6   36 37 18 S   142 27 58 E

433 Natimuk Lake Caravan Park ☎ 0407 800 753
Caravan Park 4 km N of Natimuk. Beside lake. Lake Rd
HEMA 58 A4   36 42 56 S   141 56 30 E

434 Philip of Sherewoods
Rest Area 9 km W of Natimuk or 61 km NE of Edenhope
HEMA 58 A4   36 46 29 S   141 51 56 E

435 Centenary Park Campground ☎ 131 963
Mount Arapiles-Tooan State Park
Camp Area 12 km W of Natimuk or 60 km NE of Edenhope. 2 km N of Wimmera Hwy along Centenary Park Rd
HEMA 58 A4   36 45 33 S   141 51 03 E

436 Jane Duff Highway Park
Picnic Area 21 km W of Natimuk or 24 km E of Goroke
HEMA 58 A3   36 43 59 S   141 43 21 E

✓ 437 Lake Ratzcastle Camp Area
Camp Area 10 km S of Goroke, 2 km off Edenhope-Goroke & Exells Rds
HEMA 58 B3   36 48 38 S   141 27 59 E

✓ 438 Goroke Accommodation Park ☎ 0429 672 791
Camp Area at Goroke. 108 Main St next to swimming pool. See noticeboard for fees
HEMA 58 A3   36 43 13 S   141 28 01 E

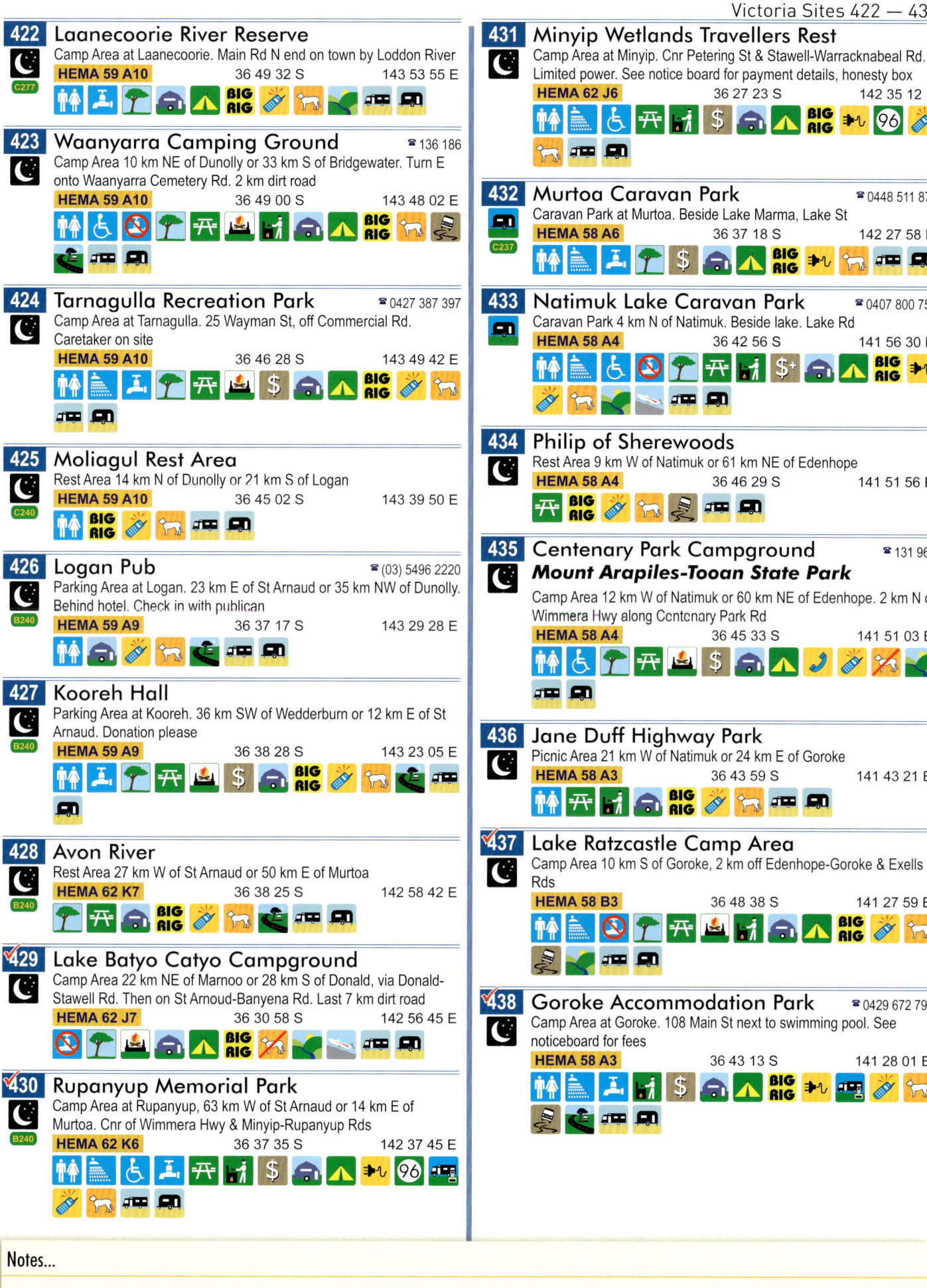

Notes...

439 Lake Charlegrark Campground ☎ (03) 5386 6281
Camp Area 33 km N of Edenhope or 23 km W of Goroke. 2 km S off C213 on Lake Charlegrark Rd
C208
HEMA 58 A2   36 46 06 S   141 14 04 E

440 Lake Bringalbert
Camp Area 5 km N of Bringalbert. on Old Bringalbert Rd. Donation welcomed
HEMA 58 B2   36 49 58 S   141 09 40 E

441 Parsons (Collins) Lake
Picnic Area. 63 km SW of Natimuk or 7 km NE of Edenhope
HEMA 58 B2   37 00 05 S   141 21 05 E

442 Johnny Mullagh Park ☎ (03) 5588 1251
Camp Area at Harrow. Blair St. S side of Harrow, beside Glenelg River. Pay at Harrows Cafe
C206
HEMA 58 C3   37 10 12 S   141 35 21 E

Melbourne to Bordertown
Western Highway

443 O'Briens Crossing ☎ 131 963
Lerderderg State Park
Camp Area 13 km NE of Greendale or 10 km SE of Blackwood. Turn E off C318, 7 km N of Greendale or 4 km S of Blackwood onto O'Briens Rd. 6 km dirt road. Not suitable for caravans. Small vehicles only
HEMA 59 D12   37 29 46 S   144 21 39 E

444 Boar Gully Campground ☎ 131 963
Brisbane Ranges National Park
Camp Area 6 km E of Mount Wallace. Turn E off C141, 18 km S of Ballan onto Brisbane Ranges Rd. Advance booking required
HEMA 59 E12   37 46 00 S   144 15 47 E

445 Mount Franklin Reserve Campground ☎ 131 963
Hepburn Regional Park
Camp Area 11 km N of Daylesford. Turn E 9 km N of Daylesford
HEMA 59 C11   37 15 47 S   144 08 57 E

446 Slaty Creek Campground ☎ 131 963
Creswick Regional Park
Camp Area 5 km SE of Creswick. Turn W off C291, 2 km SE of Creswick onto Slaty Creek Rd. 3 km dirt road. There are 2 other camp areas within 400m with no facilities
HEMA 59 D10   37 27 46 S   143 54 15 E

447 Trawalla State Forest Rest Area
Rest Area 4 km W of Trawalla or 4 km E of Beaufort
A8
HEMA 59 D9   37 26 08 S   143 25 20 E

448 Red Kangaroo Roadhouse ☎ (03) 5349 3180
Parking Area 3 km W of Beaufort or 17 km E of Buangor. Fee for shower
A8
HEMA 59 D9   37 25 28 S   143 21 14 E

449 Middle Creek Campground ☎ 131 963
Mt Buangor State Park
Camp Area 20 km NW of Beaufort or 16 km NE of Buangor. Turn N off Western Hwy 12 km NW of Beaufort or 8 km SE of Buangor onto Ferntree Gully Rd. 8 km dirt road
HEMA 59 D8   37 19 57 S   143 14 47 E

450 Langi Ghiran Rest Area
Rest Area 14 km E of Ararat. Eastbound only
A8
HEMA 59 D8   37 20 17 S   143 06 13 E

451 Langi Ghiran Campground ☎ 131 963
Langi Ghiran State Park
Camp Area 15 km NW of Buangor or 17 km SE of Ararat. Turn N off Western Hwy 10 km NW of Buangor or 12 km SE of Ararat onto Langi Ghiran Picnic Ground Rd. 5 km dirt road
HEMA 59 C8   37 17 23 S   143 05 30 E

452 Green Hill Lake Reserve
Camp Area 19 km W of Buangor or 3 km E of Ararat. 500m N of Hwy. Turn at offical sign to the lake & cross railway line to track. Donation requested
A8
HEMA 59 C8   37 17 47 S   142 58 53 E

453 Cathcart Rest Area
Rest Area 6 km W of Ararat, on Ararat-Pomonal Rd
C222
HEMA 58 C7   37 17 43 S   142 52 42 E

454 Moyston Sports Ground
Camp Area at Moyston. Entry off Moyston-Great Western Rd. Please place fee in honesty box
HEMA 58 C7   37 17 54 S   142 45 55 E

455 Great Western Racing & Recreation Reserve ☎ 0438 532 557
Camp Area at Great Western. Entry off Moyston-Great Western Rd. Fees apply if you use facilities or power
HEMA 58 C7   37 09 38 S   142 51 00 E

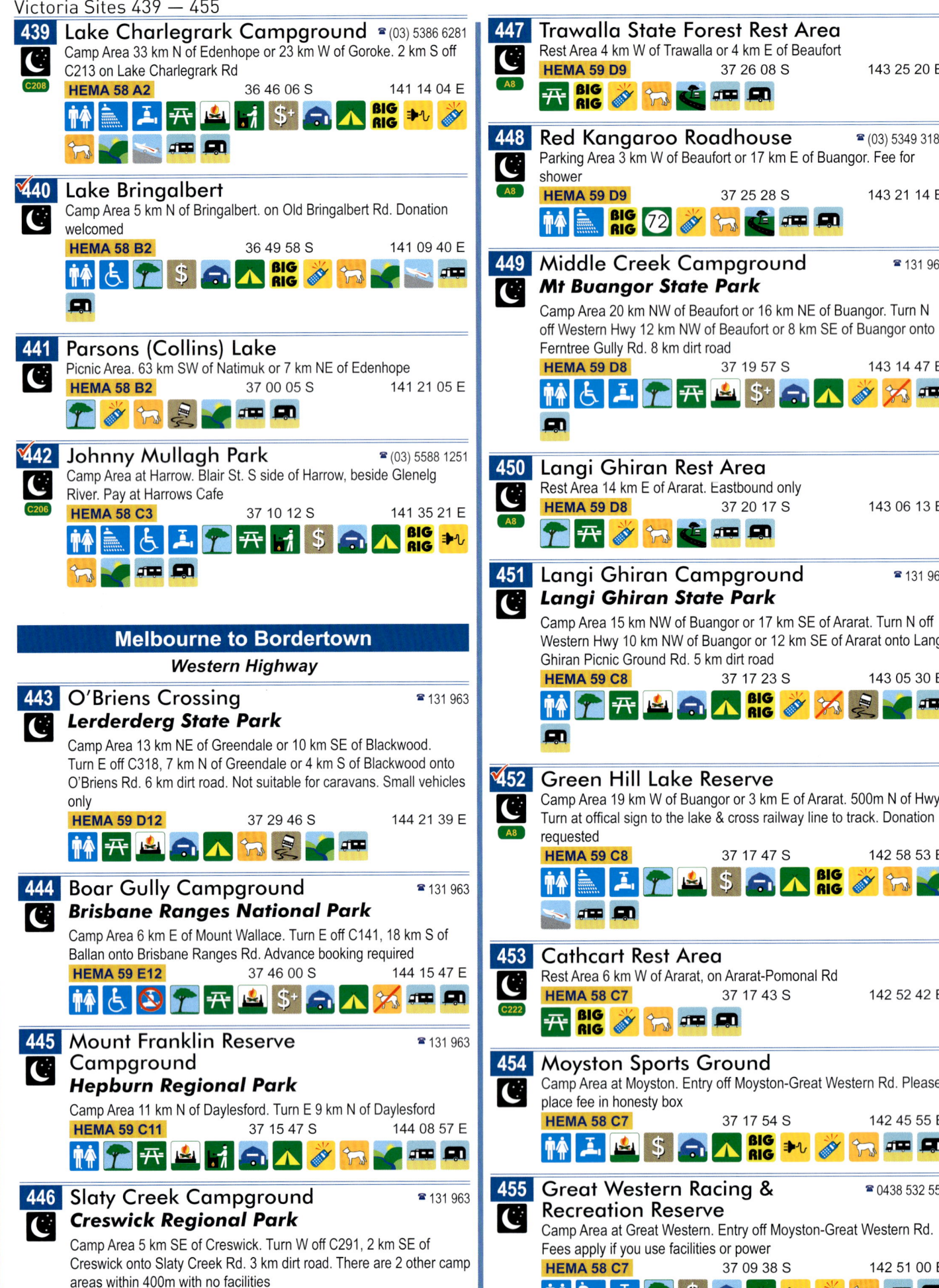

456 Great Western Rest Area
Rest Area 1 km N of Great Western or 13 km SE of Stawell
HEMA 58 C7 A8 37 08 41 S 142 50 32 E

457 Federation Park
Rest Area at Stawell. Cnr Western Hwy & Grampians Rd. Self Contained Vehicles only
HEMA 58 B7 37 03 39 S 142 45 27 E

458 Kelleys Beach
Picnic Area 17 km SW of Stawell or 7 km NE of Pomonal. Kellys Beach Rd
HEMA 58 C6 37 08 36 S 142 36 45 E

459 Canadian Gully Bushland Reserve ☎ 131 963
Rest Area 8 km NW of Stawell turnoff or 21 km SE of Dadswells Bridge
HEMA 58 B7 A8 37 00 22 S 142 42 31 E

460 Dadswells Bridge South Rest Area
Rest Area 22 km NW of Stawell turnoff or 7 km SE of Dadswells Bridge
HEMA 58 B6 A8 36 57 15 S 142 34 45 E

461 Grampians Edge Caravan Park ☎ (03) 5359 5241
Caravan Park at Dadswells Bridge. Caravan Park Rd
HEMA 58 B6 36 55 00 S 142 30 29 E

462 Plantation Campground ☎ 131 963
Grampians National Park
Camp Area 10 km N of Halls Gap Info Centre. Turn N off C216 before bridge onto Mt Zero Rd for 8.8 km. Dirt road for 8.4 km
HEMA 58 B6 37 03 34 S 142 30 53 E

463 Stapylton Campground ☎ 131 963
Grampians National Park
Camp Area 33 km SE of Horsham. Turn S off Western Hwy 17 km SE of Horsham onto Northern Grampians Rd for 14 km, then E along Olive Plantation Rd for 2 km (dirt road). Permit required. Small vehicles only
HEMA 58 B6 36 55 28 S 142 23 00 E

464 Borough Huts Campground ☎ 131 963
Grampians National Park
Camp Area 11 km S of Halls Gap. Access via Grampians Rd near Fyans Creek. Advance booking required
HEMA 58 C6 C216 37 13 27 S 142 32 25 E

465 Jimmy Creek Campground ☎ 131 963
Grampians National Park
Camp Area 29 km S of Halls Gap, via Grampians Rd. Advance booking required
HEMA 58 D6 C216 37 22 19 S 142 30 11 E

466 Wannon Crossing Campground ☎ 131 963
Grampians National Park
Camp Area 35 km S of Halls Gap, access via Grampians Rd at Knight Bridge on Wannon River. Small vehicles only
HEMA 58 D6 37 26 00 S 142 28 33 E

✓467 Boreang Campground ☎ (03) 5361 4000
Grampians National Park
Camp Area 18 km SW of Halls Gap. Access via Mount Victory Rd & Glenelg River Rd. Dirt road. Not suitable for caravans. Advance booking required
HEMA 58 C6 37 10 27 S 142 25 07 E

468 Smiths Mill Campground ☎ (03) 5361 4000
Grampians National Park
Camp Area 17 km NW of Halls Gap. Turn N off C222 onto Wartook Rd (C228), then R onto Old Mill Rd for 1 km, then L onto Smiths Rd (dirt road). Advance bookings required
HEMA 58 C6 37 06 28 S 142 25 24 E

469 Green Lake
Rest Area 24 km NW of Dadswells Bridge or 13 km SE of Horsham
HEMA 58 A5 A8 36 47 14 S 142 17 55 E

470 Burnt Creek
Rest Area 32 km NW of Dadswells Bridge or 5 km SE of Horsham
HEMA 58 A5 A8 36 45 39 S 142 15 01 E

471 Wail Picnic Area
Parking Area 12 km S of Dimboola or 24 km N of Horsham
HEMA 62 J4 A8 36 30 35 S 142 06 11 E

472 Dimboola Recreation Reserve
Parking Area at Dimboola, Lloyd St. Self Contained Vehicles only
HEMA 62 J4 36 27 30 S 142 01 44 E

Notes...

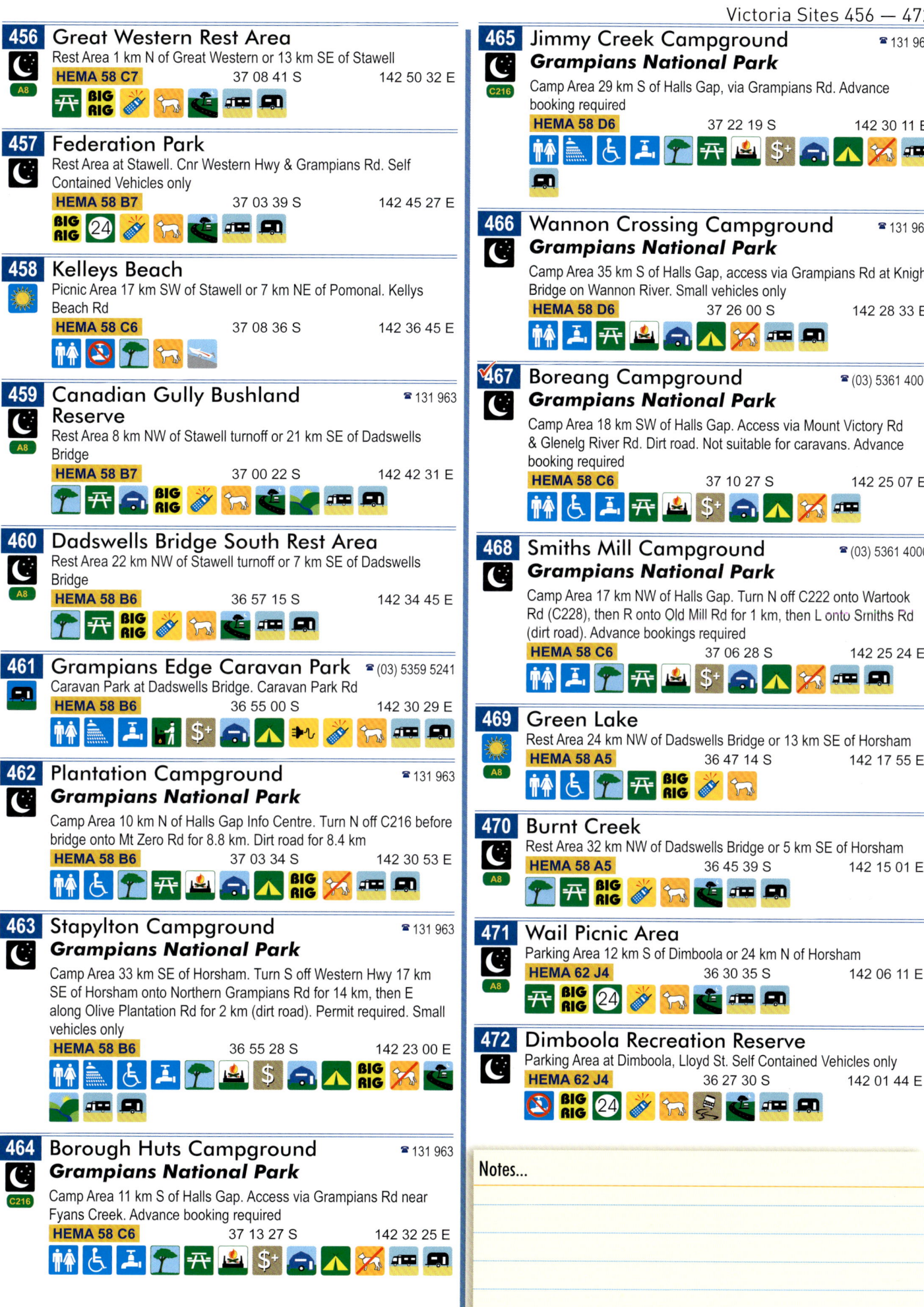

VICTORIA

473 Ackle Bend
☎ 131 963
Little Desert National Park
Camp Area 6 km S of Dimboola. Access via Riverside Rd & Horseshoe Bend Rd. 3 km dirt road. Advance booking required
HEMA 62 J4   36 30 10 S   142 01 11 E

474 Horseshoe Bend
☎ 131 963
Little Desert National Park
Camp Area 7 km S of Dimboola. Access via Riverside Rd & Horseshoe Bend Rd. 4 km dirt road. Advance booking required
HEMA 62 J4   36 29 51 S   142 01 05 E

475 Kiata Campground
☎ 131 963
Little Desert National Park
Camp Area 12 km S of Kiata, via Kiata South Rd. Signposted. 4 km dirt road
HEMA 62 J3   36 26 51 S   141 47 53 E

476 Lochiel Rest Area
Rest Area 6 km W of Dimboola or 32 km E of Nhill
HEMA 62 J4   36 25 06 S   141 58 52 E
A8

477 Nhill Aerodrome RV Stop
Camp Spot 3 km N of Nhill. Via Propodollah & Aerodrome Rds. Self Contained Vehicles only
HEMA 62 J3   36 18 27 S   141 38 53 E

478 Lawloit Rest Area
Rest Area 14 km W of Nhill or 27 km E of Kaniva
HEMA 62 J3   36 23 18 S   141 30 36 E
A8

479 Kaniva Caravan Park
☎ 0458 687 054
Caravan Park at Kaniva. Baker St
HEMA 62 J2   36 22 54 S   141 14 25 E

✓ 480 Serviceton Recreational Reserve
☎ 0419 032 418
Camp Spot at Serviceton, S of township on Baldocks-Grossers Rd. Call for access to facilities & payment
HEMA 62 J1   36 23 16 S   140 58 56 E

481 Tolmer Reserve
Rest Area 25 km W of Kaniva or 18 km E of Bordertown at Vic/SA border
HEMA 62 J1   36 20 40 S   140 57 58 E
A8

Melbourne to Mt Gambier
Princes Highway

482 Geelong Showground
☎ (03) 5221 1707
Parking Area at Geelong. Breakwater Rd, East Geelong. Contact Caretaker Bill 0457 921 264
HEMA 56 G3   38 10 17 S   144 22 20 E

483 Waurn Ponds Rest Area
Rest area 11 km SW of Geelong. Located on both sides of the Princes Hwy. Sectioned area for caravans.
HEMA 56 H2   38 13 01 S   144 16 13 E

484 Winchelsea RV Parking
Parking Area at Winchelsea. Cnr Barwon Tce & Mercer St. Self Contained Vehicles only
HEMA 61 E12   38 14 19 S   143 59 20 E
48

485 Barwon Hotel
☎ (03) 5267 2046
Parking Area at Winchelsea. Main Rd. Check in with publican on arrival
HEMA 61 E12   38 14 34 S   143 59 27 E

✓ 486 Meredith Park
Camp Area 12 km N of Colac or 11 km S of Beeac. Turn W off C146 10 km N of Colac or 9 km S of Beeac. Beside Lake Colac
HEMA 61 E9   38 16 07 S   143 36 38 E

487 Central Caravan Park
☎ (03) 5231 3586
Caravan Park at Colac. Bruce St. At showground. Not available show weekend in November
HEMA 61 F9   38 20 09 S   143 36 12 E

488 Pirron Yallock West Rest Area
Rest Area 2 km W of Pirron Yallock or 7 km E of Stoneyford. Both sides of road
HEMA 61 F8   38 20 49 S   143 24 45 E
A1

489 Floating Islands Lagoon Nature Reserve
Rest Area 3 km W of Pirron Yallock or 6 km E of Stoneyford
HEMA 61 F8   38 20 56 S   143 23 57 E
A1

490 Lake Bullen Merri Reserve
Rest Area 4 km SW of Camperdown. Turn W on to Naroghid Rd, N on to Bullen-Merri Rd
HEMA 60 E6   38 15 43 S   143 05 50 E

Notes...

VICTORIA

491 Lake Elingamite
Camp Area 7 km SW of Cobden. Turn W off Cobden-Warrnambool Rd 5 km SW of Cobden onto Oates Rd. 2 km dirt road
HEMA 60 F6   38 20 56 S   143 00 56 E

492 Brucknell Park Scout Camp ☎ (03) 5566 5205
Camp Area 30 km E of Allansford or 12 km W of Timboon on Timboon-Nullawarre Rd. Prebooking essential
HEMA 60 G5   38 28 14 S   142 51 26 E

493 Terang Apex Caravan Park ☎ (03) 5592 1687
Caravan Park at Terang. Princes Hwy. 1 km W of PO
HEMA 60 E5   38 14 31 S   142 54 34 E

494 Panmure Rest Area
Rest Area at Panmure, Princes Hwy
HEMA 60 F4   38 20 11 S   142 43 39 E

495 Woolsthorpe National Hotel ☎ (03) 5569 2391
Parking Area at Woolsthorpe. Pre booking essential, free with hotel patronage
HEMA 60 D2   38 11 10 S   142 25 51 E

496 Hawkesdale Apex Park
Camp Spot at Hawkesdale. Penshurst-Warrnambool Rd
HEMA 60 D1   38 06 15 S   142 19 19 E

497 Koroit-Tower Hill Caravan Park ☎ (03) 5565 7926
Caravan Park at Koroit. High St. 500m SE of PO
HEMA 60 E2   38 17 48 S   142 22 09 E

498 Killarney Beach Camping Reserve ☎ 0428 314 823
Camp Area at Killarney. Mahoneys Rd. 2 km S of Hwy
HEMA 60 F1   38 21 19 S   142 18 28 E

499 Martins Point
Picnic Area at Port Fairy. S end of Gipps St
HEMA 60 F1   38 23 25 S   142 14 34 E

500 Macarthur Recreation Reserve ☎ (03) 5576 1113
Camp Spot at Macarthur. 700m S of town off Port Fairy-Hamilton Rd, entry to reserve just S of river crossing. Self Contained Vehicles only
HEMA 58 G4   38 02 15 S   142 00 27 E

501 Mount Eccles Campground ☎ 131 963
Mt Eccles National Park
Camp Area 10 km SW of Macarthur via Mt Eccles Rd
HEMA 58 G4   38 03 28 S   141 55 26 E

502 Yambuk Caravan Park ☎ 0419 006 201
Caravan Park 4 km S of Yambuk via Carrolls Rd
HEMA 58 H5   38 20 22 S   142 03 16 E

503 Fitzroy River Reserve
Camp Area 26 km NW of Yambuk or 11 km SE of Tyrendarra. Turn S off A1, 22 km NW of Yambuk or 7 km SE of Tyrendarra onto Thompsons Rd, signposted "River Outlet". At river mouth
HEMA 58 H4   38 15 29 S   141 50 51 E

504 Sawpit Picnic Area ☎ 136 186
Mt Clay State Forest
Picnic Area 4 km NW of Narrawong. Turn N 1 km W of Narrawong onto Boyers Rd for 3 km
HEMA 58 H4   38 14 07 S   141 41 17 E

505 Henty Park
Parking Area at Portland, Bentinck St near Vintage Cable Tram depot
HEMA 58 H3   38 21 16 S   141 36 22 E

506 Surrey Ridge Picnic & Camp Area ☎ 136 186
Cobboboonee National Park
Camp Area 18 km W of Heywood. Turn W off A1, 6 km S of Heywood or 21 km N of Portland onto Coffeys Lane. Left at Jackys Swamp Rd, then R at Cut Out Dam Rd. 9 km dirt road
HEMA 58 G3   38 11 02 S   141 30 15 E

507 Jackass Fern Gully Picnic & Camp Area ☎ 136 186
Cobboboonee National Park
Camp Area 24 km NW of Heywood. Turn W off A1, 7 km NW of Heywood onto Sinclair Settlement Rd, Mt Deception Rd & T&W Rd. Alternative route via T&W Rd off A1, 5 km SE of Greenwald. 9 km dirt road
HEMA 58 G3   38 04 29 S   141 25 32 E

Notes...

508 Wrights Campground
☎ 131 963
Cobboboonee National Park
Camp Area 34 km NW of Heywood. Take Pacific Hwy NW for 29 Km turn S into Wrights Swamp Rd, 5 km to camp area
HEMA 58 G3   38 02 07 S   141 23 24 E

509 Heywood RV Stop
Parking Area at Heywood. Self Contained Vehicles only
HEMA 58 G3   38 07 51 S   141 37 57 E

510 Annya Road Picnic Area
☎ 136 186
Annya State Forest
Picnic Area 15 km NW of Heywood or 25 km S of Digby. Turn E off C195, 7.5 km NW of A1/C195 jcn or 24.5 km S of Digby onto Annya Rd. 500m off Hwy. Dirt road
HEMA 58 G3   38 01 07 S   141 34 58 E

511 Hotspur Bridge (Crawford River)
Camp Spot 20 km NW of A1/C195 jcn or 13 km S of Digby
HEMA 58 F3   37 55 33 S   141 33 40 E
C195

512 Digby Hotel
☎ (03) 5579 3281
Camp Spot at Digby Hotel. Portland Casterton Rd. Check in with publican. Self Contained Vehicles only
HEMA 58 F3   37 48 17 S   141 31 51 E
C195

513 Hiscocks Crossing
☎ 131 963
Crawford River Regional Park
Picnic Area 16 km W of Hotspur. Turn W off C195, 600m N of Hotspur Bridge onto Mill Rd & The Boulevard. Dirt road. Bush camping beside river. Alternative route from Greenwald not suitable for caravans. 9 km dirt road
HEMA 58 F3   37 56 19 S   141 26 47 E

514 Fort O'Hare Campground
Camp Area at Dartmoor. 500m E of PO, beside river. Donation requested
HEMA 58 F2   37 55 33 S   141 17 06 E

515 Pinaster Picnic Area
Rest Area 33 km W of Dartmoor or 17 km E of Mt Gambier, near VIC/SA border
HEMA 58 F1   37 50 29 S   140 58 42 E
A1

Portland to Mt Gambier
via Nelson

516 Cape Bridgewater
Rest Area 24 km W of Portland. Beachside car park at Surf Club
HEMA 58 H3   38 22 08 S   141 24 23 E
C193

517 Cape Bridgewater Coastal Camp
☎ (03) 5526 7247
Camp Area at Cape Bridgewater. 25 Peacock Rd
HEMA 58 H3   38 22 15 S   141 24 05 E

518 Swan Lake Campground
☎ (08) 8738 4051
Discovery Bay Coastal Park
Camp Area 36 km W of Portland or 45 km E of Nelson. Turn S onto Swan Lake Rd 30 km W of Portland or 38 km E of Nelson. 6 km to campsite. Dirt road, steep in places. Advance booking required. Not recommended for caravans
HEMA 58 H2   38 12 54 S   141 18 41 E

519 Lake Monibeong Campground
☎ (08) 8738 4051
Discovery Bay Coastal Park
Camp Area 72 km W of Portland or 23 km E of Nelson. Turn S onto Lake Monibeong Rd 65 km W of Portland or 16 km E of Nelson. 7 km to campsite. Advance booking required. Not suitable for caravans
HEMA 58 G2   38 08 02 S   141 11 08 E

520 Dartmoor Turnoff Rest Area
Rest Area 54 km NW of Portland or 15 km E of Nelson
HEMA 58 G2   38 04 31 S   141 09 54 E
C192

521 Pritchards Campground - Southern Shore
☎ (08) 8738 4051
Lower Glenelg National Park
Camp Area 18 km NW of Kentbruck, 21 km E of Nelson or 21 km S of Winnap. Turn N off C192, 12 km W of Kentbruck or 15 km E of Nelson. Access via Winnap-Nelson Rd. 1.5 km dirt road. Advance booking required
HEMA 58 G2   38 03 23 S   141 13 05 E

522 Moleside Creek Picnic Area
☎ 131 963
Lower Glenelg National Park
Picnic Area 23 km NW of Kentbruck, 26 km E of Nelson or 14 km S of Winnap. Turn N 12 km W of Kentbruck or 15 km E of Nelson. Access via Winnap-Nelson Rd
HEMA 58 G2   38 03 16 S   141 16 17 E

523 Forest Camp
☎ 131 963
Lower Glenelg National Park
Camp Area 26 km E of Nelson off Winnap-Nelson Rd. 8 km dirt road. Permit required
HEMA 58 G2   38 01 52 S   141 08 18 E

524 Wilson Hall Camping Area - Northern Shore
☎ (08) 8738 4171
Lower Glenelg National Park

Camp Area on North Shore. Signposted access off Wanwin Rd turn S onto Wilson Hall Track. Dirt road. Small to medium vehicles. Some low trees. Advance booking required

HEMA 58 G2　　　　　38 01 09 S　　　　141 06 25 E

525 River Vu Park
☎ (08) 8738 4123

Caravan Park at Nelson. Kellett St

HEMA 58 G1　　　　　38 02 57 S　　　　141 00 27 E

526 Princess Margaret Rose Caves - Northern Shore
☎ (08) 8738 4171
Lower Glenelg National Park

Camp Area 16 km N of Nelson or 28 km SE of Mt Gambier. Turn N 4 km W of Nelson or S 10 km E of Mt Gambier off the A1. Permit required

HEMA 58 G1　　　　　37 59 12 S　　　　140 59 31 E

Ballarat to Mt Gambier
Glenelg Highway

527 Haddon Woady Lions Park

Parking Area at Haddon off Racecourse Rd. Self Contained Vehicles only. Maximum stay 5 days. Envelopes on toilet block for your donation

HEMA 59 E10　　　　37 35 26 S　　　　143 42 54 E

528 Smythesdale Gardens Rest Area
☎ (03) 5342 8752

Camp Area at Smythesdale. Garden St. Donation please

HEMA 59 E10　　　　37 38 21 S　　　　143 41 09 E

529 Woady Yaloak Creek Rest Area

Rest Area 2 km W of Scarsdale or 7 km E of Linton

HEMA 59 E10　　　　37 40 41 S　　　　143 38 19 E
B160

530 Berringa Recreation Reserve
☎ (03) 5342 2367

Camp Area at Berringa. Entry off Derwent Jacks Rd. Caretaker collects fee

HEMA 61 A10　　　　37 46 22 S　　　　143 41 49 E

531 J C Stretch Memorial Park

Rest Area at Pitfield. Near Jcn of C143 & C171

HEMA 59 F9　　　　　37 48 28 S　　　　143 35 08 E
C143

532 East Beach Reserve
☎ (03) 5350 2204

Camp Area 4 km SE of Lake Bolac. Turn S off B160, E Beach rd Bolac. Ranger collects fees

HEMA 58 E7　　　　　37 43 17 S　　　　142 52 43 E

533 Lake Bolac Foreshore
☎ (03) 5350 2204

Camp Area 2 km S of Lake Bolac, via Sago Rd & Frontage Rd. Various sites on W side of lake. Ranger collects fee

HEMA 58 E7　　　　　37 43 16 S　　　　142 51 22 E

534 Wickliffe Rest Area

Rest Area at Wickliffe. 12 km W of Bolac or 34 km E of Dunkel

HEMA 58 E7　　　　　37 41 28 S　　　　142 43 23 E

535 Lake Buninjon

Rest Area 7 km SW of Maroona or 8 km NE of Willaura. Donation appreciated

HEMA 58 D7　　　　　37 29 05 S　　　　142 47 38 E
B180

536 Willaura Recreation Grounds
☎ 0429 953 150

Camp Area at Willaura, Delacome Way. Limited powered sites, call caretaker on arrival

HEMA 58 E7　　　　　37 32 41 S　　　　142 44 36 E

537 Yupperchair Park (Nine Mile Creek)

Rest Area 6 km W of Glenthompson or 12 km E of Dunkeld

HEMA 58 E6　　　　　37 38 08 S　　　　142 28 58 E
B160

538 Dunkeld Caravan Park
☎ (03) 5577 2578

Caravan Park at Dunkeld. Cnr of Victoria Valley Rd & Glenelg Hwy

HEMA 58 E6　　　　　37 38 59 S　　　　142 20 44 E

539 Mt Sturgeon Rest Area

Rest Area 1 km W of Dunkeld or 27 km NE of Hamilton

HEMA 58 E5　　　　　37 39 15 S　　　　142 19 12 E
B160

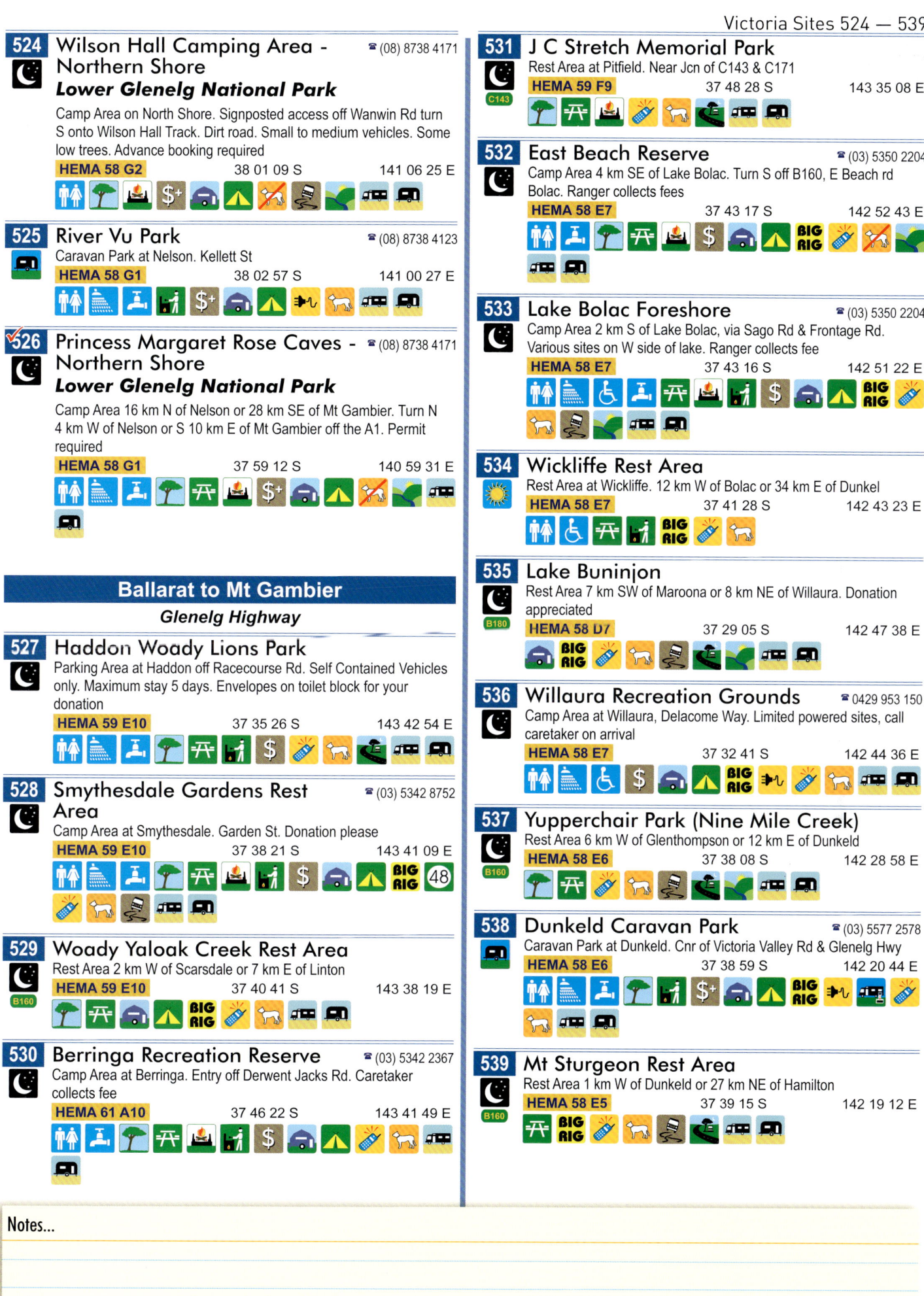

Notes...

VICTORIA

540 Nigretta Falls Scenic Reserve

Picnic Area 15 km NW of Hamilton. Turn N off B160, 7 km NW of Hamilton onto Nigretta Rd for 4 km, then W onto Wannon-Nigretta Falls Rd for 4.5 km

HEMA 58 E4	37 39 25 S	141 55 26 E

541 Wannon Falls Campground ☎ 1800 807 056

Camp Area 15 km NW of Hamilton or 17 km SE of Coleraine. Entry via Camerons Rd or Wannon Falls Rd 1 km S of Wannon

HEMA 58 E4	37 40 27 S	141 50 49 E

542 Coleraine Caravan Park ☎ (03) 5575 2268

Caravan Park at Coleraine. Cnr of Turnbull & Winter Sts, behind PO. Pay at PO

HEMA 58 E3	37 35 50 S	141 41 29 E

543 Wando Vale Memorial Hall ☎ (03) 5582 0272

Camp Area at Wando Vale. 687 Casterton-Edenhope Rd, 6.8 km N of Glenelg Hwy. Essential to call prior to arrival

HEMA 58 E3	37 30 43 S	141 26 40 E

544 Casterton Caravan Park ☎ 0457 414 187

Caravan Park at Casterton. Malcolm Carmichael Dr off Murray St, adjacent to swimming pool. Phone manager to arrange payment & key access.

HEMA 58 E3	37 34 58 S	141 24 19 E

545 Ess Lagoon

Camp Spot in Casterton. Ess Lagoon Rd. Self Contained Vehicles only. Maximum stay 1 month

HEMA 58 E3	37 34 51 S	141 23 56 E

546 Carmichael Track

Camp Spot 11 km W of Casterton. Signposted off Penola Rd

HEMA 58 E2	37 35 28 S	141 17 22 E

547 Mill Swamp - Wilkin Flora & Fauna Reserve

Camp Area 12 km E of Strathdownie. On Grubbed Rd, access via the Glenelg Hwy. Signposted

HEMA 58 E2	37 42 08 S	141 13 29 E

Notes...

548 Baileys Rocks Campground ☎ 131 963
Dergholm State Park

Camp Area 45 km NW of Casterton or 27 km SE of Langkoop. Turn E 9 km N of Dergholm or 25 km SE of Langkoop onto Baileys Rocks Rd. 3 km dirt road

HEMA 58 D2	37 17 17 S	141 10 38 E

Geelong to Hamilton
Hamilton Highway

549 Leigh River

Rest Area 28 km W of Geelong or 1 km E of Inverleigh. Only on the E of river/bridge

HEMA 61 D12	38 05 58 S	144 03 47 E

550 Browns Water Hole Caravan Park ☎ 0439 983 679

Caravan Park at Lismore. High St. Contact caretaker for key, alternative number 0439 036 265

HEMA 61 B8	37 57 16 S	143 20 48 E

551 Lismore Town Park

Rest Area at Lismore

HEMA 61 B8	37 57 14 S	143 20 38 E

552 Lake Tooliorook ☎ 0487 337 946

Camp Area 6 km S of Lismore. Turn W off C165, 5 km S of Lismore. 1 km dirt road. Good idea to check availability with caretaker

HEMA 60 C7	37 58 38 S	143 17 05 E

✓ 553 Derrinallum Recreation Reserve

Camp Area at Derrinallum. Hamilton Hwy E end of town

HEMA 60 B7	37 56 56 S	143 13 39 E

554 Deep Lake Recreation Reserve ☎ 0407 201 735

Camp Area 5 km NW of Derrinallum via Chatsworth Rd at W end of town. Pay fees at cafe

HEMA 60 B7	37 55 53 S	143 10 37 E

555 Mortlake Caravan Park ☎ 0409 428 870

Caravan Park at Mortlake. Jamieson Ave. 1 km E of PO

HEMA 60 D4	38 05 01 S	142 48 32 E

556 Tea Tree Lake

Rest Area at Mortlake. Terang Mortlake Rd

HEMA 60 D4	38 04 54 S	142 48 33 E

557 Penshurst Caravan Park ☎ (03) 5576 5220
Caravan Park at Penshurst. Cox St, 100m from PO. Pay at PO
HEMA 60 B1   37 52 26 S   142 17 26 E

Geelong to Warrnambool
Great Ocean Road

558 Hammond Road Campground ☎ 131 963
Great Otway National Park
Camp Area 8 km NW of Aireys Inlet. Access from Aireys Inlet, via Bambra Rd & Hammonds Rd. Dirt road
HEMA 61 F12   38 23 55 S   144 01 23 E

559 Big Hill Track Camping ☎ 131 963
Great Otway National Park
Camp Area 12 km NW of Lorne or 13 km SE of Deans Marsh Lorne Rd on Big Hill track. Signposted. Only open November to April
HEMA 61 G11   38 28 29 S   143 55 57 E

560 Wye River Road Campground ☎ 131 963
Great Otway National Park
Camp Area 4 km N of Wye River. Via Great Ocean & Wye Rds
HFMA 61 H11   38 37 25 S   143 54 10 E

561 Wye River Foreshore Reserve ☎ (03) 5289 0412
Camp Area at Wye River. Bookings essential for peak periods. Only open November to April
HEMA 61 H11   38 38 02 S   143 53 32 E

562 West Barwon Reservoir
Picnic Area 1 km S of Forrest or 5 km N of Barramunga. 700m off Hwy
HEMA 61 G10   38 31 52 S   143 43 15 E

563 Stevenson Falls Scenic Reserve ☎ 136 186
Great Otway State Park
Camp Area 5 km W of Barramunga. Turn W off C119, 26 km N of Apollo Bay or 8 km S of C119/C154 jcn onto Upper Gellibrand Rd. Narrow winding dirt road
HEMA 61 G10   38 33 49 S   143 39 23 E

564 Dandos Campground ☎ 136 186
Great Otway National Park
Camp Area 13 km SE of Gellibrand. Turn E off C155, 1 km S of Gellibrand onto Gellibrand East Rd, Lardners Track & Sayers Track. Dirt road. Camping beside river
HEMA 61 G9   38 33 16 S   143 37 05 E

565 Beauchamp Falls Reserve ☎ 131 963
Great Otway National Park
Camp Area 4 km SE of Beech Forest. Turn S off C159, 1 km E of Beech Forest onto Aire Valley Rd & Beauchamp Falls Rd. Dirt road
HEMA 61 H9   38 39 05 S   143 36 24 E

566 Blanket Bay Campground ☎ 131 963
Great Otway National Park
Camp Area 36 km W of Apollo Bay. Turn S onto Cape Otway Lighthouse Rd, then Blanket Bay Rd. Advance booking required
HEMA 61 K9   38 49 41 S   143 34 58 E

567 Aire River East Campground ☎ 131 963
Great Otway National Park
Camp Area 29 km W of Apollo Bay or 29 km SE of Lavers Hill. Turn S off B100, 24 km W of Apollo Bay or 24 km SE of Lavers Hill onto Hordern Vale Rd. 4.5 km to campsites. 2 km dirt road. First camp on R, larger camp area over bridge. Advance booking required
HEMA 61 K9   38 48 02 S   143 28 55 E

568 Aire River West Campground ☎ 131 963
Great Otway National Park
Camp Area 38 km W of Apollo Bay or 20 km S of Lavers Hill. Turn S off B100, 33 km W of Apollo Bay or 15 km S of Lavers Hill onto Sand Rd. 5 km narrow dirt track. Beside river. Advance booking required
HEMA 61 J8   38 48 06 S   143 28 40 E

569 Johanna Beach Campground ☎ 131 963
Great Otway National Park
Camp Area 15 km S of Lavers Hill. Turn W off B100, 38 km W of Apollo Bay or 10 km S of Lavers Hill, onto Red Johanna Rd. Advance booking required
HEMA 61 J8   38 45 44 S   143 22 44 E

570 Princetown Recreation Reserve ☎ 0429 985 176
Camp Area 1 km S of Princetown. 93 Old Coach Rd, beside Gellibrand River
HEMA 60 J7   38 41 56 S   143 09 31 E

Notes...

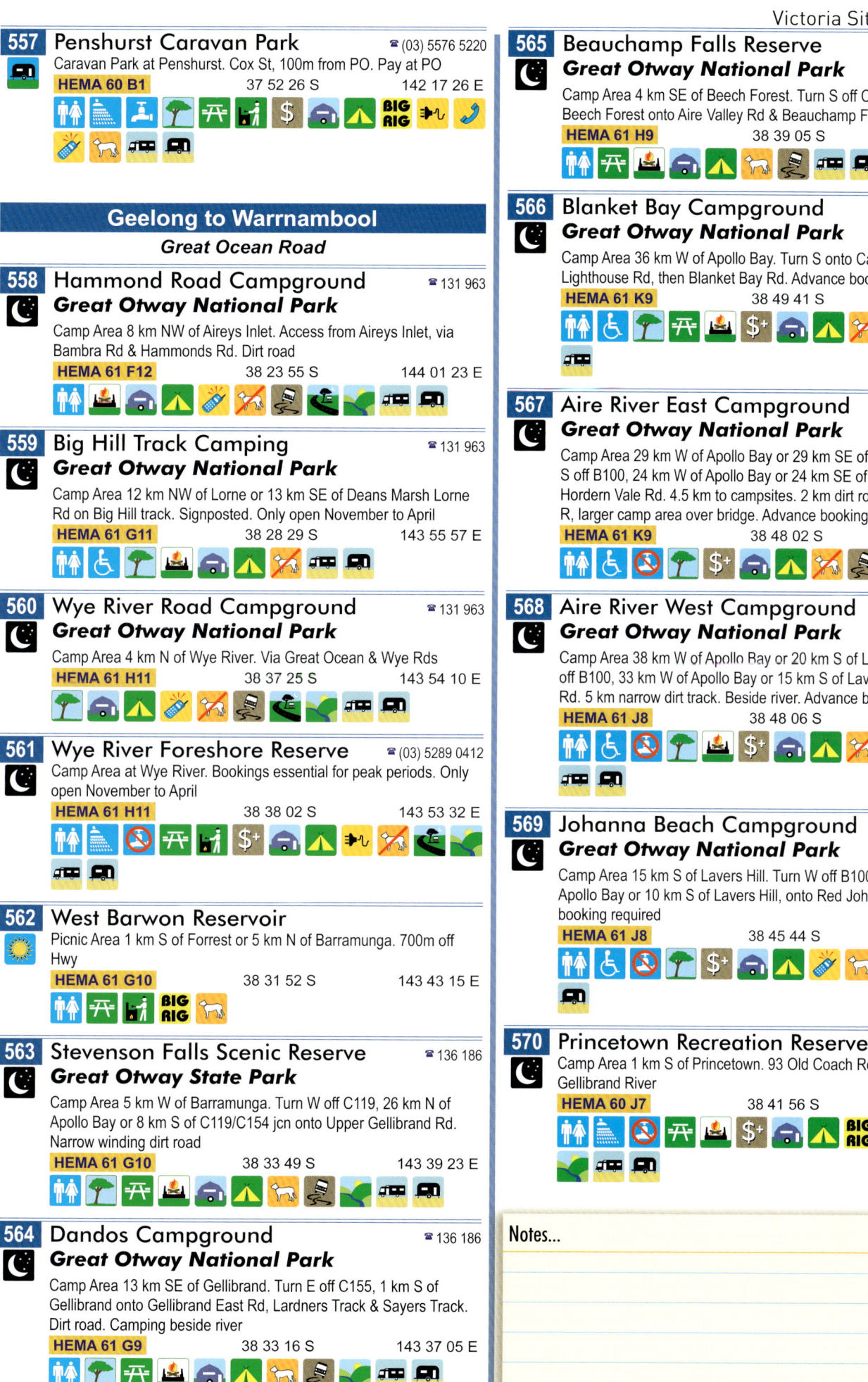

571 Port Campbell Recreation Reserve ☎ 0407 666 610
Camp Area at Port Campbell. Entry off Desaily St
HEMA 60 H6   38 36 58 S   143 00 06 E

Lascelles to Portland
Henty Highway

572 Lascelles Camping Ground ☎ (03) 5081 6242
Camp Area at Lascelles. Call into Minapre Hotel for payment
HEMA 62 F6   35 36 26 S   142 34 47 E
B220

573 Hopetoun Rest Area
Rest Area 1 km NE of Hopetoun
HEMA 62 G5   35 43 21 S   142 21 53 E
B200

574 Hopetoun Caravan Park ☎ 0417 237 587
Caravan Park at Hopetoun. Austin St
HEMA 62 G5   35 43 33 S   142 22 02 E

575 Lake Lascelles
Rest Area at Hopetoun. E end of Austin St. Turn N at the end of Austin St, follow track around lake to Eastern Foreshore. 1.5 km dirt road
HEMA 62 G5   35 43 31 S   142 22 29 E

576 Mallee Bush Retreat Campers Haven ☎ 0439 529 973
Camp Area at Hopetoun. E end of Austin St on the lake
HEMA 62 G5   35 43 39 S   142 22 15 E

577 Wonga Campground
Wyperfeld National Park ☎ 131 963
Camp Area 28 km N of Yaapeet. Turn W 3 km N of Yaapeet, then N after 3 km onto Wyperfeld Entrance. Advance booking required
HEMA 62 F4   35 35 12 S   142 03 02 E

578 O.T.I.T Campground
Lake Albacutya Regional Park ☎ 131 963
Camp Area 8 km NW of Yaapeet. W end of Rifle Butts Rd. 2 km dirt road past "OTIT Well" sign. Lake can be dry
HEMA 62 G4   35 43 40 S   141 59 30 E

579 Yaapeet Beach Campground
Lake Albacutya Regional Park ☎ 131 963
Camp Area 4 km W of Yaapeet. Via Yaapeet West Rd. Dirt road. Lake can be dry
HEMA 62 G4   35 46 01 S   142 00 23 E

580 Yaapeet Camp Ground ☎ (03) 5395 7243
Camp Area at Yaapeet. Sites are at rear of hall, honesty box or pay at school. Entry off Yaapeet-Kenmare Rd
HEMA 62 G4   35 46 01 S   142 03 07 E

581 Western Beach Campground
Lake Albacutya Regional Park ☎ 131 963
Camp Area 17 km NW of Rainbow. Access via Western Beach Rd off Albacutya Rd. Lake can be dry
HEMA 62 G4   35 46 50 S   141 56 08 E

582 Rainbow Caravan Park ☎ (03) 5395 1062
Caravan Park at Rainbow. Railway St. 1 km SW of PO
HEMA 62 G4   35 54 17 S   141 59 35 E
C227

583 The Wattles
Lake Hindmarsh Lake Reserve ☎ 131 963
Camp Area 16 km SW of Rainbow on Rainbow-Nhill Rd
HEMA 62 G4   35 56 41 S   141 52 27 E

584 Schulzes Beach
Lake Hindmarsh Lake Reserve ☎ 131 963
Camp Area 22 km SW of Rainbow on Rainbow-Nhill Rd. Beside lake, sandy track
HEMA 62 H4   36 02 46 S   141 51 25 E

585 Four Mile Beach Camping Ground
Lake Hindmarsh Lake Reserve ☎ 131 963
Camp Area 7 km W of Jeparit on Nhil Jeparit Rd
HEMA 62 H4   36 08 01 S   141 55 41 E

586 Beulah Caravan Park ☎ (03) 5390 2430
Caravan Park at Beulah. Higgbotham St, in sportsground. Payment & keys from Cafe 67 Phillip St
HEMA 62 G5   35 56 28 S   142 25 01 E

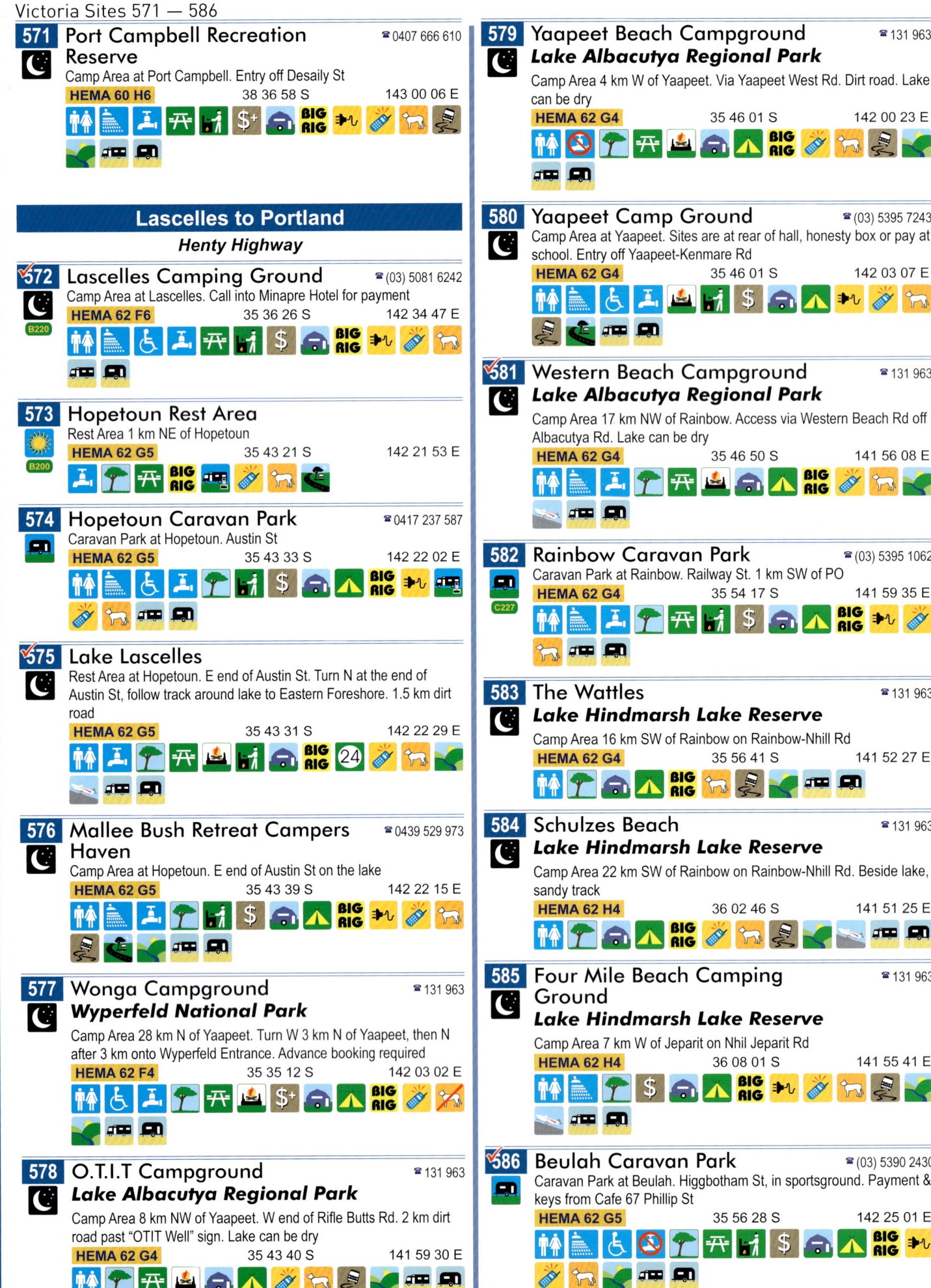

587 Jeparit Caravan Park ☎ 0408 107 851
Caravan Park at Jeparit. Peterson Ave. 500m SW of PO. See noticeboard for caretaker details
HEMA 62 H4   36 08 41 S   141 59 03 E

588 Brim Lakeside Park ☎ (03) 5390 4212
Camp Area 1 km W of Brim, via Swann St. Fee for power, payable Dixon Garage
HEMA 62 H5   36 04 32 S   142 24 26 E

589 Warracknabeal Caravan Park ☎ 0400 915 125
Caravan Park at Warracknabeal. Lyle St (Dimboola Rd). 1 km SW of PO
HEMA 62 H5   36 15 11 S   142 23 15 E

590 Balmoral Mural Square
Parking Area at Balmoral via Glendinning St. Self Contained Vehicles only
HEMA 58 C4   37 14 53 S   141 50 24 E

591 Brodies Campground
Rocklands Reservoir
Camp Area 20 km E of Balmoral off Rocklands-Cherrypool Rd. Dirt road
HEMA 58 C4   37 15 00 S   141 59 37 E

592 Glendinning Campground
Rocklands Reservoir
Camp Area 20 km SE of Balmoral, via Yarramyljup or Glendinning Rds
HEMA 58 D4   37 17 51 S   141 59 57 E

593 Mountain Dam Campground
Rocklands Reservoir
Camp Area 23 km SW of Cherrypool. Turn W off A200, 49 km S of Horsham or 55 km N of Cavendish, then L at HGH Cnr after 7 km. Dirt road
HEMA 58 C5   37 13 39 S   142 05 16 E

594 Cherrypool Highway Park
Rest Area at Cherrypool, 49 km S of Horsham or 55 km N of Cavendish. On Henty Hwy, along Glenelg River near Glenelg River bridge
HEMA 58 C5   37 06 29 S   142 11 14 E

595 Hynes Camping Reserve
Rocklands Reservoir
Camp Area 9 km W of Glenisla. Turn W off A200, 63 km S of Horsham or 41 km N of Cavendish
HEMA 58 C5   37 13 29 S   142 06 18 E

596 Buandik Campground ☎ 131 963
Grampians National Park
Camp Area 10 km E of Glenisla. Turn E off A200, 66 km S of Horsham or 38 km N of Cavendish onto Billiwing Rd, Harrop Trk & Goat Trk. 9 km dirt road
HEMA 58 C5   37 15 09 S   142 16 43 E

597 Fergusons Campground
Rocklands State Forest
Camp Area 38 km N of Cavendish. Turn W off A200, 78 km S of Horsham or 26 km N of Cavendish onto Gartons Rd. After 3.7 km turn N then after 5 km turn W follow to campsite. Dirt road
HEMA 58 D5   37 17 44 S   142 03 36 E

598 Cavendish Recreation Reserve ☎ 0499 048 184
Camp Spot 1 km N of Cavendish. Cadden St. 300m E of Hwy, next to picnic area. Pay at Hotel or see notice board
HEMA 58 E5   37 31 20 S   142 02 38 E

599 Branxholme Rest Area
Rest Area at Branxholme. Next to Recreation Reserve
HEMA 58 F4   37 51 29 S   141 48 09 E

Notes...

HELP SAVE THE FREE CAMP SITES!

All travellers have a responsibility to remove their own rubbish, but we also unfortunately need to clean up after other non-considerate travellers who leave rubbish behind.

SIMPLE WAYS TO HELP CLEAN UP!
- Always travel with a 'picker & pack of tough bags'
- If there are no bins to dispose of rubbish
  - Take it with you, to dispose of in a bin.
  - Burn the rubbish (watch for fire bans)
  - Bury the rubbish

PICKER

TOUGH BAGS

Thank you for cleaning up Australia and saving free camping areas

WINEGLASS BAY, FREYCINET NATIONAL PARK (69 B7) PHOTO: ROB BOEGHEIM

INSET on map 78

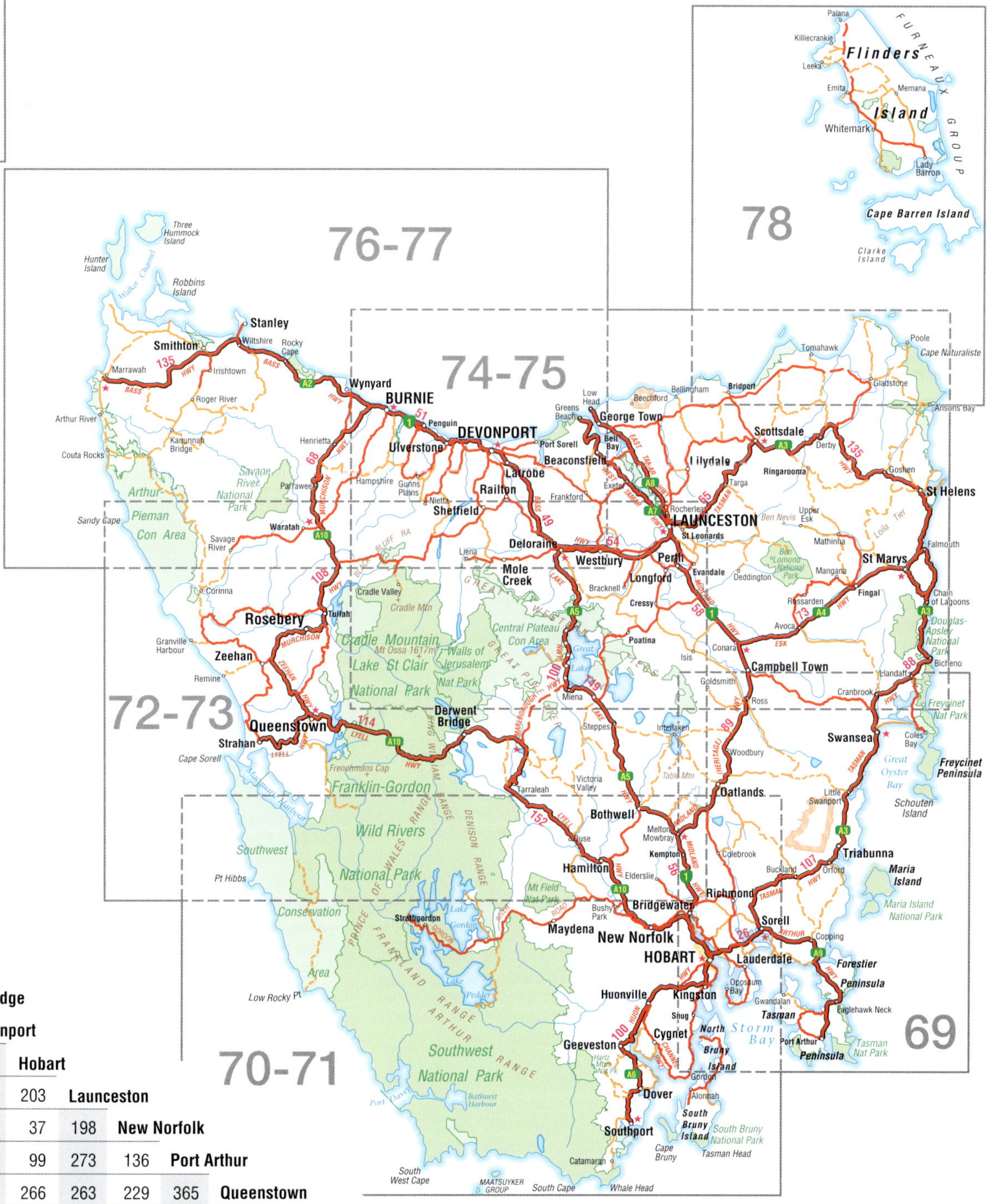

76-77

74-75

78

72-73

70-71

69

Burnie												
226	**Derwent Bridge**											
51	175	**Devonport**										
305	178	254	**Hobart**									
139	179	88	203	**Launceston**								
300	141	249	37	198	**New Norfolk**							
404	277	353	99	273	136	**Port Arthur**						
163	88	202	266	263	229	365	**Queenstown**					
109	142	148	320	209	283	419	54	**Rosebery**				
331	204	280	26	200	63	73	292	346	**Sorell**			
405	278	354	100	303	137	199	366	420	126	**Southport**		
302	288	251	253	163	250	300	376	375	227	353	**St Helens**	
79	323	130	384	218	379	483	235	181	410	484	381	**Stanley**
275	249	224	133	141	170	180	349	327	107	233	120	354	**Swansea**

Distances are shown in kilometres and follow the most direct major sealed route where possible.

Places of Interest

1. Allport Library & Museum of Fine Arts C2
2. Battery Point Area C2
3. Blundstone Arena C4
4. Cat & Fiddle Arcade C2
5. Designed Objects Tasmania B1
6. Federation Concert Hall C2
7. Franklin Square C2
8. Gasworks Cellar Door C2
9. Hobart Town Hall C2
10. International Wall of Friendship C2
11. Kelly Steps C2
12. Maritime Museum of Tasmania C2
13. Markree House Museum & Gardens C2
14. Military Museum of Tasmania C2
15. Narryna Heritage Museum C2
16. Parliament House C2
17. Penitentiary Chapel Historic Site C2
18. Peppermint Bay Cruises C2
19. Royal Tasmanian Botanical Gardens B2
20. Runnymede A1
21. Salamanca Market (Saturday) C2
22. Tasmanian Museum & Art Gallery C2
23. Theatre Royal C2
24. Village Cinemas C2
25. Wrest Point Casino D2

Accommodation

26. Best Western Hobart C2
27. Blue Hills Motel D2
28. City View Motel A4
29. Customs House Waterfront Hotel C2
30. Davey Place Holiday Town Houses D1
31. Fountainside Hotel C2
32. Graham Court Apartments A1
33. Grosvenor Court Apartments D2
34. Hadleys Hotel C2
35. Henry Jones Art Hotel C2
36. Hobart Tower Motel A1
37. Hotel Grand Chancellor C2
38. Lenna of Hobart C2
39. Macquarie Manor C2
40. Mayfair Plaza Motel D2
41. Montgomery's Hotel Hobart C2
42. Quest Waterfront C2
43. Rydges Hobart B1
44. Salamanca Inn C2
45. Somerset on the Pier C2
46. St Ives Motel Apartments D2
47. The Lodge on Elizabeth B1
48. The Old Woolstore C2
49. Travelodge Hobart C2
50. Woolmers Inn D2
51. Wrest Point Hotel Casino D2

Services

54. Police Headquarters C2
Post Office C2,D2
55. RACT C2
56. Royal Hobart Hospital C2
57. Tasmanian Visitor Information Centre C2

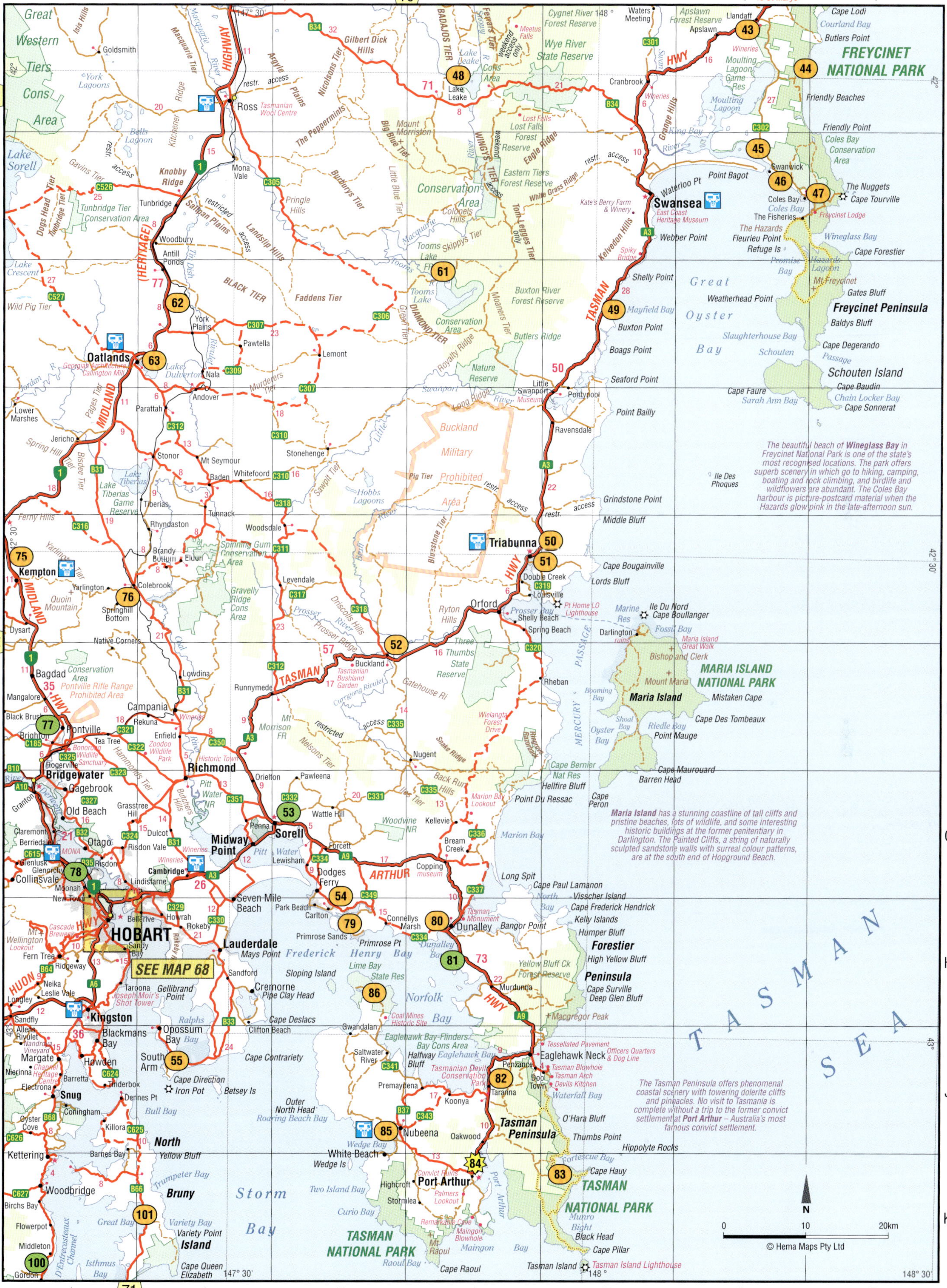
SEE MAP 68
HOBART
The beautiful beach of Wineglass Bay in Freycinet National Park is one of the state's most recognised locations. The park offers superb scenery in which go to hiking, camping, boating and rock climbing, and birdlife and wildflowers are abundant. The Coles Bay harbour is picture-postcard material when the Hazards glow pink in the late-afternoon sun.
Maria Island has a stunning coastline of tall cliffs and pristine beaches, lots of wildlife, and some interesting historic buildings at the former penitentiary in Darlington. The Painted Cliffs, a string of naturally sculpted sandstone walls with surreal colour patterns, are at the south end of Hopground Beach.
The Tasman Peninsula offers phenomenal coastal scenery with towering dolerite cliffs and pinnacles. No visit to Tasmania is complete without a trip to the former convict settlement at Port Arthur – Australia's most famous convict settlement.
0 10 20km
© Hema Maps Pty Ltd

Southern Tasmania

The wilderness area of the Southwest covers about 20% of Tasmania and is a UNESCO World Heritage Area. It is a land of temperate rainforests, rugged mountain ranges, wild rivers, pristine lakes, and many rare and threatened species of flora and fauna. The region is virtually uninhabited and hardly visited, except by experienced bushwalkers.

© Hema Maps Pty Ltd

Central Tasmania

© Hema Maps Pty Ltd

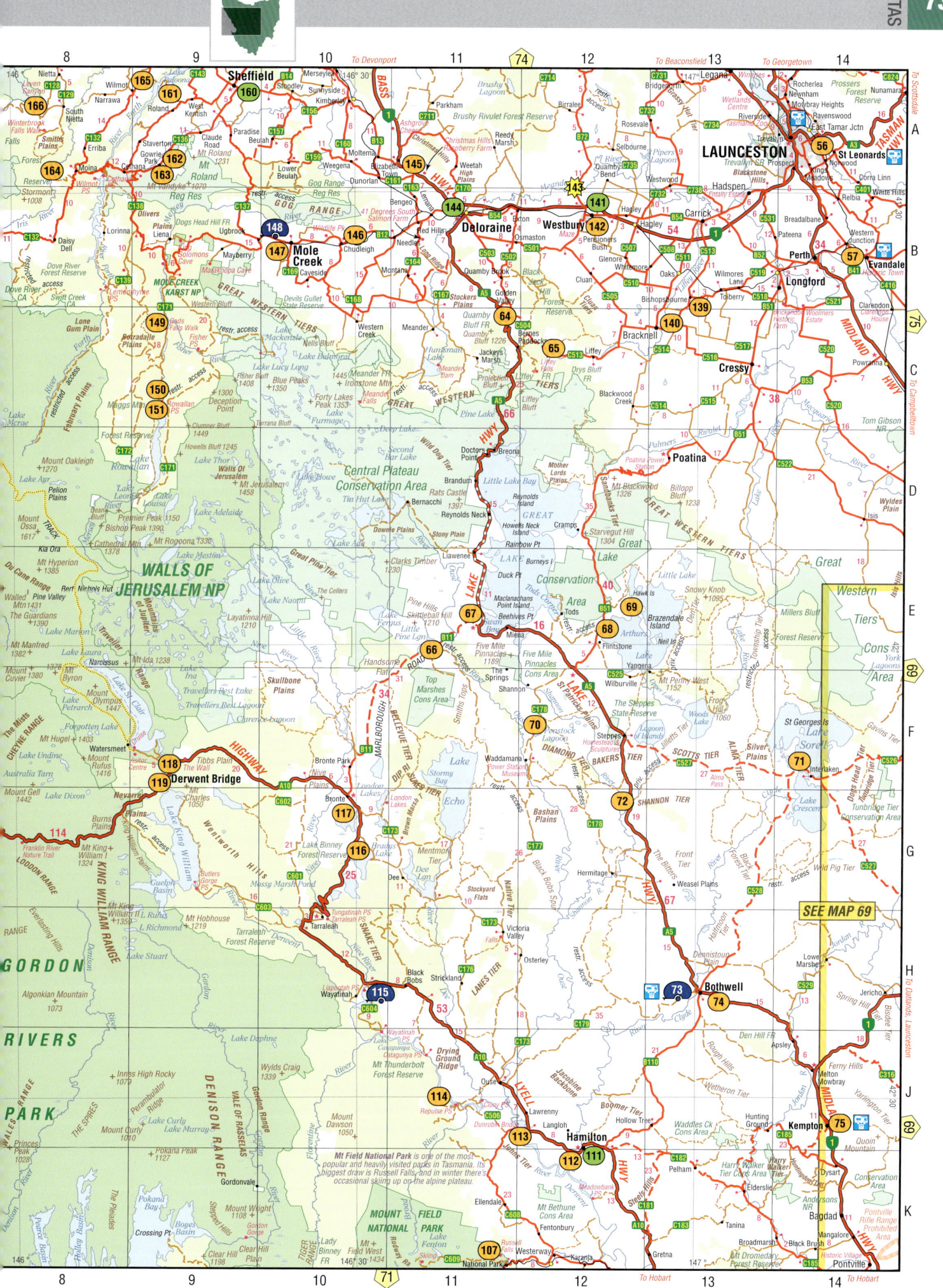

Most roads in State Forests are 'private roads', but Forestry Tasmania generally permits the public to have right of access. Forestry activities may result in certain roads and tracks being closed either on a temporary or permanent basis.

For more information on the ferry from Devonport to Melbourne, Phone 1800 634 906 www.spiritoftasmania.com.au

B a s s

Tasmania's second-largest city and the commercial heart of the north, Launceston has some fine old buildings. A big attraction is Cataract Gorge, the spectacular final stretch of the South Esk River, which is lit up at night for special effect.

The Low Head Lighthouse has been in use since 1805 and is Australia's oldest continuously operating pilot station.

© Hema Maps Pty Ltd

0   10   20   30km

N

Burnie is the fourth-largest city in Tasmania and its main deep-water port. It's an important industrial centre, and the surrounding scenery is attractive.

BURNIE
Somerset
Heybridge
Penguin
Ulverstone
DEVONPORT
Latrobe
Railton
Sheffield
Port Sorell
Beaconsfield
GEORGE TOWN
Beauty Point
Deloraine
Westbury
Mole Creek
Carrick
Bracknell
Poatina

NARAWNTAPU NATIONAL PARK

CRADLE MOUNTAIN-LAKE ST CLAIR NATIONAL PARK

WALLS OF JERUSALEM NP

Granite Tor Conservation Area

Central Plateau Conservation Area

GREAT WESTERN TIERS

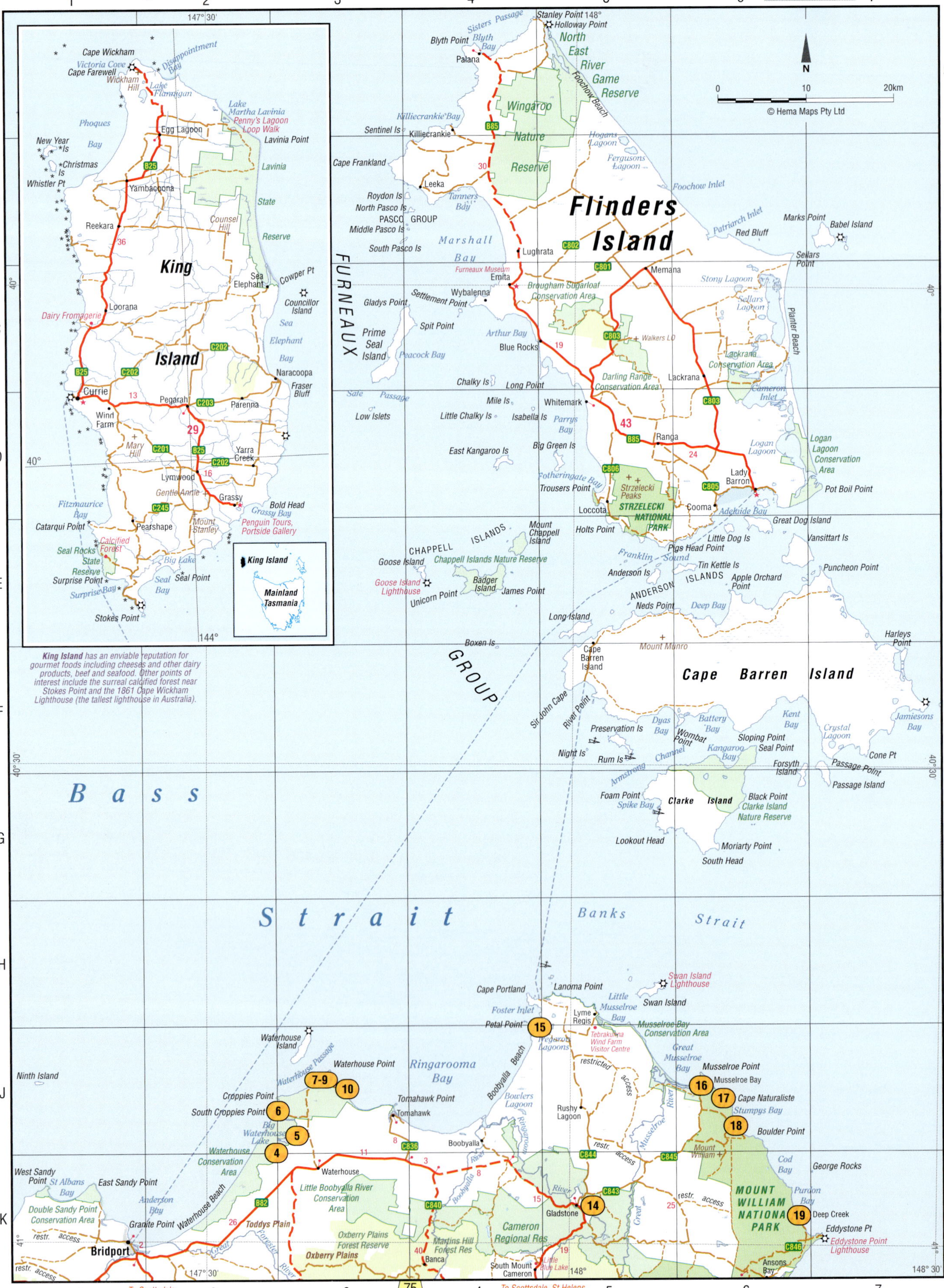

Flinders & King Islands, Tasmania

© Hema Maps Pty Ltd

King Island has an enviable reputation for gourmet foods including cheeses and other dairy products, beef and seafood. Other points of interest include the surreal calcified forest near Stokes Point and the 1861 Cape Wickham Lighthouse (the tallest lighthouse in Australia).

King Island

Flinders Island

Cape Barren Island

Clarke Island

Bass Strait

Banks Strait

FURNEAUX GROUP

ANDERSON ISLANDS

CHAPPELL ISLANDS

STRZELECKI NATIONAL PARK

MOUNT WILLIAM NATIONAL PARK

Tasmania Highway Index

Tasmania Alphabetic Site Index

Tasmania Alphabetic Site Index

TASMANIA

Launceston - St Helens - Hobart

Tasman Highway

1 Lilydale Falls

B81

Camp Area 2 km N of Lilydale

HEMA 75 D8 41 13 47 S 147 12 34 E

24

2 Myrtle Park Recreation Ground ☎(03) 6399 3368

A3

Camp Area 32 km NE of Launceston or 31 km SW of Scottsdale, beside St Patricks River. Maximum stay 7 days

HEMA 75 E9 41 18 31 S 147 21 55 E

BIG RIG

3 Northeast Park

A3

Camp Area at Scottsdale. Ringarooma Rd, 1 km E of PO. Maximum stay 7 days. Donation & hot showers gold coin

HEMA 75 D10 41 09 56 S 147 31 23 E

BIG RIG

4 Blackmans Lagoon Camping Area ☎(03) 6356 1173

Waterhouse Conservation Area

Camp Area 26.5 km NE of Bridport. Turn N off the B82, 24 km NE of Bridport. 2.5 km dirt road. Camping beside pine forest. Small vehicles only. Maximum stay 1 month

HEMA 75 B10 40 54 46 S 147 35 44 E

5 Big Waterhouse Lake Camping Area ☎(03) 6356 1173

Waterhouse Conservation Area

Camp Area 34 km NE of Bridport. Turn N off the B82, 27 km NE of Bridport onto Homestead Rd, then L after 4.3 km for 2.5 km. 7 km dirt road. Maximum stay 1 month

HEMA 75 B10 40 53 32 S 147 36 57 E

6 South Croppies Point Camping Area ☎(03) 6356 1173

Waterhouse Conservation Area

Camp Area 37 km NE of Bridport. Turn N off the B82, 27 km NE of Bridport onto Homestead Rd, then L after 6.3 km for 4 km. 10 km dirt road. Camping beside road just after fork. Maximum stay 1 month

HEMA 75 B10 40 51 56 S 147 35 37 E

7 Waterhouse Point Camping Area ☎(03) 6356 1173

Waterhouse Conservation Area

Camp Area 40 km NE of Bridport. Turn N off the B82, 27 km NE of Bridport onto Homestead Rd, then L after 12.4 km for 800m. 13 km dirt road. Small vehicles only. Beachfront. Maximum stay 1 month

HEMA 75 A11 40 49 39 S 147 40 08 E

8 Village Green Camping Area ☎(03) 6356 1173

Waterhouse Conservation Area

Camp Area 41 km NE of Bridport. Turn N off the B82, 27 km NE of Bridport onto Homestead Rd, then L after 12.4 km for 1.6 km. 14 km dirt road. Maximum stay 1 month

HEMA 75 A11 40 49 35 S 147 39 39 E

9 Mathers Camping Area

Waterhouse Conservation Area

Camp Area 40 km NE of Bridport. Turn N off the B82, 27 km NE of Bridport onto Homestead Rd, follow signs. 13 km dirt road. Beachfront. Maximum stay 1 month

HEMA 75 A11 40 49 40 S 147 40 09 E

10 Ransons Beach Camping Area ☎(03) 6356 1173

Waterhouse Conservation Area

Camp Area 41.4 km NE of Bridport. Turn N off the B82, 27 km NE of Bridport onto Homestead Rd for 14.4 km of dirt road. Beachfront. Maximum stay 1 month

HEMA 75 A11 40 50 24 S 147 41 14 E

11 Branxholm Camping Ground ☎(03) 6354 6168

A3

Camp Area at Branxholm, beside swimming pool. Bookings & payment at the IGA supermarket

HEMA 75 D11 41 10 06 S 147 44 15 E

BIG RIG

12 Derby Park

A3

Camp Spot at Derby. W end of town, beside tennis courts & river

HEMA 75 D11 41 08 31 S 147 47 52 E

BIG RIG

13 Derby Works Depot

A3

Parking Area at Derby. E end of town, beside council depot

HEMA 75 D11 41 09 00 S 147 48 16 E

BIG RIG

14 Gladstone Hall

B32

Parking Area at Gladstone. 3 Edward St

HEMA 75 B13 40 57 36 S 148 00 32 E

BIG RIG

15 Petal Point Campground

C844

Camp Area 21 km N of Gladstone, via Cape Portland Rd. Dirt road

HEMA 75 A12 40 46 38 S 147 57 02 E

BIG RIG

16 Musselroe Bay ☎(03) 6356 1173

C845

Musselroe Bay Conservation Area

Camp Area 24 km NE of Gladstone, via C843, C845 & Forester Kangaroo Dr. 800m N of Musselroe Bay fire station. Mostly dirt road. Oceanfront

HEMA 75 A14 40 50 07 S 148 10 39 E

17 Top Camp Campground
☎ (03) 6356 1173
Mt William National Park
Camp Area 27 km NE of Gladstone, via C843, C845 & Forester Kangaroo Dr. Turn E 300m N of Musselroe Bay township for 2.5 km. Mostly dirt road. Narrow access track. Oceanfront

HEMA 75 A14   40 50 34 S   148 12 12 E

18 Stumpys Bay Campground
☎ (03) 6356 1173
Mt William National Park
Camp Area 26 km NE of Gladstone, via C843, C845 & Forester Kangaroo Dr. Mostly dirt road. Turn E 6 km N of park entrance. Small vehicles only. 6 camp areas

HEMA 75 B14   40 52 16 S   148 13 19 E

19 Deep Creek Campground
☎ (03) 6356 1173
Mt William National Park
Camp Area 37 km E of Gladstone. Turn N off C846, 34 km E of Gladstone at Eddystone Point Rd jcn for 3 km. Mostly dirt road. Small vehicles only

HEMA 75 B14   40 58 11 S   148 18 44 E

20 Policemans Point Campground
☎ (03) 6376 1550
Bay of Fires Conservation Area
Camp Area 40 km E of Gladstone. Turn S off C843, 35 km E of Gladstone at South Ansons Bay Rd for 5 km. Mostly dirt road. Maximum stay 1 month

HEMA 75 C14   41 03 44 S   148 17 27 E

✓ 21 Weldborough Hotel & Campground
☎ (03) 6354 2223
A3
Camp Spot at Weldborough, 21 km E of Derby or 44 km NW of St Helens. Behind Hotel. Must book in advance for powered sites

HEMA 75 D12   41 11 38 S   147 54 16 E

22 Pub in the Paddock
☎ (03) 6373 6121
Camp Spot at Pyengana. 750m W of the Pyengana Dairy Company. Self Contained Vehicles only

HEMA 75 E12   41 17 32 S   147 59 49 E

23 Pyengana Recreation Ground
Camp Area at Pyengana. 400m W of the Pyengana Dairy Company. Self Contained Vehicles only. Donations at the gate

HEMA 75 E13   41 17 31 S   148 00 03 E

24 Moulting Bay Camping Area
☎ (03) 6376 1550
Humbug Point Nature Recreation Area
Camp Area 8 km NE of St Helens, via Binalong Bay Rd (C850). Turn E off C850 after 7 km. 1 km dirt road. Beside bay. Maximum stay 1 month

HEMA 75 E14   41 16 48 S   148 16 57 E

25 Dora Point Camping Area
☎ (03) 6376 1550
Humbug Point Nature Recreation Area
Camp Area 13 km NE of St Helens, via Binalong Bay Rd (C850). Turn E off C850 after 8.2 km. 4.7 km dirt road to various sites behind sand dunes. Beside bay. Cold showers. Maximum stay 1 month

HEMA 75 E14   41 16 37 S   148 19 36 E

26 Grants Lagoon
☎ (03) 6376 1550
Bay of Fires Conservation Area
C848
Camp Area 10 km NE of St Helens, via Binalong Bay Rd (C850) & The Gardens Rd (C848). Turn E off C848, 9.5 km NE of St Helens, then R after 300m. Near lagoon. Maximum stay 1 month

HEMA 75 D14   41 15 17 S   148 17 25 E

27 Jeanneret Beach Campground
☎ (03) 6376 1550
Bay of Fires Conservation Area
C848
Camp Area 12 km NE of St Helens, via Binalong Bay Rd (C850) & The Gardens Rd (C848). Turn E off C848, 11.4 km NE of St Helens. Beachfront. Maximum stay 1 month

HEMA 75 D14   41 14 13 S   148 17 27 E

✓ 28 Swimcart Beach Campground
☎ (03) 6376 1550
Bay of Fires Conservation Area
C848
Camp Area 13 km NE of St Helens, via Binalong Bay Rd (C850) & The Gardens Rd (C848). Turn E off C848, 12.3 km NE of St Helens. 1 km dirt road. Beachfront. Maximum stay 1 month

HEMA 75 D14   41 13 46 S   148 17 04 E

29 Cosy Corner South Camp Ground
☎ (03) 6376 1550
Bay of Fires Conservation Area
C848
Camp Area 14 km NE of St Helens, via Binalong Bay Rd (C850) & The Gardens Rd (C848). Turn E off C848, 13.6 km NE of St Helens. 500m dirt road. Beachfront. Maximum stay 1 month

HEMA 75 D14   41 13 23 S   148 16 59 E

✓ 30 Cosy Corner North Camp Ground
☎ (03) 6376 1550
Bay of Fires Conservation Area
C848
Camp Area 15 km NE of St Helens, via Binalong Bay Rd (C850) & The Gardens Rd (C848). Turn E off C848, 13.9 km NE of St Helens. 500m dirt road. Beachfront. Maximum stay 1 month

HEMA 75 D14   41 13 16 S   148 16 55 E

31 St Helens Sporting Complex
Camp Area at St Helens. Tully St. Self Contained motorhomes & campervans

HEMA 75 E14   41 19 00 S   148 14 08 E

Notes...

TASMANIA

32 Dianas Basin ☎ (03) 6376 1550
St Helens Point State Rec Area

Camp Area 9 km S of St Helens or 4 km N of Beaumaris. Turn E 8 km S of St Helens or 3 km N of Beaumaris for 900m. Turn L after 500m. Waterfront. Maximum stay 1 month

| HEMA 75 E14 | 41 22 34 S | 148 17 16 E |

33 Paddys Island Campground ☎ (03) 6376 1550
Scamander Conservation Area

Camp Area 10.5 km S of St Helens or 2.5 km NW of Beaumaris. Small area, limited sites. Beachfront

| HEMA 75 F14 | 41 23 43 S | 148 17 21 E |

34 Shelly Point ☎ (03) 6376 1550

Camp Area 2 km S of Beaumaris or 3 km N of Scamander Bridge. 400m off Hwy. No camping on oceanfront

| HEMA 75 F14 | 41 26 05 S | 148 16 36 E |

35 Scamander Forest Reserve (Trout Creek) ☎ (03) 6374 2102

Camp Area 11 km W of Beaumaris, via Upper Scamander Rd, Eastern Creek Rd & Trout Rd. Dirt road. Beside river

| HEMA 75 F14 | 41 26 08 S | 148 13 30 E |

36 South Esk River Picnic Area

Camp Spot 3 km N of Mathinna. Turn N at Mathinna, then W onto Griffin Rd after bridge. Camp Spot at jcn

| HEMA 75 F12 | 41 27 49 S | 147 53 21 E |

37 Griffin Camping Area ☎ (03) 6352 6520

Camp Area 5.5 km W of Mathinna. Turn N at Mathinna, then W onto Griffin Rd for 2.5 km. Signposted access tracks to various campsites. Beside river

| HEMA 75 F12 | 41 27 57 S | 147 51 10 E |

38 Fingal Park

Parking Area at Fingal. Talbot St, located behind toilet block at the Info Board. Fee for shower

| HEMA 75 G12 | 41 38 17 S | 147 58 06 E |

39 St Marys Sportsground & Golf Course

Camp Area at St Marys. 22 Harefield Rd. Fee for hot shower

| HEMA 75 G13 | 41 35 05 S | 148 11 02 E |

40 Little Beach Campground ☎ (03) 6256 7000
Little Beach Conservation Area

Camp Area 17 km S of A3/A4 jcn or 5.5 km N of Chain of Lagoons. 200m off Hwy. Beachfront. Maximum stay 1 month

| HEMA 75 G14 | 41 37 35 S | 148 18 44 E |

✓ 41 Lagoons Beach ☎ (03) 6256 7000
Lagoons Beach Conservation Area

Camp Area 20 km S of A3/A4 jcn or 2.5 km N of Chain of Lagoons. 300m off Hwy. Beachfront. Maximum stay 1 month

| HEMA 75 G14 | 41 38 48 S | 148 17 52 E |

42 Douglas River Cabins ☎ (03) 6375 1164

Camp Area 31 km S of St Marys or 13 km N of Bicheno on the Tasman Hwy. Prebook & obtain directions before arrival. Must have chemical toilet

| HEMA 75 J14 | 41 46 57 S | 148 15 22 E |

43 The Pondering Frog Tearoom ☎ 0412 631 299

Parking Area 11 km S of Bicheno. Entry 400m S of Coles Bay turn off. Self Contained Vehicles only. Donation requested

| HEMA 69 A6 | 41 56 35 S | 148 12 51 E |

44 Friendly Beaches Campground ☎ (03) 6256 7000
Freycinet National Park

Camp Area 13 km S of A3/C302 jcn. Turn E off C302, 9 km S of jcn. 3 km dirt road. Beachfront

| HEMA 69 A6 | 41 59 27 S | 148 17 15 E |

✓ 45 River and Rocks Campground ☎ (03) 6256 7000

Camp Area 19 km S of A3/C302 jcn or 8 km N of Coles Bay, via River & Rocks Rd. 1 km dirt road W of Hwy

| HEMA 69 B6 | 42 05 12 S | 148 14 03 E |

46 Freycinet Golf Club ☎ (03) 6257 0053

Parking Area at Coles Bay, Swanwick Rd. Pay fees at clubhouse. Self Contained Vehicles only. Maximum stay 5 days. Toilet only open when club house open

| HEMA 69 B6 | 42 05 45 S | 148 14 40 E |

47 Richardsons Beach Campground ☎ (03) 6256 7000
Freycinet National Park

Camp Area at Coles Bay. Adjacent to National Parks Visitors Centre. Beachfront. Bookings essential. Small vehicles only. Maximum stay 14 days

| HEMA 69 B6 | 42 07 27 S | 148 17 46 E |

48 Lake Leake Campground ☎ (03) 6381 1319

Camp Area 39 km NW of Swansea or 32 km E of Campbell Town, via Lake Leake Rd. 4 km dirt road. Limited space

| HEMA 69 A4 | 42 00 44 S | 147 48 02 E |

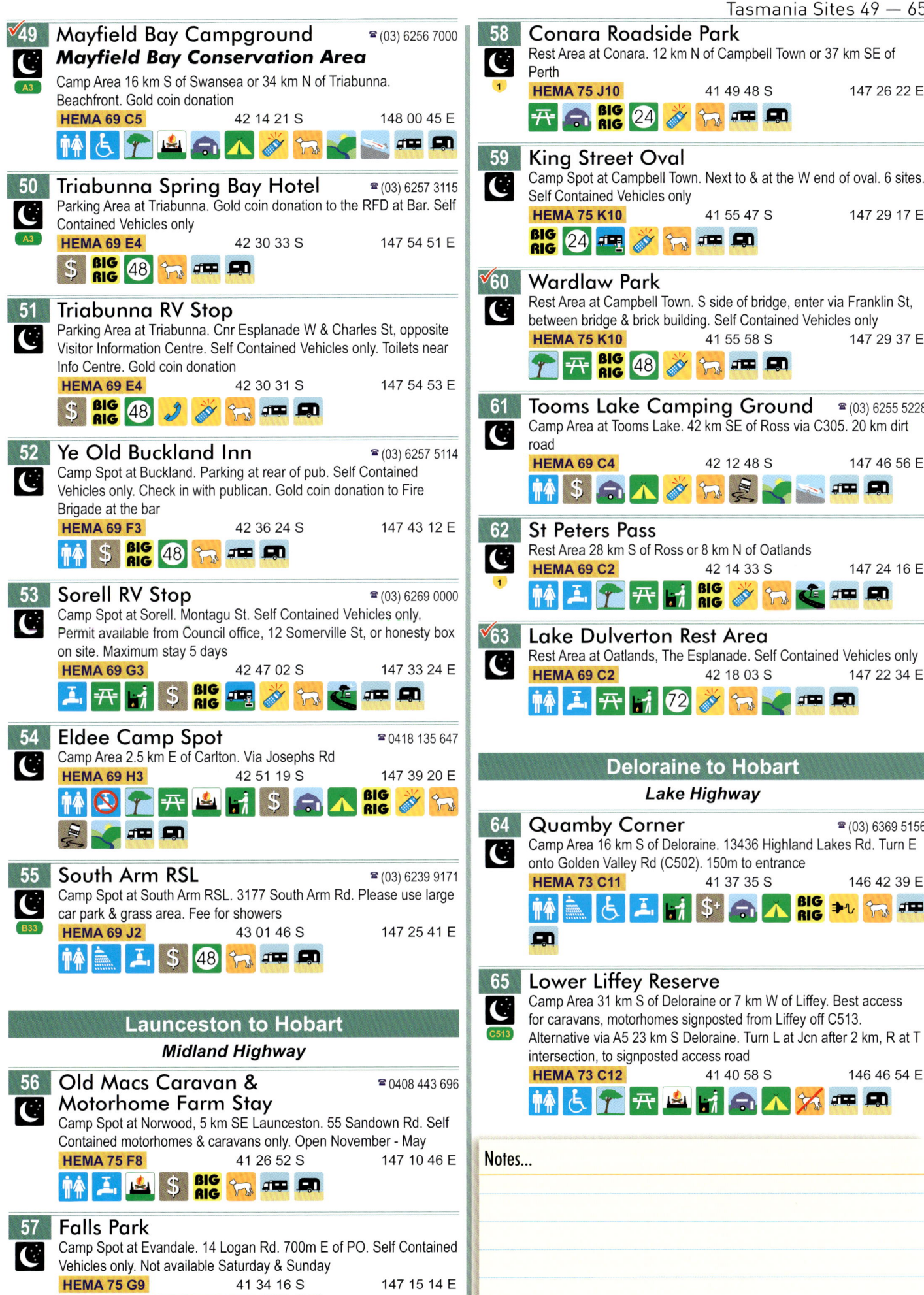

49 Mayfield Bay Campground ☎ (03) 6256 7000
Mayfield Bay Conservation Area
Camp Area 16 km S of Swansea or 34 km N of Triabunna.
Beachfront. Gold coin donation
HEMA 69 C5   42 14 21 S   148 00 45 E

50 Triabunna Spring Bay Hotel ☎ (03) 6257 3115
Parking Area at Triabunna. Gold coin donation to the RFD at Bar. Self
Contained Vehicles only
HEMA 69 E4   42 30 33 S   147 54 51 E

51 Triabunna RV Stop
Parking Area at Triabunna. Cnr Esplanade W & Charles St, opposite
Visitor Information Centre. Self Contained Vehicles only. Toilets near
Info Centre. Gold coin donation
HEMA 69 E4   42 30 31 S   147 54 53 E

52 Ye Old Buckland Inn ☎ (03) 6257 5114
Camp Spot at Buckland. Parking at rear of pub. Self Contained
Vehicles only. Check in with publican. Gold coin donation to Fire
Brigade at the bar
HEMA 69 F3   42 36 24 S   147 43 12 E

53 Sorell RV Stop ☎ (03) 6269 0000
Camp Spot at Sorell. Montagu St. Self Contained Vehicles only.
Permit available from Council office, 12 Somerville St, or honesty box
on site. Maximum stay 5 days
HEMA 69 G3   42 47 02 S   147 33 24 E

54 Eldee Camp Spot ☎ 0418 135 647
Camp Area 2.5 km E of Carlton. Via Josephs Rd
HEMA 69 H3   42 51 19 S   147 39 20 E

55 South Arm RSL ☎ (03) 6239 9171
Camp Spot at South Arm RSL. 3177 South Arm Rd. Please use large
car park & grass area. Fee for showers
HEMA 69 J2   43 01 46 S   147 25 41 E

Launceston to Hobart
Midland Highway

56 Old Macs Caravan & ☎ 0408 443 696
Motorhome Farm Stay
Camp Spot at Norwood, 5 km SE Launceston. 55 Sandown Rd. Self
Contained motorhomes & caravans only. Open November - May
HEMA 75 F8   41 26 52 S   147 10 46 E

57 Falls Park
Camp Spot at Evandale. 14 Logan Rd. 700m E of PO. Self Contained
Vehicles only. Not available Saturday & Sunday
HEMA 75 G9   41 34 16 S   147 15 14 E

58 Conara Roadside Park
Rest Area at Conara. 12 km N of Campbell Town or 37 km SE of
Perth
HEMA 75 J10   41 49 48 S   147 26 22 E

59 King Street Oval
Camp Spot at Campbell Town. Next to & at the W end of oval. 6 sites.
Self Contained Vehicles only
HEMA 75 K10   41 55 47 S   147 29 17 E

60 Wardlaw Park
Rest Area at Campbell Town. S side of bridge, enter via Franklin St,
between bridge & brick building. Self Contained Vehicles only
HEMA 75 K10   41 55 58 S   147 29 37 E

61 Tooms Lake Camping Ground ☎ (03) 6255 5228
Camp Area at Tooms Lake. 42 km SE of Ross via C305. 20 km dirt
road
HEMA 69 C4   42 12 48 S   147 46 56 E

62 St Peters Pass
Rest Area 28 km S of Ross or 8 km N of Oatlands
HEMA 69 C2   42 14 33 S   147 24 16 E

63 Lake Dulverton Rest Area
Rest Area at Oatlands, The Esplanade. Self Contained Vehicles only
HEMA 69 C2   42 18 03 S   147 22 34 E

Deloraine to Hobart
Lake Highway

64 Quamby Corner ☎ (03) 6369 5156
Camp Area 16 km S of Deloraine. 13436 Highland Lakes Rd. Turn E
onto Golden Valley Rd (C502). 150m to entrance
HEMA 73 C11   41 37 35 S   146 42 39 E

65 Lower Liffey Reserve
Camp Area 31 km S of Deloraine or 7 km W of Liffey. Best access
for caravans, motorhomes signposted from Liffey off C513.
Alternative via A5 23 km S Deloraine. Turn L at Jcn after 2 km, R at T
intersection, to signposted access road
HEMA 73 C12   41 40 58 S   146 46 54 E

Notes...

66 Little Pine Lagoon ☎ (03) 6261 8050
Camp Area 10 km SW of Miena or 24 km NE of Bronte Park, via B11. Dirt road
B11
HEMA 73 E11   41 59 57 S   146 36 44 E

67 Great Lake Hotel ☎ (03) 6259 8163
Camp Area at Hotel. 3096 Marlborough Hwy, Miena
A5
HEMA 73 E11   41 58 49 S   146 40 36 E

68 Pumphouse Bay Campground ☎ (03) 6259 4049
Arthurs Lake Recreation Area
Camp Area 7 km NE of A5/B51 jcn or 35 km S of Poatina. Turn E off B51, 6 km N of jcn or 34 km S of Poatina. 1 km dirt road. Beside lake. Closed May, June, July
HEMA 73 E12   41 59 05 S   146 51 41 E

69 Jonah Bay Campground ☎ (03) 6259 4049
Arthurs Lake Recreation Area
Camp Area 15 km NE of A5/B51 jcn or 40 km S of Poatina. Turn E off B51,10 km N of jcn or 30 km S of Poatina, then R at Y jcn. 5 km dirt road. Beside lake. Closed May, June, July
HEMA 73 E12   41 57 31 S   146 54 10 E

70 Penstock Lagoon
Camp Spot at Penstock Lagoon. Turn W off A5 10 km S of Miena or 47 km N of Bothwell onto Waddamana Rd. 9 km to camp spot on W shore. Dirt road
C178
HEMA 73 F12   42 04 58 S   146 46 05 E

71 Dago Point Campground ☎ (03) 6259 4049
Camp Area 26 km E of Steppes or 1.4 km W of Interlaken. Turn N 600m W of Interlaken. Dirt road. Lakeside. Big rigs at boat ramp. Closed May, June, July
HEMA 73 F14   42 07 57 S   147 10 07 E

72 Blackburn Creek
Parking Area 9 km S of Steppes or 25 km N of Bothwell. Beside creek
A5
HEMA 73 G12   42 10 21 S   146 54 17 E

73 Bothwell Caravan Park ☎ (03) 6259 5503
Caravan Park at Bothwell. Market Place, behind Info Centre
HEMA 73 H13   42 22 58 S   147 00 29 E

74 Pub With No Beer
Parking Area 3 km E of Bothwell or 17 km NW of Melton Mowbray
A5
HEMA 73 H13   42 23 18 S   147 02 36 E

75 The "Blue Place"
Rest Area at Kempton, beside the "Blue Place". Self Contained Vehicles only. Fee for use of showers, toilets & power. Maximum stay for a powered site is 24hrs
HEMA 69 E1   42 31 55 S   147 12 08 E

76 Colebrook Tavern ☎ (03) 6259 7164
Camp Spot at Colebrook. 1 km N of PO. Self Contained Vehicles only. Please purchase drink at the bar. Meals available Fri & Sat
HEMA 69 E1   42 31 34 S   147 21 32 E

77 Pontville Park RV Stop ☎ (03) 6268 7000
Parking Area at Pontville. Entry off Glen Lea Rd. Self Contained Vehicles only
HEMA 69 F1   42 41 12 S   147 15 37 E

78 Hobart Showgrounds ☎ (03) 6272 6812
Camp Area 2 Howard Rd Glenorchy. Report to Administration building, if closed use online booking form. Closed during October for show
HEMA 69 G1   42 50 02 S   147 17 06 E

Sorell to Port Arthur
Arthur Highway

79 Primrose Sands RSLA Club ☎ (03) 6265 5655
Parking Area at Primrose Sands, 22 km SE of Sorell. Self Contained Vehicles only. Toilets available during Club opening hours
HEMA 69 H3   42 53 09 S   147 40 09 E

80 Dunalley Hotel ☎ (03) 6253 5101
Camp Spot at Dunalley, Arthur Hwy
HEMA 69 H4   42 53 36 S   147 48 18 E

81 Sunset Beach Holiday Spot ☎ (03) 6253 5257
Camp Area 4 km S of Dunalley. 3532 Arthur Hwy. Phone ahead to book
HEMA 69 H4   42 55 02 S   147 49 27 E

82 Taranna Cottages & Self Contained Campers Park ☎ (03) 6250 3436
Camp Spot at Taranna. 19 Nubeena Rd, near Cnr of Arthur Hwy. Self Contained Vehicles only
HEMA 69 J4   43 03 45 S   147 51 43 E

Notes...

83 Fortescue Bay Campground
Tasman National Park
☎(03) 6250 2433

C344

Camp Area 17 km E of Port Arthur. Turn E off the A9, 6 km S of Taranna or 5 km N of Port Arthur. 12 km dirt road. Bookings necessary, need to purchase tokens for the shower

HEMA 69 K5   43 008 32 S   147 58 002 E

84 Stewarts Bay State Reserve
Picnic Area 1 km N of Port Arthur, via Stewarts Bay Rd

HEMA 69 K4   43 08 14 S   147 51 13 E

✓85 Tasman RSL Club Nubeena
☎(03) 6250 2135

Parking Area at Nubeena. Cnr Main & Alfred St. Next to RSL Club. Self Contained Vehicles only. Fee for use of showers

HEMA 69 J3   43 06 28 S   147 44 45 E

86 Lime Bay Campground
☎(03) 6250 3497

C341

Camp Area 16 km N of Premaydena. 6 km dirt road. Waterfront

HEMA 69 H3   42 57 27 S   147 42 16 E

Hobart to Cockle Creek
Huon Highway

87 Rivers Edge Camping
☎0439 760 007

Camp Area 28 km W of Huonville. 1322 Lonnavale Rd. Turn W, S of Houn bridge into Glen Houn Rd (C619) travel 14 km, turn W into Lonnavale Rd for 14 km to campground. Open weekends only in June, July & August

HEMA 71 E10   42 56 50 S   146 48 01 E

✓88 Franklin Foreshore Reserve
A6

Camp Spot at Franklin. Opposite the hotel behind fire station beside river. Fees collected

HEMA 71 F11   43 05 34 S   147 00 33 E

✓89 Shipwrights Point Regatta Ground
☎(03) 6264 0300

A6

Camp Area at Port Huon. Just N of wharf area, beside river. Fee collected

HEMA 71 G11   43 09 31 S   146 58 47 E

90 Geeveston Ex Servicemen & Womens Club
☎(03) 6297 1105

Parking Area at Geeveston. Memorial Dr, 1 km S of town. Donations requested

HEMA 71 G11   43 10 06 S   146 55 40 E

91 Heritage Park
Parking Area at Geeveston. Arve Rd, entry opposite roadhouse. Fees collected

HEMA 71 G11   43 09 51 S   146 55 29 E

92 Arve River Picnic Area
C631

Picnic Area 13 km W of Geeveston. Small vehicles only, unlevel surface

HEMA 71 G10   43 09 31 S   146 48 22 E

93 Tahune Forest Reserve
☎(03) 6295 7170

C631

Camp Spot 29 km W of Geeveston at Air Walk Info Centre. In overflow car park

HEMA 71 F10   43 05 43 S   146 43 49 E

94 Southport Hotel & Caravan Park
☎(03) 6298 3144

Caravan Park at Southport. 8777 Huon Hwy

HEMA 71 J11   43 25 29 S   146 58 22 E

95 Gilhams Beach Campground
Recherche Bay Nature Recreation Area
☎(03) 6264 8460

C636

Camp Area 21 km S of A6/C635 jcn. Dirt road. Maximum stay 30 days

HEMA 71 K11   43 32 36 S   146 53 25 E

96 Finns Beach Campground
Recherche Bay Nature Recreation Area
☎(03) 6264 8460

C636

Camp Area 22 km S of A6/C635 jcn. Dirt road. Maximum stay 30 days

HEMA 71 K11   43 32 56 S   146 53 14 E

97 Catamaran River Campground
Recherche Bay Nature Recreation Area
☎(03) 6264 8460

Camp Area 23 km S of A6/C635 jcn, via Cockle Creek Rd. Signposted. Dirt road. Maximum stay 30 days

HEMA 71 K11   43 33 20 S   146 53 14 E

98 Cockle Creek Campground
Recherche Bay Nature Recreation Area
☎(03) 6264 8460

C636

Camp Area 26 km S of A6/C635 jcn. Dirt road. Maximum stay 30 days

HEMA 71 K11   43 34 42 S   146 53 12 E

Notes...

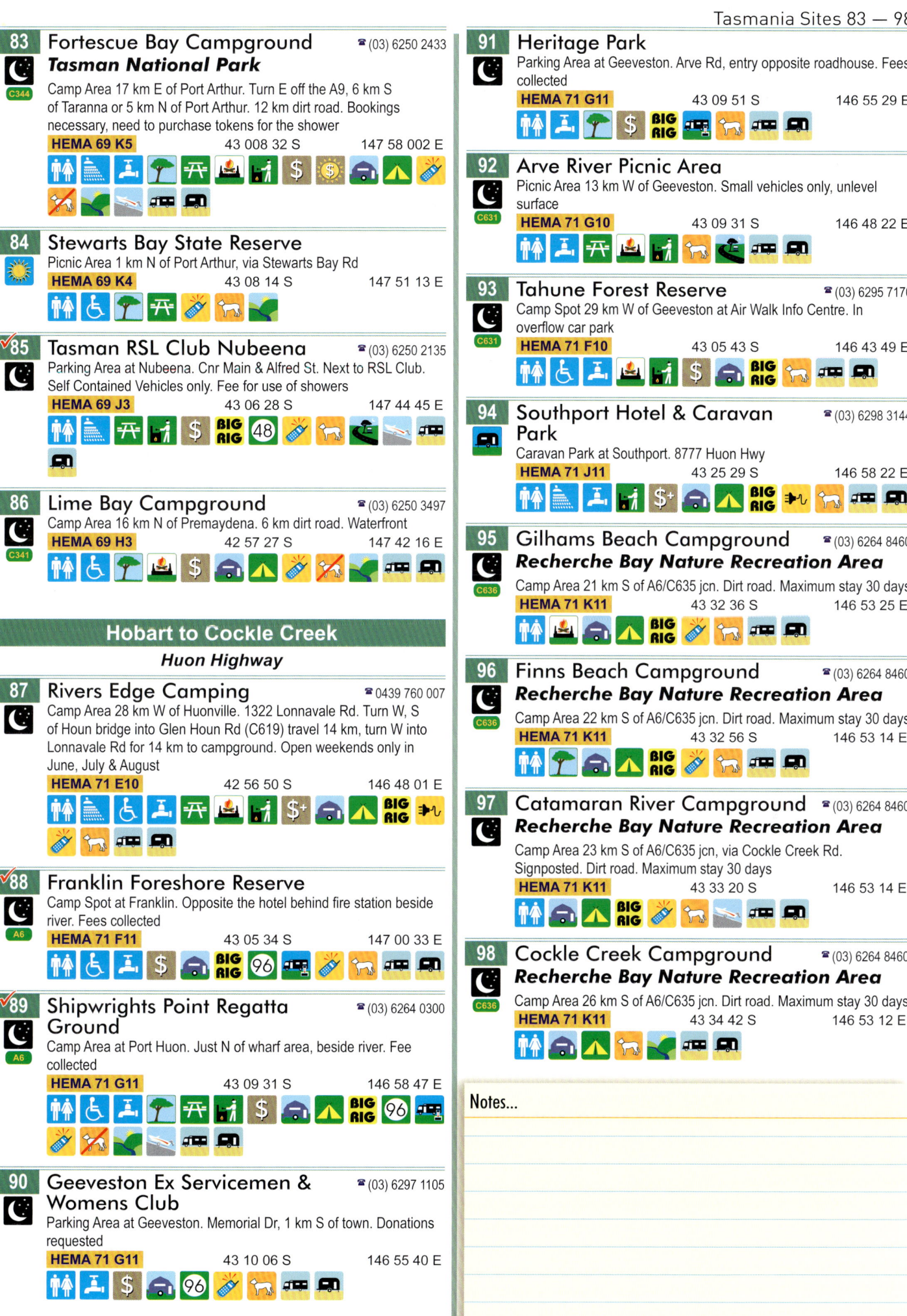

TASMANIA

99 Boltons Green Campground ☎ (03) 6264 8460
Southwest National Park

C636

Camp Area 27 km S of A6/C635 jcn. Dirt road. 5 tonne load limit on bridge. Maximum stay 30 days

HEMA 71 K11   43 34 58 S   146 53 42 E

100 Gordon Foreshore Reserve ☎ (03) 6211 8200

B68

Camp Area at Gordon. Channel Hwy. Honesty box on Hwy side of toilet block

HEMA 71 G12   43 15 42 S   147 14 33 E

101 Bruny Island Landscape ☎ (03) 6260 6380

Parking Area 15 Km S of Ferry on B66. 1751 Bruny Island Main Rd

HEMA 69 K2   43 11 55 S   147 23 11 E

102 The Neck Campground ☎ (03) 6293 1419

B66

Camp Area on Bruny Island. Lutregala Rd, 26 km S of ferry terminal. 2 km S of Penguin Rookery

HEMA 71 H13   43 17 27 S   147 19 44 E

103 Hotel Bruny ☎ (03) 6293 1148

Parking Area at Alonnah. Check in with hotel staff. Self Contained Vehicles only

HEMA 71 H12   43 19 18 S   147 14 32 E

104 Jetty Beach Camp Area ☎ (03) 6293 1419
South Bruny National Park

C629

Camp Area 57 km S of Ferry Terminal. 17 km SW of Lunawanna on the Old Jetty Rd, off Lighthouse Rd. Permit required

HEMA 71 J12   43 27 33 S   147 09 10 E

105 Cloudy Bay Corner Camp Area ☎ (03) 6293 1419
South Bruny National Park

C644

Camp Area 49 km S of Ferry Terminal. 9 km S of Lunawanna on Cloudy Bay Rd. Beach access only, approximately 3 km, check tides for access. Permit required. 4WD only recommended

HEMA 71 J12   43 27 55 S   147 15 09 E

106 The Pines Camp Area ☎ (03) 6293 1419
South Bruny National Park

C644

Camp Area 49 km S of Ferry Terminal. 8 km S of Lunawanna on Cloudy Bay Rd. Permit required. Small area

HEMA 71 J12   43 26 15 S   147 14 48 E

New Norfolk to Strathgordon
Gordon River Road

107 Mount Field Campground ☎ (03) 6288 1149
Mt Field National Park

C609

Camp Area at Mount Field National Park, via Lake Dobson Rd. 66 Lake Dobson Rd. Limited sites

HEMA 71 C10   42 40 56 S   146 43 06 E

108 Edgar Campground ☎ 1300 360 441

Camp Area off Scotts Peak Dam Rd, S end of Lake Pedder. 30 km dirt road. Signposted off B61, 42 km E of Strathgordon or 51 km W of Westerway

HEMA 71 F8   43 01 52 S   146 20 35 E

109 Huon Campground ☎ (03) 6288 1149

Camp Area 7 km W of Edgar Campground. Turn L off Scotts Peak Rd opposite dam. 1 km to camping area. Small vehicles only

HEMA 70 F7   43 02 18 S   146 17 57 E

110 Teds Beach Campground ☎ (03) 6288 1149

B61

Camp Area 4 km E of Strathgordon

HEMA 70 D6   42 47 13 S   146 03 39 E

Hobart-Queenstown-Burnie
Lyell, Zeehan and Murchison Highways

111 Hamilton Camping Ground ☎ (03) 6286 3202

A10

Camp Area at Hamilton. W end of town, beside river

HEMA 73 J12   42 33 33 S   146 49 50 E

112 Hamilton Inn ☎ (03) 6286 3204

Parking Area at Hamilton. Parking at rear of hotel, check in at the bar. Pre booking essential. Toilets open during Inn hours

HEMA 73 J12   42 33 39 S   146 49 44 E

✓113 Bethune Park ☎ 1300 360 441

Camp Area 10 km W of Hamilton. Turn S off A10 onto C608 8 km W of Hamilton or 7 km SE of Ouse. On W side of Lake Meadowbank. Maximum stay 7 days

HEMA 73 J12   42 32 11 S   146 43 49 E

114 Lake Repulse Bush Camping ☎ (03) 6233 7449

A10

Camp Area 20 km SW of Ouse. Turn W onto Ellendale Rd 7 km S of Ouse, then onto Dawson Rd for 11 km to forest & track on R to lakefront. Various tracks to sites. 4WD recommended. Not suitable for caravans

HEMA 73 J11   42 29 59 S   146 37 10 E

115 Wayatinah Lakeside Caravan Park
☎ (03) 6289 3317

A10

Caravan Park 24 km NW of Ouse or 16 km S of Tarraleah. Turn S 23 km W of Ouse or 15 km S of Tarraleah. 1.2 km sealed road from Lyell Hwy

HEMA 73 H10 42 23 09 S 146 30 19 E

116 Bradys Lake ✓

A10

Camp Spot 17 km N of Tarraleah or 8 km S of A10/B11 jcn. 800m dirt road E of Hwy. Beside lake. Maximum stay 7 days

HEMA 73 G10 42 13 57 S 146 29 46 E

117 Bronte Lagoon Camping Area
☎ 1300 360 441

A10

Camp Area 26 km N of Tarraleah. Turn S 250m S of A10/B11 jcn. 2 km to campsites. Signposted. Limited space, small vehicles only. Maximum stay 7 days

HEMA 73 G10 42 11 12 S 146 28 49 E

118 Derwent Bridge Hotel
☎ (03) 6289 1144

A10

Parking Area at Derwent Bridge. Self Contained Vehicles only in hotel car park. Must check in with publican

HEMA 73 F9 42 08 11 S 146 13 48 E

119 Lake King William

A10

Parking Area 2 km W of Derwent Bridge or 85 km E of Queenstown. Left at fork after narrow access track. 100m off Hwy beside lake

HEMA 73 F9 42 08 47 S 146 13 07 E

120 Collingwood River Reserve
☎ (03) 6471 7122

A10

Franklin Gordon Wild Rivers National Park

Camp Area 43 km E of Queenstown or 45 km W of Derwent Bridge. Lyell Hwy, entry 100m W of Collingwood River bridge

HEMA 72 G7 42 09 44 S 145 55 37 E

121 Lake Burbury Campground
☎ (03) 6471 2762

A10

Camp Area 23 km E of Queenstown. Turn N 86 km W of Derwent Bridge or 22 km E of Queenstown. 800m off Hwy

HEMA 72 F6 42 05 47 S 145 40 27 E

122 Thureau Hills Camping Area
☎ (03) 6471 5880

Camp Area 76 km W of Derwent Bridge or 20 km E of Queenstown. Turn S 72 km W of Derwent Bridge or 16 km E of Queenstown. 3.5 km to lakeside camping

HEMA 72 F6 42 08 37 S 145 39 03 E

123 Lake Burbury South Boat Ramp

Picnic Area 23 km SW of Queenstown. On Mt Jukes Rd

HEMA 72 G6 42 12 24 S 145 37 08 E

124 Lake Burbury Foreshore

A10

Parking Area 12 km E of Queenstown. Turn N 77 km W of Derwent Bridge or 11 km E of Queenstown. W side of lake, 800m N of Hwy along old bitumen road

HEMA 72 F6 42 04 25 S 145 38 17 E

125 Gravel Oval

B24

Camp Spot at Queenstown. Wilsdon St, off Batchelor St. Self Contained Vehicles only

HEMA 72 F5 42 04 30 S 145 33 32 E

126 Strahan Golf Course
☎ (03) 6471 7242

B24

Parking Area at Strahan. Access via Meredith St only. Permit required, register in Clubhouse. 400m W of Clubhouse via gravel road. Self Contained Vehicles only

HEMA 72 G4 42 08 46 S 145 18 59 E

127 Ocean Beach Coastal Reserve

C250

Picnic Area 7 km W of Strahan. 3 km dirt road

HEMA 72 G4 42 08 41 S 145 15 53 E

128 Macquarie Heads Campground ✓
☎ (03) 6471 7382

C251

Camp Area 15 km S of Strahan, via Ocean Beach Rd. 12 km dirt road

HEMA 72 G4 42 13 16 S 145 13 44 E

129 Zeehan Bush Camp & Caravan Park
☎ (03) 6471 6633

Hurst St, enter off Dodd St. 1 km NE of PO

HEMA 72 E4 41 52 40 S 145 19 59 E

130 Stitt Park

A10

Parking Area at Rosebery. Murchison Hwy. S end of town. Self Contained Vehicles only

HEMA 72 D5 41 46 57 S 145 32 25 E

131 Lake Rosebery Foreshore

A10

Parking Area 12 km E of Rosebery or 3 km S of Tullah. Turn W 50m N of Murchison Bridge or 200m S of Murchison Dam Rd intersection. Sharp turn from S. 200m off Hwy. Limited space

HEMA 72 D6 41 45 39 S 145 37 08 E

Notes...

132 Lake Mackintosh Camping
Camp Spot 2 km N of Mackintosh Dam. Signposted from Tullah, via Mackintosh Dam Rd. Access over Mackintosh Dam wall. No access when dam spilling. Maximum stay 7 days

HEMA 72 C6   41 41 07 S   145 39 23 E

133 Reece Dam
C252
Parking Area 44 km NW of Zeehan or 58 km W of Tullah. At boat ramp, off Pieman Rd

HEMA 72 C3   41 43 51 S   145 08 05 E

134 Corinna Campground   ☎ (03) 6446 1170
C249
Camp Area 49 km NW of Zeehan or 26 km SW of Savage River. Dirt road from Savage River. Limited small campsites, reservations essential. Access from S by barge. Barge maximum length 9m is from mid front hub to mid rear hub

HEMA 72 C3   41 39 03 S   145 04 39 E

135 Trial Harbour
Camp Spot at Trial Harbour. 24 km W of Zeehan, via Trial Harbour Rd. Winding access road, not suitable large caravans or motorhomes

HEMA 72 E3   41 55 39 S   145 10 21 E

136 Waratah Camping Ground   ☎ (03) 6439 7100
B23
Camp Area at Waratah, Smith St behind council offices. Key required for access to facilities

HEMA 72 A5   41 26 44 S   145 31 58 E

137 Fossey River Rest Area
A10
Rest Area 38 km N of Tullah or 2 km S of A10/B23 jcn

HEMA 72 A6   41 27 04 S   145 37 16 E

138 Hellyer Gorge Rest Area
A10
Rest Area 25 km N of A10/B23 jcn or 24 km S of Yolla

HEMA 77 H8   41 16 25 S   145 36 54 E

Launceston to Stanley
Bass Highway

139 Bishopsbourne RV Stop
C513
Camp Spot at Bishopsbourne. Bishopsbourne Rd, W side of reserve. Self Contained Vehicles only

HEMA 74 G7   41 36 59 S   146 59 41 E

140 Riverside Park
Parking Area at Bracknell. 700m E of general store, via Louisa St & Esplanade

HEMA 74 G7   41 39 00 S   146 57 01 E

141 Andys Bakery Café   ☎ (03) 6393 1846
B54
Camp Spot at Westbury. Meander Valley Rd, E end of town. Self Contained Vehicles only

HEMA 74 G6   41 31 32 S   146 50 42 E

142 Westbury Sports Ground
Parking Area at Westbury. Entry off Franklin Street. Toilets are open 8am to 5pm daily

HEMA 74 G6   41 31 38 S   146 50 07 E

143 Egmont Reserve
B54
Picnic Area 4 km N of Westbury, beside river

HEMA 74 F6   41 29 43 S   146 49 01 E

144 Deloraine East Overnight Park   ☎ (03) 6393 5300
B54
Camp Spot at Deloraine. 700m E of PO. Turn N off A5 at Police Station, E side of river. Travel 200m over railway line, then turn R. Self Contained Vehicles only

HEMA 74 G5   41 31 19 S   146 39 43 E

145 Christmas Hills Raspberry Farm   ☎ (03) 6362 2186
A1
Parking Area at Elizabeth Town. 3 km S on Bass Hwy, Christmas Hills Rd. Limited parking in cafe car park for 5 customer vehicles. Self Contained Vehicles only. Register with the Cafe during opening hours

HEMA 74 F5   41 28 58 S   146 35 49 E

146 Chudleigh Showground
B12
Camp Area at Chudleigh. Burnett & Sorrel St. Self Contained Vehicles only. Payment at Chudleigh General store

HEMA 74 G4   41 33 25 S   146 28 58 E

147 Mole Creek Hotel   ☎ (03) 6363 1102
B12
Parking Area at Mole Creek. Pioneer Dr at W end of town. Fee for power, check in at bar. Self Contained Vehicles only

HEMA 74 G4   41 33 21 S   146 24 02 E

148 Mole Creek Caravan Park   ☎ (03) 6363 1150
B12
Caravan Park 4 km W of Mole Creek. Beside creek

HEMA 74 G4   41 33 04 S   146 21 37 E

149 Lake Parangana Recreation Area
C171
Camp Spot 29 km SW of Mole Creek. 1 km S of dam wall, via picnic area. Beside lake

HEMA 74 G3   41 38 43 S   146 13 35 E

150 Lake Rowallan Bridge
C171
Parking Area 39 km SW of Mole Creek. 1 km N of dam wall, beside river. Small vehicles only. 4 km dirt road

HEMA 74 H3   41 43 23 S   146 13 09 E

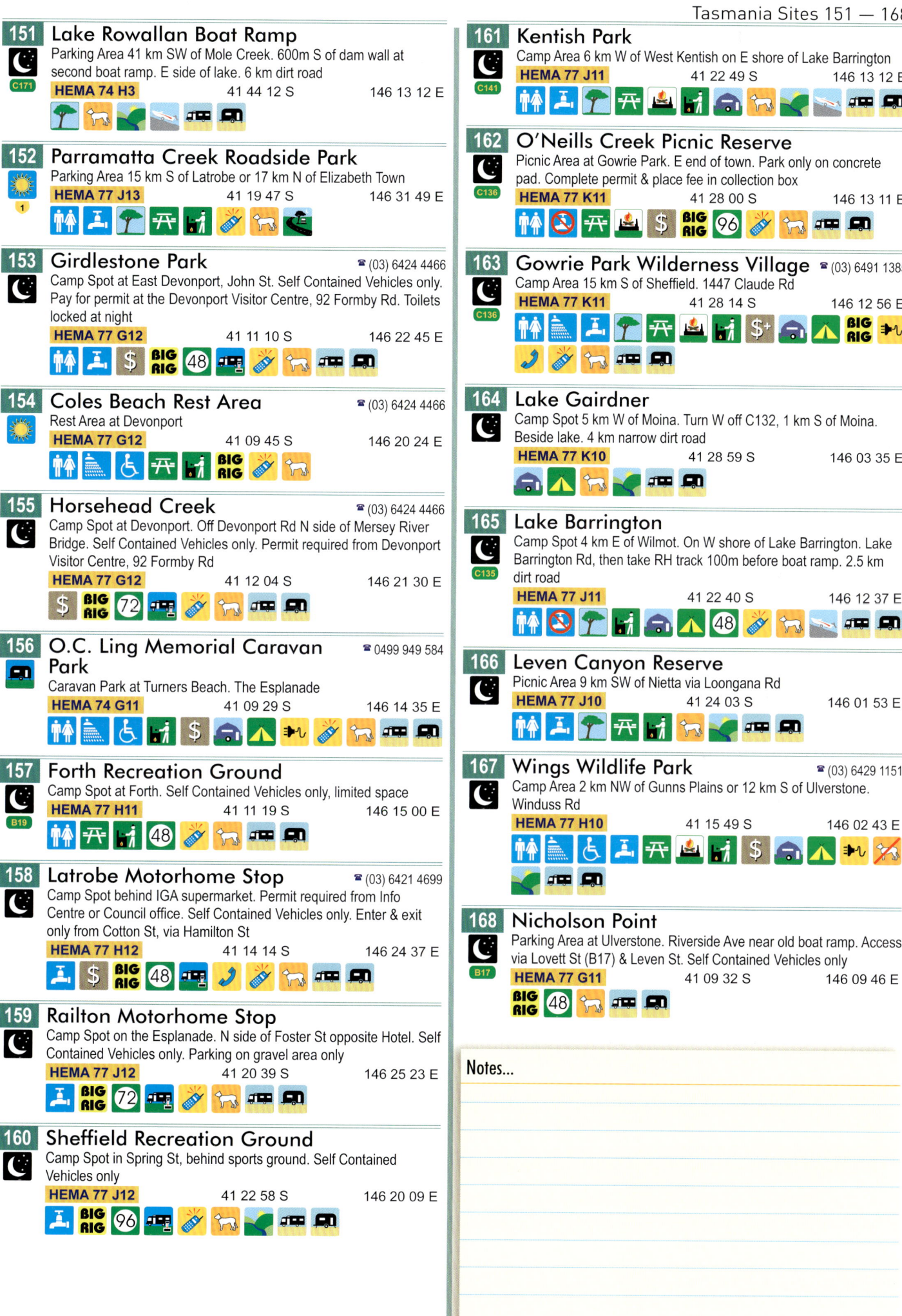

151 Lake Rowallan Boat Ramp
C171
Parking Area 41 km SW of Mole Creek. 600m S of dam wall at second boat ramp. E side of lake. 6 km dirt road
HEMA 74 H3   41 44 12 S   146 13 12 E

152 Parramatta Creek Roadside Park
1
Parking Area 15 km S of Latrobe or 17 km N of Elizabeth Town
HEMA 77 J13   41 19 47 S   146 31 49 E

153 Girdlestone Park   ☎ (03) 6424 4466
Camp Spot at East Devonport, John St. Self Contained Vehicles only. Pay for permit at the Devonport Visitor Centre, 92 Formby Rd. Toilets locked at night
HEMA 77 G12   41 11 10 S   146 22 45 E

154 Coles Beach Rest Area   ☎ (03) 6424 4466
Rest Area at Devonport
HEMA 77 G12   41 09 45 S   146 20 24 E

155 Horsehead Creek   ☎ (03) 6424 4466
Camp Spot at Devonport. Off Devonport Rd N side of Mersey River Bridge. Self Contained Vehicles only. Permit required from Devonport Visitor Centre, 92 Formby Rd
HEMA 77 G12   41 12 04 S   146 21 30 E

156 O.C. Ling Memorial Caravan Park   ☎ 0499 949 584
Caravan Park at Turners Beach. The Esplanade
HEMA 74 G11   41 09 29 S   146 14 35 E

157 Forth Recreation Ground
B19
Camp Spot at Forth. Self Contained Vehicles only, limited space
HEMA 77 H11   41 11 19 S   146 15 00 E

158 Latrobe Motorhome Stop   ☎ (03) 6421 4699
Camp Spot behind IGA supermarket. Permit required from Info Centre or Council office. Self Contained Vehicles only. Enter & exit only from Cotton St, via Hamilton St
HEMA 77 H12   41 14 14 S   146 24 37 E

159 Railton Motorhome Stop
Camp Spot on the Esplanade. N side of Foster St opposite Hotel. Self Contained Vehicles only. Parking on gravel area only
HEMA 77 J12   41 20 39 S   146 25 23 E

160 Sheffield Recreation Ground
Camp Spot in Spring St, behind sports ground. Self Contained Vehicles only
HEMA 77 J12   41 22 58 S   146 20 09 E

161 Kentish Park
C141
Camp Area 6 km W of West Kentish on E shore of Lake Barrington
HEMA 77 J11   41 22 49 S   146 13 12 E

162 O'Neills Creek Picnic Reserve
C136
Picnic Area at Gowrie Park. E end of town. Park only on concrete pad. Complete permit & place fee in collection box
HEMA 77 K11   41 28 00 S   146 13 11 E

163 Gowrie Park Wilderness Village   ☎ (03) 6491 1385
C136
Camp Area 15 km S of Sheffield. 1447 Claude Rd
HEMA 77 K11   41 28 14 S   146 12 56 E

164 Lake Gairdner
Camp Spot 5 km W of Moina. Turn W off C132, 1 km S of Moina. Beside lake. 4 km narrow dirt road
HEMA 77 K10   41 28 59 S   146 03 35 E

165 Lake Barrington
C135
Camp Spot 4 km E of Wilmot. On W shore of Lake Barrington. Lake Barrington Rd, then take RH track 100m before boat ramp. 2.5 km dirt road
HEMA 77 J11   41 22 40 S   146 12 37 E

166 Leven Canyon Reserve
Picnic Area 9 km SW of Nietta via Loongana Rd
HEMA 77 J10   41 24 03 S   146 01 53 E

167 Wings Wildlife Park   ☎ (03) 6429 1151
Camp Area 2 km NW of Gunns Plains or 12 km S of Ulverstone. Winduss Rd
HEMA 77 H10   41 15 49 S   146 02 43 E

168 Nicholson Point
B17
Parking Area at Ulverstone. Riverside Ave near old boat ramp. Access via Lovett St (B17) & Leven St. Self Contained Vehicles only
HEMA 77 G11   41 09 32 S   146 09 46 E

Notes...

TASMANIA

169 Riana Pioneer Park Campground ☎ (03) 6437 6137
Camp Area 1.5 km S of Riana, via Pine Rd. Limited sites. Maximum stay 4 weeks. Caretaker collects fees
B17
HEMA 77 H10   41 12 56 S   145 59 56 E

170 Preservation Bay
Rest Area on E side of Penguin Surf Club. Self Contained Vehicles only
HEMA 77 G10   41 06 07 S   146 03 09 E

171 Midway Point
Camp Spot 1 km E of Sulphur Creek or 3.5 km W of Penguin, off Preservation Dr. Self Contained Vehicles only
HEMA 77 G10   41 05 48 S   146 02 25 E

172 Hall Point
Camp Spot at Sulphur Creek 8 km W of Penguin. 700m E of shop. Oceanfront. Self Contained Vehicles only
HEMA 77 G10   41 05 38 S   146 01 42 E

173 Cooee Point Reserve ☎ (03) 6431 1033
Parking Area 3 km W of Burnie, via Cooee Point Rd. Oceanfront. Self Contained Vehicles only. Permit required from Info Centre or Council offices in Wilson St. Maximum stay 5 days
HEMA 77 F9   41 02 19 S   145 52 37 E

174 Wynyard Showgrounds ☎ (03) 6442 3079
Camp Spot at Wynyard. Jackson St. N side of town. Self contained motorhomes only. No caravans. Not available during major sporting or show events
HEMA 77 F8   40 59 13 S   145 43 37 E

175 Sisters Beach ☎ (03) 6443 8333
Picnic Area at Sisters Beach, 8 km W of Boat Harbour
C233
HEMA 77 F8   40 54 58 S   145 33 44 E

176 Rocky Cape Tavern & Caravan Park ☎ (03) 6443 4110
Caravan Park at Rocky Cape Tavern. 19375 Bass Hwy. Check in at Tavern Bar
A2
HEMA 76 E7   40 53 07 S   145 27 56 E

177 Peggs Beach Campground ☎ (03) 6458 1480
Camp Area 2.3 km W of Port Latta or 11.5 km E of A2/B21 jcn. Closed 01 May - 31 October
A2
HEMA 76 E6   40 51 04 S   145 21 10 E

178 Black River Campground ☎ (03) 6458 1480
Camp Area 4.8 km W of Port Latta or 9 km E of A2/B21 jcn. 1 km of dirt road N of Hwy. Maximum stay 30 days
HEMA 76 E6   40 50 36 S   145 19 00 E

179 Stanley Recreation Ground ☎ (03) 6458 1266
Parking Area at Stanley, Marine Esplanade, beach side of the road adjacent to Golf Club. Self Contained Vehicles only. Fees collected by site manager. Maximum stay 7 nights
HEMA 76 D6   40 45 51 S   145 17 22 E

180 Smithton Esplanade
Parking Area. W Esplanade. Self Contained Vehicles only
C215
HEMA 76 E5   40 50 20 S   145 07 12 E

181 Tall Timbers Hotel ☎ (03) 6452 9000
Parking Area at Smithston. 5/15 Scotchtown Rd. Self Contained Vehicles only. Maximum stay 72 hours in any 14 day period. Available October 1 - 31 May
HEMA 76 E5   40 51 24 S   145 07 10 E

182 Montagu Camping Ground ☎ (03) 6452 4800
Camp Area 20 km NW of Smithton. Turn N off C215, 16 km NW of Smithton, onto Old Port Rd. 4 km dirt road. Open from 01 Nov- 30 April, caretaker collects fees
HEMA 76 D4   40 44 40 S   144 58 44 E

183 Marrawah Green Point Beach Camping Area
Camp Area 3 km W of Marrawah, via Green Point Rd & Beach Rd. Outside cold shower. Oceanfront
HEMA 76 F3   40 54 35 S   144 40 45 E

184 Manuka Campground ☎ (03) 6457 1225
Arthur-Pieman Conservation Area
Camp Area 15 km S of Marrawah or 1 km N of Arthur River
C214
HEMA 76 G3   41 02 41 S   144 40 04 E

185 Peppermint Campground ☎ (03) 6457 1225
Arthur-Pieman Conservation Area
Camp Area at Arthur River. Next to Ranger Station. Not suitable for caravans or motorhomes. Cold Showers
C214
HEMA 76 G3   41 02 53 S   144 40 03 E

186 Prickly Wattles Campground ☎ (03) 6457 1225
Arthur-Pieman Conservation Area
Camp Area 2 km S of Arthur River. 4 entry points, 2 & 3 easiest access for caravans
C214
HEMA 76 G3   41 03 36 S   144 40 45 E

187 Nelson Bay
☎ (03) 6457 1225
Arthur-Pieman Conservation Area
Camp Spot at Nelson Bay. 15 km S of Arthur River. Turn R at beach, past fishing boats. Camp on beach side of road

HEMA 76 G3 41 07 39 S 144 40 19 E

188 Julius River Forest Reserve
☎ (03) 6452 4900

C218

Camp Spot 10 km E of Kanunnah Bridge. 600m E of picnic area. 7 km gravel road. Toilets at picnic area

HEMA 76 G5 41 09 08 S 145 02 02 E

George Town to Beaconsfield
East/West Tamar Highways

189 George Town Rest Area

A8

Rest Area at George Town. Main Rd, behind Info Centre. Self Contained Vehicles only. Pay fees at Info Centre.

HEMA 74 C6 41 06 33 S 146 50 18 E

190 Beaconsfield Recreation Ground
☎ (03) 6383 6350

A7

Camp Spot at Beaconsfield. E end of Grubb St. 1700 - 0900 hrs. Self Contained Vehicles only

HEMA 74 D6 41 11 57 S 146 49 19 E

191 Greens Beach Caravan & Holiday Park
☎ (03) 6383 9222

A7

Caravan Park at Greens Beach. Greens Beach Rd

HEMA 74 C6 41 05 08 S 146 44 49 E

192 Paper Beach Reserve
Rest Area at Paper Beach. Turn E 2 km S of Exeter. Only open between 1700 - 0900 hrs. Self Contained Vehicles only

HEMA 74 D7 41 15 12 S 146 57 55 E

193 Rose Bay Park

C728

Rest Area at Gravelly Beach. S end of town, beside river. Self Contained Vehicles only. 6 sites available between 1700 - 0900 hrs

HEMA 74 E7 41 17 38 S 146 58 20 E

194 Horse Yards Campground
☎ (03) 6428 6277
Narawntapu National Park

C740

Camp Area 12.5 km N of B71/C740 jcn. 1 km dirt road

HEMA 74 D5 41 09 14 S 146 36 31 E

195 Springlawn Campground
☎ (03) 6428 6277
Narawntapu National Park

C740

Camp Area 13.5 km N of B71/C740 jcn. 2 km dirt road

HEMA 74 D5 41 08 52 S 146 36 09 E

196 Bakers Point Campground (3)
☎ (03) 6428 6277
Narawntapu National Park

C740

Camp Area 18 km N of B71/C740 jcn. 6 km dirt road

HEMA 74 D5 41 09 44 S 146 34 05 E

Notes...

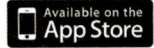

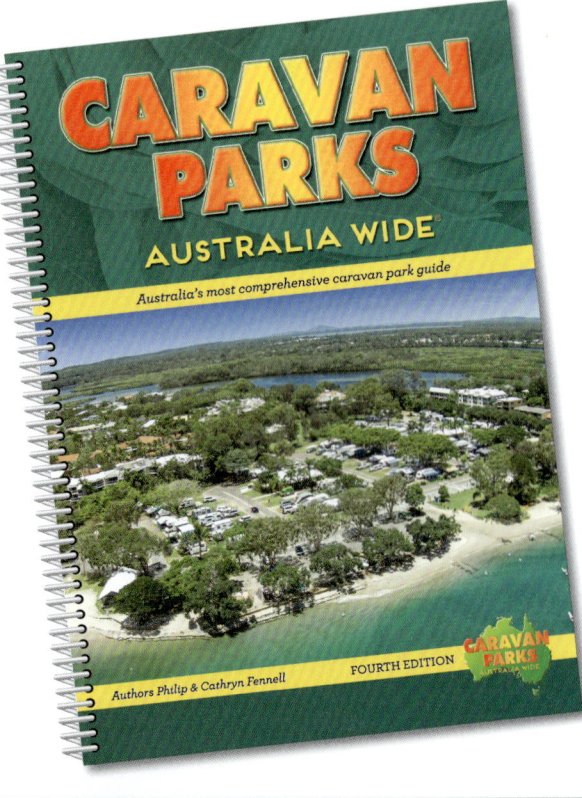

REMARKABLE ROCKS, KANGAROO ISLAND (88 J5)

PHOTO: © ISTOCK.COM/YEKORZH

92-93

90-91

94-95

96-97

86

For more detail see pages 82-83 and 84-85

88-89

87

98

Adelaide														
290	**Bordertown**													
1179	1388	**Birdsville (QLD)**												
498	707	1203	**Broken Hill (NSW)**											
772	981	1365	872	**Ceduna**										
844	1053	887	944	1006	**Coober Pedy**									
1058	1267	420	1079	1241	917	**Innamincka**								
1257	1466	1300	1357	1419	413	1330	**Kulgera (NT)**							
667	876	517	686	848	370	547	783	**Marree**						
428	180	1607	926	1204	1272	1486	1685	1095	**Mt Gambier**					
1039	1248	920	1139	1201	195	950	389	403	1467	**Oodnadatta**				
240	132	1419	738	1012	1084	1298	1497	907	312	1279	**Pinnaroo**			
305	514	898	405	467	539	774	952	381	690	734	545	**Port Augusta**		
648	857	1241	748	401	882	1117	1295	724	1033	1077	888	343	**Port Lincoln**	
253	288	1234	549	903	975	1110	1388	717	468	1170	156	436	779	**Renmark**
1252	1461	1845	1352	480	1486	1721	1899	1328	1680	1681	1492	947	881	1383	**WA-SA Border Village**

Distances are shown in kilometres and follow the most direct major sealed route where possible.

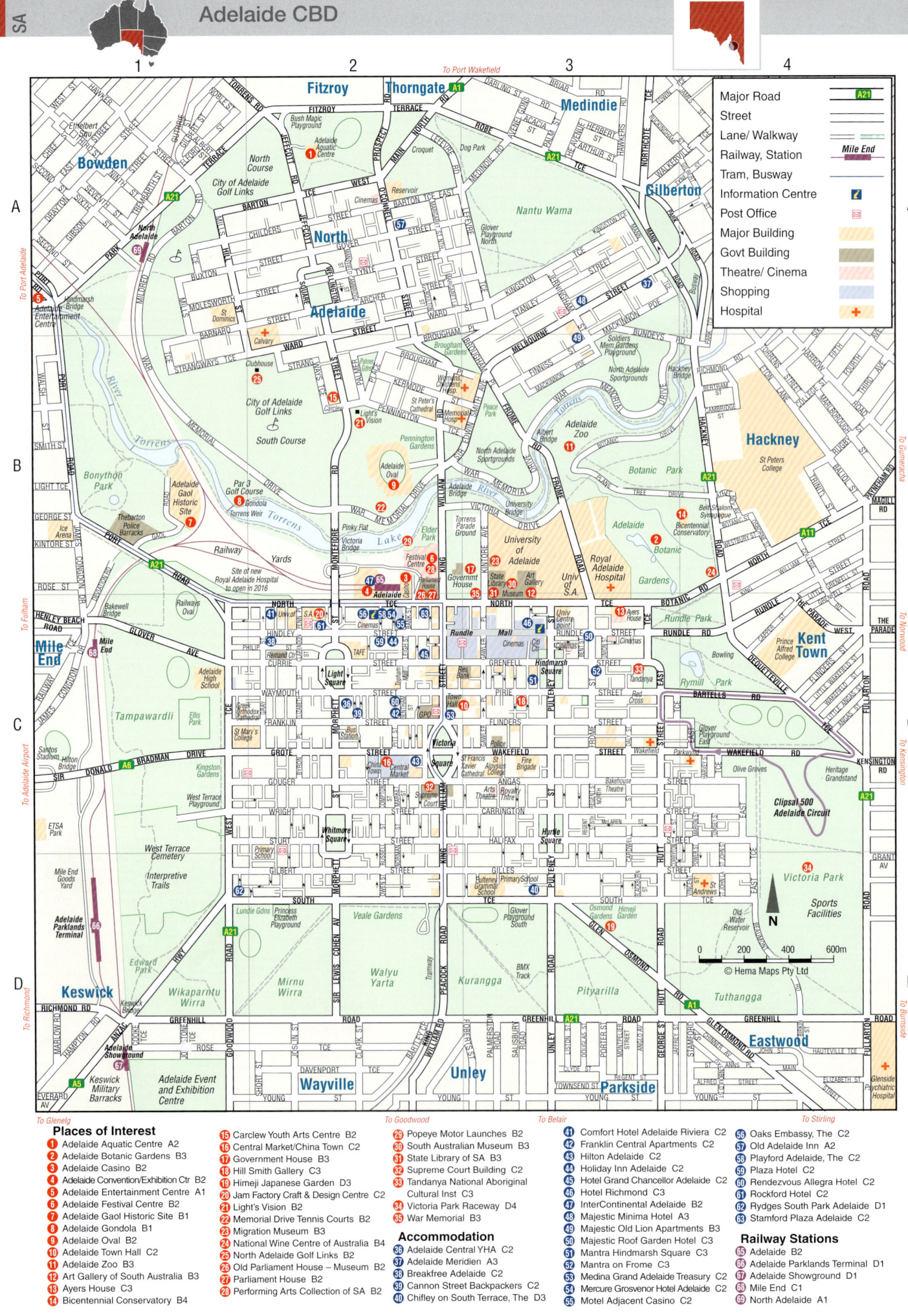

Adelaide CBD

Places of Interest
1 Adelaide Aquatic Centre A2
2 Adelaide Botanic Gardens B3
3 Adelaide Casino B2
4 Adelaide Convention/Exhibition Ctr B2
5 Adelaide Entertainment Centre A1
6 Adelaide Festival Centre B2
7 Adelaide Gaol Historic Site B1
8 Adelaide Gondola B1
9 Adelaide Oval B2
10 Adelaide Town Hall C2
11 Adelaide Zoo B3
12 Art Gallery of South Australia B3
13 Ayers House C3
14 Bicentennial Conservatory B4

15 Carclew Youth Arts Centre B2
16 Central Market/China Town C2
17 Government House B3
18 Hill Smith Gallery C3
19 Himeji Japanese Garden D3
20 Jam Factory Craft & Design Centre C2
21 Light's Vision B2
22 Memorial Drive Tennis Courts B2
23 Migration Museum B3
24 National Wine Centre of Australia B4
25 North Adelaide Golf Links B2
26 Old Parliament House – Museum B2
27 Parliament House B2
28 Performing Arts Collection of SA B2

29 Popeye Motor Launches B2
30 South Australian Museum B3
31 State Library of SA B3
32 Supreme Court Building C2
33 Tandanya National Aboriginal
 Cultural Inst C3
34 Victoria Park Raceway D4
35 War Memorial B3

Accommodation
36 Adelaide Central YHA C2
37 Adelaide Meridien A3
38 Breakfree Adelaide C2
39 Cannon Street Backpackers C2
40 Chifley on South Terrace, The D3

41 Comfort Hotel Adelaide Riviera C2
42 Franklin Central Apartments C2
43 Hilton Adelaide C2
44 Holiday Inn Adelaide C2
45 Hotel Grand Chancellor Adelaide C2
46 Hotel Richmond C3
47 InterContinental Adelaide B2
48 Majestic Minima Hotel A3
49 Majestic Old Lion Apartments B3
50 Majestic Roof Garden Hotel C3
51 Mantra Hindmarsh Square C3
52 Mantra on Frome C3
53 Medina Grand Adelaide Treasury C2
54 Mercure Grosvenor Hotel Adelaide C2
55 Motel Adjacent Casino C2

56 Oaks Embassy, The C2
57 Old Adelaide Inn A2
58 Playford Adelaide, The C2
59 Plaza Hotel C2
60 Rendezvous Allegra Hotel C2
61 Rockford Hotel C2
62 Rydges South Park Adelaide D1
63 Stamford Plaza Adelaide C2

Railway Stations
65 Adelaide B2
66 Adelaide Parklands Terminal D1
67 Adelaide Showground D1
68 Mile End C1
69 North Adelaide A1

To Port Wakefield To Gawler

1 2 3 4 5 6 7

A B C D E F G H J K

237

Elizabeth
Elizabeth East
Defence Science and Technology Organisation
Penfield Golf Club
Elizabeth Grove
Lyell McEwin Hosp
John Rice Av
Hillbank
Little Para Reservoir

St Kilda
Salt Crystallization Pans
Waterloo Corner
Burton
Waterloo Corner
Salisbury North
Salisbury
Salisbury Heights
Greenwith

Pt Grey
Pelican Pt
Snapper Point
LeFevre Peninsula
Paralowie
Salisbury Downs
Brahma Lodge
Salisbury East
Golden Grove
Cobbler Creek Recreation Park

Outer Harbor
North Haven
Parafield Gardens
Salisbury South
Salisbury
Yatala Vale

Osborne
Taperoo
Largs Bay
Green Fields
Globe Derby Park
Parafield Airport
Parafield
Wynn Vale
Surrey Downs
Fairview Park

Largs Bay
Peterhead
Garden Island
Salt Crystallization Pans
Mawson Lakes
Technology Park
Univ. of S.A.
Para Hills
Modbury Heights
Redwood Park
Banksia Park

Semaphore
Birkenhead
Dean Rifle Range
Pooraka
Modbury North
Ridgehaven

Pt Malcolm
Semaphore Park
Port Adelaide
Ottoway
Wingfield
Cavan
Dry Creek
Ingle Farm
Para Vista
St Agnes
Modbury
Tea Tree Gully
Anstey Hill Recreation Park

West Lakes
Royal Park
St Clair
Cheltenham
Alberton
Rosewater
Athol Park
Regency Park
Gepps Cross
Enfield
Valley View
Hope Valley
Vista

West Lakes
Seaton
Woodville
Ferryden Park
Kilburn
Blair Athol
Clearview
Northfield
Hillcrest
Gilles Plains
Holden Hill
Highbury

Tennyson
Grange
Findon
Woodville South
Croydon
Dudley Park
Prospect
Nailsworth
Greenacres
Klemzig
Windsor Gardens
Dernancourt
Paradise
Athelstone
Black Hill Conservation Park

Henley Beach
Fulham Gardens
Kidman Park
Flinders Park
Allenby Gdns
Brompton
Fitzroy
Walkerville
Campbelltown
Newton
Montacute

Grange
Fulham
Lockleys
Torrensville
Hindmarsh
Thebarton
North Adelaide
SEE MAP 80
Royston Park
St Peters
Payneham
Felixstow
Hectorville
Rostrevor
Magill
Norton Summit

West Beach
Brooklyn Park
Mile End
ADELAIDE
Hackney
Norwood
Kensington
Trinity Gdns
Beulah Park
Kensington Gardens
Auldana
Teringie
Skye

Adelaide Airport
Netley
Marleston
Richmond
Wayville
Unley
Parkside
Toorak Gardens
Dulwich
Burnside
Stonyfell
Ashton

Kurralta Park
Black Forest
Millswood
Goodwood
Malvern
Glenunga
Glenside
Hazelwood Park
Greenhill
Summertown
Uraidla

Plympton
Glandore
Clarence Gdns
Westbourne Park
Kingswood
Fullarton
Myrtle Bank
Glen Osmond
Waterfall Gully
Cleland Conservation Park
Crafers
Piccadilly

Glenelg North
Novar Gardens
Plympton Park
Melrose Park
Clapham
Mitcham
Springfield
Eagle on the Hill
Crafers West
Stirling

Glenelg
Glengowrie
Morphettville
Park Holme
Edwardstown
Panorama
Belair National Park
Aldgate

Somerton Park
Oaklands Park
Clovelly Park
St Marys
Belair
Glenalta
Upper Sturt
Heathfield

Warradale
Marion
Eden Hills
Hawthorndene
Longwood

Brighton
Seacombe Gardens
Bedford Park
Flinders University
Blackwood
Bellevue Heights
Coromandel Valley
Coromandel East
Ironbank
Loftia Park

Seacliff
Seaview Downs
Seacliff Park
Darlington
Marino

GULF ST VINCENT
Holdfast Bay
Largs Bay
Torrens Island
Barker Inlet
Port Adelaide River

To Aldinga, Victor Harbor To Clarendon To Mylor
To Chain of Ponds To Mannum To Lobethal To Murray Bridge To Mylor

0 1 2 3 4km
N
© Hema Maps Pty Ltd

© Hema Maps Pty Ltd

0 1 2 3 km

N

GULF ST VINCENT

Salt Crystallization Pans

Salt Crystallization Pans

Beagle Hole Rd

Waterloo Corner

To Port Wakefield

To Gawler

86

FATCHED NORTHERN EXPRESSWAY

Penfield

Bolivar

Edinburgh RAAF Base

Edinburgh Defence Science and Technology Organisation

National Military Vehicle Museum

Elizabeth West

Elizabeth

Elizabeth South

PRINCES HWY

Direk

Burton

Salisbury North

Salisbury

Salisbury Park

St Kilda

237

The Tramway Museum

Mangrove Trail & Interpretive Centre

Salt Crystallization Pans

Bolivar Sewage Treatment Works

Bolivar

Paralowie

Salisbury Downs

Salisbury Plain

Brahma Lodge

Univ. of SA

GULF

ST

VINCENT

Pt Grey

Pelican Pt

Snapper Point

LeFevre Peninsula

Outer Harbor

North Haven

Torrens Is Golf Park

Barker Inlet

Linson Reach

Torrens Reach

Quarantine Station

Swan Alley Ck

Parafield Gardens

Globe Derby Park

Salisbury South

Parafield Airport

Classic Jets Fighter Museum

Parafield

Osborne

Taperoo

Largs North

Torrens Island

Garden Island

Salt Crystallization Pans

Green Fields

Para Hills West

Para Hills

Largs Bay

Peterhead

Birkenhead

Exeter

Semaphore

Semaphore South

Mawson Lakes

Pooraka

Ingle Farm

Para Vista

Valley View

Dry Creek

Cavan

Gepps Cross

SALISBURY HWY

Wingfield

Gillman

Port Adelaide

Ottoway

Ethelton

Glanville

Semaphore Park

West Lakes Shore

Queenstown

Rosewater

Pennington

Athol Park

Angle Park

Mansfield Park

Regency Park

Kilburn

Blair Athol

Clearview

Enfield

Northfield

Oakden

Gilles Plains

West Lakes

Royal Park

Albert Park

Hendon

Cheltenham

Woodville North

Woodville Gardens

Ferryden Park

Sefton Park

Broadview

Nailsworth

Manningham

Hampstead Gardens

Green Acres

Windsor Gardens

Tennyson

Seaton

Woodville West

Woodville

Woodville Park

Kilkenny

West Croydon

Croydon

Renown Pk

Devon Park

Prospect

Collinswood

Medindie

Walkerville

Vale Park

Klemzig

Campbelltown

Felixstow

Marden

Grange

East Grange

Royal Adelaide

Findon

Beverley

Allenby Gdns

Brompton

Bowden

Ovingham

Thorngate

Fitzroy

North Adelaide

Medindie Gdns

Royston Park

St Peters

Joslin

Payneham

Gilberton

Glynde

Hectorville

Henley Beach

Fulham Gardens

Kidman Park

Flinders Park

West Hindmarsh

Hindmarsh

SEE MAP 80

College Pk

Evandale

Maylands

Trinity Gdns

St Morris

Payneham South

Firle

Tranmere

SEE MAP 80

84

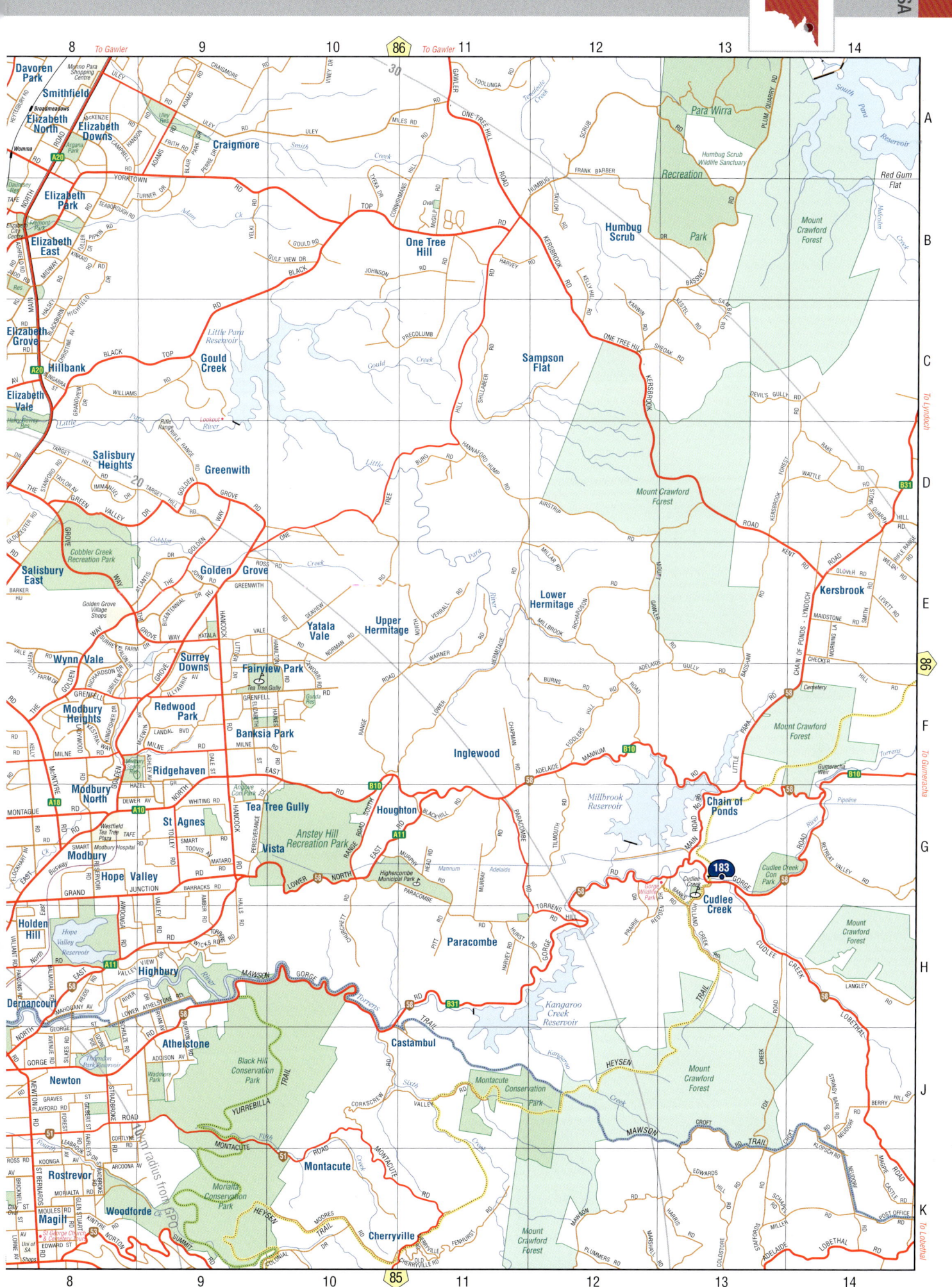

Adelaide Suburbs, South Australia

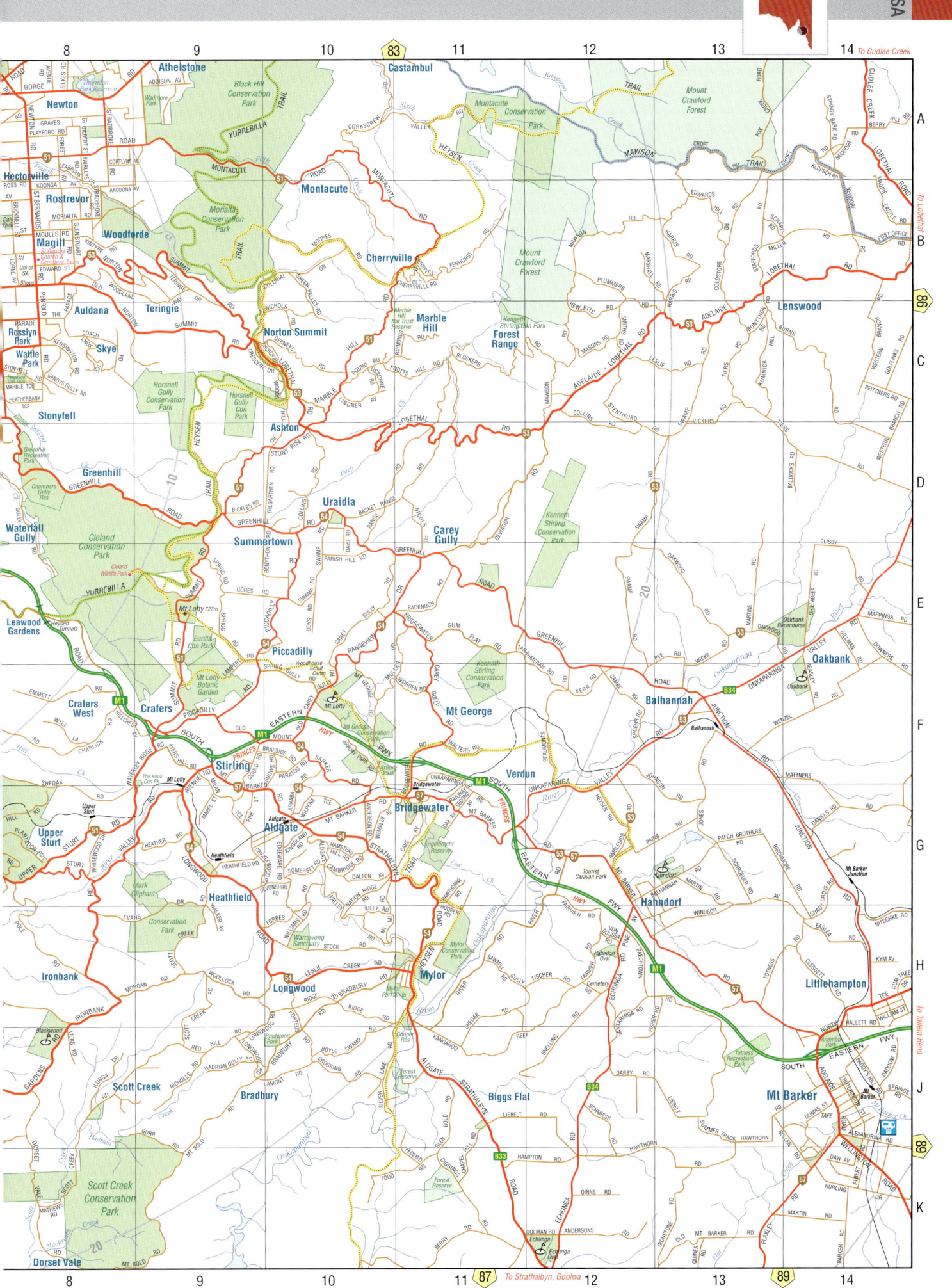

Adelaide to Barossa Region, South Australia

N

0   5   10 km

© Hema Maps Pty Ltd

138°30'

Barabba

Stockport

Gilbert River

Hamley Bridge

155

Light River

Kapunda

+ Bald Hill

St Kitts

Koonunga

138°45'

238

Mallala

Mallala Motor Sport Park

Red Banks

Wasleys

Templers

Freeling

32

MAWSON

HEYSEN

153

Stockwell

154

Greenock

Light Pass

Nuriootpa

HWY

Korunye

Reeves Plains

Roseworthy College

Roseworthy

Kangaroo Flat

A32

12

STURT

29

Shebak Log

Daveyston

Maranaga

Seppeltsfield

Wineries

Barossa

Penrice

Angaston

B19

Tanunda

Valley

22

Bethany

Menglers Hill

Sculpture Park & Lookout

Collingrove Historic Homestead

Two Wells

Lewiston

21

Gawler Airfield

Gawler

Sandy Creek

15

Gomersal

Rosedale

Concordia

North Para

Rowland Flat

Lyndoch

Sappy Ck Con Park

Kaiserstuhl Con Park

Craneford

34°30'

Buchfelde

Hillier

Evanston

Cockatoo Valley

B31

Mt Crawford Forest

179

Eden Valley

Salt Ck

PORT WAKEFIELD ROAD

PRINCES HWY

A1

To Port Wakefield

Angle Vale

Kudla

Munno Para

16

Uleybury

Bilbaringa

Barossa

Yattalunga

Whispering Wall

Barossa Res

176

Mt Crawford Forest

Williamstown

36

89

Virginia

Smithfield

Blakeview

Para Wirra Rec Park

The Knob

Warren Con Park

Mt Crawford

Forest HQ

Mt Crawford

177

Springton

Port Gawler Con Park

Port Gawler

FATCHEN ROAD

NORTHERN EXPRESSWAY

M20

Penfield

Bolivar

Broadmeadows

Elizabeth

SEE MAP 82-83

One Tree Hill

South Para Reservoir

Mt Crawford Con Park

Warren Res

Mt Crawford Forest

178

Mt Pleasant +

34°45'

St Kilda

237

Equestrian Centre

The Tramway Museum

Adelaide Int. Raceway

Edinburgh RAAF Base

Defence Science & Technology Organisation

Direk

Burton

30

GMH

Salisbury

Little Para Reservoir

Mt Crawford + Forest

Mt Gawler + Forest

Kersbrook

20

Cromer Con Park

180

181

Mt Pleasant

Outer Harbor

Torrens Is Con Park

North Haven

Bolivar

MAIN ROAD

A20

Parafield Airport

Golden Grove

17

Para Hills

Upper Hermitage

Lower Hermitage

Inglewood

Chain of Ponds

Mt Crawford Forest

Forreston

To Walker Flat

Semaphore

Largs Bay

Largs North

Fort Granville Con Park

Port Adelaide

Garden Island

A9

Cavan

Parafield

Univ of SA

Pooraka

Ingle Farm

A13

A18

Modbury

Tea Tree Gully

Hope Valley

30

58

Lower Hermitage

Gumeracha

Toy Factory

B10

Birdwood

McVittie Hill +

Kenton Valley

Torrens River

18

Cudlee Creek

Cudlee Creek Con Pk

McVittie Motor Museum

Tungkillo

West Lakes

Tennyson

Sports Park

Gepps Cross

Kilburn

Northfield

Gilles Plains

Highbury

Anstey Hill Rec Park

183

Paracombe

Kangaroo Creek Res

Mt Crawford Forest

58

Mt Torrens

182

Seaton

Grange

Findon

Woodville

Alberton

Wingfield

A16

Enfield

A10

A17

Campbelltown

A11

Gastambul

Torrens

32

Athelstone

Black Hill Con Park

MAWSON

+ Fenders Hill

Mt Lofty Ranges

Henley Beach

Fulham

Lockleys

Croydon

14

A7

Thebarton

Hindmarsh

Prospect

Walkerville

Payneham

St Peters

Magill

Rostrevor

Montacute Con Park

Morialta Con Park

Montacute

Cherryville

Marble Hill

Lenswood

Lobethal

29

Charleston

Charleston Con Pk

+ Murray Hill

West Beach

Holdfast Bay

ANZAC HWY

Richmond

A6

ADELAIDE

Norwood

Burnside

Kensington

Stonyfell

Horsnell Gully Con Park

Norton Summit

Basket Range

Forest Range

53

20

+ Mt Beevor

Glenelg

Adelaide Airport

A14

A5

Parkside

Unley

Fullarton

Glen Osmond

A17

SEE MAP 84-85

Cleland Con Park

Ashton

Uraidla

Summertown

Carey Gully

Woodside

Heritage Park

Oakbank

Harrogate

Rockleigh

35°00'

Somerton Park

Park Holme

Mitcham

14

57

Crafers

M1

Piccadilly

Kenneth Stirling Con Park

Balhannah

Racecourse

Army Camp

Brukunga

Marion

A15

A13

Belair

Belair National Park

Stirling

M1

Verdun

Ambleside

Hahndorf

Mt Barker Ctr

Nairne

Dawesley

Brighton

Seacliff

Eden Hills

Shepherds Hill Rec Park

Bellevue Heights

Blackwood

Aldgate

Bridgewater

Heathfield

Longwood

Mylor

Littlehampton

EASTERN FREEWAY

Bremer River

+ Disher Hill

Marino

Marino Con Park

Hallett Cove Con Park

Hallett Cove

M2

O'Halloran Hill Rec Park

Sturt Gorge Rec Park

Flagstaff Hill

Coromandel Valley

Ironbank

Scott Creek

Bradbury

Scott Creek Con Park

Biggs Flat

Mylor Con Park

M1

Totness Rec Park

Mt Barker

Kanmantoo

138°30'

Aberfoyle Park

Cherry Gardens

Happy Valley

A13

Dorset Vale

138°45'

139°00'

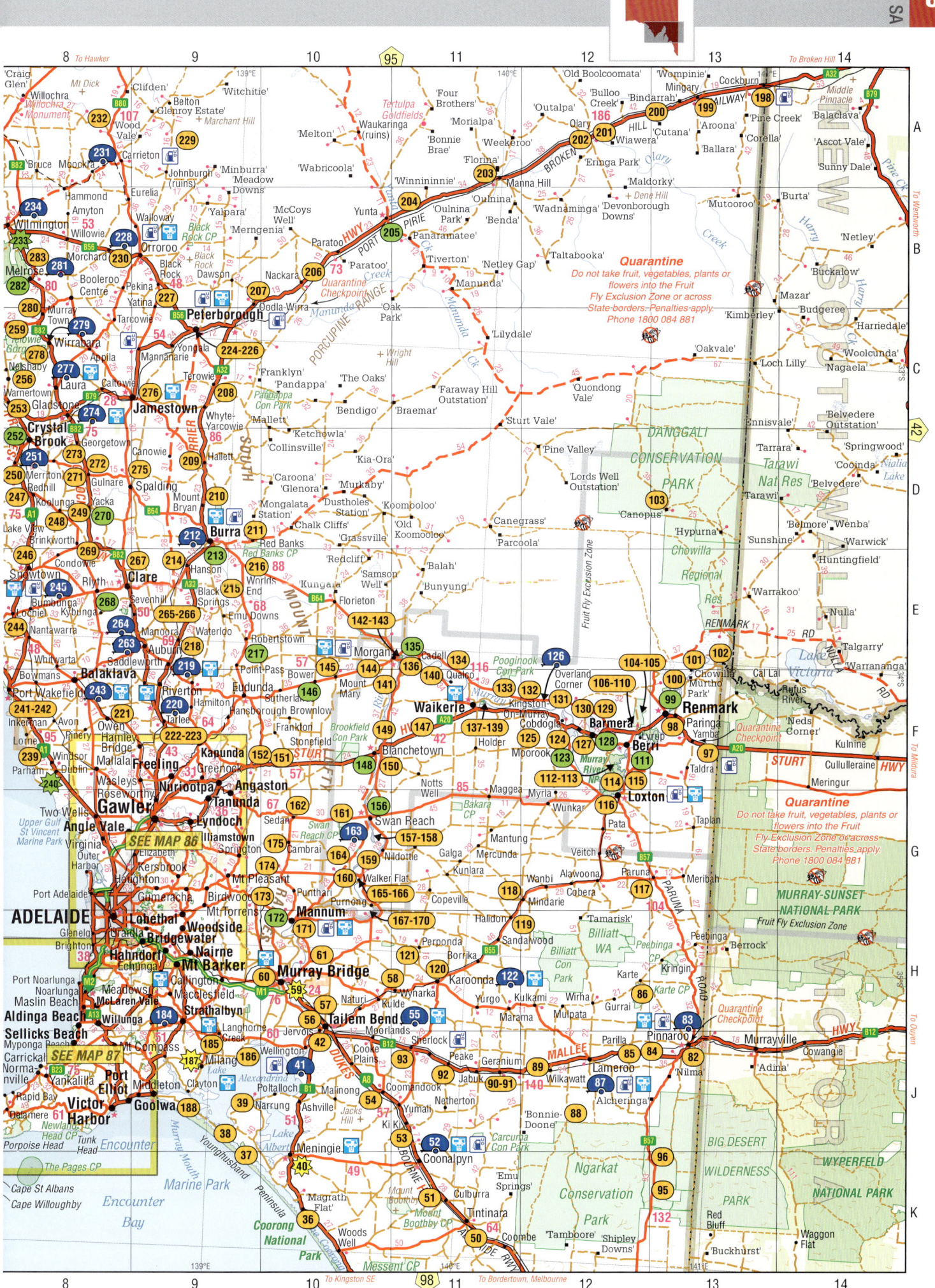

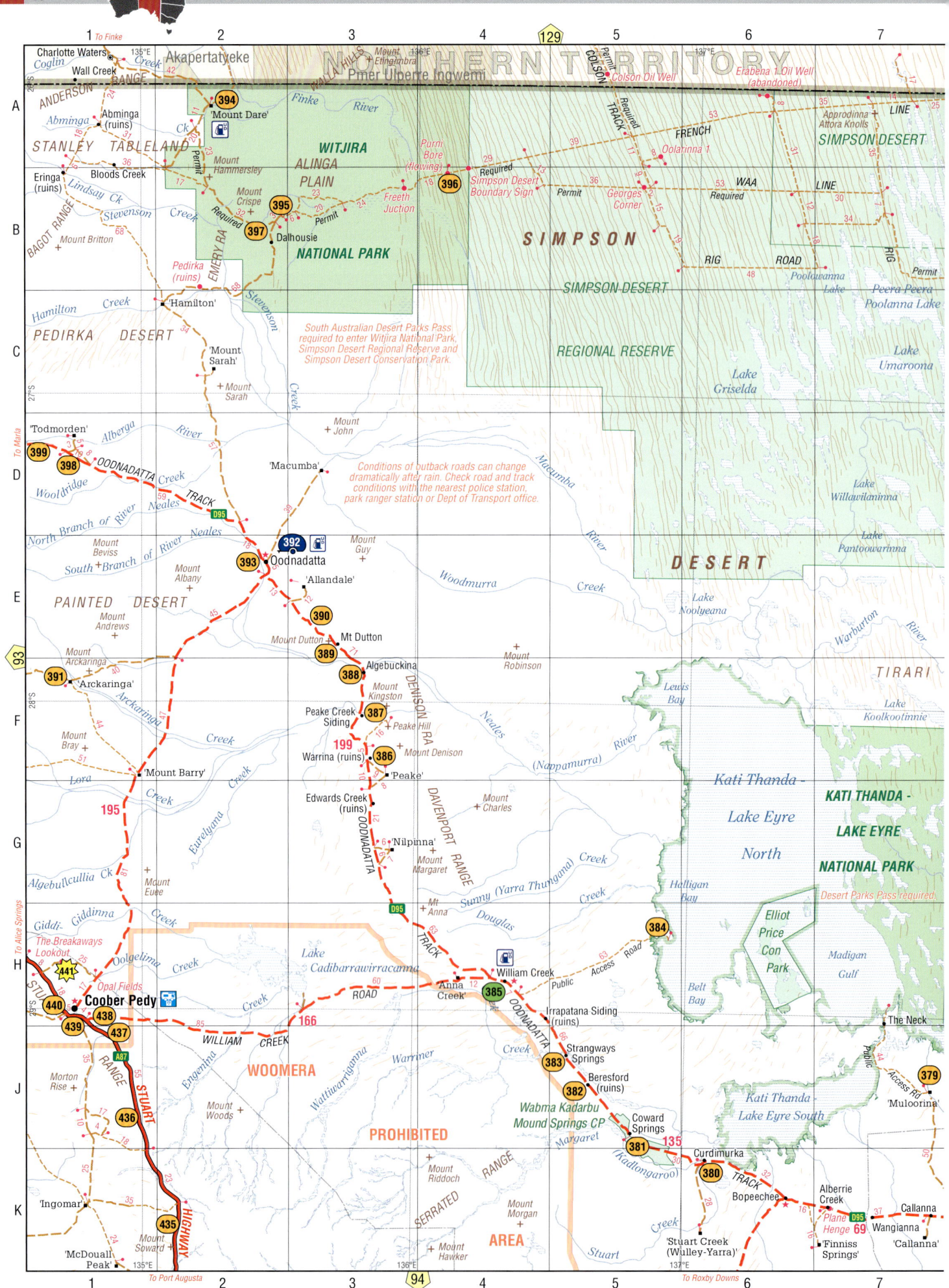

Entry Permit required for all roads and tracks in this area.

196

To Alice Springs

'Victory Downs'

Illyomba (No 22)

Johnston Geodetic Station

Mount Cavenagh

Goyder Creek

Mount Grundy

Charlotte Waters
Wall Creek

BEDDOME RANGE

ANDERSON RANGE

Akapertatyeke

'Mount Dare'

WITJIRA

Mount Hammersley

NATIONAL

PARK

Mount Crispe

EMERY RA

Donalds Well

Boomdoolyanna

Gosse Bore

Ilykuwaratja

'Sundown Outstation'

Mount Mead

Coglin

Abminga

Abminga (ruins)

STANLEY TABLELAND

Arrelumbercumma Hill

Mt Treloar

Eringa (ruins)

Bloods Creek

Mount
Howe

Marrat Range

Pine Ridge

Echo Hill

Mount Mair

Echo Hill

Yunyarinyi (Kenmore Park)

Marryat

'Agnes Creek'

Mount Tieyon

'Tieyon'

Mount Irwin

'Mount Irwin'

BAGOT RANGE

Mount Britton

Pedirka (ruins)

'Hamilton'

Warrabillinna

Centre Bore

Ironwood Bore

Corkwood Bore

Moolduldie Bores

Targoonyinna Hill

Moorilyanna Hill

Indulkana (Iwantja)

'Granite Downs'

Chandler

Alberga

River

Creek

'Lambina'

Hamilton

Creek

PEDIRKA DESERT

Conditions of outback roads can change dramatically after rain. Check road and track conditions with the nearest police station, park ranger station or Dept of Transport office.

'Mount Sarah'

Mount Sarah

Tunton Bore

Perentie Bore

Mimili (Everard Park)

Jimmy Well

Creek

Mount Weir

Mount Handolph

OODNADATTA

Creek

'Todmorden'

Neales River

Kulitjara

Victory Well

Mt Etitinna

Blue Hill

Davey Well

Ammaroodinna Creek

Gap Bore

Gecko Bore

Marla

'Welbourn Hill'

Mount Todmorden

North Branch of River Neales

TRACK

Pocket Well

Sandy Bore

Teeta Bore

Maynard Bore

Wildcat Bore

Mintabie

Private Track

Wintinna

'Wintinna'

Wooldridge

Hemietta Creek

South Branch

Mount Beviss

Mount Albany

Oodnadatta

To William Creek

Creek

'Wallatinna'

Entry Permit required for all roads and tracks in this area.

STUART

Mount Willoughby

Mount Andrews

PAINTED DESERT

Cadney Park

'Copper Hill'

'Mount Willoughby'

San Marino Hut

Mount Arckaringa

'Arckaringa'

WOOMERA

Automated Weather Station

Emu Junction (ruins)

ANNE

BEADELL

TALLARINGA

Desert Parks Pass required.

CONSERVATION

234

CENTRAL AUSTRALIA RAILWAY

Kulvegalinna Creek

'Evelyn Downs'

Mount Bray

Mount Gillen

Pootnoura

Poolnoura

Algebullcullia Creek

Restricted

Woorang

Mount Barry

195

Eurelyama Creek

Mount Euee

276

Len Beadell Marker

HIGHWAY

Required

HIGHWAY

101

Access

'Mabel Creek'

Manguri

Mount Clarence

Giddi-Giddinna Creek

The Breakaways Lookout

441

440

Opal Fields

Coober Pedy

Oolgelima Creek

PROHIBITED

Park

Mount Igy

Dog Fence

Mabel Creek

Long Creek

439

438

437

WILLIAM CREEK ROAD

RANGE

STUART

Engenina Creek

Dog Fence

To William Creek

DESERT

AREA

Wirrida

Morton Rise

Mount Woods

436

'Ingomar'

Mount Soward

435

HWY

'Comet'

'McDouall Peak'

To Port Augusta

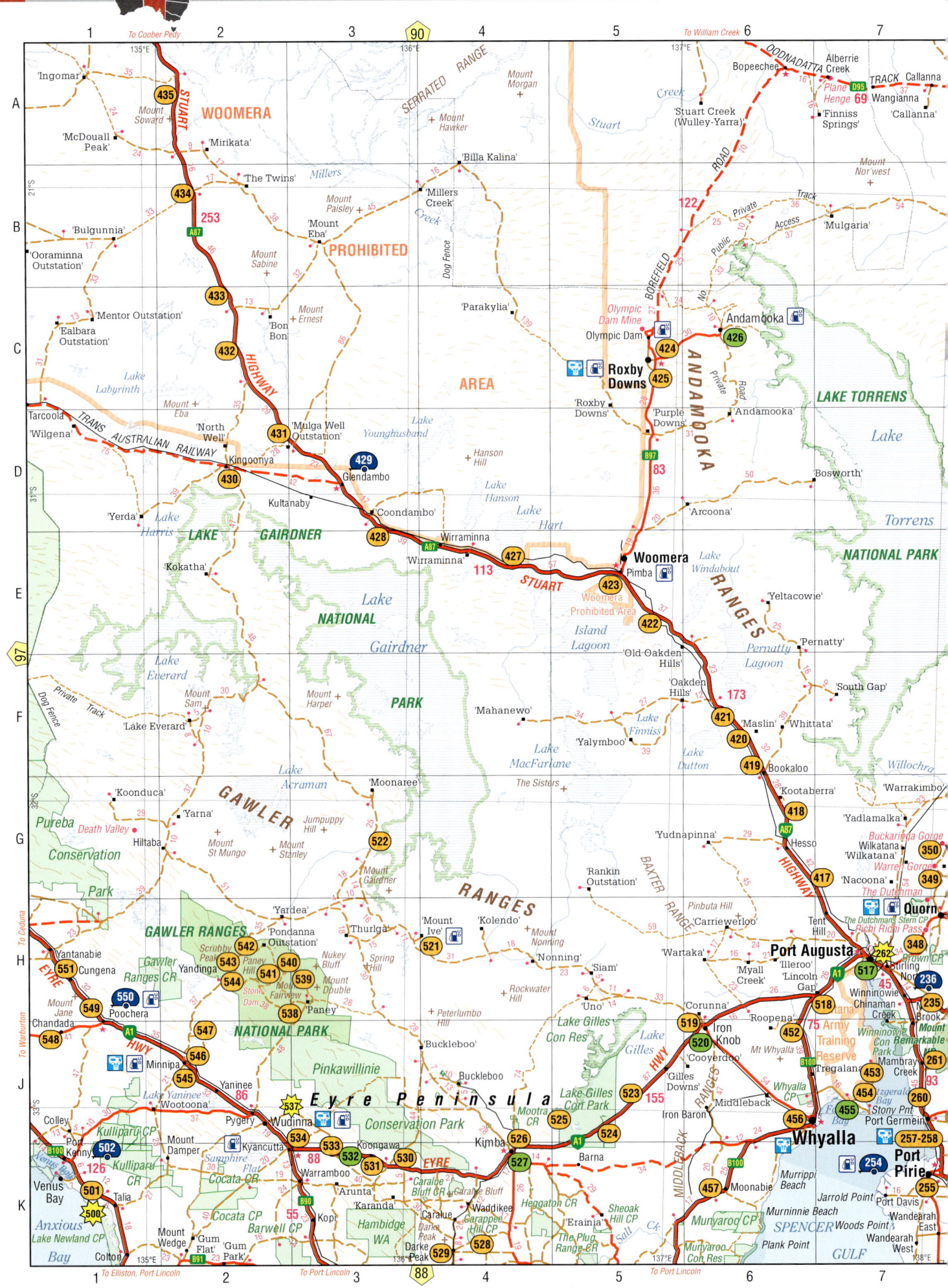

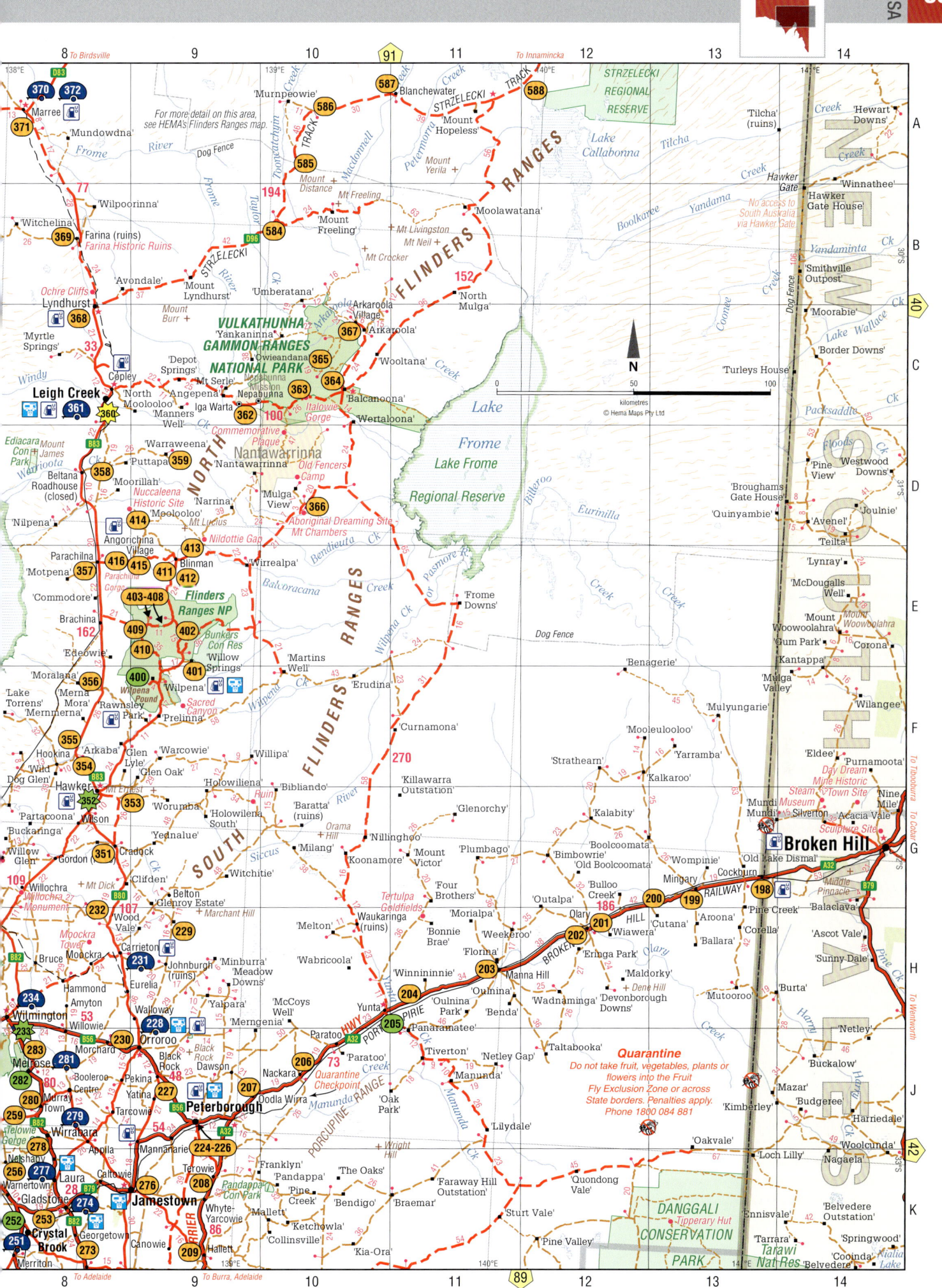

South Australia Highway Index

South Australia Alphabetic Site Index

South Australia Alphabetic Site Index

SOUTH AUSTRALIA

Mt Gambier to Tailem Bend
Princes Highway

1 Kromelite Rd Rest Area
Rest Area 23 km W of Mumbannar or 16 km E of Mt Gambier. 1 km W of SA/VIC border
HEMA 98 J6   37 50 46 S   140 55 14 E

2 Mt Gambier Showgrounds   ☎ 0408 492 182
Camp Area at Mt Gambier, Pick Ave. Caretaker on site. Maximum stay 28 days
HEMA 98 J6   37 50 16 S   140 47 51 E

3 Donovans Landing
Picnic Area 31 km SE of Mt Gambier or 7 km W of Nelson. Turn E 27 km SE of Mt Gambier or turn N 4 km NW of Nelson onto Glenelg River Rd
HEMA 98 J6   38 00 40 S   140 57 36 E

4 Brown Bay Car Park
Parking Area 13 km E of MacDonnell. On Eight Mile Creek Rd. Self Contained Vehicles only. Cold water shower
HEMA 98 K6   38 02 24 S   140 50 07 E

5 Cape Northumberland
Parking Area 4 km W of Port MacDonnell. Self Contained Vehicles only
HEMA 98 K6   38 03 31 S   140 39 44 E

✓6 Cape Banks Lighthouse   ☎ (08) 8735 1177
Canunda National Park
Camp Area 4 km N of Carpenter Rocks, via Cape Banks Rd
HEMA 98 J5   37 53 51 S   140 22 37 E

7 Carpenter Rocks Community Assoc Camp
Camp Area Carpenter Rocks. Next to community hall & tennis courts. Pay at Store or at payment box at the store. Self Contained Vehicles only
HEMA 98 J5   37 54 49 S   140 23 55 E

8 Tantanoola East
Parking Area 31 km NW of Mt Gambier or 19 km SE of Millicent. Opposite SAFF Service Station
HEMA 98 J5   37 42 21 S   140 29 54 E

9 Railway Reserve Tantanoola
Parking Area at Tantanoola, opposite hotel Tantanoola Rd
HEMA 98 J5   37 41 46 S   140 27 20 E

10 Millicent South
Parking Area 45 km NW of Mt Gambier or 5 km S of Millicent
HEMA 98 J5   37 38 01 S   140 23 29 E

11 Hillview Caravan Park   ☎ (08) 8733 2806
Caravan Park. 2.6 km S of Millicent. Dalton St
HEMA 98 J5   37 36 42 S   140 22 19 E

12 Millicent Lakeside Caravan Park   ☎ (08) 8733 1188
Caravan Park at Millicent. 12 Park Tce. 1 km S of PO
HEMA 98 J5   37 35 28 S   140 20 22 E

13 Millicent North
Parking Area 4 km N of Millicent or 103 km S of Kingston SE
HEMA 98 H5   37 33 50 S   140 21 16 E

14 Drain M
Parking Area 23 km N of Millicent or 84 km S of Kingston SE
HEMA 98 H5   37 23 37 S   140 14 17 E

15 Greenways West
Parking Area 65 km N of Millicent or 42 km S of Kingston SE
HEMA 98 H5   37 06 55 S   140 06 13 E

16 Reedy Creek South
Parking Area 77 km N of Millicent or 30 km S of Kingston SE
HEMA 98 G5   37 00 49 S   140 00 34 E

17 Southend Sands Caravan Park   ☎ (08) 8735 6200
Caravan Park at Southend. Cnr of Leake & Eliza Sts
HEMA 98 J5   37 34 07 S   140 07 38 E

✓18 Kotgee Camping Area   ☎ (08) 8735 177
Canunda National Park
Camp Area at Southend. Entry off Boozy Gully Rd, 2 km sandy dirt road. Small caravans only. E-Permit required. Maximum stay 5 days
HEMA 98 J5   37 34 50 S   140 08 14 E

19 Geltwood Beach Campground   ☎ (08) 8735 1177
Canunda National Park
Camp Area 14 km W of Millicent, via Canunda Causeway Rd, Oil Rig Square track. Small caravans only. E-Permit required, maximum stay 5 days
HEMA 98 J5   37 39 28 S   140 13 31 E

20 **Three Mile Bend Campground** ☎(08) 8735 1177
Beachport Conservation Park

Camp Area 5 km N of Beachport, via Five Mile Rd. Small vehicles only. 2 km dirt road. Permit required

HEMA 98 H5   37 27 09 S   139 59 31 E

21 **Springs Road**

Parking Area 36 km N of Beachport or 14 km S of Robe. 400m N of The Springs Rd turnoff

B101

HEMA 98 H4   37 12 49 S   139 53 17 E

22 **Robe RV Stop**

Parking Area 5.5 km N of Robe. On Southern Ports Hwy

HEMA 98 H4   37 09 12 S   139 48 27 E

23 **Old Man Lake** ☎(08) 8735 1177
Little Dip Conservation Park

Camp Area 10 km N of Nora Creina or 13 km S of Robe, via Nora Creina Dr. Some dirt road. Small vehicles only. Low trees. Permit required

HEMA 98 H4   37 15 38 S   139 49 18 E

24 **Long Gully Campground** ☎(08) 8735 1177
Little Dip Conservation Park

Camp Area 12 km N of Nora Creina or 14 km S of Robe, via Nora Creina Dr. 6 km dirt road. Permit required

HEMA 98 H4   37 15 17 S   139 48 03 E

25 **The Gums Campground** ☎(08) 8735 1177
Little Dip Conservation Park

Camp Area 3 km S of Robe, via Robe St. Small vehicles only not suitable for caravans. Some dirt road. Permit required

HEMA 98 H4   37 11 14 S   139 46 02 E

26 **Wrights Bay Bush Camping** ☎0428 340 717

Camp Spot at Wrights Bay. Turn W into Wrights Bay Rd 19 km N of Robe or 25 km S of Kingston. See caretaker

HEMA 98 G4   37 02 31 S   139 44 33 E

27 **Kingston South**

Parking Area 32 km N of Robe or 12 km S of Kingston SE

B101

HEMA 98 G4   36 55 30 S   139 49 16 E

28 **Pinks Beach**

Parking Area 6 km S of Kingston SE on Pinks Beach Rd (Cnr Marine Pde). Maximum stay 5 nights

HEMA 98 G4   36 52 23 S   139 48 52 E

29 **Kingston S.E. RV Park**

Parking Area at Kingston SE, Marine Parade. Cold shower. No tents

HEMA 98 G4   36 49 38 S   139 51 03 E

30 **Mt Scott Conservation Park**

Camp Area 24 km NE of Kingston SE. Turn SE off Desert Camp-Kingston Rd (Rowney Rd) 19 km NE of Kingston SE. 5 km dirt road

HEMA 98 G5   36 46 49 S   140 03 19 E

31 **The Granites**

Parking Area 21 km N of Kingston SE. Turn W off Princes Hwy 18 km N of Kingston SE onto Old Coorong Rd for 2.3 km, then S on Granites Rd West Range for 1 km

HEMA 98 G4   36 39 28 S   139 51 17 E

32 **Coorong Rest Area**

Rest Area 25 km N of Kingston SE or 59 km S of Salt Creek

B1

HEMA 98 G4   36 37 15 S   139 52 36 E

33 **Old Coorong Road Campgrounds** ☎(08) 8735 1177
Coorong National Park

Camp Area 39 km N of Kingston SE or 45 km S of Salt Creek. Many campsites beside Old Coorong Rd (dirt road). Permit required

HEMA 98 F4   36 23 20 S   139 45 51 E

34 **42 Mile Crossing Campground** ☎(08) 8735 1177
Coorong National Park

Camp Area 69 km N of Kingston SE or 21 km S of Salt Creek. Turn W 66 km N of Kingston SE or 18 km S of Salt Creek. 3 km dirt road. Permit required

HEMA 98 F4   36 17 15 S   139 42 42 E

35 **Adventures Rest Camp Ground** ☎(08) 8575 7021

Camp Area at Salt Creek. Next to roadhouse

B1

HEMA 98 F4   36 07 38 S   139 38 55 E

36 **Parnka Point** ☎(08) 8735 1177
Coorong National Park

Camp Area 42 km N of Salt Creek or 28 km S of Meningie. Turn W 38 km N of Salt Creek or 24 km S of Meningie. 3 km dirt road. Permit required. 2 camp areas

HEMA 89 K10   35 53 49 S   139 24 05 E

Notes...

South Australia Sites 37 — 55

37 Long Point
Coorong National Park
☎ (08) 8735 1177
Camp Area 23 km W of Meningie. Permit required
HEMA 89 K9   35 41 40 S   139 09 49 E

38 Mark Point
Coorong National Park
☎ (08) 8735 1177
Camp Area 34 km W of Meningie. 11 km unsealed road, tracks to camp sites on sandy track. 4WD recommended
HEMA 89 J9   35 37 30 S   139 04 37 E

39 Narrung Jetty Reserve
Rest Area at Narrung, beside ferry terminal. W side
HEMA 89 J9   35 30 49 S   139 11 04 E

40 Meningie Lions Jubilee Park
Rest Area at Meningie
HEMA 89 K10   35 41 07 S   139 20 21 E

41 Wellington Caravan Park
☎ (08) 8572 7302
Caravan Park at Wellington. Main Rd
HEMA 89 J10   35 19 50 S   139 22 55 E

42 Tailem Bend South Rest Area
Rest Area 45 km N of Meningie or 7 km S of Tailem Bend
HEMA 89 J10   35 18 16 S   139 25 51 E

Bordertown to Adelaide
Dukes Highway

43 Mundulla Showground
Camp Area at Mundulla. Cnr North Tce & Mile Ln. Honesty box
HEMA 98 F6   36 21 30 S   140 41 25 E

44 Poocher Swamp Rest Area
Rest Area 8 km W of Bordertown, via Crocker St from Shell Station & Cannawigara Rd
HEMA 98 F6   36 17 55 S   140 40 56 E

45 Brimbago Rest Area
Rest Area 29 km NW of Bordertown or 16 km SE of Keith
HEMA 98 F5   36 10 19 S   140 28 52 E

46 Cockatoo Downs Farmstay
☎ (08) 8756 7042
Camp Area 14 km S of Keith or 34 km N of Bordertown. Eckerts Rd. Signposted
HEMA 98 F5   36 09 21 S   140 28 44 E

47 Keith Caravan Park
☎ (08) 8755 1957
Caravan Park at Keith. Naracoorte Rd
HEMA 98 F5   36 06 04 S   140 21 04 E

48 Keith Showgrounds
☎ 0407 392 231
Camp Area at Keith. Enter via Showgrounds Rd. No camping during Show Week October
HEMA 98 F5   36 05 44 S   140 21 30 E

49 Keith Town Park
Rest Area at Keith. Heritage St. N end of town
HEMA 98 F5   36 05 45 S   140 21 08 E

50 Tintinara South Rest Area
Rest Area 29 km NW of Keith or 8 km S of Tintinara
HEMA 89 K11   35 56 17 S   140 07 27 E

51 Culburra North Rest Area
Rest Area 3 km NW of Culburra, 14 km NW of Tintinara or 13 km SE of Coonalpyn
HEMA 89 K11   35 47 49 S   139 56 37 E

52 Coonalpyn Soldiers Memorial Caravan Park
☎ 0427 399 089
Caravan Park at Coonalpyn. Richards Tce
HEMA 89 K11   35 41 33 S   139 51 27 E

53 Ki Ki South Rest Area
Rest Area 10 km NW of Coonalpyn or 6 km SE of Ki Ki
HEMA 89 J11   35 36 52 S   139 48 43 E

54 Coomandook Rest Area
Rest Area at Coomandook. Toilet across the road
HEMA 89 J10   35 28 16 S   139 41 49 E

55 Rivers Edge Caravan Park
☎ (08) 8572 3307
Caravan Park at Tailem Bend. Princes Hwy. 2 km NW of PO
HEMA 89 H10   35 14 25 S   139 26 26 E

304 CAMPS AUSTRALIA WIDE 9

56 Tailem Bend Football Oval ☎ 0419 187 446
Parking Area at Tailem Bend. Cnr Granite Rd & Second Ave. Access to amenities on request
HEMA 89 H10   35 14 56 S   139 27 20 E

57 Old Tailem Town Village ☎ (08) 8572 3838
Parking Area 5 km N of Tailem Bend. Pacific Hwy. Park in front car park. Self Contained Vehicles only
A1
HEMA 89 H10   35 13 26 S   139 25 21 E

58 Wynarka Oval
Parking Area at Wynarka. 16 km W of Karoonda or 32 km E of Tailem Bend
HEMA 89 H11   35 07 49 S   139 43 49 E

59 Sturt Reserve
Picnic Area at Murray Bridge. 1 km E of PO. Beside Murray River
HEMA 89 H10   35 07 20 S   139 17 10 E

60 Murray Bridge Showgrounds ☎ 0410 147 475
Camp Area at Murray Bridge East, Princess Hwy. Self Contained Vehicles only. Closed during show week Sept
HEMA 89 H10   35 06 50 S   139 18 11 E

61 Mulga Wildlife Sanctuary & Park ☎ (08) 8538 2862
Parking Area 20 km NE of Murray Bridge on Bowhill Rd. Self Contained Vehicles only. Bookings essential
HEMA 89 H10   35 02 40 S   139 26 43 E

Mt Gambier to Keith
Riddoch Highway

62 Kalangadoo Railway Reserve Park
Parking Area at Kalangadoo. Railway Tce. Self Contained Vehicles only
HEMA 98 J6   37 33 44 S   140 41 58 E

63 Tarpeena Football Club
Parking Area at Tarpeena. Edward St. Self Contained Vehicles only. Donation box
HEMA 98 J6   37 37 39 S   140 47 52 E

64 Forestry Information Stop
Rest Area 4 km N of Nangwarry or 15 km S of Penola
A66
HEMA 98 H6   37 30 39 S   140 49 06 E

65 Penola South Rest Area
Rest Area 10 km S of Penola or 8 km N of Nangwarry
HEMA 98 H6   37 28 30 S   140 49 46 E

✓66 Greenrise Lake
Picnic Area 18 km N of Nangwarry or 1 km S of Penola. 800m off Hwy. Self Contained Vehicles only. Donation appreciated for upkeep of facilities at the Info Centre in town
A66
HEMA 98 H6   37 23 48 S   140 50 11 E

67 Whiskas Woolshed ☎ 0418 854 505
Camp Area 12 km W of Penola. 78 Yallum Rd
HEMA 98 H6   37 25 10 S   140 43 27 E

68 Bellwether Wines & Campground ☎ 0417 080 945
Camp Area at Winery. 14183 Riddoch Hwy, 7 km N of Coonawarra. Limited sites, call ahead
HEMA 98 H6   37 13 51 S   140 51 05 E

69 Bool Lagoon Turnoff Rest Area
Rest Area 33 km N of Penola or 17 km S of Naracoorte
A66
HEMA 98 H6   37 06 09 S   140 47 35 E

70 Bool Lagoon Game Reserve ☎ (08) 8762 3412
Camp Area 43 km N of Penola or 27 km S of Naracoorte. Turn W 33 km N of Penola or 17 km S of Naracoorte, via Bool Lagoon Rd. Permit required
HEMA 98 H6   37 06 18 S   140 43 11 E

71 Wirreanda Campground ☎ (08) 8204 1910
Naracoorte Caves National Park
Camp Area 45 km N of Penola or 13 km SE of Naracoorte. Turn E onto Caves Rd 41 km N of Penola or 9 km S of Naracoorte. Permit required
HEMA 98 H6   37 02 34 S   140 48 05 E

72 Ardune Range Rest Area
Rest Area 6 km S of Lucindale. At jcn of Robe & Naracoorte Rds
HEMA 98 G5   37 01 32 S   140 22 17 E

73 Lucindale Caravan Park ☎ (08) 8766 2038
Caravan Park at Lucindale. Oak Ave
HEMA 98 G5   36 58 08 S   140 21 59 E

Notes...

SOUTH AUSTRALIA

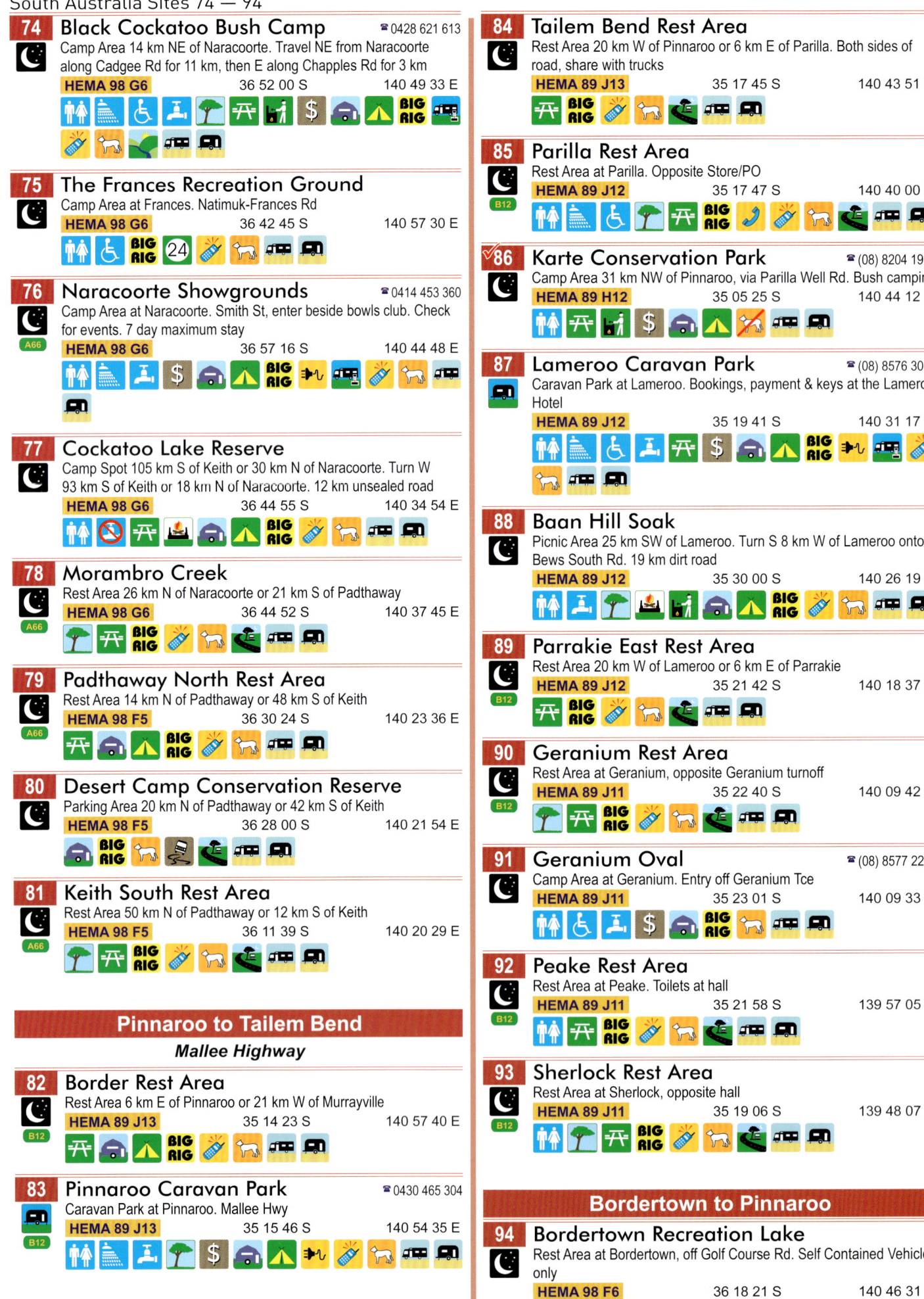

74 Black Cockatoo Bush Camp ☎ 0428 621 613
Camp Area 14 km NE of Naracoorte. Travel NE from Naracoorte along Cadgee Rd for 11 km, then E along Chapples Rd for 3 km
HEMA 98 G6 · 36 52 00 S · 140 49 33 E

75 The Frances Recreation Ground
Camp Area at Frances. Natimuk-Frances Rd
HEMA 98 G6 · 36 42 45 S · 140 57 30 E

76 Naracoorte Showgrounds ☎ 0414 453 360
Camp Area at Naracoorte. Smith St, enter beside bowls club. Check for events. 7 day maximum stay
HEMA 98 G6 · 36 57 16 S · 140 44 48 E

77 Cockatoo Lake Reserve
Camp Spot 105 km S of Keith or 30 km N of Naracoorte. Turn W 93 km S of Keith or 18 km N of Naracoorte. 12 km unsealed road
HEMA 98 G6 · 36 44 55 S · 140 34 54 E

78 Morambro Creek
Rest Area 26 km N of Naracoorte or 21 km S of Padthaway
HEMA 98 G6 · 36 44 52 S · 140 37 45 E

79 Padthaway North Rest Area
Rest Area 14 km N of Padthaway or 48 km S of Keith
HEMA 98 F5 · 36 30 24 S · 140 23 36 E

80 Desert Camp Conservation Reserve
Parking Area 20 km N of Padthaway or 42 km S of Keith
HEMA 98 F5 · 36 28 00 S · 140 21 54 E

81 Keith South Rest Area
Rest Area 50 km N of Padthaway or 12 km S of Keith
HEMA 98 F5 · 36 11 39 S · 140 20 29 E

Pinnaroo to Tailem Bend
Mallee Highway

82 Border Rest Area
Rest Area 6 km E of Pinnaroo or 21 km W of Murrayville
HEMA 89 J13 · 35 14 23 S · 140 57 40 E

83 Pinnaroo Caravan Park ☎ 0430 465 304
Caravan Park at Pinnaroo. Mallee Hwy
HEMA 89 J13 · 35 15 46 S · 140 54 35 E

84 Tailem Bend Rest Area
Rest Area 20 km W of Pinnaroo or 6 km E of Parilla. Both sides of road, share with trucks
HEMA 89 J13 · 35 17 45 S · 140 43 51 E

85 Parilla Rest Area
Rest Area at Parilla. Opposite Store/PO
HEMA 89 J12 · 35 17 47 S · 140 40 00 E

86 Karte Conservation Park ☎ (08) 8204 1910
Camp Area 31 km NW of Pinnaroo, via Parilla Well Rd. Bush camping
HEMA 89 H12 · 35 05 25 S · 140 44 12 E

87 Lameroo Caravan Park ☎ (08) 8576 3006
Caravan Park at Lameroo. Bookings, payment & keys at the Lameroo Hotel
HEMA 89 J12 · 35 19 41 S · 140 31 17 E

88 Baan Hill Soak
Picnic Area 25 km SW of Lameroo. Turn S 8 km W of Lameroo onto Bews South Rd. 19 km dirt road
HEMA 89 J12 · 35 30 00 S · 140 26 19 E

89 Parrakie East Rest Area
Rest Area 20 km W of Lameroo or 6 km E of Parrakie
HEMA 89 J12 · 35 21 42 S · 140 18 37 E

90 Geranium Rest Area
Rest Area at Geranium, opposite Geranium turnoff
HEMA 89 J11 · 35 22 40 S · 140 09 42 E

91 Geranium Oval ☎ (08) 8577 2257
Camp Area at Geranium. Entry off Geranium Tce
HEMA 89 J11 · 35 23 01 S · 140 09 33 E

92 Peake Rest Area
Rest Area at Peake. Toilets at hall
HEMA 89 J11 · 35 21 58 S · 139 57 05 E

93 Sherlock Rest Area
Rest Area at Sherlock, opposite hall
HEMA 89 J11 · 35 19 06 S · 139 48 07 E

Bordertown to Pinnaroo

94 Bordertown Recreation Lake
Rest Area at Bordertown, off Golf Course Rd. Self Contained Vehicles only
HEMA 98 F6 · 36 18 21 S · 140 46 31 E

95 Comet Bore Campground ☎ (08) 8204 1910
Ngarkat Conservation Park
B57
Camp Area 61 km S of Pinnaroo or 72 km N of Bordertown. 4WD. Not suitable caravans. Permit required
HEMA 98 E6   35 44 37 S   140 48 03 E

96 Pertendi Hut Campground ☎ (08) 8204 1910
Ngarkat Conservation Park
B57
Camp Area 48 km S of Pinnaroo or 84 km N of Bordertown. Permit required
HEMA 98 E6   35 38 24 S   140 46 43 E

Renmark to Adelaide
Sturt Highway

97 Yamba East Rest Area
A20
Rest Area 119 km W of Mildura or 23 km E of Renmark. 5 km W of VIC/SA border. S area quieter
HEMA 89 F13   34 16 07 S   140 54 13 E

98 Bert Dix Memorial Park
A20
Picnic Area 1 km W of Paringa. SE side of bridge, beside river. Self Contained Motorhomes only, no caravans, camper trailers or tents
HEMA 89 F13   34 10 59 S   140 46 37 E

99 Renmark Swimming Pool Car Park
Parking Area at Renmark. Cnr Cowra & Fifteenth St. In swimming pool car park. Self Contained Motorhomes only
HEMA 89 F13   34 10 08 S   140 44 41 E

100 Murtho Forest Landing ☎ (08) 8586 6704
Camp Area 17 km NE of Paringa, via Paringa-Murtho Rd & Headings Rd. 4 km dirt road. Beside river
HEMA 89 F13   34 03 56 S   140 46 49 E

101 Little Gums Campground ☎ (08) 8204 1910
Chowilla Game Reserve
Camp Area 32 km NE of Renmark, via Old Wentworth Rd. Turn S onto signposted road to park entrance (6.5 km). Dirt road. 4WD only. Permit required
HEMA 89 E13   34 00 28 S   140 51 22 E

102 Border Cliffs Campground ☎ (08) 8204 1910
Chowilla Game Reserve
Camp Area 30 km NE of Paringa. Take road E of river, Murtho Rd to campsite. Permit available at general store
HEMA 89 E13   33 58 24 S   140 57 28 E

103 Black Oak Campground ☎ (08) 8580 1800
Danggali Conservation Park
Camp Area 120 km N of Renmark, near Canopus Homestead. Self registration
HEMA 89 D13   33 29 52 S   140 42 20 E

104 Plushs Bend ☎ (08) 8586 6704
Camp Area 6 km S of Renmark. Turn S 2 km SW of Renmark for 4 km along Twenty-Third St. 1 km dirt road. Beside river. Maximum stay 7 days
HEMA 89 F13   34 12 31 S   140 45 15 E

105 T M Price Rotary Park
A20
Rest Area 6 km W of Renmark or 12 km E of Berri. Self Contained Motorhomes only
HEMA 89 F13   34 12 23 S   140 42 10 E

106 Black Box Campground ☎ (08) 8580 1800
Murray River National Park
Camp Area 2.5 km NE of Lyrup. Turn S 8 km SW of Renmark or 8 km E of Berri. 3 km dirt road. Bush camping beside river. Low trees. Permit required
HEMA 89 F13   34 14 39 S   140 39 44 E

107 Tea Tree Campground ☎ (08) 8580 1800
Murray River National Park
Camp Area 1.5 km N of Lyrup. Turn S 9 km SW of Renmark or 6 km E of Berri. Entrance next to ferry crossing. 500m dirt road. Bush camping beside river. Permit required
HEMA 89 F12   34 14 57 S   140 39 07 E

108 S.S. Ellen Park
Rest Area at Lyrup. S side of river. W of ferry crossing. Self Contained Vehicles only
HEMA 89 F12   34 15 14 S   140 38 52 E

109 Lyrup Turnoff
A20
Parking Area 12 km W of Renmark or 6 km E of Berri
HEMA 89 F12   34 14 14 S   140 38 33 E

110 Colligans Campground ☎ (08) 8580 1800
Murray River National Park
Camp Area 17 km W of Renmark. Turn S 12 km W of Renmark (just past Renmark Country Club). Bush camping next to river. 5 km dirt road. Permit required
HEMA 89 F12   34 15 14 S   140 41 49 E

Notes...

SOUTH AUSTRALIA

111 Martins Bend Campground ☎ (08) 8582 2423
Camp Area 3 km E of Berri, via Riverview Rd. Beside river. Maximum stay 21 days. Obtain permit from caretaker before set-up
HEMA 89 F12   34 17 24 S   140 37 49 E

112 Lock 4 Section Katarapko ☎ (08) 8580 1800
Murray River National Park
Camp Area 5 km SW Berri. Via Draper Rd, under Murray River Bridge, 4.5 km dirt road to park entrance. Designated sites. Permit required
HEMA 89 F12   34 19 06 S   140 34 16 E

113 Eckerts Creek Campground ☎ (08) 8580 1800
Murray River National Park
Camp Area 13 km SW of Berri. From Old Sturt Hwy turn S onto Lower Winkie Rd (3.5 km) & E onto Migga Rd taking the R fork to park entry (1 km). Bush camping beside river. Permit required
HEMA 89 F12   34 20 09 S   140 32 47 E

114 Thiele's Sandbar
Camp Area 3.5 km NE of Loxton via Bookpurnong Rd. Turn W at water tower (Tower Dr). At crossroads turn R, 1.5 km dirt track to river. GPS at entry
HEMA 89 F12   34 26 29 S   140 35 02 E

115 Rilli Reserve
Camp Spot 7 km N of Loxton. Turn W onto Briers Rd 6.5 km N of Loxton, 2 km to reserve. Bush camping by the river
HEMA 89 G12   34 23 37 S   140 34 57 E

116 Loxton Golf Club ☎ (08) 8584 1490
Camp Area at Loxton North. Edward St
HEMA 89 G12   34 25 26 S   140 38 45 E

117 Paruna Comfort Stop
Camp Area at Paruna. Railway Tce. Honesty box for fees
HEMA 89 G13   34 43 11 S   140 43 44 E

118 Mindarie
Parking Area at Mindarie. 500m W of town
HEMA 89 G12   34 48 59 S   140 12 50 E
B55

119 Halidon Parking Area
Parking Area 1 km W of Halidon
HEMA 89 H11   34 53 02 S   140 09 49 E
B55

120 Karoonda East
Parking Area 15 km SW of Borrika or 1 km E of Karoonda
HEMA 89 H11   35 05 14 S   139 54 34 E
B55

121 Perponda Oval
Parking Area at Perponda. 16 km N of Karoonda
HEMA 89 H11   34 59 06 S   139 48 55 E

122 Karoonda Cabin & Caravan Park ☎ (08) 8578 1004
B55
Caravan Park at Karoonda, next to oval
HEMA 89 H11   35 05 47 S   139 53 23 E

✓ 123 Moorook Riverfront Camping & Picnic Area ☎ (08) 8584 7221
Camp Area at Moorook. Loxton Rd, beside Murray River. Honesty box for fees. Maximum stay 10 nights. Limited power sites
HEMA 89 F12   34 17 17 S   140 22 06 E

124 Moorook Game Reserve ☎ (08) 8580 1800
Camp Area 4 km N of Moorook. 1 km dirt road. Bush campsites by river. Permit required
HEMA 89 F12   34 15 59 S   140 22 10 E

125 Kaiser Strip Campground ☎ (08) 8580 1800
Loch Luna Game Reserve
Camp Spot 2 km W of Cobdogla, via Shueard Dr. Various sites either side of Hwy along river. Permit required
HEMA 89 F12   34 14 00 S   140 23 16 E

126 Kingston-on-Murray Caravan Park ☎ (08) 8583 0209
Caravan Park at Kingston-on-Murray. 461 Holmes Rd
HEMA 89 F12   34 13 22 S   140 21 06 E

127 Cobdogla Pump Station
Camp Spot 2 km S of Cobdogla. From Shueard Rd turn S onto Park Tce, Schell Rd for 2 km. Turn W across causeway to Pump Station. Camping N & S of station
HEMA 89 F12   34 15 45 S   140 24 02 E

128 Barmera RV Park (Bruce Oval)
Camp Spot at Barmera. Sims St. Pay at Visitor Information Centre. Self Contained Vehicles only
HEMA 89 F12   34 15 13 S   140 28 03 E

129 Lake Bonney Reserve ☎ (08) 8582 1922
Camp Area 11 km NW of Barmera, via Morgan Rd, Nappers Bridge & Queen Elizabeth Dr. 200m E of Nappers Bridge, beside lake. Sandy area, walk in first to check
HEMA 89 F12   34 11 43 S   140 25 37 E

130 Campground 10 ☎ (08) 8580 1800
Loch Luna Game Reserve
Camp Area 18 km NW of Barmera, via Morgan Rd. 7 km W of Nappers Bridge. Dirt road. Bush camping by Chambers Creek. Other sites available, signposted
HEMA 89 F12   34 13 20 S   140 23 39 E

131 Herons Bend
Overland Corner Conservation Reserve
Camp Spot at Overland Corner. 1.2 km W of Overland Corner Hotel. Bush camping by river. GPS at entry point
HEMA 89 F12   34 09 07 S   140 20 26 E

132 Morgan East Rest Area 1
Rest Area 12 km W of Overland Corner or 57 km E of Morgan
B64   HEMA 89 F12   34 09 01 S   140 13 00 E

133 Pooginook Conservation Park ☎ (08) 8580 1800
Camp Area 45 km E of Morgan or 43 km W of B64/Sturt Hwy Jcn. Signposted, 1.9 km N to campsite. GPS at entrance
HEMA 89 F11   34 08 21 S   140 07 17 E

134 Morgan East Rest Area 2
Rest Area 44 km W of Overland Corner or 25 km E of Morgan. Both sides of Hwy
B64   HEMA 89 E11   34 03 29 S   139 53 52 E

135 Cadell Recreation Ground ☎ 0497 799 284
Camp Area at Cadell, via Heinrich, Dalzell Rds. Caretaker on site. Fee for showers
HEMA 89 E11   34 02 16 S   139 45 26 E

136 Graeme Claxton Reserve
Camp Spot at Cadell. Via Cadell Valley Rd & Kings Riverside Dr. Veer R at boat ramp
HEMA 89 E11   34 01 36 S   139 45 35 E

137 Lowbank Landing
Camp Spot 10 km E of Waikerie. Turn N off Sturt Hwy into Lowbank Rd. 1 km dirt road. Follow to riverbank
A20   HEMA 89 F11   34 11 01 S   140 04 08 E

138 Maize Island Lagoon Conservation Park ☎ (08) 8580 1800
Camp Area 7 km E of Waikerie. Turn N 3 km E of Waikerie onto Holder Top Rd for 4 km. Turn R at T intersection, then take R fork dirt road. Bush camping along river bank
HEMA 89 F11   34 09 58 S   140 00 42 E

139 Holder Bend Reserve & Boat Ramp
Camp Spot 5 km E of Waikerie. Turn N 3 km E of Waikerie onto Holder Top Rd (300m), NW onto Holder Bottom Rd (1 km), then W into Reserve via dirt road. Camping along river bank. 7 day limit
HEMA 89 F11   34 11 04 S   140 00 48 E

✓140 Hogwash Bend ☎ (08) 8541 2332
Picnic Area 25 km NW of Waikerie or 22 km E of Morgan, via Morgan-Waikerie Rd. Turn N 23 km NW of Waikerie or 20 km E of Morgan. 2 km dirt road. Bush camping by river
HEMA 89 F11   34 03 55 S   139 51 12 E

141 Cordola Camping Area - Pelican Point
Camp Area 11 km SW of Morgan. Turn S off B81 onto Blanchetown Rd for 8.5 km then turn E onto Pelican Point Rd for 2 km. S into property gate (500m). Follow River Rd to camp spots along river. Honesty box
HEMA 89 F10   34 07 47 S   139 39 54 E

142 Morgan Conservation Park North Section ☎ (08) 8580 1800
Camp Area 1 km E of Morgan, via Morgan-Cadell Rd. Signposted 750m E of ferry crossing. Various tracks. Permit required, self registration. GPS at entrance
HEMA 89 E11   34 02 19 S   139 40 57 E

143 Morgan Conservation Park South Section ☎ (08) 8580 1800
Camp Area 1.6 km E of Morgan. 1.2 km S of ferry crossing, via Tennanabie St. E side of river. Dirt road. Small area only. Permit required, self registration
HEMA 89 E11   34 02 43 S   139 41 04 E

144 Morgan West
Parking Area 7 km W of Morgan or 26 km E of Bower
B81   HEMA 89 F10   34 03 52 S   139 35 09 E

145 Mount Mary Hotel ☎ (08) 8581 0581
Camp Area at Mount Mary Hotel. 22 km W of Morgan or 11 km E of Bower. Limited powered sites
B81   HEMA 89 F10   34 06 16 S   139 26 22 E

146 Bower Reserve
Camp Area at Bower. Next to tennis court. Fee for power & use of dump point. Fee box near BBQ
B81   HEMA 89 F10   34 07 23 S   139 21 11 E

Notes...

147 Stockyard Plain Rest Area
Rest Area 20 km SW of Waikerie or 22 km NE of Blanchetown
HEMA 89 F11   34 15 55 S   139 48 21 E
A20

148 Blanchetown Oval
Camp Area at Blanchetown. Entry off South Tce
HEMA 89 F10   34 21 19 S   139 37 00 E

149 Roonka Water Activities Centre   ☎ (08) 8339 3333
Camp Area at McBean Pond 11 km N of Blanchetown. 354 Morgan Rd. Bookings preferred
HEMA 89 F10   34 17 42 S   139 37 55 E

150 Old Ferry Landing
Parking Area at Blanchetown. The Parade. Self Contained Vehicles only
HEMA 89 F10   34 20 50 S   139 36 53 E

151 Truro East Rest Area
Rest Area 8 km E of Truro or 38 km W of Blanchetown
HEMA 89 F10   34 24 09 S   139 12 47 E
A20

152 Truro Hotel   ☎ (08) 8564 0218
Parking Area at Truro. Check in with publican
HEMA 89 F9   34 24 29 S   139 07 28 E

153 Stockwell Rest Area
Rest Area 6 km E of Nuriootpa or 9 km W of Truro
HEMA 86 B7   34 25 31 S   139 03 27 E
A20

154 Greenock Oval
Camp Area at Greenock. Entry off Martin Lane, small fee
HEMA 86 B6   34 27 32 S   138 55 43 E

155 Hamley Bridge Community & Sports Centre
Parking Area at Hamley Bridge, entry off Stockport Rd
HEMA 86 A3   34 21 14 S   138 40 53 E

Blanchetown to Murray Bridge

✓156 Tenbury - Hunter Reserve   ☎ (08) 8569 0100
Camp Area at Swan Reach, take ferry N across to W side of river. Bush camping on river bank. 500m E of ferry crossing. Maximum stay 5 nights
HEMA 89 G10   34 33 43 S   139 36 01 E

157 Big Bend River
Camp Spot 6 km S of Swan Reach or 17 km N of Nildottie, turn W onto Old Loxton Rd, dirt road for 4 km, bush camping beside Murray River
HEMA 89 G10   34 38 12 S   139 36 50 E

158 Big Bend Lookout
Rest Area 10 km S of Swan Reach or 5 km N of Nildottie. E side of river
HEMA 89 G10   34 37 56 S   139 39 56 E

159 Len Kroehn Lookout
Parking Area 8 km S of Nildottie or 6 km N of Walker Flat turnoff. E side of river
HEMA 89 G10   34 42 13 S   139 35 16 E

160 Forster Lookout
Parking Area 1 km E of Walker Flat (ferry crossing). E side of river. Walkers Flat Rd
HEMA 89 G10   34 45 19 S   139 34 26 E

161 Swan Reach Conservation Park   ☎ (08) 8576 3690
Camp Spot 14 km W of Swan Reach or 16 km E of Sedan. 2 km of dirt road S of Hwy
HEMA 89 G10   34 34 29 S   139 28 44 E

162 Sedan Recreation Reserve   ☎ (08) 8565 2252
Parking Area at Sedan. Ridley Rd. Pay at Sedan Hotel
HEMA 89 G10   34 34 38 S   139 17 28 E

163 Punyelroo Caravan Park   ☎ (08) 8570 2021
Caravan Park 10 km S of Swan Reach. W side of river. 7 km dirt road
HEMA 89 G10   34 36 13 S   139 36 08 E

164 John S Christian Reserve   ☎ (08) 8569 0100
Camp Spot 19 km NW of Walker Flat, via Walker Flat- Mt Pleasant Rd (10 km), Mannum-Swan Reach Rd (5 km N) & Black Hill Rd (4 km W). 9 km dirt road
HEMA 89 G10   34 41 56 S   139 29 11 E

165 Walker Flat Boat Ramp Reserve   ☎ (08) 8569 0100
Camp Spot at Walker Flat. 1 km N of ferry crossing on W side of river
HEMA 89 G10   34 45 08 S   139 33 43 E

166 Hettner Landing   ☎ (08) 8569 0100
Camp Spot at Walker Flat. Bush camping 50m N of General Store. Access track opposite Walkers Flat Rd
HEMA 89 G10   34 45 01 S   139 33 16 E

167 Caurnamont Reserve
☎ (08) 8569 0100

Parking Area at Caurnamont. 100m N of Purnong ferry crossing on W side of river

HEMA 89 G10   34 51 17 S   139 36 55 E

168 Caurnamont North

Parking Area 3.5 km N of Purnong Ferry on W side of river

HEMA 89 G10   34 50 32 S   139 35 11 E

169 Lakeside Camping Ground
☎ (08) 8570 4309

Camp Area 5.5 km SE of Caurnamont Ferry. From ferry follow road through Caurnamont for 3.5 km. Turn SE into Craignook Rd. 2 km dirt road

HEMA 89 G10   34 51 25 S   139 36 28 E

170 Purnong Reserve
☎ (08) 8569 0100

Parking Area at Purnong. E side of river, beside ferry crossing

HEMA 89 G10   34 51 15 S   139 37 02 E

171 Bolto Reserve
☎ (08) 8569 0100

Camp Area 1 km SE of Mannum, via Khartoum Rd. E side of river. S of ferry crossing. Maximum stay 5 nights. Permit required, pay machine

HEMA 89 H10   34 54 54 S   139 18 58 E

✓172 Haythorpe Reserve
☎ (08) 8569 0100

Camp Area 1 km NE of Mannum, on Bowhill Rd. E side of river. N of ferry crossing. Permit required, pay machine at toilet block

HEMA 89 H10   34 54 33 S   139 19 24 E

173 Palmer Oval

Parking Area at Palmer. Cnr Olive Grove & Randell Rd. Please park on the gravel ring road

HEMA 89 G9   34 51 11 S   139 09 44 E

174 Saunders Gorge Sanctuary
☎ (08) 8569 3032

Camp Area 22 km NE of Palmer. Saunders Rd

HEMA 89 G9   34 44 31 S   139 12 51 E

175 Marne River Reserve

Picnic Area 1.7 km S of Cambrai or 34 km N of Mannum

HEMA 89 G10   34 39 59 S   139 16 56 E

Notes...

Adelaide Greater Area

176 Williamstown Queen Victoria Jubilee Park
☎ (08) 8524 6363

Caravan Park at Williamstown. Springton Rd. 1 km E of PO

HEMA 86 E5   34 40 26 S   138 54 15 E

177 Rocky Paddock Campground
Mount Crawford Forest
☎ (08) 8521 1700

Camp Area 8 km SE of Williamstown, via Warren Rd. 1 km S of Forest Info Centre, via Tower Rd. Permit required. Closed Dec 01 - 31 March, fire season

HEMA 86 F6   34 43 01 S   138 56 26 E

178 Chalks Campground
Mount Crawford Forest
☎ (08) 8521 1700

Camp Area 3.5 km from Mount Crawford Forest Information Centre. Turn into Chalks Rd, dirt road. Permit Required. Closed 01 Dec - 31 Mar, fire season

HEMA 86 F6   34 44 18 S   138 57 34 E

179 Murray Recreation Park (Eden Valley Showgrounds)
☎ 0412 085 557

Caravan Park at Eden Valley. On the Eden Valley-Springton Rd. 1.2 km S of PO

HEMA 86 E7   34 39 15 S   139 06 07 E

180 Totness Inn Hotel
☎ (08) 8568 2346

Parking Area at Mount Pleasant. 143 Melrose St in the middle of town. Check in with manager at bar, toilet only open during hotel hours. Self Contained Vehicles only

HEMA 86 F7   34 46 18 S   139 03 07 E

181 Talunga Park Caravan Park (Showgrounds)
☎ (08) 8568 1934

Caravan Park at Mount Pleasant. Melrose St. At showground

HEMA 86 F7   34 46 34 S   139 02 34 E

182 Mount Torrens Hotel
☎ (08) 8389 4252

Parking Area at Mount Torrens. Check in with publican, limited parking for Self Contained Vehicles only. Toilet access only during pub hours

HEMA 86 H6   34 52 32 S   138 57 31 E

183 Cudlee Creek Tavern Caravan Park
☎ (08) 8389 2319

Caravan Park at Cudlee Creek, 30 km E of Adelaide. Gorge Rd

HEMA 83 G13   34 50 23 S   138 48 58 E

SOUTH AUSTRALIA

184 Strathalbyn Caravan Park ☎ (08) 8536 3681
Caravan Park at Strathalbyn. Ashbourne Rd
HEMA 89 H9   35 15 33 S   138 53 09 E

185 Frank Potts Reserve
Rest Area 1 km E of Langhorne Creek
HEMA 89 J9   35 17 56 S   139 02 33 E

186 Tolderol Game Reserve ☎ (08) 8575 1200
Camp Area 14 km SE of Langhorne Creek, via Langhorne Creek-Wellington Rd & Dog Lake Rd. Turn S 5 km E of Langhorne Creek. Dirt road. Permit required
HEMA 89 J9   35 22 31 S   139 08 55 E

187 Milang Foreshore
Picnic Area at Milang. Coin-operated showers
HEMA 89 J9   35 24 26 S   138 58 29 E

188 Mundoo Island Station ☎ (08) 8555 2242
Camp Area on Mundoo Island via Hindmarsh Island. This is a PRE BOOK site only. Campers will be instructed to meet at the barrages and will be guided to the camp site
HEMA 89 J9   35 31 55 S   138 54 05 E

189 Bristow-Smith Park
Picnic Area at Barrage Road, Goolwa South
HEMA 87 G7   35 30 51 S   138 47 04 E

190 Crabtree Farm ☎ 0409 554 266
Camp Area 3 km W of Goolwa. Kessel Rd. Bookings essential
HEMA 87 G7   35 30 02 S   138 44 43 E

191 Chookarloo Campground
Kuitpo Forest Reserve ☎ (08) 8391 8800
Camp Area 5 km SW of Meadows. Permit available from Kuitpo Forest Info Centre. Closed December to March
HEMA 87 C7   35 12 15 S   138 42 55 E

192 Port Elliot Showground ☎ 0417 218 029
Camp Area at Port Elliot. Cameron St, entry off Kurramin Ct. Must call ahead as gates can be locked
HEMA 87 G6   35 31 30 S   138 40 40 E

193 Waitpinga Campground
Newland Head Conservation Park ☎ (08) 8552 0300
Camp Area 17 km SE of Victor Harbour. Access via Waitpinga Rd. Small vehicles only, not suitable for caravans. Self registration
HEMA 87 H5   35 37 41 S   138 29 59 E

194 Stringybark Campground
Deep Creek Conservation Park ☎ (08) 8598 0263
Camp Area 9 km SE of Delamere, via Tapanappa Rd. Dirt road. Payment & bookings online only
HEMA 87 H2   35 36 24 S   138 14 20 E

195 Trig Campground
Deep Creek Conservation Park ☎ (08) 8598 0263
Camp Area 12 km S of Delamere, via Tent Rock Rd. Dirt road. Payment & bookings online only
HEMA 87 J2   35 38 59 S   138 12 54 E

196 Rapid Bay Camping Area ☎ (08) 8598 3003
Camp Area at Rapid Bay. Outside cold shower
HEMA 87 G1   35 31 29 S   138 11 30 E

197 Cape Jervis Station Caravan & Camping ☎ (08) 8598 0288
Camp Area at Cape Jervis Station. Main South Rd
HEMA 87 H1   35 36 19 S   138 07 41 E

Broken Hill to Adelaide
Barrier Highway

198 Cockburn Village ☎ (08) 8091 1634
Camp Area in Cockburn. Elder Tce. Book in at Cockburn Hotel opposite the water tower
HEMA 95 G13   32 04 37 S   140 59 46 E

199 Mingary Siding
Parking Area 25 km SW of Cockburn or 42 km NE of Olary
HEMA 95 G13   32 07 43 S   140 44 27 E

200 Cutana Rest Area
Rest Area 32 km SW of Cockburn or 35 km NE of Olary. Both sides of the road
HEMA 95 G13   32 11 10 S   140 34 56 E

201 Olary Creek
Rest Area 2 km E of Olary. 65 km SW of Cockburn or 39 km NE of Mannahill
HEMA 95 H12   32 16 08 S   140 20 46 E

202 Olary Rest Area
Rest Area at Olary. Cnr Barrier Hwy & High St
HEMA 95 H12   32 16 53 S   140 19 39 E

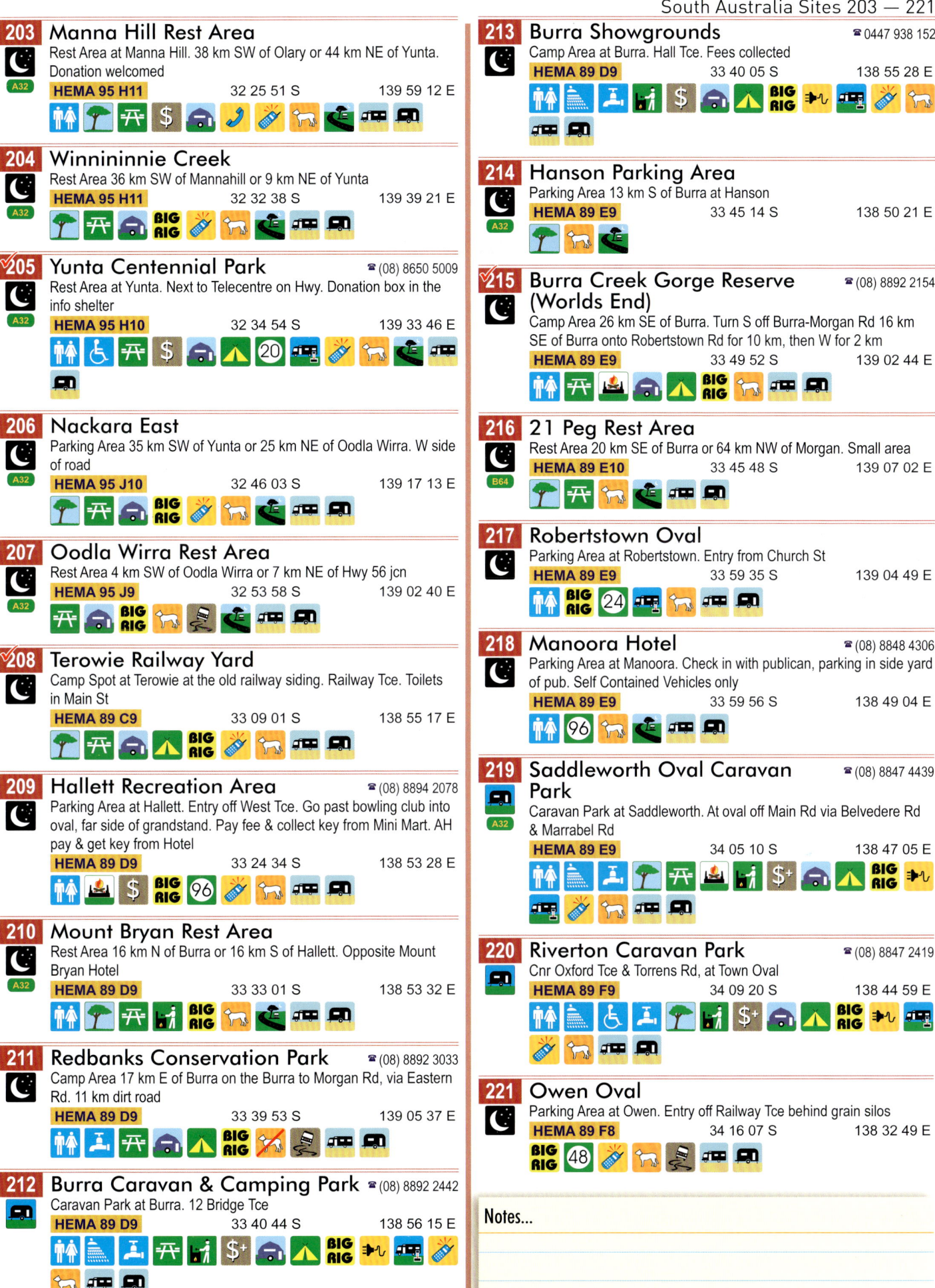

203 Manna Hill Rest Area
Rest Area at Manna Hill. 38 km SW of Olary or 44 km NE of Yunta. Donation welcomed
A32
HEMA 95 H11   32 25 51 S   139 59 12 E

204 Winnininnie Creek
Rest Area 36 km SW of Mannahill or 9 km NE of Yunta
A32
HEMA 95 H11   32 32 38 S   139 39 21 E

✓205 Yunta Centennial Park ☎ (08) 8650 5009
Rest Area at Yunta. Next to Telecentre on Hwy. Donation box in the info shelter
A32
HEMA 95 H10   32 34 54 S   139 33 46 E

206 Nackara East
Parking Area 35 km SW of Yunta or 25 km NE of Oodla Wirra. W side of road
A32
HEMA 95 J10   32 46 03 S   139 17 13 E

207 Oodla Wirra Rest Area
Rest Area 4 km SW of Oodla Wirra or 7 km NE of Hwy 56 jcn
A32
HEMA 95 J9   32 53 58 S   139 02 40 E

✓208 Terowie Railway Yard
Camp Spot at Terowie at the old railway siding. Railway Tce. Toilets in Main St
HEMA 89 C9   33 09 01 S   138 55 17 E

209 Hallett Recreation Area ☎ (08) 8894 2078
Parking Area at Hallett. Entry off West Tce. Go past bowling club into oval, far side of grandstand. Pay fee & collect key from Mini Mart. AH pay & get key from Hotel
HEMA 89 D9   33 24 34 S   138 53 28 E

210 Mount Bryan Rest Area
Rest Area 16 km N of Burra or 16 km S of Hallett. Opposite Mount Bryan Hotel
A32
HEMA 89 D9   33 33 01 S   138 53 32 E

211 Redbanks Conservation Park ☎ (08) 8892 3033
Camp Area 17 km E of Burra on the Burra to Morgan Rd, via Eastern Rd. 11 km dirt road
HEMA 89 D9   33 39 53 S   139 05 37 E

212 Burra Caravan & Camping Park ☎ (08) 8892 2442
Caravan Park at Burra. 12 Bridge Tce
HEMA 89 D9   33 40 44 S   138 56 15 E

213 Burra Showgrounds ☎ 0447 938 152
Camp Area at Burra. Hall Tce. Fees collected
HEMA 89 D9   33 40 05 S   138 55 28 E

214 Hanson Parking Area
Parking Area 13 km S of Burra at Hanson
A32
HEMA 89 E9   33 45 14 S   138 50 21 E

✓215 Burra Creek Gorge Reserve (Worlds End) ☎ (08) 8892 2154
Camp Area 26 km SE of Burra. Turn S off Burra-Morgan Rd 16 km SE of Burra onto Robertstown Rd for 10 km, then W for 2 km
HEMA 89 E9   33 49 52 S   139 02 44 E

216 21 Peg Rest Area
Rest Area 20 km SE of Burra or 64 km NW of Morgan. Small area
B64
HEMA 89 E10   33 45 48 S   139 07 02 E

217 Robertstown Oval
Parking Area at Robertstown. Entry from Church St
HEMA 89 E9   33 59 35 S   139 04 49 E

218 Manoora Hotel ☎ (08) 8848 4306
Parking Area at Manoora. Check in with publican, parking in side yard of pub. Self Contained Vehicles only
HEMA 89 E9   33 59 56 S   138 49 04 E

219 Saddleworth Oval Caravan Park ☎ (08) 8847 4439
Caravan Park at Saddleworth. At oval off Main Rd via Belvedere Rd & Marrabel Rd
A32
HEMA 89 E9   34 05 10 S   138 47 05 E

220 Riverton Caravan Park ☎ (08) 8847 2419
Cnr Oxford Tce & Torrens Rd, at Town Oval
HEMA 89 F9   34 09 20 S   138 44 59 E

221 Owen Oval
Parking Area at Owen. Entry off Railway Tce behind grain silos
HEMA 89 F8   34 16 07 S   138 32 49 E

Notes...

SOUTH AUSTRALIA

222 Tarlee Rest Area
Rest Area 1 km N of Tarlee. 54 km S of Clare or 39 km N of Gawler
HEMA 89 F9 A32
34 16 15 S 138 45 52 E

223 Tarlee Recreation Ground
Parking Area at Tarlee. Horrocks Hwy. Honesty Box or pay at store
HEMA 89 F9
34 16 21 S 138 46 08 E

Peterborough to Port Augusta

224 Peterborough West RV Stop
☎ (08) 8651 2708
Parking Area at Peterborough, Tripney Ave, W of Steamtown Heritage Rail Centre. Self Contained Vehicles only
HEMA 89 C9
32 58 31 S 138 49 23 E

225 Willangi Bush Escapes
☎ 0427 014 215
Camp Area at Peterborough. Bookings essential. Must collect key, map & directions at the office in Peterborough, Hurlstone St extension, past the Hospital. Bond payable
HEMA 89 C9
32 59 04 S 138 49 53 E

226 Peterborough Rest Area
Rest Area 2 km E of Peterborough
HEMA 89 C9 B56
32 58 11 S 138 51 45 E

227 Black Rock South
Parking Area 15 km NW of Peterborough or 22 km SE of Orroroo
HEMA 89 B9 B56
32 51 45 S 138 44 14 E

228 Orroroo Caravan Park
☎ (08) 8658 1444
Caravan Park at Orroroo. 1 Second St
HEMA 89 B9 B56
32 43 57 S 138 36 36 E

229 Bendleby Ranges Bush Camping & Accommodation
☎ (08) 8658 9064
Camp Area 50 km N of Orroroo. Take Jonburgh Rd for 42 km, turn E onto Crotta Rd. 8 km to station. Bookings required
HEMA 89 A9
32 21 15 S 138 47 33 E

230 Orroroo Rest Area
Rest Area 8 km W of Orroroo or 5 km E of Morchard
HEMA 89 B8 B56
32 44 02 S 138 32 13 E

231 Carrieton Caravan Park
☎ (08) 8658 9090
Caravan Park at Carrieton. Fourth St
HEMA 89 A8 B80
32 25 29 S 138 31 55 E

232 Almerta Station
☎ (08) 8658 9076
Camp Area at Almerta Station. 18 km N of Carrieton or 65 km S of Hawker on the RM Williams Way. Turn W 12 km N of Carrieton onto Carrieton Quorn Rd, 6 km dirt road. Signposted
HEMA 89 A8
32 17 02 S 138 27 24 E

233 Wilmington Centenary Park
Rest Area at Wilmington. E end of town
HEMA 89 B8 B56
32 39 13 S 138 06 06 E

234 Stony Creek Bush Camp Caravan Park
☎ 0488 156 850
Caravan Park 4 km E of Wilmington, via Second St & Stony Creek Rd. 1 km dirt road
HEMA 89 B8
32 38 54 S 138 08 06 E

235 Horrocks Pass
Parking Area 7 km NW of Wilmington or 36 km SE of Port Augusta
HEMA 88 B7 B56
32 38 29 S 138 02 15 E

236 Spear Creek Caravan Park
☎ 0428 822 644
Caravan Park 25 km SE of Port Augusta. On Old Wilmington Rd
HEMA 88 B7
32 34 10 S 137 59 23 E

Adelaide to Port Augusta

237 St Kilda Adventure Park
Parking Area at St Kilda. Cockle St, check in at Tackle & Tucker Store for permit. Self Contained Vehicles only
HEMA 82 C3
34 44 31 S 138 32 00 E

238 Mallala Sports Ground
Camp Area at Mallala. Wasleys Rd. 200m E of PO. Fee for showers
HEMA 86 B1 A1
34 26 18 S 138 30 49 E

239 Port Parham Foreshore
Camp Spot at Port Parham, on the Esplanade. Limit 5 Tonne
HEMA 89 F8
34 25 34 S 138 15 20 E

240 Dublin Lions Park
Rest Area at Dublin. Old Port Wakefield Rd
HEMA 89 F8
34 27 07 S 138 21 05 E

241 Dublin North Rest Area
Rest Area 21 km N of Dublin or 14 km S of Port Wakefield. Northbound only
HEMA 89 F8 A1
34 17 29 S 138 14 30 E

242 Port Wakefield South Rest Area
Rest Area 25 km N of Dublin or 10 km S of Port Wakefield.
Southbound only
A1
HEMA 89 F8   34 15 19 S   138 13 22 E

243 Balaklava Caravan Park   ☎ 0400 264 075
Caravan Park at Balaklava. Short Tce. Next to swimming pool
HEMA 89 F8   34 08 57 S   138 25 08 E

244 Lochiel Memorial Hall
Parking Area at Lochiel. Princes Hwy next to Hotel N end of town.
Self Contained Vehicles only
HEMA 89 E8   33 55 37 S   138 09 40 E

✓245 Snowtown Centenary Park   ☎ (08) 8865 2252
Caravan Park
Caravan Park at Snowtown. North Tce. See notice board for payment
details & keys
HEMA 89 E8   33 46 42 S   138 12 59 E

246 Snowtown (North) Rest Area
Rest Area 3 km N of Snowtown or 13 km S of Lake View
A1
HEMA 89 E8   33 44 45 S   138 12 36 E

247 Redhill RV Area   ☎ (08) 8636 7020
Parking Area at Redhill. On Ellis St between railway line & Mundoora
Tce. Gold coin donation appreciated, drop at Redhill Corner Store.
Self Contained Vehicles only. Toilets 100m from site
A1
HEMA 89 D8   33 32 16 S   138 13 10 E

248 Bunyip Park
Camp Area at Koolunga. 45 km NE of Clare or 11 km SW of Red Hill.
Park at S end of town. Limited power sites. Key from garage or hotel
HEMA 89 D8   33 35 20 S   138 20 01 E

249 White Cliffs Reserve
Camp Spot 5 km E of Koolunga, via Koolunga-Yacka Rd. Dirt road
HEMA 89 D8   33 35 29 S   138 23 38 E

250 Merriton Rest Area
Rest Area 2 km N of Merriton or 8 km SW of Crystal Brook
A1
HEMA 89 D8   33 24 59 S   138 09 36 E

251 Crystal Brook Caravan Park   ☎ (08) 8636 2640
Caravan Park at Crystal Brook. Eyre Rd. 1 km N of PO
HEMA 89 D8   33 20 48 S   138 12 13 E

252 Jubilee Park
Rest Area at Crystal Brook. Railway Tce. Self Contained Vehicles only
HEMA 89 D8   33 21 13 S   138 12 23 E

253 Bowman Park
Parking Area 5 km NE of Crystalbrook, via Huddlestone Rd &
Bowman Park Dr. Self Contained Vehicles only. Donation appreciated
HEMA 89 D8   33 19 54 S   138 14 24 E

254 Rangeview Caravan & Cabin   ☎ (08) 8634 4221
Park
Caravan Park at Port Pirie. Hwy A1
A1
HEMA 88 C7   33 10 06 S   138 04 06 E

255 Port Pirie Overnight Parking   ☎ (08) 8633 9777
Area
Parking Area at Port Pirie. Warnertown Rd, E of Globe Oval, in
service lane. Self Contained Vehicles only. Limited spaces
HEMA 88 C7   33 11 14 S   138 01 43 E

256 Lawrie Park
Camp Spot 10 km NE of Port Pirie. Turn E off Port Augusta Hwy onto
Nelshaby Rd for 5 km then E onto Flinders View Dr. Signposted. Self
Contained Vehicles only
HEMA 95 K8   33 07 43 S   138 06 37 E

257 Port Germein South Rest Area 2
Rest Area 21 km N of Port Pirie turnoff or 4 km S of Port Germein
turnoff. Northbound only
A1
HEMA 88 C7   33 02 46 S   138 01 51 E

258 Port Germein South Rest Area 1
Rest Area 22 km N of Port Pirie turnoff or 3 km S of Port Germein
turnoff. Southbound only
A1
HEMA 88 C7   33 02 31 S   138 01 48 E

259 Germein Gorge
Parking Area 9 km E of Port Germein turnoff, 20 km W of Murray
Town or 17 km W of B82 Hwy jcn. 200m S along Telowie Gorge Rd
HEMA 89 C8   32 59 07 S   138 04 52 E

Notes...

260 Baroota Rodeo Ground & Camping Area ☎ 0427 878 017

Camp Area near Baroota, 6 km N of Port Germein turnoff or 14 km S of Mambray Creek Roadhouse. 1 km W of Hwy. Dirt road. Call the number if gate is locked to gain access

HEMA 88 C7   32 57 39 S   137 58 33 E

261 Mambray Creek Campground ☎ (08) 8841 3400
Mount Remarkable National Park

Camp Area 26 km NE of Port Germein. Turn E 46 km S of Port Augusta or 21 km N Port Germein. Signposted

HEMA 88 B7   32 50 26 S   138 02 14 E

262 Bird Lake

Picnic Area 4 km SE of Port Augusta. Power Station Rd

HEMA 88 A7   32 30 31 S   137 47 17 E

Gawler to Wilmington
Main North Road

263 Auburn Community Caravan Park ☎ 0417 550 781

Caravan Park at Auburn. Turn E into Ford St. Signposted

HEMA 89 E9   34 01 42 S   138 41 30 E

264 Leasingham Village Cabins & Caravan Park ☎ (08) 8843 0136

Caravan Park at Leasingham. 6 km N of Auburn or 14 km S of Clare. Main North Rd

HEMA 89 E9   33 58 56 S   138 39 01 E

265 Farrell Flat Oval

Parking Area at Farrell Flat. Entry off Cameron Tce. Self Contained Vehicles only

HEMA 89 E9   33 49 40 S   138 47 36 E

266 Farrell Flat Hotel ☎ (08) 8843 8187

Parking Area Farrell Flat. Napier St, at rear of hotel. Check in with publican, its a fee or spend in the bar

HEMA 89 E9   33 49 48 S   138 47 40 E

267 Clare Valley Racecourse ☎ (08) 8842 1033

Camp Area at Clare. Main North Rd heading N, entrance off Stradbroke Rd. Must make an advance booking to stay. Limited 10 amp power outlets

HEMA 89 E8   33 47 13 S   138 35 16 E

268 Blyth Sportsground ☎ 0428 445 218

Parking Area at Blyth. Entry off South Tce. Self Contained Vehicles only. Donation welcome

HEMA 89 E8   33 50 53 S   138 29 24 E

269 Brinkworth Travellers Overnight Stay ☎ (08) 8846 2173

Camp Area at Brinkworth. Turn E onto Edgar St. Entry off East Tce (next to entrance to the bowling club)

HEMA 89 D8   33 41 33 S   138 24 18 E

270 Yackamoorundie Park ☎ (08) 8846 4077

Camp Area at Yacka. N side of town on banks of Broughton River. Cnr of Main N Rd & North Tce. Key required, see info on gate

HEMA 89 D8   33 34 06 S   138 26 43 E

271 Gulnare Hotel ☎ (08) 8662 6202

Camp Area at Gulnare. 18 Railway Tce

HEMA 89 D8   33 28 04 S   138 26 35 E

272 James Ainsworth Horrock Monument Rest Area

Rest Area 5 km N of turnoff to Gulnare. 1.5 km S of Crystal Brook turnoff

HEMA 89 D8   33 27 34 S   138 25 58 E

273 Georgetown RV Parking Area

Parking Area at Georgetown. Memorial Playground Cnr James St & Horrocks Hwy. Self Contained Vehicles only. Donation welcomed for upkeep

HEMA 89 D8   33 21 38 S   138 23 37 E

274 Gladstone Caravan Park ☎ (08) 8662 2522

Caravan Park at Gladstone. West Tce. S side of town

HEMA 89 C8   33 16 08 S   138 21 05 E

275 Barbed Wire Pub ☎ (08) 8845 2006

Parking Area at Spalding. Area behind Pub, check in with publican on arrival during opening hours. Self Contained Vehicles only

HEMA 89 D8   33 29 49 S   138 36 29 E

276 Robinson Park ☎ (08) 8664 0070

Parking Area at Jamestown. Vohr St (RM Williams Way). Self Contained Vehicles only. Permit required from Foodland in Ayr St

HEMA 89 C9   33 12 06 S   138 36 12 E

SOUTH AUSTRALIA

277 Laura Community Caravan Park ☎ (08) 8663 2296
B82
Caravan Park at Laura. Mill St. N side of town
HEMA 89 C8   33 10 54 S   138 18 02 E

278 Ippinitchie Campground ☎ (08) 8668 5000
Camp Area 8 km SW of Wirrabara, via Wirrabara-Forest Rd. Dirt road. Permit required
HEMA 89 C8   33 04 01 S   138 13 58 E

279 Wirrabara Oval Caravan Park ☎ (08) 8668 4250
B82
Caravan Park at Wirrabara. Via Crew Rd. 400m dirt road. N end of town. Key at Wirrabara Craft House
HEMA 89 C8   33 01 51 S   138 15 53 E

280 Murray Town Park ☎ (08) 8666 4253
Camp Area at Murray Town. Main North Rd. Honesty box
HEMA 89 C8   32 56 10 S   138 14 26 E

281 Melrose Caravan Park ☎ (08) 8666 2060
B82
Caravan Park at Melrose. Joes Rd
HEMA 89 B8   32 49 30 S   138 11 11 E

282 Melrose Showground ☎ 0428 662 140
B82
Camp Area 2 km N of Melrose. Main Nth Rd
HEMA 89 B8   32 48 36 S   138 11 46 E

283 Goyder's Line Memorial
B82
Parking Area 3 km N of Melrose or 22 km S of Wilmington
HEMA 89 B8   32 48 06 S   138 12 31 E

Yorke Peninsula

284 Paskeville Oval
Camp Spot at Paskeville. Railway Tce South at oval. Fees collected. Self Contained Vehicles only. Maximum stay 14 days
HEMA 88 E7   34 02 22 S   137 54 15 E

Notes...

285 Price Caravan Park ☎ (08) 8837 6311
Caravan Park at Price. Fowler Tce
HEMA 88 F7   34 17 14 S   137 59 48 E

286 Ardrossan RV Stop
Parking Area in Ardrossan. West Tce. Self Contained Vehicles only. Park in designated bays only. Donations at information centre
HEMA 88 F7   34 25 28 S   137 54 52 E

287 Parara ☎ 1800 202 445
Camp Area 4 km S of Ardrossan. Via Yorke Hwy & Parara Rd. Camp sites are located S of the Whale Memorial. Permit Required
HEMA 88 F7   34 27 37 S   137 54 32 E

288 Pine Point Caravan Park ☎ (08) 8838 2239
Caravan Park at Pine Point. Main Coast Rd
HEMA 88 G7   34 34 28 S   137 52 40 E

289 Black Point Camping Area (Harvey Campground) ☎ (08) 8838 2239
Camp Area 4 km S of Pine Point. Black Point Rd, next to boat ramp. Caretaker collects fees
HEMA 88 G7   34 36 26 S   137 52 55 E

290 Port Julia Oval (Reichenbach Memorial Park) ☎ (08) 8853 8115
B98
Camp Spot at Port Julia, via Osprey St. Caretaker collects fees in the afternoon
HEMA 88 G7   34 39 46 S   137 52 38 E

291 Curramulka Sports Complex
Parking Area at Curramulka. Mount Rat Rd, next to the bowling club & tennis courts. Self Contained Vehicles only
HEMA 88 G7   34 41 52 S   137 42 24 E

292 Oyster Point Drive Caravan Park ☎ (08) 8852 4171
Caravan Park at Stansbury. Oyster Point Dr. 2 km S of PO
HEMA 88 G7   34 55 00 S   137 47 46 E

293 Yorketown Community Caravan Park ☎ 0499 213 605
Caravan Park at Yorketown. Memorial Dr
HEMA 88 H6   35 01 13 S   137 36 37 E

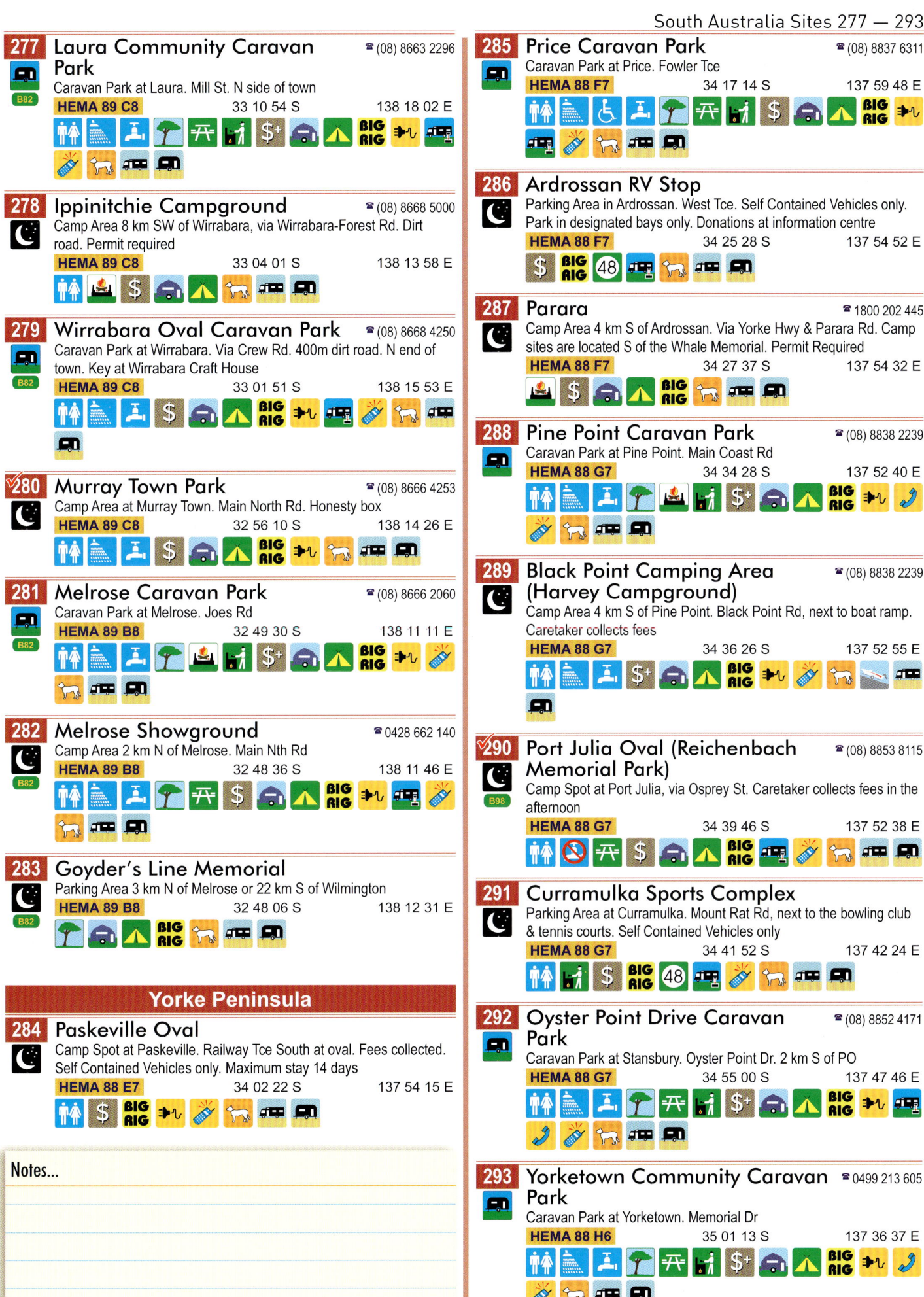

SOUTH AUSTRALIA

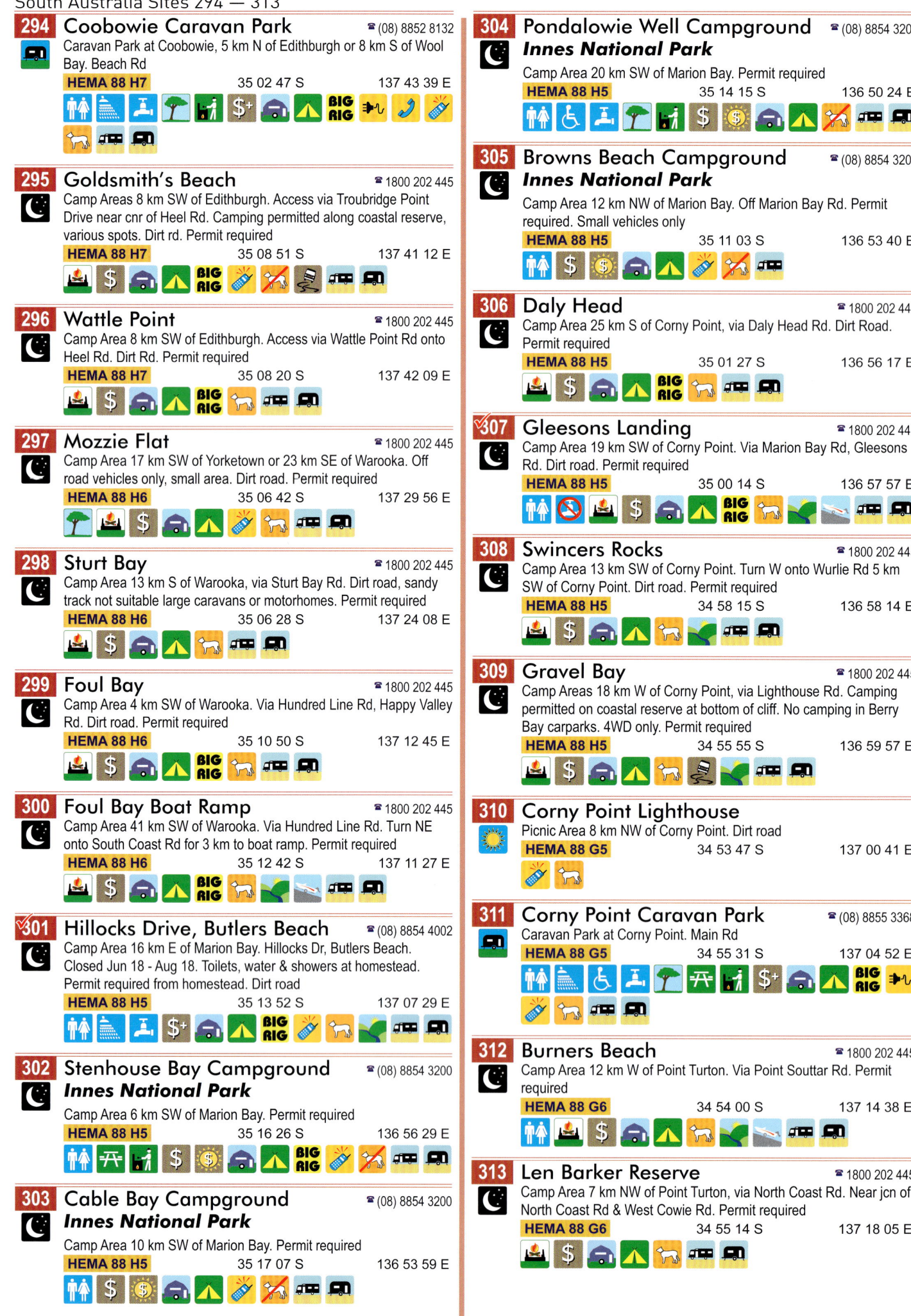

294 Coobowie Caravan Park ☎ (08) 8852 8132
Caravan Park at Coobowie, 5 km N of Edithburgh or 8 km S of Wool Bay. Beach Rd
HEMA 88 H7   35 02 47 S   137 43 39 E

295 Goldsmith's Beach ☎ 1800 202 445
Camp Areas 8 km SW of Edithburgh. Access via Troubridge Point Drive near cnr of Heel Rd. Camping permitted along coastal reserve, various spots. Dirt rd. Permit required
HEMA 88 H7   35 08 51 S   137 41 12 E

296 Wattle Point ☎ 1800 202 445
Camp Area 8 km SW of Edithburgh. Access via Wattle Point Rd onto Heel Rd. Dirt Rd. Permit required
HEMA 88 H7   35 08 20 S   137 42 09 E

297 Mozzie Flat ☎ 1800 202 445
Camp Area 17 km SW of Yorketown or 23 km SE of Warooka. Off road vehicles only, small area. Dirt road. Permit required
HEMA 88 H6   35 06 42 S   137 29 56 E

298 Sturt Bay ☎ 1800 202 445
Camp Area 13 km S of Warooka, via Sturt Bay Rd. Dirt road, sandy track not suitable large caravans or motorhomes. Permit required
HEMA 88 H6   35 06 28 S   137 24 08 E

299 Foul Bay ☎ 1800 202 445
Camp Area 4 km SW of Warooka. Via Hundred Line Rd, Happy Valley Rd. Dirt road. Permit required
HEMA 88 H6   35 10 50 S   137 12 45 E

300 Foul Bay Boat Ramp ☎ 1800 202 445
Camp Area 41 km SW of Warooka. Via Hundred Line Rd. Turn NE onto South Coast Rd for 3 km to boat ramp. Permit required
HEMA 88 H6   35 12 42 S   137 11 27 E

301 Hillocks Drive, Butlers Beach ☎ (08) 8854 4002
Camp Area 16 km E of Marion Bay. Hillocks Dr, Butlers Beach. Closed Jun 18 - Aug 18. Toilets, water & showers at homestead. Permit required from homestead. Dirt road
HEMA 88 H5   35 13 52 S   137 07 29 E

302 Stenhouse Bay Campground ☎ (08) 8854 3200
Innes National Park
Camp Area 6 km SW of Marion Bay. Permit required
HEMA 88 H5   35 16 26 S   136 56 29 E

303 Cable Bay Campground ☎ (08) 8854 3200
Innes National Park
Camp Area 10 km SW of Marion Bay. Permit required
HEMA 88 H5   35 17 07 S   136 53 59 E

304 Pondalowie Well Campground ☎ (08) 8854 3200
Innes National Park
Camp Area 20 km SW of Marion Bay. Permit required
HEMA 88 H5   35 14 15 S   136 50 24 E

305 Browns Beach Campground ☎ (08) 8854 3200
Innes National Park
Camp Area 12 km NW of Marion Bay. Off Marion Bay Rd. Permit required. Small vehicles only
HEMA 88 H5   35 11 03 S   136 53 40 E

306 Daly Head ☎ 1800 202 445
Camp Area 25 km S of Corny Point, via Daly Head Rd. Dirt Road. Permit required
HEMA 88 H5   35 01 27 S   136 56 17 E

307 Gleesons Landing ☎ 1800 202 445
Camp Area 19 km SW of Corny Point. Via Marion Bay Rd, Gleesons Rd. Dirt road. Permit required
HEMA 88 H5   35 00 14 S   136 57 57 E

308 Swincers Rocks ☎ 1800 202 445
Camp Area 13 km SW of Corny Point. Turn W onto Wurlie Rd 5 km SW of Corny Point. Dirt road. Permit required
HEMA 88 H5   34 58 15 S   136 58 14 E

309 Gravel Bay ☎ 1800 202 445
Camp Areas 18 km W of Corny Point, via Lighthouse Rd. Camping permitted on coastal reserve at bottom of cliff. No camping in Berry Bay carparks. 4WD only. Permit required
HEMA 88 H5   34 55 55 S   136 59 57 E

310 Corny Point Lighthouse
Picnic Area 8 km NW of Corny Point. Dirt road
HEMA 88 G5   34 53 47 S   137 00 41 E

311 Corny Point Caravan Park ☎ (08) 8855 3368
Caravan Park at Corny Point. Main Rd
HEMA 88 G5   34 55 31 S   137 04 52 E

312 Burners Beach ☎ 1800 202 445
Camp Area 12 km W of Point Turton. Via Point Souttar Rd. Permit required
HEMA 88 G6   34 54 00 S   137 14 38 E

313 Len Barker Reserve ☎ 1800 202 445
Camp Area 7 km NW of Point Turton, via North Coast Rd. Near jcn of North Coast Rd & West Cowie Rd. Permit required
HEMA 88 G6   34 55 14 S   137 18 05 E

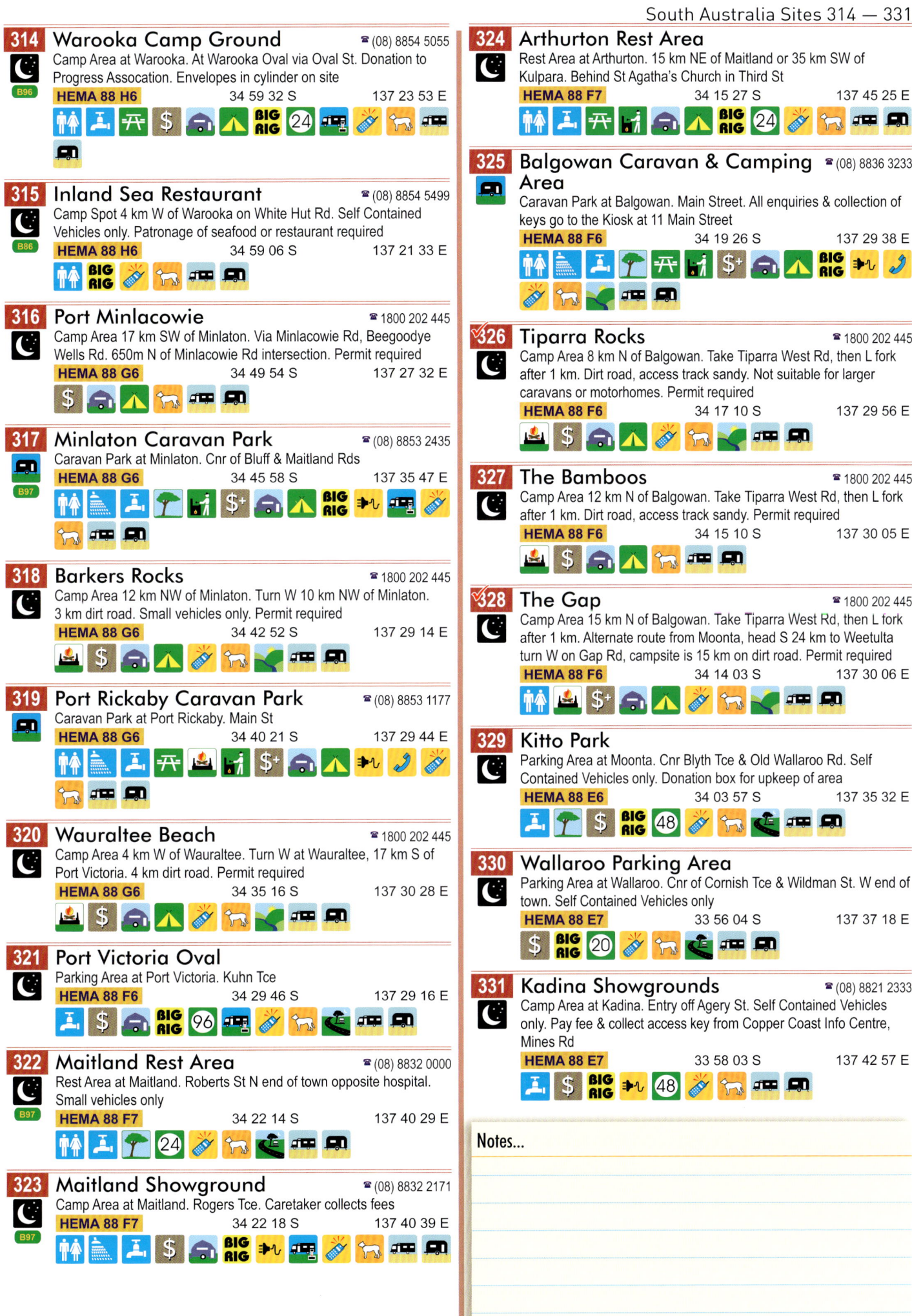

314 Warooka Camp Ground ☎ (08) 8854 5055
Camp Area at Warooka. At Warooka Oval via Oval St. Donation to Progress Assocation. Envelopes in cylinder on site
B96
HEMA 88 H6   34 59 32 S   137 23 53 E

315 Inland Sea Restaurant ☎ (08) 8854 5499
Camp Spot 4 km W of Warooka on White Hut Rd. Self Contained Vehicles only. Patronage of seafood or restaurant required
B86
HEMA 88 H6   34 59 06 S   137 21 33 E

316 Port Minlacowie ☎ 1800 202 445
Camp Area 17 km SW of Minlaton. Via Minlacowie Rd, Beegoodye Wells Rd. 650m N of Minlacowie Rd intersection. Permit required
HEMA 88 G6   34 49 54 S   137 27 32 E

317 Minlaton Caravan Park ☎ (08) 8853 2435
Caravan Park at Minlaton. Cnr of Bluff & Maitland Rds
B97
HEMA 88 G6   34 45 58 S   137 35 47 E

318 Barkers Rocks ☎ 1800 202 445
Camp Area 12 km NW of Minlaton. Turn W 10 km NW of Minlaton. 3 km dirt road. Small vehicles only. Permit required
HEMA 88 G6   34 42 52 S   137 29 14 E

319 Port Rickaby Caravan Park ☎ (08) 8853 1177
Caravan Park at Port Rickaby. Main St
HEMA 88 G6   34 40 21 S   137 29 44 E

320 Wauraltee Beach ☎ 1800 202 445
Camp Area 4 km W of Wauraltee. Turn W at Wauraltee, 17 km S of Port Victoria. 4 km dirt road. Permit required
HEMA 88 G6   34 35 16 S   137 30 28 E

321 Port Victoria Oval
Parking Area at Port Victoria. Kuhn Tce
HEMA 88 F6   34 29 46 S   137 29 16 E

322 Maitland Rest Area ☎ (08) 8832 0000
Rest Area at Maitland. Roberts St N end of town opposite hospital. Small vehicles only
B97
HEMA 88 F7   34 22 14 S   137 40 29 E

323 Maitland Showground ☎ (08) 8832 2171
Camp Area at Maitland. Rogers Tce. Caretaker collects fees
B97
HEMA 88 F7   34 22 18 S   137 40 39 E

324 Arthurton Rest Area
Rest Area at Arthurton. 15 km NE of Maitland or 35 km SW of Kulpara. Behind St Agatha's Church in Third St
HEMA 88 F7   34 15 27 S   137 45 25 E

325 Balgowan Caravan & Camping Area ☎ (08) 8836 3233
Caravan Park at Balgowan. Main Street. All enquiries & collection of keys go to the Kiosk at 11 Main Street
HEMA 88 F6   34 19 26 S   137 29 38 E

326 Tiparra Rocks ☎ 1800 202 445
Camp Area 8 km N of Balgowan. Take Tiparra West Rd, then L fork after 1 km. Dirt road, access track sandy. Not suitable for larger caravans or motorhomes. Permit required
HEMA 88 F6   34 17 10 S   137 29 56 E

327 The Bamboos ☎ 1800 202 445
Camp Area 12 km N of Balgowan. Take Tiparra West Rd, then L fork after 1 km. Dirt road, access track sandy. Permit required
HEMA 88 F6   34 15 10 S   137 30 05 E

328 The Gap ☎ 1800 202 445
Camp Area 15 km N of Balgowan. Take Tiparra West Rd, then L fork after 1 km. Alternate route from Moonta, head S 24 km to Weetulta turn W on Gap Rd, campsite is 15 km on dirt road. Permit required
HEMA 88 F6   34 14 03 S   137 30 06 E

329 Kitto Park
Parking Area at Moonta. Cnr Blyth Tce & Old Wallaroo Rd. Self Contained Vehicles only. Donation box for upkeep of area
HEMA 88 E6   34 03 57 S   137 35 32 E

330 Wallaroo Parking Area
Parking Area at Wallaroo. Cnr of Cornish Tce & Wildman St. W end of town. Self Contained Vehicles only
HEMA 88 E7   33 56 04 S   137 37 18 E

331 Kadina Showgrounds ☎ (08) 8821 2333
Camp Area at Kadina. Entry off Agery St. Self Contained Vehicles only. Pay fee & collect access key from Copper Coast Info Centre, Mines Rd
HEMA 88 E7   33 58 03 S   137 42 57 E

Notes...

SOUTH AUSTRALIA

332 Alford Community Park
Camp Area at Alford opposite tennis courts in South Tce. Donation please

HEMA 88 E7   33 49 01 S   137 49 18 E

333 Tickera North
Parking Area 4.5 km N of Tickera on the Coast Rd. Turn W to beach

HEMA 88 E7   33 45 37 S   137 43 49 E

334 Bute Caravan Park   ☎ (08) 8826 2011
Caravan Park at Bute. Railway Tce

HEMA 88 E7   33 51 57 S   138 00 22 E

335 Clement Gap Old School
Camp Spot 19.5 km NE of Port Broughton or 10.5 km SW of Merriton. Camp site in old school grounds, close to Clements Gap Conservation Park

HEMA 88 D7   33 29 45 S   138 05 04 E

Kangaroo Island

336 Antechamber Bay West Campground   ☎ (08) 8553 4444
Lashmar Conservation Park

Camp Area 17.5 km NE of Penneshaw. 5 sites. Booking & permit required

HEMA 88 K7   35 47 02 S   138 04 01 E

337 Antechamber Bay East Campground   ☎ (08) 8553 2381
Lashmar Conservation Park

Camp Area 20 km NE of Penneshaw. 5 sites. Booking & permit required

HEMA 88 K7   35 47 11 S   138 03 59 E

338 Browns Beach Campground   ☎ (08) 8553 4500
Camp Area at Browns Bay. Permit required. Self registration

HEMA 88 K7   35 47 38 S   137 51 27 E

339 D'Estrees Bay Campground   ☎ (08) 8553 4444
Cape Gantheaume Conservation Park

Camp Area in Cape Gantheaume Conservation Park. Permit required. Booking ahead essential. Dirt road

HEMA 88 K6   35 57 58 S   137 36 19 E

340 Murray Lagoon Campground   ☎ (08) 8553 2381
Cape Gantheaume Conservation Park

Camp Area in Cape Gantheaume Conservation Park. Permit required. Booking ahead essential

HEMA 88 K6   35 55 26 S   137 33 40 E

341 Vivonne Bay Campground   ☎ (08) 8553 4500
Camp Area at Vivonne Bay. Self registration. Some powered sites

HEMA 88 K6   35 59 04 S   137 10 37 E

342 Parndana Hotel   ☎ (08) 8559 6071
Camp Area at Parndana. Cnr Wedgwood Rd & Cook St

HEMA 88 K6   35 47 27 S   137 15 51 E

343 Rocky River Camping Area   ☎ (08) 8553 4470
Flinders Chase National Park

Camp Area at Rocky River. 300m S of Visitor Information Centre. Bookings essential

HEMA 88 K5   35 57 11 S   136 44 07 E

344 Western River Cove   ☎ (08) 8553 4500
Camp Area at Western River Cove. Via Western River Cove Rd, 29 km W of Parndana. Dirt road. Steep in places. Small vehicles only. Self registration

HEMA 88 J5   35 40 40 S   136 58 18 E

345 Stokes Bay   ☎ (08) 8559 2277
Camp Area at Stokes Bay. Via Stokes Bay Rd, 4 km W of Parndana. Behind café, check-in & pay at café

HEMA 88 J6   35 37 30 S   137 12 23 E

346 Discovery Lagoon Camping Grounds   ☎ (08) 8553 5220
Camp Area 3 km S of Emu Bay or 12 W of Kingscote. 948 North Coast Rd

HEMA 88 J6   35 37 25 S   137 31 23 E

347 American River Campground   ☎ (08) 8553 4500
Camp Area at American River. Permit required. Self registration. Small vehicles only

HEMA 88 K7   35 47 15 S   137 46 14 E

Notes...

Port Augusta to Birdsville

348 Woolshed Flat
Parking Area 16 km N of Stirling North or 18 km S of Quorn
HEMA 94 H7   32 27 45 S   137 58 07 E

349 Warren Gorge   ☎ (08) 8648 6031
Camp Area 21 km N of Quorn, via Arden Vale Rd. Dirt road last 8 km
HEMA 94 G7   32 10 57 S   138 00 26 E

350 Argadells Homestead   ☎ (08) 8648 6246
Camp Area 25 km N of Quorn, via Arden Vale Rd. Bookings essential. Dirt road
HEMA 94 G7   32 08 20 S   138 02 25 E

351 Cradock Hotel
Parking Area at Cradock. 27 km SE of Hawker or 43 km N of Carrieton. Free camp with a beer. Gold coin donation for showers
HEMA 95 G8   32 04 10 S   138 29 36 E

352 Hawker Town Park
Rest Area at Hawker. Elder Tce
HEMA 95 G8   31 53 15 S   138 25 16 E

353 Flinders Bush Retreats - Willow Waters Gorge Bush Camping   ☎ (08) 8648 4441
Camp Area 20 km E of Hawker. Take Cradock Rd for 7.4 km then signposted road to Willow Waters. Follow road for 6 km, turn L at first house on L. Pre-booking essential
HEMA 95 G9   31 54 27 S   138 33 41 E

354 Nooltana Creek Parking Area
Parking Area 13 km N of Hawker or 76 km S of Parachilna
HEMA 95 F8   31 48 33 S   138 22 01 E

355 Hookina Creek
Rest Area 18 km N of Hawker or 71 km S of Parachilna, near Wonoka Ruins. Entrance track 500m N of creek crossing. GPS at entrance track
HEMA 95 F8   31 45 26 S   138 19 57 E

356 Merna Mora Station   ☎ (08) 8648 4717
Camp Area Merna Mora Station. 47 km N of Hawker. 3 km W off the Hwy opposite the Moralana Scenic Dr
HEMA 95 F8   31 32 46 S   138 23 28 E

357 Parachilna Campground   ☎ (08) 8648 4895
Camp Area at Parachilna. Payment & keys at Prairie Hotel if no caretaker onsite
HEMA 95 E8   31 07 52 S   138 23 42 E

358 Beltana Station   ☎ (08) 8675 2256
Camp Area at Beltana Station. 10 km E of Beltana Roadhouse. Pets permitted only with prior authorisation. Honesty box for fees. Two camp areas, bush camping & powered sites at the Woolshed
HEMA 95 D8   30 49 18 S   138 22 17 E

359 Warraweena Conservation Park   ☎ (08) 8675 2770
Camp Area at Warraweena. 35 km E of Beltana Roadhouse. Pets permitted only with prior authorisation. Must call at homestead prior to camping. Dirt road
HEMA 95 D9   30 46 04 S   138 38 12 E

360 Leigh Creek Junction
Parking Area at Leigh Creek
HEMA 95 C8   30 35 47 S   138 24 13 E

361 Leigh Creek Caravan Park   ☎ 0429 012 445
Caravan Park at Leigh Creek. Acacia Dr
HEMA 95 C8   30 35 17 S   138 24 29 E

362 Iga-Warta Community Campground   ☎ (08) 8648 3737
Camp Area at Iga-Warta. 62 km E of Copley. Bookings required. Dirt road
HEMA 95 C9   30 35 45 S   138 56 05 E

363 Italowie Gap Campground   ☎ (08) 8648 5300
Vulkathunha-Gammon Ranges National Park
Camp Area 22 km E of Nepabunna or 17 km W of the Park HQ, via the Copley - Arkaroola Rd. Self registration required
HEMA 95 C10   30 33 22 S   139 10 11 E

364 Weetootla Gorge Campground   ☎ (08) 8648 5300
Vulkathunha-Gammon Ranges National Park
Camp Area 110 km W of Copley. Turn N at Balcanoona into Arkaroola Rd, turn W 2.3 km N of Balcanoona. 4.5 km to campsites. Small vehicles only. Self registration required
HEMA 95 C10   30 29 49 S   139 15 33 E

Notes...

SOUTH AUSTRALIA

365 Grindells Hut Campground
☎ (08) 8648 5300

Vulkathunha-Gammon Ranges National Park

Camp Area 118 km W of Copley. Turn N 9.3 km N of Balcanoona into Arkaroola Rd, camp site is 17 km along this road. 4WD & camper trailers only

HEMA 95 C10   30 28 30 S   139 12 51 E

366 Chambers Gorge

Camp Area 27 km NE of Wirrealpa. 4WD recommended

HEMA 95 D10   30 57 12 S   139 12 53 E

367 Arkaroola Wilderness Sanctuary
☎ (08) 8648 4848

Camp Area at Arkaroola.130 km E of Leigh Creek. Bush camping also available

HEMA 95 C10   30 18 42 S   139 20 10 E

368 Lyndhurst Hotel Motel
☎ (08) 8675 7781

Camp Area at Lyndhurst

B47

HEMA 95 C8   30 17 16 S   138 21 08 E

369 Farina Station Campground
☎ (08) 8675 7790

Camp Area at Farina Station. 26 km N of Lyndhurst. Turn W 25 km N of Lyndhurst or 56 km S of Marree. Signposted

HEMA 95 B8   30 03 41 S   138 16 22 E

370 Oasis Caravan Park
☎ (08) 8675 8352

Caravan Park at Marree. Railway Tce South

1

HEMA 91 K8   29 38 49 S   138 03 46 E

371 Marree Hotel
☎ (08) 8675 8344

Camp Spot at Marree. Fee for showers

HEMA 91 K8   29 38 54 S   138 03 52 E

372 Drovers Run Tourist Park
☎ (08) 8675 8248

Caravan Park at Marree. Cnr Birdsville Track & Oodnadatta Track

HEMA 91 K8   29 39 11 S   138 04 25 E

Notes...

Birdsville to Marree

Birdsville Track

This road is seasonal and more suitable to 4WD vehicles, camper trailers and off road caravans. Road conditions phone 1300 361 033

373 Lake Harry Ruins

Camp Spot 38 km NE of Marree or 168 km SW of Mungerannie Roadhouse

HEMA 91 K8   29 26 03 S   138 14 46 E

374 Clayton Station
☎ (08) 8675 8311

Camp Area at Clayton Station. 54 km NE of Marree or 152 km S of Mungerannie Roadhouse. Honesty box by toilets

HEMA 91 J8   29 16 32 S   138 22 17 E

375 Cooper Creek
☎ (08) 8675 9591

Camp Area 146 km NE of Marree or 60 km S of Mungerannie Roadhouse

HEMA 91 H9   28 37 25 S   138 42 36 E

376 Mungerannie Hotel
☎ (08) 8675 8317

Camp Area at Mungerannie, 206 km NE of Marree or 308 km SW of Birdsville. Beside Derwent River

HEMA 91 F9   28 01 07 S   138 39 47 E

377 Cowarie Station
☎ (08) 8675 8304

Camp Area at Cowarie Station. 51 km NW of Mungerannie Hotel. Bookings essential

HEMA 91 E8   27 42 06 S   138 20 08 E

378 Tippipila Creek Bush Camp

Camp Spot 134 km N of Mungerannie or 181 km S of Birdsville

HEMA 91 C10   26 59 42 S   139 01 01 E

Marree to Marla

Oodnadatta Track

This road is seasonal and more suitable to 4WD vehicles, camper trailers and off road caravans. Road conditions phone 1300 361 033

379 Muloorina Station
☎ (08) 8675 8386

Camp Area at Muloorina Station. 54 km NW of Marree. Turn N off Oodnadatta Track 2 km W of Maree. Honesty box

HEMA 90 J7   29 14 20 S   137 54 23 E

380 Curdimurka Railway Siding

Parking Area 104 km W of Marree or 100 km SE of William Creek. Parking around the ruins

HEMA 90 K6   29 28 36 S   137 05 04 E

381 Coward Springs Campground ☎ (08) 8675 8336
Camp Area 131 km W of Marree or 73 km SE of William Creek
HEMA 90 J5   29 24 14 S   136 48 44 E

382 Beresford Siding
Parking Area 154 km W of Marree or 50 km SE of William Creek
HEMA 90 J5   29 14 34 S   136 39 23 E

383 Strangways Siding
Parking Area 167 km W of Marree or 37 km SE of William Creek
HEMA 90 J5   29 09 23 S   136 34 21 E

384 Halligan Bay Campground ☎ (08) 8648 5300
Kati Thanda - Lake Eyre National Park
Camp Area at Halligan Bay. Turn N 7 km SE of William Creek onto
Halligan Bay access track (57 km). High clearance 4WD only. Check
conditions, desert pass required
HEMA 90 H5   28 45 49 S   136 56 23 E

385 William Creek Camping Ground ☎ (08) 8670 7880
Camp Area at William Creek Hotel
HEMA 90 H4   28 54 28 S   136 20 18 E

386 Warrina Siding
Parking Area 108 km NW of William Creek or 95 km S of Oodnadatta
HEMA 90 F3   28 11 38 S   135 49 42 E

387 Peake Creek Siding
Parking Area 130 km NW of William Creek or 73 km S of Oodnadatta
HEMA 90 F3   28 01 33 S   135 48 15 E

388 Algebuckina Bridge, Neals Creek
Camp Spot 145 km NW of William Creek or 58 km S of Oodnadatta
HEMA 90 F3   27 54 06 S   135 48 37 E

389 Mt Dutton Siding
Parking Area 160 km NW of William Creek or 43 km S of Oodnadatta
HEMA 90 E3   27 48 56 S   135 43 37 E

390 North Creek
Camp Spot 175 km NW of William Creek or 28 km S of Oodnadatta,
N side of road by old railway bridge
HEMA 90 E3   27 44 15 S   135 36 15 E

391 Arckaringa Station ☎ (08) 8670 7992
Camp Area at Arckaringa Station. 140 km N of Coober Pedy or 86 km
SW of Oodnadatta
HEMA 90 F1   27 56 12 S   134 44 18 E

392 The Pink Roadhouse Caravan Park ☎ (08) 8670 7822
Caravan Park at Oodnadatta. Behind the roadhouse
HEMA 90 E2   27 32 56 S   135 26 53 E

393 Oodnadatta Town Camp
Camp Spot at Oodnadatta. Opposite Health Service
HEMA 90 E2   27 32 42 S   135 26 48 E

394 Mt Dare Hotel ☎ (08) 8670 7835
Camp Area at Mt Dare. 75 km SE of Finke or 70 km NW of Dalhousie
Springs
HEMA 90 A2   26 04 10 S   135 14 52 E

395 Dalhousie Springs Campground ☎ (08) 8648 5328
Witjira National Park
Camp Area at Dalhousie Springs 183 km NE of Oodnadatta or
68 km S of Mt Dare Hotel. Turn N 18 km from Oodnadatta, 91 km
to Hamilton HS then turn NE 71 km to Dalhousie. Turn E 3 km. Dirt
road. 4WD only
HEMA 90 B2   26 25 23 S   135 30 13 E

396 Purni Bore ☎ (08) 8648 5328
Witjira National Park
Camp Area 248 km NE of Oodnadatta or 65 km E of Dalhousie
Springs. Campground on the Spring Creek Track. Dirt road. 4WD
only. Desert Parks Pass required
HEMA 90 B4   26 17 03 S   136 05 54 E

397 3 O'Clock Creek Campground ☎ (08) 8648 5328
Witjira National Park
Camp Area 183 km NE of Oodnadatta or 58 km S of Mt Dare Hotel.
Turn N 18 km from Oodnadatta, 91 km to Hamilton HS then turn NE
71 km to Dalhousie. Turn W 3 km. Dirt road. 4WD only
HEMA 90 B2   26 27 34 S   135 24 41 E

398 Kathleen Creek
Camp Spot 89 km NW of Oodnadatta or 129 km E of Marla. Tracks
along creek
HEMA 90 D1   27 12 17 S   134 45 13 E

399 Olarinna Creek
Camp Spot 104 km NW of Oodnadatta or 114 km E of Marla. Turn N
on W side of creek, follow track
HEMA 90 D1   27 09 48 S   134 37 09 E

Ikara-Flinders Ranges National Park

400 Wilpena Pound Resort
☎ (08) 8648 0048

Camp Area at Wilpena. Bookings taken at Visitor Centre or Resort

HEMA 95 F9   31 31 37 S   138 36 23 E

401 Willow Springs Station
☎ (08) 8648 0016

Camp Area at Willow Springs Station. 21 km NE of Wilpena. Some dirt road

HEMA 95 E9   31 26 56 S   138 45 32 E

402 Dingly Dell Campground
☎ (08) 8648 0049

Ikara-Flinders Ranges National Park

Camp Area 28 km N of Wilpena, on Blinman Rd. Signposted

HEMA 95 E9   31 21 19 S   138 42 20 E

403 Youngoona Campground
☎ (08) 8648 0048

Ikara-Flinders Ranges National Park

Camp Area 36 km N of Wilpena. Turn W 33 km N of Wilpena turnoff or 29 km S of Blinman onto Brachina Gorge Geological Trail for 3 km. Dirt road. 4 sites only

HEMA 95 E9   31 19 51 S   138 39 21 E

404 Trezona Campground
☎ (08) 8648 0048

Ikara-Flinders Ranges National Park

Camp Area 45 km N of Wilpena. Turn W 33 km N of Wilpena onto Brachina Gorge Geological Trail for 6 km, then turn N. Dirt road

HEMA 95 E9   31 19 51 S   138 37 42 E

405 Brachina East Campground
☎ (08) 8648 0048

Ikara-Flinders Ranges National Park

Camp Area 38 km NW of Wilpena. Turn W 5 km N of Wilpena turnoff onto Bunyeroo Valley Scenic Dr. Then turn W at T-intersection of Brachina Gorge Rd for 1 km. Dirt road

HEMA 95 E9   31 20 01 S   138 34 46 E

406 Teamsters Campground
☎ (08) 8648 0048

Ikara-Flinders Ranges National Park

Camp Area 42 km NW of Wilpena. Turn W 5 km N of Wilpena turnoff onto Bunyeroo Valley Scenic Dr. Then turn W at T-intersection of Brachina Gorge Rd for 4.5 km. Dirt road

HEMA 95 E9   31 20 18 S   138 32 59 E

407 Koolamon Campground
☎ (08) 8648 0048

Ikara-Flinders Ranges National Park

Camp Area 53 km N of Wilpena. Turn W 33 km N of Wilpena turnoff or 29 km S of Blinman onto Brachina Geological Trail for 10 km. Then turn N onto Aroona Rd for 4.6 km. Dirt road

HEMA 95 E9   31 17 32 S   138 35 08 E

408 Aroona Ruins Campground
☎ (08) 8648 0048

Ikara-Flinders Ranges National Park

Camp Area 54 km N of Wilpena. Turn W 33 km N of Wilpena turnoff or 29 km S of Blinman onto Brachina Geological Trail for 10 km. Then turn N onto Aroona Rd for 6 km. Dirt road

HEMA 95 E9   31 16 45 S   138 34 45 E

409 Cambrian Campground
☎ (08) 8648 0048

Ikara-Flinders Ranges National Park

Camp Area 33 km NW of Wilpena. Turn W 5 km N of Wilpena turnoff onto Bunyeroo Valley Scenic Dr. Dirt road

HEMA 95 E9   31 21 26 S   138 34 57 E

410 Acraman Campground
☎ (08) 8648 0048

Ikara-Flinders Ranges National Park

Camp Area 28 km NW of Wilpena. Turn W 5 km N of Wilpena turnoff onto Bunyeroo Valley Scenic Dr. Dirt road. 4 sites only. Not suitable caravans

HEMA 95 E9   31 24 35 S   138 33 42 E

411 Alpana Station
☎ (08) 8648 4626

Camp Area at Alpana Station. 59 km N of Wilpena Pound or 5 km S of Blinman off Wilpena Rd

HEMA 95 E9   31 08 25 S   138 41 04 E

412 Blinman Hotel
☎ (08) 8648 4867

Camp Area 59 km N of Wilpena or 32 km E of Parachilna, at hotel. Dirt road from Parachilna

HEMA 95 E9   31 05 37 S   138 40 40 E

413 Angorichina Station
☎ (07) 8648 4863

Camp Area at Angorichina Station. 9 km E of Blinman turn E approx 2.2 km S of Blinman into N Flinders Rd. Bookings essential. Pets on request

HEMA 95 E9   31 05 42 S   138 44 25 E

414 Moolooloo Station
☎ (08) 8648 4861

Camp Area at Moolooloo Station. 21 km NW of Blinman. Glass Gorge Rd. Variety of sites. Bookings essential

HEMA 95 D9   30 59 24 S   138 34 42 E

415 Angorichina Tourist Village
☎ (08) 8648 4842

Camp Area 17 km E of Parachilna or 16 km W of Blinman

HEMA 95 E9   31 07 35 S   138 33 39 E

SOUTH AUSTRALIA

416 Parachilna Gorge
Camp Area 10 km E of Parachilna. Various sites on riverbank
HEMA 95 E8   31 08 06 S   138 31 48 E

Port Augusta to Kulgera
Stuart Highway

417 North Tent Hill Rest Area
Rest Area 35 km NW of Port Augusta or 136 km SE of Pimba
HEMA 94 G6   32 14 30 S   137 32 45 E
A87

418 Ranges View Rest Area
Rest Area 62 km NW of Port Augusta or 108 km SE of Pimba
HEMA 94 G6   32 02 02 S   137 26 42 E
A87

419 Bookaloo Rest Area
Rest Area 79 km NW of Port Augusta or 91 km SE of Pimba
HEMA 94 F6   31 52 31 S   137 20 52 E
A87

420 Maslin Rest Area
Rest Area 94 km NW of Port Augusta or 76 km SE of Pimba
HEMA 94 F6   31 46 25 S   137 17 23 E
A87

421 Monalena Lagoon Rest Area
Rest Area 102 km NW of Port Augusta or 68 km SE of Pimba
HEMA 94 F6   31 43 06 S   137 13 47 E
A87

422 Island Lagoon Lookout
Rest Area 153 km NW of Port Augusta or 17 km SE of Pimba
HEMA 94 E5   31 22 45 S   136 55 24 E
A87

423 Pimba Roadhouse Rest Area
Rest Area at Pimba, adjacent to the roadhouse. Showers (cold) available for a fee
HEMA 94 E5   31 15 23 S   136 48 16 E
A87

424 Roxby Downs
Camp Spot 1.8 km E of Roxby Downs & Andamooka Turnoff. Large open bush area with many tracks
HEMA 94 C5   30 32 50 S   136 56 24 E
B97

425 Roxby Downs South
Parking Area 2 km S of Roxby Downs
HEMA 94 C5   30 34 30 S   136 53 38 E

426 Apoma Camping Ground   ☎ (08) 8672 7023
Camp Area at Andamooka, Water Way. Honesty box for donation
HEMA 94 C6   30 27 11 S   137 09 39 E

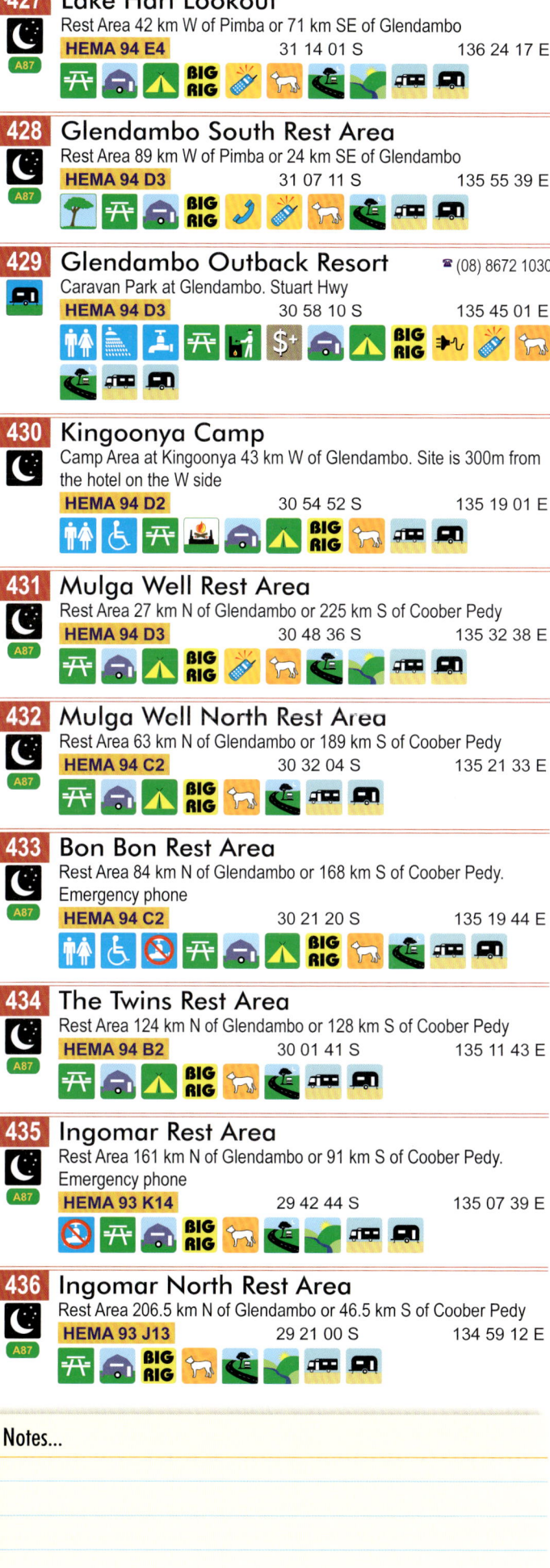

427 Lake Hart Lookout
Rest Area 42 km W of Pimba or 71 km SE of Glendambo
HEMA 94 E4   31 14 01 S   136 24 17 E
A87

428 Glendambo South Rest Area
Rest Area 89 km W of Pimba or 24 km SE of Glendambo
HEMA 94 D3   31 07 11 S   135 55 39 E
A87

429 Glendambo Outback Resort   ☎ (08) 8672 1030
Caravan Park at Glendambo. Stuart Hwy
HEMA 94 D3   30 58 10 S   135 45 01 E

430 Kingoonya Camp
Camp Area at Kingoonya 43 km W of Glendambo. Site is 300m from the hotel on the W side
HEMA 94 D2   30 54 52 S   135 19 01 E

431 Mulga Well Rest Area
Rest Area 27 km N of Glendambo or 225 km S of Coober Pedy
HEMA 94 D3   30 48 36 S   135 32 38 E
A87

432 Mulga Well North Rest Area
Rest Area 63 km N of Glendambo or 189 km S of Coober Pedy
HEMA 94 C2   30 32 04 S   135 21 33 E
A87

433 Bon Bon Rest Area
Rest Area 84 km N of Glendambo or 168 km S of Coober Pedy. Emergency phone
HEMA 94 C2   30 21 20 S   135 19 44 E
A87

434 The Twins Rest Area
Rest Area 124 km N of Glendambo or 128 km S of Coober Pedy
HEMA 94 B2   30 01 41 S   135 11 43 E
A87

435 Ingomar Rest Area
Rest Area 161 km N of Glendambo or 91 km S of Coober Pedy. Emergency phone
HEMA 93 K14   29 42 44 S   135 07 39 E
A87

436 Ingomar North Rest Area
Rest Area 206.5 km N of Glendambo or 46.5 km S of Coober Pedy
HEMA 93 J13   29 21 00 S   134 59 12 E
A87

Notes...

South Australia Sites 437 — 454

437 Hutchison Memorial
Parking Area 240 km N of Glendambo or 12 km S of Coober Pedy.
Fireplace on lower level
A87
HEMA 93 J13   29 04 30 S   134 51 12 E

438 William Creek Road
Parking Area 10 km E of Coober Pedy on William Creek Rd. Dirt road
HEMA 93 H13   29 02 03 S   134 49 20 E

439 The Clothes Barn
Parking Area at Coober Pedy. Marquardt Rd, see caretaker on arrival.
Limited space
HEMA 93 H13   28 59 59 S   134 45 23 E

440 Venushill B&B   ☎ (08) 8672 3060
Camp Area at Coober Pedy. Lot 1528 Amorosi Dr, via Seventeen Mile
Rd. Call prior to arrival
HEMA 93 H13   29 00 09 S   134 43 27 E

441 Breakaways Lookout
Parking Area 31 km N of Coober Pedy. Turn E 22 km N of Coober
Pedy or 128 km S of Cadney Roadhouse. 9 km of dirt road
HEMA 93 H13   28 50 44 S   134 42 27 E

442 Pootnoura Rest Area
Rest Area 75 km N of Coober Pedy or 75 km S of Cadney
Roadhouse. Emergency phone
A87
HEMA 93 G12   28 33 17 S   134 15 19 E

443 Evelyn Downs Rest Area
Rest Area 90 km N of Coober Pedy or 60 km S of Cadney Roadhouse
A87
HEMA 93 G12   28 25 32 S   134 11 07 E

444 Mathesons Bore
Parking Area 110 km N of Coober Pedy or 40 km S of Cadney
Roadhouse
A87
HEMA 93 G12   28 15 29 S   134 09 04 E

445 Cadney Homestead Caravan Park   ☎ (08) 8670 7994
Caravan Park at Cadney Roadhouse
HEMA 93 F12   27 54 18 S   134 03 24 E

446 Marla South Rest Area
Rest Area 46 km NW of Cadney Roadhouse or 35 km SE of Marla
A87
HEMA 93 E11   27 33 21 S   133 49 13 E

447 Marla Travellers Rest Caravan Park   ☎ (08) 8670 7001
Caravan Park at Marla. Stuart Hwy
HEMA 93 D11   27 18 15 S   133 37 20 E

448 Tarcoonyinna Rest Area
Rest Area 53 km N of Marla or 125 km S of Kulgera
A87
HEMA 93 C10   26 53 47 S   133 22 51 E

449 Agnes Creek Rest Area
Rest Area 85 km N of Marla or 93 km S of Kulgera
A87
HEMA 93 B10   26 38 14 S   133 16 45 E

450 The Marryat Rest Area
Rest Area 120 km N of Marla, 39 km S of NT Border or 58 km S of
Kulgera. Emergency phone
A87
HEMA 93 B10   26 20 29 S   133 12 04 E

451 Marryat Creek North Rest Area
Rest Area 128 km N of Marla or 31 km S of NT Border. 52 km S of
Kulgera
A87
HEMA 93 A10   26 16 42 S   133 11 20 E

Eyre Peninsula
Lincoln and Flinders Highways

452 Half Way Rest Area
Rest Area 40 km S of Port Augusta or 34 km N of Whyalla. Both sides
of Hwy
B100
HEMA 88 B6   32 43 33 S   137 30 38 E

453 Shingles Beach Ridges   ☎ (08) 8645 7900
Camp Area at Fitzgerald Bay. Turn E off B100 onto Port Bonython
Rd, 65 km SW of Port Augusta or 8 km N of Whyalla, then N after
16 km to the end of bitumen. Turn L, then 2 km dirt road. Site on R.
Signposted
HEMA 88 B7   32 55 17 S   137 44 57 E

454 Fitzgerald Bay Bush Camp
Camp Area at Fitzgerald Bay. Turn E off B100 onto Port Bonython Rd,
65 km SW of Port Augusta or 8 km N of Whyalla, then N after 16 km
to the end of bitumen. Turn L, then 3.7 km dirt road. Track on R.
Signposted. Limited space, small vehicles only
HEMA 88 B7   32 54 25 S   137 45 18 E

Notes...

455 Point Lowly
☎ (08) 8645 7900

Camp Area at Point Lowly, 35 km NE of Whyalla. Turn E off B100, 65 km SW of Port Augusta or 8 km N of Whyalla onto Point Lowly Rd. Adjacent to toilet block, near boat ramp. Dump Point 500m N campsite. Maximum stay 14 days

HEMA 88 C7 · 32 59 34 S · 137 46 51 E

456 Stuart Park (Weeroona Bay Football Club)
☎ 0458 600 036

Camp Area at Whyalla. 8 km W of PO. Access off Cartledge Ave via McDouall Stuart Ave. Self Contained Vehicles only. Caretaker will collect fee

HEMA 88 C6 · 33 01 54 S · 137 30 50 E

457 Hancocks Shaft Rest Area

Rest Area 49 km S of Whyalla or 57 km N of Cowell

HEMA 88 C6 · 33 15 55 S · 137 12 34 E

458 Cowell RV Park

Camp Area at Cowell. Wellington Rd, S end of town. Self Contained Vehicles only. Dump Point is at Brooks Dr

HEMA 88 D5 · 33 41 40 S · 136 55 20 E

✓459 The Knob Beach Park Area

Parking Area 19 km S of Cowell, via Beach Rd or via Port Gibbon. Rough corrugated dirt road

HEMA 88 E5 · 33 48 00 S · 136 50 44 E

460 Port Gibbon Foreshore
☎ (08) 8629 2019

Rest Area at Port Gibbon Foreshore. Access from B100 at Port Gibbon sign, through Igloo Rd. 6 km dirt road. $5 fee at Honesty box

HEMA 88 E5 · 33 48 07 S · 136 48 06 E

461 Yeldulknie Weir

Picnic Area 37 km W of Cowell or 5 km E of Cleve. Donation requested

HEMA 88 D4 · 33 41 35 S · 136 32 39 E

462 Cleve Showgrounds
☎ (08) 8628 2004

Camp Area at Cleve. Rudall Rd

HEMA 88 D4 · 33 42 03 S · 136 29 26 E

463 Cleve Hotel
☎ (08) 8628 2011

Parking Area at Cleve. 32 Fourth St, check in with publican. Self Contained Vehicles only

HEMA 88 D4 · 33 42 12 S · 136 29 37 E

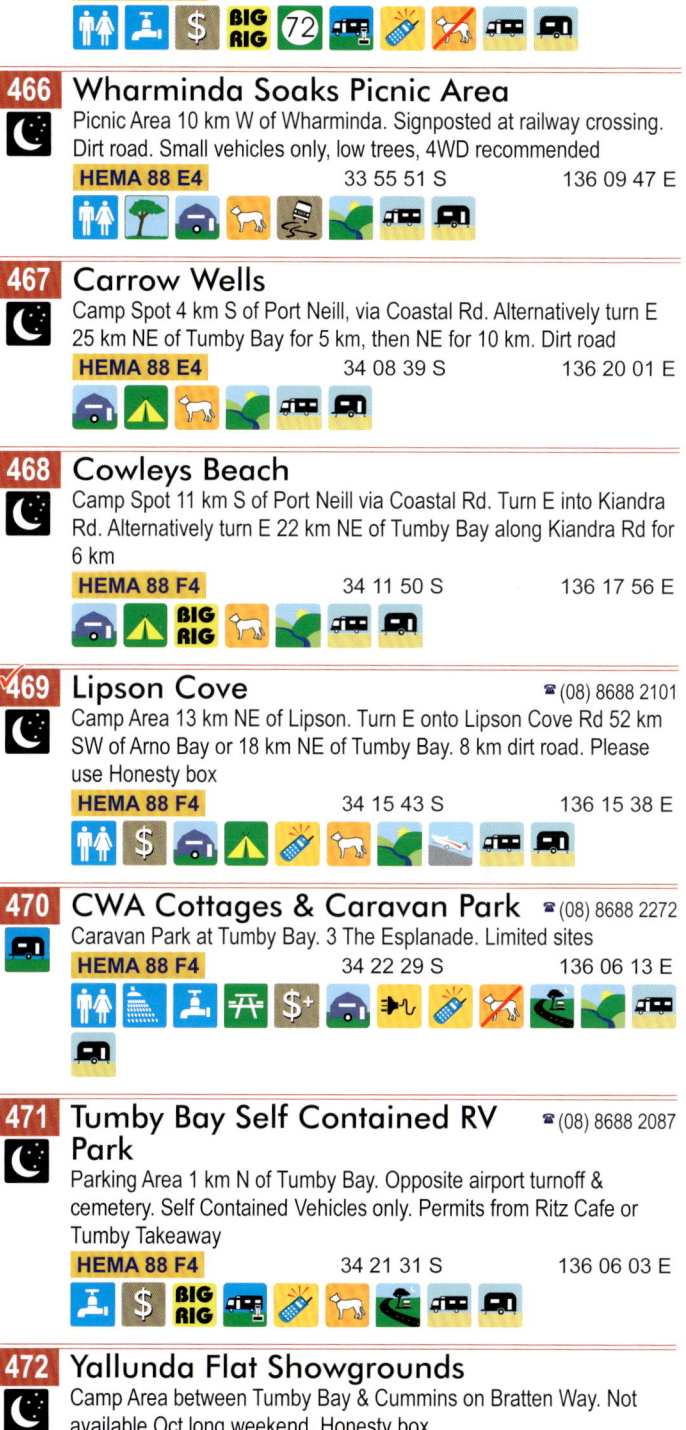

464 Birdseye Roadhouse Caravan Park
☎ (08) 8628 2019

Caravan Park at Cleve. 1 Cowell Rd

HEMA 88 D4 · 33 42 08 S · 136 29 59 E

465 The Arno Bay Hotel
☎ (08) 8628 0001

Parking Area at Arno Bay. Tel El Kebir Tce, foreshore end. Parking at rear of hotel, check in at hotel for payment. Self Contained Vehicles only

HEMA 88 E4 · 33 54 59 S · 136 34 22 E

466 Wharminda Soaks Picnic Area

Picnic Area 10 km W of Wharminda. Signposted at railway crossing. Dirt road. Small vehicles only, low trees, 4WD recommended

HEMA 88 E4 · 33 55 51 S · 136 09 47 E

467 Carrow Wells

Camp Spot 4 km S of Port Neill, via Coastal Rd. Alternatively turn E 25 km NE of Tumby Bay for 5 km, then NE for 10 km. Dirt road

HEMA 88 E4 · 34 08 39 S · 136 20 01 E

468 Cowleys Beach

Camp Spot 11 km S of Port Neill via Coastal Rd. Turn E into Kiandra Rd. Alternatively turn E 22 km NE of Tumby Bay along Kiandra Rd for 6 km

HEMA 88 F4 · 34 11 50 S · 136 17 56 E

✓469 Lipson Cove
☎ (08) 8688 2101

Camp Area 13 km NE of Lipson. Turn E onto Lipson Cove Rd 52 km SW of Arno Bay or 18 km NE of Tumby Bay. 8 km dirt road. Please use Honesty box

HEMA 88 F4 · 34 15 43 S · 136 15 38 E

470 CWA Cottages & Caravan Park
☎ (08) 8688 2272

Caravan Park at Tumby Bay. 3 The Esplanade. Limited sites

HEMA 88 F4 · 34 22 29 S · 136 06 13 E

471 Tumby Bay Self Contained RV Park
☎ (08) 8688 2087

Parking Area 1 km N of Tumby Bay. Opposite airport turnoff & cemetery. Self Contained Vehicles only. Permits from Ritz Cafe or Tumby Takeaway

HEMA 88 F4 · 34 21 31 S · 136 06 03 E

472 Yallunda Flat Showgrounds

Camp Area between Tumby Bay & Cummins on Bratten Way. Not available Oct long weekend. Honesty box

HEMA 88 F3 · 34 20 51 S · 135 52 49 E

SOUTH AUSTRALIA

473 Louth Bay
☎ (08) 8676 0400
Camp Area 27 km SW of Tumby Bay. Turn E 25 km SW of Tumby Bay or 21 km N of Port Lincoln for 2 km. First L past golf club. Only 5 sites
HEMA 88 F3   34 32 30 S   135 55 47 E

474 McKechnie Springs Farmstay
☎ 0421 062 697
Camp Area 12 km NW of Port Lincoln. Head W on Flinders Hwy, turn N onto Wine Shanty Rd, then onto Green Patch Rd. Continue along Greenpatch Rd then turn NE onto McFarlane Rd. At Y intersection veer R. Entrance 200m from the Y jcn. 12 km dirt road. Minimum 2 night stay
HEMA 88 G3   34 35 23 S   135 46 22 E

475 Axel Stenross Boat Ramp
☎ 1300 788 378
Parking Area in Port Lincoln. N end of town. Upper car park only, limited turning space. Motorhomes only, must be self contained. Permit required
HEMA 88 G3   34 42 14 S   135 51 14 E

476 Billy Lights Point Boat Ramp
☎ 1300 788 378
Parking Area in Port Lincoln. Via Ravendale Rd, Marina Dr & St Andrews Dr. Car park area adjacent to bush. Motorhomes only, must be self contained. Permit required
HEMA 88 G3   34 44 43 S   135 53 28 E

477 Horse Rock Campground
Lincoln National Park
☎ (08) 8688 3111
Camp Area 9 km NE of Park Entrance on Access Rd. Dirt road. Pay at park entry. Small sites
HEMA 88 G3   34 48 28 S   135 51 44 E

478 Taylors Landing Campground
Lincoln National Park
☎ (08) 8688 3111
Camp Area 24 km SE of Park Entrance on Access Rd. Dirt road. Pay at park entry
HEMA 88 G3   34 51 16 S   135 57 32 E

479 Surfleet Cove Campground
Lincoln National Park
☎ (08) 8688 3111
Camp Area 22 km NE of Park Entrance on Access Rd. Dirt road. Pay at park entry
HEMA 88 G3   34 45 57 S   135 57 25 E

480 Fishermans Point Campground
Lincoln National Park
☎ (08) 8688 3111
Camp Area 24 km NE of Park Entrance on Access Rd. Dirt road. Pay at park entry
HEMA 88 G3   34 45 25 S   135 59 09 E

481 September Beach Campground
Lincoln National Park
☎ (08) 8688 3111
Camp Area 28 km NE of Park Entrance on Access Rd. Dirt road. Pay at park entry
HEMA 88 G3   34 44 02 S   135 59 47 E

482 Donington Beach Campground
Lincoln National Park
☎ (08) 8688 3111
Camp Area 29 km NE of park entrance. 500m from Access Rd. Pay at park entry
HEMA 88 G3   34 43 45 S   135 59 20 E

483 Engine Point Campground
Lincoln National Park
☎ (08) 8688 3111
Camp Area 25 km NE of Park Entrance on Access Rd. Pay at park entry
HEMA 88 G3   34 44 21 S   135 59 20 E

484 Mikkira Station
☎ (08) 8685 6020
Camp Area at Mikkira Station. 30 km SW of Port Lincoln via Fishery Bay Rd
HEMA 88 G3   34 50 18 S   135 40 51 E

485 Whaling Station
Parking Area 31 km SW of Port Lincoln. Whaling Station Rd
HEMA 88 G3   34 54 39 S   135 41 21 E

486 Yangie Bay Campground
Coffin Bay National Park
☎ (08) 8688 3111
Camp Area 19 km W of Coffin Bay. Some dirt road. Permit required
HEMA 88 G2   34 38 24 S   135 21 38 E

487 Mt Dutton Bay Woolshed
☎ (08) 8685 4031
Camp Area at Mount Dutton Bay Woolshed, 5 km W of Wangary
HEMA 88 F2   34 31 53 S   135 25 58 E

488 Farm Beach Campground
☎ (08) 8676 0400
Camp Area 10 km NW of Wangary, via Farm Beach Rd. Payment box on site
HEMA 88 F2   34 29 48 S   135 23 52 E

489 Nyroca Camp & Function Centre
Camp Area 10 km N of Wangary on Flinders Hwy
HEMA 88 F2   34 27 48 S   135 27 30 E

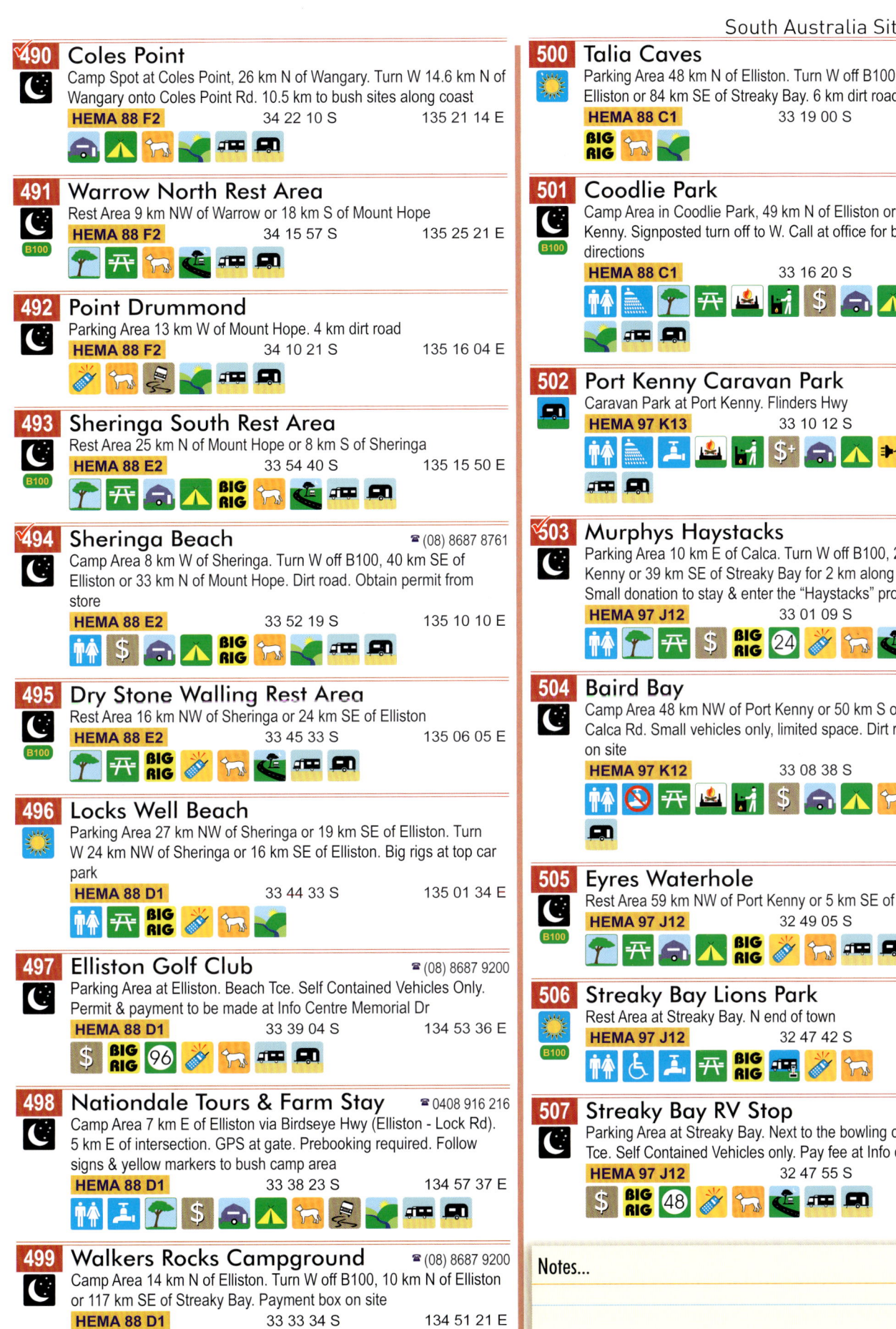

490 Coles Point
Camp Spot at Coles Point, 26 km N of Wangary. Turn W 14.6 km N of Wangary onto Coles Point Rd. 10.5 km to bush sites along coast
HEMA 88 F2   34 22 10 S   135 21 14 E

491 Warrow North Rest Area
Rest Area 9 km NW of Warrow or 18 km S of Mount Hope
HEMA 88 F2   34 15 57 S   135 25 21 E
B100

492 Point Drummond
Parking Area 13 km W of Mount Hope. 4 km dirt road
HEMA 88 F2   34 10 21 S   135 16 04 E

493 Sheringa South Rest Area
Rest Area 25 km N of Mount Hope or 8 km S of Sheringa
HEMA 88 E2   33 54 40 S   135 15 50 E
B100

494 Sheringa Beach ☎ (08) 8687 8761
Camp Area 8 km W of Sheringa. Turn W off B100, 40 km SE of Elliston or 33 km N of Mount Hope. Dirt road. Obtain permit from store
HEMA 88 E2   33 52 19 S   135 10 10 E

495 Dry Stone Walling Rest Area
Rest Area 16 km NW of Sheringa or 24 km SE of Elliston
HEMA 88 E2   33 45 33 S   135 06 05 E
B100

496 Locks Well Beach
Parking Area 27 km NW of Sheringa or 19 km SE of Elliston. Turn W 24 km NW of Sheringa or 16 km SE of Elliston. Big rigs at top car park
HEMA 88 D1   33 44 33 S   135 01 34 E

497 Elliston Golf Club ☎ (08) 8687 9200
Parking Area at Elliston. Beach Tce. Self Contained Vehicles Only. Permit & payment to be made at Info Centre Memorial Dr
HEMA 88 D1   33 39 04 S   134 53 36 E

498 Nationdale Tours & Farm Stay ☎ 0408 916 216
Camp Area 7 km E of Elliston via Birdseye Hwy (Elliston - Lock Rd). 5 km E of intersection. GPS at gate. Prebooking required. Follow signs & yellow markers to bush camp area
HEMA 88 D1   33 38 23 S   134 57 37 E

499 Walkers Rocks Campground ☎ (08) 8687 9200
Camp Area 14 km N of Elliston. Turn W off B100, 10 km N of Elliston or 117 km SE of Streaky Bay. Payment box on site
HEMA 88 D1   33 33 34 S   134 51 21 E

500 Talia Caves
Parking Area 48 km N of Elliston. Turn W off B100, 42 km N of Elliston or 84 km SE of Streaky Bay. 6 km dirt road
HEMA 88 C1   33 19 00 S   134 47 09 E

501 Coodlie Park ☎ (08) 8687 0411
Camp Area in Coodlie Park, 49 km N of Elliston or 16 km S of Port Kenny. Signposted turn off to W. Call at office for bush camp site directions
HEMA 88 C1   33 16 20 S   134 47 17 E

502 Port Kenny Caravan Park ☎ (08) 8625 5076
Caravan Park at Port Kenny. Flinders Hwy
HEMA 97 K13   33 10 12 S   134 41 32 E

503 Murphys Haystacks
Parking Area 10 km E of Calca. Turn W off B100, 22 km NW of Port Kenny or 39 km SE of Streaky Bay for 2 km along Benbarber Rd. Small donation to stay & enter the "Haystacks" property
HEMA 97 J12   33 01 09 S   134 29 28 E

504 Baird Bay ☎ (08) 8626 1001
Camp Area 48 km NW of Port Kenny or 50 km S of Streaky Bay, via Calca Rd. Small vehicles only, limited space. Dirt road. Payment box on site
HEMA 97 K12   33 08 38 S   134 21 47 E

505 Eyres Waterhole
Rest Area 59 km NW of Port Kenny or 5 km SE of Streaky Bay
HEMA 97 J12   32 49 05 S   134 14 46 E
B100

506 Streaky Bay Lions Park
Rest Area at Streaky Bay. N end of town
HEMA 97 J12   32 47 42 S   134 13 05 E
B100

507 Streaky Bay RV Stop
Parking Area at Streaky Bay. Next to the bowling club Montgomerie Tce. Self Contained Vehicles only. Pay fee at Info centre
HEMA 97 J12   32 47 55 S   134 12 32 E

Notes...

SOUTH AUSTRALIA

SOUTH AUSTRALIA

508 Speeds Point Campground
☎ (08) 8626 1001
Camp Area 16 km S of Streaky Bay. Small vehicles only. Dirt road. Honesty box
HEMA 97 J12   32 55 51 S   134 07 45 E

509 Tractor Beach
☎ (08) 8626 1001
Camp Area 17 km SW of Streaky Bay, via Westall Way Scenic Dr. Dirt road. Honesty box. Small vehicles only
HEMA 97 J12   32 52 13 S   134 06 47 E

510 Perlubie Beach
☎ (08) 8626 1001
Camp Area 21 km N of Streaky Bay or 49 km SE of Smoky Bay. Camping only allowed on beach, don't use old parking area this is private property. Beware of tide & soft sand
B100
HEMA 97 H12   32 39 40 S   134 17 41 E

511 Haslam Rest Area
Rest Area 3 km S of Haslam Hwy exit, 39 km N of Streaky Bay or 31 km SE of Smoky Bay
B100
HEMA 97 H12   32 30 45 S   134 14 25 E

512 Haslam Camping Area
Camp Area at Haslam. Cnr Main St & South Tce. Maximum stay 10 days
HEMA 97 H12   32 30 32 S   134 12 50 E

513 Acraman Creek Conservation Park
☎ (08) 8625 3144
Camp Area 23 km SE of Smoky Bay. Turn W 12 km NW of Haslam turnoff or 17 km SE of Smoky Bay for 6 km of dirt road. 4WD only. Small vehicles only. Permit required
HEMA 97 H12   32 27 15 S   134 04 12 E

514 Smoky Rd Rest Area
Rest Area 2.5 km SE of the Smoky Bay turn off
HEMA 97 12H   32 23 25 S   133 59 26 E

515 Laura Bay Conservation Park
☎ (08) 8625 3144
Camp Spot 19 km NW of Smoky Bay or 21 km SE of Ceduna. 3 km dirt road. Limited space
HEMA 97 G11   32 14 32 S   133 49 47 E

516 Wittelbee Conservation Park
☎ (08) 8625 3144
Camp Area 10 km SE of Ceduna, via Decres Bay Rd. Signposted
HEMA 97 G11   32 12 22 S   133 44 17 E

Port Augusta to Eucla
Eyre Highway

517 Port Augusta Motorhome Park
Camp Spot behind the Port Augusta Sports & Recreation facility, Power Station Rd. 4 km E of Port Augusta. Self Contained Vehicles only. Maximum stay 14 days
HEMA 88 A7   32 30 40 S   137 47 09 E

518 Lincoln/Eyre Highway Junction
Rest Area 25 km SW of Port Augusta or 42 km E of Iron Knob
A1
HEMA 88 B7   32 36 58 S   137 34 26 E

519 Iron Knob Rest Area
Rest Area 1 km W of Iron Knob, at Hwy A1 jcn
A1
HEMA 88 B6   32 43 15 S   137 08 54 E

520 Knobbies Camping & Caravan Area
Camp Area at Iron Knob. Dickenson St. Donation requested, donation box near dump point
HEMA 88 B6   32 43 56 S   137 09 02 E

521 Mt Ive Station
☎ (08) 8648 1817
Camp Area at Mt Ive Station. 126 km W of Iron Knob via Kingoonya - Iron Knob Rd
HEMA 88 A4   32 26 18 S   136 04 05 E

522 Waltumba Camping Area
Lake Gairdner National Park
Camp Area 30 km NW of N Mt Ive Station on Moonaree Station Rd. Access via Mt Ive Station by private access road enquires & gate key available from Mt Ive Station (08) 8648 1817. 4WD vehicle access
HEMA 94 G3   32 07 20 S   135 53 46 E

523 Iron Knob West Parking Area
Parking Area 37 km SW of Iron Knob or 50 km NE of Kimba
A1
HEMA 88 C5   32 57 50 S   136 53 16 E

524 Kimba East Parking Area
Parking Area 52 km SW of Iron Knob or 35 km E of Kimba
A1
HEMA 88 C5   33 02 56 S   136 46 09 E

525 Lakes Edge Camping Area
☎ (08) 8688 3111
Lake Gillies Conservation Park
Camp Area 76 km W of Iron Knob. Turn N off Eyre Hwy 67 km W of Iron Knob or 17 km E of Kimba. 9 km track to camp area. Suitable for off road caravans & camper trailers. Signposted
HEMA 88 C5   33 02 09 S   136 35 55 E

526 Kimba Apex-Lions Park
Rest Area at Kimba, Park Tce, next to swimming pool. Donation for upkeep of facilities
A1
HEMA 88 C4   33 08 20 S   136 25 00 E

527 Kimba Recreation Reserve ☎ (08) 8627 2026
Camp Area at Kimba. Buckleboo Rd, extension of North Tce. Entry through archway Kima Pioneer Memorial. Coin shower. Donation welcome for upkeep, maximum stay 5 nights
A1
HEMA 88 C4   33 08 04 S   136 24 54 E

528 Carappee Hill Campground ☎ (08) 8688 3111
Carappee Hill Conservation Park
Camp Area 8 km NE of Darke Peak or 42 km SW of Kimba. 4WD only access
HEMA 88 D4   33 25 56 S   136 16 20 E

529 Darke Peak Hotel ☎ (08) 8620 7009
Camp Spot at Darke Peak. Cnr Howard Tce & Balumbah Kinnard Rd
HEMA 88 D4   33 28 13 S   136 11 57 E

530 Koongawa East
Parking Area 44 km W of Kimba or 45 km E of Kyancutta
A1
HEMA 88 C3   33 11 49 S   135 59 57 E

531 Darkes Memorial Rest Area
Rest Area 55 km W of Kimba or 34 km E of Kyancutta
A1
HEMA 88 C3   33 09 56 S   135 53 12 E

✓532 Kooma View Old Farmhouse
Camp Area 65 km W of Kimba or 24 km E of Kyancutta. Donation welcome
HEMA 88 C3   33 08 58 S   135 48 37 E

533 Goyders Line Memorial Parking Area
Parking Area 11 km W of Koongawa or 20 km E of Kyancutta
A1
HEMA 88 C3   33 08 47 S   135 45 21 E

534 Polkdinney Park
Parking Area at Kyancutta, next to Kyancutta general store
A1
HEMA 88 C2   33 07 59 S   135 33 09 E

535 Lock Caravan Park ☎ (08) 8689 1020
Caravan Park at Lock. South Tce, near town centre. Pay at PO during week or Caretaker on weekends
B90
HEMA 88 D3   33 34 10 S   135 45 24 E

536 Peachna Rest Area
Rest Area 26 km S of Lock or 55 km N of Cummins
B90
HEMA 88 E3   33 46 54 S   135 42 47 E

537 Polda Rock
Parking Area 8 km NE of Wudinna, via Standley Rd. Dirt road
HEMA 88 C2   33 01 16 S   135 32 00 E

538 Waganny Campground ☎ (08) 8688 3111
Gawler Ranges National Park
Camp Area 63 km NW of Widunna. Access via Old Paney Scenic Route. Signposted. 3 km S to campsite. 4WD only, suitable for off road caravans & camper trailers
HEMA 88 B2   32 42 20 S   135 32 00 E

539 Chillunie Campground ☎ (08) 8688 3111
Gawler Ranges National Park
Camp Area 70 km N of Wudinna. Via Barns Rd, Loop Track. Signposted turn off 9.8 km N of Paney Homestead, 3.6 km track to campsites. 4WD only, suitable for off road caravans & camper trailers
HEMA 88 B2   32 34 33 S   135 34 06 E

540 Kolay Hut Campground ☎ (08) 8688 3111
Gawler Ranges National Park
Camp Area 69 km N of Wudinna. Via Barns Rd, Loop track. 13 km N of Paney Homestead, signposted. 4WD only, suitable for off road caravans & camper trailers
HEMA 88 B2   32 33 25 S   135 35 18 E

541 Mattera Campground ☎ (08) 8688 3111
Gawler Ranges National Park
Camp Area 80km NW of Wudinna. Via Old Paney Scenic Route, Loop Track & Mattera Track. Signposted. 4WD only, suitable for off road caravans & camper trailers, 3 km very narrow track
HEMA 88 B2   32 34 00 S   135 28 22 E

542 Kododo Campground ☎ (08) 8688 3111
Gawler Ranges National Park
Camp Area 46 km N of Minnipa via Yardea Rd. Turn off 12.7 km N of Old Paney Scenic Route intersection onto Pine Lodge Track. Signposted. 1.2 km to campground. 4WD only
HEMA 88 A2   32 29 34 S   135 22 00 E

Notes...

SOUTH AUSTRALIA

543 Scrubby Peak Campground ☎ (08) 8688 3111
Gawler Ranges National Park
Camp Area 41 km N of Minnipa via Yardea Rd. Signposted turn off
8 km N of Old Paney Scenic Route intersection. 4WD only, suitable
for off road caravans and camper trailers
HEMA 88 A2   32 31 42 S   135 20 00 E

544 Yandinga Campground ☎ (08) 8688 3111
Gawler Ranges National Park
Camp Area 36 km N of Minnipa via Yardea Rd. Signposted turn off
3 km N of Old Paney Scenic Route intersection. 500m to campground
HEMA 88 B2   32 33 41 S   135 19 28 E

545 Minnipa Apex Park
Rest Area at Minnipa. Cnr Crabb R & Eyre Hwy. Donation requested
HEMA 88 B2   32 51 16 S   135 09 03 E

546 Tcharkuldu Rock
Camp Area E of Minnipa, via Bockelberg Rd. Dirt road. 7 day
maximum stay. Donation requested
HEMA 88 B2   32 50 50 S   135 11 45 E

547 Pildappa Rock
Camp Area 15 km NE of Minnipa. Via Pildappa Rd. Donation
requested
HEMA 88 B2   32 45 03 S   135 13 47 E

548 Chandada Pioneer Park
Rest Area 15 km W of Poochera or 46 km E of Streaky Bay
HEMA 88 B1   32 45 16 S   134 40 24 E

549 Poochera Parking Area
Parking Area 2 km W of Poochera or 45 km SE of Wirrulla
HEMA 88 B1   32 42 39 S   134 49 22 E

550 Poochera Hotel Caravan Park ☎ (08) 8626 3257
Caravan Park at Poochera. Barnes St
HEMA 88 B1   32 43 10 S   134 50 12 E

551 Yantanabie South Rest Area
Rest Area 25 km NW of Poochera or 22 km SE of Wirrulla
HEMA 88 A1   32 33 12 S   134 40 21 E

552 Wirrulla Caravan Park ☎ (08) 8626 8019
Caravan Park at Wirrulla. Shower key at general store or hotel
HEMA 97 H13   32 24 16 S   134 31 57 E

553 Wirrulla West Rest Area
Rest Area 9 km W of Wirrulla or 84 km E of Ceduna
HEMA 97 H12   32 24 41 S   134 26 32 E

554 Old Perlubie School Site
Rest Area 13 km W of Wirrulla or 80 km E of Ceduna
HEMA 97 H12   32 24 44 S   134 24 10 E

555 Puntabie East Rest Area
Rest Area 48 km W of Wirrulla or 45 km E of Ceduna
HEMA 97 G12   32 12 38 S   134 07 56 E

556 A1 Cabins & Caravan Park ☎ (08) 8625 2578
Caravan Park at Ceduna. 41 McKenzie St
HEMA 97 G11   32 07 25 S   133 40 49 E

557 Koonibba Parking Area
Parking Area 33 km W of Ceduna or 40 km E of Penong
HEMA 97 G10   31 57 05 S   133 25 09 E

558 Watraba Parking Area
Parking Area 51 km W of Ceduna or 25 km E of Penong
HEMA 97 G10   31 56 26 S   133 16 31 E

559 Penong Caravan Park ☎ (08) 8625 1111
Caravan Park at Penong. 3 Stiggants Rd
HEMA 97 G10   31 55 31 S   133 00 32 E

560 Cactus Beach Point Sinclair ☎ (08) 8625 1036
Camp Area 21 km S of Penong. Via Point Sinclair Rd. Dirt road
HEMA 97 G10   32 05 19 S   132 59 00 E

561 Cohen Old School Site
Parking Area 14 km W of Penong or 65.5 km E of Nundroo. N side of
the road, 2.2 km E of Cohen Rest Area
HEMA 97 F9   31 52 16 S   132 53 02 E

562 Cohen Rest Area
Rest Area 16 km W of Penong or 63 km E of Nundroo
HEMA 97 F9   31 51 40 S   132 51 50 E

563 Scotts Point ☎ (08) 8625 3144
Fowler Bay Conservation Park
Camp Spot 13 km W of Fowlers Bay. Via Fowlers Bay Corrabie Rd,
then S onto Scotts Bay Rd for 6.6 km. W end behind dunes, sand
tracks
HEMA 97 G8   32 00 15 S   132 23 05 E

564 Coorabie Farm ☎ (08) 8625 6126
Camp Area at Coorabie. 15 km SE of Nundroo, turn S 5 km E of Nundroo into Fowlers Bay Rd. 10 km gravel, turn R into farm just before Coorabie
HEMA 97 G8   31 53 28 S   132 17 19 E

565 Nundroo East Rest Area
A1
Rest Area 69 km W of Penong or 10 km E of Nundroo
HEMA 97 F8   31 49 34 S   132 18 51 E

566 Nundroo Hotel Motel Caravan Park ☎ (08) 8025 6120
A1
Caravan Park at Nundroo Roadhouse
HEMA 97 F8   31 47 33 S   132 13 29 E

567 Nallanippi Parking Area
Parking Area 6 km W of Nundroo or 56 km E of Yalata. Cnr of Nallanippi Rd
HEMA 97 F8   31 45 11 S   132 11 02 E

568 Colona Rest Area
A1
Rest Area 27 km W of Nundroo or 25 km E of Yalata
HEMA 97 F8   31 36 21 S   132 02 09 E

569 Yalata East Parking Area
Parking Area 44 km W of Nundroo or 18 km E of Yalata. Share with trucks, caravan parking at rear of sealed area
HEMA 96 F7   31 31 44 S   131 53 36 E

570 Yalata West Rest Area
A1
Rest Area 11 km W of Yalata or 70 km E of Nullarbor Roadhouse
HEMA 96 E7   31 24 34 S   131 36 51 E

571 Red Gate Tank Parking Area
Parking Area 41 km W of Yalata or 42 km E of Nullarbor Roadhouse. Share with trucks
HEMA 96 E6   31 21 38 S   131 18 45 E

572 222k Peg Rest Area
Rest Area 54 km W of Yalata or 37 km E of Nullarbor Roadhouse
HEMA 96 E6   31 21 55 S   131 15 58 E

573 164k Peg Rest Area
A1
Rest Area 20 km W of Nullarbor Roadhouse or 164 km E of Border Village
HEMA 96 F5   31 32 05 S   130 41 32 E

574 157k Peg Rest Area
A1
Rest Area 27 km W of Nullarbor Roadhouse or 157 km E of Border Village
HEMA 96 F5   31 33 02 S   130 37 03 E

575 Mallabie Parking Area
Parking Area 29 km W of Nullarbor Roadhouse or 155 km E of Border Village. Large gravel area, caravans at the back
HEMA 96 F4   31 33 04 S   130 35 55 E

576 Koonalda Homestead ☎ (08) 8625 3144
A1
Camp Spot at Koonalda homestead. Turn N 94 km W Nullarbor Roadhouse or 88 km E of Border Village. 14 km to old Homestead
HEMA 96 F3   31 27 22 S   129 51 28 E

577 85k Peg Rest Area
A1
Rest Area 100 km W of Nullarbor Roadhouse or 84 km E of Border Village
HEMA 96 F3   31 34 49 S   129 52 27 E

578 81k Peg Rest Area
A1
Rest Area 103 km W of Nullarbor Roadhouse or 81 km E of Border Village
HEMA 93 F3   31 35 16 S   129 50 03 E

579 Bunda Cliffs Scenic Lookout
A1
Parking Area 109 km W of Nullarbor Roadhouse or 75 km E of Border Village. 600m S of Hwy
HEMA 96 F3   31 36 24 S   129 46 36 E

580 38k Peg Parking Bay
A1
Parking Area 146 km W of Nullarbor Roadhouse or 38 km E of Border Village
HEMA 96 F2   31 38 17 S   129 23 19 E

581 17k Peg Parking Bay
A1
Parking Area 167 km W of Nullarbor Roadhouse or 17 km E of Border Village
HEMA 96 F2   31 39 27 S   129 10 04 E

582 13k Peg Parking Bay
A1
Parking Area 171 km W of Nullarbor Roadhouse or 13 km E of Border Village
HEMA 96 F2   31 39 35 S   129 07 52 E

Notes...

SOUTH AUSTRALIA

583 10k Peg Parking Area
Parking Area 174 km W of Nullarbor Roadhouse or 10 km E of Border Village
A1
HEMA 96 F2   31 38 54 S   129 05 59 E

Lyndhurst to Innamincka
Strzelecki Track
This road is seasonal and more suitable to 4WD vehicles, camper trailers and off road caravans. Road conditions phone 1300 361 033

584 Freeling Rest Area
Rest Area 76 km NE of Lyndhurst or 387 km SW of Innamincka
HEMA 95 B10   29 59 48 S   139 00 28 E

585 Dog Fence Rest Area
Rest Area 104 km NE of Lyndhurst or 338 km SW of Innamincka
HEMA 95 A10   29 47 21 S   139 05 22 E

586 Murnpeowie Rest Area
Rest Area 126 km NE of Lyndhurst or 338 km SW of Innamincka. Opposite Murnpeowie Station turnoff
HEMA 91 K10   29 37 01 S   139 08 57 E

✓587 Blanchewater Ruins
Camp Spot 158 km NE of Lyndhurst or 307 km SW of Innamincka. W side of creek on the N side of road
HEMA 91 K11   29 33 01 S   139 27 01 E

588 Art Baker Rest Area
Rest Area 209 km NE of Lyndhurst or 255 km SW of Innamincka
HEMA 91 K11   29 29 37 S   139 55 47 E

✓589 Montecollina Bore Rest Area
Rest Area 222 km NE of Lyndhurst or 223 km SW of Innamincka
HEMA 91 K12   29 23 43 S   139 59 35 E

590 Strzelecki Creek Rest Area
Rest Area 273 km NE of Lyndhurst or 192 km SW of Innamincka. 2 km S of creek crossing
HEMA 91 J12   28 57 37 S   140 07 40 E

591 Moomba Lookout
Parking Area 174 km NE of Montecollina Bore or 105 km SW of Innaminka on New Strzelecki Track or 86 on Old Strzelecki Track
HEMA 91 F12   28 07 57 S   140 12 41 E

✓592 Innamincka Town Common   ☎ (08) 8675 9901
Camp Area 1 km S of township on banks of Cooper Creek. Signposted, honesty box at entrance
HEMA 91 F13   27 45 05 S   140 43 58 E

593 Policemans   ☎ (08) 8648 5328
Camp Area on the 15 Mile Track SW of Innamincka. At 3.5 km turn R to Policeman's Water Hole. Desert Parks Pass required, fees payable at Innamincka Store
HEMA 91 F13   27 45 31 S   140 42 12 E

594 Ski Beach   ☎ (08) 8648 5328
Camp Area on the 15 Mile Track SW of Innamincka. 5.6 km turn R to Ski Beach. Desert Parks Pass required, fees payable at Innamincka Store
HEMA 91 F13   27 45 52 S   140 41 06 E

✓595 Kings Site   ☎ (08) 8648 5328
Camp Area on the 15 Mile Track SW of Innamincka. 7 km turn R to King's Site Campground. Desert Parks Pass required, fees payable at Innamincka Store
HEMA 91 F13   27 46 42 S   140 40 33 E

596 Minkie Waterhole   ☎ (08) 8648 5328
Camp Area on the 15 Mile Track SW of Innamincka. 10.8 km turn R to Minkie Waterhole. Desert Parks Pass required, fees payable at Innamincka Store
HEMA 91 F13   27 46 45 S   140 38 19 E

597 Scrubby Camp   ☎ (08) 8648 5328
Camp Spot on the Coongie Lake track NW of Innamincka. 43.5 km turn L into camp site. Desert Parks Pass required, fees payable at Innamincka Store
HEMA 91 E13   27 39 38 S   140 23 03 E

598 Kudriemitchie Campground   ☎ (08) 8648 5328
Camp Spot on the Coongie Lake track NW of Innamincka. 83 km turn L into camp site. Desert Parks Pass required, fees payable at Innamincka Store
HEMA 91 E12   27 21 41 S   140 12 15 E

599 Coongie Lakes Campground   ☎ 1800 816 078
Malkumba-Coongie Lakes National Park
Camp Spot on the Coongie Lake track NW of Innamincka. 104 km turn L into camp site. Desert Parks Pass required, fees payable at Innamincka Store. Subject to flooding, check ahead to make sure road is open
HEMA 91 D12   27 11 27 S   140 09 12 E

600 Cullyamurra Waterhole   ☎ (08) 8648 5328
Camp Area Take Innamincka - Nappa Merrie Rd E from Innaminka. Turn N 14 km. Desert Parks Pass required, fees payable at Innamincka Store
HEMA 91 E14   27 42 07 S   140 50 20 E

Notes...

PURNULULU NATIONAL PARK (117 G13)

PHOTO: © ISTOCK.COM/SARAH WINTER

Distances are shown in kilometres and follow the most direct major sealed route where possible.

1400	1999	413	1546	958	3575	1892	865	799	476	1276	358	2594	**Albany**
3223	609	2217	1048	1654	1049	842	2314	1992	2703	1457	2592	**Broome**
1593	1800	178	1347	723	3372	1693	770	600	669	1077	**Bunbury**
2344	862	899	1237	815	2438	634	1459	477	1600	**Carnarvon**
924	2108	737	1655	1049	3684	2268	389	1275	**Esperance**
1867	1327	422	964	338	2983	1093	982	**Geraldton**
909	1719	596	1266	660	3295	1879	**Kalgoorlie**
2788	238	1515	631	1219	1867	**Karratha**
4206	1590	3198	2029	2635	**Kununurra**
1569	1059	563	606	**Mount Magnet**
2175	453	1169	**Newman**
1445	1622	**Perth**
2628	**Port Hedland**
WA-SA Border Village		

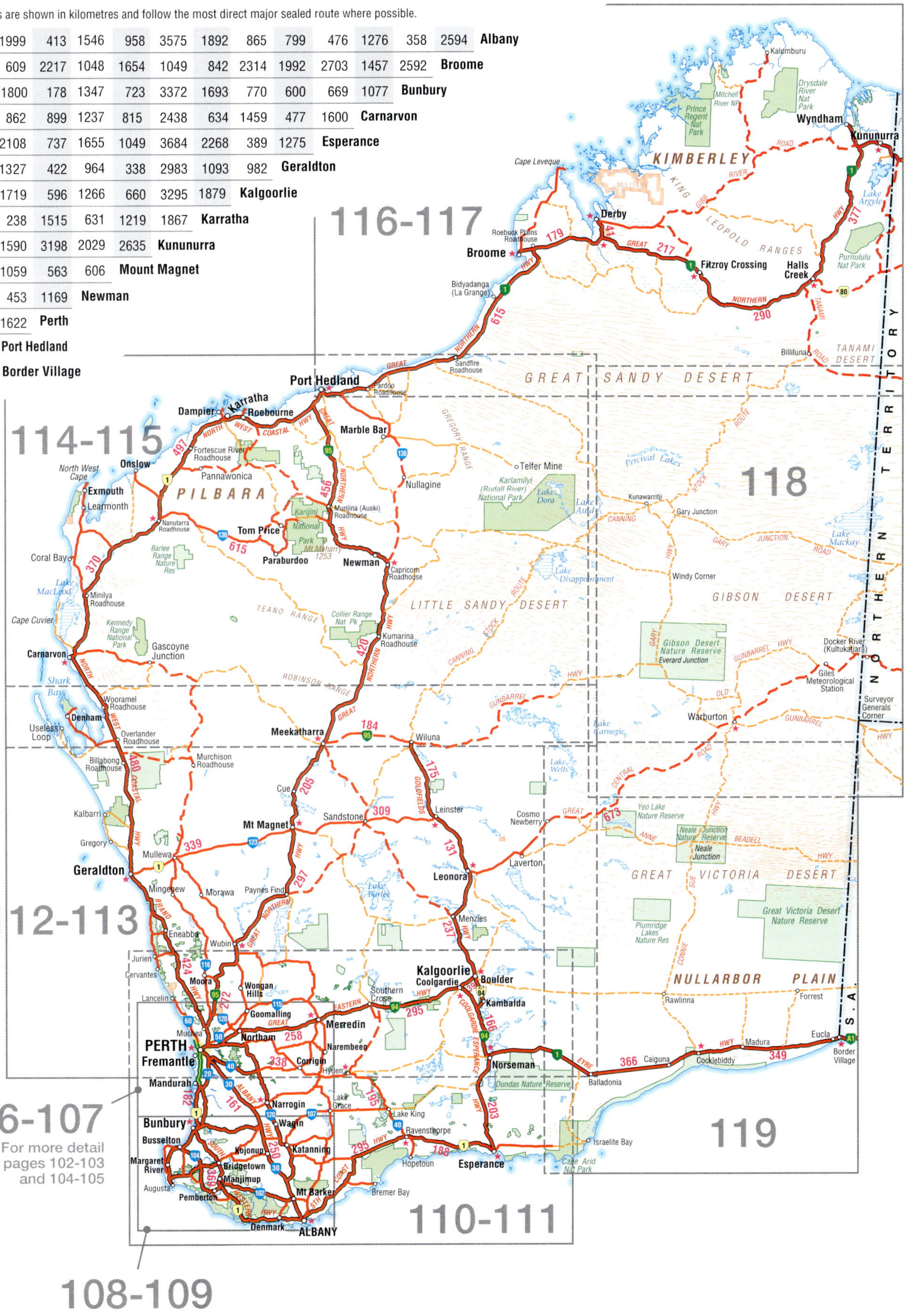

116-117

114-115

112-113

106-107
For more detail
see pages 102-103
and 104-105

108-109

110-111

118

119

Perth CBD

Points of Interest

1. Art Gallery of Western Australia A3
2. Barracks Archway B1
3. Cloisters, The B2
4. Deanery, The B3
5. Government House B3
6. Hay Street Mall B2
7. His Majesty's Theatre B2
8. Horseshoe Bridge B2
9. King Street Arts Centre B2
10. Kings Park B1
11. Kings Park Lookout C1
12. Langley Park C3
13. Murray Street Mall B2
14. NIB Stadium A4
15. Old Council House B3
16. Old Court House B3
17. Old Mill C1
18. Old Perth Boys School B2
19. Old Perth Observatory B1
20. Parliament House B1
21. Perth Arena A2

22. Perth Concert Hall B3
23. Perth Convention Exhibition Ctr B2
24. Perth Inst of Contemporary Arts A3
25. Perth Mint B4
26. Perth Town Hall B3
27. Perth Zoo E2
28. St George's Cathedral B3
29. St Mary's RC Cathedral B3
30. Scitech Discovery Centre A1
31. State Library of Western Aust A3
32. State War Memorial C1
33. Swan Bells C2
34. Wellington Square B4
35. Western Australian Museum A3

Accommodation
38. Aarons All Suites B3
39. Aarons Hotel Perth B3
40. Adina Apartment Hotel Perth B2
41. Citadines St Georges Terrace Perth B2
42. Comfort Hotel Perth City C4
43. Comfort Inn Wentworth Plaza Hotel Perth B2

44. Criterion Hotel B3
45. Crowne Plaza Perth C4
46. Duxton Hotel Perth, The B3
47. Four Points by Sheraton Perth A2
48. Globe Backpackers and City Oasis Resort B2
49. Goodearth Hotel C4
50. Grand Central Backpackers B3
51. Holiday Inn Perth City Centre B2
52. Hotel Ibis Perth B3
53. Hyatt Regency Perth C4
54. Ibis Styles Perth A3
55. Kings Perth Hotel B3
56. Mantra on Hay C4
57. Mantra on Murray B2
58. Marque Hotel Perth B1
59. Melbourne Hotel, The B2
60. Mercure Hotel B3
61. Mounts Bay Waters Apartments B1
62. New Esplanade Hotel Perth, The B2
63. Novotel Perth Hotel Langley C3
64. Parmelia Hilton Perth Hotel B2

65. Perth Ambassador Hotel C4
66. Perth City YHA B3
67. Quest West End B2
68. River View on Mount Street B1
69. Rydges Perth B2
70. Seasons of Perth B3
71. Sheraton Perth Hotel C3
72. Sullivans Hotel C1
73. Travelodge Perth Hotel B3

Travel Information
75. City West Train Station A1
76. Claisebrook Train Station A4
77. East Perth Train Station A4
78. Elizabeth Quay Station B2
79. McIver Train Station B3
80. Perth Train Station B3
81. Perth Underground Station B2
82. Perth Visitor Centre B2
83. RAC Office A1
84. Roe Street Temporary Bus Station A2
85. Wellington Street Temporary Bus Station A2

Legend
- Freeway/Tunnel — FREEWAY
- Main Road
- Secondary — ROAD
- RoadMinor Road — STREET
- Lane/Footbridge
- Metropolitan Route — 22
- One Way Street
- Railway — Underground
- Park/Garden
- Railway Station
- Major Building
- Government Building
- Theatre/Cinema
- Shopping
- Post Office
- Accredited Information
- 24hr Fuel

To Quinns Rocks 1   To Lancelin 2   3   4   5   6   7

The Vines

0   1.25   2.5   5
kilometres
© Hema Maps

N

To Geraldton

Joondalup
Lakeside Shopping Centre
TAFE
Edith Cowan Univ.
Wanneroo
Jandabup
Ellenbrook

Ocean Reef
Edgewater
Hocking
Gnangara
Lexia
Swan Valley Cuddly Animal Farm   John St   All Saints Church
Henley Brook
WA Reptile Park   Henley St

Mullaloo
Beldon
Woodvale
Wanneroo Markets
Wangara
Gnangara
Brabham
Herne Hill

Mullaloo Beach
Craigie
Yellagonga Regional Park
Landsdale
Kingsway

Kallaroo
Woodvale
Aboriginal Cultural Complex
Gnangara Lake
Gnangara Park

Pinaroo Point
Padbury
Kingsley
Alexander Heights
Cullacabardee
Whiteman Park
West Swan
Swan Valley
Middle Swan

Hillarys
Sorrento
Greenwood
Marangaroo
Whiteman
Caversham Wildlife Park
Ballajura
Bennett Springs
Dayton

Hillarys Boat Harbour
Duncraig
Warwick
Girrawheen
Koondoola
Malaga
Beechboro

Sorrento Beach
Marmion
Carine
Hamersley
Balga
Mirrabooka
Noranda
Morley
Caversham
Midland

Marmion Marine Park
North Beach
Balcatta
Stirling
Westminster
Nollamara
Marshall
Mirrabooka Square
Eden Hill
Lockridge

Watermans Bay
Karrinyup
Dianella
Morley
Bassendean
Guildford
Bellevue

North Beach
Scarborough
Innaloo
Tuart Hill
Yokine
Dianella Plaza
Galleria Morley
Ashfield
South Guildford
Hazelmere

Trigg Island
Trigg
Woodlands
Osborne Park
Joondanna
Coolbinia
Inglewood
Bedford
Maylands
Bayswater
PERTH AIRPORT
Kalamunda

Scarborough Beach
Wembley Downs
Mt Hawthorn
North Perth
Mt Lawley
Ascot
Ascot Racecourse
Redcliffe
T4 Domestic Terminal

Brighton Beach
City Beach
Floreat
Wembley
Highgate
Northbridge
Belmont
High Wycombe
Maida Vale

Floreat Beach
Jolimont
Subiaco
West Perth
East Perth
Burswood
Rivervale
Cloverdale

INDIAN OCEAN
Shenton Park
Mt Claremont
Nedlands
Crawley
PERTH
Kings Park
Victoria Park
East Victoria Park
Carlisle
Kewdale
Welshpool
Forrestfield

Swanbourne
Claremont
Karrakatta
South Perth
Como
Kensington
Cannington
Beckenham
Wattle Grove

Cottesloe
Peppermint Grove
Dalkeith
Applecross
Manning
Bentley
Waterford
Welshpool

Mosman Park
Bicton
Attadale
Mt Pleasant
Salter Point
Shelley
Riverton
Ferndale
Langford
Kenwick
Orange Grove

North Fremantle
East Fremantle
Alfred Cove
Rossmoyne
Riverton Forum
Parkwood
Maddington

Fremantle
Melville
Booragoon
Winthrop
Bull Creek
Willetton
Thornlie

Palmyra
White Gum Valley
O'Connor
Kardinya
Leeming
Canning Vale
Huntingdale
Gosnells

South Fremantle
Hilton
Samson
Murdoch
Murdoch University
Metropolitan Markets
Southern River
Westfield

Hamilton Hill
Spearwood
Bibra Lake
Jandakot Airport
Jandakot
South Lake

To Rockingham 1   To Rockingham 2   To Kwinana, Mandurah 3   4   To Oakford 5   To Armadale   To Bunbury, Albany 7

SEE MAP 100

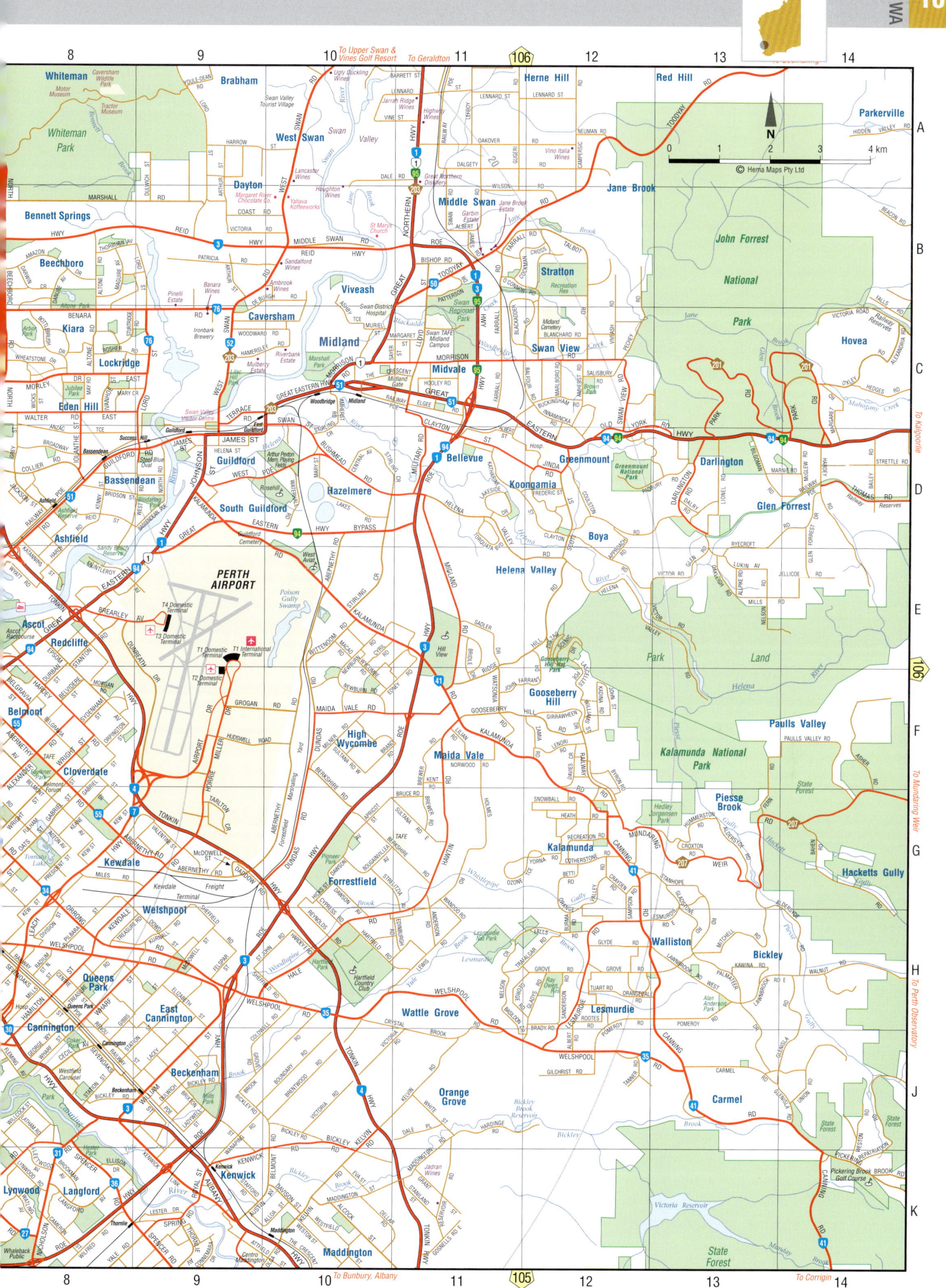

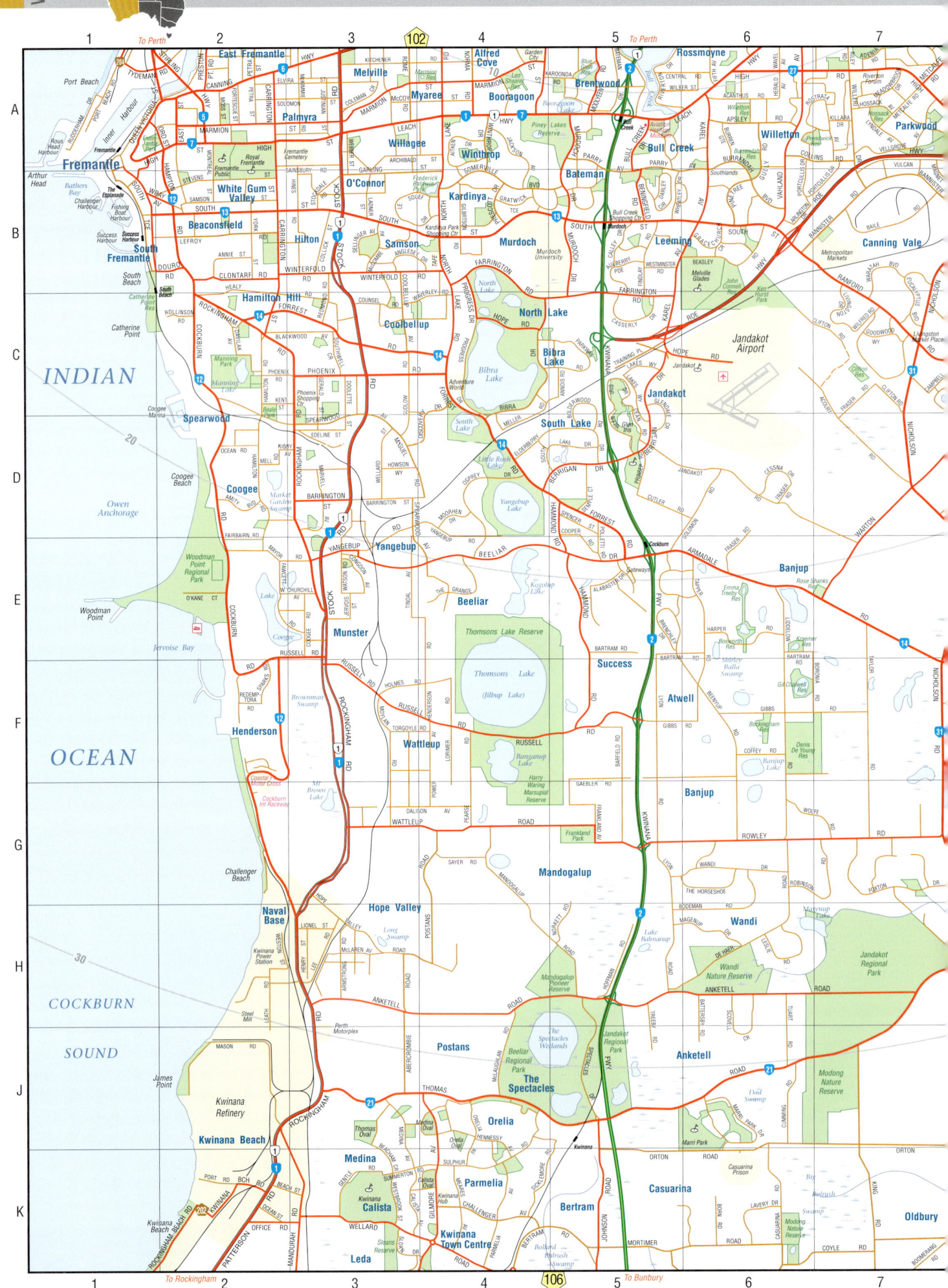

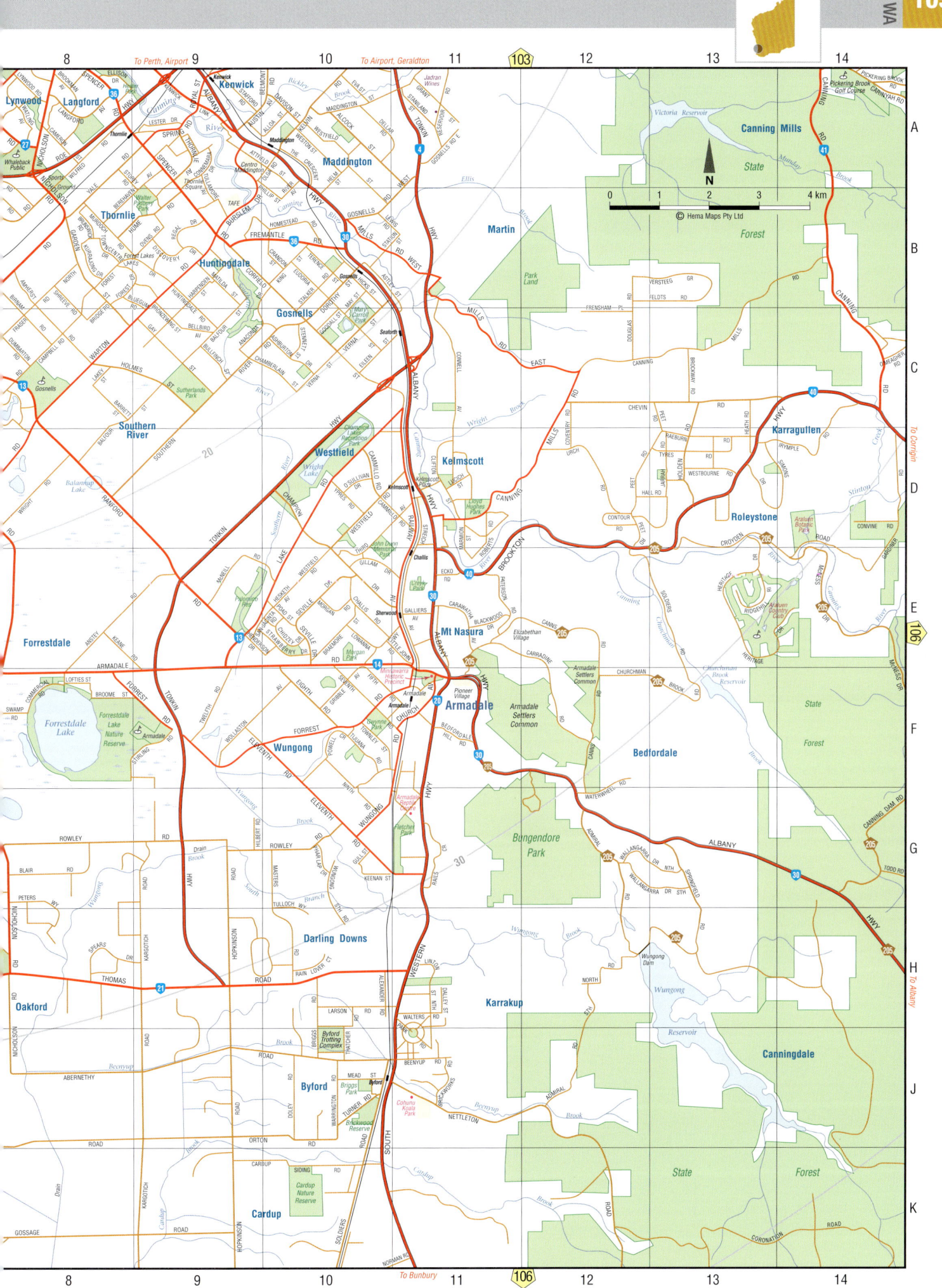

South West and South Coast, Western Australia

© Hema Maps Pty Ltd

SEE MAP 106-107
SEE MAP 108-109
For more detail on this area, see HEMA's Perth and Region map.
For more detail on this area, see HEMA's Southwest WA map.
For more detail on this area, see HEMA's South West Corner (Margaret River & Southern Forests) map.
INDIAN
OCEAN
PERTH
Fremantle
Rockingham
Mandurah
Bunbury
Busselton
Dunsborough
Margaret River
Augusta
Albany
Denmark
Mt Barker
Katanning
Kojonup
Wagin
Narrogin
Northam
York
Merredin
Moora
Collie
Bridgetown
Manjimup
Pemberton
Walpole
Harvey
Pinjarra
Waroona
Boddington
Mundaring
Kwinana
Capel
Donnybrook
Cervantes
Jurien Bay
Lancelin
Dalwallinu
Wongan Hills
Kellerberrin
Cunderdin
Tammin
Quairading
Corrigin
Kondinin
Hyden
Lake Grace
Bruce Rock
Narembeen
Pingelly
Brookton
Williams
Darkan
Gnowangerup
Tambellup
Cranbrook
Frankland River
Nannup
Northcliffe
Rottnest Island
Geographe Bay
Flinders Bay
Stirling Range NP
Leeuwin-Naturaliste NP
D'Entrecasteaux National Park
Walpole & Nornalup Inlets Marine Park
Ngari Capes Marine Park
Jurien Bay MP
Marmion Marine Park
Shoalwater Islands MP
To Geraldton
To Mt Magnet
116°E
118°E
32°S
34°S

© Hema Maps Pty Ltd

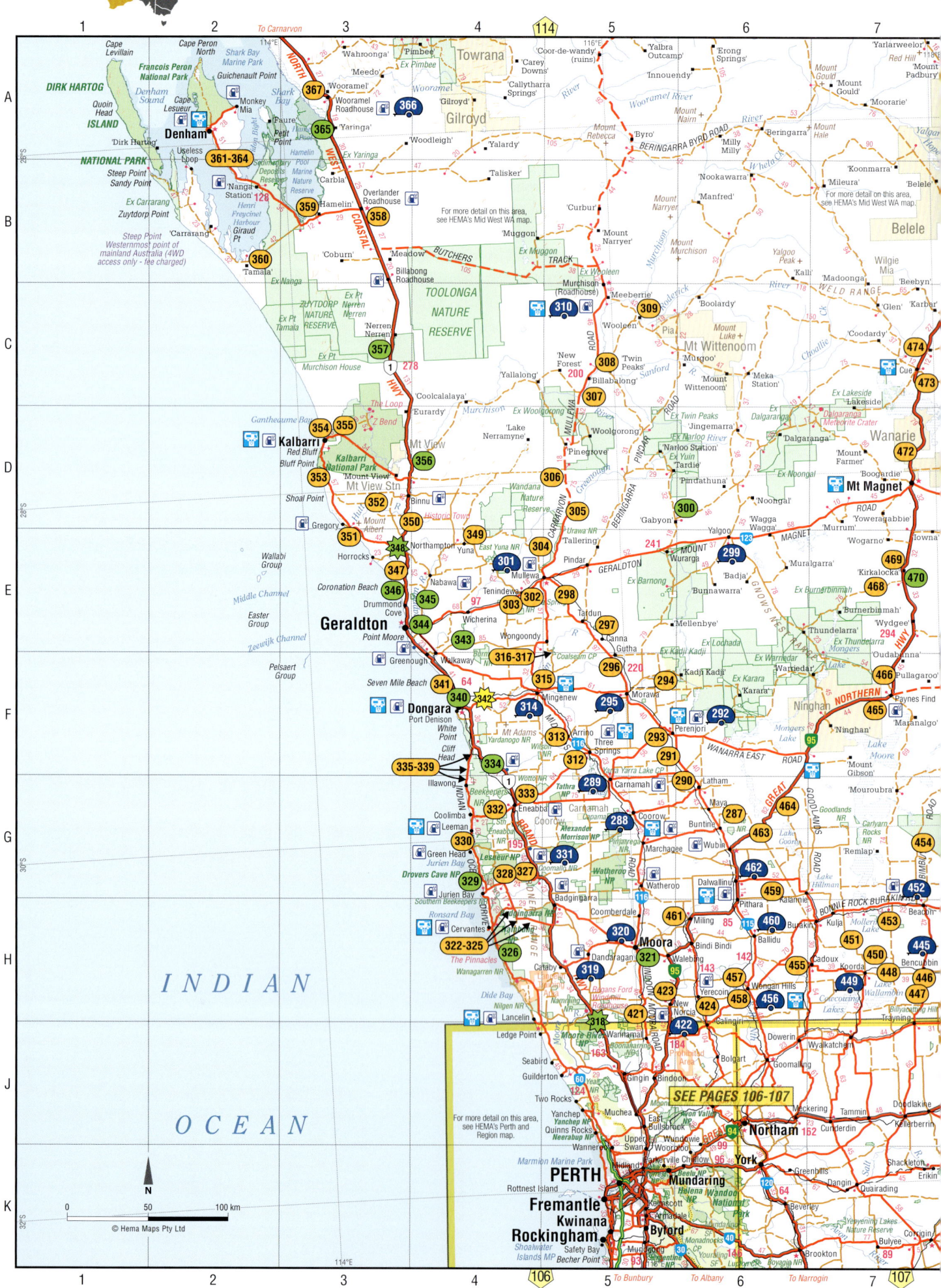

The Pilbara, Western Australia

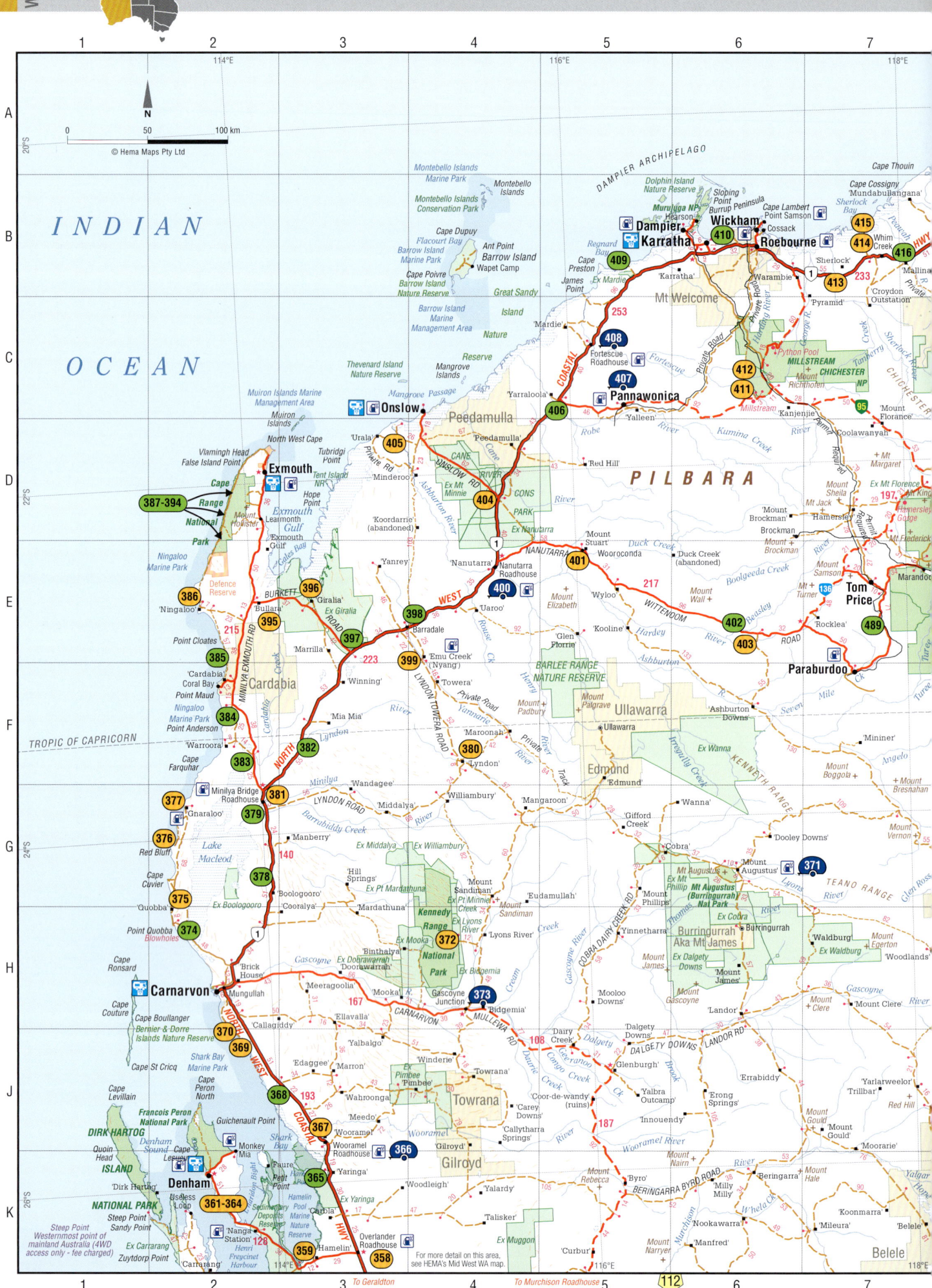

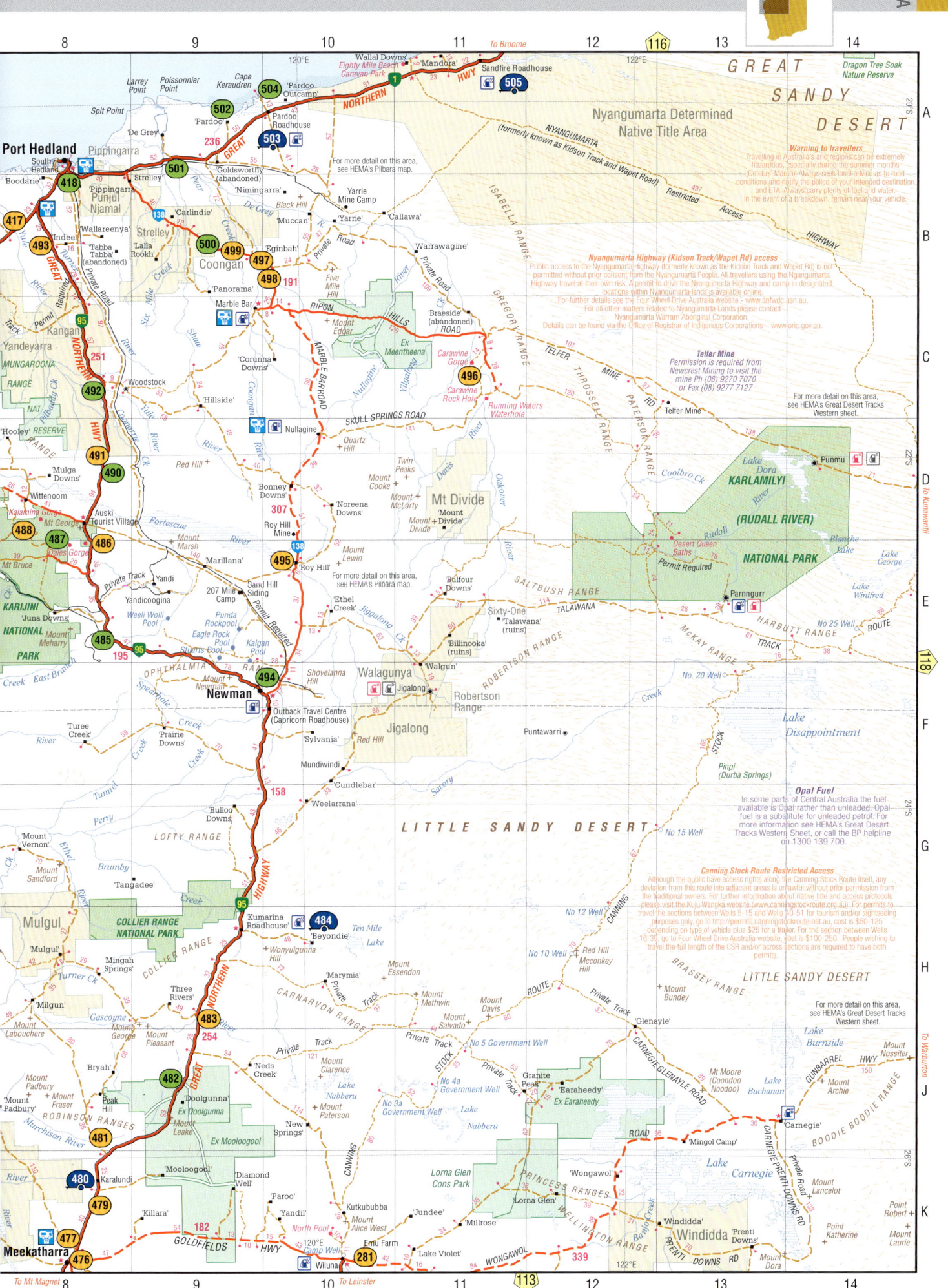

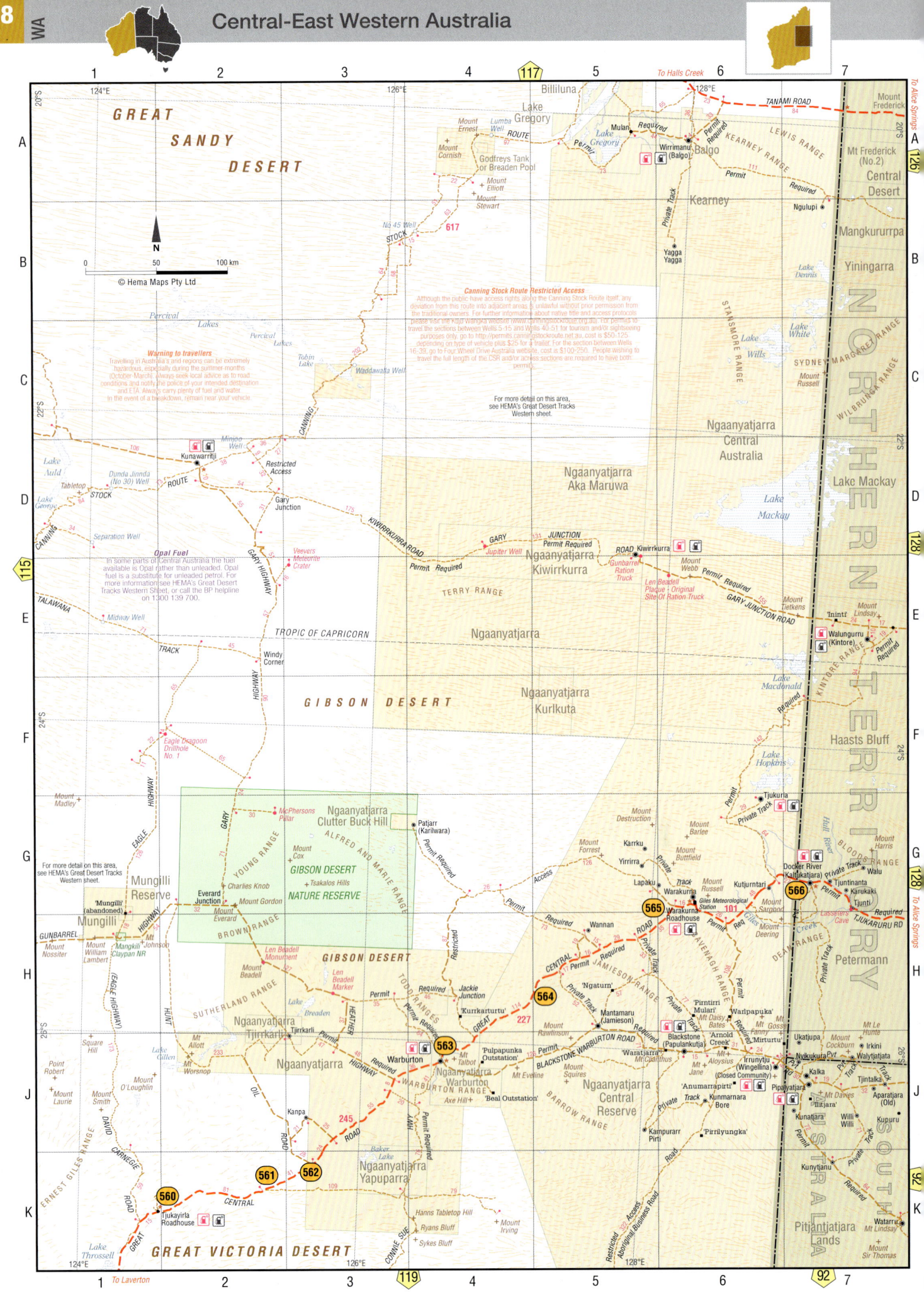

GREAT VICTORIA DESERT

Ngaanyatjarra Yapuparra

Ngaanyatjarra Central Reserve

Farquharson Tableland

ERNEST GILES RANGE

DAVID CARNEGIE ROAD

GREAT CENTRAL ROAD

Lake Wells

Lyell + Brown Bluff

Holroyd Bluff

Lake Wells

Tjukayirla Roadhouse

Lake Throssell

Lake Thross

De La Poer Range Nature Reserve

Cosmo Newberry (North)

YEO LAKE NATURE RESERVE

Yeo Lake

Yeo Station (abandoned)

Cosmo Newberry (West)

Cosmo Newberry

Permit Required

Permit Req

Salvation

'Yamarna' (abandoned)

ANNE

Cosmo Newberry (South)

Cosmo Newberry (East)

BAILEY RANGE

'White Cliffs'

Permit

Prohibited Area

Permit Required

BEADELL

Lake Rason

Saunders + Point

Point Lilian

SAUNDERS RANGE

SUE

CONNIE

Neale Junction

NEALE JUNCTION NATURE RESERVE

Light Aircraft Wreck

'Ilkurlka' (Roadhouse)

Restricted

ANNE

BEADELL

HIGHWAY

Len Beadell Border Plaque

SOUTH AUSTRALIA

GREAT VICTORIA DESERT

For more detail on this area, see HEMA's Great Desert Tracks Western sheet.

'Coglia Well Outcamp'

Lightfoot Lake

Lake Minigwal

PLUMRIDGE LAKES NATURE RESERVE

RASON LAKE ROAD

CABLE HAUL ROAD

Jubilee Lake

Tjuntjuntjara (Closed Community)

Aboriginal

Permit Required

GREAT VICTORIA DESERT NATURE RESERVE

Business

Road

'Kirgella Rocks'

Lake Rebecca

QUEEN VICTORIA SPRING NATURE RESERVE

NIPPON

BASELINE HWY

PNC

Yakadunia

Yackadunyah

Decoration Cave

SUE

CONNIE

Sleeper Camp

NULLARBOR PLAIN

Cundeelee Mission

Cundeelee (abandoned)

Emu Rocks

SPINIFEX RANGE

Ponton

Permit Required

'Premier Downs' (abandoned)

'Seemore Downs'

'Kinclaven'

'Kanandah'

CABLE HAUL ROAD

Coonana

Coonana

Zanthus

TRANS ACCESS

Creek

913 Mile

Naretha

'Rawlinna'

'Balgair'

Rawlinna

Haig

Nurina

'Kybo'

Private Track

Loongana

Forrest

Reid

TRANS

Deakin

No Access

ANKETELL

ROAD

ACCESS

Private Road

Deakin ROAD

Deakin Obelisk

Trans Access Road
The Trans Access Road between Haig (WA) and Lyons (SA) is officially closed. No travel permissions will be granted.

For more detail on this area, see HEMA's Great Desert Tracks Western sheet.

COCKLEBIDDY-RAWLINNA ROAD

Private Track

MUNDRABILLA ROAD

FORREST

EUCLA

REID ROAD

NULLARBOR REGIONAL RESERVE

NULLARBOR NP

Border Quarantine Checkpoint

Border Village

To Adelaide

Wilson Bluff

'Pondana'

'Arubiddy'

Cocklebiddy Cave

'Moonera'

'Madura'

Madura

Mundrabilla

Mundrabilla Motel

'Moopina'

Eucla

NULLARBOR NP

Cocklebiddy Motel

Eyre Bird Observatory

HAMPTON TABLELAND

ROE PLAINS

Quarantine
Do not take fruit, vegetables, plants or flowers across State and quarantine borders. Penalties Apply. Ph 1800 084 881 or email info@agric.wa.gov.au (WA Pest and Disease Information Service)

EYRE

'Noondoonia'

'Woorlba'

Balladonia Roadhouse

OLD COACH/TELEGRAPH RD

DUNDAS NATURE RESERVE

'Nanambinia'

Longest straight stretch in Australia (146.6km)

EYRE HIGHWAY

Caiguna

Caiguna Blowhole

Baxter Cliffs

Point Dover

Kanidal Beach

Twilight Cove

Scorpion Bight

Red Rocks Point

BALLADONIA ROAD

PARMANGO ROAD

NUYTSLAND NATURE RESERVE

Toolinna Cove

Point Culver

GREAT AUSTRALIAN BIGHT

Tower Peak

Mount Dean

Point Dempster

CAPE ARID NP

Mount Baring

Israelite Bay

Boyatup

Mount Arid

Point Malcolm

Sandy Bight

Cape Arid

Cape Pasley

North East Point

SOUTHERN OCEAN

N

0   50   100 km

© Hema Maps Pty Ltd

Western Australia Highway Index

Western Australia Alphabetic Site Index

WESTERN AUSTRALIA

Eucla to Esperance

Eyre and Coolgardie-Esperance Highways

1 Eucla Motor Hotel & Caravan Park ☎ (08) 9039 3468
Caravan Park at Eucla. Eyre Hwy
HEMA 119 G7   31 40 37 S   128 53 04 E

2 Najada Rockhole
Rest Area 30 km W of Eucla or 35 km E of Mundrabilla
HEMA 119 G7   31 44 46 S   128 36 01 E

3 Hearder Hill
Parking Area 36 km W of Eucla or 29 km E of Mundrabilla
HEMA 119 H6   31 46 02 S   128 31 42 E

4 Mundrabilla Roadhouse Caravan Park ☎ (08) 9039 3465
Caravan Park at Mundrabilla. Eyre Hwy
HEMA 119 H6   31 49 06 S   128 13 31 E

5 Kuthala Tank
Parking Area 3 km W of Mundrabilla or 113 km E of Madura. 500m S of Hwy
HEMA 119 H6   31 49 53 S   128 11 43 E

6 Jallah Rockhole
Rest Area 10 km W of Mundrabilla or 106 km E of Madura
HEMA 119 H6   31 50 26 S   128 07 49 E

7 Boolaboola Parking Area
Parking Area 54 km W of Mundrabilla or 62 km E of Madura
HEMA 119 H6   31 53 33 S   127 39 42 E

8 Carlabeencabba Rockhole
Parking Area 69 km W of Mundrabilla or 47 km E of Madura. Emergency phone
HEMA 119 H6   31 55 14 S   127 31 09 E

9 Moodini Bluff
Rest Area 90 km W of Mundrabilla or 26 km E of Madura
HEMA 119 H5   31 54 35 S   127 17 15 E

10 Madura Pass Roadhouse Motel & Caravan Park ☎ (08) 9039 3464
Caravan Park at Madura. Eyre Hwy
HEMA 119 H5   31 53 58 S   127 01 10 E

11 Olwolgin Bluff
Parking Area 24 km W of Madura or 66 km E of Cocklebiddy
HEMA 119 H5   31 55 40 S   126 46 43 E

12 Moonera Tank
Parking Area 47 km W of Madura or 43 km E of Cocklebiddy. Emergency phone
HEMA 119 H4   31 59 23 S   126 32 50 E

13 Observatory Turnoff
Parking Area 73 km W of Madura or 17 km E of Cocklebiddy. 1 km E of Eyre Bird Observatory turnoff
HEMA 119 H4   32 00 10 S   126 16 38 E

14 Jillbunya Rockhole
Parking Area 44 km W of Cocklebiddy or 21 km E of Caiguna
HEMA 119 H3   32 10 25 S   125 40 25 E

15 Oomblegabby Rest Area
Rest Area 39 km W of Caiguna or 143 km E of Balladonia
HEMA 119 H3   32 19 17 S   125 04 30 E

16 Baxter Rest Area
Rest Area 67 km W of Caiguna or 115 km E of Balladonia
HEMA 119 H3   32 21 26 S   124 47 14 E

17 Woorlba East Parking Area
Parking Area 97 km W of Caiguna or 85 km E of Balladonia
HEMA 119 H2   32 23 39 S   124 28 21 E

18 Woorlba Homestead Rest Area
Rest Area 132 km W of Caiguna or 50 km E of Balladonia. Emergency phone
HEMA 119 H2   32 26 12 S   124 06 17 E

19 90 Mile Sign
Parking Area 147 km W of Caiguna or 35 km E of Balladonia
HEMA 119 H2   32 27 12 S   123 57 17 E

20 Afghan Rock
Parking Area 177 km W of Caiguna or 5 km E of Balladonia
HEMA 119 H1   32 22 42 S   123 39 54 E

21 Harms Lake
Rest Area 25 km W of Balladonia or 167 km E of Norseman
HEMA 119 H1   32 13 28 S   123 22 34 E

22 Newman Rock
Camp Spot 50 km W of Balladonia or 142 km E of Norseman. Turn N at sign follow track for 1 km

| HEMA 119 H1 | 32 06 58 S | 123 10 04 E |

23 Mt Pleasant
Parking Area 82 km W of Balladonia or 110 km E of Norseman. Emergency phone

| HEMA 111 D14 | 32 01 20 S | 122 50 50 E |

24 Fraser Range Station ☎ (08) 9039 3210
Camp Area at Fraser Range Station. 90 km W of Balladonia 103 km E of Norseman. Signposted

| HEMA 111 D13 | 32 01 45 S | 122 47 40 E |

25 Fraser Range Rest Area
Rest Area 108 km W of Balladonia or 84 km E of Norseman

| HEMA 111 D13 | 32 04 24 S | 122 35 36 E |

26 Ten Mile Rocks
Rest Area 113 km W of Balladonia or 79 km E of Norseman

| HEMA 111 D13 | 32 04 04 S | 122 33 34 E |

27 Dundas Reserve Parking Area
Parking Area 125 km W of Balladonia or 67 km E of Norseman. Emergency phone

| HEMA 111 D13 | 32 04 01 S | 122 25 32 E |

28 Ken Lanceley Parking Area
Parking Area 145 km W of Balladonia or 47 km E of Norseman. Emergency phone

| HEMA 111 D12 | 32 03 41 S | 122 12 52 E |

29 Buldania Rocks
Camp Spot 162 km W of Balladonia or 30 km E of Norseman. Turn N, at approx 52 04 54S 122 02 14E, follow track to rocks

| HEMA 111 D12 | 32 04 43 S | 122 02 13 E |

30 Norseman East Parking Area
Parking Area 176 km W of Balladonia or 16 km E of Norseman

| HEMA 111 D12 | 32 06 36 S | 121 54 06 E |

31 Norseman Rest Area
Rest Area at Norseman. At Tourist Information Centre. Fee for use of dump point

| HEMA 111 D12 | 32 11 46 S | 121 46 51 E |

32 Norseman Recreation Reserve
Parking Area at Norseman. Entry via Sinclair St, W end. Self Contained Vehicles only

| HEMA 111 D13 | 32 11 46 S | 121 46 35 E |

33 Brockway Parking Area
Parking Area 15 km S of Norseman or 56 km N of Kumarl

| HEMA 111 D12 | 32 19 54 S | 121 45 34 E |

34 Dundas Rocks
Camp Spot 25 km S of Norseman or 46 km N of Kumarl. 2 km E of Hwy. 2 km dirt road, signposted. Access track narrows towards site, small vehicles only. Larger vehicles side tracks to stop in before rocks

| HEMA 111 E12 | 32 23 25 S | 121 46 23 E |

35 Bromus Dam
Camp Spot 32 km S of Norseman or 39 km N of Kumarl. Signposted

| HEMA 111 E12 | 32 27 31 S | 121 41 03 E |

36 Peak Charles Campground ☎ (08) 9083 2100
Peak Charles National Park
Camp Area 106 km SW of Norseman or 46 km W of Kumarl. Turn W off Coolgardie Esperance Hwy 56 km S of Norseman onto Lake King-Norseman Rd for 29 km, then S onto Peak Charles Rd for 21 km. 50 km dirt road. 4WD recommended

| HEMA 111 F11 | 32 52 45 S | 121 10 25 E |

37 Kumarl Siding
Rest Area 73 km S of Norseman or 24 km N of Salmon Gums

| HEMA 111 E12 | 32 47 16 S | 121 33 16 E |

38 Salmon Gums Community Caravan Park
Caravan Park at Salmon Gums. 31 Hicks St. Caretaker collects fees

| HEMA 111 F12 | 32 58 55 S | 121 38 53 E |

39 Grass Patch Park & Stay ☎ (08) 9075 7046
Caravan Park at Grass Patch, behind tavern in Shepherd St. Enquires at the tavern, after hours park & pay later

| HEMA 111 F12 | 33 13 44 S | 121 42 52 E |

40 Gibson Soak Hotel RV Parking ☎ (08) 9075 4020
Parking Area at Hotel. 26 km N of Esperance. See publican before parking. Self Contained Vehicles only

| HEMA 111 G12 | 33 39 05 S | 121 48 49 E |

Notes...

WESTERN AUSTRALIA

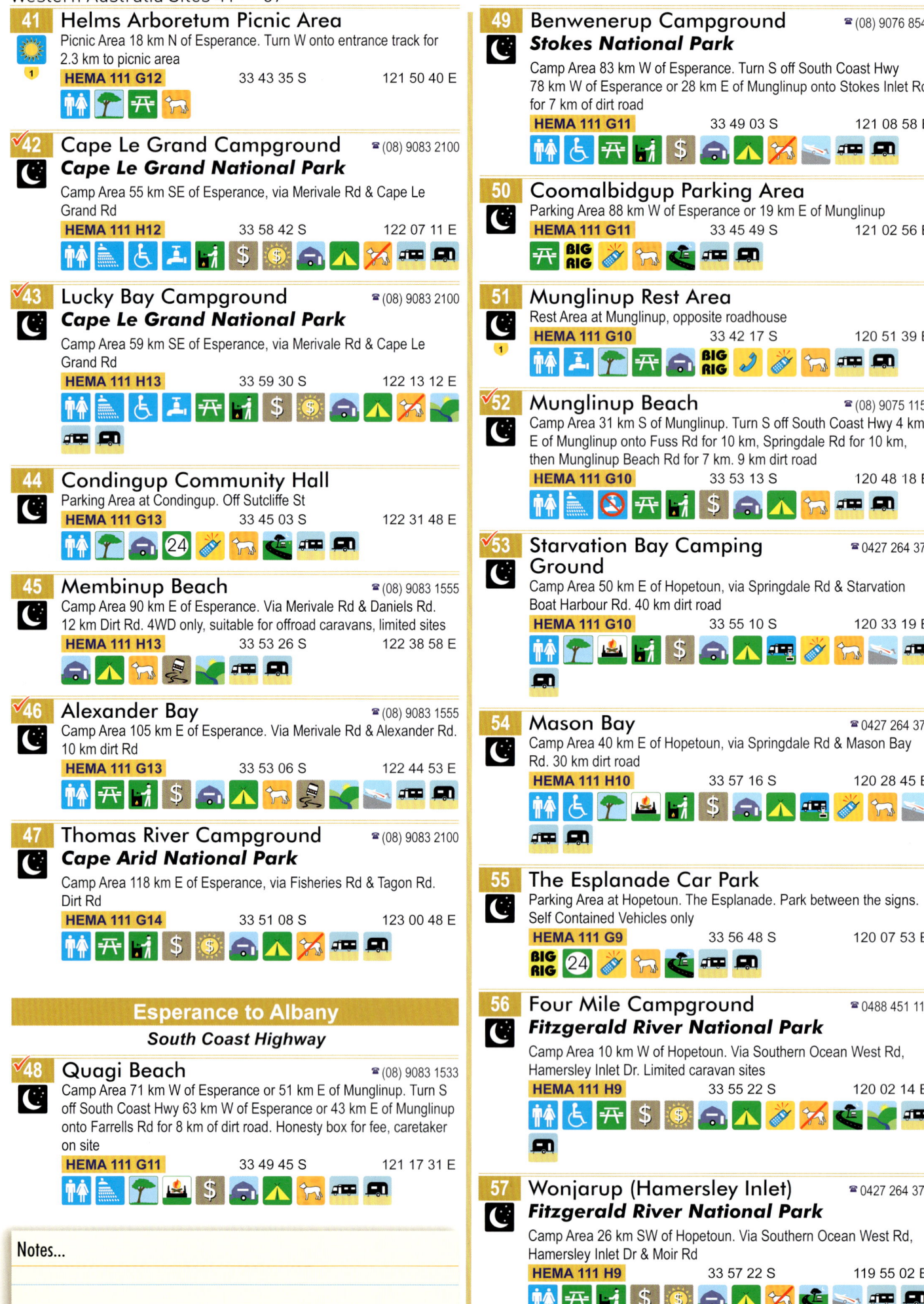

41 Helms Arboretum Picnic Area

Picnic Area 18 km N of Esperance. Turn W onto entrance track for 2.3 km to picnic area

| HEMA 111 G12 | 33 43 35 S | 121 50 40 E |

42 Cape Le Grand Campground ☎ (08) 9083 2100
Cape Le Grand National Park

Camp Area 55 km SE of Esperance, via Merivale Rd & Cape Le Grand Rd

| HEMA 111 H12 | 33 58 42 S | 122 07 11 E |

43 Lucky Bay Campground ☎ (08) 9083 2100
Cape Le Grand National Park

Camp Area 59 km SE of Esperance, via Merivale Rd & Cape Le Grand Rd

| HEMA 111 H13 | 33 59 30 S | 122 13 12 E |

44 Condingup Community Hall

Parking Area at Condingup. Off Sutcliffe St

| HEMA 111 G13 | 33 45 03 S | 122 31 48 E |

45 Membinup Beach ☎ (08) 9083 1555

Camp Area 90 km E of Esperance. Via Merivale Rd & Daniels Rd. 12 km Dirt Rd. 4WD only, suitable for offroad caravans, limited sites

| HEMA 111 H13 | 33 53 26 S | 122 38 58 E |

46 Alexander Bay ☎ (08) 9083 1555

Camp Area 105 km E of Esperance. Via Merivale Rd & Alexander Rd. 10 km dirt Rd

| HEMA 111 G13 | 33 53 06 S | 122 44 53 E |

47 Thomas River Campground ☎ (08) 9083 2100
Cape Arid National Park

Camp Area 118 km E of Esperance, via Fisheries Rd & Tagon Rd. Dirt Rd

| HEMA 111 G14 | 33 51 08 S | 123 00 48 E |

Esperance to Albany
South Coast Highway

48 Quagi Beach ☎ (08) 9083 1533

Camp Area 71 km W of Esperance or 51 km E of Munglinup. Turn S off South Coast Hwy 63 km W of Esperance or 43 km E of Munglinup onto Farrells Rd for 8 km of dirt road. Honesty box for fee, caretaker on site

| HEMA 111 G11 | 33 49 45 S | 121 17 31 E |

Notes...

49 Benwenerup Campground ☎ (08) 9076 8541
Stokes National Park

Camp Area 83 km W of Esperance. Turn S off South Coast Hwy 78 km W of Esperance or 28 km E of Munglinup onto Stokes Inlet Rd for 7 km of dirt road

| HEMA 111 G11 | 33 49 03 S | 121 08 58 E |

50 Coomalbidgup Parking Area

Parking Area 88 km W of Esperance or 19 km E of Munglinup

| HEMA 111 G11 | 33 45 49 S | 121 02 56 E |

51 Munglinup Rest Area

Rest Area at Munglinup, opposite roadhouse

| HEMA 111 G10 | 33 42 17 S | 120 51 39 E |

52 Munglinup Beach ☎ (08) 9075 1155

Camp Area 31 km S of Munglinup. Turn S off South Coast Hwy 4 km E of Munglinup onto Fuss Rd for 10 km, Springdale Rd for 10 km, then Munglinup Beach Rd for 7 km. 9 km dirt road

| HEMA 111 G10 | 33 53 13 S | 120 48 18 E |

53 Starvation Bay Camping Ground ☎ 0427 264 377

Camp Area 50 km E of Hopetoun, via Springdale Rd & Starvation Boat Harbour Rd. 40 km dirt road

| HEMA 111 G10 | 33 55 10 S | 120 33 19 E |

54 Mason Bay ☎ 0427 264 377

Camp Area 40 km E of Hopetoun, via Springdale Rd & Mason Bay Rd. 30 km dirt road

| HEMA 111 H10 | 33 57 16 S | 120 28 45 E |

55 The Esplanade Car Park

Parking Area at Hopetoun. The Esplanade. Park between the signs. Self Contained Vehicles only

| HEMA 111 G9 | 33 56 48 S | 120 07 53 E |

56 Four Mile Campground ☎ 0488 451 119
Fitzgerald River National Park

Camp Area 10 km W of Hopetoun. Via Southern Ocean West Rd, Hamersley Inlet Dr. Limited caravan sites

| HEMA 111 H9 | 33 55 22 S | 120 02 14 E |

57 Wonjarup (Hamersley Inlet) ☎ 0427 264 377
Fitzgerald River National Park

Camp Area 26 km SW of Hopetoun. Via Southern Ocean West Rd, Hamersley Inlet Dr & Moir Rd

| HEMA 111 H9 | 33 57 22 S | 119 55 02 E |

58 Kundip Rest Area
Rest Area 19 km S of Ravensthorpe or 30 km N of Hopetoun
HEMA 111 G9   33 41 25 S   120 11 10 E

59 Ravensthorpe Parking Area
Parking Area at Ravensthorpe. Cnr Morgans & Queen St. Self Contained Vehicles only
HEMA 111 G9   33 34 55 S   120 02 41 E

60 Meridian Rest Area
Rest Area 4 km W of Ravensthorpe or 109 km E of Jerramungup
HEMA 111 G9   33 34 26 S   120 00 08 E

61 Phillips River Crossing
Camp Spot 15 km W of Ravensthorpe or 98 km E of Jerramungup. 1 km E of the bridge turn S onto old detour road
HEMA 111 G12   33 36 10 S   119 53 06 E

62 Fitzgerald River (Jacup)
Parking Area 80 km W of Ravensthorpe or 33 km E of Jerramungup
HEMA 111 H8   33 49 53 S   119 15 13 E

63 Needilup Rest Area
Rest Area 14 km W of Jerramungup or 25 km E of Ongerup, behind hall
HEMA 110 H7   33 57 09 S   118 46 19 E

64 Ongerup Gardens Caravan Park ☎ 0428 282 127
Caravan Park at Ongerup. Cnr Walker & Lamont Sts
HEMA 110 H7   33 58 04 S   118 29 12 E

65 Gnowangerup Caravan Park ☎ (08) 9827 1635
Caravan Park at Gnowangerup. Richardson St. Pay at CRC or IGA. AH 0473 194 524
HEMA 109 E14   33 56 31 S   118 00 36 E

66 Louis Lookout Rest Area - North Borden
Rest Area 4 km N of Borden at Great Southern Hwy jcn
HEMA 110 H7   34 01 31 S   118 16 22 E

67 Borden Rest Area
Rest Area at Borden. Opposite General Store
HEMA 110 H7   34 04 16 S   118 15 46 E

68 Borden Recreation Ground
Parking Area at Borden. Stone St
HEMA 110 H6   34 04 22 S   118 15 31 E

69 Moingup Springs Campground ☎ (08) 9842 4500
Stirling Range National Park
Camp Area 76 km N of Albany, 65 km N of Bakers Junction or 45 km S of Borden, off Chester Pass Rd
HEMA 109 G14   34 24 03 S   118 06 08 E

70 Millers Point Reserve ☎ (08) 9835 1022
Camp Area 20 km E of Boxwood Hill or 53 km W of Bremer Bay. Turn S off Borden Bremer Bay Rd 14 km E of Boxwood Hill onto Millers Point Rd. 6 km dirt road. Small vehicles only
HEMA 110 J7   34 27 14 S   118 52 42 E

71 Quaalup Homestead Wilderness Retreat ☎ (08) 9837 4124
Camp Area 77 km SW of Jerramungup or 48 km N of Bremer Bay. From Jerramungup turn E after 28 km onto Devil Creek Rd. Dirt road. Limited solar power, no generators permitted, no credit cards
HEMA 111 H8   34 15 37 S   119 24 35 E

72 St Mary Inlet ☎ 0488 451 119
Fitzgerald River National Park
Camp Area 97 km SE of Jerramungup. Via Devils Creek Rd, Collets Rd, Pableup Dr & Point Ann Rd
HEMA 111 H9   34 09 51 S   119 34 35 E

73 Pallinup River
Rest Area 67 km S of Jerramungup or 15 km NE of Wellstead. 5 km S of Bremer Bay intersection
HEMA 110 J7   34 24 24 S   118 43 35 E

74 Cape Riche Campground ☎ (08) 9847 3088
Camp Area 18 km SE of Wellstead, via Sandalwood Rd. Limited space for big rigs. Dirt road
HEMA 110 J7   34 35 52 S   118 44 56 E

75 Green Range Rest Area
Rest Area 25 km SW of Wellstead or 73 km NE of Albany
HEMA 110 J7   34 37 41 S   118 22 51 E

76 Normans Beach ☎ (08) 9842 4500
Camp Spot 14 km S of Manypeaks. Turn SE off South Coast Hwy 3 km SW of Manypeaks or 36 km NE of Albany onto Homestead Rd for 9 km, then onto Normans Beach Rd for 2 km. 6 km dirt road
HEMA 110 J7   34 55 17 S   118 12 51 E

Notes...

WESTERN AUSTRALIA

77 Bettys Beach ☎ (08) 9842 4500
Camp Spot 17 km S of Manypeaks. Turn SE off South Coast Hwy 3 km SW of Manypeaks or 36 NE of Albany onto Homestead Rd for 9 km then onto Bettys Beach Rd for 5 km. 9 km dirt road. Limited space. Closed 15 Feb - 30 Apr for salmon season

| HEMA 110 J7 | 34 56 12 S | 118 12 30 E |

78 Napier Creek
Parking Area 25 km N of Albany or 23 km S of Porongurup. S of Napier Bridge on L

| HEMA 109 J14 | 34 49 51 S | 117 57 36 E |

Albany-Bunbury-Perth
South Western Highway

79 Torbay Inlet ☎ (08) 9841 9333
Camp Area 28 km W of Albany or 38 km E of Denmark. Turn S off Lower Denmark Rd 24 km W of Albany or 34 E of Denmark onto Perkins Beach Rd & Torbay Inlet Rd. Dirt road for 4 km. Small area. Maximum stay 7 days

| HEMA 109 K13 | 35 02 22 S | 117 40 47 E |

✓ 80 Cosy Corner (East)
Camp Area 30 km W of Albany or 38 km E of Denmark. Turn S off Lower Denmark Rd 25 km W of Albany or 33 km E of Denmark onto Cosy Corner Rd. Maximum stay 7 days

| HEMA 109 K13 | 35 03 33 S | 117 38 44 E |

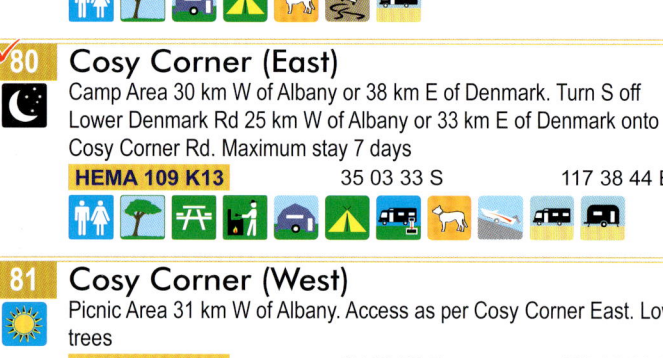

81 Cosy Corner (West)
Picnic Area 31 km W of Albany. Access as per Cosy Corner East. Low trees

| HEMA 109 K13 | 35 03 53 S | 117 38 36 E |

82 Shelley Beach Camping Area ☎ (08) 9844 4090
West Cape Howe National Park
Camp Area 38 km W of Albany. Access via Cosy Corner, Coombes & Shelley Bch Rds. 5.5 km dirt road, very steep descent. No caravans permitted, small vehicles only, small area

| HEMA 109 K12 | 35 06 32 S | 117 37 46 E |

83 Parry Beach ☎ (08) 9848 2055
Camp Area 28 km W of Denmark or 43 km E of Walpole. Turn S 22 km W of Denmark or 43 km E of Walpole onto Parry Rd for 6 km. Maximum stay 3 weeks. Maximum height limit 2.75m. Small vehicles only. Large vehicle overflow now adjacent with no facilities, fee applies time limit for overflow area is 24 hours

| HEMA 109 K10 | 35 02 25 S | 117 09 42 E |

84 Boat Harbour Camping & Chalets ☎ (08) 9840 8212
Camp Area 26 km W of Denmark on the South Coast Hwy, turn S into Boat Harbour Rd

| HEMA 109 K10 | 35 00 08 S | 117 06 01 E |

85 Ayr Sailean Chalets Camping Cottages ☎ (08) 9840 8098
Camp Area 35 km W of Denmark or 7 km E of Bow Bridge. 1 Tindale Rd (cnr S Coast Hwy). Fee for pets

| HEMA 109 J10 | 34 57 09 S | 117 01 08 E |

86 Walpole West Rest Area
Rest Area 16 km W of Walpole or 104 km SE of Manjimup

| HEMA 109 J8 | 34 57 16 S | 116 35 39 E |

87 Crystal Springs Campground ☎ (08) 9840 0400
D'Entrecasteaux National Park
Camp Area 13 km W of Walpole, turn S onto Mandalay Beach Rd. No caravans

| HEMA 109 K8 | 34 59 00 S | 116 36 21 E |

88 Fernhook Falls Campground ☎ (08) 9840 0400
Mount Frankland South National Park
Camp Area 39 km NW of Walpole or 88 km SE of Manjimup. Turn E 35 km NW of Walpole or 83 km SE of Manjimup onto Beardmore Rd for 5 km. Small sites, no caravans

| HEMA 109 K8 | 34 49 01 S | 116 35 28 E |

89 Mt Burnside Rest Area
Rest Area 56 km NW of Walpole or 64 km SE of Manjimup

| HEMA 109 H8 | 34 39 10 S | 116 29 42 E |

90 Quinninup Eco Tourist Park ☎ (08) 9773 1329
Caravan Park at Quinninup. Lot 11 Wheatley Coast Rd

| HEMA 108 G7 | 34 26 11 S | 116 14 44 E |

91 Greens Island ☎ (08) 9771 1831
Camp Spot via Graphite Rd, 26 km W of Manjimup. Turn N into Donnelly Dr 1.7 km past bridge, then onto Greens Island Rd. 2 km dirt road. Small vehicles only

| HEMA 108 F5 | 34 11 58 S | 115 56 45 E |

92 Jayes Bridge
Picnic Area 15 km S of Boyup Brook. Turn W off Boyup Brook-Kojonup Rd 6 km S of Boyup Brook onto Aegers Bridge Rd (dirt road). Beside Blackwood River

| HEMA 108 E7 | 33 54 48 S | 116 24 25 E |

93 Querijup Pool
Camp Spot 6 km SE of Mayanup. Travel E on Blackwood Rd for 1.1 km, turn S onto Scotts Brook Rd for 5.5 km. Track to camp spots, small vehicles only

| HEMA 109 E8 | 33 58 00 S | 116 30 39 E |

94 Boyup Brook Flaxmill Caravan Park ☎ (08) 9765 1200
Caravan Park at Boyup Brook. Jackson St. E end of town. AH number 0427 651 437
HEMA 108 D7   33 50 06 S   116 23 59 E

95 Harvey Dickson's Country Music Centre Campground ☎ (08) 9765 1125
Camp Area 5 km NE of Boyup Brook on the Arthur River Rd
HEMA 108 D7   33 48 25 S   116 25 18 E

96 Trigwell Bridge
Parking Area 24 km SW of Moodiarrup or 36 km NE of Boyup Brook
HEMA 109 C8   33 40 27 S   116 35 54 E

97 Maranup Ford Caravan Park ☎ (08) 9761 1200
Caravan Park 20 km W of Bridgetown. Turn N onto Maranup Ford Rd or 10 km S of Greenbushes, turn S on Maranup Ford Rd. Entrance opposite 5 Gates Rd
HEMA 108 E5   33 56 12 S   116 01 27 E

98 Willow Springs
Picnic Area 31 km SW of Bridgetown or 27 km E of Nannup. Turn S 25 km W of Bridgetown or 22 km E of Nannup, onto Gold Gully Rd. 5 km dirt road
HEMA 108 E5   34 02 52 S   115 55 24 E

99 Karri Gully Picnic Site
Picnic Area on the Brockman Hwy. 19 km E of Nannup or 27 km W of Bridgetown. Small area
HEMA 108 E5   34 00 28 S   115 56 28 E

100 Workmans Pool ☎ (08) 9752 5555
St Johns Brook Conservation Park
Camp Area 8 km NW of Nannup. Turn W 2 km N of Nannup onto Mowen Rd, Brook Rd. Signposted
HEMA 108 E4   33 57 14 S   115 41 16 E

101 Barrabup Pool ☎ (08) 9752 5555
St Johns Brook Conservation Park
Camp Area 9 km NW of Nannup. Turn W 2 km N of Nannup onto Mowen Rd, Brook Rd. Signposted. Small vehicles only
HEMA 108 E4   33 56 38 S   115 41 34 E

102 Wrights Bridge ☎ (08) 9731 6232
Camp Area 29 km NE of Nannup or 11 km SW of Balingup, on Balingup-Nannup Rd, beside Blackwood River
251
HEMA 108 D5   33 50 45 S   115 55 07 E

103 Balingup Transit Park ☎ (08) 9764 1051
Camp Area at Balingup. 1 km NE of PO. Turn R onto Jayes Rd, then L onto Walter St. Beside Balingup Brook
1
HEMA 108 D5   33 46 55 S   115 59 10 E

104 Greenbushes Rest Area
Rest Area 2 km N of Greenbushes or 8 km S of Balingup, near N exit to Greenbushes. Near the sportsground
1
HEMA 108 D6   33 50 16 S   116 02 54 E

105 Wattle Ridge Vineyard ☎ (08) 9764 3594
Camp Spot at Greenbushes. On Greenbushes - Boyup Brook Rd. 2 km E of Greenbushes
HEMA 108 D6   33 49 45 S   116 04 16 E

106 Grimwade Settlement
Camp Spot 13 km NE of Balingup or 16 km E of Kirup, via Grimwade Rd, Preston Rd
HEMA 108 D6   33 42 00 S   116 03 02 E

107 Kirup Caravan Park ☎ (08) 9731 6311
Caravan Park at Kirup. 47 South Western Hwy
HEMA 108 D5   33 42 28 S   115 53 34 E

108 Donnybrook Transit Park ☎ (08) 9731 1897
Caravan Park at Donnybrook. 18 Reserve Rd, entry at W end of the oval. Must book in at BP & collect key
HEMA 108 C5   33 34 16 S   115 49 12 E

109 Thomson Brook Wines ☎ (08) 9731 0590
Parking Area 5.5 km E of Donnybrook. Via Donnybrook - Boyup Brook & Thompson Rd. Self Contained Vehicles only. Check in at the Cellar door on arrival
HEMA 108 C5   33 34 12 S   115 52 36 E

110 Ironstone Gully Falls
Camp Area 18 km SW of Donnybrook or 17 km SE of Capel on Goodwood Rd. Limited space
HEMA 108 C4   33 39 12 S   115 42 12 E

111 Buffalo Road Rest Area
Rest Area 25 km N of Bunbury or 81 km S of Mandurah
1
HEMA 108 A4   33 11 58 S   115 43 02 E

Notes...

112 Belvidere Campground ☎ (08) 9735 1988

Leschenault Peninsula Conservation Park

Camp Area 25 km N of Bunbury or 14 km NW of Australind. Follow Buffalo Rd, along Preston Lake, continue along dirt road to campsites for 4.4 km

HEMA 108 A4   33 14 07 S   115 41 48 E

113 Martins Tank Lake ☎ (08) 9405 0750

Yalgorup National Park

Camp Area 74 km N of Bunbury or 58 km S of Mandurah. Turn W off Bunbury Hwy 61 km N of Bunbury or 45 km S of Mandurah onto Preston Beach Rd for 12 km. 5 km dirt road. Small vehicles only. Bookings essential

HEMA 106 J2   32 50 44 S   115 40 02 E

114 John Tognela Rest Area

Rest Area 32 km S of Ravenswood. 2 areas, one for N & S bound traffic

HEMA 106 J2   32 48 52 S   115 44 28 E

Ravensthorpe-Hyden-Perth

Brookton Highway

115 Overshot Hill Nature Reserve

Rest Area 9 km N of Ravensthorpe or 61 km S of Lake King, on Ravensthorpe-Lake King Rd

HEMA 111 G9   33 31 39 S   119 59 36 E

116 Lake King Caravan Park ☎ (08) 9874 4048

Caravan Park at Lake King, Critchley Ave. Register & pay at tavern across road

HEMA 111 F9   33 05 02 S   119 41 18 E

117 Varley Chicken Ranch

Parking Area at Varley. Seward Ave, via Pitt St. Donation box

HEMA 111 E8   32 47 41 S   119 30 35 E

118 Tressies Museum & Caravan Park ☎ (08) 9889 5043

Caravan Park at Karlgarin. 4313 Kondinin-Hyden Rd

HEMA 110 E7   32 29 44 S   118 42 43 E

119 The Forrestania Plots

Camp Spot 64.5 km E of Hyden on Hyden-Norseman Rd. Dirt road. Signposted

HEMA 111 E8   32 24 55 S   119 32 01 E

120 The Breakaways

Camp Area 137.4 km E of Hyden on Hyden-Norseman Rd. Signposted follow track for 500m to sites. Dirt road

HEMA 111 D10   32 16 34 S   120 15 46 E

121 McDermid Rock

Camp Area 192 km E of Hyden, or 141 km W of Norseman on Hyden-Norseman Rd. Turn N, travel 1.5 km to rock

HEMA 111 D10   32 01 18 S   120 44 20 E

122 Lake Johnston

Camp Area 200 km E of Hyden or 102 km W of Norseman on the Hyden-Norseman Rd. Access track S side of road

HEMA 111 D10   32 00 37 S   120 47 22 E

123 Disappointment Rock

Camp Area 87 km W of Norseman or 246 km E of Hyden on the Hyden-Norseman Rd. Narrow access track, limited space

HEMA 111 D11   32 07 48 S   120 55 44 E

124 Woodlands Picnic Area

Picnic Area 48 km W of Norseman or 285 km E of Hyden on the Hyden-Norseman Rd

HEMA 111 D11   32 11 15 S   121 20 16 E

125 Kulin Caravan Park ☎ 0439 469 850

Caravan Park at Kulin. 82 Johnson St

HEMA 107 H13   32 40 02 S   118 09 31 E

126 Kulin Overnight Stop ☎ (08) 9880 1204

Camp Spot at Kulin. Johnston St (Southside), entry between toilets & skate park. Self Contained Vehicles only

HEMA 107 H13   32 40 13 S   118 09 20 E

127 Harrismith Caravan Park ☎ (08) 9883 1010

Caravan Park at Harrismith. Cnr Railway Ave & Baylon St. Check in at the pub

HEMA 107 J12   32 56 10 S   117 51 44 E

128 Kondinin Caravan Park ☎ (08) 9889 1006

Caravan Park at Kondinin. Gordon St. Key & payment at Shire office or at roadhouse

HEMA 107 G13   32 29 43 S   118 15 49 E

129 Town Hall Parking Area

Parking Area at Kondinin. Jones St opposite Town Hall. Up to 11m. Self Contained Vehicles only

HEMA 107 G14   32 29 45 S   118 16 04 E

130 Gorge Rock Pool

Picnic Area 20 km SE of Corrigin or 28 km W of Kondinin

HEMA 107 G12   32 27 25 S   117 59 45 E

WESTERN AUSTRALIA

131 Narembeen Caravan Park ☎ (08) 9064 7308
Caravan Park at Narembeen. Currall St
HEMA 107 E14   32 03 49 S   118 23 46 E

132 Bruce Rock Caravan Park ☎ (08) 9061 1377
Caravan Park at Bruce Rock, Dunstall St, next to swimming pool. AH
call 0428 611 401
HEMA 107 D13   31 52 26 S   118 09 05 E

133 Bruce Rock Sporting Complex ☎ (08) 9061 1687
Parking Area at Bruce Rock, Dunstall St, veer R after entry,
signposted. Self Contained Vehicles only, permit required
HEMA 107 D13   31 52 23 S   118 09 04 E

134 Kokerbin Rock
Picnic Area 47 km W of Bruce Rock or 43 km E of Quairading. Turn N
off Bruce Rock-Quairading Rd 40 km W of Bruce Rock or 36 km E of
Quairading onto Kwolyin Rd West for 7 km
HEMA 107 D11   31 53 12 S   117 42 34 E

✓135 Kwolyin Camp
Camp Area at Kwolyin. Situated on the Old Kwolyin township site off
the Bruce Rock-Quairading Rd
HEMA 107 D11   31 55 56 S   117 45 46 E

136 Quairading Caravan Park ☎ (08) 9645 1001
Caravan Park at Quairading. McLennan St. AH 0427 392 407
HEMA 107 E10   32 00 44 S   117 24 09 E

137 Toapin Weir
Rest Area 8 km N of Quairading. Signposted, turn W from Cunderdin-
Quairading Rd 5.5 km N of Quairading. 3 km gravel road to weir.
Small caravans only
HEMA 107 E9   31 58 44 S   117 21 36 E

138 Wamenusking Sports Club
Parking Area 36 km N of Corrigin. 2789 Corrigin-Quairading Rd
HEMA 107 E10   32 08 50 S   117 37 04 E

139 Aldersyde Parking Area
Parking Area 28 km E of Brookton or 63 km W of Corrigin
HEMA 107 F10   32 19 11 S   117 16 30 E

140 Boyagin Rock
Picnic Area 36 km SW of Brookton. Turn S 19 km W of Brookton onto
York Williams Rd for 10 km then E onto Boyagin Rd & Perch Rd
HEMA 106 G7   32 28 15 S   116 53 11 E

Lake King to Bunbury

141 Lake Grace Caravan Park ☎ (08) 9865 1263
Caravan Park at Lake Grace. Mather St
HEMA 107 K14   33 05 59 S   118 27 33 E

142 Kukerin Caravan Park
Caravan Park at Kukerin. 31 Bath St. Bookings & keys avaliable from
Kukerin Tavern
HEMA 107 K13   33 11 09 S   118 04 59 E

143 Dumbleyung Caravan Park ☎ (08) 9863 4012
Caravan Park at Dumbleyung, Harvey St. Opposite Shire office.
Caretaker AH 0458 851 709
HEMA 109 B13   33 18 49 S   117 44 25 E

144 Stubbs Park
Parking Area in Dumbleyung. Bahr Rd. Self Contained Vehicles only
HEMA 109 B13   33 19 04 S   117 44 36 E

145 Darkan Caravan Park ☎ (08) 9736 2222
Caravan Park at Darkan. Lot 274 Coalfield Rd. 1 km W of PO. AH
0427 362 970
HEMA 109 B9   33 20 03 S   116 43 29 E

✓146 Stockton Lake Recreation Area ☎ (08) 9735 1988
Camp Area 8 km E of Collie. Turn S off Hwy 107, 53 km W of Darkan
or 6 km E of Collie, onto Piavanini Rd
HEMA 108 B6   33 23 05 S   116 13 43 E

147 Glen Mervyn Dam
Camp Spot at Glen Mervyn Dam. Camping on the W side only. 18 km
S of Collie on the Collie - Mumballup Rd. Small vehicles only
HEMA 108 B6   33 30 18 S   116 05 50 E

148 Minningup Pool
Picnic Area 5 km SW of Collie, via Patterson St & Mungalup Rd
HEMA 108 B6   33 22 35 S   116 08 15 E

Notes...

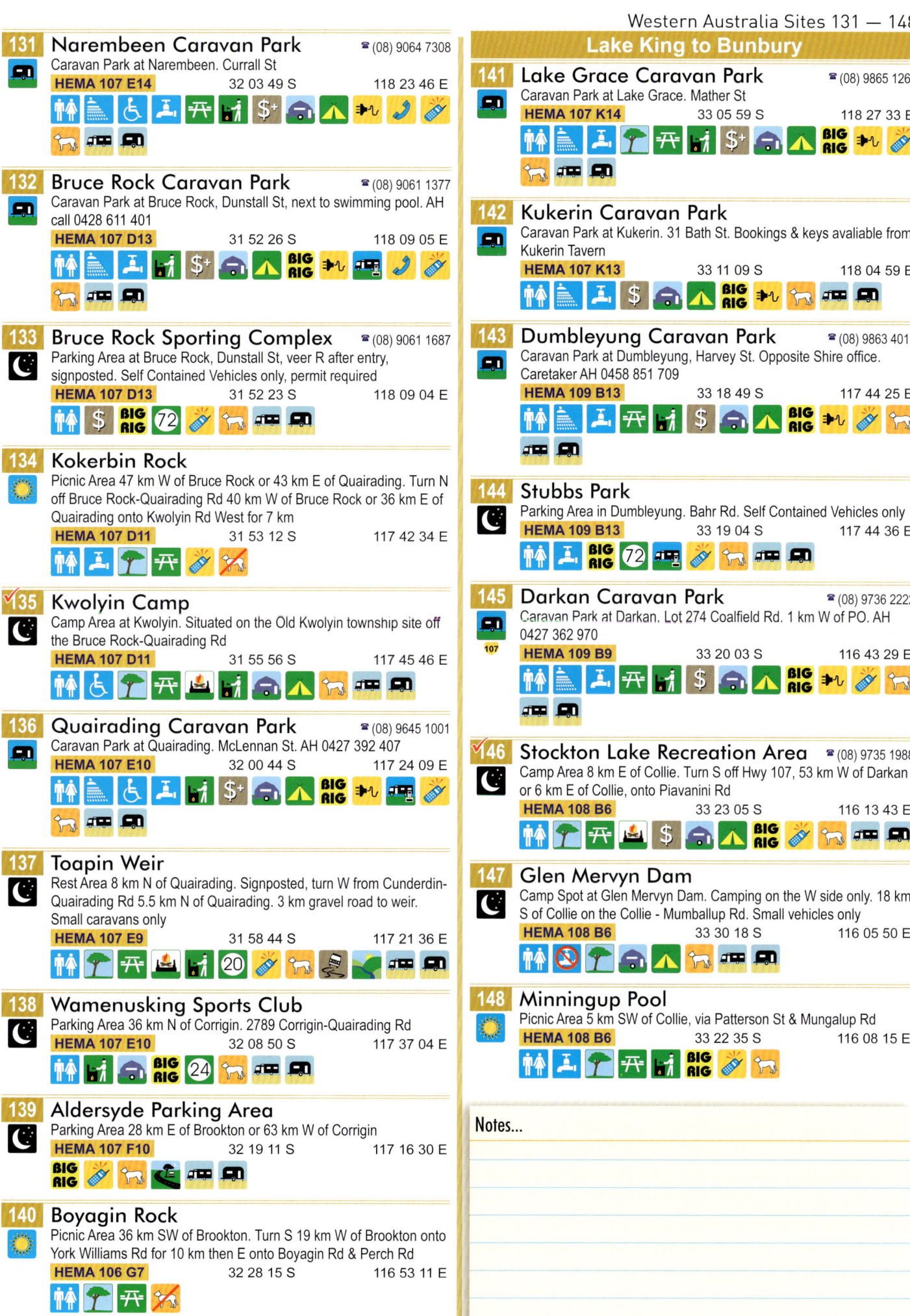

WESTERN AUSTRALIA

149 Potters Gorge ☎ (08) 9735 1988
Wellington National Park
Camp Area 29 km W of Collie, via Coalfields Rd, Wellington Dam Rd & Tom Jones Dr
HEMA 108 B5   33 23 25 S   115 58 55 E

150 Honeymoon Pool (Stones Brook) ☎ (08) 9735 1988
Wellington National Park
Camp Area 28 km W of Collie, via Coalfields Rd, Wellington Dam Rd & River Rd. Windy road small vehicles only. No caravans allowed
HEMA 108 B5   33 22 48 S   115 56 12 E

151 Coalfields Road Rest Area
Rest Area 23 km W of Collie or 13 km E of South West Hwy/ Coalfields Rd jcn
HEMA 108 B5   33 17 30 S   115 56 56 E

Cranbrook to Northam

Great Southern Highway

152 Nyabing Recreation Reserve ☎ (08) 9829 1051
Camp Area at Nyabing, Martin St. Key at Shire office
HEMA 110 G6   33 32 45 S   118 08 48 E

153 Pingrup Caravan Park ☎ (08) 9820 1101
Caravan Park at Pingrup. 18 Sanderson St. Payment at CRC, AH see notice board
HEMA 110 G7   33 32 05 S   118 30 40 E

154 Wagin Caravan Park ☎ 0419 611 057
Caravan Park at Wagin. Cnr of Arthur Rd & Scadden St. 1 km W of PO
HEMA 109 B11   33 18 39 S   117 20 05 E

155 Wagin Showgrounds ☎ (08) 9861 1177
Camp Area at Wagin. Entry via Ballagin St. Self Contained Vehicles only
HEMA 109 B11   33 18 20 S   117 20 10 E

156 Wickepin Caravan Park ☎ (08) 9888 1089
Caravan Park at Wickepin. Wogolin Rd, behind Police Station
HEMA 107 H10   32 46 52 S   117 30 12 E

157 Wickepin RV Stop ☎ (08) 9888 1005
Parking Area at Wickepin. Wogolin Rd, behind 24 hour fuel depot. Self Contained Vehicles only
HEMA 107 H10   32 46 53 S   117 29 59 E

158 Lake Yealering Caravan Park ☎ (08) 9888 7014
Caravan Park at Yealering. Beside lake
HEMA 107 H10   32 35 37 S   117 37 32 E

159 Cuballing RV Parking Area ☎ (08) 9883 6031
Parking Area at Cuballing, Western side of road between the Hwy & Railway line
HEMA 107 J9   32 49 15 S   117 10 48 E

160 Yornaning Dam
Picnic Area at Yornaning. Entry off Yornaning Rd N end of town
HEMA 107 H9   32 44 19 S   117 09 21 E

161 LazeAway Holiday Farm & Caravan Park ☎ (08) 9887 5027
Caravan Park. Great Southern Hwy, Popanyinning. 4 km S of PO
HEMA 107 H8   32 41 34 S   117 08 40 E

162 Pingelly Caravan Park ☎ (08) 9887 1351
Caravan Park at Pingelly. 26 Sharrow St
HEMA 107 G8   32 32 09 S   117 05 07 E

163 Kulyalling Picnic Area
Picnic Area 10 km N of Pingelly or 10 km S of Brookton
HEMA 107 G8   32 27 37 S   117 02 55 E

164 Brookton Caravan Park & Camping Ground ☎ (08) 9642 1106
Caravan Park at Brookton. Brookton Hwy. Behind recreation ground. Caretaker 0474 497 618
HEMA 108 E6   32 22 07 S   117 00 08 E

165 Beverley Caravan Park ☎ 0457 344 434
Caravan Park at Beverley. Council Rd, off main Hwy. N end of town
HEMA 107 E8   32 06 28 S   116 55 25 E

166 Apex Park
Rest Area at Beverley. Cnr Vincent & Lukin Sts. Self Contained Vehicles only. Donation box
HEMA 107 E8   32 06 27 S   116 55 52 E

167 White Gum Farm ☎ 0408 906 520

Camp Area 20 km E of York. 680 Cameron Rd. Via Northam-York Rd, Goldfields Rd. Permission required for pets prior to arrival

HEMA 107 D8   31 52 10 S   116 57 31 E

168 Gwambygine Park

Picnic Area 23 km N of Beverley or 10 km S of York. Self Contained Vehicles only

HEMA 106 E7   31 58 20 S   116 48 35 E

169 Avon Park

Parking Area at York. Lowe St. Self Contained Vehicles only

HEMA 106 D7   31 53 19 S   116 46 13 E

Albany to Perth

Albany Highway

170 Mount Barker RV Stop

Parking Area at Mount Barker. Muir St, bitumen area to the W of the Hall. Self Contained Vehicles only

HEMA 109 H13   34 37 29 S   117 39 45 E

171 Sturdee Road Rest Area

Rest Area 12 km N of Mt Barker or 94 km S of Kojonup

HEMA 109 H12   34 32 05 S   117 36 05 E

172 Cranbrook RV Stop

Parking Area at Cranbrook. Gathorne St, opposite the hotel, behind the museum. Fees payable to the Shire office. Self Contained Vehicles only

HEMA 109 F12   34 17 42 S   117 33 19 E

173 Lake Nunijup

Picnic Area 39 km NW of Mount Barker. Turn W 19 km N of Mount Barker or 20 km S of the Albany Hwy/Great Southern Hwy jcn onto Martagallup Rd

HEMA 109 G12   34 24 19 S   117 24 20 E

174 Lake Poorrarecup ☎ (08) 9826 1008

Camp Area 42 km SW of Cranbrook. Turn S off Cranbrook-Frankland Rd 33 km W of Cranbrook or 13 km E of Frankland onto Poorrarecup Rd. 9 km dirt road. Fees apply during peak periods

HEMA 109 G11   34 25 06 S   117 14 08 E

175 Frankland River Caravan Park ☎ 0428 302 489

Caravan Park at Frankland. Off the Wingebellup Rd, behind town hall. Caretaker collects fees

HEMA 109 G10   34 21 42 S   117 04 57 E

176 Tone Bridge Rest Area

Rest Area 1.5 km NW of Tonebridge, via Cranbrook - Boyup Brook Rd. S side of bridge, by river

HEMA 109 F9   34 13 40 S   116 42 16 E

177 Muirs Bridge Rest Area

Rest Area 11 km W of Rocky Gully or 87 km E of Manjimup, beside Frankland River

HEMA 109 G9   34 28 38 S   116 54 07 E

178 Lake Muir Observatory

Rest Area 34 km W of Rocky Gully or 64 km E of Manjimup

HEMA 109 G8   34 26 25 S   116 38 58 E

179 Katanning Caravan Park & BP Roadhouse ☎ (08) 9821 1155

Caravan Park at Katanning. 68 Cornwall St

HEMA 109 C12   33 42 04 S   117 33 36 E

180 Lions Park RV Parking Area

Parking Area at Katanning, via Clive & Albion Sts. Marked parking bays, Self Contained Vehicles only. Donation welcomed

HEMA 109 C12   33 41 43 S   117 33 01 E

181 Woodanilling Caravan Park ☎ (08) 9823 1681

Caravan Park at Woodanilling. Cnr Robinson Rd & Great Southern Hwy

HEMA 109 C12   33 33 51 S   117 25 26 E

182 Woodanilling Recreation Reserve ☎ (08) 9823 1506

Parking Area in Woodanilling, Yairabin St. Self Contained Vehicles only. Limited sites. Donation required

HEMA 109 C12   33 33 36 S   117 25 59 E

183 Queerarrup Lake ☎ (08) 9823 1506

Camp Area 28 km NW of Woodanilling. Turn N off Robinson Rd 15 km W of Woodanilling onto Reshke Rd, follow for 3 km turn L onto Douglas Rd, R onto Queerarrup Rd, turn R at T jcn. Self Contained Vehicles only

HEMA 109 C11   33 30 55 S   117 13 27 E

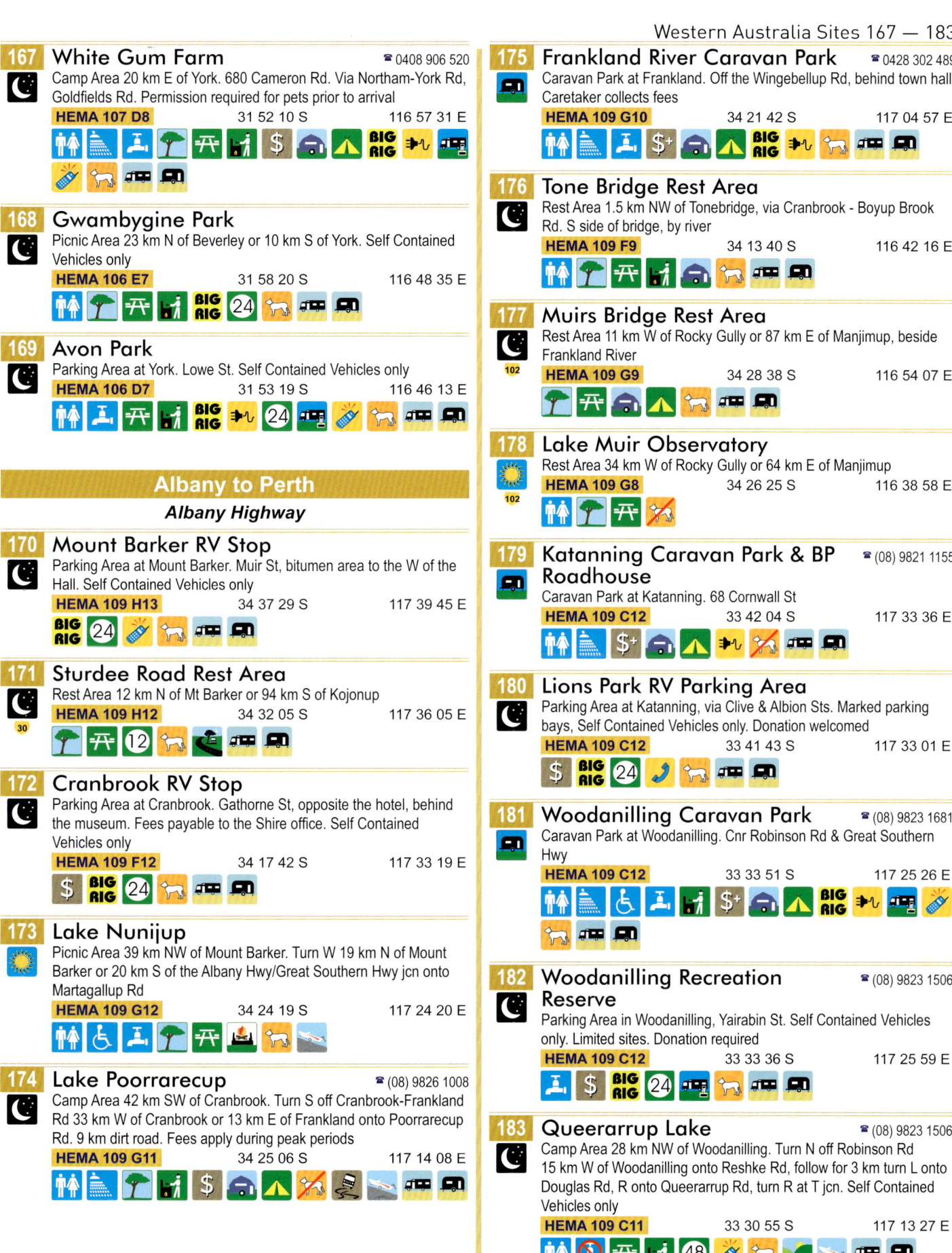

Notes...

184 Kojonup Rest Area ☎ (08) 9831 0500

Rest Area at Kojonup. Gordon St S end of town. Permit required from Info Centre 143 Albany Hwy. Self Contained Vehicles only

HEMA 109 D10   33 50 13 S   117 09 32 E

185 Martup Pool

Camp Spot 32 km N of Kojonup or 24 km S of Arthur River. Some low trees, follow track to riverside camping

HEMA 109 C10   33 32 47 S   117 05 07 E

186 Lakeside Camping (Lake Towerrinning) ☎ (08) 9863 1040

Camp Area 40 km SW of Arthur River or 64 km NE of Boyup Brook. 2 km N of Moodiarrup, via Darkan Rd S

HEMA 109 C9   33 35 02 S   116 47 32 E

187 Eulin Crossing

Camp Spot 20 km SW of Moodiarrup or 49 km NE of Boyup Brook. Turn SE 16 km from Moodiarrup or 45 km from Boyup Brook onto Kulikup N Rd for 4.3 km. Turn W into Eulin Crossing Rd. Follow for 1 km, track down to camp spot. Small vehicles only

HEMA 109 C8   33 42 02 S   116 40 28 E

188 Congelin Campground
Dryandra Woodland ☎ (08) 9881 9200

Camp Area 27 km N of Williams, via York-Williams Rd. Turn N off Hwy 30, 3 km NW of Williams onto York-Williams Rd. Signposted

HEMA 107 J7   32 49 15 S   116 53 20 E

189 Gnaala Mia Campground
Dryandra Woodland ☎ (08) 9881 9200

Camp Area 27 km N of Williams via Albany Hwy. Turn N off Hwy 3 km NW of Williams onto York-Williams Rd, then Godfrey Rd

HEMA 106 H7   32 48 34 S   116 52 25 E

190 Pumphreys Bridge Lions Park

Camp Spot at Pumphreys Bridge. Via Wandering - Narrogin Rd, 43 km N Narrogin. NW side of the CWA building

HEMA 106 H7   32 39 45 S   116 54 17 E

191 Wandering Caravan Park ☎ (08) 9884 1056

Caravan Park at Wandering. Cheetaning St. Payment at Shire office, after hours at tavern.

HEMA 106 H6   32 41 03 S   116 40 29 E

192 Armoin Nature Based Campground ☎ 0437 906 510

Camp Area 6 km S of Crossman or 34 km N of Williams on the Albany Hwy. Bookings essential, additional fee for use of toilets if required

HEMA 106 J6   32 49 26 S   116 36 53 E

193 Boddington RV Stop

Parking Area at Boddington. In Old School Grounds off Waraming Way. Self Contained Vehicles only

HEMA 106 H6   32 47 59 S   116 28 25 E

194 Bannister Parking Area

Parking Area 11 km N of Crossman or 4 km S of Bannister

HEMA 106 H6   32 42 47 S   116 32 47 E

195 Jarrahdale Old Mill

Parking Area at Jarradale. Millars Rd off Jarradale Rd. Self Contained Vehicles only

HEMA 106 F4   32 20 03 S   116 04 07 E

Perth to Bunbury
South Western Highway

196 Frank Lupino Memorial Park

Picnic Area 16 km S of Armadale or 42 km N of Pinjarra. 2 km N of Jarrahdale turnoff

HEMA 106 F4   32 17 04 S   116 00 45 E

197 Pinjarra RV Parking Area

Parking Area at Pinjarra. Cnr South Western Hwy & Pinjarra Williams Rd. Opposite Premier Hotel. Self Contained Vehicles only

HEMA 106 H3   32 37 41 S   115 52 43 E

198 Herron Point

Camp Area near Lake Clifton. Turn N off Old Bunbury Rd 16 km SW of Pinjarra or 14 km E of Old Coast Rd/Old Bunbury Rd jcn onto Herron Point Rd. Onsite caretaker for fees

HEMA 106 H2   32 44 28 S   115 42 38 E

199 Marrinup Townsite Campground ☎ (08) 9538 1078

Camp Spot 5 km NW of Dwellingup. Turn N 2.2 km W of Dwellingup or 25 km E of Pinjarra onto Grey Rd. Travel 2.7 km, cross railway line follow signposted track up hill to open camping area

HEMA 106 H4   32 42 07 S   116 01 40 E

200 Nanga Mill
Lane Pool Reserve ☎ (08) 9538 1078

Camp Area 18 km S of Dwellingup, via Nanga Rd. Dirt road

HEMA 106 H4   32 48 10 S   116 06 14 E

201 Chuditch Campground
Lane Pool Reserve ☎ (08) 9538 1078

Camp Area 16 km S of Dwellingup. 8.5 km from entry station, via Murray Valley Rd. Small vehicles only, limited caravan sites. Bookings essential

HEMA 106 H4   32 47 18 S   116 06 43 E

202 Baden Powell Campground ☎ (08) 9538 1078
Lane Pool Reserve

Camp Area 9 km S of Dwellingup & 1.5 km from entry station, via Nanga Rd. Bookings essential

HEMA 106 H4   32 46 18 S   116 05 12 E

203 Charlies Flat Campground ☎ (08) 9538 1078
Lane Pool Reserve

Camp Area 14.5 km S of Dwellingup & 7 km from entry station on River Rd, via Nanga Rd. Dirt road. Small vehicles only, limited caravan sites. Bookings essential

HEMA 106 H4   32 48 56 S   116 06 21 E

204 The Stringers Campground ☎ (08) 9538 1078
Lane Pool Reserve

Camp Area 19 km S of Dwellingup, via Nanga Rd & Murray Valley Rd. Dirt road. Tents only, no caravans or camper trailers. Bookings essential

HEMA 106 H4   32 48 08 S   116 06 24 E

205 Yarragil Campground ☎ (08) 9538 1078
Lane Pool Reserve

Camp Area 20 km S of Dwellingup, via Nanga Rd. Dirt road. Tents only, no caravans or camper trailers. Bookings required

HEMA 106 H4   32 48 13 S   116 07 22 E

206 Lake Navarino Spillway Picnic Area

Picnic Area at Waroona Dam 8 km E of Waroona. Access via Nanga Brook Rd, Scarp Rd & Invarell Rd. Past Navarino Resort over dam wall, turn R at T jcn

HEMA 106 J3   32 50 58 S   115 59 00 E

207 Navarino Lakeside Camping ☎ (08) 9733 3000

Camp Area at Waroona Dam. Access via Navarino Resort. Fees payable at resort. Bookings necessary for powered site

HEMA 106 J3   32 50 29 S   115 59 52 E

208 Wagerup Parking Area

Parking Area 6 km N of Yarloop or 6 km S of Waroona

HEMA 106 J3   32 53 36 S   115 54 30 E

209 Hoffman Mill ☎ (08) 9735 1988

Camp Area 22 km E of Yarloop. Turn E 5 km S of Yarloop or 9 km N of Harvey, onto Logue Brook Dam Rd & Clarke Rd. 11 km dirt road. Closed between Easter & end October

HEMA 106 J4   33 00 15 S   116 04 59 E

210 Logue Brook Campground ☎ (08) 9733 5402
Dwellingup State Forest

Camp Area at Lake Brockman. Turn E on to Logue Brook Dam Rd off South Western Hwy 6 km S of Yarloop, then onto Scarp Rd. Must call at Tourist Park kiosk to pay fees. Bookings preferred

HEMA 106 J3   33 00 19 S   115 58 26 E

211 Lake Brockman Bush Camping ☎ (08) 9735 1988

Camp Area at Lake Brockman NW side. 20 km NE of Harvey. Turn E on to Logue Brook Dam Rd off SW Hwy 6 km S of Yarloop. Continue over dam wall and then 3 km to end of the road. Bush camping. Ranger collects fees

HEMA 106 J3   32 59 17 S   115 58 49 E

Bunbury-Margaret River-Northcliffe
Bussell, Brockman and Vasse Highways

212 Pine Plantation Picnic Area

Picnic Area 6 km SW of Capel, on Ludlow Tuart Forest Dr. No fires

HEMA 108 C3   33 36 00 S   115 29 17 E

213 Canebrake Pool ☎ (08) 9752 5555
Rapids Conservation Park

Camp Area 25 km E of Margaret River. Turn E 4 km N of Margaret River or 7 km S of Cowaramup, onto Osmington, Canebrake & Crossing Rds. 5 km dirt road

HEMA 108 D2   33 52 55 S   115 16 52 E

214 Wharncliffe Mill Bush Retreat ☎ (08) 9758 8227

Camp Area at Margaret River. Carters Rd

HEMA 108 E1   33 56 05 S   115 04 39 E

215 Big Valley Campsite ☎ (08) 9757 5020

Camp Area 12 km SE of Margaret River on a sheep farm. Via Bussell Hwy 2 km, turn E onto Rosa Brook Rd 7 km & S onto Wallis Rd for 2 km

HEMA 108 E2   33 59 04 S   115 09 18 E

216 Warner Glen (Chapman Pool) ☎ (08) 9752 5555
Blackwood River National Park

Camp Area 15 km SE of Witchcliffe or 21 km NE of Karridale. Turn E 6 km S of Witchcliffe or turn N 11 km E of Karridale onto Warner Glen Rd for 8 km

HEMA 108 E2   34 05 33 S   115 12 23 E

Notes...

217 Conto Chuditch Campground ☎ (08) 9757 7025
Leeuwin-Naturaliste National Park
Camp Area 19 km SW of Margaret River or 20 km NW of Karridale. Turn W off Caves Rd 16 km SW of Margaret River or 18 km NW of Karridale onto Conto Rd
HEMA 108 E1   34 04 50 S   115 00 43 E

218 Conto Quenda Campground ☎ (08) 9757 7025
Leeuwin-Naturaliste National Park
Camp Area 19 km SW of Margaret River. Turn W off Caves Rd onto Conto Rd
HEMA 108 E1   34 04 57 S   115 00 47 E

219 Boranup Campground ☎ (08) 9752 5555
Leeuwin-Naturaliste National Park
Camp Area 35 km SW of Margaret River or 8 km NW of Karridale, via Caves Rd & Boranup Dr. Small vehicles only
HEMA 108 F1   34 10 41 S   115 04 04 E

220 Alexandra Bridge Camping Area ☎ (08) 9780 5679
Camp Area 10 km E of Karridale or 65 km SW of Nannup. Veer L into Clarke Dr, beside Blackwood River. Generators allowed. Cold Showers
HEMA 108 F2   34 09 51 S   115 11 10 E

221 Sues Bridge Campground ☎ (08) 9752 5555
Blackwood River National Park
Camp Area 40 km NE of Karridale. Turn N 30 km E of Karridale or 46 km SW of Nannup onto Sues Rd for 9 km
HEMA 108 E3   34 04 37 S   115 23 24 E

222 Grass Tree Hollow Campground ☎ (08) 9776 1207
D'Entrecasteaux National Park
Camp Area 84 km E of Karridale or 25 km NW of Pemberton. Turn S into Boat Landing Rd. Limited tent only sites, small vehicles only. 2 km dirt road
HEMA 108 G4   34 25 33 S   115 48 20 E

223 Big Brook Arboretum ☎ (08) 9776 1207
Camp Area 10 km N of Pemberton, via Club Rd, Pump Hill Rd, Tramway Trail & Rainbow Trail. Small vehicles only
HEMA 108 G5   34 24 14 S   116 00 14 E

224 Moons Crossing
Warrens State Forest
Camp Spot 17 km SE of Pemberton via Spring Gully & Moons Crossing Rds. 4WD recommended
HEMA 108 G5   34 30 23 S   116 08 45 E

225 Windy Harbour Campground ☎ (08) 9776 8398
D'Entrecasteaux National Park
Camp Area at Windy Harbour, 28 km SW of Northcliffe. Maximum stay 3 months
HEMA 108 J6   34 50 19 S   116 01 27 E

Norseman to Perth
Coolgardie-Esperance and Great Eastern Highways

226 Mt Thirsty
Parking Area 15 km N of Norseman or 151 km S of Coolgardie
HEMA 111 D12   32 06 03 S   121 41 40 E

227 Cave Hill Nature Reserve
Camp Spot 50 km SW of Widgiemooltha or 87 km S of Coolgardie. Turn W on to Higginsville Pump Station Rd. 4WD only, small off road caravans
HEMA 111 C11   31 39 41 S   121 13 25 E

228 Kambalda West RV Stop
Parking Area at Kambalda West. Behind Rec centre off Barnes Dr, facilites at Rec centre during opening hours
HEMA 111 B12   31 12 23 S   121 37 17 E

229 Lake Douglas Recreation Reserve
Camp spot 12 km SW of Kalgoorlie or 26 km NE Coolgardie. Turn S & follow signs for 3.5 km. 2 km dirt road
HEMA 111 B11   30 50 38 S   121 23 35 E

230 Centennial Park ☎ 1800 004 653
Rest Area at Kalgoorlie. Cnr Hannan St & Patroni Rd. Self Contained Vehicles only
HEMA 111 A11   30 45 45 S   121 27 27 E

231 Burra Rock ☎ (08) 9080 5555
Goldfields Woodlands National Park
Camp Spot 59 km S of Coolgardie, via Hunt St & Burra Rock Rd. 33 km dirt road
HEMA 111 C11   31 23 03 S   121 12 02 E

232 Victoria Rock ☎ (08) 9080 5555
Goldfields Woodlands National Park
Camp Spot 45 km SW of Coolgardie. From Coolgardie, via Jobson St & Victoria Rock Rd. Dirt road
HEMA 111 B11   31 17 35 S   120 55 32 E

233 Railway Museum
Parking Area at Coolgardie. Woodward St. Self Contained Vehicles only
HEMA 111 B11   30 57 22 S   121 09 40 E

234 Yerdani Well
Rest Area 56 km W of Coolgardie or 129 km E of Southern Cross
HEMA 111 B10   31 08 22 S   120 37 41 E

235 Wallaroo Rock   ☎ (08) 9080 5555
Wallaroo Conservation Park
Camp Area 103 W of Coolgardie. Turn N off Hwy 64 km W of Coolgardie or 123 km E of Southern Cross at the Old Woolgangie Township sign. 39 km 4WD track to rock
HEMA 111 B10   31 03 29 S   120 17 53 E

236 Boondi Lookout
Parking Area 75 km W of Coolgardie or 109 km E of Southern Cross. S side of road, follow old road
HEMA 111 B10   31 11 21 S   120 26 43 E

237 Boondi Rest Area
Rest Area 76 km W of Coolgardie or 108 km E of Southern Cross
HEMA 111 B10   31 11 18 S   120 25 45 E

238 Boondi Rock   ☎ (08) 9080 5555
Goldfields Woodlands National Park
Camp Area 83 km W of Coolgardie or 107 km E of Southern Cross. Turn N 81 km W of Coolgardie or 105 km E of Southern Cross for 3 km of dirt road. 7.5 km E of Boorabbin-Jaurdi Rd. Signposted
HEMA 111 B10   31 10 52 S   120 23 04 E

239 Boorabbin Memorial
Rest Area 90 km W of Coolgardie or 96 km E of Southern Cross
HEMA 111 B9   31 12 26 S   120 18 33 E

240 Boorabbin Rest Area
Rest Area 114 km W of Coolgardie or 68 km E of Southern Cross
HEMA 111 B9   31 16 08 S   120 01 00 E

241 Karalee Rock & Dam   ☎ (08) 9049 1001
Camp Area 137 km W of Coolgardie or 52 km E of Southern Cross. Turn N 133 km W of Coolgardie or 48 km E of Southern Cross for 5 km of dirt road. Signposted
HEMA 111 B9   31 15 03 S   119 50 24 E

242 Southern Cross Parking Area
Parking Area at Southern Cross. Cnr Great Eastern Hwy & Three Boys Rd. Self Contained Vehicles only
HEMA 111 B8   31 14 06 S   119 19 09 E

243 Bodallin Pioneers Park
Rest Area at Bodallin
HEMA 110 C7   31 22 12 S   118 51 23 E

244 Carrabin Roadhouse Motel & Caravan Park   ☎ (08) 9046 7162
Caravan Park at Carrabin
HEMA 110 C7   31 22 44 S   118 40 41 E

245 Westonia Caravan Park   ☎ (08) 9046 7063
Caravan Park at Westonia. Wolfram St
HEMA 110 B7   31 18 16 S   118 41 50 E

246 St Lukes Church Parking Area   ☎ (08) 9046 7063
Parking Area in Westonia, 69 Wolfram St. Self Contained Vehicles only
HEMA 110 B7   31 17 59 S   118 41 50 E

247 Rabbit Proof Fence Parking Bay
Parking Area 6 km W of Walgoolan or 2 km E of Burracoppin
HEMA 107 B14   31 23 23 S   118 30 05 E

248 Burracoppin Centenary Park
Rest Area at Burracoppin, centre of town
HEMA 107 B14   31 23 54 S   118 28 46 E

249 Merredin Peak Reserve
Parking Area at Merredin. Entry at Benson & Watson Rds. Self Contained Vehicles only
HEMA 107 B13   31 28 42 S   118 17 25 E

250 Kellerberrin Caravan Park   ☎ 0428 138 474
Caravan Park at Kellerberrin. Cnr of Moore & George St
HEMA 107 C11   31 37 30 S   117 43 01 E

251 Meckering Memorial Park
Rest Area at Meckering. Kelly St. Donation requested
HEMA 107 C8   31 37 58 S   117 00 26 E

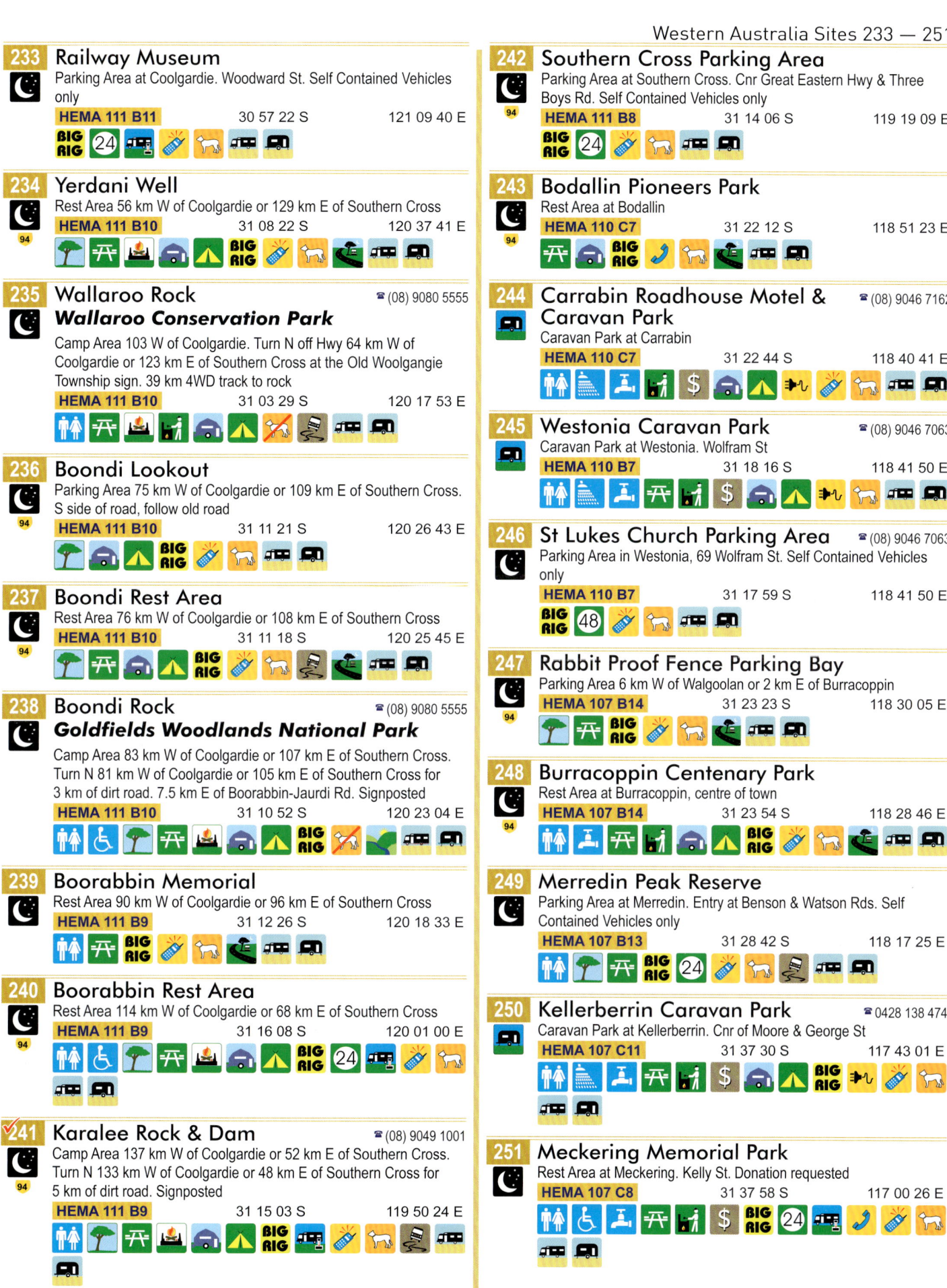

Notes...

WESTERN AUSTRALIA

252 Eadine Springs Picnic Area

Picnic Area 14 km SW of Northam or 32 km NE of The Lakes. 1 km dirt road off Hwy. Unlevel area

| HEMA 106 C6 | 31 42 45 S | 116 32 23 E |

253 Viveash Reserve

Parking Area 14 km S of Toodyay via Northam-Toodyay Rd. Cnr Katrine Rd

| HEMA 106 C6 | 31 37 03 S | 116 33 13 E |

254 Homestead Campground
Avon Valley National Park
☎ (08) 9571 1371

Camp Area 40 km W of Toodyay or 35 km N of Gidgegannup. Turn W off Toodyay Rd 24 km S of Toodyay or 19 km N of Gidgegannup onto Morangup Rd for 5 km, then onto Quarry Rd for 9 km, then Governors Dr for 2 km

| HEMA 106 C4 | 31 36 36 S | 116 14 29 E |

255 Drummonds Campground
Avon Valley National Park
☎ (08) 9571 1371

Camp Area 43 km W of Toodyay or 38 km N of Gidgegannup. Turn W off Toodyay Rd 24 km S of Toodyay or 19 km N of Gidgegannup onto Morangup Rd for 5 km, then onto Quarry Rd for 9 km, then Governors Dr for 5 km. Small vehicles only

| HEMA 106 C4 | 31 36 21 S | 116 13 45 E |

256 Bald Hill Campground
Avon Valley National Park
☎ (08) 9571 1371

Camp Area 44 km W of Toodyay or 39 km N of Gidgegannup. Turn W off Toodyay Rd 24 km S of Toodyay or 19 km N of Gidgegannup onto Morangup Rd for 5 km, then onto Quarry Rd for 9 km, then Governors Dr for 6 km. Small vehicles only

| HEMA 106 C4 | 31 26 21 S | 116 13 24 E |

257 Valley Campground
Avon Valley National Park
☎ (08) 9571 1371

Camp Area 41 km W of Toodyay or 36 km N of Gidgegannup. Turn W off Toodyay Rd 24 km S of Toodyay or 19 km N of Gidgegannup onto Morangup Rd for 5 km, then onto Quarry Rd for 9 km, then 41 Mile Rd for 3 km. Small vehicles only

| HEMA 106 C4 | 31 35 15 S | 116 14 34 E |

258 Lake Leschenaultia
☎ (08) 9295 0202

Camp Area at Chidlow 12 km NE of Mundaring. Bookings essential. Small vehicles only No caravans or motorhomes, vehicle size limit applies, ring for details

| HEMA 106 D5 | 31 51 01 S | 116 15 08 E |

Coolgardie-Leonora-Meekatharra

259 Ora Banda Historical Inn
☎ (08) 9024 2444

Camp Area 70 km NW of Kalgoorlie. Turn W 40 km N of Kalgoorlie onto Broad Arrow - Ora Banda Rd. 10 km dirt road

| HEMA 113 G11 | 30 22 34 S | 121 03 41 E |

260 Rowles Lagoon Conservation Park
☎ (08) 9080 5555

Camp Area 70 km N of Coolgardie, via Coolgardie North Rd through Kunanalling & Kintore. Dirt road

| HEMA 113 G11 | 30 25 38 S | 120 51 50 E |

261 Credo Homestead
☎ (08) 9080 5555

Camp Area 75 km NW of Coolgardie. Via Coolgardie North Rd through Kununalling & Kintore. Bookings essential at DEC Kalgoorlie. Caretaker (08) 9024 2063

| HEMA 113 H11 | 30 27 55 S | 120 49 38 E |

262 Baden Powell Mine Rest Area

Rest Area 67 km N of Kalgoorlie or 64 km S of Menzies

| HEMA 113 G11 | 30 13 28 S | 121 12 02 E |

263 Goongarrie Homestead
☎ (08) 9080 5555

Camp Area 104 km NW of Kalgoorlie. Signposted turnoff 90 km N of Kalgoorlie or 43 km S of Menzies. Bookings essential at DEC Kalgoorlie

| HEMA 113 G11 | 29 58 56 S | 121 02 43 E |

264 Menzies Caravan Park
☎ (08) 9024 2702

Caravan Park at Menzies. Shenton St. AH 0448 242 041

| HEMA 113 F11 | 29 41 38 S | 121 01 44 E |

265 Lake Ballard

Camp Area 55 km W of Menzies. Road closes with rain, check at Menzies before travelling

| HEMA 113 F11 | 29 26 56 S | 120 36 11 E |

266 Mt Elvire Reserve
☎ (08) 9080 5555

Camp Area 179 km NW of Menzies. Travel W on Menzies-Evanston Rd for 137 km turn N near Bullfinch Rd for 42 km. Signposted. 4WD access only. Book ahead

| HEMA 113 F9 | 29 21 47 S | 119 35 51 E |

267 Kookynie Well Rest Area

Rest Area 32 km N of Menzies or 72 km S of Leonora

| HEMA 113 F11 | 29 29 14 S | 121 15 25 E |

Notes...

268 Morapoi Station ☎ (08) 9031 3380
Camp Area at Morapoi Station. 53 km NE of Menzies or 74 km S of Leonora. Turn E into Kookynie Mount Remarkable Rd 42 km N of Menzies. 10 km dirt road
HEMA 113 F12   29 24 18 S   121 22 49 E

269 Kookynie Rest Area
Rest Area 47 km N of Menzies or 57 km S of Leonora
HEMA 113 F11   29 21 29 S   121 16 15 E

270 Niagara Dam ☎ (08) 9024 2041
Camp Area 60 km NE of Menzies, via Kookynie Rd, Niagara Dam Rd
HEMA 113 F12   29 24 15 S   121 25 40 E

271 Grand Kookynie Hotel ☎ (08) 9031 3010
Camp Area at Kookynie. Malcom Rd. Facilities are at main hotel next door
HEMA 113 F12   29 20 10 S   121 29 27 E

272 Malcolm Dam ☎ (08) 9037 6044
Camp Spot 13 km E of Leonora. Turn N 10 km along Laverton-Leonora Rd. 3 km dirt road, veer R at fork for spots along edge of dam
HEMA 113 E12   28 52 44 S   121 26 49 E

273 Gwalia Museum ☎ (08) 9037 7122
Parking Area 3.7 km S side of Leonora. Sign posted Museum & Hoover House, follow road to the end, turn L up the hill. Please register at Museum. Fully Self Contained Vehicles only
HEMA 113 E11   28 54 52 S   121 19 59 E

274 Ford Run Rest Area
Rest Area 52 km S of Leinster or 79 km N of Leonora
HEMA 113 D11   28 13 40 S   121 05 08 E

275 Leinster South
Parking Area 3 km S of Leinster turn off 128 km N of Leonora
HEMA 113 D11   27 57 03 S   120 43 01 E

276 Leinster Caravan Park ☎ (08) 9037 9218
Caravan Park at Leinster. Mainsbridge St. Payment at Leinster Tavern
HEMA 113 D11   27 55 07 S   120 41 53 E

277 Peter Denny Lookout
Rest Area 114 km W of Leinster or 39 km E of Sandstone
HEMA 113 D9   27 56 21 S   119 37 55 E

278 Lake Mason ☎ (08) 9080 5555
Camp Area 56 km N of Sandstone & 5 km off the Gidgee Mine Rd. Bookings essential at DEC Kalgoorlie. 4WD access only
HEMA 113 C9   27 35 16 S   119 31 13 E

279 Jones Creek Parking Area
Rest Area 58 km N of Leinster or 114 km S of Wiluna. Small area, parking for larger vehicles 100m N on W side road
HEMA 113 C10   27 28 45 S   120 32 12 E

280 Lake Way Rest Area
Rest Area 117 km N of Leinster or 58 km S of Wiluna
HEMA 113 C10   27 02 25 S   120 24 40 E

281 Gunbarrel Laager Travellers Rest ☎ (08) 9981 7161
Camp Area 11.8 km E of Wiluna. Signposted off Gunbarrel Hwy
HEMA 113 B10   26 36 01 S   120 20 26 E

Perth to Lancelin

282 Henry White Oval ☎ (08) 9303 7759
Yanchep National Park
Camp Area 50 km N of Perth CBD off Indian Ocean Dr. Turn R into Yanchep National Park. Signposted. Must register
HEMA 106 C2   31 32 55 S   115 41 07 E

283 Jarrahs End
Parking Area 7 km N of Yanchep NP turnoff or 28 km S of Guilderton turnoff
HEMA 106 B2   31 30 01 S   115 41 09 E

284 Wilbinga Grove
Rest Area 23 km N of Yanchep NP turnoff or 12 km SE of Guilderton turnoff
HEMA 106 B2   31 22 23 S   115 37 15 E

285 Sandy Lake Farm ☎ 0428 288 422
Camp Area 22 km W of Gingin. 344 Tangletoe Rd Muckenburra. Self Contained Vehicles only
HEMA 106 B2   31 20 57 S   115 46 20 E

286 Moore River Bridge
Rest Area 33 km N of Yanchep NP turnoff or 2 km SE of Guilderton turnoff
HEMA 106 B1   31 18 12 S   115 33 18 E

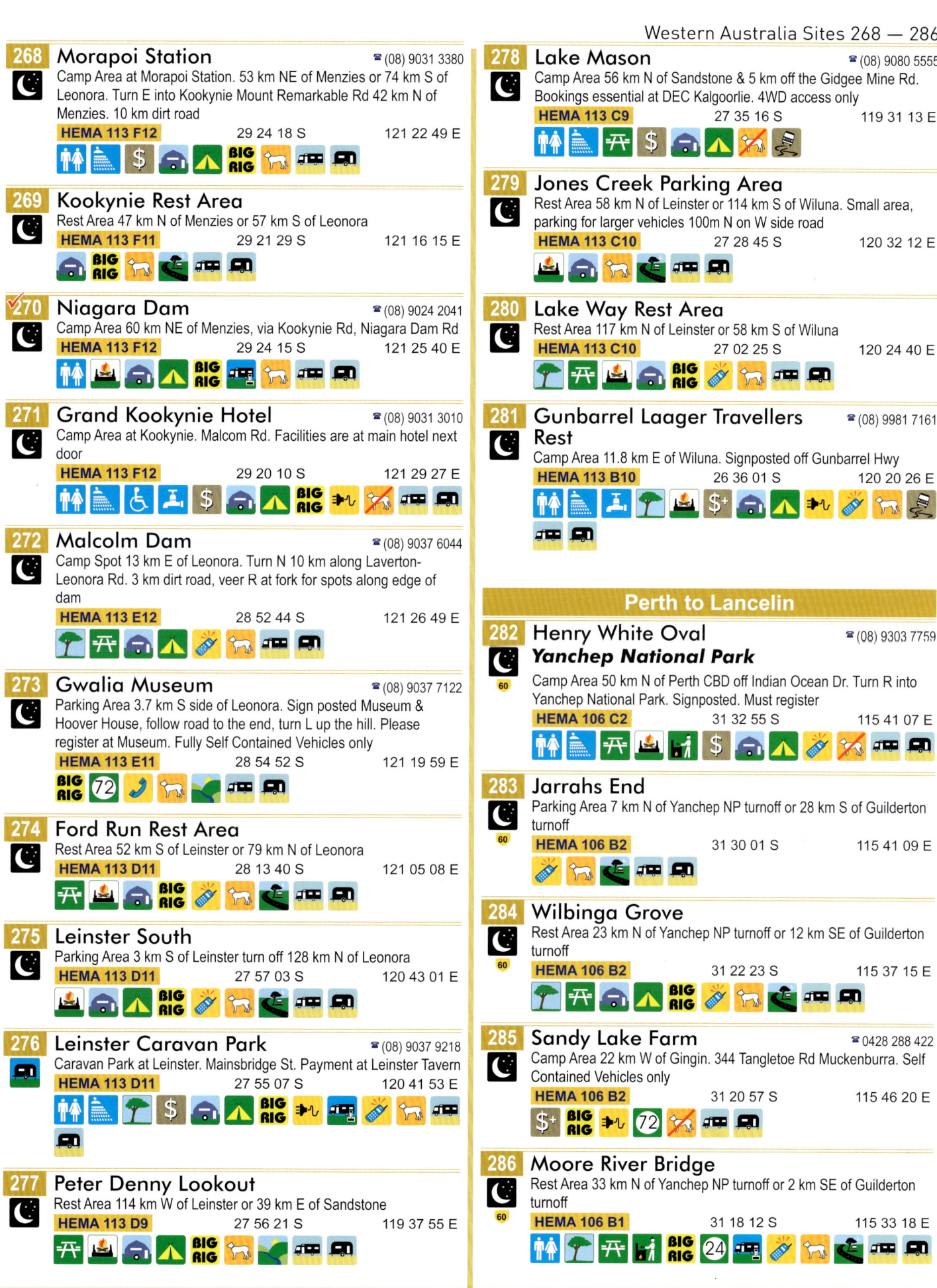

Notes...

Wubin - Mullewa - Geraldton

287 Buntine Rocks
Camp Spot 18 km NW of Wubin or 25 km SE of Latham, via Buntine East Rd. 3 km dirt Rd
HEMA 112 G6 — 29 58 13 S — 116 35 07 E

288 Coorow Caravan Park ☎ (08) 9952 0100
Caravan Park at Station St
HEMA 112 G5 — 29 52 51 S — 116 01 02 E

289 Carnamah Caravan Park ☎ (08) 9951 1785
Caravan Park At Carnamah. King St. Next to Niven Park
HEMA 112 G5 — 29 41 10 S — 115 53 28 E

290 Bunjil Rocks
Camp Spot 57 km N of Wubin or 29 km S of Perenjori. At the Bunjil Rocks signpost turn W for 1 km onto Iona Rd, then into signposted track on R. Dirt road
HEMA 112 G6 — 29 39 56 S — 116 22 18 E

291 Caron Dam Reserve
Camp Spot 13 km S of Perenjori or 65 km N of Wubin. Turn W at Caron Dam sign follow for 1 km
HEMA 112 F5 — 29 33 56 S — 116 18 57 E

292 Perenjori Caravan Park ☎ (08) 9973 1193
Caravan Park at Perenjori. Crossing Rd
HEMA 112 F5 — 29 26 09 S — 116 17 17 E

293 Perenjori Rest Area
Rest Area at Perenjori. Mullewa-Wubin Rd, between Anzac Memorial & Village Green. Self Contained Vehicles only
HEMA 112 F5 — 29 26 30 S — 116 17 11 E

294 Koolanooka Springs
Camp Spot 30 km E of Morawa, via Morawa-Yalgoo Rd, Munckton Rd, Fallon Rd, Kalanooka Rd & Mungada Rd. 16 km dirt road
HEMA 112 F5 — 29 11 25 S — 116 14 19 E

295 Morawa Caravan Park ☎ (08) 9971 1204
Caravan Park at Morawa. White Ave
HEMA 112 F5 — 29 12 31 S — 116 00 27 E

296 Ross Road Parking Bay
Parking Area 23 km NW of Morawa or 75 km SE of Mullewa
HEMA 112 F5 — 29 01 02 S — 115 56 20 E

297 Canna Hall ✓
Camp Area at Canna. Turn off the Wubin - Mullewa Rd into Offszanka Rd, travel 3 km to Hall. Box at hall for power fee
HEMA 112 E5 — 28 53 51 S — 115 51 50 E

298 Wilroy Nature Reserve
Rest Area 79 km NW of Morawa or 19 km SE of Mullewa
HEMA 112 E5 — 28 38 25 S — 115 38 56 E

299 Yalgoo Caravan Park ☎ (08) 9962 8472
Caravan Park at Yalgoo. 200 Gibbons St
HEMA 112 E6 — 28 20 40 S — 116 40 54 E

300 Gabyon Station ☎ (08) 9963 7993
Camp Area at Gabyon Station. 54 km W of Yalgoo or 99 km E of Mullewa. Turn N onto Gabyon - Tardie Rd off the Geraldton Mt Magnet Rd. 17 km of gravel road. Signposted. GPS at entrance
HEMA 112 D5 — 28 15 01 S — 116 20 29 E

301 Mullewa Caravan Park ☎ (08) 9961 1161
Caravan Park at Mullewa. Pay at service station
HEMA 112 E4 — 28 32 19 S — 115 30 14 E

302 Tenindewa Pioneer Well (Woolya)
Picnic Area 22 km W of Mullewa or 84 km E of Geraldton. Turn N off Hwy 123 on to Yuna Rd, 18 km W of Mullewa or 80 km E of Geraldton for 500m, turn R into Well Site Rd for 1.1 km
HEMA 112 E4 — 28 36 38 S — 115 21 52 E

303 Indarra
Parking Area 22 km W of Mullewa or 76 km E of Geraldton
HEMA 112 E4 — 28 38 37 S — 115 19 19 E

304 Curara Farm Bush Camp ☎ (08) 9961 1461
Camp Spot 22 km NW of Mullewa. 19 km N of Mullewa on the Carnarvon Mullewa Rd turn W into Urawa Rd, 3 km on turn W into Nangerwalla Rd. 4.5 km dirt Rd. Signposted. Donation appreciated in the box on site
HEMA 112 E4 — 28 22 47 S — 115 33 21 E

305 Greenough River
Parking Area 47 km N of Mullewa or 161 km S of Murchison Roadhouse
HEMA 112 D5 — 28 11 03 S — 115 41 14 E

WESTERN AUSTRALIA

306 Wandina Station Stay
☎ (08) 9962 9597

Camp Area at Wandina Station. 70 km N of Mullewa. Turn W onto Wandina Rd. 4 km dirt road. Limited power

HEMA 112 D5   27 59 10 S   115 37 53 E

307 Ballinyoo Bridge

Parking Area 132 km N of Mullewa or 76 km S of Murchison Roadhouse. Various tracks along river, N side better. Dirt road

HEMA 112 C5   27 31 35 S   115 46 29 E

308 Stock Well 9

Camp Spot 53 km S of Muchison Settlement or 148 km N of Mullewa. Turn E, follow track to well

HEMA 112 C5   27 20 40 S   115 53 41 E

309 Wooleen Station
☎ (08) 9963 7973

Camp Area at Wooleen Station. 50 km SE of Muchison Settlement. Sign posted on Carnarvon Mullewa Rd. Open 1st April to 31st October. Booking recommended

HEMA 112 C5   27 05 14 S   116 09 36 E

310 Murchison Oasis Roadhouse & Caravan Park
☎ (08) 9961 3875

Caravan Park at Murchison Settlement

HEMA 112 C5   26 53 46 S   115 57 26 E

Bindoon to Dongara
Midlands Road

311 Wannamal (Robert Hindmarsh) Rest Area

Rest Area 26 km N of Bindoon or 59 km S of Moora, opposite the community hall

HEMA 106 A4   31 09 54 S   116 03 29 E

312 Three Springs Short Stay Parking
☎ (08) 9954 1001

Parking Area at Three Springs. Next to sports oval, facilities open during daylight hours

HEMA 112 F5   29 32 15 S   115 45 39 E

313 Arrino Siding

Rest Area at Arrino, 18 km N of Three Springs or 35 km S of Mingenew

HEMA 112 F5   29 26 22 S   115 37 41 E

314 Mingenew Spring Caravan Park
☎ (08) 9928 1019

Caravan Park at Mingenew. Lee Steere St. 1 km SW of PO

HEMA 112 F4   29 11 34 S   115 26 17 E

315 Enanty Barn

Parking Area 3.5 km NE of Mingenew via Mingenew-Mullewa Rd. Self Contained Vehicles only

HEMA 112 F4   29 10 19 S   115 27 27 E

316 Breakaway Campground
Coalseam Conservation Park
☎ (08) 9921 5955

Camp Area 34 km N of Mingenew or 50 km S of Mullewa. Access from Mingenew is dirt road, access from Mullewa is steep in places. Maximum stay 3 nights between August - October

HEMA 112 E5   28 57 01 S   115 32 23 E

317 Miners Camp
Coalseam Conservation Park
☎ (08) 9964 0901

Camp Area 35 km N of Mingenew or 52 km S of Mullewa. Access from Mingenew is dirt road, access from Mullewa is steep in places. Maximum stay 3 nights between August - October

HEMA 112 E5   28 57 29 S   115 33 15 E

Perth to Port Hedland
Brand and North West Coastal Highways

318 Regans Ford

Rest Area 43 km N of Gingin or 32 km S of Cataby. Beside Moore River. Toilets only at Northern area

HEMA 110 B2   30 59 20 S   115 42 17 E

319 Dandaragan Transit Caravan Park
☎ (08) 9651 4071

Caravan Park at Dandaragan. Pioneer Park

HEMA 110 A2   30 40 13 S   115 42 12 E

320 Moora Shire Caravan Park
☎ (08) 9651 0000

Caravan Park at Moora. Dandaragan St. Next to Apex Park

HEMA 110 A3   30 38 17 S   116 00 16 E

321 Moora RV Short Stay
☎ (08) 9651 0000

Parking Area at Moora. Robert St. Oversized RV's only. All other vehicles must stay in Caravan Park

HEMA 110 A3   30 38 16 S   116 00 18 E

Notes...

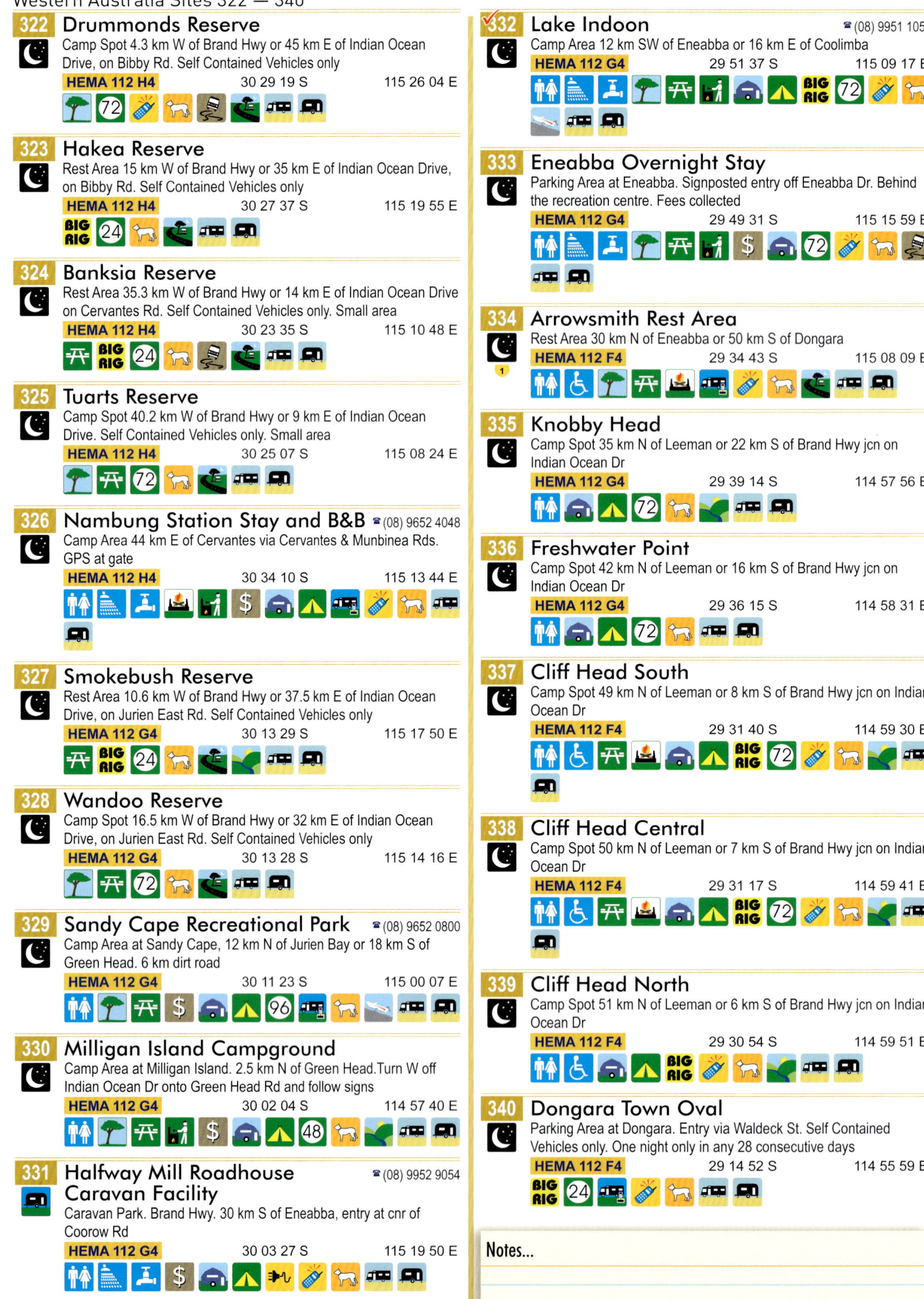

WESTERN AUSTRALIA

322 Drummonds Reserve
Camp Spot 4.3 km W of Brand Hwy or 45 km E of Indian Ocean Drive, on Bibby Rd. Self Contained Vehicles only
HEMA 112 H4   30 29 19 S   115 26 04 E

323 Hakea Reserve
Rest Area 15 km W of Brand Hwy or 35 km E of Indian Ocean Drive, on Bibby Rd. Self Contained Vehicles only
HEMA 112 H4   30 27 37 S   115 19 55 E

324 Banksia Reserve
Rest Area 35.3 km W of Brand Hwy or 14 km E of Indian Ocean Drive on Cervantes Rd. Self Contained Vehicles only. Small area
HEMA 112 H4   30 23 35 S   115 10 48 E

325 Tuarts Reserve
Camp Spot 40.2 km W of Brand Hwy or 9 km E of Indian Ocean Drive. Self Contained Vehicles only. Small area
HEMA 112 H4   30 25 07 S   115 08 24 E

326 Nambung Station Stay and B&B   ☎ (08) 9652 4048
Camp Area 44 km E of Cervantes via Cervantes & Munbinea Rds. GPS at gate
HEMA 112 H4   30 34 10 S   115 13 44 E

327 Smokebush Reserve
Rest Area 10.6 km W of Brand Hwy or 37.5 km E of Indian Ocean Drive, on Jurien East Rd. Self Contained Vehicles only
HEMA 112 G4   30 13 29 S   115 17 50 E

328 Wandoo Reserve
Camp Spot 16.5 km W of Brand Hwy or 32 km E of Indian Ocean Drive, on Jurien East Rd. Self Contained Vehicles only
HEMA 112 G4   30 13 28 S   115 14 16 E

329 Sandy Cape Recreational Park   ☎ (08) 9652 0800
Camp Area at Sandy Cape, 12 km N of Jurien Bay or 18 km S of Green Head. 6 km dirt road
HEMA 112 G4   30 11 23 S   115 00 07 E

330 Milligan Island Campground
Camp Area at Milligan Island. 2.5 km N of Green Head. Turn W off Indian Ocean Dr onto Green Head Rd and follow signs
HEMA 112 G4   30 02 04 S   114 57 40 E

331 Halfway Mill Roadhouse Caravan Facility   ☎ (08) 9952 9054
Caravan Park. Brand Hwy. 30 km S of Eneabba, entry at cnr of Coorow Rd
HEMA 112 G4   30 03 27 S   115 19 50 E

332 Lake Indoon   ☎ (08) 9951 1055
Camp Area 12 km SW of Eneabba or 16 km E of Coolimba
HEMA 112 G4   29 51 37 S   115 09 17 E

333 Eneabba Overnight Stay
Parking Area at Eneabba. Signposted entry off Eneabba Dr. Behind the recreation centre. Fees collected
HEMA 112 G4   29 49 31 S   115 15 59 E

334 Arrowsmith Rest Area
Rest Area 30 km N of Eneabba or 50 km S of Dongara
HEMA 112 F4   29 34 43 S   115 08 09 E

335 Knobby Head
Camp Spot 35 km N of Leeman or 22 km S of Brand Hwy jcn on Indian Ocean Dr
HEMA 112 G4   29 39 14 S   114 57 56 E

336 Freshwater Point
Camp Spot 42 km N of Leeman or 16 km S of Brand Hwy jcn on Indian Ocean Dr
HEMA 112 G4   29 36 15 S   114 58 31 E

337 Cliff Head South
Camp Spot 49 km N of Leeman or 8 km S of Brand Hwy jcn on Indian Ocean Dr
HEMA 112 F4   29 31 40 S   114 59 30 E

338 Cliff Head Central
Camp Spot 50 km N of Leeman or 7 km S of Brand Hwy jcn on Indian Ocean Dr
HEMA 112 F4   29 31 17 S   114 59 41 E

339 Cliff Head North
Camp Spot 51 km N of Leeman or 6 km S of Brand Hwy jcn on Indian Ocean Dr
HEMA 112 F4   29 30 54 S   114 59 51 E

340 Dongara Town Oval
Parking Area at Dongara. Entry via Waldeck St. Self Contained Vehicles only. One night only in any 28 consecutive days
HEMA 112 F4   29 14 52 S   114 55 59 E

Notes...

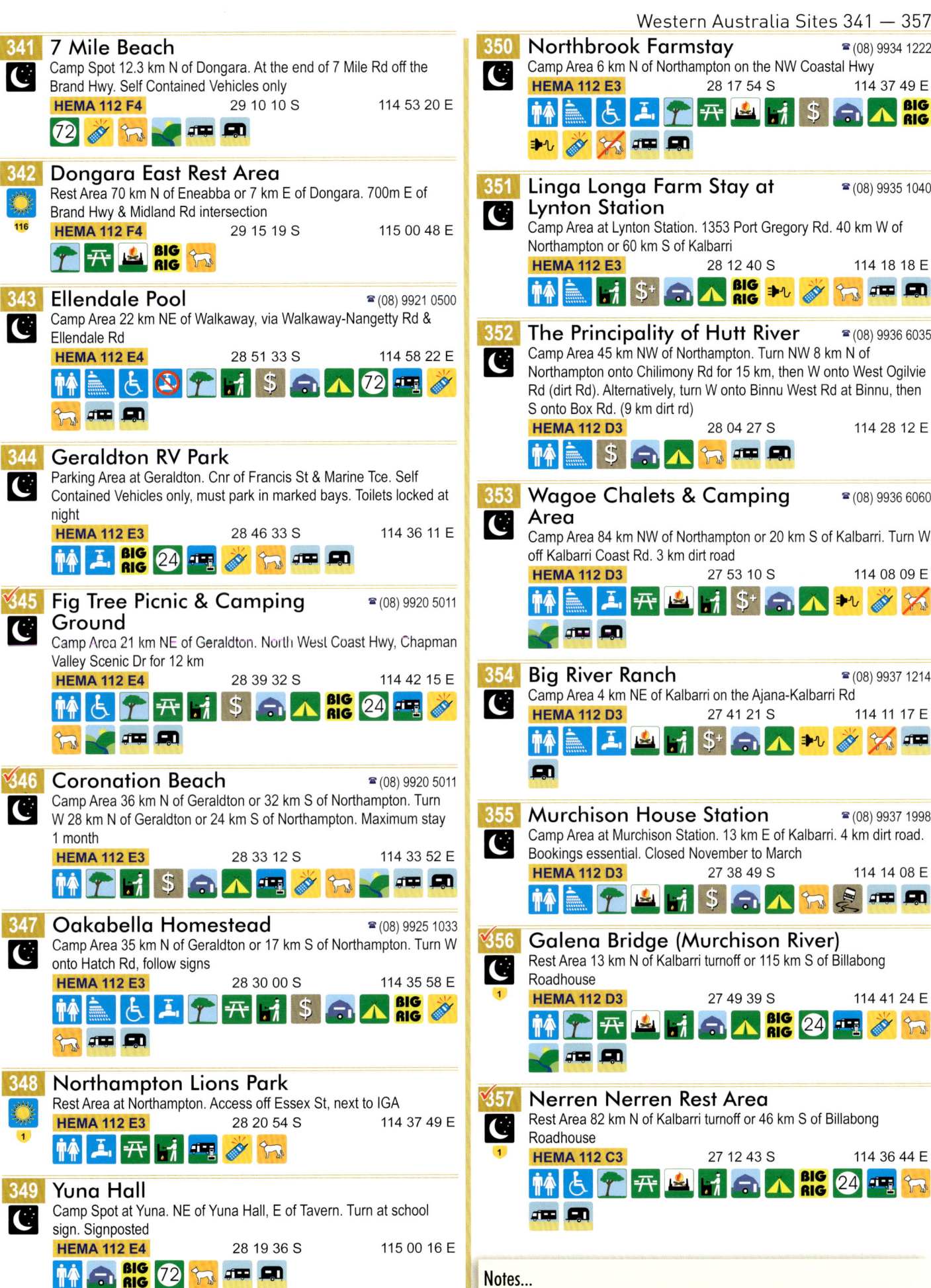

341 7 Mile Beach
Camp Spot 12.3 km N of Dongara. At the end of 7 Mile Rd off the Brand Hwy. Self Contained Vehicles only
HEMA 112 F4   29 10 10 S   114 53 20 E

342 Dongara East Rest Area
Rest Area 70 km N of Eneabba or 7 km E of Dongara. 700m E of Brand Hwy & Midland Rd intersection
HEMA 112 F4   29 15 19 S   115 00 48 E

343 Ellendale Pool   ☎ (08) 9921 0500
Camp Area 22 km NE of Walkaway, via Walkaway-Nangetty Rd & Ellendale Rd
HEMA 112 E4   28 51 33 S   114 58 22 E

344 Geraldton RV Park
Parking Area at Geraldton. Cnr of Francis St & Marine Tce. Self Contained Vehicles only, must park in marked bays. Toilets locked at night
HEMA 112 E3   28 46 33 S   114 36 11 E

345 Fig Tree Picnic & Camping Ground   ☎ (08) 9920 5011
Camp Area 21 km NE of Geraldton. North West Coast Hwy, Chapman Valley Scenic Dr for 12 km
HEMA 112 E4   28 39 32 S   114 42 15 E

346 Coronation Beach   ☎ (08) 9920 5011
Camp Area 36 km N of Geraldton or 32 km S of Northampton. Turn W 28 km N of Geraldton or 24 km S of Northampton. Maximum stay 1 month
HEMA 112 E3   28 33 12 S   114 33 52 E

347 Oakabella Homestead   ☎ (08) 9925 1033
Camp Area 35 km N of Geraldton or 17 km S of Northampton. Turn W onto Hatch Rd, follow signs
HEMA 112 E3   28 30 00 S   114 35 58 E

348 Northampton Lions Park
Rest Area at Northampton. Access off Essex St, next to IGA
HEMA 112 E3   28 20 54 S   114 37 49 E

349 Yuna Hall
Camp Spot at Yuna. NE of Yuna Hall, E of Tavern. Turn at school sign. Signposted
HEMA 112 E4   28 19 36 S   115 00 16 E

350 Northbrook Farmstay   ☎ (08) 9934 1222
Camp Area 6 km N of Northampton on the NW Coastal Hwy
HEMA 112 E3   28 17 54 S   114 37 49 E

351 Linga Longa Farm Stay at Lynton Station   ☎ (08) 9935 1040
Camp Area at Lynton Station. 1353 Port Gregory Rd. 40 km W of Northampton or 60 km S of Kalbarri
HEMA 112 E3   28 12 40 S   114 18 18 E

352 The Principality of Hutt River   ☎ (08) 9936 6035
Camp Area 45 km NW of Northampton. Turn NW 8 km N of Northampton onto Chilimony Rd for 15 km, then W onto West Ogilvie Rd (dirt Rd). Alternatively, turn W onto Binnu West Rd at Binnu, then S onto Box Rd. (9 km dirt rd)
HEMA 112 D3   28 04 27 S   114 28 12 E

353 Wagoe Chalets & Camping Area   ☎ (08) 9936 6060
Camp Area 84 km NW of Northampton or 20 km S of Kalbarri. Turn W off Kalbarri Coast Rd. 3 km dirt road
HEMA 112 D3   27 53 10 S   114 08 09 E

354 Big River Ranch   ☎ (08) 9937 1214
Camp Area 4 km NE of Kalbarri on the Ajana-Kalbarri Rd
HEMA 112 D3   27 41 21 S   114 11 17 E

355 Murchison House Station   ☎ (08) 9937 1998
Camp Area at Murchison Station. 13 km E of Kalbarri. 4 km dirt road. Bookings essential. Closed November to March
HEMA 112 D3   27 38 49 S   114 14 08 E

356 Galena Bridge (Murchison River)
Rest Area 13 km N of Kalbarri turnoff or 115 km S of Billabong Roadhouse
HEMA 112 D3   27 49 39 S   114 41 24 E

357 Nerren Nerren Rest Area
Rest Area 82 km N of Kalbarri turnoff or 46 km S of Billabong Roadhouse
HEMA 112 C3   27 12 43 S   114 36 44 E

Notes...

WESTERN AUSTRALIA

358 Overlander Roadhouse ☎ (08) 9942 5916
Camp Area at Roadhouse. North West Coastal Hwy
| HEMA 112 B3 | 26 24 42 S | 114 27 50 E |

✓ 359 Hamelin Station Stay ☎ (08) 9948 5145
Camp Area at Hamelin Station. 30 km W of Overlander Roadhouse or 100 km SE of Denham. Shark Bay Rd
| HEMA 112 B3 | 26 26 03 S | 114 12 00 E |

360 Tamala Station ☎ (08) 9948 3994
Camp Area at Tamala Station, southern end of the Shark Bay Marine Park. Various sites off Useless Loop Rd. Must call ahead, cash only. GPS at homestead. 4WD only
| HEMA 112 B2 | 26 41 47 S | 113 42 54 E |

361 Goulet Bluff ☎ (08) 9948 1590
Camp Area 95 km W of Overlander Roadhouse or 38 km SE of Denham. Turnoff 93 km W of Overlander Roadhouse or 36 km SE of Denham. 2 km dirt road W of Hwy. Phone for permit or call by the Shark Bay Visitor Centre, Knight Tce Denham. Permits are booked on the day required, no advance bookings taken
| HEMA 112 B2 | 26 12 52 S | 113 41 36 E |

362 Whalebone Bay ☎ (08) 9948 1590
Camp Area 102 km W of Overlander Roadhouse or 27 km SE of Denham. 1 km dirt road W of Hwy. Phone for permit or call by the Shark Bay Visitor Centre, Knight Tce Denham. Permits are booked on the day required, no advance bookings taken
| HEMA 112 B2 | 26 07 46 S | 113 38 27 E |

363 Fowlers Camp ☎ (08) 9948 1590
Camp Area 109 km W of Overlander Roadhouse or 24 km SE of Denham. Turnoff 107 km W of Overlander Roadhouse or 22 km SE of Denham. 2 km dirt road W of Hwy. Phone for permit or call by the Shark Bay Visitor Centre, Knight Tce Denham. Permits are booked on the day required, no advance bookings taken
| HEMA 112 B2 | 26 06 21 S | 113 37 13 E |

364 Eagle Bluff ☎ (08) 9948 1590
Camp Area 114 km W of Overlander Roadhouse or 23 km SE of Denham. Turnoff 110 km W of Overlander Roadhouse or 19 km SE of Denham. 4 km dirt road W of Hwy. Phone for permit or call by the Shark Bay Visitor Centre, Knight Tce Denham. Permits are booked on the day required, no advance bookings taken
| HEMA 112 B2 | 26 04 28 S | 113 34 56 E |

✓ 365 Gladstone Campground ☎ (08) 9942 5952
Camp Area 61 km N of Overlander Roadhouse or 27 km S of Wooramel Roadhouse. Turn W opposite Yaringa Homestead, 55 km N of Overlander Roadhouse or 21 km S of Wooramel Roadhouse. 6 km dirt road
| HEMA 112 A3 | 25 57 08 S | 114 14 55 E |

366 Wooramel Roadhouse Caravan Park ☎ (08) 9942 5910
Caravan Park at Wooramel Roadhouse. 70 km N of Overlander Roadhouse or 124 km S of Carnarvon
| HEMA 112 A3 | 25 46 13 S | 114 17 40 E |

✓ 367 Wooramel Station ☎ 0499 425 888
Camp Area at Wooramel Station. Turn E 120 km S of Carnarvon or 2.6 km N of Wooramel Roadhouse. Signposted. Closed 01st Dec to 28th Feb.
| HEMA 114 J3 | 25 44 27 S | 114 17 02 E |

368 Edaggee Rest Area
Rest Area 43 km N of Wooramel Roadhouse or 81 km S of Carnarvon
| HEMA 114 J3 | 25 27 34 S | 114 03 31 E |

369 New Beach ☎ (08) 9941 0030
Camp Area 99 km N of Wooramel Roadhouse or 41 km S of Carnarvon. Turn W 91 km N of Wooramel Roadhouse or 33 km S of Carnarvon. 8 km dirt road. Low lying, check tide charts. Chemical toilet required
| HEMA 114 J2 | 25 09 22 S | 113 47 53 E |

370 Bush Bay ☎ (08) 9941 0030
Camping Area 101 km N of Wooramel Roadhouse or 43 km S of Carnarvon. Turn W 91 km N of Wooramel Roadhouse or 33 km S of Carnarvon. 6 km N of New Beach. 10 km dirt road. Low lying, check tide charts. Chemical toilet required
| HEMA 114 J2 | 25 07 50 S | 113 45 14 E |

371 Mount Augustus Tourist Park ☎ (08) 9943 0527
Caravan Park 280 km NE of Gascoyne Junction via Dairy Creek or 360 km NW of Meekatharra
| HEMA 114 G6 | 24 18 29 S | 116 54 32 E |

372 Temple Gorge Campground ☎ (08) 9941 3754
Kennedy Range National Park
Camp Area 59 km N of Gascoyne Junction. Turn W 47 km N of Gascoyne Junction onto Ullawarra Rd for 12 km. Mostly dirt road
| HEMA 114 H4 | 24 39 38 S | 115 10 57 E |

373 Junction Pub & Tourist Park ☎ (08) 9943 0868
Caravan Park at Gascoyne Junction
| HEMA 114 H4 | 25 03 13 S | 115 12 25 E |

Notes...

✓ 374 Blowholes (Point Quobba)
☎ 0408 942 945

Camp Area 72 km N of Carnarvon. Turn W off North West Coastal Hwy 24 km N of Carnarvon or 115 km S of Minilya Roadhouse. Must have chemical toilet. 30 day maximum stay

HEMA 114 H2   24 29 16 S   113 24 44 E

375 Quobba Station
☎ (08) 9948 5098

Camp Area at Quobba Station. 82 km N of Carnarvon. Turn W off North West Coastal Hwy 24 km N of Carnarvon or 115 km S of Minilya Roadhouse. 10 km dirt road N of Blowholes

HEMA 114 H2   24 23 43 S   113 24 19 E

✓ 376 Red Bluff
☎ (08) 9948 5098

Quobba Station

Camp Area 54 km N of Quobba Homestead via Gnaraloo Rd. Signposted turnoff 44 km N of station, 10 km sometimes rough dirt road to campsite. Suitable off road caravans

HEMA 114 G2   24 01 56 S   113 26 56 E

377 Gnaraloo Station - 3 Mile Camp
☎ (08) 9948 5000

Camp Area at Gnaraloo Station. 150 km N of Cararvon, via Blowholes Rd

HEMA 114 G2   23 52 29 S   113 29 48 E

378 Lake MacLeod Rest Area

Rest Area 49 km S of Minilya Roadhouse or 90 km N of Carnarvon

HEMA 114 G2   24 14 57 S   114 02 11 E

379 Minilya River

Rest Area 500m S of Minilya Roadhouse S side of Minilya River Bridge or 141 km N of Carnarvon

HEMA 114 G2   23 49 01 S   114 00 38 E

380 Lyndon Station
☎ (08) 9943 0540

Camp Area 110 km E Lyndon or 159 km E Milnilya Roadhouse via Lyndon-Towera Rd. Bookings required

HEMA 114 F4   23 38 13 S   115 14 45 E

381 Minilya Bridge Roadhouse
☎ (08) 9942 5922

Camp Area at Roadhouse

HEMA 114 G2   23 48 53 S   114 00 34 E

382 Lyndon River

Rest Area 48 km NE of Minilya Roadhouse or 179 km SW of Nanutarra Roadhouse

HEMA 114 F3   23 28 58 S   114 16 32 E

383 Lyndon River (West)

Rest Area 32 km N of Minilya Roadhouse or 190 km S of Exmouth on Minilya-Exmouth Rd

HEMA 114 F2   23 32 32 S   113 57 47 E

✓ 384 Warroora Station - The 14 Mile

Camp Area At Warroora Station. 84 km N of Minilya Roadhouse or 166 km S of Exmouth. Turn W 75 km N of Minilya Roadhouse or 155 km S of Exmouth, 5 km sandy dirt road to camp entrance, then 6 km to campsites. Report to caretaker. Must have chemical toilet. Approach from the N entrance as the S entry is sandy

HEMA 114 F2   23 17 35 S   113 50 39 E

385 Bruboodjoo (9 Mile Camp)
☎ (08) 9942 5935

Camp Area 19 km north of Coral Bay. Turn off is approx 15 km N of Coral Bay off Minilya-Exmouth Rd. Sandy dirt road. Report to caretaker before setting up. Beach camping. Must have chemcial toilet

HEMA 114 F2   22 58 32 S   113 49 32 E

386 Ningaloo Station Wilderness Camping
☎ (08) 9942 5936

Camp Areas at Ningaloo Station. Turn W 40 km N of the Coral Bay turn off onto Ningaloo Rd. All campers must register at Homestead to collect key & map. Bond payable. Must have chemical toitelt, Eco toilet hire available. Suitable off road caravans only

HEMA 114 E2   22 41 46 S   113 40 32 E

387 Neds Campground
☎ (08) 9949 2808

Cape Range National Park

Camp Area within National Park. Limited sites. No generators allowed. Public phone & dump point at Milyering Visitor Centre

HEMA 114 D2   22 00 01 S   113 55 58 E

388 Mesa Campground
☎ (08) 9949 2808

Cape Range National Park

Camp Area within National Park. Limited sites. Generators allowed. Public phone & dump point at Milyering Visitor Centre

HEMA 114 D2   22 00 24 S   113 55 38 E

389 Tulki Beach Campground
☎ (08) 9949 2808

Cape Range National Park

Camp Area within National Park. Limited sites. Generators allowed. Public phone & dump point at Milyering Visitor Centre

HEMA 114 D2   22 04 31 S   113 53 56 E

390 Kurrajong Campground
☎ (08) 9949 2808

Cape Range National Park

Camp Area within National Park. Limited sites. No generators allowed. Public phone & dump point at Milyering Visitor Centre

HEMA 114 D2   22 10 44 S   113 51 34 E

391 North Kurrajong ☎ (08) 9949 2808
Cape Range National Park
Camp Area within National Park. Limited sites. No generators allowed. Public phone & dump point at Milyering Visitor Centre
HEMA 114 D2   22 10 24 S   113 51 39 E

392 Bungarra ☎ (08) 9949 2808
Cape Range National Park
Camp Area within National Park. Limited sites. No generators. Public phone & dump point at Milyering Visitor Centre
HEMA 114 D2   22 14 49 S   113 50 24 E

✓ 393 Osprey Bay Campground ☎ (08) 9949 2808
Cape Range National Park
Camp Area within National Park. Limited sites. Generators allowed. Public phone & dump point at Milyering Visitor Centre
HEMA 114 D2   22 14 19 S   113 50 21 E

394 Yardie Creek Campground ☎ (08) 9949 2808
Cape Range National Park
Camp Area within National Park. Limited sites. Generators allowed. Public phone & dump point at Milyering Visitor Centre
HEMA 114 D2   22 19 13 S   113 48 53 E

395 Bullara Station ☎ (08) 9942 5938
Camp Area At Bullara Station. 86 km S of Exmouth or 60 km N of Coral Bay. 8 km E of NW Coastal Hwy intersection. Signposted
HEMA 114 E2   22 40 39 S   114 03 15 E

396 Giralia Station ☎ (08) 9942 5937
Camp Area at Giralia Station. 125 km S of Exmouth or 110 km N of Coral Bay. 45 km E of NW Coastal Hwy intersection. Limited power. 4 km dirt road
HEMA 114 E3   22 42 31 S   114 20 20 E

397 Burkett Road Rest Area
Rest Area 116 km NE of Minilya Roadhouse or 111 km SW of Nanutarra Roadhouse. 1 km N of Exmouth turnoff
HEMA 114 E3   22 59 01 S   114 36 47 E

✓ 398 Barradale Rest Area
Yannarie River
Rest Area 156 km NE of Minilya Roadhouse or 70 km SW of Nanutarra Roadhouse
HEMA 114 E3   22 51 49 S   114 57 05 E

399 Emu Creek Station ☎ (08) 9943 0534
Camp Area at Emu Creek Station. Turn E onto Nyang Rd 156 km N of Minilya Roadhouse or 49 km S of Nanutarra Roadhouse. 22 km to station. Dirt road
HEMA 114 E4   23 01 54 S   115 02 31 E

400 Nanutarra Roadhouse Caravan Park ☎ (08) 9943 0521
Caravan park at Nanutarra Roadhouse
HEMA 114 E4   22 32 34 S   115 30 03 E

401 House Creek Bridge
Rest Area 62 km E of Nanutarra Roadhouse or 162 km W of Paraburdoo/Wittenoom Rd jcn
HEMA 114 E5   22 27 51 S   116 02 12 E

402 Beasley River Rest Area
Rest Area 171 km E of Nanutarra Roadhouse or 53 km W of Paraburdoo/Wittenoom Rd jcn
HEMA 114 E6   22 56 56 S   116 58 40 E

403 Cheela Plains Station ☎ (08) 9789 8084
Camp Area 181 km E of Nanutarra Roadhouse via Nanutarra-Wittenoom Rd or 43 km W of Paraburdoo/Wittenoom Rd jcn. GPS at Gate
HEMA 114 E6   22 57 26 S   116 59 02 E

404 Onslow Turnoff
Parking Area 44 km N of Nanutarra Roadhouse or 119 km S of Fortesque River Roadhouse. 1 km S of turnoff
HEMA 114 D4   22 09 03 S   115 32 28 E

405 Three Mile Pool
Camp Spot 36 km S of Onslow or 5 km S of Old Onslow Township. Turn W 64 km NW of Hwy 1 jcn or 17 km S of Onslow, onto Twitchen Rd & Old Onslow Rd. 19 km dirt road
HEMA 114 D3   21 45 44 S   114 57 05 E

406 Robe River
Rest Area 117 km N of Nanutarra Roadhouse or 43 km S of Fortescue River Roadhouse
HEMA 114 C5   21 36 55 S   115 55 21 E

407 Pannawonica Transit Park ☎ (08) 9184 1038
Caravan Park at Pannawonica. Sports Way, next to Tony Lyons Park. Book & pay at the Library
HEMA 114 C5   21 38 12 S   116 19 29 E

408 Fortescue River Roadhouse Caravan Park ☎ (08) 9184 5126
Caravan Park at Roadhouse
HEMA 114 C5   21 17 42 S   116 08 17 E

409 Gnoorea Point (40 Mile) ☎ (08) 9186 8555
Camp Area at Forty Mile Beach. Turn W 54 km N of Fortescue River Roadhouse or 40 km S of Karratha Roadhouse. Turn off is 200m S of Devil Creek Bridge. 12 km dirt road. Fees apply 1 May - 30 Sep, maximum stay 28 days. Offpeak maximum stay is 3 days per 28 days. Chemical toilet required to stay here
HEMA 114 B5   20 50 26 S   116 20 51 E

410 Cleaverville Beach ☎ (08) 9186 8555
Camp Area 26 km NW of Roebourne or 33 km NE of Karratha. Turn N 28 km E of Karratha Roadhouse or 14 km W of Roebourne. 13 km dirt road. Fees apply 1 May - 30 Sep, maximum 28 day stay. Offpeak maximum stay is 3 days per 28 days. Chemical toilet required to stay here
HEMA 114 B6   20 39 40 S   116 59 53 E

411 Miliyana Campground ☎ (08) 9184 5144
Millstream Chichester National Park
Camp Area 144 km S of Roebourne. Turn S 27 km E of Roebourne or 55 km W of Whim Creek, then SE after 79 km, then SW for 18 km. Alternative access via Pannawonica, 92 km dirt road
HEMA 114 C6   21 35 18 S   117 04 22 E

412 Stargazers Campground ☎ (08) 9184 5144
Millstream Chichester National Park
Camp Area 144 km S of Roebourne. Turn S 27 km E of Roebourne or 55 km W of Whim Creek, then SE after 79 km, then SW for 18 km. Alternative access via Pannawonica, 92 km dirt road
HEMA 114 C6   21 35 40 S   117 05 17 E

413 Sherlock River
Camp Spot 56 km E of Roebourne or 27 km W of Whim Creek. Turn N 100m W of bridge. Small area
HEMA 114 B7   20 56 41 S   117 36 41 E

414 Coorinjinna Pool
Camp Spot 20 km N of Whim Creek. Turn N opposite old hotel site, travel 14 km, then R (opposite old gravel pit) onto track for 1 km. Various sites along river. 15 km dirt road
HEMA 114 B7   20 43 22 S   117 48 00 E

415 Balla Balla Inlet
Camp Spot 25 km N of Whim Creek. Turn N opposite old hotel site, follow Rd to end. Limited spots on higher ground, tidal
HEMA 114 B7   20 40 29 S   117 46 59 E

416 Peawah River
Rest Area 26 km NE of Whim Creek or 92 km SW of Port Hedland
HEMA 114 B7   20 50 51 S   118 04 06 E

417 Herbert Parker (Yule River)
Rest Area 56 km NE of Whim Creek or 62 km SW of Port Hedland. Limited space
HEMA 115 B8   20 42 00 S   118 18 00 E

418 Port Hedland Racecourse ☎ (08) 9173 1711
Parking Area at Port Hedland. Enter via McGregor St opposite Civic Centre. Self Contained Vehicles only. Only Open 1 May to August 31
HEMA 115 A8   20 18 31 S   118 36 45 E

Perth to Port Hedland
Great Northern Highway

419 Bindoon Transit Park ☎ (08) 9576 1020
Camp Area at Bindoon. Recreation Oval S end of town on Great Northern Hwy, entry near PO. Must call into PO for payment
HEMA 106 B4   31 23 08 S   116 05 52 E

420 Bindoon Hill
Rest Area 9 km N of Bindoon or 38 km S of New Norcia
HEMA 106 B4   31 19 35 S   116 09 15 E

421 Mogumber Hall
Camp Spot at Mogumber. Bindoon-Moora Rd N of town at the sports ground
HEMA 112 H5   31 02 04 S   116 02 38 E

422 New Norcia Roadhouse Caravan Park ☎ (08) 9654 8020
Caravan Park at New Norcia. Facilities in roadhouse
HEMA 110 B3   30 58 25 S   116 12 45 E

423 New Norcia ☎ (08) 9654 8056
Parking Area at New Norcia. Great Northern Hwy near Oval S of Monastery. Self Contained Vehicles only. Pay at Visitor Centre
HEMA 110 B3   30 58 24 S   116 12 48 E

Notes...

WESTERN AUSTRALIA

424 Yerecoin Wayside Rest Area
Parking Area at Yerecoin. Yerecoin SE Road. Payment at Yerecoin Traders
HEMA 112 H6   30 55 33 S   116 23 44 E

425 Calingiri Caravan Park   ☎ (08) 9628 7004
Caravan Park at Calingiri. 21 Cavell St. Caretaker 0428 149 174
HEMA 106 A5   31 05 25 S   116 26 54 E

426 Bolgart Caravan Park   ☎ (08) 9627 5220
Caravan Park at Bolgart. George St
HEMA 106 A6   31 16 17 S   116 30 31 E

427 Goomalling Caravan Park   ☎ (08) 9629 1183
Caravan Park at Goomalling. Throssel St. 1 km SE of PO
HEMA 106 B7   31 17 59 S   116 49 57 E

428 Oak Park & Gnamma Holes
Picnic Area 17 km NE of Goomalling on Oak Park Rd
HEMA 106 A7   31 08 15 S   116 52 37 E

429 Dowerin Motel & Caravan Park   ☎ (08) 9631 1135
Caravan Park at Dowerin. Goomalling-Merredin Rd. Pay at the Roadhouse. Limited sites
HEMA 107 A8   31 11 43 S   117 01 55 E

430 Dowerin Field Days Site   ☎ (08) 9631 1662
Parking Area at Dowerin. Memorial Ave. Self Contained Vehicles only, not available on Field Days
HEMA 107 A8   31 11 31 S   117 02 08 E

431 Minnivale Rest Area
Rest Area at Minnivale. Turn N off the Goomalling-Wyalkatchem Rd 15 km E of Dowerin or 20 km W of Wyalkatchem, along Cunderdin-Minnivale Rd for 5 km. Next to disused tennis courts. Self Contained Vehicles only
HEMA 107 A9   31 08 20 S   117 11 04 E

432 Wyalkatchem Travellers Park   ☎ 0427 814 042
Caravan Park at Wyalkatchem. Lot 408 Hands Dr (Goomalling-Merredin Rd)
HEMA 107 A9   31 10 59 S   117 22 46 E

433 Shire of Trayning Caravan Park   ☎ 0428 997 156
Caravan Park at Trayning. Enter from Bencubbin-Kellerberrin Rd, behind the swimming pool
HEMA 107 A11   31 06 38 S   117 47 37 E

434 Nungarin Recreation Ground   ☎ (08) 9046 5006
Camp Area at Nungarin. Danberrin Rd, Brown Drive. At rear of oval near the playground
HEMA 107 A13   31 11 29 S   118 05 29 E

435 Danberrin Rock
Camp Spot 15.5 km S of Nungarin via Danberrin Rd, Baird Rd West. Signposted
HEMA 107 A12   31 16 51 S   118 03 08 E

436 Talgomine Reserve
Camp Spot 24 km E of Nungarin. Via Nungarin-Chandler Rds, Talgomine Reserve Rd. Signposted
HEMA 107 A13   31 12 39 S   118 17 45 E

437 Eaglestone Rock
Camp Spot 21 km NE of Nungarin towards Lake Brown. Via Danberrin Rd, Knungajin Rd & Lake Brown South Rd. 4.5 km dirt road
HEMA 110 B6   31 04 31 S   118 14 48 E

438 Mangowine Homestead   ☎ (08) 9046 5149
Camp Area in Homestead grounds. 14.5 km N of Nungarin on Karomin Rd, or 24 km S of Mukinbudin
HEMA 110 B6   31 02 55 S   118 06 21 E

439 Weira Reserve
Camp Spot 13 km E of Mukinbudin. Via Koorda-Bullfinch Rd. Signposted
HEMA 110 B7   30 59 40 S   118 23 13 E

440 Mukinbudin Caravan Park   ☎ 0429 471 103
Caravan Park at Mukinbudin. Cruickshank St
HEMA 110 B6   30 55 08 S   118 12 21 E

441 Baladjie Rock
Camp Spot 74 km E of Mukinbudin or 21 km W of Bullfinch, via Koorda-Southern Cross Rd. 5 km dirt road N of main road
HEMA 110 B7   30 57 14 S   118 52 51 E

Notes...

442 Elachbutting Rock
Camp Spot at Elachbutting Rock. 100 km N of Westonia. GPS at entrance, follow signposted track around rock to camping area
HEMA 110 A7   30 35 27 S   118 36 25 E

443 Beringbooding Rock
Camp Spot at Beringbooding Rock. Via Beringbooding Rd & Cunderdin Rd
HEMA 110 A7   30 33 30 S   118 29 32 E

444 Datjoin Well & Rock Reserve
Camp Spot 5 km W of Wialki. Buralin-Wialki Rd. Signposted
HEMA 110 A6   30 27 44 S   118 04 07 E

445 Bencubbin Caravan Park   ☎ (08) 9685 1202
Caravan Park at Bencubbin. Kellerberrin Rd
HEMA 110 B6   30 49 07 S   117 51 44 E

446 Bencubbin Recreation Ground
Camp Area in Bencubbin. Marsh St off Hammond St. Temporary site due to Caravan Parks closure. Maximum stay 14 days
HEMA 110 B6   30 48 42 S   117 51 31 E

447 Marshall Rock Camping
Camp Area 10km S of Bencubbin, via Mukinbudin Rd & Marshall Rock South Rd. 1.7 km dirt Rd
HEMA 110 B6   30 50 19 S   117 54 15 E

448 Gabbin
Camp Spot at Gabbin, Cnr Scarlett and Brindle Sts. Next to Community Heritage Hall
HEMA 110 B5   30 48 01 S   117 40 48 E

449 Koorda Caravan Park   ☎ (08) 9684 1219
Caravan Park at Koorda. Scott St. 1 km N of PO
HEMA 110 B5   30 49 20 S   117 29 12 E

450 Koorda Native Flora Reserve
Camp Area 16 km N of Koorda, via Koorda-Mollerin Rd, Mulji Rd. Signposted
HEMA 110 A5   30 44 25 S   117 33 10 E

451 Newcarlbeon Rock
Camp Area 20 km N of Koorda via Koorda-Kulja Rd, Newcarlbeon Rd. Signposted
HEMA 110 A5   30 39 59 S   117 25 05 E

452 Beacon Caravan Park   ☎ 0488 025 853
Caravan Park at Beacon. Lucas St
HEMA 110 A6   30 27 07 S   117 52 13 E

453 Mollerin Rock
Camp Area 45 km N of Koorda. Via Koorda-Mollerin Rd, Kulja-Mollerin Rock Rd. Signposted
HEMA 110 A5   30 32 19 S   117 33 57 E

454 Billiburning Rock
Camp Area 34 km N of Beacon, via Ingleton Rd & White Rd. 18 km dirt road
HEMA 112 G7   30 10 20 S   117 55 04 E

455 Cadoux Rest Area   ☎ (08) 9673 1040
Rest Area at Cadoux. Dowerin Kalannie Rd. Payment & access key at Cadoux Trader
HEMA 110 B5   30 46 18 S   117 08 00 E

456 Wongan Hills Caravan Park   ☎ (08) 9671 1009
Caravan Park at Wongan. 65 Wongan Rd
HEMA 110 B4   30 53 21 S   116 42 53 E

457 The Gap
Camp Spot 12 km W of Wongan Hills or 36 km E of Waddington on the Waddington-Wongan Hills Rd. Signposted on the L from Wongan Hills. Self Contained Vehicles only
HEMA 110 B4   30 49 49 S   116 38 02 E

458 Lake Ninan Rest Area
Rest Area 10 km SW of Wongan Hills on the Calingiri Wongan Hill Rd
HEMA 110 B4   30 57 07 S   116 39 31 E

459 Petrudor Rock
Camp Spot 31 km E of Pithara. Turn S off Pithara East Rd onto Petrudor Rd. 8 km dirt road
HEMA 110 A4   30 25 30 S   116 58 00 E

460 Ballidu Caravan Park   ☎ (08) 9674 1114
Caravan Park at Ballidu. Wallis St. Payment & caretaker info at site
HEMA 110 A4   30 35 44 S   116 46 22 E

461 Miling Sports Reserve   ☎ (08) 9654 1013
Camp Area at Miling. Miling East Rd. Pay & get code at Miling General Store or phone
HEMA 110 A3   30 29 22 S   116 22 03 E

462 Dalwallinu Caravan Park ☎ (08) 9661 1253

Caravan Park at Dalwallinu. Dowie St

| HEMA 112 G6 | 30 16 27 S | 116 40 08 E |

463 Jibberding Nature Reserve

Rest Area 22 km NE of Wubin or 131 km SW of Paynes Find. 200m N of Rabbit Proof Fence Rd. Follow track to open area

| HEMA 112 G6 | 30 00 09 S | 116 49 29 E |

95

464 White Wells

Parking Area 47 km NE of Wubin or 107 km SW of Paynes Find

| HEMA 112 G6 | 29 50 10 S | 116 56 45 E |

95

465 Paynes Find Roadhouse & Tavern ☎ (08) 9963 6111

Camp Area at Roadhouse. On Great Northern Hwy 145 km S of Mt Magnet

| HEMA 112 F7 | 29 15 48 S | 117 41 09 E |

95

466 Paynes Find Camp

Camp Spot 12 km N of Paynes Find or 132 km S of Mt Magnet. From Paynes Find turn W 1.2 km before parking area, several access tracks. From Mt Magnet turn W 1.2 km S of parking area, veer L into access track, follow to various campsites

| HEMA 112 F7 | 29 09 55 S | 117 42 22 E |

95

467 Narndee Station ☎ (08) 9963 5414

Camp Area 80 km NE of Paynes Find via Great Northern Hwy & Narndee West Rd. Signposted

| HEMA 113 E8 | 28 56 54 S | 118 10 34 E |

468 Nalbarra Station ☎ (08) 9963 5829

Camp Area at Nalbarra Station. 80 km SW of Mt Magnet. Turn W off the Great Northern Hwy 63 km S of Mt Magnet or 70 km N of Paynes Find, then 17 km to station. Signposted, dirt road

| HEMA 112 E7 | 28 38 55 S | 117 36 29 E |

469 Kirkalocka Station ☎ (08) 9963 5827

Camp Area at Kirkalocka Station. 60 km S of Mt Magnet or 84 km N of Paynes Find. Turn E at signpost. Limited power available

| HEMA 112 E7 | 28 33 42 S | 117 46 40 E |

470 Kirkalocka Rest Area

Rest Area 64 km S of Mt Magnet or 80 km N of Paynes Find. Overnight area is behind the toilets

| HEMA 112 E7 | 28 35 50 S | 117 46 51 E |

471 Windsor Rest Area

Rest Area 77 km W of Sandstone or 76 km E of Mt Magnet on Mt Magnet Sandstone Rd

| HEMA 113 D8 | 28 01 39 S | 118 31 29 E |

472 Old Wynyangoo Parking Area

Parking Area 20 km N of Mt Magnet or 60 km S of Cue. Tracks away from road

| HEMA 112 D7 | 27 53 38 S | 117 51 40 E |

473 Garden Rock

Camp Spot 16 km SE from Cue. Signposted from Cue on Cue to Sandstone Rd. Dirt road. 4WD when wet

| HEMA 112 C7 | 27 29 21 S | 118 01 36 E |

474 Lake Nallan Nature Reserve

Camp Spot 20 km N of Cue or 96 km SW of Meekatharra. Only camp in the 2 designated areas

1

| HEMA 112 C7 | 27 15 41 S | 117 59 07 E |

475 Bluebird Parking Area

Parking Area 19 km S of Meekatharra or 106 km N of Cue

| HEMA 113 B8 | 26 44 36 S | 118 24 14 E |

476 Lions Park

Parking Area at Meekatharra. Cnr Hill & Savage Sts. Self Contained Vehicles only

| HEMA 113 B8 | 26 35 35 S | 118 29 49 E |

477 Peace Gorge

Picnic Area 3.4 km W of Meekatharra. Turn N 1.5 km W of Meekatharra on the Landor Meekatharra Rd onto Peace Gorge Rd for 1.9 km

| HEMA 113 B8 | 26 34 46 S | 118 28 45 E |

478 Barlangi Rock

Parking Area 79 km SE of Meekatharra or 114 km NW of Sandstone

| HEMA 113 C8 | 27 10 52 S | 118 50 09 E |

479 25 Mile Well

Camp Spot 41 km N of Meekatharra or 215 km S of Kumarina Roadhouse

95

| HEMA 113 B8 | 26 15 54 S | 118 39 31 E |

480 Karalundi Caravan & Camping Park ☎ (08) 9981 2933

Caravan Park 55 km N of Meekatharra on Great Northern Hwy

| HEMA 113 A8 | 26 07 42 S | 118 41 09 E |

Notes...

481 Bilyuin Pool
Camp Spot 88 km N of Meekatharra. Turn W 74 km N of Meekatharra or 182 km S of Kumarina Roadhouse onto Ashburton Downs Rd. On L after Murchison River, follow tracks for 1 km to sites on river. 14 km dirt road

HEMA 115 J8   25 54 15 S   118 39 47 E

482 Gascoyne River (South Branch)
Rest Area 148 km NW of Meekatharra, 276 km S of Newman or 108 km S of Kumarina Roadhouse

HEMA 115 J9   25 34 44 S   119 14 13 E

483 Gascoyne River (Middle Branch)
Rest Area 192 km NW of Meekatharra, 230 km S of Newman or 64 km S of Kumarina Roadhouse

HEMA 115 H9   25 12 05 S   119 20 06 E

484 Kumarina Roadhouse Caravan Park   ☎ (08) 9981 2930
Caravan Park at Kumarina Roadhouse

HEMA 115 H10   24 42 38 S   119 36 27 E

485 Mt Robinson Rest Area
Rest Area 109 km NW of Newman or 86 km SE of Auski Roadhouse. 800m E of Hwy

HEMA 115 E8   23 02 34 S   118 50 57 E

486 Albert Tognolini Rest Area
Rest Area 179 km NW of Newman or 17 km S of Auski Roadhouse. 2 km E of Hwy. Follow tracks to the R along ridge

HEMA 115 E8   22 29 23 S   118 44 09 E

487 Dales Gorge Campground   ☎ (08) 9189 8121
Karijini National Park

Camp Area 8 km E of Karijini Visitors Centre. Generators allowed. Showers at Info Centre for fee

HEMA 115 E8   22 28 30 S   118 33 05 E

488 Karijini Eco Resort   ☎ (08) 9425 5591
Camp Area 35 km W of Karijini Visitors Centre or 79 km NE of Tom Price via Karijini Dr, Banjima Dr & Weano Gorge Rd. Dirt road

HEMA 115 D8   22 23 10 S   118 15 46 E

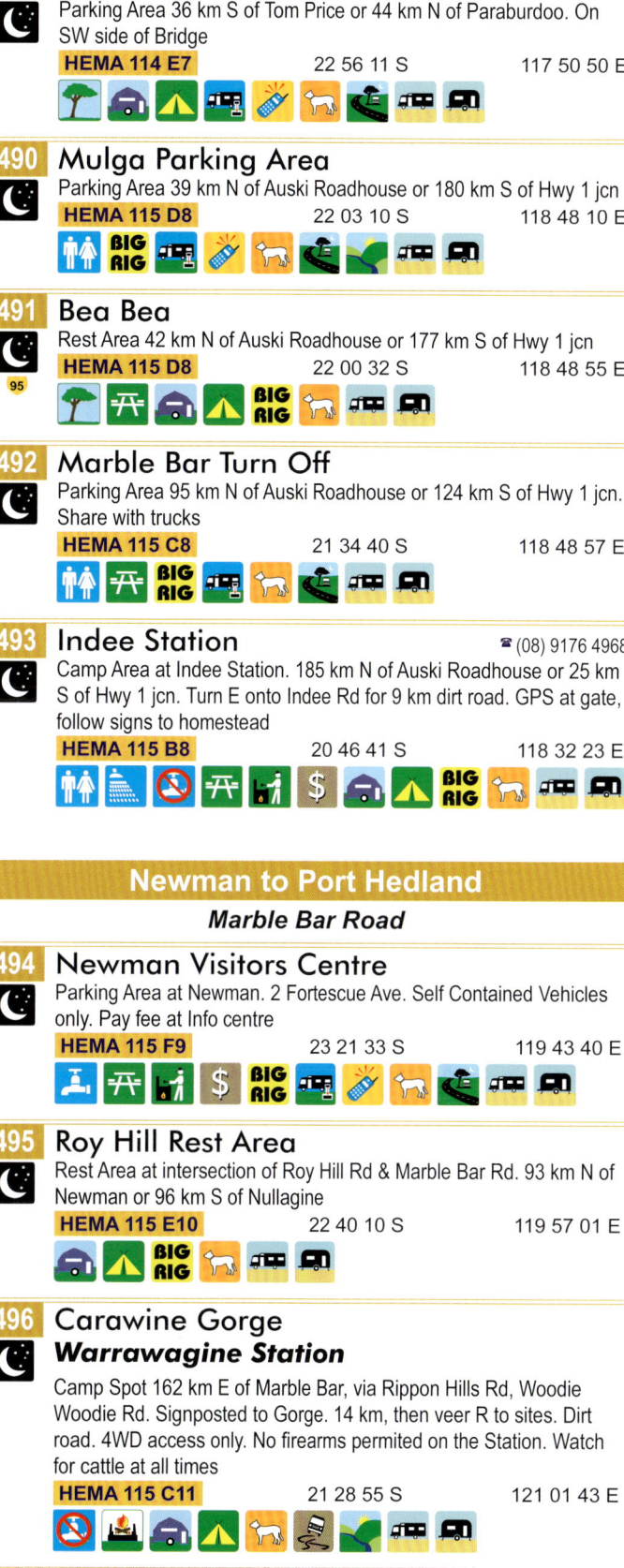

489 Halfway Bridge
Parking Area 36 km S of Tom Price or 44 km N of Paraburdoo. On SW side of Bridge

HEMA 114 E7   22 56 11 S   117 50 50 E

490 Mulga Parking Area
Parking Area 39 km N of Auski Roadhouse or 180 km S of Hwy 1 jcn

HEMA 115 D8   22 03 10 S   118 48 10 E

491 Bea Bea
Rest Area 42 km N of Auski Roadhouse or 177 km S of Hwy 1 jcn

HEMA 115 D8   22 00 32 S   118 48 55 E

492 Marble Bar Turn Off
Parking Area 95 km N of Auski Roadhouse or 124 km S of Hwy 1 jcn. Share with trucks

HEMA 115 C8   21 34 40 S   118 48 57 E

493 Indee Station   ☎ (08) 9176 4968
Camp Area at Indee Station. 185 km N of Auski Roadhouse or 25 km S of Hwy 1 jcn. Turn E onto Indee Rd for 9 km dirt road. GPS at gate, follow signs to homestead

HEMA 115 B8   20 46 41 S   118 32 23 E

Newman to Port Hedland
Marble Bar Road

494 Newman Visitors Centre
Parking Area at Newman. 2 Fortescue Ave. Self Contained Vehicles only. Pay fee at Info centre

HEMA 115 F9   23 21 33 S   119 43 40 E

495 Roy Hill Rest Area
Rest Area at intersection of Roy Hill Rd & Marble Bar Rd. 93 km N of Newman or 96 km S of Nullagine

HEMA 115 E10   22 40 10 S   119 57 01 E

496 Carawine Gorge
Warrawagine Station

Camp Spot 162 km E of Marble Bar, via Rippon Hills Rd, Woodie Woodie Rd. Signposted to Gorge. 14 km, then veer R to sites. Dirt road. 4WD access only. No firearms permited on the Station. Watch for cattle at all times

HEMA 115 C11   21 28 55 S   121 01 43 E

497 Coongan Pool
Camp Spot 110 km SE of the Great Northern Hwy or 33 km N of the Marble Bar turn off. Turn NE opposite parking area, on Marble Bar side of river, follow tracks to Y jcn veer L. Small vehicles only, dirt track

HEMA 115 B10   20 54 18 S   119 47 25 E

Notes...

WESTERN AUSTRALIA

498 Doolena Gorge
Camp Spot 109 km SE of the Great Northern Hwy or 34 km N of Marble Bar turn off. Turn S dirt track on Port Hedland side of river. Follow track for 1.5 km. Watch for overhanging trees

HEMA 115 B10   20 55 32 S   119 47 08 E

499 Pear Creek
Camp Spot 89 km SE of the Great Northern Hwy or 55 km NW of the Marble Bar turn off. Turn NE on Marble Bar side of creek & follow track. Small vehicles only, limited space

HEMA 115 B9   20 50 24 S   119 36 38 E

500 Des Streckfuss Rest Area
Rest Area 74 km NW of Marble Bar or 79 km SE of Hwy 1 jcn. 129 km SE of Port Hedland

HEMA 115 B9   20 49 33 S   119 30 44 E

Port Hedland to Kununurra
Great Northern Highway

501 De Grey River
Rest Area 82 km NE of Port Hedland or 71 km SW of Pardoo Roadhouse

HEMA 116 K2   20 18 28 S   119 15 11 E

502 Pardoo Station
☎ (08) 9176 4930

Camp Area at Pardoo Station. 133 km N of Port Hedland or 44 km S of Pardoo Roadhouse. Turn N onto Pardoo Station Rd 32 km S of Roadhouse or 120 km N of Port Hedland. 13 km dirt road

HEMA 116 K2   20 06 23 S   119 34 46 E

503 Pardoo Roadhouse Caravan Park
☎ (08) 9176 4916

Caravan Park at Pardoo Roadhouse. 153 km N of Port Hedland

HEMA 116 K2   20 03 14 S   119 49 39 E

504 Cape Keraudren
☎ (08) 9176 4979

Camp Area 11 km NW of Pardoo Roadhouse. Turn N off Hwy 1 at Pardoo Roadhouse. Dirt road. Maximum stay 28 Days

HEMA 116 K2   19 57 26 S   119 46 07 E

505 Sandfire Roadhouse Caravan Park
☎ (08) 9176 5944

Caravan Park at Sandfire Roadhouse. 291 km N of Port Headland

HEMA 116 K4   19 46 07 S   121 05 26 E

506 Stanley Rest Area
Rest Area 108 km NE of Sandfire Roadhouse or 181 km SW of Roebuck Plains Roadhouse. 4 km N of Nita Downs turnoff

HEMA 116 H5   19 02 36 S   121 39 56 E

507 Nillibubica (Goldwire) Rest Area
Rest Area 168 km NE of Sandfire Roadhouse or 121 km SW of Roebuck Plains Roadhouse

HEMA 116 H5   18 36 14 S   121 57 59 E

508 Barn Hill Station
☎ (08) 9192 4975

Camp Area at Barn Hill Station. 205 km N of Sandfire Roadhouse or 95 km SW of Roebuck Plains Roadhouse. Turn W off Hwy 1, 195 km N of Sandfire Roadhouse or 95 km S of Roebuck Plains Roadhouse for 10 km of sand & dirt road. Closed Nov to April

HEMA 116 G5   18 22 05 S   122 02 27 E

509 Roebuck Plains Rest Area
Parking Area 267 km N of Sandfire Roadhouse or 22 km SW of Roebuck Plains Roadhouse

HEMA 116 G6   18 00 51 S   122 35 42 E

510 Broome's Gateway
☎ 0437 525 485

Caravan Park 29 km E of Broome or 5 km W of Roebuck Plains Roadhouse

HEMA 116 G6   17 51 22 S   122 27 24 E

511 Broome Pistol Club & Caravan Overflow
Camp Area at Broome. Port Dr. Overflow facility which will only open when all the caravan parks are full. CLOSED September - Re open June

HEMA 116 G5   17 59 15 S   122 12 28 E

512 Mango Camping Ground
☎ (08) 9192 1366

Camp Area at Broome. 91 Walcott St. Overflow for Roebuck Caravan Park. Closed in Wet Season

HEMA 116 G5   17 58 16 S   122 14 05 E

513 Buckleys Bush Retreat
☎ 0438 085 350

Camp Area 19 km N of Broome via Broome-Cape Leveque Rd & McGuigan Rd. Self Contained Vehicles only

HEMA 116 G5   17 51 57 S   122 13 54 E

Notes...

514 Willie Creek
(08) 9191 3456

Camp Spot 35 km N of Broome. Turn N 9 km E of Broome, along Cape Leveque Rd & Manari Rd, Willie Creek Rd. Follow red markers around lake. Camping area just past picnic shelter, veer R. Small vehicles only. Dirt road. 4WD recommended

HEMA 116 G5 17 45 33 S 122 12 40 E

72

515 Barred Creek
(08) 9191 3456

Camp Spot 39 km N of Broome. Turn N 9 km E of Broome, along Cape Leveque Rd & Manari Rd then turn W 9 km N of Willie Creek Rd, follow 1.5 km to various sites

HEMA 116 F5 17 39 42 S 122 12 07 E

72

516 Quondong
(08) 9191 3456

Camp Spot 45 km N of Broome. Turn N 9 km E of Broome, along Cape Leveque Rd & Manari Rd. Dirt road. 4WD recommended

HEMA 116 F5 17 35 28 S 122 10 11 E

72

517 Prices Point
(08) 9191 3456

Camp Spot 58 km N of Broome. Turn N 9 km E of Broome, along Cape Leveque Rd & Manari Rd. Dirt road. 4WD recommended

HEMA 116 F5 17 29 15 S 122 08 39 E

72

518 Banana Well Getaway
(08) 9192 4040

Camp Area 135 km N of Broome. Travel along Cape Leveque Rd for approx 109 km, turn W at sign called Loongabid (Steve Arrow Rd), 7 kms to signpost, then 6 km to site

HEMA 116 E6 16 58 35 S 122 35 18 E

BIG RIG

519 Gnylmarung Retreat
(08) 9192 4097

Camp Area approx 150 km N of Broome. Travel along Cape Leveque Rd for 134 km, turn W onto Middle Lagoon Rd, follow signs for 28 km

HEMA 116 E6 16 51 40 S 122 37 15 E

520 Nature's Hideaway at Middle Lagoon
(08) 9192 4002

Camp Area 180 km N of Broome. Travel 134 km along Cape Leveque Rd, turn W onto Middle Lagoon Rd, follow signs. 40 km to site. Open 01 Apr - 31 October

HEMA 116 E6 16 46 26 S 122 34 37 E

521 Whalesong Cafe & Campground
(08) 9192 4000

Camp Area 175 km N of Broome. Follow the Cape Leveque Rd for 134 km, turn W onto Middle Lagoon Rd, then follow the Whalesong signs for 30 km. Reservations essential, limited sites

HEMA 116 E6 16 47 59 S 122 37 22 E

522 Goombaragin Eco Retreat
0429 505 347

Camp Area 175 km N of Broome. Follow the Cape Leveque Rd for 134 km, turn W onto Middle Lagoon Rd, turn R after 16 km, follow signs. Reservations essential, limited sites

HEMA 116 E6 16 47 43 S 122 39 58 E

523 Chile Creek
(08) 9192 4141

Camp Area 190 km N of Broome, 7 km S of Lombadina Community. Turn onto Diaradgin Rd, follow signs, 6 km of sandy access track, suitable for 4WD, camper trailers & tents

HEMA 116 E6 16 32 06 S 122 52 22 E

524 Kooljaman at Cape Leveque
(08) 9192 4970

Camp Area at Cape Leveque, 220 km N of Broome. Small campervans only, no caravans. Minimum stay 2 nights

HEMA 116 E6 16 23 47 S 122 55 38 E

525 Gambanan
0488 440 817

Camp Area 4.5 km NW of One Arm Point. Signposted, 1.5 km track

HEMA 116 E6 16 25 14 S 123 01 54 E

526 Nillibubbica Rest Area

Rest Area 71 km E of Roebuck Plains Roadhouse or 60 km W of Willare Bridge Roadhouse

1

HEMA 116 F7 17 39 21 S 123 07 57 E

BIG RIG 24

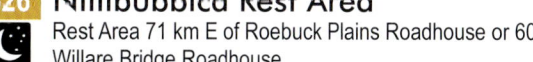

527 Willare Bridge Roadhouse & Caravan Park
(08) 9191 4775

Caravan Park at Willare Bridge 14 km SW of Derby turn off or 165 km E of Broome

1

HEMA 116 G7 17 43 35 S 123 39 15 E

BIG RIG

528 Myroodah Crossing

Camp Spot 38 km S of Camballin Rd & Grt Northern Hwy intersection. At 3 way intersection continue straight ahead to River Crossing. Various campspots both sides of river. Dirt road

HEMA 117 G8 18 04 44 S 124 13 18 E

72

529 The Boab Rest Area

Rest Area 55 km SE of Derby turnoff or 158 km W of Fitzroy Crossing

1

HEMA 117 G8 17 49 26 S 124 14 04 E

BIG RIG

530 The Lake Ellendale

Camp Spot 118 km SE of Derby turnoff or 95 km W of Fitzroy Crossing. Entry is 6.4 km W of Ellendale rest area

HEMA 117 G9 17 55 52 S 124 47 00 E

BIG RIG

WESTERN AUSTRALIA

531 Ellendale Rest Area
Rest Area 125 km SE of Derby turnoff or 88 km W of Fitzroy Crossing
HEMA 117 G9   17 57 38 S   124 50 10 E

532 Windjana Gorge Campground ☎ (08) 9195 5500
Windjana Gorge National Park
Camp Area 144 km E of Derby or 146 km NW of Fitzroy Crossing. Turn S off Gibb River Rd 125 km E of Derby for 18 km or turn N 43 km W of Fitzroy Crossing onto Leopold Downs Rd for 105 km. Dirt road. Generators allowed in separate campground. Closed during wet season
HEMA 117 F9   17 24 42 S   124 56 33 E

✓ 533 RAAF Boab Quarry
Camp Spot 54 km NW of Fitzroy Crossing. Turn N onto Leopold Downs Rd 43 km W of Fitzroy Crossing. 11 km to Y jcn, take RH fork 700m down track to various campspots. 58 km S of Tunnel Creek turnoff. Dirt road
HEMA 117 G9   17 54 44 S   125 17 48 E

534 Ngumpan Cliff Lookout
Rest Area 96 km SE of Fitzroy Crossing or 192 km W of Halls Creek
HEMA 117 H10   18 44 53 S   126 06 31 E

535 Larrawa Nature Stay & Bush Camping ☎ (08) 9191 7025
Camp Area 143 km E of Fitzroy Crossing or 147 km W of Halls Creek. 4 km on dirt road to station. Open 01 April - 30 September. GPS at gate
HEMA 117 H11   18 47 57 S   126 32 04 E

✓ 536 Mary Pool (Mary River)
Rest Area 180 km E of Fitzroy Crossing or 108 km W of Halls Creek
HEMA 117 H11   18 43 37 S   126 52 19 E

537 Caroline Pool
Camp Spot 15 km SE of Halls Creek, via Duncan Rd. Turn E 13 km SE of Halls Creek. Dirt - Sandy road, small area limited turning space
HEMA 117 H13   18 13 36 S   127 45 35 E

538 Palm Springs
Picnic Spot 40 km SE of Halls Creek, via Duncan Rd. Small area close to road
HEMA 117 H13   18 25 12 S   127 50 42 E

539 Sawpit Gorge
Camp Spot 46 km SE of Halls Creek, via Duncan Rd. Last 3 km winding & corrugated. Small vehicles only. Small area
HEMA 117 H13   18 25 30 S   127 49 14 E

540 Little Panton River
Parking Area 46 km N of Halls Creek or 117 km S of Turkey Creek
HEMA 117 G13   17 52 32 S   127 49 54 E

✓ 541 Leycesters Rest - Ord River
Rest Area 100 km N of Halls Creek or 63 km S of Turkey Creek
HEMA 117 F13   17 28 45 S   127 57 04 E

542 Spring Creek
Rest Area 107 km NE of Halls Creek or 56 km SW of Turkey Creek. Big rigs at top car park
HEMA 117 F13   17 25 59 S   127 59 21 E

543 Muluks Rest Area
Rest Area 121 km N of Halls Creek or 39 km S of Turkey Creek
HEMA 117 F13   17 20 19 S   128 03 08 E

544 Kurrajong Campground ☎ (08) 9168 4200
Purnululu National Park
Camp Area 7 km N of Visitors Centre. 56 km rough dirt road. Accessed by 4X4 vehicle & high clearance, single axle, towable units, caravan & camper trailers
HEMA 117 F13   17 23 20 S   128 19 50 E

545 Walardi Campground ☎ (08) 9168 4200
Purnululu National Park
Camp Area 12 km S of Visitors Centre. 56 km rough dirt road. Accessed by 4X4 vehicle & high clearance, single axle, towable units, caravan & camper trailers
HEMA 117 G13   17 31 16 S   128 18 02 E

546 Dunham River
Rest Area 118 km N of Turkey Creek or 35 km S of Victoria Hwy jcn
HEMA 117 E13   16 07 54 S   128 22 52 E

547 Wuggubun Aboriginal Community Campground
Camp Area 157 km N of Turkey Creek or 40 km SW of Kununurra. Turn W off Hwy. Signposted. Open April - October
HEMA 117 D13   15 57 13 S   128 22 45 E

548 Cockburn Rest Area

Rest Area at Victoria Hwy jcn or 152 km N of Turkey Creek, 56 km S of Wyndham or 45 km W of Kununurra

HEMA 117 D13   15 52 07 S   128 22 17 E

549 Maggie Creek

Rest Area 28 km N of Victoria Hwy jcn or 28 km S of Wyndham. Area not level

HEMA 117 D13   15 40 42 S   128 14 50 E

550 Diggers Rest Station   ☎ (08) 9161 1029

Camp Area 38 km N of Victoria Hwy jcn or 34 km SW Wyndham. King River Rd, Signposted on Great Northern Hwy. 4WD recommended

HEMA 117 D13   15 38 19 S   128 04 48 E

551 Mambi Island

Camp Area 54 km NW Kununurra. Turn N onto Valentine Springs Rd, travel 14.5 km to Parrys Creek Rd, turn L travel 31.5 km. Signposted access to camp. Dirt road. Steep entry

HEMA 117 D14   15 34 58 S   128 28 24 E

Leonora to Yulara (NT)

Great Central Road

This road is seasonal and more suitable to 4WD vehicles, camper trailers and off road caravans. Road conditions phone 1800 013 314. Permits are required to travel on this road

✓552 Giles Breakaway

Camp Spot 50 km N of Laverton or 262 km SW of Tjukayirla Roadhouse. At Outback Way sign turn S onto track to Breakaway

HEMA 113 D13   28 16 49 S   122 42 03 E

553 Giles Breakaway Parking Area

Parking Area 56 km N of Laverton or 256 km SW of Tjukayirla Roadhouse

HEMA 113 D13   28 14 49 S   122 43 10 E

554 Limestone Well Parking Area (The Pines)

Parking Area 120 km NE of Laverton or 191 km SW of Tjukayirla Roadhouse

HEMA 119 B1   27 54 55 S   123 10 41 E

555 Minnie Creek Rd Parking Area

Parking Area 197 km NE of Laverton or 115 km SW of Tjukayirla Roadhouse

HEMA 119 B2   27 50 32 S   123 55 03 E

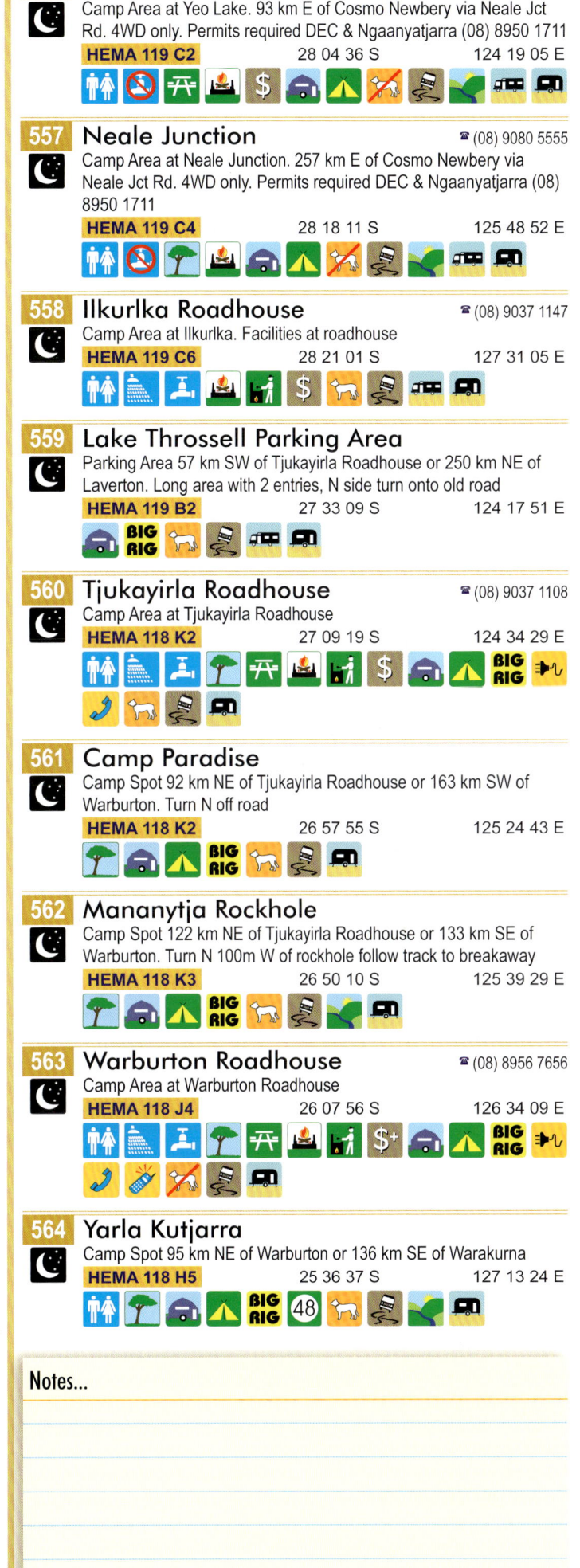

556 Yeo Lake   ☎ (08) 9080 5555

Camp Area at Yeo Lake. 93 km E of Cosmo Newbery via Neale Jct Rd. 4WD only. Permits required DEC & Ngaanyatjarra (08) 8950 1711

HEMA 119 C2   28 04 36 S   124 19 05 E

557 Neale Junction   ☎ (08) 9080 5555

Camp Area at Neale Junction. 257 km E of Cosmo Newbery via Neale Jct Rd. 4WD only. Permits required DEC & Ngaanyatjarra (08) 8950 1711

HEMA 119 C4   28 18 11 S   125 48 52 E

558 Ilkurlka Roadhouse   ☎ (08) 9037 1147

Camp Area at Ilkurlka. Facilities at roadhouse

HEMA 119 C6   28 21 01 S   127 31 05 E

559 Lake Throssell Parking Area

Parking Area 57 km SW of Tjukayirla Roadhouse or 250 km NE of Laverton. Long area with 2 entries, N side turn onto old road

HEMA 119 B2   27 33 09 S   124 17 51 E

560 Tjukayirla Roadhouse   ☎ (08) 9037 1108

Camp Area at Tjukayirla Roadhouse

HEMA 118 K2   27 09 19 S   124 34 29 E

561 Camp Paradise

Camp Spot 92 km NE of Tjukayirla Roadhouse or 163 km SW of Warburton. Turn N off road

HEMA 118 K2   26 57 55 S   125 24 43 E

562 Mananytja Rockhole

Camp Spot 122 km NE of Tjukayirla Roadhouse or 133 km SE of Warburton. Turn N 100m W of rockhole follow track to breakaway

HEMA 118 K3   26 50 10 S   125 39 29 E

563 Warburton Roadhouse   ☎ (08) 8956 7656

Camp Area at Warburton Roadhouse

HEMA 118 J4   26 07 56 S   126 34 09 E

564 Yarla Kutjarra

Camp Spot 95 km NE of Warburton or 136 km SE of Warakurna

HEMA 118 H5   25 36 37 S   127 13 24 E

Notes...

565 Warakurna Roadhouse ☎ (08) 8956 7344
Camp Area at Warakurna Roadhouse
HEMA 118 G6   25 02 34 S   128 18 12 E

566 Kaltukatjara Campground (Docker River) NT
Camp Area at Kaltukatjara. 1 km W of town turnoff
HEMA 118 G7   24 51 48 S   129 03 41 E

Gibb River Road

This road is seasonal and more suitable to 4WD vehicles, camper trailers and off road caravans. Road conditions phone 1800 013 314

567 Home Valley Station ☎ (08) 9161 4322
Camp Area at Home Valley Station. 66 km W of Wyndham-Kununurra turnoff. 1.7 km off Gibb River Rd
HEMA 117 D13   15 43 15 S   127 49 24 E

568 Ellenbrae Station ☎ (08) 9161 4325
Camp Area at Ellenbrae Station. 171 km W of Wyndham-Kununurra turnoff & 180 km E of Mt Barnett Roadhouse. 5 km N of Gibb River Rd. Pay fees at homestead
HEMA 117 D12   15 57 27 S   127 03 47 E

569 Russ Creek
Camp Spot at Russ Creek 46 km W of Ellenbrae Station turnoff or 43 km E of Kalumburu Rd. On N side of road E of the creek
HEMA 117 D11   16 02 53 S   126 42 04 E

570 Drysdale River Station - Homestead Campground ☎ (08) 9161 4326
Camp Area at Drysdale River Station. 59 km N of Gibb River Rd & Kalumburu Rd intersection. Limited powered sites. Register & pay at the shop or bar prior to setting up
HEMA 117 D11   15 42 13 S   126 22 45 E

571 Drysdale River Station - Miners Pool ☎ (08) 9161 4326
Camp Area Drysdale Station. 5 km N of Drysdale River Station. Pay fees at Drysdale River Station. Register & pay at the shop or bar prior to setting up
HEMA 117 D11   15 40 45 S   126 24 10 E

572 King Edward River Campground No 1 ☎ (08) 9168 4200
Camp Spot 8.5 km W of Kalumburu Rd along the Mitchell Plateau/ Port Warrender Rd
HEMA 117 C11   14 53 04 S   126 12 02 E

573 King Edward River Campground No 2 ☎ (08) 9168 4200
Camp Spot 8.2 km W of Kalumburu Rd along the Mitchell Plateau/ Port Warrender Rd
HEMA 117 C11   14 53 03 S   126 12 05 E

574 Mitchell Falls Campground ☎ (08) 9168 4200
Mitchell River National Park
Camp Area 16.2 km W of the Mitchell Plateau/Port Warrender Rd
HEMA 117 C10   14 49 12 S   125 43 06 E

575 Hann River
Rest Area 53.8 km W of Kalumburu Rd jcn or 54.2 km E of Mount Barnett Roadhouse
HEMA 117 E11   16 30 51 S   126 21 20 E

576 Mt Elizabeth Station ☎ (08) 9191 4644
Camp Area at Mt Elizabeth Station. 38 km NE of Mt Barnett Roadhouse or 70 km S of the Kalumburu Rd jcn, then 30 km N to campsite
HEMA 117 E10   16 25 10 S   126 06 17 E

577 Manning Gorge Camping Area ☎ (08) 9191 7007
Camp Area at Manning Gorge. 7 km N of Mt Barnett Roadhouse. Permit required, fees payable at Roadhouse
HEMA 117 E10   16 39 25 S   125 55 39 E

578 Charnley River Station ☎ (08) 9191 4646
Camp Area at Charnley River Station. Turn N 27 km NE of Imintji Store or 47 km SW of Mount Barnett Roadhouse. Travel N for 42 km to Station
HEMA 117 E10   16 42 53 S   125 27 29 E

✓579 Mornington Wilderness Camp ☎ (08) 9191 7406
Camp Area 90 km S of Gibb River Rd. Turn S 25 km E of Imintji Store or 53 km W of Mt Barnett Roadhouse. Must report in at radio booth before entering to check availability. No generators or fires
HEMA 117 F10   17 30 29 S   126 06 45 E

580 March Fly Glen Rest Area
Rest Area 9.7 km W of Silent Grove Rd or 220 km E of Derby. Small vehicles only
HEMA 117 F9   17 09 47 S   125 18 37 E

581 Silent Grove Camping Area ☎(08) 9192 5500
King Leopold Ranges Conservation Park
Camp Area 20 km N of Gibb River Rd on Silent Grove Rd. Turn N
8 km W of Imintji Roadhouse or 95 E of Gibb River Rd/ Leopold
Downs Rd jcn
HEMA 117 F9   17 03 59 S   125 14 57 E

582 Mt Hart Wilderness Lodge ☎(08) 9191 4645
Camp Area at Mt Hart Station. Turn N 65 km E of Leopold Downs Rd
jcn or 38 km W of Imintji Store. 49 km to Station
HEMA 117 E9   16 49 06 S   124 55 14 E

583 Lennard River Rest Area
Rest Area 72 km W of Silent Grove Rd or 128 km E of Derby
HEMA 117 F9   17 23 34 S   124 45 22 E

584 Birdwood Downs ☎(08) 9191 1275
Camp Area 18 km E of Derby on the Gibb River Rd. Bush camping.
No generators allowed
HEMA 116 F7   17 21 28 S   123 46 06 E

Notes...

NORTHERN TERRITORY
key map

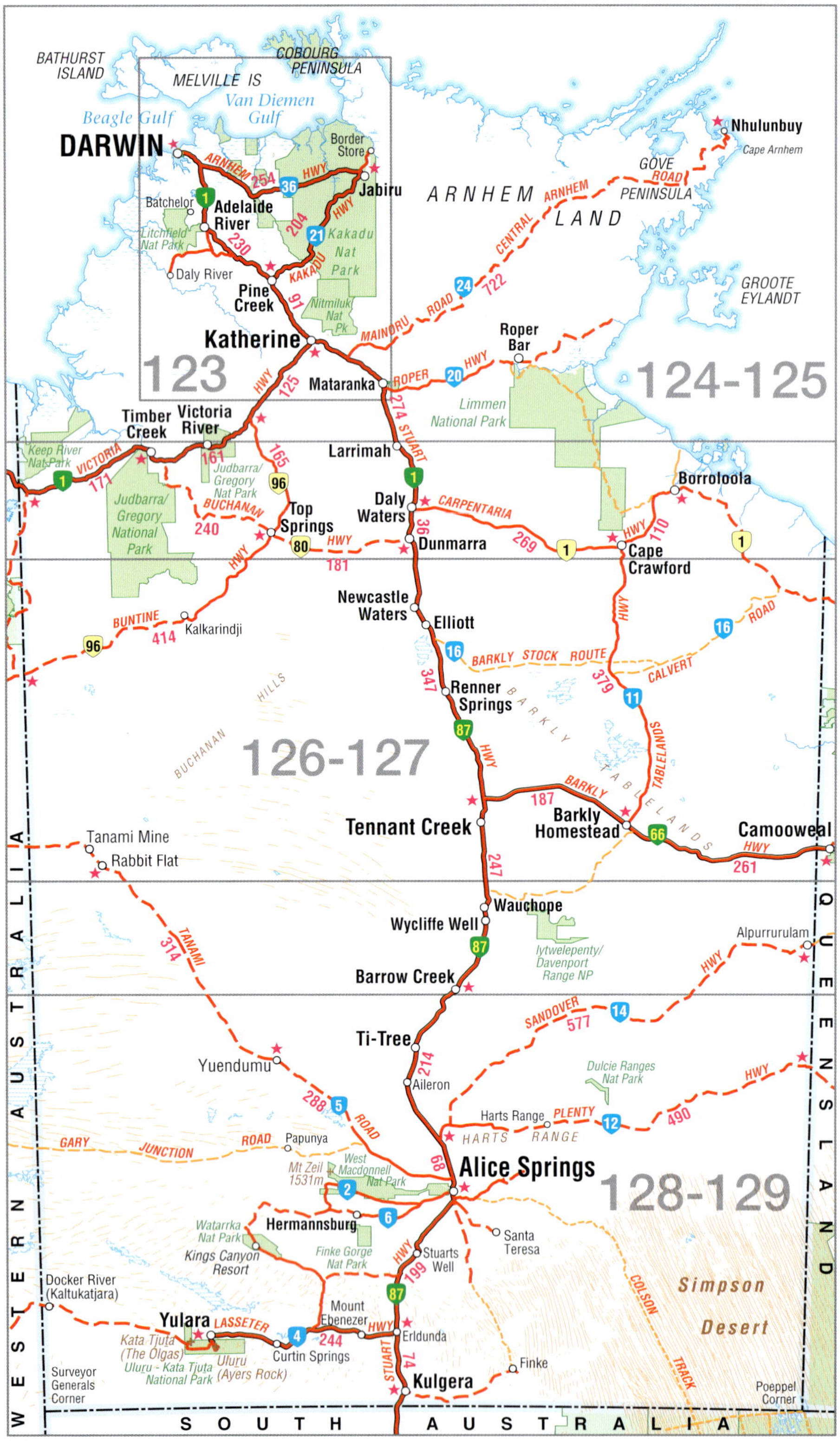

MINDIL BEACH (122 G1)

WANGI FALLS, LITCHFIELD NP (124 E3)

(Map of Northern Territory showing major towns, highways, national parks, and key map grid sections 123, 124-125, 126-127, 128-129.)

	Alice Springs	Barrow Creek	Borroloola	Camooweal	Darwin	Halls Creek	Jabiru	Katherine	Kulgera	Kununurra	Mataranka	Nhulunbuy
Barrow Creek	284											
Borroloola	893	1177										
Camooweal	721	694	978									
Darwin	1412	940	1210	1494								
Halls Creek	1187	543	1143	1310	1046							
Jabiru	1169	251	1394	922	1192	1476						
Katherine	299	865	317	1095	623	893	1177					
Kulgera	1451	1750	1320	1768	1252	1451	558	274				
Kununurra	1678	512	811	358	829	1449	1049	1247	1404			
Mataranka	624	1339	112	411	977	429	983	511	781	1065		
Nhulunbuy	739	1241	2078	729	1028	1594	1046	1722	1250	1520	1804	
Uluru (Ayers Rock)	2267	1528	1867	337	1640	1939	1509	1957	1441	1640	747	463
Tennant Creek	970	1297	558	1024	781	670	969	1118	987	471	747	223

Distances are shown in kilometres and follow the most direct major sealed route where possible.

2 To Cullen Bay
3 To Botanic Gardens

Legend

Major Road	
Minor Road	
One Way Road	→
Major Building	
Govt Building	
Theatre/Cinema	
Shopping	
Information	*i*
Post Office	✉
24hr Fuel	⛽

Points of Interest

1 Aboriginal Fine Arts Gallery B2
2 Aquascene Fish Feeding A1
3 Cenotaph / War Memorial, The C1
4 Chung Wah Temple and Museum C3
5 Crocosaurus Cove B2
6 Darwin Convention Centre D3
7 Darwin Entertainment Centre A2
8 Darwin Theatre Company C2
9 Darwin Wave Lagoon D2
10 Deckchair Cinema, The C1
11 Indo Pacific Marine D3
12 Leichhardt Memorial B1
13 Lyons Cottage (B.A.T. House) B1
14 Old Admiralty House C1
15 Old Court House, The C2
16 Old Town Hall, The C2
17 Survivors Lookout D2
18 Tree of Knowledge, The C2
19 USS Peary Memorial / USAAF Memorial A1
20 WWII Oil Storage Tunnels D2

Accommodation

1 Adina Apartment Hotel Darwin D2
2 Alatai Holiday Apartments A3
3 Argus Apartments C3
4 Banyan View Lodge A2
5 Cavenagh Hotel Motel, The C2
6 Chilli's Backpackers B2
7 City Gardens Apartments A3
8 Darwin Central Hotel B2
9 Darwin City YHA A2
10 Dingo Moon Lodge A2
11 DoubleTree by Hilton Hotel Darwin A1
12 Frogshollow Backpackers B3
13 Hilton Darwin C2
14 Luma Luma Holiday Apartments C3
15 Mantra on the Esplanade B1
16 Mantra Pandanas B3
17 Marrakai Apartments A2
18 Mediterranean All Suite Hotel A2
19 Melaleuca On Mitchell Backpackers B2
20 Novotel Atrium Darwin B1
21 Palms City Resort C1
22 Poinciana Inn A2
23 Quest Serviced Apartments B2
24 Travelodge Mirambeena Resort B2
25 Value Inn B2
26 Vibe Hotel Darwin Waterfront D2
27 Youth Shack, The B2

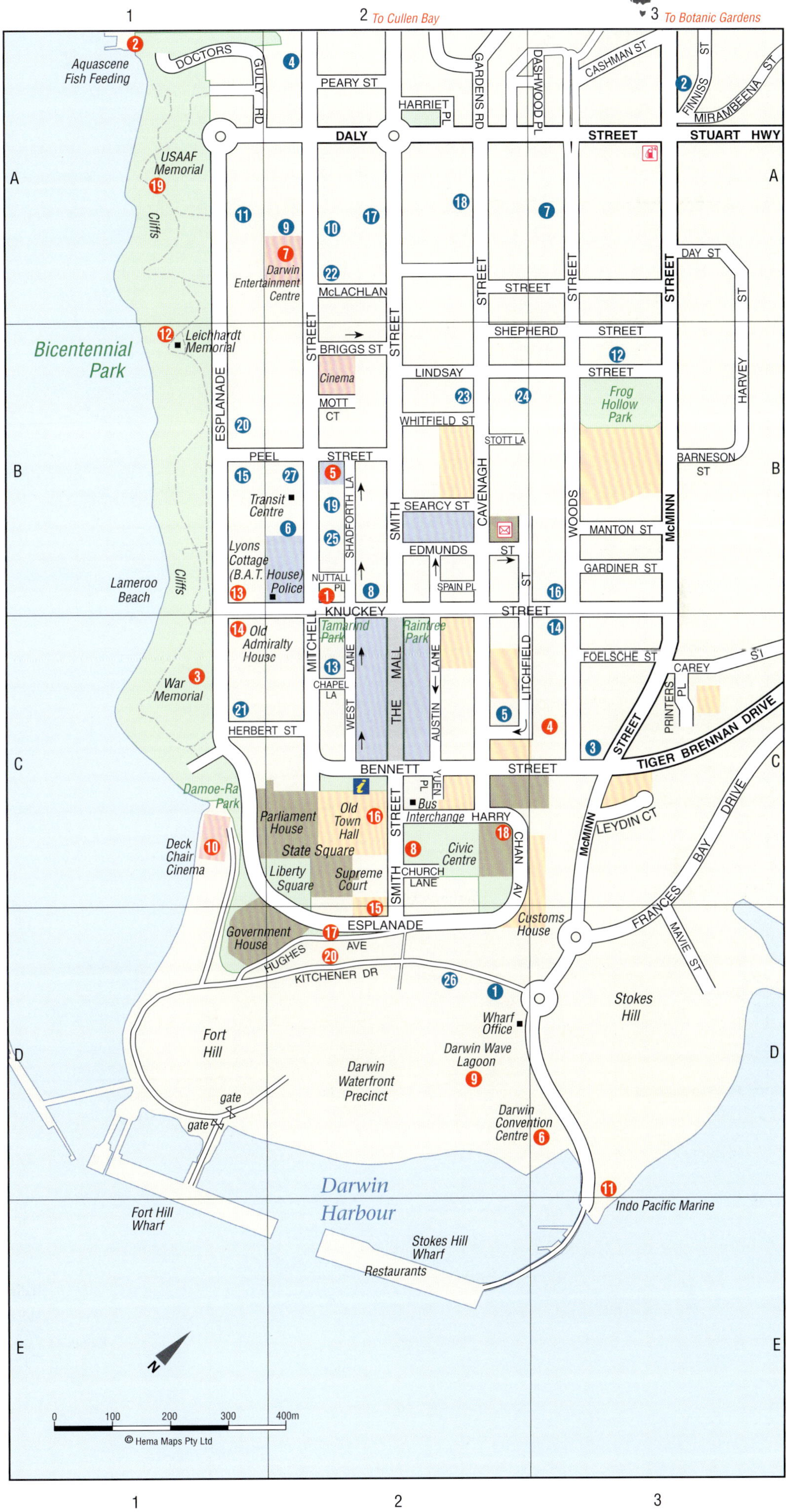

© Hema Maps Pty Ltd

© Hema Maps Pty Ltd

N

SEE MAP 121

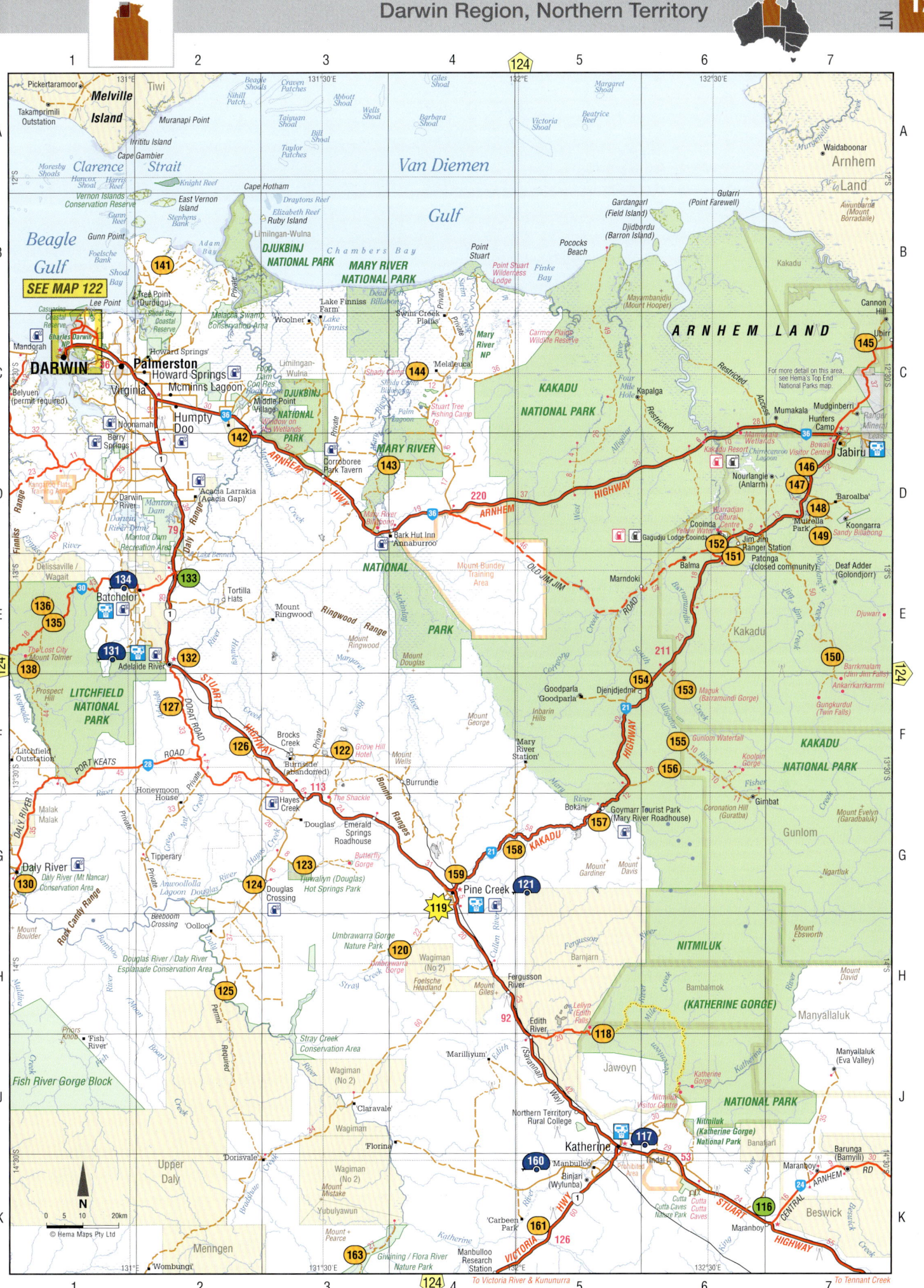

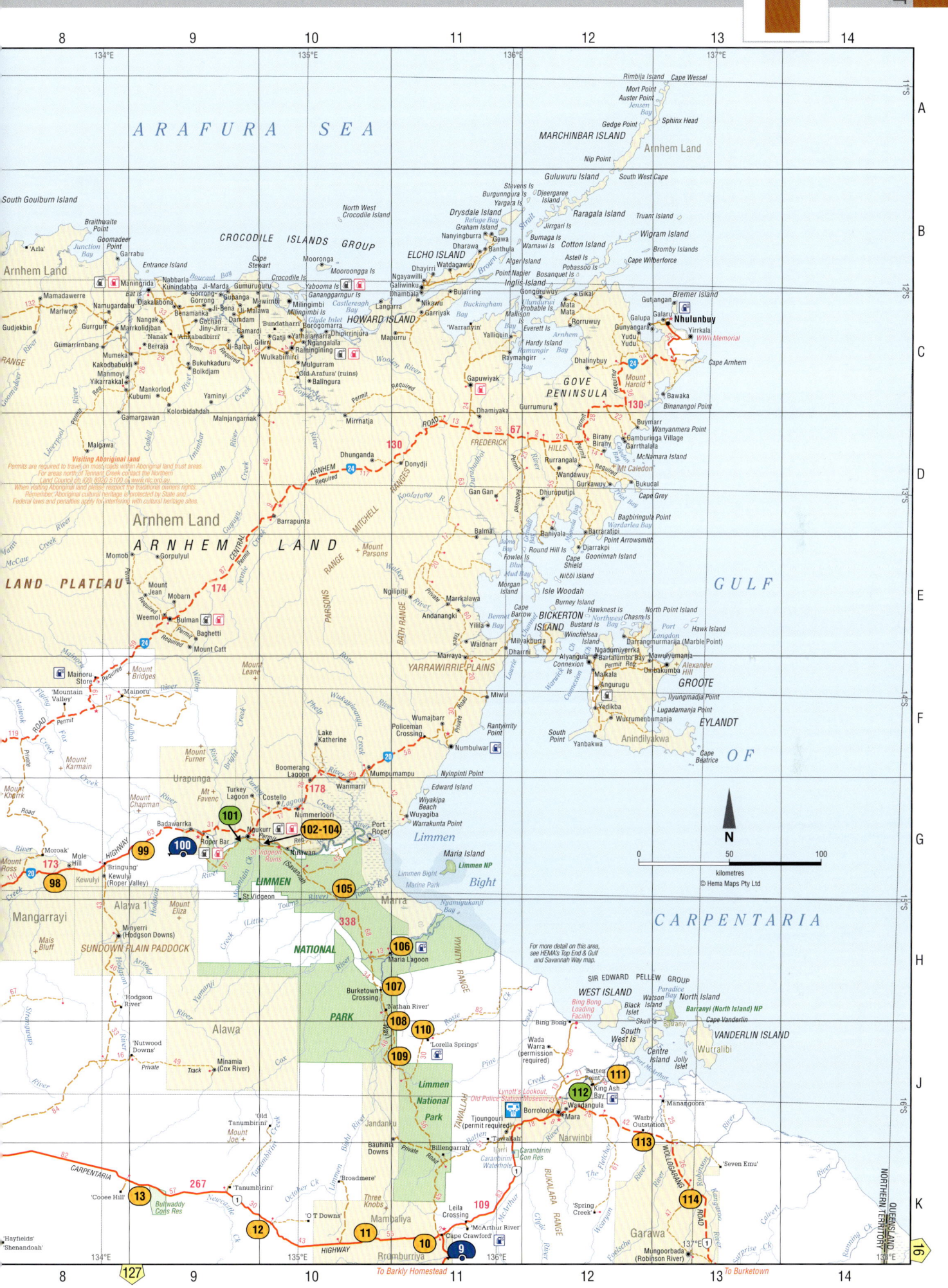

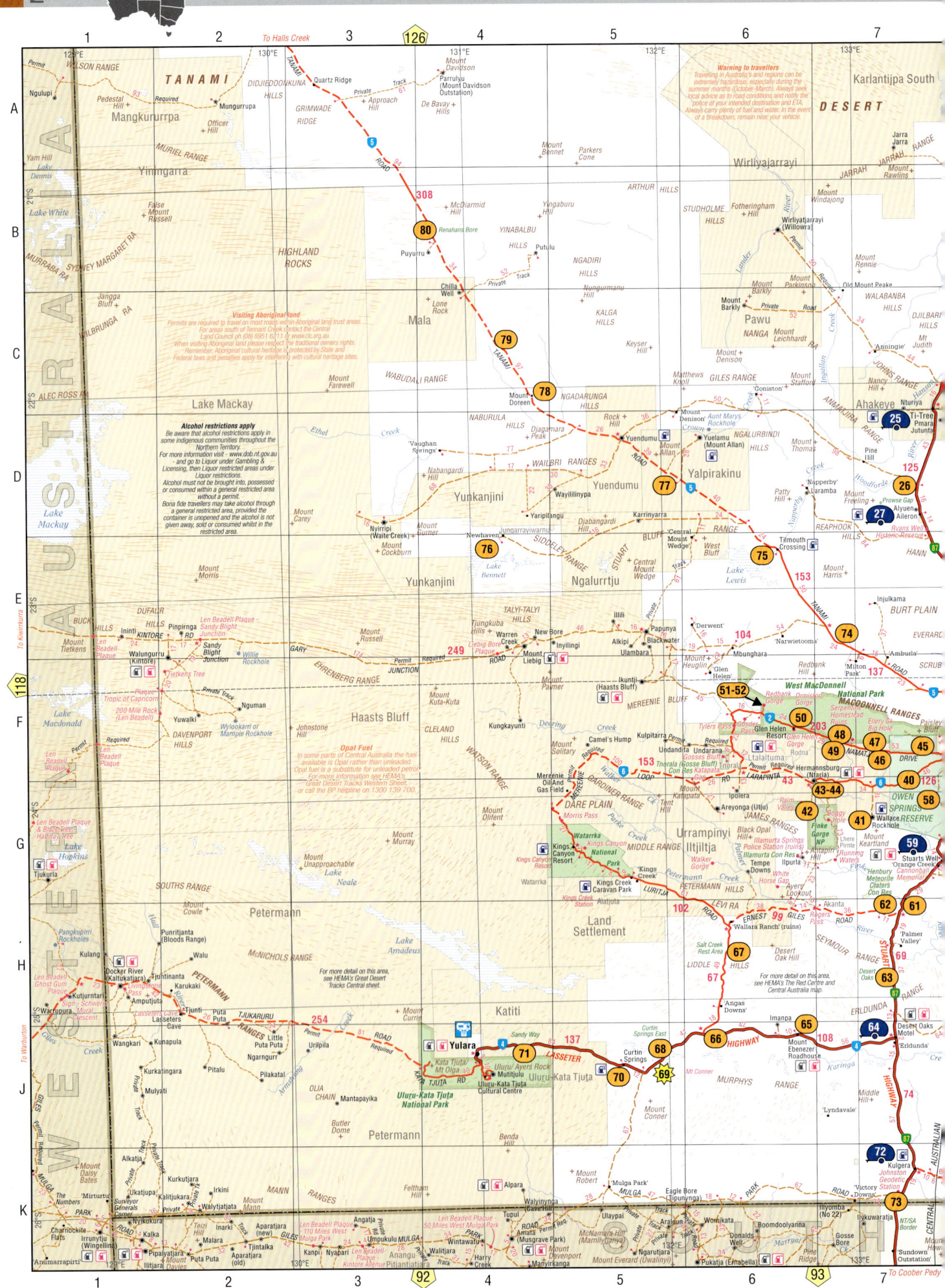

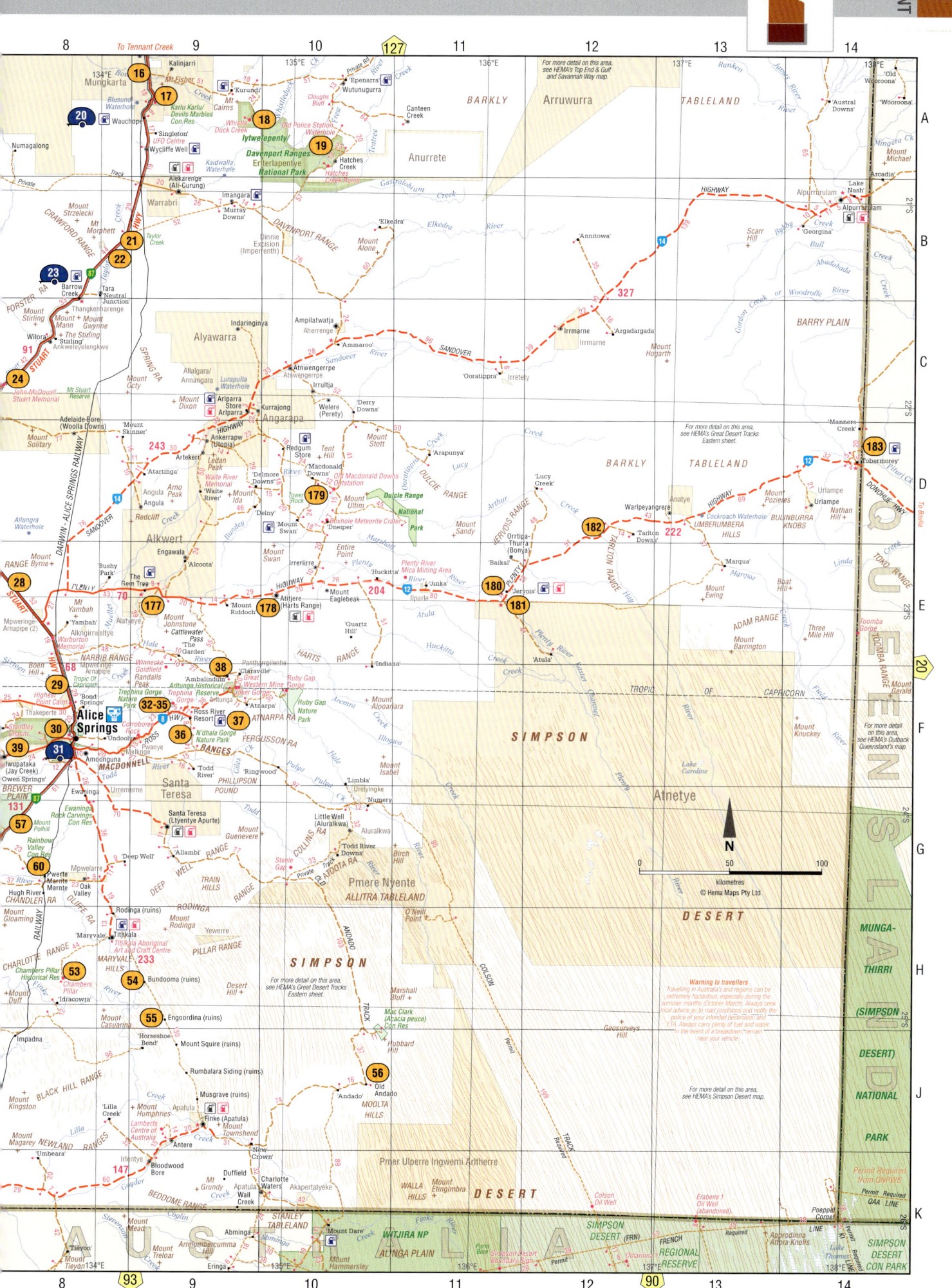

Northern Territory Highway Index

Northern Territory Alphabetic Site Index

Northern Territory Alphabetic Site Index

Camooweal to Three Ways
Barkly Highway

1 Avon Downs Rest Area
Rest Area 69 km W of Camooweal or 66 km E of Soudan
HEMA 127 H13   20 01 30 S   137 29 23 E

2 Soudan Bore Rest Area
Rest Area 66 km W of Avon Downs or 32 km E of Wunara Store.
16 km W of Soudan Station
HEMA 127 H13   20 04 25 S   136 52 43 E

3 Wonarah Bore
Rest Area 56 km W of Wunara Store or 43 km E of Barkly Homestead
HEMA 127 H11   19 50 33 S   136 09 23 E

4 Barkly Homestead   ☎ (08) 8964 4549
Caravan Park 99 km W of Wunara Store or 187 km E of Three Ways
HEMA 127 G11   19 42 38 S   135 49 39 E

5 Frewena Rest Area
Rest Area 55 km W of Barkly Homestead or 132 km E of Three Ways
HEMA 127 G10   19 25 59 S   135 24 04 E

6 41 Mile Bore
Rest Area 117 km W of Barkly Homestead or 70 km E of Three Ways
HEMA 127 G10   19 19 13 S   134 51 03 E

Barkly Homestead - Borroloola - Daly Waters
Tablelands and Carpentaria Highways

7 Brunette Downs Rest Area
Rest Area 145 km N of Barkly Homestead or 232 km S of Cape
Crawford. At windmill
HEMA 127 E11   18 28 27 S   135 58 46 E

8 Kiana Turnoff Rest Area
Rest Area 271 km N of Barkly Homestead or 107 km S of Cape
Crawford
HEMA 127 D11   17 31 41 S   135 41 02 E

9 Heartbreak Hotel Caravan Park   ☎ (08) 8975 9928
Caravan Park at Cape Crawford. Jcn of Carpentaria Hwy &
Tablelands Hwy
HEMA 127 B11   16 40 59 S   135 43 36 E

10 Little River
Camp Spot 10 km W of Cape Crawford or 259 km E of Daly Waters.
E side of bridge, beside river
HEMA 127 B11   16 42 00 S   135 38 22 E

11 Goanna Creek Rest Area
Rest Area 39 km W of Cape Crawford or 230 km E of Daly Waters.
100m N of Hwy
HEMA 127 B10   16 42 16 S   135 22 03 E

12 October Creek Rest Area
Rest Area 99 km W of Cape Crawford or 170 km E of Daly Waters
HEMA 127 B10   16 37 54 S   134 51 31 E

13 Bullwaddy Rest Area
Rest Area 179 km W of Cape Crawford or 90 km E of Daly Waters
HEMA 127 B9   16 27 03 S   134 11 40 E

Three Ways to Kulgera
Stuart Highway

14 Kunjarra (The Pebbles)
Parking Area 19 km S of Three Ways or 17 km N of Tennant Creek.
Turn W off Stuart Hwy 13 km S of Three Ways or 11 km N of Tennant
Creek, (just N of Telegraph Station) for 4 km, then L at jcn for 2 km.
6 km dirt road. Signposted
HEMA 127 G8   19 31 57 S   134 10 49 E
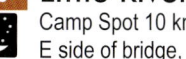

15 Tingkkarli / Lake Mary Ann
Picnic Area 5 km NE of Tennant Creek. Turn E off Stuart Hwy 3 km N
of Tennant Creek or 21 km S of Three Ways for 2 km
HEMA 127 G9   19 36 30 S   134 12 41 E

16 Bonney Well Rest Area
Rest Area 87 km S of Tennant Creek or 27 km N of Wauchope
HEMA 127 J9   20 25 48 S   134 14 46 E

17 Karlu Karlu / Devils Marbles Campground   ☎ (08) 8962 4599
Camp Area 104 km S of Tennant Creek or 10 km N of Wauchope.
1 km E of Hwy
HEMA 127 J9   20 34 05 S   134 15 51 E

Notes...

18 Whistleduck Creek ☎ (08) 8962 4599
Iytwelepenty / Davenport Ranges National Park
Camp Area 87 km S of Tennant Creek. Turn E onto Kurundi Rd for 69 km, then turn S for 25 km. Dirt road. 4WD essential
HEMA 127 J9   20 38 11 S   134 46 46 E

19 Old Police Station Waterhole ☎ (08) 8962 4599
Iytwelepenty / Davenport Ranges National Park
Camp Area 87 km S of Tennant Creek. Turn E onto Kurundi Rd for 119 km, then turn S for 43 km. Dirt road. 4WD essential
HEMA 127 J10   20 45 15 S   135 11 12 E

20 Devils Marbles Hotel ☎ (08) 8964 1963
Caravan Park at Wauchope behind Hotel
HEMA 127 J9   20 38 26 S   134 13 20 E

21 Taylor Creek
Rest Area 52 km S of Wycliffe Well or 40 km N of Barrow Creek. Limited space
HEMA 129 B8   21 14 52 S   134 06 53 E

22 Barrow Creek WWII Staging Area
Camp Spot 28 km N of Barrow Creek or 15 km S of Davenport. Signposted, 1 km off the Hwy. GPS at entrance
HEMA 129 B8   21 18 07 S   134 03 07 E

23 Barrow Creek Roadhouse & Caravan Park ☎ (08) 8956 9753
Caravan Park at Barrow Creek
HEMA 129 B8   21 31 52 S   133 53 21 E

24 McDouall Stuart Memorial
Rest Area 68 km S of Barrow Creek or 21 km N of Ti-Tree
HEMA 129 C8   21 57 38 S   133 29 48 E

25 Ti-Tree Roadhouse Caravan Park ☎ (08) 8956 9741
Caravan Park at Ti-Tree
HEMA 128 D7   22 07 53 S   133 25 00 E

26 Prowse Gap
Rest Area 45 km S of Ti-Tree or 14 km N of Aileron
HEMA 128 D7   22 31 52 S   133 19 44 E

27 Aileron Hotel & Roadhouse ☎ (08) 8956 9703
Caravan Park at Aileron
HEMA 128 D7   22 38 38 S   133 20 43 E

28 Connors Well
Rest Area 38 km S of Aileron or 95 km N of Alice Springs
HEMA 129 E8   22 57 02 S   133 32 35 E

29 Tropic of Capricorn Rest Area
Rest Area 103 km S of Aileron or 30 km N of Alice Springs
HEMA 129 F8   23 26 29 S   133 49 57 E

30 Blatherskite Park ☎ (08) 8955 5197
Camp Area in Alice Springs. Len Kittle Dr, 5 km S of city centre. Available for oversized vehicles (buses, mobile homes) & travellers with animals. Only able to take caravans if the local parks are fully booked. Prior bookings preferred
HEMA 129 F8   23 44 07 S   133 51 45 E

31 Temple Bar Caravan Park ☎ 0455 922 533
Caravan Park at 875 Ilparpa Rd. Metered power
HEMA 129 F8   23 45 37 S   133 47 13 E

32 Gorge Campground ☎ (08) 8951 8250
Trephina Gorge Nature Park
Camp Area 85 km E of Alice Springs. Turn N into Trephina Gorge Nature Park 76 km E of Alice Springs for 9 km. 5 km dirt road
HEMA 129 F9   23 31 18 S   134 23 48 E

33 Panorama Campground ☎ (08) 8951 8250
Trephina Gorge Nature Park
Camp Area 85 km E of Alice Springs. Turn N onto Trephina Gorge Nature Park 76 km E of Alice Springs. 10 km to camp area. 5 km dirt road
HEMA 129 F9   23 31 20 S   134 23 49 E

34 Bluff Campground ☎ (08) 8951 8250
Trephina Gorge Nature Park
Camp Area 85 km E of Alice Springs. Turn N into Trephina Gorge Nature Park 76 km E of Alice Springs for 9 km. 5 km dirt road. No caravans or trailers, limited space
HEMA 129 F9   23 32 10 S   134 23 48 E

Notes...

NORTHERN TERRITORY

35 John Hayes Rockhole ☎ (08) 8951 8250
Trephina Gorge Nature Park
Camp Area 85 km E of Alice Springs. Turn N into Trephina Gorge Nature Park 76 km E of Alice Springs. 4 km to Info Centre, turn W along rough track. High clearance 4WD only. Small area
HEMA 129 F9   23 32 24 S   134 21 18 E

36 N'Dhala Gorge Conservation Area ☎ (08) 8951 8250
Camp Area 90 km E of Alice Springs. Signposted off Ross Hwy. 11 km of 4WD track, 3 water crossings, first one deepest
HEMA 129 F9   23 38 19 S   134 27 47 E

37 Ross River Resort ☎ (08) 8956 9711
Camp Area 86 km E of Alice Springs via Ross Hwy
HEMA 129 F9   23 35 34 S   134 29 35 E

38 Hale River Homestead at Old Ambalindum ☎ (08) 8956 9993
Camp Area at Homestead. 135 km NE of Alice Springs on Arltunga Tourist Dr. 22 km N of Old Arltunga Hotel. Dirt road
HEMA 129 F9   23 23 05 S   134 41 00 E

39 Angkerle Atwatye / Standley Chasm ☎ (08) 8956 7440
Camp Area at Standley Chasm. First night fee includes Chasm entrance, reduces for additional nights. Gates close at 1700 hrs
HEMA 129 F8   23 43 17 S   133 28 10 E

40 Mueller Creek
Rest Area 70 km SW of Alice Springs or 56 km E of Hermannsburg. 23 km SW of Namatjira Dr jcn
HEMA 128 G7   23 55 54 S   133 17 34 E

41 Wallace Rockhole Campground ☎ (08) 8956 7993
Camp Area at Wallace Rockhole
HEMA 128 G7   24 07 25 S   133 05 09 E

42 Palm Valley Campground ☎ (08) 8951 8250
Finke Gorge National Park
Camp Area 147 km W of Alice Springs via Larapinta Dr. Turn S just W of Hermannsburg. 21 km dirt road. High clearance 4WD only
HEMA 128 G6   24 03 29 S   132 44 49 E

43 Ntaria Campground ☎ (08) 8956 7480
Camp Area at Hermannsburg. Collect keys & pay at supermarket opposite
HEMA 128 G6   23 56 33 S   132 46 50 E

44 Hermannsburg Historic Precinct ☎ (08) 8956 7402
Camp Area at Hermannsburg. 800m past sports oval. Bookings & payment at precinct entrance
HEMA 128 G6   23 56 39 S   132 46 30 E

45 Hugh River Bush Camping
Camp Spot along Hugh River. Turn N off Namatjira Dr 9.4 km W of Larapinta Dr jcn, onto access track, 200m to info board & then 1 km to dispersed bush camps along river. Access track suitable for off road caravans for approx first 5 km. GPS at entrance
HEMA 128 F7   23 48 40 S   133 23 07 E

46 Point Howard Lookout
Rest Area 78 km W of Alice Springs or 53 km E of Glen Helen, on Namatjira Dr. Steep access to lookout
HEMA 128 F7   23 48 15 S   133 10 34 E

47 Ellery Creek Big Hole ☎ (08) 8956 7799
Tjoritja / West MacDonnell National Park
Camp Area 80 km W of Alice Springs or 43 km E of Glen Helen. 2 km N of Hwy. Small vehicles only. Dirt road. Emergency phone
HEMA 128 F7   23 46 48 S   133 04 22 E

48 Serpentine Chalet Bush Camping ☎ (08) 8956 7799
Tjoritja / West MacDonnell National Park
Camp Area 108 km W of Alice Springs or 23 km E of Glen Helen. 600m to 2WD camping. 4WD only beyond. No caravans
HEMA 128 F7   23 45 01 S   132 54 56 E

49 Neil Hargrave Lookout
Rest Area 107 km W of Alice Springs or 24 km E of Glen Helen. 800m S off Hwy
HEMA 128 F7   23 45 02 S   132 54 19 E

50 Ormiston Gorge ☎ (08) 8956 7799
Tjoritja / West MacDonnell National Park
Camp Area 135 km W of Alice Springs or 12 km NE of Glen Helen. Turn N 4 km E of Glen Helen
HEMA 128 F6   23 37 57 S   132 43 29 E

Notes...

NORTHERN TERRITORY

51 Woodland Camping Area - Redbank Gorge
☎ (08) 8956 7799
Tjoritja / West MacDonnell National Park
Camp Area 23 km NW of Glen Helen. Turn N for 5 km off Namatjira Dr 20 km W of Glen Helen
HEMA 128 F6   23 35 25 S   132 30 46 E

52 Ridgetop Camping Area - Redbank Gorge
☎ (08) 8956 7799
Tjoritja / West MacDonnell National Park
Camp Area 24 km NW of Glen Helen. Turn N for 6 km off Namatjira Dr 20 km W of Glen Helen. Small vehicles only
HEMA 128 F6   23 34 58 S   132 30 52 E

53 Chambers Pillar Historical Reserve
☎ (08) 8951 8211
Camp Area 164 km S of Alice Springs off the Old Ghan Railway track. Turn W at Rodinga Ruins travel 57 km to site. 4WD only, steep sections. Suitable for off road caravans
HEMA 129 H8   24 52 22 S   133 49 41 E

54 Bundooma Siding
Parking Area 151 km S of Alice Springs or 94 km N of Finke on the Old Ghan Railway track. 4WD only
HEMA 129 H9   24 53 34 S   134 15 34 E

55 Engoordina Ruins
Parking Area 173 km S of Alice Springs or 72 km N of Finke on the Old Ghan Railway track. 4WD only
HEMA 129 H9   25 04 10 S   134 21 51 E

56 Old Andado Homestead Camping
☎ (08) 8956 0812
Camp Area at Old Andado Station, 123 km E of Finke. 4WD only
HEMA 129 J10   25 22 49 S   135 26 30 E

57 Mt Polhill Rest Area
Rest Area 68 km S of Alice Springs or 132 km N of Erldunda. 32 km N of Stuarts Well. Small area, limited space
HEMA 129 G8   24 06 30 S   133 33 28 E

58 Redbank Waterhole
☎ (08) 8956 7300
Owen Springs Reserve
Camp Spot 66 km S Alice Springs or 25 km N of Stuarts Well. Access off Stuart Hwy, signposted Owen Springs Reserve. 6 km to waterhole, follow signs. GPS at entrance. 4WD only, suitable off road caravans & campervans
HEMA 128 G7   24 09 09 S   133 30 40 E

59 Stuarts Well Roadhouse
☎ (08) 8956 0808
Caravan Park 90 km S of Alice Springs or 104 km N of Erldunda
HEMA 128 G7   24 20 26 S   133 27 31 E

60 Rainbow Valley Conservation Reserve
☎ (08) 8951 8250
Camp Area. Turn off 75 km S of Alice Springs or 14 km N of Stuarts Well. 22 km dirt road, sandy patches. 4WD recommended
HEMA 129 G8   24 19 51 S   133 37 57 E

61 Finke River Rest Area
Rest Area 126 km S of Alice Springs or 75 km N of Erldunda. Beside river
HEMA 128 H7   24 33 05 S   133 14 20 E

62 Henbury Meteorite Conservation Reserve
☎ (08) 8951 8250
Camp Area 147 km S of Alice Springs. Turn W off Stuart Hwy 131 km S of Alice Springs or 70 km N of Erldunda onto Ernest Giles Rd for 11 km, then N for 5 km. Dirt road
HEMA 128 H7   24 34 16 S   133 08 35 E

63 Desert Oaks Rest Area
Rest Area 169 km S of Alice Springs or 32 km N of Erldunda
HEMA 128 H7   24 54 18 S   133 11 46 E

64 Erldunda Roadhouse
☎ (08) 8956 0984
Caravan Park at Erldunda. Cnr Stuart Hwy & Lasseter Hwy
HEMA 128 J7   25 11 50 S   133 12 03 E

65 Mt Ebenezer Roadhouse
☎ (08) 8956 2904
Camp Area at Mt Ebenezer Roadhouse
HEMA 128 J6   25 10 44 S   132 40 37 E

66 Kernot Range Rest Area
Rest Area 101 km W of Erldunda or 59 km E of Curtin Springs. 7 km E of Luritja Rd jcn
HEMA 128 J6   25 10 37 S   132 15 06 E

67 Salt Creek Rest Area
Rest Area 48 km N of Lasseter Hwy. On Luritja Rd, 20 km S of Ernest Giles Rd jcn
HEMA 128 H6   24 46 21 S   132 18 24 E

68 Curtin Springs East Rest Area

Rest Area 136 km W of Erldunda or 27 km E of Curtin Springs. 25 km W of Luritja Rd jcn

HEMA 128 J5   25 15 57 S   131 58 43 E

69 Mt Connor Lookout

Rest Area 142 km W of Erldunda or 21 km E of Curtin Springs. 31 km W of Luritja Rd jcn

HEMA 128 J5   25 18 21 S   131 56 23 E

70 Curtin Springs Wayside Inn & Cattle Station

☎ (08) 8956 2906

Camp Area 163 km W of Erldunda or 84 km E of Yulara. Limited powered sites. Fee for power & showers, unpowered camping free

HEMA 128 J5   25 18 52 S   131 45 27 E

71 Sandy Way Rest Area

Rest Area 56 km W of Curtin Springs or 28 km E of Yulara. Tracks over dune to camp spots

HEMA 128 J4   25 13 13 S   131 13 47 E

72 Kulgera Roadhouse & Caravan Park

☎ (08) 8956 0973

Caravan Park at Kulgera Roadhouse

HEMA 128 K7   25 50 22 S   133 18 01 E

73 NT-SA Border

Rest Area 159 km N of Marla or 19 km S of Kulgera

HEMA 128 K7   25 59 54 S   133 11 47 E

Alice Springs to Halls Creek - Tanami Track

Tanami Road

This road is seasonal and more suitable to 4WD vehicles, camper trailers and off road caravans. Road conditions phone 1800 246 199 (NT) or 1800 013 314 (WA)

74 Charley Creek Rest Area

Rest Area 123 km NW of Alice Springs or 62 km SE of Tilmouth Well Roadhouse

HEMA 128 E7   23 16 15 S   132 55 06 E

75 Tilmouth Well Roadhouse

☎ (08) 8956 8777

Camp Area at Tilmouth Well Roadhouse. Limited powered sites

HEMA 128 E6   22 48 35 S   132 35 54 E

76 Newhaven Wildlife Sanctuary

☎ (08) 8964 6000

Camp Area 358 km NW of Alice Springs off the Tanami Track. Bookings essential. Limited sites. Cash only. Open April - September. Suitable for 4WD only

HEMA 128 E4   22 47 15 S   131 05 03 E

77 Yuelamu Roadside Stop

Rest Area S side of road opposite turnoff to Yuelamu Community

HEMA 128 D5   22 28 00 S   132 06 09 E

78 Mt Doreen Ruins

Camp Spot 101 km SE of Renahans Bore or 162 km N of Tilmouth Well Roadhouse

HEMA 128 C4   22 02 29 S   131 20 03 E

79 Floodout Creek

Rest Area 69 km SE of Renahans Bore or 194 km NW of Tilmouth Well Roadhouse

HEMA 128 C4   21 48 22 S   131 10 38 E

80 Renahans Bore Rest Area

Rest Area 152 km SE of Rabbit Flat or 263 km NW of Tilmouth Well Roadhouse. Tracks to bore off road

HEMA 128 B4   21 16 39 S   130 50 57 E

81 Border Rest Area

Rest Area on N.T. side of border N side of road

HEMA 126 H1   19 53 50 S   129 01 22 E

82 Sturt Creek

Camp Spot on creek bank 46 km SE of Wolfe Creek Crater turnoff or 176 km S of Halls Creek

HEMA 117 J12   19 33 36 S   127 41 37 E

83 Wolfe Creek Camp

☎ (08) 9168 4200

Wolfe Creek Crater National Park

Camp Area. Turnoff 130 km SE of Halls Creek. 20 km to campsite from Tanami Rd

HEMA 117 J12   19 10 35 S   127 47 10 E

Notes...

Three Ways to Mataranka
Stuart Highway

84 Attack Creek (Stuart Monument)
Rest Area 47 km N of Three Ways or 87 km S of Renner Springs
HEMA 127 F8   19 01 24 S   134 08 29 E

85 Banka Banka Station ☎ (08) 8964 4511
Camp Area at Banka Banka Station. 74 km N of Three Ways or 60 km S of Renner Springs
HEMA 127 F8   18 47 32 S   134 01 50 E

86 Renner Springs Desert Inn ☎ (08) 8964 4505
Caravan Park at Renner Springs. At roadhouse
HEMA 127 E8   18 19 08 S   133 47 43 E

87 Site Closed

88 Newcastle Waters Rest Area
Rest Area 25 km N of Elliott or 77 km S of Dunmarra. Just S of Newcastle Waters turnoff. Limited space
HEMA 126 D7   17 22 31 S   133 26 22 E

89 Dunmarra Wayside Inn ☎ (08) 8975 9922
Caravan Park at Dunmarra
HEMA 126 B7   16 40 47 S   133 24 45 E

90 Top Springs Hotel ☎ (08) 8975 0767
Caravan Park at Top Springs. Buntine & Buchanan Hwy intersection. Limited powered sites
HEMA 126 B5   16 32 36 S   131 47 49 E

91 Kalkarindji (Wave Hill) ☎ (08) 8975 0788
Camp Area at Kalkarindji. Next to general store
HEMA 126 D4   17 26 49 S   130 50 03 E

92 Daly Waters Hi-Way Inn ☎ (08) 8975 9925
Caravan Park at the jcn of Stuart & Carpentaria Hwys, Daly Waters
HEMA 124 K7   16 18 28 S   133 23 06 E

93 The Daly Waters Pub ☎ (08) 8975 9927
Caravan Park at Daly Waters. Stuart St, 3 km W of Hwy
HEMA 124 K7   16 15 14 S   133 22 11 E

94 Larrimah Wayside Inn Caravan Park ☎ (08) 8975 9931
Caravan Park at Larrimah, beside hotel
HEMA 124 H7   15 34 27 S   133 12 52 E

95 Warloch Rest Area
Rest Area 41 km N of Larrimah or 37 km S of Mataranka
HEMA 124 H7   15 14 12 S   133 06 53 E

Mataranka to Borroloola
Roper Highway

96 Jalmurark Campground ☎ (08) 8975 4560
Elsey National Park
Camp Area 18 km E of Mataranka, via Homestead Rd & John Hauser Dr
HEMA 124 G7   14 57 18 S   133 13 09 E

97 Elsey Rest Area
Rest Area 31 km E of Stuart Hwy or 140 km W of Roper Bar. 1 km E of Elsey Station turnoff
HEMA 124 G7   14 59 06 S   133 20 53 E

98 Mt Price Rest Area
Rest Area 75 km E of Stuart Hwy or 96 km W of Roper Bar
HEMA 125 G8   14 54 48 S   133 42 35 E

99 Roper Valley East Rest Area
Rest Area 136 km E of Stuart Hwy or 35 km W of Roper Bar
HEMA 125 G9   14 45 41 S   134 11 22 E

100 Leichhardt's Caravan Park ☎ (08) 8975 4636
Caravan Park at Roper Bar, 175 km E of Stuart Hwy. 2 km from store. Pay fees at the store. 40 km dirt road. Closed during wet season
HEMA 125 G9   14 42 50 S   134 30 39 E

101 Munbililla Campground (Tomato Island)
Limmen National Park
☎ (08) 8975 9940

Camp Area 45 km SE of Roper Bar or 293 km N of Cape Crawford
HEMA 125 G9   14 44 49 S   134 41 31 E

102 Yurrlmundji (Bullshark) Campground
Limmen National Park
☎ (08) 8975 9940

Camp Area 57 km E of Roper Bar or 281 km N of Cape Crawford
HEMA 125 G10   14 45 36 S   134 47 13 E

103 Mountain Creek
Limmen National Park
☎ (08) 8975 9940

Camp Area 60 km E of Roper Bar or 278 km N of Cape Crawford
HEMA 125 G10   14 46 28 S   134 48 23 E

104 Didi Baba (Jacana) Campground
Limmen National Park
☎ (08) 8975 9940

Camp Area 63 km E of Roper Bar or 275 km N of Cape Crawford
HEMA 125 G10   14 46 28 S   134 50 11 E

105 Towns River
Limmen National Park
☎ (08) 8975 9940

Camp Area 117 km SE of Roper Bar or 221 km N of Cape Crawford. Sandy access to sites on S side of river for 1.5 km. Small vehicles only
HEMA 125 G10   15 02 10 S   135 13 10 E

106 Limmen Bight Fishing Camp
☎ (08) 8975 9844

Camp Area 176 km SE of Roper Bar or 162 km N of Cape Crawford
HEMA 125 H11   15 15 52 S   135 30 05 E

107 Limmen Bight River Campground
Limmen National Park
☎ (08) 8975 9940

Camp Area 180 km S of Roper Bar or 158 N of Cape Crawford
HEMA 125 H10   15 28 36 S   135 24 22 E

108 Butterfly Falls
Limmen National Park
☎ (08) 8975 9940

Camp Area 199 km S of Roper Bar or 139 km N of Cape Crawford. Turn E. Signposted Butterfly Springs, camp 2 km along dirt track. Small vehicles only
HEMA 125 J11   15 37 36 S   135 27 36 E

109 Southern Lost City
Limmen National Park
☎ (08) 8975 9940

Camp Area 224 km S of Roper Bar or 114 km N of Cape Crawford. Turn N at sign follow track for 4 km. 4WD recommended
HEMA 125 J11   15 48 31 S   135 27 21 E

110 Lorella Springs Wilderness Park
☎ (08) 8975 9917

Camp Area 265 km SE of Roper Bar or 165 km NW of Borroloola. Turn E off Savannah Way 236 km SE of Roper Bar or 101 km N of Cape Crawford, 30 km to entrance
HEMA 125 J11   15 43 15 S   135 38 26 E

111 Batten Point

Camp Spot at Batten Point, 5 km from King Ash Bay, via Batten Rd. Pay fees to King Ash Bay caretaker
HEMA 125 J12   15 53 44 S   136 31 53 E

112 King Ash Bay Fishing Club
☎ (08) 8975 9800

Camp Area 42 km NE of Borroloola at King Ash Bay. Turn SE off Bing Bong Rd after 21 km to Batten Point. Beside McArthur River. 28 km dirt road
HEMA 125 J12   15 56 08 S   136 28 44 E

113 Wearyan River

Camp Spot 55 km SE of Borroloola or 223 km NW of Wollogorang. Tracks along both sides of river
HEMA 125 J12   16 10 01 S   136 45 22 E

114 Robinson River Crossing

Camp Spot 105 km SE of Borroloola or 149 km NW of Wollogorang. Tracks 100m on the NW side of Robinson River crossing
HEMA 125 K13   16 28 10 S   137 02 52 E

115 Calvert Creek

Camp Spot 177 km E of Borroloola or 85 km W of QLD border. Tracks on both sides of the river
HEMA 127 C13   16 56 01 S   137 21 29 E

Notes...

NORTHERN TERRITORY
Northern Territory Sites 116 — 131

Mataranka to Darwin

Stuart Highway

116 King Rest Area
Rest Area 59 km N of Mataranka or 46 km S of Katherine. 4 km S of King River bridge
HEMA 123 K6 14 38 38 S 132 37 56 E
BIG RIG 24

117 North Bank Park ☎ (08) 8972 1430
Caravan Park at Katherine. Lot 478 Arndt Rd
HEMA 123 J5 14 28 19 S 132 15 09 E

118 Leliyn (Edith Falls) Campground ☎ (08) 8975 4852
Nitmiluk National Park
Camp Area 61 km N of Katherine. Turn E 42 km N of Katherine or 49 km S of Pine Creek
HEMA 123 H5 14 10 46 S 132 11 10 E

119 Copperfield Dam
Picnic Area 5 km S of Pine Creek. Turn W off Stuart Hwy 3 km S of Pine Creek. 2 km dirt road
HEMA 123 G4 13 50 42 S 131 49 03 E
BIG RIG

120 Umbrawarra Gorge Nature Park ☎ (08) 8976 0282
Camp Area 24 km SW of Pine Creek. Turn W off Stuart Hwy 3 km S of Pine Creek. 21 km dirt road. Limited space
HEMA 123 H4 13 57 56 S 131 41 52 E

121 Pine Creek Service Station Caravan Park ☎ (08) 8976 1217
Caravan Park at Pine Creek. Moule St
HEMA 123 G4 13 49 29 S 131 50 06 E

122 The Grove Hill Heritage Hotel & Museum ☎ (08) 8978 2489
Camp Area at Grove Hill Siding via Goldfields Rd. 85 km N of Pine Creek or 69 km SE of Adelaide River
HEMA 123 F3 13 28 53 S 131 33 29 E
BIG RIG

123 Tjuwaliyn (Douglas) Hot Springs Park ☎ (08) 8976 0282
Camp Area 43 km SW of Hayes Creek. Turn W off Stuart Hwy 6 km NW of Hayes Creek or 62 km SE of Adelaide River onto Dorat Rd for 5 km, then SW onto Oolloo Rd for 25 km, then SE for 7 km of dirt road
HEMA 123 G3 13 45 53 S 131 26 22 E
BIG RIG

124 Douglas River Esplanade Conservation Area ☎ (08) 8978 2479
Camp Area 2 km S of Douglas Daly Tourist Park. Various camp spots along Daly River. Must check in at Tourist Park office for site allocation. Small vehicles only. Fee includes use of toilet & shower facilities in the tourist park
HEMA 123 G3 13 47 14 S 131 21 09 E

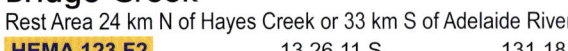

125 Oolloo Crossing
Camp Spot 37 km S of Douglas Daly Tourist Park on Oolloo Rd. Various camp spots on Daly River bank. Small vehicles only. 28 km dirt road
HEMA 123 H2 14 04 09 S 131 15 02 E

126 Bridge Creek
Rest Area 24 km N of Hayes Creek or 33 km S of Adelaide River
HEMA 123 F2 13 26 11 S 131 18 48 E
BIG RIG 24

127 Robin Falls
Rest Area 59 km NW of Hayes Creek or 14 km S of Adelaide River, via Dorat Rd. 500m W of road. Dirt road. Small vehicles only, limited space & turnaround
HEMA 123 F2 13 21 10 S 131 08 01 E

128 Sinclairs Fishing Retreat ☎ (08) 8978 2267
Camp Area 13 km N of Daly River. Lot 4034 Cemetery Rd
HEMA 124 E3 13 42 11 S 130 40 14 E
BIG RIG

129 Lee & Jenny's Bushcamp ☎ 0427 030 556
Camp Area 18 km N of Daly River. Wooliana Rd
HEMA 124 E3 13 39 53 S 130 39 25 E
BIG RIG

130 Mount Nancar Wilderness Retreat ☎ 0427 014 714
Camp Area 6 km SE of Daly River off Nancar Rd. 4WD access. Open April to September
HEMA 123 G1 13 47 57 S 130 43 32 E

131 Adelaide River Show Society Caravan Park ☎ (08) 8976 7032
Caravan Park 2 km SW of Adelaide River. Dorat Rd
HEMA 123 E2 13 14 49 S 131 06 36 E
BIG RIG

NORTHERN TERRITORY

132 Mount Bundy Station
☎ (08) 8976 7009
Camp Area at Mount Bundy Station. 5.5 km NW of Adelaide River.
Turn NW on to Haynes Rd 1 km S of Adelaide River
HEMA 123 E2   13 13 39 S   131 08 02 E

133 Coomalie Creek RV Park
☎ (08) 8976 0501
Camp Area at Coomalie Creek. 25 km N of Adelaide River or 88 km
S of Darwin
HEMA 123 E2   13 01 09 S   131 07 20 E

134 Pandanus on Litchfield
☎ (08) 8976 0242
Caravan Park. 275 Litchfield Park Rd. 9 km W of Batchelor via Rum
Jungle Rd
HEMA 123 E1   13 01 35 S   130 59 17 E

135 Buley Rockhole Campground
☎ (08) 8976 0282
Litchfield National Park
Camp Area 43 km W of Batchelor. Small vehicles only, no caravans
HEMA 123 E1   13 06 46 S   130 47 10 E

136 Florence Falls Campground
☎ (08) 8976 0282
Litchfield National Park
Camp Area 43 km W of Batchelor. 4WD, small vehicles only, no
caravans
HEMA 123 E1   13 05 49 S   130 47 04 E

137 Wangi Falls Campground
☎ (08) 8976 0282
Litchfield National Park
Camp Area 66 km SW of Batchelor
HEMA 124 D3   13 09 44 S   130 40 50 E

138 Tjaynera Falls (Sandy Creek) Campground
☎ (08) 8976 0282
Litchfield National Park
Camp Area 57 km W of Batchelor or 7 km S of Wangi Falls. 9 km dirt
road. 4WD only
HEMA 123 E1   13 15 00 S   130 44 41 E

139 Sand Palms Roadhouse & Tavern
☎ (08) 8978 2822
Camp Area at Bynoe. Via Cox Peninsular Rd, Fog Bay Rd to Bynoe
Haven Rd. 1.5 km dirt road
HEMA 124 D3   12 48 29 S   130 37 01 E

140 Dundee Downs Bush Resort
☎ (08) 8978 2900
Camp Area 90 km SW of Darwin. Lot 3040 Barramundi Dr off Fog
Bay Rd. Bookings essential
HEMA 124 D3   12 46 15 S   130 29 37 E

141 Leader Creek Fishing Camp
☎ (08) 8983 5009
Camp Area 49 km N of the Stuart Hwy & Howard Springs Rd
intersection. Signposted off Gunn Point Rd. 39 km of dirt rd. Bookings
recommended
HEMA 123 B2   12 13 26 S   131 05 33 E

Darwin-Jabiru-Pine Creek
Arnhem and Kakadu Highways

142 Beatrice Hill Parking Area
Parking Area 30 km E of Stuart Hwy jcn or 53 km W of Bark Hut Inn.
1 km W of Windows on the Wetlands
HEMA 123 C2   12 38 35 S   131 18 35 E

143 Couzens Lookout & Camping Area
☎ (08) 8978 8986
Mary River National Park
Camp Area. Turn N off Arnhem Hwy 19 km E of Bark Hut Inn or
117 km W of Jabiru onto Point Stuart Rd then Rock Hole. 35 km dirt
road
HEMA 123 D3   12 44 03 S   131 40 07 E

144 Shady Camp
☎ (08) 8978 8986
Mary River National Park
Camp Area. Turn N off Arnhem Hwy 19 km E of Bark Hut Inn or
117 km W of Jabiru onto Point Stuart Rd, then Harold Knowles Rd,
Shady Camp Rd. 53 km dirt road
HEMA 123 C4   12 28 59 S   131 43 31 E

145 Merl Campground
☎ (08) 8938 1120
Kakadu National Park
Camp Area 36 km N of Jabiru turnoff. Near Ubirr Rock
HEMA 123 C7   12 25 30 S   132 57 26 E

Notes...

146 Malabanjbanjdju Campground ☎ (08) 8938 1120
Kakadu National Park
Camp Area 16 km S of Jabiru turnoff or 32 km N of Cooinda
HEMA 123 D7   12 45 56 S   132 45 17 E

147 Burdulba Campground ☎ (08) 8938 1120
Kakadu National Park
Camp Area 17 km S of Jabiru turnoff or 31 km N of Cooinda
HEMA 123 D7   12 46 18 S   132 44 53 E

148 Djarradjin Billabong (Muirella Park) Campground ☎ (08) 8938 1120
Kakadu National Park
Camp Area 34 km S of Jabiru. Turn E 28 km S of Jabiru turnoff or 20 km NE of Cooinda for 6 km
HEMA 123 D7   12 51 15 S   132 45 18 E

149 Sandy Billabong Campground ☎ (08) 8938 1120
Kakadu National Park
Camp Area 6 km S of Muirella Park. Dirt road
HEMA 123 D7   12 54 02 S   132 46 25 E

150 Garnamarr Campground ☎ (08) 8938 1120
Kakadu National Park
Camp Area 95 km S of Bowali Centre. Turn E 43 km S of Bowali Centre, 52 km dirt road. 4WD only
HEMA 123 E7   13 13 04 S   132 48 58 E

151 Jim Jim Billabong Campground ☎ (08) 8938 1120
Kakadu National Park
Camp Area 5 km SE of Cooinda. Turn E just N of Cooinda turnoff for 3 km, then S for 2 km of dirt road
HEMA 123 D6   12 56 38 S   132 33 11 E

152 Mardugal Campground ☎ (08) 8938 1120
Kakadu National Park
Camp Area 2 km S of Cooinda turnoff or 96 km NE of Mary River Roadhouse. 500m W of Hwy
HEMA 123 E6   12 55 47 S   132 32 16 E

153 Maguk Campground ☎ (08) 8938 1120
Kakadu National Park
Camp Area 58 km S of Cooinda turnoff or 65 km NE of Mary River Roadhouse. Turn E 46 km S of Cooinda turnoff or 53 km NE of Mary River Roadhouse. 12 km dirt road. 4WD recommended
HEMA 123 F6   13 18 12 S   132 26 00 E

154 Gungural Campground ☎ (08) 8938 1120
Kakadu National Park
Camp Area 51 km S of Cooinda turnoff or 47 km NE of Mary River Roadhouse
HEMA 123 F6   13 17 25 S   132 20 08 E

155 Gunlom Campground ☎ (08) 8938 1120
Kakadu National Park
Camp Area 124 km S of Cooinda turnoff or 48 km NE of Mary River Roadhouse. Turn E 87 km S of Cooinda turnoff or 11 km NE of Mary River Roadhouse, onto Gunlom Rd. 36 km dirt road
HEMA 123 F6   13 26 05 S   132 24 53 E

156 Kambolgie Campground ☎ (08) 8938 1120
Kakadu National Park
Camp Area 100 km S of Cooinda turnoff or 24 km NE of Mary River Roadhouse. Turn E 87 km S of Cooinda turnoff or 11 km NE of Mary River Roadhouse onto Gunlom Rd. 10 km dirt road
HEMA 123 F6   13 30 13 S   132 23 37 E

157 Mary River Roadhouse ☎ (08) 8975 4229
Camp Area at Mary River Roadhouse 200m S of Kakadu National Park S entrance
HEMA 123 G5   13 36 20 S   132 13 10 E

158 Harriet Creek
Rest Area 32 km SW of Mary River Roadhouse or 26 km NE of Pine Creek. 500m E of Hwy
HEMA 123 G5   13 40 42 S   131 59 06 E

159 Pussy Cat Flats ☎ (08) 8976 1355
Camp Area 56 km SW of Mary River Roadhouse or 2 km E of Pine Creek on Kakadu Rd
HEMA 123 G4   13 48 29 S   131 50 18 E

Katherine to NT/WA Border
Victoria Highway

160 Manbulloo Homestead Caravan Park ☎ (08) 8972 1559
Caravan Park 11 SW of Katherine. Turn N off Victoria Hwy 9 km W of Katherine onto Murnburlu Rd, follow signs
HEMA 123 K5   14 31 09 S   132 11 57 E

161 King West Rest Area
Rest Area 33 km SW of Katherine or 163 km NE of Victoria River
HEMA 123 K5   14 40 38 S   132 05 11 E

162 Vince Connolly Crossing
Rest Area 58 km SW of Katherine or 138 km NE of Victoria River
HEMA 124 G5   14 49 42 S   131 55 00 E

163 Lorrngurl Campground   ☎ (08) 8973 8888
Giwining / Flora River Nature Park
Camp Area 132 km SW of Katherine. Turn NW 86 km SW of Katherine or 110 km NE of Victoria River. 46 km dirt road. Closed between November & May
HEMA 123 K3   14 45 30 S   131 35 46 E

164 Mathison Rest Area
Rest Area 104 km SW of Katherine or 92 km NE of Victoria River
HEMA 124 H5   15 08 23 S   131 41 01 E

165 Sullivan Creek Campground   ☎ (08) 8975 0888
Judbarra / Gregory National Park
Camp Area 178 km SW of Katherine or 18 km E of Victoria River. Pets allowed in campground only
HEMA 124 H4   15 35 13 S   131 16 29 E

166 Victoria River Roadhouse Caravan Park   ☎ (08) 8975 0744
Caravan Park at Roadhouse. 90 km E of Timber Creek
HEMA 124 J4   15 36 57 S   131 07 38 E

167 Charlies Crossing
Camp Spot 55 km S of the Victoria Hwy & Buchanan Hwy intersection or 157 km N of Top Springs. Dirt road
HEMA 124 J3   16 01 51 S   130 48 10 E

168 Bullita Homestead Campground   ☎ (08) 8975 0888
Judbarra / Gregory National Park
Camp Area 60 km SE of Timber Creek. Turn S 12 km SE of Timber Creek onto Binns Track. 48 km dirt road. 4WD recommended
HEMA 124 J3   16 06 46 S   130 25 25 E

169 Limestone Gorge Campground   ☎ (08) 8975 0888
Judbarra / Gregory National Park
Camp Area 60 km SE of Timber Creek. Turn S 12 km SE of Timber Creek onto Binns Track for 39 km then turn W for 9 km. Dirt road. High clearance 4WD only, some riverbed driving
HEMA 124 J3   16 02 50 S   130 23 00 E

170 Wirib Tourism Park & Store   ☎ (08) 8975 0602
Camp Area at Timber Creek. Victoria Hwy
HEMA 124 J3   15 39 46 S   130 28 52 E

171 Big Horse Creek Campground   ☎ (08) 8975 0888
Judbarra / Gregory National Park
Camp Area 10 km W of Timber Creek, 216 km E of Kununurra or 177 km E of NT/WA border. Pets allowed in campground only. Not suitable for large caravans
HEMA 124 H3   15 36 44 S   130 24 09 E

172 East Baines River
Rest Area 57 km W of Timber Creek, 169 km E of Kununurra or 130 km E of NT/WA border
HEMA 124 J2   15 46 02 S   130 01 35 E

173 Saddle Creek
Rest Area 117 km W of Timber Creek, 109 km E of Kununurra or 70 km E of NT/WA border
HEMA 124 J2   15 57 26 S   129 33 42 E

174 Zebra Rock Mine Campground   ☎ 0400 767 650
Camp Area at Zebra Rock Mine. Turn S onto Duncan Rd off Victoria Hwy 10 km E of WA border or 170 km W of Timber Creek. Travel 5 km, turn R onto access road. 10 km dirt road. Open April - Sept. Signposted. GPS at entry road
HEMA 124 J1   16 06 13 S   129 05 06 E

175 Goorrandalng Campground   ☎ (08) 9167 8827
Keep River National Park
Camp Area 202 km W of Timber Creek. Turn N 184 km W of Timber Creek or 3 km E of NT/WA border. 18 km rough, dirt road
HEMA 124 J1   15 52 31 S   129 03 05 E

176 Jarnem Campground   ☎ (08) 9167 8827
Keep River National Park
Camp Area 215 km W of Timber Creek. Turn N 184 km W of Timber Creek or 3 km E of NT/WA border. 32 km rough, dirt road
HEMA 124 J1   15 45 44 S   129 05 57 E

Notes...

Plenty Highway

This road is seasonal and more suitable to 4WD vehicles, camper trailers and off road caravans. Road conditions phone 1800 246 199 (NT)

177 Mud Tank Zircon Field Fossicking Area

Camp Spot 17 km SE of Gemtree. Turn S off Plenty Hwy 7.5 E of Gemtree onto Alatyeye Rd, travel 9 km to access gate. Bush camp spots 500m after gate. 4WD recommended

HEMA 129 E9   23 00 45 S   134 16 13 E

178 Spotted Tiger Bore Campground
☎ (08) 8956 9722

Camp Area 8 km S of Harts Range Police Station. Turn S 500m W of Police Station onto Racecourse Rd. Follow for 8 km to campground

HEMA 129 E10   23 02 21 S   134 55 04 E

179 Mac & Rose Chalmers Conservation Reserve (Tower Rock)
☎ (08) 8956 9097

Camp Area 75 km N of Plenty Hwy. Turn N 20 km E of Harts Range Police Station or 335 km W of QLD border. 75 km to campground. 4WD only. Alt phone (08) 8956 9745

HEMA 129 D10   22 28 08 S   135 05 01 E

180 Jervois Station
☎ (08) 8956 6307

Camp Area at Jervois Station. 202 km E of Stuart Hwy or 222 km W of NT/QLD border. Dirt road

HEMA 129 E11   22 57 04 S   136 08 39 E

181 Marshall River Rest Area

Rest Area 202 km E of Stuart Hwy or 222 km W of NT/QLD border. Beside river. Dirt road

HEMA 129 E11   22 57 12 S   136 09 06 E

182 Arthur River

Camp Spot 62 km NE of Jervois Station or 159 km W of NT/QLD Border. Tracks beside creek. Dirt road

HEMA 129 D12   22 40 11 S   136 37 51 E

183 Tobermorey Station
☎ (07) 4748 4996

Camp Area at Tobermorey Station. 218 km E of Jervois Station or 4 km W of NT/QLD border

HEMA 129 D14   22 17 02 S   137 57 53 E

Notes...

HELP SAVE THE FREE CAMP SITES!

All travellers have a responsibility to remove their own rubbish, but we also unfortunately need to clean up after other non-considerate travellers who leave rubbish behind.

SIMPLE WAYS TO HELP CLEAN UP!

- Always travel with a 'picker & pack of tough bags'
- If there are no bins to dispose of rubbish
  - Take it with you, to dispose of in a bin.
  - Burn the rubbish (watch for fire bans)
  - Bury the rubbish

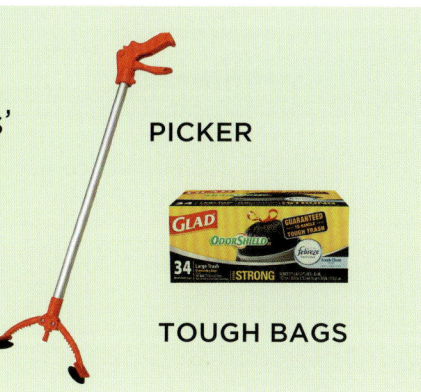

PICKER

TOUGH BAGS

Thank you for cleaning up Australia and saving free camping areas

PUBLIC DUMP POINTS

With environmental issues becoming more of a concern to travellers, the disposal of grey and black water is of major importance. A comprehensive public dump point list has been compiled to assist you in locating the facilities for responsible disposal of your waste water.

The list is alphabetical by town within each State or Territory, with location details and contact phone numbers where available. Note that public dump points are also indicated on the maps. See "Symbols used on the maps" below for an explanation of the meaning of these map symbols.

Be aware that some situations may change and the accuracy of accessibility and type of facility cannot be guaranteed.

The use of chemicals in 'black water' is of concern, so it is advisable to use those which are biodegradable and eco-friendly rather than those containing chemicals such as formaldehyde.

Most of the dump points accessible by big rigs would require the use of a waste hose, preferably 3 metres or more in length.

Please leave the facility clean and tidy, otherwise the use may be withdrawn if abused.

Where the information is available, listings show whether the dump point is suitable for cassettes or holding tanks and whether big rigs can access it.

Please respect the courtesy extended to you if you avail yourself of this service.

Explanation of a sample Public Dump Point listing

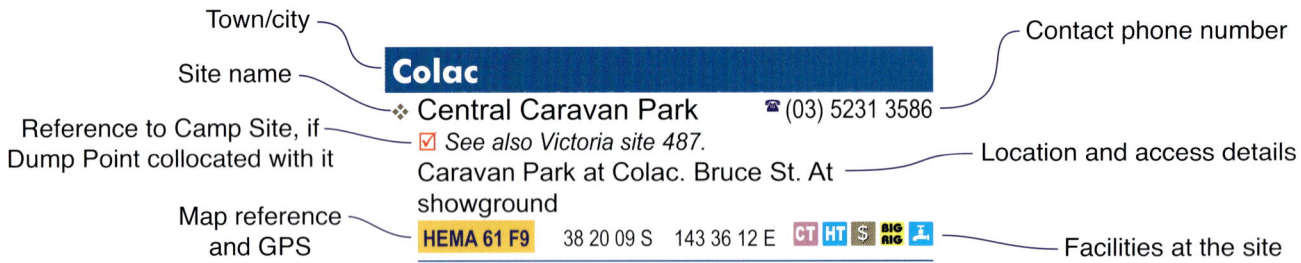

Town/city — Site name — Reference to Camp Site, if Dump Point collocated with it — Map reference and GPS

Colac
❖ Central Caravan Park   ☎ (03) 5231 3586
☑ *See also Victoria site 487.*
Caravan Park at Colac. Bruce St. At showground
HEMA 61 F9   38 20 09 S   143 36 12 E   CT HT $ BIG RIG 🚰

Contact phone number — Location and access details — Facilities at the site

Symbols used in listing

 **CT** Cassette toilet use   **HT** Holding tank use

 **BIG RIG** Access suitable for big rigs   **$** Fees applicable

🚰 Water available

Symbols used on the maps

 **30** Day Use Site with Public Dump Point

115 Camping/Parking Site with Public Dump Point

 Public Dump Point not at a Listed Site

Queensland

Adels Grove

❖ Adels Grove Dumpoint   ☎ (07) 4748 5502
Adels Grove Airfield, outside the Airport fence. GPS is approximate
HEMA 16 G1   18 41 29 S   138 31 53 E   CT HT

Agnes Water

❖ Council Depot
Agnes Water - 1770 Rd. 4.2 km N of Round Hill Rd intersection. Turn L at SES HQ sign
HEMA 15 J12   24 10 49 S   151 52 59 E   CT HT BIG RIG

Allora

❖ Allora Apex Park
New England Hwy, S end of town near Anglican Church, opposite Dalrymple Rd
HEMA 10 G1   28 02 09 S   151 59 18 E   CT HT BIG RIG

Alpha

❖ Alpha Dump Point
Clermont- Alpha Rd, opposite showgrounds
HEMA 14 H4   23 38 47 S   146 38 11 E   CT HT BIG RIG

Aramac

❖ Aramac Shire Caravan   ☎ (07) 4652 9999
Park & Camping Grounds
☑ *See also Queensland site 348.*
Booker St. Public access
HEMA 21 E10   22 58 02 S   145 14 20 E   CT HT

Atherton

❖ Atherton Sewerage   ☎ (07) 4091 7937
Works
Grove St, off Tolga Rd, over railway. N end of town
HEMA 18 F3   17 15 18 S   145 28 49 E   CT HT BIG RIG

Augathella

❖ Augathella Dump Point
Brassington Park, Bendee St - Old Charleville Augathella Rd
HEMA 21 J12   25 48 08 S   146 35 18 E   CT HT BIG RIG

Ayr

❖ Shell Burdekin Travel Centre
Cnr Bruce Hwy & Bower St
HEMA 14 A6   19 34 59 S   147 23 56 E   CT HT BIG RIG

Babinda

❖ Babinda Rotary Park   ☎ (07) 4067 1008
☑ *See also Queensland site 10.*
Rest Area at Babinda. Just east of town over railway. S end of Howard Kennedy Dr
HEMA 18 G6   17 20 54 S   145 55 35 E   CT HT BIG RIG

Baralaba

❖ Baralaba Dump Point   ☎ (07) 4992 9500
Wooroonah St, near caravan park, behind the showgrounds
HEMA 15 J9   24 11 08 S   149 48 56 E   CT HT BIG RIG

Barcaldine

❖ Barcaldine Showgrounds   ☎ (07) 4651 5600
☑ *See also Queensland site 346.*
Capricorn Hwy, E end of town
HEMA 21 F10   23 33 02 S   145 17 37 E   CT HT BIG RIG

❖ Lloyd Jones Weir
☑ *See also Queensland site 347.*
15 km SW of Barcaldine. Turn W off Landsborough Hwy 5 km S of Barcaldine for 9 km. 1 km dirt Rd
HEMA 21 F10   23 39 00 S   145 12 57 E   CT HT BIG RIG

Beaudesert

❖ Beaudesert Caravan &   ☎ (07) 5541 1368
Tourist Park
Albert Street. Public access, fee applies. Must call at office first
HEMA 11 G9   27 59 31 S   153 00 16 E   CT HT $ BIG RIG

Bedourie

❖ Bedourie Dump Point
Diamantina Development Rd. 500m N of Roadhouse
HEMA 20 G3   24 21 07 S   139 28 05 E   CT HT BIG RIG

Bedourie Area

❖ Cuttaburra Crossing Rest Area
☑ *See also Queensland site 396.*
Rest Area 121 km N of Birdsville or 68 km S of Bedourie
HEMA 20 H3   24 54 49 S   139 38 58 E   CT HT BIG RIG

❖ Monkira Rest Area
☑ *See also Queensland site 397.*
Rest Area on Diamantina Development Rd, 121 km E of Eyre Develpment Rd Jcn or 138 km W of Birdsville Development Rd Jcn
HEMA 20 H4   24 49 11 S   140 32 28 E   CT HT BIG RIG

❖ No 3 Bore Rest Area
☑ *See also Queensland site 398.*
Rest Area on Diamantina Development Rd. 28 km E of Eyre Development Rd Jcn
HEMA 20 G3   24 28 31 S   139 48 33 E   CT HT BIG RIG

Beenleigh

❖ Hugh Muntz Park   ☎ (07) 3412 3412
☑ *See also Queensland site 644.*
Reisers Rd
HEMA 11 D11   27 43 01 S   153 12 33 E   CT HT

Beerwah

❖ Beerwah Sportsground   ☎ (07) 5494 0513
☑ *See also Queensland site 190.*
Entry off Simpson St, off roundabout
HEMA 9 E9   26 51 50 S   152 57 21 E   CT HT BIG RIG

❖ Gowinta Farms Caravan   ☎ 0488 500 728
Park
205 Burys Rd, Beerwah. Public access
HEMA 9 E9   26 52 30 S   152 58 43 E   CT HT BIG RIG

Benaraby

❖ Boyne River Rest Area
☑ *See also Queensland site 109.*
At Rest Area 49 km SE of Mount Larcom or 49 km N of Miriam Vale. 1 km S of Benaraby
HEMA 15 J11   24 00 39 S   151 20 26 E   CT HT BIG RIG

Betoota

❖ Betoota Rest Area
☑ *See also Queensland site 392.*
At rest area
HEMA 22 A3   25 41 36 S   140 44 52 E   CT HT BIG RIG

❖ Morney Rest Area
☑ *See also Queensland site 389.*
Rest Area 108 km W of Windorah or 95 km E of Betoota on the Diamantina Development Rd
HEMA 20 J6   25 22 50 S   141 37 24 E   CT HT BIG RIG

Biggenden

❖ Biggenden Dump Point   ☎ (07) 4217 1177
Isis Hwy. 50m W of caravan park
HEMA 13 B12   25 30 52 S   152 02 20 E   CT HT BIG RIG

Biloela

❖ Rural Hinterland Visitor   ☎ (07) 4992 2400
Information Centre
Heritage Park complex, Exhibition Avenue, NW end of town
HEMA 15 J10   24 24 15 S   150 30 04 E   CT HT BIG RIG

Birdsville

❖ Birdsville Dump Point
Adelaide St, South side of Rd past the Airstrip
HEMA 22 A1   25 54 14 S   139 20 41 E   CT HT BIG RIG

❖ Birdsville East Dump Point
E side of Birdsville. 500m E of windmill on Eyre Development Rd
HEMA 22 A1   25 54 28 S   139 22 39 E   CT HT BIG RIG

Blackall

❖ Blackall Dump Point   ☎ (07) 4657 4637
Corner Garden St & Blackall - Isisford Rd. Opposite Barcoo River Camp
HEMA 14 J3   24 25 31 S   145 27 45 E   CT HT BIG RIG

❖ Blackall Showgrounds
Blackall-Jericho Rd
HEMA 14 J3   24 25 33 S   145 28 29 E   CT HT BIG RIG

Blackbutt

❖ Blackbutt Showgrounds   ☎ (07) 4163 0633
☑ *See also Queensland site 489.*
Bowman Rd, by water tanks
HEMA 8 E2   26 52 52 S   152 06 08 E   CT HT BIG RIG

Blackwater

❖ Blackwater Dump Point
Turpentine St, near the Showgrounds
HEMA 15 H8   23 35 35 S   148 52 31 E   CT HT BIG RIG

Bluewater

❖ Bluewater Park
☑ *See also Queensland site 36.*
Rest Area at Bluewater, 80 km S of Ingham or 29 km N of Townsville
HEMA 17 H12   19 10 35 S   146 33 05 E   CT HT BIG RIG

Bollon

❖ Bollon Dump Point   ☎ (07) 4620 8844
William St
HEMA 12 H3   28 01 51 S   147 28 40 E   CT HT BIG RIG

Boonah

❖ Boonah Showgrounds   ☎ (07) 5463 4080
☑ *See also Queensland site 684.*
Entry via Melbourne St
HEMA 10 G7   27 59 51 S   152 41 06 E   CT HT BIG RIG

Boulia
❖ Boulia Dump Point
West side of Diamantina Hwy, 1 km N of Boulia
HEMA 20 E3   22 54 28 S   139 54 15 E   CT HT BIG RIG

Bowen
❖ Bowen Showground ☎ (07) 4786 5353
Mt Nutt Rd, N side of town
HEMA 14 B7   19 59 42 S   148 13 42 E   CT HT BIG RIG

Bundaberg
❖ Hinkler Lions Park
☑ See also Queensland site 129.
Isis Hwy, opposite airport. if locked, key at Waste Transfer Station
HEMA 13 A12   24 53 49 S   152 18 51 E   CT HT BIG RIG

Burketown
❖ Burketown Dump Point
Sloman St. Opposite caravan park
HEMA 16 F3   17 44 31 S   139 32 48 E   CT HT BIG RIG

Caboolture
❖ Caboolture Showgrounds ☎ (07) 5495 2030
☑ See also Queensland site 193.
4 km N of Town Centre
HEMA 9 G9   27 04 04 S   152 56 55 E   CT HT BIG RIG

Cairns
❖ Cairns Wastewater Depot ☎ (07) 4044 8200
8-38 Macnamara St, Manunda
HEMA 18 D4   16 54 46 S   145 45 00 E   CT HT BIG RIG

Calliope
❖ Calliope Dump Point
Cnr Taragoola Rd & Dawson Hwy
HEMA 15 J11   24 00 27 S   151 12 02 E   CT HT BIG RIG

Caloundra
❖ Caloundra Dump Point ☎ (07) 5420 6240
Behind the Information Centre, Caloundra Rd. If locked, key at Info Centre
HEMA 9 E10   26 47 53 S   153 06 51 E   CT HT

Camooweal
❖ Camooweal Dump Point
E end of town, opposite the water tower
HEMA 16 J1   19 55 18 S   138 07 27 E   CT HT BIG RIG

Capalaba
❖ John Fredericks Park ☎ (07) 3829 8999
2 -14 Old Cleveland Rd
HEMA 7 D14   27 31 09 S   153 11 19 E   CT HT BIG RIG

Capella
❖ Bridgeman Park Showground
Hibernia Rd, in SW corner of grounds near horse stables
HEMA 14 G6   23 05 21 S   148 00 58 E   CT HT BIG RIG

Carmila Beach
❖ Carmila Beach ☎ 1300 472 227
☑ See also Queensland site 88.
6 km E of Carmila. 1 km dirt Rd. Last 300m narrow, sandy track
HEMA 15 E9   21 54 50 S   149 27 47 E   CT HT BIG RIG

Carnarvon National Park
❖ Takarakka Bush Resort ☎ (07) 4984 4535
Carnarvon Gorge Rd. Fee for all users
HEMA 12 A4   25 04 13 S   148 16 17 E   CT $

Cecil Plains
❖ Cecil Plains Rural Retreat Caravan Park ☎ 0428 913 779
☑ See also Queensland site 572.
Taylor St, in caravan park. Public access
HEMA 13 G10   27 31 59 S   151 11 45 E   CT HT BIG RIG

Charleville
❖ Charleville Dump Point ☎ (07) 4656 8355
Qantas Drive (Airport access Rd)
HEMA 23 B14   26 24 59 S   146 15 07 E   CT HT BIG RIG

Charters Towers
❖ Columbia Mine Poppet Head ☎ (07) 4761 5533
Flinders Hwy Bypass
HEMA 14 B4   20 04 21 S   146 16 35 E   CT HT BIG RIG 👤

Charters Towers Area
❖ Fletcher Creek
☑ See also Queensland site 289.
Rest Area 42 km N of Charters Towers or 157 km SE of Greenvale
HEMA 14 B4   19 48 57 S   146 03 14 E   CT HT BIG RIG

Childers
❖ Childers Rest Area
☑ See also Queensland site 135.
Crescent St, behind Post Office
HEMA 13 B12   25 14 06 S   152 16 44 E   CT HT BIG RIG

Chillagoe
❖ Chillagoe Rodeo Grounds ☎ (07) 4094 7119
☑ See also Queensland site 214.
From Queen St turn W onto Frew St, entrance 700m on R
HEMA 17 E9   17 09 29 S   144 30 58 E   CT HT BIG RIG

Chinchilla
❖ Chinchilla Dump Point ☎ (07) 4662 7056
Park St (Chinchilla-Wondai Rd)
HEMA 13 E9   26 44 07 S   150 37 50 E   CT HT BIG RIG

Clairview
❖ Clairview Rest Area
☑ See also Queensland site 92.
N end of Colonial Dr
HEMA 15 E9   22 06 17 S   149 31 36 E   CT HT BIG RIG

Clermont
❖ Clermont Dump Point ☎ (07) 4983 1133
Lime St, next to bowls club
HEMA 14 G6   22 49 08 S   147 38 40 E   CT HT BIG RIG

Clermont Area
❖ Theresa Creek Dam ☎ (07) 4983 2327
☑ See also Queensland site 423.
22 km SW of Clermont
HEMA 14 G6   22 58 16 S   147 33 13 E   CT HT BIG RIG

Cleveland
❖ William St Marine Facility ☎ (07) 3829 8999
William St, off Shore St Nth
HEMA 11 B11   27 30 53 S   153 17 13 E   CT HT BIG RIG 👤

Clifton
❖ Clifton Recreation Grounds ☎ 131 872
☑ See also Queensland site 667.
N side of town in Morton St, via Clark & Devonport Sts
HEMA 10 F1   27 55 34 S   151 54 45 E   CT HT BIG RIG 👤

Cloncurry
❖ Terry Smith Lookout
☑ See also Queensland site 280.
Rest Area 103 km S of Burke & Wills Roadhouse or 78 km N of Cloncurry
HEMA 16 J4   20 04 49 S   140 13 39 E   CT HT BIG RIG

Coen
❖ Coen Dump Point ☎ (07) 4060 1135
Peninsula Developmental Rd, N side of town. E side of Rd. S side of Library
HEMA 19 G3   13 56 43 S   143 12 06 E   CT HT BIG RIG

Collinsville
❖ Collinsville Showgrounds ☎ (07) 4785 5795
☑ See also Queensland site 51.
Entry from Railway Rd next to Showgrounds
HEMA 14 C6   20 33 24 S   147 50 57 E   CT HT BIG RIG

Cooktown
❖ Cooktown Dump Point ☎ (07) 4069 5444
Access from Charlotte St, opposite Sovereign Hotel
HEMA 17 B10   15 27 58 S   145 14 57 E   CT HT

Cooroy
❖ Cooroy RV Stop ☎ (07) 5485 3244
☑ See also Queensland site 184.
7 Mary River Rd, enter at driveway between Car Club & Horse & Pony Club
HEMA 9 A8   26 24 49 S   152 54 25 E   CT HT BIG RIG

Croydon
❖ Croydon Dump Point
Alldridge St, outside the caravan park
HEMA 16 G6   18 12 05 S   142 10 43 E   CT HT BIG RIG

Cunnamulla
❖ Cunnamulla Council Dump Point
Williams St, adjacent to showground fence
HEMA 23 F13   28 04 05 S   145 41 49 E   CT HT BIG RIG

Dalby
❖ Dalby Dump Point
5 Black St
HEMA 13 F10   27 10 34 S   151 14 41 E   CT HT BIG RIG

Dalveen
❖ Jim Mitchell Park
☑ See also Queensland site 676.
Rest Area at Dalveen. Mountain Park Rd
HEMA 13 J11   28 29 21 S   151 58 14 E   CT HT BIG RIG

Dirranbandi
❖ Dirranbandi Dump Point ☎ (07) 4620 8844
Theodore St, beside showground
HEMA 12 J4   28 34 33 S   148 13 52 E   CT

Duaringa
❖ Duaringa Rest Area
☑ See also Queensland site 324.
Rest Area at Duaringa. E end of town
HEMA 15 H9   23 43 18 S   149 40 20 E   CT HT BIG RIG

Dululu
❖ Dululu Rest Area
☑ See also Queensland site 433.
Bryant St, next to toilet block
HEMA 15 H10   23 50 54 S   150 15 40 E   CT HT BIG RIG

Eidsvold
❖ Eidsvold Dump Point ☎ (07) 4166 9918
Cnr Burnett Way & Esplanade St
HEMA 13 B10   25 22 18 S   151 07 24 E   CT HT BIG RIG

Einasleigh
❖ Einasleigh Dump Point
Baroota St
HEMA 17 G9   18 30 55 S   144 05 36 E   CT HT BIG RIG

Emerald
❖ Emerald Showgrounds   ☎ 0428 396 448
☑ See also Queensland site 334.
Capricorn Hwy
HEMA 14 H7   23 31 23 S   148 09 07 E   CT HT BIG RIG

Eulo
❖ Eulo Dump Point
Bulloo Development Rd, outside Airport adjacent to toilets
HEMA 23 F12   28 09 46 S   145 02 43 E   CT HT BIG RIG

Eumundi
❖ Eumundi RV Stop Over   ☎ 0412 566 671
☑ See also Queensland site 187.
Parking Area at Eumundi, Cnr Albert St & Napier St
HEMA 9 B9   26 28 34 S   152 57 13 E   CT HT BIG RIG ⛴

Fernvale
❖ Fernvale Dump Point
Clive St
HEMA 10 B6   27 27 14 S   152 39 01 E   CT HT BIG RIG

Forsayth
❖ Forsayth Rest Area
Einasleigh-Forsayth Rd, next to the public toilet block
HEMA 17 G8   18 35 10 S   143 36 10 E   CT

Gatton
❖ Gatton Showgrounds
Woodlands Rd, Behind toilet block, near grassed area at rear of grounds
HEMA 10 B4   27 33 31 S   152 16 51 E   CT HT BIG RIG

Gayndah
❖ Zonhoven Park
☑ See also Queensland site 456.
Burnett Hwy. E end of town
HEMA 13 B11   25 37 44 S   151 37 33 E   CT HT

Georgetown
❖ Georgetown Dump Point
Normanton St, opposite toilets in Heritage Park
HEMA 17 G8   18 17 30 S   143 32 53 E   CT HT BIG RIG

Gin Gin
❖ Gin Gin Dump Point
Bruce Hwy, N end of town. LH side of gravel parking area opposite service stations
HEMA 13 A11   24 59 02 S   151 57 01 E   CT HT

Glenden
❖ Glenden Dump Point
Gilbert Ave, at Golf Club
HEMA 14 D7   21 21 01 S   148 07 23 E   CT HT BIG RIG

Goomeri
❖ Goomeri Showgrounds   ☎ 0419 720 407
☑ See also Queensland site 472.
Cnr Burnett Hwy & Laird St. S end of town
HEMA 13 D12   26 11 11 S   152 04 09 E   CT HT BIG RIG

Goondiwindi
❖ Caltex Truck Stop   ☎ (07) 4671 0999
Boundary Rd, E end of town
HEMA 13 J8   28 31 42 S   150 18 37 E   CT HT BIG RIG

❖ Redmond Park
Anderson St, near the driver reviver area
HEMA 13 J8   28 33 01 S   150 19 12 E   CT HT BIG RIG

Gregory Downs
❖ Council Dump Point   ☎ (07) 4745 5100
Wills Development Rd, next to the toilets
HEMA 16 G2   18 38 59 S   139 15 14 E   CT BIG RIG

Gympie
❖ Archery Park
Cnr Cross St & Bruce Hwy. 4 km N of town centre
HEMA 13 D13   26 11 19 S   152 39 13 E   CT HT BIG RIG

❖ Six Mile Creek Rest Area
☑ See also Queensland site 162.
Bruce Hwy, 6 km S of Gympie
HEMA 13 D13   26 13 54 S   152 41 49 E   • CT BIG RIG

Hervey Bay
❖ Hervey Bay RV Stop Info Centre   ☎ 1800 811 728
☑ See also Queensland site 140.
Hervey Bay Information Centre. Cnr Urraween Rd & Hervey Bay Rd
HEMA 13 B13   25 17 59 S   152 48 34 E   CT HT BIG RIG

Home Hill
❖ Home Hill Dump Point
Sixth St. W of railway crossing
HEMA 14 A6   19 39 59 S   147 24 52 E   CT BIG RIG

Hughenden
❖ Hughenden Dump Point   ☎ (07) 4741 1958
Corner of McLaren St & Swanston St. Near white tower
HEMA 14 C1   20 51 03 S   144 11 32 E   CT HT BIG RIG ⛴

❖ Hughenden RV Parking Area   ☎ (07) 4741 2970
☑ See also Queensland site 303.
Parking Area at Hughenden. E end of Stansfield St on N side of road
HEMA 14 C1   20 50 41 S   144 12 20 E   CT HT BIG RIG ⛴

Ilfracombe
❖ Ilfracombe Dump Point   ☎ (07) 4658 2233
Murray St, opposite caravan park
HEMA 14 H1   23 29 27 S   144 30 37 E   CT HT BIG RIG

Imbil
❖ Imbil Showgrounds
Imbil Brooloo Rd
HEMA 8 A7   26 27 50 S   152 40 42 E   CT HT BIG RIG ⛴

Ingham
❖ Tyto Wetlands RV Stop   ☎ (07) 4776 4792
☑ See also Queensland site 28.
Cnr Bruce Hwy & Cooper St. S of town on W side of Hwy
HEMA 17 G11   18 39 18 S   146 09 11 E   CT HT BIG RIG

Inglewood
❖ Inglewood Rest Area
Brook St, off Cunningham Hwy. E end of town
HEMA 13 J9   28 24 51 S   151 05 02 E   CT HT BIG RIG

Injune
❖ Injune Truck Stop   ☎ (07) 4626 1581
Hutton St, near Roadhouse
HEMA 12 C5   25 50 24 S   148 34 03 E   CT HT BIG RIG

Innisfail
❖ Innisfail Dump Point   ☎ (07) 4063 2655
Haddrell Park, Bruce Hwy. Opposite Barrier Reef Motel. S side of town
HEMA 18 H6   17 32 01 S   146 01 47 E   CT HT BIG RIG

Ipswich
❖ Ipswich Showgrounds   ☎ (07) 3281 1577
☑ See also Queensland site 553.
Cnr Warwick & Salisbury Rds
HEMA 6 H2   27 37 38 S   152 45 33 E   CT HT BIG RIG

Isisford
❖ Barcoo River Nature Park   ☎ (07) 4658 8900
☑ See also Queensland site 639.
Saint Francis St. At toilet block, SE end of town
HEMA 21 G9   24 15 28 S   144 26 36 E   CT HT

Jandowae
❖ Jandowae Dump Point
Dalby St, between High & Hickey Sts. Adjacent to Lions Park, N side of town
HEMA 13 E10   26 46 45 S   151 06 33 E   CT HT BIG RIG

❖ Jandowae Showgrounds   ☎ (07) 4668 5268
☑ See also Queensland site 579.
Warra St
HEMA 13 E10   26 47 13 S   151 06 38 E   CT HT BIG RIG

Jericho
❖ Jericho Showground   ☎ (07) 4651 4129
☑ See also Queensland site 342.
1 km NE of Jericho, at E end of town, turn N just E of railway crossing
HEMA 21 F11   23 35 42 S   146 07 54 E   CT HT BIG RIG

Jondaryan
❖ Jondaryan Woolshed   ☎ (07) 4692 2229
☑ See also Queensland site 570.
264 Jondaryan Evanslea Rd. 3 km S of Jondaryan
HEMA 13 F11   27 23 32 S   151 34 30 E   CT HT BIG RIG

Julia Creek
❖ Julia Creek Dump Point
Hickman St, near Junction of Allison St
HEMA 16 K6   20 39 10 S   141 44 30 E   CT HT BIG RIG

❖ Julia Creek Racecourse
In the Racecourse off Kynuna Road. Near the blue toilet block. GPS at entry
HEMA 16 K6   20 39 50 S   141 44 32 E   CT HT BIG RIG

Jundah
❖ Jundah Dump Point   ☎ (07) 4658 6133
800m N of Jundah on Thomson Developmental Rd, near turn off to outpatient entrance
HEMA 20 H7   24 49 23 S   143 03 43 E   CT HT BIG RIG

Kalbar
❖ Kalbar Showground   ☎ 0499 970 119
☑ See also Queensland site 682.
George St. N end of town
HEMA 10 F6   27 56 15 S   152 37 32 E   CT BIG RIG

Karumba
❖ Truck Stop   ☎ (07) 4745 2240
Cnr Yappar St & Karumba Development Rd
HEMA 16 F4   17 29 29 S   140 50 07 E   CT HT BIG RIG ⛴

Kenilworth
- Kenilworth Show & Recreation Grounds ☎ 0438 849 947
  - ☑ See also Queensland site 177.
  - Elizabeth St. S side of town
  - **HEMA 8 C7** 26 35 56 S 152 43 34 E CT HT BIG RIG

Kia Ora
- Standown Caravan Park ☎ (07) 5486 5144
  - ☑ See also Queensland site 155.
  - 91 Radtke Rd. Public access for fee
  - **HEMA 13 D13** 26 02 08 S 152 47 32 E CT HT $ BIG RIG

Kingaroy
- Lions Park ☎ (07) 4162 6230
  - Baron St, off Kingaroy St
  - **HEMA 13 E11** 26 32 47 S 151 50 16 E CT

Laidley
- Laidley Dump Point
  - John St, near swimming pool
  - **HEMA 10 C4** 27 37 55 S 152 23 34 E CT HT BIG RIG

Lawnton
- Pine Rivers Showground ☎ 0459 023 346
  - ☑ See also Queensland site 198.
  - Gympie Rd
  - **HEMA 5 D8** 27 17 07 S 152 59 13 E CT HT BIG RIG

Longreach
- Longreach Dump Point
  - Cnr Landsborough Hwy & Kite St
  - **HEMA 21 F9** 23 26 24 S 144 14 57 E CT HT BIG RIG
- Longreach Showground ☎ (07) 4658 1745
  - Sandpiper St, off Eagle St. W end of town
  - **HEMA 21 F9** 23 26 20 S 144 14 56 E CT HT BIG RIG

Lowood
- Lowood Showgrounds & Caravan Park ☎ 0455 187 201
  - ☑ See also Queensland site 510.
  - Station St. Turn L at entry, between buildings
  - **HEMA 10 B6** 27 27 45 S 152 35 01 E CT HT BIG RIG

Mackay
- Mackay Rest Area
  - At the Information Centre, Bruce Hwy. Access from Nthbound only. Turn in between BP & Information Centre. Dump is on the left
  - **HEMA 15 D8** 21 09 56 S 149 09 14 E CT BIG RIG

Mareeba
- Eales Park Dump Point ☎ (07) 4092 5674
  - Doyle St, opposite Davies Park. W side of town
  - **HEMA 18 E2** 16 59 42 S 145 24 50 E CT HT BIG RIG

Maroochydore
- Maroochydore Dump Point
  - Commercial Rd
  - **HEMA 9 C10** 26 39 09 S 153 03 34 E CT HT BIG RIG

Maryborough
- Airport
  - Access via Airport Dr off Saltwater Creek Rd. Follow signs around to right. 2 km from town on Rd to Hervey Bay
  - **HEMA 13 B13** 25 31 06 S 152 42 33 E CT HT

- Maryborough Showground & Equestrian Park ☎ 1300 794 929
  - ☑ See also Queensland site 145.
  - Bruce Hwy. N end of town. Veer R past entry gates
  - **HEMA 13 B13** 25 30 22 S 152 39 46 E CT HT BIG RIG 🛈

McKinlay
- McKinlay Dump Point
  - Middleton St, at the truck stop
  - **HEMA 20 C5** 21 16 14 S 141 17 23 E CT HT BIG RIG

Meandarra
- Leo Gordon Apex Park
  - Cnr Meandarra & Dillon Sts
  - **HEMA 12 F7** 27 19 24 S 149 52 50 E CT

Miles
- Miles Council Dump Point
  - Industry Lane, via Leichhardt Hwy (Sth), Waterworks Rd
  - **HEMA 13 E8** 26 39 59 S 150 11 07 E CT HT BIG RIG

Millmerran
- Millmerran Showgrounds ☎ 0427 957 176
  - ☑ See also Queensland site 662.
  - Millmerran-Cecil Plains Rd
  - **HEMA 13 G10** 27 51 37 S 151 16 40 E CT HT BIG RIG
- Walpole Park
  - ☑ See also Queensland site 661.
  - Charles St, between Walpole & Charlotte Sts. Dump Point opposite park
  - **HEMA 13 G10** 27 52 17 S 151 16 28 E CT HT BIG RIG

Mirani
- Mirani Dump Point ☎ 1300 622 529
  - Victoria St, opposite Council Customer Service Centre
  - **HEMA 15 D8** 21 09 34 S 148 51 52 E CT HT BIG RIG

Miriam Vale
- Granite Creek (Bernie Christensen) Rest Area
  - ☑ See also Queensland site 117.
  - Rest Area 36 km S of Miriam Vale or 63 km N of Gin Gin
  - **HEMA 15 K12** 24 36 44 S 151 40 04 E CT

Mission Beach
- Mission Beach Dump Point
  - Porter Promenade, outside caravan park
  - **HEMA 18 K6** 17 51 53 S 146 06 29 E CT HT BIG RIG

Mitchell
- Mitchell Showgrounds ☎ (07) 4623 8171
  - Alice St, near entrance
  - **HEMA 12 D4** 26 29 47 S 147 58 45 E CT BIG RIG

Monto
- Monto Community Rest Stop
  - ☑ See also Queensland site 444.
  - Railway Yard, Gladstone-Monto Rd
  - **HEMA 13 A10** 24 51 46 S 151 07 15 E CT HT
- Monto Showground ☎ (07) 4166 9918
  - Oxley St, W side of town
  - **HEMA 13 A10** 24 51 57 S 151 06 53 E CT HT BIG RIG 🛈

Morven
- Morven Recreation Ground ☎ (07) 4654 8281
  - ☑ See also Queensland site 611.
  - S side of town via Victoria St
  - **HEMA 12 D2** 26 25 06 S 147 06 58 E CT HT BIG RIG

Mossman
- Mossman Dump Point
  - Cnr Foxton Ave & Park St (Outside Aquatic Centre)
  - **HEMA 18 A1** 16 27 18 S 145 22 18 E CT HT BIG RIG

Mount Isa
- Mount Isa Dump Point
  - Cnr George St & East St
  - **HEMA 16 K3** 20 43 16 S 139 30 10 E CT HT BIG RIG 🛈

Mount Molloy
- Rifle Creek Rest Area
  - ☑ See also Queensland site 206.
  - Rest Area 1 km N of Mt Molloy, 33 km S of Mossman or 41 km N of Mareeba
  - **HEMA 18 C2** 16 39 58 S 145 19 42 E CT

Mount Perry
- Mount Perry Dump Point ☎ (07) 4156 3850
  - 54 Heusman Street, in front of the caravan park
  - **HEMA 13 B11** 25 10 29 S 151 38 24 E CT HT BIG RIG

Mount Surprise
- Mount Surprise Dump Point ☎ (07) 4062 1233
  - Main Rd, outside toilet block
  - **HEMA 17 F9** 18 08 50 S 144 19 03 E CT HT BIG RIG

Moura
- Moura Dump Point
  - Moura Bindaree Rd, E end of town
  - **HEMA 15 K9** 24 33 54 S 149 58 27 E CT HT BIG RIG

Mt Isa
- Gunpowder Rest Area
  - ☑ See also Queensland site 318.
  - Rest Area 50 km NW of Mt Isa or 139 km E of Camooweal. Near monument on Barkly Hwy
  - **HEMA 16 K2** 20 22 23 S 139 15 50 E CT HT BIG RIG

Mundubbera
- Mundubbera Dump Point ☎ (07) 4165 5700
  - Bauer St, near the Lyons St intersection & the tennis courts
  - **HEMA 13 B10** 25 35 33 S 151 18 03 E CT HT BIG RIG

Mungallala
- Mungallala RV Stop
  - ☑ See also Queensland site 609.
  - Camp Spot at Mungallala. Warrego Hwy
  - **HEMA 12 D3** 26 26 44 S 147 32 29 E CT HT BIG RIG

Murgon
- Murgon RV Stop ☎ (07) 4189 9387
  - ☑ See also Queensland site 513.
  - 3 Krebs St
  - **HEMA 13 D11** 26 14 32 S 151 56 17 E CT HT BIG RIG

Murgon Area
- Bjelke Petersen Dam.
  - Via Haager Dr, Yallakool Park in parking area opposite tennis courts
  - **HEMA 13 D11** 26 18 12 S 151 59 44 E CT BIG RIG

Muttaburra

❖ Muttaburra Caravan Park ☎ (07) 4658 7191
☑ See also Queensland site 351.
Caravan Park at Muttaburra. Cnr Mary & Bridge Sts
HEMA 21 D9   22 35 36 S   144 33 07 E   CT HT BIG RIG

Nambour

❖ Nambour Dump Point
Off Bli Bli Rd. Located in the side road on the Sth side of the roundabout when taking the Western exit off Bruce Hwy. Signposted. Locked, call number on gate for combination
HEMA 9 C9   26 36 59 S   152 58 44 E   CT HT BIG RIG

Nanango

❖ Tipperary Flat Park
☑ See also Queensland site 478.
Rest Area at Nanango. 1.5 km S of PO. Next to BP service station
HEMA 8 C1   26 40 48 S   151 59 47 E   CT HT BIG RIG

Nebo

❖ Nebo Rest Area
☑ See also Queensland site 79.
Peak Downs Hwy
HEMA 14 E7   21 40 58 S   148 41 34 E   CT HT BIG RIG

Nindigully

❖ Nindigully
☑ See also Queensland site 718.
At the rear of new toilet block, near hotel
HEMA 12 H5   28 21 17 S   148 49 15 E   CT HT BIG RIG

Normanton

❖ Bang Bang Rest Area
☑ See also Queensland site 265.
Rest Area 112 km S of Normanton or 90 km N of Burke & Wills Roadhouse
HEMA 16 G4   18 31 36 S   140 39 11 E   CT HT BIG RIG

❖ Normanton Council Depot ☎ (07) 4745 2200
Old Hospital Rd. Business hours only
HEMA 16 F5   17 40 51 S   141 04 36 E   CT HT BIG RIG

Oakey

❖ Oakey Dump Point
Cnr York St & Lorrimer St next to Works Depot
HEMA 13 G11   27 26 27 S   151 43 27 E   CT HT BIG RIG

Petrie

❖ Wyllie Park Rest Area
☑ See also Queensland site 196.
Old Bruce Hwy, beside North Pine River. Gates open 8.00am - 6.00pm
HEMA 5 D8   27 16 22 S   152 58 49 E   CT HT BIG RIG

Pittsworth

❖ Pittsworth Dump Point
Railways St, outside Showgrounds next to SES building
HEMA 13 G11   27 42 41 S   151 38 31 E   CT HT BIG RIG

Pomona

❖ Pomona Showgrounds ☎ (07) 5485 1477
☑ See also Queensland site 175.
Exhibition St
HEMA 9 A8   26 21 36 S   152 51 28 E   CT HT BIG RIG

Proserpine

❖ Proserpine Dump Point ☎ (07) 4945 1554
79 Anzac Rd. On road outside caravan park
HEMA 14 C7   20 24 14 S   148 34 17 E   CT HT BIG RIG

Quilpie

❖ Quilpie Dump Point ☎ (07) 4995 8657
John Waugh Park. Quarrion St
HEMA 21 K9   26 36 57 S   144 15 46 E   CT HT BIG RIG

Rainbow Beach

❖ Rainbow Beach Sewerage Works ☎ (07) 5481 0800
By sewerage pumping station. Clarkson Drive (Inskip Point Rd)
HEMA 13 C13   25 54 03 S   153 05 18 E   CT HT BIG RIG

Ravenshoe

❖ Ravenshoe Dump Point ☎ (07) 4096 2244
Outside sewerage works, Ascham St
HEMA 18 H3   17 36 55 S   145 28 49 E   CT HT BIG RIG

Redcliffe

❖ Redcliffe Showgrounds ☎ (07) 3283 0405
Scarborough Rd, near hospital. Daylight hours only
HEMA 5 B12   27 13 30 S   153 06 22 E   CT HT BIG RIG

Richmond

❖ Richmond RV Parking Area
☑ See also Queensland site 305.
At 72 hr RV parking Area. 300m off Main Rd, via Harris St & Hillier St
HEMA 16 K7   20 43 44 S   143 08 36 E   CT HT BIG RIG

Rockhampton

❖ Music Bowl Park
Nuttall Street, off bruce Hwy, N of city. Across from sports fields
HEMA 15 H10   23 19 08 S   150 30 51 E   CT HT BIG RIG

Rolleston

❖ Beazley Park
In Rest Area, Beazley Park, Meteor St & Dawson Hwy
HEMA 14 J7   24 27 48 S   148 37 28 E   CT HT BIG RIG

Rollingstone

❖ Balgal Beach
☑ See also Queensland site 34.
At Rest Area 6 km E of Rollingstone. Turn E off Bruce Hwy 1 km S of Rollingstone. 5 km E of Hwy. N end of town near boat ramp
HEMA 17 H12   19 00 37 S   146 24 18 E   CT HT BIG RIG

❖ Bushy Parker Park
☑ See also Queensland site 33.
Rest Area at Rollingstone. Turn E off Bruce Hwy just N of Rollingstone, across railway line
HEMA 17 H11   19 02 46 S   146 23 37 E   CT HT BIG RIG

Roma

❖ Roma Dump Point ☎ (07) 4622 1266
Station St, between Lewis & Major Sts. In front of council Depot
HEMA 12 D5   26 34 34 S   148 47 46 E   CT HT BIG RIG

❖ Roma Showgrounds ☎ 0408 988 002
☑ See also Queensland site 595.
Northern Rd. N end of town
HEMA 12 D5   26 33 13 S   148 47 06 E   CT HT BIG RIG

Sapphire

❖ Sapphire Reserve
☑ See also Queensland site 337.
Rifle Range Rd, opposite general store
HEMA 14 H6   23 27 57 S   147 43 13 E   CT HT BIG RIG

Sarina

❖ Sarina Dump Point ☎ (07) 4956 2251
Tourist Centre, Railway Square off the Bruce Hwy
HEMA 15 D8   21 25 33 S   149 13 02 E   CT HT BIG RIG

Scarborough

❖ Scarborough Boat Ramp
Thurecht Parade. Next to public toilets, raised off the ground
HEMA 5 A12   27 11 39 S   153 06 15 E   CT

Shorncliffe

❖ Shorncliffe Boat Ramp
In boat ramp car park, off Sinbad St. Next to toilet block. Cassettes only, raised off ground
HEMA 5 F11   27 20 02 S   153 04 50 E   CT

Springsure

❖ Springsure Dump Point ☎ (07) 4984 1166
At toilet block near museum
HEMA 14 J7   24 07 05 S   148 05 22 E   CT

❖ Springsure Showgrounds ☎ 0427 841 612
☑ See also Queensland site 426.
Barcoo St. S side of town
HEMA 14 J7   24 07 19 S   148 05 02 E   CT HT BIG RIG

St George

❖ St George Showground ☎ (07) 4620 8844
McGahan St, behind E end of showground
HEMA 12 H5   28 01 39 S   148 35 27 E   CT HT BIG RIG

St Lawrence

❖ St Lawrence Recreational Reserve ☎ 1300 472 227
☑ See also Queensland site 93.
1 km W of St Lawrence
HEMA 15 F9   22 21 04 S   149 31 11 E   CT HT BIG RIG

Stanthorpe

❖ Apex Park ☎ (07) 4681 5500
Folkestone St, off Maryland St at toilet block
HEMA 13 J11   28 39 29 S   151 55 55 E   CT HT BIG RIG

Stonehenge Area

❖ Isisford Road Rest Area
☑ See also Queensland site 378.
Rest Area 121 km S of Longreach or 96 km N of Jundah
HEMA 21 G8   24 14 01 S   143 33 27 E   CT HT BIG RIG

Surat

❖ Surat Fishing & Restocking Club Park ☎ (07) 4626 5058
☑ See also Queensland site 755.
Carnarvon Hwy, 1 km N of Surat
HEMA 12 F6   27 08 57 S   149 04 23 E   CT BIG RIG

Tambo

❖ Tambo Lake
☑ See also Queensland site 630.
Landsborough Hwy, S end of town
HEMA 21 H11   24 52 55 S   146 15 35 E   CT HT BIG RIG

Tara Lagoon
❖ Tara Lagoon
☑ See also Queensland site 551.
In Camp Area at Tara Lagoon
`HEMA 13 F8` 27 16 21 S 150 27 36 E `CT` `HT` `BIG RIG`

Taroom
❖ Taroom Dump Point
Wolsey St. 700m N of Post Office, between Rose Rd & North St. Outside Council Depot
`HEMA 12 B7` 25 38 03 S 149 47 56 E `CT` `HT` `BIG RIG`

Texas
❖ Texas Dump Point ☎ (07) 4652 1444
Flemming St, outside Council Depot
`HEMA 13 K10` 28 51 12 S 151 10 25 E `CT` `HT` `BIG RIG` `image`

Thallon
❖ Thallon Recreation ☎ 0427 259 095
Ground
☑ See also Queensland site 719.
Henry St
`HEMA 12 J5` 28 37 58 S 148 51 59 E `CT` `HT` `BIG RIG`

Thargomindah
❖ Thargomindah Dump Point
Watts St off Adventure Way. N of town, Opposite council building near cooling ponds
`HEMA 23 F9` 27 59 23 S 143 49 11 E `CT` `HT` `BIG RIG`

Theodore
❖ Theodore Dump Point ☎ (07) 4992 9500
Eastern Lane, off 7th Avenue. Next to Tennis Courts
`HEMA 13 A8` 24 56 43 S 150 04 36 E `CT` `HT` `BIG RIG`

Thuringowa
❖ Ross River Dam ☎ (07) 4773 8411
At entrance to Ross River Dam Park, Upper Ross River Rd, via Kelso
`HEMA 14 A5` 19 24 27 S 146 44 00 E `CT` `HT` `BIG RIG`

Tin Can Bay
❖ Tin Can Bay Dump Point
Snapper Creek Rd, turning point at tip
`HEMA 13 C13` 25 55 24 S 152 59 27 E `CT` `HT` `BIG RIG`

Toogoolawah
❖ Toogoolawah ☎ 0419 706 617
Showgrounds
☑ See also Queensland site 505.
Ivory Creek Rd
`HEMA 8 G4` 27 04 41 S 152 22 31 E `CT` `HT` `BIG RIG`

Toowoomba
❖ Toowoomba ☎ (07) 4634 7400
Showground
☑ See also Queensland site 567.
Glenvale Rd. 8.00am-5.00pm Monday to Friday
`HEMA 10 C1` 27 33 36 S 151 53 04 E `CT` `HT` `$` `BIG RIG`

Townsville
❖ BP Bohle's Little Acre
900 Ingham Rd. 'Daylight hours only'. $10.00 Key deposit, dump point at rear of service station
`HEMA 14 A5` 19 15 43 S 146 42 53 E `CT` `HT` `BIG RIG`

❖ Willows Shopping Centre
Kern Brothers Dr. In shopping centre car park, S side on far right
`HEMA 17 H12` 19 19 02 S 146 43 31 E `CT` `HT` `BIG RIG` `image`

Tully
❖ Tully Showground ☎ 07 4068 2288
☑ See also Queensland site 18.
Butler St, outside Showgrounds
`HEMA 18 K5` 17 56 02 S 145 55 47 E `CT` `HT` `BIG RIG`

Wallumbilla
❖ Wallumbilla Showgrounds
☑ See also Queensland site 594.
Main Rd at the W end of town
`HEMA 12 E6` 26 35 14 S 149 11 01 E `CT` `HT` `BIG RIG`

Wandoan
❖ Wandoan Dump Point
28-30 Jerrard St
`HEMA 13 C8` 26 07 21 S 149 57 35 E `CT` `HT` `BIG RIG`

❖ Wandoan Water Tower ☎ (07) 4627 5148
Jerrard St, near tower
`HEMA 13 C8` 26 07 21 S 149 57 35 E `CT` `HT` `BIG RIG`

Warwick
❖ Matilda Roadhouse ☎ (07) 4661 7450
Cnr Cunningham Hwy & Ogilvie Rd. Nth end of town
`HEMA 10 J2` 28 11 41 S 152 02 39 E `CT` `HT` `BIG RIG`

Weipa
❖ Weipa Dump Point
Kerr Point Rd, outside Weipa Camping Ground
`HEMA 19 E1` 12 38 23 S 141 51 42 E `CT` `HT` `BIG RIG`

Windorah
❖ Windorah Dump Point
Diamantina Development Rd (near water tower). E side of Town
`HEMA 20 J7` 25 25 04 S 142 39 35 E `CT` `HT` `BIG RIG`

Winton
❖ Winton Dump Point
In Riley St parking area. Cnr of Riley & Jundah Rd
`HEMA 20 D7` 22 23 30 S 143 02 23 E `CT` `HT` `BIG RIG` `image`

❖ Winton Recreation ☎ (07) 4657 1188
Ground
Vindex St, next to skate park
`HEMA 20 D7` 22 23 14 S 143 01 56 E `CT` `BIG RIG` `image`

Wondai
❖ Wondai RV Stop ☎ (07) 4189 9251
☑ See also Queensland site 515.
Haly St, adjacent to Old Rail Station
`HEMA 13 D11` 26 19 02 S 151 52 26 E `CT` `HT` `BIG RIG`

Woodford
❖ Woodford Showgrounds ☎ 0437 390 862
☑ See also Queensland site 500.
Camp Area at Woodford. Neurem Rd
`HEMA 8 F7` 26 56 51 S 152 46 12 E `CT` `HT` `BIG RIG` `image`

Wyandra
❖ Wyandra Dump Point
Mack St, near Cooper St
`HEMA 23 D13` 27 14 44 S 145 58 43 E `CT` `HT` `BIG RIG`

Yeppoon
❖ Merv Anderson Park ☎ (07) 4939 4888
Yeppoon Emu Park Rd, 200m E of Visitor Info Centre
`HEMA 15 G11` 23 08 16 S 150 45 00 E `CT` `HT` `BIG RIG`

Yowah
❖ Yowah Rest Area
☑ See also Queensland site 736.
Rest Area at Yowah. Gemwood St, first turn L after school.
`HEMA 23 F11` 27 58 01 S 144 37 59 E `CT` `HT` `BIG RIG`

Yungaburra
❖ Yungaburra Dump Point
Lot 550 Mulgrave Rd. On road outside sewerage works
`HEMA 18 G3` 17 15 45 S 145 34 44 E `CT` `HT` `BIG RIG`

New South Wales

Aberdeen
❖ Taylor Park
☑ See also New South Wales site 174.
New England Hwy. N end of town. At fence on N side of park
`HEMA 37 C9` 32 09 39 S 150 53 17 E `CT` `HT` `BIG RIG`

Adelong
❖ Adelong Dump Point
Travers St, off Snowy Mountain Hwy
`HEMA 43 H13` 35 18 24 S 148 03 42 E `CT` `HT` `BIG RIG`

Albury
❖ Albury City Dump Point ☎ 1300 252 879
Railway Place. Enter at Cnr Smollett & Young St to Railway Station, turn S to dump location
`HEMA 43 J11` 36 05 07 S 146 55 26 E `CT` `HT` `BIG RIG`

Appin
❖ Appin Park Rest Area
Appin Road
`HEMA 35 H9` 34 11 53 S 150 47 19 E `CT` `HT` `BIG RIG`

Armidale
❖ Armidale Dump Point
Galloway St. Approx 1 km S of City off Waterfall Way. Follow signs for Arboretum
`HEMA 39 G9` 30 31 15 S 151 38 47 E `CT`

Ashford
❖ Ashford Caravan Park ☎ (02) 6725 4014
☑ See also New South Wales site 244.
57 km N of Inverell. Bukkulla St
`HEMA 39 D8` 29 19 24 S 151 05 52 E `CT` `HT` `BIG RIG`

Balranald
❖ Swimming Pool Car Park
☑ See also New South Wales site 780.
Church St. In car park next to water tower
`HEMA 42 F6` 34 38 07 S 143 33 43 E `CT` `HT` `BIG RIG`

Baradine
❖ Baradine Dump Point
Lions Park, cnr Wellington & Darling Sts
`HEMA 38 H3` 30 56 59 S 149 04 00 E `CT` `HT` `BIG RIG`

❖ Camp Cypress ☎ (02) 6843 1035
☑ See also New South Wales site 811.
1 km W of PO at showground. Lachlan St
`HEMA 38 H3` 30 56 49 S 149 03 21 E `CT` `HT` `BIG RIG`

Barraba
❖ Council Works Depot
77 Cherry St. Outside depot
HEMA 38 G6 30 22 49 S 150 36 46 E `CT` `HT` `BIG RIG`

Batehaven
❖ City Park
Beach Rd, in car park opposite shops
HEMA 44 E5 35 43 53 S 150 11 57 E `CT` `HT`

Bathurst
❖ Bathurst Council Depot ☎ (02) 6336 6011
205 Morrisset St. Mon-Fri only 0900-1600
HEMA 36 F6 33 24 10 S 149 34 26 E `CT` `HT` `BIG RIG`

❖ Bathurst Showground ☎ (02) 6331 1349
☑ See also New South Wales site 464.
Kendell Ave
HEMA 36 F6 33 25 05 S 149 35 22 E `CT` `HT` `BIG RIG`

Batlow
❖ Batlow Dump Point
Memorial Avenue, opposite Wakehurst Ave Jcn
HEMA 44 E1 35 31 12 S 148 09 00 E `CT` `HT` `BIG RIG`

Bega
❖ Bega Showgrounds
☑ See also New South Wales site 601.
Upper St. Next to the toilets
HEMA 44 H5 36 40 46 S 149 50 52 E `CT` `HT` `BIG RIG`

Bellingen
❖ Bellingen Dump Point ☎ (02) 6655 2310
Black St, opposite Bellingen Showground
HEMA 39 G12 30 26 55 S 152 53 54 E `CT` `HT`

Bendeela
❖ Bendeela Recreation Area
☑ See also New South Wales site 578.
In Camp Area 7 km W of Kangaroo Valley. Dump point near toilet block in campgrounds 1 & 2. Cassette only
HEMA 44 C6 34 44 21 S 150 28 15 E `CT`

Berridale
❖ Berridale Dump Point
At rear of the Southern Cross Motor Inn. Access off Middlingbank Rd
HEMA 44 G2 36 21 35 S 148 49 52 E `CT` `HT` `BIG RIG`

Berrigan
❖ Berrigan Dump Point
Hayes Park, Jerilderie St
HEMA 43 J10 35 39 38 S 145 48 50 E `CT` `HT`

Berry
❖ Berry Showground ☎ 0427 605 200
☑ See also New South Wales site 577.
500m S of PO. Alexandra St
HEMA 44 C7 34 46 46 S 150 41 46 E `CT` `HT` `BIG RIG`

Bingara
❖ Bingara Showground ☎ (02) 6724 0066
Bowen St, inside 2nd entrance gate
HEMA 38 E6 29 52 00 S 150 33 20 E `CT` `BIG RIG`

Blayney
❖ Blayney Showground ☎ (02) 6368 2104
Western Hwy
HEMA 36 G5 33 31 06 S 149 15 31 E `CT` `BIG RIG`

❖ Henry St Toilet Block ☎ (02) 6368 2104
Henry St. S end, behind PO
HEMA 36 G5 33 31 58 S 149 15 23 E `CT` `HT`

Boggabri
❖ Jubilee Park ☎ (02) 6799 6760
Hull St, next to the entrance
HEMA 38 H5 30 42 20 S 150 02 56 E `CT` `HT` `BIG RIG`

Bomaderry
❖ Bomaderry Country Winnebago ☎ (02) 4421 0122
314 Princes Hwy. Enter at rear via Cambewarra Rd, near McDonalds. Business hours only
HEMA 44 C6 34 50 36 S 150 35 43 E `CT`

Bombala
❖ Bombala Caravan Park ☎ (02) 6458 3817
☑ See also New South Wales site 627.
Monaro Hwy. Public access, pay fee to office
HEMA 44 J3 36 54 30 S 149 14 20 E `CT` `HT` `S`

Boorowa
❖ Boorowa Dump Point
Park St, next to caravan park
HEMA 36 J4 34 26 01 S 148 43 12 E `CT` `HT` `S` `BIG RIG`

Bourke
❖ Back O Bourke Information Centre ☎ (08) 6872 1321
Kidman Way
HEMA 41 D10 30 04 51 S 145 57 00 E `CT` `HT` `BIG RIG`

Braidwood
❖ Braidwood Dump Point ☎ (02) 4842 9231
Cnr of Kingsway & McKellar Sts, N side of town
HEMA 44 E5 35 26 24 S 149 48 07 E `CT` `HT` `BIG RIG`

Branxton
❖ Branxton Oval
☑ See also New South Wales site 189.
John Rose Ave
HEMA 45 F4 32 39 18 S 151 21 05 E `CT` `HT` `BIG RIG`

Brewarrina
❖ Brewarrina Dump Point
At rear of the Information Centre on Bathurst Rd. Only accessible when info centre open. 0830-1700 weekdays
HEMA 41 C11 29 57 35 S 146 51 28 E `CT` `HT`

Broken Hill
❖ Broken Hill Information Centre ☎ (08) 8088 9700
Cnr Bromide & Blende Sts. Key at Information Centre
HEMA 40 H2 31 57 34 S 141 27 39 E `CT` `HT` `BIG RIG`

❖ Broken Hill Racecourse ☎ 0437 250 286
☑ See also New South Wales site 945.
5 km NE of Broken Hill, Racecourse Rd, off Tibooburra Rd. Fee if not staying at Racecourse
HEMA 40 H2 31 54 48 S 141 28 51 E `CT` `HT` `S` `BIG RIG`

Bulahdelah
❖ Bulahdelah Showgrounds ☎ (02) 4997 4981
☑ See also New South Wales site 89.
Cnr Stuart & Prince Sts. Near helipad
HEMA 37 D12 32 24 18 S 152 12 16 E `CT` `HT` `BIG RIG`

Bungendore
❖ Bungendore Showground ☎ 0455 174 463
☑ See also New South Wales site 644.
On the Bungendore - Sutton Rd. See Caretaker
HEMA 44 D4 35 14 30 S 149 24 37 E `CT` `HT` `BIG RIG`

Burren Junction
❖ Burren Junction Bore Baths ☎ (02) 6828 1399
☑ See also New South Wales site 370.
Kamilaroi Hwy
HEMA 38 F3 30 06 52 S 148 59 44 E `CT` `HT` `BIG RIG`

Burrinjuck
❖ Burrinjuck Waters ☎ (02) 6227 8114
☑ See also New South Wales site 548.
Burrinjuck Dam, State Park, 25 km S of Bookham
HEMA 44 C2 34 58 46 S 148 37 11 E `CT` `HT`

Bylong
❖ Bylong Community Sportsground
☑ See also New South Wales site 408.
Bylong Valley Way, opposite store
HEMA 36 C7 32 24 58 S 150 06 52 E `CT` `HT` `BIG RIG`

Canowindra
❖ Canowindra Caravan Park ☎ 0428 233 769
☑ See also New South Wales site 480.
Tilga St. Next to swimming pool. 300m S of PO. Public access
HEMA 36 G4 33 34 08 S 148 39 50 E `CT` `HT` `BIG RIG`

Casino
❖ Casino Showground ☎ (02) 6660 0300
Grafton Rd, S end of town
HEMA 39 C12 28 53 02 S 153 02 48 E `CT` `HT` `BIG RIG`

Cessnock
❖ Abermain Bowling & Recreation Club ☎ (02) 4930 4285
☑ See also New South Wales site 193.
Entry via Goulburn St. Key at reception
HEMA 45 H4 32 48 26 S 151 25 36 E `CT` `HT` `BIG RIG`

❖ Cessnock Showground ☎ 0412 235 447
☑ See also New South Wales site 194.
Access gates beside indoor sports centre Mount View Rd. Close Feb & early Mar for show. Fee if not staying at showground
HEMA 45 J4 32 49 51 S 151 20 26 E `CT` `HT` `BIG RIG`

Clarence Town
❖ Bridge Reserve ☎ (02) 4984 2680
Durham St
HEMA 37 D11 32 34 58 S 151 46 56 E `CT` `HT` `BIG RIG`

Cobar
❖ Cobar Visitors Centre ☎ (02) 6836 2448
Barrier Highway
HEMA 41 G9 31 29 53 S 145 50 33 E `CT` `HT` `BIG RIG`

Cobargo
❖ Cobargo Hotel ☎ (02) 6493 6423
☑ See also New South Wales site 600.
Princes Hwy
HEMA 44 G5 36 23 22 S 149 53 09 E `CT` `HT`

New South Wales

Coffs Harbour
❖ **Coffs Harbour Dump Point** ☎ (02) 6648 4000
Phil Hawthorne Dr, off Stadium Dr roundabout. S of town off Pacific Hwy
`HEMA 39 G12` 30 19 26 S 153 05 47 E `CT` `HT` `BIG RIG`

Coleambally
❖ **The Coly Club** ☎ (02) 6954 4170
☑ *See also New South Wales site 988.*
Entry from Kingfisher Ave & Kidman Way
`HEMA 43 G10` 34 47 52 S 145 52 46 E `CT` `BIG RIG`

Collarenebri
❖ **Collarenebri Primitive Campground**
☑ *See also New South Wales site 263.*
Gwydir Hwy, E end of town. Next to football grounds. Beside toilet block
`HEMA 38 D2` 29 32 56 S 148 34 55 E `CT`

Conargo
❖ **Bills Park** ☎ (03) 5880 1200
☑ *See also New South Wales site 871.*
Rest Area at Conargo. W end of town, near school
`HEMA 43 H8` 35 18 24 S 145 10 38 E `CT` `HT` `BIG RIG`

Condobolin
❖ **River View Caravan Park** ☎ (02) 6895 2611
☑ *See also New South Wales site 975.*
Diggers Ave. S end of town. Public access
`HEMA 43 C12` 33 05 40 S 147 08 50 E `CT` `HT` `BIG RIG` 🛥

Coolongolook
❖ **Coolongolook Dump Point**
King St, off Pacific Hwy. Cassette only
`HEMA 37 C12` 32 13 08 S 152 19 21 E `CT`

Cooma
❖ **Cooma Dump Point**
Cnr of Geebung St & Polo Flat Rd
`HEMA 44 G3` 36 13 30 S 149 08 52 E `CT` `HT` `BIG RIG` 🛥

Coonabarabran
❖ **Neilson Park**
☑ *See also New South Wales site 819.*
Rest Area at Coonabarabran. Essex St, Eastern end of park
`HEMA 38 J3` 31 16 16 S 149 16 46 E `CT` `HT` `BIG RIG`

Coonamble
❖ **Coonamble Riverside Caravan Park** ☎ (02) 6822 1926
138 Castlereagh St. Inside caravan park, public access. Big Rigs call ahead
`HEMA 38 H1` 30 57 48 S 148 23 21 E `CT` `HT` `BIG RIG`

Cootamundra
❖ **Cootamundra Dump Point**
Apex Park, Hurley St off Olympic Hwy. Near toilet block
`HEMA 36 K3` 34 38 40 S 148 01 30 E `CT` `HT` `BIG RIG`

Corowa
❖ **Corowa Dump Point**
Rowers Park, Bridge Rd. Near the toilets
`HEMA 43 J10` 36 00 15 S 146 23 38 E `CT` `HT` `BIG RIG`

Cowra
❖ **Cowra Overnight Rest Area**
☑ *See also New South Wales site 477.*
Lachlan Valley Way
`HEMA 36 G4` 33 50 08 S 148 40 55 E `CT` `HT` `BIG RIG`

Crookwell
❖ **Crookwell Caravan Park** ☎ 0408 250 652
☑ *See also New South Wales site 451.*
Caravan Park at Crookwell. Laggan Rd
`HEMA 36 J6` 34 27 17 S 149 28 03 E `CT` `HT` `BIG RIG`

Cumnock
❖ **Cumnock Showgrounds** ☎ 0403 054 754
☑ *See also New South Wales site 906.*
Baldry Road
`HEMA 36 E4` 32 55 43 S 148 44 46 E `CT` `HT` `BIG RIG`

Dareton
❖ **Dareton Dump Point**
Tiltao St, next to service station
`HEMA 42 E3` 34 05 44 S 142 02 29 E `CT`

Darlington Point
❖ **Darlington Point Lions Park** ☎ (02) 6968 4166
Darlington St. N side of town, 200m E of caravan park
`HEMA 43 F10` 34 34 00 S 146 00 29 E `CT` `BIG RIG`

Delungra
❖ **Delungra Recreation Ground** ☎ (02) 6724 8275
☑ *See also New South Wales site 248.*
Reedy St, W end of town
`HEMA 38 E7` 29 39 04 S 150 49 33 E `CT` `HT` `BIG RIG`

Deniliquin
❖ **Deniliquin Rest Area**
☑ *See also New South Wales site 513.*
Cobb Hwy, N side of Town, adjacent to public toilet
`HEMA 43 H8` 35 31 31 S 144 58 41 E `CT` `HT` `BIG RIG`

Dorrigo
❖ **Dorrigo Dump Point**
Waterfall Way (Armidale Rd) S of showground
`HEMA 39 G11` 30 20 29 S 152 42 02 E `CT` `HT` `BIG RIG`

Dubbo
❖ **Western Plains Zoo**
At Western Plains Zoo. Turn R after entering through main gate. In caravan parking area
`HEMA 36 C4` 32 16 18 S 148 35 09 E `CT` `HT` `BIG RIG`

Dunedoo
❖ **Dunedoo Dump Point**
156 Bolaro St, next to Town Hall
`HEMA 36 B6` 32 00 58 S 149 23 24 E `CT` `HT` `BIG RIG`

Dungog
❖ **Dungog Showground** ☎ (02) 4992 1810
☑ *See also New South Wales site 322.*
Chapman St
`HEMA 37 D11` 32 24 19 S 151 45 03 E `CT` `HT` `BIG RIG`

Eugowra
❖ **Byrnes Park**
☑ *See also New South Wales site 486.*
Byrne's Park, Myall St, adjacent to bridge
`HEMA 36 F3` 33 25 40 S 148 22 11 E `CT` `HT` `BIG RIG`

Euston
❖ **Euston Dump Point** ☎ (03) 5026 4244
Nixon St, entrance between Euston Club & Motel. If locked key at club
`HEMA 42 F4` 34 34 47 S 142 44 41 E `CT` `HT` `BIG RIG`

New South Wales

Evans Head
❖ **Evans Head Industrial Estate** ☎ (02) 6682 4392
Memorial Airport Dr, near council depot, between Winjeel Dr & Sir Valston Hancock Dr
`HEMA 39 C13` 29 06 15 S 153 25 20 E `CT` `HT` `BIG RIG`

Finley
❖ **Finley RV Stop**
☑ *See also New South Wales site 876.*
Endeavour St, beside old railway station
`HEMA 43 J9` 35 38 41 S 145 34 37 E `CT` `HT` `BIG RIG`

Forbes
❖ **Forbes Lions Park**
☑ *See also New South Wales site 844.*
Rest Area at Forbes. Cnr of Lachlan & Junction Sts. 500m S of PO, beside lake
`HEMA 36 F3` 33 23 22 S 148 00 14 E `CT` `HT` `BIG RIG`
❖ **Shire Works Depot** ☎ (02) 6850 1300
Newell Hwy. Near BP Roadhouse, Fitzgeralds Bridge. 1.5 km S of PO. Business hours only
`HEMA 36 F3` 33 24 07 S 147 59 05 E `CT` `HT` `BIG RIG`

Glen Innes
❖ **Glen Innes Anzac Park**
☑ *See also New South Wales site 140.*
Cnr East Ave & Ferguson St
`HEMA 39 E9` 29 44 03 S 151 44 04 E `CT` `HT` `BIG RIG`

Gloucester
❖ **Gloucester Holiday Park** ☎ (02) 6558 1720
Denison St. 700m W of PO. Call at reception for payment & directions
`HEMA 37 B12` 32 00 23 S 151 57 12 E `CT` `$`

Goolgowi
❖ **Goolgowi Caravan Park** ☎ (02) 6965 1900
☑ *See also New South Wales site 504.*
Combo St. 1 km NE of PO
`HEMA 43 E9` 33 58 47 S 145 42 22 E `CT` `HT` `BIG RIG`
❖ **Goolgowi Dump Point**
Napier St, in the lane beside the fire station
`HEMA 43 E9` 33 58 47 S 145 42 28 E `CT` `HT`

Goulburn
❖ **Marsden Weir Park**
Fitzroy Street off Crookwell Rd. Limited access
`HEMA 44 B4` 34 44 08 S 149 42 25 E `CT`

Grafton
❖ **Grafton Greyhound Racing Club Campground** ☎ (02) 6642 3713
☑ *See also New South Wales site 32.*
Cranworth St
`HEMA 39 E12` 29 40 27 S 152 55 32 E `CT` `BIG RIG`
❖ **Grafton Showground** ☎ 0468 482 919
☑ *See also New South Wales site 33.*
Prince & Dobie St
`HEMA 39 E12` 29 41 03 S 152 56 24 E `CT` `HT` `BIG RIG`

Grenfell
❖ **Grenfell Old Railway Station** ☎ (02) 6343 1212
☑ *See also New South Wales site 492.*
West St, near old railway station. Take 2nd driveway from cnr of Camp St
`HEMA 36 H3` 33 53 43 S 148 09 21 E `CT` `HT` `BIG RIG`

Griffith
❖ Willow Park ☎ (02) 6962 4145
☑ *See also New South Wales site 984.*
Kookora St toilet block
`HEMA 43 F10` 34 17 16 S 146 01 55 E `CT` `BIG RIG`

Gulgong
❖ Gulgong Dump Point ☎ (02) 6374 1202
Saleyards Lane off Station St, front of shire depot
`HEMA 36 C6` 32 21 30 S 149 32 46 E `CT` `HT` `BIG RIG` `▲`

❖ Gulgong Showground ☎ (02) 6374 1255
☑ *See also New South Wales site 403.*
Entrance on Cnr of Grevillia & Guntawang Rds
`HEMA 36 C6` 32 22 15 S 149 31 41 E `CT` `HT` `BIG RIG`

Gundagai
❖ Gundagai Dump Point
Railway Parade
`HEMA 43 G13` 35 03 55 S 148 06 45 E `CT` `HT` `BIG RIG`

Gunnedah
❖ Gunnedah Lions RV Park
Oxley Highway (Mullaley Rd)
`HEMA 38 H6` 30 58 43 S 150 14 24 E `CT` `HT` `BIG RIG`

❖ Gunnedah Showground ☎ (02) 6740 2125
South St. Located just inside entrance
`HEMA 38 H6` 30 58 48 S 150 14 53 E `CT` `HT` `BIG RIG`

Guyra
❖ Mother of Ducks Lagoon
☑ *See also New South Wales site 143.*
Rest Area at Guyra. White St. S end of town, turn W off Hwy into McKie Parkway
`HEMA 39 F9` 30 13 21 S 151 40 10 E `CT` `HT` `BIG RIG`

Harden
❖ Harden-Murrumburrah Showgrounds ☎ 0488 509 977
☑ *See also New South Wales site 613.*
Woolrych St
`HEMA 44 B1` 34 32 45 S 148 21 27 E `CT` `HT` `BIG RIG`

Hay
❖ Hay Showground ☎ (02) 6993 1087
☑ *See also New South Wales site 507.*
Dunera Way, N end of town. Outside emergency service building. 200m W of showground
`HEMA 43 F8` 34 29 51 S 144 50 17 E `CT` `HT` `BIG RIG`

Henty
❖ Henty Dump Point
Henty Pleasant Hills Rd, behind the library
`HEMA 43 H12` 35 30 57 S 147 01 58 E `CT` `HT` `BIG RIG`

Hillston
❖ Hillston Lions Park
Kidman Way, next to the caravan park
`HEMA 43 D9` 33 28 47 S 145 32 04 E `CT` `HT` `BIG RIG`

Holbrook
❖ Holbrook Motor Village ☎ (02) 6036 3100
Bardwell St, off Hume Hwy. Public access. Must advise park office
`HEMA 43 J12` 35 43 46 S 147 18 30 E `CT` `HT`

Howlong
❖ Lowe Square Recreation Reserve
Riverina Hwy, between High & Larmer Sts. Near toilet block.
`HEMA 43 J11` 35 58 50 S 146 38 02 E `CT` `HT` `BIG RIG`

Inverell
❖ Inverell Showground ☎ (02) 6722 3435
☑ *See also New South Wales site 241.*
1 km E of town, enter off Tingha Rd, in between Sporting Complex & Pioneer Village
`HEMA 39 E8` 29 46 57 S 151 07 14 E `CT` `HT` `BIG RIG`

Jamberoo
❖ Jamberoo Dump Point
Kevin Walsh Oval. Churchill St
`HEMA 37 K9` 34 38 49 S 150 46 28 E `CT` `HT`

Jerilderie
❖ Lakeside Parking Area ☎ (03) 5886 1200
Newell Hwy car park, 100m W of Civic Centre, beside church
`HEMA 43 H9` 35 21 19 S 145 43 23 E `CT` `HT` `BIG RIG`

Jugiong
❖ Jugiong Showground
☑ *See also New South Wales site 550.*
Riverside Dr. Donation requested for use
`HEMA 43 G14` 34 49 24 S 148 19 34 E `CT` `HT` `BIG RIG`

Junee
❖ Laurie Daley Oval ☎ (02) 6924 8100
Park Lane, 70m from entry
`HEMA 36 K2` 34 51 34 S 147 34 24 E `CT` `HT` `BIG RIG`

Kempsey
❖ Kempsey Showgrounds ☎ (02) 6562 5231
☑ *See also New South Wales site 54.*
19 Sea St
`HEMA 39 J11` 31 04 24 S 152 49 45 E `CT` `HT` `BIG RIG`

Kew
❖ Kew Information & Community Centre ☎ (02) 6559 4400
133 Nancy Bird Walton Dr
`HEMA 37 A13` 31 38 07 S 152 43 20 E `CT` `HT` `BIG RIG`

Khancoban
❖ Khancoban Dump Point ☎ (02) 6948 9100
Scott St, near cnr Mitchell Ave
`HEMA 43 K13` 36 13 03 S 148 07 24 E `CT` `HT` `BIG RIG`

Kurri Kurri
❖ Kurri Kurri Central Oval
☑ *See also New South Wales site 192.*
10 Allworth St
`HEMA 45 H5` 32 49 24 S 151 28 51 E `CT` `HT` `BIG RIG`

Kyogle
❖ Kyogle Showground ☎ 0459 537 601
☑ *See also New South Wales site 205.*
N end of town. Fee if not staying at showground
`HEMA 39 B12` 28 36 57 S 153 00 00 E `CT` `HT` `$` `BIG RIG`

Lake Cargelligo
❖ Lake Cargelligo Shire Dump Point ☎ (02) 6895 1900
Narrandera St
`HEMA 43 C10` 33 18 17 S 146 22 23 E `CT`

Lake George
❖ Anderson VC Rest Area
☑ *See also New South Wales site 651.*
7 km N of Bungendore turn off
`HEMA 44 C4` 35 06 01 S 149 22 36 E `CT` `HT` `BIG RIG`

Leeton
❖ Leeton Showground ☎ (02) 6953 6481
☑ *See also New South Wales site 753.*
Racecourse Rd
`HEMA 43 F10` 34 33 49 S 146 23 58 E `CT` `HT` `BIG RIG` `▲`

Lightning Ridge
❖ Lightning Ridge Dump Point ☎ (02) 6829 1670
Onyx St
`HEMA 41 B13` 29 25 32 S 147 58 21 E `CT` `BIG RIG`

Lithgow
❖ Lithgow Showground ☎ (02) 6353 1775
Entry off George Coates Ave. Daylight hours
`HEMA 34 C2` 33 28 51 S 150 08 42 E `CT` `HT` `BIG RIG`

Lockhart
❖ Lockhart Caravan Park ☎ 0458 205 303
☑ *See also New South Wales site 743.*
Green St. 300m W of PO
`HEMA 43 H11` 35 13 13 S 146 42 46 E `CT`

Lyndhurst
❖ Lyndhurst Primitive Campground ☎ 0427 201 824
☑ *See also New South Wales site 471.*
Camp Area at Lyndhurst. In Recreation Ground, entrance off Harrow St
`HEMA 36 G5` 33 40 24 S 149 02 20 E `CT` `HT` `BIG RIG`

Macksville
❖ Gumma Crossing Reserve ☎ (02) 6568 2555
☑ *See also New South Wales site 47.*
Camp Area 7.5 km E of Macksville
`HEMA 39 H12` 30 42 24 S 152 59 00 E `CT` `HT` `BIG RIG` `▲`

Maclean
❖ Maclean Showground
☑ *See also New South Wales site 27.*
At Maclean Showground, entry off Cameron St
`HEMA 39 D13` 29 27 50 S 153 11 58 E `CT` `HT` `BIG RIG` `▲`

Manildra
❖ Manildra Showground ☎ 0428 697 685
☑ *See also New South Wales site 901.*
Orange St
`HEMA 36 F4` 33 10 38 S 148 41 16 E `CT` `HT` `BIG RIG` `▲`

Manilla
❖ Manilla Park ☎ (02) 6785 1304
Charles St
`HEMA 38 H7` 30 44 21 S 150 42 57 E `CT` `HT` `BIG RIG`

Mathoura
❖ Mathoura Dump Point
Laneway behind Bowling Club. Enter off Mitchell St. Drive through
`HEMA 43 J8` 35 48 30 S 144 53 56 E `CT` `HT` `BIG RIG`

New South Wales

Menindee
- ❖ Menindee Lakes Caravan Park ☎ (08) 8091 4315
  ☑ See also New South Wales site 1010.
  Menindee Lakes Shore Drive. Public access, pay fee at reception
  HEMA 40 J3 32 21 15 S 142 24 12 E `CT` `HT` `S` `BIG RIG`

Merriwa
- ❖ Merriwa Dump Point ☎ (02) 6548 2607
  Blaxland St, next to caravan park
  HEMA 37 C8 32 08 17 S 150 21 03 E `CT` `HT` `BIG RIG`

Milton
- ❖ Milton Showground ☎ 0429 934 067
  ☑ See also New South Wales site 586.
  Milton Showground. Croobyar Rd
  HEMA 44 D6 35 19 09 S 150 25 48 E `CT` `HT` `BIG RIG`

Moama
- ❖ Rich River Golf Club Resort ☎ (03) 5481 3333
  ☑ See also New South Wales site 520.
  Twenty Four Lane, via Perricoota Rd. ID required, report to reception for key
  HEMA 43 K8 36 04 35 S 144 43 35 E `CT` `HT` `BIG RIG`

Moree
- ❖ Moree Dump Point
  Web Ave, off Newell Hwy
  HEMA 38 D5 29 27 26 S 149 50 40 E `CT` `BIG RIG`

Moruya
- ❖ Moruya Dump Point
  Shore St. Near sewer pump station opposite tennis courts. Via Church St off Princes Hwy
  HEMA 44 F5 35 54 27 S 150 04 35 E `CT` `BIG RIG`

Moulamein
- ❖ Moulamein Dump Point
  Moulamein Rd, between Tallow St & Sainsberry St
  HEMA 42 G6 35 05 16 S 144 01 53 E `CT` `HT` `BIG RIG`

Mudgee
- ❖ Mudgee Showground ☎ (02) 6372 3828
  ☑ See also New South Wales site 401.
  Douro St, 200m from cnr Nicolson St. Phone first to check if dump open
  HEMA 36 D6 32 36 10 S 149 34 53 E `CT` `HT` `BIG RIG`

Mulwala
- ❖ Purtle Park
  Melbourne St
  HEMA 43 J10 35 59 08 S 146 00 34 E `CT` `HT` `BIG RIG`

Mungindi
- ❖ WH Smith Park
  Cnr Wirrah & Loftus Sts
  HEMA 38 B3 28 58 53 S 148 59 30 E `CT` `HT` `BIG RIG`

Murrurundi
- ❖ Wilson Memorial Park
  New England Hwy. Best entrance via Mount St through back gate
  HEMA 37 B9 31 45 51 S 150 50 11 E `CT` `HT` `BIG RIG`

Nambucca Heads
- ❖ Nambucca Heads Visitor Information Centre ☎ (02) 6568 6954
  Cnr Pacific Hwy & Riverside Dr. Key available between 0900- 700
  HEMA 39 H12 30 39 09 S 152 59 25 E `CT`

Narrabri
- ❖ Cameron Park
  ☑ See also New South Wales site 800.
  Rest Area at Narrabri. 700m S of Information Centre
  HEMA 38 F5 30 19 37 S 149 46 43 E `CT`

- ❖ Narrabri Showground ☎ (02) 6792 3913
  ☑ See also New South Wales site 801.
  Belar St
  HEMA 38 F5 30 20 19 S 149 45 48 E `CT` `HT` `BIG RIG`

Narrandera
- ❖ Narrandera Showground ☎ 0407 105 846
  ☑ See also New South Wales site 747.
  Elizabeth St, E side of town. Behind hall in grounds
  HEMA 43 G11 34 44 57 S 146 33 52 E `CT` `BIG RIG`

Newcastle Area
- ❖ Australian Motorhomes, Bennetts Green Dump Point ☎ (02) 4948 0433
  At rear of Australian Motorhomes, enter via Groves Rd, Statham St, 2nd driveway on R. Mon - Fri 0900-1700
  HEMA 33 C14 32 59 50 S 151 41 25 E `CT` `BIG RIG`

Norah Head
- ❖ Norah Head Holiday Park ☎ (02) 4396 3935
  Victoria St. Fee for non guests
  HEMA 33 G13 33 17 00 S 151 33 58 E `CT` `HT` `S`

Nowra
- ❖ Nowra Showground ☎ 1300 662 808
  ☑ See also New South Wales site 581.
  West St
  HEMA 44 C6 34 52 30 S 150 35 31 E `CT` `HT` `BIG RIG`

Nyngan
- ❖ Teamsters Rest Area
  ☑ See also New South Wales site 917.
  Teamsters Rest Area, Pangee St. Approx 300m W of Information Centre
  HEMA 41 G12 31 33 43 S 147 11 40 E `CT` `HT` `BIG RIG`

Oberon
- ❖ Jenolan Caravan Park ☎ (02) 6336 0344
  Cunynghame St. Public access
  HEMA 36 G7 33 42 06 S 149 51 28 E `CT` `HT` `S`

Orange
- ❖ Total Park
  Bathurst Rd, behind service station. E end of town
  HEMA 36 F5 33 17 27 S 149 06 34 E `CT` `HT` `BIG RIG`

Parkes
- ❖ Kelly Reserve
  ☑ See also New South Wales site 839.
  Rest Area at Parkes. N end of town
  HEMA 36 E3 33 07 28 S 148 10 23 E `CT`

- ❖ Parkes Showground ☎ (02) 6862 2580
  ☑ See also New South Wales site 840.
  Victoria St. Not available during show August or Elvis Festival 1-14 Jan
  HEMA 36 E3 33 07 52 S 148 09 47 E `CT` `HT` `BIG RIG`

Peak Hill
- ❖ Peak Hill Dump Point
  Warrah St, between Mingelo St & Bogan St. W side of Hwy
  HEMA 36 D3 32 43 38 S 148 11 10 E `CT` `HT` `BIG RIG`

New South Wales

Picton
- ❖ Picton Dump Point
  Walton Street, next to the car park. Off Menangle St W
  HEMA 35 H8 34 10 04 S 150 36 40 E `CT` `HT`

Port Macquarie
- ❖ Port Macquarie Dump Point
  Chestnut Rd, off Lake Rd. Adjacent to sewer pumping station
  HEMA 39 K12 31 27 06 S 152 53 23 E `CT`

Portland
- ❖ Kremer Park
  ☑ See also New South Wales site 462.
  Kiln St
  HEMA 36 F7 33 21 11 S 149 58 28 E `CT` `HT` `BIG RIG`

Quirindi
- ❖ Rose Lee Park
  Kamilaroi Highway
  HEMA 38 K6 31 31 04 S 150 40 34 E `CT` `HT` `BIG RIG`

Rylstone
- ❖ Rylstone Caravan Park ☎ 0448 251 440
  6 Carwell St. Public access. Fee applies
  HEMA 36 E7 32 48 02 S 149 58 04 E `CT` `HT` `S` `BIG RIG`

Seal Rocks
- ❖ Seal Rocks Dump Point
  Seal Rocks Rd, opposite entry to caravan park. Near public toilets
  HEMA 37 D13 32 25 57 S 152 31 28 E `CT` `BIG RIG`

South West Rocks
- ❖ Trial Bay Gaol Dump Point ☎ (02) 6566 6168
  Next to amenities block in day use area. $10 deposit & key collection from office at campground
  HEMA 39 H12 30 52 37 S 153 04 19 E `CT`

Talbingo
- ❖ Talbingo Dump Point ☎ (02) 6941 2555
  Murray Jackson Dr, between Lampe & Bridle Sts. At entrance to water depot station
  HEMA 43 H14 35 34 43 S 148 17 59 E `CT`

Tamworth
- ❖ South Tamworth Rest Area
  Lions Park Rest Area, 470 Goonoo Goonoo Rd (New England Hwy), opposite power sub-station
  HEMA 38 J7 31 07 57 S 150 55 22 E `CT` `HT` `BIG RIG`

- ❖ Tamworth Airport Rest Area
  ☑ See also New South Wales site 157.
  On Hwy opposite airport
  HEMA 38 J7 31 04 40 S 150 51 02 E `CT` `HT` `BIG RIG`

- ❖ Tamworth Rest Area ☎ (02) 6755 4555
  3 km NE of Tamworth on New England Hwy. Limited turning circle
  HEMA 38 J7 31 06 30 S 150 57 16 E `CT` `HT`

Tarcutta
- ❖ Tarcutta Dump Point
  Sydney St. In "Truck changeover bay". Beside toilets
  HEMA 43 H13 35 16 33 S 147 44 17 E `CT` `HT` `BIG RIG`

Taree
❖ **Taree Rotary Park**
☑ *See also New South Wales site 76.*
Manning River Dr, via Victoria St. Just W of Information Centre
HEMA 37 B13   31 53 57 S   152 29 27 E   CT HT BIG RIG

Temora
❖ **Temora Dump Point**   ☎ (02) 6980 1100
Northern end of Airport St. Approx 200m from Hwy
HEMA 36 J2   34 25 40 S   147 31 09 E   CT HT BIG RIG

❖ **Temora Showground**   ☎ 0427 280 339
☑ *See also New South Wales site 853.*
Entry via Mimosa St
HEMA 43 F12   34 26 23 S   147 31 17 E   CT HT BIG RIG

Tenterfield
❖ **Tenterfield Showground**   ☎ (02) 6736 3666
☑ *See also New South Wales site 128.*
Miles St. Entry at back gate
HEMA 39 C10   29 03 25 S   152 00 55 E   CT HT BIG RIG

The Rock
❖ **The Rock Recreation Ground**
☑ *See also New South Wales site 726.*
Parking Area at the Rock. Wilson St, via Urana & Cornwall Sts
HEMA 43 H12   35 15 55 S   147 06 37 E   CT HT BIG RIG

Tocumwal
❖ **Town Beach**   ☎ (03) 5874 2517
☑ *See also New South Wales site 878.*
From Tocumwal - Corawa Rd turn W onto Hennessy St then S on Town Beach Rd. 700m dirt Rd
HEMA 43 J9   35 49 06 S   145 33 43 E   CT HT BIG RIG

Tooleybuc
❖ **Tooleybuc Recreation Reserve**
Lockhart Rd
HEMA 42 G5   35 01 22 S   143 20 17 E   CT HT BIG RIG

Trundle
❖ **Trundle Showgrounds**   ☎ (02) 6892 1260
☑ *See also New South Wales site 841.*
Camp Area at Trundle Showgrounds, Austral St
HEMA 36 E2   32 55 33 S   147 42 06 E   CT HT BIG RIG

Tullamore
❖ **Tullamore Showground**   ☎ (02) 6892 5194
☑ *See also New South Wales site 843.*
Camp Area at Tullamore. Cornet St
HEMA 36 D2   32 37 39 S   147 34 11 E   CT HT BIG RIG

Tumbarumba
❖ **Tumbarumba Dump Point**
Cnr Cape & Bridge Sts. 100m from Visitors Centre
HEMA 43 J13   35 46 37 S   148 00 33 E   CT HT BIG RIG

Tumut
❖ **Tumut Dump Point**   ☎ (02) 6941 2555
Elm Drive
HEMA 44 D1   35 18 11 S   148 13 42 E   CT HT

Ungarie
❖ **Ungarie Showground**
☑ *See also New South Wales site 978.*
Camp Area at Ungarie, Crown Camp Rd, entrance beyond school. Behind toilets, signposted
HEMA 43 D11   33 38 07 S   146 58 43 E   CT HT BIG RIG

Uralla
❖ **Uralla Dump Point**
John St, at the Pioneer Cemetery
HEMA 39 G8   30 38 31 S   151 29 35 E   CT HT BIG RIG

Uranquinty
❖ **Uranquinty Rest Area**
Rest Area, main street
HEMA 43 H12   35 11 34 S   147 14 46 E   CT HT BIG RIG

Urunga
❖ **Urunga Recreation Reserve**
Morgo St, S of town centre heading to Hungry Head. 250m S of intersection with South St E
HEMA 39 G12   30 30 06 S   153 01 16 E   CT HT BIG RIG

Wagga Wagga
❖ **Wagga Wagga Showgrounds**   ☎ (02) 6925 2180
Urana St. Fee if not staying at showgrounds
HEMA 43 G12   35 07 35 S   147 21 15 E   CT HT $ BIG RIG

❖ **Wilks Park**
☑ *See also New South Wales site 723.*
Rest Area at Wagga Wagga. Turn E off Olympic Hwy at Travers St, across bridge to Hampden Ave. N side of town, E side of Murrumbidgee River
HEMA 43 G12   35 05 59 S   147 22 17 E   CT HT BIG RIG

Walcha
❖ **Walcha Dump Point**
North St, in front of Council depot
HEMA 39 H9   30 58 40 S   151 35 18 E   CT HT BIG RIG

Walgett
❖ **Alex Trevallion Park**
☑ *See also New South Wales site 372.*
Castlereagh Hwy. S end of town
HEMA 38 E1   30 02 04 S   148 06 55 E   CT HT BIG RIG

Wallerawang
❖ **Lake Wallace**
☑ *See also New South Wales site 461.*
Barton Ave, beside lake. Turn N off Great Western Hwy 8 km W of Lithgow or 57 km E of Bathurst
HEMA 34 B1   33 24 56 S   150 04 24 E   CT HT BIG RIG

Warialda
❖ **Saleyards Rest Area**
☑ *See also New South Wales site 253.*
Saleyards Rest Area, Gwydir Hwy. E side of town
HEMA 38 D6   29 32 44 S   150 34 53 E   CT HT BIG RIG

Warragamba
❖ **Warragamba Picnic Area**
Off Warradale Rd
HEMA 34 F7   33 53 37 S   150 36 06 E   CT HT

Warren
❖ **Warren Dump Point**
Oxley Park, Coonamble Rd. Near the water tower
HEMA 36 A2   31 41 48 S   147 50 23 E   CT BIG RIG

Wauchope
❖ **Wauchope Showgrounds**   ☎ 0475 111 074
☑ *See also New South Wales site 290.*
Camp Area at Wauchope, enter via High St
HEMA 39 K11   31 27 28 S   152 43 27 E   CT HT BIG RIG

Wee Waa
❖ **Dangar Park**   ☎ (02) 6799 6760
Cnr Cowper & George Sts, next to toilet block
HEMA 38 F4   30 13 25 S   149 26 39 E   CT HT BIG RIG

Wellington
❖ **Wellington Showground**
Bushrangers Creek Rd
HEMA 36 D5   32 33 15 S   148 56 03 E   CT HT BIG RIG

Wentworth
❖ **Fort Courage Caravan Park**   ☎ (03) 5027 3097
☑ *See also New South Wales site 1024.*
20 km W of Wentworth on Old Renmark Rd. Beside Murray River
HEMA 42 E2   34 05 03 S   141 43 53 E   CT HT BIG RIG

West Wyalong
❖ **Ace Caravan Park**   ☎ (02) 6972 3061
Cnr Newell & Mid Western Hwy's. Fee applies
HEMA 36 H1   33 55 23 S   147 11 55 E   CT $

❖ **West Wyalong Showground**   ☎ 0428 518 329
☑ *See also New South Wales site 849.*
At the showground. Entry by Duffs Rd only off the West Wyalong bypass Rd
HEMA 43 E12   33 56 18 S   147 12 50 E   CT HT BIG RIG

White Cliffs
❖ **Opal Pioneer Caravan & Camping Tourist Park**   ☎ (08) 8091 6688
☑ *See also New South Wales site 939.*
Johnstone St
HEMA 40 E5   30 50 58 S   143 05 23 E   CT HT BIG RIG

Wilcannia
❖ **Wilcannia Dump Point**
Myers St
HEMA 40 G5   31 33 23 S   143 22 29 E   CT HT BIG RIG

Wingham
❖ **Wingham Showground**   ☎ 0427 570 229
☑ *See also New South Wales site 78.*
Gloucester Rd
HEMA 37 B13   31 52 25 S   152 21 43 E   CT HT BIG RIG

Woodburn
❖ **Woodburn Dump Point**   ☎ (02) 6660 0267
Pacific Hwy. Beside public toilets next to Coraki turnoff
HEMA 39 C13   29 04 25 S   153 20 20 E   CT

Woodenbong
❖ **Woodenbong Campground**   ☎ (02) 6635 1300
☑ *See also New South Wales site 198.*
W end of town, next to swimming pool. Deposit for key at Ampol
HEMA 39 A11   28 23 20 S   152 36 21 E   CT HT BIG RIG

Wyalong
❖ **Cooinda Reserve**
Copeland St, off Newell Hwy
HEMA 43 E12   33 55 27 S   147 14 06 E   CT HT BIG RIG

New South Wales

Wyangala Dam
- Wyangala Waters Holiday Park   ☎ (02) 6345 0877
  ☑ See also New South Wales site 472.
  Day fee to enter park. See reception
  HEMA 36 H5   33 57 46 S   148 57 17 E   CT $ BIG RIG

Canberra
- Epic Exhibition Park
  Federal Hwy, Lyneham. Adjacent to camping area. Call ahead as site often closed during Dec - Jan/ Easter
  HEMA 47 C5   35 13 36 S   149 08 55 E   CT HT BIG RIG

Alexandra
- Leckie Park
  23 Station St
  HEMA 66 B3   37 11 11 S   145 42 54 E   CT HT BIG RIG

Ararat
- Ararat Dump Point
  Alexandra Ave, enter via Queen St
  HEMA 58 C7   37 16 50 S   142 55 59 E   CT HT BIG RIG

Avoca
- Avoca Caravan Park   ☎ (03) 5465 3073
  Liebig St. 1.2 km W of PO. Dump is outside caravan park
  HEMA 59 C9   37 05 36 S   143 28 07 E   CT HT BIG RIG

Ballarat
- Eureka Stockade Caravan Park   ☎ (03) 5331 2281
  104 Stawell Street South. Public access, must stop at reception, fee applies
  HEMA 59 E10   37 33 49 S   143 53 09 E   CT HT $ BIG RIG

Beechworth
- Lake Sambell Caravan Park   ☎ (03) 5728 1421
  Peach Dr. 1.5 km from PO. Must call at reception first
  HEMA 64 C5   36 21 28 S   146 42 00 E   CT HT $ BIG RIG

Benalla
- Benalla Dump Point
  Off Samaria Rd, at old Airport Terminus Building. Signposted
  HEMA 64 C3   36 33 11 S   145 59 50 E   CT HT BIG RIG

Bendigo
- Bendigo Showgrounds
  Holmes Rd. 2 km N of PO. Not available during major events
  HEMA 63 K10   36 44 18 S   144 16 23 E   CT HT BIG RIG

Birchip
- Birchip Dump Point
  At Community Leisure Centre, access from Cnr Morrison & Johnson Rds. Veer L to toilet block
  HEMA 62 G6   35 58 46 S   142 54 41 E   CT HT BIG RIG

Boort
- Boort Park Showground   ☎ (03) 5455 2282
  ☑ See also Victoria site 347.
  Malone St
  HEMA 63 H9   36 06 37 S   143 43 46 E   CT HT BIG RIG ⚓

Public Dump Points

Wyong
- Caltex Service Station   ☎ (02) 4352 2944
  Both sides of F3 Freeway. Go through truck parking to find the site
  HEMA 33 G12   33 15 10 S   151 24 12 E   CT

Yass
- Yass Dump Point
  1428 Yass Valley Way, outside council depot
  HEMA 44 C2   34 49 18 S   148 54 21 E   CT HT BIG RIG

Australian Capital Territory

Victoria

Bridgewater
- Bridgewater Recreation Reserve
  ☑ See also Victoria site 353.
  Bridgewater-Maldon Rd. Key from Bridgewater Bakery, 6 Main St
  HEMA 63 K9   36 36 23 S   143 56 41 E   CT HT BIG RIG ⚓

Bruthen
- Bruthen Caravan Park   ☎ (03) 5157 5753
  Tambo Upper Rd. 600m E of PO. Pay fee at reception
  HEMA 65 H8   37 42 43 S   147 50 08 E   CT HT $ BIG RIG

Cann River
- Cann River Rainforest Caravan Park   ☎ (03) 5158 6369
  ☑ See also Victoria site 5.
  7536 Princes Hwy, just W of Cann River Bridge
  HEMA 65 G12   37 33 59 S   149 08 46 E   CT

Casterton
- Casterton Caravan Park   ☎ 0457 414 187
  ☑ See also Victoria site 544.
  Caravan Park at Casterton. M Carmichel Dr off Murray St, adjacent to swimming pool. Next to amenities block. Public access
  HEMA 58 E3   37 34 58 S   141 24 19 E   CT BIG RIG

Charlton
- Travellers Rest Caravan Park   ☎ 0448 276 631
  ☑ See also Victoria site 346.
  43-45 High Street
  HEMA 63 H8   36 16 02 S   143 21 05 E   CT

Chiltern
- Chiltern Dump Point
  Lake Anderson Dr, adjacent to caravan park
  HEMA 64 B5   36 09 08 S   146 36 44 E   CT HT BIG RIG

Clunes
- Clunes Dump Point
  70 Bailey St. Key at bottle museum
  HEMA 59 C10   37 17 37 S   143 46 50 E   CT

Cobram
- Cobram Dump Point
  Cobram Showgrounds, entrance from Banks St into Ivy St. Follow past tennis courts to southern corner
  HEMA 64 A2   35 55 18 S   145 39 09 E   CT HT BIG RIG

Victoria

Young
- Young Showground   ☎ (02) 6382 2079
  ☑ See also New South Wales site 711.
  In showground at Young. Entry from Whitman Ave
  HEMA 36 J3   34 18 58 S   148 18 50 E   CT HT BIG RIG ⚓

Cohuna
- Cohuna Dump Point
  Cohuna Island Rd, near caravan park
  HEMA 63 G10   35 48 17 S   144 13 33 E   CT HT BIG RIG

Colac
- Central Caravan Park   ☎ (03) 5231 3586
  ☑ See also Victoria site 487.
  Caravan Park at Colac. Bruce St. At showground
  HEMA 61 F9   38 20 09 S   143 36 12 E   CT HT $ BIG RIG ⚓

Corop
- Greens Lake Recreation Reserve
  ☑ See also Victoria site 408.
  Camp Area 16 km W of Stanhope or 24 km E of Elmore
  HEMA 63 J12   36 26 16 S   144 49 42 E   CT HT BIG RIG

Corryong
- Corryong Dump Point
  Next to toilet block at Saleyards, Donaldson St (School Lane)
  HEMA 65 B8   36 11 17 S   147 53 56 E   CT BIG RIG

Cullulleraine
- Bushmans Rest Caravan Park   ☎ (03) 5028 2252
  ☑ See also Victoria site 310.
  70 Sturt Hwy
  HEMA 62 B3   34 16 23 S   141 35 13 E   CT HT BIG RIG

Daylesford
- Daylesford Victoria Caravan Park   ☎ (03) 5348 3821
  Cnr Ballan Rd & Burrall St. Key at the reception office, deposit required
  HEMA 59 D11   37 21 31 S   144 08 23 E   CT HT $ BIG RIG

Dimboola
- Dimboola Dump Point   ☎ (03) 5391 4444
  Wimmera St, near caravan park entrance
  HEMA 62 J4   36 27 24 S   142 01 30 E   CT

Dinner Plain
- Scrubbers End Overnight Parking   ☎ 1800 444 066
  ☑ See also Victoria site 141.
  Parking Area at Dinner Plain Alpine Village. Enter via Big Muster Dr & Scrubbers End Lane, E side of village
  HEMA 64 E6   37 01 28 S   147 14 36 E   CT

Donald
❖ Donald Apex Park
Rest Area at Donald. N end of town
HEMA 62 J7 36 22 03 S 142 58 39 E CT HT BIG RIG

Eagle Point
❖ Eagle Point Caravan ☎ (03) 5156 1183
Park
☑ See also Victoria site 38.
Camp Park Rd. 12 km S of Bairnsdale.
Opposite reception
HEMA 65 H8 37 53 32 S 147 40 53 E CT HT BIG RIG

Echuca
❖ Echuca Rotary Park RV Stop
☑ See also Victoria site 272.
Rotary Park. Entry Cnr Rose & Crossen Sts
HEMA 63 H11 36 08 43 S 144 44 02 E CT HT BIG RIG

Elmore
❖ Aysons Reserve ☎ (03) 5481 2200
(Campaspe River)
☑ See also Victoria site 409.
At Camp Area 8 km NE of Elmore. Turn N
off Midland Hwy 32 km W of Stanhope or
5 km NE of Elmore along Burnewang Rd
for 3 km
HEMA 63 J11 36 27 34 S 144 40 08 E CT HT BIG RIG

Euroa
❖ Euroa Freeway Service Centre
At Service Centre, off M31
HEMA 64 D2 36 44 38 S 145 35 27 E CT HT BIG RIG

❖ Kirkland Ave Rest Area
Kirkland Ave East. Adjacent to caravan park
HEMA 64 D2 36 45 15 S 145 34 34 E CT

Foster
❖ Foster Dump Point
Cnr Main St & Nelson St, at service station
HEMA 66 H5 38 39 08 S 146 12 13 E CT HT BIG RIG

Girgaree
❖ Girgarre Town Park
☑ See also Victoria site 406.
Corner of Winter Rd & Station St. Dump
beside hall near toilets
HEMA 63 J12 36 23 53 S 144 58 48 E CT HT BIG RIG

Harcourt
❖ Harcourt Dump Point
Cnr High & Bridge Sts
HEMA 59 B12 36 59 40 S 144 15 43 E CT HT BIG RIG

Heathcote
❖ Heathcote Dump Point ☎ (03) 5433 3121
Barrack St, outside of Queen Meadow
Caravan Park
HEMA 59 B13 36 55 24 S 144 42 47 E CT HT BIG RIG

Heyfield
❖ Heyfield RV Rest Stop ☎ 0418 108 691
☑ See also Victoria site 48.
700m SE of Heyfield Post Office, cnr
MacFarlane & Clark Sts
HEMA 66 E6 37 59 06 S 146 47 15 E HT

Heywood
❖ Heywood RV Stop
☑ See also Victoria site 509.
Hunter St East
HEMA 58 G3 38 07 51 S 141 37 57 E CT HT BIG RIG

Hollands Landing
❖ Hollands Landing Dump ☎ (03) 5142 3333
Point
Hollands Landing Rd. Near public toilets at
the jetty
HEMA 64 J7 38 03 13 S 147 27 36 E CT BIG RIG

Hopetoun
❖ Hopetoun Rest Area
☑ See also Victoria site 573.
At Rest Area 1 km NE of Hopetoun
HEMA 62 G5 35 43 21 S 142 21 53 E CT BIG RIG

Horsham
❖ Horsham Dump Point
Firebrace St, outside caravan park
HEMA 58 A5 36 43 21 S 142 11 58 E CT HT BIG RIG

Jeparit
❖ Jeparit Dump Point
Dimboola - Rainbow Rd, outside the shire
depot
HEMA 62 H4 36 08 24 S 141 59 23 E CT HT BIG RIG

Kaniva
❖ Kaniva Caravan Park ☎ 0458 687 054
☑ See also Victoria site 479.
Caravan Park at Kaniva. Baker St. Dump is
near Dungey St gates. Public access
HEMA 62 J2 36 22 54 S 141 14 25 E CT BIG RIG

Kerang
❖ Kerang Dump Point
Markets Rd
HEMA 63 G9 35 44 14 S 143 55 39 E CT HT BIG RIG

Korumburra
❖ Korumburra ☎ (03) 5655 2326
Showgrounds Dump
Point
Victoria St. Rear entrance gate, next to
toilet block. Key must be collected from
Korumburra Tourist Park in Bourke St.
Deposit required for key
HEMA 57 K13 38 25 40 S 145 49 02 E CT HT BIG RIG

Kyabram
❖ Kyabram Dump Point ☎ (03) 5852 2883
Fauna Park Road, off Lake Rd. Next to toilet
block. If locked, obtain key from Fauna Park
office
HEMA 63 J12 36 19 16 S 145 02 52 E CT

Kyneton
❖ South Kyneton Mineral Springs
☑ See also Victoria site 369.
Parking Area 3.5 km W of Kyneton on
Burton Ave
HEMA 59 C12 37 14 09 S 144 25 10 E CT HT BIG RIG

Lake Bolac
❖ Lake Bolac Dump Point
In service Rd, next to the Glenelg Hwy
HEMA 58 E7 37 42 40 S 142 50 32 E CT HT BIG RIG

Lakes Entrance
❖ Lakes Entrance-Gippsland Lakes
Fishing Club
Opposite Information Centre. Bullock Island
Rd
HEMA 65 H8 37 52 58 S 147 58 18 E CT HT BIG RIG

Leitchville
❖ Leitchville Dump Point
Leitchville Recreation Reserve, Cohuna -
Leitchville Rd
HEMA 63 G10 35 54 13 S 144 17 55 E CT HT BIG RIG

Leongatha
❖ Leongatha Apex ☎ (03) 5662 2753
Caravan Park
14 Turner St. 800m N of PO. Fee for non
guests
HEMA 57 K14 38 28 18 S 145 56 52 E CT $

Lockington
❖ Lockington Travellers ☎ 0447 787 581
Stopover
☑ See also Victoria site 274.
In Camp Area at Lockington, Main St
HEMA 63 H11 36 16 15 S 144 32 08 E CT HT

Lorne
❖ Lorne Dump Point ☎ 1300 891 152
Behind Lorne Visitors Centre. Turn into
Otway St, follow road towards the spit.
Dump is on the RH side at 2nd toilet block
HEMA 61 G12 38 32 06 S 143 58 37 E CT

Macarthur
❖ Macarthur Recreation ☎ (03) 5576 1113
Reserve
☑ See also Victoria site 500.
700m S of town, off Port Fairy-Hamilton
Rd, entry to reserve just S of river crossing.
Signposted
HEMA 58 G4 38 02 15 S 142 00 27 E CT HT BIG RIG

Maffra
❖ Gippsland Vehicle ☎ (03) 5147 3223
Collection
1A Sale Rd. Access by arrangement
HEMA 66 E7 37 58 24 S 146 59 05 E CT HT $ BIG RIG

Mallacoota
❖ Mallacoota Dump Point
Buckland Drive, next to toilet block
HEMA 65 G13 37 33 20 S 149 45 21 E CT

❖ Mallacoota Foreshore ☎ (03) 5158 0300
Holiday Park
☑ See also Victoria site 3.
Allan Drive
HEMA 65 G13 37 33 26 S 149 45 32 E CT HT BIG RIG

Mansfield
❖ Mansfield Dump Point ☎ 1800 039 049
Stock Route off High St, N side of rail trail.
200 metres W of Info Centre
HEMA 66 A4 37 03 00 S 146 04 43 E CT HT BIG RIG

Maryborough
❖ Maryborough dump Point
Reservoir Rd, off the Ballarat - Maryborough
Rd
HEMA 59 B10 37 03 52 S 143 43 55 E CT HT BIG RIG

Meeniyan
❖ Meeniyan Dump Point
Meeniyan Recreation Reserve, Nerrena Rd
HEMA 66 H4 38 34 32 S 146 00 44 E CT HT BIG RIG

Mildura
❖ Mildura Dump Point   ☎ (03) 5018 8450
Benetook Avenue, between 11th & 14th Sts. Front of council depot, opposite TAFE
HEMA 62 A4   34 12 17 S   142 10 06 E   CT HT BIG RIG

Mirboo North
❖ BP Service Station
Ridgway St, Mirboo North. Key from attendant, fee if no fuel purchased
HEMA 66 G4   38 24 04 S   146 09 39 E   CT HT $ BIG RIG

Murrabit
❖ Murrabit Recreation Reserve
☑ See also Victoria site 290.
Browning Ave, inside Rec Reserve
HEMA 63 F9   35 31 49 S   143 57 09 E   CT HT BIG RIG

Murtoa
❖ Murtoa Dump Point
Lake St, near the showground & caravan park
HEMA 58 A6   34 37 20 S   142 27 59 E   CT HT BIG RIG

Nathalia
❖ Nathalia Dump Point
Weir St, next to the toilets
HEMA 63 H13   36 03 20 S   145 12 03 E   CT HT BIG RIG

Neerim South
❖ Neeerim South Recreation Reserve
Neerim East Rd
HEMA 66 E4   38 00 59 S   145 57 24 E   CT HT BIG RIG

Newstead
❖ Newstead Racecourse &   ☎ (03) 5476 2360 Rec Reserve
☑ See also Victoria site 359.
Racecourse Rd
HEMA 59 C11   37 07 01 S   144 03 23 E   CT HT BIG RIG

Nhill
❖ Nhill Aerodrome RV Stop
☑ See also Victoria site 477.
3 km N of Nhill. Via Propodollah & Aerodrome Rds
HEMA 62 J3   36 18 27 S   141 38 53 E   CT HT BIG RIG

Nicholson
❖ Nicholson River Reserve
☑ See also Victoria site 37.
Toilet block at boat ramp car park. Cassette only
HEMA 65 H8   37 49 02 S   147 44 24 E   CT

Numurkah
❖ Numurkah Showgrounds
Enter via Tunnock Rd. Locked, key at Visitor Information Centre or adjacent caravan park. $20 deposit
HEMA 64 B1   36 05 38 S   145 26 45 E   CT HT BIG RIG

Nyah
❖ Nyah Recreation Reserve
☑ See also Victoria site 296.
River St, adjacent to Harness Club
HEMA 63 E8   35 10 18 S   143 22 53 E   CT BIG RIG

Orbost
❖ Orbost Dump Point
Forest Road behind the truck wash
HEMA 65 H10   37 42 28 S   148 27 05 E   CT HT

Oxley
❖ Oxley Recreation Reserve
☑ See also Victoria site 170.
Rest Area 3 km S of Oxley, via Oxley Meadowcreek Rd
HEMA 64 C4   36 28 14 S   146 23 06 E   CT HT

Paynesville
❖ Paynesville Progress   ☎ (03) 5153 9500 Jetty
Toilet block on The Esplanade
HEMA 65 H8   37 55 09 S   147 43 10 E   CT

Port Albert
❖ Port Albert Parking Area
☑ See also Victoria site 90.
In Parking Area Wharf St, near boat ramp. Collect key from Port Albert General Store
HEMA 66 H6   38 40 22 S   146 41 38 E   CT HT BIG RIG

Portland
❖ Henty Park
☑ See also Victoria site 505.
Henty Park, adjacent to amenities block, near the Cable Tram depot
HEMA 58 H3   38 21 16 S   141 36 22 E   CT HT BIG RIG

Pyramid Hill
❖ Pyramid Hill Caravan   ☎ 0438 557 012 Park
☑ See also Victoria site 275.
Caravan Park at Pyramid Hill. 1 km E of PO. At the rear of the amenities block
HEMA 63 H10   36 03 19 S   144 07 30 E   CT HT BIG RIG

Rainbow
❖ Rainbow Dump Point
Park St, off the Rainbow - Nhill Rd. Next to the bowling club
HEMA 62 G4   35 54 05 S   141 59 30 E   CT HT BIG RIG

Rawson
❖ Rawson Dump Point
Pinnacle Drive
HEMA 66 E5   37 57 22 S   146 23 49 E   CT HT BIG RIG

Robinvale
❖ Robinvale Dump Point
Riverside Park, Robin St
HEMA 62 C6   34 34 52 S   142 46 24 E   CT HT BIG RIG

Rosebud
❖ Capel Sound Foreshore   ☎ (03) 5986 4382 Reserve
Port Nepean Rd, entry at section B just N of Elizabeth Ave. Near amentities block 3
HEMA 56 J7   38 21 49 S   144 52 24 E   CT

Rosedale
❖ Rosedale Bowling Club
1 Dawson St. Near Wood St
HEMA 66 F6   38 09 21 S   146 46 49 E   CT

Rupanyup
❖ Rupanyup Memorial Park
☑ See also Victoria site 430.
Cnr of Wimmera Hwy & Minyip-Rupanyup Rds
HEMA 62 K6   36 37 35 S   142 37 45 E   CT HT

Sale
❖ Port of Sale
Canal Rd, behind Council Office. Cassettes only, access via steps behind toilet block
HEMA 64 J6   38 06 45 S   147 03 46 E   CT

❖ Sale Showground   ☎ (03) 5144 6432 Caravan & Motorhome Park
☑ See also Victoria site 42.
Sale-Maffra Rd
HEMA 64 J6   38 05 31 S   147 03 58 E   CT HT BIG RIG

❖ Wellington Visitor   ☎ 1800 677 520 Information Centre
8 Foster Street
HEMA 64 J6   38 06 44 S   147 03 27 E   CT BIG RIG

Sea Lake
❖ Sea Lake Recreation   ☎ 0427 701 261 Reserve Caravan Park
☑ See also Victoria site 337.
71-91 Calder Hwy
HEMA 62 F6   35 30 11 S   142 50 57 E   CT HT BIG RIG

Seymour
❖ Seymour Dump Point
Cnr Wallis & High Street's
HEMA 59 B14   37 01 14 S   145 08 05 E   CT HT

Shepparton
❖ Ken Muston Automotive   ☎ (03) 5821 6688 Dump Point
At the rear of business. Enter via Florence St or Doyles Rd into laneway, then through gates, signposted. Business hours only, donation required
HEMA 64 B1   36 23 08 S   145 25 41 E   CT HT $ BIG RIG

St Arnaud
❖ St Arnaud Sports Club   ☎ (03) 5495 1268
Dunstan St, off Charlton St Arnaud Rd, behind sports club
HEMA 59 A8   36 36 32 S   143 15 34 E   CT HT BIG RIG

Stawell
❖ Stawell Dump Point
Scallen St, near public toilets
HEMA 58 C7   37 03 15 S   142 46 52 E   CT

Strathmerton
❖ Strathmerton Dump Point
Murray Valley Hwy, lane behind toilet block. Opposite pub
HEMA 63 G13   35 55 33 S   145 28 46 E   CT HT BIG RIG

Sunshine
❖ Sunshine 7 Eleven   ☎ (03) 9310 2694 Service Station
Western Ring Road, Northbound. Take truck lane, past diesel pumps. Marked as Bus Effluent point
HEMA 52 G4   37 48 16 S   144 48 16 E   CT BIG RIG

❖ Sunshine 7 Eleven   ☎ (03) 9310 2615 Service Station
Western Ring Road, Southbound. Take truck lane, past diesel pumps. Marked as Bus Effluent point
HEMA 52 G4   37 48 16 S   144 48 33 E   CT BIG RIG

Swan Hill
❖ Swan Hill Showgrounds
Entry via Stradbroke Ave. Left of the grandstand
HEMA 63 E8   35 20 20 S   143 22 04 E   CT HT BIG RIG

Victoria

Tallangatta
❖ Tallangatta Showgrounds ☎ (02) 6071 2621
☑ See also Victoria site 108.
Camp Area at Tallangatta. Weramu St. Gold coin donation for water
HEMA 64 B6   36 13 10 S   147 10 05 E   CT HT BIG RIG

Tatura
❖ Tatura Park
Hastie St, entrance opposite Davy St
HEMA 64 C1   36 26 44 S   145 13 58 E   CT BIG RIG

Tidal River
❖ Tidal River ☎ 131 963
☑ See also Victoria site 94.
At Camp Area
HEMA 66 K5   39 01 48 S   146 19 16 E   CT HT

Wahgunyah
❖ Wahgunyah
Victoria St, opposite Main St
HEMA 64 A4   36 00 44 S   146 24 04 E   CT HT BIG RIG

Walwa
❖ Walwa Dump Point
Ohalloran St, off River Rd. At the football oval
HEMA 65 A8   35 57 44 S   147 44 11 E   CT HT BIG RIG

Warracknabeal
❖ Warracknabeal Caravan Park ☎ 0400 915 125
☑ See also Victoria site 589.
2 Lyle St. Public access
HEMA 62 H5   36 15 11 S   142 23 15 E   CT HT

Warrnambool
❖ Surfside Holiday Park ☎ (03) 5559 4700
Pertobe St. Public access. Call first, fee for non guests
HEMA 60 F2   38 23 31 S   142 29 02 E   CT HT S

Wedderburn
❖ Wedderburn Pioneer Caravan Park ☎ (03) 5494 3301
Caravan Park at Wedderburn. Hospital St. 1 km E of PO. Public access, report to office
HEMA 63 J8   36 24 47 S   143 36 59 E   CT HT BIG RIG

Winchelsea
❖ Barwon Hotel ☎ (03) 5267 2046
☑ See also Victoria site 485.
Palmer St. Locked, see Hotel or information on sign
HEMA 61 E12   38 14 34 S   143 59 27 E   CT HT

Tasmania

Wulgulmerang
❖ Wulgulmerang Recreation Reserve ☎ (03) 5155 0253
☑ See also Victoria site 24.
Snowy River Rd
HEMA 65 E9   37 04 06 S   148 15 37 E   CT HT BIG RIG

Wycheproof
❖ Wycheproof Caravan Park ☎ (03) 5493 7278
☑ See also Victoria site 342.
Caravan Park at Wycheproof. Calder Hwy 500m N of PO
HEMA 62 H7   36 04 10 S   143 13 33 E   CT HT BIG RIG

Yarram
❖ Yarram Recreation Reserve
Railway Ave, via Buckley St
HEMA 66 H6   38 33 25 S   146 40 25 E   CT HT BIG RIG

Yarrawonga
❖ Yarrawonga Showgrounds ☎ (03) 5744 1989
Dunlop St. Next to cream brick amenities block
HEMA 64 A3   36 01 03 S   146 00 32 E   CT HT BIG RIG

Yea
❖ Yea Water Discovery Centre ☎ (03) 5797 2663
2 Hood St
HEMA 66 B2   37 12 36 S   145 25 37 E   CT HT BIG RIG

Tasmania

Arthur River
❖ Arthur River Dump Point ☎ (03) 6452 4800
S side of river, turn R to Gardiner Point. Dump point is situated at the end of the road at the "Edge of the World Lookout"
HEMA 76 G3   41 03 27 S   144 39 37 E   CT BIG RIG

Beaconsfield
❖ Beaconsfield Recreation Ground ☎ (03) 6383 6350
☑ See also Tasmania site 190.
York St, off Grubb St. E side of town
HEMA 74 D6   41 11 57 S   146 49 19 E   CT HT BIG RIG

Bicheno
❖ Bicheno Dump Point ☎ (03) 6375 1333
Cnr of the The Esplanade & Fraser Sts
HEMA 75 J14   41 52 19 S   148 18 25 E   CT HT BIG RIG

Bothwell
❖ Bothwell Dump Point ☎ (03) 6259 5503
Market Place, rear of Council CP, behind golf museum
HEMA 73 H13   42 22 59 S   147 00 31 E   CT

Burnie
❖ Cooee Point Reserve ☎ (03) 6431 1033
☑ See also Tasmania site 173.
Cooee Point. 3 km W of Burnie, via Turrung St & Cooee Point Rd
HEMA 77 F9   41 02 19 S   145 52 37 E   CT HT BIG RIG

❖ South Burnie Dumpoint
Esplanade, Reeve St public toilets near yacht club
HEMA 77 G9   41 03 44 S   145 54 54 E   CT HT

Cambridge
❖ Cambridge Memorial Oval ☎ (03) 6245 8600
Cambridge Rd
HEMA 69 G2   42 50 10 S   147 26 41 E   CT HT BIG RIG

Campbell Town
❖ King Street Oval
☑ See also Tasmania site 59.
King St, Western end of oval
HEMA 75 K10   41 55 47 S   147 29 17 E   CT HT BIG RIG

Cradle Mountain
❖ Cradle Mountain Dump Point
Behind the Visitor Information Centre, near the bus car park
HEMA 72 B7   41 34 52 S   145 56 16 E   CT HT BIG RIG

Cygnet
❖ Burtons Reserve ☎ (03) 6264 8448
Off Charlton St, S end of town. Adjacent to toilet block
HEMA 71 G12   43 09 48 S   147 04 55 E   CT HT BIG RIG

Deloraine
❖ Deloraine East Overnight Park ☎ (03) 6393 5300
☑ See also Tasmania site 144.
Racecourse Dr, near tennis courts
HEMA 74 G5   41 31 19 S   146 39 43 E   CT HT BIG RIG

Devonport
❖ Devonport South Dump Point
Miandetta-Devonport Rd, at the sewerage facility next to bridge near Horsehead Creek
HEMA 77 G12   41 11 59 S   146 21 19 E   CT HT BIG RIG

Devonport East
❖ Girdlestone Park ☎ (03) 6424 4466
☑ See also Tasmania site 153.
Car park at football ground in John St
HEMA 77 G12   41 11 10 S   146 22 45 E   CT HT BIG RIG

Evandale
❖ Morven Park
Barclay St. W end of town. Behind clubhouse
HEMA 75 G9   41 34 04 S   147 14 38 E   CT HT BIG RIG

Fingal
❖ Fingal Park
☑ See also Tasmania site 38.
Talbot St, beside public toilets
HEMA 75 G12   41 38 17 S   147 58 06 E   CT BIG RIG

Franklin
❖ Franklin Foreshore Reserve
☑ See also Tasmania site 88.
Adjacent to toilet block
HEMA 71 F11   43 05 34 S   147 00 33 E   CT HT BIG RIG

Geeveston
❖ Heritage Park
☑ See also Tasmania site 91.
Parking Area at Geeveston. Arve Rd, entry opposite roadhouse
HEMA 71 G11   43 09 51 S   146 55 29 E   CT HT BIG RIG

George Town
❖ George Town Rest Area
☑ See also Tasmania site 189.
Main Rd. S end of town, behind information centre
HEMA 74 C6   41 06 33 S   146 50 18 E   CT HT BIG RIG

Gordon
❖ Gordon Foreshore Reserve ☎ (03) 6211 8200
☑ See also Tasmania site 100.
At Reserve, Channel Hwy
HEMA 71 G12 43 15 42 S 147 14 33 E `CT` `HT` `BIG RIG`

Hamilton
❖ Hamilton Camping Ground ☎ (03) 6286 3202
☑ See also Tasmania site 111.
W end of town. Beside river
HEMA 73 J12 42 33 33 S 146 49 50 E `CT` `HT` `BIG RIG`

Hobart
❖ BP Service Station ☎ (03) 6234 3549
200 Brooker Hwy
HEMA 68 B2 42 52 12 S 147 19 18 E `CT`

❖ Hobart Showgrounds ☎ (03) 6272 6812
☑ See also Tasmania site 78.
Howard Rd, Glenorchy
HEMA 69 G1 42 50 02 S 147 17 06 E `CT` `HT` `BIG RIG`

❖ Montrose Bay Reserve
Foreshore Rd, off Brooker Hwy
HEMA 69 G1 42 49 17 S 147 16 08 E `CT` `HT` `BIG RIG`

Huonville
❖ Huonville Foreshore ☎ (03) 6264 0326
Channel Hwy. Next to the toilets
HEMA 71 F11 43 02 06 S 147 03 02 E `CT` `HT` `BIG RIG`

Kempton
❖ Victoria Memorial Hall ☎ (03) 6259 3011
Old Hunting Ground Rd, off Main St
HEMA 73 J14 42 31 54 S 147 12 01 E `CT`

Kingston
❖ Kingston Wetlands Site ☎ (03) 6211 8242
At entrance to Wetlands Reserve, Channel Hwy
HEMA 69 H1 42 58 27 S 147 18 50 E `CT` `HT` `BIG RIG`

Latrobe
❖ Latrobe Motorhome Stop ☎ (03) 6421 4699
☑ See also Tasmania site 158.
Rear of Wells Supermarket, access off Cotton St
HEMA 77 H12 41 14 14 S 146 24 37 E `CT` `HT` `BIG RIG`

Launceston
❖ Inveresk Showgrounds (York Park Precinct) ☎ (03) 6323 3383
Forster St, off Invermay Rd. In all day parking area near the Round House. Entry near South St
HEMA 75 F8 41 25 22 S 147 08 24 E `CT` `HT` `BIG RIG`

Narawntapu National Park
❖ Bakers Point Campground (3) ☎ (03) 6428 6277
☑ See also Tasmania site 196.
In Camp Area 18 km N of B71/C740 junction. 6 km dirt road
HEMA 74 D5 41 09 44 S 146 34 05 E `CT`

❖ Springlawn Campground ☎ (03) 6428 6277
☑ See also Tasmania site 195.
In Camp Area 13.5 km N of B71/C740 junction. 2 km dirt road
HEMA 74 D5 41 08 52 S 146 36 09 E `CT`

New Norfolk
❖ New Norfolk Dump Point
Page Ave, next to caravan park
HEMA 71 D11 42 46 34 S 147 03 57 E `CT` `HT` `BIG RIG`

Nubeena
❖ Nubeena Dump Point ☎ (03) 6251 2400
Nubeena Rd, opposite Police Station. N end of town
HEMA 69 J3 43 05 44 S 147 44 36 E `CT` `HT` `BIG RIG`

Oatlands
❖ Oatlands Dump Point
Cnr William & Wellington Sts
HEMA 69 C2 42 17 52 S 147 21 58 E `CT` `HT` `BIG RIG`

Penguin
❖ Penguin Dump Point ☎ (03) 6429 8979
Cnr of Main & Johnsons Beach Rds, on the beach side. If locked, key at Information Centre
HEMA 77 G10 41 06 36 S 146 04 10 E `CT` `HT` `BIG RIG`

Pontville
❖ Pontville Park RV Stop ☎ (03) 6268 7000
☑ See also Tasmania site 77.
Glen Lea Rd, off the Midland Hwy
HEMA 69 F1 42 41 12 S 147 15 37 E `CT` `HT` `BIG RIG`

Port Huon
❖ Shipwrights Point Regatta Ground ☎ (03) 6264 0300
☑ See also Tasmania site 89.
In Camp Area at Port Huon. Just N of wharf area, beside river. Signposted
HEMA 71 G11 43 09 31 S 146 58 47 E `CT` `HT` `BIG RIG`

Port Sorell
❖ Port Sorell Jetty ☎ (03) 6426 2693
Darling St. N end, next to caravan park
HEMA 77 G13 41 09 51 S 146 33 23 E `CT` `HT` `BIG RIG`

Queenstown
❖ Queenstown Dump Point
Lyell Hwy (Batchelor St), near Mary St beside works building
HEMA 72 F5 42 04 38 S 145 33 34 E `CT` `BIG RIG`

Railton
❖ Railton Motorhome Stop
☑ See also Tasmania site 159.
At Camp Spot on the Esplanade. N side of Foster St opposite Hotel
HEMA 77 J12 41 20 39 S 146 25 23 E `CT` `HT` `BIG RIG`

Rosebery
❖ Rosebery Dump Point
Park Rd, opposite the caravan park
HEMA 72 D5 41 46 38 S 145 32 06 E `CT` `HT` `BIG RIG`

Ross
❖ Ross Caravan Park ☎ (03) 6381 5224
In the Caravan Park, the Esplanade, off High St. Locked, pay fee at office
HEMA 69 A2 42 01 50 S 147 29 26 E `CT` `HT` `$` `BIG RIG`

Scottsdale
❖ Northeast Park
☑ See also Tasmania site 3.
Ringarooma Rd. 1 km E of Post Office
HEMA 75 D10 41 09 56 S 147 31 23 E `CT` `BIG RIG`

Sheffield
❖ Sheffield Recreation Ground
☑ See also Tasmania site 160.
Spring St, on road to Recreation Grounds
HEMA 77 J12 41 22 58 S 146 20 09 E `CT` `HT` `BIG RIG` `[icon]`

Sisters Beach
❖ Sisters Beach Dump Point
Behind Fire Station, cnr Honeysuckle Ave & Cumming St
HEMA 77 F8 40 55 05 S 145 33 54 E `CT`

Smithton
❖ Smithton Esplanade
☑ See also Tasmania site 180.
West Esplanade, on W side of Duck River Bridge. RH side
HEMA 76 E5 40 50 20 S 145 07 12 E `CT` `HT` `BIG RIG`

Sorell
❖ Sorell RV Stop ☎ (03) 6269 0000
☑ See also Tasmania site 53.
Montague St
HEMA 69 G3 42 47 02 S 147 33 24 E `CT` `BIG RIG`

St Helens
❖ St Helens Sporting Complex
☑ See also Tasmania site 31.
Tully St
HEMA 75 E14 41 19 00 S 148 14 08 E `CT` `HT` `BIG RIG` `[icon]`

St Leonards
❖ St Leonards Park Dump Point
Station Rd, off Johnston Rd
HEMA 75 F8 41 27 45 S 147 11 35 E `CT` `HT` `BIG RIG`

St Marys
❖ St Marys Sportsground & Golf Course
☑ See also Tasmania site 39.
22 Harefield St
HEMA 75 G13 41 35 05 S 148 11 02 E `CT` `HT` `BIG RIG`

Stanley
❖ Stanley Public Dump Point
Tatlow's Wharf Rd, beyond caravan park, next to toilet block
HEMA 76 D6 40 45 50 S 145 17 45 E `CT` `HT` `[icon]`

Strahan
❖ Council Depot
96 Harvey St (Ocean Beach Rd), outside depot
HEMA 72 G4 42 08 59 S 145 18 48 E `CT` `HT` `BIG RIG`

Swansea
❖ Boat Ramp Car Park ☎ (03) 6257 8155
The Esplanade, near toilets & play ground
HEMA 69 B5 42 07 51 S 148 04 28 E `CT` `HT` `BIG RIG`

Triabunna
❖ Triabunna Dump Point ☎ (03) 6257 4772
Via Boyle St, Esplanade East. Veer L over bridge
HEMA 69 E4 42 30 33 S 147 55 10 E `CT` `HT` `BIG RIG`

Tullah
❖ Tullah Dump Point
Farrell St. GPS approximate
HEMA 72 C6 41 44 14 S 145 37 00 E `CT`

Tasmania

Ulverstone
❖ Ulverstone Dump Point ☎ (03) 6425 2839
Cnr of Victoria St & Beach Rd. In car park, access can be limited if busy
HEMA 77 G11 41 09 06 S 146 10 27 E CT

Waratah
❖ Waratah Dump Point ☎ (03) 6443 8342
Annie St. Opposite Council Works Depot
HEMA 72 A5 41 26 36 S 145 31 51 E CT HT BIG RIG

Public Dump Points

Wynyard
❖ Wynyard Solid Waste ☎ (03) 6443 8342
Transfer Station
Goldie St (W end). Business hours only
HEMA 77 F9 40 59 33 S 145 43 01 E CT HT BIG RIG

South Australia

Zeehan
❖ Zeehan Dump Point
Mulchahy - Packer St, off B27 300m from intersection on RHS
HEMA 72 E4 41 53 25 S 145 20 45 E CT HT BIG RIG

South Australia

❖ Port Victoria Oval
☑ See also South Australia site 321.
Kuhn Tce
HEMA 88 F6 34 29 46 S 137 29 16 E CT HT BIG RIG 🛈

Alford
❖ Alford Community Park
☑ See also South Australia site 332.
Camp Area at Alford opposite tennis courts in South Tce
HEMA 88 E7 33 49 01 S 137 49 18 E CT HT BIG RIG

Andamooka
❖ Apoma Camping Ground ☎ (08) 8672 7023
☑ See also South Australia site 426.
Camp Area 1 km W of Andamooka
HEMA 94 C6 30 27 11 S 137 09 39 E CT HT BIG RIG 🛈

Ardrossan
❖ Ardrossan RV Stop
☑ See also South Australia site 286.
Cnr Second St & West Tce at rear of Bowling Club & Tennis Courts, enter from West Tce
HEMA 88 F7 34 25 28 S 137 54 52 E CT HT BIG RIG

Arno Bay
❖ The Arno Bay Hotel ☎ (08) 8628 0001
☑ See also South Australia site 465.
Camp Area at Arno Bay. Tel El Kebir Tce, foreshore end
HEMA 88 E4 33 54 59 S 136 34 22 E CT HT BIG RIG 🛈

Balaklava
❖ Balaklava Caravan Park ☎ 0400 264 075
☑ See also South Australia site 243.
Short Tce. Next to swimming pool
HEMA 89 F8 34 08 57 S 138 25 08 E CT HT BIG RIG

Barmera
❖ Barmera RV Park (Bruce Oval)
☑ See also South Australia site 128.
Sims St
HEMA 89 F12 34 15 13 S 140 28 03 E CT HT BIG RIG 🛈

Beachport
❖ Surf Beach
Millicent - Beachport Rd. In car park 500m W of Robe turnoff (Southern Ports Hwy)
HEMA 98 H5 37 28 26 S 140 01 52 E CT HT BIG RIG

Berri
❖ Martins Bend ☎ (08) 8582 2423
Campground
☑ See also South Australia site 111.
At Camp Area 3 km E of Berri, via Riverview Rd. Follow signs. See caretaker before using
HEMA 89 F12 34 17 24 S 140 37 49 E CT

Blanchetown
❖ Blanchetown Oval
☑ See also South Australia site 148.
South St at Lower Blanchetown Oval
HEMA 89 F10 34 21 19 S 139 37 00 E CT HT BIG RIG

Blyth
❖ Blyth Sportsground ☎ 0428 445 218
☑ See also South Australia site 268.
Parking Area at Blyth. Entry off South Tce
HEMA 89 E8 33 50 53 S 138 29 24 E CT HT BIG RIG

Border Village
❖ Border Village Caravan ☎ (08) 9039 3474
Park
Eyre Hwy. Outside entrance
HEMA 96 F2 31 38 18 S 129 00 12 E CT HT BIG RIG

Bordertown
❖ Bordertown Recreation Lake
☑ See also South Australia site 94.
Off Golf Rd, at Rest Area
HEMA 98 F6 36 18 21 S 140 46 31 E

Bower
❖ Bower Reserve
☑ See also South Australia site 146.
Camp Area at Bower. Next to tennis court. Fee for use, put in donation box
HEMA 89 F10 34 07 23 S 139 21 11 E CT HT $ BIG RIG

Burra
❖ Burra Caravan & ☎ (08) 8892 2442
Camping Park
☑ See also South Australia site 212.
12 Bridge Tce. Fee for use, see reception
HEMA 89 D9 33 40 44 S 138 56 15 E CT HT $ BIG RIG

❖ Burra Showgrounds ☎ 0447 938 152
☑ See also South Australia site 213.
Hall Tce
HEMA 89 D9 33 40 05 S 138 55 28 E CT HT $ BIG RIG

Bute
❖ Bute Dump Point
Railway Tce. Near toilets
HEMA 88 E7 33 51 54 S 138 00 32 E CT BIG RIG

Cadell
❖ Cadell Recreation ☎ 0497 799 284
Ground
☑ See also South Australia site 135.
Dalzell Rd
HEMA 89 E11 34 02 16 S 139 45 26 E CT HT BIG RIG

Callington
❖ Callington Recreation Grounds
Callington Rd
HEMA 89 H9 35 06 47 S 139 02 22 E CT HT BIG RIG

Ceduna
❖ BP Service Station ☎ (08) 8625 3407
Eyre Hwy. W end of town at Fruit Fly Checkpoint
HEMA 97 G11 32 06 48 S 133 40 21 E CT HT BIG RIG

Clayton Bay
❖ Clayton Bay Dump Point
Island View Dr, next to Boat Club entrance
HEMA 89 J9 35 29 33 S 138 55 21 E CT HT BIG RIG

Cleve
❖ Cleve Dump Point
Rudall Road. 1.8 km W of PO
HEMA 88 D4 33 41 52 S 136 28 33 E CT HT BIG RIG

Coffin Bay
❖ Coffin Bay Boat Ramp
Entry from Esplanade, near toilets
HEMA 88 G2 34 36 58 S 135 27 51 E CT HT BIG RIG

Coober Pedy
❖ Coober Pedy Dump Point
Hutchinson St, next to Information Centre
HEMA 90 H1 29 00 55 S 134 45 22 E CT HT BIG RIG 🛈

Coonalpyn
❖ Coonalpyn Soldiers ☎ 0427 399 089
Memorial Caravan Park
☑ See also South Australia site 52.
Richards Tce
HEMA 89 K11 35 41 33 S 139 51 27 E CT HT BIG RIG

Cowell
❖ Cowell Showgrounds
Cnr Brooks Drive & North Terrace
HEMA 88 D5 33 40 48 S 136 55 32 E CT HT BIG RIG

Crystal Brook
❖ Jubilee Park
☑ See also South Australia site 252.
Railway Tce. Between Cunningham & Bowman Sts
HEMA 89 D8 33 21 13 S 138 12 23 E CT HT BIG RIG

Cummins
❖ Cummins Community ☎ (08) 8676 2011
Caravan Park
62 Bruce Tce. 2 km S of PO
HEMA 88 F3 34 16 15 S 135 43 23 E CT HT BIG RIG

Curramulka
❖ Curramulka Sports Complex
☑ See also South Australia site 291.
Mount Rat Rd
HEMA 88 G7 34 41 52 S 137 42 24 E CT HT BIG RIG

Dublin
❖ Dublin Lions Park
☑ *See also South Australia site 240.*
In Rest Area. Old Port Wakefield Rd. Behind toilet block
HEMA 89 F8   34 27 07 S   138 21 05 E   CT HT BIG RIG

Edithburgh
❖ Edithburgh Dump Point
Blanche St, opposite caravan park
HEMA 88 H7   35 05 24 S   137 44 44 E   CT HT BIG RIG

Elliston
❖ Eliston Dump Point
Beach Tce, at Info Centre
HEMA 88 D1   33 38 51 S   134 53 28 E   CT HT BIG RIG 🛈

Gladstone
❖ Gladstone Dump Point
Main North Rd, behind caravan park
HEMA 89 C8   33 16 06 S   138 20 59 E   CT HT BIG RIG

Hamley Bridge
❖ Hamley Bridge Community & Sports Centre
☑ *See also South Australia site 155.*
Stockport Rd
HEMA 86 A3   34 21 14 S   138 40 53 E   CT HT BIG RIG 🛈

Hawker
❖ Hawker Town Park
☑ *See also South Australia site 352.*
Rest Area at Hawker. Elder Tce
HEMA 95 G8   31 53 15 S   138 25 16 E   CT HT BIG RIG

Iron Knob
❖ Knobbies Camping & Caravan Area
☑ *See also South Australia site 520.*
Dickens St
HEMA 88 B6   32 43 56 S   137 09 02 E   CT HT $ BIG RIG

Jamestown
❖ Jamestown Dump Point   ☎ (08) 8664 0077
130 Ayr St. Outside caravan park
HEMA 89 C9   33 12 19 S   138 36 03 E   CT HT BIG RIG

Kadina
❖ Kadina Dump Point   ☎ (08) 8821 1600
Doswell Tce, opposite medical centre
HEMA 88 E7   33 57 32 S   137 43 16 E   CT HT BIG RIG

Kangaroo Island
❖ American River Dump Point
Tangara Dr, in front of toilet block
HEMA 88 K7   35 47 15 S   137 46 15 E   CT HT BIG RIG

❖ Christmas Cove - Penneshaw
Christmas St, off Howard Dr. Cassette only, access is limited
HEMA 88 K7   35 43 09 S   137 56 02 E   CT

❖ Kingscote
Third St. Adjacent to Nepean Bay Tourist Park
HEMA 88 J6   35 40 15 S   137 36 42 E   CT HT BIG RIG

❖ Parndana Dump Point   ☎ (08) 8553 4500
Jubilee Ave, adjacent to Health Centre
HEMA 88 K6   35 47 17 S   137 15 38 E   CT BIG RIG

❖ Western KI Caravan   ☎ (08) 8559 7201
Park & Wildlife Reserve
South Coast Rd. 3 km E of Flinders Chase. Fee for non guests, must call into reception
HEMA 88 K5   35 57 39 S   136 48 28 E   CT HT $ BIG RIG

Kapunda
❖ Kapunda Harness   ☎ 0428 956 462
Racing Club
Hancock Rd
HEMA 86 A5   34 20 26 S   138 54 08 E   HT BIG RIG 🛈

Karoonda
❖ Karoonda Cabin &   ☎ (08) 8578 1004
Caravan Park
☑ *See also South Australia site 122.*
Entry off Karoonda Rd, follow track to behind Oval toilet block. Signposted
HEMA 89 H11   35 05 47 S   139 53 23 E   CT HT BIG RIG

Keith
❖ Keith Caravan Park   ☎ (08) 8755 1957
☑ *See also South Australia site 47.*
Naracoorte Rd. Public access
HEMA 98 F5   36 06 04 S   140 21 04 E   CT HT

Kimba
❖ Kimba Recreation   ☎ (08) 8627 2026
Reserve
☑ *See also South Australia site 527.*
Buckleboo Rd, extension of North Tce. Entry through archway
HEMA 88 C4   33 08 04 S   136 24 54 E   CT HT BIG RIG

Kingston SE
❖ Kingston SE Dump Point
Railway Tce, off Cape Jaffa/ Robe Hwy, at Sale Yards
HEMA 98 G4   36 50 03 S   139 51 45 E   CT HT BIG RIG

Lameroo
❖ Lake Roberts
500m E of PO, entry to day use & caravan park
HEMA 89 J12   35 19 41 S   140 31 17 E   CT HT BIG RIG

Langhorne Creek
❖ Langhorne Creek Dump Point
Meechi Rd, adjacent to public toilets. 85 m N of Bridge Rd intersection
HEMA 89 J9   35 17 44 S   139 02 11 E   CT HT

Laura
❖ Laura Dump Point
North Tce, on road outside Laura Caravan Park
HEMA 89 C8   33 10 54 S   138 18 03 E   CT HT BIG RIG

Leigh Creek
❖ Leigh Creek Caravan   ☎ 0429 012 445
Park
☑ *See also South Australia site 361.*
Acacia Dr. Public access
HEMA 95 C8   30 35 17 S   138 24 29 E   CT HT BIG RIG

Lock
❖ Lock Caravan Park   ☎ (08) 8689 1020
☑ *See also South Australia site 535.*
Caravan Park at Lock. South Tce, near town centre
HEMA 88 D3   33 34 10 S   135 45 24 E   CT HT BIG RIG 🛈

Loxton
❖ Loxton Dump Point   ☎ (08) 8584 8071
AW Traeger Drive. Opposite Loxton Sporting Club
HEMA 89 G12   34 27 06 S   140 34 42 E   CT HT BIG RIG

❖ Loxton Lions Park   ☎ (08) 8584 8071
Reserve
Grant Schubert Dr
HEMA 89 G12   34 26 53 S   140 33 01 E   CT HT BIG RIG

Lucindale
❖ Lucindale Dump Point
Centenary Ave, in the Sports Oval near the toilets via Western entrance before the Agriculture Field grounds
HEMA 98 G5   36 58 18 S   140 21 51 E   CT HT BIG RIG

Maitland
❖ Maitland Showground   ☎ (08) 8832 2171
☑ *See also South Australia site 323.*
Rogers Tce. Signposted, near shed on right
HEMA 88 F7   34 22 18 S   137 40 39 E   CT HT BIG RIG

Mannum
❖ Haythorpe Reserve   ☎ (08) 8569 0100
☑ *See also South Australia site 172.*
In parking area 1 km NE of Mannum, on Bowhill Rd. E side of river. N of ferry crossing
HEMA 89 H10   34 54 33 S   139 19 24 E   CT

❖ Mannum Caravan Park   ☎ (08) 8569 1402
Purnong Rd. Public access. Fee if not a guest, must contact office
HEMA 89 H10   34 54 31 S   139 19 02 E   CT HT $ BIG RIG

Marla
❖ Marla Dump Point
Cockatoo Crescent
HEMA 93 D11   27 18 08 S   133 37 22 E   CT HT BIG RIG

Meadows
❖ Meadows Recreation Ground
Access from Mawson Rd. Not available during sports or events
HEMA 87 C7   35 10 47 S   138 45 35 E   CT HT BIG RIG

Melrose
❖ Melrose Showground   ☎ 0428 662 140
☑ *See also South Australia site 282.*
Main North Rd. N end of town
HEMA 89 B8   32 48 36 S   138 11 46 E   CT HT BIG RIG

Meningie
❖ Meningie Dump Point
Princes Hwy, in parking bay at Southern entrance to town
HEMA 89 K10   35 41 40 S   139 20 12 E   HT BIG RIG

Millicent
❖ Millicent Information   ☎ (08) 8733 0904
Centre
1 Mt Gambier St, behind Info centre
HEMA 98 J5   37 35 50 S   140 21 27 E   CT HT BIG RIG

Minnipa
❖ Minnipa Dump Point
Minnipa Oval. Mosley Tce
HEMA 88 B2   32 51 24 S   135 09 24 E   CT HT

Moonta
❖ Moonta Dump Point
Cnr of Blyth & Frances Terraces
`HEMA 88 E6` 34 03 43 S 137 35 15 E CT HT BIG RIG

Moorook
❖ Moorook Riverfront
Camping & Picnic Area ☎ (08) 8584 7221
☑ See also South Australia site 123.
Kingston-Loxton Rd
`HEMA 89 F12` 34 17 17 S 140 22 06 E CT HT

Morgan
❖ Morgan Dump Point
Morgan Oval, North East Tce
`HEMA 89 E10` 34 01 46 S 139 40 08 E CT HT BIG RIG

Mount Barker
❖ Mount Barker Dump Point
Alexandrina Rd
`HEMA 85 J14` 35 04 26 S 138 51 43 E CT

Mount Gambier
❖ Mt Gambier
Showgrounds ☎ 0408 492 182
☑ See also South Australia site 2.
Pick Ave
`HEMA 98 J6` 37 50 16 S 140 47 51 E CT HT $ BIG RIG

Mount Pleasant
❖ Talunga Park Caravan
Park (Showgrounds) ☎ (08) 8568 1934
☑ See also South Australia site 181.
Melrose St. At showground
`HEMA 86 F7` 34 46 34 S 139 02 34 E CT HT BIG RIG

Murray Bridge
❖ Murray Bridge Dump Point
Railway Tce. 200m NE of PO
`HEMA 89 H10` 35 06 57 S 139 16 25 E CT HT BIG RIG

Naracoorte
❖ Naracoorte
Showgrounds ☎ 0414 453 360
☑ See also South Australia site 76.
Smith St
`HEMA 98 G6` 36 57 16 S 140 44 48 E CT HT BIG RIG

Orroroo
❖ Orroroo Caravan Park ☎ (08) 8658 1444
☑ See also South Australia site 228.
Second St. 200m W of PO. At back of the
park. Call at reception to pay fee
`HEMA 89 B9` 32 43 57 S 138 36 36 E CT $ BIG RIG

Penola
❖ McCorquindale Park
Off Cameron St, entrance between Portland
St & Gordon St
`HEMA 98 H6` 37 22 29 S 140 50 27 E CT HT BIG RIG

Peterborough
❖ Peterborough Dump Point
Don Ferguson Drive, entry beside Tourist
Information Centre
`HEMA 89 C9` 32 58 25 S 138 50 02 E CT HT BIG RIG

Pinnaroo
❖ Pinnaroo
Cnr Mallee Hwy & Homburg Tce
`HEMA 89 J13` 35 15 37 S 140 54 46 E CT HT BIG RIG

Point Lowly
❖ Point Lowly ☎ (08) 8645 7900
☑ See also South Australia site 455.
Port Bonython Rd, S side past gas plant.
500m from camp spot
`HEMA 88 C7` 32 59 34 S 137 46 51 E CT HT BIG RIG

Port Augusta
❖ Port Augusta Motorhome Park
☑ See also South Australia site 517.
Power Station Rd
`HEMA 88 A7` 32 30 40 S 137 47 09 E CT HT BIG RIG

Port Broughton
❖ Port Broughton Dump
Point ☎ (08) 8635 2107
Cnr Mundoora & Bute Rds, next to council
depot
`HEMA 88 D7` 33 36 10 S 137 56 09 E CT HT BIG RIG

Port Germein
❖ Port Germein Recreation Grounds
West Tce, adjacent to First St
`HEMA 88 C7` 33 01 09 S 137 59 39 E CT HT BIG RIG

Port Gibbon
❖ Port Gibbon Foreshore ☎ (08) 8629 2019
☑ See also South Australia site 460.
Port Gibbon Foreshore Access from B100 at
Port Gibbon sign, through Igloo Rd
`HEMA 88 E5` 33 48 07 S 136 48 06 E CT HT BIG RIG

Port Julia
❖ Port Julia Oval
(Reichenbach Memorial
Park) ☎ (08) 8853 8115
☑ See also South Australia site 290.
Osprey St, behind toilets. Fee if not staying
`HEMA 88 G7` 34 39 46 S 137 52 38 E CT $

Port Lincoln
❖ Port Lincoln Dump Point
Windsor Ave, off Proper Bay Road. Next to
Ravendale Sportsgrounds
`HEMA 88 G3` 34 44 35 S 135 51 18 E CT HT BIG RIG

Port Pirie
❖ Port Pirie Dump Point
Globe Oval, Geddes Rd
`HEMA 88 C7` 33 11 09 S 138 01 25 E CT HT BIG RIG

Quorn
❖ Quorn Dump Point
Silo Rd
`HEMA 88 A7` 32 20 26 S 138 02 52 E CT HT BIG RIG

Renmark
❖ Renmark Swimming Pool Car Park
☑ See also South Australia site 99.
Cnr Cowra & Fifteenth St. In swimming pool
car park
`HEMA 89 F13` 34 10 08 S 140 44 41 E CT HT BIG RIG

Riverton
❖ Riverton Caravan Park ☎ (08) 8847 2419
☑ See also South Australia site 220.
Cnr Oxford Tce & Torrens Rd, at Town Oval.
Fee if not a guest
`HEMA 89 F9` 34 09 20 S 138 44 59 E CT HT $

Robe
❖ Robe Dump Point
Corner White & Robe Sts
`HEMA 98 H4` 37 10 30 S 139 45 40 E CT HT BIG RIG

Robertstown
❖ Robertstown Oval
☑ See also South Australia site 217.
Parking Area at Robertstown. Entry from
Church St
`HEMA 89 E9` 33 59 35 S 139 04 49 E CT HT BIG RIG

Roxby Downs
❖ Roxby Downs Dump Point
Near BP Service Station, Olympic Hwy.
$10.00 key deposit
`HEMA 94 C5` 30 33 15 S 136 53 36 E CT HT BIG RIG

Saddleworth
❖ Saddleworth Oval
Caravan Park ☎ (08) 8847 4439
☑ See also South Australia site 219.
off Main Rd via Belvedere Rd & Marrabel
Rd
`HEMA 89 E9` 34 05 10 S 138 47 05 E CT HT BIG RIG

Snowtown
❖ Snowtown Centenary
Park Caravan Park ☎ (08) 8865 2252
☑ See also South Australia site 245.
In Caravan Park at Snowtown. North Tce.
Use Eastern entry for higher vehicles
`HEMA 89 E8` 33 46 42 S 138 12 59 E CT HT BIG RIG

Southend
❖ Southend Dump Point
Bridges Dr, behind the public toilet at beach
car park
`HEMA 98 J5` 37 34 14 S 140 07 05 E CT BIG RIG

St Kilda
❖ St Kilda Adventure Park
☑ See also South Australia site 237.
Parking Area at St Kilda, via Mangrove St.
Dump is W end of boat ramp car park. Key
at Kiosk
`HEMA 82 C3` 34 44 31 S 138 32 00 E CT

Stansbury
❖ Stansbury Dump Point
Anzac Parade, just past caravan park rear
entrance
`HEMA 88 G7` 34 54 48 S 137 48 12 E CT HT BIG RIG

Streaky Bay
❖ Streaky Bay Lions Park
☑ See also South Australia site 506.
East Tce, off Flinders Hwy
`HEMA 97 J12` 32 47 42 S 134 13 05 E CT HT BIG RIG

Swan Reach
❖ Tenbury - Hunter
Reserve ☎ (08) 8569 0100
☑ See also South Australia site 156.
Take ferry N across to W side of river. 500m
E of ferry crossing. Next to toilets
`HEMA 89 G10` 34 33 43 S 139 36 01 E CT HT BIG RIG

Tailem Bend
❖ Tailem Bend Dump Point
Main Rd, in parking bay at S end of town
`HEMA 89 H10` 35 16 07 S 139 27 30 E CT HT BIG RIG

Tantanoola
❖ Railway Reserve Tantanoola
☑ See also South Australia site 9.
Opposite hotel in rest area
`HEMA 98 J5` 37 41 46 S 140 27 20 E CT HT BIG RIG

South Australia

Tumby Bay
❖ Tumby Bay Self Contained RV Park ☎ (08) 8688 2087
☑ See also South Australia site 471.
Northern Access Rd. N end of town
HEMA 88 F4 34 21 31 S 136 06 03 E CT HT BIG RIG

Waikerie
❖ Waikerie Dump Point
Corner of Civic Ave & Dowling St, access off Civic Ave
HEMA 89 F11 34 10 56 S 139 59 14 E CT HT BIG RIG

Wallaroo
❖ Wallaroo Dump Point ☎ (08) 8823 2023
Owen Tce. Next to Mobil Service Station
HEMA 88 E7 33 56 04 S 137 37 53 E CT HT BIG RIG

Whyalla
❖ Foreshore Rest Area
Lincoln Hwy. 350m S of McDouall Stuart Ave
HEMA 88 C6 33 02 46 S 137 31 35 E CT HT BIG RIG

Public Dump Points

❖ Jubilee Park Dump Point (Whyalla Showgrounds)
Jenkins Ave. Signposted at entry. Daytime only, gates locked at night
HEMA 88 C6 33 02 20 S 137 30 31 E CT HT BIG RIG

William Creek
❖ William Creek Camping Ground ☎ (08) 8670 7880
☑ See also South Australia site 385.
At public toilets just outside campground
HEMA 90 H4 28 54 28 S 136 20 18 E CT

Wilmington
❖ Wilmington Centenary Park
☑ See also South Australia site 233.
Melrose Tce
HEMA 89 B8 32 39 13 S 138 06 06 E CT HT BIG RIG

Wilpena Pound
❖ Wilpena Pound Dump Point
At Wilpena Pound. At the back of the long term car park. GPS approximate
HEMA 95 F9 31 31 40 S 138 36 29 E CT BIG RIG

Western Australia

Wudinna
❖ Gawler Ranges Motel & Caravan Park ☎ (08) 8680 2090
Eyre Hwy. 1 km E from PO. Behind the caravan park ablution block
HEMA 88 C2 33 03 20 S 135 28 01 E CT HT BIG RIG

Yacka
❖ Yackamoorundie Park ☎ (08) 8846 4077
☑ See also South Australia site 270.
Cnr of Main Nth Rd & North Tce
HEMA 89 D8 33 34 06 S 138 26 43 E CT BIG RIG

Yankalilla
❖ Yankalilla Dump Point
Arthur St
HEMA 87 F3 35 27 31 S 138 21 06 E CT HT BIG RIG

Yunta
❖ Yunta Centennial Park ☎ (08) 8650 5009
☑ See also South Australia site 205.
Rest Area at Yunta. Next to Telecentre on Hwy
HEMA 95 H10 32 34 54 S 139 33 46 E CT HT BIG RIG

Western Australia

Albany
❖ Albany Dump Point
At Information Bay, Albany Hwy N of town. S of Drome Rd
HEMA 109 J13 34 59 28 S 117 51 21 E CT HT BIG RIG

❖ Brig Amity Park ☎ (08) 9841 9290
Off Princess Royal Dr, Amity Quay
HEMA 109 J13 35 01 44 S 117 52 45 E CT HT BIG RIG

Balladonia Area
❖ Baxter Rest Area
☑ See also Western Australia site 16.
At Rest Area 67 km W of Caiguna or 115 km E of Balladonia
HEMA 119 H3 32 21 26 S 124 47 14 E CT HT BIG RIG

❖ Woorlba Homestead Rest Area
☑ See also Western Australia site 18.
Rest Area 132 km W of Caiguna or 50 km E of Balladonia
HEMA 119 H2 32 26 12 S 124 06 17 E CT HT BIG RIG

Beasley River
❖ Beasley River Rest Area
☑ See also Western Australia site 402.
Rest Area 171 km E of Nanutarra Rdhouse or 53 km W of Paraburdoo/Wittenoom Rd junction
HEMA 114 E6 22 56 56 S 116 58 40 E CT HT BIG RIG

Beverley
❖ Beverley Dump Point
Council Dr. Just past & opposite the caravan park entrance
HEMA 107 E8 32 06 27 S 116 55 26 E CT HT BIG RIG

Bindoon
❖ Bindoon Transit Park ☎ (08) 9576 1020
☑ See also Western Australia site 419.
Next to toilets at the oval
HEMA 106 B4 31 23 08 S 116 05 52 E CT HT BIG RIG

Boddington
❖ Boddington RV Stop
☑ See also Western Australia site 193.
1 Wuraming Ave
HEMA 106 H6 32 47 59 S 116 28 25 E CT HT BIG RIG

Boyup Brook
❖ Boyup Brook Flaxmill Caravan Park ☎ (08) 9765 1200
☑ See also Western Australia site 94.
Jackson St, east end of town. Public Access. Turn R at entry, white post marked "Dump"
HEMA 108 D7 33 50 06 S 116 23 59 E CT

Broome
❖ Roebuck Bay Caravan Park ☎ (08) 9192 1366
91 Walcott St. 2 km S of PO. Have to park outside, cassette only, must see reception
HEMA 116 G5 17 58 15 S 122 14 02 E CT $

Bruce Rock
❖ Bruce Rock Caravan Park ☎ (08) 9061 1377
☑ See also Western Australia site 132.
Dunstall St. Public access
HEMA 107 D13 31 52 26 S 118 09 05 E CT HT BIG RIG

Brunswick Junction
❖ Brunswick Junction Showgrounds ☎ (08) 9726 1244
At Showgrounds, Ridley St. Turn R inside grounds. Key at Eziway Supermarket, business hours
HEMA 108 A5 33 15 11 S 115 50 14 E CT HT BIG RIG

Busselton
❖ Busselton Dump Point ☎ (08) 9781 0444
Behind Churchill Park Hall, Adelaide St. Call to receive access code to unlock
HEMA 108 C2 33 38 47 S 115 21 03 E CT HT BIG RIG

Capel
❖ Capel Park
Buchanan Rd. Locked, Key & refundable deposit payable at Colroys Cafe
HEMA 108 C4 33 33 10 S 115 33 44 E CT HT BIG RIG

Carnarvon
❖ Carnarvon Dump Point ☎ (08) 9941 1146
Hill St, off Robinson St
HEMA 114 H2 24 52 55 S 113 39 34 E CT HT BIG RIG

Carnarvon Area
❖ Blowholes (Point Quobba) ☎ 0408 942 945
☑ See also Western Australia site 374.
At Camp Area 72 km N of Carnarvon. Turn W off North West Coastal Hwy 24 km N of Carnarvon or 115 km S of Minilya Roadhouse
HEMA 114 H2 24 29 16 S 113 24 44 E CT

Cervantes
❖ Waste Transfer Station ☎ (08) 9652 0806
Seville St, entry at Estella Pl. Limited opening hours
HEMA 112 H4 30 29 52 S 115 04 48 E CT HT BIG RIG

Cleaverville Beach
❖ Cleaverville Beach ☎ (08) 9186 8555
☑ See also Western Australia site 410.
At Camp Area. Turn N 28 km E of Karrratha Rdhouse or 14 km W of Roebourne. 13 km dirt Rd. Open May - Sep
HEMA 114 B6 20 39 40 S 116 59 53 E CT

Collie
❖ Collie River Valley Tourist Park ☎ (08) 9734 5088
Porter St. 2 km W of PO. Please call in at reception first
HEMA 108 B6 33 21 44 S 116 08 44 E CT

Coolgardie
❖ Railway Museum
☑ See also Western Australia site 233.
Woodward St, cnr of Lefroy St
HEMA 111 B11 30 57 22 S 121 09 40 E CT HT BIG RIG

Coorow
❖ Coorow Caravan Park ☎ (08) 9952 0100
☑ See also Western Australia site 288.
Station St. Public access
HEMA 112 G5 29 52 51 S 116 01 02 E CT HT BIG RIG

Coronation Beach
❖ Coronation Beach ☎ (08) 9920 5011
☑ *See also Western Australia site 346.*
At Camp Area. Turn W 28 km N of Geraldton or 24 km S of Northampton
HEMA 112 E3   28 33 12 S   114 33 52 E   CT

Corrigin
❖ Corrigin Dump Point ☎ (08) 9063 2203
Walton St, behind toilet block
HEMA 107 F12   32 19 51 S   117 52 23 E   CT

Cuballing
❖ Cuballing RV Parking Area ☎ (08) 9883 6031
☑ *See also Western Australia site 159.*
Parking Area at Cuballing, Western Side of road between the Hwy & Railway line
HEMA 107 J9   32 49 15 S   117 10 48 E   CT HT 🛁

Cue
❖ Cue Dump Point
Dowley St, next to shire hall
HEMA 112 C7   27 25 21 S   117 53 46 E   CT HT BIG RIG

Dalwallinu
❖ Dalwallinu Caravan Park ☎ (08) 9661 1253
☑ *See also Western Australia site 462.*
Dowie St. Public access
HEMA 112 G6   30 16 27 S   116 40 08 E   CT $

De Grey River
❖ De Grey River
☑ *See also Western Australia site 501.*
At rest area 82 km NE of Port Hedland or 71 km SW of Pardoo Roadhouse
HEMA 116 K2   20 18 28 S   119 15 11 E   CT

Denham
❖ Denham Dump Point
Denham - Hamelin Rd, in info bay on approach to town
HEMA 114 K2   25 55 37 S   113 32 36 E   CT HT BIG RIG

Denmark
❖ Cosy Corner (East)
☑ *See also Western Australia site 80.*
At Camp Area 30 km W of Albany or 38 km E of Denmark
HEMA 109 J11   35 03 33 S   117 38 44 E   CT

❖ Denmark Dump Point ☎ (08) 9848 2055
17 Ocean Beach Rd, at the Information Centre
HEMA 106 J11   34 57 46 S   117 21 01 E   CT HT BIG RIG 🛁

Derby
❖ Kimberley Entrance Caravan Park ☎ (08) 9193 1055
Rowan St. See reception, donation to RFDS
HEMA 116 F7   17 18 25 S   123 37 45 E   CT HT BIG RIG

Dongara
❖ Dongara Dump Point
Waldeck St, next to the Oval
HEMA 112 F4   29 14 51 S   114 55 58 E   CT HT BIG RIG 🛁

Donnybrook
❖ Donnybrook Transit Park ☎ (08) 9731 1897
☑ *See also Western Australia site 108.*
Reserve St, W end of oval
HEMA 108 C5   33 34 16 S   115 49 12 E   CT HT BIG RIG

Dowerin
❖ Dowerin Dump Point
Stewart St, opposite the hotel
HEMA 107 A8   31 11 43 S   117 01 50 E   CT HT BIG RIG

Dumbleyung
❖ Stubbs Park
☑ *See also Western Australia site 144.*
Bahrs Rd, in oval
HEMA 109 B13   33 19 04 S   117 44 36 E   CT HT BIG RIG 🛁

Eighty Mile Beach Area
❖ Stanley Rest Area
☑ *See also Western Australia site 506.*
Rest Area 108 km NE of Sandfire Roadhouse or 181 km SW of Roebuck Plains Roadhouse. 5 km N of Nita Downs turnoff
HEMA 116 H5   19 02 36 S   121 39 56 E   CT HT BIG RIG

Eneabba
❖ Arrowsmith Rest Area
☑ *See also Western Australia site 334.*
Rest Area 30 km N of Eneabba or 50 km S of Dongarra
HEMA 112 F4   29 34 43 S   115 08 09 E   CT HT BIG RIG

Esperance
❖ Esperance Dump Point
Shelden Rd, off Norseman Rd
HEMA 111 G12   33 50 35 S   121 53 54 E   CT HT BIG RIG

Exmouth
❖ Sports & Recreation Ground ☎ (08) 9949 1176
Murat Rd, in recreation reserve near visitors centre. Directions available at visitors centre
HEMA 114 D2   21 55 56 S   114 07 47 E   CT HT BIG RIG

Fitzroy Crossing Area
❖ Ellendale Rest Area
☑ *See also Western Australia site 531.*
Rest Area 125 km SE of Derby turnoff or 88 km W of Fitzroy Crossing
HEMA 117 G9   17 57 38 S   124 50 10 E   CT BIG RIG

❖ Ngumpan Cliff Lookout
☑ *See also Western Australia site 534.*
Rest Area 96 km SE of Fitzroy Crossing or 192 km W of Halls Creek
HEMA 117 H10   18 44 53 S   126 06 31 E   CT HT BIG RIG

Geraldton
❖ Geraldton RV Park
☑ *See also Western Australia site 344.*
Parking Area at Geraldton. Cnr of Francis St & Marine Tce
HEMA 112 E3   28 46 33 S   114 36 11 E   CT HT BIG RIG 🛁

Geraldton Area
❖ Fig Tree Picnic & Camping Ground ☎ (08) 9920 5011
☑ *See also Western Australia site 345.*
Camp Area 21 km NE of Geraldton. North West Coast Hwy, Chapman Valley Scenic Drive for 12 km
HEMA 112 E4   28 39 32 S   114 42 15 E   CT

Gnoorea Point (40 Mile)
❖ Gnoorea Point (40 Mile) ☎ (08) 9186 8555
☑ *See also Western Australia site 409.*
Near Camp area at Forty Mile Beach. Turn W 54 km N of Fortescue River Roadhouse or 40 km S of Karratha Roadhouse. 12 km dirt Rd. Open May - Sep
HEMA 114 B5   20 50 26 S   116 20 51 E   CT HT BIG RIG

Gnowangerup
❖ Gnowangerup Caravan Park ☎ (08) 9827 1635
☑ *See also Western Australia site 65.*
Richardson St
HEMA 109 E14   33 56 31 S   118 00 36 E   CT

Goomalling
❖ Goomalling Caravan Park ☎ (08) 9629 1183
☑ *See also Western Australia site 427.*
Throssel St. 1 km SE of PO
HEMA 106 B7   31 17 59 S   116 49 57 E   CT HT BIG RIG

Harrismith
❖ Harrismith Caravan Park ☎ (08) 9883 1010
☑ *See also Western Australia site 127.*
Caravan Park at Harrismith. Cnr Railway Ave & Baylon St
HEMA 107 J12   32 56 10 S   117 51 44 E   CT HT BIG RIG

Hopetoun
❖ Hopetoun Dump Point ☎ (08) 9839 0000
Cnr Hopetoun-Ravensthorpe Rd & Senna Rd. 3 km N of Hopetoun
HEMA 111 H9   33 55 08 S   120 08 13 E   CT HT BIG RIG 🛁

Jarradale
❖ Jarrahdale Old Mill
☑ *See also Western Australia site 195.*
Parking Area at Jarradale, Millars Rd off Jarradale Rd
HEMA 106 F4   32 20 03 S   116 04 07 E   CT HT BIG RIG 🛁

Jurien Bay
❖ Sandy Cape Recreational Park ☎ (08) 9652 0800
☑ *See also Western Australia site 329.*
2 km N of Jurien Bay or 18 km S of Green Head. 6 km dirt road
HEMA 112 G4   30 11 23 S   115 00 07 E   CT

Kalbarri
❖ Kalbarri Dump Point
Porter St, 1.7 km from turn off, in industrial area
HEMA 112 D3   27 42 08 S   114 10 03 E   CT HT BIG RIG

Kalgoorlie
❖ Boulder Dump Point
Hamilton St, between Piesse & Richardson Sts
HEMA 111 H11   30 47 00 S   121 29 29 E   CT HT BIG RIG

❖ Kalgoorlie Dump Point ☎ (08) 9021 1966
Forrest St. N of railway station
HEMA 111 A11   30 44 38 S   121 28 12 E   CT HT BIG RIG

Kambalda
❖ Kambalda West RV Stop
☑ *See also Western Australia site 228.*
Parking Area at Kambalda West. Behind Rec centre off Barnes Drive
HEMA 111 B12   31 12 23 S   121 37 17 E   CT HT BIG RIG

Karratha
❖ **Karratha Dump Point**
North Coast Hwy, near intersection of De Witt Rd
HEMA 114 B6   20 47 36 S   116 51 47 E   CT HT BIG RIG

❖ **Karratha Outback Travel Dump Point**   ☎ (08) 9143 0116
At the Outback Travel Centre, Cnr of Dampier Hwy & Exploration Dr
HEMA 114 B6   20 44 13 S   116 45 58 E   CT HT BIG RIG

Katanning
❖ **All Ages Playground**
Cnr Clive St & Great Southern Hwy
HEMA 109 C12   33 41 47 S   117 32 52 E   CT HT

Kojonup
❖ **Kojonup Rest Area**   ☎ (08) 9831 0500
☑ See also Western Australia site 184.
Gordon St. S end of town
HEMA 109 D10   33 50 13 S   117 09 32 E   CT HT BIG RIG

Kondinin
❖ **Kondinin Caravan Park**   ☎ (08) 9889 1006
☑ See also Western Australia site 128.
Gordon St
HEMA 107 G13   32 29 43 S   118 15 49 E   CT HT BIG RIG

Kookynie
❖ **Niagara Dam**   ☎ (08) 9024 2041
☑ See also Western Australia site 270.
Downstream from dam wall
HEMA 113 F12   29 24 15 S   121 25 40 E   CT HT

Kulin
❖ **Kulin Overnight Stop**   ☎ (08) 9880 1204
☑ See also Western Australia site 126.
Johnston St at the public toilets
HEMA 107 H13   32 40 13 S   118 09 20 E   CT BIG RIG

Kununurra
❖ **Kununurra Dump Point**   ☎ (08) 9169 1188
5 Messmate Way, BP Ord River Roadhouse, key required
HEMA 117 D14   15 46 42 S   128 44 25 E   CT HT $

Lake Grace
❖ **Lake Grace Dump Point**
Sport Precinct, Stubbs St
HEMA 107 K14   33 06 03 S   118 27 22 E   CT HT BIG RIG

Lake Macleod
❖ **Lake MacLeod Rest Area**
☑ See also Western Australia site 378.
Rest Area 49 km S of Minilya Roadhouse or 90 km N of Carnarvon
HEMA 114 G2   24 14 57 S   114 02 11 E   CT HT BIG RIG

Lancelin
❖ **Lancelin Dump Point**
Rock Way off Gingin Rd
HEMA 112 H4   31 01 13 S   115 19 59 E   CT HT BIG RIG

Learmonth
❖ **Burkett Road Rest Area**
☑ See also Western Australia site 397.
16 km NE of Minilya Roadhouse or 111 km SW of Nanutarra Roadhouse. 1 km N of Exmouth turnoff
HEMA 114 E3   22 59 01 S   114 36 47 E   CT HT BIG RIG

Leeman
❖ **Leeman Dump Point**
Wann Park Oval, Rudduck St
HEMA 112 G4   29 56 42 S   114 58 52 E   CT HT BIG RIG 🚐

Leonora
❖ **Leonora Dump Point**
Goldfields Hwy, at the Information bay, S of town
HEMA 113 E11   28 53 37 S   121 19 47 E   CT HT BIG RIG

Mandurah
❖ **Mandurah Dump Point**
Cnr Sholl St & Hackett St. In car park
HEMA 106 G2   32 31 42 S   115 43 21 E   CT HT BIG RIG

Marble Bar
❖ **Marble Bar Dump Point**
At Rest Area in General St. Near the General Store & Service Station
HEMA 115 C9   21 10 17 S   119 44 37 E   CT HT BIG RIG

Marble Bar Area
❖ **Des Streckfuss Rest Area**
☑ See also Western Australia site 500.
Rest Area 74 km NW of Marble Bar or 79 km SE of Hwy 1 junction.
HEMA 115 B9   20 49 33 S   119 30 44 E   CT HT BIG RIG

Margaret River
❖ **Margaret River Dump Point**
Gloucester Park access Rd, off Wallcliffe Rd. Behind Youth Zone Room. Locked, key available at Civic Admin Centre or Margaret River Recreation Centre
HEMA 108 E1   33 57 14 S   115 04 12 E   CT HT BIG RIG

Mary River
❖ **Mary Pool (Mary River)**
☑ See also Western Australia site 536.
Rest Area 180 km E of Fitzroy Crossing or 108 km W of Halls Creek
HEMA 117 H11   18 43 37 S   126 52 19 E   CT

Meckering
❖ **Meckering Memorial Park**
☑ See also Western Australia site 251.
Kelly St
HEMA 107 C8   31 37 58 S   117 00 26 E   CT HT BIG RIG 🚐

Meekatharra
❖ **Meekatharra Dump Point**   ☎ (08) 9981 1002
In lane way between Savage & Porter St's behind Shire Office
HEMA 113 B8   26 35 37 S   118 29 45 E   CT HT

Meekatharra Area
❖ **Gascoyne River (South Branch)**
☑ See also Western Australia site 482.
Rest Area 148 km NW of Meekatharra, 276 km S of Newman or 108 km S of Kumarina Roadhouse
HEMA 115 J9   25 34 44 S   119 14 13 E   CT HT BIG RIG

Merredin
❖ **Merredin Tourist Park**   ☎ (08) 9041 1535
2 Oats St. Public access
HEMA 107 B13   31 29 05 S   118 17 29 E   CT HT

Mingenew
❖ **Mingenew Dump Point**
Midlands Rd, in parking bay 100m W of Palm Roadhouse
HEMA 112 F4   29 11 25 S   115 26 19 E   CT HT BIG RIG 🚐

Minilya
❖ **Lyndon River**
☑ See also Western Australia site 382.
Rest Area 48 km NE of Minilya Roadhouse or 179 km SW of Nanutarra Roadhouse
HEMA 114 F3   23 28 58 S   114 16 32 E   CT HT BIG RIG

❖ **Lyndon River (West)**
☑ See also Western Australia site 383.
Rest Area 32 km N of Minilya Roadhouse or 190 km S of Exmouth on Minilya-Exmouth Rd
HEMA 114 F2   23 32 32 S   113 57 47 E   CT HT BIG RIG

❖ **Minilya River**
☑ See also Western Australia site 379.
Rest Area 1 km S of Minilya Roadhouse or 141 km N of Carnarvon
HEMA 114 G2   23 49 01 S   114 00 38 E   CT HT BIG RIG

Minnivale
❖ **Minnivale Rest Area**
☑ See also Western Australia site 431.
Cnr of Amery Benjaberring & Berry Rd. Next to disused tennis courts
HEMA 107 A9   31 08 20 S   117 11 04 E   CT HT BIG RIG

Moora
❖ **Moora RV Short Stay**   ☎ (08) 9651 0000
☑ See also Western Australia site 321.
Robert St at Apex Park
HEMA 110 A3   30 38 16 S   116 00 18 E   CT HT BIG RIG

Moore River
❖ **Moore River Bridge**
☑ See also Western Australia site 286.
Rest Area 33 km N of Yanchep NP turnoff or 2 km SE of Guilderton turnoff
HEMA 106 B1   31 18 12 S   115 33 18 E   CT HT BIG RIG

Mount Barker
❖ **Mount Barker Visitors Centre**   ☎ (08) 9851 1163
Albany Highway
HEMA 109 H13   34 37 38 S   117 39 49 E   CT HT BIG RIG

Mount Magnet
❖ **Mount Magnet Caravan Park**   ☎ (08) 9963 4198
Lot 397 Hepburn St
HEMA 112 D7   28 03 42 S   117 50 58 E   CT $

Mount Magnet Area
❖ **Kirkalocka Rest Area**
☑ See also Western Australia site 470.
Rest Area 64 km S of Mt Magnet or 80 km N of Paynes Find
HEMA 112 E7   28 35 50 S   117 46 51 E   CT HT BIG RIG

Mukinbudin
❖ **Mukinbudin Caravan Park**   ☎ 0429 471 103
☑ See also Western Australia site 440.
Cruickshank St
HEMA 110 B6   30 55 08 S   118 12 21 E   CT HT

Munjina (Auski)
❖ **Mulga Parking Area**
☑ See also Western Australia site 490.
Parking Area 39 km N of Auski Roadhouse or 180 km S of Hwy 1 junction
HEMA 115 D8   22 03 10 S   118 48 10 E   CT HT BIG RIG

Murchison
❖ Murchison Oasis   ☎ (08) 9961 3875
Roadhouse & Caravan Park
☑ *See also Western Australia site 310.*
Murchison Settlement
HEMA 112 C5   26 53 46 S   115 57 26 E   CT HT BIG RIG

Nannup
❖ Nannup Dump Point
Brockman St, next to the caravan park
HEMA 108 E4   33 58 34 S   115 45 47 E   CT HT BIG RIG

Narrogin
❖ Narrogin Dump Point   ☎ (08) 9881 2064
Cnr Park & Fairway Sts, behind Dryandra
Country Visitor Centre
HEMA 107 J9   32 56 14 S   117 10 46 E   CT HT

Nerren Nerren
❖ Nerren Nerren Rest Area
☑ *See also Western Australia site 357.*
Rest Area 82 km N of Kalbarri turnoff or
46 km S of Billabong Roadhouse
HEMA 112 C3   27 12 43 S   114 36 44 E   CT

Newdegate
❖ Newdegate Rest Area
Maley St
HEMA 111 F8   33 05 34 S   119 01 27 E   CT

Newman
❖ Newman Visitors Centre
☑ *See also Western Australia site 494.*
2 Fortescue Ave. Key required from
Information centre open 8.00am - 5.00pm
daily
HEMA 115 F9   23 21 33 S   119 43 40 E   CT HT BIG RIG

Newman Area
❖ Mt Robinson Rest Area
☑ *See also Western Australia site 485.*
Rest Area 109 km NW of Newman or 86 km
SE of Auski Roadhouse. 800m E of Hwy
HEMA 115 E8   23 02 34 S   118 50 57 E   CT HT BIG RIG

Norseman
❖ Norseman Rest Area
☑ *See also Western Australia site 31.*
68 Roberts St, Key required from Tourist
Information Centre. Open business hours
HEMA 111 D12   32 11 46 S   121 46 51 E   CT

Norseman Area
❖ Fraser Range Rest Area
☑ *See also Western Australia site 25.*
Rest Area 109 km W of Balladonia or 83 km
E of Norseman
HEMA 111 D13   32 04 24 S   122 35 36 E   CT HT BIG RIG

Northam
❖ Northam Dump Point   ☎ (08) 9622 2100
Peel Terrace, opposite Caltex Service
Station
HEMA 106 C6   31 38 59 S   116 40 38 E   CT HT BIG RIG

Northhampton
❖ Northampton Lions Park
☑ *See also Western Australia site 348.*
Access off Essex St, near public toilets in
caravan parking area, next to supermarket
HEMA 112 E3   28 20 54 S   114 37 49 E   CT HT

Northhampton Area
❖ Galena Bridge (Murchison River)
☑ *See also Western Australia site 356.*
Rest Area 13 km N of Kalbarri turnoff or
115 km S of Billabong Roadhouse
HEMA 112 D3   27 49 39 S   114 41 24 E   CT HT BIG RIG

Nullagine
❖ Nullagine
Cnr Cooke & Walter Sts, in the Rest Stop
HEMA 115 C10   21 53 10 S   120 06 28 E   CT HT BIG RIG

Nungarin
❖ Nungarin Dump Point
Main St, opposite Heritage Machinery &
Army Museum
HEMA 107 A13   31 11 05 S   118 06 10 E   CT HT BIG RIG

Onslow
❖ Onslow Dump Point   ☎ (08) 9184 6644
Cameron Avenue, adjacent to basketball
court. S of PO
HEMA 114 C4   21 38 28 S   115 06 47 E   CT HT BIG RIG

Ord River
❖ Spring Creek
☑ *See also Western Australia site 542.*
Rest Area 107 km NE of Halls Creek or
56 km SW of Turkey Creek
HEMA 117 F13   17 25 59 S   127 59 21 E   CT HT BIG RIG

Paynes Find Area
❖ Mount Gibson Rest Area
Rest Area 82 km N of Wubin or 74 km S of
Payes Find
HEMA 112 F6   29 36 32 S   117 08 32 E   CT HT BIG RIG

Peaceful Bay
❖ Peaceful Bay Dump Point
Peaceful Bay Rd, near public toilets
HEMA 109 K10   35 02 30 S   116 55 40 E   CT HT BIG RIG

Perenjori
❖ Perenjori Caravan Park   ☎ (08) 9973 1193
☑ *See also Western Australia site 292.*
Caravan Park at Perenjori. Crossing Rd
HEMA 112 F5   29 26 09 S   116 17 17 E   CT HT BIG RIG

Pingelly
❖ Pingelly Dump Point   ☎ (08) 9887 1066
Hall Street, behind caravan park
HEMA 107 G8   32 32 05 S   117 05 06 E   CT HT BIG RIG

❖ Pingelly Recreation Ground
Entry off Somerset St. Near swimming pool
HEMA 107 G8   32 31 53 S   117 05 25 E   CT HT BIG RIG

Pinjarra
❖ Pinjarra RV Parking Area
☑ *See also Western Australia site 197.*
Visitor Information Centre. Cnr SW Hwy &
Pinjarra Williams Rd opposite Exchange
Hotel
HEMA 106 H3   32 37 41 S   115 52 43 E   CT HT BIG RIG

Port Hedland
❖ Port Hedland   ☎ (08) 9173 1711
Racecourse
☑ *See also Western Australia site 418.*
Enter via McGregor St opposite Civic Centre
HEMA 115 A8   20 18 31 S   118 36 45 E   CT HT BIG RIG

Port Hedland Area
❖ Mundabullangana
At Rest Area, cnr Great Northern Hwy &
North West Coastal Hwy 40 km S of Port
Hedland
HEMA 115 B8   20 34 27 S   118 26 18 E   CT HT BIG RIG

Port Smith Area
❖ Nillibubica (Goldwire) Rest Area
☑ *See also Western Australia site 507.*
Rest Area 168 km NE of Sandfire
Roadhouse or 121 km SW of Roebuck
Plains Roadhouse
HEMA 116 H5   18 36 14 S   121 57 59 E   CT HT BIG RIG

Quairading
❖ Quairading Dump Point   ☎ (08) 9645 1001
Next to public toilets, stockyards on
Quairading - York Rd. W side of town
HEMA 107 E10   32 00 43 S   117 23 42 E   CT HT BIG RIG

Ravensthorpe
❖ Ravensthorpe Dump Point
42 Dunn Street, next to CRC Centre
HEMA 111 G9   33 34 50 S   120 02 46 E   CT HT BIG RIG

Regans Ford
❖ Regans Ford
☑ *See also Western Australia site 318.*
Rest Area 43 km N of Gingin or 32 km S of
Cataby
HEMA 110 B2   30 59 20 S   115 42 17 E   CT HT BIG RIG

Robe River
❖ Robe River
☑ *See also Western Australia site 406.*
Rest Area 117 km N of Nanutarra
Roadhouse or 43 km S of Fortescue River
Roadhouse
HEMA 114 C5   21 36 55 S   115 55 21 E   CT HT BIG RIG

Roebuck Plains Area
❖ Nillibubbica Rest Area
☑ *See also Western Australia site 526.*
At rest area 71 km E of Roebuck Plains
Roadhouse or 60 km W of Willare Bridge
Roadhouse
HEMA 116 F7   17 39 21 S   123 07 57 E   CT HT BIG RIG

Southern Cross
❖ Southern Cross Dump Point
Corner of Achernar & Sirius Sts. Eastern
end near old Shire yards
HEMA 111 B8   31 13 50 S   119 19 51 E   CT HT BIG RIG

Southern Cross Area
❖ Boorabbin Rest Area
☑ *See also Western Australia site 240.*
Rest Area 114 km W of Coolgardie or 68 km
E of Southern Cross
HEMA 111 B9   31 16 08 S   120 01 00 E   CT HT BIG RIG

❖ Karalee Rock & Dam   ☎ (08) 9049 1001
☑ *See also Western Australia site 241.*
At Camp Area 137 km W of Coolgardie or
52 km E of Southern Cross. Turn N 133 km
W of Coolgardie or 48 km E of Southern
Cross. 5 km of dirt Rd
HEMA 111 B9   31 15 03 S   119 50 24 E   CT HT BIG RIG

Three Springs
❖ Three Springs Dump Point
Hall St, adjacent to council building
HEMA 112 F5   29 32 10 S   115 45 52 E   CT HT BIG RIG

Western Australia

Tom Price Area
❖ Halfway Bridge
☑ *See also Western Australia site 489.*
Parking Area 36 km S of Tom Price or 44 km N of Paraburdoo
`HEMA 114 E7` 22 56 11 S 117 50 50 E `CT`

Trayning
❖ Shire of Trayning Caravan Park ☎ 0428 997 156
☑ *See also Western Australia site 433.*
Caravan Park at Trayning. Entry off Bencubbin-Kellerberrin Rd, behind the swimming pool. Public Access
`HEMA 107 A11` 31 06 38 S 117 47 37 E `CT` `HT` `BIG RIG`

Wagin
❖ Wagin Showgrounds ☎ (08) 9861 1177
☑ *See also Western Australia site 155.*
Great Southern Hwy
`HEMA 109 B11` 33 18 20 S 117 20 10 E `CT` `HT` `BIG RIG`

Walkaway
❖ Ellendale Pool ☎ (08) 9921 0500
☑ *See also Western Australia site 343.*
At Camp Area 22 km NE of Walkaway, via Walkaway-Nangetty Rd & Ellendale Rd
`HEMA 112 E4` 28 51 33 S 114 58 22 E `CT`

Walpole
❖ Walpole Visitor Information Centre
South Coast Hwy
`HEMA 109 J9` 34 58 32 S 116 43 55 E `CT` `HT`

Waroona
❖ Waroona Memorial Oval ☎ (08) 9733 1506
Enter from Millar St, off South Western Hwy. Adjacent to the Walmsley Memorial Pavilion toilets
`HEMA 106 J3` 32 50 42 S 115 55 25 E `CT` `HT` `BIG RIG`

Public Dump Points

Wellstead
❖ Wellstead Dump Point
South Coast Hwy, in truck stop
`HEMA 110 J7` 34 29 36 S 118 36 15 E `CT` `HT` `BIG RIG`

Westonia
❖ Westonia Dump Point
Cnr Westonia - Carrabin & Boodarockin Rds
`HEMA 113 J8` 31 17 48 S 118 41 21 E `CT` `HT` `BIG RIG`

Whim creek area
❖ Peawah River
☑ *See also Western Australia site 416.*
26 km NE of Whim Creek or 92 km SW of Port Hedland
`HEMA 114 B7` 20 50 51 S 118 04 06 E `CT`

Wickepin
❖ Wickepin Caravan Park ☎ (08) 9888 1089
☑ *See also Western Australia site 156.*
At caravan park at Wickepin. Wogolin Rd, behind Police Station
`HEMA 107 H10` 32 46 52 S 117 30 12 E `CT` `HT`

Wongan Hills
❖ Wongan Hills Dump Point ☎ (08) 9671 1973
Wongan Hills Rd. At Information Centre
`HEMA 110 B4` 30 53 35 S 116 42 59 E `CT` `HT` `BIG RIG`

Woodanilling
❖ Woodanilling Recreation Reserve ☎ (08) 9823 1506
☑ *See also Western Australia site 182.*
Parking Area in Woodanilling, Yairabin St
`HEMA 109 C12` 33 33 36 S 117 25 59 E `CT` `HT` `BIG RIG`

Northern Territory

Wooramel Area
❖ Edaggee Rest Area
☑ *See also Western Australia site 368.*
Rest Area 43 km N of Wooramel Roadhouse or 81 km S of Carnarvon
`HEMA 114 J3` 25 27 34 S 114 03 31 E `CT` `HT` `BIG RIG`

Wyndham
❖ Cockburn Rest Area
☑ *See also Western Australia site 548.*
Rest Area at Victoria Hwy junction or 152 km N of Turkey Creek, 56 km S of Wyndham or 45 km W of Kununurra
`HEMA 117 D13` 15 52 07 S 128 22 17 E `CT` `HT` `BIG RIG`

Yannarie River
❖ Barradale Rest Area
☑ *See also Western Australia site 398.*
Rest Area 156 km NE of Minilya Roadhouse or 70 km SW of Nanutarra Roadhouse
`HEMA 114 E3` 22 51 49 S 114 57 05 E `CT` `HT` `BIG RIG`

Yealering
❖ Lake Yealering Caravan Park ☎ (08) 9888 7014
☑ *See also Western Australia site 158.*
Sewell Rd. Public access
`HEMA 107 H10` 32 35 37 S 117 37 32 E `CT` `HT` `BIG RIG`

York
❖ Avon Park
☑ *See also Western Australia site 169.*
Lowe St at rear of public toilets
`HEMA 106 D7` 31 53 19 S 116 46 13 E `CT` `HT` `BIG RIG`

Yule River
❖ Marble Bar Turn Off
☑ *See also Western Australia site 492.*
Parking Area 95 km N of Auski Roadhouse or 124 km S of Hwy 1 junction
`HEMA 115 C8` 21 34 40 S 118 48 57 E `CT` `HT` `BIG RIG`

Northern Territory

Adelaide River
❖ Adelaide River Dump Point ☎ (08) 8976 0058
Hopwell St, adjacent to the fire station
`HEMA 123 E3` 13 14 13 S 131 06 13 E `CT` `HT`

Alice Springs
❖ Alice Springs Dump Point ☎ 1800 645 199
Commonage Rd, S of The Gap. LHS of Rd, next to Blatherskite Park
`HEMA 129 F8` 23 43 57 S 133 51 37 E `CT` `HT` `BIG RIG`

Batchelor
❖ Batchelor Dump Point ☎ (08) 8976 0058
Nurndina St, adjacent to public toilets
`HEMA 123 E2` 13 02 49 S 131 01 43 E `CT` `HT` `BIG RIG`

Borroloola
❖ Tamarind Park ☎ 1800 245 091
Broad St, near airport gate
`HEMA 125 J12` 16 04 19 S 136 18 22 E `CT` `HT`

Coomalie
❖ Coomalie Creek RV Park ☎ (08) 8976 0501
☑ *See also Northern Territory site 133.*
Camp Area at Coomalie Creek. 25 km N of Adelaide River or 88 km S of Darwin
`HEMA 123 E2` 13 01 09 S 131 07 20 E `CT` `HT` `BIG RIG`

Darwin
❖ Winnellie Greyhound Club ☎ (08) 8936 2499
Hook Rd, Winnellie
`HEMA 122 F5` 12 25 41 S 130 53 40 E `CT` `HT` `BIG RIG`

Jabiru
❖ Jabiru Dump Point ☎ (08) 8979 2230
Jabiru Dr, 300m past tourist information board, opposite turnoff to cemetery
`HEMA 123 D7` 12 39 52 S 132 50 19 E `CT` `HT` `BIG RIG`

Katherine
❖ Katherine Dump Point
200m from Information Centre. 300m along Lindsay St, just beyond Second St
`HEMA 123 J5` 14 27 53 S 132 16 02 E `CT` `HT` `BIG RIG`

Katherine Area
❖ Vince Connolly Crossing
☑ *See also Northern Territory site 162.*
Rest Area 58 km SW of Katherine or 138 km NE of Victoria River
`HEMA 124 G5` 14 49 42 S 131 55 00 E `CT` `HT` `BIG RIG`

King River
❖ King Rest Area
☑ *See also Northern Territory site 116.*
Rest Area 59 km N of Mataranka or 46 km S of Katherine
`HEMA 123 K6` 14 38 38 S 132 37 56 E `CT` `HT` `BIG RIG`

Larrimah Area
❖ Warloch Rest Area
☑ *See also Northern Territory site 95.*
Rest Area 41 km N of Larrimah or 37 km S of Mataranka
`HEMA 124 H7` 15 14 12 S 133 06 53 E `CT` `HT` `BIG RIG`

Mataranka
❖ Mataranka Dump Point
Cnr Stuart Hwy & Martin Rd, near white tower
`HEMA 124 G7` 14 55 17 S 133 03 56 E `CT` `HT` `BIG RIG`

Pine Creek
❖ Pine Creek Dump Point ☎ 1800 245 091
Ward St, outside council depot
`HEMA 123 G4` 13 49 28 S 131 49 55 E `CT` `HT` `BIG RIG`

Tennant Creek
❖ Tennant Creek Dump Point ☎ (08) 8962 3388
Ambrose St, near showgrounds
`HEMA 127 G9` 19 38 36 S 134 11 34 E `CT` `HT` `BIG RIG`

Victoria River Area

❖ Mathison Rest Area
  ☑ *See also Northern Territory site 164.*
  Rest Area 104 km SW of Katherine or 92 km NE of Victoria River
  `HEMA 124 H5` 15 08 23 S   131 41 01 E   CT HT BIG RIG

Yulara

❖ Yulara Dump Point   ☎ (08) 8956 2171
  Cnr Berry Ed & Tuit Crescent, off Giles St. Behind AAT Kings depot, on the ground under metal plate
  `HEMA 128 J4` 25 13 24 S   130 58 31 E   CT HT BIG RIG

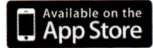

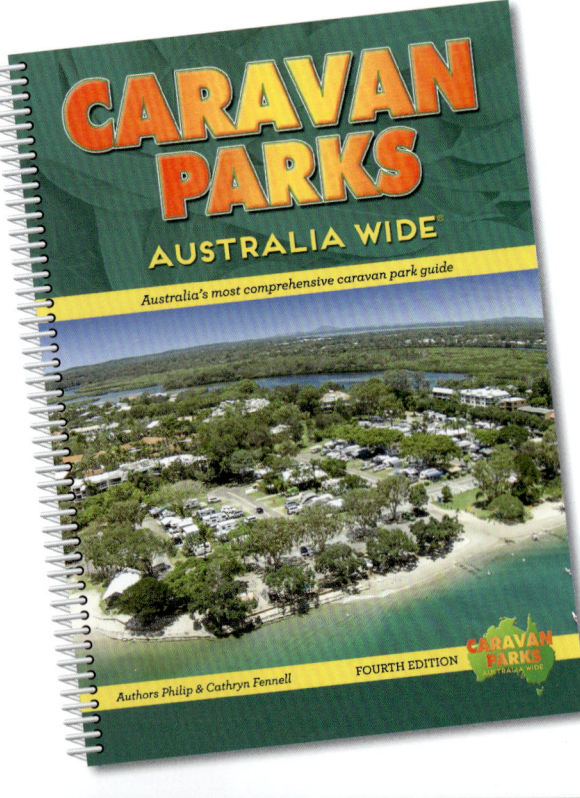

ACKNOWLEDGEMENTS

Special Acknowledgements

Barry Blair

Kym & Lyn Hutton

Robert, Ann & Rosie McGregor

Wendy & Grahame Roberts

Sheng Yee

Acknowledgements

Kate & Ralf

Lation

Robin & Nola

Sandy & Robbo

Margitta Ackers

Di Agnew

Vicki Allard

Wendy Allwood

Tim Ambrose

Dianne Ashlin

Henry Baltus

John Bamford

Leonie Beaulieu

Charlotte Bench

Ernie Bennett

Richard Bloomfield

Lynton Bolland

Mick Bourke

Terry & Rhonda Boyce

Mark & Annette Bullen

John Burges

Steve Campbell

Lee Caulfield

Malita Cognet

Richard Courtis

Margaret Covey

Cheryl Crick

Jim Crowe

Garryl Cumming

Laurie & Maxine Dagg

Julie Davey

Querida David

John Davidson

Lyn Davidson

Chloe Davis

Margaret de Hall

Graham Dempster

Don Deutscher

David Dewar

Norman Drew

Margaret Earnshaw

Warwick Erskine

Mandy Gilmore

Margaret Glover

Sutherland Graeme

David Gray

Roy & June Hargraves

Belinda Hazzledine

John Hobbins

Ian Hodgson

Dianne Hudson

Chris Hyland

Rob Janoska

Kevin Jarick

Julie Johnson

Ingrid Kaineder

Colin Kalman

Margo King

Brian Lambert

Shane & Trish Little

Robert Longmore

Bob & Sandra Lyons

Sandra Lyons

Julie Macklin

Neil & Shelagh Matthews

White Maz

Pauline McGee

Bob McKerrow

Philippa McNamara

Annette Meyer

Peter Mills

Mark Mingay

Philip Minotti

Damian Modra

Robert Moolenaar

Debis Moore

Peter Moorton

Tony North

Barry Nudd

Dennis & Colleen O'Brien

Ray Packwood

Ken Paget

Murray & Joy Pennifold

Paul Plowman

Ted & Susan Pointing

Kelvin Quinn

John Rochford

Jenny Rodwell

Trevor Schaefer

Dan Scheiwe

Brian Searle

Todd Simpson

Kenneth Smith

Alan Staley

Kevin Standen

Bryan & Marliese Stanley

Joy Stevens

Bill Stratton

Lauren & Mark Sulis

David Svensson

Liz Sykes

John Tener

Joy Travers

David & Margo Wade

Sue Wedlock

Marian White

Charles & Zillah Williams

Jennifer Williams

Liz Wright

Maurie Young

Ronald Young

Sample of a Site Listing

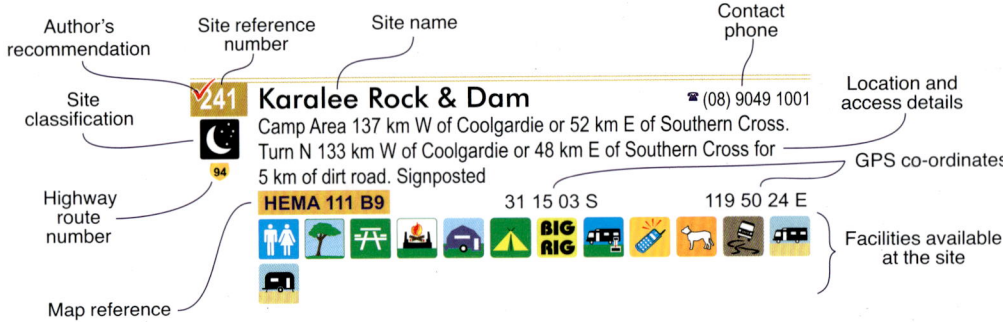

- Author's recommendation
- Site reference number
- Site name
- Contact phone
- Site classification
- Location and access details
- Highway route number
- GPS co-ordinates
- Map reference
- Facilities available at the site

241 Karalee Rock & Dam ☎ (08) 9049 1001
Camp Area 137 km W of Coolgardie or 52 km E of Southern Cross.
Turn N 133 km W of Coolgardie or 48 km E of Southern Cross for
5 km of dirt road. Signposted
HEMA 111 B9   31 15 03 S   119 50 24 E

Explanation of Symbols In Site Listings
(A detailed explanation is available starting at page 12)

Toilets	Showers (usually hot)	Boat ramp available
Disabled access (toilets and showers)	Water (drinkable)	Site suitable for tents
Water not drinkable	Suitable for camper trailer	Dry weather access only
Shade	Picnic table	Site close to road
Fireplace	Barbeque	Pets NOT allowed
Fees applicable	Fees above specified limit	Pets allowed
Site suitable for big rigs	Day use fee applicable	Mobile phone service
Power	Maximum stay (hours)	Public phone
Pleasant outlook or vista	Dump point for toilet waste	Suitable for caravan
Suitable for motorhome	✓ Author's Recommendation	

Site symbols used in listings
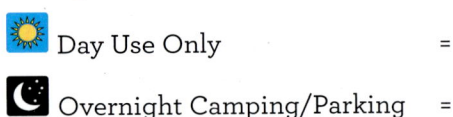

Day Use Only =
Overnight Camping/Parking =
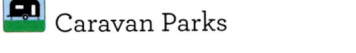
Caravan Parks =

Equivalent site symbols used on maps
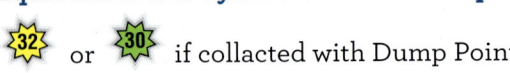

32 or 30 if collacted with Dump Point
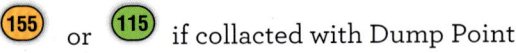
155 or 115 if collacted with Dump Point
121

Explanation of a sample Public Dump Point listing

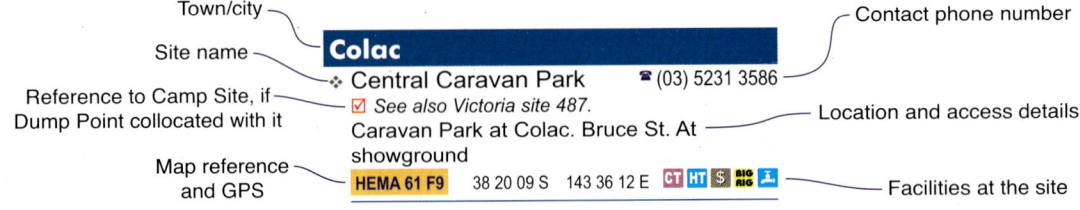

- Town/city
- Site name
- Reference to Camp Site, if Dump Point collocated with it
- Map reference and GPS
- Contact phone number
- Location and access details
- Facilities at the site

Colac
❖ Central Caravan Park   ☎ (03) 5231 3586
☑ See also Victoria site 487.
Caravan Park at Colac. Bruce St. At showground
HEMA 61 F9   38 20 09 S   143 36 12 E   CT HT $ BIG RIG 🚰

Explanation of Public Dump Point Symbols

Symbols used in listing

CT Cassette toilet use   HT Holding tank use
BIG RIG Access suitable for big rigs $ Fees applicable
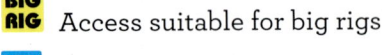
Water available

Symbols used on the maps
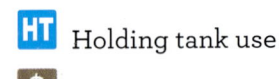

30 Day Use Site with Public Dump Point

115 Camping/Parking Site with Public Dump Point

Public Dump Point not at a Listed Site